LONGMAN WordWise Dictionary

CW00541756

2nd EDITION

Pearson Education Limited
Edinburgh Gate
Harlow
Essex CM20 2JE
England
and Associated Companies throughout the world

Visit our website at: http://www.longman.com/dictionaries

© Pearson Education Limited 2001, 2008
All rights reserved: no part of this publication may be reproduced, stored in a retrieval system, or transmitted in any form or by any means, electronic, mechanical, photocopying, recording or otherwise, without the prior written permission of the Publishers.

First published 2001
Second edition 2008

British Library Cataloguing-in-Publication data
A catalogue record for this book is available from the British Library

ISBN 978 1 4058 8078 7

Words that editors have reason to believe constitute trademarks have been described as such. However, neither the presence nor the absence of such a description should be regarded as affecting the legal status of any trademark.

Typeset by Letterpart, UK
Printed in China
GCC/01

Acknowledgements

Editorial Director
Michael Mayor

Senior Publisher
Laurence Delacroix

Managing Editor
Stephen Bullon

Senior Associate Lexicographer
Chris Fox

Associate Lexicographer
Elizabeth Manning

Senior Lexicographer
Evadne Adrian-Vallance

Senior Editor
Michael Murphy

Lexicographers
Elizabeth Beizai
Rosalind Combley
Sheila Dignen
Laura Wedgeworth
Deborah Yuill

Project Manager
Alan Savill

Production Manager
David Gilmour

Editorial Manager
Paola Rocchetti

Production Editor
Karin Fischer-Buder

Pronunciation Editor
Dinah Jackson

Proofreaders
Barbara Burge
Philippa Logan
Ruth Noble
Carol Osborne

Computational Linguists
Allan Ørsnes
Andrew Roberts

Database Administrator
Denise McKeough

Keyboarder
Pauline Savill

Administrative Assistance
Angela Wright

Design
Michael Harris

Illustrations
Jo Blake (Beehive Illustrations)
John Dillon (Beehive Illustrations)
Donald Harley (B.L. Kearley)
The Maltings Partnership
Mayumi Noguchi
Chris Pavely
Joanna Williams (B.L. Kearley)

Picture Research
Sarah Purtill

Photo Credits
Hemera Stock Photo Objects (Royalty Free)
iStockphoto.com (Royalty Free)
PhotoDisc (Sports and Recreation)
iStockphoto.com for page A13
Dorling Kindersley for page A4

Contents

How *Longman WordWise* can help students of English

The second edition of the *Longman WordWise Dictionary* provides new practical solutions for students at pre-intermediate to intermediate level. It contains 38,000 words, phrases, and examples that will help students learn the language more quickly and effectively.

Research has shown that if students learn 2000 basic words of English, they will be able to understand 80% of the English language. Based on their frequency in the 300 million-word Longman Corpus Network, including the Learners' Corpus, we have carefully selected 2000 words that form the core vocabulary of English. The **WordWise 2000** include difficult verbs such as *see*, *get*, and *feel* that students need to know well to progress in English.

Clear definitions written using a limited number of simple words.

The 2000 most **commonly used words in English** are shown in red.

The **irregular forms** of verbs are shown: past tense and past participle.

The most important **grammar patterns** are shown first, so that students can find and use them more easily.

Thousands of **natural, authentic example sentences** show how words are really used in spoken and written English.

bee /biː/ *noun* a black and yellow flying insect that makes HONEY → see picture at INSECT

be·gin /bɪˈgɪn/ *verb* (**began** /bɪˈgæn/ **begun** /bɪˈgʌn/ **beginning**)

KEY PATTERNS
begin something
begin to do something
begin doing something
begin with something
begin by looking/saying/discussing

to start doing something, or to start to happen SYNONYM **start**: *I began piano lessons when I was five.* • *The exam will begin at nine o'clock.* • *She* ***began to*** *cry.* • *When did you begin having these headaches?* • *The band* ***began with*** *one of their most famous hits.* • *Let's* ***begin by*** *looking at page 25.*

PHRASES
to begin with **a)** used to introduce the first or most important point: *They made a lot of mistakes.* ***To begin with,*** *they spelt my name wrong.* **b)** at the start of something: ***To begin with,*** *we all introduced ourselves.*

WORD CHOICE
begin or **start**?
• **Begin** and **start** mean the same.
• **Begin** is used more in formal English: *The concert will* ***begin*** *at 7.30.*
• **Start** is used especially in informal, spoken English: *What time does your class* ***start****?*

big /bɪɡ/ *adjective* (**bigger**, **biggest**)
1 large ANTONYM **small**: *a big black car* • *the biggest city in the world*
2 important or serious ANTONYM **small**: *We have some pretty big problems.* • *It was the biggest mistake of my life.*
3 (informal) very successful: *His last film was a big hit.* • *That band is not as big as it used to be.*

THESAURUS
large: *A large parcel arrived in the post* (=big).
huge: *She has a **huge** house in Los Angeles* (=very big).
enormous: *Two enormous dogs stood behind the gate* (=extremely big).
vast: *the vast open spaces of Australia* (=extremely big)

fault /fɔːlt/ *noun*
1 a problem with a machine or piece of equipment that stops it working correctly: *The fire was caused by an **electrical fault**.*
2 a bad part of someone's character: *In spite of her faults, Bet is a good friend.*

PHRASES
be someone's fault if a mistake is your fault, you are responsible for it: *The accident **was** partly **my fault**.* • *These problems **are your own fault**.*

WORD CHOICE
fault or **mistake**?
• A **fault** is something that is wrong with a machine or equipment: *My computer developed a **fault**.*
• A **mistake** is something that you do that is wrong: *We are sorry about the mistake.*
• You use the phrase **to be someone's fault** when saying who was responsible for causing something bad to happen: *The accident was the other driver's **fault**.*

e·quip·ment /ɪˈkwɪpmənt/ *noun* (no plural)
the things that you use for a particular activity: *We use the most modern scientific equipment.* • *an expensive **piece of equipment*** → see Thesaurus at MACHINE

GRAMMAR
Equipment is not used in the plural.
✘ Don't say 'equipments'.
When talking about a single thing, you say **a piece of equipment**.

The **comparative** and **superlative** forms of adjectives are shown.

Thousands of **synonyms** and **antonyms**.

Thesaurus boxes help students to expand their vocabulary. Instead of using the same words all the time, they can learn how to use related words.

The different meanings of words are listed in order of frequency. The most common meaning is shown first.

Word Choice notes explain the difference between pairs of words that are similar in meaning.

Grammar notes help students to avoid common grammatical mistakes.

Usage notes help students to avoid common mistakes with English usage.

Spelling notes help students to avoid common spelling mistakes.

Both **British** and **American spellings** are shown.

Pronunciation is shown after the word using the *International Phonetic Alphabet*.

Words with the same spelling but different parts of speech are shown separately with different numbers.

Pronunciation notes also help students avoid common pronunciation problems.

de·li·cious /dɪˈlɪʃəs/ *adjective* delicious food tastes very good: *This soup is delicious!*

USAGE
✘ Don't say 'It's very delicious'. Just say **It's delicious**.

ex·ag·ge·rate /ɪɡˈzædʒəreɪt/ *verb* to say that something is better, larger, worse etc than it really is: *"This dog was as big as a lion!" "Don't exaggerate!"* • *I think people exaggerate the risks of the sport.*

SPELLING
This word is often spelled wrongly. The correct spelling is: **exaggerate**.

fa·vour *BrE*, **favor** *AmE* /ˈfeɪvə $ ˈfeɪvər/ *noun* something kind or helpful that you do for someone else: *Sarah made my wedding dress for me, as a favour.*

PHRASES

do someone a favour to do something kind or helpful for someone: *Could you* ***do*** *me* ***a favour*** *and lend me your bike?*

ask someone a favour, ask a favour of someone to ask someone to do something kind or helpful for you: *John, can I* ***ask*** *you* ***a favour****?*

be in favour of something to support a plan or an idea ANTONYM **be against something**: *Most of the students* ***are in favour of*** *having an end-of-term party.*

in someone's favour (formal) if a court or official group makes a decision in your favour, it decides that you are right: *After a long discussion, the judges* ***decided in our favour****.*

con·tract¹ /ˈkɒntrækt $ ˈkɑntrækt/ *noun* a formal written agreement between two people, companies etc: *She's just signed a contract with a record company.*

con·tract² /kənˈtrækt/ *verb* (formal)
1 to become smaller ANTONYM **expand**: *Metal contracts as it becomes cooler.*
2 to get a serious illness: *How did he contract the disease?*

PRONUNCIATION
You pronounce the noun **CONtract**, with the stress on the first syllable. You pronounce the verb **conTRACT**, with the stress on the second syllable.

a /ə; strong eɪ/ *determiner* (**an** *before a vowel sound* /ən; strong æn/)
1 used before a noun to show that you are talking about a general type of person or thing: *I saw **a** young boy on **a** bicycle. • Do you need **a** pencil? • Lucy wants to be **a** teacher. • We went to see **a** movie on Friday.*
2 one: ***a** thousand pounds • Add **an** egg to the mixture.*
3 used before words that show how much of something there is: *There were **a** lot of people there. • **A** few magazines were on the table. • I like **a** little milk in my tea.*
4 once a week, £5 an hour etc one time each week, £5 each hour etc: *Henry makes £21,000 **a** year.*

WORD CHOICE
a or **an**?
• You use **an** before a word that begins with a vowel – **a, e, i, o, u** –, for example: *an orange • an unusual present*
• You use **a** before a word that begins with a consonant – **b, c, d, f, g** etc –, for example: *a cat • a year*
• You use **an** before a word that begins with **h** if the **h** is not pronounced, for example: *an hour • an honest man*. If the **h** is pronounced, you use **a**, for example: *a hotel.*
• You use **a** before a word that begins with **u** that is pronounced like "you", for example: *a university • a unique place*

a•ban•don /ə'bændən/ *verb* to leave someone or something and never return to them: *She abandoned her baby outside the police station.*

ab•bey /'æbi/ *noun* a large church: *Westminster Abbey*

ab•bre•vi•a•tion /əˌbriːvi'eɪʃən/ *noun* a shorter way of writing a word: *Rd. is a written abbreviation for Road.*

ab•do•men /'æbdəmən/ *noun* (formal) the part of your body between your chest and the top of your legs: *I felt a sharp pain in my abdomen.*

ab•duct /əb'dʌkt/ *verb* (written) to take someone to a place, using force SYNONYM **kidnap**: *Two men abducted him and kept him prisoner.*

a•bil•i•ty /ə'bɪləti/ *noun* (plural **abilities**)

KEY PATTERNS
have the ability to do something

power or knowledge that makes you able to do something ANTONYM **inability**: *He **has the ability to** understand difficult ideas. • students of different ages and abilities*

THESAURUS
skill: *I was impressed by the goalkeeper's **skill*** (=his ability to do something well).
talent: *She sang well and it was clear that she had **talent*** (=a natural ability to do something).

a•blaze /ə'bleɪz/ *adjective* (written) burning with a lot of flames: *Soon the whole building was ablaze.*

a•ble /'eɪbəl/ *adjective*
1 be able to do something if you are able to do something, you can do it: *She might not **be able to** reach the top shelf. • You'll **be able to** meet all my friends at the party.*
2 (formal) intelligent: *Jo is a very able student.*

ab•norm•al /æb'nɔːməl $ æb'nɔrməl/ *adjective* not normal, especially in a way that is strange or dangerous: *The doctors found some abnormal cells in her body.*

a•board /ə'bɔːd $ ə'bɔrd/ *adverb, preposition* on or onto a ship, plane, train, or bus: *"Welcome aboard," the Captain said. • Thirty passengers were aboard the plane when it crashed.*

a•bol•ish /ə'bɒlɪʃ $ ə'bɑlɪʃ/ *verb* to officially stop or end something, using a law: *In Britain, the government abolished the death penalty many years ago.*

A B C D E F G H I J K L M N O P Q R S T U V W X Y Z

a·bor·tion /əˈbɔːʃən $ əˈbɔrʃən/ *noun* an operation to stop a baby developing inside its mother, by removing the baby while it is too small to live: *She decided not to have an abortion.*

a·bout¹ /əˈbaʊt/ *preposition*
1 used to show the subject of a book, talk, or film: *a book about dinosaurs* • *The film is about a group of people who get lost in a jungle.* • *We were talking about you.*
2 used to show why someone is happy, worried, upset etc: *I'm quite worried about Jack.* • *She's upset about missing the party.*

PHRASES
what about, how about (spoken) used to make a suggestion: *"I don't know what to give him." "**What about** a book?"* • ***How about** going by train?*

THESAURUS
on: *I want to buy a book **on** playing the guitar* (=about).
concerning/regarding (formal): *I am writing to you **concerning** your son's behaviour at school* (=about).

about² *adverb, adjective*
1 used to show that an amount or time is not exact: *There were about 40 people at the party.* • *It costs about £200.* • *Come over to my house at about 7.*
2 everywhere in a place SYNONYM **around** *BrE*: *The kids were running about in the yard.*
3 somewhere in a place SYNONYM **around** *BrE*: *"Is Colin about?" "Yes, he's here somewhere."*

PHRASES
be about to do something if you are about to do something, you are going to do it very soon: *I **was about to** leave when the phone rang.* • *She looked as if she **was about to** cry.*
just about almost: *We've **just about** finished.*

THESAURUS
around: *Around 50 people came to the meeting* (=about).
approximately (formal): *It takes **approximately** 20 minutes to get to the city centre* (=about).
roughly: *We've lived here a long time. **Roughly** 20 years* (=about).

above

The picture is hanging above the fireplace.

The plane is flying over the mountains.

a·bove /əˈbʌv/ *preposition, adverb*
1 higher than something, or on top of it ANTONYM **below**: *There was a light above the door.* • *We lived in a flat above the shop.* • *His office is on the floor above.*
2 more than a particular amount ANTONYM **below**: *In summer the temperature often rises above 40 degrees.*

PHRASES
above all (formal) used to say strongly that something is more important than anything else: *I would like to thank my teachers, my friends, and **above all**, my parents.*

WORD CHOICE
above or **over**?
• **Above** means "in a higher position than another thing": *His office is **above** mine on the other side of the building.*
• **Over** means "directly above another thing": *There was a big sign **over** the door.*
• **Over** also means "moving in the air above something": *The plane was flying **over** the ocean.*

a·broad /əˈbrɔːd/ *adverb* in a foreign country or going to a foreign country: *I spent six months **travelling abroad**.* • *Jane is interested in **working** or **studying abroad**.*

GRAMMAR
You **go abroad**.
✘ Don't say 'go to abroad'.

a•brupt /ə'brʌpt/ *adjective* sudden and unexpected: *I was surprised by the abrupt change of plan.*

ab•sence /'æbsəns/ *noun* (no plural) when you are not in the place where you usually are or where you should be ANTONYM **presence**: *Jo has only had two days' absence from work this year.*

ab•sent /'æbsənt/ *adjective* someone who is absent is not where they usually are or where they should be ANTONYM **present**: *Your parents must send a letter if you are absent from school.*

ab•sen•tee /ˌæbsən'tiː/ *noun* (formal) someone who is not where they usually are or where they should be: *There were several absentees.*

ab•sen•tee•is•m /ˌæbsən'tiːɪzəm/ *noun* (no plural) (formal) when people are often not at work or at school when they should be there: *Absenteeism at the school is becoming a real problem.*

ˌabsent-'minded *adjective* an absent-minded person often forgets things or does not notice things: *He's a bit absent-minded; he never even knows what day it is!*

ab•so•lute /'æbsəluːt/ *adjective* complete and total: *She's an absolute idiot!*

ab•so•lute•ly /'æbsəluːtli/ *adverb* **1** completely or totally: *I'll be absolutely amazed if we win.* • *You will absolutely love Venice.*
2 *There's* ***absolutely nothing*** *to do in this town* (=nothing at all). • *We can do* ***absolutely anything*** *we like* (=anything at all).

ab•sorb /əb'sɔːb $ əb'sɔrb/ *verb* **1** if an object absorbs water or a similar substance, the water goes into it through its surface and stays there: *Your skin will absorb most of the cream very quickly.* **2 be absorbed in something** to be very interested in something that you are doing, watching, or reading SYNONYM **engrossed**: *The kids were completely absorbed in their game.*

ab•sor•bent /əb'sɔːbənt $ əb'sɔrbənt/ *adjective* absorbent material easily takes in water through its surface: *absorbent towels*

ab•stain /əb'steɪn/ *verb* **1** (formal) if you abstain from doing something, you do not do it even though you want to: *I managed to abstain from smoking for a month.* **2** if you abstain during a vote on something, you deliberately do not vote: *Four members of the committee abstained.*

ab•stract /'æbstrækt/ *adjective* abstract ideas are difficult to describe because they are about things that you cannot see or things that are not real: *Children of this age begin to understand abstract concepts such as right and wrong.*

ab•surd /əb'sɜːd $ əb'sɚd/ *adjective* (formal) very silly SYNONYM **ridiculous**: *Don't be so absurd!* • *an absurd idea*

a•bun•dant /ə'bʌndənt/ *adjective* if something is abundant, there is a large amount of it SYNONYM **plentiful**: *There were abundant supplies of fresh vegetables.*

a•buse[1] /ə'bjuːs/ *noun* **1** when someone uses their power or authority in a way that is wrong: *This was an abuse of your power as a doctor.* **2** (no plural) bad or cruel treatment of someone: *The prisoners suffered physical abuse.* **3** (no plural) rude things that someone says to another person: *The truck driver shouted abuse at us.*

a•buse[2] /ə'bjuːz/ *verb* **1** to treat someone very badly or cruelly: *Several elderly patients had been abused.* **2** if someone abuses their power or authority, they use it in a way that is wrong: *Two police officers were accused of abusing their position.*

PRONUNCIATION
Be careful how you pronounce this word:
abuse[1] (*noun*) is pronounced with an 's' sound at the end
abuse[2] (*verb*) is pronounced with a 'z' sound at the end

a•bu•sive /ə'bjuːsɪv/ *adjective* abusive words are rude: *He was told to leave the class for using abusive language.*

ac•a•dem•ic[1] /ˌækə'demɪk/ *adjective* **1** connected with education: *Our school has excellent academic results.* **2 academic year** the period of time, usually from September to July, when colleges and universities are open

A B C D E F G H I J K L M N O P Q R S T U V W X Y Z

academic² *noun* someone who teaches and studies in a college or university

a·cad·e·my /əˈkædəmi/ *noun* (plural **academies**) a school or college where students learn a special subject or skill: *the Royal Academy of Art*

ac·cel·e·rate /əkˈseləreɪt/ *verb* if the driver of a car accelerates, they make the car go faster: *I accelerated and passed the truck in front.*

SPELLING
This word is often spelled wrongly. The correct spelling is: **accelerate**.

ac·cel·e·ra·tor /əkˈseləˌreɪtə $ əkˈseləˌreɪtɚ/ *noun* the thing that you press with your foot in a car to make it go faster

ac·cent /ˈæksənt $ ˈæksent/ *noun* your accent is the way that you speak a language. Your accent often shows where you were born or where you live: *She speaks English with a strong French accent.*

ac·cept /əkˈsept/ *verb*

KEY PATTERNS
accept an offer/invitation
accept that

1 to say 'yes' when someone gives or offers you something ANTONYM **refuse**: *Are you going to accept the job?* • *It is a generous gift, but I can't accept it.* • *Mary decided to* ***accept the invitation*** *to the party.*
2 to agree that something is true: *He will not* ***accept that*** *he has done anything wrong.*
3 to treat someone in a friendly way: *The other children did not accept him because he was different.*
4 accept responsibility, accept the blame (formal) to admit that you did something bad: *No one has yet* ***accepted responsibility for*** *the explosion.* • *I am not going to* ***accept the blame for*** *something I didn't do.*

ac·cept·a·ble /əkˈseptəbəl/ *adjective* (formal)

KEY PATTERNS
it is acceptable to do something

1 if your work is acceptable, it is satisfactory ANTONYM **unacceptable**: *This work is not of an acceptable standard.* → see Thesaurus at SATISFACTORY
2 if something is acceptable, most people approve of it or think it is normal ANTONYM **unacceptable**: *Do you think smoking in restaurants is acceptable?* • *It isn't acceptable to be late every day.*

ac·cept·ed /əkˈseptɪd/ *adjective* (formal) an accepted idea or way of doing something is one that most people agree is right: *the accepted rules of the game*

ac·cess¹ /ˈækses/ *noun* (no plural) if you have access to something, you have the chance or ability to use it: *Access to the Internet is available from all the hotel rooms.* • *The building allows easy access for people in wheelchairs* (=people in wheelchairs can get in easily).

access² *verb* to find and use information, especially on a computer: *You can access your bank account online.*

ac·ces·si·ble /əkˈsesəbəl/ *adjective* an accessible place is easy to get to: *Some beaches are only accessible by boat.*

ac·ces·so·ry /əkˈsesəri/ *noun* (plural **accessories**) something such as a belt or jewellery that you wear because it looks nice with your clothes

ac·ci·dent /ˈæksədənt/ *noun*

KEY PATTERNS
have an accident

1 if someone has an accident, they are hurt, for example when their car crashes: *He's* ***had an accident*** *and damaged the car.* • *I saw a* ***bad accident*** *on my way to school.* • *A man has died in a* ***car accident****.*
2 if something is an accident, no one planned it or wanted it to happen: *They said my father's death* ***was an accident****, but I did not believe them.*
3 by accident if something happens by accident, no one planned it or expected it to happen: *We met* ***by accident*** *in the street.*

THESAURUS
crash: *The crash happened because he was driving too fast* (=an accident in a car).

collision: *A collision between two trains injured hundreds of people* (=a violent accident in which one vehicle hit another).
pile-up: *Eleven cars were involved in a **pile-up** on the motorway* (=an accident with a number of cars or lorries).
wreck *AmE: Two people died in the **wreck*** (=a bad accident in a car, train, or plane).

ac·ci·den·tal /ˌæksəˈdentl/ *adjective* happening by chance, without being planned ANTONYM **deliberate**: *I'm sure the mistake was accidental.*

ac·ci·den·tal·ly /ˌæksəˈdentl-i/ *adverb*
if you accidentally do something, you do it without meaning to do it or planning to do it ANTONYM **deliberately**: *I accidentally deleted an important file from the computer this morning.* • *The police think the fire was started accidentally.*

ac·com·mo·date /əˈkɒmədeɪt $ əˈkɑməˌdeɪt/ *verb* (formal) to have enough space for a particular number of people or things: *The hall can only accommodate about 70 people.*

ac·com·mo·da·tion /əˌkɒmə ˈdeɪʃən $ əˌkɑməˈdeɪʃən/ noun, also *plural* **accommodations** *AmE*
a place that you can live or stay in: *I need to find some cheap accommodation.* • *The price includes flights and hotel accommodation.*

SPELLING
This word is often spelled wrongly. The correct spelling is: **accommodation**.

ac·com·pa·ny /əˈkʌmpəni/ *verb* (**accompanied, accompanies**)
1 (formal) to go with someone to a place: *It's a good idea if someone can accompany you to the hospital.* **2** to play a musical instrument while someone else plays or sings the main tune: *Simon accompanied me on the guitar.*

ac·com·plish /əˈkʌmplɪʃ $ əˈkɑmplɪʃ/ *verb* (formal) to succeed in doing something: *There's a prize for the first group to accomplish the task.*

ac·com·plished /əˈkʌmplɪʃt $ əˈkɑmplɪʃt/ *adjective* very good at doing a particular thing: *an accomplished violinist*

ac·com·plish·ment /əˈkʌmplɪʃmənt $ əˈkɑmplɪʃmənt/ *noun* **1** (no plural) when you succeed in doing something difficult SYNONYM **achievement**: *We all felt a sense of accomplishment when we finished the project.* **2** (formal) something that you can do well: *Singing was one of her many accomplishments.*

ac·cord /əˈkɔːd $ əˈkɔrd/ *noun* **do something of your own accord** if you do something of your own accord, you do it even though no one has asked you or told you to do it: *She didn't lose her job; she left of her own accord.*

ac·cord·ance /əˈkɔːdns $ əˈkɔrdns/ *noun* **in accordance with** (formal) if something happens in accordance with a particular rule or law, it happens in the way the rule or law says it should: *The company finished the building work in accordance with the contract.*

ac·cord·ing·ly /əˈkɔːdɪŋli $ əˈkɔrdɪŋli/ *adverb* (formal) in a way that is suitable for a particular situation: *He broke the law and was punished accordingly.*

ac'cording to *preposition*
used to show who said something: *According to Rachel, Keith started the fight* (=Rachel says that Keith started the fight). • *According to the TV programme, our climate is changing* (=the programme said that our climate is changing).

WORD CHOICE
according to or **in my opinion**?
• Don't use **according to** when talking about your own opinion.
• Use **in my opinion**: *In my opinion, there are too many cars on the road these days.*

ac·count¹ /əˈkaʊnt/ *noun*

KEY PATTERNS
give an account of something
take money out of an account
pay money into an account

1 if you give an account of something, you describe what happened: *The police asked him to **give an account of** what he'd seen.*

A B C D E F G H I J K L M N O P Q R S T U V W X Y Z

A B C D E F G H I J K L M N O P Q R S T U V W X Y Z

2 if you have an account with a bank, you can leave money there or take it out, pay bills etc: *a* ***bank account*** • *She took ten pounds out of her account.* • *I will pay the money straight into my account.*
3 accounts a record of the money that a business or person has received and spent during a particular time: *the company's annual accounts*

PHRASES

open an account to start to use a bank account: *I would like to* ***open a*** *new* ***account****.*

take something into account, take account of something to think about a particular fact when you are deciding what to do, so that it affects what you decide: *The judges of the competition will* ***take*** *your age* ***into account****.* • *Before you rent an apartment,* ***take account of*** *the bills you will have to pay.*

account² *verb* **account for something** to give a reason for something that is unusual or wrong SYNONYM **explain**: *How do you account for these figures?*

ac•count•a•ble /əˈkaʊntəbəl/ *adjective* (formal) if you are accountable for the things that you do, you are responsible for them, and you must be able to explain why you did them: *Children gradually learn to be accountable for their actions.*

ac•coun•tan•cy /əˈkaʊntənsi/ *noun* (no plural) *BrE* the job of being an accountant SYNONYM **accounting**

ac•coun•tant /əˈkaʊntənt/ *noun* someone whose job is to keep records of how much money a business has received and spent

ac•count•ing /əˈkaʊntɪŋ/ *noun* ACCOUNTANCY

ac•cu•mu•late /əˈkjuːmjəleɪt/ *verb*
1 to gradually get more and more of something: *During his life he had accumulated a huge amount of money.*
2 if something accumulates, it gradually increases: *Her problems started to accumulate after the baby was born.*

ac•cu•ra•cy /ˈækjərəsi/ *noun* (no plural) when something is exactly correct: *I was amazed at the accuracy of his answers.*

ac•cu•rate /ˈækjərət/ *adjective* exactly correct ANTONYM **inaccurate**: *The police gave an accurate description of the man.* —**accurately** *adverb*: *This watch keeps time very accurately.*

ac•cu•sa•tion /ˌækjəˈzeɪʃən/ *noun* when someone says that another person has done something wrong: *They made accusations of dishonesty against the President.*

ac•cuse /əˈkjuːz/ *verb* to say that someone has done something wrong: *The manager of the shop accused her of stealing.* —**accuser** *noun*: *His accusers say he is lying.*

ac•cus•ing /əˈkjuːzɪŋ/ *adjective* showing that you think someone has done something wrong: *"Where have you been?" asked Jenny in an accusing voice.* —**accusingly** *adverb*: *He looked at me accusingly.*

ac•cus•tomed /əˈkʌstəmd/ *adjective* (formal) if you are accustomed to something, it is not strange or unusual to you SYNONYM **used**: *I soon became accustomed to the heat.*

> **SPELLING**
> This word is often spelled wrongly. The correct spelling is: **accustomed**.

ace¹ /eɪs/ *adjective* (informal) excellent: *He's an ace goalkeeper.*

ace² *noun* one of four playing cards in a pack that can have either the highest or lowest value in a game of cards: *the ace of diamonds*

ace

ache¹ /eɪk/ *verb* if part of your body aches, it hurts slightly for a long time: *My back's aching after lifting all those boxes.* → see Thesaurus at HURT¹

ache² *noun* a slight pain that does not go away quickly: *Mum was complaining of an ache in her shoulder.*

a•chieve /əˈtʃiːv/ *verb* to succeed in doing or getting something you want: *Our local team* *achieved another win last weekend. • He achieved a lot in his life.*

a·chieve·ment /ə'tʃiːvmənt/ *noun* something important or difficult that you do successfully: *Winning the tournament was a great achievement.*

ac·id /'æsɪd/ *noun* a strong chemical that can burn things: *The acid left a green stain on the metal.*

ˌacid 'rain *noun* (no plural) rain that contains acid and that damages plants, trees, and rivers

ac·knowl·edge /ək'nɒlɪdʒ $ ək'nɑlɪdʒ/ *verb* to say or show that something is true or correct: *He finally acknowledged that I was right. • She refused to acknowledge the problem.*

ac·knowl·edge·ment, acknowledgment /ək'nɒlɪdʒmənt $ ək'nɑlɪdʒmənt/ *noun* when you show that you agree that something is true or correct: *Maggie listened and nodded in acknowledgement.*

ac·ne /'ækni/ *noun* (no plural) a skin disease that makes a lot of red spots appear on your face: *I had terrible acne in my teens.*

acorn /'eɪkɔːn $ -ɔːrn/ *noun* a small nut which will grow into an OAK tree → see picture on page A10

ac·quaint·ance /ə'kweɪntəns/ *noun* someone you have met but do not know well: *There were several acquaintances of mine at the party.*

ac·quaint·ed /ə'kweɪntɪd/ *adjective* (formal) if you are acquainted with someone, you know them but not very well: *I see that you two are acquainted with each other already.*

ac·quire /ə'kwaɪə $ ə'kwaɪɚ/ *verb* (formal) to get or buy something: *She'd acquired some valuable furniture over the years.*

> **SPELLING**
> This word is often spelled wrongly. The correct spelling is: **acquire**.

a·cre /'eɪkə $ 'eɪkɚ/ *noun* a measurement of land, equal to 4,047 square METRES or 4,840 square YARDS

ac·ro·bat /'ækrəbæt/ *noun* someone who performs in a CIRCUS, doing difficult jumps or balancing their body in difficult positions

acrobat

ac·ro·nym /'ækrənɪm/ *noun* a word that is made from the first letters of a group of words. For example, EFL is an acronym for 'English as a Foreign Language'.

a·cross /ə'krɒs $ ə'krɔs/ *adverb, preposition*
1 from one side of something to the other: *A boy suddenly ran across the road. • They are building a bridge across the river.*
2 on the other side of something: *Her best friend lived across the road from her.*

act¹ /ækt/ *verb*

> **KEY PATTERNS**
> **act like a child/an idiot**
> **act in a play/film**

1 to do something: *When someone has a heart attack, you need to act quickly.*
2 to behave in a particular way: *Stop acting like a child. • Peter is acting very strangely.*
3 to perform in a play or film: *Johnny Depp has acted in a lot of really good films.*

act² *noun*

> **KEY PATTERNS**
> **an act of something**

1 something that you do, especially something that shows how you feel: *As an act of rebellion, she refused to go to school. • acts of kindness* **2** a law that the government has made: *Parliament has passed a new Education Act.* **3** one of the main parts of a play: *The ghost appears in Act 1, Scene 2.* **4** a short piece of entertainment in a television or theatre show: *a comedy act*

act·ing /'æktɪŋ/ *noun* (no plural) performing in plays or films: *He's brilliant at acting.*

A B C D E F G H I J K L M N O P Q R S T U V W X Y Z

ac·tion /'ækʃən/ *noun*
1 something that you do: *He said he was sorry for his actions.* • *Sally's quick action stopped the fire from spreading.*
2 if you take action, you do something in order to deal with a problem: *The police are **taking action against** car crime.*
3 (formal) something that you do to deal with a situation: *Cancelling our trip seemed the best **course of action**.*
4 to start using a plan: *It's time to **put** our plans **into action**.*

ˌaction 'replay *noun BrE* when an interesting part of a sports event is shown again on film or television immediately after it happens SYNONYM **instant reply** *AmE*: *The action replay showed that the ball crossed the line.*

ac·tiv·ate /'æktəveɪt/ *verb* (formal) to make something start to work: *Pressing this button will activate the car alarm.*

ac·tive¹ /'æktɪv/ *adjective*
1 someone who is active is always busy, especially doing a lot of physical activity ANTONYM **inactive**: *As you get older, it's important to keep active.* • *Having three very active teenagers in the house sure keeps us busy.*
2 in grammar, if a verb or sentence is active, the person or thing doing the action is the subject of the verb. In the sentence 'The boy kicked the ball', the verb 'kick' is active.

active² *noun* **the active (voice)** the active form of a verb

ac·tive·ly /'æktɪvli/ *adverb* if you are actively doing something, you are doing things to try and make something happen: *Are you actively trying to find work?*

ac·tiv·ist /'æktəvɪst/ *noun* someone who works hard to change society or a political situation they do not agree with: *a political activist*

ac·tiv·i·ty /æk'tɪvəti/ *noun* (plural **activities**)
the things that someone does: *The town offers plenty of opportunity for sporting activities.* • *Criminal activity in the area is increasing.*

ac·tor /'æktə $ 'æktɚ/ *noun* someone who performs in plays or films: *He wants to be an actor when he grows up.*

ac·tress /'æktrəs/ *noun* (plural **actresses**) a woman who performs in plays or films: *Kate Winslet is a famous actress.*

ac·tu·al /'æktʃuəl/ *adjective* real, rather than what you believed or expected: *The actual number of people at the party was higher than we had thought.*

ac·tu·al·ly /'æktʃuəli/ *adverb*
1 really: *Do you actually believe that?* • *I wish I knew what she was actually thinking.*
2 used to say in a polite way that someone is wrong: *"Hi Jo." "My name is Jane, actually."*

SPELLING
This word is often spelled wrongly. The correct spelling is: **actually**.

WORD CHOICE
actually or **at the moment**?
• Don't use **actually** when talking about the situation now. Use **at the moment**: *He's on holiday **at the moment**.*

a·cute /ə'kjuːt/ *adjective* **1** very serious or bad: *She suffers from acute headaches.* **2** an acute angle is less than 90 degrees

AD /ˌeɪ 'diː/ an abbreviation for 'Anno Domini'; used in dates to mean after the birth of Christ: *the first century AD*

ad /æd/ (informal) an ADVERTISEMENT
→ see Thesaurus at ADVERTISEMENT

ad·a·mant /'ædəmənt/ *adjective* (formal) determined not to change your opinion or decision: *Sarah was adamant that she would stay.*

a·dapt /ə'dæpt/ *verb* **1** to change the way you do things because you are in a new situation: *She never really adapted to living abroad.* **2** to change something so that you can use it for a different purpose: *The book has been adapted for people learning English.*

a·dapt·a·ble /ə'dæptəbəl/ *adjective* someone who is adaptable is good at changing the way they do things when they are in a new situation: *We're looking for someone lively and adaptable to join our team.*

ad·ap·ta·tion /ˌædæpˈteɪʃən/ *noun* a play or film that is based on a book: *The film is a modern adaptation of 'Romeo and Juliet'.*

a·dapt·er, adaptor /əˈdæptə $ əˈdæptɚ/ *noun* something that you use to connect two pieces of equipment when you cannot connect them together directly: *an electrical adapter*

add /æd/ *verb*

KEY PATTERNS
add an egg to the mixture
add 2 and 4 together
add that

1 to put something with another thing: *Add more garlic **to** the sauce.* • *Fluoride **is added to** water to prevent tooth decay.*
2 also **add up** to put numbers together to get the total: *Add the two numbers together and divide them by three.* • ***Add up** the prices of all the things you bought.* → see Thesaurus at CALCULATE
3 to say more about something: *He told me what Sue had done but **added that** it was not her fault.* • *"Come to my house – and don't be late," he added.*

ad·dict /ˈædɪkt/ *noun* **1** someone who cannot stop taking harmful drugs: *a drug addict* **2** (informal) someone who likes something very much and does it a lot: *I'm a TV addict.*

ad·dic·ted /əˈdɪktɪd/ *adjective* not able to stop doing something, especially taking a harmful drug: *People who become addicted to drugs need help.*

ad·dic·tion /əˈdɪkʃən/ *noun* the problem someone has when they need to take alcohol or harmful drugs regularly: *Heroin addiction is a problem in many cities.*

ad·dic·tive /əˈdɪktɪv/ *adjective* an addictive drug is one that makes you need it more and more: *Nicotine is addictive.*

ad·di·tion /əˈdɪʃən/ *noun* (no plural) **1** adding numbers or amounts together to get the total: *Mark's very good at addition and subtraction.* **2 in addition to** as well as: *We won a holiday for four, in addition to the prize money.*

ad·di·tion·al /əˈdɪʃənəl/ *adjective* additional numbers or amounts of something are more than you already have SYNONYM **extra**: *We always need additional staff over the New Year.*

ˈadd-on *noun* an extra piece of software or other equipment for a computer, MP3 player, etc

ad·dress¹ /əˈdres $ ˈædres/ *noun* (plural **addresses**)
the number of the house and the name of the street and town where you live: *My address is 37 King Street, London.*

SPELLING
This word is often spelled wrongly. The correct spelling is: **address**.

PRONUNCIATION
British people pronounce this word 'adDRESS'.
American people pronounce this word 'ADDress'.

address² /əˈdres/ *verb*
1 (formal) to speak to a group of people: *The President addressed a crowd of thousands of people.*
2 be addressed to someone if a letter is addressed to someone, their name is on it because it is for them: *The letter **was addressed to** my mother.*
3 (formal) to try to deal with a problem: *There are serious problems that we need to address.*

ad·ept /ˈædept $ əˈdept/ *adjective* (formal) good at doing something SYNONYM **skilful**: *I'm not very adept at typing.*

ad·e·quate /ˈædɪkwət/ *adjective* good enough for a particular purpose ANTONYM **inadequate**: *The government should provide adequate public transport.* → see Thesaurus at SATISFACTORY

ad·ja·cent /əˈdʒeɪsənt/ *adjective* (formal) next to something: *The garden is adjacent to the river.*

ad·jec·tive /ˈædʒəktɪv/ *noun* a word that describes something. 'Big', 'funny', and 'hot' are all adjectives

ad·join·ing /əˈdʒɔɪnɪŋ/ *adjective* (formal) next to or connected to another building, room etc: *The hotel has adjoining rooms for families.*

ad·just /əˈdʒʌst/ *verb* to change or move something slightly to make it better: *How do you adjust the colour on the TV?* • *You may need to adjust your seat belt.*

ad·just·a·ble /əˈdʒʌstəbəl/ *adjective* something that is adjustable can be changed or moved slightly to make it better: *adjustable car seats*

ad·just·ment /əˈdʒʌstmənt/ *noun* a small change that you make to something: *We had to make a few adjustments to our plan.*

ad·min·is·ter /ədˈmɪnəstə $ ədˈmɪnəstɚ/ *verb* (formal) to organize or manage something: *A special committee will administer the scheme.*

ad·min·is·tra·tion /ədˌmɪnəˈstreɪʃən/ *noun* (no plural) the work of organizing or managing the work in a company or organization: *a career in university administration*

ad·min·is·tra·tive /ədˈmɪnəstrətɪv $ ədˈmɪnəˌstreɪtɪv/ *adjective* connected with organizing or managing the work in a company or organization: *The company has thirteen administrative staff.*

ad·min·is·tra·tor /ədˈmɪnəstreɪtə $ ədˈmɪnəˌstreɪtɚ/ *noun* someone whose job is to help organize a particular area of work in a company or organization

ad·mi·ra·ble /ˈædmərəbəl/ *adjective* (formal) something that is admirable is good and deserves your respect: *He had many admirable qualities, especially honesty.*

ad·mi·ral /ˈædmərəl/ *noun* an officer who has a very high rank in the Navy

ad·mi·ra·tion /ˌædməˈreɪʃən/ *noun* (no plural) when you admire something or someone: *I have great admiration for his skill as a player.*

ad·mire /ədˈmaɪə $ ədˈmaɪɚ/ *verb*

KEY PATTERNS
admire someone for their skill/intelligence
admire someone for working hard

1 to think that someone is very good or clever: *Many people admired the way she ran the organization.* • *I* ***admired*** *Paula* ***for*** *being honest with her father.*

2 to look at something and think that it is very good: *We stopped for a moment to admire the view.*

ad·mis·sion /ədˈmɪʃən/ *noun* **1** (no plural) the amount of money you have to pay to go to a film, sports event, concert etc: *Admission to the exhibition is $9.50.* **2** when you are allowed to study at a university or get treatment in a hospital: *Lucy is applying for admission to Harvard next year.*

ad·mit /ədˈmɪt/ *verb* (**admitted, admitting**)

KEY PATTERNS
admit that
admit to lying/stealing/cheating

1 to accept and say that something is true, although you do not want to ANTONYM **deny**: *We know you stole the money. Why won't you admit it?* • ***I admit that*** *I did not like Sarah when I first met her.* • *Ian will never* ***admit to*** *being wrong.*
2 to allow someone to go into a place or join a college, university etc: *The club admits women for half price on Wednesdays.*

ad·o·les·cence /ˌædəˈlesəns/ *noun* (no plural) the time when a young person is developing into an adult, usually between the ages of 12 and 17: *Adolescence is a difficult time for young people.*

ad·o·les·cent /ˌædəˈlesənt/ *noun* a young person between the ages of about 12 and 17, who is developing into an adult SYNONYM **teenager** —**adolescent** *adjective*: *Many adolescent girls worry about their appearance.*

a·dopt /əˈdɒpt $ əˈdɑpt/ *verb* to legally make someone else's child your own son or daughter: *They adopted Sam when he was a baby.* —**adopted** *adjective*: *their adopted son*

a·dop·tion /əˈdɒpʃən $ əˈdɑpʃən/ *noun* when someone adopts a child

a·dor·a·ble /əˈdɔːrəbəl/ *adjective* very attractive: *What an adorable baby girl!*

a·dore /əˈdɔː $ əˈdɔr/ *verb* to love someone very much, or to like something very much: *She had always adored her father.* • *I just adore pizza!*

a·dren·a·lin /ə'drenl-ɪn/ *noun* (no plural) a substance that your body produces when you are frightened, excited, or angry, and which gives you more energy

ad·ult /'ædʌlt $ ə'dʌlt/ *noun* a person or animal that has finished growing: *When you are an adult you have a lot of responsibilities.* —**adult** *adjective*: *I've lived in London all my adult life.*

a·dul·ter·y /ə'dʌltəri/ *noun* (no plural) when someone who is married has sex with someone who is not their husband or wife: *She accused her husband of adultery.*

ad·ult·hood /'ædʌlthʊd $ ə'dʌlthʊd/ *noun* the time when someone is an adult: *Children who had the disease often did not reach adulthood.*

ad·vance[1] /əd'vɑːns $ əd'væns/ *noun* **1 in advance** before a particular time or event starts: *You should always plan your journey in advance.* **2** something new and important that someone discovers: *There have been great advances in technology.*

advance[2] *verb* (written) to move forward to a new position ANTONYM **retreat**: *The animal advanced slowly towards her.*

advance[3] *adjective* before an event happens: *For advance tickets, call the number below.* • *We got no advance warning that there was a problem.*

ad·vanced /əd'vɑːnst $ əd'vænst/ *adjective*
very modern and new ANTONYM **primitive**: *the most advanced medical equipment*

ad·van·tage /əd'vɑːntɪdʒ $ əd'væntɪdʒ/ *noun*

KEY PATTERNS
an advantage of this car/computer
an advantage of living/working here
have an advantage over something
give someone an advantage

something that makes things better or easier for you ANTONYM **disadvantage**: *An advantage of this school is that you can learn Chinese.* • *The* ***advantage of*** *living in a town is that there is lots to do.* • *The new system* ***has*** *many* ***advantages over*** *the old one.* • *Did having a famous father* ***give*** *you* ***an advantage*** *as an actor?*

PHRASES
take advantage of something to use a situation to help you get what you want: *The thief* ***took advantage of*** *a door that someone left open.*
take advantage of someone to behave unfairly towards someone to help you get what you want: *Because she's a kind person, people often* ***take advantage of*** *her.*

ad·van·ta·geous /ˌædvən'teɪdʒəs/ *adjective* (formal) helpful to you and likely to make you more successful: *The new deal will be advantageous to both companies.*

ad·vent /'ædvent/ *noun* (no plural) when something important first starts to exist: *Since the advent of computers, offices have changed completely.*

ad·ven·ture /əd'ventʃə $ əd'ventʃɚ/ *noun* an unusual, exciting, or dangerous thing that happens to someone: *It's a book about Johnson's adventures at sea.*

ad·ven·tur·ous /əd'ventʃərəs/ *adjective* an adventurous person likes doing new and exciting things: *an adventurous little boy*

ad·verb /'ædvɜːb $ 'ædvɚb/ *noun* a word that describes or adds to the meaning of a verb, an adjective, another adverb, or a sentence. For example, 'quietly' is an adverb in 'He spoke quietly' and 'very' is an adverb in 'It was very difficult'

ad·verse /'ædvɜːs $ əd'vɚs/ *adjective* (formal) bad and causing problems: *The illness had an adverse effect on her schoolwork.* • *Adverse weather conditions caused the accident.*

ad·vert /'ædvɜːt $ 'ædvɚt/ *noun BrE* an ADVERTISEMENT: *Have you seen that advert for Nike sportswear?*

ad·ver·tise /'ædvətaɪz $ 'ædvɚˌtaɪz/ *verb* **1** to put pictures and information about something in newspapers, on television, on walls etc in order to persuade people to buy it or use it: *They're advertising the new car on TV.* **2** to put a notice in a newspaper saying that you are looking for someone to do a particular job: *The school is advertising for a new head teacher.*

A B C D E F G H I J K L M N O P Q R S T U V W X Y Z

ad·ver·tise·ment /əd'vɜːtɪsmənt $ ˌædvə'taɪzmənt/ *noun* **1** a notice in a newspaper, a short film on television etc, which tries to persuade people to buy something: *an advertisement for a cellphone* **2** a notice in a newspaper that gives information about a job that is available: *I saw an advertisement for a driver in the paper.*

USAGE
You say **an advertisement for** something.
✘ Don't say 'an advertisement about something'.

THESAURUS
ad (informal): *I've seen an ad for a fantastic new computer* (=an advertisement).
commercial: *I hate that commercial for washing powder* (=an advertisement on TV or radio).
poster: *Have you seen the poster for the new James Bond film* (=a large advertisement on a wall)?
junk mail: *You can throw any junk mail in the bin* (=letters containing advertisements, which you do not want to get).

ad·ver·tis·ing /'ædvətaɪzɪŋ $ 'ædvəˌtaɪzɪŋ/ *noun* (no plural) the business of advertising things on television, in newspapers etc: *My father works in advertising.*

ad·vice /əd'vaɪs/ *noun* (no plural)

KEY PATTERNS
advice on/about something
advice on how to do something

when you suggest what someone should do: *I need some **advice about** university courses.* • *Do you have any **advice on** how to remove coffee stains?* • *My mother is always **giving** me **advice**.*

PHRASES
take someone's advice, follow someone's advice to do what someone suggests you should do: *I **took** your **advice** and phoned her.* • *If you **follow** my **advice**, you will be all right.*
ask someone's advice to ask someone what they think you should do: *Can I **ask** your **advice about** something?*

GRAMMAR
Advice is not used in the plural.
✘ Don't say 'advices'.
You usually say **some advice** or **a piece of advice**: *He gave me some useful **advice**.* • *I want to give you a **piece of advice**.*
✘ Don't say 'an advice'.

ad·vis·a·ble /əd'vaɪzəbəl/ *adjective* (formal) something that is advisable is something that you should do in order to avoid problems: *It's advisable to book your ticket early.*

ad·vise /əd'vaɪz/ *verb*

KEY PATTERNS
advise someone to do something
advise someone against doing something
advise someone on something

to tell someone what you think they should do: *His lawyer **advised** him **to** say nothing.* • *I **advised** her **against** going out with Andy* (=said she should not). • *Can you **advise** me **on** what to wear?*

WORD CHOICE
advise or **advice**?
• **Advise** is a verb: *The doctor **advised** him to get plenty of rest.*
• **Advice** is a noun: *I wanted to ask you for your **advice**.*

ad·vis·er, **advisor** /əd'vaɪzə $ əd'vaɪzə/ *noun* someone whose job is to give advice to a company, government etc: *a financial adviser*

ad·vo·cate¹ /'ædvəkeɪt/ *verb* (formal) to say that you support a particular plan or method: *Doctors advocate a sensible diet and plenty of exercise.*

ad·vo·cate² /'ædvəkət/ *noun* (formal) **1** someone who supports a particular plan or method: *He was an advocate of political reform.* **2** a lawyer who tries to show that someone is not guilty of a crime

aer·i·al¹ /'eəriəl $ 'eriəl/ *adjective* from a plane or happening in the air: *an aerial photograph of the island*

aerial² *noun BrE* an object on top of a building or television that sends or receives radio or television signals SYNONYM **antenna** *AmE*: *The TV aerial blew down in the storm.*

ae·ro·bic /eəˈrəʊbɪk $ əˈroʊbɪk/ *adjective* aerobic exercise is any exercise that makes your heart and lungs strong, such as running or swimming: *an aerobic workout*

aer·o·bics /eəˈrəʊbɪks $ əˈroʊbɪks/ *plural noun* a type of physical exercise that you do with music, especially in a class: *She teaches aerobics.*

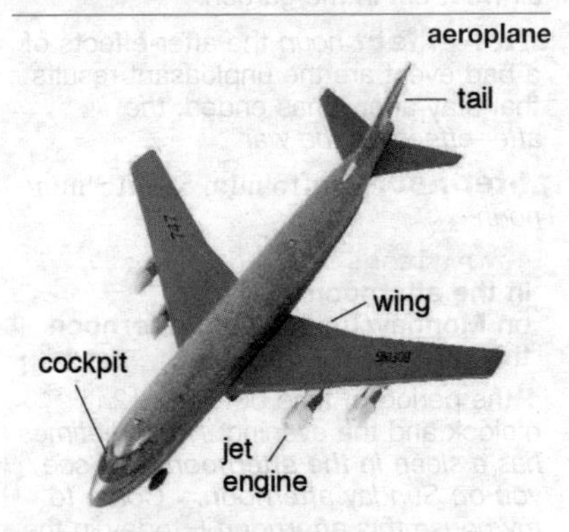

aer·o·plane /ˈeərəpleɪn $ ˈerəˌpleɪn/ *noun BrE* a vehicle with wings and an engine that flies in the air SYNONYM **airplane** *AmE* SYNONYM **plane**: *The aeroplane has landed on time.* → see picture on page A11

aer·o·sol /ˈeərəsɒl $ ˈerəˌsɔl/ *noun* a small metal container with a liquid inside. You press a button on the container to make the liquid come out: *an aerosol deodorant spray*

af·fair /əˈfeə $ əˈfer/ *noun* **1** if two people have an affair, they have a sexual relationship, especially one that is secret because they are married to other people: *She had an affair with her husband's best friend.* **2** a situation that everyone knows about, especially one that involves bad things that important people have done: *Several teachers had to resign over the affair.* **3 affairs** things that are connected with a particular subject, especially business or politics: *He never talked about his business affairs.*

af·fect /əˈfekt/ *verb* to make something or someone different or change in some way: *I hope this new job will not affect your schoolwork.* • *How did the divorce affect the children?*

WORD CHOICE
affect or **effect**?
• **Affect** is a verb: *Smoking* ***affects*** *your health.*
• **Effect** is usually a noun: *The drug has a lot of harmful* ***effects****.*

af·fec·tion /əˈfekʃən/ *noun* a feeling of liking someone and caring about them: *I've always had a great affection for Tim.*

af·fec·tion·ate /əˈfekʃənət/ *adjective* showing that you like or love someone: *He gave her an affectionate hug.* —**affectionately** *adverb*: *He patted his son on the head affectionately.*

af·fin·i·ty /əˈfɪnəti/ *noun* a feeling that you like and understand a person or animal: *He had a remarkable affinity with horses.*

af·fir·ma·tive /əˈfɜːmətɪv $ əˈfɝmətɪv/ *adjective* (formal) meaning 'yes' ANTONYM **negative**: *an affirmative reply*

af·flict /əˈflɪkt/ *verb* (formal) **be afflicted by something** to be badly affected by a serious disease or problem: *a country that is afflicted by disease and famine*

af·flic·tion /əˈflɪkʃən/ *noun* (formal) something that makes people suffer: *Bad eyesight is a common affliction.*

af·flu·ent /ˈæfluənt/ *adjective* having a lot of money and possessions SYNONYM **wealthy**, **rich**: *our affluent western society*

af·ford /əˈfɔːd $ əˈfɔrd/ *verb*

KEY PATTERNS
can afford to do something
can't afford it

to have enough money to buy something: *Can you* ***afford to*** *buy a computer?* • *I want to go on holiday but I* ***can't afford it****.*

af·ford·a·ble /əˈfɔːdəbəl $ əˈfɔrdəbəl/ *adjective* something that is affordable is not too expensive, and you are able to buy it: *It was difficult to find affordable accommodation.*

af·front /əˈfrʌnt/ *noun* (no plural) (formal) something that someone says or does that offends or upsets you: *The people saw the remark as an affront to their religion.*

a•fraid /əˈfreɪd/ *adjective*

KEY PATTERNS
afraid of snakes/heights
afraid that
afraid of making a mistake

1 frightened SYNONYM **scared**: *Don't be afraid, I won't hurt you.* • *Some people are **afraid of** spiders.* → see Thesaurus at FRIGHTENED
2 worried that something may happen: *I was **afraid that** no one would like my paintings.* • *He was **afraid of** offending my father.*

a•fresh /əˈfreʃ/ *adverb* **start afresh** to start again from the beginning: *You'd better start afresh on a clean piece of paper.*

A•fri•can A•mer•i•can /ˌæfrɪkən əˈmerɪkən/ *noun* an American whose family originally came from Africa —**African-American** *adjective*

af•ter¹ /ˈɑːftə $ ˈæftɚ/ *preposition*
1 when something has happened or finished ANTONYM **before**: *I felt much better after my holiday.* • *I'll meet you after school* (=when the school day has finished).
2 when a period of time has passed: *We left after half an hour.*
3 *AmE* later than a particular hour: *It's ten after five* (=it's ten minutes after five o'clock).
4 following someone: *His little sister ran after him.* → see Thesaurus at FOLLOW

PHRASES
after all **a)** used to say that what you expected did not happen: *It didn't rain **after all**.* **b)** used when saying something that shows why you are right: *The accident could have been worse – **after all** no one was killed.*
one after the other with each person or animal following the one in front: *The children went downstairs, **one after the other**.*
day after day, year after year etc (written) used to say that something happens for a long time: ***Day after day** he stayed in his room, studying.*

WORD CHOICE
after or **in**?
• You use **in** when talking about a time in the future: *I'll see you **in** a few days.*
• You use **after** when talking about a period of time in the past: ***After** a few weeks she felt well enough to go back to school.*

after² *conjunction*
when someone has done something or something has finished ANTONYM **before**: *I'll come and talk to you after I've finished this.* • *After we'd had lunch, we all went out in the garden.*

ˈafter-efˌfect *noun* the after-effects of a bad event are the unpleasant results that stay after it has ended: *the after-effects of the war*

af•ter•noon /ˌɑːftəˈnuːn $ ˌæftɚˈnun/ *noun*

KEY PATTERNS
in the afternoon
on Monday/Tuesday etc afternoon
this afternoon

1 the period of time between 12 o'clock and the evening: *He sometimes has a sleep **in the afternoon**.* • *I'll see you **on** Sunday **afternoon**.* • *Come to my house **this afternoon*** (=today in the afternoon). • *There's a good film on TV **tomorrow afternoon**.* • *She's been crying **all afternoon**.*
2 (Good) Afternoon (spoken) used when you meet someone in the afternoon: *Good afternoon, everyone.*

af•ter•shave /ˈɑːftəʃeɪv $ ˈæftɚˌʃeɪv/ *noun* a liquid with a nice smell that a man puts on his skin: *Are you wearing aftershave?*

af•ter•thought /ˈɑːftəθɔːt $ ˈæftɚˌθɔt/ *noun* if you do something as an afterthought, you do it after doing other things, because you forgot to do it earlier: *She invited me to the party, but only as an afterthought.*

af•ter•wards /ˈɑːftəwədz $ ˈæftɚwɚdz/ also **afterward** *AmE* *adverb*
after something has happened: *There will be party games and a disco afterwards.* • *They married, but two years afterwards he died in a car crash.*

THESAURUS
next/then: *First, I told my parents the news. **Next**, I told my best friend, Sam* (=after that).
later: *It's only 2 o'clock. We can go to the shops **later*** (=after the present time).

a·gain /ə'gen/ *adverb*
1 one more time: *I'd like to see that film again.* • *The beaches were very crowded so I don't think I'll go there again.*
2 when you do something or feel something as before: *He should be back at school again soon* (=he should return to school soon). • *There are lots of things I want to do when I'm well again* (=when I'm no longer ill).
PHRASES
all over again used to say that you have to do something for a second time, and that this is a bad thing: *We're going to have to paint the room **all over again**.*
again and again very many times: *I've tried calling him **again and again** but he's never home.* ➔ see Thesaurus at OFTEN

a·gainst /ə'genst/ *preposition*
KEY PATTERNS
against doing something
against the idea of doing something
1 if you are against a plan or action, you do not agree with it: *I'm against testing chemicals on animals* (=I do not think people should do it). • *Philip was against the idea of selling the house.*
2 used to show who someone is fighting or is competing with: *the war against Spain* • *Italy will play in the final against Brazil.*
3 used to show what someone is trying to stop: *The government must take action against homelessness.* • *the war against drugs*
4 used to show that something is touching a surface it is next to: *He leaned his bike against a tree.* • *The cat rubbed itself against my legs.*
PHRASES
against the law, against the rules: *You can't park here, it's **against the law*** (=not allowed by the law).
have nothing against someone to not dislike someone: *I **have nothing against** him personally, but I do not think he is right for the job.*

age¹ /eɪdʒ/ *noun*
your age is the number of years you have lived: *What age were you when your father died?* • *Louise is the same age as me.* • *When you get to my age, you'll understand.* • *people of all different ages*
PHRASES
ten, 40 etc years of age (formal) if someone is ten, 40 etc years of age, they have been alive for ten, 40 etc years: *His sister was born when he was five **years of age**.*
for your age if someone is big, clever etc for their age, they are bigger, more clever etc than other people who are the same age: *Grace is not very big **for her age**.*
under age not old enough to do something legally: *You cannot drive if you are **under age**.*
USAGE
When talking about someone's age, you say *She's six.* or *She's six **years old**.*

age² *verb* if someone ages, they become older and weaker: *Jim had aged a lot since I last saw him.*
—**ageing** *BrE*, **aging** *AmE adjective*: *the country's ageing population*

aged¹ /eɪdʒd/ *adjective* **aged five, aged 15 etc** five, 15 etc years old: *His son is now aged four.*

a·ged² /'eɪdʒɪd/ *adjective* (formal) very old: *his aged mother* ➔ see Thesaurus at OLD

a·gen·cy /'eɪdʒənsi/ *noun* (plural **agencies**) a business that arranges services for people: *I booked my holiday via the travel agency's website.*

a·gen·da /ə'dʒendə/ *noun* a list of the things that people are going to discuss at a meeting: *The next item on the agenda is the school trip.*

a·gent /'eɪdʒənt/ *noun* **1** a person or company that arranges services or does work for other people: *Our company has an agent in Madrid.*
2 someone who tries to get secret information about another government or organization SYNONYM **spy**: *a secret agent*

ag·gra·vate /'ægrəveɪt/ *verb* (formal) **1** to make a bad situation worse: *He aggravated the injury by playing football before he was better.* **2** to annoy someone: *It aggravates me when she doesn't listen to what I say.*

A B C D E F G H I J K L M N O P Q R S T U V W X Y Z

—**aggravating** *adjective*: *Having the radio on all day at work is really aggravating.*

ag·gres·sion /əˈgreʃən/ *noun* (no plural) angry or violent behaviour or feelings: *Sometimes he was bad-tempered and couldn't control his aggression.*

ag·gres·sive /əˈgresɪv/ *adjective* behaving angrily, as if you want to fight or attack someone: *He is very aggressive when he plays football.*
—**aggressively** *adverb*: *He shouted at me aggressively.*

a·gile /ˈædʒaɪl $ ˈædʒəl/ *adjective* able to move quickly and easily: *He was young and agile, and climbed the tree easily.*

a·gi·ta·ted /ˈædʒəteɪtɪd/ *adjective* very worried or upset: *Mum gets very agitated when I'm late.*

a·go /əˈgəʊ $ əˈgoʊ/ *adverb*
use **ago** after a period of time to say how far back in the past something happened: *Rob and Di got married two years ago.* • *Carl left a few moments ago.* • *A very long time ago, this area was covered with trees and grass.*

ag·o·nize also **agonise** *BrE* /ˈægənaɪz/ *verb* to think and worry for a long time about something you have to do: *Don't agonize for too long about any of the exam questions.*

ag·o·niz·ing also **agonising** *BrE* /ˈægənaɪzɪŋ/ *adjective* **1** very painful: *an agonizing injury* **2** making you feel very worried or nervous: *Waiting for the result was agonizing.*

ag·o·ny /ˈægəni/ *noun* very bad pain: *I was in agony before the operation.*

a·gree /əˈgriː/ *verb*

KEY PATTERNS
agree on/about something
agree with someone
agree that
agree to an idea/plan
agree to do something
agree with doing something

1 to have the same opinion as someone else ANTONYM **disagree**: *Paul and I don't* ***agree on*** *everything.* • *I* ***agree about*** *the colour – it's awful.* • *I want you to tell me if you don't* ***agree with*** *me.* • *We all* ***agreed that*** *it was a bad idea.*
2 to say 'yes' when someone asks you to do something: *Do you think she will* ***agree to*** *our plan?* • *Tracy* ***agreed to*** *help her mother.*
3 to think that something is right: *I don't* ***agree with*** *hitting children.*

GRAMMAR
You **agree with** someone or **agree with** someone's opinion.
✘ Don't say 'agree someone' ✘ or 'agree someone's opinion'.
When you are agreeing with a negative statement, you use **no**: *"It isn't very warm today." "****No****, it isn't."*

a·gree·a·ble /əˈgriːəbəl/ *adjective* (formal) pleasant or enjoyable: *a very agreeable meal*

a·greed /əˈgriːd/ *adjective* **1** an agreed amount or arrangement is one that people have all accepted: *The agreed price for the bike was $50.*
2 be agreed on if people are agreed on something, they all accept it: *Are we all agreed on the date for the party?*

a·gree·ment /əˈgriːmənt/ *noun*

KEY PATTERNS
an agreement between people
an agreement to do something

an arrangement or promise between people, countries, or organizations, agreeing to do something: *a trade* ***agreement between*** *Europe and the US* • *We* ***made an agreement*** *to help each other.*

PHRASES
come to an agreement, reach an agreement if two or more people come to an agreement, or if they reach an agreement, they agree about what they are going to do: *I'm sure that we can* ***come to an agreement*** *about this.* • *The company has* ***reached an agreement*** *with the bank.*
in agreement if two or more people are in agreement, they have the same opinion: *If we are all* ***in agreement****, we can start the work tomorrow.*

ag·ri·cul·tural /ˌægrɪˈkʌltʃərəl/ *adjective* related to or used in agriculture: *agricultural machinery*

ag·ri·cul·ture /ˈægrɪˌkʌltʃə $ ˈægrɪˌkʌltʃɚ/ *noun* (no plural) growing crops and keeping animals on farms: *Agriculture in Britain is changing.*

Mark is ahead of Chris.

a•head /ə'hed/ *adverb*

KEY PATTERNS
ahead of someone

1 in front of someone or further forward than someone ANTONYM **behind**: *Lucy and Dave ran on ahead.* • *I could see the mountains **ahead of** us.*
2 going to happen in the future: *I think we have a lot of problems ahead.* • *We have a busy day **ahead of** us tomorrow.*
3 more successful than someone else in a competition ANTONYM **behind**: *The Reds are **ahead of** us in the championship* (=the Reds are more successful than us).

aid /eɪd/ *noun* **1** (no plural) help such as money or food that an organization gives to people: *We are sending aid to the victims of the war.* **2 with the aid of something** using something to help you: *I opened the jar with the aid of a knife.* **3** a thing that helps you do something: *Computers in the classroom are an important teaching aid.*

AIDS /eɪdz/ *noun* (no plural) Acquired Immune Deficiency Syndrome; a very serious disease that stops your body from protecting itself against other diseases

ail•ment /'eɪlmənt/ *noun* an illness that is not very serious: *He misses too much school because of minor ailments.*

aim¹ /eɪm/ *verb*

KEY PATTERNS
aim for success
aim to win/achieve something
aim a gun/camera at something

1 to plan or want to do something: *The government is **aiming for** 100% employment.* • *He says he's **aiming to** win the competition.*
2 to point something in a particular direction: ***Aim** the arrow **at** the target.*

PHRASES
be aimed at someone if something is aimed at a particular group of people, it has been made or designed for them: *Many magazines **are aimed at** teenagers.*
be aimed at doing something if something is aimed at getting a particular result, it is done in a way that will get that result: *The course **is aimed at** building up people's self-confidence.*

aim² *noun*
something that you want to do or get: *My aim is to start my own business.* • *The aim of the game is to get 100 points.* ➔ see Thesaurus at PURPOSE

ain't /eɪnt/ (spoken) a short form of 'am not', 'is not', 'are not', 'has not', or 'have not' that many people think is not correct: *It ain't true!*

air¹ /eə $ er/ *noun* (no plural)
the gases around the Earth which we breathe: *The air is very clean in the mountains.*

PHRASES
fresh air air from outside: *Open the window, I need some **fresh air**.*
the air the space above the ground or around things: *I threw my hat into **the air**.*
an air of something a general appearance or feeling: *There was **an air of** tension in the room.*

air² *verb* (formal) to tell other people your opinions or feelings: *Everyone got a chance to air their complaints.*

'air con,ditioning *noun* (no plural) a system that keeps the air in a building or vehicle at the correct temperature

air•craft /'eəkrɑːft $ 'erkræft/ *noun* (plural **aircraft**) a plane or any vehicle that can fly: *The aircraft can carry 600 passengers.*

air•fare /'eəfeə $ 'erfer/ *noun* the price of a plane trip: *I couldn't afford the airfare to New York.*

'air force *noun* the part of a country's military organization that uses planes to fight: *He's an officer in the air force.*

'air ,hostess *noun BrE* (plural **air hostesses**) a woman whose job is to

A B C D E F G H I J K L M N O P Q R S T U V W X Y Z

help and serve the passengers on a plane SYNONYM **flight attendant**

air·line /ˈeəlaɪn $ ˈerlaɪn/ *noun* a company that carries passengers by plane: *Which airline are you travelling with?*

air·mail /ˈeəmeɪl $ ˈermeɪl/ *noun* (no plural) the system of sending letters and packages by plane: *I sent the letter by airmail.*

air·plane /ˈeəpleɪn $ ˈerpleɪn/ the American word for AEROPLANE ➔ see picture on page A11

air·port /ˈeəpɔːt $ ˈerpɔrt/ *noun* the place where you arrive and leave when you travel by plane: *The plane landed at Sydney airport.*

> **SPELLING**
> This word is often spelled wrongly. The correct spelling is: **airport**.

air·strip /ˈeəˌstrɪp $ ˈerˌstrɪp/ *noun* a long narrow piece of land where planes can come down: *We landed at a small airstrip near Canterbury.*

air·tight /ˈeəˌtaɪt $ ˈerˌtaɪt/ *adjective* completely closed so that air cannot get in or out: *an airtight jar*

aisle /aɪl/ *noun* a long space between rows of seats in a theatre, church, or plane: *Please do not block the aisle.*

a·jar /əˈdʒɑː $ əˈdʒɑr/ *adjective* a door or window that is ajar is not completely closed: *I could hear their conversation because the door was ajar.*

a·larm¹ /əˈlɑːm $ əˈlɑrm/ *noun* **1** (no plural) a feeling of fear because something dangerous might happen: *The police told us there was no cause for alarm.* **2** something that makes a loud noise or produces a bright light that warns people of danger: *The fire alarm started to ring.* • *I'm having an alarm fitted to the house to stop burglars.* **3 false alarm** a warning that something dangerous will happen that you discover later was a mistake or not true: *We thought there was a fire, but it was a false alarm.*

alarm² *verb* to make someone feel very worried or frightened —**alarmed** *adjective*: *Please don't be alarmed, I'm fine.* —**alarming** *adjective*: *An alarming sound downstairs woke me up.*

a'larm clock *noun* a clock that makes a noise to wake you up

alarm clock

al·bum /ˈælbəm/ *noun* **1** a record, CD, or tape that has several songs on it: *Do you want to listen to the new album I bought?* **2** a book with special pages where you can stick photographs or stamps

al·co·hol /ˈælkəhɒl $ ˈælkəˌhɔl/ *noun* (no plural) drinks such as beer and wine, that can make you drunk: *I never drink alcohol.*

al·co·hol·ic¹ /ˌælkəˈhɒlɪk $ ˌælkəˈhɔlɪk/ *adjective* containing alcohol ANTONYM **non-alcoholic**: *an alcoholic drink*

alcoholic² *noun* someone who cannot stop drinking too much alcohol: *He won't admit he's an alcoholic.*

al·co·hol·is·m /ˈælkəhɒlɪzəm $ ˈælkəhɔˌlɪzəm/ *noun* (no plural) the medical condition of being an alcoholic: *Alcoholism is a serious problem.*

a·lert¹ /əˈlɜːt $ əˈlɚt/ *adjective* always watching and ready to act: *The danger seems to have passed, but we must remain alert.*

alert² *verb* to warn someone about a problem or danger: *Police found a bomb and alerted the public.*

alert³ *noun* **be on the alert** to be ready to notice and deal with a problem: *The school warned parents to be on the alert for any signs of illness.*

A lev·el /ˈeɪ ˌlevəl/ *noun* an examination in a particular subject that students take when they are 18 in England, Wales, and Northern Ireland: *I have A levels in French and English.*

al·ge·bra /ˈældʒəbrə/ *noun* (no plural) a type of mathematics that uses letters and signs to show amounts

a·li·as¹ /ˈeɪliəs/ *preposition* used to give another name that someone uses, after giving their real name: *the writer Eric Blair, alias George Orwell*

alias² *noun* (plural **aliases**) a false name, usually used by a criminal: *Bates sometimes uses the alias John Smith.*

al·i·bi /ˈæləbaɪ/ *noun* proof that someone was not at the place where a crime happened: *He has an alibi for the night of the murder.*

a·li·en¹ /ˈeɪliən/ *adjective* very different and strange: *Some tourists may find our culture alien to them at first.*

alien² *noun* **1** a creature that comes from another world: *a film about aliens from Mars* **2** (formal) someone who is not a citizen of the country where they live: *Many illegal aliens are employed in Texas.*

a·li·en·ate /ˈeɪliəneɪt/ *verb* to make someone feel that they do not belong to your group: *We don't want to alienate young people from society.*

a·light /əˈlaɪt/ *adjective* **set something alight** to make something start burning: *The crowd set the building alight.*

a·like /əˈlaɪk/ *adjective* similar or the same: *All the sisters look alike.* → see Thesaurus at SIMILAR

a·live /əˈlaɪv/ *adjective* living and not dead: *The doctors struggled to **keep** him **alive**. • A man was brought out of the wreckage alive.*

all¹ /ɔːl/ *determiner, pronoun*

KEY PATTERNS
all of something
all of us/them

1 the whole of an amount: *Have you done all your homework? • I've spent **all of** my money.*
2 every person or thing: *All children are different. • This affects **all of us**. • We **all** felt sorry for him. • I've lost all my books.*

PHRASES
all day, all year etc for the whole of a day, year etc: *I lay awake **all night**. • It's the best film I've seen **all year**.*
not at all, none at all etc: *I **wasn't at all** worried* (=I wasn't even slightly worried). • *We had **no** money **at all*** (=we didn't have any money).
all the time continuously or very often: *I think about him **all the time**.* → see Thesaurus at ALWAYS

GRAMMAR
Use **all** with a singular verb when you are using a noun that you cannot count: *All the wine is finished.*
Use **all** with a plural verb when you are using a plural noun: *All my friends are coming to the party.*

all² *adverb* **1** (spoken) completely or very: *They were **all alone**. • She got **all** upset.* **2** used to show that two players or teams have an equal amount of points or GOALS: *The score was two all at half time.*

PHRASES
all over in every part of a place: *We looked for him **all over** the house. • He had chocolate **all over** his face.*
→ see Thesaurus at EVERYWHERE
all along from the beginning: *I knew **all along** that we could win.*
all through through the whole time that something continues: *They talked **all through** the film.*

ˈall-around the American word for ALL-ROUND

al·lay /əˈleɪ/ *verb* **allay someone's worries, allay someone's fears** (formal) to make someone feel less worried or frightened: *I tried to allay his fears by telling him the facts.*

ˌall ˈclear *noun* **the all clear** when someone tells you that it is safe to do something: *The pilot got the all clear to take off.*

al·le·ga·tion /ˌælɪˈgeɪʃən/ *noun* if you make an allegation about something, you say that someone has done something bad but you do not prove that it is true SYNONYM **accusation**: *There were allegations that he stole the money.*

al·lege /əˈledʒ/ *verb* to say that someone has done something bad, but not to prove that it is true: *She alleges that he was violent towards her.*

al·le·giance /əˈliːdʒəns/ *noun* loyalty to a leader, country, or team: *They swore allegiance to the king.*

al·ler·gic /əˈlɜːdʒɪk $ əˈlɚdʒɪk/ *adjective* if you are allergic to something, you become ill if you touch, eat, or breathe it: *I am allergic to peanuts.*

al·ler·gy /ˈælədʒi $ ˈælɚdʒi/ *noun* (plural **allergies**) a medical condition that makes you ill when you eat, touch, or breathe a particular thing: *He has an allergy to cats.*

A B C D E F G H I J K L M N O P Q R S T U V W X Y Z

al·ley /ˈæli/ also **al·ley·way** /ˈæliweɪ/ *noun* a narrow path between buildings

al·li·ance /əˈlaɪəns/ *noun* an agreement between countries or groups of people to support each other: *Environmental groups formed an alliance to stop the new road being built.*

al·li·ga·tor /ˈæləgeɪtə $ ˈæləˌgeɪtɚ/ *noun* a large animal with a long body, sharp teeth, and short legs, that lives in hot wet areas

al·lo·cate /ˈæləkeɪt/ *verb* (formal) to decide to use an amount of money, time etc for a particular purpose: *The school has allocated £5,000 for new computers.*

al·low /əˈlaʊ/ *verb*

> KEY PATTERNS
> **allow someone to do something**
> **be allowed to do something**
> **allow something to happen**

1 to say that someone can do something because they have permission: *My father won't **allow** me **to** stay out late.* • *Are you **allowed to** smoke in here?* • *I'd love to come to your party, but I'm not allowed.* ➔ see Thesaurus at FORBID
2 to make it possible for something to happen: *I earned some money, which **allowed** me **to** travel around Europe.*

> THESAURUS
> **let**: *Will your Mum **let** you come to the party* (=allow you to come)?
> **permit** (formal): *Smoking is not **permitted** in this building* (=allowed).

al·low·ance /əˈlaʊəns/ *noun*
1 money that someone gives you regularly or for a special purpose: *Her parents give her a clothes allowance.*
2 make allowances for someone/something to be kinder than usual towards someone when you judge their behaviour because they have a problem: *They made no allowances for her age.*

all right, **al·right** /ɔːlˈraɪt/ *adjective* (spoken) **1** satisfactory or acceptable, but not good SYNONYM **ok**: *"How was your holiday?" "It was all right, but it did rain quite a lot."* ➔ see Thesaurus at SATISFACTORY **2** safe and not hurt or upset SYNONYM **ok**: *Don't worry, I'm sure the kids will be all right.* **3** used to say that you agree to do something SYNONYM **ok**: *"I think we should leave." "All right, we'll go now if you want to."*
4 that's all right a) used to reply to someone who has just thanked you: *"Thanks for the lift." "That's all right."*
b) used to tell someone you are not angry when they tell you something or say they are sorry: *"I'm sorry, but I don't really want to go to a club." "That's all right!"*

ˈall-round *adjective BrE* good at doing many different things, especially in sports SYNONYM **all-around** *AmE*: *an all-round athlete*

al·lude /əˈluːd/ *verb* (formal) **allude to something** to mention something, without saying it directly or clearly: *I think he was alluding to your problems at school.*

al·ly /ˈælaɪ/ *noun* (plural **allies**) a country that helps another country, especially in a war ANTONYM **enemy**: *the US and its European allies*

almond /ˈɑːmənd $ ˈɑː-/ *noun* a flat nut which you can eat ➔ see picture on page A7

al·most /ˈɔːlməʊst $ ˈɔlmoʊst/ *adverb* nearly: *Almost everyone did well in the test* (=only a few people didn't do well). • *I almost forgot to go to my music lesson* (=I remembered just in time). • *I've almost finished* (=I will finish soon). • *It was almost dark.*

> SPELLING
> This word is often spelled wrongly. The correct spelling is: **almost**.

> GRAMMAR
> You usually use **almost** with **all**, **everyone**, or **everything**: *Almost all Japanese people like sushi.* • *Almost everyone agreed that it was a good idea.*
> ✘ Don't say 'Almost Japanese people like sushi.'
> You also use **almost** with a verb, when saying that you have nearly done something: *I've **almost** finished my homework.*

a·lone /əˈləʊn $ əˈloʊn/ *adjective, adverb*
1 not having anyone with you or helping you: *She didn't like being alone in the house.* • *He lives alone now.* • *We*

can't do this alone (=without other people helping us). • *She was* **all alone** *in a strange country* (=completely alone).
2 without anything else: *This disease cannot be cured by drugs alone.*

WORD CHOICE
alone or **lonely**?
• **Alone** means "with no other people": *He lives* **alone**.
• **Lonely** means "unhappy because you do not have people to talk to": *I felt* **lonely** *in my first week at college.*

a·long¹ /əˈlɒŋ $ əˈlɔːŋ/ *preposition* following a road, river, or line: *We were walking along the road, talking.* • *the path along the river* • *Cut along this line.*

along² *adverb*
1 going forward: *He was driving along quite quickly.*
2 (spoken) going somewhere with someone: *Can I* **come along** (=come with you)? • *She'd* **brought** *a couple of friends* **along** (=she'd brought a couple of friends with her).
PHRASES
along with someone or something (written) with someone or something else, at the same time: *Jack was chosen for the team,* **along with** *both his brothers.*

a·long·side /əˌlɒŋˈsaɪd $ əˌlɔːŋˈsaɪd/ *adverb, preposition* close to the side of something: *A police car stopped alongside us.*

a·loud /əˈlaʊd/ *adverb* speaking so that people can hear you SYNONYM **out loud**: *We read our essays aloud.*

al·pha·bet /ˈælfəbet/ *noun* a set of letters that you use to write a language: *the Russian alphabet*

al·pha·bet·i·cal /ˌælfəˈbetɪkəl/ *adjective* arranged in the order of the letters of the alphabet: *The words in this dictionary are in alphabetical order.* —**alphabetically** /-kli/ *adverb*: *The books are arranged alphabetically.*

al·read·y /ɔːlˈredi/ *adverb*
1 before: *I've seen that film already.* • *He's already won three titles this year.* • *When they went in the shop, they had already decided what to buy.*
2 now, rather than later: *I can't wait for Christmas, I'm getting excited already.* • *It was only 11.30, but Pat was already feeling hungry.*

WORD CHOICE
already or **yet**?
• You use **already** in positive statements: *She has* **already** *visited the US three times.*
• You usually use **yet** in negative sentences and questions: *I haven't finished my homework* **yet**. • *Are you in bed* **yet**?
• **Yet** usually comes at the end of a sentence.

al·right /ˌɔːlˈraɪt/ another spelling of ALL RIGHT

al·so /ˈɔːlsəʊ $ ˈɒlsoʊ/ *adverb* use **also** when you want to add a new fact to what you have said or to show that something is true about two people or things: *Jan plays the guitar, and she* **also** *plays the piano.* • *I'd* **also** *like some stamps, please.* • *The sports centre has a large swimming pool, and it* **also** *has a small pool for children.* • *Sophie was tall, and her sister was also.*

WORD CHOICE
also or **not either**?
• You use **also** in positive statements. You use it before a main verb, or after the verb **be**: *She can sing and she can* **also** *play the piano.* • *He's a good actor. He's* **also** *very good looking.*
• In negative sentences you use **not... either**: *She* **doesn't** *play tennis. She* **doesn't** *play badminton* **either**.

WORD CHOICE
also or **too/as well**?
• **Too** and **as well** mean the same as **also**. They are used especially in spoken English. You use them at the end of a sentence: *Can we come too?* • *I like modern music, but I like classical music* **as well**.

al·tar /ˈɔːltə $ ˈɒltər/ *noun* a raised area or table that someone uses to perform a religious ceremony, for example in a church

al·ter /ˈɔːltə $ ˈɒltər/ *verb* to change, or to make something or someone change: *Her tone of voice altered slightly.* • *They had to alter their plans.*
➔ see Thesaurus at CHANGE¹

A B C D E F G H I J K L M N O P Q R S T U V W X Y Z

al·ter·a·tion /ˌɔːltəˈreɪʃən $ ˌɔltəˈreɪʃən/ *noun* if you make an alteration, you change something slightly: *She made a few alterations to the letter.*

al·ter·nate¹ /ɔːlˈtɜːnət $ ˈɔltərnət/ *adjective* **1** happening or arranged in a regular way, first one thing, then the other thing: *The rug had alternate stripes of red, black, and blue.*
2 alternate days, alternate weeks etc if you do something on alternate days, weeks etc, you do it on one of every two days, weeks etc: *We visit my grandma on alternate weekends.* **3** an American word for ALTERNATIVE
—**alternately** *adverb*: *We spend the summers in France and England alternately.*

al·ter·nate² /ˈɔːltəneɪt $ ˈɔltərˌneɪt/ *verb* if two things alternate, first one thing happens, then the other, and this process continues: *She alternated between shouting and crying.*
—**alternating** *adjective*: *alternating periods of sun and rain*

al·ter·na·tive¹ /ɔːlˈtɜːnətɪv $ ɔlˈtərnətɪv/ *adjective* **1** an alternative plan, idea etc can be used instead of another one: *Leave your car at home and use an alternative method of transport.* **2** different from what is usual or accepted: *alternative medicine, such as aromatherapy*

alternative² *noun* something you can choose to do or use instead of something else: *Yoghurt is a healthy alternative to cream.*

al·ter·na·tive·ly /ɔːlˈtɜːnətɪvli $ ɔlˈtərnətɪvli/ *adverb* used to suggest something that someone could do or use instead of something else: *I could call you, or alternatively I could come to your house.*

al·though /ɔːlˈðəʊ $ ɔlˈðoʊ/ *conjunction*
1 in spite of something: *Although she is only seven, she can speak three languages.* • *He lent his friend £20 although he didn't have much money himself.*
2 but: *You can copy my answers, although I'm not sure they're right.*

al·ti·tude /ˈæltətjuːd $ ˈæltəˌtud/ *noun* the height of something above sea level: *Breathing is more difficult at high altitudes.*

al·to /ˈæltəʊ $ ˈæltoʊ/ *noun* a female singer with a low voice or a male singer with a high voice

al·to·geth·er /ˌɔːltəˈgeðə $ ˌɔltəˈgeðər/ *adverb* **1** completely: *Should we allow smoking in certain areas, or ban it altogether?* • *I'm not altogether sure that you're right.*
2 considering everything or including the whole amount: *The bill came to $45 altogether.*

WORD CHOICE
altogether or **all together**?
• You use **all together** when saying that people all do something as a group: *The children jumped up **all together** and ran towards the door.*

al·u·min·i·um /ˌæləˈmɪniəm/ *BrE*, **a·lu·mi·num** /əˈluːmənəm/ *AmE noun* (no plural) a light silver metal

al·ways /ˈɔːlwəz $ ˈɔlweɪz/ *adverb*
1 every time: *You should always clean your teeth after eating sweet things.* • *I always forget her name* (=I never remember her name).
2 for a long time: *I've always wanted to visit Australia.*
3 for ever: *You'll always be my friend.*
4 happening very often: *My dad is always losing his car keys.*

SPELLING
This word is often spelled wrongly. The correct spelling is: **always**.

THESAURUS
all the time: *They seem to argue all the time* (=very often or continuously, especially in an annoying way).
the whole time: *I know he hasn't phoned, because I've been here the whole time* (=continuously).

am /əm; strong æm/ the first person singular present tense of the verb BE

am, a.m. /ˌeɪ ˈem/ **7 am, 9 am etc** 7 or 9 o'clock in the morning, not in the afternoon or evening: *I get up at 8 am.* • *It's 5 a.m.*

am·a·teur /ˈæmətə $ ˈæmətʃər/ *noun* someone who does a particular activity because they enjoy it, not because it is their job ANTONYM **professional**: *He's not* *a professional athlete, but he's a very good amateur.* —**amateur** *adjective*: *an amateur photographer*

a•maze /ə'meɪz/ *verb* if something amazes you, it surprises you a lot SYNONYM **astonish**: *Her skill amazed me.* —**amazed** *adjective*: *I'm amazed that she invited you.* ➔ see Thesaurus at SURPRISED

a•maze•ment /ə'meɪzmənt/ *noun* (no plural) the feeling of being very surprised SYNONYM **astonishment**: *To my amazement, he remembered me.*

a•maz•ing /ə'meɪzɪŋ/ *adjective* very surprising or very good: *Their apartment is amazing.* —**amazingly** *adverb*: *an amazingly high score*

> **USAGE**
> ✘ Don't say 'It's very amazing.' Just say *It's amazing* or *It's absolutely amazing.*

am•bas•sa•dor /æm'bæsədə $ æm'bæsədɚ/ *noun* an important person who lives and works in a foreign country, and whose job is to represent their own country and people there: *the Dutch ambassador to Brazil*

am•bi•ence, **ambiance** /'æmbiəns/ *noun* (no plural) the type of feeling you have because of the place you are in and the people who are there SYNONYM **atmosphere**: *The club has a friendly ambience.*

am•big•u•ous /æm'bɪgjuəs/ *adjective* something that is ambiguous has more than one possible meaning: *His answer was rather ambiguous.*

am•bi•tion /æm'bɪʃən/ *noun* **1** something that you want to achieve in the future: *My ambition is to become a doctor.* **2** (no plural) a strong determination to be successful or powerful: *You need a lot of ambition to succeed as a musician.*

am•bi•tious /æm'bɪʃəs/ *adjective* determined to be successful or powerful: *We are looking for ambitious, hard-working young people.*

am•biv•a•lent /æm'bɪvələnt/ *adjective* (formal) if you feel ambivalent about something, you are not sure whether you like it or not: *Young people may feel ambivalent about leaving home.*

am•bu•lance /'æmbjələns/ *noun* a special vehicle for taking ill people to hospital: *I asked a neighbour to call an ambulance.*

am•bush /'æmbʊʃ/ *noun* (plural **ambushes**) a sudden attack by people who have been waiting and hiding: *Three US soldiers were killed in an ambush.* —**ambush** *verb*: *Two men ambushed him in the forest.*

a•mend /ə'mend/ *verb* (formal) to make small changes to a law, rule, system, or piece of writing: *The examination system has been amended several times.*

a•mend•ment /ə'mendmənt/ *noun* a change made in a law or document: *We made a few amendments to the contract.*

a•mends /ə'mendz/ *noun* **make amends** to do something to show that you are sorry for hurting or upsetting someone: *I sent my mom chocolates to make amends for not visiting her.*

a•me•ni•ty /ə'miːnəti $ ə'menəti/ *noun* (formal) (plural **amenities**) something useful or enjoyable in a place that makes it nice to live there: *The town's amenities include a sports ground and cinemas.*

A•mer•i•can[1] /ə'merəkən/ *adjective* **1** from or connected with the United States: *American cars* **2** **North American, South American** from or connected with one of the countries in North America or South America

American[2] *noun* someone from the United States: *She married an American.*

A,merican 'football *noun* (no plural) *BrE* a game played in the US in which two teams wearing special clothes to protect them carry, kick, and throw a ball SYNONYM **football** *AmE* ➔ see picture on page A14

am•i•ca•ble /'æmɪkəbəl/ *adjective* (formal) done in a friendly way, without arguing: *My parents' divorce was quite amicable.*

a•miss /ə'mɪs/ *adjective* **be amiss** (formal) if something is amiss, there is a problem SYNONYM **be wrong**: *I checked the house, but nothing was amiss.*

A B C D E F G H I J K L M N O P Q R S T U V W X Y Z

am·mu·ni·tion /ˌæmjəˈnɪʃən/ *noun* (no plural) bullets that people fire from a weapon such as a gun: *The soldiers had no ammunition left.*

am·nes·ty /ˈæmnəsti/ *noun* (plural **amnesties**) a period of time when a government lets some people leave prison or does not punish people: *The new government announced an amnesty for political prisoners.*

a·mong /əˈmʌŋ/ also **a·mongst** /əˈmʌŋst/ *preposition*
1 used to say which group of people is affected by something: *The disease is quite common among young people.* • *There is a lot of concern among parents about this problem.*
2 (written) surrounded by things: *He hid among the bushes.*
3 used to say that part of something is given to each person in a group: *She shared the sweets among the children.*

PHRASES

among yourselves with each other: *Just talk* ***among yourselves*** *until I'm ready to begin the lesson* (=talk to each other). • *The soldiers ended up fighting* ***among themselves*** (=fighting with each other).

> **WORD CHOICE**
> **among** or **between**?
> • **Among** means "surrounded by people or things": *The letter was hidden* ***among*** *the other things on my desk.*
> • **Between** means "with one thing or person on each side": *The bank is* ***between*** *the cinema and the post office.*

a·mount¹ /əˈmaʊnt/ *noun*

> **KEY PATTERNS**
> **an amount of money/time/goods**

a quantity of something, for example money: *A large* ***amount of*** *jewellery was stolen.* • *Kevin gets £5 a week from his parents, but Jo gets half that amount.*

amount² *verb* **amount to a)** to be the same as something or to have the same effect: *What she said* ***amounted to*** *a criticism of her father.* **b)** to add up to a particular total: *My debts* ***amount to*** *over £500.*

amp /æmp/ *noun* **1** also **am·pere** /ˈæmpeə $ æmpɪr/ a unit for measuring an electric current **2** (informal) an AMPLIFIER

am·ple /ˈæmpəl/ *adjective* more than enough: *There was ample food for everyone.*

am·pli·fi·er /ˈæmpləfaɪə $ ˈæmpləˌfaɪɚ/ *noun* a piece of electronic equipment that you use to make music louder

am·pu·tate /ˈæmpjəteɪt/ *verb* to cut off a part of someone's body for medical reasons: *His leg was amputated after a car crash.*

a·muse /əˈmjuːz/ *verb* if something amuses you, it makes you laugh or smile: *His jokes always amuse me.* —**amused** *adjective*: *He was highly amused by my story.* —**amusing** *adjective*: *an amusing joke* ➔ see Thesaurus at FUNNY

a·muse·ment /əˈmjuːzmənt/ *noun* (no plural) the feeling that you want to laugh or smile: *They watched with amusement as I tried to catch the cat.*

aˈmusement ˌpark *noun* a large park where people can enjoy themselves, for example by riding on big machines such as ROLLER COASTERS

an·aes·thet·ic *BrE*, **anesthetic** *AmE* /ˌænəsˈθetɪk/ *noun* a drug that stops you feeling pain, used during a medical operation: *You will have an anaesthetic before the operation.*

a·naes·the·tist *BrE*, **anesthetist** *AmE* /əˈniːsθətɪst $ əˈnestətɪst/ *noun* a doctor whose job is to give anaesthetics to people

an·a·gram /ˈænəgræm/ *noun* a word or phrase that you make by changing the order of the letters in another word or phrase: *'Dear' is an anagram of 'read'.*

a·nal·o·gy /əˈnælədʒi/ *noun* (plural **analogies**) a way of explaining one thing by showing how it is similar to another thing: *He made an analogy between the brain and a computer.*

an·a·lyse *BrE*, **analyze** *AmE* /ˈænl-aɪz/ *verb* to examine something carefully so that you understand what it is or why it happens: *Scientists are still analysing the results of the experiment.*

a·nal·y·sis /əˈnæləsəs/ *noun* (plural **analyses** /-siːz/) a careful examination of something so that you understand more about it: *an analysis of blood samples*

an·a·lyst /ˈænl-ɪst/ *noun* **1** someone whose job is to analyse a subject and explain it to other people: *a political analyst* **2** a PSYCHOANALYST

an·ar·chist /ˈænəkɪst $ ˈænərkɪst/ *noun* someone who believes that there should be no government or laws

an·ar·chy /ˈænəki $ ˈænərki/ *noun* (no plural) a situation in which people do not obey the rules or laws and no one has control: *For a time, the country was close to political anarchy.*

a·nat·o·my /əˈnætəmi/ *noun* (no plural) the scientific study of the structure of the body

an·ces·tor /ˈænsəstə $ ˈænˌsestər/ *noun* a person in your family who lived a very long time ago: *Her ancestors came from Ireland.*

an·ces·try /ˈænsəstri $ ˈænˌsestri/ *noun* (no plural) your ancestors, or the place they came from: *He is of German ancestry.*

an·chor /ˈæŋkə $ ˈæŋkər/ *noun* **1** a heavy metal object on a chain or rope that you put into the water to stop a ship or boat moving: *They sailed into the harbour, then dropped anchor.* **2** a NEWSREADER

an·cient /ˈeɪnʃənt/ *adjective* many hundreds of years old: *an ancient temple* ➔ see Thesaurus at OLD

and /ən, ənd; strong ænd/ *conjunction* **1** used when adding something to what you are saying: *I have one brother and two sisters.* • *The house was large and very old.* • *She finished her homework and went to bed.* • *He fell over and hurt his arm.* **2** used when adding numbers SYNONYM **plus**: *What's eight and seventeen?*

an·ec·dote /ˈænɪkdəʊt $ ˈænɪkˌdoʊt/ *noun* an interesting or funny story about something that really happened: *He told a funny anecdote about his day at work.*

anesthetic the American spelling of ANAESTHETIC

anesthetist the American spelling of ANAESTHETIST

an·gel /ˈeɪndʒəl/ *noun* **1** in the Christian religion, an angel is a SPIRIT who lives with God in heaven **2** (spoken) someone who is very good or kind: *Joe is such a little angel.*

an·ger¹ /ˈæŋɡə $ ˈæŋɡər/ *noun* (no plural) a strong feeling of wanting to shout at someone or hurt them because they have done something bad: *I felt such anger when I saw what the burglars had done.*

anger² *verb* (formal) to make someone feel angry: *The school's decision has angered parents.*

an·gle /ˈæŋɡəl/ *noun* **1** the space between two lines or surfaces that meet, measured in degrees: *an angle of 45°* **2 at an angle** not straight or flat: *The painting was hanging at an angle.* **3** a way of thinking about something: *Let's look at the problem from a different angle.*

an·gling /ˈæŋɡlɪŋ/ *noun* (no plural) the activity of trying to catch fish with a hook on the end of a line SYNONYM **fishing**

an·gry /ˈæŋɡri/ *adjective* (**angrier**, **angriest**)

KEY PATTERNS
angry about something
angry with someone
angry that

if you are angry, you feel anger towards someone who has done something bad: *My father was* ***angry about*** *the broken window.* • *I was* ***angry with*** *him for laughing at me.* • *Will Simon be* ***angry that*** *I forgot his birthday?*
—**angrily** *adverb*: *"It's not funny," my mother said angrily.*

THESAURUS
furious: *He was* ***furious*** *when he saw the damage to his car* (=very angry).
mad (spoken): *My parents will be mad with me when they see what's happened to their car* (=very angry).
annoyed: *I was* ***annoyed*** *with him for being late* (=slightly angry).
bad-tempered: *The taxi driver was a* ***bad-tempered*** *old man* (=he often behaved in an unfriendly and angry way).

A B C D E F G H I J K L M N O P Q R S T U V W X Y Z

an·guish /ˈæŋgwɪʃ/ *noun* (no plural) (written) very great pain or worry: *She suffered the anguish of losing her baby in the accident.*

an·gu·lar /ˈæŋgjələ $ ˈæŋgjələr/ *adjective* something that is angular has sharp corners

an·i·mal /ˈænəməl/ *noun* a living thing that can move around and is not a bird, insect, or fish: *farm animals* • *The children went to see the animals in the zoo.* ➔ see pictures on page A8 and A9

ˌanimal ˈrights *noun* the idea that people should not hurt animals or use them to do things such as test medicines etc

an·i·mat·ed /ˈænəmeɪtɪd/ *adjective* **1** interesting and with lots of energy: *We had a lively and animated discussion about music.* **2** an animated film is one in which drawings of people or things seem to move and talk

an·i·ma·tion /ˌænəˈmeɪʃən/ *noun* (no plural) the process of making films or computer games with drawings that seem to move and talk

an·kle /ˈæŋkəl/ *noun* the part of your body where your foot joins your leg: *I tripped and hurt my ankle.* ➔ see picture on page A5

an·nexe *BrE*, **annex** *AmE* /ˈæneks/ *noun* a separate building that is attached to a bigger one: *Our house has a separate annexe where my grandparents live.*

an·ni·hi·late /əˈnaɪəleɪt/ *verb* (formal) to destroy something or defeat someone completely: *In 1314, the English army was annihilated by the Scots.*

an·ni·ver·sa·ry /ˌænəˈvɜːsəri $ ˌænəˈvɜrsəri/ *noun* (plural **anniversaries**) a date that is special because it is exactly a year or a number of years after an important event: *Today is my parents' 25th wedding anniversary* (=today, it is exactly 25 years since their wedding).

an·nounce /əˈnaʊns/ *verb*

> KEY PATTERNS
> **announce the result**
> **announce that**

to say something in public: *The judges are ready to announce the winner.* • *He suddenly* ***announced that*** *he was leaving.*

an·nounce·ment /əˈnaʊnsmənt/ *noun* an official statement about something important: *They're going to make an announcement this afternoon.*

an·noy /əˈnɔɪ/ *verb* if someone or something annoys you, they make you feel slightly angry SYNONYM **irritate**: *Stop annoying your father.* • *It really annoys me when people are late.* —**annoying** *adjective*: *She has an annoying laugh.*

an·noy·ance /əˈnɔɪəns/ *noun* (no plural) the feeling of being annoyed: *I tried not to show my annoyance.*

an·noyed /əˈnɔɪd/ *adjective* slightly angry SYNONYM **irritated**: *She gets annoyed with me for being untidy.* • *I'm annoyed that he didn't reply.* ➔ see Thesaurus at ANGRY

an·nu·al /ˈænjuəl/ *adjective* happening once each year SYNONYM **yearly**: *the school's annual concert* • *The annual fee is £25.*

a·non·y·mous /əˈnɒnəməs $ əˈnɑnəməs/ *adjective* someone who is anonymous does not tell you what their name is: *The person who complained wishes to remain anonymous.* —**anonymously** *adverb*: *He wrote anonymously to the newspaper.*

an·o·rex·i·a /ˌænəˈreksiə/ *noun* (no plural) a mental illness that makes someone stop eating because they believe they are fat: *Many teenage girls suffer from anorexia.*

an·o·rex·ic /ˌænəˈreksɪk/ *adjective* someone who is anorexic is very thin and ill because they have anorexia

an·oth·er /əˈnʌðə $ əˈnʌðər/ *determiner, pronoun*
1 an additional thing or person: *Have another biscuit.* • *I think we will stay for another week.* ➔ see Thesaurus at MORE
2 a different thing or person: *She's trying to find another job.* • *students from another country*

> WORD CHOICE
> **another** or **other**?
> • You use **another** with a singular noun: *Do you want* ***another*** *coffee?*

• You use **other** with a plural noun: *People often move to **other** countries.*
✘ Don't say 'People often move to another countries.'

an·swer¹ /ˈɑːnsə $ ˈænsɚ/ *verb*

KEY PATTERNS
answer a question
answer someone
answer that

1 to say something after someone has asked you a question: *"How old is Brian?" "I don't know," Mary answered.* • *He refused to **answer my questions**.* • *She thought for a minute before answering him.* • *When I asked his name, she **answered that** she could not remember.*
2 to say or write something in reply to a question in a test or competition: *I didn't have time to answer all the questions.*

PHRASES
answer the telephone to pick up the telephone when it rings and speak into it
answer the door to go to open the door when someone knocks or rings the bell

GRAMMAR
You **answer someone** or **answer a question or a letter**.
✘ Don't say 'answer to a question/letter'.

answer² *noun*

KEY PATTERNS
an answer to a question
give someone an answer
an answer to a problem

1 a reply to something that someone asks you: *I don't know the **answer to** your question.* • *I will **give** you my **answer** tomorrow.*
2 a reply to a question in a test or competition: *What is the **answer to** the first question?*
3 something that solves a problem SYNONYM **solution**: *Could this be the **answer to** all our problems?*

ˈanswering maˌchine also **an·swer·phone** /ˈɑːnsəfəʊn $ ˈænsɚˌfoʊn/ *BrE noun* a machine that answers the telephone for you and records messages from the people who are calling: *I left a message on his answering machine.*

ant /ænt/ *noun* a small red or black insect that lives in large groups

An·tarc·tic /ænˈtɑːktɪk $ ænˈtɑrktɪk/ *noun* **the Antarctic** the most southern part of the world, where it is very cold

an·ten·na /ænˈtenə/ *noun* **1** (plural **antennae**) one of two long thin parts on an insect's head that it uses to feel things **2** the American word for AERIAL

an·them /ˈænθəm/ *noun* a serious song that people sing at special events: *We stood up to sing the national anthem* (=a song that belongs to a country and its people).

an·thro·pol·o·gy /ˌænθrəˈpɒlədʒi $ ˌænθrəˈpɑlədʒi/ *noun* (no plural) the scientific study of people and their origins, customs, beliefs etc: *I'm interested in African anthropology.*

an·ti·bi·ot·ic /ˌæntɪbaɪˈɒtɪk $ ˌæntɪbaɪˈɑtɪk/ *noun* a medicine that doctors give to people who are ill with an infection, to make them better again: *The doctor gave me some antibiotics for my cold.*

an·tic·i·pate /ænˈtɪsəpeɪt/ *verb* to expect something to happen: *We anticipate about 1,000 visitors at the exhibition.*

an·tic·i·pa·tion /ænˌtɪsəˈpeɪʃən/ *noun* (no plural) a hopeful or slightly nervous feeling that you have when something exciting is going to happen: *The audience waited in eager anticipation.*

an·ti·cli·max /ˌæntɪˈklaɪmæks/ *noun* (plural **anticlimaxes**) something that is not as exciting as you expected: *It was an exciting film, but the end was an anticlimax.*

an·ti·clock·wise /ˌæntɪˈklɒkwaɪz $ ˌæntɪˈklɑkwaɪz/ *adjective, adverb BrE* moving in the opposite direction to the hands of a clock SYNONYM **counterclockwise** *AmE* ANTONYM **clockwise**: *Turn the handle anticlockwise.*

an·tics /ˈæntɪks/ *plural noun* funny, silly, or annoying behaviour: *We laughed at the children's antics.*

A B C D E F G H I J K L M N O P Q R S T U V W X Y Z

an·ti·dote /ˈæntɪdəʊt $ ˈæntɪˌdoʊt/ *noun* **1** something that makes a bad situation better: *Laughter can be an antidote to stress.* **2** a substance that stops a poison harming or killing someone

an·tique /ˌænˈtiːk/ *noun* an old piece of furniture, jewellery etc that costs a lot of money: *My grandmother wears an antique wedding ring.* —**antique** *adjective*: *an antique chair* ➔ see Thesaurus at OLD ➔ see picture at OLD

an·ti·sep·tic /ˌæntɪˈseptɪk/ *noun* a substance that kills harmful BACTERIA, for example on your skin —**antiseptic** *adjective*: *antiseptic cream*

an·ti·so·cial /ˌæntɪˈsəʊʃəl $ ˌæntiˈsoʊʃəl/ *adjective* antisocial behaviour upsets or annoys other people: *It's considered very antisocial to drop litter in the street.*

ant·ler /ˈæntlə $ ˈæntlɚ/ *noun* one of the two horns on the head of male DEER

antler

antlers

an·to·nym /ˈæntənɪm/ *noun* a word that means the opposite of another word in the same language: *'Finish' is an antonym of 'start'.*

a·nus /ˈeɪnəs/ *noun* (formal) the hole near your bottom from which solid waste material leaves your body

anx·i·e·ty /æŋˈzaɪəti/ *noun* (plural **anxieties**) a strong feeling of worry that something bad may happen: *He has caused his family a lot of anxiety.*

anx·ious /ˈæŋkʃəs/ *adjective*

KEY PATTERNS
anxious about something
anxious for someone to do something
anxious to do something
anxious that

1 very worried: *Many students get anxious about exams.* • *the children's anxious faces* ➔ see Thesaurus at WORRIED
2 wanting something to happen very much SYNONYM **keen**: *She was anxious for everyone to enjoy the food.* • *Police are anxious to interview a man who was seen running away.* • *We are anxious that nobody should be upset.*

an·y[1] /ˈeni/ *determiner, pronoun*
1 use **any** in negative statements when there is not even a small amount or not even one thing: *There weren't any children playing in the street.* • *I don't have any money with me.* • *No thanks, I don't want any.* • *She didn't eat any of her dinner.*
2 use **any** in questions to mean 'some', when you do not know what the answer will be: *Is there any cake left?* • *Did he bring any pictures of his holiday?*
3 use **any** to talk about each one of the people or things in a group, when it is not important to say exactly which one: *You can buy the magazine at any good bookstore.* • *I'm sure any student would use this a lot.* • *If any of you are interested in going, call Debbie.*

WORD CHOICE
all, **any**, or **every**?
• If something is true about everyone in a group, you use **all** or **every**: *All parents love their children.* or *Every parent loves their children.*
✘ Don't say 'Any parents love their children.'

any[2] *adverb*
1 use **any** in negative sentences to emphasize what you are saying: *I couldn't walk any further.* • *It doesn't make the job any easier.*
2 use **any** in questions to mean 'at all' or 'in any way': *Are you feeling any better?*

an·y·bod·y /ˈeniˌbɒdi $ ˈeniˌbɑdi/ *pronoun* anyone

an·y·how /ˈenihaʊ/ *adverb* (informal) anyway

any more, **an·y·more** /ˌeniˈmɔː $ ˌeniˈmɔr/ *adverb* **not anymore** if something does not happen any more, it used to happen in the past but it does not happen now: *I don't go out with him any more.*

an·y·one /ˈeniwʌn/ *pronoun* any person: *Would anyone like some more cake?* • *I cannot see anyone I* *know.* • *Don't tell* **anyone else** (=any other person) *about this.* • *It's easy – anyone can do it.*

an·y·place /ˈenipleɪs/ *adverb AmE* anywhere

an·y·thing /ˈeniθɪŋ/ *pronoun* one thing of any kind: *Did he seem worried about anything?* • *Do you need* **anything else***?* (=any other thing) • *She couldn't think of anything to say.* • *I'll do anything that needs doing.*

an·y·way /ˈeniweɪ/ also **anyhow** *adverb*
1 in spite of something: *Catherine wasn't sure the book was the right one, but she bought it anyway.* • *We might not take any pictures, but we'll take the camera anyway.*
2 used when changing the subject you are talking about: *So we all had a great time. Anyway, what have you been doing?*
3 used when adding another reason for something: *I didn't buy the suit because I couldn't afford it, and anyway it was the wrong colour.*

an·y·where /ˈeniweə $ ˈeniˌwer/ *adverb* in any one place: *I can't find my purse anywhere.* • *You can sit anywhere you like.* • *If you could travel anywhere in the world, where would you go?*

a·part /əˈpɑːt $ əˈpɑrt/ *adverb* not together: *I get very sad when we are apart.* • *My mother and father live apart.* • *Kim* **sat apart from** *the rest of the children.*

PHRASES

apart from except for: *Everyone came to the party* **apart from** *Sue.* • **Apart from** *a wooden table, the room was empty.*

5 cm apart, three days apart etc separated by 5 cm, three days etc: *Plant the seeds three inches apart.* • *Our birthdays are only two days apart.*

take something apart to separate something into parts: *The mechanic* **took** *the engine* **apart***.*

fall apart, come apart to break into many pieces: *She wore the coat until it* **fell apart***.*

a·part·ment /əˈpɑːtmənt $ əˈpɑrtmənt/ *noun* a set of rooms on one floor of a large building, where someone lives SYNONYM **flat** *BrE*: *Let's meet at your apartment.*

> **SPELLING**
> This word is often spelled wrongly. The correct spelling is: **apartment**.

ap·a·thet·ic /ˌæpəˈθetɪk/ *adjective* not interested in anything and not wanting to try: *People here are too apathetic to run a youth club.*

ap·a·thy /ˈæpəθi/ *noun* (no plural) when people are not interested and do not want to try: *There's a lot of apathy about politics nowadays.*

ape /eɪp/ *noun* a large monkey without a tail, such as a GORILLA

a·pol·o·get·ic /əˌpɒləˈdʒetɪk $ əˌpɑləˈdʒetɪk/ *adjective* saying that you are sorry for something bad you have done: *He was really apologetic about the mess.* —**apologetically** /-kli/ *adverb*

a·pol·o·gize also **apologise** *BrE* /əˈpɒlədʒaɪz $ əˈpɑləˌdʒaɪz/ *verb*

> **KEY PATTERNS**
> **I apologize**
> **apologize for doing something**
> **apologize for something**
> **apologize to someone**

to tell someone that you are sorry for something bad that you did: *I have behaved very badly, and I apologize.* • *She apologized for her bad behaviour.* • *He came in,* **apologizing for** *being late.* • *I think you should* **apologize to** *your teacher.*

> **GRAMMAR**
> You **apologize to** someone **for** something.
> ✘ Don't say 'apologize someone'.

a·pol·o·gy /əˈpɒlədʒi $ əˈpɑlədʒi/ *noun* (plural **apologies**) something that you say or write to show that you are sorry for something bad you have done: *She forgot my birthday so I'm expecting an apology.* • *a letter of apology*

a·pos·tro·phe /əˈpɒstrəfi $ əˈpɑstrəfi/ *noun* **1** the sign (') used to show that one or more letters are missing, such as in the word 'don't' (=do not) **2** the sign (') used before or after the letter 's' to show that

A B C D E F G H I J K L M N O P Q R S T U V W X Y Z

something belongs to someone: *Lucy's friends* • *my parents' house*

USAGE
You use an apostrophe (') when you miss out part of a word or number: *aren't* (=are not) • *I'd* (=I would) • *'08* (=2008)
You use an apostrophe to show that something belongs to someone or is concerned with something: ***George's** house* • *the **company's** image*
You use an apostrophe when something belongs to or is for a group of people: *the **teachers'** room* • ***women's** magazines*
If something is part of a building, or belongs to an organization, you often do not use an apostrophe.
You say **the hotel restaurant**.
✘ Don't say 'the hotel's restaurant'.
You say **the school bus**.
✘ Don't say 'the school's bus'.

ap·pal *BrE*, **appall** *AmE* /əˈpɔːl/ *verb* (**appalled**, **appalling**) if something appals you, it shocks you because it is so unpleasant SYNONYM **horrify**: *The idea of killing animals appals me.*
—**appalled** *adjective*: *We were appalled at the price of the meal.*
—**appalling** *adjective*: *appalling cruelty*

ap·pa·ra·tus /ˌæpəˈreɪtəs $ ˌæpəˈrætəs/ *noun* (plural **apparatus** or **apparatuses**) a set of equipment or tools that you use for a particular purpose: *The school needs new science apparatus.*

ap·par·ent /əˈpærənt/ *adjective*
1 easy to see or understand SYNONYM **clear**: *From her behaviour, it was apparent that she liked him.* **2** seeming to be true or real: *He found the apparent cause of the problem.*

ap·par·ent·ly /əˈpærəntli/ *adverb* used to say that something seems to be true or you have heard it is true: *Apparently, he doesn't like his job.*

ap·peal¹ /əˈpiːl/ *verb*

KEY PATTERNS
appeal for help/money
appeal to someone to help
something appeals to someone

1 to ask people for something publicly: *The organization is **appealing for** more money to help the earthquake victims.* • *The police **appealed to** local people **to** help.*
2 if something appeals to you, you like it: *Camping has never **appealed to** me.*

appeal² *noun*

KEY PATTERNS
an appeal for help/money
the appeal of something

1 when an organization asks for something such as money or help: *Oxfam launched **an appeal for** food and clothing* (=announced). • *The police appeal for information was successful.*
2 the quality of something that makes you like it or want it: *Just what is **the appeal of** fast motorbikes?*

ap·peal·ing /əˈpiːlɪŋ/ *adjective* attractive or interesting: *That's an appealing idea.*

ap·pear /əˈpɪə $ əˈpɪr/ *verb*

KEY PATTERNS
appear to think/feel/be

1 to seem: *She **appeared to** think I was joking.* • *You **appear to** be very nervous.* • *Everyone appeared very relaxed.* → see Thesaurus at SEEM
2 if something appears, you see it for the first time ANTONYM **disappear**: *Clouds started to appear in the sky.*

ap·pear·ance /əˈpɪərəns $ əˈpɪrəns/ *noun*
1 your appearance is what you look like, for example your hair colour and height: *He worries about his appearance.* • *The wig completely changed her appearance.*
2 when someone or something arrives: *The crowd cheered as the band **made their appearance** on stage.*

ap·pen·di·ci·tis /əˌpendəˈsaɪtəs/ *noun* (no plural) an illness in which your appendix hurts a lot

ap·pen·dix /əˈpendɪks/ *noun* **1** a small organ inside your body, near your stomach **2** (plural **appendixes** or **appendices** /-dɪsiːz/) a part at the end of a book that has additional information: *There is a list of dates in the appendix.*

ap·pe·tite /ˈæpətaɪt/ *noun* the feeling that makes you want to eat: *That walk has given me an appetite.*

ap·plaud /ə'plɔːd/ *verb* to hit your hands together to show that you have enjoyed a performance SYNONYM **clap**: *Everyone applauded after the speech.*

ap·plause /ə'plɔːz/ *noun* (no plural) the sound of people hitting their hands together to show that they have enjoyed a performance: *There was applause from the fans as the team left the field.*

ap·ple /'æpəl/ *noun* a hard round red or green fruit that is white inside
➔ see picture on page A7

ap·pli·ance /ə'plaɪəns/ *noun* a piece of electrical equipment that people use in their homes: *kitchen appliances*
➔ see Thesaurus at MACHINE

ap·plic·a·ble /ə'plɪkəbəl $ 'æplɪkəbəl/ *adjective* concerning or involving a particular person or situation: *Question 8 on the form is only applicable to married people.*

ap·pli·cant /'æplɪkənt/ *noun* someone who has formally asked for a job, a place at a college etc: *We have too many applicants for the course.*

ap·pli·ca·tion /ˌæplɪ'keɪʃən/ *noun* **1** a letter or other document in which someone officially asks for a job, place at a college etc: *The college lost my application.* **2** a way in which something can be used: *His new invention has many different applications.* **3** a computer program

ˌappli'cation ˌform *noun* a document on which you give answers to questions about yourself. You complete an application form when you are asking for something officially: *You can fill in the job application form online.* • *I had to complete an application form to get my passport.*

ap·ply /ə'plaɪ/ *verb* (**applied**, **applies**)

KEY PATTERNS
apply for a job/place
apply to students/employees
apply paint to a wall

1 to ask for something in writing, such as a job, a place at a college etc: *I* ***applied for*** *a place on the computing course.*
2 to concern or affect a particular person or situation: *This rule* ***applies to*** *both girls and boys.*
3 to spread something such as paint or a cream on a surface: *Stir the paint well, then apply it to the wall.* • *Don't forget to apply sun cream.*

ap·point /ə'pɔɪnt/ *verb* to choose someone for an important job: *They have appointed a new school principal.*

ap·point·ment /ə'pɔɪntmənt/ *noun* **1** a meeting that has been arranged for a particular time and place: *I made an appointment with the doctor.* **2** when someone is chosen for an important job: *the appointment of a new Finance Minister*

ap·pre·ci·ate /ə'priːʃieɪt/ *verb* **1** to understand what something is really like, especially how good it is: *Being at college made me appreciate my family more.* **2** to be grateful for something: *Thanks, I appreciate your help.*

ap·pre·ci·a·tion /əˌpriːʃi'eɪʃən/ *noun* the feeling of being grateful to someone because they have helped you: *I gave her some flowers to show my appreciation.*

ap·pre·cia·tive /ə'priːʃətɪv/ *adjective* showing that you have enjoyed something or feel grateful for it: *The audience was very appreciative.*

ap·pre·hen·sive /ˌæprɪ'hensɪv/ *adjective* worried or nervous about something you have to do in the future: *I'm apprehensive about taking my driving test.*

ap·pren·tice /ə'prentɪs/ *noun* someone who works for an employer for an agreed amount of time in order to learn a skill

ap·proach[1] /ə'prəʊtʃ $ ə'proʊtʃ/ *verb* **1** to move closer to someone or something: *A man approached me and asked me the time.* **2** (formal) to ask someone for something: *I approached my father for some money.*

approach[2] *noun* (plural **approaches**) a way of doing something or dealing with a problem: *a new approach to language teaching*

ap·proach·a·ble /ə'prəʊtʃəbəl $ ə'proʊtʃəbəl/ *adjective* friendly and easy to talk to: *Our school principal is very approachable.*

ap·pro·pri·ate /ə'prəʊpri-ət $ ə'proʊpri-ət/ *adjective* suitable or

A B C D E F G H I J K L M N O P Q R S T U V W X Y Z

right for a particular time, situation, or purpose ANTONYM **inappropriate**: *It is not appropriate to shout in church.* • *I chose an appropriate gift.* • *Those clothes are not appropriate for a job interview.* —**appropriately** *adverb*: *Make sure you are dressed appropriately.*

ap·prov·al /əˈpruːvəl/ *noun* (no plural)

KEY PATTERNS
approval for a plan/idea

1 an official statement saying that someone allows you to do something: *We are waiting for* ***approval for*** *our project.*
2 someone's approval is their opinion that someone or something is good: *She was desperate for her teacher's approval.*

ap·prove /əˈpruːv/ *verb*

KEY PATTERNS
approve of doing something
approve of someone
approve of someone doing something

1 to think that something or someone is good or suitable ANTONYM **disapprove**: *She doesn't* ***approve of*** *eating meat.* • *Mum has never* ***approved of*** *any of my girlfriends.* • *Do you* ***approve of*** *people smoking in public places?*
2 to officially agree to something: *The committee approved the plan.*

ap·prox /əˈprɒks $ əˈprɑks/ *adverb* the written abbreviation of 'approximately'

ap·prox·i·mate /əˈprɒksəmət $ əˈprɑksəmət/ *adjective* nearly right but not exact: *The approximate cost of the building will be £500,000.*

ap·prox·i·mate·ly /əˈprɒksəmətli $ əˈprɑksəmətli/ *adverb* a little more or less than an exact number, amount etc SYNONYM **about, roughly**: *It will take approximately 15 minutes to walk to the station.* ➔ see Thesaurus at ABOUT²

SPELLING
This word is often spelled wrongly. The correct spelling is: **approximately**.

A·pril /ˈeɪprəl/ (written abbreviation **Apr**) *noun* the fourth month of the year

a·pron /ˈeɪprən/ *noun* a piece of clothing that you wear to protect your clothes, for example when you are cooking

ap·ti·tude /ˈæptətjuːd $ ˈæptəˌtud/ *noun* a natural ability to do something well: *They tested our aptitude for computing.*

a·quar·i·um /əˈkweəriəm $ əˈkweriəm/ *noun* **1** a clear glass container that you use to keep fish or other water animals **2** a building where people go to look at fish or other water animals

aquarium

Ar·ab /ˈærəb/ *noun* someone whose family comes from the Middle East or North Africa

Ar·a·bic /ˈærəbɪk/ *noun* the language of Arab people or the religious language of ISLAM

ar·bi·tra·ry /ˈɑːbətrəri $ ˈɑrbəˌtreri/ *adjective* arbitrary decisions or rules seem unfair because there are not good reasons for them: *The rules of English spelling sometimes seem arbitrary to students.*

arc /ɑːk $ ɑrk/ *noun* a curved line

ar·cade /ɑːˈkeɪd $ ɑrˈkeɪd/ *noun* **1** a large room or building where people go to play VIDEO GAMES etc **2** *BrE* a building where there are many shops: *a new shopping arcade*

arch /ɑːtʃ $ ɑrtʃ/ *noun* (plural **arches**) a curved structure at the top of a door, bridge etc, or something that has this curved shape

ar·chae·o·log·i·cal also **archeological** *AmE* /ˌɑːkiəˈlɒdʒɪkəl $ ˌɑrkiəˈlɑdʒɪkəl/ *adjective* relating to archaeology: *an archaeological site*

ar·chae·ol·o·gist also **archeologist** *AmE* /ˌɑːkiˈɒlədʒɪst $ ˌɑrkiˈɑlədʒɪst/ *noun* someone who digs up and examines ancient buildings and objects in order to study them

ar·chae·ol·o·gy also **archeology** *AmE* /ˌɑːkiˈɒlədʒi $ ˌɑrkiˈɑlədʒi/ *noun* (no plural) the study of ancient societies by digging up and examining ancient buildings and objects: *She wants to study archaeology.*

ar·cha·ic /ɑːˈkeɪ-ɪk $ ɑrˈkeɪ-ɪk/ *adjective* very old-fashioned: *the archaic language of Shakespeare*

arch·bish·op /ˌɑːtʃˈbɪʃəp $ ˌɑrtʃˈbɪʃəp/ *noun* the most important priest in a country, in some Christian religions

archeologist the American spelling of ARCHAEOLOGIST

archeology the American spelling of ARCHAEOLOGY

ar·cher·y /ˈɑːtʃəri $ ˈɑrtʃəri/ *noun* (no plural) the sport of shooting ARROWS from a BOW

ar·chi·tect /ˈɑːkətekt $ ˈɑrkəˌtekt/ *noun* someone whose job is to design buildings: *Her dad is an architect.*

ar·chi·tec·tur·al /ˌɑːkəˈtektʃərəl $ ˌɑrkəˈtektʃərəl/ *adjective* relating to architecture

ar·chi·tec·ture /ˈɑːkətektʃə $ ˈɑrkəˌtektʃɚ/ *noun* (no plural) **1** the style and design of buildings: *The city has some beautiful architecture.* **2** the skill or job of designing buildings: *He's studying architecture.*

Arc·tic /ˈɑːktɪk $ ˈɑrktɪk/ *noun* **the Arctic** the most northern part of the world, where it is very cold

ar·dent /ˈɑːdənt $ ˈɑrdnt/ *adjective* admiring or supporting something very strongly: *an ardent fan of Manchester United*

ar·du·ous /ˈɑːdjuəs $ ˈɑrdʒuəs/ *adjective* needing a lot of effort and hard work: *an arduous journey*

are /ə $ ɚ; *strong* ɑː $ ɑr/ the present tense plural and second person singular of BE

ar·e·a /ˈeəriə $ ˈeriə/ *noun*

KEY PATTERNS
an area of a city/country
an area for someone to work/play
the area of a square/room

1 part of a place or building: *Camden is my favourite area of London.* • *We want a garden with a big area for children to play.*
2 the size of a flat surface that you calculate by multiplying its length by its width: *The area of the room is six square metres.*

THESAURUS
region: *The northwest* ***region*** *has a lot more snow* (=a large area of a country).
zone: *This street is in a no-parking* ***zone*** (=an area that is different from the area around it).
suburb: *Our house was in a* ***suburb*** *of Liverpool* (=an area outside the centre of a city, where people live).
neighbourhood *BrE*, **neighborhood** *AmE*: *We soon got to know some other people living in the* ***neighbourhood*** (=an area of a town where people live).

ˈarea ˌcode another phrase for DIALLING CODE

a·re·na /əˈriːnə/ *noun* a building with a large flat area inside with seats all around it, used for watching something such as a sports game: *The concert will be at Wembley arena.*

aren't /ɑːnt $ ˈɑrənt/ **a)** the short form of 'are not': *We aren't going to the party.* **b)** the short form of 'am not', used when asking questions: *I'm lucky, aren't I?*

ar·gue /ˈɑːgjuː $ ˈɑrgju/ *verb*

KEY PATTERNS
argue about something
argue with someone
argue that
argue for/against something

1 if people argue, they shout or say angry things because they do not agree about something: *I hate it when Mum and Dad argue.* • *Some of the kids started* ***arguing about*** *which was the best band.* • *He always* ***argues with*** *the teacher.*
2 to explain why you think something is true: *Joe* ***argued that*** *it is better to use public transport.* • *The students* ***argued for*** *more time to prepare for the exam.* • *The local people* ***argued against*** *the proposal for a new road.*

THESAURUS
have an argument: *Let's discuss this sensibly, not* ***have an argument*** (=talk about it in an angry way).

A B C D E F G H I J K L M N O P Q R S T U V W X Y Z

quarrel: *My brother and I were always* ***quarrelling*** *(=arguing).*

ar·gu·ment /'ɑːgjəmənt $ 'ɑrgjəmənt/ *noun*

KEY PATTERNS
have an argument with someone
an argument about something
an argument for/against something
an argument that

1 if you have an argument with someone, you shout or say angry things to them because you do not agree with them SYNONYM **row** *BrE*: *I* ***had*** *a big* ***argument with*** *my girlfriend.* • *There was an* ***argument about*** *who was going to pay for the meal.* ➔ see Thesaurus at ARGUE

argument

They are having an argument.

2 the reasons that you give to show that something is right or wrong: *Kate explained her* ***arguments for*** *banning smoking.* • *So what are the* ***arguments against*** *experiments on animals?* • *She doesn't accept the* ***argument that*** *16-year-olds are not old enough to vote.*

SPELLING
This word is often spelled wrongly. The correct spelling is: **argument**.

ar·gu·men·ta·tive /ˌɑːgjə'mentətɪv $ ˌɑrgjə'mentətɪv/ *adjective* someone who is argumentative often argues with other people: *Don't be so argumentative.*

a·rise /ə'raɪz/ *verb* (formal) (**arose** /ə'rəʊz $ ə'roʊz/ **arisen** /ə'rɪzən/) if a problem arises, it begins to happen: *We are prepared for any difficulties that arise.*

ar·is·toc·ra·cy /ˌærə'stɒkrəsi $ ˌærə'stɑkrəsi/ *noun* the people belonging to the highest social class in some countries, who usually have a lot of land, money, and power SYNONYM **nobility**

ar·is·to·crat /'ærɪstəkræt $ ə'rɪstəˌkræt/ *noun* someone who is a member of the aristocracy

a·rith·me·tic /ə'rɪθmətɪk/ *noun* (no plural) the skill of working with numbers by adding, dividing, multiplying etc: *I'm no good at arithmetic.*

arm¹ /ɑːm $ ɑrm/ *noun*
1 the long part of your body between your shoulder and your hand: *He put his arms around me.* ➔ see picture on page A5
2 the part of a piece of clothing that covers your arm: *It's a nice jacket but the arms are too long.*
3 arms weapons: *Britain still sells arms to some countries.*

arm² *verb* to give someone weapons: *Should we arm the police?*

arm·chair /'ɑːmtʃeə $ 'ɑrmtʃer/ *noun* a comfortable chair with sides where you can rest your arms ➔ see picture at CHAIR¹

armed /ɑːmd $ ɑrmd/ *adjective* carrying weapons: *armed police* • *Armed with a knife, the man stole jewellery worth £2,000.*

ˌarmed 'forces *plural noun* **the armed forces** a country's military organizations such as its army

ar·mour *BrE*, **armor** *AmE* /'ɑːmə $ 'ɑrmɚ/ *noun* (no plural) metal or leather clothing that men wore in the past to protect themselves in fights: *a knight's armour*

ar·moured *BrE*, **armored** *AmE* /'ɑːməd $ 'ɑrməd/ *adjective* an armoured vehicle has a strong layer of metal on it to protect it against bullets or bombs

arm·pit /'ɑːmˌpɪt $ 'ɑrmˌpɪt/ *noun* the hollow place under your arm where it joins your body: *The dress is too tight under my armpits.*

ar·my /'ɑːmi $ 'ɑrmi/ *noun* (plural **armies**) the part of a country's military force that is trained to fight on land: *My brother joined the army.*

a·ro·ma /ə'rəʊmə $ ə'roʊmə/ *noun* a strong pleasant smell: *the aroma of baking bread* ➔ see Thesaurus at SMELL²

arose the past tense of ARISE

around

The family was sitting around the table.

a•round /əˈraʊnd/ *adverb, preposition*
1 also **round** *BrE* surrounding something: *There was a high fence around the school.* • *She had a gold chain around her neck.*
2 also **round** *BrE* in or to many parts of a place: *The puppy ran around the sitting room.* • *They showed us around their new house* (=took us to every part of their new house). • *People around the world admire his singing* (=in every part of the world).
3 (informal) somewhere in a place: *I've got a pen around here somewhere.* • *I went to the house, but there was no one around* (=no one was there).
→ see Thesaurus at NEARBY
4 also **round** *BrE* moving in a circle: *The Earth goes around the sun.* • *The wheels spin around very quickly.*
5 used when mentioning an amount or time that is not exact SYNONYM **about**: *These machines cost around £60 in the shops.* • *We should be ready by around 10 o'clock.* → see Thesaurus at ABOUT[2]

ar•range /əˈreɪndʒ/ *verb*

KEY PATTERNS
arrange a meeting/appointment/trip
arrange to go/meet/see
arrange for someone to go/meet/see

1 to make plans so that something can happen: *I've arranged a football practice for tomorrow.* • *Sorry I can't come, I've* ***arranged to*** *meet my sister tonight.* • *Susan* ***arranged for*** *the whole class* ***to go*** *out for a meal.*
2 to put things in a particular order or pattern: *We arranged the chairs so that everyone could see the screen.*

ar•range•ment /əˈreɪndʒmənt/ *noun*

KEY PATTERNS
make the arrangements for a party/trip
have an arrangement with someone

1 if you make arrangements, you organize things so that something can happen: *Have you* ***made*** *all the* ***arrangements for*** *the wedding?* • *He is in charge of security arrangements for the concert.* • *What are your travel arrangements?*
2 something that two people or groups have agreed to do: *I* ***have an arrangement with*** *my sister that we share some of our clothes.*

ar•rears /əˈrɪəz $ əˈrɪrz/ *plural noun*
be in arrears to owe someone money and not make a payment when you should: *The family are in arrears with the rent.*

ar•rest[1] /əˈrest/ *verb* if the police arrest someone, they take them away because they believe that the person is guilty of a crime: *They arrested her for stealing.*

arrest

arrest[2] *noun*
1 when a police officer takes someone away and guards them because they may have done something illegal: *He was interviewed for two hours after his arrest.* **2 be under arrest** if someone is under arrest, the police have arrested them: *The policewoman told me that I was under arrest.*

ar•riv•al /əˈraɪvəl/ *noun* (no plural)

KEY PATTERNS
arrival in a city/country
arrival at the station/airport/hospital

1 when you get to a place you were going to ANTONYM **departure**: *Someone will meet you on your* ***arrival in*** *Madrid.* • *Julie met Mike a few days after her* ***arrival at*** *college.*
2 the arrival of someone/something when a new thing or person first starts

A B C D E F G H I J K L M N O P Q R S T U V W X Y Z

A B C D E F G H I J K L M N O P Q R S T U V W X Y Z

to exist: *The arrival of the World Wide Web changed everything.* • *the arrival of a new baby*

ar•rive /əˈraɪv/ *verb*

KEY PATTERNS
arrive at the station/airport/hotel
arrive in a city/country
arrive home

1 to get to a place after a journey: *We **arrived at** the party just as Lee was leaving.* • *The next train to **arrive at** platform 2 is the 10:10 to London.* • *If the train is on time, we will **arrive in** Frankfurt by eight.* • ***Arriving home** was really great after three months abroad.* • *The parcel took two weeks to arrive.*
2 if a particular event or time arrives, it comes or happens: *At last the day of the party arrived.* • *The time has arrived for me to leave.*
3 to begin to exist: *Contacting people was much slower before email arrived.*

THESAURUS
get to: *What time will you **get to** New York* (=arrive there)?
reach: *It took us five hours to **reach** the top of the mountain* (=arrive there, usually after a long or difficult journey).
turn up (informal): *Fred **turned up** at the party an hour late.*

ar•ro•gant /ˈærəgənt/ *adjective* believing that you are very important, clever etc: *He's so arrogant that he was sure he would win.*

ar•row /ˈærəʊ $ ˈæroʊ/ *noun* **1** a thin straight weapon with a point at one end that you shoot from a BOW **2** a sign (→), used to show the direction or position of something

ar•son /ˈɑːsən $ ˈɑrsən/ *noun* (no plural) the crime of deliberately burning something, especially a building: *He was accused of arson.*

art /ɑːt $ ɑrt/ *noun*
1 (no plural) things that you can look at such as drawings or paintings, that are beautiful or express ideas: *She went to college to study art.* • *Do you like modern art?*
2 arts school subjects such as history and English, that are not sciences
3 the arts art, music, theatre, film, literature etc: *I am interested in the arts.*

PHRASES
a work of art something such as a painting that is an example of art: *The building is full of expensive works of art.*

ar•te•ry /ˈɑːtəri $ ˈɑrtəri/ *noun* (plural **arteries**) one of the tubes that takes blood from your heart to the rest of your body

ar•thri•tis /ɑːˈθraɪtəs $ ɑrˈθraɪtəs/ *noun* (no plural) a disease that causes pain and swelling in the joints of your body: *She suffers from arthritis.*

ar•ti•cle /ˈɑːtɪkəl $ ˈɑrtɪkəl/ *noun* **1** a piece of writing in a newspaper, magazine etc: *I read an interesting article about the technology of the future.* **2** a thing, especially one of a group of things SYNONYM **item**: *an article of clothing* **3** in grammar, the word 'the' (=the definite article), or the word 'a' or 'an' (=the indefinite article)

ar•tic•u•late¹ /ɑːˈtɪkjələt $ ɑrˈtɪkjələt/ *adjective* able to express your thoughts and feelings clearly: *He's clever, but not very articulate.*

ar•tic•u•late² /ɑːˈtɪkjəleɪt $ ɑːrˈtɪkjəˌleɪt/ *verb* to be able to say what you think or feel SYNONYM **express**: *Men can find it hard to articulate their feelings.*

ar•ti•fi•cial /ˌɑːtəˈfɪʃəl $ ˌɑrtəˈfɪʃəl/ *adjective* not real or natural, but made by people: *The room was decorated with artificial flowers.*

SPELLING
This word is often spelled wrongly. The correct spelling is: **artificial**.

THESAURUS
synthetic: *A lot of clothes are made from **synthetic** materials* (=not natural).
fake: *Some kids try to use **fake** identity cards* (=not real and made to deceive people).
imitation: *a handbag made of **imitation** leather* (=something that looks like leather but is not)
virtual: *You can have a **virtual** tour of the building* (=on a computer or the Internet, not in the real world).

ˌartificial inˈtelligence *noun* (no plural) the science of making computers do things that people can do, such as understand language

art·ist /ˈɑːtɪst $ ˈɑrtɪst/ *noun* someone who makes art, for example a painter, musician, or dancer: *It is hard to make money as an artist.*

ar·tis·tic /ɑːˈtɪstɪk $ ɑrˈtɪstɪk/ *adjective* **1** good at making things such as paintings or drawings: *I'm not very artistic.* **2** connected with art or with being an artist: *Denis is the film's artistic director.*

as /əz; strong æz/ *adverb, preposition, conjunction*

KEY PATTERNS
be as tall/old/intelligent as someone
be as cold/hard/tough as something
work as a doctor/builder

1 used when comparing people or things: *He's **as tall as** his father now* (=he and his father are now the same height). • *Her hands were **as cold as** ice* (=her hands were very cold, like ice). • *I worked **as hard as** I could.*
2 used to show what job someone does: *She worked as a teacher for a while.*
3 used to show what something is used for: *He used the piece of wood as a bridge across the stream.*
4 (written) when: *He fell as he was walking up the steps.* • *Mary arrived **just as** I was leaving* (=I was just leaving when Mary arrived).
5 because: *As we've got some time left, I'll give you a short test.*

PHRASES
as if, as though: *She looked **as though** she'd been crying* (=the way she looked made me think she'd been crying). • *It looks **as if** it's been raining.*
as well also SYNONYM **too**: *Can I have a drink **as well**?*

asap /ˌeɪ es eɪ ˈpiː/ *adverb* (informal) the abbreviation of 'as soon as possible': *I will let you know asap.*

as·cend /əˈsend/ *verb* (formal) to move up or towards the top of something ANTONYM **descend**: *The plane ascended rapidly.*

as·cent /əˈsent/ *noun* (formal) when someone moves or climbs up or to the top of something ANTONYM **descent**: *The ascent of Mount Everest is difficult and dangerous.*

ash /æʃ/ *noun* (plural **ashes**) the soft grey powder that is left after something has burned: *cigarette ash*

a·shamed /əˈʃeɪmd/ *adjective*

KEY PATTERNS
ashamed of/about something
ashamed to say/admit something
ashamed of myself/yourself

feeling embarrassed or guilty about something: *I felt **ashamed of** the way I had lied to him.* • *Doug was **ashamed to** tell his family what had happened.* • *She was ashamed of herself for shouting at the kids.*

WORD CHOICE
ashamed/embarrassed
• **Ashamed** means "feeling very guilty about something bad that you have done": *I felt **ashamed** that I had been so rude to her.*
• **Embarrassed** means "worried about what other people will think of you, especially when you make a silly mistake": *She was **embarrassed** that she had forgotten his birthday.*

a·shore /əˈʃɔː $ əˈʃɔr/ *adverb* onto or towards the side of a lake, river, or ocean: *We swam ashore.*

ash·tray /ˈæʃtreɪ/ *noun* a small dish where you put finished cigarettes

a·side /əˈsaɪd/ *adverb* **1 move aside, step aside** to move to the side: *She moved aside to let me pass.* **2 put something aside, set something aside** to keep or save something so that you can use it later: *We set aside some of the fruit to eat later.*

ask /ɑːsk $ æsk/ *verb*

KEY PATTERNS
ask a question
ask someone a question
ask someone about someone/something
ask someone why/when etc
ask someone their advice/opinion
ask someone for help/money
ask someone to help

1 to say to someone that you want them to tell you something: *"Where have you been?" asked my mother.* • *Can I **ask a question**?* • *He wanted to*

A B C D E F G H I J K L M N O P Q R S T U V W X Y Z

A B C D E F G H I J K L M N O P Q R S T U V W X Y Z

ask his girlfriend something. • *Tess kept* ***asking*** *me* ***about*** *you.* • *Just* ***ask*** *him* ***why*** *he doesn't want to come.* • *The police* ***asked*** *her* ***whether*** *she had seen him before.*
2 to say to someone that you want them to help you or give you something: *She often asks my advice.* • *If you don't understand, just ask.* • *I had to* ***ask*** *my parents* ***for*** *money.* • *He* ***asked*** *me* ***to*** *give him a lift into town.*
PHRASES
ask someone in to invite someone to come into your house: *She* ***asked*** *me* ***in*** *for coffee.*
ask someone out to ask someone to go with you for a meal, drink etc because you like them: *Leo* ***asked*** *me* ***out*** *but I said no.*

GRAMMAR
You **ask someone** about something.
✘ Don't say 'ask to someone'.

THESAURUS
order: *The waiter came over and we* ***ordered*** *our meal* (=asked for particular types of food and drink).
demand: *One customer got angry and* ***demanded*** *to see the manager* (=asked in a strong, determined way).
request: *You have to* ***request*** *permission to leave school early* (=ask for it in an official way).
inquire/enquire (formal): *I'm writing to* ***inquire*** (=ask for information) *about the job you advertised.*
beg: *Lucy* ***begged*** *her mother to let her have a cat* (=asked in a way that showed that she wanted a cat very much).

a·sleep /ə'sliːp/ *adjective* **1** sleeping ANTONYM **awake**: *Dad was asleep in his chair.* **2 fall asleep** to begin to sleep: *I fell asleep in class.*

as·pect /'æspekt/ *noun* one of the separate parts of something: *My work and my family are two important aspects of my life.*

as·phyx·i·ate /æs'fɪksieɪt/ *verb* (formal) to stop someone breathing: *The thick smoke asphyxiated three children in an upstairs bedroom.*

as·pi·rin /'æsprɪn/ *noun* (no plural) a drug that stops pain: *She took some aspirin for her headache.*

as·sai·lant /ə'seɪlənt/ *noun* (formal) someone who attacks another person SYNONYM **attacker**: *He did not know his assailant.*

as·sas·sin·ate /ə'sæsəneɪt/ *verb* to murder an important person: *a plot to assassinate the Pope* → see Thesaurus at KILL[1]

as·sas·sin·ation /əˌsæsə'neɪʃən/ *noun* when someone murders an important person: *the assassination of John F Kennedy*

as·sault¹ /ə'sɔːlt/ *noun* a violent attack: *He was accused of several assaults on women.*

assault² *verb* to attack someone violently: *A gang of boys assaulted him.*

as·sem·ble /ə'sembəl/ *verb* to come together in the same place: *The students assembled in the school yard.*

as·sem·bly /ə'sembli/ *noun* (plural **assemblies**) **1** a regular meeting of all the students and teachers in a school: *Assembly begins at 9.30.* **2** a group of people who have come together for a particular purpose: *the United Nations General Assembly*

as·sert /ə'sɜːt $ ə'sɜ˞t/ *verb* **1 assert your rights, assert your authority** (formal) to say strongly that you have rights or authority: *My father decided to assert his authority by refusing to let me go out.* **2 assert yourself** to say what you think or ask for what you want in a confident and determined way

as·ser·tive /ə'sɜːtɪv $ ə'sɜ˞tɪv/ *adjective* saying or asking for something in a confident and determined way: *Be polite but assertive when you make a complaint.*

as·sess /ə'ses/ *verb* to examine something and make a decision about it SYNONYM **judge**: *We assess the students' work throughout the year.*

as·set /'æset/ *noun* something or someone that helps you to succeed: *Tom is a real asset to the team.*

as·sign·ment /ə'saɪnmənt/ *noun* a piece of work that someone gives you to do: *a homework assignment*

as·sist /ə'sɪst/ *verb* (formal) to help someone to do something: *The porter will assist you with your bags.* ➔ see Thesaurus at HELP[1]

as·sist·ance /ə'sɪstəns/ *noun* (no plural) (formal) help: *Students can get financial assistance from the government.*

as·sis·tant /ə'sɪstənt/ *noun* **1** someone whose job is to help customers in a shop: *I asked the assistant for a bigger size.* **2** someone who helps someone else to do their work: *My assistant answers the phone and arranges meetings.*

as·so·ci·ate /ə'səʊʃieɪt $ ə'soʊʃiˌeɪt/ *verb* **be associated with** to be connected or related to something: *A lot of health problems are associated with smoking.*

as·so·ci·a·tion /əˌsəʊsi'eɪʃən $ əˌsoʊsi'eɪʃən/ *noun* **1** an organization for people who do the same work or have the same interests: *the Association of University Teachers* **2 in association with someone** working with another organization or person: *The school is building a new library in association with local companies.*

as·sort·ment /ə'sɔːtmənt $ ə'sɔrtmənt/ *noun* a mixture of various different types of thing: *an assortment of cookies*

as·sume /ə'sjuːm $ ə'sum/ *verb* to think that something is true although you have no proof: *I assume his girlfriend went to the party with him.*

as·sump·tion /ə'sʌmpʃən/ *noun* something that you think is true although you have no proof: *I made the assumption that he would agree with me.*

as·sur·ance /ə'ʃʊərəns $ ə'ʃʊrəns/ *noun* a definite statement or promise: *The company gave me an assurance that they would replace the broken washing machine.*

as·sure /ə'ʃʊə $ ə'ʃʊr/ *verb* to tell someone that something will definitely happen or is definitely true, so that they are less worried: *The doctor assured me that the injection would not hurt.*

as·te·risk /'æstərɪsk/ *noun* a mark like a star (*), used to show that there is a note about a particular word or phrase

asth·ma /'æsmə $ 'æzmə/ *noun* (no plural) an illness that makes it difficult for you to breathe: *Both sisters suffer from asthma.*

as·ton·ish /ə'stɒnɪʃ $ ə'stɑnɪʃ/ *verb* to surprise someone very much SYNONYM **amaze**: *He astonished everybody with his skill.*

as·ton·ished /ə'stɒnɪʃt $ ə'stɑnɪʃt/ *adjective* very surprised SYNONYM **amazed**: *I was astonished at how easy the test was.* ➔ see Thesaurus at SURPRISED

as·ton·ish·ing /ə'stɒnɪʃɪŋ $ ə'stɑnɪʃɪŋ/ *adjective* very surprising: *It is astonishing that so many students failed.* ➔ see Thesaurus at SURPRISING —**astonishingly** *adverb*: *It was astonishingly simple.*

as·ton·ish·ment /ə'stɒnɪʃmənt $ ə'stɑnɪʃmənt/ *noun* (no plural) very great surprise SYNONYM **amazement**: *My parents stared at me in astonishment.*

as·tound /ə'staʊnd/ *verb* to surprise or shock someone very much: *She astounded me by saying she was getting married.* —**astounded** *adjective*: *They were astounded at his decision to leave.* ➔ see Thesaurus at SURPRISED

as·tound·ing /ə'staʊndɪŋ/ *adjective* very surprising or shocking: *A car went past at an astounding speed.* ➔ see Thesaurus at SURPRISING

a·stray /ə'streɪ/ *adverb* **1 go astray** to become lost: *My letter went astray in the post.* **2 lead someone astray** to make someone do bad things by encouraging them: *Don't let the older girls lead you astray.*

as·trol·o·gy /ə'strɒlədʒi $ ə'strɑlədʒi/ *noun* (no plural) the study of the position of stars and PLANETS, and the effect that they might have on people's lives: *Do you believe in astrology?*

A B C D E F G H I J K L M N O P Q R S T U V W X Y Z

as·tro·naut /ˈæstrənɔːt/ *noun* someone who travels in a spacecraft

astronaut

as·tron·o·my /əˈstrɒnəmi $ əˈstrɑnəmi/ *noun* (no plural) the scientific study of stars and PLANETs

as·tute /əˈstjuːt $ əˈstut/ *adjective* clever and quick to understand situations and people: *an astute politician*

at /ət; strong æt/ *preposition*
1 used to say where someone or something is: *Her aunt met her at the station.* • *You should be at school.* • *His mother was standing at the bottom of the stairs.*
2 used to mention the time when something happens: *We arrived at three o'clock.* • *I'll see you at the weekend.*
3 used to mention an event when something happens: *They met at a party.*
4 used to say where something is thrown, kicked etc: *She threw the cushion at him.* • *The two men shot at police officers.*
5 used to say who someone is looking or shouting towards: *The man was staring at her.* • *Don't shout at me!*
6 used to say how fast something is moving: *The car was going at about 60 miles an hour* (=its speed was about 60 miles an hour).

ate the past tense of EAT

a·the·ist /ˈeɪθi-ɪst/ *noun* someone who does not believe that God exists —**atheism** *noun*

ath·lete /ˈæθliːt/ *noun* someone who takes part in sports such as running: *You can earn a lot of money as a professional athlete* (=someone who is paid to play a sport).

ath·let·ic /æθˈletɪk/ *adjective* physically strong and good at sport

ath·let·ics /æθˈletɪks/ *noun* **1** *BrE* sports such as running races and jumping: *We play hockey in winter and do athletics in summer.* **2** *AmE* sports and physical exercise in general

at·las /ˈætləs/ *noun* (plural **atlases**) a book of maps: *an atlas of Europe*

ATM /ˌeɪ tiː ˈem/ (Automated Teller Machine) the American word for CASH MACHINE

ATM

at·mo·sphere /ˈætməsfɪə $ ˈætməsˌfɪr/ *noun* (no plural) **1** the kind of feeling that you get when you are in a place: *The town has a nice friendly atmosphere.*
2 the atmosphere the mixture of gases surrounding the Earth

at·om /ˈætəm/ *noun* the smallest part that a substance can be divided into

a·tom·ic /əˈtɒmɪk $ əˈtɑmɪk/ *adjective* **1** using the power that is produced by dividing atoms SYNONYM **nuclear**: *an atomic bomb* **2** related to atoms

a·tro·cious /əˈtrəʊʃəs $ əˈtroʊʃəs/ *adjective* very bad SYNONYM **awful**: *His handwriting is atrocious.*

a·troc·i·ty /əˈtrɒsəti $ əˈtrɑsəti/ *noun* (formal) (plural **atrocities**) a very cruel and violent action: *Both sides in the war committed atrocities.*

at·tach /əˈtætʃ/ *verb*

KEY PATTERNS
attach something to something

1 to fix one thing to another: *Please attach a photograph **to** your application form.* • *The cat had a bell **attached to** its collar.* → see Thesaurus at FASTEN
2 to connect a document to an email in order to send them together: *I've attached some photos of the party.*

at·tached /əˈtætʃt/ *adjective* **be attached to someone/something** to like someone or something very much: *I've lived here for ten years and I'm very attached to this house.*

at·tach·ment /əˈtætʃmənt/ *noun* **1** (formal) a strong feeling of liking or loving someone or something: *A baby quickly forms a strong attachment to its mother.* **2** a document, picture etc that you connect to an email and send with it

at·tack¹ /əˈtæk/ *verb* **1** to try to hurt or kill someone: *Two men attacked him and took his car.* • *The soldiers planned* *to attack the village at night.* **2** to criticize someone very strongly: *She attacked politicians for not doing enough for young people. • All the newspapers attacked the President.* **3** to kick or throw a ball forward during a game in order to get a GOAL or point

attack² *noun* **1** a violent action that someone does to hurt or kill someone: *Two men were killed in the attack.* **2** a very strong criticism of someone: *In his speech he made an attack on all journalists.* **3** a sudden short period of illness: *an attack of coughing* **4** *BrE* the players in a game such as football who try to get points

at·tack·er /əˈtækə $ əˈtækɚ/ *noun* someone who attacks someone else: *Her attacker ran off.*

at·tempt¹ /əˈtempt/ *verb*

KEY PATTERNS
attempt something
attempt to do something

to try to do something difficult or dangerous: *You should* ***attempt to*** *answer all the questions. • Few people have climbed this mountain, although many have attempted it.* → see Thesaurus at TRY¹

attempt² *noun*

KEY PATTERNS
an attempt to do something
an attempt at doing something
an attempt at something

if you make an attempt to do something, you try to do it: *Despite our* ***attempts to*** *stop him, he decided to leave school. • She* ***made no attempt to*** *be polite. • This was my first* ***attempt at*** *baking a cake. • Was that an* ***attempt at*** *a joke?*

at·tend /əˈtend/ *verb* **1** (formal) to go to a meeting, school, church etc: *About 300 students attended the lecture.* **2** **attend to someone/something** to give care or attention to something or someone: *The doctor will attend to you in a moment.*

at·tend·ance /əˈtendəns/ *noun* when you go to a meeting, school, church etc: *Your attendance at classes is obligatory.*

at·ten·tion /əˈtenʃən/ *noun* (no plural)

KEY PATTERNS
give attention to something/someone

when you watch, listen to, or think about something carefully: *He was a brilliant teacher who knew how to get the kids' attention. • She* ***gives*** *a lot of* ***attention to*** *her clothes.*

PHRASES

pay attention to listen or watch carefully: *The boy's mother was not* ***paying attention to*** *him.*

attract attention if someone or something attracts attention, people notice them: *I waved to try and* ***attract*** *his* ***attention****. • Her new dress was* ***attracting*** *a lot of* ***attention****.*

draw attention to something to make people notice or think about something: *The programme* ***drew attention to*** *the problems of traffic in our cities.*

the centre of attention the person that everyone is looking at: *Naomi is shy and hates being* ***the centre of attention****.*

at·ten·tive /əˈtentɪv/ *adjective* listening or watching carefully: *The students were very attentive.* —**attentively** *adverb*: *They all listened attentively.*

at·tic /ˈætɪk/ *noun* a room at the top of a house, inside the roof: *I keep my old clothes in the attic.*

at·ti·tude /ˈætətjuːd $ ˈætəˌtuːd/ *noun*

KEY PATTERNS
an attitude to/towards something
someone's attitude to/towards someone else

what you think and feel about something or someone, and how you show this in your behaviour: *I think it's good to have a relaxed* ***attitude to*** *life. • I don't like her* ***attitude towards*** *me. • The team coach encourages players to have a positive attitude before the match.*

at·tor·ney /əˈtɜːni $ əˈtɝni/ the American word for LAWYER

at·tract /əˈtrækt/ *verb*

KEY PATTERNS
attract someone
attract someone to a job/subject

1 if something attracts you, you like it or feel interested in it: *What* ***attracted***

A B C D E F G H I J K L M N O P Q R S T U V W X Y Z

you **to** *teaching?* • *She* ***was attracted by*** *the idea of living in a big city.*
2 be attracted to someone to feel interested in someone in a sexual way: *I like him, but I* ***am not attracted to*** *him.*
3 if a place or thing attracts people, it makes them want to go there or see it: *Disneyland attracts millions of visitors each year.*

at·trac·tion /əˈtrækʃən/ *noun*
1 something that people like to see or do because it is interesting or enjoyable: *Buckingham Palace is one of London's most popular tourist attractions.* **2** when you feel interested in someone in a sexual way: *There was a strong physical attraction between us.*

at·trac·tive /əˈtræktɪv/ *adjective*

KEY PATTERNS
attractive to someone

1 pretty or pleasant to look at: *His new girlfriend is very attractive.*
2 if something is attractive, people want to see it, go to it, or have it: *The new theatre will make the town more* ***attractive to*** *tourists.*

THESAURUS
pretty: *Sally's a really* ***pretty*** (=attractive) *girl.* You use **pretty** about a girl or woman.
beautiful: *His wife was tall, slim, and* ***beautiful*** (=extremely attractive). You use **beautiful** about a woman or a young child.
good-looking: *Do you think Jamie is* ***good-looking*** (=attractive)? You use **good-looking** about a man or a woman.
handsome: *The photography showed a* ***handsome*** (=attractive) *man with dark hair.* You use **handsome** about a man or boy.
gorgeous: *Matt's new girlfriend is absolutely* ***gorgeous*** (=very attractive).

au·ber·gine /ˈəʊbəʒiːn $ ˈoʊbərʒin/ *noun* a large vegetable with smooth shiny purple skin SYNONYM **eggplant** *AmE* → see picture on page A6

au·burn /ˈɔːbən $ ˈɔbərn/ *adjective* auburn hair is a reddish brown colour

auc·tion /ˈɔːkʃən/ *noun* an event at which things are sold to the person who offers the most money: *We bought the furniture at an auction.*

au·di·ble /ˈɔːdəbəl/ *adjective* loud enough to be heard: *His words were clearly audible.*

audience

au·di·ence /ˈɔːdiəns/ *noun* the people who watch or listen to a performance: *The audience stood up and cheered at the end of the performance.*

au·di·o /ˈɔːdiəʊ $ ˈɔdioʊ/ *adjective* relating to recording and broadcasting sound: *The audio equipment wasn't working, so we couldn't hear properly.*

au·di·o·vis·u·al /ˌɔːdiəʊˈvɪʒuəl $ ˌɔdioʊˈvɪʒuəl/ *adjective* having recorded pictures and sound: *The children learn with CD-ROMs and other audiovisual materials.*

au·di·tion /ɔːˈdɪʃən/ *noun* a short performance to test whether an actor or singer is good enough to be in a play or concert: *I have an audition tomorrow for a part in 'Annie'.*

au·di·to·ri·um /ˌɔːdɪˈtɔːriəm/ *noun* the part of a theatre where people sit

Au·gust /ˈɔːgəst/ (written abbreviation **Aug**) *noun* the eighth month of the year: *It's Friday August 10th.* • *My birthday's in August.*

aunt /ɑːnt $ ænt/ also **aunt·ie** /ˈɑːnti $ ˈænti/ *noun* the sister of your father or mother, or the wife of your uncle: *I'm going to stay with my aunt.* • *Auntie Mary is here.*

PRONUNCIATION
British people pronounce **aunt** like 'aren't'.
American people pronounce **aunt** like 'ant'.

au pair /əʊ ˈpeə $ oʊ ˈper/ *noun* a young woman who stays with a family in a foreign country and cares for their children: *I worked for a year as an au pair.*

au·ral /ˈɔːrəl/ *adjective* connected with hearing and listening: *visual and aural sensations*

aus·tere /ɔːˈstɪə $ ɔˈstɪr/ *adjective* (formal) plain and simple: *The room was very austere.*

aus·ter·i·ty /ɔːˈsterəti/ *noun* (no plural) (formal) bad economic conditions in which people do not have enough money: *There was a period of austerity after the war.*

au·then·tic /ɔːˈθentɪk/ *adjective* not copying or pretending to be something else: *The restaurant serves authentic Chinese food.* • *Is it an authentic Van Gogh painting?*

au·thor /ˈɔːθə $ ˈɔθɚ/ *noun* the writer of a book: *Who is the author of 'Pride and Prejudice'?*

au·thor·i·tar·i·an /ɔːˌθɒrəˈteəriən $ əˌθɔrəˈteriən/ *adjective* strict and not allowing people much freedom: *Her father is very authoritarian.*

au·thor·i·ty /ɔːˈθɒrəti $ əˈθɔrəti/ *noun*

KEY PATTERNS
have the authority to do something
authority over someone

1 (no plural) if someone has authority, they have the right to make important decisions and control people: *The manager* ***has the authority to*** *stop people entering the club.* • *My father wanted complete* ***authority over*** *us.*
2 an organization or government department that controls something: *the local health authority*

PHRASES
in authority with the right to make important decisions and control people: *Only leave the building if you are told to do so by someone* ***in authority.***
the authorities organizations such as the police who control people: *If you see anything suspicious, inform* ***the*** *airport* ***authorities.***

au·thor·ize also **authorise** *BrE* /ˈɔːθəraɪz/ *verb* to officially allow someone to do something: *You can't go in unless I authorize it.*

au·to·bi·o·graph·i·cal /ˌɔːtəbaɪəˈgræfɪkəl/ *adjective* about someone's own life: *The film is based on the autobiographical novel by Joseph Ackerley.*

au·to·bi·og·ra·phy /ˌɔːtəbaɪˈɒgrəfi $ ˌɔtəbaɪˈɑgrəfi/ *noun* (plural **autobiographies**) a book that someone writes about their own life: *His autobiography caused a lot of embarrassment to the government.*

au·to·graph /ˈɔːtəgrɑːf $ ˈɔtəˌgræf/ *noun* if a famous person gives you their autograph, they sign their name for you: *Can I have your autograph?*

au·to·mat·ic /ˌɔːtəˈmætɪk/ *adjective* an automatic machine works by itself without much human control: *an automatic washing machine*
—**automatically** /-kli/ *adverb*: *The camera flashes automatically.*

au·to·mo·bile /ˈɔːtəməbiːl/ the American word for CAR

au·top·sy /ˈɔːtɒpsi $ ˈɔˌtɑpsi/ *noun* (plural **autopsies**) an examination of a dead body to discover why the person died SYNONYM **post-mortem**: *Doctors performed an autopsy on the body.*

au·tumn /ˈɔːtəm/ *noun*

KEY PATTERNS
in autumn
in the autumn

the season when the leaves fall off the trees SYNONYM **fall** *AmE*: *This shrub has orange berries* ***in autumn.*** • *His new book will be published* ***in the autumn.***
→ see picture on page A13

SPELLING
This word is often spelled wrongly. The correct spelling is: **autumn**.

aux·il·ia·ry /ɔːgˈzɪljəri $ ɔgˈzɪləri/ *adjective* **auxiliary nurse, auxiliary worker** someone whose job is to give additional help to other nurses or other workers

auxˌiliary ˈverb *noun* a verb used with another verb to make questions, negative sentences, and tenses. In English the auxiliary verbs are 'be', 'do', and 'have'.

a·vail·a·bil·i·ty /əˌveɪləˈbɪləti/ *noun* when you can get, buy, or use something: *I rang to ask about the availability of tickets.*

A B C D E F G H I J K L M N O P Q R S T U V W X Y Z

a•vail•a•ble /ə'veɪləbəl/ *adjective*

KEY PATTERNS
available to someone
available for use/sale/work
available from a shop/department

if something is available, you can buy it, use it, or have it: *Tickets will be* ***available to*** *the public next week.* • *Have you got any bikes* ***available for*** *sale?* • *The books are* ***available from*** *all good booksellers.*

av•a•lanche /'ævəlɑːnʃ $ 'ævəˌlæntʃ/ *noun* a large amount of snow that falls down a mountain: *He was killed in an avalanche.*

avalanche

av•e•nue /'ævənjuː $ 'ævəˌnu/ *noun* a road in a town: *The hotel is on 11th Avenue.* ➔ see Thesaurus at ROAD

av•e•rage¹ /'ævərɪdʒ/ *noun* the amount that you get when you add several figures together and then divide the result by the number of figures: *The* ***average of*** *ten, five, and three is six.* • *The girls spend* ***an average of*** *£10 a week on clothes.*

PHRASES
on average: *I see my grandmother once a month* ***on average*** (=I usually see her once a month).
above average, below average higher or lower than the usual level or amount: *Her intelligence is well* ***above average.***

average² *adjective* **1** the average amount is the amount you get when you add several figures together and then divide the result by the number of figures: *The average age of the students is 14.* **2** typical or normal: *The average person doesn't know much about computers.* ➔ see Thesaurus at NORMAL

average³ *verb* to be a particular amount as an average: *Her test results average 60%.*

a•vert /ə'vɜːt $ ə'vət/ *verb* (written) to stop something unpleasant from happening SYNONYM **prevent**: *The government acted quickly to avert the crisis.*

a•vi•a•tion /ˌeɪvi'eɪʃən/ *noun* (no plural) (formal) the activity of flying in planes, or making planes: *an expert in aviation*

av•id /'ævɪd/ *adjective* liking something a lot, or doing a lot of something SYNONYM **keen**: *Doug's an avid fan of American football.*

av•o•ca•do /ˌævə'kɑːdəʊ $ ˌævə'kɑdoʊ/ *noun* a fruit with a thick green or purple skin and a soft green part inside that you eat

a•void /ə'vɔɪd/ *verb*

KEY PATTERNS
avoid something/someone
avoid doing something

1 if you avoid something bad, you try to make sure it does not happen: *She avoided trouble by keeping quiet.* • *I left early to avoid getting stuck in traffic.*
2 to deliberately try not to see or meet someone: *Were you trying to avoid me at the party?*
3 to deliberately not do something: *Avoid using informal language when you are writing an essay.*

a•wait /ə'weɪt/ *verb* (formal) to wait for something to happen or arrive: *The soldiers made a camp and awaited their orders.*

a•wake¹ /ə'weɪk/ *adjective* not sleeping ANTONYM **asleep**: *Mum was still awake when I got home.* • *His music* ***kept*** *me* ***awake*** *all night.* • *I tried to* ***stay awake*** *to watch the film but couldn't.*

PHRASES
lie awake to be unable to sleep when you are in bed, especially because you are worried: *She* ***lay awake*** *wondering what to tell Toby.*
wide awake: *I was* ***wide awake*** (=completely awake) *at five this morning.*

awake² *verb* (written) (**awoke** /ə'wəʊk $ ə'woʊk/ **awoken** /ə'wəʊkən $ ə'woʊkən/) to stop sleeping SYNONYM **wake up**: *Richard was there when she awoke.*

a•ward¹ /ə'wɔːd $ ə'wɔrd/ *verb* to officially give someone a prize: *She was awarded the Nobel Peace Prize.*

award² *noun* a prize for something good that you have done: *The fireman won an award for bravery.*

a•ware /əˈweə $ əˈwer/ *adjective*

KEY PATTERNS
aware of something/someone
aware that

if you are aware of something, you know about it or realize that it is there ANTONYM **unaware**: *I was aware of someone standing behind me.* • *Everyone* ***is aware that*** *it is dangerous to smoke.*

a•wash /əˈwɒʃ $ əˈwɑʃ/ *adjective* (written) covered with water: *The streets were awash with flood water.*

a•way /əˈweɪ/ *adverb*
1 further from a place: *We walked* ***away from*** *the building.* • *She waved goodbye before driving away.* • *The paper boat floated away down the river.* • *Go away! I'm busy!*
2 used to show how far something is from a place: *The nearest town was ten miles away.* • *The huge animal was only two metres* ***away from*** *me.*
3 not at home, work, or school: *He's away on holiday at the moment.* • *Fiona's been* ***away from*** *school for a week.*
4 used to show how long it will be before something happens: *The exams are only two weeks away* (=they will happen after two weeks).

awe /ɔː/ *noun* **in awe, with awe** when you feel that you admire something or someone a lot: *I looked back in awe across the mountains.*

awe•some /ˈɔːsəm/ *adjective* very big or important: *It's an awesome achievement.*

aw•ful /ˈɔːfəl/ *adjective* very bad or unpleasant SYNONYM **terrible**: *What awful food!* • *My hair looks awful.* → see Thesaurus at BAD

awk•ward /ˈɔːkwəd $ ˈɔkwəd/ *adjective* **1** difficult to deal with: *He kept asking awkward questions.*
2 embarrassed and shy: *I felt awkward going there by myself.*
—**awkwardness** *noun* (no plural): *She looked away quickly to hide her awkwardness.*

awoke the past tense of AWAKE

awoken the past participle of AWAKE

axe also **ax** *AmE* /æks/ *noun* a tool that you use for breaking wood into smaller pieces, or for cutting down trees

ax•is /ˈæksɪs/ *noun* (plural **axes** /ˈæksiːz/) a line at the side or bottom of a GRAPH, where you write the measurements

ax•le /ˈæksəl/ *noun* the bar that joins two wheels on a vehicle

Bb

BA /ˌbiː ˈeɪ/ *noun* Bachelor of Arts; a university degree in a subject such as history or literature: *She has a BA in French.*

ba·by /ˈbeɪbi/ *noun* (plural **babies**) **1** a very young child who has not learned to talk yet: *The baby's crying.* ➔ see Thesaurus at CHILD **2 have a baby** to give birth to a baby: *Lucy recently had a baby.*

baby

ˈbaby ˌcarriage also **ˈbaby ˌbuggy** the American word for a PRAM

baby·sit /ˈbeɪbisɪt/ *verb* (past tense and past participle **babysat** /-sæt/ **babysitting**) to look after children while their parents go out: *Can you babysit tomorrow night?* —**babysitter** *noun*: *I'm Sarah's babysitter.*

bach·e·lor /ˈbætʃələ $ ˈbætʃələr/ *noun* **1** a man who is not married: *His son is 32 and still a bachelor.* **2 Bachelor of Arts, Bachelor of Science** the title of a first university degree

back¹ /bæk/ *noun*

KEY PATTERNS
the back of the room/house/car

1 the part of your body from your neck and shoulders down to your bottom: *Billy lay on his back and looked at the sky.* • *I hurt my back when I was moving the computer.* • *Jilly leapt lightly onto the horse's back.*
2 the part of something that is furthest away from the front ANTONYM **front**: *Sam and Steve always sit at the back of the class.* • *Put your bags in the back of the car.*

back

He's got his shirt on back to front.

I sat in the back of the car.

PHRASES
back to front *BrE* in the wrong position, so that the front is where the back should be: *He's got his shirt on* ***back to front.***
in back of something *AmE* if something is in back of another thing, it is behind it: *There's a football field* ***in back of*** *the school.*
out back *AmE* if a person is out back, they are outside, behind a building: *Mom's* ***out back*** *in the yard.*
behind someone's back if you do something unkind behind someone's back, you do it secretly, so that they do not know you did it: *Carole's been talking about me to the teacher behind my back.*

back² *adverb*
1 to the place where someone or something was before: *Tracey ran back to the house to get her umbrella.* (=ran to the house she had just left). • *She put the magazine back in her bag* (=she put the magazine in the bag she had taken it from).
2 in the direction that is behind you: *He stepped back from the edge of the road.* • *Jane turned and looked back.*
3 doing the same thing to someone that they have done to you: *Stephanie waved to me, and I waved back.* • *I'll phone you back later.* • *When are you going to give me that money back?*

back³ *verb*

KEY PATTERNS
back a person/idea/plan
back a car into somewhere
back a car out of somewhere

1 to support someone or something, for example by voting for them or agreeing with them in a meeting: *I'm backing Peter in the election for school president.* • *Most people backed the plan to ban smoking in public places.* **2** to make a vehicle move in the direction that is behind you SYNONYM **reverse**: *I can't **back** the car **into** that tiny space!* • *Joe **backed** his truck **out of** the garage.*

PHRASAL VERBS

back away
to move slowly backwards because you are afraid, shocked etc: *When he saw the dog, he started to **back away**.*

back down
to stop saying that you are right about something and admit that you are wrong: *She had to **back down** because I knew she was lying.*

back off
to move away from someone in order to avoid a problem: *I thought he was going to hit me but he **backed off**.*

back out
if you back out of something that you agreed to do, you decide not to do it: *You can't **back out of** the holiday now.*

back up
1 back someone/something up to support someone or show that what they are saying is true: *Will you **back** me **up** in the meeting?*
2 back something up to make a copy of information on a computer: *You should **back up** all your data at least once a week.*

back⁴ *adjective* **1** behind or furthest from the front of something ANTONYM **front**: *There's someone at the back door.* • *Tim and I always sit on the back row at the cinema.* **2 back street, back road** a street or road that is away from the main streets of a town

back·ache /ˈbækeɪk/ *noun* pain in your back: *I've got terrible backache.*

back·bone /ˈbækbəʊn $ ˈbækboʊn/ *noun* the bone down the middle of your back SYNONYM **spine**: *He damaged his backbone in a car accident.* ➔ see picture on page A5

back·break·ing /ˈbækˌbreɪkɪŋ/ *adjective* backbreaking work is very difficult physical work that makes you tired: *Moving the piano was backbreaking work.*

back·fire /ˌbækˈfaɪə $ ˈbækfaɪə˞/ *verb* if something you do backfires, it has the opposite result to the one you wanted: *The plan backfired when I realised I didn't have enough money.*

back·ground /ˈbækgraʊnd/ *noun* **1** your background is the type of education you had and the family you belong to: *Jo and I come from very different backgrounds.* **2 in the background** in the part of a picture or scene that is behind the main part: *In the background of the painting there is a river.*

back·ing /ˈbækɪŋ/ *noun* (no plural) money or support that a person or organization gives you in order to help you achieve something: *The government gives financial backing to many small businesses.*

back·log /ˈbæklɒg $ ˈbæklɔg/ *noun* a lot of work that you should have done earlier: *We have a huge backlog of letters to answer.*

back·pack /ˈbækpæk/ *noun* a large bag that you carry on your back when you go walking or camping SYNONYM **rucksack** *BrE*: *I carried everything including my tent in a backpack.* —**backpacker** *noun*: *a hostel for backpackers*

back·pack·ing /ˈbækˌpækɪŋ/ *noun* (no plural) an occasion when you go walking and camping carrying a backpack: *We're going backpacking in Nepal.*

back·side /ˈbæksaɪd/ *noun* (informal) the part of your body that you sit on SYNONYM **bottom**

back·slash /ˈbækslæʃ/ *noun* a line (\) that is used to separate numbers, letters etc, for example in names of computer files

back·stage /ˌbækˈsteɪdʒ/ *adverb, adjective* in the area behind the stage in a theatre: *We're hoping to go backstage and talk to the actors.*

back·stroke /ˈbækstrəʊk $ ˈbækstroʊk/ *noun* (no plural) a style of swimming on your back: *Can you do backstroke?*

A B C D E F G H I J K L M N O P Q R S T U V W X Y Z

ˌback-to-ˈback *adjective, adverb* with the backs of two people or things facing each other: *Stand back-to-back and we'll see who's tallest.*

back·up /ˈbækʌp/ *noun* a copy of a document, especially a computer FILE, that you can use if you lose or damage the original one: *Do you have a backup of this file?*

back·ward /ˈbækwəd $ ˈbækwərd/ *adjective* towards the direction that is behind you: *a backward glance*

back·wards /ˈbækwədz $ ˈbækwərdz/ also **backward** *adverb*
1 towards the direction that is behind you ANTONYM **forward**: *He fell over backwards.*
2 starting at the end, instead of the beginning: *'Pan' spelled backwards is 'nap'.*
3 backwards and forwards first in one direction, then in the other direction, many times: *I travel **backwards and forwards** to London several times a week.*

back·yard /ˌbækˈjɑːd $ ˌbækˈjɑrd/ *noun* a small area behind a house: *The kids are playing in the backyard.*

ba·con /ˈbeɪkən/ *noun* (no plural) long thin pieces of meat from a pig: *Would you like bacon and eggs for breakfast?*

bac·te·ri·a /bækˈtɪəriə $ bækˈtɪriə/ *plural noun* very small living things that can cause disease: *This cleaning product kills bacteria.*

bad → see box on page 49

badge /bædʒ/ *noun* a piece of metal or plastic with a sign or writing on it that you wear on your clothes: *The policeman showed me his badge.*

bad·ger /ˈbædʒə $ ˈbædʒər/ *noun* an animal with black and white fur that lives under the ground

bad·ly /ˈbædli/ *adverb* (**worse** /wɜːs $ wərs/ **worst** /wɜːst $ wərst/)
1 not done in the correct or a good way ANTONYM **well**: *The team played badly. • badly made clothes*
2 very much or very seriously: *She needs some sleep badly. • Was anyone badly injured?*

bad·min·ton /ˈbædmɪntən/ *noun* (no plural) a game in which you hit a SHUTTLECOCK (=a small object with feathers) over a net: *Who wants a game of badminton?*

ˌbad-ˈtempered *adjective* someone who is bad-tempered gets annoyed easily: *Why is Tim so bad-tempered today?* → see Thesaurus at ANGRY

baf·fle /ˈbæfəl/ *verb* if something baffles you, you cannot understand it: *Question 4 baffled the whole class.*
—**baffled** *adjective*: *We were completely baffled by her behaviour.*

bag /bæg/ *noun*

KEY PATTERNS
a bag of sugar/flour/sweets

1 a container made of paper, plastic, cloth etc that you use for carrying things: *She brought her lunch in a paper bag. • You can take one bag on the plane with you. • She put the vegetables in her shopping bag.*
2 the amount that you can fit in a bag: *He put **a** whole **bag of** sugar in the cake.*

bag·gage /ˈbægɪdʒ/ *noun* (no plural) the bags that you carry when you are travelling SYNONYM **luggage**: *The porter will help you with your baggage.*

bag·gy /ˈbægi/ *adjective* (**baggier, baggiest**) baggy clothes are big and loose ANTONYM **tight**: *She wore a baggy T-shirt.*

bail¹ /beɪl/ *noun* (no plural) money that you pay to a court so that a prisoner does not have to stay in prison before the TRIAL starts: *They released him on £10,000 bail this morning.*

bad /bæd/ *adjective* (**worse** /wɜːs $ wɚs/, **worst** /wɜːst $ wɚst/)

1 not good or nice ANTONYM **good**: *bad weather* • *I've had a really **bad** day.* • *Unfortunately, I've got some **bad** news for you.*

THESAURUS
awful/dreadful/horrible: *There's an **awful** smell in here* (=very bad or unpleasant).
terrible: *They had a **terrible** journey and arrived a day late* (=extremely bad).
horrific: *a **horrific** crime* (=very bad and shocking)
disgusting/revolting: *The fish tasted **disgusting*** (=so bad that it made me feel ill).

2 of a low standard or quality ANTONYM **good**: *I've never read such a **bad** essay.* • *That was the **worst** party I've ever been to.*

3 not useful or suitable ANTONYM **good**: *That's a **bad** idea.*

4 someone who is bad at something does not do it well or find it easy ANTONYM **good**: *I'm pretty **bad at** maths.* • *Gary's **worse** than me **at** getting up early.*

5 serious or severe: *She had a **bad** cough.* • *Was the traffic **bad** this morning?*

6 not morally good ANTONYM **good**: *Her husband was a **bad** man, and the children were afraid of him.*

THESAURUS
wrong: *It's **wrong** to steal* (=very bad).
immoral: *I think cruelty to animals is **immoral*** (=very bad).
wicked: *a story about a **wicked** witch* (=she did bad things)
evil: *The man was an **evil** killer* (=he did extremely bad things).

7 something that is bad for you is not healthy for your body or mind ANTONYM **good**: *Fatty foods such as chips are **bad for** you.*

PHRASES

not bad *BrE* (spoken)
*"Was the food good?" "**Not bad*** (=it was fairly good; okay)*."*

too bad (spoken)
used to say that you do not care what someone thinks or feels: *"I think you should stay at home this evening." "**Too bad**, I want to go out!"*

feel bad
to feel ashamed or sorry: *I **feel bad that** I wasn't there when you needed me.*

bail² *verb* **bail someone out** to help someone who is in trouble, especially by giving them money: *She asked her dad to* ***bail*** *her* ***out****.*

bait /beɪt/ *noun* food that you use to attract fish or animals so that you can catch them: *We used worms for bait.*

bake /beɪk/ *verb* to make things such as bread and cakes: *Mom bakes her own bread.*

ˌbaked ˈbeans *plural noun* white beans cooked with tomato sauce and sold in TINS

bak·er /ˈbeɪkə $ ˈbeɪkɚ/ *noun*
1 someone whose job is making bread
2 baker's a shop that sells bread and cakes: *Is there a baker's near here?*

bak·er·y /ˈbeɪkəri/ *noun* (plural **bakeries**) a place where people make or sell bread

bal·ance¹ /ˈbæləns/ *noun* (no plural)
1 when you are able to stay steady while you are standing up: *These drugs may affect your balance.*
2 when you give the right amount of attention to two different things, rather than giving too much attention to one of them: *It's important to* ***find a balance between*** *work and play.*

PHRASES

lose your balance: *I* ***lost my balance*** *and fell off the wall* (=was unable to stay steady).

off balance when you are not steady, for example because you are standing on one leg: *The wind caught him* ***off balance*** *and he fell over.*

on balance used to tell someone your opinion after considering all the facts: ***On balance****, the new test is probably fairer.*

balance² *verb* to stay in a steady position, without falling to one side or the other: *Can you balance on this beam?*

bal·anced /ˈbælənst/ *adjective* **1** a balanced opinion, view etc is sensible and fair: *He has a very balanced attitude to the situation.* **2** a balanced meal, way of living etc includes a variety of different things that you need to make you healthy or happy: *Eat a balanced diet with plenty of fresh fruit and vegetables.*

bal·co·ny /ˈbælkəni/ *noun* (plural **balconies**) a small area outside an upstairs window, where you can sit or stand: *The room had a balcony overlooking the harbour.*

balcony

bald /bɔːld/ *adjective* having little or no hair on your head: *He's going bald.*

bale /beɪl/ *noun* a large amount of dried grass that has been tied together: *a bale of hay*

ball /bɔːl/ *noun*
1 a round object that you throw, hit, or kick in a game: *She threw a tennis ball at me.* • *a golf ball*
2 any round object: ***a ball of*** *string*
→ see picture at YARN
3 a large formal party where people dance: *a Christmas ball*

bal·lad /ˈbæləd/ *noun* a long song that tells a story

bal·le·ri·na /ˌbæləˈriːnə/ *noun* a female ballet dancer: *I wanted to be a ballerina when I grew up.*

bal·let /ˈbæleɪ $ bæˈleɪ/ *noun* **1** (no plural) a type of dancing that dancers do on a stage in a theatre, which tells a story with music and actions but no words: *I've been doing ballet for a year.* **2** a dance done in this style: *Swan Lake is my favourite ballet.*

bal·loon /bəˈluːn/ *noun* a coloured rubber object that you fill with air and use as a decoration

bal·lot /ˈbælət/ *verb* to find out what a group of people wants by asking them to vote in secret: *The trade union will ballot its members next week, asking them if they want to take strike action* (=asking them if they want to officially stop working). —**ballot** *noun*: *We held a ballot to decide who would be the new chairman.*

ball·park /ˈbɔːlpɑːk $ ˈbɒlˌpɑrk/ *noun* *AmE* a field for playing baseball, with seats for people to watch the game

ball·point pen /ˌbɔːlpɔɪnt ˈpen/ *noun* a pen with a very small ball in the end that controls the flow of ink

ball·room /ˈbɔːlruːm/ *noun* a large room for formal dances: *the hotel ballroom*

bam·boo /ˌbæmˈbuː/ *noun* a tall plant with hard hollow stems that are used to make furniture: *a set of bamboo chairs*

ban¹ /bæn/ *noun* an official order saying that people cannot do something: *They put a ban on nuclear tests.* ➔ see Thesaurus at RULE¹

ban² *verb* (**banned, banning**) to officially say that people cannot do something SYNONYM **prohibit**: *Britain has banned cigarette advertising.* ➔ see Thesaurus at FORBID

ba·nal /bəˈnɑːl $ bəˈnæl/ *adjective* (formal) ordinary and not interesting: *a banal conversation*

ba·na·na /bəˈnɑːnə $ bəˈnænə/ *noun* a long curved yellow fruit: *a bunch of bananas* ➔ see picture at BUNCH¹ ➔ see picture on page A7

band¹ /bænd/ *noun*

KEY PATTERNS
be/play in a band

1 a group of musicians who play popular music together: *He plays drums in a band.* • *Which is your favourite band?*
2 a thin flat piece of material that you use to keep something in a particular position: *She wore a white hair band.* • *a pack of rubber bands*

band² *verb* **band together (to do something)** to join with other people to do something: *We all banded together to organize the party.*

ban·dage /ˈbændɪdʒ/ *noun* a long piece of cloth that you use to cover a wound —**bandage** *verb*: *The nurse bandaged my leg.*

ˈ**Band-Aid** *AmE* (trademark) the American word for a PLASTER¹

ban·dit /ˈbændɪt/ *noun* someone who robs people who are travelling: *The bandits stole money and cameras from the tourists.*

band·width /ˈbændwɪdθ/ *noun* the amount of information that can be carried through a computer connection or a telephone wire at one time: *an old telephone modem with a bandwidth of 512 K*

bang¹ /bæŋ/ *verb*

KEY PATTERNS
bang on a door/table
bang the phone/a glass down
bang your head/knee on something

1 to make a loud noise by hitting something hard: *Someone's **banging on** the door.* • *The door **banged shut*** (=it made a loud sound as it closed). • *Lucy **banged** the phone **down** angrily.* ➔ see Thesaurus at HIT¹
2 to hit a part of your body against something by mistake: *Don't bang your head on the ceiling.*

bang² *noun*

KEY PATTERNS
with a bang
a bang on the head/knee

1 a sudden loud noise: *He slammed the door **with a** loud **bang**.* • *I heard a bang, and the car engine started smoking.*
2 when you hit part of your body against something hard by mistake: *a painful **bang on** the knee*
3 bangs the American word for FRINGE: *My bangs are getting long.*

bang³ *adverb* (informal) exactly: *He arrived bang on time.*

ban·gle /ˈbæŋgəl/ *noun* a band of metal or wood that you wear around your wrist: *silver bangles* ➔ see picture at JEWELLERY

ban·ish /ˈbænɪʃ/ *verb* to punish someone by making them go away somewhere: *My mother banished me to my bedroom.*

ban·is·ter /ˈbænəstə $ ˈbænəstɚ/ *noun* the long piece of wood at the side of stairs that you can hold onto as you go up them ➔ see picture at STAIRCASE

ban·jo /ˈbændʒəʊ $ ˈbændʒoʊ/ *noun* a musical instrument with four or more strings and a round body

bank¹ /bæŋk/ *noun*
1 an organization where you can keep your money safely until you need it. You can also borrow or change money

in a bank: *You can change your money into pounds* ***at the bank***. • *I need to go to the bank to get some money.*
2 land along the side of a river or lake: *We went for a walk along the* ***river bank***. → see Thesaurus at SHORE
3 a place where a large amount of something is kept until someone needs it: *a* ***data bank***

bank² *verb* **bank on someone/something** to depend on someone for something SYNONYM **count on**: *We were banking on your help.*

bank·er /ˈbæŋkə $ ˈbæŋkɚ/ *noun* someone who works in a bank at a high level

ˌbank ˈholiday *noun BrE* an official holiday when banks and most companies are closed SYNONYM **public holiday** *AmE*: *Next Monday is a bank holiday.*

bank·ing /ˈbæŋkɪŋ/ *noun* (no plural) the business that is done by a bank: *I'd like a career in banking.*

bank·note /ˈbæŋknəʊt $ ˈbæŋkˌnoʊt/ *noun* a piece of paper money SYNONYM **bill** *AmE*

bank·rupt /ˈbæŋkrʌpt/ *adjective* not able to pay your debts, and therefore not able to continue in business: *Many small businesses go bankrupt.*
—**bankrupt** *verb*: *This tax increase could bankrupt us.*

bank·rupt·cy /ˈbæŋkrʌptsi/ *noun* (plural **bankruptcies**) when someone goes bankrupt: *A series of business failures led to bankruptcy.*

ban·ner /ˈbænə $ ˈbænɚ/ *noun* a long piece of cloth with writing on it: *They waved banners reading 'Welcome home'.*

ban·quet /ˈbæŋkwɪt/ *noun* a very formal meal for a lot of people: *a state banquet*

bap·tis·m /ˈbæptɪzəm/ *noun* a religious ceremony in which a priest puts water on someone to make them a member of the Christian Church

bap·tize also **baptise** *BrE* /bæpˈtaɪz $ ˈbæptaɪz/ *verb* to put water on someone in a religious ceremony to make them a member of the Christian Church: *This is the priest who baptized me.*

bar¹ /bɑː $ bɑr/ *noun*

KEY PATTERNS
at a bar
in a hotel/restaurant bar
a bar of something

1 a place where you can buy and drink alcohol: *Steve was standing* ***at the bar*** *with a glass of beer.* • *I just met a really old friend in the hotel bar* (=a place in a hotel where you can buy drinks).
2 coffee bar/sandwich bar etc a place where you can buy and drink coffee, buy and eat a sandwich etc: *a coffee bar*
3 a small block of something solid: *a* ***bar of soap*** • *a chocolate bar*
4 a long thin piece of metal or wood: *The man attacked us with an iron bar.*
5 a part of a piece of music, which consists of several notes or beats: *She played* ***a few bars of*** *the song on her guitar.*

bar² *verb* (**barred**, **barring**) to officially stop someone from doing something: *He was barred from playing football for six months.*

bar·bar·ic /bɑːˈbærɪk $ bɑrˈbærɪk/ *adjective* violent and cruel: *This was a barbaric crime.*

bar·be·cue /ˈbɑːbɪkjuː $ ˈbɑrbɪˌkju/ *noun* **1** an occasion when you cook and eat hot food outdoors, on a fire or a special piece of equipment: *We had a barbecue on the beach.* **2** a piece of equipment that you use for cooking food outdoors: *Put some more sausages on the barbecue.*
—**barbecue** *verb*: *Dad barbecued all the food.*

ˌbarbed ˈwire /ˌbɑːbd ˈwaɪə $ ˌbɑːrbd ˈwaɪɚ/ *noun* (no plural) wire with short sharp points on it, to stop people from getting into a place: *a fence with barbed wire on top*

barbed wire

bar·ber /ˈbɑːbə $ ˈbɑrbɚ/ *noun* a man whose job is to cut men's hair

ˈbar code *noun* a row of black lines printed on products sold in a shop, that a computer reads when you buy the product

bare /beə $ ber/ *adjective* **1** not covered by clothes: *It's too cold to go out with bare legs.* **2** empty: *The classroom looked very bare without any desks.* ➔ see Thesaurus at EMPTY[1]

bare·foot /ˌbeəˈfʊt $ ˈberfʊt/ *adjective, adverb* not wearing any shoes or socks: *They walked barefoot on the grass.*

barefoot

bare·ly /ˈbeəli $ ˈberli/ *adverb* almost not: *I could barely understand her.*

bar·gain¹ /ˈbɑːɡən $ ˈbɑrɡən/ *noun* something you buy for a price that is cheaper than normal: *In the market you can often find a bargain.*

bargain² *verb* to discuss with someone how much you are willing to pay for something, or how much money you want to be paid for something, until you both agree about it SYNONYM **haggle**: *In Egypt they expect you to bargain over the price you pay.*

barge¹ /bɑːdʒ $ bɑrdʒ/ *verb* (informal) to walk somewhere quickly, pushing past people or things: *He barged past me into the room.*

barge² *noun* a long narrow boat with a flat bottom

bark¹ /bɑːk $ bɑrk/ *verb* if a dog barks, it makes several short loud sounds: *I knocked on the door and a dog barked inside.*

bark

bark² *noun* **1** the sound that a dog makes **2** (no plural) the material that covers the surface of a tree ➔ see picture on page A10

bar·ley /ˈbɑːli $ ˈbɑrli/ *noun* (no plural) a grain used to make food and alcoholic drinks

bar·maid /ˈbɑːmeɪd $ ˈbɑrmeɪd/ *noun BrE* a woman whose job is to serve drinks in a bar SYNONYM **bartender** *AmE*

bar·man /ˈbɑːmən/ *noun BrE* (plural **barmen** /-mən/) a man whose job is to serve drinks in a bar SYNONYM **bartender** *AmE*

barn /bɑːn $ bɑrn/ *noun* a building on a farm for keeping crops or animals in

bar·racks /ˈbærəks/ *plural noun* a group of buildings where soldiers live

bar·rage /ˈbærɑːʒ $ bəˈrɑʒ/ *noun* when there are a lot of complaints, questions, sounds etc that happen very quickly after each other: *We faced a barrage of criticism after announcing the winner.*

bar·rel /ˈbærəl/ *noun* a large container for liquids such as beer: *I've ordered ten barrels of beer.*

bar·ren /ˈbærən/ *adjective* if land is barren, plants cannot grow on it ANTONYM **fertile**: *a barren desert*

bar·ri·cade /ˈbærəkeɪd/ *noun* an object that is put across a road or a door to stop people from going through: *The police put barricades across the road.* —**barricade** *verb*: *The kids had barricaded themselves into their bedroom.*

bar·ri·er /ˈbæriə $ ˈbæriɚ/ *noun* a fence that stops people from entering an area: *The police put up barriers to hold back the crowds.*

bar·tend·er /ˈbɑːˌtendə $ ˈbɑrˌtendɚ/ *noun AmE* someone whose job is to serve drinks in a bar SYNONYM **barman** *BrE* SYNONYM **barmaid** *BrE*

bar·ter /ˈbɑːtə $ ˈbɑrtɚ/ *verb* to pay for goods or services by giving other goods or services, instead of using money: *They bartered food for coal.*

base¹ /beɪs/ *verb*

KEY PATTERNS
based in/at a place

to live somewhere most of the time, or use it as your main place of business: *The actress was born in Wales but **is based in** Los Angeles now. • The New York City ballet **is based at** the Lincoln Center. • Where are you based?*

PHRASAL VERBS

base on

base something on something to develop an idea, story etc from particular information or facts: *The film **is based on** events in the director's life.*

A B C D E F G H I J K L M N O P Q R S T U V W X Y Z

base² *noun*

KEY PATTERNS
the base of a tree/mountain/dish
a base for walking/touring/exploring

1 the lowest part of something SYNONYM **bottom**: *They planted flowers around* ***the base of*** *the tree.* • *We had to repair the base of the boat.*
2 a place where people in the army, navy etc live and work: *There is a US* ***military base*** *near here.*
3 a place that you stay in because it is close to other places that you want to go to: *We used the campsite* ***as a base for*** *exploring the mountains.*
4 one of the four places that a player must run to in order to get a point in the game of baseball

base·ball /ˈbeɪsbɔːl/ *noun* **1** (no plural) a game in which two teams try to get points by hitting a ball and running around four bases: *Who's your favourite baseball player?* **2** the ball used in this game

base·ment /ˈbeɪsmənt/ *noun* the rooms in a building that are below the level of the ground: *We keep our wine in the basement.*

bases the plural of BASIS

bash /bæʃ/ *verb* to hit something hard: *I bashed my leg on the table.*

bash·ful /ˈbæʃfəl/ *adjective* embarrassed and shy: *Why are you looking so bashful?*

ba·sic /ˈbeɪsɪk/ *adjective*
1 you use 'basic' to describe things that are the simplest and most important part of something: *I know some basic vocabulary in Greek.* • *His basic problem is that he's lazy.*
2 if something is basic, it has only the things you need and nothing more: *The science equipment in the school is very basic.*

ba·si·cally /ˈbeɪsɪkli/ *adverb*
1 (spoken) you use 'basically' to explain a situation or describe something simply: *Basically, the team didn't play well enough.*
2 in the most important ways: *She gave basically the right answer.*

ba·sics /ˈbeɪsɪks/ *plural noun* the most important skills or facts of something: *I don't even know the basics of first aid.*

ba·sin /ˈbeɪsən/ *noun BrE* the round container in a bathroom for washing your hands and face SYNONYM **washbasin**

ba·sis /ˈbeɪsəs/ *noun* (plural **bases** /-siːz/)
1 on the basis of something for a particular reason or because of a particular piece of information: ***On the basis of*** *her interview she got a place at college.* • *The doctor decided to admit Jean to hospital* ***on the basis of*** *her symptoms.*
2 on a weekly basis, on a regular basis etc: *We meet regularly,* ***on a monthly basis*** (=we meet every month). • *He runs several miles* ***on a daily basis*** (=every day). • *I go swimming* ***on a regular basis*** (=regularly).
3 the basis for something the information or ideas that you use to develop an idea or plan: *The work he did at university* ***formed the basis for*** *his first book.*

bask /bɑːsk $ bæsk/ *verb* to enjoy lying somewhere warm: *The cat was basking in the sun.*

baskets

bas·ket /ˈbɑːskɪt $ ˈbæskɪt/ *noun* a container made from thin pieces of wood, plastic, or wire: *She brought me a basket of fruit.* • *a woman with a shopping basket full of groceries*

bas·ket·ball /ˈbɑːskɪtbɔːl $ ˈbæskɪtˌbɔl/ *noun* **1** a game in which two teams try to win points by throwing a ball through a net: *I'm not very good at basketball.* **2** the ball used in this game → see picture on page A14

bass¹ /beɪs/ *adjective* a bass instrument plays low musical notes: *He plays the bass guitar.*

bass² *noun* **1** a singer or instrument that sings or plays notes that are the lowest in the range **2** a DOUBLE BASS

bas·soon /bəˈsuːn/ *noun* a long wooden musical instrument that makes a low sound

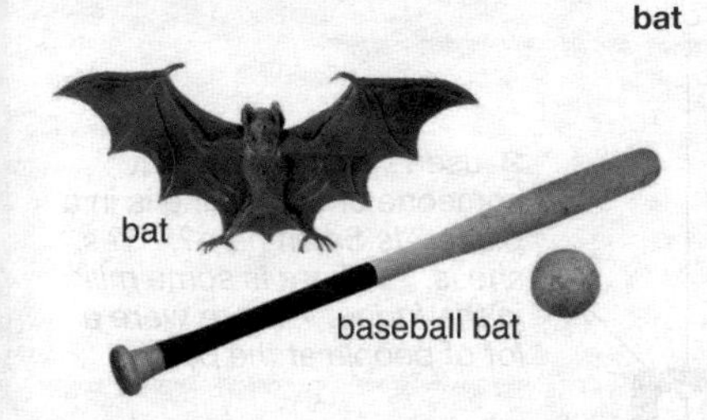

bat¹ /bæt/ *noun* **1** a piece of wood that you use to hit the ball in some games: *a baseball bat* **2** a small animal like a mouse with wings, that flies around at night

bat² *verb* (**batted**, **batting**) to hit the ball with a bat in a game: *It's your turn to bat.*

batch /bætʃ/ *noun* (plural **batches**) a group of things that arrive together: *I've just received my first batch of replies.*

bath¹ /bɑːθ $ bæθ/ *noun* *BrE* a long container that you sit in to wash yourself SYNONYM **bathtub** *AmE*: *Sally's **in the bath**.*

PHRASES

have a bath *BrE*, **take a bath** *AmE* to wash yourself in a bath: *I think I'll have a nice hot bath.*

bath² *verb* *BrE* to wash someone in a bath: *I'll help you bath the baby.*

bathe /beɪð/ *verb* **1** to wash a wound or a part of your body: *Bathe the cut with warm water.* **2** *AmE* to wash yourself in a bath: *I usually bathe in the morning.*

bathing suit /ˈbeɪðɪŋ ˌsuːt/ *noun* a SWIMSUIT

bath·robe /ˈbɑːθrəʊb $ ˈbæθroʊb/ *noun* a piece of clothing like a coat that you wear after you have a bath

bath·room /ˈbɑːθruːm $ ˈbæθrum/ *noun* **1** the room in a house where you wash yourself **2** **go to the bathroom** *AmE* to use the toilet

bath·tub /ˈbɑːθtʌb $ ˈbæθtʌb/ an American word for a BATH¹

bats·man /ˈbætsmən/ (plural **batsmen** /-mən/) *noun* the person who is trying to hit the ball in CRICKET

bat·tal·ion /bəˈtæljən/ *noun* a large group of soldiers that consists of several smaller groups

bat·ter¹ /ˈbætə $ ˈbætɚ/ *noun* **1** a mixture of flour, milk, and eggs: *They served fish in batter.* **2** the person who is trying to hit the ball in baseball

batter² *verb* to hit something many times: *The waves battered against the rocks.*

bat·tered /ˈbætəd $ ˈbætɚd/ *adjective* old and damaged: *a battered old book*

bat·ter·y /ˈbætəri/ *noun* (plural **batteries**) an object that provides the electrical power for a machine, toy, car etc: *I need to recharge the batteries for my camera.* • *The car's got a **flat battery*** (=one that doesn't work anymore).

bat·tle¹ /ˈbætl/ *noun* **1** a fight between two armies: *Many soldiers were killed in the battle.* **2** a situation in which people try to do something difficult: *The police in many cities are fighting a battle against crime.*

battle² *verb* to try very hard to do or get something SYNONYM **fight**: *We had to battle to get new computers for the school.*

bat·tle·field /ˈbætlfiːld/ also **bat·tle·ground** /ˈbætlgraʊnd/ *noun* a place where a battle has been fought

bat·tle·ship /ˈbætlˌʃɪp/ *noun* a very large ship used in wars

bawl /bɔːl/ *verb* (informal) to shout or cry loudly: *The baby was bawling for most of the journey.*

bay /beɪ/ *noun* a part of the coast where the land curves inwards: *I know a bay that's great for surfing.*

ba·zaar /bəˈzɑː $ bəˈzɑr/ *noun* a sale to collect money for an organization: *I bought this book at a school bazaar.*

BC /ˌbiː ˈsiː/ *adverb* an abbreviation for 'Before Christ'; used in dates to mean before the birth of Christ: *Alexander the Great died in 323 BC.*

be → see box on page 56

be /biː/ *verb*

1 used when describing someone or something: *I'm very tired.* • *My brothers* ***are*** *older than me.* • *The movie* ***wasn't*** *very good.* • *The next meeting* ***will be*** *on Friday.* • *It* ***has been*** *a good day.*

2 used when saying that someone or something is in a place: *"Is Sarah here?" "Yes, she* ***is****."* • ***There is*** *some milk in the fridge.* • ***There were*** *a lot of people at the party.*

3 used when talking about the time, the day, or the date: ***It's*** *ten o'clock.* • ***Is it*** *Tuesday today?*

4 used to form the progressive of a verb: *It* ***is*** *raining.* • *What* ***are*** *you doing?*

5 used to form the passive of a verb: *The house* ***was*** *built in 2005.* • *He***'s** *called John.*

6 used when saying how someone should behave, or how someone is behaving: ***Be*** *careful!* • *Stop* ***being*** *silly!*

GRAMMAR

there is or **there are**?

- Use **there is** with a singular noun: *There is a car outside our house.*
- Use **there are** with a plural noun: *There are too many cars on the roads.*

✗ Don't say 'There is too many cars.'

Don't forget **a**.

- Always use **a** when **be** is followed by a singular noun: *My mother is a doctor.*

✗ Don't say 'My mother is doctor.'

VERB FORMS

Present tense

Singular	Plural
I **am** (I**'m**)	we **are** (we**'re**)
you **are** (you**'re**)	you **are** (you**'re**)
he, she, it **is** (he**'s**, she**'s**, it**'s**)	they **are** (they**'re**)

Past tense

Singular	Plural
I **was**	we **were**
you **were**	you **were**
he, she, it **was**	they **were**

present participle: **being**
past participle: **been**
negative short forms: **aren't, isn't, wasn't, weren't**

beach /biːtʃ/ *noun* (plural **beaches**) an area of sand next to the sea: *Shall we go to the beach?* ➔ see Thesaurus at SHORE

bea•con /ˈbiːkən/ *noun* a light that flashes to guide boats or planes

bead /biːd/ *noun* a small round ball of plastic or glass used in jewellery: *She wore a string of beads around her neck.*

bead•y /ˈbiːdi/ *adjective* (**beadier**, **beadiest**) beady eyes are small and dark: *an old woman with beady eyes*

beak /biːk/ *noun* the hard pointed mouth of a bird ➔ see picture at BIRD

beam¹ /biːm/ *noun* **1** a line of light shining from something: *A beam of light shone through the curtains.* **2** a long heavy piece of wood or metal that is used to support something in a building: *I banged my head on a wooden beam.*

beam² *verb* to smile very happily: *Gary beamed at us as he went to collect his prize.* ➔ see Thesaurus at SMILE¹

bean /biːn/ *noun* **1** the seed of a plant that you can cook and eat, or the seed and the case together: *green beans* **2** the seed of a plant that is used to make a drink: *coffee beans*

bear¹ /beə $ ber/ *verb* (**bore** /bɔː $ bɔr/ **borne** /bɔːn $ bɔrn/)

KEY PATTERNS
can bear something
can bear to do something
can bear doing something

1 to be able to accept or deal with something unpleasant: *Some people can bear pain better than others.* • *Dad loved the house and he* ***couldn't bear to sell it.*** • *When she died, I didn't think* ***I could bear*** *living alone.*
2 to turn or go in a particular direction: *Go straight on until you reach a church, then* ***bear right.***
3 (formal) to carry or bring something: *George came in bearing a message.*

PHRASES
bear in mind that, bear something in mind to consider something or someone carefully when you are making a decision about something: ***Bear in mind that*** *the journey may take longer in bad weather.* • *I hope you'll* ***bear me in mind*** *if any jobs come up.*
can't bear (doing) something, can't bear it to hate something very much: *I* ***can't bear*** *the food we get at school.* • *Mum* ***can't bear*** *travelling by plane.* • *It's so hot here – I can't bear it!*
bear the blame, bear the responsibility to accept that you are responsible for something bad that has happened: *The school must* ***bear some responsibility for*** *the accident.*
bear a grudge to feel angry with someone for a long time because of something they have done: *Mark was the sort of person who* ***bore a grudge*** *for months after an argument.*

PHRASAL VERBS
bear out
bear something out to show that something is true: *There is no evidence* ***to bear out*** *this idea.*

bear² *noun* a large strong animal with thick fur: *There are wild bears around here.* ➔ see picture on page A9

bear•a•ble /ˈbeərəbəl $ ˈberəbəl/ *adjective* if a situation is bearable, it is difficult but you are able to accept it or deal with it: *I don't enjoy the work but it is bearable.*

beard /bɪəd $ bɪrd/ *noun* the hair that grows on a man's chin: *He has shaved his beard off.*

bear•ing /ˈbeərɪŋ $ ˈberɪŋ/ *noun*
1 have a bearing on something to affect something: *Recent events have had a bearing on his decision.*
2 lose your bearings to become lost: *The boat lost its bearings in the fog.*

beast /biːst/ *noun* (written) a wild or dangerous animal

beat¹ /biːt/ *verb* (**beat**, **beaten** /ˈbiːtn/)

KEY PATTERNS
beat a player/team
beat someone at tennis/golf/cricket
beat a drum

A B C D E F G H I J K L M N O P Q R S T U V W X Y Z

beat the eggs/mixture
beat on the roof/windows

1 to defeat someone in a game or competition: *Our team beat theirs easily.* • *I* **beat** *Dad* **at** *tennis for the first time today.*
2 to hit someone or something many times with your hand, a stick etc: *They beat him and robbed him.* • *One man marched in front* **beating a drum.**
➔ see Thesaurus at HIT[1]
3 to mix food together quickly using a fork, spoon etc: **Beat the eggs** *and pour them into a pan.* ➔ see Thesaurus at MIX[1] ➔ see picture on page A4
4 to make a regular sound or movement: *I can hear your* **heart beating.** • *The rain* **beat on** *the roofs of the little houses all night.*

PHRASAL VERBS
beat up
beat someone up to hit someone many times so that they are badly hurt: *A gang of men* **beat** *him* **up** *and left him.*

THESAURUS
defeat (formal): *France were* **defeated** *in the final game* (=beaten).
win: *Who do you think will* **win** *the election* (=beat all the other people)?

beat² *noun* a regular movement or sound: *the slow beat of a drum*

beat·en /ˈbiːtn/ *adjective* **off the beaten track** far away from places that people usually visit: *We want to stay somewhere off the beaten track.*

beau·ti·ful /ˈbjuːtəfəl/ *adjective*
1 a woman, girl, or child who is beautiful is very attractive: *Some of the models were incredibly beautiful.*
➔ see Thesaurus at ATTRACTIVE
2 something that is beautiful is very attractive or pleasant: *That's a beautiful picture.* • *The music was really beautiful.* —**beautifully** *adverb*: *She sings beautifully.*

SPELLING
This word is often spelled wrongly. The correct spelling is: **beautiful**.

beau·ty /ˈbjuːti/ *noun* (no plural) the quality of being beautiful: *He was amazed by her beauty.* • *the beauty of the morning sunrise*

became the past tense of BECOME

be·cause¹ /bɪˈkɒz, bɪkəz $ bɪˈkɔz, bɪkəz/ *conjunction*
used to give the reason for something: *I like history because it's interesting.* • *She left the party early because she felt ill.*

because² *preposition*
because of something used to give the reason for something: *He did badly in his exams* **because of** *problems at home.*

beck·on /ˈbekən/ *verb* (formal) to move your hand or arm to show that you want someone to come to you: *He beckoned me over to him.*

be·come /bɪˈkʌm/ *verb* (**became** /bɪˈkeɪm/ **become**)
1 (formal) to start to be or do something SYNONYM **get**: *The weather had become colder.* • *It is becoming difficult to find a parking space.* • *Dad started to become angry.*
2 if someone becomes a doctor, teacher etc, they start to be a doctor, teacher etc: *At the age of only 35 he became a judge.*

THESAURUS
get: *It's* **getting** *dark outside* (=becoming dark).
go: *Have you* **gone** *crazy* (=become crazy)?
turn: *In autumn, the tree's leaves* **turn** *yellow* (=become yellow).
grow (formal): *The others* **grew** *tired and went home* (=became tired).

WORD CHOICE
become or **get**?
• **Become** and **get** mean the same when they are used with an adjective.
• **Get** is the usual word to use in conversation: *I'm* **getting** *tired.* • *It's* **getting** *cold in here.*
• **Become** is used especially in formal English: *The Earth's temperature is* **becoming** *warmer.*

bed /bed/ *noun* **1** a piece of furniture that you sleep on at night: *It's time to go to bed.* • *I bought a new bed.* **2** the ground at the bottom of the sea or a river: *The boat's now lying on the sea bed.*

bed·clothes /ˈbedkləʊðz $ ˈbedkloʊðz/ *plural noun* the sheets and other covers that are on a bed

A B C D E F G H I J K L M N O P Q R S T U V W X Y Z

bed·rid·den /ˈbedˌrɪdn/ *adjective* unable to get out of bed because you are old or ill: *My grandmother's bedridden and can't go out.*

bed·room /ˈbedruːm/ *noun* a room that you sleep in at night: *a house with four bedrooms*

bed·side /ˈbedsaɪd/ *noun* the area next to a bed: *His mother stayed at his bedside all night.*

bed·sit /ˌbedˈsɪt/ also **bed·sit·ter** /ˌbedˈsɪtə $ ˌbedˈsɪtɚ/ *noun BrE* a room that you rent to live and sleep in: *I had a bedsit in London.*

bed·spread /ˈbedspred/ *noun* a large cloth cover that goes on top of a bed

bed·time /ˈbedtaɪm/ *noun* the time when you usually go to bed: *It's past my bedtime.*

bee /biː/ *noun* a black and yellow flying insect that makes HONEY → see picture at INSECT

beef /biːf/ *noun* (no plural) meat from a cow

beef·bur·ger /ˈbiːfˌbɜːgə $ ˈbifˌbɚgɚ/ *noun BrE* a BURGER

bee·hive /ˈbiːhaɪv/ *noun* a place where you keep BEES to make HONEY

been /biːn, bɪn $ bɪn/ **1** the past participle of BE **2** a past participle of GO

beep /biːp/ *verb* to make a short high noise: *My mobile phone beeps when there's a message for me.* —**beep** *noun*: *I heard the beep of a car horn.*

beep·er /ˈbiːpə $ ˈbipɚ/ *noun* a PAGER

beer /bɪə $ bɪr/ *noun* (no plural) a drink that contains alcohol, made from grain: *a bottle of beer*

bee·tle /ˈbiːtl/ *noun* an insect with a hard round black back → see picture at INSECT

beet·root /ˈbiːtruːt/ *BrE*, **beet** /biːt/ *AmE noun* a dark red root of a plant that you can cook and eat

be·fore¹ /bɪˈfɔː $ bɪˈfɔr/ *preposition*
1 earlier than ANTONYM **after**: *I got up before 7 o'clock.* • *We arrived before the others.*
2 when something has not yet happened or started ANTONYM **after**: *I felt very tired before my holiday.* • *We met in a pub before the show.*

PHRASES
before long soon: *First my sister caught the flu, and* ***before long*** *everyone in the family had it.* → see Thesaurus at SOON

before² *adverb*
used to show that something has already happened once, at an earlier time: *I had seen the film before.* • *I think I've met you before.*

PHRASES
the day before, the year before etc the previous day, year etc: *I spoke to her yesterday and* ***the day before.*** • *His mother had died* ***the year before.***
two weeks before, many years before etc two weeks, many years etc before a time or event in the past: *He was unable to take part in the game because he had injured his leg* ***two weeks before.***
the same as before if something is the same as before, it has not changed: *When I came home, everything was just the same as before.*

> **WORD CHOICE**
> **before** or **ago**?
> • You use **ago** when saying how long it is since something happened: *My grandfather died a long time* ***ago.***
> • You use **before** when saying how long before a time in the past something happened: *The first men landed on the moon in 1969. Of course people had imagined doing this many years* ***before.***

before³ *conjunction*
if you do something before doing something else, you do the first thing at

an earlier time than the second thing ANTONYM **after**: *I always brush my teeth before going to bed.* • *You should wash the walls before you paint them.*

be·fore·hand /bɪˈfɔːhænd $ bɪˈfɔrˌhænd/ *adverb* (formal) before a particular time or event: *Our teacher told us beforehand that the test would be difficult.*

beg /beg/ *verb* (**begged**, **begging**)
1 to ask for something in a way that shows you want or need it very much: *She begged me to stay.* → see Thesaurus at ASK **2** to ask someone for food or money because you are very poor: *Children were begging in the street.*

began the past tense of BEGIN

beg·gar /ˈbegə $ ˈbegɚ/ *noun* someone who lives by asking people for food and money

be·gin /bɪˈgɪn/ *verb* (**began** /bɪˈgæn/ **begun** /bɪˈgʌn/ **beginning**)

> KEY PATTERNS
> **begin something**
> **begin to do something**
> **begin doing something**
> **begin with something**
> **begin by looking/saying/discussing**

to start doing something, or to start to happen SYNONYM **start**: *I began piano lessons when I was five.* • *The exam will begin at nine o'clock.* • *She **began to** cry.* • *When did you begin having these headaches?* • *The band **began with** one of their most famous hits.* • *Let's **begin by** looking at page 25.*

PHRASES
to begin with **a)** used to introduce the first or most important point: *They made a lot of mistakes. **To begin with**, they spelt my name wrong.* **b)** at the start of something: ***To begin with**, we all introduced ourselves.*

> WORD CHOICE
> **begin** or **start**?
> • **Begin** and **start** mean the same.
> • **Begin** is used more in formal English: *The concert will **begin** at 7.30.*
> • **Start** is used especially in informal, spoken English: *What time does your class **start**?*

be·gin·ner /bɪˈgɪnə $ bɪˈgɪnɚ/ *noun* someone who has just started to do or learn something: *This French class is for complete beginners.*

be·gin·ning /bɪˈgɪnɪŋ/ *noun*

> KEY PATTERNS
> **the beginning of something**
> **at the beginning of something**
> **in the beginning**

the start or first part of something ANTONYM **end**: *I didn't like **the beginning of** the book.* • *We moved house **at the beginning of** the year.* • ***In the beginning**, the company was very successful.* • *Can we start again **from the beginning**?*

> SPELLING
> This word is often spelled wrongly. The correct spelling is: **beginning**.

be·grudge /bɪˈgrʌdʒ/ *verb* if you begrudge someone something, you do not want them to have it, usually because it is something you want: *I don't begrudge him his money.*

begun the past participle of BEGIN

be·half /bɪˈhɑːf $ bɪˈhæf/ *noun* **on behalf of someone, on someone's behalf** instead of someone, or in order to help someone: *Will you go to the meeting on my behalf?*

be·have /bɪˈheɪv/ *verb*
1 to do or say things in a particular way: *Some boys behaved badly at the party.*
2 to act politely and not cause trouble ANTONYM **misbehave**: *I hope you **behave yourself** while your mother is away.* • *Children, please behave.*

be·hav·iour *BrE*, **behavior** *AmE* /bɪˈheɪvjə $ bɪˈheɪvjɚ/ *noun* (no plural) your behaviour is the way that you act or do things: *I thought Paul's behaviour was very rude.*

be·hind[1] /bɪˈhaɪnd/ *preposition, adverb*
1 at or near the back of something SYNONYM **in front (of)**: *The car behind us was driving too close.* • *His diary had fallen behind the sofa.* • *There are some empty seats in the row behind.*
2 less successful than someone in a competition SYNONYM **ahead (of)**: *Our team is still behind theirs in the championship.*

3 responsible for something that has happened: *Who is behind the bombing?*

behind² *adjective*
behind with something if you are behind with your work, you have not done as much work as you should have done: *I can't come out, I'm a bit behind with my homework this week.*

beige /beɪʒ/ *adjective, noun* a pale brown colour: *a beige carpet*

be·ing /ˈbiːɪŋ/ *noun* **1** a creature or person: *The film is about beings from outer space.* **2 come into being** to begin to exist: *A lot of new towns came into being in the 1960s.*

be·lat·ed /bɪˈleɪtɪd/ *adjective* a belated letter, action etc is sent or done late: *Myra sent me a belated birthday card.*

belch /beltʃ/ BURP

be·lief /bəˈliːf/ *noun*

KEY PATTERNS
belief that
a belief in progress/science/education
someone's belief in someone

1 (no plural) the feeling that something is true or right: *There is a general **belief that** parents know what is best for their children.* • *We share **a belief in** the importance of education.*
2 (no plural) a feeling of respect or trust for someone or something, because you think that they are good: *She never lost her **belief in** him.*
3 an idea that you think is true: *What are your religious beliefs?*

be·liev·a·ble /bəˈliːvəbəl/ *adjective* easy to believe SYNONYM **convincing**: *His story is very believable.*

be·lieve /bəˈliːv/ *verb*

KEY PATTERNS
believe something/someone
believe that
believe someone/something to be something

1 to feel sure that something is true: *No one believed his story about what had happened.* • *I can't believe they're brothers.* • *The police **believed that** they had found the killer.* • *His family **believed** him **to be** dead.*
2 if you believe someone, you are sure that they are telling the truth: *I told her what happened, but she didn't believe me.*
3 to think that something might be true, without being completely sure: *I believe that her name is Lucy Gray.*

PHRASAL VERBS
believe in
believe in something/someone a) to feel sure that something or someone exists: *Do you **believe in** love at first sight?* **b)** to trust or respect someone or something because you think that they are good: *We **believe in** you.* • *The revolutionaries **believed in** liberty, freedom, and equality.*

SPELLING
This word is often spelled wrongly. The correct spelling is: **believe**.

bell /bel/ *noun* **1** a piece of electrical equipment that makes a noise as a signal or warning: *Just then, I heard the door bell.* • *At last the bell rang and the lesson was over.* **2** a metal object that makes a musical sound when you move it: *He rang a bell to attract our attention.* • *church bells*

bel·low /ˈbeləʊ $ ˈbeloʊ/ *verb* to shout something in a very loud low voice: *"Come here," he bellowed.*

ˈbell ˌpepper the American word for a PEPPER

bel·ly /ˈbeli/ *noun* (informal) (plural **bellies**) your stomach: *I've got a pain in my belly.*

ˈbelly ˌbutton *noun* (informal) NAVEL

be·long /bɪˈlɒŋ $ bɪˈlɔːŋ/ *verb*

KEY PATTERNS
belong in a place

if something belongs somewhere, it is in the correct place or situation: *Some of the new buildings do not **belong in** such a beautiful town.* • *Where does this book belong?*

PHRASAL VERBS
belong to
1 belong to something if you belong to a group, you are a member of it: *I don't **belong to** any political parties.*
2 belong to someone if something belongs to you, you own it: *That bike **belongs to** my sister.*

A B C D E F G H I J K L M N O P Q R S T U V W X Y Z

be·long·ings /bɪˈlɒŋɪŋz $ bɪˈlɔːŋɪŋz/ *plural noun* the things that you own or take with you somewhere SYNONYM **possessions**: *She packed her belongings into a suitcase.* → see Thesaurus at PROPERTY

be·lov·ed /bɪˈlʌvɪd/ *adjective* (written) loved very much: *He never recovered from the death of his beloved wife.*

be·low /bɪˈləʊ $ bɪˈloʊ/ *adverb, preposition*
1 lower than something, or under it ANTONYM **above**: *When I looked out of the plane window, I could see the fields below us.* • *They skied down the mountain to the valley below.*
2 less than a particular amount ANTONYM **above**: *The temperature dropped to below zero at night.*

belt /belt/ *noun* a band of leather or cloth that you wear around your waist, for example to stop your trousers or skirt from falling down: *a leather belt*

be·mused /bɪˈmjuːzd/ *adjective* (written) slightly confused: *She looked bemused by what he was saying.*

bench /bentʃ/ *noun* (plural **benches**) a long wooden seat for two or more people: *a garden bench*

bend¹ /bend/ *verb* (past tense and past participle **bent** /bent/)

KEY PATTERNS
bend down/over
bend something

1 to move the top part of your body and your head down: *His back hurts when he bends.* • *She bent down to pat the dog.* • *In this exercise you have to* ***bend over*** *and touch your toes.*
→ see picture on page A2

bend

2 to move a part of your body so that it is no longer straight ANTONYM **straighten**: *This jacket's so tight that I can't bend my arms.*
3 if something bends, or if you bend it, it does not have its normal shape any more ANTONYM **straighten**: *You've bent the wheel.* • *Plastic bends easily.*

bend² *noun* a curve in a road or river: *There was a sharp bend in the road.*

be·neath /bɪˈniːθ/ *adverb, preposition* (written)
under or below something: *These animals live in tunnels beneath the ground.* • *We stood on the hill and looked down at the fields beneath.*

ben·e·fi·cial /ˌbenəˈfɪʃəl/ *adjective* (formal) helpful or useful: *It might be beneficial to talk to someone about your problems.*

ben·e·fit¹ /ˈbenəfɪt/ *noun*

KEY PATTERNS
have/get the benefit of something

1 an advantage that you get from something: *Nowadays we* ***have the benefits of*** *cheaper flights.* • *I went outside to* ***get the benefit of*** *the sun.*
2 money that the government gives you when you are ill or when you do not have a job: *Her boyfriend is unemployed and* ***on benefit*** (=receiving this money).

PHRASES
for someone's benefit, for the benefit of someone: *For the benefit of people who arrived late, I'll repeat what I said* (=in order to help them).
give someone the benefit of the doubt to believe what someone says even though they might be wrong or not telling the truth: *I find it difficult to believe, but I'll* ***give you the benefit of the doubt*** *this time.*

benefit² *verb* (**benefited** or **benefitted**, **benefiting** or **benefitting**) if something benefits someone, it helps them: *Will the changes in the law benefit us?*

bent¹ the past tense and past participle of BEND¹

bent² /bent/ *adjective* curved and no longer flat or straight: *I can't sew with this needle, it's bent.*

be·reaved /bɪˈriːvd/ *adjective* (formal) if you are bereaved, someone that you love has died: *a support group for bereaved parents*

be·reave·ment /bɪˈriːvmənt/ *noun* the situation when someone you love has died: *He is away from work because of a family bereavement.*

be•ret /ˈbereɪ $ bəˈreɪ/ *noun* a soft round flat hat → see picture at HAT

ber•ry /ˈberi/ *noun* (plural **berries**) a small soft fruit with very small seeds

ber•serk /bɜːˈsɜːk $ bɚˈsɚk/ *adjective* **go berserk** (informal) to become very angry and violent in a crazy way: *He went berserk and started hitting Sue.*

be•set /bɪˈset/ *verb* (formal) (past tense and past participle **beset**, **besetting**) if someone is beset by problems, they have a lot of problems: *The company has been beset by financial difficulties.*

be•side /bɪˈsaɪd/ *preposition* next to or very close to someone or something: *His dog walked beside him.* • *There is a picnic area beside the river.*

be•sides /bɪˈsaɪdz/ *preposition, adverb* in addition to someone or something: *Besides painting, she enjoys reading and sewing.* • *Who will be there besides you and me?*

be•siege /bɪˈsiːdʒ/ *verb* if you are besieged by people or things, you have to deal with a lot of them: *They were besieged by journalists as they left the building.*

best¹ /best/ *adjective*
1 better than anyone or anything else ANTONYM **worst**: *This is the best Chinese restaurant in town.* • *Where's **the best** place to leave my bike?*
2 your best friend, her best friend etc the friend someone knows and likes the most: *Susan's my **best friend**.*

best² *adverb*
1 most: *Which bit of the film did you like best?* • *His brother **knew** him **best**.*
2 in a way that is better than any other: *Which of the children draws best?* • *Michael **did best in** the spelling test* (=was most successful).

best³ *noun* **1 the best** the person or thing that is better than any others ANTONYM **the worst**: *There are a lot of good players on the team, but he is **the best**.* **2 do your best, try your best** to try very hard to succeed: *She **tried her best** but she still didn't pass the exam.*
→ see Thesaurus at TRY¹

ˌbest ˈman *noun* a friend of a man who is getting married, who helps him to get ready and stands next to him during the wedding

best•sel•ler /ˌbestˈselə $ ˌbestˈselɚ/ *noun* a book that a lot of people have bought

bet¹ /bet/ *verb* (past tense and past participle **bet**, **betting**)

KEY PATTERNS
bet money/$50/£10 etc
bet on a horse/race
bet someone $20/£5 etc that

to try to win money by saying what the result of a game or competition will be: *He **bet** a lot of **money** and lost it all.* • *My Dad used to **bet on** the horses* (=on the result of horse races). • *That guy just **bet $100 on** the last race.* • ***I bet** you five pounds **that** I can run faster than you!*

PHRASES
I bet (spoken) used to say that you are sure something is true or happened: *I wonder what time it is? **I bet** it's past midnight.* • ***I bet** she was surprised when she saw you at the party!*
You bet! (spoken) used to say 'yes' in a very definite way: *"Would you like to come?" "**You bet!**"*

bet² *noun*

KEY PATTERNS
have a bet on something

if you have a bet on something, you try to win money by saying what the result of a game or competition will be. You can also place or lay a bet: *I might **have a bet on** the match.* • *Tom **won** his **bet**.*

PHRASES
a good bet something that is likely to be useful or successful: *This shop is always **a good bet** for presents.*

be•tray /bɪˈtreɪ/ *verb* to behave dishonestly towards someone who loves you or trusts you: *She felt her husband had betrayed her by lying to her.*

be•tray•al /bɪˈtreɪəl/ *noun* when someone betrays you: *The film is a story of betrayal and murder.*

bet•ter¹ /ˈbetə $ ˈbetɚ/ *adjective*

KEY PATTERNS
better at maths/football/spelling
one thing is better than another

1 more useful, interesting, skilful etc than something or someone else ANTONYM **worse**: *We need a better*

A B C D E F G H I J K L M N O P Q R S T U V W X Y Z

A B C D E F G H I J K L M N O P Q R S T U V W X Y Z

computer. • *My sister's got much* **better at** *maths since she moved to a new school.* • *Sitting on the beach is definitely* **better than** *working!*
2 less ill than you were, or no longer ill ANTONYM **worse**: *Are you* **feeling a bit better** *today?* • *I had a cold, but I'm* **better** *now.* ➔ see Thesaurus at HEALTHY

PHRASES

get better to improve: *His English* **is getting better**.
the sooner the better, the bigger the better: *He should stop smoking,* **the sooner the better** (=as soon as possible). • *Fetch a large bowl,* **the bigger the better** (=as big as possible).

better² *adverb*
1 more: *I think this jacket* **suits me better**. • *I* **knew** *her* **better than** *anyone else did.*
2 in a more skilful way: *He speaks English* **better than** *I do.*

PHRASES

you'd better, we'd better etc (spoken) used to tell someone what you think they should do: **You'd better** *not annoy him.* • **We'd better** *start packing up now.*

better³ *noun* **get the better of someone** if a feeling gets the better of you, you do not control it when you should: *His anger got the better of him and he lashed out at me.*

better 'off *adjective* **1 be better off doing something** (informal) if you say that someone would be better off doing something, you are advising them to do it: *You'd be better off sitting the exam next year, when you're ready for it.* **2** if you are better off, you have more money now than in the past ANTONYM **worse off**: *My father worked hard and in a few years we were a bit better off.*

be·tween /bɪ'twiːn/ *preposition, adverb*
1 also **in between** with one thing or person on each side: *He sat between the two women on the sofa.*
2 used to show that a place is in the middle, with other places at a distance from it: *Oxford is between London and Birmingham.*
3 also **in between** after one event or time and before another: *I didn't see my parents at all between Christmas and Easter.* • *He had a year off between leaving school and going to university.* • *You shouldn't eat in between meals.* • *I have a lesson at nine o'clock and another at three o'clock, but nothing* **in between**.
4 also **in between** used to show a range of amounts, by giving the largest and smallest: *My journey to school takes between 30 and 40 minutes.* • *children aged between 7 and 11*
5 used to show who is involved in a relationship, agreement, fight etc: *There has always been a friendly relationship between these two countries.* • *an agreement between the company and the trade unions* • *the war between England and France*
6 used to say that part of something is given to each person in a group: *They shared the prize money between the three winners.*

PHRASES

have something between you if people have an amount of money between them, that is the total amount they have: *We only* **had** *ten dollars* **between us**.

bev·er·age /'bevərɪdʒ/ *noun* (formal written) a drink: *Alcoholic beverages are not allowed in the theatre.*

be·ware /bɪ'weə $ bɪ'wer/ *verb* used to warn someone to be careful: *Beware of the dog!* • *There are some very difficult questions, so beware.*

be·wil·dered /bɪ'wɪldəd $ bɪ'wɪldərd/ *adjective* confused and not sure what to do or think: *The children looked lost and bewildered.*

be·yond /bɪ'jɒnd $ bɪ'jɑnd/ *preposition, adverb*
1 if something is beyond a place, it is on the side of it that is farthest away from you: *Beyond the stream was a small wood.*
2 past a particular time or date: *The project will continue beyond June.*
3 if something is beyond repair, beyond control etc, you cannot repair it, control it etc: *The television is* **beyond repair**. • *The evidence proved her innocence* **beyond doubt** (=there was no doubt that she was innocent).

PHRASES

it's beyond me (informal, spoken): **It's beyond me** *why she's so popular* (=I can't understand).

bi·as /ˈbaɪəs/ *noun* **have a bias against someone** to have an unfair opinion about someone that affects the way you treat them: *Some employers have a bias against older workers.*

bi·ased /ˈbaɪəst/ *adjective* preferring one person, group, idea etc to another, in an unfair way ANTONYM **impartial**: *I think Harvard is the best university, but I'm biased because I went there.*

bib /bɪb/ *noun* a piece of cloth or plastic that you tie under a baby's chin to protect its clothes while it is eating

bi·ble, **Bible** /ˈbaɪbəl/ *noun* the holy book of the Christian religion: *Do you ever read the Bible?*

bib·li·og·ra·phy /ˌbɪbliˈɒgrəfi $ ˌbɪbliˈɑgrəfi/ *noun* (plural **bibliographies**) a list of books on a particular subject

bick·er /ˈbɪkə $ ˈbɪkɚ/ *verb* to argue about something that is not very important SYNONYM **squabble**: *The kids were bickering about who was the fastest runner.*

bi·cy·cle /ˈbaɪsɪkəl/ *noun* a vehicle with two wheels that you ride by pushing the PEDALS with your feet SYNONYM **bike**: *Did you come by bicycle?* ➔ see picture on page A11

bid /bɪd/ *verb* (past tense and past participle **bid**, **bidding**) to offer to pay a particular price for one particular thing that several people want to buy: *Mr Jones bid $50,000 for the painting.* —**bid** *noun*: *We received three bids on the house.*

big /bɪg/ *adjective* (**bigger**, **biggest**)
1 large ANTONYM **small**: *a big black car • the biggest city in the world*
2 important or serious ANTONYM **small**: *We have some pretty big problems. • It was the biggest mistake of my life.*
3 (informal) very successful: *His last film was a big hit. • That band is not as big as it used to be.*

THESAURUS
large: *A large parcel arrived in the post* (=big).
huge: *She has a huge house in Los Angeles* (=very big).
enormous: *Two enormous dogs stood behind the gate* (=extremely big).
vast: *the vast open spaces of Australia* (=extremely big)

big·head·ed /ˌbɪgˈhedɪd/ *adjective* someone who is bigheaded thinks that they are better than other people ➔ see Thesaurus at PROUD

big·ot /ˈbɪgət/ *noun* a person who has strong and unreasonable opinions about people who are different from them

big·ot·ed /ˈbɪgətɪd/ *adjective* someone who is bigoted has strong and unreasonable opinions about people who belong to a different race, religion, or political group: *Some people are very bigoted about the Irish. • a bigoted old man*

bike /baɪk/ *noun* a bicycle or a MOTORCYCLE: *He fell off his bike. • I came here by bike.*

bik·er /ˈbaɪkə $ ˈbaɪkɚ/ *noun* (informal) someone who rides a MOTORCYCLE, especially as part of a group: *This road is popular with bikers.*

bi·ki·ni /bɪˈkiːni/ *noun* a piece of clothing in two parts that women wear on the beach when it is hot

bi·lin·gual /baɪˈlɪŋgwəl/ *adjective*
1 able to speak two languages very well: *Philippe and Jane's children are bilingual.* **2** spoken or written in two languages: *a bilingual dictionary*

bill /bɪl/ *noun*
1 a list of things that you have bought or that someone has done for you, showing how much you have to pay for them: *Have you* ***paid*** *the electricity bill? • I'm expecting to get a* ***big phone bill*** (=a bill asking for a lot of money to pay for your phone calls).
2 the American word for NOTE: *a ten-dollar bill*
3 a plan for a new law: *The new education* ***bill was passed*** (=became law) *last week.*

bill·board /ˈbɪlbɔːd $ ˈbɪlbɔrd/ *noun* a big sign next to a road, that is used to advertise something

bill·fold /ˈbɪlfəʊld $ ˈbɪlˌfoʊld/ the American word for WALLET

bil·lion /ˈbɪljən/ *number* (plural **billion** or **billions**) 1,000,000,000: *two billion pounds • There are billions of stars in the universe.* —**billionth** *number*

A B C D E F G H I J K L M N O P Q R S T U V W X Y Z

GRAMMAR
You use the plural form **billion** after a number.
You use the plural form **billions** before **of**.

bil·low /ˈbɪləʊ $ ˈbɪloʊ/ *verb* if smoke billows, a lot of it rises into the air: *Smoke billowed out of the chimneys.*

bin /bɪn/ *noun*
1 a large container where you put small things that you no longer want: *She threw the letter in the bin.*
2 a container that you use to store things: *a bread bin*

bind /baɪnd/ *verb* (past tense and past participle **bound** /baʊnd/) to tie something together firmly, with string or rope: *I wrapped up the parcel and bound it with string.*

binge /bɪndʒ/ *noun* an occasion when you eat, drink, or spend a lot in a very short time: *a week-long shopping binge* —**binge** *verb*: *Sometimes I binge on chocolate and sweets.*

bi·noc·u·lars /bɪˈnɒkjələz $ bɪˈnɑkjələ˞z/ *plural noun* an object like a large pair of glasses that you hold up and look through to see things that are far away: *a pair of binoculars*

bi·o·de·grad·a·ble /ˌbaɪəʊdɪˈgreɪdəbəl $ ˌbaɪoʊdɪˈgreɪdəbəl/ *adjective* able to be destroyed by natural processes, in a way that does not harm the environment: *Plastic is not biodegradable.*

bi·og·ra·pher /baɪˈɒgrəfə $ baɪˈɑgrəfə˞/ *noun* a person who writes someone's biography

bi·og·ra·phy /baɪˈɒgrəfi $ baɪˈɑgrəfi/ *noun* (plural **biographies**) a book about a person's life: *He wrote a biography of Nelson Mandela.*

bi·o·lo·gi·cal /ˌbaɪəˈlɒdʒɪkəl $ ˌbaɪəˈlɑdʒɪkəl/ *adjective* connected with biology: *The company does biological research.*

bi·ol·o·gist /baɪˈɒlədʒɪst $ baɪˈɑlədʒɪst/ *noun* someone whose job involves studying biology

bi·ol·o·gy /baɪˈɒlədʒi $ baɪˈɑlədʒi/ *noun* (no plural) the scientific study of living things: *Biology is my favourite subject.*

birch /bɜːtʃ $ bɜ˞tʃ/ *noun* a tree with smooth BARK and thin branches, which is grown for its pale-coloured wood

bird /bɜːd $ bɜ˞d/ *noun* an animal with wings and feathers that can usually fly. Female birds produce eggs. → see picture on page A8

ˌbird of ˈprey *noun* (plural **birds of prey**) a bird that kills and eats other birds and small animals: *The eagle is a bird of prey.*

bi·ro /ˈbaɪərəʊ $ ˈbaɪroʊ/ *noun BrE* (trademark) a type of pen

birth /bɜːθ $ bɜ˞θ/ *noun*

KEY PATTERNS
the birth of a baby
at birth

the time when a baby comes out of its mother's body: *They celebrated the birth of their first child.* • *She weighed 3 kg at birth* (=when she was born).

PHRASES
give birth if a woman gives birth, she produces a baby from her body: *Jenni gave birth on Tuesday.* • *She's just given birth to her fifth son.*
date of birth: *Write down your name, address, and **date of birth*** (=the date when you were born).

ˈbirth conˌtrol *noun* (no plural) methods of stopping a woman becoming PREGNANT SYNONYM **contraception**

birth·day /ˈbɜːθdeɪ $ ˈbɜ˞θdeɪ/ *noun*

KEY PATTERNS
on someone's birthday

the date in each year on which you were born: *It's my birthday next week.* • *What did you do **on your birthday**?* • *I got ten birthday cards.* • *Happy birthday* (=said to someone on their birthday)!

birth·mark /ˈbɜːθmɑːk $ ˈbɜ˞θmɑrk/ *noun* an unusual mark on someone's skin that is there when they are born

birth·place /ˈbɜːθpleɪs $ ˈbɜ˞θpleɪs/ *noun* the place where someone was born: *Stratford-upon-Avon is the birthplace of William Shakespeare.*

bis·cuit /ˈbɪskɪt/ *noun* **1** *BrE* a thin dry sweet cake SYNONYM **cookie** *AmE*: *Who wants a chocolate biscuit?*
2 *AmE* a kind of bread that you bake in small round shapes

bi·sex·u·al /baɪˈsekʃuəl/ *noun* someone who is sexually attracted to men and women —**bisexual** *adjective*

bish·op /ˈbɪʃəp/ *noun* a priest with a high rank who is in charge of the churches and priests in a large area: *The Bishop of Durham conducted the service.*

bi·son /ˈbaɪsən/ *noun* an animal that looks like a large cow with long hair on the front part of its body, and lives in the United States SYNONYM **buffalo**

bit[1] /bɪt/ *noun*
1 a small piece or amount of something: *Can I have a **bit of** paper to write on?* • *I've got a **bit of** work to do.* • *All I want is a **bit of** fun.*
2 a part of something: *The best bit in the film was the car chase.*

PHRASES
a bit slightly: *I felt **a bit** embarrassed.* • *It tastes **a bit like** cabbage.* • *Turn the sound up **a bit**.* • *I hadn't seen Yolanda for 20 years and she **hadn't changed a bit*** (=she hadn't changed, not even slightly).
a bit of a shock, a bit of a surprise *BrE* (spoken): *The news **came as a bit of a** shock* (=a slight shock).
for a bit, after a bit (informal) following or taking a short amount of time: ***After a bit**, he got used to the idea.* • *I waited **for a bit** and then tried phoning again.*
tear something to bits, smash something to bits, blow something to bits to destroy something completely: *The car **was blown to bits** in the explosion.*

bit[2] the past tense of BITE[1]

bite[1] /baɪt/ *verb* (**bit** /bɪt/ **bitten** /ˈbɪtn/)

KEY PATTERNS
be bitten by a dog/spider
bite into an apple/sandwich

1 to cut or crush something with your teeth: *Sophie was **bitten by** a dog.* • *I can't stop **biting** my fingernails.* • *James **bit into** the apple.*
2 if an insect bites you, it pushes a sharp point into your skin and it hurts: *I think I've been bitten by ants.*

bite[2] *noun*

KEY PATTERNS
have a bite of a sandwich/apple
take a bite out of something

1 if you take a bite of something, you use your teeth to remove part of it: *Can I have **a bite of** your sandwich?* • *He **took a big bite out of** his apple.*
2 a wound made when an animal or insect bites you: *Have you got any cream for mosquito bites?*

bitten the past participle of BITE[1]

bit·ter /ˈbɪtə $ ˈbɪtɚ/ *adjective*
1 angry for a long time because you feel that something bad or unfair has happened to you: *She's very bitter about losing her job.* **2** having a strong taste, like coffee without sugar —**bitterness** *noun* (no plural)

bit·ter·ly /ˈbɪtəli $ ˈbɪtɚli/ *adverb*
1 in a way that shows that you are very unhappy: *"You tricked me," she said bitterly.* **2 bitterly cold/disappointed/ashamed** very cold, disappointed etc: *We were bitterly disappointed to lose.*

bi·zarre /bɪˈzɑː $ bɪˈzɑr/ *adjective* very unusual and strange: *As a teenager, his behaviour became more and more bizarre.* —**bizarrely** *adverb*

black[1] /blæk/ *adjective*
1 something that is black is as dark as it can be, like the colour of the sky at night: *a black horse*
2 someone who is black has dark skin: *two young black kids*
3 black coffee or tea does not have milk in it: *I'll have two black coffees and one white, please* (=with milk in it).

WORD CHOICE
dark brown eyes or **a black eye**?
• **Dark brown eyes** are very dark in colour.
• **A black eye** is a bruise around someone's eye.

black[2] *noun*
the darkest colour, like the colour of the sky at night: *He was dressed in black.*

black·ber·ry /ˈblækbəri $ ˈblækˌberi/ *noun* (plural **blackberries**) a small sweet black fruit that grows on a bush ➔ see picture on page A7

blackberries

black·board /ˈblækbɔːd $ ˈblækˌbɔrd/ *noun* a dark smooth board that you write on with CHALK: *The teacher wrote the date on the blackboard.* ➔ see picture at BOARD[1] ➔ see Thesaurus at BOARD[1]

black·cur·rant /ˌblækˈkʌrənt $ ˌblækˈkɚənt/ *noun* a small black fruit, often used to make drinks: *blackcurrant juice*

ˌblack ˈeye *noun* an area of dark skin around someone's eye where someone has hit them: *How did you get that black eye?*

ˌblack ˈmagic *noun* (no plural) a type of magic used to do bad or evil things

black·mail /ˈblækmeɪl/ *noun* (no plural) when someone makes you do what they want by saying that they will tell secrets about you: *"Give me the money or I'll tell the police." "That's blackmail!"* —**blackmail** *verb*: *Jeremy tried to blackmail his boss.*

ˌblack ˈmarket *noun* when people buy and sell things illegally: *They probably bought the guns on the black market.*

black·out /ˈblækaʊt/ *noun* when you suddenly cannot see, hear, or feel anything for a short time, for example because you are ill or have hit your head: *I had a blackout and couldn't remember anything.*

black·smith /ˈblækˌsmɪθ/ *noun* someone who makes and repairs metal things

blad·der /ˈblædə $ ˈblædɚ/ *noun* the part of your body where URINE stays before it leaves your body

blade /bleɪd/ *noun* **1** the flat sharp cutting part of a knife or tool: *The blade of this knife is completely blunt* (=not sharp). **2** a single piece of grass

blame[1] /bleɪm/ *verb*

KEY PATTERNS
blame someone for a death/failure/problem
blame a death/problem/failure on someone
blame yourself

if you blame someone, you say or think that they are responsible for something bad that has happened: *They **blamed** the captain **for** the team's defeat.* • *He **blamed** his bad results **on** his teachers.* • *Don't blame yourself for what happened – it was an accident.*

PHRASES

I don't blame you (spoken) used to say that you think that someone is being reasonable, although other people might criticize them: *"I was so angry!" "**I don't blame you.** He treated you really badly."*

be to blame to be responsible for something bad: *I know who's to blame for this.*

blame[2] *noun* (no plural)

KEY PATTERNS
get/take the blame for something
put the blame on someone

if you get the blame for something bad, other people say you are responsible for it: *I always **get the blame for** things that go wrong.* • *He tried to **put the blame on** his brother* (=he said that his brother was responsible). • *She **took the blame for** causing the problem* (=people said that she was responsible).

bland /blænd/ *adjective* bland food has very little taste: *The vegetables were overcooked and tasted very bland.* —**blandness** *noun* (no plural)

blank[1] /blæŋk/ *adjective* **1** a blank sheet of paper, DVD etc has nothing written or recorded on it: *She started writing on a blank page.* **2 go blank** if your mind goes blank, you suddenly cannot remember something: *When she saw the exam questions, her mind went blank.*

blank[2] *noun* an empty space on a piece of paper, for you to write a word or letter in: *Fill in the blanks on this quiz.*

blan·ket /ˈblæŋkɪt/ *noun* **1** a thick warm cover for a bed ➔ see picture

A B C D E F G H I J K L M N O P Q R S T U V W X Y Z

at BED **2** (written) a thick layer of something: *A blanket of snow covered the mountains.*

blare /bleə $ bler/ also **blare out** *verb* to make a very loud unpleasant noise: *Music blared out from the house next door.*

blast¹ /blɑːst $ blæst/ *noun* an explosion: *Five people were killed in the blast.*

blast² *verb* to break rock into pieces using explosives: *They blasted a tunnel through the side of the mountain.*

bla·tant /ˈbleɪtnt/ *adjective* easy to notice, in a way that is shocking: *What a blatant insult!* **—blatantly** *adverb*: *It was blatantly obvious he was lying.*

blaze¹ /bleɪz/ *noun* a large fire: *The blaze was caused by a cigarette.* → see Thesaurus at FIRE¹

blaze² *verb* (written) to burn or shine very brightly and strongly: *A fire was blazing in the hearth.*

bleach¹ /bliːtʃ/ *noun* (no plural) a chemical used to clean things or make them whiter

bleach² *verb* to make something white or lighter in colour, using bleach: *She's bleached her hair.*

bleach·ers /ˈbliːtʃəz $ ˈblitʃɚz/ *plural noun AmE* long rows of wooden seats where people sit to watch sports games: *We could only afford to sit in the bleachers.*

bleak /bliːk/ *adjective* **1** cold and unattractive: *It was a bleak December day.* **2** a bleak situation seems very bad and is not likely to get better: *Without a job, the future seemed bleak.*

blear·y-eyed /ˌblɪəri ˈaɪd $ ˌblɪri ˈaɪd/ *adjective* someone who is bleary-eyed looks tired or as if they have been crying: *At breakfast, Louisa looked bleary-eyed.*

bleat /bliːt/ *verb* if a sheep or goat bleats, it makes a high noise

bled the past tense and past participle of BLEED

bleed /bliːd/ *verb* (past tense and past participle **bled** /bled/) if you bleed, blood comes out of a cut on your body: *The cut on his arm started bleeding again.*

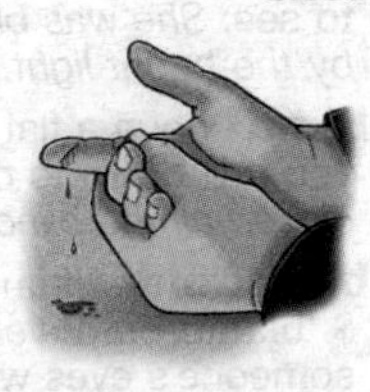

bleed

bleed·ing /ˈbliːdɪŋ/ *noun* (no plural) the flow of blood from a wound: *She pressed on the wound to stop the bleeding.*

bleep /bliːp/ *verb* to make a high electronic sound: *The alarm clock was bleeping.* **—bleep** *noun*: *You'll hear a bleep when you have a new text message.*

bleep·er /ˈbliːpə $ ˈblipɚ/ *noun BrE* a PAGER

blem·ish /ˈblemɪʃ/ *noun* (formal) (plural **blemishes**) a small mark that spoils something: *This is a good cream for hiding blemishes on your skin.* → see Thesaurus at MARK²

blend /blend/ *verb* to mix two or more things together thoroughly: *Blend the butter and the flour.* → see Thesaurus at MIX¹ **—blend** *noun*: *You have to get the right blend of flavours.*

blend·er /ˈblendə $ ˈblendɚ/ *noun* a small electric machine that you use to mix food

bless /bles/ *verb* **1** to ask God to make something holy: *The priest blessed the bread and wine.* **2 bless you!** (spoken) what you say to someone when they SNEEZE

blew the past tense of BLOW¹

blind¹ /blaɪnd/ *adjective* a blind person cannot see because their eyes are damaged: *She **is going blind*** (=becoming). • *Some of the children **were born blind*** (=they were blind when they were born).

PHRASES

turn a blind eye to pretend you have not noticed something bad that is happening: *The school used to **turn a blind eye to** smoking, but not any more.* **—blindness** *noun* (no plural): *a new treatment for some forms of blindness*

blind² *verb* to make someone unable to see: *She was blinded for a moment by the bright light.*

blind³ *noun* a flat piece of cloth that you pull down to cover a window: *We closed all the blinds.*

blind·fold¹ /ˈblaɪndfəʊld $ ˈblaɪndfoʊld/ *verb* to cover someone's eyes with a piece of cloth so that they cannot see: *They blindfolded him and locked him in a room.*

blindfold² *noun* a piece of cloth that you put over someone's eyes to stop them being able to see

blind·ing /ˈblaɪndɪŋ/ *adjective* very bright: *There was a blinding flash as the car exploded.*

blink /blɪŋk/ *verb* **1** to open and close your eyes quickly: *He blinked as he stepped into the sunlight.* **2** if a light blinks, it goes on and off: *The red warning light was blinking.*

bliss /blɪs/ *noun* (no plural) complete happiness: *Swimming in the sea on a hot day is my idea of bliss.*

blis·ter¹ /ˈblɪstə $ ˈblɪstɚ/ *noun* a small area of raised skin that is painful and full of liquid because something has rubbed or burnt it: *My new shoes were rubbing and I had blisters on my feet.*

blister² *verb* to become covered with blisters: *The skin on my hand blistered where I had burnt it.* • *The sun had blistered her back.*

blitz /blɪts/ *noun* when you use a lot of effort to do something in a short time: *Let's have a blitz on cleaning the house.*

bliz·zard /ˈblɪzəd $ ˈblɪzɚd/ *noun* a storm with a lot of wind and snow

bloat·ed /ˈbləʊtɪd $ ˈbloʊtɪd/ *adjective* feeling very full and uncomfortable: *I'd eaten so much I felt bloated.*

blob /blɒb $ blɑb/ *noun* a small drop of a thick liquid: *Dad had some cake with a blob of cream on top.*

block¹ /blɒk $ blɑk/ *noun*
1 a large piece of heavy solid material with straight sides: *a* ***block of*** *concrete* • *a* ***block of*** *ice*
2 *BrE* a large building with many homes or offices in it: *a* ***block of flats*** • *a new* ***office block***
3 *AmE* a group of buildings with streets on all four sides: *I lived two blocks away from the station.*

block² *verb*
1 also **block up** if something blocks a space, it is in that space and things cannot get past it: *Two large men were blocking the entrance.*
2 if something blocks your view, it is in front of you and stops you from seeing something: *From the hotel window, some trees* ***were blocking our view*** *of the sea.*
3 if your nose is blocked up, it is difficult for you to breathe because air cannot easily pass in and out: *I've got a cold and my nose is blocked up.*
4 to stop something being done or being finished: *Local residents successfully blocked the plan to build a prison near the village.*

PHRASAL VERBS

block off
block something off to completely close a road or entrance: *The police* ***blocked off*** *the road where the accident happened.*

block·ade /blɒˈkeɪd $ blɑˈkeɪd/ *noun* when an army or navy surrounds a place to stop people getting in or out

block·age /ˈblɒkɪdʒ $ ˈblɑkɪdʒ/ *noun* something that blocks a tube or pipe

block·bust·er /ˈblɒkˌbʌstə $ ˈblɑkˌbʌstɚ/ *noun* (informal) a book or film that is very successful: *the latest Hollywood blockbuster*

ˌblock ˈcapitals also **ˌblock ˈletters** *noun* big letters, for example 'A' instead of 'a'

blog /blɒg $ blɑg/ *noun* a webpage in which someone writes about their opinions, activities etc, which has the newest information first SYNONYM **weblog**: *He writes about his trip in his blog.* **—blogger** *noun* **—blogging** *noun*

bloke /bləʊk $ bloʊk/ *noun BrE* (informal) a man SYNONYM **guy**

blonde¹, **blond** /blɒnd $ blɑnd/ *adjective* **1** blonde hair is pale or yellow **2** someone who is blonde has pale or yellow hair: *She's small, blonde, and very attractive.*

blonde² *noun* (informal) a woman who has pale or yellow hair: *All his girlfriends have been blondes.*

blood /blʌd/ *noun* (no plural) the red liquid that your heart pushes around your body: *I cut my finger and there was blood everywhere!*

blood·bath /ˈblʌdbɑːθ $ ˈblʌdbæθ/ *noun* when a lot of people are killed violently

blood·cur·dling /ˈblʌdˌkɜːdlɪŋ $ ˈblʌdˌkɚdlɪŋ/ *adjective* bloodcurdling sounds are very frightening: *a bloodcurdling scream*

blood·shed /ˈblʌdʃed/ *noun* (no plural) (formal) when people are killed in fighting: *The war finally ended after four years of bloodshed.*

blood·shot /ˈblʌdʃɒt $ ˈblʌdʃɑt/ *adjective* bloodshot eyes look slightly red

blood·stream /ˈblʌdstriːm/ *noun* your blood as it flows around your body: *If you don't treat the infection, it may get into your bloodstream.*

blood·thirst·y /ˈblʌdˌθɜːsti $ ˈblʌdˌθɚsti/ *adjective* someone who is bloodthirsty enjoys violence

ˈblood ˌvessel *noun* one of the tubes in your body that blood flows through

blood·y /ˈblʌdi/ *adjective* **1** covered in blood: *Her hands were all bloody.* **2** violent, and killing or wounding a lot of people: *a bloody battle*

bloom¹ /bluːm/ *noun* **in bloom** a plant that is in bloom has flowers that are fully open: *The roses are in bloom.*

bloom² *verb* if plants bloom, their flowers open: *Daffodils bloom early in the spring.*

blos·som¹ /ˈblɒsəm $ ˈblɑsəm/ *noun* the flowers on a tree or bush: *apple blossom* → see picture on page A10

blossom² *verb* **1** if trees blossom, they produce flowers **2** if someone blossoms, they become happier, more successful, more attractive etc: *Elsa made a lot of friends at college, and she really blossomed there.*

blot¹ /blɒt $ blɑt/ *verb* (**blotted**, **blotting**) **blot something out** to stop yourself from thinking about something: *It was a terrible experience and she tried to blot it out.*

blot² *noun* a drop of liquid such as ink that has fallen on a piece of paper: *The letter was dated 1950, and was covered in ink blots.*

blotch /blɒtʃ $ blɑtʃ/ *noun* (plural **blotches**) a mark on something: *There were red blotches on his face.*

blouse /blaʊz $ blaʊs/ *noun* a shirt for women → see picture at CLOTHES

blow

The wind is blowing. He is blowing a whistle.

blow¹ /bləʊ $ bloʊ/ *verb* (**blew** /bluː/, **blown** /bləʊn $ bloʊn/)

KEY PATTERNS
blow away/down/over
the wind blows something away/down/over
the wind blows from the north/east etc
blow towards someone
blow on/through something

1 if the wind blows something somewhere, or if it blows there, the wind moves it there: *It was so windy the tent nearly* ***blew away****!* • *The door* ***blew shut****.* • *The wind* ***blew*** *the fence* ***down****.*
2 if the wind blows, the air moves: *A cold wind* ***was blowing from*** *the north.* • *The breeze* ***blew towards*** *us.*
3 to send a thin stream of air out through your mouth: *She* ***blew through*** *the tube.* • *John* ***blew on*** *his cold fingers.*
4 if a musical instrument or whistle blows, or if you blow it, it makes a

sound when you send air through it from your mouth: *Joe blew the trumpet as hard as he could.* • *The guard's whistle blew and the train started to leave.*
5 to violently move or destroy something with an explosion or bullet: *The explosion **blew** the windows **out**.* • *The bomb **blew** a hole **in** the wall.*

PHRASES

blow your nose to force air through your nose in order to clear it
blow it, blow a chance (informal) to lose a good opportunity because you make a mistake: *He had a great chance of scoring a goal but he **blew it**.*
blow money on something (informal) to spend a lot of money quickly in a careless way: *He **blew** all his **money on** presents for his new girlfriend.* • *I **blew** £140 **on** a new pair of trainers.*

PHRASAL VERBS

blow out
blow something out if you blow out a flame, or if a flame blows out, your breath or the wind stops it burning: *She **blew out** the candle.* • *The match **blew out** as soon as I lit it.*
blow over
if an argument blows over, it ends: *Don't worry, it'll soon **blow over**.*
blow up
1 blow something up if something blows up, or if someone blows it up, it is destroyed in an explosion: *They had only just escaped when the car **blew up**.* • *The soldiers **blew up** the bridge.*
2 blow something up if you blow up a BALLOON or car tyre, you fill it with air SYNONYM **inflate**

blow² *noun* **1** a hard hit: *He gave the handle several blows with his hammer.* **2** something that disappoints or upsets you: *Her mother's death was a terrible blow.*

ˈblow dry *verb* (**blow dried**, **blow dries**) to dry your hair using a HAIRDRYER

blown the past participle of BLOW¹

blue¹ /bluː/ *adjective* something that is blue is the colour of a clear sky on a nice day: *She had blue eyes.* • *a dark-blue sweater*

blue² *noun* **1** the colour of a clear sky on a nice day: *Blue is my favourite colour.* **2 blues** a slow sad style of music that came from the southern US: *I like jazz and blues.*

ˈblue-ˌcollar *adjective* blue-collar workers do jobs such as repairing machines and making things in factories

bluff /blʌf/ *verb* to pretend that you are going to do something, when this is not true: *She was only bluffing when she said she would leave college.* —**bluff** *noun*: *He said he would go to the police, but it was just a bluff.*

blun·der /ˈblʌndə $ ˈblʌndɚ/ *noun* a careless or stupid mistake that causes serious problems

blunt /blʌnt/ *adjective* **1** a blunt object is not sharp: *This knife's blunt!* **2** someone who is blunt says exactly what they think, even if it upsets people: *John can be very blunt sometimes.*

blur /blɜː $ blɚ/ *noun* something that you cannot see or remember clearly: *The crash is all a blur in my mind.*

blurred /blɜːd $ blɚd/ *adjective* blurred shapes, pictures, or thoughts are not clear: *The photograph was rather blurred.*

blurt /blɜːt $ blɚt/ **blurt something out** *verb* (informal) to say something suddenly and without thinking, especially something you should have tried to keep quiet or secret: *I had promised not to tell anyone else, but I blurted it out by mistake.*

blush /blʌʃ/ *verb* if you blush, your face becomes red because you feel embarrassed: *Rosie blushed when she realized she had pronounced his name wrongly.*

blus·ter·y /ˈblʌstəri/ *adjective* blustery weather is very windy

board¹ /bɔːd $ bɔrd/ *noun*

> KEY PATTERNS
> **put/pin something on the board**
> **be on the board of a company**

1 a flat piece of wood or plastic that is fixed on a wall and used to show information for everyone to see: *He **pinned** the notice **up on the board**.* • *Copy the picture from the board.*

A B C D E F G H I J K L M N O P Q R S T U V W X Y Z

boards

2 a thin flat piece of wood or plastic that is used for a particular purpose: *a chess board*
3 the group of people in an organization who make the rules and important decisions: *He's **on the board** of two companies.* • *a board meeting*

PHRASES
on board on a plane, ship, train, or bus: *Everyone **on board** the plane survived the crash.*

THESAURUS
blackboard: *The teacher wrote the date on the **blackboard*** (=a dark board that you write on with chalk).
whiteboard: *Many modern classrooms now have **whiteboards*** (=white boards that you write on with a special pen).
noticeboard *BrE*, **bulletin board** *AmE: All your exam results will be on the **noticeboard*** (=a board on a wall where you put information).

board² *noun* **board and lodging** *BrE* a room to sleep in and meals to eat SYNONYM **room and board** *AmE*: *They charge £100 a week for board and lodging.*

board³ *verb* **1** (formal) to get on a plane, ship, train, or bus: *Passengers may now board the plane.* **2** if a plane or ship is boarding, passengers are getting on it: *Flight 207 for Paris is now boarding.* **3 board something up** to cover a window or door with wooden boards: *The shop is empty and boarded up.*

'boarding school *noun* a school where students live as well as study

board·room /ˈbɔːdruːm $ ˈbɔrdrum/ *noun* a room where the important people in an organization have meetings

boast /bəʊst $ boʊst/ *verb* to talk too proudly about yourself and tell other people how good or clever you are SYNONYM **brag**: *He's always boasting about his rich friends.*

boast·ful /ˈbəʊstfəl $ ˈboʊstfəl/ *adjective* if you are boastful, you talk too proudly about yourself and tell other people how good or clever you are ANTONYM **modest**: *He was not popular at school because he was very boastful.*

boats

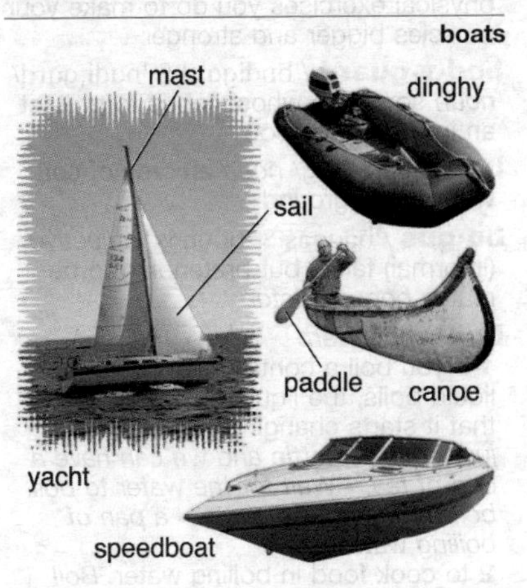

boat /bəʊt $ boʊt/ *noun*

KEY PATTERNS
by boat

something that people sit in to travel across water: *a sailing boat* • *We went to the island **by boat**.*

THESAURUS
ship: *The ship sailed into the harbour and all the passengers got off* (=a big boat for a lot of people).
ferry: *You can get a **ferry** across the river* (=a boat that regularly takes people a short distance).
yacht: *First prize in the round-the-world race was won by the yacht 'Tinka'* (=a boat with sails).

bob /bɒb $ bɑb/ *verb* (**bobbed, bobbing**) **bob up and down** to move up and down in water

bod·i·ly /ˈbɒdəli $ ˈbɑdl-i/ *adjective* (written) related to someone's body SYNONYM **physical**: *He did not suffer any bodily harm.*

A B C D E F G H I J K L M N O P Q R S T U V W X Y Z

bod·y /ˈbɒdi $ ˈbɑdi/ *noun* (plural **bodies**)
1 the physical structure of a person or animal: *Our bodies need vitamins to stay healthy.* • *the human body* → see picture on page A5
2 a dead person SYNONYM **corpse**: *Two bodies were found in the car.*
3 (formal) an official group of people who work together: *the public body responsible for safety at work*

ˈbody ˌbuilding *noun* (no plural) physical exercises you do to make your muscles bigger and stronger

bod·y·guard /ˈbɒdigɑːd $ ˈbɑdiˌgɑrd/ *noun* someone whose job is to protect an important person

bog /bɒg $ bɑg/ *noun* an area of soft wet muddy ground

bo·gus /ˈbəʊgəs $ ˈboʊgəs/ *adjective* (informal) false, but pretending to be real: *a bogus doctor*

boil¹ /bɔɪl/ *verb*
1 if you boil a container of liquid, or if liquid boils, the liquid becomes so hot that it starts changing into steam: *I'll just **boil the kettle** and we can have a cup of tea.* • *Wait for the water to boil before adding the pasta.* • *a pan of boiling water*
2 to cook food in boiling water: *Boil the potatoes for 20 minutes.* • *a boiled egg* → see picture at COOK¹ → see picture on page A4

PHRASES
it all boils down to something: ***It all boils down to*** *trust* (=the most important thing is trust).

boil² *noun* **1 bring something to the boil** *BrE*, **bring something to a boil** *AmE* to heat something in a pan until it boils: *Bring the potatoes **to the boil**.*
2 a small area of your skin that has become red and painful because it is infected: *He has a boil on his chin.*

boil·er /ˈbɔɪlə $ ˈbɔɪlɚ/ *noun* a piece of equipment that heats a large amount of water for people to use

boil·ing /ˈbɔɪlɪŋ/ also **ˌboiling ˈhot** *adjective* very hot: *a boiling hot day* → see Thesaurus at HOT¹

ˈboiling ˌpoint *noun* the temperature at which a liquid gets so hot that it starts changing into steam: *The boiling point of water is 100 degrees Celsius.*

bois·ter·ous /ˈbɔɪstərəs/ *adjective* noisy and full of energy: *a boisterous four-year-old*

bold /bəʊld $ boʊld/ *adjective*
1 confident and willing to take risks ANTONYM **timid**: *a bold decision* • *He was a bold soldier and a great leader of men.* **2** writing, shapes, or colours that are bold are very clear or bright
—**boldly** *adverb*

bol·lard /ˈbɒləd $ ˈbɑlɚd/ *noun BrE* a thick post that is fixed in the ground to stop cars going onto a piece of land or road

bolt¹ /bəʊlt $ boʊlt/ *noun* **1** a metal bar that you slide across in order to keep a door or window shut **2** a type of screw, which is used with a NUT to hold pieces of metal or wood together

bolt² *verb* **1** to run away suddenly: *The man bolted before the police could catch him.* **2** to close a door or window with a bolt **3** also **bolt down** to eat something very quickly SYNONYM **gobble**: *I bolted down my breakfast.*

bomb¹ /bɒm $ bɑm/ *noun* a container filled with a substance that will explode: *a nuclear bomb*

> PRONUNCIATION
> In this word you do not pronounce the **b** at the end of the word.

bomb² *verb* **1** to attack a place with bombs: *The city was bombed during the war.* **2** (informal) if a play or film bombs, it is not successful

bom·bard /bɒmˈbɑːd $ bɑmˈbɑrd/ *verb* **1** to attack a place with bombs or guns: *Enemy planes bombarded the capital throughout the night.*
2 bombard someone with questions, bombard someone with information to ask someone too many questions or give them too much information

bomb·er /ˈbɒmə $ ˈbɑmɚ/ *noun* **1** a plane that drops bombs **2** (informal) someone who puts a bomb somewhere: *the hunt for the bombers*

bond¹ /bɒnd $ bɑnd/ *noun* a shared feeling or interest that makes people feel love and loyalty towards each other: *There's a strong bond between the two brothers.*

bond² *verb* **1** to develop a special loving relationship with someone: *It*

takes time to bond with a new baby.
2 to join or glue things together firmly

bone /bəʊn $ boʊn/ *noun* one of the hard parts in the frame of your body: *She broke a bone in her leg.*

ˌ**bone 'dry** *adjective* completely dry: *After the long, hot summer, the ground was bone dry.*

bonfire

bon·fire /'bɒnfaɪə $ 'bɑnˌfaɪər/ *noun* a large outdoor fire that someone has under their control → see Thesaurus at FIRE[1]

bon·net /'bɒnɪt $ 'bɑnɪt/ *noun* **1** *BrE* the part at the front of a car that covers the engine SYNONYM **hood** *AmE* **2** a hat that you tie under your chin

bo·nus /'bəʊnəs $ 'boʊnəs/ *noun*
1 money that is added to someone's usual pay: *All members of staff get a Christmas bonus.* **2** something good that you did not expect: *Getting a free printer with the computer was a bonus.*

bon·y /'bəʊni $ 'boʊni/ *adjective* (informal) (**bonier**, **boniest**) bony people are very thin

boo /buː/ *verb* to shout 'boo' to show that you do not like someone's performance or speech —**boo** *noun*

boo·by prize /'buːbi ˌpraɪz/ *noun* a prize given as a joke to the person who finishes last in a competition

'**booby ˌtrap** *noun* a bomb or other dangerous thing that is hidden in something that seems harmless

book¹ /bʊk/ *noun*

KEY PATTERNS
a book on/about something

1 a set of printed pages fastened together in a cover so that you can read them: *Have you read any good books recently?* • *The new dictionary is a useful* ***reference book*** (=a book that you use for finding information). • ***a book on*** *shells and fishes* • *Jim had some* ***school books*** *under his arm* (=books that you use at school).
2 small sheets of paper fastened together in a thin cover: *a cheque book* • *an address book* • ***a book of*** *stamps*
3 books written records of the financial accounts of a business

book² *verb*
1 *BrE* to arrange to have or do something at a particular time: *He* ***booked a table*** *at the restaurant for eight o'clock.* • *We've booked a band to play at the wedding.* • *The hotel was* ***fully booked*** (=all the rooms were being used).
2 (informal) to ARREST someone: *The policeman booked me for speeding.*

PHRASAL VERBS
book in, book into something *BrE* to arrive at a hotel and collect your key SYNONYM **check in**: *We* ***booked into*** *a hotel for the night.* • *I'll call you as soon as I've* ***booked in***.

book·case /'bʊk-keɪs/ *noun* a piece of furniture with shelves for books

book·ing /'bʊkɪŋ/ *noun BrE* an arrangement that you make to have a hotel room, a seat on a plane etc at a future time: *Please can I make a booking?*

book·let /'bʊklət/ *noun* a small book that contains information

book·mak·er /'bʊkmeɪkə $ 'bʊkˌmeɪkər/ *noun* someone whose job is to serve people who want to BET on the result of a game or competition

book·mark /'bʊkmɑːk $ 'bʊkmark/ *noun* a piece of paper that you put in a book so that you can find the page you want

book·shelf /'bʊkʃelf/ *noun* (plural **bookshelves** /-ʃelvz/) a shelf that has books on it

book·shop /'bʊkʃɒp $ 'bʊkʃɑp/ *BrE*, **book·store** /'bʊkstɔː $ 'bʊkstɔr/ *AmE noun* a shop that sells books

boom /buːm/ *verb* to become very successful or popular: *Britain's economy is booming.* —**boom** *noun*: *There's been a boom in the sale of health foods.*

A B C D E F G H I J K L M N O P Q R S T U V W X Y Z

boost¹ /buːst/ *noun* something that helps you become more successful or feel more confident and happy: *His promotion was a great boost to his confidence.*

boost² *verb* to increase the value or amount of something: *The hot weather boosted sales of ice cream* (=more people bought ice cream than usual).

boot¹ /buːt/ *noun* **1** a type of strong shoe that covers your foot and the lower part of your leg: *a pair of boots* → see picture at SHOE **2** *BrE* a covered space in the back of a car, used for carrying bags, boxes etc SYNONYM **trunk** *AmE* **3 get the boot, give someone the boot** (informal) to be forced to leave your job, or to force someone to leave their job

boot² *verb* (informal) to kick something hard: *She booted the ball as hard as she could.*

booth /buːð $ buθ/ *noun* a small space surrounded by thin walls: *a telephone booth*

booze /buːz/ *noun* (no plural) (informal) alcoholic drink

bor·der¹ /ˈbɔːdə $ ˈbɔrdɚ/ *noun*

KEY PATTERNS
the border between two countries

1 the official line that separates two countries: *The train crossed the* ***border between*** *Russia and Poland at night.* **2** a narrow area or piece around the edge of something: *The flag was blue with a white border.*

border² *verb* **1** to be in a line along the edge of something: *Large trees border the park.* **2** to be next to another country: *Iraq borders on Iran.* **3 border on something** to be very nearly something bad or unpleasant: *His behaviour bordered on rudeness.*

bore¹ /bɔː $ bɔr/ *verb* **1** to make someone feel bored: *It was a terrible journey, but I won't bore you with a description of it.* • *Sorry, am I boring you?* **2 bore a hole** to make a deep round hole in the ground or under the sea

bore² *noun* someone or something that you find dull and uninteresting: *I'm not asking that bore to the party!*

bore³ the past tense of BEAR¹

bored

bored /bɔːd $ bɔrd/ *adjective*

KEY PATTERNS
bored with something

unhappy and impatient because something is not interesting or you have nothing to do: *She soon got* ***bored with*** *the game.* • *Most of the students* ***looked bored.***

PHRASES
be bored stiff, be bored to tears to be very bored

WORD CHOICE
bored or **boring**?
• **Bored** means "unhappy because something is not interesting": *You look bored!*
• **Boring** means "not interesting or enjoyable": *The film was* ***boring.***

bore·dom /ˈbɔːdəm $ ˈbɔrdəm/ *noun* (no plural) the feeling you have when you are bored

bor·ing /ˈbɔːrɪŋ/ *adjective* not interesting in any way: *The programme was so boring she fell asleep.*

THESAURUS
not very interesting: *I watched the programme but it* ***wasn't very interesting.***
dull: *It was raining so we spent a* ***dull*** *day indoors* (=boring).
monotonous: *I don't want a* ***monotonous*** *office job* (=one that is boring and always the same).

born¹ /bɔːn $ bɔrn/ *verb*

KEY PATTERNS
be born in 1998/April etc
be born in London/Australia etc

be born to come out of your mother and begin life: *I* ***was born in*** *1996.* • *Where* ***were*** *you* ***born?***

GRAMMAR
You say **I was born in 1992.**
✘ Don't say 'I borned in 1992' ✘ or 'I born in 1992.'

born² *adjective* a born leader, teacher etc is someone who has a natural ability to lead, teach etc

borne the past participle of BEAR¹

bor•row /ˈbɒrəʊ $ ˈbɑroʊ/ *verb*

KEY PATTERNS
borrow something from someone

to take and use something that belongs to someone else and give it back to them later: *He* ***borrowed*** *£2,000* ***from*** *his father.* • *She borrowed her friend's jacket.*

bos•om /ˈbʊzəm/ *noun* (formal) a woman's breasts

boss¹ /bɒs $ bɔs/ *noun* (plural **bosses**) your boss at work is the person who tells you what work to do: *I get on well with my boss.*

boss² *verb* **boss someone around** to tell someone to do things in an unfriendly way, especially when you have no authority over them

boss•y /ˈbɒsi $ ˈbɔsi/ *adjective* (**bossier**, **bossiest**) always telling other people what to do, in a way that is annoying

both /bəʊθ $ boʊθ/ *determiner, pronoun, conjunction*
1 two people or things: *Both the boys had dark hair.* • *"Which of these shirts do you like best?" "I like both."* • *Jump with both feet together.* • *They are both learning to play the piano.*
2 both ... and not only one person or thing, but also the other: *I like both pop and jazz.* • *Both Hannah and Clare are coming to the party.*

both•er¹ /ˈbɒðə $ ˈbɑðɚ/ *verb*

KEY PATTERNS
bother someone
bother to do something

1 to make someone stop what they are doing in order to ask them for something: *How can I work when people keep bothering me?* • *Sorry to bother you, but have you seen Ian anywhere?*
2 if something bothers you, it makes you feel slightly worried or upset: *Something's obviously bothering her.*
3 to make the effort to do something: *He didn't* ***bother to*** *lock the door.*

PHRASES
can't be bothered to do something *BrE* (informal) to not have enough interest or energy to do something: ***I can't be bothered to*** *go out tonight.*
not bothered (spoken) if you are not bothered about something, it is not important to you: *"Do you want tea or coffee?" "I'm* ***not bothered.****"*

bother² *noun* (no plural) problems or trouble that you have to spend time and effort on: *This new car has caused me a lot of bother.*

bot•tle¹ /ˈbɒtl $ ˈbɑtl/ *noun* a glass or plastic container with a narrow top, used for liquids: *a wine bottle*

bottle² *verb* **1** to put a liquid into a bottle: *This wine is bottled in France.*
2 bottle something up to keep a feeling hidden and not show it: *Don't bottle your anger up.*

ˈbottle ˌbank *noun* a large container in a public place where people leave empty glass bottles so that the glass can be used again

bot•tled /ˈbɒtld $ ˈbɑtld/ *adjective* bottled water has been put in a bottle so that people can buy it and drink it

bot•tle•neck /ˈbɒtlnek $ ˈbɑtlˌnek/ *noun* a place in a road where the traffic cannot pass easily, so that cars are delayed

bot•tom¹ /ˈbɒtəm $ ˈbɑtəm/ *noun*
1 the lowest part of something ANTONYM **top**: *Her mother was standing* ***at the bottom of*** *the stairs.* • *The bucket had a hole in the bottom.* ➔ see picture at TOP¹
2 (informal) the part of your body that you sit on SYNONYM **backside**

bottom² *adjective*
in the lowest place or position ANTONYM **top**: *The juice is on the bottom shelf.*

bought the past tense and past participle of BUY

boul•der /ˈbəʊldə $ ˈboʊldɚ/ *noun* a very large rock

boule•vard /ˈbuːlvɑːd $ ˈbʊləvɑrd/ *noun* a wide road in a town or city

A B C D E F G H I J K L M N O P Q R S T U V W X Y Z

A B C D E F G H I J K L M N O P Q R S T U V W X Y Z

bounce¹ /baʊns/ *verb* **1** if something bounces, it hits a surface and then immediately moves away from it again: *The ball bounced off the wall.* **2** if you write a cheque and it bounces, your bank will not pay the amount written on the cheque because there is not enough money in your bank account **3** to run or walk quickly because you are happy: *She bounced into the office.* **4** if an email bounces, the other person does not receive it and it comes back to the sender, usually because of a technical problem: *He gave me the wrong address and the email bounced.*

bounce

bounce² *noun* when something bounces: *You have to hit the ball after the first bounce.*

bounc·er /ˈbaʊnsə $ ˈbaʊnsɚ/ *noun* (informal) someone whose job is to keep people who behave badly out of a club or bar

bounc·y /ˈbaʊnsi/ *adjective* (**bouncier**, **bounciest**) something that is bouncy bounces easily: *a bouncy ball*

bound¹ the past tense and past participle of BIND

bound² /baʊnd/ *adjective*

> **KEY PATTERNS**
> **be bound to do something**
> **be bound for somewhere**
> **be bound up with something**

1 to be certain to do something: *Fiona is bound to win the competition – she's brilliant!*
2 (written) a ship, plane etc that is bound for a particular place is going there: *A ship **bound for** Singapore had just left.* • *a Paris-bound flight*
3 to be closely connected with something: *Her success **was bound up with** the success of the team.*

bound³ *noun* **1** (written) a long or high jump **2 out of bounds** if somewhere is out of bounds, you are not allowed to go there: *This area is out of bounds to the prisoners.*

bound·a·ry /ˈbaʊndəri/ *noun* (plural **boundaries**) the line that marks the edge of an area of land: *The river forms the boundary between the two states.*

bou·quet /bəʊˈkeɪ $ boʊˈkeɪ/ *noun* a number of flowers fastened together, that you give to someone

bout /baʊt/ *noun* a short period of illness: *a bout of flu*

bou·tique /buːˈtiːk/ *noun* a small shop that sells fashionable clothes

bow¹ /baʊ/ *verb* **1** to bend your head or the top part of your body forward: *The musicians stood up and bowed.* **2 bow to pressure/demand/opinion** to finally agree to do something that other people want you to do: *The school has bowed to public pressure and agreed to allow the pop concert.*

bow² /baʊ/ *noun* **1** when someone bows **2** also **bows** the front part of a ship ANTONYM **stern**

> **PRONUNCIATION**
> Be careful how you pronounce this word:
> **bow¹** (*verb*) is pronounced like 'cow'
> **bow²** (*noun*) is pronounced like 'cow'
> **bow³** (*noun*) is pronounced like 'go'

bow³ /bəʊ $ boʊ/ *noun* **1** a thin band of cloth or string that you tie to form two circles and use as a decoration or to tie your shoes: *Jenny had a big red bow in her hair.* **2** a weapon that you use for shooting ARROWS **3** a thing that you use for playing instruments with strings, such as a VIOLIN

bow·el /ˈbaʊəl/ *noun* the part inside your body that carries solid waste food away from your stomach and out of your body SYNONYM **intestine**

bowl¹ /bəʊl $ boʊl/ *noun* **1** a round container in which you put food or liquid: *a bowl of rice* **2 bowls** an outdoor game, in which you roll large wooden balls towards a smaller ball

bowl² *verb* to throw a ball towards the BATSMAN in CRICKET —**bowler** *noun*

bow-legged /ˈbəʊˌlegɪd $ ˈboʊˌlegɪd/ *adjective* a bow-legged person has legs that curve out at their knees

bowl·ing /ˈbəʊlɪŋ $ ˈboʊlɪŋ/ also **ten pin bowling** *noun* (no plural) an indoor game in which you roll a heavy ball along a wooden track in order to knock over pieces of wood

bow tie /ˌbəʊ ˈtaɪ $ ˈboʊ taɪ/ *noun* a man's tie that he fastens to form two small circles at the front of his neck

bow tie

box¹ /bɒks $ bɑːks/ *noun* (plural **boxes**) **1** a container for putting things in, especially one with four straight sides: *a large cardboard box • a box of chocolates* → see picture at CONTAINER **2** a small space surrounded by thin walls: *a telephone box* **3** a small square on a page where you write a figure or other information: *Sign your name in the box below.* **4 the box** *BrE* (informal) television: *What's on the box tonight?*

box² *verb* to take part in the sport of boxing

box·er /ˈbɒksə $ ˈbɑːksər/ *noun* someone who does boxing as a sport

ˈ**boxer ˌshorts** *noun* loose cotton underwear for men → see picture at UNDERWEAR

box·ing /ˈbɒksɪŋ $ ˈbɑːksɪŋ/ *noun* (no plural) a sport in which two people wearing big leather GLOVEs hit each other

ˈ**Boxing Day** *noun BrE* the 26th December, the day after Christmas Day, which is a national holiday in the UK

ˈ**box ˌoffice** *noun* a place in a theatre, cinema etc where you buy tickets

boy /bɔɪ/ *noun* a male child or a young man: *She is married now and has two boys.*

boy·cott /ˈbɔɪkɒt $ ˈbɔɪkɑːt/ *verb* to refuse to buy, use, or take part in something as a protest: *Several countries threatened to boycott the Olympic Games.* —**boycott** *noun*

boy·friend /ˈbɔɪfrend/ *noun* a boy or man with whom you have a romantic relationship

SPELLING
This word is often spelled wrongly. The correct spelling is: **boyfriend**.

boy·hood /ˈbɔɪhʊd/ *noun* (no plural) the time during a man's life when he is a boy

boy·ish /ˈbɔɪ-ɪʃ/ *adjective* like a young man: *She had a slim, boyish figure.*

bra /brɑː/ *noun* a piece of underwear that a woman wears to support her breasts → see picture at UNDERWEAR

brace /breɪs/ *verb* **brace yourself** to prepare yourself for something unpleasant

brace·let /ˈbreɪslət/ *noun* a piece of jewellery that you wear around your wrist → see picture at JEWELLERY

bra·ces /ˈbreɪsɪz/ *plural noun* **1** *BrE* two narrow bands that you wear over your shoulders and fasten to your trousers to stop them from falling down SYNONYM **suspenders** *AmE*: *a pair of red braces* **2** also **brace** *BrE* a wire frame that some children wear to make their teeth straight

brack·et /ˈbrækɪt/ *noun* **1** one of the pairs of signs [ ] or ( ) that you sometimes put around less important words: *Please give your age (in brackets) after your name.* **2** a piece of metal or wood fixed to a wall to support a shelf

brag /bræg/ *verb* (**bragged, bragging**) to talk too proudly about yourself SYNONYM **boast**: *He's always bragging about how much he earns.*

braid /breɪd/ *verb* to twist three long pieces of hair, rope etc together to make one long piece SYNONYM **plait** *BrE* —**braid** *noun* → see picture at HAIRSTYLE

Braille /breɪl/ *noun* (no plural) a type of printing that blind people can read by touching the page

brain /breɪn/ *noun* **1** the part of your body inside your head which you use to think and control everything you do: *Scientists don't fully understand how the human brain works. • He had suffered some brain damage in the accident.* **2 brains** the ability to think well

brain·storm¹ /ˈbreɪnstɔːm $ ˈbreɪnstɔrm/ *verb* to get together in a group in order to think of new ideas —**brainstorming** *noun*: *They had a*

A B C D E F G H I J K L M N O P Q R S T U V W X Y Z

brainstorming session to think of a new name for the company.

brainstorm² *noun* **1** *AmE* if you have a brainstorm, you suddenly think of a clever idea SYNONYM **brainwave** *BrE* **2** *BrE* if you have a brainstorm, you cannot think clearly or sensibly

brain·wash /ˈbreɪnwɒʃ $ ˈbreɪnwɑʃ/ *verb* to force someone to believe something that is not true by telling them many times that it is true

brain·wave /ˈbreɪnweɪv/ *noun BrE* a very good idea that you have suddenly SYNONYM **brainstorm** *AmE*

brain·y /ˈbreɪni/ *adjective* (informal) (**brainier**, **brainiest**) clever and good at learning

brake¹ /breɪk/ *noun* the part of a vehicle that makes it go more slowly or stop

brake² *verb* to make a vehicle go more slowly or stop, using its brake: *The car in front braked as it went around the corner.*

bran /bræn/ *noun* (no plural) the crushed skin of wheat and other grain, often used in bread

branch¹ /brɑːntʃ $ bræntʃ/ *noun* (plural **branches**)
1 a part of a tree that grows out from the main part: *Joe climbed up the tree and sat on one of the branches.*
➔ see picture at TREE ➔ see picture on page A10
2 one part of an organization: *That shop has branches in most big towns.*

branch² *verb* **branch off** to leave a main road or path: *We branched off the road onto a small track.*

brand¹ /brænd/ *noun* **1** a product that a particular company makes: *What brand of washing powder do you use?* **2** a particular type of something: *I'm not sure I like his brand of humour.*

brand² *verb* **brand someone as something** to describe someone as a very bad type of person: *You can't brand all football fans as violent.*

bran·dish /ˈbrændɪʃ/ *verb* (written) to wave something around, especially a weapon: *The man was brandishing a knife.*

ˌbrand-ˈnew *adjective* completely new and not used at all: *a brand-new house*

bran·dy /ˈbrændi/ *noun* a strong alcoholic drink made from wine

brash /bræʃ/ *adjective* a brash person seems too confident and speaks too loudly

brass /brɑːs $ bræs/ *noun* **1** (no plural) a shiny yellow metal that is a mixture of COPPER and ZINC **2 the brass (section)** the part of a band that plays instruments made of brass, such as TRUMPETS

brat /bræt/ *noun* (informal) a badly behaved child

bra·va·do /brəˈvɑːdəʊ $ brəˈvɑdoʊ/ *noun* (no plural) (formal) behaviour that is meant to show that you feel brave and confident, even though you do not

brave¹ /breɪv/ *adjective* behaving with courage in a frightening or difficult situation: *Only Gary was brave enough to stand up and say what he thought.* —**bravely** *adverb*: *She smiled bravely in spite of the pain.*

brave² *verb* (written) to be brave enough to do something difficult, dangerous, or unpleasant: *We braved the cold weather to go and watch the match.*

brav·e·ry /ˈbreɪvəri/ *noun* (no plural) the quality of being brave ANTONYM **cowardice** SYNONYM **courage**: *He was awarded a medal for his bravery.*

bra·vo /ˈbrɑːvəʊ $ ˈbrɑvoʊ/ a word you shout to show that you like something

brawl /brɔːl/ *noun* a noisy fight —**brawl** *verb*: *Two men were brawling in the street.*

breach /briːtʃ/ *noun* when you break a law, rule, or agreement: *If he leaves his job, he will be in breach of contract.*

bread /bred/ *noun* (no plural) a common food made by baking a mixture of flour and water: *He bought a loaf of bread.* • *She cut another slice of bread.*

breadth /bredθ/ *noun* (no plural) the distance from one side of something to the other SYNONYM **width**: *First we had to guess the breadth of the river.*

bread·win·ner /ˈbredˌwɪnə $ ˈbredˌwɪnɚ/ *noun* the person in a family who earns most of the money that the family needs: *Mum was the breadwinner after Dad became ill.*

break¹ ➔ see box on pages 82 and 83

break² *noun*

> KEY PATTERNS
> **a break in something**

1 if you take a break, you stop what you are doing for a short time in order to rest or eat: *OK, let's* ***take a break*** *for a few minutes. • It's time for my* ***lunch break.***
2 a short holiday: *I need a break. • a weekend break by the sea*
3 a pause or opening in the middle of something: *He stopped to wait for* ***a break in*** *the traffic.*
4 a chance to become successful: *Her* ***big break*** *was being chosen to star in a TV series.*
5 a part of something where it has been broken: *My arm always hurts where I had that break in my elbow.*

break·age /ˈbreɪkɪdʒ/ *noun* (written) something that has been broken or when something is broken: *You will have to pay for any breakages.*

break·down /ˈbreɪkdaʊn/ *noun*
1 when something stops working successfully: *a breakdown in the relationship between the two countries*
2 when a car stops working **3** if someone has a breakdown, they become seriously ill in their mind because they cannot deal with the problems in their life: *After his wife left he had a breakdown.*

break·fast /ˈbrekfəst/ *noun*

> KEY PATTERNS
> **have breakfast**
> **have something for breakfast**

the meal that you eat when you get up in the morning: *I haven't* ***had breakfast*** *yet. • What would you like* ***for breakfast****?*

ˈbreak-in *noun* when someone breaks a door or window to enter a building and steal things: *There was a break-in at the school over the weekend.*

break·through /ˈbreɪkθruː/ *noun* an important new discovery or change: *a breakthrough in the treatment of cancer*

break·up /ˈbreɪkʌp/ *noun* **1** when a marriage or romantic relationship ends
2 when an organization or country is forced to separate into smaller parts: *the breakup of the Soviet Union*

breast /brest/ *noun* **1** one of the two round raised parts on a woman's chest that can produce milk for babies **2** the front of a bird's body, or the meat from this: *chicken breast*

breast·stroke /ˈbrest-strəʊk $ ˈbreststroʊk/ *noun* (no plural) a way of swimming on your front in which you push your arms forward and move them round towards your sides

breath /breθ/ *noun*
the air that comes out of your lungs when you breathe: *I could smell garlic on his breath.*

PHRASES

take a breath to take air into your lungs: *He* ***took*** *a deep* ***breath*** *and dived into the water.*

be out of breath to have difficulty breathing, for example because you have been running: *After climbing to the top of the tower, we were all* ***out of breath.***

hold your breath to deliberately stop breathing for a short time while keeping air in your lungs: *I* ***held*** *my* ***breath*** *and swam under the boat.*

get your breath back, catch your breath to rest after doing something such as running until you can breathe normally again: *I'll have to stop for a moment and* ***get*** *my* ***breath back.***

under your breath if you say something under your breath, you say it quietly, so that other people cannot hear: *He said something angrily* ***under his breath*** *as he walked away.*

> WORD CHOICE
> **breath** or **breathe**?
> • **Breath** is a noun: *She took a long deep* ***breath.***
> • **Breathe** is a verb: *The room was so hot that I found it difficult to* ***breathe.***

breathe /briːð/ *verb*
to take air in through your nose or mouth and let it out again: *The room was so crowded I could hardly breathe. • "Is she still breathing?" asked Doctor May.*

break /breɪk/ *verb* (past tense **broke** /brəʊk $ broʊk/, past participle **broken** /'brəʊkən $ 'broʊkən/)

1 to damage something so that it separates into pieces: *Someone threw a stone and* ***broke*** *one of our windows.* • *Be careful with those eggs, or you'll* ***break*** *them.* • *He fell off his bike and* ***broke*** *his arm.*

break

3 to make a machine stop working properly: *I think I've* ***broken*** *my computer.*

2 to become damaged and separate into pieces: *The chair broke when he sat on it.* • *A branch* ***broke off*** *the tree.* • *I dropped the plate and it* ***broke into pieces.***

I dropped the plate and it broke into pieces.

THESAURUS

smash: *The thieves* ***smashed*** *the window* (=broke it by hitting it with a lot of force). • *The plate fell and* ***smashed*** *on the kitchen floor* (=it broke with a lot of force, because it hit a hard surface).

shatter: *A ball came through the window and the glass shattered* (=broke into a lot of small pieces).

crack: *I'm sorry – I've cracked this plate* (=damaged it so that a line appears on the surface).

burst: *Suddenly the balloon burst* (=broke).

A ball came through the window and the glass ***shattered.***

I'm sorry – I've ***cracked*** *this plate.*

PHRASES

break a law/rule
to disobey a law or rule: *If you* ***break the law****, you will be punished.*

break loose/break free
to escape: *He managed to* ***break free*** *of his attacker.*

break someone's heart
to make someone very unhappy: *He* ***broke my heart*** *when he left me.*

break a promise
if someone breaks a promise, they do not do what they have promised to do: *You've* ***broken your promise*** *again!*

break a record
to do something faster or better than anyone has ever done it before: *He was trying to* ***break the record*** *for the 10,000 metres.*

PHRASAL VERBS

break down
1 if a car or a machine breaks down, it stops working: *The car* ***broke down*** *on the way home.*
2 if someone breaks down, they start crying: *She* ***broke down*** *in tears.*

She broke down in tears.

break in
to use force to get into a building: *Burglars* ***broke in*** *last night and took two computers.*

break into
to use force to get into a building: *Someone* ***broke into*** *our house and stole the TV.*

Someone broke into our house and stole the TV.

break out
if a disease, fire, war etc breaks out, it starts: *A fire had* ***broken out*** *at the airport.*

break through
to use force to get through something that is stopping you from moving forward: *The crowd* ***broke through*** *the police barriers.*

break up
1 to separate something into many pieces: ***Break*** *the biscuit* ***up*** *into pieces.*

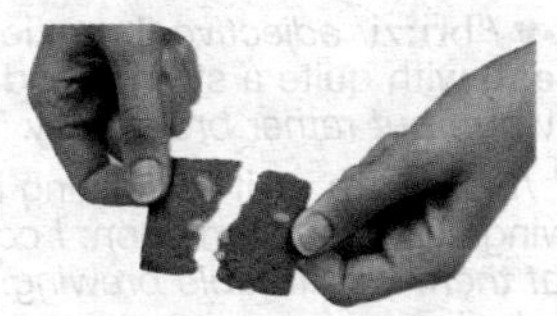

Break the biscuit up into pieces.

2 to end a relationship with a husband, wife, boyfriend etc: *She and her boyfriend* ***broke up*** *last week.* • *I've* ***broken up*** *with Gary.*
3 *BrE* to start the school holiday: *We* ***break up*** *at the end of the week.*

A B C D E F G H I J K L M N O P Q R S T U V W X Y Z

PHRASAL VERBS

breathe in

breathe in, breathe something in to take air in through your nose or mouth: *I tried not to **breathe in** the smoke.*

breathe out

to let air out through your nose or mouth: *Now **breathe out** slowly.*

breath·er /'bri:ðə $ 'briðɚ/ *noun* (informal) a short rest: *Let's stop for a breather.*

breath·less /'breθləs/ *adjective* if you are breathless, you are finding it difficult to breathe normally

breath·tak·ing /'breθˌteɪkɪŋ/ *adjective* very beautiful, exciting, or surprising: *a breathtaking view of the Grand Canyon*

bred the past tense and past participle of BREED[1]

breed[1] /bri:d/ *verb* (past tense and past participle **bred** /bred/) **1** if animals breed, they have babies **2** if you breed animals, you keep them in order to produce young ones

breed[2] *noun* a particular type of dog, horse etc

breeze /bri:z/ *noun* a light gentle wind ➔ see Thesaurus at WIND[1]

breez·y /'bri:zi/ *adjective* (**breezier**, **breeziest**) with quite a strong wind: *It was a warm but rather breezy day.*

brew[1] /bru:/ *verb* **1** if something bad is brewing, it will happen soon: *I could see that there was trouble brewing.* **2** to make beer

brew·er·y /'bru:əri/ *noun* (plural **breweries**) a place where beer is made, or a company that makes beer

bribe[1] /braɪb/ *noun* money that someone gives to a person in an official position to persuade them to do something dishonest

bribe[2] *verb* to pay money to someone to persuade them to help you by doing something dishonest: *He was sent to prison for trying to bribe the judge.*

brib·er·y /'braɪbəri/ *noun* (no plural) when someone offers or accepts bribes

brick /brɪk/ *noun* a hard block of baked clay used for building

brid·al /'braɪdl/ *adjective* relating to a bride or a wedding: *a bridal shop*

bride /braɪd/ *noun* a woman who is getting married

bride·groom /'braɪdgru:m/ *noun* a man who is getting married

brides·maid /'braɪdzmeɪd/ *noun* a woman or girl who helps a BRIDE at her wedding

bridge /brɪdʒ/ *noun* a special road that is built over a river or a busy road so that people or vehicles can cross the river or busy road: *They are building a new bridge over the river.*

brief /bri:f/ *adjective* (written) **1** continuing for only a short time: *There was a brief silence.* **2** using only a few words: *She gave the police a brief description of the man.* • *There isn't much time, so I'll be brief.* —**briefly** *adverb*: *He told us briefly what had happened.*

brief·case /'bri:fkeɪs/ *noun* a thin flat case that you use to carry papers or books to work or college ➔ see picture at CASE

briefs /bri:fs/ *plural noun* underwear that you wear between your waist and the top of your legs SYNONYM **pants** *BrE*: *a pair of cotton briefs*

bri·gade /brɪ'geɪd/ *noun* a large group of soldiers who are part of an army

bright /braɪt/ *adjective* **1** something that is bright shines a lot or has a lot of light: *the bright flames of the candles* • *a nice bright room* **2** bright colours are strong and not dark: *a bunch of bright yellow flowers* **3** intelligent: *Maria is one of the brightest students in the school.* ➔ see Thesaurus at INTELLIGENT —**brightness** *noun* (no plural) —**brightly** *adverb*

bright·en /'braɪtn/ also **brighten up** *verb* **1** to become happier: *Kate brightened up a bit when Tim arrived.* **2** to make a place more colourful or attractive: *I put some posters on the walls to brighten the room up.* **3** to become brighter: *The weather brightened up in the afternoon.*

bril·liant /'brɪljənt/ *adjective* **1** very bright: *brilliant yellows and reds* **2** very intelligent or skilful: *a brilliant mathematician* ➔ see Thesaurus at INTELLIGENT **3** *BrE* (spoken) very good

or enjoyable: *We had a brilliant time!*
→ see Thesaurus at GOOD[1]
—**brilliantly** *adverb*: *brilliantly coloured flowers • a brilliantly sunny day*

brim[1] /brɪm/ *noun* **1** the bottom part of a hat that turns out **2 be full to the brim** to be as full as possible: *The cup was absolutely full to the brim.*

brim[2] *verb* (**brimmed**, **brimming**)
1 be brimming with confidence, be brimming with excitement to be very confident or very excited: *At the start of the match, the team was brimming with confidence.* **2 brim over** if a bowl or cup brims over, it is so full that liquid is coming out

bring → see box on page 86

brink /brɪŋk/ *noun* **be on the brink of something** if you are on the brink of something exciting or terrible, it will happen soon: *The country is on the brink of war.*

brisk /brɪsk/ *adjective* quick and determined: *She walked at a brisk pace.*

bris•tle[1] /ˈbrɪsəl/ *noun* one of many short stiff hairs, wires etc growing or placed together: *the bristles on a toothbrush*

Brit•ish[1] /ˈbrɪtɪʃ/ *adjective* from or connected with Great Britain

British[2] *plural noun* **the British** the people of Great Britain

Brit•on /ˈbrɪtn/ *noun* someone from Great Britain

brit•tle /ˈbrɪtl/ *adjective* hard and easily broken: *The wood was dry and brittle.*

broach /brəʊtʃ $ broʊtʃ/ *verb* **broach a subject** to mention a subject that may be embarrassing or unpleasant: *It can be difficult to broach the subject of death with young children.*

broad /brɔːd/ *adjective*
1 wide ANTONYM **narrow**: *He had a broad smile on his face. • a long, broad river*
2 including many different things or people: *The university offers a broad range of subjects.*
3 concerning the main ideas or parts of something, rather than the small details: *I support the broad aims of the group.*

broad•band /ˈbrɔːdbænd/ *noun* a system for connecting computers to the Internet, which makes it possible to send and receive large amounts of information very quickly: *Do you have a broadband connection at home?*

broad•cast[1] /ˈbrɔːdkɑːst $ ˈbrɔdkæst/ *noun* a programme on radio or television: *a live broadcast of the concert*

broadcast[2] *verb* (past tense and past participle **broadcast**) to send out a radio or television programme
—**broadcaster** *noun*

broad•en /ˈbrɔːdn/ *verb* **1** to make something include more kinds of things or people: *Travel broadens your knowledge of the world.* **2** also **broaden out** to become wider: *The river broadens out here.*

broad•ly /ˈbrɔːdli/ *adverb* in a general way: *I broadly agree with what you are saying.*

broad-mind•ed /ˌbrɔːd ˈmaɪndɪd/ *adjective* willing to accept behaviour or ideas that are different from your own ANTONYM **narrow-minded**

broc•co•li /ˈbrɒkəli $ ˈbrɑkəli/ *noun* (no plural) a thick green vegetable with green or purple flowers that you cook
→ see picture on page A6

bro•chure /ˈbrəʊʃə $ broʊˈʃʊr/ *noun* a thin book that gives information or advertises something: *a holiday brochure*

broke[1] /brəʊk $ broʊk/ *adjective* (informal) if you are broke, you have no money at all

broke[2] the past tense of BREAK[1]

bro•ken[1] /ˈbrəʊkən $ ˈbroʊkən/ *adjective*
1 something that is broken is damaged or in pieces because it has been hit, dropped etc: *a broken window • Their best player now has a broken leg.*
2 a machine or piece of equipment that is broken does not work: *a broken TV set*

A B C D E F G H I J K L M N O P Q R S T U V W X Y Z

bring /brɪŋ/ *verb* (past tense and past participle **brought** /brɔːt/)

1 to take something with you to the place where you are now, or to the place that you are going to with someone: *Can you **bring** me another glass of water?* • *Did you remember to **bring** your passport?* • *Is it all right if I **bring** a friend **with** me to the party?*

KEY PATTERNS

bring someone a present
bring your passport/some money
bring someone/something with you

bring

3 to move something to a different place: *She **brought out** a laptop from her bag.* • *We **brought** the box down from the upstairs bedroom.*

2 to make something happen or cause a particular result: *New technology **brings** new problems.* • *His music **brought** joy to many people.*

WORD CHOICE

bring or **take**?

- You **bring** something here, or to the place that you are going to with someone: *Did you remember to **bring** your passport?*
- You **take** something with you when you go to another place: *I always **take** my camera with me when I go on holiday.*

PHRASAL VERBS

bring back
1 to start using something again that was used in the past: *They should **bring back** the old system.* • *a vote on whether to **bring** the death penalty **back***
2 to make someone remember something: *That song **brought back** some happy memories for me.* • *Talking about it just **brings** it all **back** again.*

bring down
to reduce the number or amount of something: *Doctors want to **bring down** the number of deaths from this disease.* • *Competition has **brought** the price of mobile phones **down**.*

bring forward
to arrange for something to happen at an earlier time than you originally planned: *The match has been **brought forward** to Wednesday.*

bring up
1 **bring someone up** to look after a child until he or she has become an adult: *She was **brought up** by her grandmother.* • *It's not easy **bringing** kids **up** on your own.*
2 **bring something up** to start to talk about something: *He wasn't sure how to **bring up** the subject.* • *Did you have to **bring** that **up** right now?*

WORD CHOICE
broken or **not working**?
• You use **broken** about small machines and small pieces of equipment: *My watch is* ***broken****.*
• For larger machines and vehicles such as cars, you use **not working**: *My car isn't working.*

broken² the past participle of BREAK¹

ˌbroken-ˈhearted *adjective* very sad, especially because someone you love has died or left you

bro·ker /ˈbrəʊkə $ ˈbroʊkɚ/ *noun* someone whose job is to buy and sell property, insurance etc for other people

bronze /brɒnz $ brɑnz/ *noun* (no plural) a metal that is a mixture of COPPER and TIN

brooch /brəʊtʃ $ broʊtʃ/ *noun* (plural **brooches**) a piece of jewellery that you fasten to your clothes with a pin

brood /bruːd/ *verb* to think about something angrily or sadly for a long time

broom /bruːm/ *noun* a brush with a long handle that you use for sweeping floors

broth·er /ˈbrʌðə $ ˈbrʌðɚ/ *noun* a boy or man who has the same parents as you: *This is my brother Dave.* • *She has two* ***older brothers****.* • *Johnny was my* ***big brother****, and I always admired him* (=older brother). • *My* ***little brother*** *is very annoying* (=younger brother).

ˈbrother-in-ˌlaw *noun* (plural **brothers-in-law**) **1** the brother of your husband or wife **2** the husband of your sister

brought the past tense and past participle of BRING

brow /braʊ/ *noun* (written) your FOREHEAD

brown /braʊn/ *adjective* something that is brown is the colour of chocolate or wood: *He had light brown hair.* —**brown** *noun*

browse /braʊz/ *verb* **1** to spend time looking at things in a shop without buying anything and without hurrying **2** to look through a book or magazine without reading it carefully **3 browse the Internet, browse the Web** to look for information on the INTERNET

brows·er /ˈbraʊzə $ ˈbraʊzɚ/ *noun* computer software that you use to look at information on the INTERNET

bruise¹ /bruːz/ *noun* a dark mark on your skin where you have hurt yourself: *She had a nasty bruise on her face.*

bruise² *verb* to cause a bruise on someone's skin: *He fell and bruised his leg.*

bru·nette /bruːˈnet/ *noun* a woman who has dark brown hair

brunt /brʌnt/ *noun* **bear the brunt of something** to suffer the worst part of something unpleasant: *The south coast bore the brunt of the storm.*

brushes

brush¹ /brʌʃ/ *noun* (plural **brushes**) a thing that you use for cleaning, painting etc, consisting of hairs fastened onto a handle: *a paint brush* • *a brush and comb*

brush² *verb*

KEY PATTERNS
brush your hair/teeth/shoes etc
brush the dirt/dust/mud etc off something
brush tears/crumbs/sand etc away
brush against someone's face/skin/shoulder etc

1 to clean or tidy something with a brush: *She brushed her hair.*
2 to remove something by moving a brush or your hand across a surface: *He* ***brushed*** *the mud* ***off*** *his boots.* • *She* ***brushed away*** *her tears.*
3 to touch someone or something lightly as you go past them: *She felt something brush her leg.* • *His coat* ***brushed against*** *her arm.*

A B C D E F G H I J K L M N O P Q R S T U V W X Y Z

PHRASAL VERBS

brush up

brush up on something to try to reach again the level of skill or knowledge that you had in the past: *I must* **brush up on** *my English before our British visitors come.*

Brus·sels sprout /ˌbrʌsəlz ˈspraʊt/ *noun* a small round green vegetable

bru·tal /ˈbruːtl/ *adjective* very cruel and violent: *a brutal murder* —**brutally** *adverb*: *She was brutally murdered.*

brute¹ /bruːt/ *noun* **1** a cruel violent man **2** a large strong animal

brute² *adjective* **brute force, brute strength** physical strength: *He uses brute force to get what he wants.*

BSc /ˌbiː es ˈsiː/ *BrE*, **B.S.** /ˌbiː ˈes/ *AmE noun* Bachelor of Science; a university degree in a science subject

bub·ble¹ /ˈbʌbəl/ *noun* a ball of air in a liquid: *The bubbles rise to the surface as the water boils.*

bubble² *verb* if a liquid bubbles, it produces bubbles, especially when it boils: *When the water bubbles, put in the pasta.*

bub·bly /ˈbʌbli/ *adjective* **1** full of bubbles **2** happy and full of energy: *a bright, bubbly girl*

buck /bʌk/ *noun AmE* (spoken) a dollar: *It cost me 50 bucks.*

buck·et /ˈbʌkɪt/ *noun* a large round container, used for carrying liquids

buck·le¹ /ˈbʌkəl/ *verb* **1** also **buckle up** to fasten something with a buckle: *He buckled his belt.* **2** if your knees buckle, they become weak and you fall down **3** if metal buckles, it bends because of heat or pressure

buckle² *noun* a thing made of metal used for fastening a belt, shoe, bag etc → see picture at FASTENING

bud /bʌd/ *noun* a young flower or leaf before it opens → see picture on page A10

Bud·dhis·m /ˈbʊdɪzəm $ ˈbudɪzəm/ *noun* (no plural) a very old religion that started in Asia, which teaches people to want fewer things so that they can be happy

Bud·dhist /ˈbʊdɪst $ ˈbudɪst/ *noun* someone whose religion is Buddhism

bud·dy /ˈbʌdi/ *noun* (informal) (plural **buddies**) a friend

budge /bʌdʒ/ *verb* (informal) to move: *I pushed on the door but it wouldn't budge.*

bud·get¹ /ˈbʌdʒɪt/ *noun* an amount of money that is available, or a careful plan of how to spend an amount of money: *We had a budget of £150 for the party.*

budget² *verb* to carefully plan and control how you will spend your money: *We've budgeted for a new car this year.*

budget³ *adjective* very low in price SYNONYM **cheap**: *budget air tickets*

buf·fa·lo /ˈbʌfələʊ $ ˈbʌfəloʊ/ *noun* (plural **buffalos**, **buffaloes**, or **buffalo**) **1** an animal that looks like a cow with very long horns that lives in Africa or Asia **2** a BISON

buf·fet /ˈbʊfeɪ $ bəˈfeɪ/ *noun* a meal in which people take food that is on a table and then move away to eat

bug¹ /bʌg/ *noun* **1** (informal) a small insect **2** (informal) a very small living thing that gets into your body and makes you ill: *We've all been ill with this horrible flu bug.* **3** a small mistake in a computer program that stops it from working correctly **4** a small piece of electronic equipment for listening to people secretly

bug² *verb* (**bugged**, **bugging**) **1** to use electronic equipment to listen to people secretly: *Someone had bugged my telephone.* **2** (spoken) to annoy someone: *Go away, you're bugging me.*

bug·gy /ˈbʌgi/ *noun* (plural **buggies**) a light folding chair on wheels that you push small children in SYNONYM **stroller** *AmE*

build¹ /bɪld/ *verb* (past tense and past participle **built** /bɪlt/)
to make something large and strong such as a building, road, bridge etc, using special materials: *They are going to build a hotel near the beach.* • *When was this house built?*

PHRASAL VERBS

build on

build on something if you build on something, you use it to make more progress or be more successful: *The* *students will* ***build on*** *the writing skills they learned last year.*

build up

build something up, build up if you build something up, or if it builds up, it gradually becomes bigger: *Nick* ***has built up*** *a huge collection of DVDs.* • *The amount of work I had to do each week seemed to* ***build up.***

build² *noun* (no plural) the shape and size of someone's body: *He is tall with a heavy build.*

build·er /ˈbɪldə $ ˈbɪldɚ/ *noun* a person or a company that builds and repairs buildings

build·ing /ˈbɪldɪŋ/ *noun* a place such as a house that has a roof and walls: *The science laboratory is in this building.*

ˈbuilding soˌciety *noun BrE* an organization similar to a bank, where you can save money or borrow money to buy a house SYNONYM **savings and loan association** *AmE*

built the past tense and past participle of BUILD¹

bulb /bʌlb/ *noun* **1** the glass part of an electric light, where the light shines from: *a 60 watt bulb* → see picture at LIGHT¹ **2** a round root that grows into a plant: *tulip bulbs* → see picture on page A10

bulge¹ /bʌldʒ/ *noun* a curved shape caused by something pushing against a flat surface

bulge² *verb* to stick out in a rounded shape: *Her bag was bulging.*

bulk /bʌlk/ *noun* **1** the large size of something or someone **2 in bulk** in large quantities: *We buy all our food in bulk.*

bulk·y /ˈbʌlki/ *adjective* big and difficult to move

bull /bʊl/ *noun* a male cow, or the male of some other large animals such as an ELEPHANT

bull·doz·er /ˈbʊldəʊzə $ ˈbʊlˌdoʊzɚ/ *noun* a large powerful vehicle that can push over buildings and move rocks

bul·let /ˈbʊlɪt/ *noun* a small piece of metal that is fired from a gun

bul·le·tin /ˈbʊlətɪn/ *noun* a short news report

ˈbulletin ˌboard *noun* **1** a board on a wall where you can put information for people to see SYNONYM **noticeboard** *BrE* → see Thesaurus at BOARD¹ **2** a place on a computer system where a group of people can leave and read messages

ˈbullet ˌpoint *noun* **1** one of a list of words or phrases, which are the most important things that someone wants to mention in a talk or a piece of writing: *A list of bullet points came up on the screen at the start of her talk.* **2** a symbol, for example a circle or a square, which comes before each word or phrase on a list of important words or phrases

bul·ly¹ /ˈbʊli/ *verb* (**bullied**, **bullies**) to frighten or threaten to hurt someone who is smaller or weaker than you

bully² *noun* (plural **bullies**) someone who frightens or threatens to hurt people who are smaller or weaker than them

bum /bʌm/ *noun* (informal) **1** *BrE* the part of your body that you sit on **2** *AmE* someone who has no home or job

bump¹ /bʌmp/ *verb* **1** to hit or knock against something, especially by accident: *I fell and bumped my head.* • *He nearly bumped into the door.* **2 bump into someone** to meet someone when you were not expecting to: *Oh, I bumped into Martha this morning.*

bump² *noun* **1** a small raised area on a surface **2** a sudden movement in which one thing hits against another thing: *Ben had a bump in the car and damaged a headlight.*

bump·er /ˈbʌmpə $ ˈbʌmpɚ/ *noun* the part across the front and back of a car that protects it if it hits anything

bump·y /ˈbʌmpi/ *adjective* (**bumpier**, **bumpiest**) a bumpy surface has a lot of raised parts on it: *The road was narrow and very bumpy.*

bun /bʌn/ *noun* **1** *BrE* a small round sweet cake **2** bread that is made in a small round shape: *hamburger buns* **3** a way of arranging long hair by fastening it on top of your head in a small round shape → see picture at HAIRSTYLE

bunch¹ /bʌntʃ/ *noun* (plural **bunches**)

KEY PATTERNS
a bunch of flowers/grapes/keys etc

1 a group of similar things that are fastened together: *He gave her a* **bunch of** *flowers.* • *I bought two* **bunches of** *bananas.*
2 *AmE* (informal) a group of people: *I invited a* **bunch of** *friends round.* • *They're an odd bunch.*
3 (informal) a large number of things or amount of something: *We visited a whole* **bunch of** *places.*

bun·dle¹ /ˈbʌndl/ *noun* a group of things that are fastened or tied together: *a bundle of old clothes*

bundle

a bundle of old letters

bundle² *verb*
1 to move someone or something quickly and roughly into a place: *They bundled him out of the room.* **2 bundle something up** to tie things into a bundle

bung /bʌŋ/ *verb BrE* (informal) to put something somewhere: *Just bung your coat on the chair.*

bun·ga·low /ˈbʌŋgələʊ $ ˈbʌŋgəˌloʊ/ *noun* a house that has only one level and no stairs

bun·gee jump /ˈbʌndʒi ˌdʒʌmp/ *noun* a jump off a high place, with a long ELASTIC rope attached to your foot so that you do not hit the ground: *One of my friends did a bungee jump off a bridge in Australia.* **—bungee jumping** *noun*

bunk /bʌŋk/ *noun* **1** a bed on a train or ship **2 bunk beds** two beds arranged so that one is above the other ➔ see picture at BED

bun·ker /ˈbʌŋkə $ ˈbʌŋkɚ/ *noun* a strongly built room or building where people can shelter from bombs

buoy /bɔɪ $ ˈbui, bɔɪ/ *noun* an object that floats on the water to show ships which areas are safe and which areas are dangerous

PRONUNCIATION
British people pronounce **buoy** like 'boy'.
American people pronounce **buoy** either like 'boo' + 'ee' or like 'boy'.

bur·den /ˈbɜːdn $ ˈbɚdn/ *noun* (formal) something difficult or worrying that you have to deal with: *Sending your children to college can be a financial burden.*

bu·reau /ˈbjʊərəʊ $ ˈbjʊroʊ/ *noun* (plural **bureaux** or **bureaus**) **1** an office, department, or organization: *the Federal Bureau of Investigation* **2** *AmE* a piece of furniture with drawers, used for keeping clothes in SYNONYM **chest of drawers** *BrE*

bu·reauc·ra·cy /bjʊəˈrɒkrəsi $ bjʊˈrɑkrəsi/ *noun* an official system that annoys and confuses people because it has too many rules

bu·reau·crat /ˈbjʊərəkræt $ ˈbjʊrəˌkræt/ *noun* a person who works for a government organization and who uses the rules in a way that annoys people

bu·reau·crat·ic /ˌbjʊərəˈkrætɪk $ ˌbjʊrəˈkrætɪk/ *adjective* involving or using too many rules

burg·er /ˈbɜːgə $ ˈbɚgɚ/ *noun* meat that has been pressed into a round flat shape and cooked SYNONYM **hamburger**

bur·glar /ˈbɜːglə $ ˈbɚglɚ/ *noun* someone who goes into buildings in order to steal things

bur·glar·ize /ˈbɜːgləraɪz $ ˈbɚgləˌraɪz/ the American word for BURGLE ➔ see Thesaurus at STEAL

bur·glar·y /ˈbɜːgləri $ ˈbɚgləri/ *noun* (plural **burglaries**) the crime of going into a building to steal things

A B C D E F G H I J K L M N O P Q R S T U V W X Y Z

bur·gle /ˈbɜːgəl $ ˈbɚgəl/ *BrE*, **burglarize** *AmE* *verb* to go into a place and steal things → see Thesaurus at STEAL

bur·i·al /ˈberiəl/ *noun* when a dead body is put into the ground

burn¹ /bɜːn $ bɚn/ *verb* (past tense and past participle **burned** or **burnt** /bɜːnt $ bɚnt/)

KEY PATTERNS
burn something
burn your finger/hand etc on something
burn a hole in something

1 if you burn something, or if it burns, it is damaged by fire or heat: *She burned the letter.* • *I* ***burned*** *my* ***hand on*** *the hot pan.* • *These dry sticks should burn well.* • *The cigarette had* ***burnt*** *a* ***hole in*** *the carpet.*
2 if a fire burns, it produces heat and flames
3 if a part of your body is burning, it hurts and feels very hot: *Her sore throat was burning.*

PHRASAL VERBS
burn down
if a building burns down, it is destroyed by fire: *The old house* ***burned down*** *a long time ago.*

burn² *noun* an injury to your skin caused by fire or heat

burnt¹ a past tense and past participle of BURN¹

burnt² /bɜːnt $ bɚnt/ *adjective* damaged or hurt by burning: *The meat was dry and burnt.*

burp /bɜːp $ bɚp/ *verb* (informal) to let air come out noisily from your stomach SYNONYM **belch** —**burp** *noun*

bur·row¹ /ˈbʌrəʊ $ ˈbɚoʊ/ *verb* to make a hole in the ground by digging: *Rabbits had burrowed under the fence.*

burrow² *noun* a hole in the ground made by an animal such as a rabbit

burst¹ /bɜːst $ bɚst/ *verb*

KEY PATTERNS
burst something
a door/window bursts open
someone bursts out of somewhere
someone bursts in/into somewhere

1 if something bursts, or if you burst it, it breaks open suddenly and something such as air or water comes out of it: *A water pipe had burst upstairs and water was coming through the ceiling.* • *I burst the balloon with a pin.* → see Thesaurus at BREAK¹
2 to move suddenly, with a lot of energy or violence: *The door* ***burst open*** *and four men ran in.* • *A woman on a horse* ***burst out of*** *the woods.* • *The class had already started when Sheila* ***burst in*** *late.*

PHRASES
be bursting with energy to have a lot of energy: *The kids* ***are*** *always* ***bursting with energy.***
burst into tears to suddenly start to cry: *She put her head on his shoulder and* ***burst into tears.*** → see Thesaurus at CRY¹
burst into flames to suddenly start to burn: *The plane crashed and* ***burst into flames.***
burst out laughing, burst out crying to suddenly start to laugh or cry: *Everyone in the room* ***burst out laughing.***

burst² *noun* a short sudden period of activity or noise: *a burst of gunfire*

burst³ *adjective* broken or torn apart: *a burst pipe*

bur·y /ˈberi/ *verb* (**buried, buries**)

KEY PATTERNS
bury someone/something
bury someone in a grave/tomb
bury something in the ground/sand
bury someone/something under a pile/heap

1 to put a dead body into a GRAVE (=a hole that has been dug in the ground for this purpose): *We* ***buried*** *my brother* ***in*** *a small country churchyard.* • *We visited the grave where Bob Marley is buried.*
2 to cover something so that no one can see it: *The wall collapsed,* ***burying*** *him* ***under*** *a pile of bricks.* • *We found the treasure* ***buried underground.***

PHRASES
bury your face in something, bury your head in something to hide your face by pressing it into something,

usually because you are upset: *She **buried her face in** her hands and began to cry.*

PRONUNCIATION
You pronounce **bury** like 'berry'.

bus /bʌs/ *noun* (plural **buses**)
a large road vehicle that people pay to travel on: *I usually **catch a bus** to college.* • *We **went** to the nightclub **by bus**.* • *We **missed the bus*** (=we were too late, so it went without us). • *a London **bus driver*** (=someone whose job is to drive a bus) ➔ see picture on page A11

USAGE
You **get on a bus**.
✘ Don't say 'get in a bus'.
You go somewhere **by bus**.

bush /bʊʃ/ *noun* (plural **bushes**)
1 a plant like a small tree with a lot of branches: *a rose bush*
2 the bush areas of Australia and Africa that are still wild: *We got lost in **the bush**.*

bush·y /ˈbʊʃi/ *adjective* bushy hair or fur grows thickly

bus·i·ly /ˈbɪzəli/ *adverb* in a busy way: *chefs busily preparing dinner*

busi·ness /ˈbɪznəs/ *noun*

KEY PATTERNS
in business
open for business
on business

1 (no plural) making, buying, or selling things: *You need a lot of money to succeed **in business**.* • *The store is **open for business** 24 hours a day.*
2 (no plural) the amount of work a company is doing, or the amount of money it is making: *The local shops have **lost business** since the new supermarket opened.*
3 (plural **businesses**) an organization that produces or sells things: *James **runs** a publishing **business**.* • *a **small family business***
4 (no plural) the work that you do as your job to earn money: *The next day, Tim went to Paris **on business*** (=as part of his job). • *Information on new products is always useful **in my business**.*

PHRASES
go out of business to close a company because it is not making enough money: *Many small firms **went out of business** last year.*
the film business, the music business etc all the companies and people that are involved in making films, music etc: *If you're lucky, you can make a lot of money in **the music business**.*
do business (with someone) if one company does business with another company, it buys things from the other company, or sells things to it: *Our firm has been **doing business with** that company for years.*
mind your own business (spoken) used to tell someone in a rude way that something is private: *"Where are you going?" **"Mind your own business!"***

THESAURUS
trade: *The new laws encouraged international **trade*** (=buying and selling).
industry: *the car **industry*** (=all the businesses that make cars in a particular country)

busi·ness·like /ˈbɪznəs-laɪk/ *adjective* sensible and practical in the way you do things

busi·ness·man /ˈbɪznəsmən/ *noun* (plural **businessmen** /-mən/) a man who works at a high level in a company or who owns his own company

busi·ness·wom·an /ˈbɪznəsˌwʊmən/ *noun* (plural **businesswomen** /-ˌwɪmɪn/) a woman who works at a high level in a company or who owns her own company

ˈbus stop *noun* a place at the side of a road where buses stop for passengers

bust¹ /bʌst/ *verb* (informal) (past tense and past participle **bust** or **busted**) to break: *You can borrow my camera but don't bust it.*

bust² *noun* the measurement around a woman's breasts and back

bust³ *adjective* (informal) **1 go bust** a business that goes bust has to close because it has lost so much money
2 broken: *This TV is bust.*

bus·tle¹ /ˈbʌsəl/ *noun* busy and noisy activity

bus·y /ˈbɪzi/ *adjective* (**busier**, **busiest**)
1 someone who is busy has a lot of things that they must do: *a busy mother of three small children • Dad was too **busy with** work to spend much time with us. • Our tutor **keeps** us **busy** in class.*
2 a busy time is a time when you have a lot of things that you must do: *Christmas is always the **busiest time** of **year**. • Have you had a **busy day** at work?*
3 full of people, vehicles etc: *We live on a very **busy road**. • It was busy in the city centre today.*
4 a telephone number that is busy is being used SYNONYM **engaged** *BrE*: *The line's busy; I'll ring back later.*

but¹ /bət; *strong* bʌt/ *conjunction*
1 used when adding something different or surprising: *He's not much good at schoolwork, but he is good at sport. • I was very tired, but I still enjoyed the party.*
2 used when giving the reason why something did not or will not happen: *I'd like to go, but I've got to finish my homework.*

but² *preposition*
except: *Everyone but me went on the trip.*

butch·er /ˈbʊtʃə $ ˈbʊtʃɚ/ *noun*
1 someone who owns or works in a shop that sells meat **2 butcher's** a shop that sells meat

butt /bʌt/ *noun* **1** the person that other people often make jokes about: *Why am I always the butt of their jokes?* **2** *AmE* (informal) your bottom **3** the end of a cigarette after it has been smoked

but·ter¹ /ˈbʌtə $ ˈbʌtɚ/ *noun* (no plural)
a solid yellow food made from cream that you spread on bread or use in cooking: *Fry the onions in butter.*

butter² *verb* to put butter on something

but·ter·fly /ˈbʌtəflaɪ $ ˈbʌtɚˌflaɪ/ *noun* (plural **butterflies**) an insect with large coloured wings ➔ see picture at INSECT

but·tocks /ˈbʌtəks/ *plural noun* the part of your body that you sit on

but·ton¹ /ˈbʌtn/ *noun* **1** a small round object that you use to fasten your clothes: *I've lost a button off my shirt.* ➔ see picture at FASTENING **2** a small part on a machine that you press to make it start, stop etc **3** *AmE* a BADGE

button² *verb* **button something up** to fasten something with buttons

but·ton·hole /ˈbʌtnhəʊl $ ˈbʌtnˌhoʊl/ *noun* a hole in a shirt, jacket etc that you push a button through to fasten it

buy /baɪ/ *verb* (past tense and past participle **bought** /bɔːt/)

> KEY PATTERNS
> **buy something**
> **buy something from a person or shop**
> **buy someone a present**
> **buy a present for someone**
> **buy something for $50/25 cents etc**

if you buy something, you give someone money and they give you the thing in return: *Where did you buy that T-shirt? • I **bought** a new computer game **from** a shop in High Street. • Can I buy you a drink? • Ken **bought** a silver necklace **for** his girlfriend. • We **bought** the apartment **for** $460,000.*

> THESAURUS
> **get**: *What shall I get Mum for her birthday* (=buy)?
> **purchase** (formal): *You can **purchase** tickets online or by phone* (=buy).

buy·er /ˈbaɪə $ ˈbaɪɚ/ *noun* someone who wants to buy something from another person: *Have you found a buyer for your car yet?*

buzz¹ /bʌz/ *verb* to make a low steady noise like the sound an insect makes: *A fly was buzzing round the bedroom.* ➔ see picture on page A1

buzz² *noun* a low steady noise like the sound an electric bell makes: *There was a buzz at the door.*

buz·zer /ˈbʌzə $ ˈbʌzɚ/ *noun* a piece of electrical equipment that makes a sudden sound to tell you that something has happened

by¹ /baɪ/ *preposition*
1 used to say who or what does something: *She was bitten by a dog* (=a dog bit her). *• I was frightened by the sudden noise. • The room was*

heated by three electric fires. • *a new book by J.K. Rowling* (=a book that J.K. Rowling wrote)
2 next to something: *There's a garage by the side of the house.* • *I'll see you by the park gates at nine.* • *the house by the river*
3 used to say which part of something you hold: *Always hold a knife by the handle, not the blade.* • *He grabbed me by the arm.*
4 used to say the latest time when something must be done or finished: *You must finish this piece of homework by Friday.* • *We need to get to the airport by six.*
5 used to show how big a difference in amount something is: *We won by ten points* (=we had ten points more than the other team). • *Prices have increased by four per cent this year.*
6 used when giving measurements: *The room was 12 foot by ten foot* (=the room was 12 foot long and ten foot wide).

PHRASES
by bus, by train, by car etc travelling in a bus, train etc: *Suzy and I went into town **by bus**.*
by phone, by email etc using the telephone etc: *He contacted me **by email**.*
by cash, by credit card etc using cash etc to pay for something: *We paid for the holiday **by credit card**.*
by yourself without anyone else: *Alec made supper for six of us **all by himself*** (=without help from anyone else). • *She lives **by herself*** (=alone).

by² *adverb*
past someone or something: *They watched the cars going by.*

bye /baɪ/ also **bye-'bye** (spoken) goodbye: *Bye Max! It was nice meeting you!*

byte /baɪt/ *noun* a unit for measuring the amount of information a computer can use: *There are one million bytes in one megabyte.*

A B C D E F G H I J K L M N O P Q R S T U V W X Y Z

Cc

C the written abbreviation of CELSIUS or CENTIGRADE

cab /kæb/ *noun* a car with a driver who you pay to take you somewhere SYNONYM **taxi**: *We took a cab to the airport.*

cab·bage /ˈkæbɪdʒ/ *noun* a large round vegetable with thick green leaves that you cook and eat ➔ see picture on page A6

cab·in /ˈkæbɪn/ *noun* **1** a room on a ship where you sleep **2** the area inside a plane where the passengers or pilots sit

cabin

cab·i·net /ˈkæbənət/ *noun* **1** a piece of furniture with shelves or drawers, that you keep things in: *a filing cabinet* **2 the Cabinet** a group of the most important members of the government

ca·ble /ˈkeɪbəl/ *noun* **1** wires that carry electricity or telephone signals: *electricity cables* **2** CABLE TELEVISION ➔ see picture on page A12

ˌcable ˈtelevision also **ˌcable TˈV** or **cable** *noun* (no plural) a way of showing television programmes by sending signals through wires under the ground: *The hotel has cable TV.* • *The movie was showing on cable.*

cac·tus /ˈkæktəs/ *noun* (plural **cacti** /-taɪ/ or **cactuses**) a plant that grows in hot dry places and is covered with small sharp points ➔ see picture at PRICKLY ➔ see picture on page A10

ca·fé, cafe /ˈkæfeɪ $ kæˈfeɪ/ *noun* a small restaurant: *We had a cup of tea in the cafe.*

> **PRONUNCIATION**
> British people pronounce this word 'CAfé'.
> American people pronounce this word 'caFÉ'.

caf·e·te·ri·a /ˌkæfəˈtɪəriə $ ˌkæfəˈtɪriə/ *noun* a restaurant where you collect your own food and take it to a table to eat it: *a self-service cafeteria*

caf·feine /ˈkæfiːn $ kæˈfin/ *noun* (no plural) the substance in coffee, tea, and some other drinks that makes people feel more awake

cage /keɪdʒ/ *noun* a box that you can keep birds or animals in, and which is made of metal bars or wires

cake /keɪk/ *noun* a sweet food that is made by mixing flour, butter, sugar, eggs etc together, and baking it: *a chocolate cake* • *Who wants a piece of cake?*

cal·ci·um /ˈkælsiəm/ *noun* (no plural) a substance that helps bones and teeth to grow strongly: *Milk contains a lot of calcium.*

cal·cu·late /ˈkælkjəleɪt/ *verb* to find out something by using numbers, for example how big something is SYNONYM **work out**: *Have you calculated what the cost will be?*

> **THESAURUS**
> **add**: *Add 7 and 5 to make 12* (=put 7 and 5 together to find the total).
> **subtract**: *If you subtract 2 from 8 you get 6* (=take away 2).
> **multiply**: *If you multiply 4 by 10, you get 40* (=add 10 4s together).
> **divide**: *Divide 10 by 5 and the answer is 2* (=calculate how many times 10 contains 5).

cal·cu·la·tion /ˌkælkjəˈleɪʃən/ *noun* when you add, multiply, or divide numbers, for example to find out the answer to a sum: *I did a quick calculation in my head.*

cal·cu·la·tor /ˈkælkjəleɪtə $ ˈkælkjəˌleɪtɚ/ also **pocket calculator** *noun* a small electronic machine that you use for adding, multiplying etc numbers

calculator

cal·en·dar /ˈkæləndə $ ˈkæləndɚ/ *noun* a list that shows the days and months of a year

calf /kɑːf $ kæf/ *noun* (plural **calves** /kɑːvz $ kævz/) **1** a young cow **2** the back of your leg between your knee and foot: *She had strong calf muscles.* → see picture on page A5

call¹ → see box on page 97

call² *noun*

> KEY PATTERNS
> **make a call**
> **give someone a call**

1 a telephone conversation: *Could I use your phone to **make a call** please? • **Give** me **a call** later. • My job involves **taking calls** from members of the public* (=answering phone calls). • *She won't **return** my **calls*** (=telephone me back after I telephoned her).
2 a shout or cry: *We could hear calls from behind the door.*

ˈcall ˌcentre *BrE*, **call center** *AmE* *noun* a large office where people answer customers' questions, try to sell people things etc, using the telephone: *Whenever I try to speak to someone at our bank, they put me through to a call centre in Scotland.*

call·er /ˈkɔːlə $ ˈkɔlɚ/ *noun* someone who makes a telephone call: *There was one caller but he didn't give me his name.*

calm¹ /kɑːm/ *adjective*
1 relaxed and not worried, angry, or upset: *It isn't easy to **keep calm** before an exam. • Gradually, she began to **feel calmer**.*
2 if an area of water or the weather is calm, there is no wind: *a calm sunny day* → see picture at CHOPPY
—**calmness** *noun* (no plural): *the calmness of the sea*

calm² *verb* **calm down, calm someone down** to become quiet again instead of being angry, excited, or upset, or to make someone do this: *She was very shocked and it took me a long time to calm her down.*

> PRONUNCIATION
> In this word you do not pronounce the **l**.

calm·ly /ˈkɑːmli/ *adverb* in a calm way that shows you are not upset, angry, or worried: *Dad **took** the news very **calmly**. • Joe was very angry, but Liz smiled calmly.*

cal·o·rie /ˈkæləri/ *noun* a unit that measures the amount of energy a particular food can produce: *Don't eat high-calorie food if you're trying to lose weight.*

calves the plural of CALF

cam·cor·der /ˈkæmˌkɔːdə $ ˈkæmˌkɔrdɚ/ *noun* a camera that you can carry with you and use for recording moving pictures and sound

came the past tense of COME

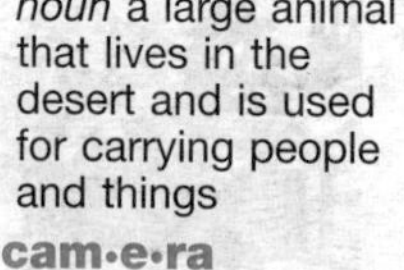

cam·el /ˈkæməl/ *noun* a large animal that lives in the desert and is used for carrying people and things

camel

cam·e·ra /ˈkæmərə/ *noun* a piece of equipment that you use for taking photographs or making films → see picture at LENS

cam·e·ra·man /ˈkæmərəmæn/ *noun* (plural **cameramen** /-men/) someone whose job is to use the camera when people are making a film or television programme

cam·ou·flage /ˈkæməflɑːʒ/ *noun* (no plural) clothes or colours that hide people, animals, or things by making them look the same as the things around them: *All the soldiers were in camouflage.* —**camouflage** *verb*: *The zebra is camouflaged by its stripes.*

camp¹ /kæmp/ *noun* **1** a place where children go to stay for a short time and do special activities: *The kids all go to summer camp in the vacation.* **2** an area of land where people sleep in tents

A B C D E F G H I J K L M N O P Q R S T U V W X Y Z

call /kɔːl/ *verb*

1 to telephone someone SYNONYM **phone**, **ring** *BrE*: *I called Sarah at her office in London.* • *Call this number if you need advice.* • *In the evenings I like to call my friends.*

GRAMMAR

✗ Don't say 'call to someone' when you are talking about telephoning them. Just say **call someone**.

call

2 to give someone or something a name: *They decided to call the baby Sarah.* • *I have a dog called Prince* (=his name is 'Prince'). • *What's the company called* (=what is its name)?

KEY PATTERNS

call someone John/Sarah etc
be called John/Sarah etc
What's she/it called?

3 to describe someone or something using a particular word or phrase: *Critics have called his latest film a great success.* • *Are you calling me a liar?*

4 to say something loudly to someone who is not near you SYNONYM **call out**: *I heard someone call my name.*

PHRASAL VERBS

call at
if a train, bus etc calls at a place, it stops there to let passengers get on or off: *This train **calls at** all local stations.*

call back
to telephone someone, after they have telephoned you: *I'm just about to eat – can I **call you back** later?* • *Mr Walters rang while you were out. He said he would **call back** later.*

call off
to decide that a planned event will not happen SYNONYM **cancel**: *The match was **called off** because of bad weather.* • *I don't know what he did, but she **called** the wedding **off**!*

call out
1 to say something loudly to someone who is not near you: *As the bus drove past, she waved and **called out** his name.*
2 to ask someone to come to a place to help you because something bad has happened: *Firefighters were **called out** to a fire in a factory.*

call up
to telephone someone: *I think you should **call her up** to thank her.* • ***Call up** a few builders and ask them how much it costs.*

camp² *verb* to put up a tent and sleep in it, especially when you are travelling somewhere: *That night we camped in the forest.*

cam•paign¹ /kæm'peɪn/ *noun* a number of things that people do in order to get a particular result, especially people in business or government: *an election campaign*

campaign² *verb* to do things to try to achieve a particular result, especially in politics: *She campaigned for nuclear disarmament.* —**campaigner** *noun*: *a human rights campaigner*

camp•ing /'kæmpɪŋ/ *noun* (no plural) the activity of sleeping in a tent, especially for a holiday: *We went camping in France in the summer.*

camp•site /'kæmpsaɪt/ *BrE*, **campground** /'kæmpgraʊnd/ *AmE* *noun* a piece of land where you can stay in a tent

cam•pus /'kæmpəs/ *noun* (plural **campuses**) an area of land where the main buildings of a university or college are: *the campus at Atlanta University*

can¹ /kən; strong kæn/ *modal verb*
1 if you can do something, you are able to do it: *Pete can speak Spanish well.* • *Can you swim?* • *I can't run any faster.*
2 used to say that something sometimes happens, or that something is generally possible: *Too much fat can be bad for you.* • *If a doctor makes a mistake, it can have terrible results.*
3 use **can't** and **cannot** to say that you do not believe that something is true: *You can't be serious!* • *She's married? That can't be true!*
4 used for asking or giving permission, or to say that someone has the right to do something: *Can Sally stay the night with us?* • *All citizens who are over 18 can vote.* • *I'm sorry, you cannot leave your bag there.*
5 used for asking for something: *Can I have another slice of cake?* • *Can my boyfriend use the computer tomorrow?* • *Can you take me home?*
6 used for offering to do something: *Can I help you?*
7 used to say that someone sees something, hears something etc: *Can you smell gas?*

GRAMMAR
The negative of **can** is **cannot** or **can't**: *She cannot walk without a stick.* • *I can't understand why she didn't call.*
To talk about ability in the past, use **could** or **was able to**: *I woke up in hospital and **couldn't** move.*
To talk about ability in the future, use **will be able to**: *The computers **will be able to** store more information.*
To talk about something that is possible in the future, use **could**: *This time next week we **could** be in France.*
To talk about something that was possible in the past but did not happen, use **could have**: *I **could have** been rich if I'd married Sam.*
To talk about having permission to do something in the past, use **be allowed to**: *We were not allowed to leave until we'd finished our work.*

can² /kæn/ *noun* a metal container containing food or drink: *a can of cola*

canal

ca•nal /kə'næl/ *noun* a long narrow area of water that has been cut into a piece of land so that boats can travel along it: *Venice is famous for its canals.*

can•cel /'kænsəl/ *verb* (**cancelled**, **cancelling** *BrE*, **canceled**, **canceling** *AmE*) if you cancel an event, meeting etc, you say that it will not happen SYNONYM **call off**: *We had to cancel the picnic because of the bad weather.*

WORD CHOICE

cancel or **postpone**?

- **Cancel** means “to decide that an event will not happen”: *Tonight’s concert has been cancelled.*
- **Postpone** means “to decide that an event should happen at a later date”: *The meeting has been **postponed** till next week.*

can·cel·la·tion /ˌkænsəˈleɪʃən/ *noun* when someone decides that they will not do something they were going to do, or that a planned event will not happen: *Bad weather forced the cancellation of the game.*

can·cer /ˈkænsə $ ˈkænsɚ/ *noun* a very serious illness in which cells in some parts of the body grow in a way that is not normal: *He died of lung cancer.*

can·di·date /ˈkændədət $ ˈkændəˌdeɪt/ *noun* **1** someone who tries to get a political position or a particular job: *the Republican party’s candidate for president* **2** *BrE* someone who takes an examination: *Candidates should write their names at the top.*

can·dle /ˈkændl/ *noun* a long piece of WAX with a piece of string through the middle, which you burn to use as a light

candle

candle

candlestick

can·dle·stick /ˈkændlˌstɪk/ *noun* an object that you put a candle in so that it stands up

can·dy /ˈkændi/ *noun* (plural **candies**) the American word for a SWEET

cane /keɪn/ *noun* **1** a long thin stick that people use to help them walk or to hit someone **2** the long hard stem of some plants that people use, for example to make furniture: *cane furniture*

can·na·bis /ˈkænəbɪs/ *noun* (no plural) an illegal drug that some people smoke SYNONYM **marijuana**

canned /kænd/ *adjective* canned food is in a special metal container called a can SYNONYM **tinned** *BrE*: *canned pears*

can·non /ˈkænən/ *noun* a large gun, usually on wheels, that was used in battles in the past

can·not /ˈkænɒt $ kænɑt/ the negative of CAN[1]

ca·noe /kəˈnuː/ *noun* a long narrow boat for one or two people that you push through the water using a short flat piece of wood called an OAR → see picture at BOAT

ca·noe·ing /kəˈnuːɪŋ/ *noun* (no plural) the sport or activity of using a canoe: *We could go canoeing this weekend.*

ˈcan ˌopener *noun* a tool for opening cans of food SYNONYM **tin opener** *BrE*

can’t /kɑːnt $ kænt/ the short form of CANNOT: *I’m sorry I can’t come to your party.*

PRONUNCIATION

British people pronounce **can’t** like ‘aren’t’.

American people pronounce **can’t** like ‘ant’.

can·teen /kænˈtiːn/ *noun* a place where the people who work in a school, factory, or office go to eat: *the college canteen*

can·vas /ˈkænvəs/ *noun* **1** (no plural) a type of strong cloth that is used to make tents, bags etc **2** a piece of canvas on which a picture is painted

can·vass /ˈkænvəs/ *verb* to try to persuade people to vote for your political party in an election: *Someone came to the house canvassing for the Labour Party.*

can·yon /ˈkænjən/ *noun* a deep narrow valley with steep sides SYNONYM **gorge**: *the Grand Canyon*

cap /kæp/ *noun*
1 a soft hat with a curved part at the front: *a Red Sox baseball cap* → see picture at HAT
2 something that covers the end or top of something, and stops other things from getting in it: *I can’t get the fuel cap off my car.*

ca·pa·ble /ˈkeɪpəbəl/ *adjective* **1** if you are capable of doing something, you are able to do it because you have the right skills or knowledge ANTONYM **incapable**: *Our team is certainly capable of winning.* **2** a capable worker is skilful and good at their job: *He's a very capable teacher.*

ca·pac·i·ty /kəˈpæsəti/ *noun* the amount that something can contain: *The theatre has a capacity of 500.*

cap·i·tal /ˈkæpətl/ *noun*
1 the most important city in a country, where the government and other big organizations are: *London is **the capital of** England.*
2 also ˌ**capital ˈletter** the large form of a letter of the alphabet, that you use at the beginning of a name or sentence: *The days of the week always begin with a capital letter.*

SPELLING
You use **capital letters** for the names of people and places: *Richard Wright • Paris, France*
You also use **capital letters** for days of the week, months of the year, and festivals: *Monday April 25th • Christmas • Easter*
You use a small letter for seasons: *winter • spring • summer • autumn/fall*

cap·i·tal·is·m /ˈkæpətl-ɪzəm/ *noun* (no plural) an economic system in which businesses and industry are owned by private owners and not by the government

ˌ**capital ˈpunishment** *noun* (no plural) when people are killed as an official punishment for a serious crime

cap·size /kæpˈsaɪz $ ˈkæpsaɪz/ *verb* if a boat capsizes, or if you capsize it, it turns over in the water

cap·tain¹ /ˈkæptən/ *noun* **1** someone who leads a team or group: *the captain of the football team* **2** the most important person working on a ship or plane **3** an officer in the army or navy

captain² *verb* to be the captain of a team or group: *She captained the school's hockey team.*

cap·tion /ˈkæpʃən/ *noun* a few words that are written under a photograph or drawing to explain what or who it is

cap·tive /ˈkæptɪv/ *noun* (written) someone who is kept as a prisoner: *The captives were released after six hours.* → see Thesaurus at PRISONER

cap·tiv·i·ty /kæpˈtɪvəti/ *noun* (no plural) when a person or animal is not free: *It's sad to see beautiful wild animals in captivity.*

cap·ture /ˈkæptʃə $ ˈkæptʃɚ/ *verb*
1 to catch a person or animal and to keep them somewhere as a prisoner: *Murray was captured in Italy, two days after his escape from a British gaol.*
2 (written) to get control of a place during a war: *The army has captured many towns and villages from the rebels.*

car /kɑː $ kɑr/ *noun*
1 a vehicle with four wheels and an engine, that carries a small number of people: *We decided to travel **by car*** (=in a car). • *I parked **my car** outside the house.* → see picture on page A11
2 one of the separate carriages on a train: *the dining car*

USAGE
You **get in a car**.
✘ Don't say 'get on a car'.
You **get out of a car**.
✘ Don't say 'get off a car'.
You go somewhere **by car**.

car·at also **karat** *AmE* /ˈkærət/ *noun* a unit for measuring how pure gold is, or how heavy jewels are: *an 18 carat gold ring*

car·a·van /ˈkærəvæn/ *noun BrE* a vehicle that can be pulled by a car, and that you can cook and sleep in when you are on holiday

car·bo·hy·drate /ˌkɑːbəʊˈhaɪdreɪt $ ˌkɑrboʊˈhaɪdreɪt/ *noun* a substance in some foods that gives your body energy: *Bread and rice contain a lot of carbohydrates.*

car·bon /ˈkɑːbən $ ˈkɑrbən/ *noun* (no plural) a chemical ELEMENT that is found in coal and petrol

carbon di·ox·ide /ˌkɑːbən daɪˈɒksaɪd $ ˌkɑrbən daɪˈɑksaɪd/ *noun* (no plural) the gas that people and animals produce when they breathe out

card /kɑːd $ kɑrd/ *noun*
1 a small piece of plastic or thick paper with information written on it: *Here's my student identity card.* • *I paid by credit card.*

2 a piece of thick folded paper with a picture on the front and a message inside that you send to people on their birthday, at Christmas etc: *a Christmas card*
3 one of a set of small pieces of thick paper with pictures or numbers on them, that you use to play games
4 cards a game that you play using a set of cards: *Do you want to **play cards**? • a **game of cards***

card•board /ˈkɑːdbɔːd $ ˈkɑrdbɔrd/ *noun* (no plural) very stiff thick paper, used especially for making boxes

car•di•gan /ˈkɑːdɪɡən $ ˈkɑrdɪɡən/ *noun* a piece of clothing that you wear on the top half of your body, and that you fasten down the front with buttons

care[1] /keə $ ker/ *verb*

KEY PATTERNS
care about someone/something
care whether/if/what etc
care that

if you care about someone or something, you feel concerned about them because you like or love them, or they are important to you: *Most young people **care about** the environment. • She didn't seem to **care whether** she passed the exam or not. • I don't **care that** he likes you better than me.*

PHRASES
who cares? (spoken) used to say that you do not think that something is important: *We came last in the race, but **who cares**? It was fun.*

PHRASAL VERBS
care for
care for someone to make sure that someone who is ill, old, or very young has the attention, food etc they need SYNONYM **look after, take care of**: *He gave up his job to **care for** his elderly mother. • women stay at home to **care for** their children*

care[2] *noun*
1 when you do something carefully in order to avoid making a mistake: *Choose your university **with care**. • He doesn't **take** enough **care over** homework.*
2 medical care, dental care etc: *Your father needs expert **medical care*** (=medical treatment).

PHRASES
take care of someone to make sure that someone who is ill, old, or very young has the attention, food etc they need: *Can you **take care of** the children while I'm out?*
take care of something **a)** to make sure that you do not damage something, by being careful: *If you **take care of** your CDs, they will last for years.* **b)** to be responsible for the work or effort that is needed to get a particular result: *I'll **take care of** all the travel arrangements.* → see Thesaurus at DEAL[2]

ca•reer /kəˈrɪə $ kəˈrɪr/ *noun* a job or profession that you do for a long time, especially one in which you can move to a higher position: *careers in business and finance.* → see Thesaurus at JOB

SPELLING
This word is often spelled wrongly. The correct spelling is: **career**.

care•free /ˈkeəfriː $ ˈkerfri/ *adjective* without any problems or worries: *At that time we were young and carefree.*

care•ful /ˈkeəfəl $ ˈkerfəl/ *adjective*

KEY PATTERNS
careful to do something
careful with something

if you are careful, you do something with a lot of attention, to avoid making a mistake or damaging something ANTONYM **careless**: *Be careful crossing the road. • Sally **was careful to** avoid getting into trouble. • You should be a bit more **careful with** your written work. • Try to keep a careful record of your spending.*

PHRASES
careful with money not spending more money than you need to —**carefully** *adverb*: *Please listen carefully to the instructions.*

THESAURUS
thorough: *Emma's work is always very **thorough*** (=careful and complete).
cautious: *Dad's a **cautious** driver* (=careful to avoid danger).

care•less /ˈkeələs $ ˈkerləs/ *adjective* if you are careless, you do not give enough attention to what you are doing, and you often make a mistake

A B C D E F G H I J K L M N O P Q R S T U V W X Y Z

or damage something ANTONYM **careful**: *Try not to be so careless in future.* • *a careless mistake* • *He was found guilty of* ***careless driving.*** —**carelessly** *adverb*: *This essay is very carelessly written.* —**carelessness** *noun* (no plural): *He might lose his job because of your carelessness.*

care·tak·er /ˈkeəˌteɪkə $ ˈkerˌteɪkɚ/ *noun BrE* someone whose job is to look after a building, especially a school SYNONYM **janitor** *AmE*

car·go /ˈkɑːgəʊ $ ˈkɑrgoʊ/ *noun* (plural **cargoes**) the things that a ship, plane etc carries from one place to another: *a cargo of grain*

car·ing /ˈkeərɪŋ $ ˈkerɪŋ/ *adjective* someone who is caring is kind and helps people: *She was a warm and caring person, always ready to help.*

car·ni·val /ˈkɑːnəvəl $ ˈkɑrnəvəl/ *noun* a big public party in the streets of a town with dancing, drinking, and entertainment: *the Venice carnival*

car·ni·vore /ˈkɑːnəvɔː $ kɑrnəvɔr/ *noun* (formal) a type of animal that eats meat: *Lions are carnivores.*

car·ol /ˈkærəl/ *noun* a song that people sing at Christmas

ˈ**car park** *noun BrE* a large area or building where people can park their cars SYNONYM **parking lot** *AmE*: *I parked in the underground car park.*

car·pen·ter /ˈkɑːpəntə $ ˈkɑrpəntɚ/ *noun* someone whose job is making and repairing wooden things

car·pen·try /ˈkɑːpəntri $ ˈkɑrpəntri/ *noun* (no plural) the work of a carpenter: *He is good at carpentry.*

car·pet /ˈkɑːpɪt $ ˈkɑrpɪt/ *noun* a material for covering the floor, that is often made of wool: *a thick bedroom carpet*

car·riage /ˈkærɪdʒ/ *noun* **1** *BrE* one of the several connected parts of a train, where the passengers sit SYNONYM **car** *AmE*: *I prefer sitting in a front carriage.* **2** a vehicle pulled by a horse, that people in the past travelled in

car·ri·er bag /ˈkæriə ˌbæg $ ˈkæriɚ ˌbæg/ *noun BrE* a plastic or paper bag for carrying things that you buy in a shop → see picture at BAG[1]

car·rot /ˈkærət/ *noun* a long thin orange vegetable that grows under the ground → see picture on page A6

car·ry /ˈkæri/ *verb* (**carried**, **carries**)

> **KEY PATTERNS**
> **carry something**
> **carry something to/into etc a place**

1 to hold something in your hands or arms, and take it somewhere: *Would you like me to carry your bag?* • *Steve* ***carried*** *a tray of drinks* ***into*** *the room.* • *Kim picked up the baby and* ***carried*** *her* ***back*** *inside.* → see picture on page A2
2 if vehicles, pipes etc carry things somewhere, they take them from one place to another: *The trucks were carrying emergency food supplies.* • *A system of channels* ***carries*** *the water* ***to*** *the fields.*

PHRASES

get carried away to become so excited that you do or say things that you would not normally do or say: *We both* ***got carried away*** *by our feelings for each other.*

PHRASAL VERBS

carry on
to continue doing something: *I tried to ask a question, but he just* ***carried on*** *talking.*

carry out
carry something out to do something that has been planned and organized, or that someone has told you to do: *Scientists are* ***carrying out*** *research into this disease.* • *Please* ***carry out*** *my instructions.*

cart /kɑːt $ kɑrt/ *noun* **1** a wooden vehicle on wheels, that a horse pulls: *a farmer with his horse and cart* **2** the American word for a TROLLEY

car·ton /ˈkɑːtn $ ˈkɑrtn/ *noun* a small strong container of thick paper that contains food or drink: *a carton of orange juice*

car·toon /kɑːˈtuːn $ kɑrˈtun/ *noun* **1** a film that is made with characters that are drawn, rather than real actors: *a Walt Disney cartoon* **2** a drawing, especially in a newspaper or magazine, that makes a joke about something or tells a story

carve /kɑːv $ kɑrv/ *verb* **1** to cut wood, stone etc into a particular shape: *The statue is carved from marble.* **2** to cut cooked meat into pieces, using a large knife: *Will you carve the chicken?*
→ see Thesaurus at CUT¹ → see picture on page A4

carve

carv·ing /ˈkɑːvɪŋ $ ˈkɑrvɪŋ/ *noun* an object that has been carved from wood, stone etc: *a wooden carving*

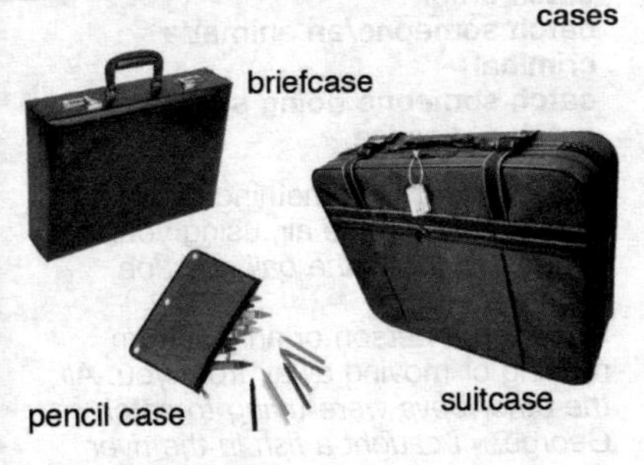

cases

case /keɪs/ *noun*

KEY PATTERNS
a case of something
in some/many cases

1 an example of a particular situation or problem: *This is the worst* ***case of*** *animal cruelty I have ever seen.* • ***In some cases****, people were given completely wrong information.*
2 a crime that the police deal with: *The police are still investigating the case.*
3 something that must be decided in a court of law: *The* ***court case*** *will continue next week.*
4 a container for storing or carrying something: *a guitar case* • *I've lost my pencil case.*
5 *BrE* a SUITCASE: *Have you packed your case?*

PHRASES

in case, just in case: *I brought some food,* ***in case*** *we get hungry later* (=because we might get hungry later). • ***Just in case*** *you don't know, all our classes are cancelled today.* (=because you might not know).

in any case used to give another reason for something: *I don't feel like going out to a bar, and* ***in any case*** *I can't afford it.*

in my case, in her case etc in my, her etc particular situation: ***In my case****, the tutor agreed that I could finish the essay later.*

cash¹ /kæʃ/ *noun* (no plural) money in the form of coins and paper notes: *I haven't got much cash. Can I pay by cheque?* → see Thesaurus at MONEY

cash² *verb* to change a cheque for money: *I went to the bank to cash a cheque.*

cash·ier /kæˈʃɪə $ kæˈʃɪr/ *noun* someone whose job is to take money from customers in a shop, or give money to customers in a bank etc

ˈcash maˌchine also **Cash·point** /ˈkæʃpɔɪnt/ *BrE* (trademark) *noun* a machine that you can get money out of, using a plastic card SYNONYM **ATM** *AmE*: *There's a cash machine next to the post office.*

ca·si·no /kəˈsiːnəʊ $ kəˈsinoʊ/ *noun* a place where people try to win money by playing games with numbers, cards etc

cas·sette /kəˈset/ *noun* a small plastic container with tape inside that you use for playing or recording sound or pictures: *a video cassette*

SPELLING
This word is often spelled wrongly. The correct spelling is: **cassette**.

casˈsette ˌplayer *noun* a machine that you use for playing and recording sound cassettes

cast¹ /kɑːst $ kæst/ *verb* (past tense and past participle **cast**) to give an actor a particular part in a film, play etc: *Because he looks tough, he is often cast as a villain.*

cast² *noun* all of the actors in a film or play: *The film has a brilliant cast.*

cas·tle /ˈkɑːsəl $ ˈkæsəl/ *noun* a large strong building that was built in the past to defend the people inside from attack

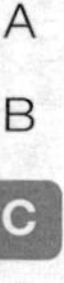

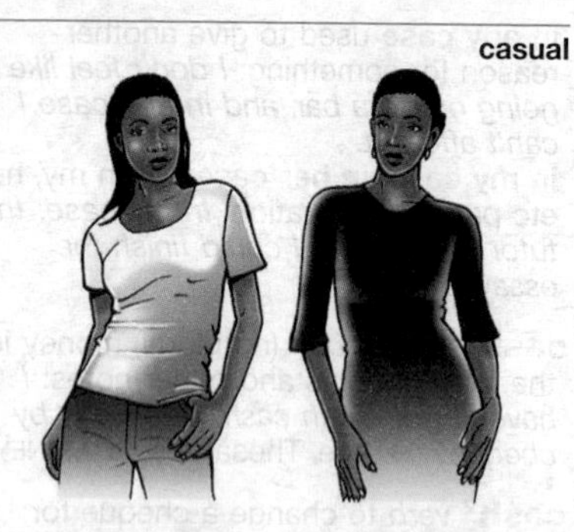

casual clothes formal clothes

cas·u·al /ˈkæʒuəl/ *adjective* **1** relaxed and not very serious: *He bent to kiss her in a casual sort of way.* **2** casual clothes are comfortable and you wear them in informal situations ANTONYM **formal**: *casual trousers* **3** casual work is temporary work that you do for a short time: *a casual part-time job* —**casually** *adverb*

cas·u·al·ty /ˈkæʒuəlti/ *noun* (plural **casualties**) **1** someone who is hurt in an accident, a war etc: *There have been 20 casualties following an accident on the motorway.* **2** (no plural) *BrE* the part of a hospital that people are taken to when they need urgent treatment SYNONYM **emergency room** *AmE*

cat /kæt/ *noun* a small animal with four legs, fur, and sharp teeth and CLAWS, that people often keep in their house as a pet → see picture on page A8

cat·a·logue *BrE*, **catalog** *AmE* /ˈkætəlɒg $ ˈkætl̩ˌɔg/ *noun* a book with pictures and information about the things you can buy from a particular company: *a children's clothes catalogue*

cat·a·pult /ˈkætəpʌlt/ *verb* (written) to make someone or something move through the air very quickly: *The horse stopped suddenly, catapulting Sam to the ground.*

ca·tas·tro·phe /kəˈtæstrəfi/ *noun* a terrible event that causes a lot of damage or death SYNONYM **disaster**: *the danger of a nuclear catastrophe*

throw catch

catch¹ /kætʃ/ *verb* (past tense and past participle **caught** /kɔːt/)

KEY PATTERNS
catch a ball
catch someone/an animal/a criminal
catch someone doing something
catch a disease

1 to get hold of something that is moving through the air, using your hands: *Bill threw the ball and Joe caught it.*
2 to stop a person or animal from running or moving away from you: *All the other boys were trying to catch George.* • *I caught a fish in the river today.*
3 if the police catch someone who has done something illegal, they find that person: *Police officers say they need help to catch the robbers.*
4 to see someone doing something wrong: *I caught him reading through my letters.*
5 to get an illness that is passed from one person to another: *Lots of students* ***catch a cold*** *at the beginning of term.*

PHRASES
catch a bus, catch a train etc to get on a bus, train etc: *We* ***caught a cab*** *to Grand Central station* (=taxi).
catch fire to start burning, especially by mistake: *We had a barbecue and somehow the fence* ***caught fire.***

PHRASAL VERBS
catch on
to become popular or fashionable: *This kind of music has really* ***caught on*** *in Britain.*
catch out
catch someone out to ask someone a question that will show that they have been lying: *The boy was far too clever*

*to be **caught out** by his father's questions.*

catch up

1 catch someone up to get to the same place as someone who is in front of you by moving faster than them: *We ran to **catch up with** our friends.* • *Ahmed was winning the race but then his brother started to **catch** him **up**.*

2 to reach the same standard or level that someone else has reached: *After my illness, it took a long time to **catch up with** the rest of the class.*

catch up on

catch up on something (informal) to do something that you have not yet had time to do: *I'm going to **catch up on** some reading during the Christmas break.*

catch² *noun* (plural **catches**) when you catch something that someone has thrown or hit: *Good catch, Paul!*

catch·ing /ˈkætʃɪŋ/ *adjective* an illness that is catching passes easily from one person to another SYNONYM **infectious**

cat·e·go·ry /ˈkætəgəri $ ˈkætəˌgɔri/ *noun* (plural **categories**) a group of people or things that are similar in some way: *These animals can be divided into four categories.* → see Thesaurus at TYPE¹

ca·ter /ˈkeɪtə $ ˈkeɪtɚ/ *verb* **cater to** also **cater for** *BrE* to provide a particular group of people with what they need or want: *We chose the hotel because it caters for small children.*

cat·er·pil·lar /ˈkætəˌpɪlə $ ˈkætɚˌpɪlɚ/ *noun* a small garden creature that eats leaves. A caterpillar later becomes a BUTTERFLY (=a flying insect with large beautiful wings).

ca·the·dral /kəˈθiːdrəl/ *noun* a very large church that is the most important one in a particular area

Cath·o·lic /ˈkæθəlɪk/ *adj* belonging or relating to the part of the Christian religion that has the Pope as its leader SYNONYM **Roman Catholic** —**Catholic** *noun*

cat·sup /ˈkætsəp/ an American word for KETCHUP

cat·tle /ˈkætl/ *plural noun* male and female cows: *a cattle ranch*

caught the past tense and past participle of CATCH¹

cau·li·flow·er /ˈkɒlɪˌflaʊə $ ˈkɔlɪˌflaʊɚ/ *noun* a vegetable with green leaves on the outside and a large firm white centre

cause¹ /kɔːz/ *verb* (written)

> KEY PATTERNS
> **cause an event/problem/illness**
> **cause someone to do something**
> **cause someone problems**

to make something happen: *Smoking causes cancer.* • *The floods were caused by heavy rain.* • *I wonder what **caused** her **to** leave so early.* • *I don't want to cause you any trouble.*

> THESAURUS
> **make**: *David's so funny – he **makes** me laugh* (=causes me to laugh).
> **result in**: *The fire **resulted in** the deaths of two children* (=caused).

cause² *noun*

> KEY PATTERNS
> **a/the cause of something**

a person, event, or thing that makes something happen: *Police are trying to find **the cause of** the fire.* • *What are **the causes of** this illness?*

PHRASES

have cause for something, have cause to do something to have reasons for feeling or behaving in a particular way: *You **have no cause for** worry because your illness is not serious.* • *I hope you won't **have cause** to regret that decision.*

for a good cause, in a good cause if you do something kind or helpful for a good cause, you do it to help people who need and deserve help: *Would you like to give a donation* (=money) *to the Children's Charity? It's all **in a good cause**.*

cau·tion /ˈkɔːʃən/ *noun* (no plural) (formal) great care when you are doing something, because it is dangerous: *The sign said 'Caution. Dangerous cliffs.'*

cau·tious /ˈkɔːʃəs/ *adjective* careful not to hurt or harm yourself → see Thesaurus at CAREFUL —**cautiously** *adverb*: *He began to climb cautiously down the tree.*

A B C D E F G H I J K L M N O P Q R S T U V W X Y Z

cav·al·ry /ˈkævəlri/ *noun* (no plural) soldiers who fought on horses in the past

cave /keɪv/ *noun* a large natural hole under the ground, or in the side of a mountain or cliff

cave·man /ˈkeɪvmæn/ *noun* (plural **cavemen** /-men/) someone who lived many thousands of years ago, when people lived in caves

cav·i·ty /ˈkævəti/ *noun* (plural **cavities**) a hole in a tooth: *The dentist said I had a cavity.*

CD /ˌsiː ˈdiː/ *noun* an abbreviation for COMPACT DISC; a small round piece of hard plastic with music or words recorded on it: *He's in his room listening to CDs.*

CˈD ˌplayer *noun* a piece of electric equipment that you play CDs on

CD-ROM /ˌsiː diː ˈrɒm $ ˌsi di ˈrɑm/ *noun* a CD with a lot of information stored on it, which you look at using a computer

cease /siːs/ *verb* (formal) to stop doing something or stop happening: *The company ceased trading in 1997.*

cease·fire /ˈsiːsfaɪə $ ˈsisˌfaɪə˞/ *noun* an agreement between two countries or enemy groups to stop fighting

cei·ling /ˈsiːlɪŋ/ *noun* the flat surface above your head in a room: *It was a big room with a high ceiling.* ➔ see picture at ROOF

> **PRONUNCIATION**
> You pronounce **cei-** like 'see'.

cel·e·brate /ˈseləbreɪt/ *verb* to do something nice because it is a special occasion, or because something good has happened: *The team celebrated by opening some bottles of champagne.*

cel·e·bra·tion /ˌseləˈbreɪʃən/ *noun* a party, meal, dance etc when you celebrate something special or good: *The wedding celebrations went on all through the night.*

ce·leb·ri·ty /səˈlebrəti/ *noun* (plural **celebrities**) a famous person, especially an actor or entertainer SYNONYM **star**: *There were lots of TV celebrities at the party.*

cel·e·ry /ˈseləri/ *noun* a vegetable with long hard pale green stems that you can cook or eat in a SALAD ➔ see picture on page A6

cell /sel/ *noun* **1** a small room in a police station or prison for keeping prisoners: *They locked him in a cell.* **2** the smallest living part of an animal or plant: *brain cells*

cel·lar /ˈselə $ ˈselə˞/ *noun* a room under the ground in a house, used especially for storing things: *He got a bottle of wine from the cellar.*

cel·lo /ˈtʃeləʊ $ ˈtʃeloʊ/ *noun* a large wooden musical instrument that you hold between your knees and play by pulling a special stick across four strings

ˈcell phone or **cel·lu·lar phone** /ˌseljələ ˈfəʊn $ ˌseljələ˞ ˈfoʊn/ the American word for MOBILE PHONE ➔ see picture on page A12

Cel·si·us /ˈselsiəs/ (abbreviation **C**) *noun* (no plural) a scale for measuring temperature, in which water freezes at 0° and boils at 100°

ce·ment /sɪˈment/ *noun* (no plural) a substance that is mixed with sand and water to make CONCRETE (=a substance for building walls and making hard surfaces): *You have to wait for the cement to dry.*

cem·e·tery /ˈsemətri $ ˈseməˌteri/ *noun* (plural **cemeteries**) an area of land where dead people are buried

cen·sor /ˈsensə $ ˈsensə˞/ *verb* to look at books, films etc and remove anything that might offend or harm people: *It was obvious that the television reports were being censored.*

cen·sor·ship /ˈsensəʃɪp $ ˈsensə˞ʃɪp/ *noun* when a government or other authority censors books, films, newspapers etc: *She believes that censorship is wrong.*

cen·sus /ˈsensəs/ *noun* (plural **censuses**) an official event when a government collects information about the number of people in the country and their ages, jobs etc

cent /sent/ *noun* a small coin used in the US. There are 100 cents in a dollar

cen·te·na·ry /senˈtiːnəri/ *BrE*, **cen·ten·ni·al** /senˈteniəl/ *AmE noun* (plural **centenaries** *BrE*) the day or year exactly 100 years after an important event: *Next year, we will be celebrating the school's centenary.*

cen·ter /ˈsentə $ sentɚ/ the American spelling of CENTRE

Cen·ti·grade /ˈsentəgreɪd/ CELSIUS

cen·ti·me·tre *BrE*, **centimeter** *AmE* /ˈsentəmiːtə $ ˈsentəˌmitɚ/ (written abbreviation **cm**) *noun*
a unit for measuring length in the METRIC system. There are 100 centimetres in a metre

cen·tral /ˈsentrəl/ *adjective*
1 in the middle of a place: *Central Europe* • *The central shopping area has the best shops.*
2 more important than anything else: *The central theme of the book is the beauty of nature.*

ˌcentral ˈheating *noun* (no plural) a system of heating buildings in which pipes carry the heat to every part of the building: *Most of these houses have central heating.*

cen·tre¹ *BrE*, **center** *AmE* /ˈsentə $ ˈsentɚ/ *noun*

KEY PATTERNS
the centre of something
a centre for research/education etc

1 the middle part or point of something: *He took her hand and led her to* ***the centre of*** *the room.* • *Find* ***the centre of*** *the circle using your ruler.*
2 a building where people go for a particular purpose: *a sports centre* • *I have an appointment at the Health Centre this afternoon.* • *the new* ***Centre for*** *Medical Research*
3 the part in the middle of a city or town where most of the shops, restaurants, clubs etc are: *We took a bus to* ***the centre of*** *Cairo.* • *a busy* ***city centre***

centre² *BrE*, **center** *AmE* *verb* **centre on, centre around** to have something or someone as the most important part: *The town centres on the university.* • *Her whole life centres around her family.*

cen·tu·ry /ˈsentʃəri/ *noun* (plural **centuries**)

KEY PATTERNS
in the 12th/18th/20th etc century

a period of 100 years, used especially for dates: *The church was built* ***in the 13th century.*** • *at the beginning of the last century* • *The rocks were formed many centuries ago.*

ce·ram·ics /səˈræmɪks/ *noun* (no plural) the art of making pots, bowls etc from clay, or things that are made from clay SYNONYM **pottery**: *Sonia teaches ceramics at Columbia College.*

ce·re·al /ˈsɪəriəl $ ˈsɪriəl/ *noun* **1** a food you eat for breakfast that is made from wheat, rice etc, and that you usually mix with milk **2** a plant such as wheat or rice that is grown for food

cer·e·mo·ny /ˈserəməni $ ˈserəˌmouni/ *noun* (plural **ceremonies**) a formal event, when people do or say something special in public: *The opening ceremony for the new theatre was performed by the Queen.* • *a wedding ceremony*

cer·tain /ˈsɜːtn $ ˈsɚtn/ *adjective*

KEY PATTERNS
certain about/of something
certain what/whether/if/how etc
certain (that)

1 if you are certain, you are completely sure about something ANTONYM **uncertain**: *One day we will be married – I* ***feel certain about*** *that.* • *We cannot be* ***certain of*** *the date of the painting.* • *Phil isn't quite* ***certain what*** *he wants to do next year.* • *Everyone seems to be* ***certain that*** *he'll win the race.*
2 used to talk about people or things without saying exactly who or what they are: *Certain people have been spreading nasty rumours.*

cer·tain·ly /ˈsɜːtnli $ ˈsɚtnli/ *adverb* without any doubt: *This match will certainly be difficult for us to win.*

cer·tif·i·cate /səˈtɪfɪkət $ sɚˈtɪfəkət/ *noun* an official document showing that something is true or correct: *We need to see your birth certificate before you can get a passport.*

CGI /ˌsiː dʒiː ˈaɪ/ *noun* the use of computers to produce images for films and video games, without using real people or things: *Films like 'Toy Story' and 'Shrek' used CGI.*

chain¹ /tʃeɪn/ *noun* **1** a line of metal rings that are connected to each other: *She wore a gold chain around her neck.* **2** a group of shops that one person or company owns: *a chain of menswear shops*

chain² *verb* to fasten one thing to another with a chain: *I chained my bicycle to a tree.*

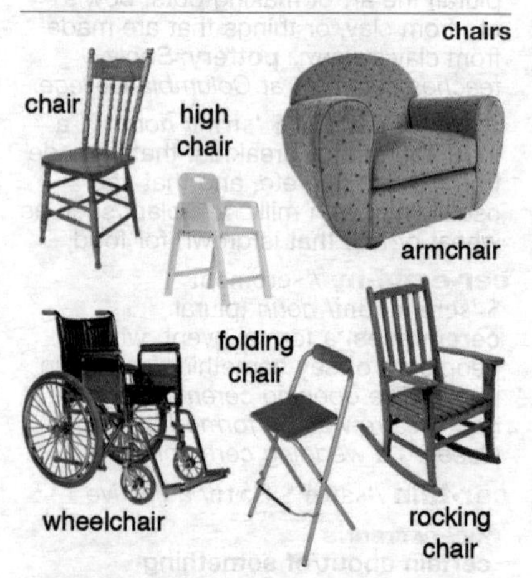

chair¹ /tʃeə $ tʃer/ *noun* a piece of furniture for one person to sit on: *a kitchen chair*

chair² *verb* to be the chairperson of a meeting or official group: *Mrs Dolan will chair the meeting.*

chair·per·son /ˈtʃeəˌpɜːsən $ ˈtʃerˌpɚsən/ also **chair·man** /ˈtʃeəmən $ ˈtʃermən/ or **chair·wom·an** /ˈtʃeəˌwʊmən $ ˈtʃerˌwʊmən/ *noun* someone who manages a meeting, official group, or company: *They elected a new chairperson.*

chalk /tʃɔːk/ *noun* (no plural) **1** soft white rock that you buy in small sticks and use for writing on a board: *Take a piece of chalk and write your name on the blackboard.* **2** soft white rock: *the chalk cliffs of Dover*

chal·lenge¹ /ˈtʃæləndʒ/ *noun* something new, exciting, or difficult that you will need a lot of determination and effort to do: *Getting students interested is a challenge for most teachers.* • *Philip gets bored easily, and enjoys meeting new challenges.*

challenge² *verb* **1** to say that you disagree with a decision or judgement and try to change it: *She's always challenging my decisions.* **2** to invite someone to compete against you: *Sam challenged me to a game of tennis.*

chal·leng·ing /ˈtʃæləndʒɪŋ/ *adjective* difficult but interesting or enjoyable: *Teaching is a very challenging job.*

cham·pagne /ʃæmˈpeɪn/ *noun* (no plural) a type of wine containing gas, that people often drink on special occasions: *Who would like a glass of champagne?*

cham·pi·on /ˈtʃæmpiən/ *noun* a person or team that wins a competition: *My ambition is to be world champion.*

cham·pi·on·ship /ˈtʃæmpiənʃɪp/ *noun* a competition to find the best player or team: *the Davis Cup tennis championship*

chance /tʃɑːns $ tʃæns/ *noun*

KEY PATTERNS
a/the chance to do something
a/no chance of doing something
a chance (that)

1 a time or situation when you can do something you wanted to do SYNONYM **opportunity**: *Have you **had a chance** to read the paper yet?* • *Fans **got the chance to** meet the band after the concert.* • *"Did you explain why you were late?" "She didn't **give me a chance** (=give me time to explain)."*
2 something that may happen SYNONYM **possibility**: *I don't think we **have** much **chance of** winning.* • *There's **a chance that** it might rain later today.* • *What are England's chances in the World Cup* (=is England likely to win or not)?

PHRASES

by chance if something happens by chance, it happens even though you did not plan or expect it: *We got lost, and found this house quite **by chance**.*

take a chance to do something that may be dangerous or may fail: *Lock the car – I don't want to **take any chances**.*

chan·cel·lor /ˈtʃɑːnsələ $ ˈtʃænsələ/ *noun* **1** the head of a university or government: *the Chancellor of York University* • *The German Chancellor has* *arrived in Britain.* **2** also **Chancellor of the Exchequer** in Britain, the government minister who is in charge of the money the government spends

chan·de·lier /ˌʃændəˈlɪə $ ˌʃændəˈlɪr/ *noun* a large decoration that holds lights and hangs from the ceiling

change¹ /tʃeɪndʒ/ *verb*

KEY PATTERNS
change something/someone
change from something to something
change a light bulb/tyre etc
change into/out of clothes
change pounds into dollars

1 if someone or something changes, or if you change them, they become different: *Getting married has changed him.* • *You can change the settings on your computer.* • *As we travelled, the view* ***changed from*** *mountains* ***to*** *fields.*
2 to replace something that is old, used, or not working properly: *It's important to be able to change a tyre on your car.* • *The hotel staff haven't changed the sheets on the bed.*
3 to remove the clothes you are wearing and put on different ones: *She went upstairs to* ***change into*** *some dry clothes.*
4 if you change some money, you give it to someone and they give back the same amount to you, but in different notes or coins: *Could you* ***change*** *500 euros* ***into*** *dollars, please?* • *She asked the shop assistant to change a £20 note.*
5 to get out of one bus, train, or plane and get into another one: *Does this train go direct to London, or do I have to change?* • *We had to* ***change planes*** *in Kuwait.*

PHRASES
change your mind to change your decision, plan, or opinion: *Has Carol* ***changed her mind about*** *having children?*
change the subject to stop talking about one thing and start talking about something else: *Ruth looked upset, so I quickly* ***changed the subject.***

THESAURUS
alter (formal): *The town has* ***altered*** *a lot in recent years* (=changed).
reform: *There are plans to* ***reform*** *the education system* (=change it so that it is better).

change² *noun*

KEY PATTERNS
a/no change in something
it makes a change (from something)
do something for a change
40p/25 cents etc in change
change for a £5 note/a twenty etc

1 when something becomes different from what it was before: *There have been huge* ***changes in*** *technology in the past five years.* • *There has been no* ***change in*** *the patient's condition.*
2 a change of clothes, a change of address etc a different set of clothes, a different address etc from the one you have now or had before: *Take a* ***change of clothes*** *in case it rains.* • *Sandy sent out cards to tell people about her* ***change of address.***
3 something that is interesting or enjoyable because it is different from what you usually do: *It* ***makes a change*** *to eat in a restaurant.* • *Let's walk to college* ***for a change.***
4 (no plural) the money someone gives back to you when you pay for something with more money than it costs: *You've given me* ***the wrong change*** (=too much or not enough money). ➔ see Thesaurus at MONEY
5 (no plural) money in the form of coins: *I had about a dollar* ***in change.*** ➔ see Thesaurus at MONEY
6 (no plural) coins or notes of small value that you give someone in exchange for a coin or note of large value: *Have you got* ***change for*** *a £10 note?*

chan·nel /ˈtʃænl/ *noun* **1** a television station: *Which channel is the film on?* • *Can we change channels to watch the football?* **2** a long narrow area that water can go along: *There are channels at the edge of the road for flood water.*

chant /tʃɑːnt $ tʃænt/ *noun* words or phrases that people sing or shout many times: *There were chants of "We want more!"* —**chant** *verb*: *The crowd chanted his name.*

cha·os /ˈkeɪ-ɒs $ ˈkeɪɑs/ *noun* (no plural) when there is no organization or order: *I left the kids alone for 10 minutes and when I came back it was chaos.*

A B C D E F G H I J K L M N O P Q R S T U V W X Y Z

cha·ot·ic /keɪˈɒtɪk $ keɪˈɑtɪk/ *adjective* without any organization or plan: *Tina has a very chaotic lifestyle.*

chap /tʃæp/ *noun BrE* (informal) a man SYNONYM **bloke**, **guy**: *Frank seems a friendly chap.*

chap·el /ˈtʃæpəl/ *noun* a small Christian church

chap·e·rone /ˈʃæpərəʊn $ ˈʃæpəroʊn/ *noun* an older person who went to places with a young person, to protect and take care of them: *Your aunt will go with you as your chaperone.*

chap·lain /ˈtʃæplən/ *noun* a priest who works for the army, a hospital, or a college: *the college chaplain*

chap·ter /ˈtʃæptə $ ˈtʃæptɚ/ *noun* one of the parts that a book is divided into: *Chapter 7 is about space travel.*

char·ac·ter /ˈkærɪktə $ ˈkærɪktɚ/ *noun*
1 the particular qualities that a person, place, or thing has SYNONYM **nature**: *The new road will spoil the quiet character of the village.*
2 a person in a book, play, film etc: *Who is your favourite character in the book?*
3 a written letter, mark, or sign: *The software can read Japanese characters.*

char·ac·ter·is·tic /ˌkærɪktəˈrɪstɪk/ *noun*
a particular quality or feature that someone or something has: *What personal characteristics should a leader have?* → see Thesaurus at QUALITY
—**characteristic** *adjective*: *He showed none of his characteristic charm.*

char·coal /ˈtʃɑːkəʊl $ ˈtʃɑrkoʊl/ *noun* (no plural) a black substance made of burned wood, that you can burn to make heat: *She put some more charcoal on the barbecue.*

charge[1] /tʃɑːdʒ $ tʃɑrdʒ/ *noun*

KEY PATTERNS
a charge of £250/$425 etc
make a charge
free of charge
arrest someone on a charge of murder/robbery etc

1 the amount of money that you must pay for a service, or to use something: *There's **a charge of** $350 for hiring the room.* • *The bank will no longer **make a charge*** (=make you pay something) *each time you use the cash machine.* • *The student guide is available **free of charge*** (=you do not have to pay for it). → see Thesaurus at COST[1]
2 an official statement by the police, saying that someone might be guilty of a crime: *The police arrested him **on a charge of** theft.*

PHRASES
be in charge if you are in charge, you control something or you are responsible for something: *Joe Taylor is **in charge of** the project.* • *Who's in charge here?*
take charge to take control of someone or something: *A police officer arrived and **took charge of** the situation.*

charge[2] *verb*

KEY PATTERNS
charge (someone) £50/$300 etc
charge for a service
charge someone with theft/ murder etc

1 to ask someone to pay a particular amount of money for something: *The university is charging students £200 in fees each term.* • *Do you **charge for** bike hire?* • *Some companies charge extra* (=ask for more money) *for supplying the software.*
2 if the police charge someone, they say officially that he or she might be guilty of a crime: *He appeared in court, **charged with** murder.*
3 to run towards someone very quickly in order to attack them: *The elephant lowered its head and started to charge.* • *Police with batons charged the demonstrators.*

cha·ris·ma /kəˈrɪzmə/ *noun* (no plural) a natural ability to make people like you: *He is a man of great charisma.*

char·is·mat·ic /ˌkærɪzˈmætɪk/ *adjective* having charisma: *President Clinton was a very charismatic leader.*

char·i·ty /ˈtʃærəti/ *noun* (plural **charities**) an organization that collects money and provides help for people who need it: *She works for the charity Oxfam.* • *I'm collecting money for charity.*

charm /tʃɑːm $ tʃɑrm/ *noun* the special quality someone or something has that makes people like them: *Oxford has a lot of charm.*

charm·ing /ˈtʃɑːmɪŋ $ ˈtʃɑrmɪŋ/ *adjective* having qualities which people think are pleasing or attractive: *What a charming child!*

chart¹ /tʃɑːt $ tʃɑrt/ *noun* a picture or DIAGRAM that shows information: *Look at the chart to find your ideal weight.*

chart² *verb* (formal) to record information about something over a period of time: *The teacher will chart your progress over the year.*

char·ter /ˈtʃɑːtə $ ˈtʃɑrtɚ/ *noun* a statement of the beliefs, duties, and purposes of an organization: *the United Nations charter*

ˈcharter ˌflight *noun* a flight that you buy from a travel company, and that is often cheaper than a flight you buy directly from an AIRLINE: *We managed to get a charter flight to Istanbul.*

chase /tʃeɪs/ *verb*

> KEY PATTERNS
> **chase someone/something down the road/round the room etc**
> **chase (after) someone**

to try to catch someone or something by following them or running towards them: *The dog **chased** the rabbit across the field.* • *The boys **chased after** her.* → see Thesaurus at FOLLOW

chat /tʃæt/ *verb* (informal) (**chatted, chatting**)

> KEY PATTERNS
> **chat to/with someone**
> **chat about something**

1 to talk in a friendly and informal way: *Pete and I were chatting in the bar.* • *Jane was **chatting to** a friend.* • *They were **chatting about** old times.*
2 to have a conversation with people on the Internet by sending and receiving messages on your computer: *He likes to spend his evenings chatting with people on the Internet.* —**chat** *noun*: *Let's meet for coffee and have a chat.*

PHRASAL VERBS

chat up
chat someone up *BrE* (informal) to talk to someone in a way that shows you think they are sexually attractive: *Eric was trying to **chat up** my girlfriend.*

châ·teau /ˈʃætəʊ $ ʃæˈtoʊ/ *noun* (plural **châteaux** /-təʊz $ -ˈtoʊz/) a castle or large country house in France

ˈchat room *noun* a place on the Internet where you can have conversations with people by writing and receiving messages: *They met in a chat room on the Internet.*

ˈchat show *noun BrE* a television or radio show on which someone talks to famous or interesting people SYNONYM **talk show** *AmE*: *All the big stars appeared as guests on her chat show.*

chat·ter /ˈtʃætə $ ˈtʃætɚ/ *verb* **1** to talk a lot about things that are not important: *Stop chattering and listen to me.* **2** if your teeth chatter, they knock together because you are cold or afraid

chat·ty /ˈtʃæti/ *adjective* (informal) (**chattier, chattiest**) a chatty person is friendly and easy to talk to: *She was very chatty on the telephone.*

chauf·feur /ˈʃəʊfə $ ˈʃoʊfɚ/ *noun* someone whose job is to drive another person's car, and take that person to the places they want to go: *My chauffeur drove me to the airport.*

cheap /tʃiːp/ *adjective* something that is cheap does not cost very much money, or costs less money than you expect ANTONYM **expensive**: *cheap rail fares* • *Houses are much cheaper there than in Britain.*
—**cheaply** *adverb*: *You can buy fruit and vegetables more cheaply in the market.*

cheat /tʃiːt/ *verb* to do something that is not fair, honest, or truthful, especially in order to win or get something you want: *Kylie and*

Grant cheated in the spelling test.
—**cheat** *noun*: *You're a cheat, changing the score like that!*

check[1] /tʃek/ *verb*

KEY PATTERNS
check something
check (that)
check what/whether/if etc
check with your doctor/parents/boss etc

1 to do something in order to make sure that everything is safe, correct, or working properly: *The firemen check all the equipment daily.* • *If your computer fails to start,* ***check that*** *you have entered your password correctly.* • *Bill* ***is checking whether*** *the trains are running on Sunday.*
2 to ask someone's advice or permission before you do something: *Before starting a diet, you should* ***check with your doctor.***

PHRASAL VERBS
check in/into
check in, check into something to go to the desk at a hotel, airport etc and say that you have arrived SYNONYM **book in**: *We have to* ***check in*** *two hours before the flight leaves.* • *We* ***checked into*** *a motel.*
check up on
check up on someone to get information about someone, for example to make sure that they are honest: *We always* ***check up on*** *new employees.*
check out
1 check something out (informal) to get information in order to discover whether something is true, correct, or acceptable: *I made a phone call to* ***check out*** *the address he gave.* • *Roy went in to* ***check out*** *the menu.*
2 check out to pay the bill and leave a hotel: *What time did he* ***check out****?*

check[2] *noun*

KEY PATTERNS
do a check
run a check on something
keep a check on something

1 an examination to find out if something is correct, true, or safe: *The police are* ***doing*** *road safety* ***checks.*** • *We* ***ran a check on*** *the network after we found a computer virus.* • *The nurses* ***kept a check on*** *him* (=kept checking his condition).
2 the American spelling of CHEQUE
3 the American word for a restaurant BILL
4 the American word for TICK

check·book /ˈtʃekbʊk/ the American spelling of CHEQUEBOOK

checked /tʃekt/ also **check** *adjective* a checked shirt, cloth etc has a regular pattern of different coloured squares: *a red and white checked tablecloth*
→ see picture at PATTERN

check·ers /ˈtʃekəz $ ˈtʃekərz/ the American word for DRAUGHTS

ˈ**check-in** *noun* **1** also ˈ**check-in ˌdesk** the place where you go to in order to show your ticket at an airport, or to report that you have arrived at a hotel: *What time do we have to be at the check-in?* **2** the process of showing your ticket at an airport, or reporting that you have arrived at a hotel: *Check-in takes only a few minutes.*

check·list /ˈtʃekˌlɪst/ *noun* a list of all the things you have to do for a job or activity: *Read the checklist to make sure you haven't forgotten anything.*

check·out /ˈtʃek-aʊt/ also ˈ**checkout ˌcounter** *AmE noun* the place in a SUPERMARKET (=large shop) where you go to pay for the things you want to buy: *Sally was working on the checkout.*

check·point /ˈtʃekpɔɪnt/ *noun* a place where an official person stops people and vehicles to examine them: *There are several checkpoints along the border.*

check·up, **check-up** /ˈtʃek-ʌp/ *noun* when a doctor or DENTIST examines you to see if you are healthy: *You should have regular checkups with your dentist.*

cheek /tʃiːk/ *noun*
1 your cheeks are the two soft round parts of your face below your eyes: *He kissed her gently on the cheek.*
2 (no plural) *BrE* (informal) when someone says or does something that shows no respect for another person: *Tom* ***had the cheek*** *to ask me for some more money.*

cheek·y /ˈtʃiːki/ *adjective BrE* (**cheekier**, **cheekiest**) someone who is cheeky says or does things that show a lack of respect for someone who is older, in a higher position at work etc SYNONYM **impertinent**: *He's a cheeky little boy.*

cheer¹ /tʃɪə $ tʃɪr/ *verb* **1** to shout in order to encourage someone or because you are enjoying what they are doing: *The crowd cheered as the players ran onto the field.* **2 cheer someone up** to make someone who is unhappy feel happier: *He bought her some flowers to cheer her up.*

cheer² *noun* a shout that shows you are happy or pleased with something ANTONYM **boo**: *You could hear the cheers from outside the theatre.*

cheer·ful /ˈtʃɪəfəl $ ˈtʃɪrfəl/ *adjective* happy and showing this by your behaviour: *Tom seems a very cheerful child.* → see Thesaurus at HAPPY —**cheerfully** *adverb*

cheer·lead·er /ˈtʃɪəˌliːdə $ ˈtʃɪrˌlidɚ/ *noun* a member of a group of young women that encourages the crowd at a sports event to cheer for a particular team

cheers /tʃɪəz $ tʃɪrz/ something you say just before you drink a glass of alcohol with someone, to show friendly feelings

cheese /tʃiːz/ *noun* (no plural) a solid white or yellow food made from milk: *Michael wants extra cheese on his pizza.*

cheese·cake /ˈtʃiːzkeɪk/ *noun* a sweet cake made with soft white cheese and fruit: *strawberry cheesecake*

chef /ʃef/ *noun* the most important cook in a restaurant

chem·i·cal¹ /ˈkemɪkəl/ *noun* a substance used in chemistry: *Some of these chemicals are very dangerous.*

chemical² *adjective* related to chemicals: *Chemical weapons were used in the war.*

chem·ist /ˈkemɪst/ *noun* **1** also **chemist's** *BrE* a shop where you can buy medicines, soap, TOOTHPASTE etc SYNONYM **drugstore** *AmE* **2** *BrE* someone whose job is to prepare drugs and medicines for sale in a shop SYNONYM **pharmacist** *AmE* **3** a scientist who studies chemistry

chem·is·try /ˈkeməstri/ *noun* (no plural) the scientific study of chemicals and what happens to them when they change or combine with each other

cheque *BrE*, **check** *AmE* /tʃek/ *noun*

> KEY PATTERNS
> **a cheque for £50/$200 etc**
> **pay by cheque**

a special printed form that you use to pay for things, using the money in your bank account. You write the amount of money, the date, and the name of the person you are paying on the cheque, and then you sign it: *He gave me a check for $300.* • *I'd like to pay by cheque.* • *Do you mind if I **write** you **a cheque*** (=pay for something with a cheque)?

cheque·book /ˈtʃekbʊk/ *noun BrE* a small book of cheques SYNONYM **checkbook** *AmE*

cher·ry /ˈtʃeri/ *noun* (plural **cherries**) a small round soft red fruit with a large seed → see picture on page A7

chess /tʃes/ *noun* (no plural) a board game for two players in which you must catch your opponent's king in order to win: *a game of chess*

chest /tʃest/ *noun* **1** the front part of your body between your neck and stomach: *He has a very broad chest.* **2** a large strong box with a lid, that you use to keep things in: *I took two blankets out of the chest.*

chest·nut /ˈtʃesnʌt/ *noun* **1** a smooth red-brown nut that you can eat: *roast chestnuts* **2** the large tree on which these nuts grow

ˌchest of ˈdrawers *noun* a piece of furniture with drawers, used for keeping clothes in: *The room had only a bed and a small chest of drawers.*

chew /tʃuː/ *verb* to crush food with your teeth before you swallow it: *He was chewing a tough piece of meat.*

ˈchewing ˌgum also **gum** *noun* (no plural) a type of sweet that you chew for a long time, but do not swallow: *a stick of chewing gum*

A B C D E F G H I J K L M N O P Q R S T U V W X Y Z

chic /ʃiːk/ *adjective* fashionable and showing good style: *We had lunch at a chic little cafe.*

chick /tʃɪk/ *noun* a baby bird: *You can hear the chicks in the nest.* → see picture at HATCH[1]

chick·en¹ /ˈtʃɪkən/ *noun* **1** a farm bird that you keep for its meat and eggs **2** (no plural) the meat from a chicken: *a chicken sandwich* → see picture on page A8

chicken² *verb* **chicken out** to decide not to do something because you do not feel brave enough: *I was going to try to swim across the lake, but I chickened out.*

chicken pox /ˈtʃɪkən ˌpɒks $ ˈtʃɪkən ˌpɑks/ *noun* (no plural) an illness that children get, that causes a fever and red spots on their skin: *Ruth's got chicken pox.*

chief¹ /tʃiːf/ *adjective*
1 highest in rank: *the company's chief executive*
2 the most important SYNONYM **main**: *I've made a list of the chief points from the lecture.*

chief² *noun* the leader of a group or organization: *the city's chief of police*

chief·ly /ˈtʃiːfli/ *adverb* mainly: *The book is aimed chiefly at women.*
→ see Thesaurus at MAINLY

child /tʃaɪld/ *noun* (plural **children** /ˈtʃɪldrən/)
1 a young person who is not yet fully grown: *I lived in the US when I was a child.* • *The children were coming out of the school gates.*
2 a son or daughter: *Lynda has three grown-up children.*

> THESAURUS
> **baby**: *The baby wouldn't stop crying* (=a very young child).
> **kid** (informal): *My kids like to watch TV after school* (=children).
> **teenager**: *Teenagers usually spend a lot of time with their friends* (=young people between 13 and 19).

child·birth /ˈtʃaɪldbɜːθ $ ˈtʃaɪldbɚθ/ *noun* (no plural) the process by which a baby is born: *Childbirth is very painful.*

child·care /ˈtʃaɪldkeə $ ˈtʃaɪldˌker/ *noun* (no plural) when someone is responsible for the care of children whose parents are at work: *The government should provide free childcare.*

child·hood /ˈtʃaɪldhʊd/ *noun* the time when you are a child: *I had a happy childhood.*

child·ish /ˈtʃaɪldɪʃ/ *adjective* an adult who is childish behaves in a silly way, like a small child: *Stop being so childish.*

child·less /ˈtʃaɪldləs/ *adjective* having no children: *The treatment has helped thousands of childless couples.*

child·mind·er /ˈtʃaɪldˌmaɪndə $ ˈtʃaɪldˌmaɪndɚ/ *noun BrE* someone who is responsible for the care of young children while their parents are at work

child·mind·ing /ˈtʃaɪldˌmaɪndɪŋ/ *noun BrE* the job of being a childminder: *I do a little childminding.*

children *noun*
the plural of CHILD

chill¹ /tʃɪl/ *verb* **1** to make something cold: *Chill the champagne before you serve it.* **2** also **chill out** (informal) to relax and rest, especially after going to a party, club etc: *We stayed there till about 3 o'clock, then went back to our place to chill.*

chill² *noun* a feeling of coldness: *There was a chill in the air.*

chil·li *BrE* also **chili** *AmE* /ˈtʃɪli/ *noun* a small thin red or green vegetable with a very hot taste

chill·y /ˈtʃɪli/ *adjective* (**chillier**, **chilliest**) cold, but not very cold: *It's a bit chilly today.* → see Thesaurus at COLD[1]

chime /tʃaɪm/ *verb* (written) if a clock or bell chimes, it makes a sound like a bell: *The clock chimed six o'clock.*
—**chime** *noun*: *The chimes of the church bells woke me up.*

chim·ney /ˈtʃɪmni/ *noun* a wide pipe that takes smoke from a fire through the roof

chim·pan·zee /ˌtʃɪmpænˈziː/ also **chimp** /tʃɪmp/ (informal) *noun* an African APE (=an animal that looks like a monkey)

chin /tʃɪn/ *noun* the front part of your face below your mouth: *a pointed chin* → see picture on page A5

chi·na /ˈtʃaɪnə/ *noun* (no plural) the hard white substance that cups and plates are made of: *a china teapot*

chip[1] /tʃɪp/ *noun* **1** *BrE* a long thin piece of potato that has been cooked in oil SYNONYM **french fry** *AmE*: *Would you like chips with your burger?* **2** the American word for a CRISP **3** a mark on something where a small piece has broken off it: *This cup has a chip in it.*

chip[2] *verb* (**chipped**, **chipping**) to break a small piece off something: *I've chipped my tooth.*

chip·munk /ˈtʃɪpmʌŋk/ *noun* a small brown animal like a SQUIRREL, that has black and white lines on its fur

chirp /tʃɜːp $ tʃɝp/ *verb* if a bird chirps, it makes short high sounds

chirp·y /ˈtʃɜːpi $ ˈtʃɝpi/ *adjective* (informal) (**chirpier**, **chirpiest**) happy, and showing this by your behaviour SYNONYM **cheerful**: *You're very chirpy this morning.*

chis·el /ˈtʃɪzəl/ *noun* a metal tool with a sharp end, used for cutting and shaping wood or stone → see picture at TOOL

choco·late /ˈtʃɒklət $ ˈtʃɑklɪt/ *noun* (no plural) a sweet hard brown food: *Can I have a piece of chocolate?* • *chocolate ice cream*

choice /tʃɔɪs/ *noun*

KEY PATTERNS
make a choice
a choice between things
a choice of things
have a/no choice

1 a decision to choose one thing or person rather than another: *It's a difficult choice, but I think I like the red dress best.* • *I had to* ***make a choice between*** *a quiet evening at home or going to the concert.*
2 (no plural) the opportunity or right to choose between two or more things: *We* ***had a choice of*** *five questions in the exam.* • *I accepted the job because I* ***had no choice*** *and I needed the money.*
3 a person or thing that you choose or can choose: *Spain is a good choice, if you want to go somewhere hot.* • *You have two choices: you can support me or you can leave.*

choir /kwaɪə $ kwaɪɚ/ *noun* a group of people who sing together: *Sue sings in the school choir.*

choke /tʃəʊk $ tʃoʊk/ *verb* if you choke, or if something chokes you, you cannot breathe properly because you are not getting enough air into your lungs: *I choked on a small piece of bone.* • *Your cigarette smoke is choking me!*

choose /tʃuːz/ *verb* (**chose** /tʃəʊz $ tʃoʊz/ **chosen** /ˈtʃəʊzən $ ˈtʃoʊzən/)

KEY PATTERNS
choose someone/something
choose from a number of things/people
choose which/whether/what etc
choose to do something

to decide to have or do one of several things that are available or possible: *Lucy chose a red dress with a white collar.* • *We were able to* ***choose from*** *over a dozen films.* • *Students can* ***choose whether*** *to study abroad or stay at home.* • *"Where would you like to go tonight?" "I'm not sure – you choose!"* • *He* ***chose to*** *ignore my advice.*

THESAURUS
pick: *I've been* ***picked*** *for the football team* (=chosen).
decide on: *Have you* ***decided on*** *a date for the wedding* (=chosen one from many possibilities)?
select (formal): *The university* ***selects*** *students very carefully* (=chooses).

choos·y /ˈtʃuːzi/ *adjective* (**choosier**, **choosiest**) someone who is choosy only likes or accepts certain things SYNONYM **fussy**, **picky**: *Cats can be choosy about their food.*

chop[1] /tʃɒp $ tʃɑp/ *verb* (**chopped**, **chopping**) also **chop up** to cut something into small pieces: *He's outside chopping firewood.* • *Shall I chop the carrots up?* → see Thesaurus at CUT[1]

chop² *noun* **lamb chop, pork chop** a small flat piece of lamb or PORK on a bone

chop·per /'tʃɒpə $ 'tʃɑpɚ/ *noun* (informal) a HELICOPTER

chop·sticks /'tʃɒpstɪks $ 'tʃɑpstɪks/ *plural noun* a pair of thin sticks used for eating food in China and Japan

chord /kɔːd $ kɔrd/ *noun* two or more musical notes that you play at the same time: *I can play a few chords on the guitar.*

chore /tʃɔː $ tʃɔr/ *noun* a job that you have to do, especially a boring one in the house or garden: *You can't go out until you've finished your chores.*

chor·e·og·ra·pher /ˌkɒri'ɒgrəfə $ ˌkɔri'ɑgrəfɚ/ *noun* someone who does the choreography for a performance

chor·e·og·ra·phy /ˌkɒri'ɒgrəfi $ ˌkɔri'ɑgrəfi/ *noun* (no plural) the art of arranging how dancers should move during a performance

cho·rus /'kɔːrəs/ *noun* the part of a song that is repeated after each VERSE: *Everyone can join in the chorus.*

chose the past tense of CHOOSE

chosen the past participle of CHOOSE

Christ /kraɪst/ *noun* Jesus Christ, who Christians believe is the son of God

chris·ten /'krɪsən/ *verb* if a priest christens someone, he gives them their name in a religious ceremony

chris·ten·ing /'krɪsənɪŋ/ *noun* a Christian ceremony in which a priest gives a baby its name

Chris·tian¹ /'krɪstʃən/ *adjective* related to Christianity: *his Christian beliefs*

Christian² *noun* someone whose religion is Christianity

Chris·ti·an·i·ty /ˌkrɪsti'ænəti/ *noun* (no plural) the religion that is based on the life and teachings of Jesus Christ

'Christian name *noun* the first name of a Christian: *His Christian name is David.*

Christ·mas /'krɪsməs/ *noun* the period around December 25th when people celebrate the birth of Christ and give and receive gifts: *We're going to my parents' house this Christmas.*

ˌChristmas 'Day *noun* December 25th, the day on which Christians celebrate the birth of Christ

ˌChristmas 'Eve *noun* the evening or the day before Christmas Day

ˌChristmas 'stocking *noun* a long sock that children leave out on the night before Christmas to be filled with presents

chrome /krəʊm $ kroʊm/ also **chro·mi·um** /'krəʊmiəm $ 'kroʊmiəm/ *noun* (no plural) a hard shiny silver metal that is used for covering objects: *The door has chrome handles.*

chron·ic /'krɒnɪk $ 'krɑnɪk/ *adjective* if a situation or illness is chronic, it is serious and likely to continue for a long time: *There is a chronic shortage of teachers.*

chron·o·log·i·cal /ˌkrɒnə'lɒdʒɪkəl $ ˌkrɑnl'ɑdʒɪkəl/ *adjective* arranged in the same order as events happened: *The children had to put the events of the war in chronological order.*

chub·by /'tʃʌbi/ *adjective* (informal) (**chubbier, chubbiest**) slightly fat: *He's a chubby little baby.*

chuck /tʃʌk/ *verb* (informal) to throw something: *I chucked the ball over the fence.* → see Thesaurus at THROW¹

chuck·le /'tʃʌkəl/ *verb* (informal) to laugh quietly: *He chuckled to himself as he read his book.* → see Thesaurus at LAUGH¹ —**chuckle** *noun*: *"This is funny," he said with a chuckle.*

chunk /tʃʌŋk/ *noun* a large piece of something solid SYNONYM **hunk**: *She broke off a large chunk of bread.* → see Thesaurus at PIECE

church /tʃɜːtʃ $ tʃɚtʃ/ *noun* (plural **churches**)

KEY PATTERNS
go to church

a building where Christians go to pray: *We always* ***go to church*** *on Sundays.*

church·yard /'tʃɜːtʃjɑːd $ 'tʃɚtʃjɑrd/ *noun* a piece of land around a church where dead people are buried

ci·der /'saɪdə $ 'saɪdɚ/ *noun* a drink containing alcohol that is made from apples

ci·gar /sɪ'gɑː $ sɪ'gɑr/ *noun* a thick tube of tobacco leaves that people smoke

cig·a·rette /ˌsɪgə'ret $ 'sɪgəˌret/ *noun* a paper tube filled with tobacco that people smoke: *Cigarettes are bad for you.*

cin·e·ma /'sɪnəmə/ *noun* *BrE* a building where you go to see films SYNONYM **movie theater** *AmE*: *Shall we go to the cinema tonight?*

cir·cle¹ /'sɜːkəl $ 'sɚkəl/ *noun* **1** a round flat shape like the letter O, or a group of people or things arranged in this shape: *Draw a circle on a piece of paper.* • *We sat* ***in a circle*** *round the table.* → see picture at SHAPE¹ **2 political circles, literary circles etc** the people who are involved in politics, literature etc

PHRASES

go round (and round) in circles to think or talk etc about something a lot without achieving anything

circle² *verb* **1** to move in a circle around something: *Our plane circled the airport for hours, waiting for the fog to clear.* **2** to draw a circle around something: *Circle the right answer.*

cir·cuit /'sɜːkɪt $ 'sɚkɪt/ *noun* **1** a track where people race cars, bicycles etc: *The racing cars go three times round the circuit.* **2** the complete circle that an electric current flows around: *an electrical circuit*

cir·cu·lar¹ /'sɜːkələ $ 'sɚkjələ/ *adjective* shaped like a circle SYNONYM **round**: *a circular table*

circular² *noun* a printed advertisement or notice that a lot of people receive at the same time: *The school sent out a circular to all the parents.*

cir·cu·late /'sɜːkjəleɪt $ 'sɚkjəˌleɪt/ *verb* to go around something: *Your blood circulates around your body.*

cir·cu·la·tion /ˌsɜːkjə'leɪʃən $ ˌsɚkjə'leɪʃən/ *noun* (no plural) the movement of blood around your body: *Exercise can improve your circulation.*

cir·cum·cise /'sɜːkəmsaɪz $ 'sɚkəmˌsaɪz/ *verb* if a man or boy is circumcised, a doctor or priest has removed the skin at the end of his PENIS

cir·cum·ci·sion /ˌsɜːkəm'sɪʒən $ ˌsɚkəm'sɪʒən/ *noun* when someone is circumcised

cir·cum·fer·ence /sə'kʌmfrəns $ sɚ'kʌmfrəns/ *noun* the distance around the outside of a circle

cir·cum·stance /'sɜːkəmstæns $ 'sɚkəmˌstæns/ *noun* (formal) something such as a particular fact that affects what happens in a situation: *We hope the circumstances of her death will eventually be discovered.*

PHRASES

in the circumstances, under the circumstances: *In certain circumstances, students will receive money towards their course fees* (=in particular conditions).

cir·cus /'sɜːkəs $ 'sɚkəs/ *noun* (plural **circuses**) a group of performers and animals that travel to different places doing tricks and other kinds of entertainment

cit·i·zen /'sɪtəzən/ *noun* **1** someone who has the legal right to live and work in a particular country: *American citizens* **2** someone who lives in a particular town, state, or country

cit·i·zen·ship /'sɪtəzənʃɪp/ *noun* (no plural) the legal right to belong to a particular country: *Peter has British citizenship.*

cit·rus fruit /'sɪtrəs ˌfruːt/ *noun* a fruit such as an orange or LEMON

cit·y /'sɪti/ *noun* (plural **cities**) a large important town: *London is the largest city in England.*

civ·il /'sɪvəl/ *adjective* **1** not connected with military or religious organizations: *The company makes civil aircraft.* • *We were married in a civil ceremony, not in church.* **2** related to laws that deal with people's rights, not laws that are related to crimes: *This is a civil case, not a criminal one.*

ci·vil·ian /sə'vɪljən/ *noun* anyone who is not a member of a military organization or the police: *He left the army and became a civilian again.*

civ·i·li·za·tion also **civilisation** *BrE* /ˌsɪvəlaɪ'zeɪʃən $ ˌsɪvələ'zeɪʃən/ *noun* a society that is well organized and developed: *We will study the ancient civilizations of Greece and Rome.*

A B C D E F G H I J K L M N O P Q R S T U V W X Y Z

A B C D E F G H I J K L M N O P Q R S T U V W X Y Z

civ·i·lized also **civilised** *BrE* /'sɪvəlaɪzd/ *adjective* **1** a civilized society is well organized and has laws and customs **2** behaving politely and sensibly: *Can't we discuss this in a civilized way?*

ˌcivil 'rights *plural noun* the legal rights that every person has

ˌcivil 'servant *noun* someone who works in the civil service

ˌcivil 'service *noun* **the civil service** all the government departments and the people who work in them

ˌcivil 'war *noun* a war between groups of people from the same country

claim¹ /kleɪm/ *verb*

KEY PATTERNS
claim (that)
claim to be someone/something
claim something
claim for something

1 to say that something is true, even though it might not be: *The manufacturers* ***claim that*** *the car is the safest you can buy.* • *He* ***claimed to be*** *a lawyer.*
2 to ask for something because you have a right to have it or because it belongs to you: *Many lost dogs are never claimed by their owners.* • *Have you* ***claimed for*** *your travel costs?*

claim² *noun*

KEY PATTERNS
a claim that

1 a statement that something is true, even though it may not be: *The police are investigating* ***claims that*** *she stole the car.*
2 a demand for something that you have a right to have: *Insurance companies receive hundreds of false claims.*

clair·voy·ant /kleə'vɔɪənt $ kler'vɔɪənt/ *noun* someone who says they can see what will happen in the future

clam·ber /'klæmbə $ 'klæmbər/ *verb* to climb over something with difficulty, using your hands and feet: *I clambered over the rocks.*

clam·my /'klæmi/ *adjective* (**clammier**, **clammiest**) wet and sticky in an unpleasant way: *clammy hands*

clam·our *BrE*, **clamor** *AmE* /'klæmə $ 'klæmər/ *verb* to demand something loudly: *All the reporters were clamouring for his attention.*

clamp /klæmp/ *verb* **1** to hold something tightly in a particular position so that it does not move: *He clamped his hand over her mouth.*
2 clamp down to become very strict in order to stop people from doing something: *The police are clamping down on drivers who go too fast.*

clang /klæŋ/ *verb* to make a loud sound like metal being hit: *The heavy gate clanged shut.*

clap /klæp/ *verb* (**clapped**, **clapping**) to hit your hands together several times to show that you enjoyed something or approve of something SYNONYM **applaud**: *We all clapped and cheered.* —**clap** *noun*

clar·i·fy /'klærəfaɪ/ *verb* (formal) (**clarified**, **clarifies**) to make something easier to understand: *Can you clarify exactly what you mean?*

clar·i·net /ˌklærə'net/ *noun* a wooden musical instrument like a long black tube, which you play by blowing into it

clash /klæʃ/ *verb* **1** to fight, argue, or disagree: *The demonstrators clashed with police.* **2** if colours or clothes clash, they do not look nice together: *That tie clashes with your shirt.* **3** if two events clash, they happen at the same time, so you cannot go to one of them: *The concert clashes with Dave's party.* —**clash** *noun*: *There was a violent clash between rival groups of supporters.*

clasps

clasp¹ /klɑːsp $ klæsp/ *noun* a small metal object used to fasten a bag or piece of jewellery: *The clasp on my necklace is broken.*

clasp² *verb* (written) to hold something tightly in your hands: *He clasped the book to his chest.*

class¹ /klɑːs $ klæs/ *noun* (plural **classes**)

KEY PATTERNS
be in someone's class/the same class
do something in class

1 a group of students who learn together: *Mary **is in the same class** as me* (=belongs to the same group of students).
2 a period of time when a group of students learn together SYNONYM **lesson** *BrE*: *I've got a French class this afternoon.* • *We are not supposed to talk **in class**.*
3 the social group that you belong to: *They live in a **working class** area.* • *Class still has a big effect on education in Britain.*

class² *verb* to decide that something belongs in a particular group SYNONYM **classify**: *They class his music as jazz.*

clas·sic¹ /ˈklæsɪk/ *adjective* very typical: *Confusing 'their' and 'there' is a classic mistake.*

classic² *noun* an important book or film that has been popular for a long time

ˌclassical ˈmusic *noun* music by people such as Beethoven and Mozart that is serious and important

clas·si·fied /ˈklæsəfaɪd/ *adjective* officially secret: *I can't tell you what he is working on – that's classified information.*

clas·si·fy /ˈklæsəfaɪ/ *verb* (**classified, classifies**) to put things into groups according to their type, size, age etc SYNONYM **class**: *They classified Bill as a problem child.*

class·mate /ˈklɑːsmeɪt $ ˈklæsmeɪt/ *noun* someone who is in the same class as you: *His classmates don't like him.*

class·room /ˈklɑːsruːm $ ˈklæsrum/ *noun*
a room in a school where students learn with a teacher

class·work /ˈklɑːswɜːk $ ˈklæswɚk/ *noun* (no plural) school work that you do in class, not at home: *Do exercises 1 to 4 as classwork.*

clat·ter /ˈklætə $ ˈklætɚ/ *verb* if hard objects clatter, they make a loud unpleasant noise when they hit against each other: *The saucepans clattered as they fell to the floor.* —**clatter** *noun*: *I heard the clatter of dishes coming from the kitchen.*

clause /klɔːz/ *noun* **1** a part of a legal document: *Read the first clause in the contract.* **2** a group of words that contains a subject and a verb, which may be a sentence or part of a sentence

claus·tro·pho·bi·a /ˌklɔːstrəˈfəʊbiə $ ˌklɔstrəˈfoʊbiə/ *noun* fear of being in a small space: *People who suffer from claustrophobia hate going in caves.*

claus·tro·pho·bic /ˌklɔːstrəˈfəʊbɪk $ ˌklɔstrəˈfoʊbɪk/ *adjective* someone who is claustrophobic suffers from claustrophobia

claw /klɔː/ *noun* a sharp curved hard part on the toe of an animal or bird: *The cat scratched the furniture with its claws.* → see picture at BIRD

clay /kleɪ/ *noun* (no plural) a type of heavy soil that is used for making pots: *He made a figure out of clay.*

clean¹ /kliːn/ *adjective*
not dirty: *He put on a clean shirt.* • *The room looked very neat and clean.*

clean² *verb* also **clean up**

KEY PATTERNS
clean something
clean something with a cloth/liquid
clean dirt off/from something

to remove dirt from something, for example by washing it: *I need to clean my boots.* • *He **cleaned** his glasses **with** his handkerchief.* • *She was **cleaning** the mud **off** her bicycle.* • *It took us two hours to **clean up** all the mess after the party.*

THESAURUS
wash: *It's your turn to **wash** the dishes* (=clean them in water).
scrub: *You'll have to **scrub** this pan to get it clean* (=clean it by rubbing it with a hard cloth or brush).

A B C D E F G H I J K L M N O P Q R S T U V W X Y Z

A B C D E F G H I J K L M N O P Q R S T U V W X Y Z

sweep: *Chris tidied the kitchen and swept the floor* (=cleaned it using a brush with a long handle).
hoover *BrE*, **vacuum**: *Don't forget to hoover in the sitting room* (=clean the carpet with a machine that sucks up dirt).

clean•er /ˈkliːnə $ ˈklinɚ/ *noun*
1 someone whose job is to clean houses or offices **2 the cleaner's** the DRY CLEANER'S

clean•li•ness /ˈklenlinəs/ *noun* (no plural) when you keep things clean SYNONYM **hygiene**: *Cleanliness is very important in the kitchen.*

cleanse /klenz/ *verb* (formal) to clean something: *The nurse cleansed the wound with warm water.*

clean-shaven

John has a beard. Mike is clean-shaven.

ˌclean-ˈshaven *adjective* a man who is clean-shaven does not have a beard

clear¹ /klɪə $ klɪr/ *adjective*

KEY PATTERNS
it is clear (that)
it is clear why/what/how etc
make it clear that

1 easy to see, hear, or understand: *His writing isn't very clear.* • *Some of the exam questions weren't very clear.*
→ see Thesaurus at NOTICEABLE
2 if something is clear, it is certain and people cannot doubt it: *It soon* ***became clear*** *that John was lying to us.* • *It's not clear how many people were hurt.* • *Sarah* ***made it clear*** *that she wanted to come with us.*
3 if a substance or liquid is clear, you can see through it SYNONYM **transparent**: *clear glass*
4 a clear sky has no clouds

clear² *verb*

KEY PATTERNS
clear an area/table etc
clear up a mess/an area etc
clear something off/from a surface
clear something away

1 also **clear up** to make a place tidy or empty by removing things from it: *Sammy helped me clear the table when we had finished eating.* • *Who's going to help me* ***clear up*** *all this mess?* • *We* ***cleared*** *the snow* ***off*** *the path.* • *I asked the children to come and* ***clear*** *their toys* ***away***.
2 (written) to jump over something such as a fence or wall without touching it: *He cleared the wall easily.*

clear³ *adverb* away from something: *Stand clear of the doors.*

ˈclear-cut *adjective* certain or definite: *There's no clear-cut answer to your question.*

clear•ing /ˈklɪərɪŋ $ ˈklɪrɪŋ/ *noun* a small area in a forest where there are no trees

clear•ly /ˈklɪəli $ ˈklɪrli/ *adverb*
1 without any doubt SYNONYM **obviously**: *Clearly, you will have to work harder if you want to pass your exam.*
2 if you say or show something clearly, you do it in a way that is easy to see or understand: *The teacher* ***explained*** *everything very* ***clearly***.
3 if you cannot think clearly, you are confused

cleav•age /ˈkliːvɪdʒ/ *noun* the space between a woman's breasts: *She wore a dress that showed her cleavage.*

clench /klentʃ/ *verb* to close your hands or your mouth tightly, especially because you are angry: *He clenched his fists and started banging the door.* • *Clenching her teeth she said, "Go away!"*

cler•gy /ˈklɜːdʒi $ ˈklɚdʒi/ *plural noun* priests and other religious leaders: *Catholic clergy are not allowed to marry.*

cler•gy•man /ˈklɜːdʒimən $ ˈklɚdʒimən/ *noun* (plural **clergymen** /-mən/) a male member of the clergy

cler•i•cal /'klerɪkəl/ *adjective* connected with office work: *We need some more clerical staff.*

clerk /klɑːk $ klɚk/ *noun* **1** someone whose job is to keep the records or accounts in an office: *A bank clerk was counting money.* **2** *AmE* someone whose job is to deal with people arriving at a hotel: *The desk clerk will give you your room keys.*

clev•er /'klevə $ 'klevɚ/ *adjective* **1** someone who is clever is able to learn and understand things quickly SYNONYM **smart**, **intelligent**: *a very clever student*
2 something that is clever has been made or done in an intelligent way, so that it is useful and effective: *What a clever idea!*

cli•ché /'kliːʃeɪ $ kli'ʃeɪ/ *noun* an expression that is used too often and no longer has any real meaning: *His speech was full of clichés like "We must take one day at a time."* ➔ see Thesaurus at PHRASE

click /klɪk/ *verb* **1** to make a short hard sound: *The door clicked open.*
2 if you click on something on a computer screen, you press a button on the mouse in order to do something: *Click on the file name to open the file.* **3 click your fingers** to make a short sound by moving your thumb quickly across your second finger —**click** *noun*: *I heard the click of the gate closing.* ➔ see picture on page A1

cli•ent /'klaɪənt/ *noun* someone who pays a person or organization for a service or advice: *Mr Dolan is an important client of this law firm.*

cli•en•tele /ˌkliːən'tel $ ˌklaɪən'tel/ *noun* (no plural) the people who regularly go to a shop or restaurant: *The shop is trying to appeal to a younger clientele.*

cliff /klɪf/ *noun* a high piece of land with a very steep side, usually next to the sea: *Don't go near the edge of the cliff.*

cli•mate /'klaɪmət/ *noun* the typical weather conditions in an area: *The climate in the Maldives is hot and sunny.*

cliff

WORD CHOICE
climate or **weather**?
• You use **climate** about the usual weather conditions in an area: *The climate in England is generally quite mild.*
• You use **weather** when saying whether it is cloudy, sunny, rainy etc at a particular time: *The weather was very hot and humid.*

cli•max /'klaɪmæks/ *noun* the most important or exciting part of something: *The competition reaches its climax tomorrow.*

climb /klaɪm/ *verb*

KEY PATTERNS
climb stairs/a hill etc
climb up something
climb into/over etc something

climb

1 to move towards the top of something: *She slowly climbed the stairs.* • *He* **climbed up** *the ladder.* • *We* **climbed up to** *the top of the hill.*
2 to move somewhere by bending your body and using your hands and feet: *He* **climbed into** *the truck.* • *We had to* **climb out of** *the window.* • *She managed to* **climb over** *the fence.*
—**climb** *noun*: *It was a long climb up to the top of the hill.* ➔ see picture on page A3 ➔ see picture on page A14

PRONUNCIATION
In this word you do not pronounce the **b**.

climb·er /ˈklaɪmə $ ˈklaɪmɚ/ *noun* someone who climbs mountains or rocks as a sport

climb·ing /ˈklaɪmɪŋ/ *noun* (no plural) the sport of climbing mountains or rocks: *We go climbing most weekends.*

cling /klɪŋ/ *verb* (past tense and past participle **clung** /klʌŋ/) to hold someone tightly, especially because you do not feel safe: *She clung to her mother.*

cling·film /ˈklɪŋfɪlm/ *noun* (no plural) *BrE* (trademark) thin clear plastic that is used for wrapping food

clin·ic /ˈklɪnɪk/ *noun* a place where people go for medical treatment: *I went to the clinic to see the doctor.*

clin·i·cal /ˈklɪnɪkəl/ *adjective* connected with medical treatment and tests: *The drug needs to have clinical trials.*

clink /klɪŋk/ *noun* the sound made when glass or metal touch each other

clip¹ /klɪp/ *noun* **1** a small metal or plastic object used to hold things together: *a hair clip* **2** a short part of a film or television programme that is shown separately: *They showed a clip from the actor's latest film before the interview.*

clip² *verb* (**clipped**, **clipping**) to fasten things together using a clip: *I clipped my papers together.*

clip·pers /ˈklɪpəz $ ˈklɪpɚz/ *plural noun* a tool used for cutting small pieces off something: *a pair of nail clippers*

clip·ping /ˈklɪpɪŋ/ *noun* a piece of writing that you cut from a newspaper or magazine SYNONYM **cutting** *BrE*: *I found an old newspaper clipping about my parents' wedding.*

clique /kliːk/ *noun* a small group of people who know each other well and are not very friendly to other people: *Jane has become part of their clique.*

cloak /kləʊk $ kloʊk/ *noun* a warm piece of clothing like a coat without sleeves that hangs from your shoulders

cloak·room /ˈkləʊkruːm $ ˈkloʊkrum/ *noun* a room in a public building where people can leave their coats

clock

watch

clock

clock /klɒk $ klɑk/ *noun* an object that shows the time: *You could hear the clock ticking.*

> WORD CHOICE
> **clock** or **watch**?
> • You wear a **watch** on your wrist. You put a **clock** on a wall or other surface.

clock·wise /ˈklɒk-waɪz $ ˈklɑk-waɪz/ *adverb, adjective* in the same direction as the moving parts on the face of a clock ANTONYM **anticlockwise**, **counterclockwise** *AmE*: *The dancers moved clockwise in a circle.* • *Turn the key in a clockwise direction.*

clock·work /ˈklɒk-wɜːk $ ˈklɑk-wɚk/ *noun* (no plural) a type of machinery that starts when you turn a key: *The child was playing with a clockwork mouse.*

clog /klɒg $ klɑg/ *verb* (**clogged**, **clogging**) also **clog up** to block something: *Leaves can clog drains.*

clone¹ /kləʊn $ kloʊn/ *noun* (formal) an exact copy of a plant or animal that a scientist develops from one of its cells

clone² *verb* to produce a plant or an animal that is a clone: *Scientists have successfully cloned sheep.*

close¹ /kləʊz $ kloʊz/ *verb*
1 if you close something such as a door or window, or if it closes, it shuts ANTONYM **open**: *Please could you close the window?* • *Jude lay on the bed and closed her eyes.* • *I heard the door close behind him as he left.*
2 if a shop, bank, or other public place closes, it is then not available for people to use ANTONYM **open**: *The shops close at 5:30.*

WORD CHOICE
close, **turn off**, or **switch off**?
- You **close** a door, window, box, or book.
- You **turn off** a tap.
- You **switch off** or **turn off** a light, an engine, the television, a computer etc.

PHRASAL VERBS
close down
if a shop or business closes down, its activities stop permanently
close off
close something off if the police close off a road, street etc, they stop people going there: *It was a bad accident, and the police* ***closed*** *the road* ***off*** *for three hours.*

close² /kləʊs $ kloʊs/ *adjective, adverb*

KEY PATTERNS
close to something/someone
be/sit/stand close together

1 near to a place or person: *We live quite* ***close to*** *the school.* • *She came a bit closer.* • *Don't get too close to the fire.* • *The two boys were standing quite* ***close together.***
2 used to say that something will happen soon: *The day of the exam was coming closer.* • *The shops were busy because it was so* ***close to*** *Christmas.*
3 if two people are close, they like or love each other very much: *We are very close friends.* • *I'm very* ***close to*** *my parents.*
4 if a competition or race is close, someone wins by a very small amount: *It was a very close game.*

close³ /kləʊz $ kloʊz/ *noun* the end of an event or period of time: *We brought the party to a close.*

PRONUNCIATION
Be careful how you pronounce this word:
close¹ (*verb*) and **close³** (*noun*) are pronounced with a 'z' sound at the end
close² (*adjective, adverb*) is pronounced with an 's' sound at the end

closed /kləʊzd $ kloʊzd/ *adjective*
1 if a shop or school is closed, it is not open to the public SYNONYM **shut**: *The school is closed for six weeks in the summer.*
2 not open SYNONYM **shut**: *The door was closed and locked.* • *Her eyes are closed, but I don't think she's asleep.*
➔ see picture at OPEN

close•ly /ˈkləʊsli $ ˈkloʊsli/ *adverb*
1 if you look at something closely, you look at it very carefully: *The teacher was watching the students closely.*
2 people who are closely related are members of the same family, for example brothers or sisters
3 if people work closely together, they work together and help each other a lot: *We have worked closely with the police to solve this crime.*

clos•et /ˈklɒzɪt $ ˈklɑzɪt/ the American word for WARDROBE

close-up /ˈkləʊs ʌp $ ˈkloʊs ʌp/ *noun* a photograph of a person or thing which seems to be taken by a camera that is very close: *a close-up of the actor's face*

clos•ing /ˈkləʊzɪŋ $ ˈkloʊzɪŋ/ *adjective* the closing part of something is the final part ANTONYM **opening**: *In the closing chapter of the book, Max dies.*

clo•sure /ˈkləʊʒə $ ˈkloʊʒɚ/ *noun* when a factory, company, school etc closes permanently: *Workers are angry at the closure of their factory.*

clot /klɒt $ klɑt/ *noun* an amount of blood that has become almost solid: *She has a blood clot in her leg.*

cloth /klɒθ $ klɔθ/ *noun* **1** (no plural) material SYNONYM **fabric**: *The bag is made from thick cloth.* **2** a piece of material that is used for cleaning: *I wiped the table with a damp cloth.*

clothe /kləʊð $ kloʊð/ *verb* (written) to provide clothes for someone: *We don't have enough money to clothe our children.*

clothed /kləʊðd $ kloʊðd/ *adjective* **fully clothed, partly clothed** with all your clothes on, or with only some of your clothes on: *She got into bed fully clothed.*

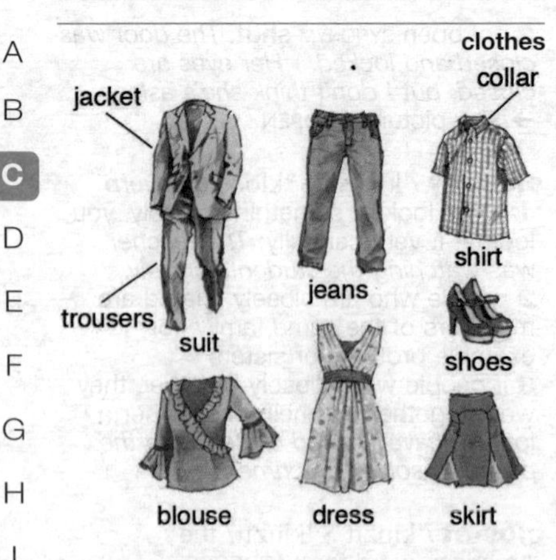

clothes /kləʊðz $ kloʊðz/ *plural noun* the things such as shirts, skirts, or trousers that you wear: *She was wearing smart clothes.* • *He* ***put on*** *some clean* ***clothes****.* • *I'm shy about* ***taking*** *my* ***clothes off*** *in front of other people.*

WORD CHOICE
clothes or **clothing**?
• You use **clothes** when talking about the things that someone wears: *I like your new* ***clothes****!*
• You use **clothing** when talking in general about things that people wear: *The shop sells men's* ***clothing****.* • *Make sure that you take plenty of warm* ***clothing****.*
• You say **a piece of clothing** when talking about one thing that someone was wearing: *The police found* ***a piece of clothing*** *in the bushes.*

clothes·line /ˈkləʊðzlaɪn $ ˈkloʊzlaɪn/ *noun* a rope that you hang clothes on so that they will dry

ˈ**clothes peg** *BrE*, **clothes·pin** /ˈkləʊðzpɪn $ ˈkloʊzpɪn/ *AmE noun* a small object that you use to fasten clothes to a clothesline

cloth·ing /ˈkləʊðɪŋ $ ˈkloʊðɪŋ/ *noun* (no plural) clothes: *You'll need to take some warm clothing.*

cloud¹ /klaʊd/ *noun* a white or grey shape in the sky that is made of small drops of water: *There were no clouds in the sky.*

cloud² *verb* to make something less easy to understand, or make someone less able to think clearly: *His own experiences had clouded his judgement.*

cloud·y /ˈklaʊdi/ *adjective* (**cloudier**, **cloudiest**) if it is cloudy, there are a lot of clouds in the sky: *It's very cloudy today.* • *a cloudy, overcast sky* → see picture on page A13

clove /kləʊv $ kloʊv/ *noun* **1** one of the parts that a GARLIC plant is made up of: *Chop up two cloves of garlic.*
2 a small dried black flower with a strong sweet smell, used in cooking

clo·ver /ˈkləʊvə $ ˈkloʊvɚ/ *noun* a small plant with white or purple flowers and three round leaves on each stem

clown /klaʊn/ *noun* someone who entertains people by dressing in strange clothes, painting their face, and doing funny things, especially in a CIRCUS

club¹ /klʌb/ *noun*
1 an organization for people who have the same interest or enjoy similar activities: *a football club* • *Are you going to* ***join*** *the film* ***club****?*
2 a place where young people go in the evening to dance SYNONYM **nightclub**: *We had a few drinks in the pub, then went to a club.*
3 a special long stick that you use in the game of golf to hit the ball
4 clubs a group of playing cards with black shapes like rounded leaves on them: *the ace of clubs*

club² *verb* (**clubbed**, **clubbing**) **club together** if a group of people club together, they all share the cost of something: *We all clubbed together to buy him a leaving present.*

club·bing /ˈklʌbɪŋ/ *noun* (no plural) when you go to a club to dance: *When we were in Ibiza, we went out clubbing every night.*

clue /kluː/ *noun*

KEY PATTERNS
a clue to something

a small piece of information or an object that helps you to understand something or know something: *The police searched the area for clues.* • *This note could be a* ***clue to*** *the identity of the murderer.* • *I don't know* *the answer to question 6 – can you give me **a clue*** (=give me a piece of information that will help me know the answer)?

PHRASES

not have a clue (informal) if you do not have a clue about something, you do not know what to do about it or you do not understand it at all: *I **haven't got a clue** what I'm going to wear.*

clump /klʌmp/ *noun* a group of trees, bushes, plants etc that are close together: *a clump of trees*

clum·sy /ˈklʌmzi/ *adjective* (**clumsier**, **clumsiest**) a clumsy person often damages things by accidentally hitting them: *I'm always breaking cups – I'm so clumsy.* —**clumsily** *adverb* —**clumsiness** *noun* (no plural)

clung the past tense and past participle of CLING

clus·ter /ˈklʌstə $ ˈklʌstɚ/ *verb* to form a group of people or things: *Everyone clustered around the television.* —**cluster** *noun*: *There's a cluster of restaurants on the main street.*

clutch¹ /klʌtʃ/ *verb* (written) to hold something tightly SYNONYM **grip**: *She was clutching a black bag.*

clutch² *noun* (plural **clutches**) the part of a car that you press with your foot when you change GEAR

clut·ter¹ /ˈklʌtə $ ˈklʌtɚ/ also **clutter up** *verb* to make something untidy by covering or filling it with things: *Books and papers cluttered his desk.*

clutter² *noun* (no plural) a lot of things scattered in an untidy way: *I hate clutter – let's put these toys away.*

cm the written abbreviation of CENTIMETRE

Co. /kəʊ $ koʊ/ the abbreviation of COMPANY: *Hilton, Brooks & Co.*

c/o the written abbreviation of 'care of'; used as part of an address when you send a letter to someone who is staying away from their home for a short time: *Michael Miles, c/o the Grand Hotel, Park Lane, London*

coach¹ /kəʊtʃ $ koʊtʃ/ *noun* (plural **coaches**) **1** someone who trains a person or team in a sport: *Jack's my tennis coach.* **2** *BrE* a bus with comfortable seats, that you go on for long journeys SYNONYM **bus** *AmE*: *Everyone got back on the coach.* • *It will take us two days, if we go by coach.* **3** another word for CARRIAGE ➔ see picture on page A11

coach² *verb* **1** to train a person or team in a sport: *Who coaches your football team?* **2** to give a student special lessons in a subject, especially to help them in an examination: *Tim earned some extra money by coaching students in French.*

coal /kəʊl $ koʊl/ *noun* (no plural) a hard black substance from under the ground that you burn to produce heat: *Put some more coal on the fire.*

coarse /kɔːs $ kɔrs/ *adjective* rough and thick, not smooth or fine: *She dried herself on a coarse old towel.*

coast /kəʊst $ koʊst/ *noun* the land next to the sea: *It gets quite cold on the coast.* • *the southern coast of the USA* ➔ see Thesaurus at SHORE

coast·al /ˈkəʊstl $ ˈkoʊstl/ *adjective* in the sea or on the land near the sea: *the coastal regions of Italy*

ˈcoast guard *noun* a person or group of people whose job is to help boats and swimmers that are in danger

coast·line /ˈkəʊstlaɪn $ ˈkoʊstlaɪn/ *noun* the edge of the coast: *You can see the rocky coastline from here.*

coat¹ /kəʊt $ koʊt/ *noun*

1 a piece of clothing that you wear over your other clothes to keep you warm: *Put your coat on before you go out.*

2 a layer of paint that covers a surface: *The doors will need two **coats of paint**.*

3 an animal's fur, wool, or hair: *Your dog has a lovely shiny coat.*

coat² *verb* to cover a surface with a thin layer of something: *Coat the chicken with oil.*

coax /kəʊks $ koʊks/ *verb* to persuade someone to do something by talking to them gently and kindly: *Mom managed to coax me into going.* ➔ see Thesaurus at PERSUADE

cob·web /ˈkɒbweb $ ˈkɑbweb/ *noun* a structure made by a SPIDER, consisting of fine threads: *The ceiling is covered in cobwebs.*

A B C D E F G H I J K L M N O P Q R S T U V W X Y Z

co•caine /kəʊˈkeɪn $ koʊˈkeɪn/ *noun* (no plural) a drug that some people take illegally for pleasure

cock /kɒk $ kɑk/ *noun BrE* a male chicken SYNONYM **rooster** *AmE*

cock•e•rel /ˈkɒkərəl $ ˈkɑkərəl/ *noun* a young male chicken

cock•pit /ˈkɒkˌpɪt $ ˈkɑkˌpɪt/ *noun* the part of a plane where the pilot sits → see picture at AEROPLANE

cock•roach /ˈkɒk-rəʊtʃ $ ˈkɑk-roʊtʃ/ *noun* (plural **cockroaches**) a large black or brown insect that lives where food is kept

cock•tail /ˈkɒkteɪl $ ˈkɑkteɪl/ *noun* an alcoholic drink that is a mixture of different drinks

cock•y /ˈkɒki $ ˈkɑki/ *adjective* (informal) (**cockier**, **cockiest**) too proud or confident about yourself, in a way that annoys other people

co•coa /ˈkəʊkəʊ $ ˈkoʊkoʊ/ *noun* (no plural) **1** a dark brown powder used to make chocolate and to make food taste of chocolate: *You need cocoa powder to make a chocolate cake.* **2** a drink made with cocoa powder: *I always have a cup of cocoa before I go to bed.*

co•co•nut /ˈkəʊkənʌt $ ˈkoʊkəˌnʌt/ *noun* a large brown nut with white flesh, which is filled with a liquid → see picture on page A7

code /kəʊd $ koʊd/ *noun* a system of words, letters, or signs that are used for sending secret messages: *They sent the message in code, so that I would be the only person who understood it.*

co-ed /ˌkəʊˈed $ ˌkoʊˈed/ *adjective* co-ed schools and colleges are ones where male and female students study together SYNONYM **mixed** *BrE*

co•erce /kəʊˈɜːs $ koʊˈɚs/ *verb* (formal) to force someone to do something by threatening them: *They coerced him into confessing.*

cof•fee /ˈkɒfi $ ˈkɔfi/ *noun*
1 (no plural) a brown powder that is made by crushing the beans of the coffee tree
2 a drink made with coffee: *a cup of coffee • Two coffees, please.*

ˈcoffee ˌtable *noun* a low table in a LIVING ROOM → see picture at TABLE

cof•fin /ˈkɒfɪn $ ˈkɔfɪn/ *noun* the box in which a dead person is buried

coil¹ /kɔɪl/ *verb* to wind or twist something into a round shape: *The snake coiled itself around the branch of the tree.*

coil² *noun* a piece of wire, rope etc that someone has wound into a round shape: *a coil of wire* → see picture at ROPE¹

coin /kɔɪn/ *noun* a piece of money made of metal: *He put a fifty pence coin into the drinks machine.*

co•in•cide /ˌkəʊɪnˈsaɪd $ ˌkoʊɪnˈsaɪd/ *verb* if one event coincides with another, the two things happen at the same time: *My birthday coincides with Paul's.*

co•in•ci•dence /kəʊˈɪnsədəns $ koʊˈɪnsədəns/ *noun* when two things happen at the same time or are the same by chance: *What a coincidence – my name's Laura too!*

cold¹ /kəʊld $ koʊld/ *adjective*

KEY PATTERNS
go/get cold

1 something that is cold has a low temperature and is not warm or hot: *Drink your soup before it* ***goes cold.*** • *Hurry up – I'm* ***getting cold.*** • *It's* ***freezing cold*** *outside today.* • *Would you like coffee, or would you prefer a cold drink?*
2 cold food is cooked, but is not eaten while it is hot: *a salad of cold chicken and rice*
3 a cold person is not very friendly or kind: *He was a cold, unsympathetic man.*

THESAURUS
cool: *The summer evenings were long and* ***cool*** (=fairly cold in a nice way).
chilly: *Take a coat – it's getting* ***chilly*** (=cold but not very cold).
freezing: *I've put the heating on – it's* ***freezing*** *in here* (=extremely cold).

cold² *noun* **1** a common illness that makes you cough and SNEEZE: *I've got a bad cold.* • *Be careful not to catch a cold.* **2 the cold** a very low temperature because the weather is cold: *He made me stay outside in the cold.*

ˌcold-'blooded *adjective* cruel and showing no feelings: *This was a cold-blooded murder.*

col·lab·o·rate /kə'læbəreɪt/ *verb* to work together to produce or achieve something: *Two companies collaborated on this project.*

col·lab·o·ra·tion /kəˌlæbə'reɪʃən/ *noun* when people work together to achieve something

col·lage /'kɒlɑːʒ $ kə'lɑʒ/ *noun* a picture that you make by sticking pieces of paper and cloth onto a surface, or putting different photographs together: *The children made a collage of their visit to the zoo.*

col·lapse /kə'læps/ *verb* to fall down suddenly: *The building collapsed in the earthquake.* • *He collapsed after running a marathon.* —**collapse** *noun*: *What caused the collapse of the bridge?*

col·lar /'kɒlə $ 'kɑlɚ/ *noun* the part of a shirt, coat, or dress that fits around your neck: *Your shirt collar is dirty.* → see picture at CLOTHES

col·lar·bone /'kɒləbəʊn $ 'kɑlɚˌboʊn/ *noun* one of two bones that go from the base of your neck to your shoulders: *I broke my collarbone playing rugby.* → see picture on page A5

col·league /'kɒliːg $ 'kɑlig/ *noun* someone who you work with: *This is Ian, a colleague of mine.*

> SPELLING
> This word is often spelled wrongly. The correct spelling is: **colleague**.

col·lect¹ /kə'lekt/ *verb*

> KEY PATTERNS
> **collect things**
> **collect (money) for a charity**
> **collect someone from school/the station etc**

1 also **collect up** to get things from different places and bring them all to one place SYNONYM **gather**: *Can you collect all the books and put them on my desk?* • *She* **collected up** *all the dirty glasses.*
2 to get and keep things that are the same in some way, because you like them and find them interesting: *He collects stamps.*
3 if you collect money, you ask people to give it for a particular purpose: *The school is* **collecting** *money* **for** *the Children in Need appeal.*
4 *BrE* to go to a place and get someone or something: *I've got to go and* **collect** *Jane* **from** *the station.*

collect² *adverb AmE* if you call someone collect, the person who gets the telephone call pays for it: *Phone me tonight – you can call collect, if you need to.* —**collect** *adjective*: *Will you accept a collect call from Chicago?*

col·lec·tion /kə'lekʃən/ *noun*

> KEY PATTERNS
> **a collection of things**
> **a collection for a person/charity**

1 a set of similar things that you keep together: *She's got a wonderful* **collection of** *books.* • *a stamp collection*
2 when you ask people for money for a particular purpose: *We* **had a collection for** *local children's homes.*

col·lec·tive /kə'lektɪv/ *adjective* a collective decision, effort etc is shared by all the members of a group together: *It was a collective decision to give you the money.* —**collectively** *adverb*

col·lege /'kɒlɪdʒ $ 'kɑlɪdʒ/ *noun* a place where students study after they leave school: *I want to go to art college.*

col·lide /kə'laɪd/ *verb* to hit something violently by crashing into it: *The car collided with a lorry.*

col·li·sion /kə'lɪʒən/ *noun* a violent crash in which one vehicle hits another: *Two trains were involved in a head-on collision.* → see Thesaurus at ACCIDENT

co·lon /'kəʊlən $ 'koʊlən/ *noun* the mark (:) used in writing to introduce a list, example etc

colo·nel /'kɜːnl $ 'kɚnl/ *noun* an officer with a high rank in the Army, the Marines, or the US Air Force

col·o·ny /'kɒləni $ 'kɑləni/ *noun* (plural **colonies**) a country or area that a more powerful country controls: *Senegal was once a French colony.*

color the American spelling of COLOUR

color-blind the American spelling of COLOUR-BLIND

colorful the American spelling of COLOURFUL

colorless the American spelling of COLOURLESS

co•los•sal /kəˈlɒsəl $ kəˈlɑsəl/ *adjective* very big SYNONYM **huge**: *Global warming is a colossal problem.*

colour[1] *BrE*, **color** *AmE* /ˈkʌlə $ ˈkʌlɚ/ *noun*

KEY PATTERNS
what colour is something?
blue/red etc in colour

1 green, blue, yellow, red etc: *The room was painted in bright colours.* • *a beautiful dark red colour* • *What colour is her hair?* • *The leaves are dark green **in colour**.*
2 (no plural) a colour photograph, film etc shows all the different colours, not just black and white: *a colour TV* • *Is the film in black and white or **in colour**?*
3 how dark or light someone's skin is: *The carnival brought together people of all colors.*

colour[2] *BrE*, **color** *AmE verb* **1** to make something a different colour: *I want to colour my hair.* **2** also **colour something in** to put colour onto a drawing or picture using coloured pencils: *He drew a picture of a house and coloured it in.*

ˈ**colour-blind** *BrE*, **color-blind** *AmE adjective* not able to see the difference between particular colours

col•oured *BrE*, **colored** *AmE* /ˈkʌləd $ ˈkʌlɚd/ *adjective* having a colour such as blue, red, or yellow: *A black dress looks good with a coloured scarf.*

col•our•ful *BrE*, **colorful** *AmE* /ˈkʌləfəl $ ˈkʌlɚfəl/ *adjective* having a lot of bright colours: *I prefer colourful clothes.*

col•our•ing *BrE*, **coloring** *AmE* /ˈkʌlərɪŋ/ *noun* (no plural) the colour of someone's hair, skin, eyes etc: *She has the same pale colouring as her sister.*

col•our•less *BrE*, **colorless** *AmE* /ˈkʌlələs $ ˈkʌlɚləs/ *adjective* not having any colour: *Water is a colourless liquid.*

col•umn /ˈkɒləm $ ˈkɑləm/ *noun* **1** numbers or words written under each other down a page: *There were six columns of names.* **2** a tall thin stone structure that supports something SYNONYM **pillar**: *Four marble columns support the roof.*

co•ma /ˈkəʊmə $ ˈkoʊmə/ *noun* when someone is unconscious for a long time, especially after an accident: *She's been in a coma for weeks.*

comb[1] /kəʊm $ koʊm/ *noun* a piece of plastic or metal with a row of thin teeth, that you use to make your hair tidy

comb[2] *verb* to make your hair tidy with a comb: *Have you combed your hair?*

PRONUNCIATION
In this word you do not pronounce the **b**.

com•bat[1] /ˈkɒmbæt $ ˈkɑmbæt/ *noun* fighting during a war: *He joined the army and was killed in combat.*

com•bat[2] /ˈkɒmbæt $ kəmˈbæt/ *verb* (**combated** or **combatted**, **combating** or **combatting**) to try to stop something bad from happening or getting worse SYNONYM **fight**: *What is the best way to combat crime?*

com•bi•na•tion /ˌkɒmbəˈneɪʃən $ ˌkɑmbəˈneɪʃən/ *noun*

KEY PATTERNS
a combination of things

two or more things that you use or mix together: *Doctors use a **combination of** drugs to treat the disease.*

com•bine /kəmˈbaɪn/ *verb*

KEY PATTERNS
combine (something) with something
combine things (together)
things combine to do something

1 if you combine two or more different things, you mix, do, or put them together: ***Combine** the eggs **with** a small amount of oil.* • *She manages to combine her career and family life quite successfully.* • *I like the way the painter has combined different shades of purple together.* → see Thesaurus at MIX[1]

2 if things combine, they come together and have a particular effect: *The interesting characters and exciting plot combine to make a perfect novel.* • *A very hot year* ***combined with*** *a lack of rain led to a very poor harvest.*

come → see box on pages 130 and 131

come·back /ˈkʌmbæk/ *noun* when someone or something becomes popular or successful again: *The 50-year-old singer is hoping to make a comeback.*

co·me·di·an /kəˈmiːdiən/ *noun* someone whose job is to tell jokes and make people laugh SYNONYM **comic**

com·e·dy /ˈkɒmədi $ ˈkɑmədi/ *noun* (plural **comedies**) a funny film or play: *All my favourite films are comedies.*

com·et /ˈkɒmɪt $ ˈkɑmɪt/ *noun* a very bright object in space like a star with a tail: *A comet flew across the sky.*

com·fort¹ /ˈkʌmfət $ ˈkʌmfɚt/ *noun*

KEY PATTERNS
do something in comfort

1 (no plural) when you feel physically relaxed, happy, and without pain: *I buy shoes for comfort rather than for their appearance.* • *We were able to sit and watch the play* ***in comfort.*** • *You can now use the Internet to do your shopping from* ***the comfort of*** *your own home.*
2 (no plural) when you feel calm and less unhappy: *Support from friends and family* ***brought*** *us a lot of* ***comfort*** *after the death of our daughter.*
3 (no plural) when you have enough money to buy all the things that you need: *They now had enough money to* ***live in comfort*** *for the rest of their lives.*
4 comforts all the things that make your life easier and more comfortable: *I really missed* ***home comforts*** *while I was travelling.*

comfort² *verb* to make someone feel happier or less worried by being kind to them: *Ruth always comforted him when he was upset.* —**comforting** *adjective*: *It's very comforting to know you're here.*

com·forta·ble /ˈkʌmftəbəl $ ˈkʌmftɚbəl/ *adjective*

1 if you are comfortable, you feel physically relaxed ANTONYM **uncomfortable**: *Are you comfortable sitting on the floor?*
2 something that is comfortable makes you feel physically relaxed ANTONYM **uncomfortable**: *a comfortable bed*
3 emotionally relaxed and not worried ANTONYM **uncomfortable**: *I feel very comfortable with Paul whenever we're together.*

com·for·ta·bly /ˈkʌmftəbli $ ˈkʌmftɚbli/ *adverb* if you are sitting or lying comfortably, you are sitting or lying in a comfortable way and feeling relaxed

com·ic /ˈkɒmɪk $ ˈkɑmɪk/ *noun*
1 someone whose job is to tell jokes and make people laugh SYNONYM **comedian**: *He's a truly great comic.*
2 *BrE* a magazine that tells a story or several stories using sets of pictures SYNONYM **comic book** *AmE*

com·i·cal /ˈkɒmɪkəl $ ˈkɑmɪkəl/ *adjective* funny in a strange or unexpected way: *It was comical to watch him trying to ride a bike.*

ˈcomic ˌbook the American word for a COMIC

ˌcomic ˈstrip *noun* a set of pictures in a newspaper or magazine that tell a short funny story

com·ing /ˈkʌmɪŋ/ *adjective* (formal) a coming event or period of time is happening soon: *We will be very busy over the coming months.*

com·ma /ˈkɒmə $ ˈkɑmə/ *noun* the mark (,) used in writing or printing to show a short pause

com·mand¹ /kəˈmɑːnd $ kəˈmænd/ *noun*

KEY PATTERNS
be in command (of an army/ship etc)
take command

1 an order that must be obeyed: *The sergeant shouted commands to his men.*
2 (no plural) if you are in command, you are responsible for deciding what people should do: *I need to talk to the officer* ***in command.*** • *The chief fire officer* ***took command*** *of the situation.*

come /kʌm/ *verb* (past tense **came** /keɪm/, past participle **come**)

1 to move towards the place where you are now: *The bus is **coming**! • Bob is **coming from** Seattle for the wedding. • I'll **come and see** you again tomorrow.*

2 to go somewhere with someone: *Can I **come with** you to the concert? • We're going to the beach this afternoon. **Would you like to come?***

3 to arrive at a place: *She **came home** very late. • The letter still hasn't **come** yet. • They **came to** a forest.*

GRAMMAR
✗ Don't say 'come to here'
✗ or 'come to home'.
Say **come here** or **come home**.

4 to happen or start to happen: *Autumn **came** early this year. • The holidays have **come and gone**.*

*Autumn **came** early this year.*

5 to reach as far as somewhere: *The snow **came up to** my knees. • Marty's jacket was too big and the sleeves **came down to** his fingertips.*

*The snow **came up** to my knees.*

6 to have a particular position in a group of people, letters, or numbers: *Jodi **came first** in the 100 metre race. • 'R' **comes after** 'Q'. • In the set '2, 4, 6, 8,' what number **comes next**?*

7 come loose/open/apart to start to be loose, open, or broken: *The box **came open** as I was carrying it upstairs. • The handle **came loose** and finally fell off.*

WORD CHOICE
come or **go**?
• **Come** means 'to move towards the place where you are now': *The bus is **coming**!*
• You use **go** when talking about moving to a different place: *Does this bus **go** to the airport?*

PHRASES

here comes Ted/Jo/Sue etc (spoken)
used when saying that someone is coming towards you: ***Here comes** your mother now.*

for years/months/days to come
years, months, days etc in the future: *The tree will still be here **for many years to come**.*

PHRASAL VERBS

come about
to happen: *How did this situation **come about**?*

come across
to meet someone or find something accidentally: *I **came across** some old photos from my high school days.*

come back
to return to a place: *What time are you **coming back** tonight?*

come down
1 to move from the top of something to the bottom: *The climbers **came down** the mountain as fast as they could when the storm arrived.*
2 if rain or snow comes down, it falls: *The rain started to **come down** more heavily.*

come from
used to talk about the place where you were born or where you first lived: *Where does Enrico **come from**? • My mother **comes from** Canada.*

come in
to enter a room or house: *It was just starting to rain when we **came in**. • Hi, Charles, **come in**.*

come off
to start being separate or removed from something: *A button **came off** my shirt.*

*A button **came off** my shirt.*

come on
1 (spoken) say this when you want someone to hurry: ***Come on**, Linda, we're going to be late.*
2 (spoken) say this when you want to encourage someone: ***Come on**, you can do it – just keep your eye on the ball.*
3 (spoken) say this when you do not believe someone: *Oh, **come on**! He'd never do that!*

come out
when the sun, moon, or stars come out, you can see them in the sky: *Finally the clouds cleared and the sun **came out**.*

come over
if someone comes over, they go to the place where you are: *Why don't you and Ron **come over** for dinner? • Jane **came over** to talk to me.*

come round *BrE*
to visit someone: *Aunt Flora **came round** last night.*

come up
1 to move to the front or the top of something: *When I call your names, please **come up** to get your essays.*

*When I call your names, please **come up** to get your essays.*

2 be coming up if an event or time is coming up, it will happen soon: *The summer holidays are **coming up** in July.*
3 when the sun or the moon comes up, you can see it in the sky for the first time in the morning or the night SYNONYM **rise** ANTONYM **go down**: *The sun doesn't **come up** until nine o'clock in the winter.*

3 an instruction to a computer to do something: *A program is a list of commands.*

command² *verb* **1** to order someone to do something: *The king commanded him to stay.* **2** to control an army or group of soldiers: *Major Fish will command the troops.*

com·mand·er /kə'mɑːndə $ kə'mændɚ/ *noun* an officer who is in charge of a military organization or group

com·mem·o·rate /kə'meməreɪt/ *verb* if something commemorates an event or group of people, it exists so that people will remember them with respect: *The monument commemorates the war.*

com·mence /kə'mens/ *verb* (formal) to begin: *The new system will commence next week.*

com·mend·a·ble /kə'mendəbəl/ *adjective* (formal) deserving praise and admiration: *It is commendable that you want to help.*

com·ment¹ /'kɒment $ 'kɑment/ *noun*

KEY PATTERNS
a comment on/about something
make a comment

an opinion that you give about someone or something: *If you have any comments on our ideas, we would be glad to hear them.* • *My teacher* ***made*** *some very useful* ***comments*** *about my work.*

comment² *verb*

KEY PATTERNS
comment on something
comment that

to give your opinion about someone or something: *The England manager refused to* ***comment on*** *rumours that he was about to resign.* • *Paul* ***commented that*** *the food was a bit disappointing.*

com·men·ta·ry /'kɒməntəri $ 'kɑmən,teri/ *noun* (plural **commentaries**) a description of an event that is on the television or radio, while the event is happening: *There will be a live commentary on the football match.*

com·men·tate /'kɒmənteɪt $ 'kɑmən,teɪt/ *verb* to describe an event on television or radio at the same time as the event happens: *He commentates on football matches for the BBC.*

com·men·ta·tor /'kɒmənteɪtə $ 'kɑmən,teɪtɚ/ *noun* someone whose job is to describe an event on television or radio at the same time as it happens: *a sports commentator*

com·merce /'kɒmɜːs $ 'kɑmɚs/ *noun* (no plural) (formal) the activity of buying and selling things in business SYNONYM **trade**: *We want to encourage commerce between Britain and France.*

com·mer·cial¹ /kə'mɜːʃəl $ kə'mɚʃəl/ *adjective* connected with the buying and selling of things and with making money: *Not all good films are a commercial success.*
—**commercially** *adverb*

commercial² *noun* an advertisement on television or radio: *He appeared in a Pepsi commercial.* → see Thesaurus at ADVERTISEMENT

com·mer·cial·ized also **comercialised** *BrE* /kə'mɜːʃəlaɪzd $ kə'mɚʃə,laɪzd/ *adjective* too concerned with making money: *The holiday resort has become too commercialized.*

com·mis·sion¹ /kə'mɪʃən/ *noun* **1** an official group whose job is to find out about something or control an activity: *The International Whaling Commission decides the limits on catching whales.* **2** money that a person or organization is paid when they sell something: *They get ten per cent commission on all the products they sell.*

commission² *verb* (formal) to ask someone to do a particular piece of work for you: *The government commissioned the report.*

com·mit /kə'mɪt/ *verb* (**committed, committing**)

KEY PATTERNS
commit a crime/murder/robbery

to do something wrong or illegal: *The police are still looking for the gang that* ***committed*** *this* ***crime.*** • *Most murders are committed by men.* • *We were* *worried that George might **commit suicide*** (=kill himself).

com·mit·ment /kəˈmɪtmənt/ *noun*
1 a promise to do something: *They made a commitment to work together.*
2 (no plural) determination to work hard and continue with something: *You need commitment to succeed in this sport.*

com·mit·ted /kəˈmɪtɪd/ *adjective* wanting to work hard at something: *He seems committed to his work.*

com·mit·tee /kəˈmɪti/ *noun* an official group of people who have meetings to decide what needs to be done about something: *Nick and Bob are both on the tennis club committee.*

SPELLING
This word is often spelled wrongly. The correct spelling is: **committee**.

com·mon¹ /ˈkɒmən $ ˈkɑmən/ *adjective*

KEY PATTERNS
common to someone/something

1 something that is common is often seen or often happens: *Rabbits are the most common wild animal in this area.* • *This is a very common spelling mistake.*
2 shared by two or more people or things: *We have a common interest in old films.* • *These problems **are common to** all schools and colleges.*

common² *noun*
have something in common if two people or things have something in common, they are similar in some way: *I don't **have a lot in common with** my brothers.* • *The two towns **have** many things **in common**.*

com·mon·ly /ˈkɒmənli $ ˈkɑmənli/ *adverb* often: *People with this illness commonly complain of headaches.*

com·mon·place /ˈkɒmənpleɪs $ ˈkɑmənˌpleɪs/ *adjective* very common and not unusual: *Divorce is now commonplace.*

ˌcommon ˈsense *noun* (no plural) the ability to do sensible things: *Just use your common sense.*

com·mo·tion /kəˈməʊʃən $ kəˈmoʊʃən/ *noun* (no plural) (formal) sudden noise or activity

com·mu·ni·cate /kəˈmjuːnəkeɪt/ *verb*

KEY PATTERNS
communicate with someone

if people communicate with each other, they give each other information, for example by writing letters, speaking on the telephone etc: *It can be difficult to **communicate with** people if you don't speak their language.* • *We usually communicate by email.*

com·mu·ni·ca·tion /kəˌmjuːnəˈkeɪʃən/ *noun* (no plural)

KEY PATTERNS
communication between people

when people talk to each other or give each other information using letters, telephones etc: *There is good **communication between** teachers and parents.*

PHRASES
means of communication: *The Internet is an important **means of communication*** (=way of talking to someone or sending information).

Com·mun·ism /ˈkɒmjənɪzəm $ ˈkɑmjənɪzəm/ *noun* (no plural) a political system based on the idea that people are equal and that the state should own companies

Com·mu·nist /ˈkɒmjənɪst $ ˈkɑmjənɪst/ *noun* someone who believes in Communism —**Communist** *adjective*: *the Communist Party*

com·mu·ni·ty /kəˈmjuːnəti/ *noun* (plural **communities**)
1 a group of people who live in the same town or area: *a small **rural community*** (=people who live in the countryside) • *The club has had a lot of help from the **local community**.*
2 a group of people who are similar in some way, for example because they have the same religion or do the same job: *The city has quite a large Jewish community.* • *the business community*

com·mute /kəˈmjuːt/ *verb* to regularly travel a long distance to work: *My Dad commutes from Oxford to London every day.*

com·mut·er /kəˈmjuːtə $ kəˈmjutɚ/ *noun* someone who travels to work each day: *The train was packed with commuters.*

com·pact /kəmˈpækt $ ˈkɑmpækt/ *adjective* small and neat

ˌcompact ˈdisc *noun* a CD

com·pan·ion /kəmˈpænjən/ *noun* someone who travels somewhere with you: *One of her travelling companions became ill.*

com·pan·ion·ship /kəmˈpænjənʃɪp/ *noun* (no plural) when you are not alone but have a friend with you: *She joined the club for companionship.*

com·pa·ny /ˈkʌmpəni/ *noun* (plural **companies**)
1 an organization that makes or sells things SYNONYM **business**, **firm**: *My father **runs** his own **company**.* • *an insurance company*
2 (no plural) when someone is with you and you are not alone: *She has a dog for company.* • *I really **enjoy** his **company*** (=like being with him).
PHRASES
keep someone company to spend time with someone so that they are not alone: *I'll stay here to **keep you company**.*

com·pa·ra·ble /ˈkɒmpərəbəl $ ˈkɑmpərəbəl/ *adjective* (formal) similar in size or importance: *He was offered a comparable job at another branch of the company.*

com·par·a·tive¹ /kəmˈpærətɪv/ *adjective* compared with something else SYNONYM **relative**: *the Prime Minister's comparative youth*

comparative² *noun* **the comparative** the form of an adjective or adverb that you use when saying that something is bigger, better, more expensive etc than another thing or than before

com·par·a·tive·ly /kəmˈpærətɪvli/ *adverb* compared with something else: *Houses in that area are comparatively cheap.*

com·pare /kəmˈpeə $ kəmˈper/ *verb*

KEY PATTERNS
compare things
compare something with something else
compare something to something else

1 if you compare things, you examine them in order to find out how they are similar or different: *We went to three different shops to compare their prices.* • *Look at this list and **compare it with** yours.* • *It would be interesting to **compare** this computer **to** one from ten years ago.* • ***Compared to** Harry, Jamie is very tall.*
2 if you compare two things, you say that they are similar in some way: *He **compared** the human brain **to** a computer.*

com·pa·ri·son /kəmˈpærəsən/ *noun* when you compare things or people: *a comparison of this year's results with last year's*

com·part·ment /kəmˈpɑːtmənt $ kəmˈpɑrtmənt/ *noun* a separate space or area inside something: *a purse with several compartments*

com·pass /ˈkʌmpəs/ *noun* (plural **compasses**)
1 an instrument that shows the direction you are travelling in, with a part that always points north
2 also **compasses** an instrument that you use for drawing circles

compass

com·pas·sion /kəmˈpæʃən/ *noun* (no plural) sympathy for someone who is suffering

com·pas·sion·ate /kəmˈpæʃənət/ *adjective* feeling sympathy for people who are suffering

com·pat·i·ble /kəmˈpætəbəl/ *adjective* **1** two people who are compatible have similar ideas or interests, and are able to have a good relationship ANTONYM **incompatible**
2 two things that are compatible are able to exist or be used together without problems ANTONYM **incompatible**: *Is the new software compatible with the old version?*

com·pel /kəmˈpel/ *verb* (formal) (**compelled**, **compelling**) to force someone to do something: *The bad weather compelled them to turn back.*

com·pel·ling /kəmˈpelɪŋ/ *adjective* **1** very interesting or exciting: *a compelling TV drama* **2** a compelling argument, reason etc is one which you can believe or accept because it is probably correct

com·pen·sate /ˈkɒmpənseɪt $ ˈkɑmpənˌseɪt/ *verb* to do something so that something bad has a smaller effect: *He bought his kids presents to compensate for being away so much.*

com·pen·sa·tion /ˌkɒmpənˈseɪʃən $ ˌkɑmpənˈseɪʃən/ *noun* **1** (no plural) money that someone is given because they have been injured or badly treated, or have lost something: *The holiday company had to pay the Taylors £1,500 compensation.* **2** something that makes a bad situation seem better: *Being unemployed has its compensations, like not having to get up early.*

com·pete /kəmˈpiːt/ *verb*

KEY PATTERNS
compete with/against someone
compete in something

to try to win something or to be more successful than someone else: *Our team* ***competes with*** *teams from other villages.* • *Small companies cannot* ***compete against*** *large international companies.* • *Ten runners will be* ***competing in*** *the race.* • *The shops are all* ***competing for*** *customers.*

com·pe·tence /ˈkɒmpətəns $ ˈkɑmpətəns/ *noun* when someone is able to do their job correctly ANTONYM **incompetence**

com·pe·tent /ˈkɒmpətənt $ ˈkɑmpətənt/ *adjective* good at your work or able to do a job well ANTONYM **incompetent**: *a highly competent doctor*

com·pe·ti·tion /ˌkɒmpəˈtɪʃən $ ˌkɑmpəˈtɪʃən/ *noun* **1** an organized event in which people or teams compete against each other: *Who won the poetry competition?* **2** (no plural) a situation in which people or organizations compete with each other: *There is a lot of competition for places at this university.*

com·pet·i·tive /kəmˈpetətɪv/ *adjective* determined to be more successful than other people —**competitiveness** *noun* (no plural)

com·pet·i·tor /kəmˈpetɪtə $ kəmˈpetɪtɚ/ *noun* a person, team, or company that competes with another

com·pi·la·tion /ˌkɒmpəˈleɪʃən $ ˌkɑmpəˈleɪʃən/ *noun* a CD containing songs from different CDs, or a book containing pieces of writing from different books: *a compilation of Madonna's hit singles*

com·pile /kəmˈpaɪl/ *verb* to make a book, list etc, using different pieces of information: *They compiled a list of the most popular activities.*

com·pla·cen·cy /kəmˈpleɪsənsi/ *noun* when you are too pleased with what you have achieved so that you no longer try to improve

com·pla·cent /kəmˈpleɪsənt/ *adjective* too pleased with what you have achieved so that you no longer try to improve: *You should do well in your exams but you mustn't get complacent.*

com·plain /kəmˈpleɪn/ *verb*

KEY PATTERNS
complain about someone/something
complain that
complain to someone
complain of pain/something bad

to say that you are not satisfied with something or not happy about something: *The children all* ***complained about*** *the food.* • *Teachers often* ***complain that*** *they do not get enough support from parents.* • *I'm going to* ***complain to*** *the manager!* • *He* ***complained of*** *a pain in his stomach.*

com·plaint /kəmˈpleɪnt/ *noun*

KEY PATTERNS
a complaint about someone/something
a complaint to someone
make a complaint

something that you say or write when you are not satisfied with something or not happy about something: *We have received a lot of* ***complaints about*** *noise.* • *My biggest complaint is that we had to wait for two hours before we saw a doctor.* • ***I made a complaint*** *to the manager.*

com·plete[1] /kəmˈpliːt/ *adjective* **1** something that is complete has all the parts that it should have ANTONYM

incomplete: *the complete works of Shakespeare • The collection is nearly complete.*
2 finished ANTONYM **incomplete**: *Work on the new bridge is almost complete.* → see Thesaurus at FINISHED
3 used when you are emphasizing something SYNONYM **total**: *The campaign was a complete failure.*

complete² *verb* to finish doing or making something: *We hope to complete the work by next month.*

com·plete·ly /kəm'pliːtli/ *adverb* in every way SYNONYM **totally**: *She set out to invent a completely new language. • He completely ignored me!*

com·plex¹ /'kɒmpleks $ kɑm'pleks/ *adjective* something that is complex has a lot of different parts and is often difficult to understand: *This is a very complex problem.*

com·plex² /'kɒmpleks $ 'kɑmpleks/ *noun* (plural **complexes**) a group of buildings or rooms used for a particular purpose: *a new shopping complex*

com·plex·ion /kəm'plekʃən/ *noun* the appearance of the skin on your face: *She had a lovely complexion.*

com·pli·cate /'kɒmpləkeɪt $ 'kɑmplə,keɪt/ *verb* to make something more difficult to do: *Bad weather complicated the attempt to rescue the climbers.*

com·pli·cat·ed /'kɒmpləkeɪtɪd $ 'kɑmplə,keɪtɪd/ *adjective* not simple or easy to understand: *These instructions are too complicated. • a complicated mathematical equation*

com·pli·ca·tion /,kɒmplə'keɪʃən $,kɑmplə'keɪʃən/ *noun* a problem that makes something more difficult to do: *We don't expect any further complications in the travel arrangements.*

com·pli·ment /'kɒmpləment $ 'kɑmplə,ment/ *verb* to say something to someone that shows you admire them: *Mr Green complimented her on her taste in music.* —**compliment** /-mənt/ *noun*: *She felt embarrassed when people paid her compliments.*

com·ply /kəm'plaɪ/ *verb* (formal) (**complied**, **complies**) to obey a rule, law, or request: *The company has failed to comply with the law.*

com·po·nent /kəm'pəʊnənt $ kəm'poʊnənt/ *noun* one of the different parts of a machine → see Thesaurus at PART¹

com·pose /kəm'pəʊz $ kəm'poʊz/ *verb* **1** to write a piece of music **2 be composed of things/people** to consist of particular things or people: *The class is composed of students of various abilities.*

com·pos·er /kəm'pəʊzə $ kəm'poʊzə/ *noun* someone who writes music, especially CLASSICAL MUSIC (=serious and important music)

com·po·si·tion /,kɒmpə'zɪʃən $,kɑmpə'zɪʃən/ *noun* (formal) **1** a piece of music that someone wrote: *a composition by Debussy* **2** (no plural) the things that something is made of: *the chemical composition of this new material*

com·pound /'kɒmpaʊnd $ 'kɑmpaʊnd/ *noun* **1** a chemical substance that consists of two or more substances **2 compound noun, compound adjective, compound word** a noun or adjective made from two or more words. 'Compact disc' is a compound noun and 'blue-eyed' is a compound adjective

com·pre·hen·sion /,kɒmprɪ'henʃən $,kɑmprɪ'henʃən/ *noun* **1** *BrE* a test of how well students understand written or spoken language **2** (no plural) the ability to understand something: *He had no comprehension of the problems facing the school.*

com·pre·hen·sive /,kɒmprɪ'hensɪv $,kɑmprɪ'hensɪv/ *adjective* including everything that is needed: *a comprehensive range of books*

compre'hensive ,school also **comprehensive** *noun* a school in Britain which teaches students aged between 11 and 18, who are of all levels of ability

com·prise /kəm'praɪz/ *verb* (formal) to consist of particular people or things: *The club comprises myself and 12 other members.*

com·pro·mise /'kɒmprəmaɪz $ 'kɑmprə,maɪz/ *noun* when people or groups who are trying to agree on

something both accept less than they really want: *Eventually the two sides reached a compromise.*
—**compromise** *verb*: *If you don't learn to compromise, you'll never succeed.*

com·pul·so·ry /kəmˈpʌlsəri/ *adjective* something that is compulsory must be done because of a rule or law ANTONYM **optional**, **voluntary**: *Some countries have compulsory military service.*

com·put·er /kəmˈpjuːtə $ kəmˈpjutɚ/ *noun* an electronic machine that can store and arrange information and that you can use to do many different things: *I do a lot of my work* ***on the computer.*** • *The results of the survey were analysed* ***by computer.*** • *Do you like playing* ***computer games****?* • *a* ***computer program*** → see picture on page A12

comˌputer-ˈliterate *noun* able to use computers: *In many cases, children are more computer-literate than their parents.*

con /kɒn $ kɑn/ *verb* (informal) (**conned**, **conning**) to trick someone in order to get something you want: *They conned me into paying for all the tickets.* —**con** *noun*: *It was just a big con.*

con·ceal /kənˈsiːl/ *verb* (formal) to hide something: *He tried to conceal the book under his jacket.*

con·cede /kənˈsiːd/ *verb* **concede defeat** (formal) to admit that you are not going to win a game, argument etc

con·ceit·ed /kənˈsiːtɪd/ *adjective* too proud of how good, clever, or attractive you are: *He's so conceited about his looks.* → see Thesaurus at PROUD

con·ceiv·a·ble /kənˈsiːvəbəl/ *adjective* possible: *We tried every conceivable way of getting the lid off the jar.*

con·ceive /kənˈsiːv/ *verb* to become PREGNANT

con·cen·trate /ˈkɒnsəntreɪt $ ˈkɑnsənˌtreɪt/ *verb*

KEY PATTERNS
concentrate on something
concentrate on doing something

1 to think very carefully about what you are doing: *Sometimes I find it hard to concentrate when I'm driving long distances.* • *Try to* ***concentrate on*** *what you are doing.*
2 to give most of your time and attention to one thing SYNONYM **focus**: *I gave up the piano so that I could* ***concentrate on*** *the violin.* • *We must* ***concentrate on*** *getting the most important tasks done first.*

con·cen·trat·ed /ˈkɒnsəntreɪtɪd $ ˈkɑnsənˌtreɪtɪd/ *adjective* a concentrated liquid is thick and strong because it does not contain much water

con·cen·tra·tion /ˌkɒnsənˈtreɪʃən $ ˌkɑnsənˈtreɪʃən/ *noun*
1 (no plural) when you think very carefully about what you are doing: *The job requires a lot of concentration.* • *I* ***lost concentration*** (=did not think carefully) *for a moment, and that's when I crashed the car.*
2 (formal) a large number of things in a small area: *The area has* ***a high concentration of*** *good schools.*

con·cept /ˈkɒnsept $ ˈkɑnsept/ *noun* (formal) a general idea: *Many films have been based on the concept of time travel.*

con·cep·tion /kənˈsepʃən/ *noun* (no plural) (formal) when a woman or female animal becomes PREGNANT

con·cern¹ /kənˈsɜːn $ kənˈsɚn/ *noun*

KEY PATTERNS
concern about someone/something
concern for someone/something
concern that

worry that you feel about something important: *Some parents have* ***expressed*** *their* ***concern about*** *the number of cars entering and leaving the school yard.* • *There is* ***growing concern for*** *the welfare of the hostages.* • *There is* ***concern that*** *he will not be fit enough to play in Monday's match.* • *My* ***only concern*** *is your safety* (=the only thing I am worried about).

PHRASES
be of concern to someone (formal) if something is of concern to you, it is important to you and worries you: *This problem* ***is of concern to*** *all of us.*

A B C D E F G H I J K L M N O P Q R S T U V W X Y Z

concern² *verb* **1** if something concerns you, it affects or involves you: *"What were you talking about?" "It doesn't concern you."* **2** to worry someone: *Helen's odd behaviour was beginning to concern us.* **3** (formal) to be about something: *Much of his work concerned the way the brain works.*

con·cerned /kənˈsɜːnd $ kənˈsɚnd/ *adjective*

KEY PATTERNS
concerned about someone/something
concerned that
concerned for someone

1 the people concerned are the people involved in something or affected by it: *The fire has been a very upsetting experience for everyone concerned.* **2** worried about something important: *The police **are very concerned about** the amount of crime in the area.* • *I'm **concerned that** she's getting too thin.* • *She **is concerned for** her children.*
→ see Thesaurus at WORRIED

con·cern·ing /kənˈsɜːnɪŋ $ kənˈsɚnɪŋ/ *preposition* (formal) about someone or something SYNONYM **regarding**: *I'm afraid I have some bad news for you concerning your son.*
→ see Thesaurus at ABOUT¹

con·cert /ˈkɒnsət $ ˈkɑnsɚt/ *noun* a performance given by musicians or singers: *We went to a concert last night.*

con·ces·sion /kənˈseʃən/ *noun* something that you agree to in order to end an argument: *She wasn't prepared to make any concessions.*

con·cise /kənˈsaɪs/ *adjective* not using too many words: *He gave a concise explanation of the problem.*

con·clude /kənˈkluːd/ *verb* **1** to decide that something is true after considering all the information you have: *The police concluded that the man was already dead when he was thrown in the river.* **2** (formal) to finish a meeting or discussion: *They concluded the meeting soon after two o'clock.*

con·clu·sion /kənˈkluːʒən/ *noun*

KEY PATTERNS
come to/reach/draw a conclusion
the conclusion (that)

1 something that you decide is true after considering all the information you have: *I've **come to the conclusion that** most people don't actually enjoy Christmas.* • *It took scientists two years to **reach** this **conclusion**.* **2** (formal) the end or final part of something: *I've nearly finished my essay – I've just got to write the conclusion.*

con·clu·sive /kənˈkluːsɪv/ *adjective* proving that something is definitely true: *There is now conclusive evidence that smoking causes cancer.*
—**conclusively** *adverb*: *The marks on his jacket prove conclusively that he was present at the scene of the crime.*

con·crete¹ /ˈkɒŋkriːt $ ˈkɑŋkrit/ *noun* (no plural) a substance used for building that is made by mixing sand, water, small stones, and CEMENT

con·crete² /ˈkɒŋkriːt $ kɑnˈkrit/ *adjective* **1** made of concrete: *a concrete floor* **2** based on facts: *We need concrete evidence before we accuse him of stealing.*

con·cus·sion /kənˈkʌʃən/ *noun* slight damage to your brain that is caused when you hit your head on something

con·demn /kənˈdem/ *verb* (written) **1** to say very strongly that you do not approve of someone or something: *Doctors have condemned the government's plans to change the hospital system.* **2** to give a severe punishment to a criminal: *He was condemned to death for bringing drugs into the country.*

con·dem·na·tion /ˌkɒndəmˈneɪʃən $ ˌkɑndəmˈneɪʃən/ *noun* (written) a statement of very strong disapproval: *There has been widespread condemnation of the bombing.*

con·den·sa·tion /ˌkɒndenˈseɪʃən $ ˌkɑndənˈseɪʃən/ *noun* (no plural) small drops of water that appear on a cold surface when warm air touches it

con·de·scend·ing /ˌkɒndɪˈsendɪŋ $ ˌkɑndɪˈsendɪŋ/ *adjective* someone who is condescending shows that they think they are better or more important than other people SYNONYM **patronizing**

con·di·tion /kənˈdɪʃən/ *noun*

KEY PATTERNS
be in good/bad condition

be in a serious/satisfactory etc condition
a condition for something to happen
on condition that

1 how damaged something is, or how well someone is: *Have you checked **the condition of** the house? • The car's engine is still **in good condition**. • The dog was **in a terrible condition** when we found her. • He was extremely tired, and **in no condition to** drive.*
2 something that you must do or agree to first, before something else can be done: *One of the **conditions for** getting a student loan is that you must have been accepted for college. • I'll come with you **on condition that** you pay for everything.*

PHRASES

working conditions, living conditions the situation in which people work or live: *The people are very poor, and their **living conditions** are very bad.*

weather conditions what the weather is like on a particular day: *The **weather conditions** made the rescue difficult.*

con·di·tion·al /kən'dɪʃənəl/ *adjective* a conditional part of a sentence begins with 'if' or 'unless'

con·di·tion·er /kən'dɪʃənə $ kən'dɪʃənɚ/ *noun* a liquid that you put on your hair after you have washed it to keep it in good condition

con·done /kən'dəʊn $ kən'doʊn/ *verb* (formal) to allow or accept behaviour that most people think is wrong: *I cannot condone lying.*

con·duct¹ /kən'dʌkt/ *verb*
1 to do something in an organized way in order to find out information or achieve something SYNONYM **carry out**: *The government is conducting a survey into the effects of smoking on young children.*
2 if a material conducts heat or electricity, it allows heat or electricity to pass along it
3 to stand in front of a large group of musicians and direct them as they play a piece of music: *Simon Rattle will be conducting the orchestra.*

con·duct² /'kɒndʌkt $ 'kɑndʌkt/ *noun* (no plural) (formal) the way that someone behaves SYNONYM **behaviour**: *His conduct has been disgraceful.*

con·duc·tor /kən'dʌktə $ kən'dʌktɚ/ *noun* **1** someone who stands in front of a large group of musicians and directs them as they play a piece of music **2** someone who works on a bus or train

cones

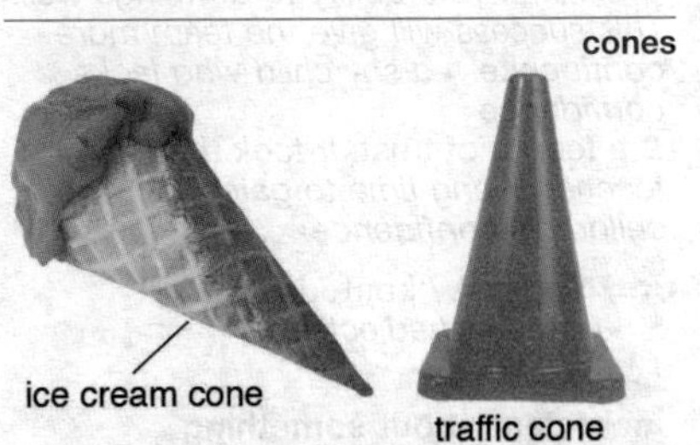

cone /kəʊn $ koʊn/ *noun* **1** an object which is round at one end and pointed at the other: *There were traffic cones preventing drivers using one side of the road. • an ice-cream cone* **2** a brown egg-shaped object containing seeds that grows on a PINE or FIR tree

con·fed·e·ra·tion /kən,fedə'reɪʃən/ also **con·fed·e·ra·cy** /kən'fedərəsi/ *noun* an official group of people, organizations, or states

con·fer /kən'fɜː $ kən'fɚ/ *verb* (formal) (**conferred**, **conferring**) **1** to discuss something with other people: *I will have to confer with my colleagues about this.* **2** to officially give someone a degree, honour etc: *His old university conferred a special degree on him.*

con·fe·rence /'kɒnfərəns $'kɑnfrəns/ *noun* a large formal meeting in which people discuss important things: *Five hundred people attended a recent conference on the environment.*

con·fess /kən'fes/ *verb* to admit that you have done something wrong or stupid: *Eventually Mitchell confessed to the robbery. • She confessed that she had forgotten to post the letter.*

con·fes·sion /kən'feʃən/ *noun* a statement in which you say that you have done something wrong

con·fet·ti /kən'feti/ *noun* (no plural) small pieces of paper that you throw over a man and woman who have just got married

A B C D E F G H I J K L M N O P Q R S T U V W X Y Z

con•fide /kən'faɪd/ *verb* if you confide in someone, you tell them a secret: *She chose to confide in her sister.*

con•fi•dence /'kɒnfədəns $ 'kɑnfədəns/ *noun* (no plural)
1 belief in your ability to do things well: *This success will **give** the team more **confidence**. • a shy child who **lacks** confidence*
2 a feeling of trust: *It took the new teacher a long time to **gain** the children's **confidence**.*

con•fi•dent /'kɒnfədənt $ 'kɑnfədənt/ *adjective*

KEY PATTERNS
confident about something
confident of doing something
confident (that)

1 sure that you can do something well: *Jenny **seems** very **confident about** her exam. • We **were** quite **confident of** winning. • a confident swimmer*
2 sure that something good is true or will happen: *I **am confident that** this is the right course for you.* —**confidently** *adverb*

con•fi•den•tial /ˌkɒnfə'denʃəl $ ˌkɑnfə'denʃəl/ *adjective* confidential information is secret: *The envelope was marked 'Confidential'.* → see Thesaurus at SECRET[1]

con•fine /kən'faɪn/ *verb* **1 be confined to someone/something** to happen in only one place, or to affect only one group of people: *This illness is not confined to older people.* **2** if you confine your activities to one thing, you do or deal with only that thing SYNONYM **restrict**: *He confined his research to monkeys.*

con•firm /kən'fɜːm $ kən'fɚm/ *verb* (formal) **1** to say or show that something is definitely true: *He confirmed that the money had been paid.* **2** to tell someone that an arrangement is now definite: *Have you confirmed the hotel booking?*

con•fir•ma•tion /ˌkɒnfə'meɪʃən $ ˌkɑnfɚ'meɪʃən/ *noun* something telling you that something is definitely true or will definitely happen: *We think Matt will be well enough to play in tomorrow's game, but we're waiting for confirmation.*

con•fis•cate /'kɒnfəskeɪt $ 'kɑnfəˌskeɪt/ *verb* if someone in authority confiscates something, they take it away from you: *The teacher confiscated the boy's mobile phone.*

con•flict[1] /'kɒnflɪkt $ 'kɑnˌflɪkt/ *noun* a disagreement or fighting: *There was often conflict between him and his brother.*

con•flict[2] /kən'flɪkt/ *verb* if two ideas or statements conflict, they are different and cannot both be true: *Her description of the man conflicted with the descriptions given by others.* —**conflicting** *adjective*: *The people who saw the accident gave conflicting descriptions of what happened.*

PRONUNCIATION
Be careful how you pronounce the noun **CONflict**, with the stress on the first syllable.
You pronounce the verb **conFLICT**, with the stress on the second syllable.

con•form /kən'fɔːm $ kən'fɔrm/ *verb* **1** to behave in the way that most other people behave: *Kids feel they have to conform.* **2** (formal) if something conforms to a rule or standard, it obeys or matches it: *Does this cycle helmet conform to the European standard?*

con•front /kən'frʌnt/ *verb* **1** if you confront a problem or difficult situation, you deal with it rather than ignoring it: *You've got to confront this problem.*
2 if you confront someone, you talk to them and try to make them admit they have done something wrong: *Richard confronted his sister about her lies.*

con•fron•ta•tion /ˌkɒnfrən'teɪʃən $ ˌkɑnfrən'teɪʃən/ *noun* a situation in which there is a lot of angry disagreement: *I try to avoid confrontations.*

con•fuse /kən'fjuːz/ *verb*

KEY PATTERNS
confuse someone
confuse one person/thing with another

1 if someone or something confuses you, you cannot think clearly or cannot understand something: *His explanation was so complicated that it confused me.*

2 to think wrongly that a person or thing is someone or something else SYNONYM **mix up**: *I'm always **confusing** Joe **with** his brother.*

con·fused /kən'fjuːzd/ *adjective*

KEY PATTERNS
confused about something

if you are confused, you do not understand something clearly: *I'm slightly **confused about** what we're supposed to be doing. • I **got confused** when Sam tried to explain what had happened.*

con·fus·ing /kən'fjuːzɪŋ/ *adjective* difficult to understand: *I find some of the maths a bit confusing.*

con·fu·sion /kən'fjuːʒən/ *noun* (no plural) **1** when people do not understand what is happening or what something means: *There was some confusion about whether the goal was allowed.* **2** when people are moving about and making a lot of noise in a confused way: *The man who fired the shot escaped in the confusion.*

con·ges·tion /kən'dʒestʃən/ *noun* (no plural) (formal) when a road is too full of vehicles: *There is a lot of congestion on the roads today.*

con·grat·u·late /kən'grætʃəleɪt/ *verb*

KEY PATTERNS
congratulate someone on something

to tell someone that you are happy because they have done something well, or something good has happened to them: *James **congratulated** me **on** passing my driving test.*

con·grat·u·la·tions /kən,grætʃə'leɪʃənz/ *plural noun*

KEY PATTERNS
congratulations on something
congratulations to someone

something you say to tell someone that you are happy because they have done something well, or something good has happened to them: ***Congratulations on** passing your exams. • **Congratulations to** everyone involved in the project. • Give him my **congratulations**. • "I got that job I applied for." "Congratulations!"*

con·gre·ga·tion /ˌkɒŋgrə'geɪʃən $ ˌkɑŋgrə'geɪʃən/ *noun* the people who are in a church for a religious ceremony

co·ni·fer /'kəʊnəfə $ 'kɑnəfɚ/ *noun* a tree that keeps its leaves in winter and which has CONEs containing its seeds → see picture on page A10

con·junc·tion /kən'dʒʌŋkʃən/ *noun* a word such as 'but', 'and', or 'while' that connects parts of sentences

con·jur·er, conjuror /'kʌndʒərə $ 'kɑndʒərɚ/ *noun* someone who does magic tricks SYNONYM **magician**

con·man /'kɒnmæn $ 'kɑnmæn/ *noun* (informal) (plural **conmen** /-men/) someone who tries to get money by tricking people

con·nect /kə'nekt/ *verb*

KEY PATTERNS
connect one object/place to another
connect things
connect something/someone with something

1 to join two things or places together: ***Connect** this wire **to** the back of the machine. • the road **connecting** the two cities*
2 to think or show that a thing or person is related to or involved in something: *The police **have** not **connected** him **with** the murder.*

con·nect·ed /kə'nektɪd/ *adjective*

KEY PATTERNS
connected with something
connected to an object/place

1 if one thing is connected with another, they are related in some way SYNONYM **linked**: *The disease may **be connected with** the type of work you do.*
2 if one thing is connected to another, it is joined to it: *The motorway **is connected to** the airport by a tunnel.*

con·nec·tion /kə'nekʃən/ *noun*

KEY PATTERNS
a connection between things
a connection with/to something

1 a relationship between things SYNONYM **link**: *There is a strong **connection between** happiness and health. • He no longer has any **connection with** the company.*

2 when two or more things are joined together, especially by an electrical wire: *Some villages still have no* ***connection to*** *an electricity supply.*
3 a bus, train, or plane that leaves a short time after the one you are on arrives, and that you must get on to continue your journey: *We missed our connection and had to wait two hours for the next train.*

PHRASES

in connection with something because of a connection with something, or relating to something: *A man has been arrested* ***in connection with*** *the murder.*

con·quer /ˈkɒŋkə $ ˈkɑŋkɚ/ *verb* to get control of a country by fighting: *The Romans conquered Britain.*

con·quest /ˈkɒŋkwest $ ˈkɑŋkwest/ *noun* when people from another country get control of a country by fighting

con·science /ˈkɒnʃəns $ ˈkɑnʃəns/ *noun* **1** the feeling that tells you whether what you are doing is morally right or wrong: *He had a guilty conscience about forgetting to feed the rabbit.* **2 on someone's conscience** if you have something on your conscience, you feel guilty about it: *I know the mistake is still on his conscience.*

con·sci·en·tious /ˌkɒnʃiˈenʃəs $ ˌkɑnʃiˈenʃəs/ *adjective* careful to do the things that need doing

con·scious /ˈkɒnʃəs $ ˈkɑnʃəs/ *adjective* **1** awake and able to understand what is happening ANTONYM **unconscious**: *The injured man was still conscious.* **2** knowing of something or always thinking about it SYNONYM **aware**: *She was always conscious of her weight.* • *fashion conscious teenagers*

con·scious·ness /ˈkɒnʃəsnəs $ ˈkɑnʃəsnəs/ *noun* **lose consciousness, regain consciousness** if someone who is ill loses consciousness, they stop being awake and are not able to understand what is happening: *He was bleeding heavily and soon lost consciousness.* • *Will she ever regain consciousness?*

con·sec·u·tive /kənˈsekjətɪv/ *adjective* happening one after the other: *He was late for school on three consecutive days.*

con·sen·sus /kənˈsensəs/ *noun* (no plural) (formal) agreement between all or most people in a group: *There was consensus on the need for change.*

con·sent /kənˈsent/ *noun* (no plural) (formal) permission: *She had taken the car without the owner's consent.*

con·se·quence /ˈkɒnsəkwəns $ ˈkɑnsəˌkwens/ *noun* something that happens as a result of something else: *You don't think about the consequences of your actions!* → see Thesaurus at RESULT[1]

con·se·quent·ly /ˈkɒnsəkwəntli $ ˈkɑnsəˌkwentli/ *adverb* (formal) as a result: *He lost his coat and consequently his wallet.*

con·ser·va·tion /ˌkɒnsəˈveɪʃən $ ˌkɑnsɚˈveɪʃən/ *noun* (no plural) the protection of natural things

con·ser·va·tion·ist /ˌkɒnsəˈveɪʃənɪst $ ˌkɑnsɚˈveɪʃənɪst/ *noun* someone who tries to protect natural things

con·ser·va·tive /kənˈsɜːvətɪv $ kənˈsɚvətɪv/ *adjective* someone who is conservative likes to continue doing things in the way they are already done, rather than making changes

con·ser·va·to·ry /kənˈsɜːvətəri $ kənˈsɚvəˌtɔri/ *noun* (plural **conservatories**) a room made of glass that is joined to the side of a house

con·sid·er /kənˈsɪdə $ kənˈsɪdɚ/ *verb*

KEY PATTERNS
consider a fact/possibility etc
consider doing something
consider how/what/whether etc
consider someone/something (to be) something

1 to think about something carefully, especially before deciding what to do: *Anna is considering studying languages at university.* • *It sounds a great idea, but have you* ***considered how much*** *it will cost?*
2 to think of someone or something in a particular way: *He seemed to* ***consider*** *himself* ***to be*** *better than other people.*

con·sid·er·a·ble /kən'sɪdərəbəl/ *adjective* great or large in amount: *I spent a considerable amount of time trying to persuade him to come.*
—**considerably** *adverb*: *He is considerably older than his girlfriend.*

con·sid·er·ate /kən'sɪdərət/ *adjective* a considerate person thinks about other people's feelings and needs ANTONYM **inconsiderate** SYNONYM **thoughtful** ➔ see Thesaurus at KIND[2]

con·sid·e·ra·tion /kənˌsɪdə'reɪʃən/ *noun* (no plural) **1** when someone thinks about other people's feelings and needs: *He shows no consideration for others.* **2** careful thought: *After much consideration, he decided to study history at university.*

con·sid·er·ing /kən'sɪdərɪŋ/ *preposition*

KEY PATTERNS
considering (that)

used to remind people of a fact that they should think about: *Maria's doing very well,* ***considering that*** *she's the youngest in her class.*

con·sist /kən'sɪst/ *verb*
consist of things if something consists of other things, those things are different parts of it: *The class consists of children from a wide range of countries.*

con·sis·ten·cy /kən'sɪstənsi/ *noun* **1** (no plural) when someone always behaves in the same way ANTONYM **inconsistency**: *You have to admire his consistency as a player.* **2** how thick or firm a mixture is: *Stir the mixture until it is the consistency of thick cream.*

con·sis·tent /kən'sɪstənt/ *adjective* always happening or behaving in the same way ANTONYM **inconsistent**: *His school work is consistent.*
—**consistently** *adverb*: *Their results are consistently good.*

con·so·la·tion /ˌkɒnsə'leɪʃən $ ˌkɑnsə'leɪʃən/ *noun* something that makes you feel better when you are sad or disappointed: *My only consolation is that everyone else found the exam hard too.*

con·sole[1] /kən'səʊl $ kən'soʊl/ *verb* if you console someone who is sad or disappointed, you try to make them feel better

con·sole[2] /'kɒnsəʊl $ 'kɑnsoʊl/ *noun* a piece of equipment with buttons on it that you connect to a computer and use when you play a game on the computer: *a games console* ➔ see picture on page A12

PRONUNCIATION
You pronounce the verb **conSOLE**, with the stress on the second syllable.
You pronounce the noun **CONsole**, with the stress on the first syllable.

con·so·nant /'kɒnsənənt $ 'kɑnsənənt/ *noun* any letter of the English alphabet except a, e, i, o, and u

con·spic·u·ous /kən'spɪkjuəs/ *adjective* very easy to notice: *Her red hair made her very conspicuous.*
➔ see Thesaurus at NOTICEABLE

con·spi·ra·cy /kən'spɪrəsi/ *noun* (plural **conspiracies**) a secret plan made by several people to do something bad or illegal ➔ see Thesaurus at PLAN[1]

con·sta·ble /'kʌnstəbəl $ 'kɑnstəbəl/ *noun* a British police officer of the lowest rank

con·stant /'kɒnstənt $ 'kɑnstənt/ *adjective* **1** happening regularly or all the time SYNONYM **continual**: *We couldn't get any work done because there were constant interruptions.* **2** a constant speed, temperature etc is always the same: *The medicine must be kept at a constant temperature.*

con·stant·ly /'kɒnstəntli $ 'kɑnstəntli/ *adverb* regularly or all the time SYNONYM **continually**: *She complained constantly about her job.*

con·stel·la·tion /ˌkɒnstə'leɪʃən $ ˌkɑnstə'leɪʃən/ *noun* a group of stars that has a name

con·ster·na·tion /ˌkɒnstə'neɪʃən $ ˌkɑnstɚ'neɪʃən/ *noun* (no plural) (written) a feeling of shock or worry

con·sti·pa·tion /ˌkɒnstə'peɪʃən $ ˌkɑnstə'peɪʃən/ *noun* (no plural) when someone is unable to remove waste food from inside their body

con·sti·tu·ent /kən'stɪtʃuənt/ *noun* (formal) one of the substances in a mixture: *The main constituent of this type of paint is oil.*

con·sti·tute /'kɒnstətjuːt $ 'kɑnstəˌtut/ *verb* (formal) to be or form something: *His action constitutes a criminal offence.* • *the people who constitute the committee*

con·sti·tu·tion /ˌkɒnstə'tjuːʃən $ ˌkɑnstə'tuʃən/ *noun* the written laws and principles of a government or organization

con·straint /kən'streɪnt/ *noun* (formal) something that stops you doing the things you want to do: *the constraints that were placed on Victorian women*

con·struct /kən'strʌkt/ *verb* to build something: *They have not finished constructing the new airport.*

con·struc·tion /kən'strʌkʃən/ *noun* **1** (no plural) the process of building something: *The construction of the road will take two years.* **2** something that has been built SYNONYM **structure**: *He had built a wooden construction to keep chickens in.* **3** a way in which words are put together in a sentence: *We learned a new grammatical construction.*

con·struc·tive /kən'strʌktɪv/ *adjective* helpful or useful: *The teacher wrote some constructive comments on Gary's essay.*

con·sult /kən'sʌlt/ *verb*

KEY PATTERNS
consult someone about something

to ask someone for advice or information: *You should **consult** your teacher **about** which course is best for you.*

con·sul·tant /kən'sʌltənt/ *noun* someone whose job is to give advice about a subject: *a management consultant*

con·sul·ta·tion /ˌkɒnsəl'teɪʃən $ ˌkɑnsəl'teɪʃən/ *noun* when someone is asked for their opinion or advice: *The decision was made after consultations with the students.*

con·sume /kən'sjuːm $ kən'sum/ *verb* to use energy, products etc: *We are still consuming too much coal and oil.*

con·sum·er /kən'sjuːmə $ kən'sumɚ/ *noun* someone who buys things or uses a service that a company provides: *Consumers are now more aware of their rights.*

con·sump·tion /kən'sʌmpʃən/ *noun* (no plural) the amount of electricity, gas etc that something uses: *This car has very low fuel consumption.*

con·tact¹ /'kɒntækt $ 'kɑntækt/ *noun* **1 get in contact/make contact** to telephone someone, write to them, or meet them SYNONYM **get in touch**: *I wanted to **get in contact with** her but she was on holiday.*
2 keep/stay in contact to meet, telephone, or write to someone regularly SYNONYM **keep in touch**: *I try to **keep in contact with** all my old friends from school.*
3 lose contact to stop meeting, telephoning, or writing to someone SYNONYM **lose touch**: *I **lost contact with** Simon when he moved to a different town.*
4 come into contact to be with someone: *You catch a cold by **coming into contact with** someone who already has one.*
5 be in contact if one thing is in contact with another, it is touching it: *Make sure the wire **is not in contact with** metal.*
6 someone whose name or email address is stored on your phone, computer etc: *I'll add your name to my list of contacts.*

contact² *verb* to telephone or write to someone: *In an emergency, you should contact the police immediately.*

'contact ˌlens *noun* (plural **contact lenses**) one of a pair of small pieces of plastic that you put on your eyes to help you see clearly

con·ta·gious /kən'teɪdʒəs/ *adjective* a contagious disease can pass directly from one person to another

con·tain /kən'teɪn/ *verb* if something contains things, those things are in it: *The suitcase contained a lot of old clothes.* • *Monday's*

A B C D E F G H I J K L M N O P Q R S T U V W X Y Z

newspaper contained several articles about the train crash.

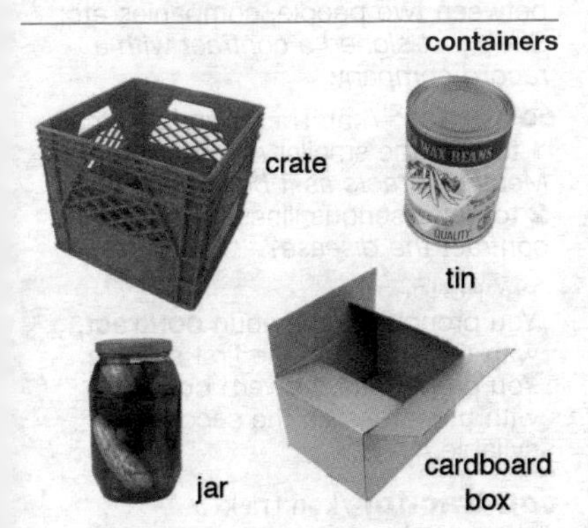

con·tain·er /kən'teɪnə $ kən'teɪnər/ *noun* something that you can put things in, for example a box or can: *She put the food in plastic containers.*

con·tam·i·nate /kən'tæməneɪt/ *verb* to add a substance that makes something dirty or dangerous: *The water was contaminated with chemicals.*

con·tam·i·na·tion /kənˌtæmə'neɪʃən/ *noun* (no plural) when a substance is added that makes something dirty or dangerous

con·tem·plate /'kɒntəmpleɪt $ 'kɑntəmˌpleɪt/ *verb* to think about something that you might do SYNONYM **consider**: *She had never even contemplated marriage.*

con·tem·po·ra·ry[1] /kən'tempərəri $ kən'tempəˌreri/ *adjective* **1** modern and belonging to the present time: *She is one of the country's best contemporary artists.* **2** happening or existing in the same period of time: *This information comes from a contemporary record of those events.*

contemporary[2] *noun* (plural **contemporaries**) a person living at the same time as someone else: *Many of Darwin's contemporaries did not agree with his theories.*

con·tempt /kən'tempt/ *noun* (no plural) a feeling that someone or something does not deserve any respect: *He showed complete contempt for the people who worked for him.*

con·tend /kən'tend/ *verb* **contend with** to try to do something in a difficult situation: *The players had to contend with very windy conditions.*

con·tend·er /kən'tendə $ kən'tendər/ *noun* someone who is competing to win a title, prize, or political job

con·tent[1] /kən'tent/ *adjective*

KEY PATTERNS
content with something
content to do something

happy and satisfied: *She seems very content with her life.* • *The children were content to spend the afternoon drawing and painting.*

con·tent[2] /'kɒntent $ 'kɑntent/ *noun*

KEY PATTERNS
the contents of something

1 the amount of a substance that something contains: *Choose foods with a lower fat content.*
2 the ideas or information in a book, programme etc: *The content of the programme was quite upsetting.*
3 contents a) the things that are inside a box, bag, house etc: *All the contents of the house were destroyed in a fire.* **b)** the list at the beginning of a book saying what things are in the book

con·tent·ed /kən'tentɪd/ *adjective* (written) happy and satisfied ANTONYM **discontented**: *He was contented with what he had.*

con·test /'kɒntest $ 'kɑntest/ *noun* a competition: *She won first prize in a beauty contest.*

con·tes·tant /kən'testənt/ *noun* someone who enters a competition

con·text /'kɒntekst $ 'kɑntekst/ *noun* **1** the situation within which something happens: *Think about the historical context of these events.* **2** the words around a word or phrase that help you understand its meaning: *What do you think the word means in this context?*

con·ti·nent /'kɒntənənt $ 'kɑntənənt/ *noun* **1** one of the large areas of land in the world, such as Africa, Asia, or Europe
2 the Continent *BrE* Europe, not

A B C D E F G H I J K L M N O P Q R S T U V W X Y Z

including Britain: *The situation is different on the Continent.*

con·ti·nen·tal /ˌkɒntəˈnentl $ ˌkɑntəˈnentl/ *adjective BrE* in or belonging to Europe, not including Britain

con·tin·u·al /kənˈtɪnjuəl/ *adjective* happening often or all the time SYNONYM **constant**: *He was in continual pain.* —**continually** *adverb*: *The phone rang continually.*

con·tin·ue /kənˈtɪnjuː/ *verb*

KEY PATTERNS
continue to do something
continue your work/a discussion etc
continue along/down etc something

1 to do something or happen for a period of time without stopping: *Lisa is **continuing to** make good progress with her French.* • *The bad weather will continue for another week.*
2 to start again, or start something again, after stopping: *The film will continue after the news.* • *We can continue our conversation later.*
3 to go further in the same direction: *Continue along this road until you come to a church.*

con·ti·nu·i·ty /ˌkɒntəˈnjuːəti $ ˌkɑntəˈnuəti/ *noun* (no plural) when something continues for a long period of time without change

con·tin·u·ous /kənˈtɪnjuəs/ *adjective* **1** continuing without stopping: *Long periods of continuous study are very tiring.* **2** the continuous form of a verb consists of 'be' and the present participle, as in 'she was reading' SYNONYM **progressive**

con·tin·u·ous·ly /kənˈtɪnjuəsli/ *adverb* without stopping: *It rained continuously for three days.*

con·tra·cep·tion /ˌkɒntrəˈsepʃən $ ˌkɑntrəˈsepʃən/ *noun* (no plural) methods of stopping a woman becoming PREGNANT SYNONYM **birth control**

con·tra·cep·tive /ˌkɒntrəˈseptɪv $ ˌkɑntrəˈseptɪv/ *noun* something that stops a woman becoming PREGNANT

con·tract¹ /ˈkɒntrækt $ ˈkɑntrækt/ *noun* a formal written agreement between two people, companies etc: *She's just signed a contract with a record company.*

con·tract² /kənˈtrækt/ *verb* (formal) **1** to become smaller ANTONYM **expand**: *Metal contracts as it becomes cooler.* **2** to get a serious illness: *How did he contract the disease?*

PRONUNCIATION
You pronounce the noun **CONtract**, with the stress on the first syllable. You pronounce the verb **conTRACT**, with the stress on the second syllable.

con·trac·tor /kənˈtræktə $ ˈkɑnˌtræktɚ/ *noun* a person or company that does work for another company: *a building contractor*

con·tra·dict /ˌkɒntrəˈdɪkt $ ˌkɑntrəˈdɪkt/ *verb* **1** if one statement contradicts another, the two are different and cannot both be true: *Their stories contradicted each other.* **2** if you contradict someone, you say that what they have just said is not true: *Don't contradict your mother!*

con·tra·dic·tion /ˌkɒntrəˈdɪkʃən $ ˌkɑntrəˈdɪkʃən/ *noun* a difference between two statements or facts, that shows they cannot both be true: *There were some obvious contradictions in what he said.*

con·tra·dic·to·ry /ˌkɒntrəˈdɪktəri $ ˌkɑntrəˈdɪktəri/ *adjective* if two statements are contradictory, they are different and cannot both be true

con·tra·ry¹ /ˈkɒntrəri $ ˈkɑnˌtreri/ *noun* (formal) **on the contrary** used to emphasize that the opposite of something is true: *He's not a strict teacher. On the contrary, he lets us do anything we like.*

contrary² *adverb* **contrary to something** used to say that something is not correct: *Contrary to earlier reports, the team captain has not resigned.*

con·trast¹ /ˈkɒntrɑːst $ ˈkɑntræst/ *noun*

KEY PATTERNS
a contrast between things
in contrast to something

a big difference between people, things, or situations: *There was a great* ***contrast between*** *the rich areas and the poor areas of the city.* • ***In contrast to*** *her brother, Tina is small and fair-haired.*

con·trast² /kən'trɑːst $ kən'træst/ *verb*

KEY PATTERNS
contrast something with something else
contrast something and something else
contrast with something

1 to show or think about how two things are different from each other: *I'd like to* ***contrast*** *Picasso's early work* ***with*** *his later style.* • ***Contrast*** *Japanese* ***and*** *British factories.*
2 if one thing contrasts with another, it is very different from it: *We chose patterned curtains, to* ***contrast with*** *the plain walls.*

con·trib·ute /kən'trɪbjuːt/ *verb*

KEY PATTERNS
contribute to/towards an event/situation
contribute (money etc) to/towards something

1 to be one of the causes of something that happens: *He thanked everyone who* ***had contributed to*** *the success of the company.* • *Smoking* ***contributed towards*** *his death.*
2 to give money or things to help pay for or achieve something: *Would you like to* ***contribute towards*** *a present for Linda's birthday?* • *Jerry* ***contributed*** *£5* ***to*** *the fund.*

con·tri·bu·tion /ˌkɒntrə'bjuːʃən $ ˌkɑntrə'bjuʃən/ *noun* if you make a contribution to something, you do or give something to help it: *Would you like to make a contribution to charity?* • *He was given a special award for his outstanding contribution to the sport.*

con·trol¹ /kən'trəʊl $ kən'troʊl/ *noun* one of the parts of a machine that you press or move to make it work: *The pilot checks all the controls before take-off.*

PHRASES
have control, be in control to have the ability to make people do what you want, or to make things happen in the way you want: *Some parents feel that they* ***have no control over*** *their children.* • *It's important that you* ***are in control of*** *your life.*
be under control, keep something under control if something is under control, you are succeeding in controlling it: *Don't worry, everything* ***is under control.*** • *Please* ***keep*** *your dog* ***under control.***
be out of control, get out of control: *The fighting got worse, and the situation* ***was soon out of control*** (=not possible to manage or control).
lose control to be unable to stay calm or manage a difficult situation any more: *The referee* ***lost control*** *and several players started a fight.*
take control to start to organize and make decisions about something that someone else was organizing before SYNONYM **take charge**: *When Rose became ill, Jim* ***took control of*** *the farm.*

control² *verb* (**controlled**, **controlling**)
1 to make someone or something do what you want: *The little girl was unable to control her horse.*
2 to have the power in an organization or place: *Britain controlled India for many years.*
3 to limit something or stop it increasing: *Modern drugs can control the disease.*
4 control yourself to make yourself behave calmly, even though you feel angry, upset, excited etc: *I couldn't control myself any longer and I started to laugh.*

con·tro·ver·sial /ˌkɒntrə'vɜːʃəl $ ˌkɑntrə'vɚʃəl/ *adjective* something that is controversial causes arguments because people do not agree about it: *Scientific testing on animals is a controversial issue.*

con·tro·ver·sy /'kɒntrəvɜːsi, kən'trɒvəsi $ 'kɑntrəˌvɚsi/ *noun* (plural **controversies**) a lot of argument about something important: *The book has caused a great deal of controversy.*

con·ve·ni·ent /kən'viːniənt/ *adjective*
1 suitable or easy to do ANTONYM **inconvenient**: *What would be a convenient time for me to come and see you?* • *Shopping by computer is convenient for many people.*

A B C D E F G H I J K L M N O P Q R S T U V W X Y Z

2 a place that is convenient is close to you: *The shops are very convenient.*

con•vent /'kɒnvənt $ 'kɑnvent/ *noun* a place where NUNS live and work

con•ven•tion•al /kən'venʃənəl/ *adjective* conventional ideas, things, and ways of behaving are of the normal or usual kind: *Conventional medicine could not help her, so she tried using herbs.*

con•ver•sa•tion /ˌkɒnvə'seɪʃən $ ˌkɑnvə˞'seɪʃən/ *noun*

KEY PATTERNS
have a conversation
a conversation with someone
a conversation about something

a talk between two or more people, especially friends: *I **had** an interesting **conversation with** Alice yesterday.* • *We **had** a long **conversation about** music.*

con•ver•sion /kən'vɜːʃən $ kən'vɚʒən/ *noun* when something changes from one form or system to another: *the conversion of the sun's heat into electrical energy*

con•vert /kən'vɜːt $ kən'vɚt/ *verb* to change something from one form or system to another, or to change like this: *The old barn has been converted into apartments.* • *Water converts to steam when it is heated.*

con•vey /kən'veɪ/ *verb* (formal) to try to help other people understand your feelings or ideas: *I tried to convey my excitement to the rest of the class.*

con•vict /kən'vɪkt/ *verb* if someone is convicted of a crime, a court of law decides that they are guilty of it: *He was convicted of murder.*

con•vic•tion /kən'vɪkʃən/ *noun* **1** when someone is convicted of a crime: *He has three convictions for theft.* **2** a strong belief or opinion

con•vince /kən'vɪns/ *verb*

KEY PATTERNS
convince someone (that)
convince yourself

to make someone believe that something is true: *In the end Mark **convinced** me **that** he was right.* • *You have to **convince yourself** that you can succeed.*

con•vinced /kən'vɪnst/ *adjective*

KEY PATTERNS
convinced (that)

sure that something is true: *I **became convinced that** Sarah was lying to me.* • *I'm convinced we're going the wrong way.*

con•vinc•ing /kən'vɪnsɪŋ/ *adjective* a convincing argument, story etc makes you believe that something is true or right: *There was convincing evidence that he was guilty.*

con•voy /'kɒnvɔɪ $ 'kɑnvɔɪ/ *noun* a group of vehicles or ships travelling together

cook¹ /kʊk/ *verb*
1 to prepare food to eat, by heating it, mixing things together etc: *Shall I cook an omelette for you?* • *You should learn to cook while you're young.*
2 if food cooks, you heat it until it is ready to eat: *How long does the rice take to cook?*

cook² *noun* someone who prepares and cooks food: *My sister is an excellent cook.*

cook•er /'kʊkə $ 'kʊkɚ/ *noun BrE* a large piece of kitchen equipment that you use for cooking food SYNONYM **stove** *AmE*

WORD CHOICE
cooker or **cook**?
• A **cook** is a person who prepares food for people to eat: *My Dad is a*

very good **cook** (=he is very good at cooking).
• A **cooker** is the equipment that you use for cooking: *I left the pan on the* **cooker** (=stove).

cook·e·ry /ˈkʊkəri/ *noun* (no plural) *BrE* the skill or activity of cooking food: *I really enjoyed cookery at school.*

cook·ie /ˈkʊki/ the American word for BISCUIT

cook·ing /ˈkʊkɪŋ/ *noun* (no plural) the activity of cooking food ➔ see picture on page A4

cool¹ /kuːl/ *adjective*
1 slightly cold, especially in a nice way ANTONYM **warm**: *It was hot in the day, but pleasantly cool at night.* • *After his run, he had a shower and a long, cool drink.* ➔ see Thesaurus at COLD¹
2 calm, rather than nervous or excited: *She tried to* **stay cool** *and not panic.*
3 (spoken, informal) if you say that someone or something is cool, you like or admire them: *It was a really cool party last night.*

cool² *verb* **1** also **cool down** to become colder, or to make something do this: *Remove the cake from the oven and allow it to cool.* **2 cool down** to become calm after being angry: *By the time we got home, I had cooled down.*

cooped up /ˌkuːpt ˈʌp/ *adjective* if you are cooped up somewhere, you are kept for too long in a place that is too small: *He kept his dogs cooped up in a kennel.*

co·op·e·rate also **co-operate** *BrE* /kəʊˈɒpəreɪt $ koʊˈɑpəˌreɪt/ *verb* to work with someone, or do what they ask you to do, in order to achieve something: *Parents are co-operating with teachers to deal with the problem of bullying in schools.*

co·op·e·ra·tion also **co-operation** *BrE* /kəʊˌɒpəˈreɪʃən $ koʊˌɑpəˈreɪʃən/ *noun* (no plural) when you work with someone else, or do what they ask you to do, in order to achieve something: *Thank you for your co-operation.*

co·op·e·ra·tive also **co-operative** *BrE* /kəʊˈɒpərətɪv $ koʊˈɑprətɪv/ *adjective* willing to help: *The children were all cooperative and polite.*

co·or·di·nate¹ also **co-ordinate** *BrE* /kəʊˈɔːdəneɪt $ koʊˈɔrdnˌeɪt/ *verb* to organize all the different things and people involved in an activity: *I'm responsible for co-ordinating training courses.*

co·or·di·nate² also **co-ordinate** *BrE* /kəʊˈɔːdənət $ koʊˈɔrdənət/ *noun* one of a set of numbers that give an exact position on a map

cop /kɒp $ kɑp/ *noun* (informal) a police officer

cope /kəʊp $ koʊp/ *verb*

KEY PATTERNS
cope with something

to manage a difficult situation successfully: *It isn't easy,* **coping with** *four kids and a job.* • *If you're having problems with college work, we're here to help you cope.*

cop·per /ˈkɒpə $ ˈkɑpɚ/ *noun* **1** (no plural) a brown metal: *copper pipes* **2** *BrE* (informal) a police officer

cop·y¹ /ˈkɒpi $ ˈkɑpi/ *noun* (plural **copies**)

KEY PATTERNS
a copy of something

something that is exactly the same as another thing, because someone has made it like that: *Could you* **make a copy of** *this report?*

copy² *verb* (**copied**, **copies**)
1 to do exactly the same thing as someone else has done: *Other companies are likely to copy the idea.*
2 to make something that is exactly the same as another thing: *She was copying a picture from a book.*

cor·al /ˈkɒrəl $ ˈkɔrəl/ *noun* (no plural) a hard substance formed from the bones of small sea animals: *Many fish live around this* **coral reef** (=large area of coral).

cord /kɔːd $ kɔrd/ *noun* **1** a type of strong thick string **2** *AmE* an electrical wire that you use to connect a piece of equipment to a supply of electricity

core /kɔː $ kɔr/ *noun* **1** the central or most important part of something: *the Earth's core* • *The core subjects we teach are English and maths.* **2** the hard part in the middle of an apple or similar fruit

A B C D E F G H I J K L M N O P Q R S T U V W X Y Z

co·ri·an·der /ˌkɒriˈændə $ ˈkɔriˌændɚ/ *noun* (no plural) *BrE* a plant with leaves or seeds that you add to food to give it a pleasant taste

cork /kɔːk $ kɔrk/ *noun* a round piece of soft wood, used to close a bottle

cork·screw /ˈkɔːkskruː $ ˈkɔrkskru/ *noun* the tool you use to pull a cork out of a bottle

corn /kɔːn $ kɔrn/ *noun* **1** (no plural) *BrE* plants such as wheat that produce seeds for making flour, or the seeds they produce: *a field of corn* **2** the American word for MAIZE

corner

There is a shop on the corner.

cor·ner /ˈkɔːnə $ ˈkɔrnɚ/ *noun* **1** the place where two edges, surfaces, or walls join each other at an angle: *Mick was sitting on his own **in a corner of** the room.* **2** the place where two roads join each other at an angle: *There's a cake shop **on the corner of** Church Lane and Mill Street.* • *Sam was waiting for me just **around the corner**.*

corn·flakes /ˈkɔːnfleɪks $ ˈkɔrnfleɪks/ *plural noun* small dry pieces of corn that you eat mixed with milk for breakfast

cor·o·na·tion /ˌkɒrəˈneɪʃən $ ˌkɔrəˈneɪʃən/ *noun* a ceremony to make someone king or queen: *the coronation of Elizabeth II*

cor·po·ral /ˈkɔːpərəl $ ˈkɔrpərəl/ *noun* a soldier who has a low rank in the army

cor·po·ra·tion /ˌkɔːpəˈreɪʃən $ ˌkɔrpəˈreɪʃən/ *noun* a large business organization

corpse /kɔːps $ kɔrps/ *noun* a dead body

cor·rect¹ /kəˈrekt/ *adjective* right or without a mistake ANTONYM **incorrect**: *In the test all my answers were correct.* • *Have you filled in the correct form?* —**correctly** *adverb*

correct² *verb* if a teacher corrects a student's work, they make marks on it to show where it is wrong: *Mrs Young was correcting the class's maths papers.*

cor·rec·tion /kəˈrekʃən/ *noun* a change that needs to be made to a piece of writing: *"Please **do** your **corrections** for homework," Mr Murray said.* • *The editor of the newspaper published a correction, apologising for the mistake.*

cor·re·spond /ˌkɒrəˈspɒnd $ ˌkɔrəˈspɑnd/ *verb* (formal) **1** if two things correspond, they are similar in some way: *Sally's description of the accident corresponded with mine.* **2** if two people correspond, they write to each other: *We started to correspond in 1989.*

cor·re·spon·dence /ˌkɒrəˈspɒndəns $ ˌkɔrəˈspɑndəns/ *noun* (no plural) (formal) letters that people write: *The company has not replied to my correspondence.*

cor·re·spon·dent /ˌkɒrəˈspɒndənt $ ˌkɔrəˈspɑndənt/ *noun* a news reporter: *an overseas correspondent*

cor·ri·dor /ˈkɒrədɔː $ ˈkɔrədɚ/ *noun* a long narrow passage in a building

cor·rupt¹ /kəˈrʌpt/ *adjective* **1** a corrupt person or organization is dishonest: *a corrupt government* **2** if a computer FILE is corrupt, the information in it is damaged and you cannot read it

corrupt² *verb* **1** to encourage someone to behave in a way that is bad, not honest, or not fair: *I think that television corrupts the young.* **2** if a computer FILE is corrupted, the information in it is damaged and you cannot read it

cor·rup·tion /kəˈrʌpʃən/ *noun* (no plural) behaviour that is not honest or fair: *The president was accused of corruption.*

cos·met·ic /kɒzˈmetɪk $ kɑzˈmetɪk/ *adjective* cosmetic products or medical treatments are designed to improve your appearance: *He had cosmetic surgery to make his nose smaller.*

cos•met•ics /kɒzˈmetɪks $ kɑzˈmetɪks/ *plural noun* products that you put on your skin to improve your appearance: *She spends a lot on cosmetics, especially lipstick.*

cost¹ /kɒst $ kɔst/ *noun* the amount of money that you have to pay in order to buy, do, or produce something: ***The cost of** accommodation in the city centre is very high.*

PHRASES

the cost of living the amount of money that people need in order to buy things they need: ***The cost of living** is increasing all the time.*

THESAURUS

price: *The prices in that shop are very high* (=the amount you must pay to buy something).
charge: *In a restaurant, there's often an extra **charge** for service* (=an amount you must pay).
fee: *The museum is open every day and the entrance **fee** is £7* (=the amount you pay to go in). • *Did you have to pay legal **fees*** (=an amount you pay a lawyer, doctor etc for the work they do for you)?
fare: *How much is the bus **fare*** (=an amount you pay to travel somewhere)?

cost² *verb* (past tense and past participle **cost**)

KEY PATTERNS

cost (someone) £10/$20 etc
it costs £10/$20 etc to do something

if something costs a particular amount, that is the amount you have to pay for it: *How much do these jeans cost?* • *This coat only cost me $30.* • ***It costs** ten pounds **to** get into the club.*

co-star /ˈkəʊ stɑː $ ˈkoʊ stɑr/ *verb* (**co-starred**, **co-starring**) if a film co-stars two people, or they co-star in it, they both have important parts in the film: *The film co-starred Brad Pitt and Angelina Jolie.* —**co-star** *noun*: *The two co-stars hated each other.*

cos•tume /ˈkɒstjʊm $ ˈkɑstum/ *noun* the clothes that an actor wears in a play or film

co•sy *BrE*, **cozy** *AmE* /ˈkəʊzi $ ˈkoʊzi/ *adjective* (**cosier**, **cosiest**) warm and comfortable: *It's really cosy in this bed.*

cot /kɒt $ kɑt/ *noun* **1** *BrE* a baby's bed with high sides SYNONYM **crib** *AmE* → see picture at BED **2** *AmE* a narrow bed that you can fold up

cot•tage /ˈkɒtɪdʒ $ ˈkɑtɪdʒ/ *noun* a small house in the country

cot•ton /ˈkɒtn $ ˈkɑtn/ *noun* (no plural) **1** cloth or thread made from the cotton plant: *a cotton dress* **2** the American word for COTTON WOOL

ˌcotton ˈwool *noun BrE* a soft piece of cotton that you use for cleaning your skin or putting liquids on it SYNONYM **cotton** *AmE*: *Wipe the wound with damp cotton wool.*

couch /kaʊtʃ/ *noun* (plural **couches**) a long comfortable seat that you can sit or lie on SYNONYM **sofa**

cough¹ /kɒf $ kɔf/ *verb* if you cough, air suddenly comes out of your throat with a short sound, for example because you are ill: *Smoking makes you cough.*

cough² *noun* **1** the action or sound of someone coughing once: *She gave a nervous cough before she spoke.* **2** an illness that makes you cough a lot: *Tom's got a really bad cough – he should see a doctor.*

PRONUNCIATION

You pronounce **cough** like 'off'.

could /kəd; strong kʊd/ *modal verb*
1 used to say that someone or something was able to do something in the past: *My brother couldn't read or write until he was eight.* • *Ellis drank his tea as fast as he could.* • *Nothing could change Dad's mind once he'd decided something.*
2 if something could happen in the future or be true, it is possible: *Don't park the car there – it could cause an accident.* • *Those berries could be poisonous.*
3 if something could have happened, it was possible in the past, but it did not happen: *What a silly thing to do! I **could have** been killed!*
4 used when asking politely: *Could I have another coffee, please?* • *Could you explain what you mean?*

5 used when suggesting something: *We could go to see a film.* • *You could ask your teacher for help.*
6 used to say that someone saw something, heard something etc: *I could hear someone in the garden last night.*

GRAMMAR
The negative of **could** is **couldn't** or **could not**.

could·n't /ˈkʊdnt/ the short form of 'could not': *I couldn't open the door.*

could·'ve /ˈkʊdəv/ the short form of 'could have': *I wish I could've spent more time with my sister.*

coun·cil /ˈkaʊnsəl/ *noun* a group of people that have been elected to do a particular job: *the UN Security Council*

coun·cil·lor *BrE*, **councilor** *AmE* /ˈkaʊnsələ $ ˈkaʊnsələr/ *noun* a member of a council: *Councillor Bill Roberts*

coun·sel·ling *BrE*, **counseling** *AmE* /ˈkaʊnsəlɪŋ/ *noun* (no plural) the job of giving people help and advice about their personal problems: *She is trained in counselling and therapy.*

coun·sel·lor *BrE*, **counselor** *AmE* /ˈkaʊnsələ $ ˈkaʊnsələr/ *noun* someone whose job is to help and advise people with personal problems

count¹ /kaʊnt/ *verb*

KEY PATTERNS
count things
count to 10/20 etc

1 also **count up** to discover the exact number of things or people in a group by adding them together: *I **counted up** the number of hours I watched TV each day.* • *There were so many cars in the car park, I couldn't count them all.*
2 to say numbers one after another in the right order: *Tom was only two, but he could already **count to** 20.*
3 to include something when you are adding up a total amount: *I have 23 CDs, counting these new ones.*
4 if something counts, it is important or accepted in a situation: *Everyone's opinion counts.*

PHRASAL VERBS
count on
count on someone/something to expect or be sure that someone will do what you need them to do or that something will happen: *If you need any help, you can **count on** me.*

count² *noun* **1 lose count** if you lose count when you are counting something, you forget the number you reached, and so do not know what the total is: *She's **lost count of** the number of cats she has owned.* **2** a man from Europe with a high social rank: *the Count of Luxembourg*

count·a·ble /ˈkaʊntəbəl/ *adjective* in grammar, a countable noun has a singular and a plural form. 'Table' (plural 'tables') and 'man' (plural 'men') are examples of countable nouns
ANTONYM **uncountable**

count·down /ˈkaʊntdaʊn/ *noun* when numbers are counted backwards to one or zero: *The countdown for the launch of the space shuttle began.*

coun·ter /ˈkaʊntə $ ˈkaʊntər/ *noun*
1 a long table in a shop where someone working in the shop serves you **2** a small round object used in some games

coun·ter·clock·wise /ˌkaʊntəˈklɒkwaɪz $ ˌkaʊntərˈklɑkwaɪz/ the American word for ANTICLOCKWISE

coun·tess /ˈkaʊntəs/ *noun* (plural **countesses**) a woman from Europe with a high social rank

count·less /ˈkaʊntləs/ *adjective* very many: *Countless lives are lost on our roads each year.*

coun·try /ˈkʌntri/ *noun* (plural **countries**)
1 an area of land that has its own government and people: *How many countries are there in Europe?*
2 the country areas that are not near towns or cities: *Do you prefer living in the town or **the country**?*

WORD CHOICE
country or **nation**?
• You use **country** about an area of land: *The company has offices all over the **country**.*
• You use **nation** about the people who live there: *President Kennedy's death shocked the whole **nation**.*

ˈcountry ˌmusic also **ˌcountry and ˈwestern** *noun* (no plural) a type of popular music from the US

coun·try·side /ˈkʌntrisaɪd/ *noun* (no plural) land that is not near towns or cities: *a walk in the countryside*

coun·ty /ˈkaʊnti/ *noun* (plural **counties**) an area in Britain, Ireland, or the US with its own local government

coup /kuː/ *noun* **1** also **coup d'é·tat** /ˌkuː deɪˈtɑː $ ˌku deˈtɑ/ when a group of people take control of a country by force: *a military coup* **2** a very good achievement: *Getting such a big star to give a talk at the school was a real coup.*

cou·ple /ˈkʌpəl/ *noun*
two people who are married or having a romantic relationship: *Sally and Dave are a nice couple.* ➔ see Thesaurus at TWO

PHRASES

a couple of people/things (spoken) two or a few people or things: *There were **a couple of** men standing at the door.* • *Linda appeared **a couple of** minutes later.* ➔ see Thesaurus at TWO

cou·pon /ˈkuːpɒn $ ˈkupɑn/ *noun* **1** a ticket that you can use instead of money: *Collect three coupons for a free jar of coffee.* **2** a printed form in a newspaper or magazine that you fill in and send to a company to order things, enter a competition etc

cour·age /ˈkʌrɪdʒ $ ˈkɚɪdʒ/ *noun* (no plural) the quality of not feeling or showing fear in difficult or dangerous situations SYNONYM **bravery**: *It takes courage to admit that you are wrong.*

cou·ra·geous /kəˈreɪdʒəs/ *adjective* very brave: *a courageous man* —**courageously** *adverb*: *The firefighters acted courageously.*

cour·gette /kʊəˈʒet $ kʊrˈʒet/ *noun* *BrE* a long green vegetable SYNONYM **zucchini** *AmE* ➔ see picture on page A6

cou·ri·er /ˈkʊriə $ ˈkʊriɚ/ *noun*
1 someone whose job is to take and deliver letters and packages **2** *BrE* someone whose job is to help people who are on holiday with a travel company

course /kɔːs $ kɔrs/ *noun*

KEY PATTERNS
a course in accountancy/ engineering etc
take/do a course

1 a set of lessons about a subject: *I'd like to **take a course in** business studies.*
2 one of the parts of a meal: *We had soup for the first course.* • *a three-course meal*
3 a place where people play golf or races take place: *We stood on the edge of the race course as the horses galloped past.*
4 the direction that a plane, ship etc moves in: *The ship **changed course** and headed west.*
5 during the course of something, in the course of something while something is happening: *We got to know each other really well **during the course of** the holiday.*

PHRASES

of course, of course not (spoken) used to say 'yes' or 'no' in a strong way: *"Can I come in?" "**Of course**, sit down."* • *"Is something wrong?" "No, **of course not**."*

of course used when something is easy to understand or not surprising: ***Of course**, she was upset when she lost the game.*

ˈcourse-book *noun* a book that students use to learn a subject and that is divided into separate lessons

court /kɔːt $ kɔrt/ *noun*

KEY PATTERNS
appear/give evidence in court

1 the people who make a legal judgment, for example about whether someone is guilty of a crime, or a place where these judgments are made: *The court rejected the charges against him.* • *Would you be willing to say that in court?*
2 an area where you play a sport such as tennis: *I've booked a squash court for tonight.*

cour·te·sy /ˈkɜːtəsi $ ˈkɚtəsi/ *noun* (no plural) (formal) polite behaviour

court·house /ˈkɔːthaʊs $ ˈkɔrthaʊs/ *noun AmE* a building containing a room or rooms in which people make legal judgments

court·room /ˈkɔːtruːm $ ˈkɔrtrum/ *noun* a room in which people make legal judgments

court·yard /ˈkɔːtjɑːd $ ˈkɔrtjɑrd/ *noun* an outdoor area surrounded by walls or buildings

A B C D E F G H I J K L M N O P Q R S T U V W X Y Z

cous·in /'kʌzən/ *noun* the son or daughter of your aunt or uncle

cov·er[1] /'kʌvə $ 'kʌvɚ/ *verb*

KEY PATTERNS
cover something with something else

1 also **cover up** to put something over the top of another thing, for example to protect or hide it: *She covered the plate with a cloth.*
2 be covered with/in something if something is covered with something, it has that thing over its whole surface: *The walls of her room* ***are covered with*** *pictures of pop stars.*
3 to lie or fit over the top or surface of something: *the cloth covering the table*
4 to include something: *Does the course cover 19th century literature?*

cover[2] *noun*
1 something that fits over another thing to protect it, keep it clean etc: *Where's the cover for this record?*
2 the front or back part on the outside of a book or magazine: *The price is usually on the back cover.*
3 covers the sheet and other pieces of cloth that cover you when you are in bed

PHRASES
take cover to go somewhere in order to be protected from bad weather or attack: *When the storm started we* ***took cover*** *in a barn.*

THESAURUS
lid: *Where's the* ***lid*** *for this saucepan* (=the cover that fits on it)?
top: *Put the* ***top*** *back on your pen when you're not using it* (=the cover that fits on it).

cov·er·age /'kʌvərɪdʒ/ *noun* (no plural) the amount and type of attention that television, radio, and newspaper reports give to a news event: *The television coverage of the race was excellent.*

cov·er·ing /'kʌvərɪŋ/ *noun* something that covers something else: *wooden floor coverings*

'cover-up *noun* an attempt to stop people finding out the truth: *The government says there has not been a cover-up.*

cow /kaʊ/ *noun* a large animal that is kept on farms for its milk and meat → see picture at HERD[1]

cow·ard /'kaʊəd $ 'kaʊɚd/ *noun* someone who is not brave and who avoids dangerous or difficult situations: *They called me a coward because I wouldn't fight.*

cow·ard·ice /'kaʊədɪs $ 'kaʊɚdɪs/ *noun* (no plural) behaviour that shows you are not brave ANTONYM **bravery**

cow·boy /'kaʊbɔɪ/ *noun* a man whose job is to look after cattle in North America

cozy the American spelling of COSY

crab /kræb/ *noun* a sea animal with a shell and ten legs that walks to the side, not forwards: *a rock pool full of tiny crabs*

crack[1] /kræk/ *verb* **1** if something cracks, or if you crack it, it starts to break and a line appears on its surface: *I dropped the cup and it cracked.* → see Thesaurus at BREAK[1] **2 crack down** to deal very firmly with a particular crime or bad behaviour: *The government plans to crack down on drug dealers.*

crack[2] *noun* **1** a thin line on something that shows it is starting to break: *There's a crack in this mug.* **2** a very narrow space: *The coin fell down a crack in the sidewalk.* **3** a sudden short noise: *the crack of a whip*

crack·down /'krækdaʊn/ *noun* a serious and firm attempt to stop a particular crime or bad behaviour: *The government announced a crackdown on drugs.*

cracked /krækt/ *adjective* a cracked object is damaged and has thin lines on its surface: *These plates are all cracked.*

crack·le /'krækəl/ *verb* (written) to make a lot of short sharp noises: *The fire crackled in the hearth.* **—crackle** *noun*: *the crackle of the radio* → see picture on page A1

cra·dle /'kreɪdl/ *noun* a small bed for a baby

craft /krɑːft $ kræft/ *noun* a skilled activity in which you make something using your hands: *traditional crafts such as woodwork and pottery*

crafts·man /ˈkrɑːftsmən $ ˈkræftsmən/ *noun* (plural **craftsmen** /-mən/) someone whose job is making things skilfully with their hands: *violins made by the country's finest craftsmen*

craft·y /ˈkrɑːfti $ ˈkræfti/ *adjective* (**craftier**, **craftiest**) a crafty person deceives people in a clever way to get what they want: *A crafty football fan had got into the game without paying.* —**craftily** *adverb*: *She had craftily hidden all her sweets.*

cram /kræm/ *verb* (**crammed**, **cramming**) **1** if you cram things into a small space, you put them there so that they completely fill it: *Sally crammed a huge slice of cake into her mouth.*
2 be crammed if a place is crammed with things or people, it is full of them: *The bus was crammed with people.* ➔ see Thesaurus at FULL

cram

cramp /kræmp/ *noun* a bad pain in your muscles

cramped /kræmpt/ *adjective* a cramped place is not big enough for the people or things in it: *Six of us lived in a tiny, cramped apartment.*

crane¹ /kreɪn/ *noun* a large machine with a long metal arm for lifting heavy things: *A crane lifted the box onto the boat.*

crane² *verb* to stretch your neck forwards in order to see something: *Mark craned forward to get a better look.*

crap /kræp/ *noun* (no plural) (informal) a rude word for something that you think is of very bad quality SYNONYM **rubbish**: *The last game I saw was crap.*

crash¹ /kræʃ/ *verb*

KEY PATTERNS
crash into a wall/car/mountain etc

1 if a car, plane etc crashes, it hits something very hard and stops: *The truck ran off the road and* ***crashed into*** *a tree.*
2 if a computer crashes, it suddenly stops working

crash² *noun* (plural **crashes**)
1 an accident in which a car, plane etc hits something hard and stops: *There was a bad crash on the motorway and two people were killed.* ➔ see Thesaurus at ACCIDENT
2 a loud noise, like something suddenly falling down or breaking: *Just then we heard a loud crash in the kitchen.*

ˈcrash ˌcourse *noun* a short course in a subject where you study the most important things very quickly: *I had a crash course in French before I went to live in Paris.*

ˈcrash ˌhelmet *noun* a hard hat that people wear on their heads when they are riding MOTORCYCLES (=bicycles with engines): *By law, motorcyclists must wear crash helmets.*

ˈcrash-land *verb* to land a damaged plane: *The pilot crash-landed in a field.*

crass /kræs/ *adjective* stupid and rude: *Paul made crass comments throughout the film.*

crate /kreɪt/ *noun* a large wooden box: *a crate of champagne* ➔ see picture at CONTAINER

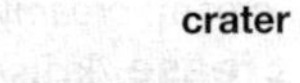

crater

cra·ter /ˈkreɪtə $ ˈkreɪtɚ/ *noun* a large hole in the ground or at the top of a VOLCANO: *Hot lava flowed from the crater.*

crawl¹ /krɔːl/ *verb*
1 to move on your hands and knees: *The baby crawled towards the fire.* **2** if an insect crawls, it moves using its legs: *The spider crawled up my leg.* ➔ see picture on page A2

crawl² *noun* (no plural) a way of swimming in which you move each arm in turn over your head and kick your legs: *Can you do the crawl?*

crayons

cray·on /ˈkreɪən $ ˈkreɪɑn/ *noun* a coloured pencil: *a picture drawn in crayon*

craze /kreɪz/ *noun* something that is very popular for a

A B C D E F G H I J K L M N O P Q R S T U V W X Y Z

short time SYNONYM **fad**: *the latest fashion craze*

cra·zy /ˈkreɪzi/ *adjective* (**crazier**, **craziest**)
strange or silly SYNONYM **mad**: *a crazy idea • He must be crazy to drive his car so fast.*

PHRASES

be crazy about someone/something (informal) to like someone or something very much: *She's crazy about one of the boys in her class.*
go crazy (informal) to become very angry or excited: *The crowd went crazy when the team scored.*

creak /kriːk/ *verb* if something creaks, it makes a long high noise when it moves: *The gate creaked in the wind.* —**creak** *noun*: *the creak of the stairs*
➔ see picture on page A1

cream¹ /kriːm/ *noun* **1** (no plural) a thick white liquid produced from milk: *coffee with cream* **2** a thick smooth substance that you put on your skin: *shaving cream*

cream² *noun, adjective* a yellowish-white colour: *a cream suit*

cream·y /ˈkriːmi/ *adjective* (**creamier**, **creamiest**) containing or looking like cream: *creamy soup*

crease /kriːs/ *verb* if you crease something, or if it creases, lines or folds appear in it: *Try not to crease your skirt. • The new dollar bills had creased in his pocket.* —**crease** *noun*: *an old man with creases around his eyes*

cre·ate /kriˈeɪt/ *verb*
to make something happen or exist: *The new rules will create a lot of problems.* ➔ see Thesaurus at INVENT

cre·a·tion /kriˈeɪʃən/ *noun*
1 something new and different that someone has made: *Her latest fashion creation is a leather skirt.* **2** when something new is made or formed: *the creation of new jobs*

cre·a·tive /kriˈeɪtɪv/ *adjective* **1** a creative person has a lot of new ideas: *a very creative artist* **2** using your imagination: *creative writing* —**creatively** *adverb*: *the ability to think creatively*

cre·a·tiv·i·ty /ˌkriːeɪˈtɪvəti/ *noun* (no plural) the ability to use your imagination: *Many of the children show great creativity in class.*

cre·a·tor /kriˈeɪtə $ kriˈeɪtɚ/ *noun* someone who makes or invents something: *Ian Fleming, the creator of James Bond*

crea·ture /ˈkriːtʃə $ ˈkritʃɚ/ *noun* an animal, fish, or insect: *A pond like this is full of all sorts of living creatures.*

crèche /kreʃ/ *noun BrE* a place where someone is responsible for babies whose parents are away for a short time: *Many shopping centres now have a crèche.*

cred·i·bil·i·ty /ˌkredəˈbɪləti/ *noun* (no plural) if someone has credibility, other people believe and trust them: *The company lost credibility with its customers.*

cred·it¹ /ˈkredɪt/ *noun* **1** (no plural) a system in which you receive things and pay for them later: *She was refused credit by all the major banks.* **2** (no plural) praise you give to someone for doing something: *They deserve a lot of credit for finishing the project on time.* **3 be in credit** if your bank account is in credit, there is money in it **4 the credits** a list of the people who made a television programme or film

credit² *verb* if someone is credited with doing something good, people say that they did it: *The film's success can be credited to its director.*

ˈcredit ˌcard *noun* a small plastic card that you use to buy things and pay for them later: *You can pay by cash or by credit card.*

creep /kriːp/ *verb* (past tense and past participle **crept** /krept/) **1** to move very quietly and slowly: *She crept outside.* **2 creep up** (written) to increase slowly: *The number of people without jobs crept up to two million.*

creeps /kriːps/ *plural noun* **give someone the creeps** (informal) to make someone feel nervous or frightened: *That man gives me the creeps!*

creep·y /ˈkriːpi/ *adjective* (**creepier**, **creepiest**) slightly frightening: *a creepy ghost story*

cre·mate /krəˈmeɪt $ ˈkrimeɪt/ *verb* to burn the body of a dead person: *He will be cremated on Saturday.*

cre·ma·tion /krɪˈmeɪʃən/ *noun* when a dead person's body is burned: *a cremation service*

crept the past tense and past participle of CREEP

cres·cent /ˈkresənt/ *noun* **1** a curved shape that is wider in the middle and pointed at the ends: *The moon was a perfect crescent shape.* **2 Crescent** used in the names of some small curved streets: *number 5, Cherry Crescent* → see picture at SHAPE[1]

crest /krest/ *noun* the top of a hill or wave: *We reached the crest of the hill and looked down.*

crev·ice /ˈkrevɪs/ *noun* a narrow crack, especially in rock: *These plants grow in crevices in rock.*

crew /kruː/ *noun* a group of people who work together: *The crew of the plane are trained in fire safety procedures.*

crib /krɪb/ the American word for COT

crick·et /ˈkrɪkɪt/ *noun* **1** (no plural) a game in which two teams of eleven players each get points by hitting a ball and running between two sets of sticks **2** an insect that makes a short loud noise by rubbing its wings together

crime /kraɪm/ *noun* an illegal action: *Anyone who* ***commits a crime*** *must be punished.* • *Crime in our cities is increasing.*

USAGE
You say **commit a crime**.
✗ Don't say 'do a crime'.

crim·i·nal[1] /ˈkrɪmənəl/ *adjective* related to crime: *criminal activities*

criminal[2] *noun* someone who has done something illegal: *The police want to catch these criminals before they hurt more people.*

crim·son /ˈkrɪmzən/ *adjective, noun* a dark red colour: *crimson lipstick*

cringe /krɪndʒ/ *verb* to feel embarrassed by something: *Some of the things she says make me cringe.*

crip·ple /ˈkrɪpəl/ *verb* **1** to hurt someone so they can no longer walk: *She was crippled in a car accident.* **2** to damage something or make it much weaker: *These policies have crippled the education system.*

cri·sis /ˈkraɪsɪs/ *noun* (plural **crises** /-siːz/)

KEY PATTERNS
be in crisis

a situation in which someone or something has very bad problems: *an economic crisis* • *He had to go and deal with a crisis at home.* • *The car industry* ***is in crisis.***

crisp[1] /krɪsp/ *adjective* **1** fresh, firm, and pleasant to eat: *Bake the pie until the top is crisp and golden.*
2 pleasantly clean and fresh: *crisp new dollar bills*

crisp[2] *noun BrE* a very thin piece of potato cooked in hot oil and eaten cold SYNONYM **chip** *AmE*: *a bag of crisps*

crisp·y /ˈkrɪspi/ *adjective* (**crispier, crispiest**) crispy food is pleasantly hard: *crispy fried bacon*

cri·te·ri·a /kraɪˈtɪəriə $ kraɪˈtɪriə/ *plural noun* (formal) facts or standards that you use to help you decide something: *What are the college's criteria for the selection of students?*

crit·ic /ˈkrɪtɪk/ *noun* someone whose job is to give their opinion about films, books etc: *The critics praised the play highly.*

crit·i·cal /ˈkrɪtɪkəl/ *adjective*
1 saying that you think a person or thing is bad or wrong: *Dad's very critical of the way I dress.* **2** very serious or important: *It's critical that you get your essays in on time.*
—**critically** /-kli/ *adverb*: *He looked critically at my crumpled dress.* • *Ged was critically ill in hospital.*

crit·i·cis·m /ˈkrɪtəsɪzəm/ *noun*

KEY PATTERNS
criticism of something

when you say that a person or thing is bad in some way ANTONYM **praise**: *She is upset by* ***criticism.*** • *He disagreed with the teacher's* ***criticisms of*** *his work.*

A B C D E F G H I J K L M N O P Q R S T U V W X Y Z

crit·i·cize also **criticise** *BrE* /ˈkrɪtəsaɪz/ *verb*

KEY PATTERNS
criticize someone/something
criticize someone for doing something

to say that someone or something is bad in some way ANTONYM **praise**: *She criticizes everything I do.* • *My parents are always **criticizing** me **for** spending too much money.*

croak /krəʊk $ kroʊk/ *verb* (written) to make a deep low sound in your throat: *"My throat is sore," she croaked.*

crockery

crock·e·ry /ˈkrɒkəri $ ˈkrɑkəri/ *noun* (no plural) cups, plates, dishes etc

croc·o·dile /ˈkrɒkədaɪl $ ˈkrɑkəˌdaɪl/ *noun* a large animal with a long body, short legs, a big mouth, and very sharp teeth, that lives mainly in water → see picture on page A9

crook /krʊk/ *noun* (informal) a criminal: *Don't trust Ben – he's a crook.*

crook·ed /ˈkrʊkɪd/ *adjective* something that is crooked is not straight, but it should be: *The picture on the wall was crooked.*

crop¹ /krɒp $ krɑp/ *noun* a plant that a farmer grows: *The main crop grown here is barley.*

crop² *verb* (**cropped**, **cropping**) **crop up** (informal) to happen suddenly: *A problem has just cropped up.*

cross¹ /krɒs $ krɔs/ *verb*

KEY PATTERNS
cross (over) a road/river/bridge etc
cross a room

1 to go from one side of a road, river, room etc to the other: *Hold Daddy's hand while we cross the road.* • *Thousands of refugees had crossed the border.* • *We had **crossed over** the bridge safely.* • *A small boy was waiting to cross, so I stopped the car.*

cross

with your legs crossed

cross-legged

2 if roads or lines cross, they go across each other: *Draw two lines that cross each other at an angle of 60 degrees.*

PHRASES

cross your legs to put one leg on top of the other, when sitting down

PHRASAL VERBS

cross off

cross something off (something) to remove something from a list: *I asked the committee to **cross** my name **off** the list of volunteers.* • *We've tidied the bookshelves and cleaned the desks, so we can **cross** them **off** the list.*

cross out

cross something out to draw a line through something that you have written because it is wrong: *If you make a mistake, just **cross it out**.*

cross² *noun* (plural **crosses**)

1 *BrE* a mark (X) that you make on paper, especially to show that something that is written is not correct: *The teacher had put a cross by three of my answers.*

2 a shape or object that is an important sign for Christians, which has a long upright part with a shorter part crossing it near the top: *He always wore a gold cross round his neck.*

cross³ *adjective BrE* angry: *Please don't be cross with me.*

ˌcross-ˈcountry *adjective* cross-country running involves running across fields and not along a road or track: *a cross-country race*

ˌcross-exˈamine *verb* to ask someone questions about something they have just said in a court of law: *The lawyer cross-examined the witness for an hour.*

ˌ**cross-'eyed** / $ '. ./ *adjective* if someone is cross-eyed, their eyes look towards their nose

cross·ing /'krɒsɪŋ $ 'krɔsɪŋ/ *noun* **1** a place where you can safely cross a road: *We waited at the crossing.* **2** a journey across the sea: *It was a rough crossing.*

cross-leg·ged /ˌkrɒs 'legɪd $ ˌkrɔs 'legɪd/ *adverb, adjective* sitting with your knees wide apart and your feet crossed: *We sat cross-legged on the floor.*

ˌ**cross-'reference** / $ '. ˌ.../ *noun* a note in a book that tells you where to look in the same book for more information

cross·roads /'krɒsrəʊdz $ 'krɔsroudz/ *noun* (plural **crossroads**) a place where two roads cross each other: *Turn right at the crossroads.*

'**cross** ˌ**section**, **cross-section** *noun* **1** a drawing of what something looks like inside by showing it as if it has been cut into two pieces: *a cross section of the ship showing all the levels* **2** a group of people or things that is similar to a larger group: *The students here are a cross-section of the local community.*

cross·walk /'krɒswɔːk $ 'krɔswɔk/ the American word for PEDESTRIAN CROSSING

cross·word /'krɒswɜːd $ 'krɔsˌwərd/ also '**crossword** ˌ**puzzle** *noun* a game in which you try to write the correct words in a pattern of spaces: *I love doing crosswords.*

crouch /kraʊtʃ/ also **crouch down** *verb* to bend your knees and back so that you are close to the ground: *He crouched behind a bush so that he couldn't be seen.* ➔ see picture on page A3

crowd /kraʊd/ *noun* a large number of people in one place: *There was a* ***crowd of*** *people waiting for the film star to come out.* ➔ see Thesaurus at GROUP[1]

crowd·ed /'kraʊdɪd/ *adjective* a place that is crowded is full of people: *a crowded beach* ➔ see Thesaurus at FULL

crown[1] /kraʊn/ *noun* a circle made of gold and jewels that a king or queen wears on their head: *The Queen only wears her crown on official occasions.*

crown[2] *verb* to place a crown on someone's head, so that they officially become king or queen: *They crowned him King of England.*

cru·cial /'kruːʃəl/ *adjective* very important: *It is crucial that we act quickly.* ➔ see Thesaurus at IMPORTANT

Cru·ci·fix·ion /ˌkruːsə'fɪkʃən/ *noun* **the Crucifixion** the death of Christ on the cross

crude /kruːd/ *adjective* **1** rude, especially about sex: *crude jokes* **2** made in a simple way from simple parts: *They made a crude shelter out of branches.*

cru·el /'kruːəl/ *adjective* (**crueller**, **cruellest** *BrE*, **crueler**, **cruelest** *AmE*) someone who is cruel deliberately treats people or animals in a very unkind way: *I think it's cruel to keep wild animals in zoos.* • *That was a really cruel thing to say.* ➔ see Thesaurus at UNKIND —**cruelly** *adverb*

cru·el·ty /'kruːəlti/ *noun* actions that deliberately hurt people or animals: ***Cruelty to*** *animals is against the law.*

cruise[1] /kruːz/ *verb* **1** to sail along slowly: *They spent the summer cruising the Mediterranean Sea.* **2** to move along at a steady speed in a car, plane etc: *The plane will be cruising at 30,000 feet.*

cruise[2] *noun* a holiday on a large ship: *They went on a Caribbean cruise.*

crumb /krʌm/ *noun* a very small piece of bread, cake etc: *She wiped the crumbs off the table.*

PRONUNCIATION
In this word you do not pronounce the **b**.

crum·ble /'krʌmbəl/ *verb* to break into small pieces: *The rocks here are crumbling into the sea.*

A B C D E F G H I J K L M N O P Q R S T U V W X Y Z

A B C D E F G H I J K L M N O P Q R S T U V W X Y Z

crum·ple /ˈkrʌmpəl/ *verb* to crush paper or cloth so that it is folded in an untidy way: *You're crumpling my shirt.* —**crumpled** *adjective*: *a crumpled handkerchief*

crumple

crunch¹ /krʌntʃ/ *verb* to make a noise like something being crushed: *The snow crunched under our feet.* ➔ see picture on page A1

crunch² *noun* (no plural) **1** a noise like something being crushed: *There was a crunch as the car hit the post.* **2 the crunch** (informal) the moment when you must make an important decision or a special effort: *The crunch came when her husband asked her to leave her job.*

crunch·y /ˈkrʌntʃi/ *adjective* (**crunchier**, **crunchiest**) food that is crunchy is pleasantly hard: *a crunchy apple*

crush¹ /krʌʃ/ *verb* to press something so hard that it breaks or is damaged: *He crushed the paper cup and threw it in the bin.* ➔ see Thesaurus at PRESS¹ ➔ see picture on page A4

crush² *noun* (plural **crushes**) **1** when a young person feels love for someone they are unlikely to have a relationship with: *She had a crush on the captain of the school football team.* **2** a crowd of people very close together: *There was a real crush by the door.*

crust /krʌst/ *noun* the hard part on the outside of something, especially bread: *He cut the crust off his sandwiches.* • *the Earth's crust*

crutch /krʌtʃ/ *noun* (plural **crutches**) a stick that you use to help you walk when you have hurt your leg: *Ian was on crutches for a month after the accident.*

cry¹ /kraɪ/ *verb* (**cried**, **cries**)

KEY PATTERNS
cry for help/mercy

1 if you are crying, tears are coming from your eyes because you are sad or hurt: *Maria read the letter and started to cry.*
2 also **cry out** (written) to shout something: *"Help!" he cried. "I can't swim!"* • *Mandy* ***cried for help****, but no-one could hear her.* ➔ see Thesaurus at SHOUT¹

cry out (written)
to make a loud sound, for example because you are afraid or hurt: *Sam fell over and* ***cried out*** *in pain.*

THESAURUS
in tears: *The little girl was* ***in tears*** *because she was lost* (=crying).
burst into tears: *She read the letter and* ***burst into tears*** (=suddenly started crying).
weep (formal): *The woman was* ***weeping*** *over her dead son* (=crying a lot because of great sadness).

cry² *noun* (written) (plural **cries**) a loud sound that a person or bird makes: *We could hear the cries of the people who were trapped in the burning building.*

cryp·tic /ˈkrɪptɪk/ *adjective* having a meaning that is not clear: *a cryptic message*

crys·tal /ˈkrɪstl/ *noun* **1** an amount of a substance in a regular shape that forms naturally: *sugar crystals* **2** (no plural) high quality glass: *a crystal vase*

cub /kʌb/ *noun* a young bear, lion etc

cube¹ /kjuːb/ *noun* **1** a solid object with six equal square sides: *ice cubes* **2** the number you get when you multiply a number by itself twice: *27 is the cube of 3.*

cube² *verb* to multiply a number by itself twice: *4 cubed is 64.*

cu·bic /ˈkjuːbɪk/ *adjective* relating to a measurement of space which is calculated by multiplying the length of something by its width and height: *A thousand cubic metres of rock fell into the bay.*

cu·bi·cle /ˈkjuːbɪkəl/ *noun* a small private area or room, for example where someone can change their clothes: *the changing cubicles at the swimming pool*

cu·cum·ber /ˈkjuːkʌmbə $ ˈkjuˌkʌmbɚ/ *noun* a long round vegetable with a dark green skin that you do not cook: *a cucumber and tomato salad* → see picture on page A6

cud·dle /ˈkʌdl/ *verb* to hold your arms around someone or something that you love: *The little girl was cuddling a doll.* —**cuddle** *noun*: *His mother gave him a cuddle.*

cuddle

cue /kjuː/ *noun* **1** a long thin stick used for hitting the ball in games such as POOL **2** an action or event that is a sign for something else to happen: *His girlfriend's arrival was our cue to leave.*

cuff /kʌf/ *noun* the end of a sleeve: *The cuffs of his shirt were dirty.*

cul-de-sac /ˈkʌl də ˌsæk/ *noun* a street which is closed at one end

cul·mi·nate /ˈkʌlməneɪt/ *verb* (formal) **culminate in something** to have an important event at the end: *The holiday culminated in a terrible argument.*

cul·prit /ˈkʌlprɪt/ *noun* a person who has done something wrong: *The man whose car was damaged was determined to find the culprits.*

cult /kʌlt/ *noun* **1** a small religion whose members have unusual views: *a member of an extreme religious cult* **2** (no plural) a film, band etc that has become very popular among a particular group of people: *It has become a cult film among students.*

cul·ti·vate /ˈkʌltəveɪt/ *verb* to prepare and use land for growing plants for food

cul·tu·ral /ˈkʌltʃərəl/ *adjective* **1** connected with a particular society and its way of life: *the cultural differences between England and Pakistan* **2** related to art, literature, music etc: *There aren't many cultural events in this town.* —**culturally** *adverb*: *a culturally diverse society*

cul·ture /ˈkʌltʃə $ ˈkʌltʃɚ/ *noun* **1** the ideas, behaviour, beliefs etc of a particular society: *You have to spend time in a country if you want to understand its culture.* • *the many differences between the two cultures* **2** (no plural) art, music, literature etc: *I prefer living in a big city, where there's plenty of culture.*

cul·tured /ˈkʌltʃəd $ ˈkʌltʃɚd/ *adjective* knowing a lot about art, literature, music etc

cum·ber·some /ˈkʌmbəsəm $ ˈkʌmbɚsəm/ *adjective* difficult to move or use: *a large, cumbersome bag*

cun·ning /ˈkʌnɪŋ/ *adjective* clever, especially in a rather dishonest way: *a cunning plan* —**cunningly** *adverb*: *He cunningly persuaded his wife to stay at home.*

cup

rim
saucer
mug
cup

cup /kʌp/ *noun* **1** a small container with a handle that you drink from: *Would you like a cup of tea?* **2** a metal container that is given as a prize in a competition, or the competition itself: *Who do you think will win the European Cup?*

cup·board /ˈkʌbəd $ ˈkʌbɚd/ *noun* a piece of furniture with a door and shelves for storing things: *I'm going to clean the kitchen cupboards.*

PRONUNCIATION
In this word you do not pronounce the **p**. The stress is on the first syllable.

curb¹ /kɜːb $ kɚb/ the American spelling of KERB

curb² *verb* to control or limit something: *You must curb your spending.*

cure¹ /kjʊə $ kjʊr/ *verb* to remove an illness or injury: *The doctors are sure they can cure him.*

cure² *noun* a medicine or treatment that can remove an illness: *We have not yet found a cure for this type of cancer.*

cu·ri·os·i·ty /ˌkjʊəriˈɒsəti $ ˌkjʊriˈɑsəti/ *noun* (no plural) the wish to know about something: *His parents showed no curiosity about where he had been.*

> **SPELLING**
> This word is often spelled wrongly. The correct spelling is: **curiosity**.

cu·ri·ous /ˈkjʊəriəs $ ˈkjʊriəs/ *adjective*

> **KEY PATTERNS**
> **curious about something**

1 if you are curious about something, you want to know or learn about it: *I was **curious about** how the system worked.* • *The children were excited and curious.*
2 strange or unusual: *There was a curious blue light in the sky.*

curl¹ /kɜːl $ kɚl/ *noun* a piece of hair which curves around: *She has beautiful blond curls.*

curl² *verb* to make hair curve around: *She curled her hair round her finger.*

PHRASAL VERBS

curl up a) to lie or sit comfortably with your legs bent close to your body: *She decided to curl up with a book.* **b)** if paper, leaves etc curl up, the edges bend upwards: *The bottom leaves began to curl up and drop off.*

curl up

curl·y /ˈkɜːli $ ˈkɚli/ *adjective* (**curlier**, **curliest**) curly hair has a lot of curls

cur·ren·cy /ˈkʌrənsi $ ˈkɚənsi/ *noun* (plural **currencies**) the type of money that a country uses: *We need to get some of the local currency before we go on holiday.* → see Thesaurus at MONEY

cur·rent¹ /ˈkʌrənt $ ˈkɚənt/ *adjective* happening or existing at the present time: *I have been in my current job for two years.* —**currently** *adverb*: *He is currently on holiday.* → see Thesaurus at NOW¹

current² *noun* **1** a flow of water or air in a particular direction: *The current swept the boat away.* **2** a flow of electricity through a wire: *an electric current that passes through a coil of wire*

cur·ric·u·lum /kəˈrɪkjələm/ *noun* (plural **curricula** /-lə/ or **curriculums**) the subjects that students learn at a school or college: *Greek will be on the curriculum next term.*

cur·ry /ˈkʌri $ ˈkɚi/ *noun* (plural **curries**) meat or vegetables cooked in a hot-tasting sauce: *chicken curry*

curse¹ /kɜːs $ kɚs/ *verb* (written) to swear in an angry way: *He put the phone down angrily and cursed.*

curse² *noun* **1** (written) a word or words that you use when you are angry: *I could hear his curses from the next room.* **2** magical words that bring someone bad luck: *The witch put a curse on him.*

cur·sor /ˈkɜːsə $ ˈkɚsɚ/ *noun* a shape on a computer screen that moves to show where you are writing: *Put the cursor on the icon and click the mouse.*

cur·tain /ˈkɜːtn $ ˈkɚtn/ *noun* a piece of hanging cloth that you can pull across a window, for example at night time: *Close the curtains.*

curve¹ /kɜːv $ kɚv/ *noun* a line or shape which gradually bends like part of a circle: *They came to a curve in the river.*

curve² *verb* to bend or move in the shape of a curve: *The ball curved through the air into the net.*

curved /kɜːvd $ kɚvd/ *adjective* having the shape of a curve: *a Japanese sword with a curved blade*

cush·ion /ˈkʊʃən/ *noun* a bag filled with soft material that you sit or lie on: *She removed the cushions from the sofa.*

cush·y /ˈkʊʃi/ *adjective* (informal) (**cushier**, **cushiest**) a cushy job or situation is very easy or pleasant

cus·tard /ˈkʌstəd $ ˈkʌstɚd/ *noun* *BrE* a thick, yellow sauce that is poured over sweet foods

cus·to·dy /ˈkʌstədi/ *noun* (no plural) the right to be responsible and care for a child: *His ex-wife has custody of the kids.*

A B C D E F G H I J K L M N O P Q R S T U V W X Y Z

cus•tom /ˈkʌstəm/ *noun*
1 something that people in a particular group or society have done for a long time, and which they continue doing because it is important to them SYNONYM **tradition**: *She follows Islamic custom by covering her hair.* ➔ see Thesaurus at HABIT
2 customs the place where officials examine your bags to make sure you do not have anything illegal in them before you enter or leave a country: *All baggage must* ***go through customs****.*

cus•tom•a•ry /ˈkʌstəməri $ ˈkʌstəˌmeri/ *adjective* usual or normal: *She caught her customary train.*

cus•tom•er /ˈkʌstəmə $ ˈkʌstəmər/ *noun* someone who buys things from a shop or company: *We try to keep our customers happy.*

cut¹ ➔ see box on page 164

cut² *noun*

> KEY PATTERNS
> **a cut in something**

1 a wound that you get when something sharp cuts your skin: *Mum put a plaster over the cut.* ➔ see Thesaurus at INJURY
2 when the size, number, or amount of something is made smaller SYNONYM **reduction**: *a* ***cut in*** *school fees*

cute /kjuːt/ *adjective* pretty or attractive: *her cute little nose*

cut•le•ry /ˈkʌtləri/ *noun* (no plural) knives, forks, and spoons

ˌcut-ˈprice also **ˌcut-ˈrate** *adjective* cheaper than normal: *a shop selling cut-price books*

cut•ting /ˈkʌtɪŋ/ *noun BrE* a piece of writing that you cut from a newspaper or magazine SYNONYM **clipping** *AmE*: *He keeps newspaper cuttings about his favourite football team.*

ˌcutting ˈedge *noun* if you are at the cutting edge of an activity, you are involved in the most recent and most exciting part of its development: *Dr Campbell's work is at the cutting edge of medical science.* —**cutting-edge** *adjective*: *cutting-edge technology*

CV /ˌsiː ˈviː/ *noun BrE* a list of your education and previous jobs that you show companies when you are trying to get a new job SYNONYM **résumé** *AmE*: *Please send an up-to-date CV with your job application.*

cy•ber•space /ˈsaɪbəspeɪs $ ˈsaɪbərˌspeɪs/ *noun* (no plural) a place that is not real where people say electronic messages go when they travel from one computer to another: *He said his email had got lost in cyberspace.*

cy•cle¹ /ˈsaɪkəl/ *noun* **1** a number of events that happen many times in the same order: *the life cycle of the frog*
2 a bicycle or MOTORCYCLE: *He went for a cycle ride.*

cycle² *verb* to ride a bicycle: *She cycled over to Jane's house.* —**cycling** *noun* ➔ see picture on page A14

> USAGE
> When talking about cycling as an activity that you do, you say **go cycling**: *We* ***went cycling*** *in the park.*

cy•clist /ˈsaɪklɪst/ *noun* someone who rides a bicycle: *This part of the road is for cyclists only.*

cy•clone /ˈsaɪkləʊn $ ˈsaɪkloʊn/ *noun* a very strong wind that moves in a circle

cyl•in•der /ˈsɪləndə $ ˈsɪləndər/ *noun* an object or container with circular ends and straight sides

cym•bal /ˈsɪmbəl/ *noun* one of a pair of round metal plates that you hit together or hit with a stick to make a musical sound: *There was a clash of cymbals.*

cyn•ic /ˈsɪnɪk/ *noun* someone who is cynical: *Don't be such a cynic!*

cyn•i•cal /ˈsɪnɪkəl/ *adjective* believing that no one does things for good or honest reasons: *I'm rather cynical about journalists who claim to be helping the public.*

cut /kʌt/ *verb* (past tense and past participle **cut**, present participle **cutting**)

KEY PATTERNS
cut something
cut something into pieces
cut something off
cut yourself/your finger etc

cut

1 to use a knife or scissors to divide something into two or more pieces: *Cut the cheese into cubes.* • *Cut off a corner of the paper.* • *Lisa had her hair cut really short.*

2 to hurt yourself with a knife or something else that is sharp: *I cut my finger chopping carrots.*

3 to make something smaller, especially a number or amount of money SYNONYM **reduce**: *The leader of the party promised to cut taxes.*

THESAURUS
chop: *First, chop the onions* (=cut them into small pieces).
slice: *Can you slice some bread for me* (=cut it into thin pieces)?
carve: *Dad carved the chicken* (=cut meat from it when it had been cooked).
peel: *Shall I peel the potatoes* (=cut the outside part off)?

PHRASAL VERBS

cut back
cut something back to make a number amount, cost, etc smaller: *Ian cut back the number of hours he was working.*

cut down
cut something down to do something less or use less of something: *Recycling bottles helps cut down on waste.*

cut off
1 **cut something off** to stop supplying something to someone: *The US cut off aid to the country.*
2 **be cut off** a) if a place is cut off, it is separated from other places, usually because of bad weather or because it is a long way from other places: *The town was cut off by floods.* b) if you are talking on the telephone and you are cut off, the telephone stops working: *I was just asking her where she was, and we were cut off.*

cut out
1 **cut something out** to remove something by cutting it with a knife or scissors: *Beth cut out pictures of movie stars from the magazine.*
2 **cut it out**, **cut that out** (spoken) used when you want someone to stop doing something that is annoying you: *Hey, Kate, cut it out! That really hurts!*

cut up
cut something up to cut something into small pieces: *Cut up the carrots into small pieces.*

Cut up the carrots into small pieces.

Dd

dab /dæb/ *verb* (**dabbed, dabbing**) to lightly touch something several times in order to dry it or put something on it: *He dabbed at the mark on his trousers.*

dad /dæd / *noun* (informal) a word for father: *My dad took me to the zoo.* • *Dad, can I borrow the car?*

dad·dy /ˈdædi/ *noun* (plural **daddies**) a word for father, used by children: *When is daddy coming home?*

daf·fo·dil /ˈdæfədɪl/ *noun* a tall yellow flower that grows in early spring → see picture at FLOWER

daft /dɑːft $ dæft/ *adjective BrE* (informal) silly: *I think it's a daft idea.*

dag·ger /ˈdægə $ ˈdægɚ/ *noun* a short knife used as a weapon

dai·ly /ˈdeɪli/ *adjective, adverb* happening or produced every day: *a daily newspaper*

dai·ry /ˈdeəri $ ˈderi/ *noun* (plural **dairies**) **1** a part of a farm where butter and cheese are made **2** a company that sells milk and other foods made from milk

dai·sy /ˈdeɪzi/ *noun* a white flower with a yellow centre. Daisies are often small and grow in grass → see picture on page A10

dam /dæm/ *noun* a wall built across a river to make a lake: *Water poured through a hole in the dam.*

dam·age¹ /ˈdæmɪdʒ/ *noun*

KEY PATTERNS
cause/do damage
damage to something

physical harm that breaks or spoils something: *The bomb **caused** a lot of damage.* • *After the fire, there was some **damage to** the ceiling and walls.*

damage² *verb*
to physically harm something, so that it breaks or no longer works properly: *The water had damaged the books in the library.* • *Our suitcase was damaged at the airport.*

THESAURUS
injure: *She fell off her horse and injured her leg* (=damaged it).
ruin: *He spilt wine on the carpet and ruined it* (=damaged it very badly).
destroy: *The bomb destroyed several buildings* (=damaged them so that they no longer existed).

damn¹ /dæm/ also **damned** /dæmd/ *adverb, adjective* (spoken) used to emphasize something in a rude way, especially when you are annoyed: *Don't be so damn stupid!* • *The damned thing's broken again.*

damn² *noun* **not give a damn** (spoken) to not care at all about something: *I don't give a damn what he thinks.*

damp /dæmp/ *adjective*
slightly wet, in an unpleasant way: *a cold, damp day* • *This bed feels a bit damp to me.* —**damp, dampness** *noun* (no plural): *Protect your computer from extreme cold and damp.* • *As he entered the old house, he could feel a slight dampness in the air.*

dance¹ /dɑːns $ dæns/ *verb*

KEY PATTERNS
dance with someone
dance to something

to move your body in a way that follows a piece of music: *They danced and drank champagne until two in the morning.* • *Sharon **danced with** Joe.* • *Witney's only three, but she loves **dancing to** pop music.* —**dancer** *noun*: *Ballet dancers practise several hours a day.*

dance² *noun*
1 an event where people go in order to dance with each other: *Did you go to the dance last Friday?*
2 a particular set of movements that you make, following a piece of music: *a traditional Russian dance*
3 when you dance with someone: *May I **have this dance*** (=will you dance with me)?

A B C D E F G H I J K L M N O P Q R S T U V W X Y Z

danc·ing /ˈdɑːnsɪŋ $ ˈdænsɪŋ/ *noun* (no plural) when people dance together: *We went dancing on New Year's Eve.*

dan·ger /ˈdeɪndʒə $ ˈdeɪndʒɚ/ *noun*

KEY PATTERNS
danger of something
be in danger of something

1 (no plural) the possibility that something bad may happen: *There is more **danger of** fire in our homes during the Christmas holidays.* • *Colin is in hospital but his life is no longer **in danger**.* • *He's **in danger of** losing his job.*
2 (plural **dangers**) something or someone that may harm you: *the dangers of the journey*

THESAURUS
risk: *If you smoke, it increases the risk of getting cancer* (=danger).
threat: *Our changing climate is a threat to wildlife* (=something that may cause it harm).

dan·ger·ous /ˈdeɪndʒərəs/ *adjective* likely to harm you: *Police say the escaped prisoner is a very dangerous man.* • *Drugs are dangerous.*
—**dangerously** *adverb*: *He stood dangerously close to the fire.*

dan·gle /ˈdæŋgəl/ *verb* to hang or swing from something: *Long earrings dangled from her ears.*

dare /deə $ der/ *verb*

KEY PATTERNS
dare (to) do something
dare someone to do something

1 to be brave enough to do something: *I didn't dare admit what I'd done.* • *No one **dared to** oppose him.*
2 to ask someone to do something brave to show they are not afraid: *I **dare you to** ask her out on a date!*
3 how dare you, how dare he, how dare they (spoken) used when you are very angry about what someone has done: *How dare you speak to me like that!*
4 don't you dare (spoken) used to tell someone not to do something: *Don't you dare tell Mum!*

GRAMMAR
The negative of **dare** is **do/does not dare, dare not**, or **daren't**: *She daren't tell him in case he gets angry* (=she does not dare).

daren't /deənt $ derənt/ the short form of 'dare not': *I daren't be late.*

dar·ing /ˈdeərɪŋ $ ˈderɪŋ/ *adjective* very brave: *a daring attempt to break the land speed record*

dark¹ /dɑːk $ dɑrk/ *adjective*
1 it is dark when it is dark, it is night time: *It's only five o'clock, and **it's** already **dark**.* • *I want to get home before **it gets dark*** (=becomes dark). • *Come inside, **it's dark out*** (=it is dark outside).
2 a dark place is one where there is little or no light ANTONYM **light**, **bright**: *a dark, quiet room* • *It was very dark in the forest and we could hardly see.*
3 a dark colour is strong and closer to black than to white ANTONYM **light**, **pale**: *a dark blue dress* • *I'd like a carpet that's a bit darker than this one.*
4 someone who is dark or who has dark hair or eyes has black or brown skin, hair, or eyes ANTONYM **fair**: *a beautiful dark-haired woman* • *Tony's dad was dark, but his mother had blonde hair.*

dark² *noun* **1 the dark** when there is no light: *When I was little, I was afraid of the dark.* **2 after dark, before dark** after or before night begins: *The town really gets lively after dark.* • *You must get home before dark.*

dark·en /ˈdɑːkən $ ˈdɑrkən/ *verb* (written) to become darker, or to make something darker: *The sky darkened very quickly.*

dark·ness /ˈdɑːknəs $ ˈdɑrknəs/ *noun* (no plural) when there is no light: *The whole house was in darkness.*

dar·ling /ˈdɑːlɪŋ $ ˈdɑrlɪŋ/ *noun* used when talking to someone you love: *You look lovely, darling.*

dart¹ /dɑːt $ dɑrt/ *noun* **1** a small pointed object that you throw in the game of darts **2 darts** a game in which you throw small pointed objects at a round board: *Let's have a game of darts.*

dart² *verb* to move suddenly and quickly in a particular direction: *The fish darted away.*

dash¹ /dæʃ/ *verb* to go somewhere very quickly SYNONYM **rush**: *When he heard about his father's accident, he dashed to the hospital.*

dash² *noun* (plural **dashes**) **1 make a dash for something** to run very quickly towards something: *I made a dash for the door.* **2** a small amount of a liquid: *Add a dash of lemon juice.* **3** a mark (-) used to separate parts of a sentence

dash·board /ˈdæʃbɔːd $ ˈdæʃbɔrd/ *noun* the part inside a car at the front which has the instruments and controls on it

da·ta /ˈdeɪtə/ *noun* facts: *The scientists do not yet have enough data to say if the pollution problem is serious.*

> **GRAMMAR**
> You can use **data** with a singular verb, or with a plural verb in formal English: *All the data* ***is*** *stored on computer.* • *These data* ***are*** *now being analysed.*
> ✘ Don't say 'datas' ✘ or 'a data'.

da·ta·base /ˈdeɪtəˌbeɪs/ *noun* a large amount of information stored in a computer system: *a database of students' names and addresses*

date¹ /deɪt/ *noun*
1 a particular day of the month or year, shown by a number. For example, 4 October 2001, 16th May, and Tuesday 1 June are all dates: *What was the date yesterday – was it the sixth?* • *I need your full name and your* ***date of birth*** (=the day, month, and year you were born). • *"What date are you travelling?" "The third of August."* • *We must* ***set a date*** *for the party* (=say which date it will happen on). • *We* ***made a date*** (=arranged a date) *to meet up.*
2 an arrangement to go to a restaurant, film etc with someone you like in a romantic way: *Alison* ***has a date with*** *Mark on Saturday night.*
3 a small sweet brown fruit → see picture on page A7

PHRASES
out of date not new or modern: *The clothes she wears are always* ***out of date.*** • *an* ***out-of-date*** *computer network*
up to date new and modern, or having the most recent information: *I try to* ***keep up to date with*** *all the latest technology developments.* • *You will need* ***up-to-date*** *software.*
to date (written) until now: *The movie has made $8.4 million* ***to date.***
at a later date (written) at a time in the future: *Details will be given to you* ***at a later date.***

> **PRONUNCIATION**
> You write **January 11th** or **11th January**. You say **January the eleventh** in British English, and **January eleventh** in American English.

date² *verb* **1** to write today's date on something: *The letter was dated May 1st, 1923.* **2** *AmE* to have a romantic relationship with someone SYNONYM **go out with**: *Do you know if he's dating anyone?* **3 date from, date back to** to have existed since a particular time: *The house dates from the 17th century.*

dat·ed /ˈdeɪtɪd/ *adjective* no longer fashionable or modern SYNONYM **old-fashioned**: *dated ideas*

daugh·ter /ˈdɔːtə $ ˈdɔtɚ/ *noun* someone's female child

> **PRONUNCIATION**
> **daughter/laughter**
> You pronounce **daughter** like 'water'. You pronounce **laughter** like 'after'.

ˈdaughter-in-ˌlaw *noun* (plural **daughters-in-law**) the wife of your son

daunt·ed /ˈdɔːntɪd/ *adjective* afraid or worried about something you have to do: *He felt daunted by the size of the job.*

daunt·ing /ˈdɔːntɪŋ/ *adjective* frightening or worrying: *Being captain of the team is a daunting responsibility.*

dawn¹ /dɔːn/ *noun* (no plural) the time of day when light first appears SYNONYM **daybreak**: *Many farmers get up before dawn.*

dawn² *verb* **it dawns on someone** if something dawns on someone, they suddenly know that it is true: *It suddenly dawned on me that Terry had been lying.*

day /deɪ/ *noun*
1 a period of time equal to 24 hours. There are seven days in a week: *Dad was away for four days on a business trip.* • *Ella's birthday is* ***on the same day*** *as Sam's.*
2 the time when it is light, between the time when the sun rises and night ANTONYM **night**: *a hot, sunny day* • *I had a headache* ***all day.***

A B C D E F G H I J K L M N O P Q R S T U V W X Y Z

A B C D E F G H I J K L M N O P Q R S T U V W X Y Z

PHRASES

a long day a day when you had to get up early and you were busy all day: *Jessie was really tired after **a long day** at work.*

one day **a)** at some time in the future: *I'd like to have children **one day**.* **b)** (written) on a particular day in the past: ***One day**, Henry decided that he wanted an adventure.*

some day at some time in the future: *I'd love to visit India **some day**.*

these days used to talk about now, rather than the past, especially when you want to say how things have changed: *You're looking very slim **these days**. Have you lost weight?*

one of these days (spoken) at some time soon, but you do not know exactly when: *I'll have to give him a call **one of these days**.*

the other day (spoken) a few days ago: *Ted gave me that book **the other day**.*

> **GRAMMAR**
> You usually use **on** with days of the week: *I saw her on Monday.*
> Don't use **on** before **next**, **last**, or **this**.
> ✗ Don't say 'on next Monday'. Just say **next Monday**.

day·break /'deɪbreɪk/ *noun* (no plural) (written) the time of day when light first appears SYNONYM **dawn**: *They left at daybreak.*

day·care cen·ter /'deɪkeə ˌsentə $ 'deɪker ˌsentɚ/ the American word for CRÈCHE

daydream

day·dream /'deɪdriːm/ *verb* to think about nice things so that you forget what you should be doing: *She was always daydreaming about being a fashion model.* —**daydream** *noun*: *He seemed to be in a daydream.*

day·light /'deɪlaɪt/ *noun* (no plural) **1** the light that comes from the sun: *She opened the curtains to let the daylight in.* **2 in broad daylight** if someone does something bad in broad daylight, they do it in the daytime, even though people may see them: *The thieves broke into the house in broad daylight.*

day·time /'deɪtaɪm/ *noun* (no plural) the part of a day when it is light ANTONYM **nighttime**

ˌday-to-'day *adjective* day-to-day activities happen every day as a regular part of your life or work: *the day-to-day running of the college*

daze /deɪz/ *noun* **in a daze** unable to think clearly: *When I heard I'd won the prize, I just sat there in a daze.*

dazed /deɪzd/ *adjective* unable to think clearly, for example because you have hit your head or you are surprised about something: *I'm still a bit dazed at the news.*

daz·zle /'dæzəl/ *verb* if a light dazzles you, it is so bright that you cannot see clearly for a short time —**dazzling** *adjective*: *a dazzling light*

dead[1] /ded/ *adjective*
1 no longer alive: *Her mother is dead.* • *There was a dead fox lying in the road.*
2 a machine or piece of equipment that is dead is not working because there is no power: *I'm afraid your car engine is completely dead.* • *Why don't you throw these dead batteries away?*
3 go dead if a piece of electrical equipment, especially a telephone, goes dead, it stops working suddenly: *We were talking on the telephone, and the line just went dead.*
4 (informal) complete or exact: *the dead center of the road* • *There was dead silence as Guy entered the room.*

dead[2] *adverb* **1** (informal) very: *We were dead tired after the long journey.* • *Mr Sampson's classes are dead boring.* **2** exactly: *You're dead right.* **3 stop dead** to suddenly stop completely: *The woman walking in front of me suddenly stopped dead.*

dead[3] *noun* **1 the dead** people who are dead ANTONYM **the living**: *You should* *not say bad things about the dead.* **2 in the dead of night** (written) in the middle of the night

ˌdead ˈend *noun* a street with no way out at one end

ˌdead ˈheat *noun* the result of a race in which two people finish at exactly the same time: *The race ended in a dead heat.*

dead·line /ˈdedlaɪn/ *noun* a date or time by which you must finish something: *Do you think we'll be able to meet the deadline?*

dead·lock /ˈdedlɒk $ ˈdedlɑk/ *noun* (no plural) when groups or countries cannot agree: *The talks ended in deadlock.*

dead·ly¹ /ˈdedli/ *adjective* (**deadlier, deadliest**) something that is deadly can kill you: *a deadly spider*

deadly² *adverb* very: *I thought he was joking but he was deadly serious.*

deaf /def/ *adjective* not able to hear: *There are several deaf students in the class.* • *My grandmother* **went deaf** (=became deaf) *when she was in her sixties.* —**deafness** *noun* (no plural): *A childhood disease caused her deafness.*

deaf·en /ˈdefən/ *verb* to be so loud that it is difficult for you to hear anything: *The music deafened us.* —**deafening** *adjective*: *a deafening explosion*

deal¹ /diːl/ *noun*

KEY PATTERNS
strike/make a deal

an agreement, especially in business or politics: *He accepted a five-year deal to become the team's coach.* • *The Democrats* **struck a deal** (=agreed to do something) *with the Republicans to get the bill passed.* • *After some negotiating, we* **made a deal**.

PHRASES

a great deal, a good deal a large amount or quantity: *The students have learned a good deal.* • *After* **a great deal of** *thought, I decided to go to university.* • *This computer costs* **a good deal more** *than this other one.*

be a good deal to be cheap or sold for a fair price: *At £8.50, the CD is a* **good deal**.

deal² *verb* (past tense and past participle **dealt** /delt/) **1 deal in something** to buy and sell a particular type of thing: *The shop deals in high-quality jewellery.* • *The police believe the men were dealing in stolen mobile phones.* **2 deal with something a)** if you deal with a problem, you do something to make sure the problem no longer exists: *We are here to deal with customer complaints.* • *There are ways of dealing with stress.* **b)** if a book, film, play etc deals with a particular subject, it is about that subject: *Chapter 2 deals with the history of the area.* **3** also **deal out** to give cards to each player in a card game: *I'd been dealt some good cards, so I was sure I'd win.*

THESAURUS
handle: *It was a difficult situation to handle* (=deal with).
take care of: *I'll take care of all the holiday arrangements* (=do the work that is necessary for the holiday to happen).

deal·er /ˈdiːlə $ ˈdilɚ/ *noun* someone who buys and sells a particular kind of thing: *a car dealer*

dealt the past tense and past participle of DEAL²

dear¹ /dɪə $ dɪr/ **oh dear** (spoken) used when something bad has happened: *Oh dear! We're going to be late.*

dear² *noun* (spoken) used when talking to someone you like or love: *Thank you, dear.*

dear³ *adjective*
1 Dear Sir, Dear Mr Smith, Dear Mrs Jones etc (written) used before the name of the person you are writing to: *Dear Miss Patterson, I am writing to you about your son.*
2 *BrE* costing a lot of money SYNONYM **expensive**: *Everything in those designer shops is so dear.*

death /deθ/ *noun* **1** the end of someone's life: *After her husband's death, she lived alone for 20 years.* • *What was the cause of death?* • *The driver of the truck bled to death before the ambulance crew could reach him.* **2 scared to death, bored to death**

A B C D E F G H I J K L M N O P Q R S T U V W X Y Z

(informal) very scared or bored: *I would be scared to death if I saw a lion.*

ˈdeath ˌpenalty *noun* **the death penalty** the legal punishment of being killed: *Britain permanently abolished the death penalty in 1969.*

de·bat·a·ble /dɪˈbeɪtəbəl/ *adjective* something that is debatable is not certain: *It is debatable whether the peace will last.*

de·bate[1] /dɪˈbeɪt/ *noun* **1** an organized discussion on an important subject: *He took part in a school debate on animal rights.* **2** (no plural) the process of discussing a subject or question: *There has been a lot of debate in the newspapers about this matter.*

debate[2] *verb* to discuss an important subject: *Scientists are still debating whether the new treatment really works.*

deb·it /ˈdebɪt/ *noun* an amount of money that you take out of your bank account: *His bank statement showed several large debits.* —**debit** *verb*: *The bank will debit the monthly payments from your account automatically.*

ˈdebit ˌcard *noun* a plastic card that you use for paying for things in shops. The money is taken directly out of your bank account: *I use my debit card to pay for almost everything these days.*

deb·ris /ˈdebriː $ dɪˈbri/ *noun* (no plural) pieces of material that are left after a crash, explosion, or large event: *After the crash, the road was covered with debris.*

debt /det/ *noun*

KEY PATTERNS
pay (off) a debt
be in debt

1 money that you owe to someone: *credit card debts* • *Last year I finally* ***paid off*** *all my* ***debts.***
2 (no plural) when you owe money to someone: *Many poor countries are* ***in debt*** *to richer countries.*

de·but /ˈdeɪbjuː $ deɪˈbju/ *noun* the first time that an actor, sports player etc performs in public: *Lee made his debut in the TV film, 'Kung Fu'.*

dec·ade /ˈdekeɪd/ *noun* a period of ten years: *The building is now four decades old.*

de·caf·fein·a·ted /diːˈkæfəneɪtəd/ *adjective* decaffeinated drinks do not contain CAFFEINE (=a substance that makes you feel more awake): *a cup of decaffeinated coffee*

de·cay /dɪˈkeɪ/ *verb* if something decays, natural processes slowly destroy it: *The body of the dead mouse had started to decay.* —**decay** *noun* (no plural): *Eating lots of sweets causes tooth decay.*

de·ceit /dɪˈsiːt/ *noun* (no plural) when someone tries to make people believe something that is not true: *The government was accused of deliberate deceit.*

de·ceive /dɪˈsiːv/ *verb* to make someone believe something that is not true: *I felt very upset when I realized that he had deceived me.* → see Thesaurus at LIE[2]

De·cem·ber /dɪˈsembə $ dɪˈsembɚ/ (written abbreviation **Dec**) *noun* the twelfth month of the year: *War began in the middle of December.*

de·cent /ˈdiːsənt/ *adjective* **1** good enough: *Everyone should have a decent education.* **2** decent people are good and honest

de·cep·tive /dɪˈseptɪv/ *adjective* something that is deceptive makes people believe something that is not true: *Advertisements should not be deceptive.*

de·cide /dɪˈsaɪd/ *verb*

KEY PATTERNS
decide to do something
decide who/what/when etc
decide (that)

to choose what you are going to do after thinking about it: *Megan* ***decided to*** *go to Denise's party.* • *Children should be allowed to* ***decide how to*** *spend their pocket money.* • *I can't* ***decide which*** *dress to wear.* • *We* ***decided that*** *we couldn't afford to go on holiday this year.* • *The date of the game has not yet been decided.*

PHRASAL VERBS
decide on
decide on something to choose one thing from a group of things: *She decided on teaching as a career.*
→ see Thesaurus at CHOOSE

de·cid·ed·ly /dɪˈsaɪdɪdli/ *adverb* (formal) very or definitely: *When I woke up the next day, I felt decidedly ill.*

dec·i·mal¹ /ˈdesəməl/ *adjective* based on the number ten: *the decimal system*

decimal² *noun* the part of a number which comes after the mark (.) and is less than one, for example in 3.5 or 0.25

ˌdecimal ˈpoint *noun* the mark (.) before a decimal

de·ci·sion /dɪˈsɪʒən/ *noun*

KEY PATTERNS
make/take/reach a decision

a choice that you make: *Ben knew he'd made the right **decision**. • The city council has not yet **reached a decision**.*

de·ci·sive /dɪˈsaɪsɪv/ *adjective* **1** a decisive event is definite or important: *the party's decisive victory in the election* **2** able to make decisions quickly ANTONYM **indecisive**: *a confident and decisive leader*

deck

deck /dek/ *noun* **1** the part of a ship where you can walk or sit outside: *Most people were out on deck, sunbathing.* **2** one of the levels on a ship or bus: *Our cabin was on the top deck.* **3** the American word for a PACK of cards

dec·la·ra·tion /ˌdekləˈreɪʃən/ *noun* an official statement about something: *a declaration of war*

de·clare /dɪˈkleə $ dɪˈkler/ *verb*

KEY PATTERNS
declare war/independence
declare something safe/open etc
declare that

1 to say officially what will happen or what you have decided: *In December 1718, England **declared war on** Spain. • The fire department declared the building unsafe.*
2 (written) to say publicly what you think or feel: *"I am very proud of the team," Coach Hall declared. • Brown **declared that** the situation was very serious.*

de·cline /dɪˈklaɪn/ *verb* to become weaker, smaller, or less good: *Her health declined rapidly.* —**decline** *noun*: *There has been a slight decline in the company's profits.*

de·cor /ˈdeɪkɔː $ ˈdeɪkɔr/ *noun* the colours, furniture etc in a room: *The restaurant had changed its decor.*

decorate

decorating the home

decorating the Christmas tree

dec·o·rate /ˈdekəreɪt/ *verb* **1** to make something look more attractive by adding things to it: *The room was decorated with balloons and coloured lights.* **2** to put paint or paper onto the walls of a room or building: *I'm going to decorate the kitchen this summer.*

dec·o·ra·tion /ˌdekəˈreɪʃən/ *noun* a pretty thing that you use to make something look more attractive: *The shop windows were already full of Christmas decorations.*

dec·o·ra·tive /ˈdekərətɪv/ *adjective* pretty and used to decorate something: *a decorative vase*

dec·o·ra·tor /ˈdekəreɪtə $ ˈdekəˌreɪtɚ/ *noun BrE* someone whose job is to decorate rooms and buildings: *The decorators finished painting the ceiling.*

de·crease /dɪˈkriːs/ *verb* to become smaller in number, amount, size etc, or to make something do this ANTONYM

increase: *The price of computers is decreasing all the time.* → see Thesaurus at REDUCE —**decrease** /ˈdiːkriːs/ *noun*: *a decrease in crime*

THESAURUS
go down: *The cost of flights has gone down again* (=become lower or less).
drop: *Last night the temperature dropped suddenly* (=became much lower).
fall: *House prices could **fall** in the autumn* (=become lower or less).

de·cree /dɪˈkriː/ *noun* an official order that a ruler or government makes

de·crep·it /dɪˈkrepɪt/ *adjective* old and in bad condition: *The office buildings were thoroughly decrepit.*

ded·i·cate /ˈdedəkeɪt/ *verb* if you dedicate a book, film, song etc to someone, you say publicly that it is for them, because you love and respect them: *This song is dedicated to my wife.*

ded·i·cat·ed /ˈdedəkeɪtɪd/ *adjective* someone who is dedicated works very hard at something because it is important to them: *Our staff are all very dedicated.*

ded·i·ca·tion /ˌdedəˈkeɪʃən/ *noun* (no plural) when you work very hard because you believe that what you are doing is important: *I was impressed by the dedication of the school staff.*

de·duce /dɪˈdjuːs $ dɪˈdus/ *verb* (written) to decide that something is true, using what you know or notice: *From his accent, I deduced that he was not English.*

de·duct /dɪˈdʌkt/ *verb* to take an amount away from a larger amount: *The tax is deducted from your salary each month.*

deed /diːd/ *noun* (formal) an action: *She was well known for her good deeds in the community.*

deep¹ /diːp/ *adjective*
1 if something is deep, there is a long distance between the top and the bottom ANTONYM **shallow**: *The snow was so deep it was nearly over Kerry's head.* • *at the bottom of the deep blue sea* → see picture at SHALLOW
2 used to talk about the distance from the top to the bottom of something: *The pool is only three feet deep at this end.* • *How deep is this river?*
3 a deep sound or voice is very low: *Ken has a nice deep voice.*
4 a deep feeling or belief is very strong: *Thompson expressed his deep concern for the missing pilot.*

PHRASES
take a deep breath to breathe a lot of air into your lungs, especially before you do something difficult or frightening: ***I took a deep breath** and climbed onto the horse.*
be in a deep sleep if someone is in a deep sleep, it is difficult to wake them up

deep² *adverb*
a long way into or inside something: *Julian thrust his hands **deep into** his pockets.* • *a hotel **deep in** the countryside*

PHRASES
deep down if you feel or know something deep down, it is what you really feel or know: *She looks fine, but **deep down** she's very unhappy.*

deep·en /ˈdiːpən/ *verb* (written) to become worse, or to make something become worse: *The president's political troubles deepened last week.*

deep·ly /ˈdiːpli/ *adverb* extremely or very much: *She had been deeply affected by what happened.*

deer /dɪə $ dɪr/ *noun* (plural **deer**) a large wild animal that lives in forests. The male has long horns that look like tree branches → see picture at HERD

de·feat¹ /dɪˈfiːt/ *verb*
if you defeat someone in a game, battle, or election, you win: *We defeated last year's champions by three goals to two.* → see Thesaurus at BEAT¹

defeat² *noun* when you lose a game, battle, or election ANTONYM **victory**: *On Saturday, the team suffered their fifth defeat in a row.*

de·fect /dɪˈfekt/ *noun* (formal) a fault in something that stops it working properly: *a defect in the plane engine* • *He's had a hearing defect since he was a child.*

de·fence *BrE*, **defense** *AmE* /dɪˈfens/ *noun* **1** (no plural) the weapons, soldiers, actions etc that a country uses to protect itself from attack: *How much does Britain spend on defence?* **2** / $ ˈdiːfens/ the players in a game such as football who try to stop the other team getting points: *The team's defence is one of the strongest in the Italian league.* **3 the defence** the lawyers who are trying to prove that someone is not guilty of a crime ANTONYM **prosecution**: *the defence lawyer*

de·fence·less *BrE*, **defenseless** *AmE* /dɪˈfensləs/ *adjective* if someone is defenceless, they are weak and cannot protect themselves: *The thugs attacked a defenceless old woman.*

de·fend /dɪˈfend/ *verb*

> KEY PATTERNS
> **defend someone/something against something**
> **defend yourself**

1 to protect someone or something from harm, danger, or an attack: *We must have a large enough army to* ***defend*** *the country* ***against*** *attack.* • *He hit me first; I* ***was defending myself.*** • *A spokesman for the government has defended the tax rises.*
2 defend the championship, defend the title etc to play in a sports competition that you won last time to try and win it again: *Stanford* ***are defending the*** *volleyball* ***title*** *today.*

de·fen·dant /dɪˈfendənt/ *noun* the person in a court of law who the police say is guilty of a crime

defense the American spelling of DEFENCE

de·fens·ive /dɪˈfensɪv/ *adjective* used or suitable for defending against an attack ANTONYM **offensive**: *We took up a defensive position behind the wall.*

de·fi·ant /dɪˈfaɪənt/ *adjective* someone who is defiant will not obey someone who is trying to make them do something —**defiantly** *adverb*: *"I won't go to school!" shouted Lisa defiantly.*

de·fi·cien·cy /dɪˈfɪʃənsi/ *noun* (plural **deficiencies**) when you do not have enough of something that you need: *a vitamin deficiency*

de·fine /dɪˈfaɪn/ *verb* to say exactly what a word means or what something is

def·i·nite /ˈdefɪnət/ *adjective*
1 completely certain and not likely to change: *I don't have any definite plans for the holidays.*
2 clear and easy to notice: *The new laws are having a definite effect.*

ˌdefinite ˈarticle *noun* in grammar, the word 'the'

def·i·nite·ly /ˈdefɪnətli/ *adverb* used to make a statement stronger: *I'll definitely phone you tonight.*

def·i·ni·tion /ˌdefəˈnɪʃən/ *noun* a phrase or sentence, for example in a dictionary, that says exactly what a word means or what something is

de·flect /dɪˈflekt/ *verb* **be deflected** if something is deflected, it hits a surface and then goes in a different direction: *The ball hit the post and was deflected.*

de·formed /dɪˈfɔːmd $ dɪˈfɔrmd/ *adjective* someone who is deformed has something wrong with the shape of their body: *Mothers who took the drug gave birth to deformed babies.*

de·frost /ˌdiːˈfrɒst $ dɪˈfrɔst/ *verb* if frozen food defrosts, or if you defrost it, it slowly stops being frozen until you can cook or eat it: *Defrost the chicken thoroughly before cooking.*

deft /deft/ *adjective* (written) movements that are deft are quick and skilful: *Katherine drew a picture with a few deft strokes of her pen.*

de·fy /dɪˈfaɪ/ *verb* (**defied, defies**) to say you will not obey someone: *Don't defy your father.*

de·grad·ing /dɪˈgreɪdɪŋ/ *adjective* something that is degrading makes people lose their respect for themselves: *It was degrading to have to ask strangers for money.*

de·gree /dɪˈgriː/ *noun*

> KEY PATTERNS
> **a degree of something**
> **to a large/small degree**
> **a degree in physics/history etc**

1 the level or amount of something: *This task requires* ***a high degree of*** *skill.* • *All the students helped* ***to some degree*** (=they all helped, but by different amounts).

A B C D E F G H I J K L M N O P Q R S T U V W X Y Z

2 a unit for measuring temperature, written (°): *It's 10 degrees below zero!*
3 a unit for measuring angles, written (°): *A right angle measures 90 degrees.* • *Turn the bottle cap 180 degrees.*
4 what you get when you successfully finish a university course: *Robbie **has** a first-class **degree in** law.* • *a history degree*

de·hy·drat·ed /ˌdiːhaɪˈdreɪtɪd $ diˈhaɪˌdreɪtɪd/ *adjective* someone who is dehydrated is ill because they do not have enough water in their body

de·lay¹ /dɪˈleɪ/ *verb* **1** to make someone or something late: *I'm sorry I'm late – I was delayed by the traffic.*
2 to do something at a later date than you planned: *We had to delay the project until the following year.*

THESAURUS
postpone: *The football match has been **postponed** until next week* (=delayed).
put off: *We had to **put off** the picnic because of the rain* (=delay).

delay² *noun* a period of time when you have to wait for something to happen: *There was a 12-hour delay before the plane took off.* • *Please accept my apologies for the delay.*

del·e·gate /ˈdeləgət/ *noun* someone that a country or organization chooses to do something for it, such as speak or vote at a meeting: *UN delegates*

del·e·ga·tion /ˌdeləˈgeɪʃən/ *noun* a small group of people that a country or organization sends to do something for it, such as vote or find out about something

de·lete /dɪˈliːt/ *verb* to remove part of a piece of writing, or to remove a document on a computer: *I deleted a file by mistake.*

de·lib·er·ate /dɪˈlɪbərət/ *adjective* a deliberate action is one that someone wants and has planned, not a mistake or an accident SYNONYM **intentional**: *The killing was deliberate.* • *Martin's jokes were a deliberate attempt to embarrass Jean.*

de·lib·er·ate·ly /dɪˈlɪbərətli/ *adverb* if you do something deliberately, you do it because you want to: *You deliberately disobeyed me!*

THESAURUS
on purpose: *It wasn't an accident – he hit me **on purpose*** (=deliberately).
intentionally: *The man said he didn't start the fire **intentionally*** (=deliberately).

del·i·ca·cy /ˈdelɪkəsi/ *noun* (plural **delicacies**) a rare or expensive food that is especially nice to eat

del·i·cate /ˈdelɪkət/ *adjective* if something is delicate, you have to be careful with it because you can easily damage or break it: *These silk dresses are very old and delicate.* • *a delicate piece of equipment*

del·i·ca·tes·sen /ˌdelɪkəˈtesən/ *noun* a shop that sells good quality cheese, cooked meat etc, as well as special food from foreign countries

de·li·cious /dɪˈlɪʃəs/ *adjective* delicious food tastes very good: *This soup is delicious!*

USAGE
✘ Don't say 'It's very delicious'. Just say **It's delicious**.

de·light¹ /dɪˈlaɪt/ *noun*

KEY PATTERNS
to someone's delight

a feeling of great happiness and excitement: *There were shouts of delight from the children.* • ***To my delight**, I passed the exam.* • ***To the delight of** the audience, the concert ended with fireworks.*

delight² *verb* (formal) to give someone great pleasure and enjoyment: *His music delights people of all ages.*

de·light·ed /dɪˈlaɪtɪd/ *adjective* very pleased about something: *She was delighted with her new car.* → see Thesaurus at HAPPY

de·light·ful /dɪˈlaɪtfəl/ *adjective* very nice or enjoyable: *a delightful party*

de·lir·i·ous /dɪˈlɪriəs/ *adjective* unable to think clearly because you are ill

de·liv·er /dɪˈlɪvə $ dɪˈlɪvɚ/ *verb*

KEY PATTERNS
deliver a letter/package etc (to someone)

to take something such as a letter or a package to a place: *Can you deliver this parcel before Christmas?* • *He got a job delivering pizzas.* • *Hot meals* ***are delivered to*** *old people in the area.*

de·liv·er·y /dɪˈlɪvəri/ *noun* (plural **deliveries**) when someone brings something to your house or office, for example letters or things you have asked for: *There's no postal delivery on Sunday.*

del·ta /ˈdeltə/ *noun* an area of low land near the sea where a large river separates into many smaller rivers

del·uge /ˈdeljuːdʒ/ *noun* (formal) a large flood, or a period of time when it rains continuously: *Weathermen warned that the deluge could continue for several days.*

de·lu·sion /dɪˈluːʒən/ *noun* (formal) something you believe, but which is not really true: *I thought he loved me, but it was only a delusion.*

de·luxe /dɪˈlʌks/ *adjective* deluxe things cost more money than others of the same kind because they are better: *We had a deluxe room with a balcony.*

delve /delv/ *verb* (written) to put your hand deep inside a bag, box etc in order to find something: *He delved into his pockets for his key.*

de·mand[1] /dɪˈmɑːnd $ dɪˈmænd/ *noun* **1** (no plural) if there is a demand for something, people want to buy it: *There was a huge demand for concert tickets.* **2** something that someone asks for in a very determined way: *The company refused the workers' demands for more pay.*

demand[2] *verb*

KEY PATTERNS
demand to do something
demand something (from someone)
demand that

to ask for something, or ask a question, in a very strong determined way: *An officer* ***demanded to*** *see my passport.* • *They are* ***demanding*** *an apology* ***from*** *the company.* • *"Where's Richard?" demanded James.* • *The hijackers* ***are demanding that*** *the plane be allowed to leave.* → see Thesaurus at ASK

de·mand·ing /dɪˈmɑːndɪŋ $ dɪˈmændɪŋ/ *adjective* a demanding job is not easy because you need a lot of skill or effort to do it: *It was very demanding work.*

de·moc·ra·cy /dɪˈmɒkrəsi $ dɪˈmɑkrəsi/ *noun* (plural **democracies**) the system in which everyone in a country has the right to choose a government by voting, or a country that has this system: *I believe in freedom and democracy.* • *We live in a democracy.*

SPELLING
This word is often spelled wrongly. The correct spelling is: **democracy**.

dem·o·crat /ˈdeməkræt/ *noun* someone who believes in or supports democracy

dem·o·crat·ic /ˌdeməˈkrætɪk/ *adjective* a democratic country, government, or system is one in which everyone has the right to choose their government by voting

de·mol·ish /dɪˈmɒlɪʃ $ dɪˈmɑlɪʃ/ *verb* to deliberately destroy a building SYNONYM **knock down**, **tear down**: *The old houses were demolished years ago.*

de·mon /ˈdiːmən/ *noun* an evil SPIRIT

dem·on·strate /ˈdemənstreɪt/ *verb*

KEY PATTERNS
demonstrate that
demonstrate against something
demonstrate how to do something
demonstrate something to someone

1 to show something clearly: *The president demonstrated great leadership.* • *Our research* ***demonstrates that*** *people do not always remember events clearly.* → see Thesaurus at SHOW[1]
2 when people demonstrate, they stand or walk together somewhere to protest about something or to support something: *The students* ***are demonstrating against*** *high course fees.* → see Thesaurus at PROTEST[2]
3 to show someone how to do something by doing it yourself: *Artists will* ***demonstrate how to*** *use oil paints.* • *We* ***demonstrated*** *our experiment* ***to*** *the rest of the class.*

dem·on·stra·tion /ˌdemənˈstreɪʃən/ *noun* **1** when a large group of people meet to protest against something or to support something: *Thousands of people took part in the demonstration against the war.* **2** if you give a demonstration, you show a group of people how to do something: *The photography club arranges lectures, demonstrations and trips to art galleries.*

dem·on·stra·tor /ˈdemənstreɪtə $ ˈdemənˌstreɪtɚ/ *noun* someone who takes part in a demonstration to protest against something or to support something: *Angry demonstrators marched through the streets.*

de·mor·a·lized also **demoralised** *BrE* /dɪˈmɒrəlaɪzd $ dɪˈmɔrəˌlaɪzd/ *adjective* feeling less confident and hopeful than before because of bad things that have happened: *After a year in the job I felt totally demoralized.*

de·mor·a·li·zing also **demoralising** *BrE* /dɪˈmɒrəlaɪzɪŋ $ dɪˈmɔrəˌlaɪzɪŋ/ *adjective* making you feel less confident and hopeful than before: *Losing the match was very demoralizing for the team.* • *The announcement had a demoralizing effect on staff.*

den /den/ *noun* the home of some wild animals such as lions and FOXES

de·ni·al /dɪˈnaɪəl/ *noun* (formal) a statement that something is not true: *his denial of guilt*

den·im /ˈdenəm/ *noun* (no plural) a type of strong cotton cloth, usually blue, used for making clothes: *denim jeans*

dense /dens/ *adjective* **1** containing a lot of trees, people etc close together: *a dense tropical jungle* • *the city's dense population* **2** dense cloud, FOG etc is thick and difficult to see through —**densely** *adverb*

dent /dent/ *noun* a hollow place in the surface of something, especially metal: *There was a dent in the can of soup.* —**dent** *verb*: *I dented the side of my car.*

dent

den·tal /ˈdentl/ *adjective* connected with teeth: *dental problems*

den·tist /ˈdentɪst/ *noun* someone whose job is to look after and repair people's teeth

den·tures /ˈdentʃəz $ ˈdentʃɚz/ *plural noun* false teeth that people wear because they do not have their own teeth: *a set of dentures*

de·ny /dɪˈnaɪ/ *verb* (**denied**, **denies**) to say that something is not true ANTONYM **admit**: *Gary denied being involved in the robbery.*

de·o·do·rant /diːˈəʊdərənt $ diˈoʊdərənt/ *noun* a substance that you put under your arms to stop your body smelling unpleasant

de·part /dɪˈpɑːt $ dɪˈpɑrt/ *verb* (formal) if a plane, train etc departs from a place, it leaves it: *Your flight will depart from Heathrow Airport at 8.30.*

de·part·ment /dɪˈpɑːtmənt $ dɪˈpɑrtmənt/ *noun* one of the parts of a large organization such as a college, government, or company: *the Modern Languages Department at Cambridge University*

deˈpartment ˌstore *noun* a large shop that sells many different types of things

de·par·ture /dɪˈpɑːtʃə $ dɪˈpɑrtʃɚ/ *noun* when a person, plane, train etc leaves a place ANTONYM **arrival**: *Our departure was delayed because of bad weather.*

de·pend /dɪˈpend/ *verb*
it depends, that depends (spoken) used to say that you are not sure about something, because you do not know what will happen: *"What time will you be back?" "**It depends**. I'm not sure what the traffic will be like."*

PHRASAL VERBS

depend on/upon
1 depend on something to change because of other things that happen: *"Will the concert be indoors or outdoors?" "**It depends on** the weather."*
2 depend on someone/something to need help from someone or something in order to do something: *We depend on the rain **for** a good harvest.* • *I hate having to depend on her **to** drive me places.*

de·pend·a·ble /dɪˈpendəbəl/ *adjective* someone or something that is dependable will always do what you need them to do SYNONYM **reliable**: *We want our employees to be dependable and loyal.* • *a dependable supply of water*

de·pen·dant *BrE*, **dependent** *AmE* /dɪˈpendənt/ *noun* (formal) a child or other person who needs someone to pay for their food, clothes etc

de·pen·dent /dɪˈpendənt/ *adjective* needing someone or something in order to live or to continue ANTONYM **independent**: *The villages are completely dependent on agriculture.*

de·port /dɪˈpɔːt $ dɪˈpɔrt/ *verb* to force someone to leave a country and return to the country they came from

de·pose /dɪˈpəʊz $ dɪˈpoʊz/ *verb* to remove a leader from their position: *an attempt to depose the King*

de·pos·it[1] /dɪˈpɒzɪt $ dɪˈpɑzɪt/ *noun* **1** part of the price of something, that you pay when you agree to buy it: *We paid a ten per cent deposit on the house.* **2** an amount of money that you pay into a bank account: *a deposit of £300*

deposit[2] *verb* to put money into a bank account

dep·ot /ˈdepəʊ $ ˈdipoʊ/ *noun* a place where buses, trains, products etc are kept until they are needed: *a bus depot*

de·press /dɪˈpres/ *verb* to make someone feel sad or not hopeful about the future: *The standard of sport in this school depresses me.*

de·pressed /dɪˈprest/ *adjective* feeling sad or not hopeful about the future: *She felt very depressed after losing her job.* ➔ see Thesaurus at SAD

de·press·ing /dɪˈpresɪŋ/ *adjective* making you feel sad or not hopeful about the future: *depressing news*

de·pres·sion /dɪˈpreʃən/ *noun* a feeling of great sadness that sometimes makes you ill and unable to live normally: *Her mother had depression for many years.*

de·prive /dɪˈpraɪv/ *verb* to stop someone having something that they need or that they normally have: *They deprived the prisoners of food.*

de·prived /dɪˈpraɪvd/ *adjective* deprived places or people do not have the good things that other places or people have: *Sylvia had a deprived childhood.* • *deprived inner city areas*

depth /depθ/ *noun* how deep something is, measured from the top to the bottom: *As part of our project, we had to measure the depth of the river.*

dep·u·ty /ˈdepjəti/ *noun* (plural **deputies**) the person in a business, school etc who has the second most important position: *the deputy head teacher*

der·e·lict /ˈderəlɪkt/ *adjective* a derelict building or piece of land is in bad condition because no one has used it for a long time: *derelict factories with broken windows and holes in the roof*

de·scend /dɪˈsend/ *verb* (formal) to go down ANTONYM **ascend**: *We watched the plane slowly descend.*

de·scen·dant /dɪˈsendənt/ *noun* someone who is related to a particular person who lived long ago: *a descendant of Abraham Lincoln*

de·scent /dɪˈsent/ *noun* (formal) when a plane, person etc goes down to a lower place ANTONYM **ascent**: *The climbers began their descent.*

de·scribe /dɪˈskraɪb/ *verb*

KEY PATTERNS
describe someone/something
describe someone/something as something
describe how/what/why etc

to say what someone or something is like or what happened: *Can you describe the car you saw?* • *The police **have described** him **as** around 25 years old, with brown hair.* • ***Describe how** you felt when you heard the news.* • *I tried to **describe what** happened next.*

SPELLING
This word is often spelled wrongly. The correct spelling is: **describe**.

de·scrip·tion /dɪˈskrɪpʃən/ *noun*

KEY PATTERNS
a description of someone/something

A B C D E F G H I J K L M N O P Q R S T U V W X Y Z

something you say or write that shows what someone or something is like: *Carson **gave** the police **a description** of the car.*

desert

de·sert¹ /ˈdezət $ ˈdezɚt/ *noun* a large area of very hot dry land where few plants grow: *the Sahara desert*

de·sert² /dɪˈzɜːt $ dɪˈzɚt/ *verb* if you desert a person or a place, you leave them and never go back SYNONYM **abandon**: *He deserted his family.*

PRONUNCIATION
You pronounce the noun **DEsert**, with the stress on the first syllable.
You pronounce the verb **deSERT**, with the stress on the second syllable.

de·sert·ed /dɪˈzɜːtɪd $ dɪˈzɚtɪd/ *adjective* a deserted place is empty and quiet: *It was midnight and the streets were deserted.* → see Thesaurus at EMPTY¹

ˌdesert ˈisland *noun* a tropical island where nobody lives

de·serve /dɪˈzɜːv $ dɪˈzɚv/ *verb*

KEY PATTERNS
deserve something
deserve to do something

if someone deserves something, they should get it because of something they have done: *After all that work, I think we deserve a cup of coffee.* • *He is guilty and **deserves to** go to prison.*

de·sign¹ /dɪˈzaɪn/ *noun* (no plural)
1 the way that something is planned or made, or the ability to plan or make things: *I like the design of this room.* • *Jill has a natural talent for design.*
2 a pattern used to decorate something: *Each plate has a different design.*

design² *verb*
1 to draw or plan something that you will make, plan, or build: *The company is designing a golf course.*
2 be designed for someone, be designed to do something to be made for a particular type of person or a particular purpose: *The game **is designed for** younger children.* • *The course **is designed to** help you improve your writing skills.*

de·sign·er¹ /dɪˈzaɪnə $ dɪˈzaɪnɚ/ *noun* someone whose job is to design new styles of clothes, cars etc: *the fashion designer Calvin Klein*

designer² *adjective* designer clothes are expensive because they were designed by a famous designer: *designer jeans*

de·sir·a·ble /dɪˈzaɪərəbəl $ dɪˈzaɪrəbəl/ *adjective* (written) if something is desirable, people want it because it is good or useful: *a desirable apartment in the centre of the city*

de·sire¹ /dɪˈzaɪə $ dɪˈzaɪɚ/ *noun* a strong feeling that you want something very much: *I had a strong desire to hit him.*

desire² *verb* (formal) to want something

desk /desk/ *noun* a table where you sit and write or work → see picture at TABLE

de·spair¹ /dɪˈspeə $ dɪˈsper/ *noun* (no plural) a very sad feeling that there is no hope any more: *I was in despair, when at last she phoned to say that she was all right.*

despair² *verb* to feel that there is no hope any more: *Don't despair – things will get better.*

des·per·ate /ˈdespərət/ *adjective*

KEY PATTERNS
desperate for something
desperate to do something

1 wanting very much to get out of a bad situation or achieve something very difficult: *Many homeless families **are desperate for** a place to live.* • ***desperate attempts** to escape* • *After five losses, the team **is desperate to** win.*

2 a desperate situation is very bad: *There is a desperate shortage of doctors.* —**desperately** *adverb*: *Simon was desperately unhappy.*

de·spise /dɪˈspaɪz/ *verb* to not like and to have no respect for someone or something: *Laura despised boys; she thought they were all stupid.*

de·spite /dɪˈspaɪt/ *preposition* although something happens or exists SYNONYM **in spite of**: *He struggled on despite the pain.*

des·sert /dɪˈzɜːt $ dɪˈzɚt/ *noun* something sweet that you eat after the main part of a meal SYNONYM **pudding** *BrE* **sweet** *BrE*: *For dessert we had ice cream and chocolate sauce.*

SPELLING
Don't confuse the spelling of **dessert** with **desert** (=a large area where it is very hot and there is a lot of sand).

des·ti·na·tion /ˌdestəˈneɪʃən/ *noun* (formal) the place that you are travelling to: *It took me five hours to reach my destination.*

des·tined /ˈdestənd/ *adjective* someone who is destined to do something will definitely do it: *He was destined to become president.*

des·ti·ny /ˈdestəni/ *noun* (plural **destinies**) the things that will happen to someone in the future SYNONYM **fate**: *Do you think we can control our own destinies?*

de·stroy /dɪˈstrɔɪ/ *verb* to damage something very badly, so that people can no longer use it, or so that it no longer exists: *The bombings have destroyed most of the city.* • *Unfortunately, all her letters were destroyed in a fire.* ➔ see Thesaurus at DAMAGE[2]

de·struc·tion /dɪˈstrʌkʃən/ *noun* (no plural) when something is destroyed: *the destruction of the Amazon rain forest*

de·tach /dɪˈtætʃ/ *verb* (formal) to remove part of something that has been made so that you can remove it: *Detach the bottom half of the page by tearing along the dotted line.*

de·tached /dɪˈtætʃt/ *adjective BrE* a detached house is not joined to another house

de·tail /ˈdiːteɪl $ dɪˈteɪl/ *noun*

KEY PATTERNS
details of something

a small fact or piece of information about something: *You will find more details of the program on our website.*

PHRASES
in detail: *Can you describe **in detail** (=thoroughly) how you did this experiment?*
someone's details your details are the facts about you that someone wants to know: *Please **fill in your details** below.*

de·tailed /ˈdiːteɪld $ dɪˈteɪld/ *adjective* a detailed description, account etc includes a lot of information: *The woman gave a detailed description of the man.*

de·tain /dɪˈteɪn/ *verb* (formal) if the police detain someone, they keep them somewhere and do not allow them to leave

de·tect /dɪˈtekt/ *verb* to find or notice something that is not easy to see, hear etc: *a machine that can detect alcohol in people's breath*

de·tec·tive /dɪˈtektɪv/ *noun* a police officer whose job is to discover who is responsible for crimes

de·tec·tor /dɪˈtektə $ dɪˈtektɚ/ *noun* a piece of equipment that tells you if there is a particular substance somewhere: *a smoke detector*

de·ten·tion /dɪˈtenʃən/ *noun* a school punishment in which you have to stay at school after the other students have left

de·ter /dɪˈtɜː $ dɪˈtɚ/ *verb* (formal) (**deterred**, **deterring**) if something deters you from doing something, it makes you not want to do it: *The long working hours deter many young people from becoming doctors.*

de·ter·gent /dɪˈtɜːdʒənt $ dɪˈtɚdʒənt/ *noun* a liquid or powder that you use for washing clothes, dishes etc

de·te·ri·o·rate /dɪˈtɪəriəreɪt $ dɪˈtɪriəˌreɪt/ *verb* (formal) to become worse: *The weather deteriorated, and by the afternoon it was raining.*

de·ter·mi·na·tion /dɪˌtɜːməˈneɪʃən $ dɪˌtɚməˈneɪʃən/ *noun* (no plural) a desire to continue trying to do something, even when it is difficult: *I really admire his determination to succeed!*

de·ter·mined /dɪˈtɜːmɪnd $ dɪˈtɝmɪnd/ *adjective*

KEY PATTERNS
determined to do something
determined (that)

wanting very much to do something, and not letting anyone or anything stop you: *No one in my family had ever gone to university, but I* ***was determined to*** *go.* • *We* ***were determined that*** *we would win the game.*

de·ter·min·er /dɪˈtɜːmɪnə $ dɪˈtɝmənɚ/ *noun* in grammar, a word you use before a noun to show which thing you mean. In the phrases 'the car' and 'some new cars', 'the' and 'some' are determiners

de·test /dɪˈtest/ *verb* (formal) to hate someone or something very much SYNONYM **loathe**: *He detests vegetables and hardly ever eats them.* → see Thesaurus at HATE[1]

det·o·nate /ˈdetəneɪt $ ˈdetnˌeɪt/ *verb* if you detonate a bomb, or if it detonates, it explodes

de·tour /ˈdiːtʊə $ ˈditʊr/ *noun* a way of going somewhere that takes longer than the usual way: *On the way home we made a detour to visit some friends.* —**detour** *verb*

dev·a·state /ˈdevəsteɪt/ *verb* if bombs, wars, storms etc devastate a place, they damage it very badly: *The storm devastated a large part of the state.*

dev·a·stat·ed /ˈdevəsteɪtɪd/ *adjective* very sad and shocked about something that has happened: *Andrew and Maria were devastated by their son's death.*

dev·a·stat·ing /ˈdevəsteɪtɪŋ/ *adjective* causing a lot of damage or shock: *The accident had a devastating effect on Stanley's life.*

de·vel·op /dɪˈveləp/ *verb*

KEY PATTERNS
develop into something
develop from something
develop something

1 if something develops, or if you develop it, it gets bigger or becomes more important: *Their business* ***has developed into*** *one of the biggest in the country.* • *Most plants* ***develop from*** *seeds.* • *We are developing close ties between our two countries.*
2 to begin to have an illness or feeling: *His wife developed cancer.*
3 to make pictures from photographic film, using special chemicals: *Photographs are developed in a dark room.*

SPELLING
This word is often spelled wrongly. The correct spelling is: **develop**.

de·vel·op·ment /dɪˈveləpmənt/ *noun*
1 the process of growing, changing, or making something: *The company spends a lot on research and development.* • ***the development of*** *a baby*
2 a new event that changes a situation: *a new development in the treatment of cancer*
3 a group of new buildings, or the work of building them: *a housing development* • *The environment is being damaged by development.*

de·vice /dɪˈvaɪs/ *noun* a machine or tool, usually a fairly complicated one → see Thesaurus at MACHINE

Dev·il /ˈdevəl/ *noun* **the Devil** an evil SPIRIT that is God's powerful enemy in some religions

de·vi·ous /ˈdiːviəs/ *adjective* clever but unpleasant and dishonest

de·vise /dɪˈvaɪz/ *verb* (formal) to think of a new way of doing something: *People are constantly devising new exercise programmes.*

de·vote /dɪˈvəʊt $ dɪˈvoʊt/ *verb* if you devote your time, energy etc to something, you spend most of your time doing it: *He devoted most of his life to scientific research.*

de·vot·ed /dɪˈvəʊtɪd $ dɪˈvoʊtɪd/ *adjective* someone who is devoted to another person, their work etc loves or cares about them a lot: *He is devoted to his family.*

de·vo·tion /dɪˈvəʊʃən $ dɪˈvoʊʃən/ *noun* (no plural) when you love or care about someone or something a lot: *her devotion to her job*

de·vour /dɪˈvaʊə $ dɪˈvaʊɚ/ *verb* (written) to eat something quickly: *Tony had already devoured half a pizza.*

de·vout /dɪˈvaʊt/ *adjective* very religious: *a devout Catholic*

dew /djuː $ duː/ *noun* (no plural) small drops of water that form on the surfaces of things that are outside during the night: *The grass was covered in dew.*

di·a·be·tes /ˌdaɪəˈbiːtiːz/ *noun* (no plural) a disease in which there is too much sugar in your blood

di·a·bet·ic /ˌdaɪəˈbetɪk/ *noun* someone who has diabetes: *Diabetics cannot eat a lot of sweet food.*

di·a·bol·i·cal /ˌdaɪəˈbɒlɪkəl $ ˌdaɪəˈbɑlɪkəl/ *adjective BrE* (spoken) very bad SYNONYM **terrible**: *This film is diabolical.*

di·ag·nose /ˈdaɪəgnəʊz $ ˌdaɪəgˈnoʊs/ *verb* to find out or say what illness someone has: *His doctor diagnosed cancer.*

di·ag·no·sis /ˌdaɪəgˈnəʊsəs $ ˌdaɪəgˈnoʊsəs/ *noun* (plural **diagnoses** /-siːz/) when a doctor says what illness someone has: *The doctor's diagnosis was wrong.*

di·ag·o·nal /daɪˈægənəl/ *adjective* a diagonal line slopes up or down

di·a·gram /ˈdaɪəgræm/ *noun* a drawing that uses simple lines: *He drew a diagram of the new bridge.*
→ see Thesaurus at PICTURE[1]

dial[1] /daɪəl/ *verb* (**dialled, dialling** *BrE*, **dialed, dialing** *AmE*) to press the buttons or turn the dial on a telephone: *I dialled her number again.*

dial[2] *noun* a round flat object on a radio or other piece of equipment that you turn to make it do something: *Turn the dial to make the oven hotter.*

dial

di·a·lect /ˈdaɪəlekt/ *noun* a form of a language that people in one part of a country speak: *Chinese people speak many different dialects.*

ˈdialling ˌcode *noun BrE* the part of a telephone number that you have to add when you are telephoning a different town or country SYNONYM **area code** *AmE*: *The dialling code for Cambridge is 01223.*

di·a·logue *BrE*, **dialog** *AmE* /ˈdaɪəlɒg $ ˈdaɪəˌlɔg/ *noun* a conversation between people in a book, film, or play

di·am·e·ter /daɪˈæmətə $ daɪˈæmətɚ/ *noun* a line that goes through the middle of a circle, or the length of this line: *The ball is about four inches in diameter.*

di·a·mond /ˈdaɪəmənd/ *noun* **1** a very valuable clear hard stone, used in jewellery: *She wore a diamond ring.* **2** a shape with four straight sides of equal length that stands on one of its points **3 diamonds** a group of playing cards with a diamond shape printed on them: *the queen of diamonds*

di·a·per /ˈdaɪəpə $ ˈdaɪpɚ/ the American word for NAPPY

di·ar·rhoea *BrE*, **diarrhea** *AmE* /ˌdaɪəˈrɪə/ *noun* (no plural) an illness in which waste from your body is not solid and comes out often: *Too much fruit can give you diarrhoea.*

di·a·ry /ˈdaɪəri/ *noun* (plural **diaries**) a book with a space for each day in which you write things that you are planning to do or things that have happened: *I'll check my diary to see if I can come Friday.*

SPELLING
Don't confuse the spelling of **diary** with **dairy** (=a place where they make butter and cheese).

dice[1] /daɪs/ *noun* (plural **dice**) a small square block with a different number of spots on each side, that you use in games: *The first player rolls the dice.*

dice[2] *verb* to cut food into small square pieces: *Dice the potato and add it to the oil.*

dic·tate /dɪkˈteɪt $ ˈdɪkteɪt/ *verb* to say words for someone to write on a piece of paper: *She used to dictate letters to her secretary.*

dic·ta·tion /dɪkˈteɪʃən/ *noun* when someone says words for someone else to write on a piece of paper: *The exam consists of a written paper and a dictation.*

dic·ta·tor /dɪk'teɪtə $ 'dɪkteɪtɚ/ *noun* a leader who has complete power: *A cruel dictator ruled the country.*

dic·ta·tor·ship /dɪk'teɪtəʃɪp $ dɪk'teɪtɚˌʃɪp/ *noun* a system in which a dictator controls a country

dic·tion·a·ry /'dɪkʃənəri $ 'dɪkʃəˌneri/ *noun* (plural **dictionaries**) a book that gives a list of words in alphabetical order, with their meanings in the same or another language: *If you don't understand a word, look it up in a dictionary.*

did the past tense of DO

did·n't /'dɪdnt/ the short form of 'did not': *I didn't want to go.*

die /daɪ/ *verb* (**dying**)

KEY PATTERNS
die of/from an illness

to stop living: *Grandmother died last year.* • *The oak trees are **dying from** some sort of disease.* • *Her dad **died of** a heart attack.*

PHRASES

be dying for something, be dying to do something (spoken) to want to have or do something very much: *I'm **dying for** a cup of tea.* • *I'm **dying to** see her new movie.*

PHRASAL VERBS

die down
if something such as a wind or fire dies down, it slowly becomes less strong: *The flames **died down** after a few minutes.*

die out
to disappear completely: *That species of bird **died out** in the early 20th century.*

GRAMMAR
You say **He died**.
✘ Don't say 'he was died'.

die·sel /'diːzəl/ *noun* (no plural) a type of FUEL used in some engines

di·et¹ /'daɪət/ *noun* **1** the kind of food that you eat each day: *a healthy diet* **2** a plan to eat only certain kinds or amounts of food, in order to become thinner: *I'm so fat I need to go on a diet.*

diet² *verb* to eat less in order to become thinner: *My mother's always dieting.*

dif·fer /'dɪfə $ 'dɪfɚ/ *verb* **1** to be different: *This book differs from his other novels.* **2** (formal) if two people differ, they have different opinions SYNONYM **disagree**: *My father and I differ on many subjects.*

dif·fe·rence /'dɪfərəns/ *noun*

KEY PATTERNS
a difference between things/people
a difference in age/size etc

a way in which one person or thing is not the same as another ANTONYM **similarity**: *The **difference between** the two students is that Ross works harder.* • *The **difference in** age doesn't affect our friendship.* • ***What's the difference between** these two computers?*

PHRASES

make a difference to have an effect on a situation: *I want to **make a difference to** society.* • *New drugs have **made a big difference** in the treatment of the disease.* • ***It makes no difference*** (=does not have an effect) *whether you're black or white.*

tell the difference to be able to see what makes two things or people different: *I still can't **tell the difference between** her twin sons.*

dif·fe·rent /'dɪfərənt/ *adjective*

KEY PATTERNS
different from something
different to something *BrE*
different than something *AmE*

not the same: *I had lived in four different houses before I was ten.* • *Each day at work was different.* • *Schools in Japan **are different from** schools in England.* • *Boys **are** definitely **different to** girls in the way they behave.* • *The hotel **was different than** I expected.* —**differently** *adverb*: *Joe and I think quite **differently from** each other.*

GRAMMAR
Teachers prefer **different from**.

dif·fi·cult /'dɪfɪkəlt/ *adjective*

KEY PATTERNS
it is difficult to do something

not easy to understand or do SYNONYM **hard**: *Skiing isn't difficult, but it takes practice.* • *Philosophy is a difficult subject.* • ***It's really difficult to** find a cheap place to live in London.* • *That's a really difficult question.*

dif·fi·cul·ty /'dɪfɪkəlti/ *noun*

KEY PATTERNS
have difficulty doing something
do something with difficulty

1 (no plural) when it is not easy to do something: *I **had difficulty** finding Kim's house.* • *He speaks slowly and **with difficulty**.*
2 a problem: *They had mechanical difficulties on the plane.*

dig

dig /dɪg/ *verb* (**dug** /dʌg/, **digging**)

KEY PATTERNS
dig a hole

to make a hole in the ground by moving the earth: *Her father was digging in the garden.* • *Dig a hole and put the rose bush in it.*

PHRASAL VERBS
dig out
dig something/someone out to get something out of earth, snow etc using a tool or your hands: *Workers **dug out** the people buried in the avalanche.*
dig up
dig something up to take something out of the ground using a tool: *We **dug up** a gold watch.*

di·gest /daɪ'dʒest/ *verb* when you digest food, it changes in your stomach into a form your body can use

di·ges·tion /daɪ'dʒestʃən/ *noun* (no plural) the process of digesting food: *He has problems with his digestion.*

di·git /'dɪdʒɪt/ *noun* (formal) a single number SYNONYM **figure**: *What's the first digit of your phone number?*

di·gi·tal /'dɪdʒɪtl/ *adjective* **1 a digital watch, a digital clock** a watch or clock that shows the time in the form of numbers → see picture at WATCH[2] **2** using a system in which information is in the form of changing electronic signals: *a digital recording of the concert*

dig·ni·fied /'dɪgnəfaɪd/ *adjective* calm, serious, and proud in a way that makes people respect you: *She remained dignified despite her husband's behaviour.*

dig·ni·ty /'dɪgnəti/ *noun* (no plural) when you act in a calm, serious way, even in difficult situations, and this makes people respect you: *She accepted her fate with great dignity.*

di·lap·i·dat·ed /də'læpədeɪtɪd/ *adjective* a dilapidated building or vehicle is old and in bad condition

di·lem·ma /də'lemə/ *noun* a situation in which you find it difficult to choose between two possible actions: *He's in a dilemma about whether to go to college or not.*

dil·i·gent /'dɪlədʒənt/ *adjective* working very hard: *Mary is a very diligent student.*

di·lute /daɪ'luːt/ *verb* to make a liquid weaker or thinner by mixing another liquid with it: *Dilute the orange juice with water.*

dim /dɪm/ *adjective* (**dimmer**, **dimmest**) not bright: *The light was becoming dimmer.*

dime /daɪm/ *noun* a coin used in the US worth 10 cents

di·men·sions /daɪ'menʃənz/ *plural noun* the size of something, including its length, width, and height: *Measure the dimensions of the room.*

di·min·ish /dɪ'mɪnɪʃ/ *verb* (formal) to become smaller SYNONYM **decrease**: *The problem diminished as time passed.*

dim·ple /'dɪmpəl/ *noun* a small hollow place on your cheek or chin: *She gets two little dimples when she smiles.*

din /dɪn/ *noun* (informal) a loud continuous unpleasant noise SYNONYM **racket**: *Stop making such a din!*

A B C D E F G H I J K L M N O P Q R S T U V W X Y Z

din•er /'daɪnə $ 'daɪnɚ/ *noun AmE* a small restaurant where you can buy cheap meals: *The diner across the road does good food.*

din•gy /'dɪndʒi/ *adjective* (**dingier**, **dingiest**) dingy buildings or places are dirty, dark, and unpleasant: *The room was small and dingy.*

'dining ˌroom *noun* a room in a house or hotel where you sit down at a table to eat

SPELLING
This word is often spelled wrongly. The correct spelling is: **dining room**.

din•ner /'dɪnə $ 'dɪnɚ/ *noun*

KEY PATTERNS
have dinner
have something for dinner

the main meal of the day, which most people eat in the evening: *They had dinner at 8.* • *We're **having** fish **for dinner**.* • *Let's **go out for dinner*** (=eat at a restaurant) *tonight.*

'dinner ˌjacket *noun* a jacket that men wear on formal occasions SYNONYM **tuxedo** *AmE*

dinosaur

di•no•saur /'daɪnəsɔː $ 'daɪnəˌsɔr/ *noun* a large animal that lived in very ancient times and no longer exists

dip¹ /dɪp/ *verb* (**dipped**, **dipping**) to put something into a liquid and quickly lift it out again: *I dipped my toe in the water.* ➔ see picture on page A4

dip² *noun* a place where the surface of something goes down suddenly: *a dip in the road*

di•plo•ma /də'pləʊmə $ dɪ'ploʊmə/ *noun* an official document showing that someone has successfully finished a course of study: *I have a diploma in French translation.*

dip•lo•mat /'dɪpləmæt/ *noun* someone who the government employs to live and work in a foreign country. Their job is to help people from their own country who are also living or visiting there

dip•lo•mat•ic /ˌdɪplə'mætɪk/ *adjective* talking to people in a way that does not offend them: *Tell her she can't come to the party, but be diplomatic.*

dire /daɪə $ daɪɚ/ *adjective* (informal) very serious or terrible: *I'm in dire trouble.*

di•rect¹ /də'rekt/ *adjective*
1 going straight towards a person, place etc ANTONYM **indirect**: *direct eye contact* • *We got a **direct flight** to LA.*
2 not involving other events, things, or people ANTONYM **indirect**: *Over 20,000 people died this year as a direct result of smoking.*

direct² *adverb* **1** without stopping and not going anywhere else first: *Can I fly to Hong Kong **direct**?* • *This train **goes direct from** London **to** Edinburgh.*
2 without asking or involving anyone else SYNONYM **directly**: *You can speak to him direct on his mobile phone.*

direct³ *verb*

KEY PATTERNS
direct someone to a place

1 to tell the actors in a film or play what to do: *Jodie Foster has directed several films.*
2 (formal) to tell someone how to get to a place: *Can you **direct** me **to** the post office?*

di•rec•tion /də'rekʃən/ *noun*
1 the way that someone is going or pointing: *Are you sure you're **going in the right direction**?* • *Half the group went one way, while the others went **in the opposite direction**.* • *Charles pointed his finger **in my direction*** (=he pointed it towards me).
2 directions instructions telling you how to go from one place to another, or how to do something: *A woman gave us directions to the theatre.* • *Cook the pasta according to the directions on the package.*

di•rect•ly /də'rektli/ *adverb* **1** without involving any other person or thing: *I bought my computer directly from the manufacturer.* **2 directly in front of**

someone/something, directly behind someone/something exactly in front of or behind someone or something SYNONYM **right**: *I sat directly in front of Jon.*

di͵rect 'object *noun* the person or thing that is directly affected by the verb in a sentence. In the sentence 'Joe ate a sandwich', the direct object is 'sandwich'.

di·rec·tor /də'rektə $ də'rektɚ/ *noun* **1** someone who controls or manages a company: *a conference for company directors* **2** someone who gives instructions to actors in a film or play: *Who was the director of 'Star Wars'?*

di·rec·to·ry /daɪ'rektəri/ *noun* (plural **directories**) **1** a book or list of names, facts etc in alphabetical order: *the telephone directory* **2** a place on a computer where you store information SYNONYM **folder**: *Do you know what directory the files are in?*

dirt /dɜːt $ dɚt/ *noun* (no plural) dust, mud, or soil that makes things dirty: *Don't get any dirt on the carpet.*

dirt·y /'dɜːti $ 'dɚti/ *adjective* (**dirtier, dirtiest**) not clean: *Don't get your clothes dirty.* • *dirty hands*

THESAURUS
muddy: *muddy walking boots* (=covered in mud)
greasy: *The cooker's all* ***greasy*** (=covered with dirty fat or oil).
dusty: *There were piles of* ***dusty*** *old books* (=covered with dust).
filthy: *The boys came home from school with* ***filthy*** *clothes* (=very dirty).

dis·a·bil·i·ty /͵dɪsə'bɪləti/ *noun* (plural **disabilities**) a physical or mental condition that makes it difficult for someone to do things that most people do easily, such as walk or see: *children with learning disabilities*

dis·a·bled /dɪs'eɪbəld/ *adjective* someone who is disabled cannot use a part of their body in the way most people are able to: *There's a lift for disabled people.*

dis·ad·van·tage /͵dɪsəd'vɑːntɪdʒ $ ͵dɪsəd'væntɪdʒ/ *noun* something that makes things more difficult to do or less pleasant for you ANTONYM **advantage**: *What are the disadvantages of living in a flat?*

dis·a·gree /͵dɪsə'griː/ *verb*

KEY PATTERNS
disagree with someone
people disagree about/on something

to think or say that someone's opinion is wrong: *I'm sorry, but I totally disagree.* • *Many students* ***disagreed with*** *their parents on the issue.* • *My dad and I* ***disagree about*** *most things.* • *We'd only been married a week, and already we* ***disagreed on*** *which car to buy.*

GRAMMAR
You **disagree with** someone or **disagree with** someone's opinion.
✘ Don't say 'disagree someone' or 'disagree someone's opinion'.

dis·a·gree·ment /͵dɪsə'griːmənt/ *noun* when you do not agree with someone: *They had a disagreement about money.*

dis·ap·pear /͵dɪsə'pɪə $ ͵dɪsə'pɪr/ *verb*

KEY PATTERNS
disappear from a place

1 if someone or something disappears, you cannot then see them or find them SYNONYM **vanish** ANTONYM **appear**: *The plane* ***disappeared from*** *the radar screens.* • *Some books have* ***disappeared from*** *the library.*
2 to stop existing: *The rain forests are disappearing quickly.*

SPELLING
This word is often spelled wrongly. The correct spelling is: **disappear**.

dis·ap·point /͵dɪsə'pɔɪnt/ *verb* to make someone unhappy because something good that they expected did not happen: *I don't want to disappoint the children by telling them we can't go on holiday.*

SPELLING
This word is often spelled wrongly. The correct spelling is: **disappoint**.

—**disappointing** *adjective*: *It was disappointing to lose the match.* • *The England team had a disappointing result against Poland.*

dis·ap·point·ed /ˌdɪsəˈpɔɪntɪd/ *adjective*

KEY PATTERNS
disappointed (that)
disappointed in someone
disappointed with something

unhappy because something good that you expected did not happen: *Julie **was disappointed that** her friends couldn't come.* • *I'm very **disappointed in** you, Mark – I thought you could do better.* • *The coach was **bitterly disappointed** (=very disappointed) **with** our performance.* ➔ see Thesaurus at SAD

SPELLING
This word is often spelled wrongly. The correct spelling is: **disappointed**.

dis·ap·point·ment /ˌdɪsəˈpɔɪntmənt/ *noun* **1** (no plural) a feeling of sadness that something good has not happened: *I couldn't hide my disappointment at missing the trip.* **2** someone or something that is not as good as you hoped: *The party was a disappointment.*

SPELLING
This word is often spelled wrongly. The correct spelling is: **disappointment**.

dis·ap·prove /ˌdɪsəˈpruːv/ *verb*

KEY PATTERNS
disapprove of someone/something

to believe that someone or something is not good or acceptable ANTONYM **approve**: *Pete's parents **disapproved of** his new girlfriend.*

dis·ar·ma·ment /dɪsˈɑːməmənt $ dɪsˈɑrməmənt/ *noun* (no plural) when a country reduces the number of soldiers and weapons it has: *nuclear disarmament*

dis·ar·ray /ˌdɪsəˈreɪ/ *noun* **be in disarray** (written) to be very untidy or not organized: *After the party, the room was in total disarray.*

di·sas·ter /dɪˈzɑːstə $ dɪˈzæstɚ/ *noun* **1** an event such as an accident, flood, or storm that causes a lot of harm SYNONYM **catastrophe**: *Forty people were killed in the rail disaster.* **2** (informal) a complete failure: *The meal was a disaster.*

di·sas·trous /dɪˈzɑːstrəs $ dɪˈzæstrəs/ *adjective* very bad or ending in complete failure: *It will be disastrous if we lose.*

dis·be·lief /ˌdɪsbəˈliːf/ *noun* (no plural) (written) a feeling that something is not true or does not exist: *He stared at the broken window in disbelief.*

disc *BrE*, **disk** *AmE* /dɪsk/ *noun* **1** a round flat shape or object: *A metal disc hung from the dog's collar.* **2** a computer DISK

dis·card /dɪˈskɑːd $ dɪˈskɑrd/ *verb* (written) to throw something away because you no longer need it: *Make sure you discard old batteries safely.*

dis·charge /dɪsˈtʃɑːdʒ $ dɪsˈtʃɑrdʒ/ *verb* to officially allow someone to leave a place or organization: *They discharged him from hospital yesterday.*

dis·ci·pline /ˈdɪsəplɪn/ *noun* (no plural) when people obey rules and orders: *Discipline is very important in this school.*

ˈdisc ˌjockey *BrE*, **disk jockey** *AmE* a DJ

dis·co /ˈdɪskəʊ $ ˈdɪskoʊ/ *noun* a place or event where people dance to popular music: *Are you going to the school disco?*

dis·com·fort /dɪsˈkʌmfət $ dɪsˈkʌmfɚt/ *noun* (no plural) slight pain, or a feeling of being physically uncomfortable: *I have a little discomfort in my back.*

dis·con·cert·ing /ˌdɪskənˈsɜːtɪŋ $ ˌdɪskənˈsɚtɪŋ/ *adjective* (formal) making you feel slightly embarrassed, confused, or worried: *It's disconcerting when someone keeps staring at you.*

dis·con·nect /ˌdɪskəˈnekt/ *verb* to take out the wire, pipe etc that connects a machine or piece of equipment to something ANTONYM **connect**: *Have you disconnected the phone?*

dis·con·tent·ed /ˌdɪskənˈtentɪd/ *adjective* (written) unhappy or not satisfied ANTONYM **contented**: *Are you discontented with your work?*

dis·co·theque /ˈdɪskətek/ *noun* a DISCO

dis·count /ˈdɪskaʊnt/ *noun* a lower price than usual: *There are discounts of*

50% on all hats (=you can buy hats for 50% less than the usual price).

dis·cour·age /dɪsˈkʌrɪdʒ $ dɪsˈkɚɪdʒ/ *verb* to try to make someone want to do something less often ANTONYM **encourage**: *The government wants to discourage people from using their cars.*

dis·cour·aged /dɪsˈkʌrɪdʒd $ dɪsˈkɚɪdʒd/ *adjective* no longer having the confidence to continue doing something SYNONYM **disheartened**: *She gets discouraged when she doesn't win.*

dis·cov·er /dɪˈskʌvə $ dɪˈskʌvɚ/ *verb*

KEY PATTERNS
discover who/what/how etc
discover that

to find or learn something that you did not know about before: *Anna discovered a secret entrance to the old house.* • *At the end of the film, you **discover who** killed her.* • *Scientists soon **discovered that** the gas is lighter than air.* ➔ see Thesaurus at FIND

dis·cov·e·ry /dɪˈskʌvəri/ *noun* (plural **discoveries**)
1 a fact or an answer to a question that people did not know before: *Doctors have **made** important new **discoveries** about the disease.*
2 (no plural) when someone finds something that was hidden: *After the **discovery of** gold in California, many people went there.*

di·screet /dɪˈskriːt/ *adjective* careful about what you say or do because you do not want other people to know or be embarrassed: *They were very discreet about their relationship.*
—**discreetly** *adverb*

di·screp·an·cy /dɪˈskrepənsi/ *noun* (formal) (plural **discrepancies**) a difference between two things that should be the same: *There's a discrepancy between your results and mine.*

di·scre·tion /dɪˈskreʃən/ *noun* (no plural) (formal) the authority to decide what is the right thing to do in a situation: *Punishment is at the discretion of your teacher.*

di·scrim·i·nate /dɪˈskrɪməneɪt/ *verb* to unfairly treat one person or group differently from another: *It is illegal to discriminate against people because of their sex.*

di·scrim·i·na·tion /dɪˌskrɪməˈneɪʃən/ *noun* (no plural) unfair treatment of someone because of the group they belong to: *The company was found guilty of racial discrimination* (=unfair treatment of someone because of their race).

dis·cus /ˈdɪskəs/ *noun* (plural **discuses**) a flat heavy object that you throw as a sport

di·scuss /dɪˈskʌs/ *verb*

KEY PATTERNS
discuss something (with someone)
discuss how/whether/what

if you discuss something, you talk with someone about it: *Tomorrow we will discuss Chapter 3 in class.* • *I can always **discuss** my problems **with** my sister.* • *The teachers **were discussing how** to deal with the situation.*

di·scus·sion /dɪˈskʌʃən/ *noun*

KEY PATTERNS
a discussion about/on something

a conversation in which people talk about something: *Several students **had a discussion about** the homework assignment.* • *The meeting ended with **a discussion on** the current political situation.*

dis·ease /dɪˈziːz/ *noun* an illness or serious medical condition: *deaths from heart disease* ➔ see Thesaurus at ILLNESS

WORD CHOICE
disease or **illness**?
• You use **disease** about illnesses that you can catch from other people: *childhood **diseases** such as measles and chickenpox*
• You can also use **disease** about illnesses that affect a particular part of your body: *heart **disease***
• You use **illness** especially about the general condition of being ill: *She died after a long **illness**.*

dis·en·chant·ed /ˌdɪsɪnˈtʃɑːntɪd $ ˌdɪsɪnˈtʃæntɪd/ *adjective* (formal) no longer believing that something is good or important SYNONYM **disillusioned**: *I'm disenchanted with my job.*

dis·fig·ure /dɪs'fɪgə $ dɪs'fɪgjɚ/ *verb* to damage someone's appearance: *His face was disfigured in the fire.*

dis·grace¹ /dɪs'greɪs/ *noun* **1** (no plural) something that is very bad: *Your homework is a disgrace.* **2 in disgrace** if you are in disgrace, people disapprove of you because you have done something wrong: *After the fight, Sam went home in disgrace.*

disgrace² *verb* to do something so bad that people lose respect for you, your family, or your group: *You have disgraced yourself and your family.*

dis·grace·ful /dɪs'greɪsfəl/ *adjective* very bad: *Your behaviour was disgraceful.* —**disgracefully** *adverb*

dis·guise /dɪs'gaɪz/ *verb* **disguise yourself (as something)** to change your usual appearance so that people will not know who you are: *He disguised himself as a policeman.* —**disguise** *noun*: *The bank robber was in disguise.*

dis·gust /dɪs'gʌst/ *noun* (no plural) a feeling of strong dislike or disapproval: *He pushed his plate away in disgust.*

dis·gus·ted /dɪs'gʌstɪd/ *adjective* feeling strong dislike or disapproval: *I'm disgusted that you had to wait so long.*

dis·gust·ing /dɪs'gʌstɪŋ/ *adjective* something that is disgusting is very unpleasant, and makes you feel ill SYNONYM **revolting**: *This stuff tastes disgusting!* • *There's a disgusting smell in the fridge.* → see Thesaurus at BAD

USAGE
✘ Don't say 'It's very disgusting'. Just say **It's disgusting** or **It's absolutely disgusting**.

dish /dɪʃ/ *noun* (plural **dishes**)
1 a round container with low sides, used for holding food: *Arrange the slices on a flat dish and put them in the oven.*
2 food cooked or prepared in a particular way: *The restaurant offers a wide range of French dishes.*
PHRASES
do the dishes, wash the dishes to wash the plates, bowls etc that have been used when eating a meal

dis·heart·ened /dɪs'hɑːtnd $ dɪs'hɑrtnd/ *adjective* unhappy because you do not think you will achieve something you have been hoping for: *Don't get disheartened if your experiment doesn't work first time.*

di·shev·elled *BrE*, **disheveled** *AmE* /dɪ'ʃevəld/ *adjective* someone who is dishevelled looks untidy: *Her hair was all dishevelled.*

dis·hon·est /dɪs'ɒnəst $ dɪs'ɑnɪst/ *adjective* likely to lie, steal, or cheat ANTONYM **honest**: *a dishonest businessman* —**dishonestly** *adverb*: *Philip had behaved very dishonestly towards his classmates.*

dis·hon·est·y /dɪs'ɒnəsti $ dɪs'ɑnəsti/ *noun* (no plural) when someone lies, steals, or cheats: *His employer accused him of dishonesty.*

dis·hon·our *BrE*, **dishonor** *AmE* /dɪs'ɒnə $ dɪs'ɑnɚ/ *noun* (no plural) (formal) when people no longer respect you or approve of you because you have done something bad: *You have brought dishonour on your family.*

dish·wash·er /'dɪʃˌwɒʃə $ 'dɪʃˌwɑʃɚ/ *noun* a machine that washes dishes: *Please empty the dishwasher.*

dis·il·lu·sioned /ˌdɪsə'luːʒənd/ *adjective* having lost your belief that someone or something is good or right: *He became disillusioned with religion.*

dis·in·fect /ˌdɪsɪn'fekt/ *verb* to clean something with a chemical that destroys BACTERIA (=small living things that cause disease): *They disinfected all the kitchen surfaces.*

dis·in·fec·tant /ˌdɪsɪn'fektənt/ *noun* a chemical that destroys BACTERIA (=small living things that cause disease): *The nurse cleaned the floor with disinfectant.*

dis·in·te·grate /dɪs'ɪntəgreɪt/ *verb* to break up into small pieces: *The boat was heading towards land when it hit a rock and disintegrated.*

disk /dɪsk/ *noun* **1** also **hard disk** the part of a computer where you store information: *I think the hard disk is full.* **2** a FLOPPY DISK **3** the American spelling of DISC

'disk drive *noun* a piece of equipment in a computer that is used to move information to or from a FLOPPY DISK

'disk ˌjockey *AmE* a DJ

dis·like /dɪs'laɪk/ *verb* to not like someone or something ANTONYM **like**: *My mother dislikes all my girlfriends.* —**dislike** *noun*: *She's always had a dislike of hard work.*

dis·lo·cate /'dɪsləkeɪt $ dɪs'loʊkeɪt/ *verb* if you dislocate a bone in your body, it comes out of its normal place because of an accident: *He's dislocated his shoulder.*

dis·loy·al /dɪs'lɔɪəl/ *adjective* (formal) not supporting your friends, family, country etc, or doing things that may harm them ANTONYM **loyal**: *It would be disloyal of me to complain about my wife.*

dis·loy·al·ty /dɪs'lɔɪəlti/ *noun* (no plural) when you do not support your friends, family, country etc, or do things that may harm them ANTONYM **loyalty**: *He showed disloyalty to his colleagues by criticizing them.*

dis·mal /'dɪzməl/ *adjective* making you feel unhappy and without hope SYNONYM **depressing**: *dismal January weather*

dis·may /dɪs'meɪ/ *noun* (no plural) (written) a strong feeling of worry, disappointment, or sadness that you have when something unpleasant happens: *She shook her head in dismay.*

dis·miss /dɪs'mɪs/ *verb* **1** to refuse to consider someone's ideas or opinions: *Why do you always dismiss my ideas?* **2** (formal) to make someone leave their job SYNONYM **fire**, **sack**: *The company dismissed him for stealing.*

dis·o·be·di·ent /ˌdɪsə'biːdiənt/ *adjective* deliberately not doing what someone tells you to do ANTONYM **obedient**: *You're a very disobedient child.*

dis·o·bey /ˌdɪsə'beɪ/ *verb* to refuse to do what someone in authority or a rule tells you to do ANTONYM **obey**: *He deliberately disobeyed my orders.*
➔ see picture at OBEY

dis·or·der /dɪs'ɔːdə $ dɪs'ɔrdɚ/ *noun* (formal) **1** (no plural) when things or people are very untidy: *The classroom was in a state of disorder.* **2** an illness that stops part of your body working properly: *She has a rare blood disorder.*

dis·or·der·ly /dɪs'ɔːdəli $ dɪs'ɔrdɚli/ *adjective* (formal) untidy or uncontrolled ANTONYM **orderly**: *The papers were in a disorderly mess.*

dis·or·gan·ized also **disorganised** *BrE* /dɪs'ɔːgənaɪzd $ dɪs'ɔrgəˌnaɪzd/ *adjective* not arranged or planned very well: *The wedding was completely disorganized.*

dis·or·i·ent·ed /dɪs'ɔːrientɪd/ also **dis·or·i·en·tat·ed** *BrE* /dɪs'ɔːriənˌteɪtɪd/ *adjective* confused and not knowing what is happening or where you are: *She felt disoriented after the accident.*

di·spatch also **despatch** *BrE* /dɪ'spætʃ/ *verb* (formal) **1** to send someone to a place as part of their job: *Troops are being dispatched to protect the airport.* **2** to send a letter, package etc to someone: *Father dispatched an angry letter to 'The Times' immediately.*

di·spense /dɪ'spens/ *verb* (formal) to provide something for people, usually when they come for it: *a machine that dispenses chocolate*

di·spens·er /dɪ'spensə $ dɪ'spensɚ/ *noun* a machine that you can get things such as drinks or money from: *I got a coffee from the drinks dispenser.* • *a cash dispenser*

di·sperse /dɪ'spɜːs $ dɪ'spɚs/ *verb* (formal) to make things or people go in different directions: *The police finally managed to disperse the crowd.*

di·spir·it·ed /dɪ'spɪrətɪd/ *adjective* sad and without hope SYNONYM **disheartened**: *After their defeat, the team felt dispirited.*

dis·play¹ /dɪ'spleɪ/ *noun*

KEY PATTERNS
a display of things

1 a set of things that are put somewhere so that people can see them: *There was a **display of** modern sculptures in the library.*
2 a public performance of skilful actions: *a display of juggling*
3 a part of an electronic machine that shows numbers, words etc: *The number you are calling is shown on the phone's display.*

PHRASES

be on display if things are on display, they have been put somewhere so that

A B C D E F G H I J K L M N O P Q R S T U V W X Y Z

people can see them SYNONYM **be on show**: *The paintings will be on display until November 30.*

display² *verb* **1** to put things where people can see them: *We will display your pictures on the wall.* **2** to show a particular feeling: *The killer has displayed no sympathy for his victims.*

dis·po·sa·ble /dɪˈspəʊzəbəl $ dɪˈspoʊzəbəl/ *adjective* disposable things are used for a short time and then thrown away: *a disposable razor*

dis·pos·al /dɪˈspəʊzəl $ dɪˈspoʊzəl/ *noun* (no plural) (formal) when you get rid of something because you no longer want it: *The council is in charge of waste disposal.*

dis·po·si·tion /ˌdɪspəˈzɪʃən/ *noun* (formal) someone's usual character SYNONYM **nature**: *He has a very trusting disposition.*

dis·prove /dɪsˈpruːv/ *verb* to show that something is false ANTONYM **prove**: *He set out to disprove my theory.*

dis·pute¹ /dɪˈspjuːt/ *noun* a serious argument or disagreement: *We're having a dispute with our neighbours about noise.*

dispute² *verb* to say that you think something is not correct or true: *I don't dispute what you're saying.*

dis·qual·i·fy /dɪsˈkwɒləfaɪ $ dɪsˈkwɑləˌfaɪ/ *verb* (**disqualified**, **disqualifies**) to stop someone taking part in an activity or competition because they have done something wrong: *The judges disqualified him for taking drugs.*

dis·re·gard /ˌdɪsrɪˈɡɑːd $ ˌdɪsrɪˈɡɑrd/ *verb* (formal) if you disregard something, you do not give it your attention because you think it is not important: *Why do you always disregard everything I say?*

dis·rupt /dɪsˈrʌpt/ *verb* to stop a situation or event from continuing normally: *I don't want to disrupt your work, but can you come to a meeting?*

dis·rup·tion /dɪsˈrʌpʃən/ *noun* when someone or something stops a situation or event from continuing normally: *After the brief disruption, the game continued.*

dis·sat·is·fied /dɪˈsætəsfaɪd/ *adjective* not satisfied: *Are you dissatisfied with the course?*

dis·sect /dɪˈsekt/ *verb* (formal) to cut up a plant or animal in order to study it: *In biology, we dissected a rat.*

> **SPELLING**
> This word is often spelled wrongly. The correct spelling is: **dissect**.

dis·ser·ta·tion /ˌdɪsəˈteɪʃən $ ˌdɪsɚˈteɪʃən/ *noun* a long piece of writing about a subject, especially one that you write as part of a university degree: *She wrote a dissertation on Shakespeare's early plays.*

dis·si·dent /ˈdɪsədənt/ *noun* someone who publicly criticizes their government

dissolve

dis·solve /dɪˈzɒlv $ dɪˈzɑlv/ *verb* if something solid dissolves, it becomes part of a liquid when you mix it with the liquid: *These tablets dissolve in water.*

dis·tance /ˈdɪstəns/ *noun* the amount of space between two places or things: *Kelly was only able to run a **short distance**.* • *Some people have to drive **long distances** to work.*

PHRASES

in the distance far away: *We could see some houses **in the distance**.*

at a distance at or from a place that is far away: *Even **at a distance**, we could see that it was Rob.*

dis·tant /ˈdɪstənt/ *adjective* **1** far away, or long ago: *The story takes place on a distant planet.* • *All these things happened in the distant past.* **2** distant relatives are not very closely related to you ANTONYM **close**: *Frances is a distant cousin of mine.*

dis·taste /dɪsˈteɪst/ *noun* (no plural) (formal) a strong dislike of something: *He has a great distaste for foreign films.*

dis•til *BrE*, **distill** *AmE* /dɪˈstɪl/ *verb* (**distilled**, **distilling**) to turn a liquid into gas and then turn the gas into liquid again, in order to make it purer or stronger —**distilled** *adjective*: *distilled water*

dis•tinct /dɪˈstɪŋkt/ *adjective* **1** clearly different or separate: *two distinct groups* **2** very easy to see or hear: *She spoke in a clear, distinct voice.*

dis•tinc•tion /dɪˈstɪŋkʃən/ *noun* a clear difference between things: *the distinction between formal and informal language*

dis•tinc•tive /dɪˈstɪŋktɪv/ *adjective* different from others and easy to recognize: *She has a distinctive style of writing.*

dis•tin•guish /dɪˈstɪŋgwɪʃ/ *verb* (formal) **1** if you can distinguish between things or people, you can recognize or understand the difference between them: *He couldn't distinguish red from green.* **2** something that distinguishes a person or thing makes them clearly different from others: *What distinguishes this book from others you have read?*

> **PRONUNCIATION**
> You pronounce **-uish** like 'wish'.

dis•tin•guished /dɪˈstɪŋgwɪʃt/ *adjective* successful and respected: *a distinguished doctor*

dis•tort /dɪˈstɔːt $ dɪˈstɔrt/ *verb* to change the shape or sound of something so it is strange or unclear: *The heat had distorted the doll's face.*

dis•tract /dɪˈstrækt/ *verb* to take someone's attention away from what they are doing: *Don't distract your sister from her homework.*

dis•tract•ed /dɪˈstræktɪd/ *adjective* anxious and not able to think clearly about what is happening around you: *You seem a little distracted.*

dis•trac•tion /dɪˈstrækʃən/ *noun* something that takes your attention away from what you are doing: *I can't work at home – there are too many distractions.*

dis•traught /dɪˈstrɔːt/ *adjective* very anxious or upset: *She was distraught because her son was missing.*

dis•tress[1] /dɪˈstres/ *noun* (no plural) very great worry or sadness: *The disagreement caused us a lot of distress.*

distress[2] *verb* to make someone feel very upset —**distressed** *adjective*: *Clare seemed very distressed.* —**distressing** *adjective*: *The funeral was very distressing.*

dis•trib•ute /dɪˈstrɪbjuːt/ *verb* to give something to each person in a group SYNONYM **give out**: *The children distributed sandwiches.*

dis•trict /ˈdɪstrɪkt/ *noun* an area of a city or country: *He works in the financial district of London.*

dis•trust /dɪsˈtrʌst/ *noun* a feeling that you cannot trust someone: *He views all businessmen with distrust.* —**distrust** *verb*: *My father distrusts all accountants.*

dis•turb /dɪˈstɜːb $ dɪˈstɚb/ *verb* **1** to stop someone doing something, for example by making a noise, asking a question etc: *Please don't disturb me while I'm working.* **2** to worry or upset someone: *The way he stared at me really disturbed me.*

dis•turb•ance /dɪˈstɜːbəns $ dɪˈstɚbəns/ *noun* something that stops you doing something you would normally do: *The builders said they would cause as little disturbance as possible.*

dis•turb•ing /dɪˈstɜːbɪŋ $ dɪˈstɚbɪŋ/ *adjective* making you feel worried or upset: *disturbing news*

ditch /dɪtʃ/ *noun* (plural **ditches**) a long narrow hole in the ground at the side of a field or road: *The car ended up in a ditch at the side of the road.*

dit•to /ˈdɪtəʊ $ ˈdɪtoʊ/ *noun* two small marks (") that you write under a word in a list so that you do not have to write the same word again

di•va /ˈdiːvə/ *noun* a very famous and successful female singer

dive /daɪv/ *verb* (**dived**, **dove** /dəʊv $ doʊv/ *AmE*) **1** to jump into water with your head and arms first: *I walked to the edge of the pool and dived in.* → see Thesaurus at JUMP[1] **2** to swim under water, using special equipment

A B C D E F G H I J K L M N O P Q R S T U V W X Y Z

to help you breathe —**dive** *noun*: *He did a perfect dive into the water.*

div·er /ˈdaɪvə $ ˈdaɪvɚ/ *noun* someone who swims under water with breathing equipment: *The divers found an old ship that had sunk.*

di·verse /daɪˈvɜːs $ dəˈvɚs/ *adjective* (formal) very different from each other: *She has a diverse range of interests.*

di·ver·sion /daɪˈvɜːʃən $ dəˈvɚʒən/ *noun* something that takes your attention away from something else: *One boy created a diversion while the other stole the CDs.*

di·vert /daɪˈvɜːt $ dəˈvɚt/ *verb* **1** to change the direction of something: *They diverted the river.* **2 divert attention from something** to stop people giving their attention to something: *The government is trying to divert attention from its mistakes.*

di·vide /dɪˈvaɪd/ *verb*

KEY PATTERNS
divide (something) into two/three etc parts
divide something between/among people
divide one number by another

1 if you divide something, or if it divides, it separates into two or more parts SYNONYM **split**: *Divide the cake into four equal pieces.* • *The class* ***divided into*** *three groups for the game.* • *Brenda* ***divided*** *the candy* ***among*** *all the children.*
2 to calculate how many times a number is contained in another number: *21* ***divided by*** *7 is 3 (21/7=3).*
→ see Thesaurus at CALCULATE

di·vine /dɪˈvaɪn/ *adjective* like God, or coming from God: *She asked for divine help.*

div·ing /ˈdaɪvɪŋ/ *noun* (no plural)
1 the activity of swimming under water, using special equipment to help you breathe **2** the activity or sport of jumping into water with your head and arms first

di·vis·i·ble /dɪˈvɪzəbəl/ *adjective* a number that is divisible by another number can be divided by it exactly: *All even numbers are divisible by 2.*

di·vi·sion /dɪˈvɪʒən/ *noun*

KEY PATTERNS
a division between things

1 (no plural) the process of calculating how many times one number is contained in another number: *multiplication and division*
2 when you separate something into two or more parts, or the way that you separate it: *the* ***division between*** *work and leisure time*
3 a part of a large company or organization: *Tony is the manager of the marketing division.*

di·vorce¹ /dɪˈvɔːs $ dɪˈvɔrs/ *noun* the legal ending of a marriage: *His parents decided to get a divorce.*

divorce² *verb* to legally end your marriage: *Julie divorced her husband.* —**divorced** *adjective*: *My parents are divorced.*

USAGE
You usually say that two people **get divorced**: *Her parents got divorced when she was 12.*

THESAURUS
separate: *Her parents have separated* (=started living apart).
split up: *She's just split up with John* (=ended their marriage or relationship).
break up: *They* ***broke up*** *after ten years together* (=ended their marriage or relationship).

diz·zy /ˈdɪzi/ *adjective* (**dizzier, dizziest**) feeling as if you cannot stand up properly, for example because you are ill: *After we danced I felt dizzy and had to sit down.* —**dizziness** *noun* (no plural)

DJ /ˌdiː ˈdʒeɪ/ *noun* someone who plays popular music records on the radio or at parties or clubs

DNA /ˌdiː en ˈeɪ/ *noun* the chemical substance that carries GENETIC information in cells in plants, animals, and humans: *You can have a DNA test to find out if you have the disease.*

do → see box on pages 194 and 195

do·cile /ˈdəʊsaɪl $ ˈdɑsəl/ *adjective* quiet and easy to control: *The horse was very docile.*

dock¹ /dɒk $ dɑk/ *noun* **1** a place where things are taken on and off ships

2 the dock *BrE* the place in a court of law where the prisoner stands SYNONYM **the stand** *AmE* **3** a piece of electronic equipment that you can connect a LAPTOP, camera, MP3 player etc to, in your home, office etc SYNONYM **docking station**: *I bought a dock for my i-Pod so I can listen to music through my speaker system.*

dock² *verb* **1** to go into the part of a HARBOUR where people and goods are taken on and off ships: *The ship was getting ready to dock.* **2** to connect a LAPTOP to a dock, so that you can use it on your desk like a normal computer

'docking ˌstation *noun* a piece of electronic equipment that you can connect a LAPTOP, MP3 player etc to, in your home, office etc SYNONYM **dock**

doc·tor /'dɒktə $ 'dɑktɚ/ *noun* someone whose job is to treat people who are sick. In writing, you use the abbreviation 'Dr' before someone's name: *Nina had to* ***go to the doctor.*** • *The letter was addressed to Dr Armand.*

> THESAURUS
> **surgeon**: *The surgeon* (=a doctor who does operations) *removed her left kidney.*
> **specialist**: *a heart* ***specialist*** (=a doctor who knows a lot about a particular medical area)
> **GP**: *If you're worried, go and see your GP* (=a doctor who deals with ordinary health problems).

doc·u·ment /'dɒkjəmənt $ 'dɑkjəmənt/ *noun* a piece of paper that has official information written on it: *a case full of important legal documents*

doc·u·men·tary /ˌdɒkjə'mentri $ ˌdɑkjə'mentri/ *noun* (plural **documentaries**) a serious film or television programme that gives facts about something: *We watched a documentary about dinosaurs.*

doc·u·men·ta·tion /ˌdɒkjəmən'teɪʃən $ ˌdɑkjəmən'teɪʃən/ *noun* (no plural) (formal) documents that prove or show that something is true: *Have you got any documentation to prove who you are?*

dodge /dɒdʒ $ dɑdʒ/ *verb* to move suddenly to the side in order to avoid someone or something: *Someone threw a stone at me and I dodged.*

dodg·y /'dɒdʒi $ 'dɑdʒi/ *adjective BrE* (informal) (**dodgier**, **dodgiest**) a person or thing that is dodgy is one that you think may be dishonest or bad: *His friend looked a bit dodgy to me.*

does /dəz ; strong dʌz/ the third person singular of the present tense of DO

does·n't /'dʌzənt/ the short form of 'does not': *She doesn't speak English.*

dog /dɒg $ dɔg/ *noun* an animal with four legs, a tail, and fur that many people keep as a pet or to protect them: *We got a big dog to frighten away burglars.* ➔ see picture on page A8

dog·mat·ic /dɒg'mætɪk $ dɔg'mætɪk/ *adjective* someone who is dogmatic has strong beliefs which they do not want to change: *He is very dogmatic about how languages should be taught.*

doing the present participle of DO

dole /dəʊl $ doʊl/ *noun* **be on the dole** *BrE* if you are on the dole, you do not have a job, so the government gives you money to help you buy food, clothes etc: *He left school at 16 and now he's on the dole.*

doll /dɒl $ dɑl/ *noun* a toy that looks like a small person: *My little sister was playing with her dolls.*

dol·lar /'dɒlə $ 'dɑlɚ/ *noun* written sign **$** the name of the unit of money in the US, Australia, Canada, New Zealand, and some other countries: *Dad gave me $5* (=five dollars) *for washing the car.*

> SPELLING
> This word is often spelled wrongly. The correct spelling is: **dollar**.

dol·phin /'dɒlfɪn $ 'dɑlfɪn/ *noun* a very intelligent sea animal that looks like a large grey fish

do·main name /də'meɪn neɪm/ *noun* the first part of the address of a website, which usually begins with 'www.' and often ends with '.com'

dome /dəʊm $ doʊm/ *noun* a building with a round roof

do·mes·tic /də'mestɪk/ *adjective* **1** connected with family relationships

A B C D E F G H I J K L M N O P Q R S T U V W X Y Z

do /du:/ *verb*

1 to perform an action or activity: *"What are you* **doing***?" "I'm mending my bike."* • *She's gone into town to* **do the shopping***.* • *Have you* **done your homework** *yet?* • *He's been* **doing** *the same* **job** *for the last 20 years.* • *I still have so much work to* **do***!*

KEY PATTERNS
do the shopping/washing/cooking/cleaning
do your work/your homework/the housework
do your job/duty
do an experiment/some research

2 used when forming negative sentences: *I* **don't** *know.* • **Don't** *be nervous. It'll be all right.* • *Michelle* **doesn't** *trust me.* • *I* **didn't** *want to get up this morning.*

3 used in questions: *Where* **do** *you live?* • *What* **did** *you say?* • *When* **did** *you and Ken first meet?* • *Why* **do** *I have to sign all these papers?*

4 used in question tags at the end of a sentence, when changing a statement into a question: *You didn't tell him what I said,* **did** *you?* • *You went to Mary's yesterday,* **didn't** *you?* • *They don't argue all the time,* **do** *they?*

5 used when you do not want to repeat another verb: *She's only eight, but she eats more than I* **do** (=she eats more than I eat). • *"I loved the movie." "So* **did** *I."*

6 used when you want to emphasize what you are saying: *You* **do** *look good in that suit* (=you look very good)*!* • *The course* **does** *sound interesting* (=it sounds very interesting).

WORD CHOICE
do, **make**, **take**, or **commit**?
Be careful which verb you choose.
- You **do** your **work** or a **job**.
- You **make** a **mistake**.
- You **take** a **test**.
- Someone **commits** a **crime**.

✗ Don't say 'make a test', 'do a mistake', or 'make a crime'.

PHRASES

I/she etc could do with something (spoken)
used when saying that someone wants or needs something: *I **could do with** some sleep.* • *You look as if you **could do with** a cup of tea.*

do well, do badly
to do something in a way that has a good or bad result: *Susan has always **done well** in school.* • *The team is **doing well** this year.* • *The business is **doing badly**.*

do your best
to do something in the best way that you can: *I hope you will always try to **do your best**.* • *She was very nice and **did her best** to help us.*

what did you do with something? (spoken)
used when asking where someone put something: *Jenny, **what did you do with** my keys?* • ***What did I do with** my pen? Oh, there it is.*

How do you do?
used when you meet someone for the first time, and want to be very polite. You say **How do you do?** as a reply, when someone has just said it to you: *"**How do you do**, Mr Mason?" said Miss Cosby. "**How do you do?** I'm pleased to meet you," replied Mr Mason.*

"How do you do?" "How do you do?"

what do you do (for a living)?
used when asking or saying what someone's job is: *"**What does** your wife **do**?" "She's a police officer."* • *I'm not sure **what** Mike **does**. I think he works in a bank.* • *I really like art, and painting is what I'd like to **do for a living**.*

"What do you do?" "I'm a teacher."

VERB FORMS

Present tense

Singular	Plural
I **do**	we **do**
you **do**	you **do**
he, she, it **does**	they **do**

Past tense

Singular	Plural
I **did**	we **did**
you **did**	you **did**
he, she, it **did**	they **did**

present participle: **doing**
past participle: **done**
negative forms: **do not, does not, did not**
negative short forms: **don't, doesn't, didn't**

and life at home: *They enjoyed 30 years of domestic happiness.* **2** a domestic animal is kept by someone, especially as a pet

dom•i•nant /ˈdɒmənənt $ ˈdɑmənənt/ *adjective* most important or most noticeable: *The dominant flavour of the stew was garlic.*

dom•i•nate /ˈdɒməneɪt $ ˈdɑməˌneɪt/ *verb* to be the most important or most noticeable person or thing: *One or two students always dominate the lesson.*

dom•i•neer•ing /ˌdɒməˈnɪərɪŋ $ ˌdɑməˈnɪrɪŋ/ *adjective* someone who is domineering tries to control other people: *Her boyfriend was very domineering.*

dom•i•no /ˈdɒmənəʊ $ ˈdɑməˌnoʊ/ *noun* (plural **dominoes**) one of a set of small pieces of wood or plastic with spots on, used for playing a game called dominoes

dominoes

do•nate /dəʊˈneɪt $ ˈdoʊneɪt/ *verb* to give something to a person or organization that needs help: *He donates money to various charities.*

do•na•tion /dəʊˈneɪʃən $ doʊˈneɪʃən/ *noun* something, especially money, that you give to help a person or organization: *I made a donation to help homeless people.*

done¹ the past participle of DO

done² /dʌn/ *adjective* finished or completed: *Is the work done yet?* → see Thesaurus at FINISHED

don•key /ˈdɒŋki $ ˈdɑŋki/ *noun* a grey or brown animal like a small horse with long ears

do•nor /ˈdəʊnə $ ˈdoʊnɚ/ *noun* **1** a person or group that gives something, especially money, to an organization in order to help people: *The youth club received £1,000 from a donor.* **2** someone who lets a doctor take out some of their blood or part of their body so that the doctor can put it in a person who is ill: *a kidney donor*

don't /dəʊnt $ doʊnt/ the short form of 'do not': *I don't know.*

donut another spelling of DOUGHNUT

doom /duːm/ *noun* (no plural) a bad situation in the future that you cannot avoid: *I had an awful sense of doom before the exam.*

doomed /duːmd/ *adjective* if something is doomed, it will certainly fail: *Our relationship was doomed from the beginning.*

door

doorbell

doorstep door handle doormat

door /dɔː $ dɔr/ *noun*
1 the thing that you open and close to get into or out of a house, room, car etc: *Peter **opened the door** and went in.* • *Be sure to **lock the door** when you leave.*
2 the entrance to a building or room: *the next person who comes through that door* • *Two men were **standing at the door*** (=near the entrance, waiting to come in).
3 next door in the room, house, or building next to the one you are in: *The Smiths **live next door to** us.* • *our **next-door neighbours*** (=the people who live in the house next to ours)

door•bell /ˈdɔːbel $ ˈdɔrbel/ *noun* a button by the door of a house that makes a sound when you press it and lets the people inside know you are there: *Someone rang the doorbell.* • *Was that the doorbell I heard?*

door•mat /ˈdɔːmæt $ ˈdɔrmæt/ *noun* a thick piece of material next to a door for you to clean your shoes on → see picture at MAT

door•step /ˈdɔːstep $ ˈdɔrstep/ *noun* a step just outside the door to a building: *We sat on the doorstep in the sunshine.*

door·way /ˈdɔːweɪ $ ˈdɔrweɪ/ *noun* the space where a door opens into a room or building: *He stood in the doorway watching us.*

dor·mi·to·ry /ˈdɔːmətəri $ ˈdɔrməˌtɔri/ *noun* (plural **dormitories**) also **dorm** /dɔːm $ dɔrm/ (informal) **1** a large room where a lot of people sleep **2** the American word for HALL OF RESIDENCE

dose /dəʊs $ doʊs/ *noun* a measured amount of medicine: *Take one dose three times a day.*

dot /dɒt $ dɑt/ *noun* **1** a small round mark or spot: *a line of dots* **2 on the dot** (informal) exactly at a particular time: *The train left at 10 o'clock on the dot.*

dot·ing /ˈdəʊtɪŋ $ ˈdoʊtɪŋ/ *adjective* loving someone very much, in a way that seems silly to other people: *His doting parents let him do whatever he likes.*

doub·le¹ /ˈdʌbəl/ *adjective* **1** twice the usual amount, size, or number: *I asked for a double portion of fries.* **2** made to be big enough for two people or things: *a double room* → see picture at BED **3** consisting of two things of the same kind: *double doors*

double² *verb* to become twice as big, or to make something become twice as big: *The number of girls at the school has doubled.* • *They have doubled the price of cigarettes.* → see Thesaurus at INCREASE¹

double³ *pronoun, adverb* used to talk about an amount that is twice the size of another amount: *This is only enough rice for two people – we'll need double for four.* • *He offered to pay me double the normal fee for the job.*

ˌdouble ˈbass *noun* a very large musical instrument, shaped like a VIOLIN, that you play standing up

double bass

ˌdouble-ˈcheck *verb* to check something again so that you are completely sure about it: *Could you just double-check that the door is locked?*

ˌdouble-ˈclick *verb* to press the button on a mouse twice with your finger, in order to choose something or tell the computer to do something: *Double-click on the picture you want and then press 'print'.*

ˌdouble-ˈdecker *noun* a bus with two levels —**double-decker** *adjective*: *a double-decker bus*

doub·les /ˈdʌbəlz/ *noun* (no plural) a game of tennis played by two teams of two people: *I prefer playing doubles.*

doub·ly /ˈdʌbli/ *adverb* twice as much: *The job was doubly difficult because of the rain.*

doubt¹ /daʊt/ *noun*

> KEY PATTERNS
> **have some doubt/doubts about something**
> **have no doubt that**
> **there is no doubt that**

the feeling that something may not be true, good, or possible: *I still **have** some serious **doubts about** Ken's plan.* • *The police **had no doubt that** Stevens was lying* (=they were sure he was lying). • ***There is no doubt that** Lorna stole the money* (=it is certain that she stole it).

PHRASES

be in doubt to be uncertain: *His future as a professional footballer **is in doubt**.*

no doubt (spoken): ***No doubt** Mike will know what to do* (=it is very likely that he will know what to do).

doubt² *verb*

> KEY PATTERNS
> **doubt something**
> **doubt that**
> **doubt whether/if**

to think that something is not true or not likely: *We had no reason to doubt Maria's story.* • ***I doubt that** many young people can afford the price of those tickets.* • *Some people **doubted whether** the team could win.*

PHRASES

I doubt it (spoken): *"Do you think Rick will join us?" "**I doubt it** (=I don't think he will)."*

> PRONUNCIATION
> You pronounce **doubt** like 'out'.

A B C D E F G H I J K L M N O P Q R S T U V W X Y Z

doubt·ful /ˈdaʊtfəl/ *adjective* **1** not likely to happen or be true: *It's doubtful whether any of the other runners can beat him.* **2** not certain about something: *Everyone looked doubtful about the idea.*

doubt·less /ˈdaʊtləs/ *adverb* (formal) used to say that something is very likely SYNONYM **no doubt**: *Students will doubtless use the Internet for some of their research.*

dough /dəʊ $ doʊ/ *noun* (no plural) a soft mixture containing flour that you bake to make bread

PRONUNCIATION
You pronounce **dough** like 'low'.

dough·nut, **donut** /ˈdəʊnʌt $ ˈdoʊnʌt/ *noun* a small cake shaped like a ring or a ball

dove¹ /dʌv/ *noun* a type of white bird often used as a sign of peace

dove² /dəʊv $ doʊv/ *AmE* a past tense of DIVE

down¹ /daʊn/ *adverb, preposition* **1** towards or in a lower place ANTONYM **up**: *Alison ran down the hill.* • *Harry bent down to pick up the shell.* • *He put his glass down on the table.*
2 used to say that something becomes or has become lower in amount ANTONYM **up**: *My weight is now down to 9 stone* (=it used to be more than 9 stone).
3 further along a road or path SYNONYM **up**: *Go down this corridor and turn left at the end.* • *There's a bread shop down the road.*
4 towards the south ANTONYM **up**: *Are you going to fly down to Arizona or drive?*

down² *adjective* **1** (informal) unhappy SYNONYM **depressed**: *She looked a bit down.* **2** a computer that is down is not working: *The network has been down all afternoon.*

down·fall /ˈdaʊnfɔːl/ *noun* (written) when someone fails or loses their good position in life: *One careless mistake led to his downfall.*

down·hill /ˌdaʊnˈhɪl/ *adverb, adjective* **1** towards the bottom of a hill ANTONYM **uphill**: *Cycling downhill is easy.* ➔ see picture at UPHILL **2 go downhill** to become worse: *After the argument our relationship quickly went downhill.*

down·load¹ /ˌdaʊnˈləʊd $ ˈdaʊnloʊd/ *verb* to move information, programs etc to your computer from the Internet or from a computer system: *You can download music and videos from the Internet for free.*

down·load² /ˈdaʊnləʊd $ ˈdaʊnloʊd/ *noun* something that you download from the Internet, for example software, a computer game, or a song: *I've got downloads of all their songs.*

down·pour /ˈdaʊnpɔː $ ˈdaʊnpɔr/ *noun* a lot of rain falling in a short time

down·right /ˈdaʊnraɪt/ *adverb* (informal) completely: *It was downright stupid to go there alone.*

down·side /ˈdaʊnsaɪd/ *noun* **the downside** a bad feature of something that is good in other ways: *The downside of the job is you have to work at weekends.*

down·stairs /ˌdaʊnˈsteəz $ ˌdaʊnˈsterz/ *adverb, adjective* on or towards a lower level of a house ANTONYM **upstairs**: *Michael came downstairs in his pyjamas.* • *the downstairs toilet*

down·stream /ˌdaʊnˈstriːm/ *adverb* in the same direction that a river or stream is flowing: *The boat floated downstream.*

ˌdown-to-ˈearth *adjective* sensible and practical: *I like Kate – she's honest and down-to-earth.*

down·town /ˌdaʊnˈtaʊn/ *adverb, adjective AmE* to or in the centre of a city or town: *She works in a bar downtown.* • *a downtown district of New York*

down·wards /ˈdaʊnwədz $ ˈdaʊnwərdz/ also **downward** *adverb* towards a lower position ANTONYM **upwards**: *Push the handle downwards.*

doze /dəʊz $ doʊz/ *verb* **1** to sleep lightly for a short time SYNONYM **snooze**: *Grandma was dozing in her chair.*
2 doze off to fall asleep SYNONYM **drop off**: *It was so boring I almost dozed off.*
—**doze** *noun*: *Grandad always has a doze after dinner.*

doz·en /ˈdʌzən/ *noun* **1** a group of 12 things: *a dozen eggs* **2 dozens of**

things/people (informal) a lot of things or people: *I've been to that pizza restaurant dozens of times.*

Dr the written abbreviation for DOCTOR

drab /dræb/ *adjective* (**drabber**, **drabbest**) dull: *The room was painted a drab brown.*

draft[1] /drɑːft $ dræft/ *noun* **1** a piece of writing, a drawing, or a plan that you have not finished yet: *This is just a first draft of my essay.* **2** the American spelling of DRAUGHT

draft[2] *verb* **1** to write a plan, letter, report etc that you will need to change before you finish it: *She drafted a letter of complaint.* **2** *AmE* if someone is drafted, the government orders them to join the army during a war: *He was drafted during the Vietnam war.*

drafty the American spelling of DRAUGHTY

drag[1] /dræg/ *verb* (**dragged**, **dragging**) **1** to pull someone or something heavy along the ground: *He dragged the table over to the window.* ➔ see Thesaurus at PULL[1] ➔ see picture at TOW **2** to move a file by CLICKing on it with your mouse and moving it across your computer screen: *You can* ***drag and drop*** *the file into the folder.* **3** if an event drags, it is boring and seems to go very slowly: *The weather was dull and grey, and the day was starting to drag.* **4 drag someone into something** to make someone get involved in a situation when they do not want to: *I didn't want to get dragged into an argument about politics.*

drag[2] *noun* **be a drag** (informal) to be boring or annoying: *It's such a drag having to work on a Sunday.*

drag·on /ˈdrægən/ *noun* a large animal in children's stories with wings and a long tail, which can breathe fire

drain[1] /dreɪn/ *verb* **1** if you drain something, you make water flow away from it so that it is less wet: *I drained the water from the pasta.* **2** if liquid drains away, it flows away: *The water in the sink slowly drained away.*

drain[2] *noun* **1** a pipe or hole that carries water away from something: *The drain is blocked with leaves again.* **2 a drain on something** something that uses too much money or strength: *Too many late nights are a drain on your energy.*

drained /dreɪnd/ *adjective* very tired SYNONYM **exhausted**: *After the exams, I felt completely drained.*

drain·pipe /ˈdreɪnpaɪp/ *noun BrE* a pipe that carries rain water down from a roof

dra·ma /ˈdrɑːmə $ ˈdræmə/ *noun* **1** a story that actors perform as a play in the theatre, or on television or radio: *He has written a new drama for the BBC.* **2** (no plural) the study of plays or acting in plays: *Miss Jay is our drama teacher.* • *the history of Greek drama*

dra·mat·ic /drəˈmætɪk/ *adjective* **1** very sudden, exciting, or noticeable: *The improvement in his behaviour was dramatic.* • *a dramatic story* **2** relating to plays and the theatre: *a dramatic society* —**dramatically** /-kli/ *adverb*: *She looked dramatically different.* • *We decided to tell our story dramatically.*

dram·a·tist /ˈdræmətɪst/ *noun* someone who writes plays SYNONYM **playwright**

dram·a·tize also **dramatise** *BrE* /ˈdræmətaɪz/ *verb* **1** to use a real event or a story from a book to write a play: *They are dramatizing her life story for TV.* **2** to make an event seem more exciting than it really is: *She tends to dramatize things.*

drank the past tense of DRINK

drapes /dreɪps/ *AmE*, (plural) *noun* heavy curtains

dras·tic /ˈdræstɪk/ *adjective* drastic actions or changes are great, sudden, and have a big effect: *The new school principal is planning to make drastic changes.* —**drastically** /-kli/ *adverb*: *The cost of fuel has increased drastically.*

draught *BrE*, **draft** *AmE* /drɑːft $ dræft/ *noun* **1** cold air blowing through a room: *Could you shut the window? There's a draught.* **2 draughts** *BrE* a game played by two people, who each have 12 round pieces on a board with 64 squares SYNONYM **checkers** *AmE*

A B C D E F G H I J K L M N O P Q R S T U V W X Y Z

draugh·ty *BrE*, **drafty** *AmE* /ˈdrɑːfti $ ˈdræfti/ *adjective* (**draughtier**, **draughtiest**) a draughty room has cold air blowing through it

draw

drawing a picture drawing the curtains

draw¹ /drɔː/ *verb* (**drew** /druː/, **drawn** /drɔːn/)

KEY PATTERNS
draw a picture/line/map
draw a picture of someone/something
draw the curtains

1 if you draw something, you use a pen or pencil to make a picture of it: *He was* ***drawing*** *a picture* ***of*** *the church.* • *I'll draw you a map of how to get there.*
2 (written) to pull something from a container or across something: *She* ***drew*** *a large envelope* ***from*** *her briefcase.* • *Helena* ***drew the curtains*** (=closed or opened the curtains).
3 *BrE* if two teams or players draw, they both get the same number of points SYNONYM **tie**: *Spain drew with Korea 2–2.*

PHRASAL VERBS
draw up
1 draw something up to think of and write a list, plan etc: *Before you go camping,* ***draw up*** *a list of equipment you'll need.*
2 draw up (written) if a car draws up somewhere, it stops there: *A large car* ***drew up*** *outside the house.*

draw² *noun* a game that ends with both teams or players having the same number of points SYNONYM **tie**

draw·back /ˈdrɔːbæk/ *noun* something that might be a problem or disadvantage: *The only drawback to living in London is the cost.*

drawer /drɔː $ drɔr/ *noun* part of a piece of furniture that is shaped like a long thin box that slides in and out. You keep things in drawers: *I keep my socks in the top drawer.*

PRONUNCIATION
You pronounce **drawer** like 'four'.

draw·ing /ˈdrɔːɪŋ/ *noun*

KEY PATTERNS
a drawing of something

1 a picture you make with a pen or pencil: *a* ***drawing of*** *a cat* → see Thesaurus at PICTURE¹
2 (no plural) when you make pictures with a pen or pencil: *Katrina loves drawing and painting.*

ˈdrawing ˈpin *noun BrE* a short pin with a wide flat top, used for fastening paper to a board SYNONYM **thumbtack** *AmE*

drawl /drɔːl/ *verb* (written) to speak slowly with long vowel sounds: *"Hi there," he drawled.* —**drawl** *noun*: *She speaks in a slow drawl.*

drawn the past participle of DRAW¹

dread /dred/ *verb* to feel very worried about something that is going to happen: *I'm really dreading the exams.*

dread·ful /ˈdredfəl/ *adjective* very bad or unpleasant SYNONYM **terrible**: *a dreadful accident* → see Thesaurus at BAD

dream¹ /driːm/ *noun*

KEY PATTERNS
a dream about something
a dream that

1 the pictures that you see in your mind when you are asleep: *I had a* ***dream about*** *my dog last night.* • *After the accident, he had* ***bad dreams*** (=unpleasant or frightening dreams). • *She often had a* ***dream that*** *someone was following her.*
2 something that you want, or that you hope will happen: *It was her dream to travel around the world.*

dream² *verb* (past tense and past participle **dreamed** or **dreamt** /dremt/)

KEY PATTERNS
dream that
dream about someone/something
dream of being/becoming/winning etc something

1 to see pictures in your mind while you are asleep: *I **dreamed that** I was flying.* • *I **dreamed about** you last night.* **2** to think about something that you hope will happen: *When I was growing up, I **dreamed of** being a movie star.* • *Shelley **had** always **dreamed that** one day she would meet him again.*

PHRASAL VERBS

dream up

dream something up to think of an unusual plan or idea: *I don't know who **dreamed up** the idea of a picnic in the middle of winter!*

> **GRAMMAR**
> You **dream of doing something**.
> ✘ Don't say 'dream to do something'.

dream³ *adjective* your dream job, house etc is the best one that you can imagine: *My dream job would be testing computer games!*

dreamt a past tense and past participle of DREAM²

drear·y /ˈdrɪəri $ ˈdrɪri/ *adjective* (**drearier**, **dreariest**) not exciting SYNONYM **dull**: *Life here is so dreary.*

drench /drentʃ/ *verb* to make something very wet SYNONYM **soak** —**drenched** *adjective*: *I got totally drenched in the rain.*

dress¹ /dres/ *verb* to put clothes on someone or on yourself: *She dressed the twins and got their breakfast ready.* • *I **got dressed** quickly and ran to the shops to get some milk.* • *Tina is three, and is learning to **dress herself*** (=put her clothes on for herself).

PHRASES

be dressed in something: *They were all **dressed in** jeans* (=they were all wearing jeans).

PHRASAL VERBS

dress up

1 to wear your best clothes for a special occasion: *Everybody **dressed up** for the party and looked really nice.* **2** to wear special clothes for fun: *When I was a kid, I loved **dressing up** as a cowboy.*

> **USAGE**
> You usually say that someone **gets dressed**: *She woke up and got dressed.*

dress² *noun* (plural **dresses**) a piece of clothing that a woman or girl wears, which covers the top of her body and part of her legs: *a summer dress* → see picture at CLOTHES

dress·er /ˈdresə $ ˈdresɚ/ *noun* **1** *BrE* a large piece of furniture with shelves for holding dishes and plates **2** an American word for CHEST OF DRAWERS

dress·ing /ˈdresɪŋ/ *noun* **1** a mixture of oil and other things that you pour over SALAD **2** a piece of material that you use to cover a wound: *The doctor put a clean dressing on the cut.*

ˈdressing ˌgown *noun BrE* a piece of clothing like a long loose coat that you wear in your home before you get dressed SYNONYM **robe**

ˈdressing ˌroom *noun* a room where an actor gets ready before going on stage or on television

drew the past tense of DRAW¹

drib·ble /ˈdrɪbəl/ *verb* **1** *BrE* if you dribble, liquid in your mouth comes out onto your chin SYNONYM **drool** **2** to move a ball forward by kicking or BOUNCING it several times in football or BASKETBALL

drier another spelling of DRYER

drift¹ /drɪft/ *verb* **1** to move along slowly in the air or water: *The leaves drifted gently in the wind.* **2 drift apart** if people drift apart, they gradually stop being friends

drift² *noun* **1** snow or sand that the wind has blown into a large pile: *Her car was stuck in a snow drift.* **2 get someone's drift** (informal) to understand the general meaning of what someone says: *I don't know much about computers but I get your drift.*

drill¹ /drɪl/ *noun* a tool or machine that you use to make small holes in something hard: *an electric drill*

drill

drill² *verb* to make a hole with a drill: *The dentist drilled a hole in my tooth.*

A B C D E F G H I J K L M N O P Q R S T U V W X Y Z

drink¹ /drɪŋk/ *verb* (**drank** /dræŋk/ **drunk** /drʌŋk/)
1 to take liquid into your mouth and swallow it: *Rob was drinking a Coke.* • *Do you want something to drink?*
2 to drink alcohol, especially regularly: *Don't drink and drive.* • *I usually drink white wine rather than red.*

THESAURUS
sip: *Jenny **sipped** her hot coffee slowly* (=drank it by taking very small amounts).
gulp (down): *He took the water from me and **gulped it down*** (=drank it very quickly by swallowing large amounts).

drink² *noun*

KEY PATTERNS
a drink of something

an amount of something such as water, juice etc that you drink: *Are you thirsty? Would you like a drink?* • *a drink of water*

drip¹ /drɪp/ *verb* (**dripped, dripping**)
1 if a liquid drips from something, it falls in drops: *Water was dripping from the tap.* → see Thesaurus at FLOW²
2 if something is dripping, drops of a liquid are falling from it: *The tap is dripping.*

drip² *noun* a small amount of a liquid that falls from something: *She wiped the drips of paint off the floor.*

drip

drive¹ /draɪv/ *verb* (**drove** /drəʊv $ droʊv/ **driven** /ˈdrɪvən/)

KEY PATTERNS
drive a car/truck/bus
drive (someone) to work/school/London etc
drive home/here/there
drive past/through/around a place

1 to make a car move in the direction you want: *I learned to drive when I was 17.* • *I think the man was driving a red car.* • *Peggy **drove to** work as usual.* • *How long did it take you to drive there?* • *It took us over an hour to drive through the city.*
2 if you drive someone somewhere, you take them there in a car: *Many parents **drive** their children **to** school.* • *They **drove** us **around** the city for a tour.*

PHRASES
drive someone crazy, drive someone mad to annoy someone a lot: *I can't remember his name, and it's **driving** me **crazy**.*

drive² *noun*
1 a trip in a car: *It's a three-hour drive to the lake.*
2 a part of a computer that can read or store information: *the **hard drive***
3 *BrE* a DRIVEWAY

ˈdrive-in *adjective* a drive-in restaurant or cinema is one where you stay in your car to collect food or watch a film —**drive-in** *noun*: *We saw a movie at the drive-in.*

driv·el /ˈdrɪvəl/ *noun* (no plural) (informal) nonsense: *Don't talk drivel!*

driven the past participle of DRIVE¹

driv·er /ˈdraɪvə $ ˈdraɪvər/ *noun* someone who drives: *a truck driver*

ˈdrive-through *adjective* a drive-through restaurant, bank etc is one that you can use without getting out of your car

drive·way /ˈdraɪvweɪ/ also **drive** *noun* a short road between your house and the street, where you put your car: *There is room to park two cars in his driveway.*

driv·ing¹ /ˈdraɪvɪŋ/ *noun* (no plural) the activity or skill of driving a car: *I love driving.* • *His driving is terrible sometimes.*

driving² *adjective* **driving rain, driving snow** rain or snow that is falling very heavily and fast

ˈdriving ˌtest *noun* an official test that you must pass in order to drive a car on the roads

driz·zle /ˈdrɪzəl/ *verb* if it is drizzling, it is raining very lightly: *It was only drizzling so I didn't take an umbrella.*

drool /druːl/ *verb* if you drool, liquid in your mouth comes out onto your chin SYNONYM **dribble** *BrE*: *The dog keeps drooling.*

A B C D E F G H I J K L M N O P Q R S T U V W X Y Z

droop /druːp/ *verb* if something droops, it hangs down because it is old or weak: *These flowers have started to droop.*

drop

Luke dropped a book.

An apple dropped from the tree.

drop¹ /drɒp $ drɑp/ *verb* (**dropped**, **dropping**)

KEY PATTERNS
drop something
drop from a tree/shelf/table etc
drop onto the ground/floor etc

1 if you drop something you are holding, you let it fall, often by accident: *She dropped a glass when she was drying the dishes.* ➔ see picture on page A2
2 to fall: *The ground was covered in apples that **had dropped from** the tree.* • *The coin dropped onto the floor and rolled away.* • *I think this plant is dying; the leaves are starting to **drop off**.*
3 also **drop someone off** to take someone to a place in a car, before going to another place: *Shall I drop you at the station?* • *She **drops** the kids **off** at school on her way to work.*
4 to become lower in level or amount SYNONYM **fall** ANTONYM **rise**: *It's warm during the day, but the temperature drops at night.* • *Pam's voice **dropped** to a whisper.* ➔ see Thesaurus at DECREASE

PHRASAL VERBS
drop in, drop by
to visit someone who does not know you are coming because you have not arranged it with them: *Doris **dropped in** just before lunchtime.*
drop off
to fall asleep: *Dad's **dropped off** in front of the telly again.*
drop out
to leave school or college before you have finished your course: *My grandfather had to **drop out of** school when he was 13 to help on the farm.*

drop² *noun*

KEY PATTERNS
a drop of water/oil/rain etc
a drop in the number/price/value etc of something

1 a very small amount of liquid: *I think I felt a few raindrops.* • *Put **a drop of** oil on the wheel.*
2 when the amount or level of something becomes lower SYNONYM **fall** ANTONYM **rise**: *There has been **a drop in** the price of computers.*

ˌdrop-down ˈmenu *noun* a list of choices that appears on a computer screen when you CLICK on part of the screen: *The drop-down menu lets you choose the language you want.*

drop·out /ˈdrɒpaʊt $ ˈdrɑp-aʊt/ *noun* someone who leaves school or college without finishing their course: *a high-school dropout*

drought /draʊt/ *noun* a long period of dry weather when there is not enough water: *The country has had two years of drought.*

PRONUNCIATION
You pronounce **drought** like 'out'.

drove the past tense of DRIVE

drown /draʊn/ *verb* if someone drowns, or if they are drowned, they die from being under water for too long: *The fishermen drowned when their boat overturned.* • *He was drowned in a diving accident.*

drow·sy /ˈdraʊzi/ *adjective* (**drowsier**, **drowsiest**) tired and almost asleep SYNONYM **sleepy**: *During the lesson I started to feel drowsy.*

drug¹ /drʌg/ *noun* **1** an illegal substance that people smoke, swallow etc to give themselves a pleasant feeling: *He has never taken drugs.* **2** a medicine: *a new drug that is being used to treat cancer* ➔ see Thesaurus at MEDICINE

drug² *verb* (**drugged**, **drugging**) to give someone drugs, usually to make them sleep: *The kidnappers drugged him and put him into the van.*

drug·store /ˈdrʌgstɔː $ ˈdrʌgstɔr/ the American word for CHEMIST[1]

drum /drʌm/ *noun* **1** a round musical instrument which you hit with your hand or a stick: *Clare plays the drums in a band.* **2** a large round container for storing liquids such as oil or chemicals: *an oil drum*

drum·mer /ˈdrʌmə $ ˈdrʌmɚ/ *noun* someone who plays the drums: *The band has a great drummer.*

drunk[1] the past participle of DRINK[1]

drunk[2] /drʌŋk/ *adjective* if someone is drunk, they have drunk too much alcohol and it makes them behave strangely ANTONYM **sober**: *He got drunk and crashed his car.*

> **WORD CHOICE**
> **drunk** or **drunken**?
> • **Drunk** is the usual word you use to describe someone who has drunk too much alcohol: *Her husband was always drunk.*
> • **Drunken** is much less common than **drunk**. It is always used before a noun, and is used especially in certain phrases: *a drunken party* • *a drunken stupor*

dry[1] /draɪ/ *adjective* (**drier**, **driest**)
1 something that is dry has no water in it or on it ANTONYM **wet**: *Get a dry towel out of the cupboard.*
2 if your mouth, throat, or skin is dry, it does not have enough of the natural liquid that is usually in it: *My skin gets so dry in the winter.*
3 if the weather is dry, there is no rain ANTONYM **wet**: *It's been a very dry summer.*

dry[2] *verb* (**dried**, **dries**)
if you dry something, or if it dries, it no longer has any water in it or on it: *Lynn dried the dishes.* • *Lay the sweater out flat to dry.*

PHRASAL VERBS

dry out
dry out, dry something out if clothing, soil etc dries out, or if you dry it out, it becomes completely dry: *It was so hot our swimsuits* ***dried out*** *quickly.*

dry up
1 dry up if a river or lake dries up, there is no longer any water in it: *The stream* ***dried up*** *during the very hot summer.*
2 dry something up *BrE* to move a cloth across dishes that have been washed so that they become dry: *Can you* ***dry*** *these dishes* ***up*** *for me?*

ˌdry-ˈclean / $ ˈ. ./ *verb* to clean clothes with chemicals instead of water

ˌdry ˈcleaner's *noun* a shop where you take clothes to be dry-cleaned

dry·er, **drier** /ˈdraɪə $ ˈdraɪɚ/ *noun* a machine that dries things, especially clothes or hair: *Put the washing in the dryer.*

du·al /ˈdjuːəl $ ˈduəl/ *adjective* (formal) having two of something, or two parts: *The interview has a dual purpose: to find out more about you, and to test your English.*

du·bi·ous /ˈdjuːbiəs $ ˈdubiəs/ *adjective* **1** if you are dubious about something, you are not sure whether it is good or true SYNONYM **doubtful**: *Her parents felt rather dubious about her new friends.* **2** not seeming real or honest: *a dubious story*

duch·ess /ˈdʌtʃɪs/ *noun* (plural **duchesses**) a woman from Europe with the highest social rank below a princess, or the wife of a DUKE

duck[1] /dʌk/ *verb* to lower your body or head very quickly to avoid something: *He threw a book at me and I ducked.*

duck

duck[2] *noun* **1** a common bird that lives in water and has short legs and a wide beak → see picture at GOOSE **2** (no plural) the meat from a duck: *duck with orange sauce*

duck·ling /ˈdʌklɪŋ/ *noun* a baby duck

due /djuː $ du/ *adjective* **1** expected to happen or arrive at a particular time: *Your essay was due in yesterday.* • *The concert was due to start at 8.00 pm.*
2 due to something if one thing is due to another, it happens as a result of it: *Her success was due to hard work.* • *The game was cancelled due to bad weather.*

PRONUNCIATION
British people pronounce the **-ue** with a 'y' sound at the start, like 'you'. American people pronounce the word 'due' like 'do'.

du•et /dju'et $ du'et/ *noun* a piece of music for two performers: *a duet for flute and violin*

dug the past tense and past participle of DIG

duke /djuːk $ duk/ *noun* a man from Europe with the highest social rank below a prince

dull /dʌl/ *adjective* not interesting or exciting: *The book was great, but the movie is dull.*
➔ see Thesaurus at BORING

dumb /dʌm/ *adjective* **1** (informal) stupid: *He's so dumb.* **2** not able to speak. Many people think this use is rude and offensive.

PRONUNCIATION
In this word you do not pronounce the **b**.

dum•my /'dʌmi/ *noun* (plural **dummies**) **1** a plastic figure of a person: *a dummy in a shop window* **2** *BrE* a rubber object that you put in a baby's mouth when they are hungry or upset SYNONYM **pacifier** *AmE*

dump¹ /dʌmp/ *verb* **1** to drop or put something somewhere in a careless way: *He always just dumps his coat on the floor, instead of hanging it up.* **2** to leave something somewhere, because you do not want it: *It is illegal to dump rubbish here.*

dump² *noun* **1** a place where you can take things you do not want and leave them there **2** (informal) a place that is unpleasant because it is dirty, ugly, or boring: *Their house is a dump.*

dune /djuːn $ dun/ *noun* a hill made of sand: *We walked over the sand dunes to the beach.*

dung /dʌŋ/ *noun* (no plural) solid waste from animals, especially large animals: *cow dung*

dun•ga•rees /ˌdʌŋgə'riːz/ *plural noun* *BrE* trousers with thin pieces that go over your shoulders and a square piece of cloth that covers your chest SYNONYM **overalls** *AmE*: *a pair of red dungarees*

dunk /dʌŋk/ *verb* to quickly put something into a liquid and then take it out again: *He dunked his biscuit in his coffee.*

dun•no /də'nəʊ $ də'noʊ/ (spoken) an informal way of saying 'I don't know': *"Where's Lucy?" "Dunno."*

dupe /djuːp $ dup/ *verb* (written) to tell lies in order to make someone believe or do something SYNONYM **trick**: *She was duped into giving the robbers her car keys.*

du•pli•cate¹ /'djuːpləkət $ 'dupləkət/ *adjective* a duplicate copy of something is made so that it is exactly the same: *a duplicate copy of the letter*
—**duplicate** *noun*: *Don't worry, I've got a duplicate of the door key in my car.*

du•pli•cate² /'djuːpləkeɪt $ 'dupləˌkeɪt/ *verb* (formal) to copy something: *Could you duplicate this letter for me?*

du•ra•tion /djʊ'reɪʃən $ dʊ'reɪʃən/ *noun* (no plural) (formal) the length of time that something continues: *The cost of cycle hire is included for the duration of your holiday.*

dur•ing /'djʊərɪŋ $ 'dʊrɪŋ/ *preposition* **1** all through a period of time: *Foxes sleep during the day and hunt at night.* • *She kept talking during the lesson.* **2** at one time in a period of time: *Their car was stolen during the night.*

WORD CHOICE
during or **for**?
• You use **during** to say when something happens: *He woke up* ***during*** *the night.* • *She made a lot of friends* ***during*** *her stay in Japan.*
• You use **for** to say how long something continues: *I studied Chinese* ***for*** *six years.* • *He's been living in the US* ***for*** *over 20 years.*

dusk /dʌsk/ *noun* (no plural) when it starts to get dark at the end of the day: *The streetlights come on at dusk.*

dust¹ /dʌst/ *noun* (no plural) very small bits of dirt or soil that look like a powder: *There was a thick layer of dust on the table.*

dust² *verb* to clean the dust from something with a cloth: *He dusted the bookshelves.*

dust·bin /ˈdʌstbɪn/ *noun BrE* a large container outside your home where you put waste so that it can be taken away SYNONYM **garbage can** *AmE*

dust·man /ˈdʌstmən/ *noun BrE* (plural **dustmen** /-mən/) someone whose job is to take away waste that people leave in containers outside their houses

dust·y /ˈdʌsti/ *adjective* (**dustier**, **dustiest**) covered with dust: *dusty old books* → see Thesaurus at DIRTY

du·ty /ˈdjuːti $ ˈduti/ *noun* (plural **duties**)
something that you should do because it is right or it is part of your job: *Parents* ***have a duty to*** *protect their children.* • *On January 10, he will begin his duties as chairman of the company.*

PHRASES

(be) on duty if a doctor, nurse, police officer etc is on duty, they are working: *I'm not* ***on duty*** *this evening.* • *Police officers may not drink alcohol while* ***on duty****.*

be off duty if a doctor, nurse, police officer etc is off duty, they are not working: *I'm afraid I can't help you, I'm off duty.*

PRONUNCIATION
British people pronounce the **-u-** like 'you'.
American people pronounce the **-u-** like 'do'.

du·vet /ˈduːveɪ $ duˈveɪ/ *noun* a thick warm cover that you put on top of you when you are in bed

DVD /ˌdiː viː ˈdiː/ *noun* a flat round object like a CD that you use on a computer or a piece of equipment called a DVD player to play films, pictures, and sounds: *I didn't see the movie at the cinema, but I bought the DVD.* → see picture on page A12

dwell /dwel/ *verb* (past tense and past participle **dwelt** /dwelt/ or **dwelled**) **dwell on, dwell upon** to think or talk for too long about something unpleasant: *I don't want to dwell on all the details of the accident.*

dwelt a past tense and past participle of DWELL

dye¹ /daɪ/ *noun* a substance you can use to change the colour of hair, cloth etc

dye² *verb* to change the colour of something using a dye: *She dyes her hair.*

dy·nam·ic /daɪˈnæmɪk/ *adjective* full of energy and ideas: *The new teacher is very dynamic.*

dy·na·mite /ˈdaɪnəmaɪt/ *noun* (no plural) a substance that can cause powerful explosions: *They blew up the building with dynamite.*

dyn·a·sty /ˈdɪnəsti $ ˈdaɪnəsti/ *noun* (plural **dynasties**) a family of rulers who controlled a country for a long time: *The Ming dynasty ruled China for 300 years.*

E the written abbreviation of EAST or EASTERN

each /iːtʃ/ *determiner, pronoun* every person or thing separately: *You have 20 minutes to answer each question.* • ***Each of** her friends gave her a present.* • ***They each** arrived separately.* • *The children were given £5 each.*

PHRASES

each other: *The two brothers hated **each other*** (=each one hated the other).

ea·ger /ˈiːɡə $ ˈiɡɚ/ *adjective*

KEY PATTERNS
eager to do something

if you are eager to do something, you want to do it very much SYNONYM **keen**: *He was **eager to** see the result of his experiment.* —**eagerly** *adverb*: *She opened the letter eagerly.*

ea·gle /ˈiːɡəl/ *noun* a big wild bird with a curved beak that eats small animals ➔ see picture on page A8

eagle

ear /ɪə $ ɪr/ *noun* your ears are the two things on your head that you hear with: *She turned and whispered something in his ear.* ➔ see picture on page A5

ear·ly /ˈɜːli $ ˈɚli/ *adjective, adverb* (**earlier**, **earliest**)
1 near the beginning of a period of time ANTONYM **late**: *It snowed in early January.* • *The postman comes early in the morning.*
2 before the usual or expected time ANTONYM **late**: *Hi, Jim, you're here a bit earlier than you were yesterday.* • *I got there early and had to wait for Debbie.*
3 near the beginning of an event or process: *Our team scored early in the game.* • *He spent the early part of his career teaching.*

WORD CHOICE
early or **on time**?
• You use **early** when saying that something happens before the expected time: *We got to the station a few minutes **early**.*
• You use **on time** when saying that something happens at the correct time and is not late: *The plane arrived **on time** at Los Angeles airport.*

earn /ɜːn $ ɚn/ *verb*
1 to get money from the work that you do: *How much do you earn a week?*
2 to get something good because you have worked hard or done something well: *He quickly earned the respect of the other members of the team.* • *I think you've earned a rest!*

THESAURUS
make: *You can **make** a lot of money as a lawyer* (=earn).
get: *How much do you **get** an hour* (=earn)?
be/get paid: *I **get paid** at the end of the month* (=receive the money for the regular work that I do).

earn·ings /ˈɜːnɪŋz $ ˈɚnɪŋz/ *plural noun* (formal) money that you get from working: *It's a good idea to save some of your earnings.* ➔ see Thesaurus at PAY[2]

ear·phones /ˈɪəfəʊnz $ ˈɪrfoʊnz/ *plural noun* small pieces of equipment connected to something such as a PERSONAL STEREO, which you put in or over your ears to listen to music

ear·plug /ˈɪəplʌɡ $ ˈɪrplʌɡ/ *noun* one of a pair of small pieces of rubber that you put into your ears to keep out noise

ear·ring /ˈɪərɪŋ $ ˈɪrɪŋ/ *noun* a piece of jewellery that you fasten to your ear: *a pair of gold earrings* ➔ see picture at JEWELLERY

ear·shot /ˈɪəʃɒt $ ˈɪrʃɑt/ *noun* **within earshot, out of earshot** near enough

A B C D E F G H I J K L M N O P Q R S T U V W X Y Z

or not near enough to hear what someone is saying: *I called her name but she was already out of earshot.*

earth, **Earth** /ɜːθ $ ɚθ/ *noun* (no plural)
1 the PLANET that we live on: *Earth is the third planet from the sun.* • *The blue whale is the largest animal **on Earth**.*
2 the dark substance on the ground that plants and trees grow in SYNONYM **soil**: *He knelt on the cold, wet earth.*

THESAURUS
the world: *Which is the highest mountain in **the world*** (=on Earth)?
the planet: *The climate of **the planet** is changing* (=of Earth).

earth·quake /ˈɜːθkweɪk $ ˈɚθkweɪk/ *noun* a sudden shaking of the Earth's surface: *More than 200 people were killed in the earthquake.*

ease /iːz/ *noun* **1 with ease** if you do something with ease, it is very easy: *He won the race with ease.* **2 at ease** comfortable and confident in a situation: *The interviewer made me feel at ease.*

eas·i·ly /ˈiːzəli/ *adverb* **1** without difficulty: *You can easily book tickets online.* **2 easily the best, easily the biggest etc** (informal) much better, bigger etc than the others: *That's easily the funniest film I've seen this year.*

east /iːst/ *noun* **1** (no plural) the direction from which the sun rises
2 the east the eastern part of a country or area: *We live to the east of the city.* —**east** *adverb, adjective*: *My bedroom faces east.*

east·bound /ˈiːstbaʊnd/ *adjective* leading towards the east or travelling towards the east: *Police have closed the eastbound lanes of the expressway.*

Eas·ter /ˈiːstə $ ˈistɚ/ *noun* a holiday in March or April when Christians remember Christ's death and his return to life: *I went to stay with my grandma at Easter.*

eas·ter·ly /ˈiːstəli $ ˈistɚli/ *adjective*
1 towards the east: *The plane was heading in an easterly direction.*
2 easterly wind an easterly wind blows from the east

east·ern /ˈiːstən $ ˈistɚn/ *adjective* **1** in or from the east part of a country or area: *Bulgaria and Romania are in Eastern Europe.* **2** also **Eastern** in or from the countries in Asia, especially China and Japan: *Eastern music*

east·ward /ˈiːstwəd $ ˈistwɚd/ also **eastwards** /ˈiːstwədz $ ˈistwɚdz/ *adjective, adverb* towards the east: *We drove in an eastward direction.*

eas·y¹ /ˈiːzi/ *adjective* (**easier, easiest**)

KEY PATTERNS
it's easy to do something
find something easy

not difficult: *Our homework was just a few easy maths problems.* • *The house is easy to find.* • ***It's not easy to** learn Chinese* (=it's difficult). • *I **found** the exam quite **easy**.*

easy² *adverb* **take it easy, take things easy** (informal) to relax and not try to do too much: *Take it easy today if you're not feeling well.*

easy·go·ing /ˌiːziˈɡəʊɪŋ $ ˌiziˈɡoʊɪŋ/ *adjective* relaxed and calm, and not often angry or upset: *I was lucky because my parents were pretty easygoing.*

eat /iːt/ *verb* (**ate** /et, eɪt $ eɪt/ **eaten** /ˈiːtn/)

KEY PATTERNS
eat something for breakfast/lunch/dinner
have/get something to eat

1 to take food into your body through your mouth: *Most of the children eat sandwiches for lunch.* • *I was so hungry I just ate and ate and ate.* • *Do you want to go and **get something to eat*** (=some food)?
2 to have a meal: *I haven't eaten yet.*

PHRASAL VERBS
eat out
to eat in a restaurant, not at home: *We sometimes **eat out** at weekends.*
eat up (spoken)
eat up, eat something up (spoken) to eat all of something: *Eat up – then you can watch TV.* • *The cake was so delicious that we ate it all up.*

eaten the past participle of EAT

ec·cen·tric /ɪkˈsentrɪk/ *adjective* someone who is eccentric behaves in an unusual way SYNONYM **odd**

—**eccentric** *noun*: *My uncle is quite an eccentric.* —**eccentrically** /-kli/ *adverb*: *She was dressed eccentrically in a man's coat.*

ech•o¹ /ˈekəʊ $ ˈekoʊ/ *noun* (plural **echoes**) a sound that you hear again because it was made, for example, in a large empty room: *If you shout into the valley you will hear an echo.*

echo² *verb* if a sound echoes, you hear it again because it was made, for example, in a large empty room: *Her voice echoed around the hall.*

e•clipse /ɪˈklɪps/ *noun* when the sun or the moon seems to disappear. The eclipse of the sun happens when the moon passes between it and the Earth. The eclipse of the moon happens when the Earth comes between it and the sun: *a total eclipse of the sun*

e•co•lo•gi•cal /ˌiːkəˈlɒdʒɪkəl $ ˌikəˈlɑdʒɪkəl/ *adjective* about the relationship between plants, animals, people, and the environment: *These farming methods have caused an ecological disaster.*

e•col•o•gist /ɪˈkɒlədʒɪst $ ɪˈkɑlədʒɪst/ *noun* someone who studies ecology

e•col•o•gy /ɪˈkɒlədʒi $ ɪˈkɑlədʒi/ *noun* (no plural) the relationship between plants, animals, people, and the environment, or the study of this: *Cutting down the forests has damaged the ecology of the area.*

ec•o•nom•ic /ˌekəˈnɒmɪk $ ˌekəˈnɑmɪk/ *adjective* related to the way that a country makes money from its industries, businesses etc: *Can the government fix the country's economic problems?*

> **WORD CHOICE**
> **economic** or **economical**?
> • **Economic** means "concerning a country's economy": *The economic situation is getting worse.*
> • **Economical** means "using very little money, petrol etc": *My car is very economical* (=it uses very little petrol).

ec•o•nom•i•cal /ˌekəˈnɒmɪkəl $ ˌekəˈnɑmɪkal/ *adjective* using money or things carefully without wasting any: *It is more economical to buy the big packets.* —**economically** /-kli/ *adverb*: *ways of heating your house more economically*

ec•o•nom•ics /ˌekəˈnɒmɪks $ ˌekəˈnɑmɪks/ *noun* (no plural) the study of the way that a country produces money and things to sell: *I want to do economics at college.*

e•con•o•mist /ɪˈkɒnəməst $ ɪˈkɑnəmɪst/ *noun* someone who studies economics

e•con•o•mize also **economise** *BrE* /ɪˈkɒnəmaɪz $ ɪˈkɑnəˌmaɪz/ *verb* to try to spend less money or the amount of something that you use: *Try to economize on water during this dry period.*

e•con•o•my /ɪˈkɒnəmi $ ɪˈkɑnəmi/ *noun* (plural **economies**) **1** the way that money and business are organized in a country or area: *The government has promised to build a strong economy. • Closing the factory has affected the local economy very badly.* **2** when you use things carefully so that you do not waste anything or spend too much: *Since Dad lost his job, we've had to make economies.*

e'conomy ˌclass *adjective* a cheap type of ticket for travel: *an economy class air ticket*

ec•sta•sy /ˈekstəsi/ *noun* (no plural) **1** a feeling of great happiness: *He had a look of ecstasy on his face.* **2** an illegal drug

ec•stat•ic /ɪkˈstætɪk/ *adjective* very happy and excited: *When they won the match, the crowd was ecstatic.*

edge

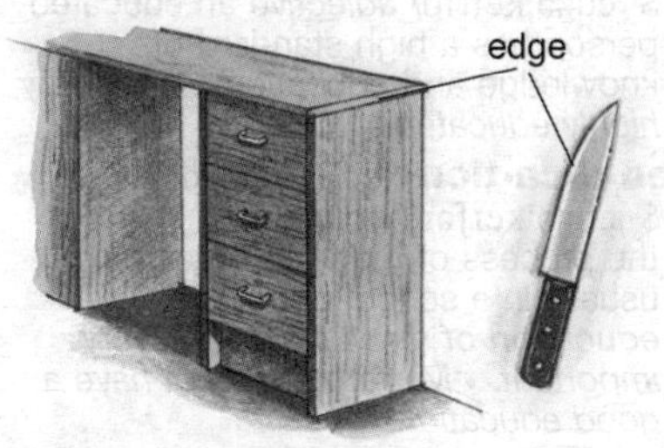

edge¹ /edʒ/ *noun*

> **KEY PATTERNS**
> **on the edge of something**
> **at the edge of somewhere**

along/around the edge of something
the edge of a knife/sword

1 the part of something that is furthest from the middle: *Dana sat* ***on the edge of*** *the bed.* • *Their house was* ***at the edge of*** *the village.* • *A hedge ran* ***around the edge of*** *the field.*
2 the thin sharp side of a tool that you use to cut things: *Make sure* ***the edge of*** *the knife is sharp.*

edge² *verb* to move slowly and carefully, or to make something do this: *People were edging away from him.* • *I edged the car into the parking space.*

ed·i·ble /ˈedəbəl/ *adjective* something that is edible can be eaten: *edible mushrooms*

ed·it /ˈedɪt/ *verb* to prepare a book, film etc by correcting mistakes and removing some parts

e·di·tion /ɪˈdɪʃən/ *noun* **1** the copies of a book, newspaper etc that are all the same: *They are bringing out a new edition of the dictionary.* **2** one of a series of television or radio programmes broadcast regularly with the same name: *the 9 o'clock edition of the news*

ed·i·tor /ˈedətə $ ˈedətɚ/ *noun* the person who decides what should be included in a book, newspaper, magazine etc: *an editor of a car magazine*

ed·u·cate /ˈedjʊkeɪt $ ˈedʒəˌkeɪt/ *verb* to teach someone, usually in a school or college: *He was educated at a private school.*

ed·u·cat·ed /ˈedjʊkeɪtɪd $ ˈedʒəˌkeɪtɪd/ *adjective* an educated person has a high standard of knowledge and education: *She is very highly educated.*

ed·u·ca·tion /ˌedjʊˈkeɪʃən $ ˌedʒəˈkeɪʃən/ *noun* the process of teaching or learning, usually in a school or college: ***The education of*** *small children is very important.* • *My father did not have a good education.*

ed·u·ca·tion·al /ˌedjʊˈkeɪʃənəl $ ˌedʒəˈkeɪʃənəl/ *adjective* involved with teaching or learning: *There are many educational television programmes for kids.*

eel /iːl/ *noun* a long thin fish that looks like a snake

ef·fect /ɪˈfekt/ *noun*

KEY PATTERNS
the effect of something
have an effect on something

a change or result that something causes: ***The effects of*** *the disease are terrible.* • *The food we eat* ***has a*** *great* ***effect on*** *our health.* • *What will be* ***the effect on*** *the environment?* → see Thesaurus at RESULT¹

PHRASES

special effects clever things that are done in a film to make things that are not real appear to exist or happen: *The* ***special effects*** *in 'Star Wars' were brilliant!*

put something into effect (formal) if you put a plan, idea etc into effect, you do what has been planned: *It is time to* ***put*** *our plan* ***into effect.***

be in effect, come into effect (formal) if a law, system etc is in effect or comes into effect, it exists: *The new law* ***has been in effect*** *for a year.* • *The changes will* ***come into effect*** *immediately.*

take effect to start to have results: *After 20 minutes, the pills* ***took effect*** *and the pain stopped.*

ef·fec·tive /ɪˈfektɪv/ *adjective* having the result that you want ANTONYM **ineffective**: *an effective way to teach reading* —**effectiveness** *noun* (no plural): *They argued about the effectiveness of putting people in jail.*

ef·fec·tive·ly /ɪˈfektɪvli/ *adverb* in a way that gets the result you want: *She controlled the class very effectively.*

ef·fi·cient /ɪˈfɪʃənt/ *adjective* working well, without wasting time or energy ANTONYM **inefficient**: *You have to find an efficient way of organizing your work.* —**efficiently** *adverb*: *This heats up the water very efficiently.*

ef·fort /ˈefət $ ˈefɚt/ *noun*

KEY PATTERNS
put a lot of effort into something
make an effort to do something
in an effort to do something

1 hard work that you do when you are trying to achieve something: *Edward* ***puts a lot of effort into*** *his studies* (=he works very hard).

2 an attempt to do something: *He failed at first, but his second effort was successful.* • *Kim **is making an effort to** lose weight.* • ***In an effort to** reduce crime, more police are being hired.*

ef·fort·less /ˈefətləs $ ˈefɚtləs/ *adjective* done in a way that looks easy: *His running looks effortless.* —**effortlessly** *adverb*: *She seems to learn new languages effortlessly.*

EFL /ˌiː ef ˈel/ (English as a Foreign Language) the teaching of English to people who speak a different language

eg, e.g. /ˌiː ˈdʒiː/ an abbreviation that means 'for example': *science subjects, eg chemistry and physics*

egg /eg/ *noun* **1** a round object with a hard surface that contains a baby bird, insect, snake etc: *The birds lay their eggs in spring.* **2** an egg from a chicken, used as food: *Do you like boiled eggs?* **3** a cell produced inside a woman or female animal that can develop into a baby

egg·plant /ˈegplɑːnt $ ˈegplænt/ the American word for AUBERGINE ➔ see picture on page A6

e·go /ˈiːgəʊ $ ˈigoʊ/ *noun* the opinion that you have about yourself: *Her remarks were not very good for my ego.*

eh /eɪ/ *BrE* (spoken) used to ask someone to say something again: *"You need a modem." "Eh?"*

eight /eɪt/ *number* 8

eigh·teen /ˌeɪˈtiːn/ *number* 18 —**eighteenth** *number*

eighth /eɪtθ/ *number* **1** 8th **2** one of eight equal parts of something; 1/8

eigh·ty /ˈeɪti/ *number* (plural **eighties**) **1** 80 **2 the eighties** the years between 1980 and 1989 **3 be in your eighties** to be aged between 80 and 89 —**eightieth** *number*: *his eightieth birthday*

ei·ther¹ /ˈaɪðə $ ˈiðɚ/ *conjunction* **either ... or** used for showing that there are two or more possibilities to choose from: *We can **either** have lunch here **or** go out.* • *Your socks must be **either** black, grey, **or** dark blue.*

either² *determiner, pronoun* one of two things or people: *Helen has a British and a Canadian passport so she can live in either country.* • *I don't like **either of** them much.* • *There's a choice of football or rugby so you can do either.*

PHRASES

on either side on both sides: *On either side of the road there were tall trees.*

> **GRAMMAR**
> **Either** is used with a singular noun and verb: *I can meet you on Wednesday or Thursday – either day is good for me.*
> **Either of** is used with a plural noun or pronoun, and the verb can be singular or plural: *Has/have either of them telephoned yet?*

either³ *adverb* used in negative sentences to mean 'also': *"I don't like him." "I don't either."*

e·ject /ɪˈdʒekt/ *verb* **1** (formal) to make someone leave a place, using force: *A few people were ejected from the club for fighting.* **2** to make something come out of a machine by pressing a button: *Press this button to eject the DVD.*

e·lab·o·rate /ɪˈlæbərət/ *adjective* something that is elaborate has a lot of small details or parts that are connected in a complicated way ANTONYM **simple**: *The plot of the film was very elaborate.* —**elaborately** *adverb*: *elaborately decorated furniture*

e·las·tic /ɪˈlæstɪk/ *noun* (no plural) a material that can stretch and then go back to its usual size, used to make clothes: *These socks have elastic around the top.*

el·bow¹ /ˈelbəʊ $ ˈelboʊ/ *noun* the joint where your arm bends: *I've hurt my elbow.* ➔ see picture on page A5

elbow² *verb* to push someone with your elbow: *He elbowed me in the ribs.* ➔ see Thesaurus at PUSH¹

A B C D E F G H I J K L M N O P Q R S T U V W X Y Z

A B C D E F G H I J K L M N O P Q R S T U V W X Y Z

el·der /'eldə $ 'eldɚ/ *adjective* someone's elder brother, daughter etc is an older one: *Her elder son is at college.*

WORD CHOICE
elder or **older**?
• You use **elder** about an older sister or brother, son or daughter etc.
✘ Don't say 'elder people'. Say **older people**.

el·der·ly /'eldəli $ 'eldɚli/ *adjective* an elderly person is old: *His parents are quite elderly.* ➔ see Thesaurus at OLD

el·dest /'eldəst/ *adjective* the eldest child, boy etc in a family is the oldest one: *My eldest sister lives in Canada.* —**eldest** *noun* (no plural): *They have four children and Tom is the eldest.*

e·lect /ɪ'lekt/ *verb* to choose someone for an official position by voting: *The country elected a new government in January.*

e·lec·tion /ɪ'lekʃən/ *noun* an occasion when people vote to choose someone for an official position: *Buffy won the election for school president.*

e·lec·tric /ɪ'lektrɪk/ *adjective* something that is electric works using electricity: *an electric light* • *He plays the electric guitar.*

e·lec·tri·cal /ɪ'lektrɪkəl/ *adjective* using or concerned with electricity: *a store selling electrical equipment*

el·ec·tri·cian /ɪˌlek'trɪʃən/ *noun* someone whose job is to repair electrical equipment

e·lec·tri·ci·ty /ɪˌlek'trɪsəti/ *noun* (no plural) the power that is carried by wires and used to make lights and machines work: *Does your cooker work by gas or electricity?*

eˌlectric 'shock *noun* a sudden painful feeling you get if you accidentally touch electricity: *I got an electric shock from my hairdryer.*

e·lec·tro·cute /ɪ'lektrəkjuːt/ *verb* to kill someone by passing electricity through their body: *He was electrocuted in an accident at the factory.*

e·lec·tron·ic /ɪˌlek'trɒnɪk $ ɪˌlek'trɑnɪk/ *adjective* using electricity and MICROCHIPS: *electronic magazines* (=magazines on the Internet, that you can read using a computer) —**electronically** /-kli/ *adverb*: *Now we can communicate electronically.*

e·lec·tron·ics /ɪˌlek'trɒnɪks $ ɪˌlek'trɑnɪks/ *noun* (no plural) the process of making electronic equipment, such as computers or televisions, or the study of this: *an electronics company*

el·e·gant /'eləgənt/ *adjective* graceful and attractive: *simple but elegant clothes* —**elegantly** *adverb*: *She was dressed very elegantly.*

el·e·ment /'eləmənt/ *noun* **1** a simple chemical substance that consists of only one kind of atom **2** a small amount of something: *There's an element of risk in every sport.*

el·e·men·tary /ˌelə'mentri/ *adjective* simple or basic: *The teacher asked a few elementary questions.*

ele'mentary ˌschool also **grade school** the American word for PRIMARY SCHOOL

el·e·phant /'eləfənt/ *noun* a very large grey animal with big ears and a very long nose called a TRUNK ➔ see picture on page A9

el·e·va·tor /'eləveɪtə $ 'eləˌveɪtɚ/ the American word for LIFT[2]

e·lev·en /ɪ'levən/ *number* 11

e·lev·enth /ɪ'levənθ/ *number* **1** 11th **2** one of eleven equal parts of something; 1/11

el·i·gi·ble /'elədʒəbəl/ *adjective* if you are eligible for something, you have the right to have it or do it: *You have to be 18 to be eligible to vote.*

e·lim·i·nate /ɪ'lɪməneɪt/ *verb* **1** to completely destroy something or someone so that it no longer exists: *We can never eliminate crime from our society.* **2 be eliminated** if you are eliminated in a sports competition, you can no longer be in it, for example because you lost a game: *We were eliminated in the very first game.*

else /els/ *adverb*
1 used when talking about something or someone who is different from the one already mentioned: *Can I get you anything else?* • *He was sitting in someone else's seat.* • *Where else could she be?*

2 or else used to threaten someone: *You'd better give it back **or else**!*

else·where /els'weə $ 'elswer/ *adverb* in another place or to another place: *You will have to smoke that cigarette elsewhere.*

ELT /ˌiː el 'tiː/ *noun* (English Language Teaching) the teaching of English to people whose first language is not English

e·mail *noun* /'iːmeɪl/ **1** (no plural) electronic mail; a system for sending messages by computer: *It's easy to keep in touch with old friends by email.* **2** a message sent by computer: *I got an email from Josie.* —**email** *verb*: *He emailed me every day.*

PRONUNCIATION
email
You write:
ian.smith@worldbusiness.com. You say: **Ian dot Smith at worldbusiness dot com**.
You write: **www.bbc.co.uk/sport**. You say: **double-u double-u double-u dot bbc dot co dot uk slash sport**.

em·bark /ɪm'bɑːk $ ɪm'bɑrk/ *verb* (formal) **1** to get on a ship SYNONYM **board** **2 embark on something** to start something new: *She left school to embark on a career as a model.*

em·bar·rass /ɪm'bærəs/ *verb* to make someone feel ashamed, stupid, or uncomfortable: *Mum embarrassed me by giving me a big kiss.*

SPELLING
This word is often spelled wrongly. The correct spelling is: **embarrass**.

em·bar·rassed /ɪm'bærəst/ *adjective*

KEY PATTERNS
be/feel embarrassed about something

if you feel embarrassed, you feel nervous or uncomfortable about what other people think of you: *I felt **embarrassed about** my dirty shoes.*

WORD CHOICE
embarrassed or **embarrassing**?
• **Embarrassed** means "feeling nervous and uncomfortable": *I always feel embarrassed when I have to give a speech.*
• **Embarrassing** means "making you feel nervous and uncomfortable": *The doctor asked me some **embarrassing** questions.*

SPELLING
This word is often spelled wrongly. The correct spelling is: **embarrassed**.

em·bar·ras·sing /ɪm'bærəsɪŋ/ *adjective*

KEY PATTERNS
it is embarrassing to do something
embarrassing for someone

if something is embarrassing, it makes you feel embarrassed: ***It was** very **embarrassing to** have to admit that I had lied.* • ***It was** so **embarrassing for** me when mum found all my letters to David.*

SPELLING
This word is often spelled wrongly. The correct spelling is: **embarrassing**.

em·bar·rass·ment /ɪm'bærəsmənt/ *noun* (no plural) the feeling of being embarrassed: *Eric went red in the face with embarrassment.*

SPELLING
This word is often spelled wrongly. The correct spelling is: **embarrassment**.

em·bas·sy /'embəsi/ *noun* (plural **embassies**) a group of officials who live and work in a foreign country, and whose job is to help people from their own country who are also living or visiting there. The building these people work in is also called an embassy: *You have to apply to the US embassy for a visa.*

em·brace /ɪm'breɪs/ *verb* (formal) to put your arms around someone and hold them in a loving way SYNONYM **hug**: *He embraced his cousin warmly.*

em·broi·der /ɪm'brɔɪdə $ ɪm'brɔɪdɚ/ *verb* to decorate cloth by sewing a picture or pattern on it: *a dress embroidered with flowers*

em·bry·o /'embriəʊ $ 'embriˌoʊ/ *noun* an animal or human that has just begun to develop inside its mother's body

em·e·rald /'emərəld/ *noun* a bright green jewel

A B C D E F G H I J K L M N O P Q R S T U V W X Y Z

e·merge /ɪˈmɜːdʒ $ ɪˈmɚdʒ/ *verb* (written) **1** to become known: *We are waiting for the facts to emerge.* **2** to appear or come out from somewhere: *The children emerged from their hiding place under the bed.*

e·mer·gen·cy /ɪˈmɜːdʒənsi $ ɪˈmɚdʒənsi/ *noun* (plural **emergencies**)

> KEY PATTERNS
> **in an emergency**

a dangerous situation that happens suddenly: *Make sure your children know what to do **in an emergency**.*

eˈmergency ˌroom the American word for CASUALTY

eˈmergency ˌservices *noun* official organizations such as the police that deal with crimes, fires, or helping people who are badly hurt

em·i·grate /ˈeməgreɪt/ *verb* to leave your own country and go to live in another country: *All of her children have emigrated to Australia.*

> WORD CHOICE
> **emigrate** or **immigrate**?
> • **Emigrate** means "to leave your home country in order to live in a different one": *He's thinking of emigrating to the United States.*
> • **Immigrate** means "to come to this country in order to live here permanently": *People have **immigrated** here from all over the world.*

em·i·nent /ˈemɪnənt/ *adjective* famous and respected: *an eminent professor*

em·i·nent·ly /ˈemɪnəntli/ *adverb* (formal) very: *The room was eminently suitable for our purposes.*

e·mo·tion /ɪˈməʊʃən $ ɪˈmoʊʃən/ *noun*

> KEY PATTERNS
> **with emotion**
> **show emotion**

a strong feeling such as love or hate: *Jennifer's voice was shaking **with** emotion. • The two boys **showed** no emotion during the trial.*

e·mo·tion·al /ɪˈməʊʃənəl $ ɪˈmoʊʃənəl/ *adjective* relating to the way people show how they feel, especially when they cry: *It was a very emotional reunion. • Dad became quite emotional when he watched me accept my gold medal.* —**emotionally** *adverb*: *She spoke emotionally about her father.*

e·mo·tive /ɪˈməʊtɪv $ ɪˈmoʊtɪv/ *adjective* making people have strong feelings: *She made an emotive speech about human rights.*

em·pe·ror /ˈempərə $ ˈempərɚ/ *noun* the ruler of an EMPIRE

em·pha·sis /ˈemfəsɪs/ *noun* (plural **emphases** /-siːz/)

> KEY PATTERNS
> **emphasis on something**

the special importance or attention that you give to something: *There was a lot of **emphasis on** sport at my school.*

em·pha·size also **emphasise** *BrE* /ˈemfəsaɪz/ *verb*

> KEY PATTERNS
> **emphasize the importance of something**
> **emphasize that**

to say strongly that something is important SYNONYM **stress**: *The teacher emphasized the importance of correct spelling. • Dad **emphasized that** I must always be home by 12 o'clock.*

em·phat·ic /ɪmˈfætɪk/ *adjective* said in a strong way that shows you are certain about something: *She was very emphatic that she did not like him.* —**emphatically** /-kli/ *adverb*: *"No way!" he said emphatically.*

em·pire /ˈempaɪə $ ˈempaɪɚ/ *noun* a group of countries that are controlled by one ruler or government

em·ploy /ɪmˈplɔɪ/ *verb* to pay someone to work for you: *The company employs 250 people. • She was employed as a cleaner.*

em·ploy·ee /ɪmˈplɔɪ-iː/ *noun* someone who is paid to work for someone else: *The canteen is for employees of the company only.*

em·ploy·er /ɪmˈplɔɪə $ ɪmˈplɔɪɚ/ *noun* your employer is a person or company that pays you to work for them: *His employer allowed him to take the day off.*

em·ploy·ment /ɪmˈplɔɪmənt/ *noun* (no plural) (formal) work that you do to earn money: *She had to leave school and find employment.*

empty

emp·ty¹ /'empti/ *adjective* (**emptier**, **emptiest**)
something that is empty has nothing or no one inside ANTONYM **full**: *an empty bottle* • *Many of the office buildings are empty.*

> THESAURUS
> **bare**: *The room was **bare** apart from a bed* (=empty because there was nothing in it).
> **deserted**: *It was very late and the streets were **deserted*** (=empty because no one was there).
> **free**: *There were still some seats **free*** (=empty because no one was using them).

empty² *verb* (**emptied**, **empties**)
1 also **empty something out** to remove everything that is inside a container, cupboard etc: *I'll empty the bins while you sweep the floor.* • *I emptied out my desk drawers looking for a pen.* **2** to become empty: *As soon as the lecture finished, the hall emptied.*

ˌempty-'handed *adjective* without getting anything: *I forgot to take any money to the shops and came back empty-handed.*

en·a·ble /ɪ'neɪbəl/ *verb* (formal) to make it possible for someone to do something: *His help enabled me to study at college.*

en·chant·ing /ɪn'tʃɑːntɪŋ $ ɪn'tʃæntɪŋ/ *adjective* very beautiful: *She looked enchanting.*

en·close /ɪn'kləʊz $ ɪn'kloʊz/ *verb*
1 to put something inside an envelope with a letter: *Please enclose a photograph of yourself.* **2** if an area of land is enclosed, it has a wall or fence all the way around it: *The prison yard was enclosed by high walls.*

en·clo·sure /ɪn'kləʊʒə $ ɪn'kloʊʒɚ/ *noun* (formal) an area that has a wall or fence all the way around it: *You must not enter the lion enclosure.*

en·core /'ɒŋkɔː $ 'ɑŋkɔr/ *noun* a piece of music that a performer adds or repeats at the end of a performance because people ask for it: *The band played one of their old hits as an encore.*

en·coun·ter¹ /ɪn'kaʊntə $ ɪn'kaʊntɚ/ *verb* (written) if you encounter difficulties or problems, they happen and you have to do something about them: *If you encounter any difficulties, give me a call.*

encounter² *noun* a meeting, especially one that you did not expect or that caused problems: *They survived an encounter with a polar bear.*

en·cour·age /ɪn'kʌrɪdʒ $ ɪn'kɚɪdʒ/ *verb*

> KEY PATTERNS
> **encourage someone**
> **encourage someone to do something**

to give someone hope and confidence in order to persuade them to do something ANTONYM **discourage**: *People work best if you encourage them.* • *The programme **encourages** kids **to** stay in school.*

en·cour·ag·ing /ɪn'kʌrɪdʒɪŋ $ ɪn'kɚɪdʒɪŋ/ *adjective* giving you hope and confidence: *She said some encouraging things about my work.* —**encouragingly** *adverb*: *"It's great," he said encouragingly.*

en·cy·clo·pe·di·a also **encyclopaedia** *BrE* /ɪnˌsaɪklə'piːdiə/ *noun* a book that contains facts about many subjects

end¹ /end/ *noun*

> KEY PATTERNS
> **the end of something**
> **at the end of the month/book/meeting etc**
> **at the end of the road/garden/field etc**

an end to the war/violence/attacks etc
come to an end

1 the last part of a period of time, activity, book, film etc ANTONYM **beginning**, **start**: *I finally reached **the end of** the book.* • *You'll get paid **at the end of** the month.*
2 the part of a place or thing that is furthest away from you: *There's a shop **at the end of** the street.* • *John dived into **the deep end of** the pool.* • *Hold the rope **at this end** and pull as hard as you can.*
3 when something finishes or stops existing SYNONYM **close**: *The Pope asked for **an end to** the violence.* • *The war has finally **come to an end**.* • *The chairman **brought** the meeting **to an end*** (=he ended it).

PHRASES
in the end after a lot of time or discussion: ***In the end,** all that hard work was worth it.*

WORD CHOICE
at the end or **in the end**?
• **At the end** means "in the last part of a book, film etc": *They get married at the end.*
• **In the end** means "after a lot of other things have happened or been said": ***In the end,** I agreed to give him the money.*

end² *verb*

KEY PATTERNS
end something
end a meeting/story/game etc with something
end in disaster/failure etc

if something ends, or if you end it, it finishes or stops: *I really think we should end this argument.* • *The priest **ended** the service **with** a prayer.* • *After 15 years, their marriage **ended in** divorce.*

PHRASAL VERBS
end up
if you end up in a particular place or situation, you are in that place or situation after a series of events that you did not plan: *I didn't like him at school, but we **ended up being** really good friends.*

en·dan·ger /ɪn'deɪndʒə $ ɪn'deɪndʒɚ/ *verb* (formal) to put someone or something in a dangerous or harmful situation SYNONYM **put at risk**: *Pollution is endangering our planet.*

end·ing /'endɪŋ/ *noun* **1** the end of a story, film etc: *I like films to have a happy ending.* **2** the last part of a word: *To make a past tense you usually add the ending '-ed'.*

end·less /'endləs/ *adjective* continuing for a very long time, especially in an annoying way: *We had endless conversations about her new job.* —**endlessly** *adverb*: *They argue endlessly.*

en·dure /ɪn'djʊə $ ɪn'dʊr/ *verb* to suffer pain or be in a difficult situation for a long time: *People had to endure terrible living conditions during the war.*

en·e·my /'enəmi/ *noun* (plural **enemies**)
someone who hates you or whom you are fighting against in a war ANTONYM **friend**, **ally**: *Friends of the dead man said that he didn't have any enemies.* • *The president has many political enemies.* • *They shot at enemy aircraft.*

en·er·get·ic /ˌenə'dʒetɪk $ ˌenɚ'dʒetɪk/ *adjective* showing or using a lot of energy: *Dancing can be very energetic.* —**energetically** /-kli/ *adverb*: *The teacher moved around the classroom energetically.*

en·er·gy /'enədʒi $ 'enɚdʒi/ *noun*

KEY PATTERNS
energy from the sun/wind/fuel
save energy

1 (no plural) the ability to do a lot of work or activity without feeling tired: *The team was excited and **full of energy**.* • *After I had the flu, I felt as if I had no energy.*
2 power from oil, coal etc that produces heat and makes machines work: ***Energy from the sun** can be used to heat homes.* • *Try to **save energy** by turning off lights.*

en·force /ɪn'fɔːs $ ɪn'fɔrs/ *verb* to make people obey a rule or law: *We are finding it difficult to enforce the 'no smoking' rule.*

en·gaged /ɪn'geɪdʒd/ *adjective* **1** if two people are engaged, they have agreed to get married: *Greg wants us to get engaged.* **2** *BrE* if a telephone line is engaged, it is already being used by someone SYNONYM **busy** *AmE*

en·gage·ment /ɪn'geɪdʒmənt/ *noun* **1** an agreement to get married: *We are having a party to celebrate our engagement.* **2** (formal) an arrangement to do something or meet someone: *His secretary keeps a diary for all his engagements.*

en·gine /'endʒɪn/ *noun* part of a vehicle or other machine that uses oil, petrol, electricity etc to make it move: *a car engine* → see picture at AEROPLANE

en·gi·neer /ˌendʒə'nɪə $ ˌendʒə'nɪr/ *noun* **1** someone whose job is to design roads, bridges, machines etc **2** *AmE* someone whose job is to drive trains

en·gi·neer·ing /ˌendʒə'nɪərɪŋ $ ˌendʒə'nɪrɪŋ/ *noun* (no plural) the work of designing roads, bridges, machines etc: *The course will introduce young people to engineering.*

En·glish[1] /'ɪŋglɪʃ/ *noun* **1** the language that people speak in Britain, the US, Australia etc: *Do you speak English?* **2 the English** the people of England: *The English are very polite to visitors.*

English[2] *adjective* **1** connected with the English language **2** connected with or coming from England: *the English countryside*

en·grave /ɪn'greɪv/ *verb* to cut words or pictures into metal, stone, or glass: *a silver mug engraved with his name*

en·grossed /ɪn'grəʊst $ ɪn'groʊst/ *adjective* if you are engrossed in something, you are so interested in it that you give it all your attention: *Bill was engrossed in the newspaper.*

en·joy /ɪn'dʒɔɪ/ *verb*
1 to get pleasure from something: *The park was lovely, and I enjoyed the walk.* • *I enjoy cooking when I have time.*
2 enjoy yourself, enjoy myself etc to be happy and have fun: *Did you enjoy yourself at the party?*

> GRAMMAR
> You **enjoy doing something**.
> ✘ Don't say 'enjoy to do something'.

en·joy·a·ble /ɪn'dʒɔɪəbəl/ *adjective* something enjoyable is fun and makes you feel happy: *It's an enjoyable movie.* • *We had a very enjoyable afternoon.* → see Thesaurus at NICE

en·large /ɪn'lɑːdʒ $ ɪn'lɑrdʒ/ *verb* to make something bigger: *There are plans to enlarge the hospital.* • *I had the photograph enlarged.*

e·nor·mous /ɪ'nɔːməs $ ɪ'nɔrməs/ *adjective* very big SYNONYM **huge**: *an enormous amount of money* → see Thesaurus at BIG

e·nor·mous·ly /ɪ'nɔːməsli $ ɪ'nɔrməsli/ *adverb* extremely or very much: *The film was enormously successful.*

enough

There isn't enough cake for everyone.

e·nough /ɪ'nʌf/ *determiner, adverb, pronoun*
as much as is necessary: *Have we got enough time for another coffee?* • *We had enough money left to buy some chocolate.* • *The car was only big enough for four people.* • *He's not clever enough to go to university.* • *You don't practise your violin enough – you should do an hour every day.* • *I keep giving him money but it's never enough.*
PHRASES
have had enough (spoken) if you have had enough, you are tired of something and want it to stop: *I've **had enough of** your complaining.* • *I've **had enough.** I'm leaving.*

> GRAMMAR
> You use **enough** after an adjective on its own: *Do you think this bag is big **enough**?*
> You use **enough** before a noun: *Make sure that you take **enough** food.*

enquire *BrE* another spelling of INQUIRE

A B C D E F G H I J K L M N O P Q R S T U V W X Y Z

enquiry *BrE* another spelling of INQUIRY

en·rol *BrE*, **enroll** *AmE* /ɪn'rəʊl $ ɪn'roʊl/ *verb* (**enrolled**, **enrolling**) to become a member of a particular school, college, class etc: *I decided to enrol on the chemistry course.*

en·rol·ment *BrE*, **enrollment** *AmE* /ɪn'rəʊlmənt $ ɪn'roʊlmənt/ *noun* when someone becomes a member of a particular school, college, class etc: *Enrollment is scheduled for September 3 to 16.*

en route /ˌɒn 'ruːt $ ɑn 'rut/ *adverb* on the way to a place: *We bought a bottle of wine en route to the party.*

en·sue /ɪn'sjuː $ ɪn'su/ *verb* (formal) to happen soon after something, often as a result of it: *One man pulled out a knife, and a fight ensued.* —**ensuing** *adjective*: *What will happen over the ensuing months?*

en·sure /ɪn'ʃʊə $ ɪn'ʃʊr/ *verb* (formal) to make certain that something happens SYNONYM **make sure**: *Please ensure that you sign the form.*

en·ter /'entə $ 'entɚ/ *verb*
1 (written) to go or come into a place: *As soon as I entered the room, I knew something was wrong.*
2 to arrange to take part in a competition, race etc: *He decided to enter the poetry competition.* • *The horse was entered in the first race.*
3 to put information somewhere, such as into a computer or a book: *Enter your name and password, then press 'return'.* • *The job involved **entering** data **into** the computer.*

GRAMMAR
You usually say **enter a place**.
✘ Don't say 'enter into a place'.

en·ter·prise /'entəpraɪz $ 'entɚˌpraɪz/ *noun* **1** (no plural) the ability to think of and try new things, especially in business: *He showed a lot of enterprise in the way he solved the problem.* **2** a company or business: *She got a loan to set up her new enterprise.* **3** something new and difficult that you plan to do: *Moving to a new city was a huge enterprise for all of us.*

en·ter·pris·ing /'entəpraɪzɪŋ $ 'entɚˌpraɪzɪŋ/ *adjective* someone who is enterprising thinks of and does things that are new: *Some enterprising students set up a book-lending scheme.*

en·ter·tain /ˌentə'teɪn $ ˌentɚ'teɪn/ *verb* if someone or something entertains people, people enjoy watching or listening to them: *He has been entertaining audiences for nearly 20 years.* • *They switched on the TV to entertain the children.*

en·ter·tain·er /ˌentə'teɪnə $ ˌentɚ'teɪnɚ/ *noun* someone whose job is to tell jokes or sing to amuse people: *a nightclub entertainer*

en·ter·tain·ing /ˌentə'teɪnɪŋ $ ˌentɚ'teɪnɪŋ/ *adjective* amusing and interesting: *a lively and entertaining speech*

en·ter·tain·ment /ˌentə'teɪnmənt $ ˌentɚ'teɪnmənt/ *noun* (no plural) things such as television, films, and shows that people like to watch or listen to: *Most teenagers love entertainment such as movies and computer games.*

en·thral *BrE*, **enthrall** *AmE* /ɪn'θrɔːl/ *verb* (**enthralled**, **enthralling**) to keep someone's attention and interest completely: *The music enthralled the audience.* —**enthralling** *adjective*: *an enthralling story*

en·thu·si·as·m /ɪn'θjuːziæzəm $ ɪn'θuziˌæzəm/ *noun* (no plural) a strong feeling of interest or excitement about something: *My teacher was full of enthusiasm for music.*

en·thu·si·ast /ɪn'θjuːziæst $ ɪn'θuziˌæst/ *noun* someone who is very interested in a particular subject or activity: *My brother is a motorbike enthusiast.*

en·thu·si·as·tic /ɪnˌθjuːzi'æstɪk $ ɪnˌθuzi'æstɪk/ *adjective*

KEY PATTERNS
enthusiastic about something

someone who is enthusiastic about something likes it a lot and is excited about it: *Her parents **were enthusiastic about** the idea.* —**enthusiastically** /-kli/ *adverb*: *The crowd cheered enthusiastically.*

en·tice /ɪn'taɪs/ *verb* (written) to persuade someone to do something by offering them something nice SYNONYM **lure**: *The shops are already enticing customers with low prices.* —**enticing** *adjective*: *an enticing suggestion*

en·tire /ɪn'taɪə $ ɪn'taɪɚ/ *adjective* whole or complete: *We spent the entire evening talking.* —**entirely** *adverb*: *It was entirely my decision to leave.*

en·ti·tle /ɪn'taɪtl/ *verb* if you are entitled to something, you have the right to do or have it: *You are entitled to have your money back if you are not satisfied.*

en·trance /'entrəns/ *noun*

KEY PATTERNS
the entrance of/to something
at/in the entrance

the way into a place ANTONYM **exit**: *I'll meet you outside **the main entrance of** the shop.* • *When I got to the restaurant, Carl was waiting **at the entrance**.*

en·tranced /ɪn'trɑːnst $ ɪn'trænst/ *adjective* feeling great pleasure and surprise because of something very beautiful: *We were entranced by her singing.*

en·trant /'entrənt/ *noun* (formal) someone who enters a competition, university, or profession

en·tre·pre·neur /ˌɒntrəprə'nɜː $ ˌɑntrəprə'nɚ/ *noun* someone who starts a company: *The bank offers loans to encourage entrepreneurs.*

en·trust /ɪn'trʌst/ *verb* (formal) if you entrust someone with something, you make them responsible for it: *I was entrusted with the care of the children for two hours.*

en·try /'entri/ *noun*

KEY PATTERNS
entry to something
gain entry
refuse someone entry

1 (no plural) (formal) when you go into a place: *Members have **free entry to** the sports centre* (=can go in without paying). • *How did the thieves **gain entry*** (=get in)? • *Anyone wearing jeans **will be refused entry*** (=will not be allowed to go in).
2 (plural) **entries** something which someone sends to be judged in a competition: *The **winning entry** comes from Katie Chandler of Birmingham.*
3 (plural) **entries** one of a number of short pieces of writing in a book: *the last entry in her diary* • *a dictionary entry*

en·ve·lope /'envələʊp $ 'envəˌloʊp/ *noun* a folded paper cover, that you put a letter in so that you can send it

en·vi·ous /'enviəs/ *adjective* wishing that you had something that someone else has: *I'm really envious of your new camera.* —**enviously** *adverb*: *"I wish I had a job like yours," she said enviously.*

en·vi·ron·ment /ɪn'vaɪərənmənt $ ɪn'vaɪɚnmənt/ *noun*
1 the environment the land, water, and air that people, animals, and plants live in: *We must protect the environment.*
2 the people and things around you that affect your life: *a friendly office environment*

en·vi·ron·ment·al /ɪnˌvaɪərən'mentl $ ɪnˌvaɪɚn'mentl/ *adjective* relating to the land, water, and air: *environmental pollution*

en·vi·ron·men·tal·ist /ɪnˌvaɪərən'mentəlɪst $ ɪnˌvaɪɚn'mentl-ɪst/ *noun* someone who wants to protect the environment

enˌvironmentally 'friendly *adjective* environmentally friendly products are designed not to harm the environment

en·vis·age /ɪn'vɪzɪdʒ/ *verb* (formal) to think that something is likely to happen in the future: *I can't envisage any problems in finding a new job.*

en·vy /'envi/ *verb* (**envied**, **envies**) if you envy someone, you wish you had something that they have: *I envy her – her parents buy her anything she wants.* —**envy** *noun* (no plural): *I was filled with envy when my best friend won.*

ep·ic /'epɪk/ *adjective* an epic story or journey is very long, exciting, or impressive: *an epic journey in the Himalayas* • *an epic novel*

ep·i·dem·ic /ˌepə'demɪk/ *noun* when a disease spreads very quickly: *the AIDS epidemic*

ep·i·sode /ˈepəsəʊd $ ˈepəˌsoʊd/ *noun* one of the parts of a television or radio story that is broadcast separately: *What happened in last night's episode? I missed it.*

ep·i·taph /ˈepətɑːf $ ˈepəˌtæf/ *noun* a short sentence describing someone who has died, often written on the stone over their GRAVE: *I read his epitaph: "A great man and much-loved husband".*

e·qual¹ /ˈiːkwəl/ *adjective*

KEY PATTERNS
equal to something

two things that are equal are the same size or have the same value: *Plant the seeds equal distances apart.* • *two apples of equal size* • *One inch is **equal to** 2.54 centimetres.*

PHRASES
equal rights, equal opportunities the same legal rights or opportunities for everyone: *Women fought for equal rights.*

equal² *verb* (**equalled**, **equalling** *BrE*, **equaled**, **equaling** *AmE*)
1 to be as large as something else: *Four plus four equals eight (4+4=8).*
2 to be as good as something else: *Nothing can equal the excitement of winning the competition.*

equal³ *noun* someone with the same abilities or rights as someone else: *Young people want adults to treat them as equals.*

e·qual·i·ty /ɪˈkwɒləti $ ɪˈkwɑləti/ *noun* (no plural) when people from different groups have the same rights and opportunities ANTONYM **inequality**: *sexual equality*

e·qual·ize also **equalise** *BrE* /ˈiːkwəlaɪz/ *verb* in a team sport, to get a point or GOAL so that you have the same number as your opponents: *Germany equalized in the last few minutes of the game.*

eq·ual·ly /ˈiːkwəli/ *adverb* **1** just as much: *Jim and his sister are equally talented.* **2** in equal parts or amounts: *We should divide the work equally.*

e·qua·tion /ɪˈkweɪʒən/ *noun* a statement in mathematics showing that two quantities are equal, for example 2y + 4 = 10

e·qua·tor /ɪˈkweɪtə $ ɪˈkweɪtɚ/ *noun* **the equator** an imaginary line around the Earth that divides it equally into its northern and southern halves → see picture at GLOBE

e·quip /ɪˈkwɪp/ *verb* (**equipped**, **equipping**) to provide the tools or equipment that someone needs to do something: *We were equipped with calculators for the exam.*

e·quip·ment /ɪˈkwɪpmənt/ *noun* (no plural)
the things that you use for a particular activity: *We use the most modern scientific equipment.* • *an expensive **piece of equipment*** → see Thesaurus at MACHINE

GRAMMAR
Equipment is not used in the plural.
✘ Don't say 'equipments'.
When talking about a single thing, you say **a piece of equipment**.

e·quiv·a·lent /ɪˈkwɪvələnt/ *adjective* equal in amount, value, rank etc to something or someone else: *The certificate is equivalent to a High School diploma.* —**equivalent** *noun*: *A car costs almost the equivalent of a year's pay.*

e·ra /ˈɪərə $ ˈɪrə/ *noun* a period of time in history: *the post-war era*

e·rad·i·cate /ɪˈrædəkeɪt/ *verb* (formal) to destroy or remove something completely: *We want to eradicate nuclear weapons by 2030.*

e·rase /ɪˈreɪz $ ɪˈreɪs/ *verb* to completely remove written or recorded information: *I erased the file from the computer.*

e·ras·er /ɪˈreɪzə $ ɪˈreɪsɚ/ the American word for RUBBER

e·rect¹ /ɪˈrekt/ *adjective, adverb* in a straight upright position: *The winners stood erect on the platform.*

erect² *verb* (formal) to build something or put it in position: *It was difficult to erect the tent because of the strong winds.*

e·rode /ɪˈrəʊd $ ɪˈroʊd/ *verb* if land is eroded, or if it erodes, it is gradually destroyed by the weather or by water: *The action of the waves slowly erodes the rocks.*

e·ro·sion /ɪˈrəʊʒən $ ɪˈroʊʒən/ *noun* (no plural) the gradual destruction of land by the weather or by water: *Planting trees will help prevent soil erosion.*

e·rot·ic /ɪˈrɒtɪk $ ɪˈrɑtɪk/ *adjective* involving or producing sexual feelings: *an erotic painting*

er·rand /ˈerənd/ *noun* a short trip somewhere, made in order to get or do something for someone: *Are there any errands I can do for you?*

er·rat·ic /ɪˈrætɪk/ *adjective* not following a regular pattern: *Your attendance at college has been rather erratic.* —**erratically** /-kli/ *adverb*: *She was driving erratically before the accident.*

er·ror /ˈerə $ ˈerɚ/ *noun* if you make an error, you make a mistake: *Owing to a computer error, his name was left off the list.* • *She **had made** several spelling **errors**.* → see Thesaurus at MISTAKE[1]

e·rupt /ɪˈrʌpt/ *verb* **1** if violence erupts, it suddenly happens: *The crowd became angry and then violence erupted.* **2** if a VOLCANO erupts, it sends smoke and fire into the sky

e·rup·tion /ɪˈrʌpʃən/ *noun* when a VOLCANO erupts and sends smoke and fire into the sky

es·ca·la·tor /ˈeskəleɪtə $ ˈeskəˌleɪtɚ/ *noun* moving stairs that carry people from one level of a building to another: *We took the escalator to the first floor of the store.*

escalator

es·cape¹ /ɪˈskeɪp/ *verb*

KEY PATTERNS
escape from somewhere
escape death/punishment

1 to succeed in getting away from an unpleasant place or situation: *He **escaped from** prison by making a tunnel.* • *an escaped prisoner* **2** (written) if you escape death, punishment etc, you are not killed, punished etc when you could have been: *She narrowly **escaped death** when a tree fell on her car.*

escape² *noun* when someone escapes from a place or a situation: *We made our escape while the guards were not looking.*

es·cort¹ /ɪˈskɔːt $ ɪˈskɔrt/ *verb* to go somewhere with someone in order to protect or guard them: *The police escorted him from the courtroom to the car.* • *Jeff agreed to escort her back to the hotel.*

es·cort² /ˈeskɔːt $ ˈeskɔrt/ *noun* a person or group of people that goes somewhere with someone to guard or protect them: *The president had a police escort.*

Es·ki·mo /ˈeskəməʊ $ ˈeskəˌmoʊ/ *noun* someone who comes from the far north of Canada, Alaska etc

ESL /ˌiː es ˈel/ (English as a Second Language) the teaching of English to students whose first language is not English, but who live in an English-speaking country

es·pe·cial·ly /ɪˈspeʃəli/ *adverb* used to say that something is more true of one person or thing than of other people or things SYNONYM **particularly**: *Teenagers can get bored, especially in small towns and villages.* • *He is especially good at maths.*

es·say /ˈeseɪ/ *noun* a short piece of writing about a particular subject: *I had to write an essay on Shakespeare.*

es·sen·tial /ɪˈsenʃəl/ *adjective* important and necessary: *If you live in the country, a car is essential.* • *It's essential to phone us if you are going to be late.* → see Thesaurus at NECESSARY

es·sen·tials /ɪˈsenʃəlz/ *plural noun* things that are important or necessary: *I packed a bag of essentials.*

es·tab·lish /ɪˈstæblɪʃ/ *verb* **1** to start a company, organization etc that will exist for a long time SYNONYM **found**: *He established the business in 1982.* **2** to find out a fact: *The police established that he was not at work that day.*

es·tab·lish·ment /ɪˈstæblɪʃmənt/ *noun* (formal) a place for education, training, or RESEARCH: *an educational establishment*

A B C D E F G H I J K L M N O P Q R S T U V W X Y Z

es•tate /ɪˈsteɪt/ *noun* **1** a large area of land in the countryside that is owned by one person or organization: *The prince has a large estate in Cornwall.* **2** *BrE* a place where a lot of the same kind of houses have been built together: *a small housing estate*

esˈtate ˌagent *noun BrE* someone whose job is to buy and sell houses and land for people SYNONYM **real estate agent** *AmE*

esˈtate car *noun BrE* a large car with a door at the back SYNONYM **station wagon** *AmE*

es•ti•mate¹ /ˈestəmeɪt/ *verb*

KEY PATTERNS
estimate that
estimate the cost/value/number etc to be something
estimate the cost/value/number etc at something
estimate someone to have or be something

to make a reasonable guess at the size, amount, or time of something: *I* ***estimate that*** *the job will be finished by Friday.* • *We* ***estimate*** *the cost of repairs* ***to be*** *£100,000.* • *The time needed for the work* ***is estimated at*** *three weeks.* • *He* ***is estimated to*** *have over £50 million.*

es•ti•mate² /ˈestəmət/ *noun*

KEY PATTERNS
an estimate of something

what someone guesses the size, amount, or time of something to be: *What is your* ***estimate of*** *their chances of success?*

etc, etc. /et ˈsetərə/ used at the end of a list to show that you could add similar things: *Bring a coat, hat, spare sweater etc.*

USAGE
You write **books, pens, paper etc.**
✘ Don't write 'and etc'.

e•ter•nal /ɪˈtɜːnl $ ɪˈtɚnl/ *adjective* (written) continuing for ever: *They made a promise of eternal love.* —**eternally** *adverb*: *No one can look eternally young.*

e•ter•ni•ty /ɪˈtɜːnəti $ ɪˈtɚnəti/ *noun* **1** (no plural) time that does not end, especially the time after you die **2 an eternity** a very long time: *It was an eternity before the phone rang.*

eth•i•cal /ˈeθɪkəl/ *adjective* involving beliefs about what is right and wrong SYNONYM **moral**: *She's a vegetarian on ethical grounds.* —**ethically** /-kli/ *adverb*: *We try to run the business ethically.*

eth•ics /ˈeθɪks/ *plural noun* rules that people use to decide what is right and wrong: *medical ethics*

eth•nic /ˈeθnɪk/ *adjective* related to a particular race of people: *people from different ethnic groups*

e-tick•et /ˈiː ˌtɪkɪt/ *noun* the abbreviation of 'electronic ticket'; a ticket that is stored on a computer, not on paper: *Her e-ticket was issued by email.*

et•i•quette /ˈetɪket $ ˈetɪkət/ *noun* (no plural) the rules of polite behaviour

EU /ˌiː ˈjuː/ *noun* **the EU** the European Union; a political and economic organization of European countries

eu•phe•mis•m /ˈjuːfəmɪzəm/ *noun* a polite word or phrase that you use to avoid saying something that might offend people: *'Passed away' is often used as a euphemism for 'died'.*

eu•ro /ˈjʊərəʊ $ ˈjʊroʊ/ *noun* a unit of money intended to be used by all the EU countries

Eu•ro•pe•an /ˌjʊərəˈpiːən $ ˌjʊrəˈpiən/ *adjective* from or connected with Europe: *the European Court of Justice* —**European** *noun*: *Most of the people in my class are Europeans.*

ˌEuropean ˈUnion *noun* **the European Union** the EU

eu•tha•na•si•a /ˌjuːθəˈneɪziə $ ˌjuθəˈneɪʒə/ *noun* (no plural) the practice of killing very old or ill people in a painless way, so that they will not suffer any more: *Euthanasia is illegal in most countries.*

e•vac•u•ate /ɪˈvækjueɪt/ *verb* to move people from a dangerous place to a safer place: *The police evacuated us after they received a bomb warning.*

e•vac•u•a•tion /ɪˌvækjuˈeɪʃən/ *noun* when people are moved from a dangerous place to a safer place: *The fire led to the evacuation of the whole street.*

e•val•u•ate /ɪˈvæljueɪt/ *verb* (formal) to decide how good or bad something or someone is by carefully considering them SYNONYM **assess**: *School inspectors evaluate the quality of teaching.*

e•vap•o•rate /ɪˈvæpəreɪt/ *verb* if a liquid evaporates, or if something evaporates it, it changes into steam: *Salt is produced by evaporating sea water.*

e•vap•o•ra•tion /ɪˌvæpəˈreɪʃən/ *noun* (no plural) the process of removing water from something, usually by heating it

eve /iːv/ *noun* **Christmas Eve, New Year's Eve** the night or day before Christmas or New Year: *What are you doing on New Year's Eve?*

e•ven¹ /ˈiːvən/ *adverb*
1 used when adding something surprising: *Even Mum liked my new hair style.* • *He keeps everything, even old bus tickets.* • *He was very helpful, and even offered to drive us home.* • *The mountains always have snow on them, even in summer.*
2 used when comparing people or things: *Then he bought an even bigger car.* • *The second book is even more exciting than the first!*

PHRASES
even so in spite of this: *He knew he could pass the exam, but* ***even so*** *he felt nervous.*
even though although: *He kept asking her out,* ***even though*** *he knew she didn't like him.*

even² *adjective*
1 not changing much: *The room was kept at an even temperature.* • *He was running slowly at an even pace.*
2 flat, level, or smooth: *Put the tray on an even surface.* → see Thesaurus at FLAT¹
3 a game or competition that is even is one where the teams are equal and as good as each other: *For the first 45 minutes the game was very even.*

PHRASES
get even (informal) to hurt someone as much as they have hurt you: *He wanted to* ***get even with*** *the boy who had tricked him.*
break even if a business breaks even, it does not lose any money, but neither does it make any money: *In the first year, the company didn't* ***break even*** (=it lost money).
even number an even number is a number that you can divide exactly by two. For example, 2, 4, 6, and 8 are all even numbers ANTONYM **odd number**

eve•ning /ˈiːvnɪŋ/ *noun*

KEY PATTERNS
in the evening
on Monday/Tuesday etc evening
this evening

1 the end of the day and the early part of the night: *We usually eat at around 7* ***in the evening.*** • *I was out* ***on Tuesday evening.*** • *Do you feel like meeting up* ***this evening*** (=today in the evening)? • *an evening performance*
2 **(Good) Evening** (formal) used to greet someone in the evening: *Good evening, Sir.*

e•ven•ly /ˈiːvənli/ *adverb* divided or spread equally: *Spread the cream evenly over the cake.*

e•vent /ɪˈvent/ *noun*
1 something that happens, especially something important, interesting, or unusual: *He described the events that took place before the fight.*
2 something that has been organized, such as a party, sports game, or show: *We are organizing an event to raise money for charity.*

PHRASES
in the event of something (formal) if something happens: ***In the event of*** *a fire, leave the school building at once.*

e•vent•ful /ɪˈventfəl/ *adjective* full of interesting or important events: *an eventful holiday*

e•ven•tu•al•ly /ɪˈventʃuəli/ *adverb* after a long time: *We eventually arrived over three hours late.*

SPELLING
This word is often spelled wrongly. The correct spelling is: **eventually**.

THESAURUS
finally: *Finally, we managed to start the car* (=eventually).
at last: *At last we found the hotel* (=after we had been looking for it for a long time).

ev·er /ˈevə $ ˈevɚ/ *adverb*
at any time: *Have you ever been to New York?* • *It was the best birthday I've ever had.* • *Nothing exciting ever happens here.* • *Don't ever lie to me again!*
PHRASES
ever since all the time since something happened: *She's been unhappy* ***ever since*** *she moved to this school.*
for ever always, from now: *I'd like to live here* ***for ever!***

ev·er·green /ˈevəgriːn $ ˈevɚˌgrin/ *adjective* an evergreen tree or plant does not lose its leaves in winter

ev·ery /ˈevri/ *determiner*
all the people or things: *Every child has the right to go to school.* • *They cut down every tree in the garden.*
PHRASES
every day, every week etc once each day, each week etc: *He phones his girlfriend* ***every day.***
every so often, every now and then (informal) sometimes, not regularly: ***Every so often*** *we meet up for a chat.*

GRAMMAR
Every is followed by a singular verb: *Every house* ***has*** *its own garage.*

ev·ery·bod·y /ˈevribɒdi $ ˈevriˌbɑdi/ *pronoun*
everyone

ev·ery·day /ˈevrideɪ/ *adjective*
ordinary, usual, or happening every day: *Make exercise part of your everyday life.*

ev·ery·one /ˈevriwʌn/ also **everybody** *pronoun*
every person: *She knew everyone at the party.*

GRAMMAR
Everyone is followed by a singular verb: *Everyone* ***is*** *pleased.*
✘ Don't say 'everyone are pleased'.

WORD CHOICE
everyone or **every one**?
• **Everyone** means "all of the people or things in a group": *Hello, everyone. I'd like to introduce you to your new teacher.*
• **Every one** means "each person or thing in a group": *I have seen* ***every one*** *of his films.*
• Both **everyone** and **every one** are followed by a singular verb.

ev·ery·thing /ˈevriθɪŋ/ *pronoun*
each thing or all things: *Everything's going to be fine.* • *He forgot about* ***everything else*** (=all other things) *when he was playing computer games.*
PHRASES
be everything to be more important than anything else: *Money* ***isn't everything.***

ev·ery·where /ˈevriweə $ ˈevriˌwer/ *adverb*
in every place or to every place: *There was broken glass everywhere.* • *Some people get taxis everywhere they go.*

THESAURUS
all over: *Jack's clothes were* ***all over*** *the floor* (=everywhere on the floor).
throughout: *The organization has branches* ***throughout*** *the country* (=in every part of it).
worldwide: *The bank has branches* ***worldwide*** (=in many parts of the world).

ev·i·dence /ˈevədəns/ *noun* (no plural)

KEY PATTERNS
evidence that
evidence of something
evidence against someone

1 things that you see, hear, or discover that make you believe that something exists or is true: *There is clear* ***evidence that*** *this disease is caused by eating too much fat.* • *There is no* ***evidence of*** *his guilt.* • *She had some* ***evidence to*** *support her statement.*
2 in a court of law, the facts and objects that a lawyer presents to the people there in order to prove that something is true: *The gun was an important* ***piece of evidence.*** • *The* ***evidence against*** *him was weak.*

GRAMMAR
Evidence is not used in the plural.
✘ Don't say 'evidences'.
When talking about a single thing, you say **a piece of evidence**.

ev·i·dent /ˈevədənt/ *adjective* (formal) clear and easily seen: *It became evident that he was not interested in the subject.* —**evidently** *adverb*: *She was evidently ill.*

e·vil /ˈiːvəl/ *adjective* very cruel or bad: *an evil killer* → see Thesaurus at BAD

ev·o·lu·tion /ˌiːvəˈluːʃən $ ˌevəˈluʃən/ *noun* (no plural) the gradual development of something, especially types of plants and animals: *the evolution of man*

e·volve /ɪˈvɒlv $ ɪˈvɑlv/ *verb* to develop gradually: *The sun is a star that has evolved over billions of years.*

ex·act /ɪgˈzækt/ *adjective*
an exact detail, description, or copy is completely correct: *I can remember his exact words.* • *The exact cause of the disease is not known.*

PHRASES
the exact opposite something that is completely different from another thing: *If you ask him to do something, he does **the exact opposite**!*

ex·act·ly /ɪgˈzæktli/ *adverb*
1 you use exactly to say strongly that something is completely right, the same etc SYNONYM **precisely**: *I know **exactly what** is going to happen.* • *Where **exactly** did you leave your bike?* • *I was born exactly two years after my sister.* • *Simon looks **exactly like** his father.*
2 (spoken) used to agree completely with someone: *"So it's a secret." "Exactly!"*

PHRASES
not exactly (spoken, informal)
a) used to say that something is not at all true: *I'm **not exactly** the world's best cook* (=I'm not a very good cook)!
b) used to say that something is only partly true: *"Are they sisters?" "**Not exactly** – they're half-sisters."*

ex·ag·ge·rate /ɪgˈzædʒəreɪt/ *verb* to say that something is better, larger, worse etc than it really is: *"This dog was as big as a lion!" "Don't exaggerate!"* • *I think people exaggerate the risks of the sport.*

SPELLING
This word is often spelled wrongly. The correct spelling is: **exaggerate**.

ex·ag·ge·ra·tion /ɪgˌzædʒəˈreɪʃən/ *noun* a statement saying that something is better, larger, worse etc than it really is: *It would be an exaggeration to call it a disaster.*

ex·am /ɪgˈzæm/ *noun*
a written or spoken test to discover how much you know about a particular subject, or how well you can do something. You take, sit, or do an exam: *How did you do **in** your **exams**?* • *I'm **taking** my history **exam** tomorrow.* • *I was amazed when I **passed** my maths **exam*** (=succeeded in getting a high enough mark). • *I have to **re-sit** the French oral **exam** tomorrow* (=do the exam again). • *She **failed** all her **exams**.*

ex·am·i·na·tion /ɪgˌzæməˈneɪʃən/ *noun* **1** when someone looks at something carefully: *a medical examination* **2** (formal) an exam: *I passed all my examinations.*

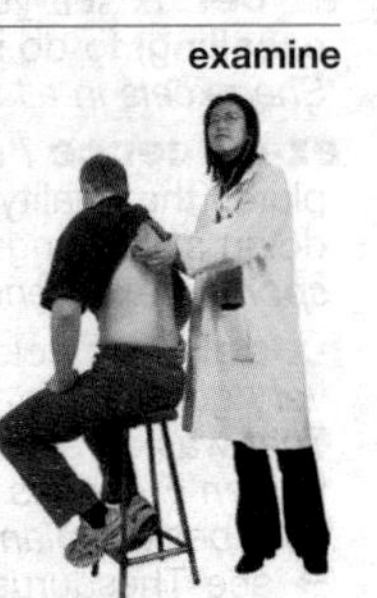
examine

ex·am·ine /ɪgˈzæmɪn/ *verb* to look at something carefully in order to find out or decide something: *The doctor examined me, but could find nothing wrong.*

ex·am·ple /ɪgˈzɑːmpəl $ ɪgˈzæmpəl/ *noun*

KEY PATTERNS
an example of something
give an example

something that helps to explain a general idea, or that shows what is typical: *Computer technology is a good **example of** how quickly things are changing.* • *I **gave** a few **examples of** animals that live in hot countries.* • *This is a **typical example of** 18th century architecture.*

PHRASES
for example used to add something to what you are saying in order to support your argument or opinion SYNONYM **for instance**: *He's so odd. **For example**, he has a rat as a pet.*

ex·as·pe·rate /ɪgˈzɑːspəreɪt $ ɪgˈzæspəˌreɪt/ *verb* to make you feel very annoyed: *His remarks clearly*

A B C D E F G H I J K L M N O P Q R S T U V W X Y Z

exasperated her. —**exasperating** *adjective*: *It's exasperating when you don't listen.*

ex·as·pe·ra·tion /ɪɡˌzɑːspəˈreɪʃən $ ɪɡˌzæspəˈreɪʃən/ *noun* (no plural) a feeling of great annoyance: *She hit the computer in exasperation.*

ex·ca·vate /ˈekskəveɪt/ *verb* to dig deeply into the ground over a large area, usually to build or find something: *Workers found an unexploded bomb while excavating the tunnel.*

ex·ca·va·tion /ˌekskəˈveɪʃən/ *noun* the activity of digging deep into the ground over a large area: *the archaeological excavation of an ancient city*

ex·ceed /ɪkˈsiːd/ *verb* (formal) to go or be above a particular number, amount, or limit: *Many drivers exceed the speed limit.* • *The cost of repairs will exceed $200.*

ex·cel /ɪkˈsel/ *verb* (formal) (**excelled**, **excelling**) to do something very well: *She excels in all scientific subjects.*

ex·cel·lence /ˈeksələns/ *noun* (no plural) the quality of being very good at doing something: *She won a prize for sporting excellence.*

ex·cel·lent /ˈeksələnt/ *adjective* very good: *He's an excellent player.* • *That was an excellent film.* • *Joe's written French is excellent, but he does not speak the language very well.*
→ see Thesaurus at GOOD[1]

SPELLING
This word is often spelled wrongly. The correct spelling is: **excellent**.

ex·cept /ɪkˈsept/ *preposition, conjunction*
not including someone or something: *Everyone was happy except Paul.* • *Put all the ingredients,* ***except for*** *the milk, in a pan.* • *I can't remember anything about the film* ***except that*** *it had a sad ending.* • *He's always bored* ***except when*** *he's playing computer games* (=the only time he isn't bored is when he's playing computer games).

SPELLING
This word is often spelled wrongly. The correct spelling is: **except**.

ex·cep·tion /ɪkˈsepʃən/ *noun* something that is not included in a general statement: *There are some exceptions to this rule.*

ex·cep·tion·al /ɪkˈsepʃənəl/ *adjective* unusually good SYNONYM **outstanding**: *an exceptional pupil* —**exceptionally** *adverb*: *an exceptionally talented musician*

ex·ces·sive /ɪkˈsesɪv/ *adjective* too much or too great: *Excessive dieting can be very harmful.*

ex·change[1] /ɪksˈtʃeɪndʒ/ *noun*
in exchange for something if you get one thing in exchange for another, you give one thing and receive something else as a result: *I gave Sue my red shoes* ***in exchange for*** *her leather belt.*

exchange[2] *verb*

KEY PATTERNS
exchange ideas/phone numbers/addresses etc
exchange one thing for another thing

to give something to someone who gives you something similar: *They exchanged addresses.* • *Do you want to exchange one of your DVDs for one of mine?*

exˈchange rate *noun* the value of the money of one country when you change it for the money of another country: *I want to buy some Japanese Yen – what's the exchange rate, please?*

ex·cit·ed /ɪkˈsaɪtɪd/ *adjective*

KEY PATTERNS
excited about/at something

very happy or interested because something good is happening or is going to happen: *Emma* ***was*** *so* ***excited about*** *the concert that she couldn't sleep.* • *He* ***was excited at*** *the thought of playing in the school team.*
—**excitedly** *adverb*

SPELLING
This word is often spelled wrongly. The correct spelling is: **excited**.

WORD CHOICE
excited or **exciting**?
• **Excited** means "very happy or interested in something": *The children were* ***excited*** *when they saw their presents.*

• **Exciting** means "very interesting and enjoyable": *People imagine that being a model is an **exciting** job.*

ex·cite·ment /ɪk'saɪtmənt/ *noun* (no plural) the feeling of being excited: *There's always a lot of excitement on the last day of term.*

ex·cit·ing /ɪk'saɪtɪŋ/ *adjective* something that is exciting makes you feel excited: *It was a pretty exciting game.*

SPELLING
This word is often spelled wrongly. The correct spelling is: **exciting**.

ex·claim /ɪk'skleɪm/ *verb* to speak suddenly and loudly because you are surprised, excited, or angry: *"What a lovely surprise!" he exclaimed.*

ex·cla·ma·tion mark /ˌekskləˈmeɪʃən ˌmɑːk $ ˌekskləˈmeɪʃən ˌmɑrk/ *BrE*, **ˌexclaˈmation ˌpoint** *AmE noun* the mark (!) that you write after words to show that something is sudden or surprising

ex·clude /ɪk'skluːd/ *verb* **1** to not allow someone to enter a place or join an organization: *People under the age of 18 are excluded from the club.* **2** to deliberately not include something: *The price of the holiday excludes flights.* • *The car is $25,000, excluding taxes.*

ex·clu·sive /ɪk'skluːsɪv/ *adjective* expensive and only available to certain people: *an exclusive London club*

ex·clu·sive·ly /ɪk'skluːsɪvli/ *adverb* only: *She writes exclusively about her own experiences.*

ex·cur·sion /ɪk'skɜːʃən $ ɪk'skɚʒən/ *noun* a short trip: *an excursion by boat to the island of Capri*

ex·cuse¹ /ɪk'skjuːz/ *verb*
1 to forgive someone for something that is not very bad: *You'll have to excuse the mess – I haven't had a chance to tidy.*
2 to allow someone not to do something that they should do: *She asked to **be excused from** games.* • *He was excused from class.*
3 to make someone's bad behaviour seem reasonable: *His situation at home doesn't excuse his violence.*

PHRASES
excuse me (spoken) **a)** used to politely get someone's attention: *Excuse me, do you need any help?* **b)** used to say sorry politely
excuse me? (spoken) *AmE* used to ask someone to repeat something: *"Have you heard from Gary?" "Excuse me?"*

ex·cuse² /ɪk'skjuːs/ *noun*

KEY PATTERNS
an excuse for being late/missing the bus etc
make an excuse about something
an excuse to do something

1 a reason that you give to explain why you behaved in a careless or annoying way: *What's your **excuse for** forgetting to do your homework?* • *He's always **making excuses about** why he's late.*
2 a reason, often one that is not true, that you give in order to do something: *She tried to think of an **excuse to go** home early.*

PHRASES
there's no excuse, that's no excuse (spoken) used to say that something is not acceptable: ***There's no excuse for** treating someone like that.* • *"I didn't mean to upset her!" **"That's no excuse!"***

PRONUNCIATION
Be careful how you pronounce this word:
excuse¹ (*verb*) is pronounced with a 'z' at the end
excuse² (*noun*) is pronounced with an 's' at the end

ex·e·cute /'eksəkjuːt/ *verb* to kill someone as an official punishment → see Thesaurus at KILL¹

ex·e·cu·tion /ˌeksə'kjuːʃən/ *noun* the act of killing someone as an official punishment

ex·ec·u·tive /ɪg'zekjətɪv/ *noun* an important manager in a company: *the chief executive*

ex·er·cise¹ /'eksəsaɪz $ 'eksɚˌsaɪz/ *noun*

KEY PATTERNS
do/take/get exercise

1 physical activities such as sport that you do in order to stay strong and healthy: *Try to **do some exercise** every day.* • *You should **take more exercise** –*

A B C D E F G H I J K L M N O P Q R S T U V W X Y Z

you're getting fat. • *He doesn't get enough exercise.* • *Walking up and down stairs is* ***good exercise.***
2 a piece of work that you do in order to learn or practise something: *Do exercise 5 in your English course book.*

SPELLING
This word is often spelled wrongly. The correct spelling is: **exercise**.

exercise² *verb* to do physical activities such as sport so that you stay strong and healthy: *I try to exercise each morning.* • *Cycling is good for exercising your leg muscles.*

ex·haust¹ /ɪg'zɔːst/ *verb* if something exhausts you, it makes you very tired: *Looking after the kids exhausts me.* —**exhausting** *adjective: a long exhausting day*

exhaust² also **ex'haust pipe** *noun* a pipe on a car that waste gas comes out of

ex·haust·ed /ɪg'zɔːstɪd/ *adjective* very tired: *I was so exhausted that I fell asleep on the couch.* → see Thesaurus at TIRED

WORD CHOICE
exhausted or **exhausting**?
• **Exhausted** means "very tired and wanting to rest": *By the end of the race I was exhausted.*
• **Exhausting** means "making you feel very tired": *Looking after young children can be exhausting.*

ex·hib·it¹ /ɪg'zɪbɪt/ *verb* to show something in a public place so that people can enjoy looking at it: *The paintings were exhibited in the city's main art gallery.* • *She exhibits her three dogs at all the big dog shows.*

exhibit² *noun* an object that is shown in a public place: *The British Museum has an enormous number of exhibits.*

ex·hi·bi·tion /ˌeksə'bɪʃən/ *noun*

KEY PATTERNS
an exhibition of something

a group of objects, paintings, photographs etc that are put in a public place so that people can enjoy looking at them: *We went to an* ***exhibition of*** *modern paintings at the art gallery.*

ex·hil·a·rat·ed /ɪg'zɪləreɪtɪd/ *adjective* feeling very happy and excited: *The team were exhilarated at their success.*

ex·hil·a·rat·ing /ɪg'zɪləreɪtɪŋ/ *adjective* making you feel very happy and excited: *an exhilarating helicopter ride*

ex·ile¹ /'eksaɪl $ 'egzaɪl/ *noun* **1 in exile** if you are living in exile, you are living in a country that is not your own because the people in authority have forced you to leave your country
2 someone who has been exiled: *political exiles*

exile² *verb* if someone is exiled from their country, the people in authority force them to leave it: *Napoleon was exiled to the island of Elba.*

ex·ist /ɪg'zɪst/ *verb* to be a real thing in the world: *The blue whale is the largest animal that has ever existed.*

ex·ist·ence /ɪg'zɪstəns/ *noun* when something exists: *At that time, no one knew of the island's existence.*

ex·ist·ing /ɪg'zɪstɪŋ/ *adjective* existing things are the ones that you use or that exist now: *The existing computer network is out of date.*

ex·it¹ /'egzɪt/ *noun* the way out of a place ANTONYM **entrance**: *He tried to leave the theatre but couldn't find the exit.*

exit² *verb* to finish using a computer program: *Exit Windows and shut down the machine.*

ex·ot·ic /ɪg'zɒtɪk $ ɪg'zɑtɪk/ *adjective* something that is exotic is unusual and interesting, often because it comes from a distant place: *the exotic music of the East*

ex·pand /ɪk'spænd/ *verb* to become bigger ANTONYM **contract**: *The world population is expanding all the time.*

ex·pect /ɪk'spekt/ *verb*

KEY PATTERNS
expect something
expect (that)
expect someone/something to do something
expect to do something

1 to think that something will happen: *The police are expecting trouble after*

the match. • *I* ***expect that*** *Keith will be at the party.* • *We* ***expected*** *John* ***to*** *pass the exam, but he failed.* • *We're* ***expecting to*** *move to the States next year.*
2 to believe that someone should do something because it is fair or right: *I* ***expect*** *everyone* ***to*** *help with the clearing up.*
3 if you are expecting something, you are waiting for it to arrive: *I'm expecting a parcel.* • *She's expecting her third child* (=going to have her third baby).

PHRASES
I expect *BrE* (spoken) used to say that you think something is probably true: *I* ***expect*** *you've heard that I'm leaving.* • *"Do you think she'd go out with me?"* ***"I expect so*** (=she probably would)."

ex·pec·tant /ɪk'spektənt/ *adjective* (written) hoping that something good will happen: *Hundreds of expectant fans waited for him to appear.* —**expectantly** *adverb*: *The dog looked up expectantly.*

ex·pec·ta·tion /ˌekspek'teɪʃən/ *noun* a strong belief or hope that something will happen: *He had no expectation of passing the exam.*

ex·pe·di·tion /ˌekspə'dɪʃən/ *noun* a carefully organized journey to a place for a particular purpose: *an expedition to the South Pole*

ex·pel /ɪk'spel/ *verb* (**expelled, expelling**) to officially order someone to leave a school, organization, or country: *The head teacher has the power to expel pupils who behave badly.*

ex·pense /ɪk'spens/ *noun* the amount of money you have to spend on something: *the expense involved in travelling abroad* • *living expenses*

ex·pen·sive /ɪk'spensɪv/ *adjective* something that is expensive costs a lot of money ANTONYM **cheap, inexpensive**: *We can't afford this – it's too expensive.* • *a very expensive car*

THESAURUS
pricey (informal): *Do you think these jeans are too* ***pricey*** (=expensive)?
overpriced: *I thought the food was very* ***overpriced*** (=more expensive than it should be).

WORD CHOICE
expensive or **high**?
• You use **high** when talking about the rent, prices, or costs: *The rent on my flat is very* ***high.*** • *Their prices are* ***high*** *compared with other shops.*
✘ Don't say 'My rent is very expensive.'

ex·pe·ri·ence¹ /ɪk'spɪəriəns $ ɪk'spɪriəns/ *noun*

KEY PATTERNS
experience of (doing) something

1 (no plural) the things that you learn when you do a particular job or activity: *The new principal has a lot of experience.* • *I* ***gained*** *a lot of valuable* ***experience*** *from working at the hospital.* • *Do you have any* ***experience of*** *working with children?*
2 something that happens to you: *Pam* ***had*** *some very bad* ***experiences*** *in the army.* • *It was his first* ***experience of*** *flying.*

experience² *verb* (formal) to be affected by something: *He experienced some pain in his leg.*

ex·pe·ri·enced /ɪk'spɪəriənst $ ɪk'spɪriənst/ *adjective* an experienced person has a lot of skill or knowledge about a particular job because they have done it for a long time ANTONYM **inexperienced**: *a very experienced soldier*

ex·per·i·ment¹ /ɪk'sperəmənt/ *noun*

KEY PATTERNS
do/carry out an experiment

a scientific test that you do in order to discover or prove something: *We* ***did*** *an* ***experiment*** *to show the effect that acid has on metal.*

ex·per·i·ment² /ɪk'sperəˌment/ *verb* to try using different things in order to find out what they are like: *Experiment with different herbs in your cooking.*

ex·pert /'ekspɜːt $ 'ekspɚt/ *noun* someone with special skills or knowledge: *Bomb experts managed to make the device safe.* —**expert** *adjective*: *an expert sailor*

ex·per·tise /ˌekspɜː'tiːz $ ˌekspɚ'tiz/ *noun* (no plural) special skills or knowledge: *legal expertise*

ex·pire /ɪk'spaɪə $ ɪk'spaɪɚ/ *verb* (formal) if a legal agreement or document expires, the period of time in which you can use it ends: *My passport expires in two weeks.*

ex·plain /ɪk'spleɪn/ *verb*

KEY PATTERNS
explain how/why/what
explain that
explain something (to someone)

1 to tell someone about something so that they can understand it: *I tried to **explain how** to play the game.* • *He **explained** the situation **to** me.*
2 to say why something happened: *I've already **explained why** I was late.* • *William **explained that** he had forgotten his key.* • *I just can't explain it* (=I don't know why it happened).
3 if a fact explains something, people accept that it is the reason for it: *This **explains why** the treatment only works with some patients.*

GRAMMAR
You **explain something to someone**.
✘ Don't say 'explain someone'.

ex·pla·na·tion /ˌeksplə'neɪʃən/ *noun*

KEY PATTERNS
an explanation of something
an explanation for something

the reason for something happening, or what someone says or writes about something that lets other people understand it: *She **gave** us a short **explanation of** the rules before we started.* • *There must be an **explanation for** these unusual results.*

ex·pli·cit /ɪk'splɪsɪt/ *adjective* clear or detailed: *explicit instructions*

ex·plode /ɪk'spləʊd $ ɪk'sploʊd/ *verb* if something explodes, it breaks apart suddenly and violently, causing a loud noise and a lot of damage: *A bomb has exploded in the shopping centre.*

ex·ploit /ɪk'splɔɪt/ *verb* to unfairly use someone's ideas, time, work etc without rewarding them for it: *The company was accused of exploiting workers.*

ex·ploits /'eksplɔɪts/ *plural noun* (written) your exploits are the brave or interesting things you have done: *My father loved telling us about his exploits in the army.*

ex·plo·ra·tion /ˌeksplə'reɪʃən/ *noun* when someone travels through a new or strange place to discover what it is like: *his **exploration of** the Antarctic*

ex·plore /ɪk'splɔː $ ɪk'splɔr/ *verb* to travel through a new or strange place to discover what it is like: *They spent the afternoon exploring the town.*

ex·plo·rer /ɪk'splɔːrə $ ɪk'splɔrɚ/ *noun* someone who travels to places that no one has ever been to

ex·plo·sion /ɪk'spləʊʒən $ ɪk'sploʊʒən/ *noun* when something explodes, or the loud noise it makes: *People heard the explosion five miles away.*

ex·plo·sive /ɪ'spləʊsɪv $ ɪk'sploʊsɪv/ *noun* a substance that can cause an explosion

ex·port¹ /ɪk'spɔːt $ ek'spɔrt/ *verb* to send and sell things to another country ANTONYM **import**: *The weapons were exported illegally.* —**exporter** *noun*

ex·port² /'ekspɔːt $ 'ekspɔrt/ *noun* the business of selling things to another country, or something that is sold ANTONYM **import**: *We produce computers for export.* • *Cloth is one of India's main exports.*

ex·pose /ɪk'spəʊz $ ɪk'spoʊz/ *verb* (formal) to remove what is covering something so that it can be seen or affected by something: *Do not expose your skin to the sun for too long.*

ex·po·sure /ɪk'spəʊʒə $ ɪk'spoʊʒɚ/ *noun* when someone is not protected from a harmful situation or substance: *Exposure to tobacco smoke can harm your children.*

ex·press¹ /ɪk'spres/ *verb* to tell people what you think or feel: *I want to express my thanks to all of you.* • *Joe finds it difficult to express his feelings.*

express² *noun* (plural **expresses**) also **ex'press train** a fast train which stops at only a few stations

ex·pres·sion /ɪk'spreʃən/ *noun*
1 a word or phrase that has a particular meaning: *What does the expression 'by yourself' mean?* → see Thesaurus at PHRASE
2 the way that your face shows how you feel: *The doctor's expression was*

A B C D E F G H I J K L M N O P Q R S T U V W X Y Z

serious. • *Richard looked at me with an expression of surprise.*

ex·pres·sive /ɪk'spresɪv/ *adjective* (written) showing what someone thinks or feels: *She had expressive brown eyes.*

ex·press·way /ɪk'spresweɪ/ *noun* *AmE* a very wide road, used for travelling fast between cities

ex·qui·site /ɪk'skwɪzɪt/ *adjective* very beautiful and delicate: *exquisite jewellery* —**exquisitely** *adverb*: *The room was exquisitely decorated.*

ex·tend /ɪk'stend/ *verb* **1** to continue over a particular distance or period of time: *The forest extends to the mountains.* **2** to make something bigger or longer: *We had the house extended to give ourselves an extra room.*

ex·ten·sion /ɪk'stenʃən/ *noun* **1** a part that you add to a building to make it bigger: *There's an extension at the back of the house.* **2** one of the telephones that is connected to a central system of telephones in a building: *What's your extension number?*

ex·ten·sive /ɪk'stensɪv/ *adjective* large in amount or area: *The bombing caused extensive damage* (=a lot of damage).

ex·tent /ɪk'stent/ *noun* (no plural) the size, amount, or importance of something: *We are trying to discover the extent of the problem.*

ex·te·ri·or /ɪk'stɪəriə $ ɪk'stɪriə˞/ *noun* the outside surface of something ANTONYM **interior**: *The exterior of the church was badly damaged.*

ex·ter·nal /ɪk'stɜːnl $ ɪk'stə˞nl/ *adjective* on the outside or related to the outside of something ANTONYM **internal**: *the external walls of the house*

ex·tinct /ɪk'stɪŋkt/ *adjective* a type of animal or plant that is extinct no longer exists

ex·tinc·tion /ɪk'stɪŋkʃən/ *noun* (no plural) when a type of animal or plant stops existing: *The white tiger is facing extinction.*

ex·tin·guish·er /ɪk'stɪŋgwɪʃə $ ɪk'stɪŋgwɪʃə˞/ a FIRE EXTINGUISHER

> PRONUNCIATION
> **extinguisher**
> You pronounce **-uish** like 'wish'.

ex·tra /'ekstrə/ *adjective, adverb* more than the usual amount: *Can I have extra fries with my burger?* • *You have to pay extra for a room with a sea view.*

ex·tract¹ /ɪk'strækt/ *verb* (formal) to remove something from a place: *I had two teeth extracted by the dentist.*

ex·tract² /'ekstrækt/ *noun* a small part of a story, poem, song etc: *She read an extract from her latest book.*

ex·tra·cur·ric·u·lar /ˌekstrəkə'rɪkjələ $ ˌekstrəkə'rɪkjələ˞/ *adjective* extracurricular activities are extra activities that students do, which are not part of the work they usually do in school or college

ex·traor·di·na·ry /ɪk'strɔːdənəri $ ɪk'strɔrdnˌeri/ *adjective* very strange, unusual, or surprising: *David told us an extraordinary story.* • *It's extraordinary how well she is doing.* ➔ see Thesaurus at SURPRISING

ex·trav·a·gant /ɪk'strævəgənt/ *adjective* spending or costing too much money: *He has an extravagant lifestyle.*

ex·treme¹ /ɪk'striːm/ *adjective* **1** very great: *Many rivers froze in the extreme cold.* **2** extreme opinions are very strong and unusual: *Some of her ideas are very extreme.* **3** farthest away from the middle of a place: *in the extreme south of the country*

extreme² *noun* the greatest amount of a quality, or something that has this: *The animals have to cope with extremes of temperature.*

ex·treme·ly /ɪk'striːmli/ *adverb* very: *I am extremely angry with you.*

ex·tro·vert, **extravert** /'ekstrəvɜːt $ 'ekstrəˌvə˞t/ *noun* someone who is confident and enjoys being with other people ANTONYM **introvert** ➔ see Thesaurus at SOCIABLE

eye /aɪ/ *noun* your eyes are the two things in your face that you see with: *Paul has green eyes and brown hair.* • *She* ***closed her eyes*** *and went to sleep.* • *You can* ***open your eyes*** *now.*

A B C D E F G H I J K L M N O P Q R S T U V W X Y Z

PHRASES

keep an eye on someone/something to watch what someone or something does in order to stop something bad happening: *I'll **keep an eye on** the baby while you go to the shop.* • ***Keep an eye on** that soup for me, please – I don't want it to boil.*

keep your eyes open to watch carefully so that you will notice something: ***Keep your eyes open** for a petrol station.*

in someone's eyes if something is true, important, wrong etc in someone's eyes, they think it is true etc, although other people may not: ***In** Steve's **eyes**, football is the most important thing in the world.*

cannot take your eyes off someone/something to keep looking at someone you find attractive or something you find interesting: *Drew **couldn't take his eyes off** Libby all evening.*

set eyes on someone, lay eyes on someone to see someone for the first time: *As soon as I **set eyes on** Ricky, I knew we would get married.* → see picture on page A5

eye·brow /ˈaɪbraʊ/ *noun* your eyebrows are the lines of short hairs above your eyes → see picture on page A5

eye·lash /ˈaɪlæʃ/ *noun* (plural **eyelashes**) your eyelashes are the small hairs that grow on the edge of your eyelids → see picture on page A5

eye·lid /ˈaɪlɪd/ *noun* your eyelids are the pieces of skin that cover your eyes when you close them

ˈeye-ˌshadow *noun* (no plural) a coloured substance that women put on their eyelids

eye·sight /ˈaɪsaɪt/ *noun* (no plural) how well you can see: *She has very good eyesight.*

eye·sore /ˈaɪsɔː $ ˈaɪsɔr/ *noun* something that is very ugly: *That building is an eyesore.*

F the written abbreviation of FAHRENHEIT

fab·ric /ˈfæbrɪk/ *noun* cloth SYNONYM **material**: *beautiful cotton fabrics*

fab·u·lous /ˈfæbjələs/ *adjective* (informal) extremely good SYNONYM **wonderful**: *We had a fabulous holiday!*

face¹ /feɪs/ *noun*

KEY PATTERNS
the look/expression on someone's face

1 the front part of your head, where your eyes, nose, and mouth are: *You have a beautiful face.* • *I washed my hands and face.* • *He had a worried look **on** his **face**.* → see picture on page A5
2 the front part of a clock or watch, which shows the time → see picture at WATCH²
PHRASES
make a face, pull a face to make your face have a funny or rude expression: *We **made faces at** the people in the car behind.*
someone's face fell if someone's face fell, they suddenly looked very disappointed: *My mother's **face fell** when I told her I'd failed all my exams.*
keep a straight face to stop yourself from smiling or laughing: *I tried hard to **keep a straight face**, but she looked really funny.*
face to face if two people do something face to face, they meet and speak to each other directly: *I'd like to **speak with** you **face to face** rather than on the phone.*
on the face of it if something seems true on the face of it, it seems true but it might not be: ***On the face of it**, it sounds like a very good job.*
to someone's face if you say something to someone's face, you say it directly to them rather than to someone else: *He called me a liar **to my face**.*

face² *verb*
1 if you face a bad situation or problem, you have to accept it or deal with it: *The president is facing a political crisis.* • *She must face the fact that she will never walk again.*
2 if you face something, you have the front of your body turned towards it: *Turn around and face the wall.*
3 if you have to face someone, you have to talk to them even though you feel upset, nervous, or embarrassed: *How can I ever face Stephen again?*
PHRASES
be faced with something if you are faced with something difficult, you have to do or deal with it: ***I was faced with** an impossible decision.*
can't face doing something (spoken) if you can't face doing something, you feel that you cannot do it because it seems too unpleasant: ***I can't face** driving for two hours in this heat.*
face up to something to accept or deal with something difficult or unpleasant instead of ignoring it: *We must **face up to** this problem.*

face·lift /ˈfeɪslɪft/ *noun* a medical operation to make your face look younger by removing loose skin

ˌface ˈvalue *noun* **take something at face value** to accept something without thinking that it might not be as good as it seems

fa·cil·i·ties /fəˈsɪlətiz/ *plural noun* rooms, equipment, or services that are available in a place: *The school has very good sporting facilities.*

fact /fækt/ *noun*

KEY PATTERNS
the fact that
a fact about something
the facts of a situation/case

something that you know is true or that you know has happened: *They won't make a decision until they know all the facts.* • *Children need to learn the **facts about** drugs.* • *The jury needs to examine the **facts of** the case.* • *John mentioned **the fact that** his family was from Germany.*

A B C D E F G H I J K L M N O P Q R S T U V W X Y Z

A B C D E F G H I J K L M N O P Q R S T U V W X Y Z

PHRASES

in fact, as a matter of fact (especially spoken) **a)** say this when you are adding information to what you are saying: *His mother just got married again; **in fact**, this is her third marriage.* • ***As a matter of fact**, I started working when I was 16.* • ***In fact**, the two schools have worked together on this project.* **b)** say this when you are correcting what someone else thinks: *"Isn't Alice a friend of yours?" "No, **as a matter of fact** I've just met her."* • *People think Ian's family is rich, but **in fact** they're not.* **c)** say this to emphasize that something is true even when it is surprising: ***As a matter of fact** it's cheaper to fly than to take the train.* • *She was, **in fact**, terrified of meeting new people.*

the fact is (that) use this to show what your main point is, especially when it shows what is really true in a situation: *People just want to turn on a computer and use it, but **the fact is that** computers are complicated machines.* • *I wanted to do it, but **the fact is**, I was scared.*

fac·tor /ˈfæktə $ ˈfæktɚ/ *noun* one of several things that affect a situation or something that happens: *The bad weather was an important factor in the crash.*

fac·to·ry /ˈfæktəri/ *noun* (plural **factories**)
a building where workers make large numbers of things to be sold: *She **works in a** chocolate **factory**.* • *There was a fire **at a** carpet **factory** just outside the city.* • *a group of **factory workers***

fac·tu·al /ˈfæktʃuəl/ *adjective* based on facts: *He gave us a factual account of what happened.*

fac·ul·ty /ˈfækəlti/ *noun* (plural **faculties**) **1** a group of university departments: *the Faculty of Engineering* **2 the faculty** *AmE* all the teachers in a school or college

fad /fæd/ *noun* something that is popular for only a short time SYNONYM **craze**: *Most of her special diets are just fads.*

fade /feɪd/ *verb* **1** if clothes or coloured objects fade, they gradually lose their colour or brightness: *The curtains have faded.* • *Her jeans had faded to a very pale blue.* **2** also **fade away** (written) to become weaker and gradually disappear: *Hopes of an end to the war are fading.* • *The memory of that day will never fade away.* —**faded** *adjective*: *She wore a pair of faded blue jeans.* → see Thesaurus at LIGHT[2]

fag /fæg/ *noun BrE* (informal) a cigarette

Fah·ren·heit /ˈfærənhaɪt/ (written abbreviation **F**) *noun* (no plural) a system for measuring temperature, in which water freezes at 32° (=0°C) and boils at 212° (=100°C)

fail[1] /feɪl/ *verb*

KEY PATTERNS
fail a test/examination
fail to do something

1 to not pass a test or examination: *She **failed** all her **exams**.* • *If you fail, you can take the test again.*
2 to not be successful ANTONYM **succeed**: *He **failed to** win the competition.* • *The attempt to save the ship failed.*
3 if a machine or a part of someone's body fails, it stops working: *If one of the plane's engines fails, the other engine will keep the plane flying.* • *Her eyesight is beginning to fail.*

fail[2] *noun* **1 without fail** if you do something without fail, you always do it: *She visits her aunt every Wednesday, without fail.* **2** used to tell someone firmly that they must do something: *You must all give your essays to me by Wednesday, without fail!*

fail·ing /ˈfeɪlɪŋ/ *noun* a fault or weakness that someone has: *His only failing is that he's always late!*

fail·ure /ˈfeɪljə $ ˈfeɪljɚ/ *noun*

KEY PATTERNS
someone's failure to do something
the failure of something

1 when you do not do something that you planned or wanted to do ANTONYM **success**: *He went to Australia after his **failure to** get a job in England.* • *We were very disappointed by **the failure of** the project.* • *The doctor said the operation had a high risk of failure* (=was very likely to fail).
2 when you do not do something that you should do: *The accident was*

caused by the train driver's ***failure to*** *notice the red signal light.*
3 when a machine or part of your body stops working: *The plane crashed because of* ***engine failure.*** • *He died of* ***heart failure.***
4 someone or something that is not successful ANTONYM **success**: *You always make me feel like a failure.* • *The party was a complete failure – no one came.*

faint¹ /feɪnt/ *adjective* **1** a faint smell, sound, or colour is not very strong: *a faint smell of perfume* **2** if you feel faint, you feel weak and as if you are about to become unconscious: *It was very hot, and I began to feel a bit faint.* **3 not have the faintest idea** to not know something at all: *I haven't got the faintest idea where she is!*

> **SPELLING**
> This word is often spelled wrongly. The correct spelling is: **faint**.

faint² *verb* to become unconscious for a short time SYNONYM **pass out**: *Some people faint when they see blood.*

fair¹ /feə $ fer/ *adjective*
1 treating everyone in an equal way, or in a way that is right according to a law or rule ANTONYM **unfair**: ***It's not fair*** *to expect me to do all the work.* • *He did not get a fair trial.*
2 reasonable and acceptable: *Is £100 a fair price for a bike?*
3 fair hair or skin is light in colour ANTONYM **dark**: *She had blue eyes and long fair hair.*

fair² *noun* an outdoor event where there are large machines to ride on and games to play SYNONYM **funfair** *BrE*: *Mum, can we go to the fair?*

fair·ly /ˈfeəli $ ˈferli/ *adverb*
1 in a reasonable or equal way: *It's important to treat everyone fairly and equally.* • *We must share the money out fairly.*
2 more than a little, but not very SYNONYM **quite**: *Matt is fairly good at tennis.* • *I am fairly sure that she will come.*

> **THESAURUS**
> **quite**: *It's quite easy* (=fairly).
> **pretty** (spoken): *He'll be OK – he's pretty tough* (=fairly).
> **rather**: *I'm rather busy at the moment* (=fairly).

fai·ry /ˈfeəri $ ˈferi/ *noun* (plural **fairies**) a creature in children's stories that looks like a small person with wings

ˈfairy tale *noun* a story for young children in which magical things happen

faith /feɪθ/ *noun* **1** (no plural) if you have faith in someone or something, you believe that you can trust them: *I have great faith in Fergus.* **2** (no plural) belief and trust in God: *Her strong faith helped her to cope.* **3** a religion: *the Jewish faith*

faith·ful /ˈfeɪθfəl/ *adjective*
1 continuing to support a person or an idea SYNONYM **loyal**: *The group has many faithful supporters.* **2** if you are faithful to your husband or wife, you do not have a sexual relationship with anyone else ANTONYM **unfaithful**

faith·ful·ly /ˈfeɪθfəli/ *adverb* **1** in a faithful way: *She supported him faithfully.* **2 Yours faithfully** *BrE* the usual polite way of ending a formal letter which begins 'Dear Sir' or 'Dear Madam'

fake¹ /feɪk/ *noun* a copy of something valuable that someone makes and pretends is real: *The painting was a fake.*

fake² *adjective* made to look like something real ANTONYM **genuine**: *a fake leather coat* → see Thesaurus at ARTIFICIAL

fake³ *verb* **1** to pretend: *He wasn't really upset – he was just faking it.*
2 to make a copy of something and pretend it is real: *Someone had faked my signature.*

fall¹ /fɔːl/ *verb* (**fell** /fel/ **fallen** /ˈfɔːlən/)

> **KEY PATTERNS**
> **rain/snow is falling**
> **fall onto/off something**
> **fall down the stairs/a hill**
> **fall down/over**

1 to drop down towards the ground: *The rain was falling heavily.* • *I slipped and* ***fell onto*** *the ice.* • *She danced round and round until she* ***fell over.*** • *I hurt my knee when I* ***fell off*** *my bike.* • *The letter* ***had fallen down*** *behind the desk.* → see picture on page A3

2 if an amount or level falls, it becomes less or lower SYNONYM **drop** ANTONYM **rise**: *Computer prices are falling all the time.* ➔ see Thesaurus at DECREASE

PHRASES

fall asleep to start to sleep: *She finally* ***fell asleep*** *after midnight.*

fall in love to begin to love someone: *My parents* ***fell in love*** *when they were 16. • I think I'm* ***falling in love with*** *you.*

be falling to pieces, be falling to bits (informal) if something is falling to pieces or falling to bits, it is in a very bad condition because it is very old: *I need some new trainers – these ones* ***are falling to bits.***

PHRASAL VERBS

fall apart
to separate into small pieces: *When I opened the book, it* ***fell apart.***

fall behind
to not make as much progress as other people: *She* ***is falling behind*** *in her school work.*

fall for
fall for someone to start to love someone: ***I fell for*** *George the first time I met him.*

fall out
to have a quarrel with a friend or someone you know well: *Those girls* ***are always falling out with*** *each other.*

> **THESAURUS**
> **slip**: *She* ***slipped*** *on the ice and broke her leg* (=slid so that she fell).
> **trip**: *Be careful not to* ***trip*** *on that step* (=hit your foot on it and fall or nearly fall).
> **stumble**: *The old man* ***stumbled*** *on the rough ground* (=put his foot on the ground in a way that made him nearly fall).

fall² *noun*

> **KEY PATTERNS**
> **a fall in the price/number of something**
> **have a fall**
> **the fall of a country/leader/empire**
> **in the fall**

1 when an amount or level becomes less or lower SYNONYM **drop**: *There has been* ***a fall in*** *the price of electricity.*

2 when someone falls: *My grandma* ***had a fall*** *and broke her leg.*

3 when someone or something is defeated or loses power ANTONYM **rise**: ***the fall of*** *the Roman empire*

4 *AmE* autumn: *We're getting married* ***in the fall.***

fallen the past participle of FALL¹

false /fɔːls/ *adjective*

1 not true or correct: *He gave false information to the police. • He may be using a false name. • The Second World War started in 1939 – true or false?* ➔ see Thesaurus at WRONG¹

2 a false object is not real, although it looks real SYNONYM **artificial**: *She was wearing false nails. • false teeth*

3 not sincere or honest: *Her enthusiasm seemed false.*

PHRASES

a false alarm when you think something bad is going to happen, but then it does not happen: *They warned us that a storm might be coming, but it was a false alarm.*

fame /feɪm/ *noun* (no plural) when everyone knows about you: *Appearing in a television series brought him instant fame.*

fa•mil•i•ar /fəˈmɪliə $ fəˈmɪljər/ *adjective*

> **KEY PATTERNS**
> **look/sound/be familiar to someone**
> **be familiar with a place/subject**

1 if something is familiar, you recognize it because you have seen or heard it before: *Do any of these people* ***look familiar to*** *you? • His face* ***is vaguely familiar*** (=I know his face, but not very well). *• 'Tina Jones' – that name* ***sounds familiar.*** *• It was nice to see some familiar faces* (=people I know) *again.*

2 if you are familiar with something, you know it well: *I* ***am*** *very* ***familiar with*** *London – I've lived there all my life.*

fa•mil•i•ar•i•ty /fəˌmɪliˈærəti/ *noun* (no plural) when you know something well or know a lot about it: *It's useful to have some familiarity with computers.*

fam•i•ly /ˈfæməli/ *noun* (plural **families**)

> **KEY PATTERNS**
> **in your family**
> **a member of a family**
> **a family of four/five people**

1 a group of people who are related to each other, especially parents and their children: *There are four girls and two boys **in my family**.* • *Who is the oldest **member of** your **family**?* • *a **family of** four* (=a family with four people in it)
2 a type of animal or plant: *The tiger is a member of the cat family.*

PHRASES
start a family to have your first child: *We're too young to **start a family**.*
run in the family if a quality or an illness runs in the family, several members of the same family have it: *Bad eyesight **runs in the family**.*

THESAURUS
relative/relation: *Some of my **relatives** are coming to stay* (=some members of my family).
folks (informal): *My **folks** wanted me to go to college* (=parents or family).
immediate family: *He told no one outside his **immediate family** about his illness* (=the people who were very closely related to him).
next of kin (formal): *The police are trying to find the dead man's **next of kin*** (=his closest relative).

fam•ine /'fæmɪn/ *noun* when a large number of people become ill and die because they do not have enough food

fa•mous /'feɪməs/ *adjective*

KEY PATTERNS
be famous for something

a famous person or thing is one that everyone knows about: *Many famous actors live in Beverly Hills.* • *Italy **is famous for** its good food.*

THESAURUS
well-known: *He's a **well-known** writer* (=known about by a lot of people).
world-famous: *Van Gogh's paintings are **world-famous*** (=famous everywhere in the world).

fan¹ /fæn/ *noun* **1** someone who likes a particular sport, kind of music, actor etc very much: *a rugby fan* • *My brother's a big fan of Madonna.* **2** a machine, or a flat object that you wave, which makes the air move so that you feel less hot

fan² *verb* (**fanned, fanning**) **fan yourself** to wave something to make the air near you move, so that you feel less hot: *She fanned herself with her hat.*

fa•nat•ic /fə'nætɪk/ *noun* **1** someone who has very strong and unreasonable beliefs about religion or politics
2 someone who likes something very much: *a football fanatic*

fan•cy¹ /'fænsi/ *adjective* (**fancier, fanciest**) special or unusual, not ordinary: *She didn't like wearing fancy clothes.* • *He took her to a fancy restaurant.*

fancy² *verb BrE* (informal) (**fancied, fancies**) **1** to want something: *Do you fancy going to the cinema?* **2** to feel sexually attracted to someone: *My brother fancies you!*

ˌfancy 'dress *noun* (no plural) *BrE* clothes that make you look like a different person and that you wear for fun or for a party

fan•fare /'fænfeə $ 'fænfer/ *noun* a short piece of music that is played loudly to introduce an important person or event

fang /fæŋ/ *noun* an animal's fangs are its long sharp teeth

fan•ta•size also **fantasise** *BrE* /'fæntəsaɪz/ *verb* to imagine that something pleasant is happening to you

fan•tas•tic /fæn'tæstɪk/ *adjective* (informal) extremely good or enjoyable: *It's a fantastic film!* → see Thesaurus at NICE, GOOD¹

USAGE
✗ Don't say 'It's very fantastic'.
Just say **It's fantastic**.

fan•ta•sy /'fæntəsi/ *noun* (plural **fantasies**) something that you think about that is pleasant but unlikely to happen: *I had fantasies about becoming a famous actress.*

far¹ /fɑː $ fɑr/ *adverb* (**further** /'fɜːðə $ 'fɚðɚ/, **farther** /'fɑːðə $ 'fɑrðɚ/ **furthest** /'fɜːðəst $ 'fɚðəst/, **farthest** /'fɑːðəst $ 'fɑrðəst/)
1 used to talk about distance: *We live **not far from** the station* (=not a great distance from the station). • ***How far** is it to your house* (=what is the distance between here and your house)? • *I want to get as **far away from** this place*

A B C D E F G H I J K L M N O P Q R S T U V W X Y Z

as possible. • *I can't walk any further – I'm too tired.* → see picture at NEAR[2]
2 very much: *He's* **far more** *intelligent* (=much more intelligent) *than I am.* • *It's* **far too** *hot to go running.*
PHRASES
(spoken) **as far as I know** used when you think something is true but are not sure about it: ***As far as I know,*** *they still live in Cambridge.*
so far until now: *I've understood everything* ***so far.***

WORD CHOICE
far or **a long way**?
• You usually use **far** in questions and negative sentences: ***How far*** *is the nearest town?* • *It's* ***not far*** *to my house.*
• You use **a long way** when saying that something is a long distance from another place: *The hotel was* ***a long way*** *from the airport.*

far[2] *adjective*
furthest away: *The principal's office is at the far end of the corridor.* • *I could see the others on the far side of the field.*

farce /fɑːs $ fɑrs/ *noun* **1** an event or situation that is very badly organized: *The meeting was a complete farce.*
2 a funny play in which a lot of silly things happen

fare /feə $ fer/ *noun* the price that you pay to travel by train, plane, bus etc: *a company that offers cheap air fares*
→ see Thesaurus at COST[1]

fare•well /feəˈwel $ ferˈwel/ *noun* (formal) goodbye

ˌfar-ˈfetched *adjective* a story that is far-fetched is very strange and not likely to be true

farm[1] /fɑːm $ fɑrm/ *noun* an area of land where people keep animals or grow food: *a large pig farm*

farm[2] *verb* to use land for growing food and keeping animals

farm•er /ˈfɑːmə $ ˈfɑrmɚ/ *noun* someone who owns a farm or is in charge of a farm

farther a COMPARATIVE form of FAR

farthest a SUPERLATIVE form of FAR

fas•ci•nate /ˈfæsəneɪt/ *verb* if something fascinates you, you think it is extremely interesting: *Japan has always fascinated me.*

fas•ci•nat•ing /ˈfæsəneɪtɪŋ/ *adjective* extremely interesting: *This is a fascinating book.*

fas•ci•na•tion /ˌfæsəˈneɪʃən/ *noun* (no plural) when you think that something is extremely interesting: *He has a fascination for old books.*

fas•cis•m /ˈfæʃɪzəm/ *noun* (no plural) an extreme political system in which the state has complete power and controls everything

fas•cist /ˈfæʃɪst/ *noun* someone who supports fascism

fash•ion /ˈfæʃən/ *noun*
the style of clothes, hair etc that is popular at a particular time: *The shop sells all* ***the latest fashions.*** • *Even young children are now becoming interested in fashion.* • *a fashion magazine*
PHRASES
be in fashion to be popular at a particular time SYNONYM **be in**: *Short skirts* ***are*** *always* ***in fashion.*** • *Long hair* ***is*** *back* ***in fashion.*** → see Thesaurus at FASHIONABLE
be out of fashion to no longer be popular: *That haircut* ***is*** *just so* ***out of fashion*** *now.* • *These hats* ***went out of fashion*** *years ago!*

fash•ion•a•ble /ˈfæʃənəbəl/ *adjective* something that is fashionable is popular at a particular time ANTONYM **unfashionable**: *Short hair is fashionable for men now.*

THESAURUS
be in fashion: *Short skirts* ***are in fashion*** *at the moment* (=are fashionable).
be in (informal): *Silver jewellery* ***is in*** (=is fashionable).
trendy (informal): *That's a very* ***trendy*** *shirt you're wearing* (=fashionable).
stylish: *She always wears* ***stylish*** *clothes* (=fashionable and attractive).

fast[1] /fɑːst $ fæst/ *adjective*
1 moving or happening quickly ANTONYM **slow**: *He has always loved fast cars.* • *This computer is much faster than my old one.* • *He is the fastest runner in the world.*

2 a clock that is fast shows a time that is later than the real time ANTONYM **slow**: *That clock is two minutes fast.*

WORD CHOICE
fast or **quick**?
• You use **fast** about things and people that can move or do things at high speed: *Her car is very fast.*
• You use **quick** when saying that someone does something for a short time: *I had a quick look at the newspaper* (=I looked at it for a short time).

fast² *adverb*
quickly ANTONYM **slowly**: *I can't run very fast.* • *You have to work faster.*
PHRASES
be fast asleep to be completely asleep: *The children are* ***fast asleep*** *in bed.*
be stuck fast to be completely stuck somewhere and unable to move: *The car* ***was stuck fast*** *in the sand.*

fast³ *verb* to eat no food or very little food for a period of time, especially for religious reasons

fas•ten /ˈfɑːsən $ ˈfæsən/ *verb*

KEY PATTERNS
fasten a zip/belt/coat
fasten one thing to another

1 if you fasten something, you join together the two sides of it so that it is completely closed ANTONYM **unfasten**: *I can't fasten the zip of these trousers.* • *Fasten your seat belt – the plane is about to take off.*
2 if you fasten something to something else, you put it on the other thing in a firm way, so that it will stay connected: *She* ***fastened*** *a rope* ***to*** *the front of the boat.* • *He* ***fastened*** *the flower* ***onto*** *the side of her hat.*

THESAURUS
tie: *I tied the boat to a tree with a rope* (=fastened it using a knot).
attach: *Please attach a photograph to your application form* (=fasten it firmly, for example with a clip).
fix *BrE: We wanted to fix the shelves to the wall* (=fasten them firmly).
join: *Join the ends of the rope together* (=fasten them so that they are connected).

PRONUNCIATION
In this word you do not pronounce the **t**.

fastenings

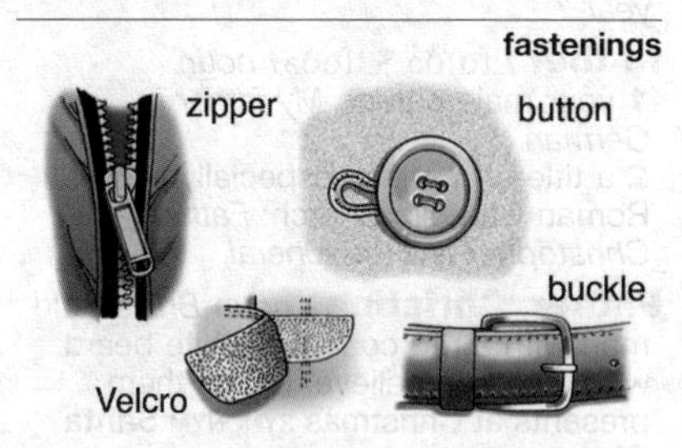

fas•ten•ing /ˈfɑːsənɪŋ $ ˈfæsənɪŋ/ *noun* something that you use to hold another thing closed

ˈfast food *noun* (no plural) hot food that a restaurant cooks and serves very quickly to customers

ˌfast-ˈforward *verb* if you fast-forward a tape, you wind it forward quickly without playing it ANTONYM **rewind**

fat¹ /fæt/ *adjective* (**fatter, fattest**)
1 someone who is fat is too wide and round ANTONYM **thin**: *I'm too fat – I must try to eat less chocolate.* • *a small fat man*
2 something that is fat is thick or wide: *a big fat book* • *a fat wallet full of money*

THESAURUS
plump: *a plump woman of about 50* (=slightly fat)
overweight: *The doctor said I was a little* ***overweight*** (=slightly heavier than I should be).
obese (formal): *Unhealthy food can cause children to become* ***obese*** (=extremely fat in a way that is dangerous for their health).

fat² *noun* (no plural) **1** the substance under the skin of people and animals which helps to keep them warm **2** an oily substance that some foods contain: *Doctors tell us we should eat less fat.*

fa•tal /ˈfeɪtl/ *adjective* something that is fatal causes someone's death: *a fatal road accident*

fate /feɪt/ *noun* **1** someone's fate is what happens to them: *The government will decide the fate of the refugees.* **2** (no plural) a power that, some people believe, controls what happens to people in their lives: *Fate brought him back to London later that year.*

fa·ther /ˈfɑːðə $ ˈfɑðɚ/ *noun*
1 your male parent: *My father is German.*
2 a title of a priest, especially in the Roman Catholic Church: *Father Christopher led the funeral.*

ˌFather ˈChristmas *noun BrE* an old man with a red coat and white beard who, children believe, brings them presents at Christmas SYNONYM **Santa Claus**

fa·ther·hood /ˈfɑːðəhʊd $ ˈfɑðɚˌhʊd/ *noun* (no plural) the state of being a father

ˈfather-in-ˌlaw *noun* (plural **fathers-in-law**) the father of your husband or wife

fa·tigue /fəˈtiːg/ *noun* (no plural) (formal) extreme tiredness

fat·ten·ing /ˈfætn-ɪŋ/ *adjective* food that is fattening is likely to make you fat

fat·ty /ˈfæti/ *adjective* (**fattier**, **fattiest**) fatty food contains a lot of fat

fau·cet /ˈfɔːsɪt/ the American word for a water TAP

fault /fɔːlt/ *noun*
1 a problem with a machine or piece of equipment that stops it working correctly: *The fire was caused by an electrical fault.*
2 a bad part of someone's character: *In spite of her faults, Bet is a good friend.*

PHRASES

be someone's fault if a mistake is your fault, you are responsible for it: *The accident **was** partly **my fault**. • These problems **are** your **own fault**.*

WORD CHOICE

fault or **mistake**?

• A **fault** is something that is wrong with a machine or equipment: *My computer developed a **fault**.*

• A **mistake** is something that you do that is wrong: *We are sorry about the **mistake**.*

• You use the phrase **to be someone's fault** when saying who was responsible for causing something bad to happen: *The accident was the other driver's **fault**.*

fault·y /ˈfɔːlti/ *adjective* not working properly: *Some of the equipment was faulty.*

fa·vour *BrE*, **favor** *AmE* /ˈfeɪvə $ ˈfeɪvɚ/ *noun*
something kind or helpful that you do for someone else: *Sarah made my wedding dress for me, as a favour.*

PHRASES

do someone a favour to do something kind or helpful for someone: *Could you **do me a favour** and lend me your bike?*

ask someone a favour, ask a favour of someone to ask someone to do something kind or helpful for you: *John, can I **ask you a favour**?*

be in favour of something to support a plan or an idea ANTONYM **be against something**: *Most of the students **are in favour of** having an end-of-term party.*

in someone's favour (formal) if a court or official group makes a decision in your favour, it decides that you are right: *After a long discussion, the judges **decided in our favour**.*

fa·vou·ra·ble *BrE*, **favorable** *AmE* /ˈfeɪvərəbəl/ *adjective* **1** showing that you like someone or something: *All the comments about her work were favourable.* **2** favourable conditions are good, and likely to make something succeed: *We were lucky because the weather conditions were favourable.*

fa·vou·rite[1] *BrE*, **favorite** *AmE* /ˈfeɪvərət/ *adjective*
your favourite thing or person is the one that you like most: *We chose Joe's favorite music for the party. • You're my favourite uncle.*

favourite[2] *BrE*, **favorite** *AmE noun*
1 the person or thing that you like more than all the others: *Which picture is your favourite?* **2** the team, runner etc that is expected to win a competition: *Who is the favourite to win the 100 metres?*

fa·vou·ri·tis·m *BrE*, **favoritism** *AmE* /ˈfeɪvərətɪzəm/ *noun* (no plural) when one person or group is unfairly treated better than others

fax /fæks/ *noun* (plural **faxes**) **1** a document that is sent down a telephone line and then printed using a

special machine: *I'll send you a fax.*
2 also **'fax ma,chine** a machine that you use for sending and receiving faxes —**fax** *verb*: *I'll fax the documents to you.*

fear¹ /fɪə $ fɪr/ *noun*

KEY PATTERNS
fear of something
fear for something/someone you care about
for fear of doing something bad

the feeling that you get when you are very afraid or worried: *He does not travel by plane because of his* ***fear of*** *flying.* • *Her mind was full of* ***fears for*** *her daughter's safety.* • *She was afraid to make a noise,* ***for fear of*** *being discovered.*

USAGE
You say **I'm afraid** or **I'm scared.**
✘ Don't say 'I have fear'.

fear² *verb*

KEY PATTERNS
fear (that)
fear for someone/something you care about

to feel very afraid or worried: *The police* ***fear that*** *he may have killed himself.* • *They feared the programme would upset people.* • *Her parents began to* ***fear for*** *her safety.*

fear·less /'fɪələs $ 'fɪrləs/ *adjective* not afraid of anything

fea·si·ble /'fiːzəbəl/ *adjective* possible: *Is it feasible to get the work finished by next month?*

feast /fiːst/ *noun* a large meal for a lot of people to celebrate a special occasion

feat /fiːt/ *noun* something that someone does that shows a lot of strength or skill

fea·ther /'feðə $ 'feðɚ/ *noun* one of the light soft things that cover a bird's body

fea·ture¹ /'fiːtʃə $ 'fitʃɚ/ *noun*

KEY PATTERNS
a feature of something
a feature on a subject

1 an important or interesting part of something: *This new software has some very useful features.* • *The use of very bright colours is a typical* ***feature of*** *his paintings.*
2 a long article in a newspaper or magazine: *The paper published a three-page* ***feature on*** *global warming.*
3 features your features are your eyes, nose, mouth etc: *a pretty woman with fine features*

feature² *verb* **1** if a film, magazine etc features someone, they are in it: *The film features Dustin Hoffman as a New York lawyer.* **2** to be an important part of something: *His photographs feature in several books on gardens.*

Feb·ru·a·ry /'februəri $ 'febju,eri/ (written abbreviation **Feb**) *noun* the second month of the year: *We went on holiday at the end of February.*

SPELLING
This word is often spelled wrongly.
The correct spelling is: **February**.

fed the past tense and past participle of FEED¹

,fed 'up *adjective* (informal) annoyed, bored, or unhappy: *I'm fed up with my job!*

fee /fiː/ *noun* **1** an amount of money that you pay a professional person for their work **2** an amount of money that you pay to do something: *school fees*
→ see Thesaurus at COST¹

fee·ble /'fiːbəl/ *adjective* extremely weak: *She is now very old and feeble.*

feed¹ /fiːd/ *verb* (past tense and past participle **fed** /fed/)

KEY PATTERNS
feed someone (food)
feed food to someone
feed animals on a type of food
animals feed on a type of food

1 to give food to a person or animal: *Have you fed the cats this morning?* • *We* ***fed*** *apples* ***to*** *the horses.* • *She sat next to Simon and fed him grapes.* • *We* ***fed*** *the puppy* ***on*** *bread and warm milk.*
2 if animals or babies feed, they eat: *Some birds* ***feed on*** *insects.*

feed² *noun* **1** (no plural) food for animals **2** *BrE* milk or food that you give to a baby: *When did he have his last feed?*

feed·back /ˈfiːdbæk/ *noun* (no plural) criticism or advice about how well or badly you have done something: *Your teacher will give you feedback on your work.*

feel¹ /fiːl/ *verb* (past tense and past participle **felt** /felt/)

KEY PATTERNS
feel sad/hungry etc
feel smooth/wet etc
it feels as if
it feels good/strange to do something
feel (that)
feel strongly about something

1 to experience something such as anger, happiness, cold, hunger etc: *I felt cold and lonely.* • *You must feel very disappointed.* • *I* ***feel better*** *now that I've had a rest.*
2 used to say how something you touch, or an experience, seems to you: *A snake's skin feels dry, not wet.* • ***It felt as if*** *the dentist was using a hammer to take my tooth out.* • ***It felt*** *good* ***to*** *be home again.* • ***How does it feel*** *to be back in England?*
3 to have an opinion about something, based on your feelings: *I felt that I should apologise.* • *Rick* ***feels strongly about*** *animal rights.* • ***How do you feel about*** *going out tonight* (=would you like to go out tonight)?
4 to touch something with your hands: *When she felt the carpet, it was wet.* • *Gill slowly* ***felt her way*** (=used her hands to find the way) *to the door.*
→ see Thesaurus at TOUCH¹

PHRASES
feel like something to want something or want to do something: *Do you* ***feel like*** *a walk?* • *Sam was being so annoying I* ***felt like*** *hitting him.*

feel² *noun* **1** the way that something feels when you touch it: *I love the feel of wool.* **2** the way that something seems to people: *The theatre has a very modern feel.*

feel·ing /ˈfiːlɪŋ/ *noun*

KEY PATTERNS
a feeling of anger/joy etc
a feeling about something

1 something that you experience in your mind or your body: *I enjoy running – it gives me a* ***good feeling.*** • *When I'm angry, it's hard to* ***hide my feelings.*** • *a* ***feeling of*** *boredom*
2 your opinion or attitude: *What are your* ***feelings about*** *the plan?*

PHRASES
have a/the feeling that to think that something is probably true or will probably happen: ***I had the feeling that*** *Jack was lying to me.* • ***I left, with the feeling that*** *I would never see him again.*

feet the plural of FOOT

fell the past tense of FALL¹

fel·low /ˈfeləʊ $ ˈfeloʊ/ *noun* (informal) a man

felt¹ the past tense and past participle of FEEL¹

felt² /felt/ *noun* (no plural) a type of soft thick cloth

ˌfelt tip ˈpen *noun* a pen that has a hard piece of felt at the end that the ink comes through

fe·male¹ /ˈfiːmeɪl/ *adjective* belonging to the sex that can have babies or produce eggs ANTONYM **male**: *a female tiger* • *female relatives* • *a female voice*

female² *noun* a person or animal belonging to the sex that can have babies or produce eggs ANTONYM **male**: *We have three cats – two females and one male.*

fem·i·nine /ˈfemənɪn/ *adjective*
1 having qualities that people think are typical of women ANTONYM **masculine**: *She never wears very feminine clothes.*
2 belonging to a group of nouns, adjectives etc in some languages that is different from the MASCULINE and NEUTER groups

fem·i·nis·m /ˈfemənɪzəm/ *noun* (no plural) the belief that women should have the same rights and opportunities as men

fem·i·nist /ˈfemənɪst/ *noun* someone who believes in feminism

fence¹ /fens/ *noun* a line of posts that are joined together around an area of land or between two areas of land: *There was a tall wooden fence around the garden.* • *He jumped easily over the fence.*

fence² *verb* **1 fence something in** to put a fence around something: *The*

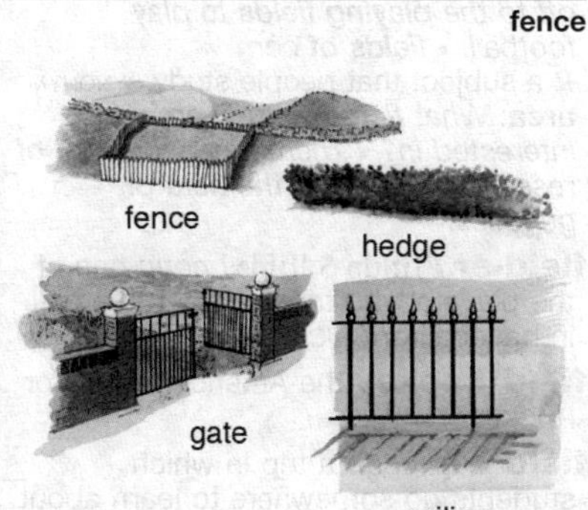

animals were all fenced in. **2 fence something off** to separate an area with a fence

fenc·ing /ˈfensɪŋ/ *noun* (no plural) a sport in which people fight with long thin swords

fend /fend/ *verb* **fend for yourself** to look after yourself without help from other people: *The children had to fend for themselves while their parents were at work.*

fend·er /ˈfendə $ ˈfendɚ/ *noun AmE* the part of a car that covers the wheels

fe·ro·cious /fəˈrəʊʃəs $ fəˈroʊʃəs/ *adjective* extremely violent and dangerous SYNONYM **fierce**: *a ferocious wild animal*

fer·ry /ˈferi/ *noun* (plural **ferries**) a boat that regularly carries people across a narrow area of water ➔ see Thesaurus at BOAT ➔ see picture on page A11

fer·tile /ˈfɜːtaɪl $ ˈfɚtl/ *adjective* **1** fertile land or soil produces a lot of healthy plants ANTONYM **infertile** **2** someone who is fertile is able to produce babies ANTONYM **infertile**

fer·ti·lize also **fertilise** *BrE* /ˈfɜːtəlaɪz $ ˈfɚtlˌaɪz/ *verb* if an egg is fertilized, the egg and a SPERM join together so that a new animal or baby can start to develop

fer·ti·liz·er also **fertiliser** *BrE* /ˈfɜːtəlaɪzə $ ˈfɚtlˌaɪzɚ/ *noun* a chemical or natural substance that you put on the soil to help plants grow

fes·ti·val /ˈfestəvəl/ *noun* **1** a time when people celebrate something, especially a religious holiday **2** an occasion when there are a lot of concerts, films, or performances: *an international music festival*

fes·tive /ˈfestɪv/ *adjective* connected with a happy celebration: *a festive occasion*

fes·tiv·i·ties /feˈstɪvətiz/ *plural noun* when people eat, drink, and dance to celebrate something

fetch /fetʃ/ *verb*

KEY PATTERNS
fetch something/someone (from a place)
fetch someone something
fetch something for someone

to go and get something or someone and bring them back: *What time is your dad coming to fetch you?* • *Would you mind fetching me some milk?* • *She **fetched** a newspaper **for** her grandma.* • *She went off to **fetch** some water **from** the well.* • *I've got to **fetch** Sally **from** the station.*

fetus the American spelling of FOETUS

feud /fjuːd/ *noun* an angry argument between two people or groups that continues for a long time: *There has been a feud between the two families for many years.*

fe·ver /ˈfiːvə $ ˈfivɚ/ *noun* an illness in which you are very hot

fe·ver·ish /ˈfiːvərɪʃ/ *adjective* someone who is feverish has a fever

few /fjuː/ *determiner, pronoun* only a small number, not more: *He has very few friends.* • *Few of the original buildings remain.*

PHRASES

a few a small number of people or things: *We had to wait for **a few** minutes.* • ***A few of** her friends were jealous.*

quite a few a fairly large number of people or things: *I've been to **quite a few** parties recently.*

fi·an·cé /fiˈɒnseɪ $ ˌfiɑnˈseɪ/ *noun* the man that a woman has promised to marry

fi·an·cée /fiˈɒnseɪ $ ˌfiɑnˈseɪ/ *noun* the woman that a man has promised to marry

A B C D E F G H I J K L M N O P Q R S T U V W X Y Z

A B C D E F G H I J K L M N O P Q R S T U V W X Y Z

fi·as·co /fiˈæskəʊ $ fiˈæskoʊ/ *noun* (plural **fiascoes** or **fiascos**) an event that is completely unsuccessful SYNONYM **disaster**

fib /fɪb/ *noun* (informal) a small unimportant lie

fi·bre *BrE*, **fiber** *AmE* /ˈfaɪbə $ ˈfaɪbɚ/ *noun* **1** a material such as cotton or NYLON, which is made of thin threads: *Nylon is a man-made fibre.* **2** one of the threads that form a material **3** (no plural) parts of plants that you eat but do not DIGEST, which help food to move through your body: *The doctor said I need more fibre in my diet.*

fic·tion /ˈfɪkʃən/ *noun* (no plural) books and stories about people and events that are not real ANTONYM **nonfiction**: *Most children enjoy reading fiction.*

fic·tion·al /ˈfɪkʃənəl/ *adjective* fictional people or events are in a book or story, and are not real SYNONYM **imaginary**

fid·dle¹ /ˈfɪdl/ *verb* **fiddle with something, fiddle around with something** to keep touching something or moving it around in your hands: *Stop fiddling with your knife and fork!*

fiddle² *noun* **1** a VIOLIN **2** *BrE* a dishonest way of getting money: *a tax fiddle*

fid·dly /ˈfɪdli/ *adjective* (**fiddlier, fiddliest**) (informal) difficult to do because you have to move very small objects: *Repairing the radio was a fiddly job.*

fid·get /ˈfɪdʒɪt/ *verb* to keep moving your hands or feet, because you are bored or nervous: *The audience were starting to fidget.*

field /fiːld/ *noun*

KEY PATTERNS
in a field
on/onto a field
a field of wheat/potatoes etc
in the field of education/medicine

1 an area of land that is used for growing food, keeping animals, or playing a sport: *There were cows **in the field**. • The crowd cheered as the players ran **onto the field**. • We went off to the playing **fields** to play football. • **fields of** corn*
2 a subject that people study SYNONYM **area**: *What **field of study** are you interested in? • There has been a lot of research recently **in the field of** genetics.*

field·er /ˈfiːldə $ ˈfildɚ/ *noun* one of the players who tries to catch the ball in baseball or CRICKET

ˈfield ˌhockey the American word for HOCKEY

ˈfield trip *noun* a trip in which students go somewhere to learn about a subject

field·work /ˈfiːldwɜːk $ ˈfildwɚk/ *noun* (no plural) the study of subjects outside, rather than in a building: *The course involves quite a lot of fieldwork.*

fiend·ish /ˈfiːndɪʃ/ *adjective* very clever in an unpleasant way: *a fiendish plot to take control of the company*

fierce /fɪəs $ fɪrs/ *adjective*
1 a fierce animal is likely to attack you SYNONYM **ferocious**: *a fierce tiger*
2 a fierce person is angry and likely to shout at people: *Miss Stewart can be quite fierce at times.*
3 involving a lot of energy or violence: *A **fierce battle** took place between the police and the protesters. • The climbers could not come down from the mountain because of a **fierce storm**.* —**fiercely** *adverb*: *The dog showed its teeth fiercely.*

fi·er·y /ˈfaɪəri/ *adjective* full of strong or angry emotion: *John has a fiery temper.*

fif·teen /ˌfɪfˈtiːn/ *number* 15 —**fifteenth** *number*

fifth /fɪfθ/ *number* **1** 5th **2** one of five equal parts of something; 1/5

fif·ty /ˈfɪfti/ *number* (plural **fifties**)
1 50 **2 the fifties** the years from 1950 to 1959 **3 be in your fifties** to be aged between 50 and 59 —**fiftieth** *number*

ˌfifty-ˈfifty *adjective, adverb* (informal)
1 if something is divided fifty-fifty, it is divided equally between two people
2 a fifty-fifty chance an equal chance that something will happen or will not happen: *She has a fifty-fifty chance of succeeding.*

fig /fɪɡ/ *noun* a small soft sweet fruit that is often dried ➔ see picture on page A7

fight¹ /faɪt/ *verb* (past tense and past participle **fought** /fɔːt/)

KEY PATTERNS
fight (with) someone
fight over something
fight (against) a country/enemy
fight for something you want
fight (against) something bad
fight to do something

1 if people fight, they hit each other: *My brother and I often fight, but we never really hurt each other.* • *Terry **was always fighting with** other boys.* • *He said he would fight anyone who said anything about his sister.* • *What are you two **fighting over**?*
2 to take part in a war: *He fought with great bravery in the war.* • *The English **fought against** the French at the Battle of Agincourt.* • *The terrorists believe that they **are fighting for** freedom.* • *The two countries **fought** a war **over** this area of land.*
3 to try hard to stop something bad or to make something good happen SYNONYM **battle**: *Everyone can help to **fight crime**.* • *We must **fight against** these harmful ideas.* • *an organization that **fights for** improvements in the environment* • *The workers at the factory **are fighting to** keep their jobs.*

PHRASAL VERBS

fight back
to fight or try hard to defeat someone who has attacked or harmed you: *Don't let them win – **fight back**!*

fight off
fight someone off to fight someone who is attacking you so that you make them go away: *She managed to **fight off** her attackers.*

fight² *noun* **1** an attempt to do something which is difficult and takes a long time SYNONYM **battle**: *the fight for democracy* • *her long fight against cancer* **2** when two people hit each other, or argue with each other: *He got drunk and got into a fight.* • *She's had a fight with her father.*

fight·er /ˈfaɪtə $ ˈfaɪtɚ/ *noun*
1 someone who takes part in a sport in which people fight each other **2** a small fast military plane that can destroy other planes

fig·ure¹ /ˈfɪɡə $ ˈfɪɡjɚ/ *noun*
1 a number that shows an amount: *The figures show that house prices are rising quickly.* • *The painting was sold for **a figure of** around $50,000.*
2 any of the written signs between 0 and 9 SYNONYM **digit**: *a four-figure number, such as 2,300*
3 the shape of a person, especially one you cannot see very well: *A dark figure was sitting alone on the beach.*
4 (formal) a shape in mathematics: *A hexagon is a six-sided figure.*

figure² *verb* **1** if a person or thing figures in something, they are included in it **2** *AmE* (spoken) to believe or think SYNONYM **reckon**: *I figured I ought to talk to her again.* **3 figure something out** (informal) to begin to understand something that is difficult to understand SYNONYM **work out**

file¹ /faɪl/ *noun*

KEY PATTERNS
(keep) a file on someone/something
be on file

1 a set of papers containing information about a particular person or thing, or the box used to store these papers: *Please fetch the file labelled 'AE'.* • *The hospital **keeps files on** all the people who come there.* • *Details of your application are **on file** in the main office.* • *All the information you need should be **in that file**.* • *We will keep all your details **on file*** (=in a file).
2 an amount of information that you store on a computer under a particular name: *You need to **create a new file**.* • *How do I **save the file**?*
3 a tool with a rough edge that you use for making things smooth

file² *verb* **1** to store papers or information in a particular place: *Her letter is filed under 'complaints'.* **2 file your nails** to rub your nails with a rough tool in order to make them smooth

filet an American spelling of FILLET

fill /fɪl/ *verb*

KEY PATTERNS
fill a container/space (with something)

a container/space fills with something

1 also **fill up** to put a large amount of something in a container or an area so that it becomes full: *We filled the car's petrol tank before we started our trip.* • ***Fill up** the holes **with** soil so that the seeds are covered.* • *Mary **filled** two glasses **with** champagne.*
2 also **fill up** to become full of something: *The concert hall was starting to **fill up with** people.* • *As the fire spread, the building **filled with** smoke.*

PHRASAL VERBS

fill in

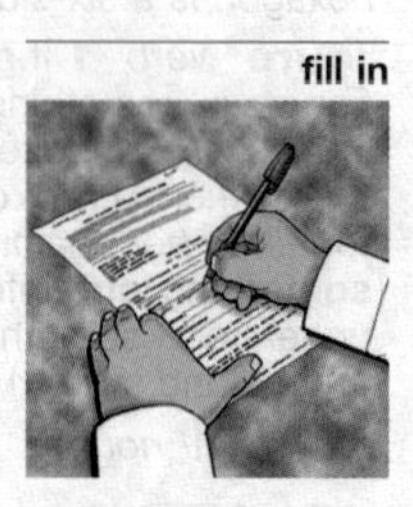
fill in

fill something in to write the information that someone wants in the spaces on a printed piece of paper: *You have to **fill** this form **in**.* • *Please **fill in** your name and address.*

fill out

fill something out to write the information that someone wants in the spaces on a printed piece of paper: *Have you **filled out** that job application form yet?*

fil·let *BrE* also **filet** *AmE* /ˈfɪlɪt $ fɪˈleɪ/ *noun* a piece of meat or fish without any bones

fill·ing¹ /ˈfɪlɪŋ/ *noun* **1** a small amount of metal that is put into a hole in your tooth **2** food that is put inside other food: *The filling had fallen out of my sandwich.*

filling² *adjective* food that is filling makes your stomach feel full

ˈfilling ˌstation *noun* a place where you can buy petrol for your car SYNONYM **petrol station**, **gas station**

film¹ /fɪlm/ *noun*

KEY PATTERNS
a film about something

1 a story told in moving pictures that is shown in a cinema or on television SYNONYM **movie** *AmE*: *'Star Wars' is my favourite film.* • *Have you **seen** any good **films** recently?* • *We **watched** a **film about** a Russian ballet dancer.*
2 the roll of thin plastic that you use in a camera to take photographs: *I must buy some film for my camera.*

film² *verb* to record moving pictures of something: *No one has ever filmed these animals before.*

ˈfilm star *noun* a famous film actor or actress

fil·ter¹ /ˈfɪltə $ ˈfɪltɚ/ *noun* a thing that removes substances that you do not want from a liquid or gas as it flows through: *the oil filter in a car*

filter² *verb* to clean a liquid or gas using a filter: *I filter all my drinking water.*

filth /fɪlθ/ *noun* (no plural) unpleasant dirt: *The old bicycle was completely covered in filth.*

filth·y /ˈfɪlθi/ *adjective* (**filthier**, **filthiest**) extremely dirty: *Your hands are filthy!* ➔ see Thesaurus at DIRTY

fin /fɪn/ *noun* one of the flat parts that stick out of a fish's body and help it to swim

fi·nal¹ /ˈfaɪnl/ *adjective*
1 the final thing is the one that is last or that happens at the end: *On the final day of our holiday, we all went out for a meal.* • *The final scene of the play has a big surprise.*
2 if a decision or offer is final, it cannot be changed: *The judge's decision is final.* • *£300 is my final offer.*

final² *noun* **1** the last part of a competition: *Tickets for the World Cup Final are hard to get.* • *He reached the finals but only came second.* **2 finals** **a)** *BrE* the examinations that students take at the end of their last year at university **b)** *AmE* the examinations that students take at the end of each class in high school and college

fi·nal·ist /ˈfaɪnl-ɪst/ *noun* one of the people or teams that reach the last part of a competition

fi·nal·ize also **finalise** *BrE* /ˈfaɪnl-aɪz/ *verb* to decide firmly on the details of a plan or arrangement: *I haven't finalized the details yet.*

fi·nal·ly /ˈfaɪnl-i/ *adverb*
1 after a long time: *We finally arrived home at 10 o'clock, over three hours late.* • *Mark finally agreed to accept the job.* ➔ see Thesaurus at EVENTUALLY

2 used when you are saying the last of a series of things SYNONYM **lastly**: *Finally, we welcome Xavier, who has joined the class today.*

fi·nance¹ /ˈfaɪnæns $ fəˈnæns/ *noun*
1 (no plural) activities connected with the spending or saving of large amounts of money: *He works in finance.* **2** (no plural) money that you get in order to pay for something important: *The government is offering finance to new small businesses.*
3 finances the money that a person or organization has: *My finances are pretty good at the moment.*

finance² *verb* to provide money for something SYNONYM **fund**: *The school agreed to finance my trip.*

fi·nan·cial /fəˈnænʃəl/ *adjective* connected with money: *The film was a financial disaster.* —**financially** *adverb*

find /faɪnd/ *verb* (past tense and past participle **found** /faʊnd/)

KEY PATTERNS
find something (for) someone
find someone something
find (that)

1 to see or get something, especially after you have been looking for it: *The boys found a gold watch buried under a tree.* • *I* ***can't find*** *my socks!* • *Phil's been trying to* ***find a job*** *for three weeks.* • *I've* ***found*** *a house* ***for*** *you.* • *Mark went outside to find us a taxi.*
2 to learn that something is true: *They* ***found that*** *men are better at reading maps than women.*

PHRASES
find something difficult, find something easy: *I* ***find*** *maths very* ***difficult*** (=maths is difficult for me). • *Jessica said she* ***found*** *the exam quite* ***easy***. • *Bill* ***finds it difficult*** *to make friends* (=it is difficult for Bill to make friends).
find your way to arrive at a place by discovering the right way to get there: *I tried to* ***find my way*** *back to the station.*
find yourself doing something to realize that you are doing something, even though you did not mean to: *He* ***found himself*** *laughing out loud during the film.*
find fault with someone/something to criticize someone or something: *My boss* ***finds fault with*** *everything I do.*

PHRASAL VERBS
find out
find something out to get information about something: *I'd like to* ***find out*** *more* ***about*** *the college music courses.* • *I did the test to* ***find out*** *how fit I was.* • *Can you* ***find out*** *what time the film starts?*

THESAURUS
discover: *Scientists have* ***discovered*** *a new planet* (=found a planet that nobody knew about before).
locate (formal): *Ned soon* ***located*** *the hotel on the map* (=found its exact position).
track down: *He managed to* ***track down*** *his old school friend* (=find him after looking for him in many places).

find·ings /ˈfaɪndɪŋz/ *plural noun* the things that people have learned as the result of an official study: *They reported their findings to the Health Minister.*

fine¹ /faɪn/ *adjective*
1 very good: *We sell fine food from around the world.* • *The team gave a fine performance.*
2 very thin, or in very small pieces or amounts: *a shampoo for fine hair* • *a scarf made from very fine silk* • *The sand here is fine and soft.*
3 (spoken) good enough SYNONYM **ok**: *"I've only got water to drink." "That's fine."*
4 (spoken) healthy and reasonably happy: *"How is your mother?" "She's fine."* → see Thesaurus at HEALTHY
5 if the weather is fine, it is sunny and not raining SYNONYM **wet**: *I hope it stays fine for the picnic.*

USAGE
✘ Don't say 'I'm very fine'.
Just say **I'm fine**.

fine² *verb* to make someone pay an amount of money as a punishment: *The judge fined him $500 for stealing.* —**fine** *noun*: *He was given a £100 fine for speeding.*

fine³ *adverb* (spoken) well: *Everything was going fine until you arrived!*

fine·ly /ˈfaɪnli/ *adverb* into very small pieces: *Chop the onion finely.*

A B C D E F G H I J K L M N O P Q R S T U V W X Y Z

A B C D E F G H I J K L M N O P Q R S T U V W X Y Z

fin·ger /ˈfɪŋɡə $ ˈfɪŋɡɚ/ *noun* one of the long parts at the end of your hand: *She wore a ring on nearly every finger.* → see picture on page A5

PHRASES

keep your fingers crossed to hope that something will happen in the way that you want it to: *The exam results come out tomorrow, so we're **keeping our fingers crossed**!*

fin·ger·nail /ˈfɪŋɡəneɪl $ ˈfɪŋɡɚˌneɪl/ *noun* the hard flat part at the end of your finger → see picture at NAIL

fin·ger·print /ˈfɪŋɡəˌprɪnt $ ˈfɪŋɡɚˌprɪnt/ *noun* a mark that someone's finger makes, which shows its pattern of lines: *The burglar left his fingerprints on the window.* → see picture at FOOTPRINT

fin·ish¹ /ˈfɪnɪʃ/ *verb*

KEY PATTERNS
finish (doing) something

1 to come to the end of doing or making something: *Just let me finish this letter.* • *I'll finish cleaning the house in the morning.*
2 to come to an end SYNONYM **end**: *What time did the party finish?*
3 to eat, drink, or use all the rest of something: *Who finished the pie?*
4 finish first, finish second etc to be the winner, come second etc at the end of a race or competition: *Kate **finished** last.*

PHRASAL VERBS

finish off
1 finish something off to do the last part of something: *David has to **finish off** his homework, and then he can go out.*
2 finish something off to eat, drink, or use all the rest of something: *Would you like to **finish off** the sandwiches?*

finish with
1 finish with something if you have finished with something, you are no longer using it and no longer need it: *You can have this magazine – I've **finished with** it.*
2 finish with someone to end a relationship with someone: *I was really upset when Paul **finished with** me.*

finish² *noun* (plural **finishes**) the end of something, especially a race: *It was a very close finish.*

fin·ished /ˈfɪnɪʃt/ *adjective*
1 completed: *The finished building will be 200 feet high.* **2** no longer able to be successful: *Most footballers are finished by the time they are 30.*

THESAURUS
complete: *By April, the project should be **complete*** (=finished – used about big or important things that people are working on).
over: *The tennis match was **over** by three o'clock* (=finished – used about events, activities, or periods of time).
done: *Katie, is your History essay **done** yet* (=finished – used about jobs or tasks that someone has to do)?

fir /fɜː $ fɚ/ also **ˈfir tree** *noun* a tree with very narrow leaves that do not fall off in winter

fire¹ /faɪə $ faɪɚ/ *noun*
1 the light and heat that something produces when it burns: *The village was completely destroyed **by fire**.* • *A **fire started** in the kitchen.*
2 a pile of wood or coal that you burn in order to make a place warm or to cook food: *They sang songs around the fire.*

PHRASES

be on fire to be burning: *One of the plane's engines **was on fire**.*
catch fire to start burning, especially by mistake: *Somehow the curtains **caught fire**.*
set fire to something, set something on fire to make something start burning: *A cigarette **set fire to** a pile of leaves.*
put out a fire to stop something burning: *Firefighters tried for three hours to **put out the fire**.*
open fire to start shooting: *The soldiers were ordered to **open fire**.*

THESAURUS
bonfire: *We made a **bonfire** on the beach* (=a large fire you make outdoors).
blaze: *Firemen fought to control the **blaze*** (=a dangerous fire).

fire² *verb*

KEY PATTERNS
fire (a bullet/gun) at/into something

1 to shoot bullets from a gun: *Police **fired into** the air.* • *The man **fired** two shots **at** the car.*

2 to tell someone that they must leave their job SYNONYM **sack** *BrE*: *The company fired her after she had worked there for only a week.*

fire aˌlarm *noun* a piece of equipment that makes a loud noise when there is a fire in a building, in order to warn people: *The fire alarm went off and we had to leave the building.*

fire·arm /ˈfaɪərɑːm $ ˈfaɪərɑrm/ *noun* (formal) a gun

fire briˌgade *BrE*, **ˈfire deˌpartment** *AmE noun* an organization of people whose job is to stop fires

ˈfire ˌengine *noun* a large vehicle that carries firefighters and their equipment

ˈfire esˌcape *noun* a set of stairs that is next to the outside wall of a building. People use the fire escape to get out of the building if there is a fire.

ˈfire exˌtinguisher *noun* a piece of equipment used for stopping small fires

fire·fight·er /ˈfaɪəˌfaɪtə $ ˈfaɪərˌfaɪtər/ *noun* someone whose job is to stop fires

fire·man /ˈfaɪəmən $ ˈfaɪərmən/ *noun* (plural **firemen** /-mən/) a man whose job is to stop fires

fire·place /ˈfaɪəpleɪs $ ˈfaɪərpleɪs/ *noun* in a room, the open place in the wall where you light a fire to heat the room → see picture at ABOVE

ˈfire truck the American word for FIRE ENGINE

fire·wall /ˈfaɪəwɔːl $ ˈfaɪərˌwɔl/ *noun* a system that protects a computer network and prevents other people from using it or damaging it: *They managed to get through the company firewall and steal information about customers.*

fire·work /ˈfaɪəwɜːk $ ˈfaɪərwərk/ *noun* an object that you light so that it explodes and produces bright lights in the sky, in order to celebrate a special event

firm¹ /fɜːm $ fərm/ *adjective*

1 something that is firm is not soft when you press it: *The fruit should be firm and not too ripe.* • *These exercises will give you a firm, flat stomach.*
→ see Thesaurus at HARD¹

2 a firm date, decision etc is not likely to change: *We have not agreed a firm date for the party.*

3 if you are firm, you say that someone must do what you want them to do: *You need to* ***be firm with*** *people when you are trying to get your money back.*

4 a tight strong way of holding something: *a strong man with a firm handshake* —**firmly** *adverb*: *"No," he said firmly.* • *Glue the pieces of wood firmly together.*

firm² *noun* a business or company: *My father works for a printing firm.*

first¹ /fɜːst $ fərst/ *number, adverb, adjective*

1 before anyone or anything else; 1st: *January is the first month of the year.* • *The band's first recording was very successful.*

2 before doing something, or before something happens: *You can borrow my clothes, but you have to ask me first.* • *First I did my homework, then I watched TV.*

3 at the beginning of something: *When Jane first met Steve, he was working in a bar.* • *Using email is easier than I first thought.*

4 the first the first person or thing: *I was* ***the first to*** *answer the question.* • *The second week of the holiday was better than* ***the first***.

PHRASES

come first a) to win a race or competition: *Lee* ***came first*** *in a skateboarding contest.* **b)** to be more important than anything else: *For me, friends* ***come first***.

at first in the beginning: *I didn't like her* ***at first***, *but now we're friends.*

in the first place at the start of a situation: *Why didn't you tell me the truth* ***in the first place***?

first of all before doing anything else: ***First of all***, *we need to decide who to invite.*

WORD CHOICE

at first, **first of all**, or **firstly**?

• You use **at first** when saying how a situation was at the beginning, when it changes later: *At first the test seemed easy, but some of the questions were quite difficult.*

• You use **first of all** when saying that you want to say or do something before anything else: *First of all I'd*

A B C D E F G H I J K L M N O P Q R S T U V W X Y Z

like to say "thank you" to everyone.
• You use **firstly** when giving a list of things, especially reasons: *There are several reasons for the team's success. **Firstly**, they have some excellent players.*

first² *noun* **1** something that has never happened before: *Their surprising victory is a sporting first.* **2** the highest level of university degree you can get in Britain: *He got a first in Economics.*

ˌfirst ˈaid *noun* (no plural) simple medical treatment that you give quickly to someone who is injured

ˈfirst-class¹ *adjective* **1** excellent: *a first-class actor* **2** of the best and most expensive type: *a first-class train ticket*

ˌfirst-ˈclass² *adverb* if someone travels or sends something first-class, they do it using the best and most expensive service: *She sent the birthday card first-class.*

ˌfirst ˈfloor *noun* **1** *BrE* the level of a building that is just above the level of the street: *The bathroom is on the first floor.* **2** *AmE* the level of a building that is level with the street SYNONYM **ground floor** *BrE*

first•hand /ˌfɜːstˈhænd $ ˌfɚstˈhænd/ *adjective* firsthand information or knowledge is what you learn or see yourself, not what you hear from other people —**firsthand** *adverb*: *He saw firsthand the conditions the poorest people were living in.*

first•ly /ˈfɜːstli $ ˈfɚstli/ *adverb* used before saying the first of several things: *"Why did you take up tennis?" "Firstly I needed the exercise and secondly I thought it would be fun."*

ˈfirst name *noun* the name chosen for you when you were born: *Miss Green's first name is Karen.*

ˈfirst person *noun* **the first person** the form of a verb that you use with 'I' and 'we'

fish¹ /fɪʃ/ *noun* **1** (plural **fish** or **fishes**) a creature without legs that swims about in water **2** (no plural) the flesh of a fish that people eat: *We had fish cooked with onions and tomatoes.*

GRAMMAR
The usual plural of **fish** is **fish**.

fish² *verb* to try to catch fish: *They are fishing for salmon.*

USAGE
When talking about fishing as an activity that you do, you say **go fishing**: *He goes fishing most weekends.*

fish•er•man /ˈfɪʃəmən $ ˈfɪʃɚmən/ *noun* (plural **fishermen** /-mən/) a man who catches fish as a job or a sport

fish•ing /ˈfɪʃɪŋ/ *noun* (no plural) the sport or job of catching fish

ˈfishing rod also **fishing ˈpole** *AmE* *noun* a long stick with string and a hook that you use for catching fish

fish•y /ˈfɪʃi/ *adjective* (informal) (**fishier**, **fishiest**) seeming bad or dishonest SYNONYM **suspicious**: *The deal sounds a bit fishy to me.*

fist /fɪst/ *noun* a hand with all the fingers curled tightly: *He banged his fist angrily on the table.*

fit¹ /fɪt/ *verb* (past tense and past participle **fitted** also **fit** *AmE*, **fitting**)

KEY PATTERNS
fit (something) in/into a container/space

1 to be the right size and shape for someone or something: *My old jeans still fit me.* • *This cover doesn't fit.*
2 if something fits in a place, or if you can fit it in there, there is enough space for it: *This book is too big to **fit in** my schoolbag.* • *He managed to **fit** all our skiing things **into** his car.*
3 to fix a piece of equipment to something: *Before you can ride that bike you need to fit new brakes.*

PHRASAL VERBS
fit in
1 fit in if you fit in, the other people in a group accept you because you are like them: *I didn't really **fit in with** the other kids in my class.*
2 fit something in (informal) to have enough time to do something: *He managed to **fit in** a game of tennis after work.*

fit² *adjective* (**fitter**, **fittest**)

KEY PATTERNS
fit to do something
fit for something

1 suitable or good enough: *He said I was not **fit to** be the team captain.* •

When will the swimming pool ***be fit for*** *use again?* • *That car is not* ***in a fit state to*** *be driven.*
2 healthy and strong ANTONYM **unfit**: *Dancing* ***keeps me fit.*** • *Owen should* ***be fit for*** *the game on Saturday.*
➔ see Thesaurus at HEALTHY

fit³ *noun* **1 have a fit, throw a fit** (informal) to be very angry and shout a lot: *Dad will have a fit when he sees what you've done to your hair!* **2** a short period of time when you cannot control what you do, for example because you are ill or angry: *She had a coughing fit.* • *In a fit of anger, he tore up the letter.* **3 be a good fit** if a piece of clothing is a good fit, it fits your body well: *Those jeans are a good fit.*

fit·ness /ˈfɪtnəs/ *noun* (no plural) when you are healthy and able to run or do physical work for a long time: *He started to go running to improve his fitness.*

five /faɪv/ *number* 5

fix /fɪks/ *verb*

KEY PATTERNS
fix something to/onto something

1 to repair something: *Harry can fix your bike for you.* ➔ see Thesaurus at REPAIR[1]
2 to decide on an exact time, place, price etc: *Have you fixed a date for the wedding?*
3 *BrE* to fasten something to something else so that it will not come off: *She* ***fixed*** *a new mirror* ***to*** *her bedroom wall.* ➔ see Thesaurus at FASTEN
4 *AmE* to get something ready SYNONYM **prepare**: *Mom was fixing dinner.*

PHRASAL VERBS
fix up
fix something up *BrE* to arrange an event or trip: *We need to* ***fix up*** *a meeting with all the parents.*

fix·ture /ˈfɪkstʃə $ ˈfɪkstʃɚ/ *noun BrE* a sports event that has been arranged

fiz·zle /ˈfɪzəl/ *verb* **fizzle out** to gradually end in a weak or disappointing way: *Their relationship just fizzled out.*

fiz·zy /ˈfɪzi/ *adjective* (**fizzier**, **fizziest**) a fizzy drink contains gas: *fizzy mineral water*

flab·ber·gas·ted /ˈflæbəˌɡɑːstɪd $ ˈflæbɚˌɡæstɪd/ *adjective* (informal) extremely surprised ➔ see Thesaurus at SURPRISED

flab·by /ˈflæbi/ *adjective* (**flabbier**, **flabbiest**) a part of your body that is flabby has too much soft loose fat: *her flabby arms*

flag /flæɡ/ *noun* a piece of cloth with a picture or pattern on it that is used as the sign of a country or as a signal: *The French flag has blue, white, and red stripes.*

flag·pole /ˈflæɡpəʊl $ ˈflæɡpoʊl/ *noun* a tall pole for a flag

flair /fleə $ fler/ *noun* a natural ability to do something very well SYNONYM **talent**: *She has a real flair for languages.*

flak /flæk/ *noun* (no plural) (informal) criticism: *She got a lot of flak for her decision to move abroad.*

flake /fleɪk/ *noun* a small flat thin piece of something: *The paint was coming off the door in flakes.*

flame /fleɪm/ *noun* **1** a bright moving yellow or orange light that you see when something is burning: *the cheerful flames of a log fire* **2 in flames** burning: *The whole house was in flames.*

flan /flæn/ *noun* a PIE with no lid that is filled with fruit etc

flan·nel /ˈflænl/ *noun* **1** *BrE* a piece of cloth that you use to wash yourself **2** (no plural) a type of soft cloth that is warm: *flannel sheets*

flap¹ /flæp/ *noun* a flat piece of cloth, paper etc that is fastened by one edge to something: *He stuck down the flap of the envelope.*

flap² *verb* (**flapped**, **flapping**) **1** if a bird flaps its wings, it moves them up and down **2** if a piece of cloth flaps, it moves backwards and forwards: *The curtains flapped in the wind.*

flare¹ /fleə $ fler/ also **flare up** *verb* (written) if trouble or anger flares, it suddenly starts or becomes more violent: *Fighting has flared up again in the city.*

flare² *noun* a thing that produces a bright light and that someone shoots into the air as a sign that they need help

flared /fleəd $ flerd/ *adjective* flared trousers or skirts become wider towards the bottom

flash¹ /flæʃ/ *verb* to shine brightly for a short time: *the flashing lights of a police car* → see Thesaurus at SHINE

flash² *noun* (plural **flashes**) **1** a sudden quick bright light: *a flash of lightning* **2** a bright light on a camera that you use to take photographs indoors

flash·back /ˈflæʃbæk/ *noun* part of a film, play, book etc that shows something that happened earlier in the story

flash·light /ˈflæʃlaɪt/ the American word for TORCH

flash·y /ˈflæʃi/ *adjective* (**flashier**, **flashiest**) too big, bright, or expensive: *She was showing off her flashy engagement ring.*

flask /flɑːsk $ flæsk/ *noun* **1** *BrE* a type of bottle in which liquids remain hot or cold for a long time: *I've brought a flask of coffee.* **2** a type of bottle used in chemistry

flat¹ /flæt/ *adjective* (**flatter**, **flattest**)
1 smooth and level, without any raised parts: *I need a flat surface to work on.* • *Holland is good for cycling because it's very flat.*
2 a tyre that is flat does not have enough air inside it
3 a drink that is flat has lost its gas: *This soda water has **gone flat**.*
4 *BrE* a BATTERY that is flat has lost its electrical power SYNONYM **dead**
5 E flat, B flat etc the musical note that is slightly lower than E, B etc ANTONYM **sharp**
6 flat shoes have very low heels

flat

THESAURUS
level: *The house has a large **level** garden* (=not sloping).
even: *Be careful here, because the ground is not very **even*** (=without any holes or small raised areas).
smooth: *A baby's skin is soft and **smooth*** (=with a nice even surface).

flat² *noun* **1** *BrE* a set of rooms for someone to live in that is part of a larger building SYNONYM **apartment** *AmE*: *They're building a new block of flats opposite us.* **2** a tyre that does not have enough air inside it

flat³ *adverb*
with no parts raised, usually in a horizontal position: *He lay flat on his back and looked at the stars.* • *My hair just won't stay flat.*

PHRASES
in ten seconds flat, in two minutes flat etc (informal) very quickly, in ten seconds, two minutes etc: *He did all his homework **in 20 minutes flat**.*
flat out (informal) as fast as possible: *She had to work **flat out** to get the house clean before her parents came back.*

flat·ly /ˈflætli/ *adverb* **flatly refuse, flatly deny** to say something in a very firm strong way: *She flatly refused to let me borrow her car.*

flat·mate /ˈflætmeɪt/ *noun BrE* someone who shares a flat with one or more other people SYNONYM **roommate** *AmE*

flat·ten /ˈflætn/ *verb* to make something flat: *The children had ridden their bikes all over the garden, flattening the flowers.*

flat·ter /ˈflætə $ ˈflætər/ *verb* **1** to say nice things to someone, sometimes when you do not really mean it: *George flattered her, saying how attractive she looked.* **2 be flattered, feel flattered** to feel pleased because someone has shown that they like or admire you: *When they asked me to join their group, I felt flattered.*

flat·ter·ing /ˈflætərɪŋ/ *adjective* something that is flattering makes someone look more attractive: *a flattering dress*

flat·ter·y /ˈflætəri/ *noun* (no plural) nice things that you say but do not really mean

flaunt /flɔːnt/ *verb* if you flaunt your money, success, beauty etc, you try to make other people notice it and admire you for it

fla·vour¹ *BrE*, **flavor** *AmE* /ˈfleɪvə $ ˈfleɪvɚ/ *noun*
1 the taste that a food or drink has: *The ice cream comes in ten different flavours.*
2 (no plural) a strong, good taste: *Salt is used to give food more flavour.*

flavour² *BrE*, **flavor** *AmE* *verb* to give food or drink a particular taste: *The sauce is flavoured with herbs.*

fla·vour·ing *BrE*, **flavoring** *AmE* /ˈfleɪvərɪŋ/ *noun* something used to give food or drink a particular taste: *This drink contains artificial flavourings.*

flaw /flɔː/ *noun* a mistake, mark, or weakness that stops something from being perfect: *She took the material back to the shop because there was a flaw in it.*

flawed /flɔːd/ *adjective* something that is flawed has mistakes or weaknesses and so is not perfect: *His theory is badly flawed.*

flea /fliː/ *noun* a very small jumping insect that bites animals and drinks their blood

fled the past tense and past participle of FLEE

flee /fliː/ *verb* (written) (past tense and past participle **fled** /fled/) to leave a place very quickly, in order to escape from danger: *People have been fleeing the country to avoid the fighting.*

fleece /fliːs/ *noun* the wool that covers a sheep

fleet /fliːt/ *noun* a group of ships or vehicles: *a fleet of trucks*

flesh /fleʃ/ *noun* (no plural) **1** the soft part of your body, between your skin and your bones **2** the soft part inside a fruit or vegetable: *A peach can have yellow or white flesh.*

flew the past tense of FLY¹

flexible

flex·i·ble /ˈfleksəbəl/ *adjective* **1** able to change or be changed easily ANTONYM **inflexible**: *One good thing about the job is the flexible working hours.* **2** easy to bend ANTONYM **rigid**: *a flexible plastic tube*

flick

flick /flɪk/ *verb*
1 to send something small through the air with a quick movement of your finger or hand: *He flicked the fly off his sleeve.* **2 flick something on/off** (informal) to press a switch in order to start or stop electrical equipment SYNONYM **flip on/off**: *I flicked on the TV.* **3 flick through something** *BrE* (informal) to look at a book, magazine etc quickly SYNONYM **flip through**: *She was flicking through a magazine.* ➔ see Thesaurus at READ —**flick** *noun*: *I had a quick flick through the book.*

flick·er /ˈflɪkə $ ˈflɪkɚ/ *verb* (written)
1 to burn or shine with an unsteady light: *The fire in the sitting room flickered gently.* **2** (written) if an expression flickers across your face, it appears for a moment: *A smile flickered across her face.*

flight /flaɪt/ *noun*
1 a journey in a plane, or the plane making a particular journey: *It was a very quick flight.* • *They* ***caught the next flight*** *home.* • *She* ***booked a flight*** *to New York.*
2 (no plural) when a bird, plane etc flies through the air: *We could see seagulls in flight.*

PHRASES

a flight of stairs, a flight of steps a set of stairs: *He climbed up the steep flight of stairs.*

ˈflight atˌtendant *noun* someone whose job is to look after passengers on a plane

A B C D E F G H I J K L M N O P Q R S T U V W X Y Z

flim·sy /ˈflɪmzi/ *adjective* (**flimsier**, **flimsiest**) **1** not strong, and easily damaged: *Their flimsy boats were destroyed in the storm.* **2** a flimsy argument or excuse is not a good one

flinch /flɪntʃ/ *verb* to make a sudden small backward movement because you are afraid, hurt, or shocked: *The boy flinched when she tried to clean his cuts.*

fling /flɪŋ/ *verb* (written) (past tense and past participle **flung** /flʌŋ/) to throw or move something quickly and with a lot of force: *She flung the ring back at him.* • *He flung open the door.* ➔ see Thesaurus at THROW[1]

flip /flɪp/ *verb* (**flipped**, **flipping**) **1 flip over** to turn over quickly: *The boat went too fast and flipped over.* **2** also **flip out** (informal) to suddenly become very angry: *I just suggested a few changes and he flipped.* **3 flip something on/off, flip a switch** (informal) to press a switch in order to start or stop electrical equipment SYNONYM **flick on/off**: *He flipped on the light.* • *Just flip this switch and the music comes on.* **4 flip through something** (informal) to look at a book, magazine etc quickly SYNONYM **flick through**: *He flipped through his diary to find a free day.* ➔ see Thesaurus at READ

ˈ**flip chart** *noun* large sheets of paper on a board to write facts or ideas on in a meeting or class

ˈ**flip-flop** *noun* a light shoe with a V-shaped band to hold your foot

flip·pant /ˈflɪpənt/ *adjective* if you are flippant about something, you speak about it in a less serious way than you should: *He was rather flippant about her problems.*

flip·per /ˈflɪpə $ ˈflɪpɚ/ *noun* **1** the flat arm or leg of a sea animal such as a SEAL **2** a large flat rubber shoe that you use for swimming under water

flip·ping /ˈflɪpɪŋ/ *adjective, adverb* *BrE* (spoken, informal) used when you are annoyed: *I tried phoning them 20 flipping times!*

flirt /flɜːt $ flɚt/ *verb* to behave as if you are sexually attracted to someone, but not in a very serious way: *She always flirted with other boys at parties.*

float

float[1] /fləʊt $ floʊt/ *verb*

KEY PATTERNS
float on/in water
float in/through the air
float somewhere

1 to stay or move on the surface of a liquid ANTONYM **sink**: *Does plastic float?* • *The paper boat* ***floated along on*** *the river.* • *There was all sorts of rubbish* ***floating in the water.***
2 if something very light floats in the air, it stays in the air or moves slowly through the air: *The feather* ***floated*** *slowly* ***to*** *the ground.*

float[2] *noun* a large vehicle that is decorated to be part of a PARADE

flock[1] /flɒk $ flɑk/ *noun* a group of sheep, goats, or birds

flock[2] *verb* (written) if people flock to a place, a lot of them go there: *People flocked to see the exhibition.*

flog /flɒg $ flɑg/ *verb* (**flogged**, **flogging**) **1** *BrE* (informal) to sell something to someone: *I'm still trying to flog my old car.* **2** to hit someone with a whip or stick as a punishment SYNONYM **beat**

flood[1] /flʌd/ *verb*

KEY PATTERNS
people/things flood somewhere

1 if something floods a place or if a place floods, the place becomes covered with water: *A pipe burst and flooded the kitchen.* • *One corner of the field flooded.*
2 if people or things flood somewhere, a very large number of them go there: *Calls* ***came flooding in*** *from worried members of the public.* • *People* ***flooded across*** *the border, trying to escape.*

PHRASES

be flooded with things to get so many letters, complaints etc that you cannot deal with them all: *We **were flooded with** complaints about the show.*

flood² *noun* a very large amount of water that covers an area that is usually dry: *Many animals have drowned in the floods.*

flood·ing /ˈflʌdɪŋ/ *noun* (no plural) when an area that is usually dry becomes covered with water: *The heavy rain caused a lot of flooding.*

flood·light /ˈflʌdlaɪt/ *noun* a large bright light that is used for lighting sports fields, public buildings etc

flood·lit /ˈflʌdlɪt/ *adjective* lit by floodlights: *floodlit tennis courts*

floor /flɔː $ flɔr/ *noun*

KEY PATTERNS
be on the ground/second/top etc floor

1 the surface that you stand on in a building: *There was a pile of books **on the floor**. • He leaves his clothes all over the floor.*
2 one of the levels in a building SYNONYM **storey**: *The toilets are **on the top floor**.*

floor·board /ˈflɔːbɔːd $ ˈflɔrbɔrd/ *noun* a long piece of wood that is part of a floor

floor·ing /ˈflɔːrɪŋ/ *noun* (no plural) a material used to make or cover floors: *They chose wooden flooring for the kitchen.*

flop¹ /flɒp $ flɑp/ *verb* (**flopped**, **flopping**) to sit down or fall in a loose heavy way: *She flopped down onto the sofa.*

flop² *noun* (informal) something that is not successful ANTONYM **hit**: *The play was a flop.*

flop·py /ˈflɒpi $ ˈflɑpi/ *adjective* (**floppier**, **floppiest**) soft and hanging loosely down: *a dog with long floppy ears*

ˌfloppy ˈdisk also **floppy** *noun* a flat piece of plastic used for storing information from a computer

flo·ral /ˈflɔːrəl/ *adjective* (written) made of flowers or having a design of flowers: *floral wallpaper*

flor·ist /ˈflɒrɪst $ ˈflɔrɪst/ also **florist's** *noun* a shop that sells flowers

floun·der /ˈflaʊndə $ ˈflaʊndɚ/ *verb* to be unsuccessful or not know what to do: *Some of the younger students seemed to be floundering a bit.*

flour /flaʊə $ flaʊɚ/ *noun* (no plural) powder made from grain which you use for making bread, cakes etc

flour·ish /ˈflʌrɪʃ $ ˈflɚrɪʃ/ *verb* to grow well or be successful: *This plant will flourish in a sunny place. • a flourishing business*

flow¹ /fləʊ $ floʊ/ *noun*

KEY PATTERNS
a/the flow of something

1 a steady continuous movement of an amount of something, for example a liquid: *The gates can be opened or closed to control **the flow of** water. • There is **a** steady **flow of** traffic through the village.*
2 the movement of something such as ideas or money from one person or place to another: *We want to encourage **the flow of** information between countries.*

flow² *verb*

KEY PATTERNS
flow somewhere

if an amount of something flows somewhere, it moves along in a steady way: *The River Don **flows through** the city centre. • The police tried to keep the traffic flowing.*

THESAURUS
pour: *A pipe burst and water **poured** through the ceiling* (=flowed quickly in large amounts).
drip: *Blood was **dripping** from his finger* (=falling in small drops).
leak: *The tank was damaged and oil was **leaking** out* (=passing through a hole or crack).

flow·er /ˈflaʊə $ ˈflaʊɚ/ *noun* one of the pretty coloured things that a plant or tree produces: *There was a vase of yellow flowers by the window.* ➔ see picture at BUNCH¹ ➔ see picture on page A10

flow·er·bed /ˈflaʊəbed $ ˈflaʊɚˌbed/ *noun* an area of ground in which someone grows flowers

A B C D E F G H I J K L M N O P Q R S T U V W X Y Z

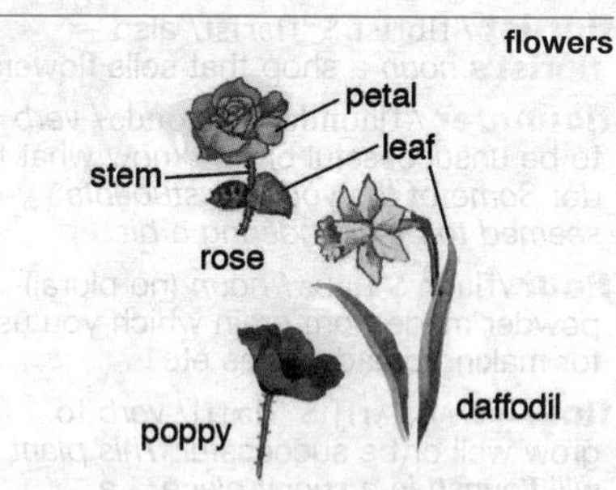

flown the past participle of FLY[1]

flu /fluː/ also **the flu** *noun* (no plural) a common illness which is like a very bad cold SYNONYM **influenza**

> USAGE
> You say **She has flu** or **She has the flu**.
> ✗ Don't say 'She has a flu.'

fluc·tu·ate /ˈflʌktʃueɪt/ *verb* (formal) if an amount fluctuates, it keeps going up and down SYNONYM **vary**: *Her weight fluctuated.*

flu·en·cy /ˈfluːənsi/ *noun* (no plural) (formal) the ability to speak a language very well

flu·ent /ˈfluːənt/ *adjective* able to speak a language quickly and well: *Hannah is fluent in three languages.* —**fluently** *adverb*: *He speaks French fluently.*

fluff /flʌf/ *noun* (no plural) soft fine amounts of thread that come off things: *I was covered in fluff from the new carpet.*

fluff·y /ˈflʌfi/ *adjective* (**fluffier**, **fluffiest**) covered with soft fur or threads: *a fluffy toy*

flu·id /ˈfluːɪd/ *noun* (formal) a liquid: *You need to drink plenty of fluids.*

fluke /fluːk/ *noun* something that only happens because of luck: *He got the ball in the net by a fluke.*

flung the past tense and past participle of FLING

flunk /flʌŋk/ *verb AmE* (informal) to fail a test or course: *I flunked all my exams last year.*

flu·o·res·cent /flʊəˈresənt $ flʊˈresənt/ *adjective* **1** a fluorescent light consists of a long glass tube containing a special gas **2** fluorescent colours are extremely bright

fluo·ride /ˈflʊəraɪd $ ˈflɔraɪd/ *noun* (no plural) a chemical that is added to water and TOOTHPASTE to help protect people's teeth

flush /flʌʃ/ *verb* **1** if you flush a toilet, you make water go through it to clean it **2** if you flush, your face becomes red because you are embarrassed or angry

flushed /flʌʃt/ *adjective* if someone is flushed, their face is red: *She looked hot and flushed.*

flus·tered /ˈflʌstəd $ ˈflʌstərd/ *adjective* confused because you are nervous or trying to do things too quickly: *She got flustered and dropped her papers.*

flute /fluːt/ *noun* a musical instrument shaped like a tube, which you play by blowing across a hole near one end

flut·ter /ˈflʌtə $ ˈflʌtər/ *verb* **1** to wave or move about gently in the air: *The flags were fluttering in the wind.*
2 if a bird or insect flutters somewhere, it goes there by moving its wings very quickly up and down: *The butterfly fluttered across the garden.*

fly[1] /flaɪ/ *verb* (**flew** /fluː/ **flown** /fləʊn $ floʊn/ **flies**)

> KEY PATTERNS
> **fly (from Paris etc) to London etc**

1 to travel somewhere by plane: *Sam flew to New York for his brother's wedding.* • *We are now flying over the Alps.*
2 to move through the air: *Penguins are birds, but they can't fly.*
3 to control a plane: *Have you ever flown this type of aircraft before?*
4 (written) to suddenly move very quickly: *Helen **flew to** the window when she heard the car arrive.* • *The door **flew open** and Tim came in.*
5 also **fly by** if time flies, it seems to pass very quickly: *The weeks flew until it was time to go back to school.*
6 if a flag is flying, it has been put at the top of a pole so that people can see it: *A white flag was flying above the building.*

fly[2] *noun* (plural **flies**) **1** a common insect with wings → see picture at INSECT **2** also **flies** *BrE* the ZIP or buttons at the front of a pair of trousers: *Your flies are undone.*

fly·ing¹ /ˈflaɪ-ɪŋ/ *noun* (no plural) travelling by plane or controlling a plane: *A lot of people are scared of flying.*

flying² *adjective* **with flying colours** if you pass a test with flying colours, you do very well in the test

ˌflying ˈsaucer *noun* an object in the sky carrying creatures from space SYNONYM **UFO**

fly·o·ver /ˈflaɪ-əʊvə $ ˈflaɪˌoʊvɚ/ *noun BrE* a bridge that carries one road over another

FM /ˌef ˈem/ *noun* (no plural) a system used for broadcasting radio programmes

foam /fəʊm $ foʊm/ *noun* (no plural) a substance with a lot of very small bubbles of air in it

fo·cus¹ /ˈfəʊkəs $ ˈfoʊkəs/ *verb* (**focused** or **focussed**, **focusing** or **focussing**) **1** to give all or most of your attention to a particular thing SYNONYM **concentrate**: *In this course we will focus on basic computer skills.*
2 to move part of a camera, TELESCOPE etc so you can see something clearly: *He focused his camera on the nearest of the birds.*

focus² *noun* **1** the person or thing that gets most attention: *The focus of teaching has changed.* • *The new student was the focus of attention.*
2 in focus, out of focus if a photograph is in focus it is clear, and if it is out of focus it is not clear

foe·tus *BrE*, **fetus** *AmE* /ˈfiːtəs/ *noun* (plural **foetuses**) a human or animal that is growing inside its mother

fog /fɒg $ fɑg/ *noun* cloudy air near the ground, which is difficult to see through: *There was thick fog early this morning.* ➔ see picture on page A13

fog·gy /ˈfɒgi $ ˈfɑgi/ *adjective* (**foggier**, **foggiest**) a foggy day is one when there is fog: *It was so foggy we couldn't see the other side of the road.*

foil /fɔɪl/ *noun* (no plural) very thin metal used for covering and wrapping food

fold¹ /fəʊld $ foʊld/ *verb*
1 also **fold up** to bend something so that one part covers another part and it becomes smaller: *He folded the letter and put it into an envelope.* • *The man **folded up** his newspaper and stood up to leave.*
2 fold your arms to bend your arms, so that they are resting across your chest

fold

fold your arms

fold² *noun* a line in paper or cloth where you have folded it: *Cut along the folds in the paper.*

fold·er /ˈfəʊldə $ ˈfoʊldɚ/ *noun* **1** a large folded piece of hard paper, in which you keep loose pieces of paper
2 a group of FILES containing information which are stored together on a computer SYNONYM **directory**

fo·li·age /ˈfəʊli-ɪdʒ $ ˈfoʊli-ɪdʒ/ *noun* (no plural) (formal) the leaves of a plant: *She arranged the flowers and foliage in a vase.*

folk /fəʊk $ foʊk/ *adjective* traditional and typical of the ordinary people who live in an area: *Do you like Scottish folk music?*

folks /fəʊks $ foʊks/ *plural noun*
1 (informal) your parents or family: *My girlfriend has never met my folks.*
➔ see Thesaurus at FAMILY
2 (spoken) used to talk to a group of people in a friendly way: *Hi folks – it's good to see you all.*

fol·low /ˈfɒləʊ $ ˈfɑloʊ/ *verb*
1 to walk or drive behind someone or something: *I **followed** her **into** the house.* • *Sam had a feeling that someone was following him.*
2 to happen or come after something else: *The floods followed three weeks of heavy rain.* • *We had roast beef, followed by apple pie.*
3 if you follow a path, road etc, you go along it: *We **followed the path** around the outside of the castle.*
4 to understand something that is said: *Were you able to follow the lecture?*

A B C D E F G H I J K L M N O P Q R S T U V W X Y Z

PHRASES

as follows used to introduce a list: *The team is* ***as follows****: Williams, Young, Hunter ...*

follow advice, follow instructions to do what someone advises or tells you to do: *I think you should* ***follow*** *your mum's* ***advice****.*

follow someone's example, follow someone's lead to do something because someone else has done it: *His friends* ***followed*** *his* ***example*** *and stopped smoking.*

PHRASAL VERBS

follow up

follow something up if you follow up some information, you try to find out more: *The scientists decided to* ***follow up*** *this discovery* ***with*** *a new set of experiments.*

> **THESAURUS**
> **run after**: *I ran after her to give her back her handbag* (=followed her, running).
> **chase**: *Police* ***chased*** *the boy down the street* (=followed him quickly in order to catch him).
> **pursue** (formal): *Two police cars* ***pursued*** *the robbers* (=chased).

fol·low·er /ˈfɒləʊə $ ˈfɑloʊɚ/ *noun* someone who believes in someone's ideas or in a religion: *His followers believe he is a god.*

fol·low·ing¹ /ˈfɒləʊɪŋ $ ˈfɑloʊɪŋ/ *adjective* after the one you have just mentioned ANTONYM **preceding**: *I was born in 1985, and my sister was born the following year.*

following² *noun* (no plural) **1** a group of people who support or admire someone such as a singer: *The band has a big following all over the world.* **2 the following** the people or things that you are going to mention next: *You will need the following: eggs, sugar, milk.*

following³ *preposition* after or as a result of something: *Following her victory yesterday, she is feeling more confident.*

fond /fɒnd $ fɑnd/ *adjective*

> **KEY PATTERNS**
> **fond of someone/something**

if you are fond of someone or something, you like them very much: *He* ***was fond of*** *his sister.* • *I'm very* ***fond of*** *chocolate.*

food /fuːd/ *noun* (no plural) things that you eat: *She was out buying food and drink for the party.*

ˈfood chain *noun* a group of different kinds of living thing, in which one kind is eaten by another, which is eaten by another etc: *the plants at the bottom of the food chain*

ˈfood ˌpoisoning *noun* (no plural) an illness that is caused by eating food that contains harmful BACTERIA (=small living things that cause disease): *I got food poisoning from eating a beefburger.*

fool¹ /fuːl/ *noun* **1** a stupid person SYNONYM **idiot**: *You're behaving like a fool!* **2 make a fool of yourself** to do something stupid, which you feel embarrassed about later: *She's always getting drunk and making a fool of herself.*

fool² *verb* to make someone believe something that is not true SYNONYM **deceive**: *It was easy to fool the teachers into believing that I was ill.*

fool·ish /ˈfuːlɪʃ/ *adjective* not sensible SYNONYM **silly**, **stupid**: *It was very foolish of you to swim so far out in the sea.* —**foolishly** *adverb*: *I've behaved very foolishly.*

fool·proof /ˈfuːlpruːf/ *adjective* certain to be successful: *a foolproof plan*

foot /fʊt/ *noun*

1 (plural **feet** /fiːt/) your feet are the parts at the end of your legs that you stand on: *My feet are cold!* → see picture on page A5

2 (plural **feet** or **foot**) a unit for measuring length, equal to 12 INCHES or 0.3048 metres: *She was sitting a few feet away from us.* • *He was well over six foot tall.*

3 (no plural) the bottom of something such as a mountain, tree, or set of stairs ANTONYM **top**: *She went to* ***the foot of*** *the stairs and called up to Robin.*

PHRASES

get to your feet, jump to your feet etc to stand up after you have been sitting down: *She* ***got to her feet*** *when we came in.*

on foot if you go somewhere on foot, you walk there: *We decided to go **on foot** rather than take the car.*
put your foot down (informal) to say very firmly that someone must not do something: *She wanted to go to the party but her dad **put** his **foot down**.*
put your foot in it (informal) to say something that upsets someone by mistake

> **USAGE**
> You usually say **on foot**.
> ✘ Don't say 'by foot'.

foot·ball /'fʊtbɔːl/ *noun* **1** (no plural) *BrE* a game in which two teams try to kick a ball between two posts at either end of a field SYNONYM **soccer**: *The children are playing football.* • *Who won the football match?* **2** (no plural) *AmE* a game in which two teams wearing special hats and clothes carry, kick, or throw a ball into an area at the end of a field to win points SYNONYM **american football** *BrE*: *Would you like to come to the football game with me?* **3** a ball that people use to play football: *He kicked the football over the fence.*
foot·bal·ler /'fʊtbɔːlə $ 'fʊtˌbɔlɚ/ *noun BrE* someone who plays football
foot·note /'fʊtnəʊt $ 'fʊtnoʊt/ *noun* a note at the bottom of a page in a book, which gives more information about something on that page: *He didn't bother reading the footnotes.*
foot·path /'fʊtpɑːθ $ 'fʊtpæθ/ *noun* a path for people to walk along: *Don't ride your bike on the footpath.*

footprint

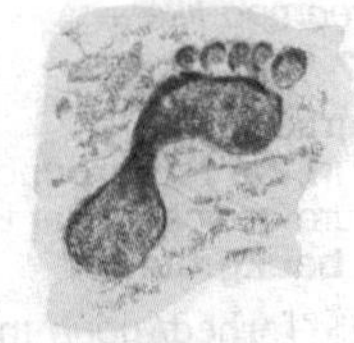
footprint

fingerprint

foot·print /'fʊtˌprɪnt/ *noun* a mark that your foot or shoe makes on the ground: *The children had made footprints in the snow.*
foot·step /'fʊtstep/ *noun* the sound of each step when someone is walking: *He heard footsteps outside.*
foot·wear /'fʊtweə $ 'fʊtwer/ *noun* (no plural) things that you wear on your feet, such as shoes or boots: *The store has a big footwear department.*
for /fə $ fɚ; strong fɔː $ fɔːr/ *preposition*
1 used to say how long something continues to happen: *I've been at this school for six years.* • *I must have slept for ten hours.*
2 used to say who will be given something or who can use something: *I have a present for you.* • *Those swings are for little children.*
3 used to say what the purpose of something is: *This knife is for cutting vegetables.* • *I need some money for my train ticket.*
4 used to say who you are helping: *I opened the door for her.* • *We raised some money for the local hospital.* • *I did a few little jobs for my grandmother.*
5 used to say where you are going: *The next morning we set off for London.* • *Is this the train for Cambridge?*
6 used to say how far someone or something goes: *We walked for five miles without seeing anyone.*
7 if you are for a plan or action, you agree with it ANTONYM **against**: *Most people were for the idea of sharing the work* (=most people thought that sharing the work was a good idea).
8 used to show how much you pay: *I bought an old television for £50.*

PHRASES
what for? why: ***What** did you do that **for**?*
for your birthday, for Christmas etc because it is your birthday, Christmas etc: *I **got** a puppy **for** my **birthday**.*

> **WORD CHOICE**
> **for** or **(in order) to**?
> • You use **for** with a noun: *He went there **for** a holiday.*
> • You use **to** or **in order to** with a verb: *She went there **to** see her family.* • *He looked at the address again **in order to** make sure it was the right one.*
> • **To** is used in everyday conversation.
> • **In order to** is used especially in formal English.

forbade the past tense of FORBID
for·bid /fə'bɪd $ fɚ'bɪd/ *verb* (formal) (**forbade** /fə'beɪd $ fɚ'bæd/ **forbidden**

/fəˈbɪdn $ fɚˈbɪdn/ **forbidding**) to order someone not to do something: *My mother has forbidden me to see you.*

THESAURUS
not allow: *You are **not allowed** to leave school without permission* (=forbidden).
ban: *The government has **banned** cigarette advertising* (=forbidden it officially).
prohibit (formal): *That sign means that parking is **prohibited*** (=forbidden officially).

for·bid·den¹ /fəˈbɪdn $ fɚˈbɪdn/ *adjective* not allowed: *It is forbidden to feed the animals.*

forbidden² the past participle of FORBID

force¹ /fɔːs $ fɔrs/ *noun*
1 an organization or group of people who have been trained to do something, especially military or police work: *the local **police force** • a United Nations **peacekeeping force** • the company's **sales force***
2 (no plural) if you use force, you use physical strength or violence: *He threatened to take the letter from her **by force**.*
3 (no plural) the strength or power of something: *We all felt **the force of** the explosion.*
4 something that has an effect on things: ***the force of** gravity*

PHRASES
be in force, come into force if a law or rule is in force, it exists and people must obey it: *The rules will **be in force** by next summer. • The new law **came into force** last month.*
join forces if two people join forces, they start working together: *The university **is joining forces with** a technology company to do research.*

force² *verb*

KEY PATTERNS
force someone to do something
force something open/back etc

1 to make someone do something that they do not want to do: *His new girlfriend **forced** him **to** stop seeing his old friends. • We **were forced to** go home early when our tent blew away.*
2 to use physical strength to move something or go somewhere: *He **forced open** the box. • The soldiers **forced** their **way into** the building.*

forced /fɔːst $ fɔrst/ *adjective* a forced smile or laugh is one that you give because you feel you have to, and not because you really want to ANTONYM **genuine**

force·ful /ˈfɔːsfəl $ ˈfɔrsfəl/ *adjective* powerful and strong: *his forceful personality*

fore·arm /ˈfɔːrɑːm $ ˈfɔrɑrm/ *noun* the part of your arm between your hand and your elbow: *She has a cut on her left forearm.* ➔ see picture on page A5

fore·cast¹ /ˈfɔːkɑːst $ ˈfɔrkæst/ *noun* a description of what is likely to happen: *Have you heard the weather forecast?*

forecast² *verb* (past tense and past participle **forecast** or **forecasted**) to say what is likely to happen SYNONYM **predict**: *The government is forecasting that unemployment will fall.*

fore·fa·ther /ˈfɔːˌfɑːðə $ ˈfɔrˌfɑðɚ/ *noun* (written) a member of your family who lived a long time ago SYNONYM **ancestor**: *the time when our forefathers arrived in America*

fore·front /ˈfɔːfrʌnt $ ˈfɔrfrʌnt/ *noun* **be at the forefront of something** to do more than other people to make, discover, or cause something new: *a British company that was at the forefront of computer design*

fore·gone con·clu·sion /ˌfɔːgɒn kənˈkluːʒən $ ˌfɔrgɔn kənˈkluʒən/ *noun* something that is certain to happen: *War now seemed like a foregone conclusion.*

fore·ground /ˈfɔːgraʊnd $ ˈfɔrgraʊnd/ *noun* **in the foreground** in the part of a picture or scene that is at the front ANTONYM **background**

fore·head /ˈfɒrəd $ ˈfɔrhed/ *noun* the part of your face above your eyes: *You've got a spot in the middle of your forehead.* ➔ see picture on page A5

for·eign /ˈfɒrɪn $ ˈfɑrɪn/ *adjective*
1 not from your own country: *He speaks three foreign languages. • The university has a lot of foreign students.*
2 dealing with other countries: *Britain's foreign policy*

for•eign•er /ˈfɒrənə $ ˈfɑrənɚ/ *noun* someone who is not from your own country: *A lot of foreigners visit our town.*

WORD CHOICE
foreigners/people from other countries
• The word **foreigners** sounds very negative. It sounds much more friendly to say **people from other countries**: *I studied languages because I wanted to be able to talk to people from other countries.*

fore•most /ˈfɔːməʊst $ ˈfɔrmoʊst/ *adjective* (formal) the most famous or important: *the world's foremost chess player*

fo•ren•sic /fəˈrensɪk/ *adjective* connected with the use of science to find out who was responsible for a crime: *There is a lot of forensic evidence, including fingerprints.*

foresaw the past tense of FORESEE

fore•see /fɔːˈsiː $ fɔrˈsi/ *verb* (**foresaw** /fɔːˈsɔː $ fɔrˈsɔ/ **foreseen** /fɔːˈsiːn $ fɔrˈsin/) to expect that something will happen in the future: *I don't foresee any problems with the new system.*

foreseen the past participle of FORESEE

fore•sight /ˈfɔːsaɪt $ ˈfɔrsaɪt/ *noun* (no plural) the ability to imagine what might happen in the future, and consider this in your plans: *Lucy was glad she had had the foresight to keep her money separate from her husband's.*

for•est /ˈfɒrɪst $ ˈfɔrɪst/ *noun* a large area of land covered with trees: *He got lost in the forest.*

THESAURUS
wood: *Behind our house, there was a wood* (=a small area of land with trees).
woodland: *Large parts of the valley are woodland* (=land that is covered with trees).
rain forest: *the beautiful rain forests of South America* (=tropical forests with tall trees)
jungle: *He disappeared into the jungle and was never seen again* (=a tropical forest with trees growing very close together).

for•ev•er /fərˈevə $ fəˈrevɚ/ *adverb* for all of the future: *I could stay here forever.* • *Those days are gone forever.*

PHRASES
take forever (informal) to take a very long time: *It's going to* ***take forever*** *to clean all this mess up!*

fore•word /ˈfɔːwɜːd $ ˈfɔrwɚd/ *noun* a short piece of writing at the beginning of a book about the book or its writer

forgave the past tense of FORGIVE

forge /fɔːdʒ $ fɔrdʒ/ *verb* to illegally produce something such as a document or picture and pretend that someone else produced it: *He forged his wife's signature.* • *forged banknotes*

for•ge•ry /ˈfɔːdʒəri $ ˈfɔrdʒəri/ *noun* (plural **forgeries**) a document, painting etc that someone has forged SYNONYM **fake**: *It was obvious that the painting was a forgery.*

for•get /fəˈget $ fɚˈget/ *verb* (**forgot** /fəˈgɒt $ fɚˈgɑt/ **forgotten** /fəˈgɒtn $ fɚˈgɑtn/ **forgetting**)

KEY PATTERNS
forget something
forget (that)
forget what/who/where etc
forget to do something
forget about something

1 to be or become unable to remember something: *I'll never forget the day I started school.* • *I* ***had forgotten that*** *you know him.* • *I've* ***forgotten what*** *her name is.*
2 if you forget to do something, you do not remember to do it: *Don't* ***forget to*** *feed the fish.* • *We* ***forgot about*** *lunch.*
3 if you forget something, you do not remember to bring it with you: *I've forgotten my purse.*
4 to stop thinking about someone or something: *Forget her – you'll find someone better.*

for•get•ful /fəˈgetfəl $ fɚˈgetfəl/ *adjective* someone who is forgetful often forgets things: *I'm getting forgetful in my old age.*

A B C D E F G H I J K L M N O P Q R S T U V W X Y Z

A B C D E F G H I J K L M N O P Q R S T U V W X Y Z

for·give /fə'gɪv $ fɚ'gɪv/ *verb* (**forgave** /fə'geɪv $ fɚ'geɪv/ **forgiven** /fə'gɪvən $ fɚ'gɪvən/)

KEY PATTERNS
forgive someone (for doing something)

to stop being angry with someone who has done something wrong: *He begged her to forgive him.* • *I'll never **forgive** her **for** lying to me.*

forgiven the past participle of FORGIVE

for·give·ness /fə'gɪvnəs $ fɚ'gɪvnəs/ *noun* (no plural) when someone forgives another person for doing something wrong: *I begged for her forgiveness.*

forgot the past tense of FORGET

forgotten the past participle of FORGET

fork /fɔːk $ fɔrk/ *noun*
1 a small tool with four points that you use for picking up food when you eat: *He put down his **knife and fork**.*
➔ see picture at CUTLERY
2 a tool with four points that you use for breaking up soil in the garden
➔ see picture at GARDENING
3 a place where a road divides into two parts: *At the next fork in the road, go left.*

for·lorn /fə'lɔːn $ fɚ'lɔrn/ *adjective* (written) sad and lonely: *She looked very forlorn sitting alone waiting for a train.*

form¹ /fɔːm $ fɔrm/ *noun*

KEY PATTERNS
a form of something

1 one type of something: *Game shows are a cheap **form of** entertainment.* • *We would welcome help **in any form**.*
2 an official piece of paper with spaces to write information in. You fill in, fill out, or complete a form: *Just **fill in** the application **form*** (=write information in the right spaces).
3 *BrE* a class in school: *He's **in the sixth form** now.*

form² *verb*
1 if something forms, it starts to exist: *A long line of people formed outside the shop.*
2 to make something or start something that is new: *In 1996, he formed a new band called 'Target'.*
3 to be something: *The river forms a natural barrier between the two countries.*

form·al /'fɔːməl $ 'fɔrməl/ *adjective*
1 official: *There will be a formal investigation into the accident.* • *He had no formal qualifications.*
2 formal words or clothes are suitable for serious or important occasions ANTONYM **informal**, **casual**: *'Good evening' is a formal way of saying hello.* • *He wasn't comfortable wearing formal clothes.* —**formally** *adverb*: *She has not yet formally applied for the job.*

for·mal·i·ty /fɔː'mæləti $ fɔr'mæləti/ *noun* (plural **formalities**) an official part of a process: *After going through the usual formalities, we got on the plane.*

for·mat¹ /'fɔːmæt $ 'fɔrmæt/ *noun* the way that something is organized or designed: *This week the show has a new format.*

format² *verb* (**formatted**, **formatting**) to organize the space on a computer DISK so that you can store information on it

for·ma·tion /fɔː'meɪʃən $ fɔr'meɪʃən/ *noun* (no plural) when something starts to exist or develop: *the formation of ice crystals*

for·mer¹ /'fɔːmə $ 'fɔrmɚ/ *adjective* used to say that a person or thing was something in the past but is not that thing now: *his former girlfriend* • *the former world champion* ➔ see Thesaurus at LAST¹

former² *noun* **the former** (formal) the first of two people or things that you have just mentioned: *He had lived in Edinburgh and London, and preferred the former.*

for·mer·ly /'fɔːməli $ 'fɔrmɚli/ *adverb* in the past SYNONYM **previously**, **once**: *This hotel was formerly a monastery.*

for·mi·da·ble /'fɔːmədəbəl $ 'fɔrmədəbəl, fɚ'mɪdəbəl/ *adjective* a formidable person is powerful and slightly frightening: *The headmistress was a formidable woman.*

for·mu·la /'fɔːmjələ $ 'fɔrmjələ/ *noun* (plural **formulas** or **formulae** /-liː/) a series of numbers or letters that show a mathematical or scientific rule: *What's the formula for calculating the area of a circle?*

for·mu·late /ˈfɔːmjəleɪt $ ˈfɔrmjəˌleɪt/ *verb* to develop a plan and decide all the details: *He soon formulated a plan of escape.*

fort /fɔːt $ fɔrt/ *noun* a strong building that soldiers use for defending a place

forth·com·ing /ˌfɔːθˈkʌmɪŋ $ ˌfɔrθˈkʌmɪŋ/ *adjective* (formal) **1** a forthcoming event will happen soon: *Who will win the forthcoming election?* **2** if something is forthcoming, someone gives it to you or offers it to you: *No offers of help have been forthcoming.*

forth·right /ˈfɔːθraɪt $ ˈfɔrθraɪt/ *adjective* saying what you think honestly and directly: *She's usually very forthright – I'm surprised she didn't tell you she was annoyed.*

fort·night /ˈfɔːtnaɪt $ ˈfɔrtnaɪt/ *noun* BrE two weeks: *The work will take about a fortnight.* • *She first became ill a fortnight ago.*

for·tress /ˈfɔːtrɪs $ ˈfɔrtrɪs/ *noun* (plural **fortresses**) a big strong building that people use for defending a place

for·tu·nate /ˈfɔːtʃənət $ ˈfɔrtʃənət/ *adjective*

KEY PATTERNS
fortunate to do/be something
fortunate in having something
fortunate (that)

lucky ANTONYM **unfortunate**: *It was a bad accident – I'm* ***fortunate to*** *be alive.* • *You are* ***fortunate in having*** *such good friends.* • ***It was fortunate*** *that they weren't caught.*

for·tu·nate·ly /ˈfɔːtʃənətli $ ˈfɔrtʃənətli/ *adverb* used to talk about something good or lucky that happens SYNONYM **luckily**: *Fortunately, the car wasn't damaged much in the accident.*

for·tune /ˈfɔːtʃən $ ˈfɔrtʃən/ *noun* **1** a lot of money: *This jacket cost a fortune.* **2** chance, or the good and bad things that happen to you: *The team's fortunes changed and they began winning games.*

for·ty /ˈfɔːti $ ˈfɔrti/ *number* (plural **forties**) **1** 40 **2 the forties** the years from 1940 to 1949 **3 be in your forties** to be aged between 40 and 49 —**fortieth** *number*

SPELLING
This word is often spelled wrongly. The correct spelling is: **forty**.

for·ward¹ /ˈfɔːwəd $ ˈfɔrwərd/ also **forwards** *adverb* towards the direction that is in front of you ANTONYM **backwards**: *They pushed the car forward a couple of feet.* • *Debbie leaned forward to speak to the taxi driver.*

forward² *adjective* **forward planning, forward thinking** when you make plans for the future: *With a little forward planning, your party should be a great success.*

ˈforward ˌslash *noun* a line (/) that is used to separate numbers, letters etc, for example on Internet addresses

fos·sil /ˈfɒsəl $ ˈfɑsəl/ *noun* the shape of an animal or plant from the past that appears in rock

fos·ter¹ /ˈfɒstə $ ˈfɔstər/ *verb* **1** to encourage a feeling or skill to develop: *We want to foster a friendly atmosphere in the office.* **2** to take care of someone else's child for a period of time, without becoming their legal parent: *They fostered two children for nearly a year.*

foster² *adjective* **foster parents, foster children** people who foster someone else's child, or children who are fostered

fought the past tense and past participle of FIGHT¹

foul¹ /faʊl/ *adjective* **1** very dirty or very unpleasant: *What's that foul smell?* **2 foul language** language that is rude and offensive: *The film contains a lot of violence and foul language.*

foul² *verb* if a sports player fouls another player, they do something that is against the rules: *He was sent off for fouling the goalkeeper.* —**foul** *noun*: *He committed a foul.*

found¹ the past tense and past participle of FIND

found² /faʊnd/ *verb* to start an organization: *Our school was founded in 1900.*

foun·da·tion /faʊnˈdeɪʃən/ *noun* **1** something basic or important on which something else is based: *Reading and writing are the foundations of learning.* **2** an organization that gives money for special purposes: *The project was funded by the Carnegie Foundation.* **3 foundations** *BrE*, **foundation** *AmE* the solid base under the ground that supports a building: *They have only built the foundations of the new office block.*

found·er /ˈfaʊndə $ ˈfaʊndɚ/ *noun* someone who starts an organization: *one of the original founders of the company*

foun·tain /ˈfaʊntən/ *noun* an object that sends water up into the air

ˈfountain pen *noun* a pen that you fill with ink

four /fɔː $ fɔr/ *number* **1** 4 **2 on all fours** if you are on all fours, your hands and knees are on the ground: *She was crawling around on all fours under the table.*

four·teen /ˌfɔːˈtiːn $ ˌfɔrˈtin/ *number* 14 —**fourteenth** *number*

fourth /fɔːθ $ fɔrθ/ *number* **1** 4th: *This is the fourth time I've asked you.* **2** the American word for QUARTER

fox /fɒks $ fɑks/ *noun* (plural **foxes**) a wild animal like a dog with red-brown fur, a pointed face, and a thick tail

foy·er /ˈfɔɪeɪ $ ˈfɔɪɚ/ *noun* a room at the entrance to a hotel, theatre, or other large building SYNONYM **lobby**: *I'll meet you in the foyer of the nightclub.*

frac·tion /ˈfrækʃən/ *noun* a number that is smaller than 1, for example ⅓ or ⅝

frac·ture /ˈfræktʃə $ ˈfræktʃɚ/ *verb* to break a bone in your body: *I've fractured my wrist.* —**fracture** *noun*: *He had a fracture in his foot.*

fra·gile /ˈfrædʒaɪl $ ˈfrædʒəl/ *adjective* easily broken or destroyed SYNONYM **delicate**: *Some of the works of art are very fragile.*

frag·ment /ˈfrægmənt/ *noun* a small piece of something: *The nurse removed the fragments of glass from my hand.*

fra·grant /ˈfreɪgrənt/ *adjective* (written) something that is fragrant smells pleasant: *fragrant flowers such as roses* —**fragrance** *noun*: *She could smell the rich fragrance of the roses.*
→ see Thesaurus at SMELL²

frail /freɪl/ *adjective* thin and weak: *My grandma's getting very old and frail now.*

frames

window frame
picture frame

frame¹ /freɪm/ *noun*
1 the wood, metal etc that is around a picture or window: *a wooden picture frame*
2 the pieces of wood, metal etc that are the main structure of something: *The frame of the chair is made of metal.*

PHRASES
frame of mind your frame of mind is the way you are feeling: *This music should put you in a relaxed **frame of mind**.*

frame² *verb* to put a picture into a frame: *It's a very good photo – why don't you frame it?*

frames /freɪmz/ *plural noun* the part of a pair of glasses that holds the two pieces of glass: *He sat on my glasses and broke the frames.*

frame·work /ˈfreɪmwɜːk $ ˈfreɪmwɚk/ *noun* the main structure around which a building or vehicle is built: *The framework of the roof was not strong enough.*

frank /fræŋk/ *adjective* someone who is frank says things in an honest and direct way: *I've always been frank with her.* —**frankness** *noun* (no plural): *Some people don't like Sue's frankness.*

fran·tic /ˈfræntɪk/ *adjective*
1 hurrying in a way that is not organized: *There was a frantic rush for tickets.* **2** very anxious or upset: *We've*

A B C D E F G H I J K L M N O P Q R S T U V W X Y Z

been frantic with worry – where have you been? —**frantically** /-kli/ *adverb*: *I tried frantically to put out the fire.*

fraud /frɔːd/ *noun* when someone deceives people to get money: *Tax fraud is a serious offence.*

fraught /frɔːt/ *adjective* (written) if something is fraught with problems, danger etc, it involves a lot of problems, danger etc: *Firefighting is a job that is fraught with risks.*

fray /freɪ/ *verb* if cloth frays, its threads become loose at the edge: *The legs of his trousers had frayed at the bottom.*

freak[1] /friːk/ *noun* **1** (informal) someone who has a very strong interest in something SYNONYM **fanatic**: *I'm an exercise freak.* **2** someone who is strange or who looks strange

freak[2] *adjective* a freak event is a very unusual one: *He was injured in a freak accident.*

freck·le /ˈfrekəl/ *noun* a small brown spot on someone's skin: *She has freckles all over her nose.*

free[1] /friː/ *adjective*

KEY PATTERNS
free to do something
free of/from something bad

1 something that is free does not cost any money: *a free gift in a magazine* • *Membership of the club is free.*
2 if people are free, they are not controlled and can do what they like: *In a free society, you can say what you like about the government.* • *You* **are free to** *do whatever you like.*
3 if you are free, you are not being held or kept somewhere: *After six years in prison, at last he was free.* • *She managed to* **get free of** *the crashed car.*
4 not busy doing other things: *I'm free every evening this week.*
5 if something is free, it is not being used: *There's a free table over there.* • *Carrying a bag on your back leaves your hands free.* ➔ see Thesaurus at EMPTY[1]
6 something that is free of something harmful or unpleasant does not have it: *These vegetables* **are free from** *chemicals.*

PHRASES
feel free (spoken) used to tell someone that they are allowed to do something: ***Feel free to*** *make suggestions.*
set someone/something free to allow someone to leave a prison or to allow a wild animal to leave a place such as a ZOO: *All the prisoners* **were set free.**
free of charge something that is free of charge does not cost any money: *This advice is* **free of charge.**

free[2] *verb*

KEY PATTERNS
free someone from a place
free someone to do something

1 if you free someone who has been unable to leave a place, you let them go or get them out: *Should they* **free** *this murderer* **from** *prison?* • *They tried to free the people who were trapped inside the burning building.*
2 also **free up** to make a person or thing available: *If nurses treat small injuries, this will* **free** *doctors* **to** *deal with more serious injuries.* • *Remove some of the files to* **free up** *space on the computer.*

free[3] *adverb*
without having to pay any money: *After four o'clock, you can get into the exhibition free.*
PHRASES
for free a) if you do something for free, you do it without being paid: *He offered to appear in the film* **for free.**
b) if you get something for free, you get it without having to pay: *I got this jacket* **for free.**

free·dom /ˈfriːdəm/ *noun* (no plural)

KEY PATTERNS
freedom of speech/action etc
the freedom to do something

1 when you are not controlled and are allowed to do what you like: *I believe in* ***freedom of choice*** (=I believe people should be able to choose what they like). • *With this diet, you have* **the freedom to** *eat as many vegetables as you want.*
2 when you are not held as a prisoner ANTONYM **captivity**: *his first day of freedom after ten years in jail*

free·lance /ˈfriːlɑːns $ ˈfrilæns/ *adjective, adverb* someone who is freelance works independently for several different organizations: *I'm a freelance writer.* • *I'm thinking of going freelance.*

free·ly /ˈfriːli/ *adverb* without anyone trying to control you or stop you doing something: *Children can move freely between classrooms.*

ˌfree ˈspeech *noun* (no plural) the right to express your opinions: *If the government believes in free speech, why does it stop us protesting?*

free·way /ˈfriːweɪ/ the American word for MOTORWAY ➔ see Thesaurus at ROAD

freeze /friːz/ *verb* (**froze** /frəʊz $ froʊz/ **frozen** /ˈfrəʊzən $ ˈfroʊzən/)
1 if water freezes, it becomes hard because it is very cold ANTONYM **melt**: *The lake had frozen.*
2 if you freeze food, you make it very cold and hard so that it stays in good condition for a long time ANTONYM **defrost**: *She froze some of the soup.*
—**frozen** *adjective*: *a packet of frozen peas*
PHRASES
freeze to death to die because you are so cold: *The climbers froze to death on the mountain.*

freez·er /ˈfriːzə $ ˈfrizɚ/ *noun* a large piece of kitchen equipment where you freeze food and keep it at a very low temperature: *There's some ice cream in the freezer.*

freez·ing[1] /ˈfriːzɪŋ/ *adjective* (informal) very cold: *I'm freezing – shall we light the fire?* • *Put your coat on – it's freezing outside.* ➔ see Thesaurus at COLD[1]

freezing[2] *noun* (no plural) 32°F or 0°C: *It was three degrees below freezing.*

freight /freɪt/ *noun* (no plural) things that are being taken from one place to another by train, road, plane, or ship: *a freight train*

French fry /ˌfrentʃ ˈfraɪ/ *noun* (plural **French fries**) a long thin piece of potato cooked in fat SYNONYM **chip** *BrE*

fren·zy /ˈfrenzi/ *noun* (no plural) when you are so anxious, excited etc that you are unable to control your behaviour: *She was shouting and swearing in a frenzy of rage.*

fre·quen·cy /ˈfriːkwənsi/ *noun* (formal) (plural **frequencies**) **1** (no plural) the number of times that something happens: *Her headaches have increased in frequency.* **2** the rate at which a sound or light wave is repeated: *We cannot hear sounds of very high frequency.*

fre·quent /ˈfriːkwənt/ *adjective* something that is frequent happens often: *She makes frequent visits to the United States.*

fre·quent·ly /ˈfrikwəntli/ *adverb* (formal) often: *He's frequently late for school.* ➔ see Thesaurus at OFTEN

fresh /freʃ/ *adjective*
1 new and different from the previous ones: *The police have received fresh information relating to the murder.* • *people with fresh new ideas*
2 fresh food has been produced or picked recently: *Eat plenty of* ***fresh fruit and vegetables.***
3 pleasantly clean: *the fresh smell of lemons* • *I need some* ***fresh air*** (=air outside a building).
4 fresh water contains no salt and can be drunk: *They had a good supply of fresh water on the boat.*
5 if you are fresh, you are not tired: *Let's do as much work as possible while we're still fresh.*
PHRASES
be fresh in your mind, be fresh in your memory if something is fresh in your mind or memory, you remember it clearly, because it happened recently: *The events of that day* ***were still fresh in her mind.***
fresh from somewhere, fresh out of somewhere someone who is fresh from a place has just left that place: *He joined the company* ***fresh from*** *college.*

fresh·ly /ˈfreʃli/ *adverb* very recently: *the smell of freshly baked bread*

fresh·man /ˈfreʃmən/ *noun AmE* (plural **freshmen** /-mən/) a student in the first year of HIGH SCHOOL or college

fric·tion /ˈfrɪkʃən/ *noun* (no plural) **1** when people disagree with each other and argue in an unfriendly way: *There seemed to be some friction between Jo and Pete.* **2** when one surface rubs against another: *Friction produces heat.*

A B C D E F G H I J K L M N O P Q R S T U V W X Y Z

Fri·day /ˈfraɪdi/ (written abbreviation **Fri**) *noun* the day of the week between Thursday and Saturday: *See you on Friday!* • *It's Friday June 22nd.*

fridge /frɪdʒ/ *noun* a large piece of kitchen equipment where you keep food at a low temperature but do not freeze it

friend /frend/ *noun*
someone that you know well and like: *She invited all her friends to the party.* • *Everyone needs a few **close friends**.* • *He used to be my **best friend*** (=my closest friend).

PHRASES

make friends to start having someone as a friend, or several people as friends: *I **made friends with** a girl in my class.* • *I **made** many **friends** there.*
be friends if two people are friends, they know each other well and like each other: *We've **been friends** for years.*

SPELLING
This word is often spelled wrongly. The correct spelling is: **friend**.

friend·ly /ˈfrendli/ *adjective* (**friendlier**, **friendliest**)

KEY PATTERNS
friendly to/towards someone
friendly with someone

1 someone who is friendly talks to people or behaves pleasantly towards them ANTONYM **unfriendly**: *Everyone in the village **was** very **friendly to** us.*
2 if you are friendly with someone, you are their friend: *She's still **friendly with** many people she knew at college.*

THESAURUS
warm: *She gave him a **warm** smile* (=friendly).
hospitable: *Everyone I met in Italy was very **hospitable*** (=friendly and happy to welcome visitors).

friend·ship /ˈfrendʃɪp/ *noun* a relationship in which two people are friends: *Our long friendship began at school.*

fries /fraɪz/ *plural noun* FRENCH FRIES: *I'll have a cheeseburger and fries.*

fright /fraɪt/ *noun* (no plural) a sudden feeling of fear: *You gave me a fright – I didn't realize you were right behind me.* • *I nearly died of fright!*

fright·en /ˈfraɪtn/ *verb*
to make someone feel afraid SYNONYM **scare**: *Being alone in the dark frightens some people.* • *If you have a cat, it will **frighten** the birds **away*** (=make them go away because they are afraid).

fright·ened /ˈfraɪtnd/ *adjective*

KEY PATTERNS
frightened of something/someone
frightened that
frightened to do something

afraid that something bad might happen: *Liz has always **been frightened of** spiders.* • *I was **frightened that** someone would fall and hurt themselves.* • *He **was frightened to** leave the house.*

THESAURUS
afraid/scared: *Some children are **afraid** of the dark* (=frightened).
terrified: *The man had a gun and everyone was **terrified*** (=very frightened).

WORD CHOICE
frightened or **frightening**?
• **Frightened** means "afraid of something": *I'm **frightened** of the dark.*
• **Frightening** means "making you feel afraid": *Travelling by helicopter was a **frightening** experience.*

fright·en·ing /ˈfraɪtn-ɪŋ/ *adjective* something that is frightening makes you feel afraid SYNONYM **scary**: *It's a very frightening film.*

frill /frɪl/ *noun* a long piece of cloth with many small folds, which you use to decorate clothing etc: *Her skirt had a frill around the bottom.*

frill·y /ˈfrɪli/ *adjective* (**frillier**, **frilliest**) decorated with pieces of cloth which have many small folds: *I don't like frilly dresses.*

fringe /frɪndʒ/ *noun BrE* the part of your hair that hangs over the part of your face above your eyes SYNONYM **bangs** *AmE*: *My fringe needs cutting.*

frisk /frɪsk/ *verb* to feel and search the clothes someone is wearing, to check that they do not have any hidden weapons or drugs: *The security guard frisked me.*

A B C D E F G H I J K L M N O P Q R S T U V W X Y Z

fri·vol·i·ty /frɪˈvɒləti $ frɪˈvɑləti/ *noun* when people behave in a way that is not serious or sensible: *My father disapproves of frivolity.*

friv·o·lous /ˈfrɪvələs/ *adjective* behaving in a silly way when you should be sensible: *She kept making frivolous comments.*

frizz·y /ˈfrɪzi/ *adjective* (**frizzier**, **frizziest**) frizzy hair is very tightly curled: *My hair's gone all frizzy.*

frog /frɒg $ frɔg/ *noun* a small, usually green animal that lives in water or near water and has long legs for jumping

frog·man /ˈfrɒgmən $ ˈfrɔgmən/ *noun* (plural **frogmen** /-mən/) someone whose job is to work under water wearing a rubber suit and special equipment for breathing SYNONYM **diver**: *Frogmen are searching for the body in the river.*

from /frəm; strong frɒm $ frʌm/ *preposition*
1 used to say what place someone or something leaves, or where something starts: *I ran all the way home from school.* • *Can you fetch a chair from the kitchen?* • *the road from Bath to Bristol*
2 used to say when something starts: *I worked from 4 o'clock until 7* (=I started work at 4 o'clock and finished at 7).
3 used to say where someone was born, lives, or works: *My mother is from Wales* (=she was born in Wales). • *We're all from Glasgow* (=we all live in Glasgow). • *This is Mr Grange from the hospital* (=Mr Grange works in the hospital). • *a group of students from the local college*
4 used when talking about the distance between one thing and another: *Our house is 1 kilometre from the station* (=the distance between our house and the station is 1 kilometre). • *The ball stopped two metres from the hole.* • *She now lives 200 miles* ***away from*** *her parents.*
5 used to say who has given or sent something: *I've just had an email from Kurt.* • *Last Christmas I got a new bike from my parents.*

front¹ /frʌnt/ *noun*
the front the part of something that is furthest forward, or that is most important ANTONYM **the back**: *Can I sit in* ***the front of*** *the car?* • *His name was on* ***the front of*** *the book in big letters.*

PHRASES

in front further forward than someone or something else: *The car* ***in front*** *stopped suddenly.* • *Tom was sitting* ***in front of*** *me in the cinema.*

in front of something/someone facing something or near the most important side of it: *She stood* ***in front of*** *the mirror.* • *There was a lake* ***in front of*** *the house.*

front

Joe ran in front of the bus.

Joe got a seat at the front of the bus.

front² *adjective* at or in the front of something ANTONYM **back**: *His brother sat in the front seat.* • *The front door was open.*

fron·tier /ˈfrʌntɪə $ frʌnˈtɪr/ *noun BrE* the place where two countries meet SYNONYM **border**: *Strasbourg is on the frontier between France and Germany.*

frost /frɒst $ frɔst/ *noun* (no plural) a white powder of ice, which forms on surfaces outside when it is very cold: *The ground was covered with frost.*

frost·bite /ˈfrɒstbaɪt $ ˈfrɔstbaɪt/ *noun* (no plural) if you get frostbite, your fingers or toes freeze and are badly damaged

frost·ing /ˈfrɒstɪŋ $ ˈfrɔstɪŋ/ the American word for ICING

frost·y /ˈfrɒsti $ ˈfrɔsti/ *adjective* (**frostier**, **frostiest**) very cold or covered with frost: *It was a frosty morning.*

froth /frɒθ $ frɔθ/ *noun* (no plural) a lot of small bubbles on top of a liquid: *He blew the froth off his coffee.*

frown /fraʊn/ *verb* to make an angry or unhappy expression, so that lines appear on your face above your eyes: *Her mother frowned when she saw what Ann was wearing.* —**frown** *noun*: *He had a worried frown on his face.*

frown

froze the past tense of FREEZE

frozen the past participle of FREEZE

fruit /fruːt/ *noun* (plural **fruit** or **fruits**) something such as an apple or orange which grows on a plant, tree, or bush, and contains seeds: *Bananas are my favourite fruit.* • *a basket of fruit* • *a tree covered in red fruits* ➔ see picture on page A7

USAGE
✘ Don't say 'a fruit'.
Say **a piece of fruit** or **some fruit**.

fruit·ful /ˈfruːtfəl/ *adjective* (formal) producing good results: *Was it a fruitful meeting?*

fruit·less /ˈfruːtləs/ *adjective* (formal) failing to produce good results, especially after much effort SYNONYM **unsuccessful**: *I spent two hours on a fruitless search for my keys.*

fruit·y /ˈfruːti/ *adjective* (**fruitier**, **fruitiest**) tasting or smelling strongly of fruit: *This wine has a fruity smell.*

frus·trate /frʌˈstreɪt $ ˈfrʌstreɪt/ *verb* if something frustrates you, it makes you feel impatient or angry because you are unable to do what you want to do: *It frustrates me when she doesn't listen to me.* —**frustrated** *adjective*: *I get frustrated when I can't do things straight away.*

frus·trat·ing /frʌˈstreɪtɪŋ $ ˈfrʌstreɪtɪŋ/ *adjective* making you feel disappointed and angry because you try to do something, but cannot do it: *It is so frustrating to play well and still lose.*

frus·tra·tion /frʌˈstreɪʃən/ *noun* the feeling of being impatient or angry because you are unable to do what you want to do: *She threw her pen on the floor in frustration.*

fry /fraɪ/ *verb* (**fried**, **fries**) to cook something in hot oil: *I'll fry the onions.* ➔ see picture at COOK[1] ➔ see picture on page A4

ˈfrying ˌpan *noun* a round flat pan with a long handle that you use for frying food ➔ see picture at PAN

ft. the written abbreviation of FOOT or FEET: *The garage is 20 ft. long.*

fu·el[1] /ˈfjuːəl/ *noun* a substance such as coal, gas, or oil, which you can burn to produce heat or power: *The plane was running out of fuel.*

fuel[2] *verb* (written) (**fuelled**, **fuelling** *BrE*, **fueled**, **fueling** *AmE*) to make a situation worse, or make someone's feelings stronger SYNONYM **increase**: *Her behaviour only fuelled his anger.*

fu·gi·tive /ˈfjuːdʒətɪv/ *noun* someone who has escaped and is trying to avoid being caught, especially by the police

ful·fil *BrE*, **fulfill** *AmE* /fʊlˈfɪl/ *verb* (formal) (**fulfilled**, **fulfilling**) **1** if you fulfil a promise, aim etc, you do something that you have promised or wanted to do: *I must fulfil my promise.* • *Will he ever fulfil his ambition to be a pilot?* **2** if someone or something fulfils a ROLE or FUNCTION, they do something that is needed: *I think he will fulfil his role as captain well.*

ful·filled /fʊlˈfɪld/ *adjective* completely satisfied with your life or your job: *It is important to feel fulfilled in your work.*

ful·fil·ling /fʊlˈfɪlɪŋ/ *adjective* making you feel satisfied SYNONYM **satisfying**: *Is your relationship a fulfilling one?*

full /fʊl/ *adjective*

KEY PATTERNS
full of things/people

1 something that is full of things or people contains a lot of them: *His house **is full of** interesting books.* • *On Saturday nights the streets **are full of** young people.* ➔ see picture at EMPTY
2 also **full up** *BrE* if something is full, there is no space left in it ANTONYM **empty**: *My suitcase was already completely full.* • *The school **is full up** this year.*
3 complete and including everything: *Could you give me your **full name** and*

A B C D E F G H I J K L M N O P Q R S T U V W X Y Z

address? • *For **full** details of our holidays, write to the address below.* **4** also **full up** *BrE* (informal) you can say that you are full when you have eaten as much food as you want: *"More ice cream, Susan?" "No thanks, I'm full."*

PHRASES

full marks *BrE* if you get full marks for work you do at school, you get the highest mark that it is possible to get: *I **got full marks** in my French test.*

at full speed, at full volume: *The train was going **at full speed** (=as quickly as it could) when the accident happened.* • *He was playing his stereo **at full volume*** (=as loudly as it could be played).

in full if you pay an amount of money in full, you pay the whole amount

THESAURUS

crammed: *The room was **crammed** with furniture* (=very full of it).

crowded: *a **crowded** café* (=full of people)

packed: *On the first night of the play, the theatre was **packed*** (=very full of people).

ˈfull-blown *adjective* fully developed: *The situation developed into a full-blown crisis.*

ˌfull-ˈgrown also **ˌfully ˈgrown** *adjective* a full-grown animal, plant, or person has developed completely and will not grow any bigger: *A full-grown blue whale can weigh 30 tons.*

ˈfull-length *adjective* **1** not shorter than the normal length: *I've seen the full-length version of the film.* **2** a full-length skirt or dress reaches the ground

ˌfull ˈmoon *noun* the moon when it looks completely round: *There's going to be a full moon tonight.*

ˈfull-scale *adjective* **1** a full-scale action or situation uses or includes everything possible: *This disagreement could lead to a full-scale war.* **2** a full-scale model, copy, or picture is the same size as the real thing: *a full-scale model of a human brain*

ˌfull ˈstop *noun BrE* a mark (.) that you use to show the end of a sentence SYNONYM **period** *AmE*

ˌfull-ˈtime *adverb, adjective* if you work or study full-time, you work or study all day during the whole week ANTONYM **part-time**: *I'm looking for a full-time job.*

ful•ly /ˈfʊli/ *adverb* completely: *I am fully aware of the situation.*

fum•ble /ˈfʌmbəl/ *verb* (written) to try with difficulty to find, move, or hold something, using your hands in an awkward way: *She fumbled in her bag for her keys.*

fume /fjuːm/ *verb* to be very angry: *I was an hour late coming home, and my mother was fuming.*

fumes /fjuːmz/ *plural noun* gas or smoke with a strong smell that is unpleasant to breathe: *They had breathed in poisonous fumes.*

fun¹ /fʌn/ *noun* (no plural) if something is fun, you enjoy doing it or being involved in it: *The party **was great fun**.*

PHRASES

have fun to enjoy yourself doing something nice: *Everyone **had fun** playing in the snow.*

for fun if you do something for fun, you do it because you enjoy it: *We slept out in the garden, just **for fun**.*

make fun of someone to say unkind things about someone and laugh at them: *The other children **made fun of** her because she was fat.*

WORD CHOICE

fun or **funny**?

• **Fun** means "enjoyable": *The class was fun.*

• **Funny** means "making you laugh": *a funny film*

fun² *adjective* (informal) enjoyable: *We had a really fun time.*

func•tion¹ /ˈfʌŋkʃən/ *noun* the purpose that something is made for: *The function of this switch is to make the screen brighter or darker.*

function² *verb* if a machine, system etc is functioning, it is working: *Scientists are not sure how our brains function.*

fund¹ /fʌnd/ *noun* **1** an amount of money that someone keeps for a particular purpose: *I put the money in my holiday fund.* **2** **funds** the money that you need to do something: *We're raising* (=collecting) *funds for our school.*

fund² *verb* to provide money for an event or activity: *A local business is funding the competition.*

fun·da·men·tal /ˌfʌndəˈmentl/ *adjective* related to the most basic and important parts of something: *What are the fundamental differences between men and women?* —**fundamentally** *adverb*: *The company is fundamentally changing the way it does business.*

fund·ing /ˈfʌndɪŋ/ *noun* money that an organization provides for something: *The sport needs more funding.*

ˈ**fund-ˌraising** *noun* (no plural) the activity of collecting money for a particular purpose: *concerts and other fund-raising activities*

fu·ne·ral /ˈfjuːnərəl/ *noun* a ceremony for someone who has just died: *I didn't go to my aunt's funeral.*

fun·fair /ˈfʌnfeə $ ˈfʌnfer/ *noun BrE* a noisy outdoor event where you can ride on machines or play games to win prizes SYNONYM **fair**

fun·gus /ˈfʌŋgəs/ *noun* (plural **fungi** /-gaɪ, -dʒaɪ/ or **funguses**) a type of plant such as a MUSHROOM, which has no leaves or flowers, and which grows on other plants or other surfaces: *Fungus was growing on the damp walls.*

funk·y /ˈfʌŋki/ *adjective* (informal) music that is funky has a good strong beat and is enjoyable to listen to

fun·ny /ˈfʌni/ *adjective* (**funnier**, **funniest**)
1 if someone or something is funny, they make you laugh: *It was one of the funniest films I've ever seen.*
2 strange or unusual SYNONYM **odd**: *There was a funny smell in the house.*
➔ see Thesaurus at STRANGE

THESAURUS
amusing: *The first chapter of the book was quite **amusing*** (=funny).
hilarious: *Sammy told me a **hilarious** joke* (=extremely funny).

fur /fɜː $ fɚ/ *noun* (no plural) the thick soft hair that covers the bodies of some animals: *I stroked the rabbit's soft fur.* • *She wore a fur coat.*

fu·ri·ous /ˈfjʊəriəs $ ˈfjʊriəs/ *adjective* very angry: *She's furious with me for kissing her boyfriend.* ➔ see Thesaurus at ANGRY

fur·nace /ˈfɜːnɪs $ ˈfɚnɪs/ *noun* an object with a very hot fire in it that is used for melting metals, burning things, or producing heat: *They burned the rubbish in a furnace.*

fur·nish /ˈfɜːnɪʃ $ ˈfɚnɪʃ/ *verb* to put furniture into a house or room: *I can't afford to furnish my new apartment.*

fur·ni·ture /ˈfɜːnɪtʃə $ ˈfɚnɪtʃɚ/ *noun* (no plural)
objects such as chairs, tables, and beds: *All our furniture is old.* • *Do you sell office furniture?*

GRAMMAR
Furniture is not used in the plural.
✘ Don't say 'furnitures'.
When talking about a single chair or table, you say **a piece of furniture**.

fur·ry /ˈfɜːri $ ˈfɚi/ *adjective* (**furrier**, **furriest**) covered with fur: *a small furry animal*

fur·ther¹ /ˈfɜːðə $ ˈfɚðɚ/ *adverb*
1 a longer distance: *He walked a few steps further away from me.* • *They wanted to move to a town further south.*
2 (formal) more: *Have you thought about your plans any further?*

further² *adjective* (formal) additional: *Do I need a further appointment?*
➔ see Thesaurus at MORE

ˌ**further eduˈcation** *noun* (no plural) *BrE* education for people who have finished school but are not at a university: *Do you want to go on to further education?*

fur·thest /ˈfɜːðəst $ ˈfɚðəst/ *adjective, adverb* the longest distance: *the planet that is furthest from the Earth*

fur·tive /ˈfɜːtɪv $ ˈfɚtɪv/ *adjective* behaving as if you want to keep something secret: *He had a furtive look at the letter which lay on the desk.* —**furtively** *adverb*

fu·ry /ˈfjʊəri $ ˈfjʊri/ *noun* (no plural) (written) extreme anger SYNONYM **rage**: *After reading the letter, she was shaking with fury.*

A B C D E F G H I J K L M N O P Q R S T U V W X Y Z

fuse¹ /fjuːz/ *noun* **1** a short wire inside a piece of electrical equipment that melts if too much electricity passes through it: *This plug needs a new fuse.* **2** a piece of string fixed to explosive that you light to make an explosion happen a short time later

fuse² *verb* if two things fuse, or if you fuse them, they join together and become one thing: *The two pieces of bone fused together.*

fuss¹ /fʌs/ *noun* **1** (no plural) when people become very excited, angry, or upset about something that is not very serious or important: *What's all the fuss about?* **2 make a fuss** to complain about something in a noisy way: *He was making a fuss because the train was late.* **3 make a fuss of someone** *BrE*, **make a fuss over someone** *AmE* to pay someone a lot of attention and do nice things for them: *My boyfriend always makes a fuss of me on my birthday.*

fuss² *verb* to behave in a nervous, anxious way, worrying over unimportant things: *Don't fuss – I'm fine.*

fuss·y /ˈfʌsi/ *adjective* (**fussier**, **fussiest**) someone who is fussy only likes a few things and does not accept things that they do not like SYNONYM **choosy**, **picky**: *I'm very fussy about what I wear.*

fu·tile /ˈfjuːtaɪl $ ˈfjutl/ *adjective* certain not to be effective or successful: *The police made a futile attempt to rescue him.*

fu·ture¹ /ˈfjuːtʃə $ ˈfjutʃɚ/ *noun*

KEY PATTERNS
in the future

1 the future the time that will come after the present time: *Young people often don't think about **the future**.* • ***In the future**, almost everyone will have a computer.*
2 what will happen to something or someone: *The future of the band was looking uncertain.* • *We all need to think about our country's future.*

PHRASES
in future starting now and continuing: *In future I'm going to work a lot harder.*

future² *adjective* future things are things that will happen or exist after the present time: *They discussed possible future projects.* • *He and his future wife* (=the woman who will be his wife) *have bought a house together.*

PHRASES
the future tense the form of a verb that we use to talk about what will happen after the present time

ˌfuture ˈperfect *noun* **the future perfect** the verb tense that you use to talk about things that will happen before a time in the future, which is formed with 'will have' and the PAST PARTICIPLE, as in 'I will have finished by five o'clock.'

fuzz·y /ˈfʌzi/ *adjective* (**fuzzier**, **fuzziest**) unclear: *The TV picture's gone fuzzy.*

gad·get /ˈgædʒɪt/ *noun* a small tool or machine that helps you do something: *a handy little gadget for opening bottles* ➔ see Thesaurus at MACHINE

gag[1] /gæg/ *verb* (**gagged**, **gagging**) to cover someone's mouth with a piece of cloth so that they cannot make any noise: *The robbers tied him up and gagged him.*

gag[2] *noun* a piece of cloth used to gag someone

gain[1] /geɪn/ *verb* **1** to get something that is important, useful, or valuable: *I want to gain more experience with computers.* • *The army gained control of the town.* **2** to get more of something ANTONYM **lose**: *She's gained a lot of weight.*

> WORD CHOICE
> **gain**, **earn**, or **win**?
> • You **gain** something important or valuable: *I gained a lot of experience.*
> • You **earn** a particular amount of money for your work: *He* **earns** *$100,000 a year.*
> • You **win** a game, competition, prize, or victory: *Our team* **won** *the game 2:1.*

gain[2] *noun* an increase in the amount or level of something ANTONYM **loss**: *What is the reason for his weight gain?*

ga·la /ˈgɑːlə $ ˈgælə/ *noun* a special public performance or celebration: *The theatre is holding a 30th anniversary gala.*

gal·ax·y /ˈgæləksi/ *noun* (plural **galaxies**) a very large group of stars: *a distant galaxy*

gale /geɪl/ *noun* a very strong wind: *Several trees blew down in the gale.* ➔ see Thesaurus at WIND[1]

gall /gɔːl/ *noun* **have the gall to do something** to do something that is rude and not right: *She had the gall to say I was being childish!*

gal·le·ry /ˈgæləri/ *noun* (plural **galleries**) a room or building where you can look at paintings: *an art gallery*

gal·lon /ˈgælən/ *noun* a unit for measuring liquid, equal to 4.5435 litres in Britain or 3.785 litres in the US: *I need ten gallons of petrol.*

gal·lop /ˈgæləp/ *verb* if a horse gallops, it runs very quickly

gam·ble[1] /ˈgæmbəl/ *verb* to try to win money by guessing the result of a competition or race, by playing cards etc: *He used to gamble on the horses* (=horse races). —**gambler** *noun*

gamble[2] *noun* something that you are not sure will succeed: *Employing someone with so little experience is a gamble.*

gam·bling /ˈgæmblɪŋ/ *noun* (no plural) the activity of trying to win money by guessing the result of a competition or race, by playing cards etc: *Many more people are now using the Internet for gambling.*

game /geɪm/ *noun*

> KEY PATTERNS
> **a game of chess/tennis etc**
> **play a game**

1 an activity, such as a sport, in which you obey rules in order to defeat someone or achieve something: *I got a new computer game for Christmas.* • *Would you like a* **game of cards** (=a game using playing cards)? • *The boys were out in the garden,* **playing a game**. • *Manchester United* **won** *last night's* **game against** *Leeds.*
2 games an important sports event where people play many different sports: *the Olympic Games*

ˈgame show *noun* a television programme in which people play games in order to win prizes

gang[1] /gæŋ/ *noun* a group of people, especially a group that causes trouble or does illegal things: *He was beaten up by a gang of youths.* ➔ see Thesaurus at GROUP[1]

gang[2] *verb* **gang up on** to join together in order to criticize or attack

A B C D E F G H I J K L M N O P Q R S T U V W X Y Z

someone: *They were always ganging up on the younger children.*

gang·ster /ˈgæŋstə $ ˈgæŋstɚ/ *noun* a member of a group of violent criminals: *Do you like gangster movies?*

gaol a British spelling of JAIL

gap

gap /gæp/ *noun*

KEY PATTERNS
a gap in something
a gap between things

1 an empty space in something or between things: *There was a huge **gap in** the roof.* • *The book had fallen into the **gap between** the couch and the wall.*
2 a difference between people, things, or ideas: *the **gap between** men's pay and women's pay*

gape /geɪp/ *verb* (written) to look at something or someone in surprise, with your mouth open: *He just stood there gaping at the mess.*

gap·ing /ˈgeɪpɪŋ/ *adjective* a gaping hole is very wide: *The crash left a gaping hole in the wall.* • *a gaping wound*

gar·age /ˈgærɑːʒ $ gəˈrɑʒ/ *noun* **1** a building where you keep your car: *The garage is big enough for two cars.* **2** a place where cars are repaired: *My car's in the garage so I can't take you home.* **3** *BrE* a place where you buy petrol SYNONYM **gas station** *AmE*

PRONUNCIATION
British people pronounce this word 'GARage'.
American people pronounce this word 'gaRAGE'.

gar·bage /ˈgɑːbɪdʒ $ ˈgɑrbɪdʒ/ an American word for RUBBISH → see Thesaurus at RUBBISH

ˈgarbage ˌcan the American word for DUSTBIN

gar·bled /ˈgɑːbəld $ ˈgɑrbəld/ *adjective* garbled information is mixed up and difficult to understand: *She left a garbled message about being late.*

gar·den /ˈgɑːdn $ ˈgɑrdn/ *noun* a piece of land next to your house where there is grass and you can grow flowers SYNONYM **yard** *AmE*: *The kids are playing in the garden.*

gar·den·er /ˈgɑːdnə $ ˈgɑrdnɚ/ *noun* someone who works in a garden: *Our gardener cuts the grass.* • *Sam is a keen gardener.*

gardening

gar·den·ing /ˈgɑːdnɪŋ $ ˈgɑrdnɪŋ/ *noun* (no plural) the activity or job of working in a garden: *We did a bit of gardening this afternoon.*

gar·gle /ˈgɑːgəl $ ˈgɑrgəl/ *verb* to clean your throat with water or a special liquid that you do not swallow: *If you have a sore throat, try gargling with salt water.*

gar·ish /ˈgeərɪʃ $ ˈgærɪʃ/ *adjective* very brightly coloured and unpleasant to look at: *The curtains are very garish.*

garland

gar·land /ˈgɑːlənd $ ˈgɑrlənd/ *noun* a ring of flowers or leaves, that people wear for decoration: *They put garlands of flowers around our necks.*

gar·lic /ˈgɑːlɪk $ ˈgɑrlɪk/ *noun* (no plural) a small plant like an onion with a very strong taste, used in cooking: *Your breath smells of garlic.* → see picture on page A6

gar·ment /ˈgɑːmənt $ ˈgɑrmənt/ *noun* (formal) a piece of clothing: *How should you wash woollen garments?*

gar·nish /ˈgɑːnɪʃ $ ˈgɑrnɪʃ/ *verb* to decorate food with a small piece of a fruit or vegetable: *I garnished the dessert with cherries.*

gas /gæs/ *noun*
1 (plural **gases**) any light substance like air that you usually cannot see or feel: *Carbon monoxide is a dangerous gas, produced by cars.*
2 (no plural) a substance like air that we use for cooking and heating: *I prefer to cook with gas rather than electricity.* • *a gas fire*
3 (no plural) the American word for PETROL SYNONYM **gasoline** *AmE*: *Do we have enough gas?*

gash /gæʃ/ *noun* (plural **gashes**) a deep cut in something: *She had a deep gash in her leg.* —**gash** *verb*: *I've gashed my knee.*

gas·o·line /ˈgæsəliːn/ also **gas** the American word for PETROL

gasp /gɑːsp $ gæsp/ *verb* (written) to make a short sudden noise when you breathe in, once or several times: *The crowd gasped when the horse fell.* • *She was gasping for breath when she finished the race.* —**gasp** *noun*: *Tom let out a gasp of surprise.*

ˈgas ˌstation the American word for PETROL STATION

gate /geɪt/ *noun* the part of a wall or fence that you can open like a door: *We went through the gate and into the field.* → see picture at FENCE[1]

gat·eau /ˈgætəʊ $ gɑˈtoʊ/ *noun BrE* (plural **gateaux** /-təʊz $ -ˈtoʊz/) a large cake, often filled and decorated with cream and fruit: *a piece of chocolate gateau*

gate·crash /ˈgeɪtkræʃ/ *verb* to go to a party or event that you have not been invited to: *People always gatecrash my parties.* —**gatecrasher** *noun*: *We don't want any gatecrashers.*

gate·way /ˈgeɪt-weɪ/ *noun* an opening in a fence or outside wall that can be closed with a gate

gath·er /ˈgæðə $ ˈgæðɚ/ *verb*

KEY PATTERNS
people gather at/outside a place
people gather round (someone/something)
gather things together

1 if people gather somewhere, they all come together in that place: *A large crowd had* ***gathered at*** *the scene of the accident.* • *The children* ***gathered round*** *to hear the story.*
2 also **gather things up** to collect things and put them in one place: *I* ***gathered*** *all the clothes* ***together***. • *He* ***gathered up*** *his papers and walked out.*

PHRASES
I gather (that) (spoken) someone has told me that: *I gather that Mary and Steve aren't going out together any more.*

gath·er·ing /ˈgæðərɪŋ/ *noun* (formal) a group of people meeting together for a particular purpose: *a room for private gatherings*

gau·dy /ˈgɔːdi/ *adjective* (**gaudier**, **gaudiest**) gaudy colours are too bright: *He was wearing a gaudy tie.*

gauge[1] /geɪdʒ/ *noun* an instrument that measures the amount or size of something: *The temperature gauge tells you how hot the engine is.*

gauge

gauge[2] *verb* to decide what someone is probably feeling or will probably do: *It's difficult to gauge how she's going to react.*

gaunt /gɔːnt/ *adjective* very thin and pale: *He was looking sick and gaunt.*

gave the past tense of GIVE

gay /geɪ/ *adjective* someone who is gay is sexually attracted to people of the same sex SYNONYM **homosexual** ANTONYM **heterosexual**

gaze /geɪz/ *verb* (written) to look at something for a long time: *She stood gazing at the lovely view.* —**gaze** *noun*: *Paul tried to avoid her gaze.*

gear /gɪə $ gɪr/ *noun* **1** the equipment in a car or other vehicle that turns

A B C D E F G H I J K L M N O P Q R S T U V W X Y Z

power from the engine into movement: *It is difficult to shift the gears in this car.* **2** (no plural) special equipment, clothing etc that you need for a particular activity: *I've forgotten my swimming gear.*

geek /giːk/ *noun* (informal) a boring unfashionable person, especially someone who is more interested in using computers than being with people: *Her brother is a bit of a geek. He seems to spend his whole life on the Internet.*

geese the plural of GOOSE

gel /dʒel/ *noun* a thick wet clear substance: *He used lots of hair gel.*

gem /dʒem/ *noun* a stone used in jewellery SYNONYM **jewel**: *The crown is covered with precious gems.*

gen·der /ˈdʒendə $ ˈdʒendɚ/ *noun* **1** (formal) whether someone is male or female SYNONYM **sex**: *You can't tell Jessie's gender from his name.* **2** (no plural) the system in some languages of dividing nouns, pronouns, and adjectives into MASCULINE, FEMININE, or NEUTER

gene /dʒiːn/ *noun* a part of a CELL in a living thing that controls what it will be like. Parents pass on genes to their children

gen·e·ral¹ /ˈdʒenərəl/ *adjective* **1** relating to the main parts of something: *This book should give you a general idea of the subject.* • *We began with a general discussion of the problems.* • *a general knowledge test* **2** including most or all people: *At the meeting, there was general agreement on what should be done.* • *The new medicine will soon be available for general use.*

PHRASES

in general used to talk about what usually happens or what is usually true: ***In general**, April is a wetter month than May.*

general² *noun* an officer with a very high rank in an army, AIR FORCE, or navy: *General Eisenhower*

ˌgeneral eˈlection *noun* an election in which all the voters in a country choose a government: *The Labour Party won the general election.*

gen·e·ral·i·za·tion also **generalisation** *BrE* /ˌdʒenərəlaɪˈzeɪʃən $ ˌdʒenərələˈzeɪʃən/ *noun* a statement about all people or things of a particular kind, which may not be true about every one: *It is silly to make generalizations about all students.*

gen·er·al·ly /ˈdʒenərəli/ *adverb* usually or mostly: *The food at that restaurant is generally quite good.* • *It is generally accepted that too much fat is bad for you.*

gen·e·rate /ˈdʒenəreɪt/ *verb* (formal) **1** to make something happen or start SYNONYM **create**: *The violence generated a lot of fear.* **2** to produce heat, electricity, or power: *Even small fires generate a lot of heat.*

gen·e·ra·tion /ˌdʒenəˈreɪʃən/ *noun* all the people who are about the same age: *People of my father's generation don't know much about computers.*

gen·e·ros·i·ty /ˌdʒenəˈrɒsəti $ ˌdʒenəˈrɑsəti/ *noun* (no plural) when you willingly give a lot of money to someone: *We appreciate your generosity.*

gen·e·rous /ˈdʒenərəs/ *adjective*

> **KEY PATTERNS**
> **it is generous of someone to do something**
> **be generous to someone**

someone who is generous gives a lot of money, presents, or help to other people ANTONYM **stingy**, **mean** *BrE*: ***It** was really **generous of** Jack **to** take us all on holiday.* • *My parents **have** always **been** very **generous to** me.*
—**generously** *adverb*: *All the bands generously gave the money from the concert to a charity.*

ge·net·ic /dʒəˈnetɪk/ *adjective* related to or caused by GENES: *Heart disease is sometimes a genetic condition.*

geˌnetically ˈmodified (abbreviation **GM**) *adjective* genetically modified plants have received GENES from another plant in a scientific process: *These burgers contain genetically modified soya.*

ge·net·ics /dʒəˈnetɪks/ *plural noun* the study of GENES

gen·i·tals /ˈdʒenətlz/ also **gen·i·ta·lia** /ˌdʒenəˈteɪljə/ *plural noun* (formal) the parts on the outside of your body that are used for having sex and producing babies

ge·ni·us /ˈdʒiːniəs/ *noun* (plural **geniuses**) someone who is very intelligent: *Einstein was a genius.*

gen·tle /ˈdʒentl/ *adjective*

KEY PATTERNS
be gentle with someone/something

1 a gentle person is kind and calm, and treats people and things carefully ANTONYM **rough**: *You have to* ***be*** *very* ***gentle with*** *young animals.*
2 not strong, loud, or rough: *There was some gentle music playing in the background.* • *a gentle breeze*
—**gently** *adverb*: *"You mustn't worry," she said gently.*

WORD CHOICE
gentle or **kind**?
• **Gentle** means "treating people and things carefully so that you do not hurt or damage them": *Please be gentle with the baby.*
• **Kind** means "caring about other people and wanting to help them": *He was very* ***kind*** *to us when we were young.*

gen·tle·man /ˈdʒentlmən/ *noun* (plural **gentlemen** /-mən/) a polite word that you can use when talking about a man: *This gentleman is Mr Wright.*

gents /dʒents/ *noun* **the gents** *BrE* a room in a public building where there are toilets for men SYNONYM **men's room** *AmE*

gen·u·ine /ˈdʒenjuɪn/ *adjective* something that is genuine is real, not pretended, false, or imagined: *Is that a genuine antique?* • *a genuine apology*

ge·og·ra·phy /dʒiˈɒgrəfi $ dʒiˈɑgrəfi/ *noun* (no plural) the study of the countries of the world, including their land, rivers, and cities

ge·ol·o·gy /dʒiˈɒlədʒi $ dʒiˈɑlədʒi/ *noun* (no plural) the study of materials such as rocks and soil

ge·o·met·ric /ˌdʒiːəˈmetrɪk/ also **ge·o·met·ric·al** /ˌdʒiːəˈmetrɪkəl/ *adjective* **1** a geometric shape or pattern has regular sides, lines, or shapes: *The rugs have geometric designs.* **2** related to geometry

ge·om·e·try /dʒiˈɒmətri $ dʒiˈɑmətri/ *noun* (no plural) the study of lines and shapes in mathematics

geranium /dʒəˈreɪniəm/ *noun* a plant with pink, red, or white flowers, which is often grown in gardens → see picture on page A10

germ /dʒɜːm $ dʒɝm/ *noun* a very small living thing that can make you ill: *This cleaning fluid kills all household germs.*

Ger·man mea·sles /ˌdʒɜːmən ˈmiːzəlz $ ˌdʒɝmən ˈmizəlz/ *noun* (no plural) a disease that causes red spots on your body: *Sam's got German measles.*

ger·mi·nate /ˈdʒɜːməneɪt $ ˈdʒɝməˌneɪt/ *verb* if a seed germinates, it begins to grow

ger·und /ˈdʒerənd/ *noun* a noun with the same form as the PRESENT PARTICIPLE of a verb, for example 'reading' in the sentence 'He enjoys reading.'

ges·ture[1] /ˈdʒestʃə $ ˈdʒestʃɚ/ *noun* **1** a movement of your head, arm, or hand that shows what you mean or how you feel: *He made a gesture towards the door to show it was time to leave.* **2** something you do to show that you care about someone or something: *It would be a nice gesture if we paid for her meal.*

gesture[2] *verb* to tell someone something by moving your arms, hands, or head: *I gestured to my friend to come inside.*

get → see box on pages 278 and 279

get·a·way /ˈgetəweɪ/ *noun* **make a getaway** to escape quickly from a place, especially after doing something illegal: *The robbers made a quick getaway after stealing the money.*

ˈget-toˌgether *noun* a friendly informal meeting or party: *We're having a family get-together tomorrow.*
→ see Thesaurus at PARTY[1]

ghast·ly /ˈgɑːstli $ ˈgæstli/ *adjective* very unpleasant SYNONYM **dreadful**: *I couldn't eat the food there – it was ghastly.*

A B C D E F G H I J K L M N O P Q R S T U V W X Y Z

get /get/ *verb* (past tense **got** /gɒt/, past participle **got** *BrE*, **gotten** *AmE* /ˈgɒtn $ ˈgɑːtn/, present participle **getting**)

1 to buy or obtain something: *Where did you **get** that shirt? • She wants to **get** a new job. • I **got** him a present. • Can you **get** some milk for me when you go to the shop?*

KEY PATTERNS
get something
get someone something
get something for someone

2 to receive something: *He **gets** lots of emails. • What did you **get** for your birthday?*

3 used in passives: *The thief **got caught** by the police. • My feet **got stuck** in the mud.*

4 to become: *It's **getting cold** outside. • Please don't **get angry** with me.*

5 to arrive somewhere: *We **got to** the airport at eight. • What time do you usually **get** home?*

KEY PATTERNS
get to your hotel/the station
get home/here/there/back

6 to bring someone or something SYNONYM **fetch**: *Can someone **get** a doctor? • I'll go and **get** you something to drink.*

7 to move somewhere: *He **got off** his chair. • How did they **get into** the house?*

8 to travel on a train, bus, plane etc SYNONYM **catch**, **take**: *I **got** the bus into town.*

9 to catch a disease: *I think I'm **getting** a cold.*

10 to make someone do something for you: *She **got** him to lower the price. • I need to **get** my hair cut* (=have someone cut my hair for me).

KEY PATTERNS
get someone to do something (for you)
get your hair cut/your car fixed etc

11 to understand someone or something: *I don't **get** what you mean.*

PHRASAL VERBS

get away
to leave a place or person: *I need to **get away from** the city for a while.*

get away with
to not be punished for something bad that you have done: *He thinks he can cheat and **get away with** it.*

get back
to return somewhere: *I'll call her as soon as I **get back**.* • *They've just **got back** from Japan.*

get in/into
1 to arrive at a place: *My plane **gets in** at 7.30.* • *The train **gets into** Paris early in the afternoon.*
2 to go into a place or a car: *She **got into** her car and drove off.* • *The hall was full and we couldn't **get in**.*

get off
to leave a bus, train, plane, or large boat: *Be careful **getting off** the bus.*

get on
1 also **get onto** to walk onto a bus, train, or plane: *I **got on** the wrong bus.*

get on

get off

2 *BrE* to be friendly with someone: *We **get on** really well.* • *I never **got on** with Jeremy's sister.*

get out
1 to leave or move from a place: *How did the dogs **get out** of the yard?* • ***Get out** of the way!*
2 to leave a car, taxi, boat etc: *He fell into the water as he was **getting out** of the boat.*

get out of
to succeed in not doing something that you do not want to do, even though you ought to do it: *He's trying to **get out of** tidying his room.*

get over
to feel better again after you have had an illness, or something bad has happened to you SYNONYM **recover from**: *It took me a long time to **get over** my cold.*

get through
1 to be able to speak to someone on the telephone: *I can't **get through** to his office.*

*I can't **get through** to his office.*

2 to finish something: *I still have a lot of work to **get through**.*
3 to use a lot of something: *We **get through** so much paper!*

get together (informal)
to meet: *Let's **get together** some time for a meal.*

get up
1 to wake up and move out of bed: *He has to **get up** at seven a.m. every morning.*

*He has to **get up** at seven a.m. every morning.*

2 to stand up: *Lisa **got up** and made a cup of tea.*

ghet·to /ˈgetəʊ $ ˈgetoʊ/ *noun* (plural **ghettos** or **ghettoes**) a part of a city where people of a particular race or class live, usually in bad conditions: *He came from the ghettos of New York.*

ghost /gəʊst $ goʊst/ *noun* the SPIRIT of a dead person that some people believe they can see: *I don't believe in ghosts.*

gi·ant¹ /ˈdʒaɪənt/ *adjective* much larger than other things of the same type: *The band performed on a giant stage.*

giant² *noun* an extremely tall strong man in children's stories

gib·ber·ish /ˈdʒɪbərɪʃ/ *noun* (no plural) things someone says or writes that have no meaning or are difficult to understand: *I tried to read the instruction book, but it was all gibberish.*

gibe another spelling of JIBE

gid·dy /ˈgɪdi/ *adjective* (**giddier**, **giddiest**) feeling unable to stand up very well, for example because you have been turning round SYNONYM **dizzy**: *If you feel giddy while exercising, then stop.*

gift /gɪft/ *noun*

KEY PATTERNS
a gift for/from someone
a gift for languages/maths etc

1 something that you give to someone as a present: *Did you* ***give*** *your mother* ***a gift****? • People* ***exchange gifts*** *at Christmas. • We received a beautiful wedding* ***gift from*** *Lisa.*
2 a natural ability to do something SYNONYM **talent**: *Sam has a great* ***gift for*** *acting.*

gift·ed /ˈgɪftɪd/ *adjective* very intelligent or having a natural ability to do something very well: *a school for gifted children • Paul's a very gifted artist.*

gig /gɪg/ *noun* (informal) a popular music or JAZZ concert

gi·gan·tic /dʒaɪˈgæntɪk/ *adjective* very big SYNONYM **huge**: *He was eating a gigantic ice cream.*

gig·gle /ˈgɪgəl/ *verb* to laugh in a silly way, especially because you are nervous or embarrassed: *The little girls wouldn't stop giggling.* ➔ see Thesaurus at LAUGH¹ —**giggle** *noun*: *I could hear giggles coming from the back of the class.*

gim·mick /ˈgɪmɪk/ *noun* something unusual that is used to make people interested in something: *The news story was just a gimmick to sell more tickets.*

gin /dʒɪn/ *noun* (no plural) a strong clear alcoholic drink: *Her favourite drink is gin and tonic.*

gin·ger¹ /ˈdʒɪndʒə $ ˈdʒɪndʒər/ *noun* (no plural) a light brown root with a strong hot taste, used in cooking

ginger² *adjective BrE* hair or fur that is ginger is bright orange-brown in colour: *a ginger cat*

gin·ger·ly /ˈdʒɪndʒəli $ ˈdʒɪndʒərli/ *adverb* (written) slowly, carefully, and gently: *She stepped gingerly onto the ice.*

gipsy a British spelling of GYPSY

gi·raffe /dʒɪˈrɑːf $ dʒəˈræf/ *noun* a tall animal that has a very long neck and dark areas on its fur, and lives in Africa ➔ see picture on page A9

gir·der /ˈgɜːdə $ ˈgɜrdər/ *noun* a long thick piece of iron or steel, used to build bridges or buildings: *Huge iron girders held up the roof.*

girl /gɜːl $ gɜrl/ *noun* a female child: *Lots of girls like riding horses.*

girl·friend /ˈgɜːlfrend $ ˈgɜrlfrend/ *noun* a girl or woman with whom you have a romantic relationship: *Has Steve got a girlfriend?*

SPELLING
This word is often spelled wrongly. The correct spelling is: **girlfriend**.

gist /dʒɪst/ *noun* the main points or general meaning of what someone says or writes: *I understood the gist of what he was saying.*

give ➔ see box on page 281

give·a·way /ˈgɪvəweɪ/ *noun* **be a giveaway, be a dead giveaway** to make it very easy for someone to know that something is true: *I knew it was Joe on the phone – the deep voice was a dead giveaway.*

given the past participle of GIVE

ˈgiven name an American word for FIRST NAME: *His given name is Simon.*

give /gɪv/ *verb* (past tense **gave** /geɪv/, past participle **given** /ˈgɪvən/)

give

1 to put something into someone's hand: *I gave him the car keys.* • *Ken **gave** the bags **to** Ellen.*

2 to let someone have something, especially as a present: *What are you **giving** Sophie for her birthday?* • *Companies often **give** money **to** political parties.*

GRAMMAR
• You **give someone a present** or **give a present to someone.**
✗ Don't say 'give to someone a present'.

3 to do something by making a movement of your hand, body etc: *She **gave a smile** when she opened the present.* • *Danny **gave** her a big **hug**.* • *He picked up the parcel and **gave** it a **shake**.*

4 to make someone have something: ***Give** me some time to think about it.* • *The constant noise was **giving** me a headache.* • *The judge **gave** him five years in prison.*

5 to tell someone something: *Will you please **give** your name **to** the secretary?* • ***Give** the doctor as much information as possible.*

PHRASES

give (someone) some advice/an explanation to provide advice or an explanation
give someone a call to telephone someone
give a concert/performance to play music or perform in public
give someone some help to help someone
give someone a lift to take someone somewhere in your car
give a party to organize a party
give someone permission to allow someone to do something
give a speech/talk/lecture to talk about something to a group of people

PHRASAL VERBS

give away
to give something to someone else, without asking for money: *The radio station is **giving away** 20 tickets to the concert.* • *"What happened to the furniture?" "We **gave** it all **away**."*

give back
to return something to the person who owns it: *I'll **give** you **back** your essays on Monday.* • *He took the twenty dollar bill and **gave back** the change.*

give in
to finally agree to do something that you did not want to do: *He kept asking for a dog until his parents **gave in** and bought him one.*

give out
to give something to each person in a group: *The teacher **gave out** the books to the class.* • *The bakery would not **give** the cookie recipe **out** to its customers.*

give up
to stop doing something: *I had almost **given up** hope.* • *Andy had to **give up** tennis when he hurt his knee.* • *Carol tries really hard – she doesn't **give up** easily.*

gla·ci·er /ˈglæsiə $ ˈgleɪʃɚ/ *noun* a large amount of ice that moves slowly down a mountain

glad /glæd/ *adjective*

KEY PATTERNS
glad (that)
glad to do something

if you are glad, you are pleased and happy about something: *I'm **glad that** Mark decided to come with us.* • *My parents **were very glad to** see me at last.* ➔ see Thesaurus at HAPPY

glad·ly /ˈglædli/ *adverb* willingly: *I'll gladly help you.*

glam·or·ous /ˈglæmərəs/ *adjective* more attractive and exciting than ordinary people or things: *a glamorous supermodel*

glam·our *BrE*, **glamor** *AmE* /ˈglæmə $ ˈglæmɚ/ *noun* (no plural) the quality of being attractive and exciting, and connected with wealth or success: *I love the glamour of Hollywood.*

glance /glɑːns $ glæns/ *verb* to look at someone or something for a short time: *He glanced towards the door.* —**glance** *noun*: *We exchanged glances* (=glanced at each other).

gland /glænd/ *noun* a small part of the body that produces a liquid, such as SWEAT or SALIVA: *The glands in her neck are swollen.*

glare¹ /gleə $ gler/ *verb* to look at someone or something in an angry way, usually for a long time: *The farmer glared at the men who were walking across his land.*

glare² *noun* **1** a bright unpleasant light which hurts your eyes: *the glare of the sun* **2** a long angry look: *She gave him an angry glare.*

glar·ing /ˈgleərɪŋ $ ˈglerɪŋ/ *adjective* bad and very easy to notice SYNONYM **obvious**: *The article in the newspaper was full of glaring mistakes.*

glass /glɑːs $ glæs/ *noun*
1 (no plural) a clear hard material that we use for making windows, bottles etc: *The ball hit the window and broke the glass.* • *a glass bowl*
2 (plural **glasses**) a cup with no handle that is made of glass: *Could you put the glasses on the table?* • *a wine glass* • *I'd like a **glass of** lemonade, please.*

glass·es /ˈglɑːsɪz $ ˈglæsɪz/ *plural noun* two pieces of special glass in a plastic or metal frame which you wear in front of your eyes to help you see better SYNONYM **spectacles**: *You might need to wear glasses.* • *a pair of glasses*

glaze /gleɪz/ also **glaze over** *verb* if your eyes glaze or glaze over, they show no expression because you are bored or tired: *As soon as he mentioned football, her eyes started to glaze over.*

gleam /gliːm/ *verb* to shine softly: *She washed the car until it was gleaming.* ➔ see Thesaurus at SHINE

glean /gliːn/ *verb* to find out information slowly and with difficulty: *It's difficult to glean any information from Dan.*

glide /glaɪd/ *verb* to move smoothly, quietly, and without effort: *The swan glided through the water.*

glim·mer /ˈglɪmə $ ˈglɪmɚ/ *verb* (written) to shine with a light that is not very bright or steady: *They could see his flashlight glimmering in the distance.* —**glimmer** *noun*: *the glimmer of street lights*

glimpse /glɪmps/ *verb* to see something for a very short time, or not completely: *I only glimpsed her face.* —**glimpse** *noun*: *He caught a glimpse of the man* (=glimpsed the man) *as he drove away.*

glint /glɪnt/ *verb* (written) if something glints, one or more flashes of light come from it: *His glasses glinted in the light.* —**glint** *noun*: *the glint of sunlight on the sea*

glis·ten /ˈglɪsən/ *verb* (written) to shine because of being wet or oily: *His face glistened with sweat.*

glit·ter /ˈglɪtə $ ˈglɪtɚ/ *verb* (written) to shine with a lot of small flashes of light SYNONYM **sparkle**: *The sand on the beach glittered in the sunshine.* ➔ see Thesaurus at SHINE —**glitter** *noun* (no plural): *the glitter of the Christmas decorations*

A B C D E F G H I J K L M N O P Q R S T U V W X Y Z

gloat /gləʊt $ gloʊt/ *verb* to show in an annoying way that you are happy about your success or about someone else's failure: *He keeps gloating about his new car.*

glo·bal /ˈgləʊbəl $ ˈgloʊbəl/ *adjective* affecting or including the whole world SYNONYM **worldwide**: *Pollution is a global problem.*

glo·bal·i·za·tion /ˌgləʊbəlaɪˈzeɪʃən $ ˌgloʊbələˈzeɪʃən/ *noun* the process in which countries all over the world are becoming connected with each other and similar to each other, because of the development of trade and communication: *Countries such as China and India have changed a lot because of globalization.*

ˌglobal ˈwarming *noun* (no plural) an increase in world temperatures, caused by an increase of CARBON DIOXIDE around the Earth: *Maybe the warmer weather is caused by global warming.*

globe /gləʊb $ gloʊb/ *noun* a round object with a map of the Earth drawn on it

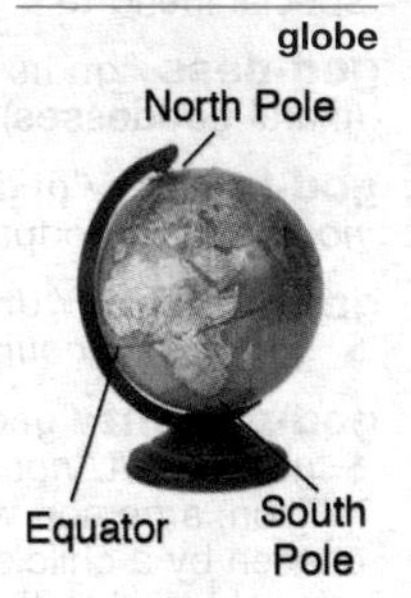

gloom /gluːm/ *noun* (no plural) almost complete darkness: *I could see almost nothing in the gloom of the tunnel.*

gloom·y /ˈgluːmi/ *adjective* (**gloomier**, **gloomiest**) **1** feeling sad because you do not have a lot of hope: *Why are you so gloomy today?* **2** dark, especially in a way that seems sad: *It was dark and gloomy in the cellar.*

glo·ri·ous /ˈglɔːriəs/ *adjective* **1** very successful: *He left the team after twelve glorious years.* **2** very enjoyable or beautiful: *It was a glorious summer's day.*

glo·ry /ˈglɔːri/ *noun* praise and honour that someone gets because of something good they have done: *the glory of an Olympic victory*

glos·sa·ry /ˈglɒsəri $ ˈglɑsəri/ *noun* (plural **glossaries**) a list of unusual words and what they mean, printed at the end of a book: *a glossary of technical terms*

gloss·y /ˈglɒsi $ ˈglɔsi/ *adjective* (**glossier**, **glossiest**) shiny and smooth: *a small dog with glossy black fur*

glove /glʌv/ *noun* gloves are pieces of clothing that you wear on your hands, which have separate parts for each finger: *I must buy a new pair of gloves.*

glow¹ /gləʊ $ gloʊ/ *noun* a soft light, for example from something that is burning gently: *A fire was burning, giving the whole room a warm glow.*

glow² *verb* to produce a soft light: *It was dark except for one small lamp glowing in the corner.* → see Thesaurus at SHINE

glow·er /ˈglaʊə $ ˈglaʊɚ/ *verb* (written) to look at someone in an angry way SYNONYM **glare**: *I started to speak but Chris glowered at me, so I stopped.*

glow·ing /ˈgləʊɪŋ $ ˈgloʊɪŋ/ *adjective* a glowing report, description etc praises someone or something a lot: *Geoff got a glowing report from his teachers last term.*

glue¹ /gluː/ *noun* a sticky substance that you use to join things together

glue² *verb* (**gluing** or **glueing**) **1** to join things together using glue SYNONYM **stick**: *I tried to glue the broken pieces back together again.* **2 be glued to something** (informal) to be watching something, especially television, with all your attention: *It was five o'clock and the kids were glued to the television.*

A B C D E F G H I J K L M N O P Q R S T U V W X Y Z

glum /glʌm/ *adjective* (**glummer**, **glummest**) sad or disappointed: *Don't look so glum!*

glut /glʌt/ *noun* too many things of the same kind coming at the same time SYNONYM **surplus** ANTONYM **shortage**: *There's a glut of violent American films around at the moment.*

gm a written abbreviation for GRAM

gnaw /nɔː/ *verb* to bite something many times in order to break part of it off or make a hole in it SYNONYM **chew**: *A dog was gnawing at a bone out in the yard.*

go[1] → see box on pages 286 and 287

go[2] /gəʊ $ goʊ/ *noun* (plural **goes**) **1 have a go, give something a go** to try doing something: *I'd never been skiing before, but I decided to have a go.* → see Thesaurus at TRY[1] **2 your go** your turn to play in a game, try to do something etc: *"It's my go now!" Billy shouted.*

'go-ahead *noun* **give someone the go-ahead** (informal) to give someone official permission to start doing something: *The council gave them the go-ahead to build the new stadium.*

goal /gəʊl $ goʊl/ *noun* **1** the space between two posts into which you try to kick or hit the ball in some sports, for example football **2** a point that you win when the ball goes into the goal: *The Russians scored three goals in sixteen minutes.* **3** something that you hope to achieve: *Our goal is to make this the best school in the country.* → see Thesaurus at PURPOSE

goal·ie /'gəʊli $ 'goʊli/ *noun* (informal) a GOALKEEPER

goal·keep·er /'gəʊlˌkiːpə $ 'goʊlˌkipɚ/ *BrE*, **goal·tend·er** /'gəʊlˌtendə $ 'goʊlˌtendɚ/ *AmE noun* the player in a sports team who tries to stop the ball from going into the goal

goal·post /'gəʊlpəʊst $ 'goʊlpoʊst/ *noun* one of the two posts on each side of the goal in games such as football

goat /gəʊt $ goʊt/ *noun* a farm animal with horns that has long hair under its chin → see picture on page A8

gob·ble /'gɒbəl $ 'gɑbəl/ also **gobble up** *verb* to eat something very quickly SYNONYM **bolt**: *Matt gobbled up his dinner and ran back outside.*

gob·lin /'gɒblɪn $ 'gɑblɪn/ *noun* a small ugly creature in children's stories, who often does bad things

go-cart an American spelling of GO-KART

god /gɒd $ gɑd/ *noun* **1 God** in some religions, the maker and ruler of the world: *She prayed to God for help.* **2** any force that people pray to and consider to be powerful: *In the past, the sun was worshipped as a god.* **3 God, my God** (spoken) used to express strong feelings of surprise, anger etc, in a way that offends some people

god·child /'gɒdtʃaɪld $ 'gɑdtʃaɪld/ *noun* (plural **godchildren** /-ˌtʃɪldrən/) in the Christian religion, a person's godchild is a child they will be a special friend to

god·dess /'gɒdɪs $ 'gɑdɪs/ *noun* (plural **goddesses**) a female god

god·fa·ther /'gɒdˌfɑːðə $ 'gɑdˌfɑðɚ/ *noun* a male godparent

god·moth·er /'gɒdˌmʌðə $ 'gɑdˌmʌðɚ/ *noun* a female godparent

god·pa·rent /'gɒdˌpeərənt $ 'gɑdˌperənt/ *noun* in the Christian religion, a person who has been chosen by a child's parents to be a special friend to that child

goes the third person singular of the present tense of GO

gog·gles /'gɒgəlz $ 'gɑgəlz/ *plural noun* large glasses that fit close to your face and protect your eyes: *You should wear goggles when cutting metal.*

go·ing[1] /'gəʊɪŋ $ 'goʊɪŋ/ *noun* **be good going, be slow going** (informal) to take a shorter time to do than usual, or a longer time to do than usual: *The journey only took two hours, which was very good going.*

going[2] *adjective* **the going rate** the usual amount that you have to pay for a service or that you get for doing a job: *What's the going rate for private lessons at the moment?*

ˌ**goings-ˈon** *plural noun* (informal) things that happen which are strange or interesting SYNONYM **happenings**: *There have been some interesting goings-on at the house next door.*

go-kart *BrE*, also **go-cart** *AmE* /ˈgəʊ kɑːt $ ˈgoʊ kɑrt/ *noun* a low vehicle with no roof and a small engine that people use in races for fun

gold¹ /gəʊld $ goʊld/ *noun* (no plural) a valuable yellow metal that is used for making jewellery, coins etc

gold

a gold ring

gold² *adjective* **1** made of gold: *a gold ring* **2** having the colour of gold: *a gold dress*

gold·en /ˈgəʊldən $ ˈgoʊldən/ *adjective* (written) **1** having a bright yellow colour: *Shelley was tall with long golden hair.* **2** made of gold: *a golden cup*

gold·fish /ˈgəʊldˌfɪʃ $ ˈgoʊldˌfɪʃ/ *noun* (plural **goldfish**) a small orange fish that people often keep as a pet ➔ see picture on page A8

golf /gɒlf $ gɑlf/ *noun* (no plural) a game in which you try to hit a small white ball into holes in the ground with a special stick called a CLUB

ˈ**golf course** *noun* an area of land where people play golf

gone the past participle of GO

good¹ ➔ see box on page 288

good² *noun* **1 be no good, do no good** to not improve a situation or not achieve anything: *I tried to start the car but it was no good – the battery was flat.* • *Complaining doesn't do any good.* **2 be no good, not be much good** to not work well, or not be of a good standard: *Can I borrow your pen? This one's no good any more.* • *I'm not much good at sport.* **3 for good** if something happens for good, the situation will not change back again SYNONYM **for ever**: *Has she stopped working for good?* **4** what is right, compared with what is bad and wrong: *our ideas of good and evil* **5 goods** (formal) things that are made for people to buy: *The shop sells a range of household goods.*

good ˌafterˈnoon used when you meet someone in the afternoon: *Good afternoon, sir.*

good·bye /gʊdˈbaɪ/ used when someone is leaving: *Goodbye Chris! See you Monday.*

good ˈevening used when you meet someone in the evening: *Good evening, everybody, and welcome!*

ˌ**good-ˈlooking** *adjective* someone who is good-looking is attractive to look at: *a very good-looking man* ➔ see Thesaurus at ATTRACTIVE

good ˈmorning used when you meet someone in the morning: *Good morning, class.*

good night, **good·night** /gʊdˈnaɪt/ used at night when someone is leaving or when they are going to bed: *Good night. Sleep well.*

goo·ey /ˈguːi/ *adjective* (informal) (**gooier**, **gooiest**) sticky and soft, and usually sweet: *a gooey chocolate cake*

goof /guːf/ also **goof up** *verb AmE* (informal) to make a silly mistake: *Sorry, I've goofed again!*

goof·y /ˈguːfi/ *adjective* (informal) (**goofier**, **goofiest**) stupid or silly: *Robby looked at me with a goofy expression.*

goose

goose duck

goose /guːs/ *noun* (plural **geese** /giːs/) a water bird that is like a duck but bigger

gorge /gɔːdʒ $ gɔrdʒ/ *noun* a very narrow valley with steep sides, sometimes with water flowing along the bottom: *The railway runs through a beautiful gorge.*

go[1] /gəʊ $ goʊ/ *verb* (past tense **went** /went/, past participle **gone** /gɒn $ gɔːn/ or **been** /biːn, bɪn $ bɪn/, third person singular **goes**)

1 to move from one place to another: *She* ***went to*** *Paris to study French.* • *To get to his office,* ***go through*** *that door and turn left.* • *The little boy wanted to* ***go home****.* • *"Where's Jim?" "He's* ***gone*** *to buy some milk."*

GRAMMAR

gone to or **been to**?

• You use **gone to** when saying that someone has gone to a place and has not come back: *"Where's Sarah?" "She's* ***gone to*** *the library."*

• You use **been to** when saying that someone has visited a place and come back from there: *I've* ***been to*** *Paris many times.*

GRAMMAR

• You say **go home** or **go back home**.

✗ Don't say 'go to home' or 'go back my home'.

• You say **go there**.

✗ Don't say 'go to there'.

2 go shopping/swimming/skiing etc to go somewhere in order to buy things, to swim, to ski etc: *Ken and Tina* ***are going skiing*** *in France.* • *We* ***went shopping*** *and found some great clothes.* • *We* ***went camping*** *in the mountains.*

GRAMMAR

• You say **go skiing**.

✗ Don't say 'go to ski'.

3 go for a walk/swim/drive etc to go somewhere in order to walk, swim, drive etc: *We* ***went for a*** *short* ***walk*** *after dinner.* • *Karen and I are* ***going for a swim*** *in the lake.*

4 go to school/class/church etc to go somewhere in order to take part in something that you do regularly SYNONYM **attend**: *Jenny* ***goes to*** *dance lessons every Monday.* • *I've been* ***going to*** *my French class since September.*

5 go deaf/grey/dark etc to become deaf, grey, dark etc: *Beethoven* ***went deaf*** *when he was 40 years old.* • *Her hair has* ***gone*** *completely white.* • *David* ***is going bald****.*

6 go well/badly/fine to happen in a particular way: *His speech* ***went well****.* • *What* ***went wrong****?* • *"How did the game* ***go****?" "We lost."*

7 used when saying where you usually put something: *The washing powder* ***goes in*** *the cupboard under the sink.* • *Where do these cups* ***go****?*

8 to disappear: *The pain has* ***gone****.*

9 to lead somewhere: *Does this road* ***go to*** *the airport?*

10 to look good or taste good with another thing: *The tie* ***goes with*** *the shirt.* • *Strawberries and cream* ***go well together****.*

PHRASES

go and do something also **go do something** *AmE* (spoken)
to move somewhere in order to do something: *Please* ***go and sit down*** *at your desks.* • *Let's* ***go see*** *a movie.*

be going to do something
used when saying that something seems certain to happen, or someone has definite plans to do something: *It's* ***going to*** *rain tomorrow.* • *Are you* ***going to*** *play basketball tonight?*

to go (spoken)
used in a restaurant when ordering food that you will take away with you: *I want a burger and fries* ***to go****.*

How's it going?/How are things going? (spoken, informal)
say this to say hello and ask someone how they are: *"Hi, Ken,* ***how's it going****?" "Fine, thanks, how about you?"*

PHRASAL VERBS

go away
to leave a place or person – used especially when you are angry or upset: ***Go away****! Can't you see that I'm busy?*

go back
to return to a place: *I* ***went back to*** *the car to get my bag.*

go down
1 when the sun goes down, you can no longer see it in the sky at the end of the day SYNONYM **set** ANTONYM **come up**: *The sun doesn't* ***go down*** *until ten o'clock in the summertime.*
2 to become lower in amount, price, level etc SYNONYM **fall**, **decrease** ANTONYM **go up**: *The number of students in the school has* ***gone down****.*

go off
1 to suddenly make a loud noise or explode: *The alarm clock* ***went off*** *at eight a.m.* • *A bomb* ***went off*** *in the city centre.*
2 if food or drink goes off, it becomes bad and you cannot eat or drink it: *The milk has* ***gone off****.*
3 to stop liking something: *I've* ***gone off*** *chocolate.*

go on
1 to continue: *I wanted to* ***go on*** *learning French after I left school.* • *The meeting* ***went on*** *for a lot longer than I expected.*
2 to happen: *What's* ***going on*** *in the next room? Who's making all that noise?*

go out
1 to leave your house to do something: *I'm* ***going out*** *for dinner with Lucy.* • *Did you* ***go out*** *last Friday?*

Did you ***go out*** *last Friday?*

2 to have a romantic relationship with someone: *She started* ***going out*** *with him when she was 16.* • *They've only been* ***going out*** *for a month.*

go through
1 to check something carefully: *The customs officer* ***went through*** *all my things.*
2 to experience something very bad SYNONYM **endure**: *She has* ***been through*** *a lot this year.*

go up
to become higher in level, price, amount etc SYNONYM **rise**, **increase** ANTONYM **go down**: *School fees have* ***gone up****.*

good /gʊd/ *adjective* (**better** /ˈbetə $ ˈbetɚ/, **best** /best/)

KEY PATTERNS
it is good to do something
good at (doing) something
good for someone
good to someone
it is good of someone to do something kind

good

1 of a high standard or quality ANTONYM **bad**: *I love wearing really **good** clothes.* • *This is the **best** hotel in the town.*

2 enjoyable or pleasant ANTONYM **bad**: *Did you have a **good** holiday?* • *I've got some **good** news!* • *It's really **good** to be home.*

3 someone who is good at something can do it well ANTONYM **bad**: *She's **very good** at her job, isn't she?* • *Martin is a **better** driver than I am.*

4 useful or suitable ANTONYM **bad**: *That's a **good** idea!* • *It's a **good** day for going to the park.*

5 someone who is good behaves well or tries to do what is right ANTONYM **bad**: *"You've all been very **good** today," our teacher said.* • *Mr Hardy was a **good**, kind man.*

6 something that is good for you makes your body or mind healthy ANTONYM **bad**: *Fresh air and exercise are **good for** you.*

7 if you are good to someone, you are kind to them, especially when they need help: *Everyone **was** very **good to** me when my husband died.* • ***It's good of** you **to** call.*

THESAURUS
great: *The party on Saturday was **great*** (=very good or enjoyable).
excellent: *She said my English homework was **excellent*** (=very good in quality).
wonderful: *We had a really **wonderful** holiday* (=very good and special).
fantastic/brilliant (informal): *My new computer game is **brilliant*** (=extremely good and enjoyable)*!*

WORD CHOICE
good or **well**?
• You use the adjective **good** to describe a person or thing: *She's a **good** player.*
• You use the adverb **well** to describe how someone does something: *She can play really **well**.*

PHRASES
good, that's good
*"There's another bus in five minutes." "Oh, **good*** (=I am pleased about that)*."*
feel bad
*"My exams start tomorrow." "**Good luck*** (=I hope you will be successful)*!"*

gor·geous /ˈɡɔːdʒəs $ ˈɡɔrdʒəs/ *adjective* (informal) very beautiful or pleasant: *Carlo was gorgeous, with dark hair and eyes.* • *It's a gorgeous day – let's have a picnic!* → see Thesaurus at ATTRACTIVE

go·ril·la /ɡəˈrɪlə/ *noun* a very large strong animal that looks like a monkey

gor·y /ˈɡɔːri/ *adjective* (**gorier**, **goriest**) a gory film, story etc has a lot of violence in it: *The ending was too gory for me.*

gos·sip¹ /ˈɡɒsɪp $ ˈɡɑsəp/ *noun* things that people say about other people's behaviour or private lives, especially things that may not be true: *I heard some gossip about Mary, but I don't believe it.*

gossip² *verb* to talk about other people's behaviour and private lives, especially in a way that is not kind: *They were gossiping about Lucy's new boyfriend.*

got the past tense and a past participle of GET

got·ten the usual American past participle of GET

gour·met /ˈɡʊəmeɪ $ ɡʊrˈmeɪ/ *noun* someone who enjoys good food and drink —**gourmet** *adjective*: *gourmet food shops*

gov·ern /ˈɡʌvən $ ˈɡʌvən/ *verb* to officially control a country or state: *The people decide who will govern the country.*

gov·ern·ment /ˈɡʌvəmənt $ ˈɡʌvəmənt/ *noun* the group of people who govern a country: *The new government promised not to increase taxes.* • *a socialist government* • *What will the government do to help the poorest people in society?*

SPELLING
This word is often spelled wrongly. The correct spelling is **government**.

gov·er·nor /ˈɡʌvənə $ ˈɡʌvənə/ *noun* **1** a person who officially controls a state, especially in the US: *the governor of Alabama* **2** a person or a member of a group of people that controls an organization: *a meeting of the school governors*

gown /ɡaʊn/ *noun* a long dress for special occasions: *She wore a pink silk gown.*

gown

GP /ˌdʒiː ˈpiː/ *noun* *BrE* a doctor who treats people for ordinary health problems: *You should go and see your GP.* → see Thesaurus at DOCTOR

grab /ɡræb/ *verb* (**grabbed**, **grabbing**) to suddenly take or hold something roughly and with force SYNONYM **seize**: *He grabbed my arm and refused to let go.* —**grab** *noun*: *She made a grab for the money* (=tried to take the money).

grace /ɡreɪs/ *noun* (no plural) when you move your body in a smooth and attractive way: *The dancers moved with grace and confidence.*

grace·ful /ˈɡreɪsfəl/ *adjective* a person or animal who is graceful moves in a smooth and attractive way: *a tall graceful woman* —**gracefully** *adverb*

gra·cious /ˈɡreɪʃəs/ *adjective* (formal) polite and kind, especially in a formal way: *The King was gracious to everyone who met him.* —**graciously** *adverb*

grade¹ /ɡreɪd/ *noun*
1 a level that tells you how good the quality of something is or how important it is: *There are five different grades of hotel.*
2 a mark that your teacher gives you for an examination or for school work, to show how good it is: *Martia got grade A in her maths exam.* • *I got some very poor* (=bad) *grades when I was at school.*
3 one of the 12 years that you are at school in the US: *Liz is in fifth grade.*
4 make the grade to succeed or reach a high level at a particular activity: *Do you think my son will* **make the grade** *as a professional footballer?*

grade² *verb* **1** to put people or things into groups according to how good, big etc they are: *The students are graded according to their level of English.*

2 the American word for MARK: *Mrs Watts still hasn't graded my homework.*

'grade ˌcrossing the American word for a LEVEL CROSSING

'grade ˌschool an American word for a PRIMARY SCHOOL

gra·di·ent /'greɪdiənt/ *noun* a slope, or how steep a slope is, especially part of a road or railway: *Ringstead Road was on a steep gradient.*

grad·u·al /'grædʒuəl/ *adjective* happening slowly or over a long time: *Learning to walk again after the accident was a very gradual process.*

grad·u·al·ly /'grædʒuəli/ *adverb* slowly, or over a long period of time ANTONYM **suddenly**: *Her work gradually improved during the year.* • *Gradually, Dick began to feel a bit better.*

grad·u·ate[1] /'grædʒuət/ *noun* **1** someone who has completed their first course at university and passed the final examinations: *a graduate in physics* • *law graduates* **2** *AmE* someone who has completed a course at a school, college, or university: *a high school graduate*

grad·u·ate[2] /'grædʒueɪt/ *verb* **1** to pass your final examinations at university: *Don graduated from York University in 1998.* **2** *AmE* to finish studying at HIGH SCHOOL

'graduate ˌstudent the American word for a POSTGRADUATE

grad·u·a·tion /ˌgrædʒu'eɪʃən/ *noun* when you complete a university degree or your education at an American HIGH SCHOOL: *My parents came to the graduation ceremony.*

graf·fi·ti /grə'fiːti/ *noun* (no plural) writing and pictures that people draw in public places illegally: *The school walls were covered with graffiti.*

graffiti

grain /greɪn/ *noun* **1** the seeds of crops such as corn, wheat, or rice that we grow for food: *The barn was full of grain.* **2** one seed or one very small piece of something: *a grain of salt*

gram, gramme /græm/ (written abbreviation **g** or **gm**) *noun* a unit for measuring weight. There are 1,000 grams in a kilogram

gram·mar /'græmə $ 'græmɚ/ *noun* (no plural) the rules of a language: *His pronunciation is good, but his knowledge of grammar is poor.*

> **SPELLING**
> This word is often spelled wrongly. The correct spelling is: **grammar**.

'grammar ˌschool *noun* a school in Britain for children between the ages of 11 and 18, who have to pass an examination to go there

gram·mat·i·cal /grə'mætɪkəl/ *adjective* related to grammar: *a grammatical mistake* —**grammatically** /-kli/ *adverb*: *The sentence is not grammatically correct.*

gran /græn/ *noun BrE* (informal) a GRANDMOTHER

grand[1] /grænd/ *adjective* very big, important, or impressive: *She gave a grand party for three hundred people.* • *Their house is very grand.*

grand[2] *noun* (informal) (plural **grand**) a thousand pounds or dollars: *He earns forty grand a year.*

gran·dad, granddad /'grændæd/ *noun* (informal) a GRANDFATHER

grand·child /'græntʃaɪld/ *noun* (plural **grandchildren** /-ˌtʃɪldrən/) the child of your son or daughter: *Rosa is his youngest grandchild.*

grand·daugh·ter /'grænˌdɔːtə $ 'grænˌdɔtɚ/ *noun* the daughter of your son or daughter

grand·fa·ther /'grænˌfɑːðə $ 'grænˌfɑðɚ/ *noun* the father of one of your parents: *My grandfather gave me this book.*

> **SPELLING**
> This word is often spelled wrongly. The correct spelling is: **grandfather**.

grand·ma /'grænmɑː/ *noun* (informal) a GRANDMOTHER

grand·moth·er /'grænˌmʌðə $ 'grænˌmʌðɚ/ *noun* the mother of one of your parents: *This is a photograph of my grandmother.*

A B C D E F G H I J K L M N O P Q R S T U V W X Y Z

SPELLING
This word is often spelled wrongly. The correct spelling is: **grandmother**.

grand·pa /ˈgrænpɑː/ *noun* (informal) a GRANDFATHER

grand·par·ent /ˈgrænˌpeərənt $ ˈgrænˌperənt/ *noun* one of your mother's or father's parents: *We visited my grandparents at the weekend.*

grand·son /ˈgrænsʌn/ *noun* the son of your son or daughter

gran·ny /ˈgræni/ *noun* (informal) (plural **grannies**) a GRANDMOTHER

grant¹ /grɑːnt $ grænt/ *verb* **1 take it for granted** to think that something is true even though you have not heard that it is definitely true: *I took it for granted that we would get a pay rise.* **2 take someone for granted** if someone takes you for granted, they expect you to help them and do things for them but they never thank you or praise you for this: *I'm fed up with my boss always taking me for granted.* **3** (formal) to give someone official permission to have or do something: *Everyone was granted an extra day's holiday.*

grant² *noun* an amount of money that an organization gives someone for a particular purpose: *She got a grant to study at college.*

gran·ule /ˈgrænjuːl/ *noun* a very small hard piece of something, especially dried coffee: *instant coffee granules*

grape /greɪp/ *noun* a small round juicy fruit that grows in bunches and is used to make wine: *a bunch of black grapes* ➔ see picture on page A7

grape·fruit /ˈgreɪpfruːt/ *noun* a yellow fruit like a big orange, but without a sweet taste ➔ see picture on page A7

graph /græf/ *noun* a drawing that shows information about numbers, measurements etc: *The graph showed how the population had increased.*

graph·ic /ˈgræfɪk/ *adjective* a graphic account, description etc is very clear and gives a lot of details: *She gave a graphic description of the accident.*

ˌgraphic deˈsign *noun* (no plural) the job or art of combining pictures with the writing in books, magazines etc

graph·ics /ˈgræfɪks/ *plural noun* drawings or pictures, especially the ones that a computer produces: *The latest computer games have brilliant graphics.*

grasp¹ /grɑːsp $ græsp/ *verb* **1** (written) to take and hold something firmly in your hands: *Rob grasped the rope and began to climb.* **2** to understand something: *She didn't seem to grasp what I was saying.*

grasp² *noun* (no plural) the ability to understand something SYNONYM **understanding**: *You need to have a good grasp of how computers work.*

grass /grɑːs $ græs/ *noun* (no plural) **1** the green plant that covers the ground in gardens, fields etc: *We lay on the grass by the river.* **2** (informal) MARIJUANA

grass·hop·per /ˈgrɑːsˌhɒpə $ ˈgræsˌhɑpɚ/ *noun* an insect with long back legs that it uses to jump and make short loud sounds ➔ see picture at INSECT

grate¹ /greɪt/ *verb* to cut food such as cheese or vegetables into small pieces by rubbing it against a GRATER (=a kitchen tool with a rough surface): *Put grated cheese on the pizza.* ➔ see picture on page A4

grate² *noun* the metal part of a fire, where you put the wood, coal etc

grate·ful /ˈgreɪtfəl/ *adjective*

KEY PATTERNS
grateful for something
grateful to someone for (doing) something

someone who is grateful wants to thank another person for something ANTONYM **ungrateful**: *I lent him the money but he didn't seem very grateful.* • *We are very* ***grateful for*** *your help.* • *I was really* ***grateful to*** *her* ***for*** *being so kind.* —**gratefully** *adverb*: *"Thank you so much for helping," she said gratefully.*

SPELLING
This word is often spelled wrongly. The correct spelling is: **grateful**.

grat·er /ˈgreɪtə $ ˈgreɪtɚ/ *noun* a kitchen tool with a rough surface and small holes. You break food into small pieces by rubbing the food against the grater

grat·i·tude /ˈgrætɪtjuːd $ ˈgrætəˌtud/ *noun* (no plural) (formal) when you want to thank someone for something ANTONYM **ingratitude**: *I'd like to express my gratitude to you all for your support.*

gra·tu·i·tous /grəˈtjuːɪtəs $ grəˈtuətəs/ *adjective* gratuitous violence, criticism etc is not necessary and is very unpleasant: *I don't like television programmes with gratuitous violence.*

grave[1] /greɪv/ *noun* the place in the ground where a dead body is buried: *Joan put some flowers on her father's grave.*

grave[2] *adjective* (formal) very serious or worrying: *Poverty is a grave problem here.*

grav·el /ˈgrævəl/ *noun* (no plural) very small stones that are used to make a surface for paths: *His boots crunched on the gravel.* —**gravel** *adjective*: *a gravel driveway* (=a path between a house and the road that cars can drive along)

grave·stone /ˈgreɪvstəʊn $ ˈgreɪvstoʊn/ *noun* a large stone that is put on a grave and shows the dead person's name and the dates they were alive SYNONYM **tombstone**

grave·yard /ˈgreɪvjɑːd $ ˈgreɪvjɑrd/ *noun* an area of ground where dead people are buried, especially beside a church

grav·i·ty /ˈgrævəti/ *noun* (no plural) the force that makes objects fall to the ground: *the Earth's gravity*

gra·vy /ˈgreɪvi/ *noun* (no plural) a liquid that you pour over meat, potatoes etc, which is usually made from the meat's juices

gray the American spelling of GREY

graze[1] /greɪz/ *verb* **1** to slightly cut the surface of your skin, for example by falling on a hard surface: *Tim fell off his bicycle and grazed his knees.* **2** if an animal grazes, it eats grass: *The sheep were grazing in a corner of the field.*

graze[2] *noun* a small cut in the surface of your skin: *His arms were covered in grazes.*

grease[1] /griːs/ *noun* (no plural) **1** fat from food that you have cooked: *The pans were all covered in grease.*
2 thick oil that you put on the moving parts of a machine to make them move smoothly

grease[2] *verb* to put fat or grease on something: *Grease the cake tin well.*

greas·y /ˈgriːsi/ *adjective* (**greasier**, **greasiest**) covered in or containing grease, oil, or a similar substance: *greasy fish and chips* • *a shampoo for greasy hair* → see Thesaurus at DIRTY

great /greɪt/ *adjective*
1 a lot of something: *Lily opened the present with great care.*
2 very good or enjoyable SYNONYM **wonderful**: *The kids were having a great time in the sea.* • *It's really great to be home.* → see Thesaurus at GOOD[1], NICE
3 very important, successful, or famous: *He is one of the greatest film directors in the world.*

PHRASES

great, that's great (spoken) used to say that you are pleased about something: *"We've decided to get married." "Oh, that's great!"*

great big (informal) very big: *a great big spider*

great·ly /ˈgreɪtli/ *adverb* (formal) very much: *I greatly admired him as a teacher.*

greed /griːd/ *noun* (no plural) when someone wants more money, food, power etc than they need: *The greed of these companies could lead to the destruction of the forest.*

greed·i·ness /ˈgriːdinəs/ *noun* (no plural) when someone wants more of something than they really need

greed·y /ˈgriːdi/ *adjective* (**greedier**, **greediest**) someone who is greedy wants more money, food, power etc than they need: *Don't be greedy – leave some pie for the rest of us!* • *greedy businessmen* —**greedily** *adverb*: *He looked greedily at the chocolate cake.*

green[1] /griːn/ *adjective* **1** something that is green is the colour of grass: *a green sweater* **2** covered with grass, trees etc: *Most towns have very few green areas nowadays.* **3** relating to

A B C D E F G H I J K L M N O P Q R S T U V W X Y Z

the protection of the environment: *We should develop greener forms of transport.*

green² *noun* **1** the colour of grass: *The skirt is also available in dark green.* **2 greens** vegetables with green leaves

ˌgreen ˈcard *noun* an official piece of paper that allows you to live and work in the US, although you are not American

green·gro·cer /ˈgriːnˌgrəʊsə $ ˈgrinˌgroʊsɚ/ *noun BrE* **1** also **greengrocer's** a shop that sells fruit and vegetables SYNONYM **grocer**: *There is a greengrocer's in the village.* **2** someone who owns a shop that sells fruit and vegetables

green·house /ˈgriːnhaʊs/ *noun* a glass building where you grow plants that must be kept warm: *She grows tomatoes in her greenhouse.*

ˈgreenhouse efˌfect *noun* **the greenhouse effect** when POLLUTION stops the sun's heat from escaping and the air around the Earth becomes warmer

greet /griːt/ *verb* **1** to welcome someone when you meet them, for example by saying "Hello": *The whole family were waiting at the door to greet me.* **2 be greeted with something** if an idea, event etc is greeted with shouts, laughter etc, that is how people react to it: *The idea was greeted with great enthusiasm.*

greet·ing /ˈgriːtɪŋ/ *noun* something friendly that you say or do when you meet someone, write to them, or telephone them: *The two men **exchanged greetings*** (=said "Hello" to each other). • *The King raised his hand in greeting.*

gre·nade /grəˈneɪd/ *noun* a small bomb that is thrown: *a hand grenade*

grew the past tense of GROW

grey¹ *BrE*, **gray** *AmE* /greɪ/ *adjective* **1** something that is grey is the colour of dark clouds, between black and white: *The house was built of old grey stone.* **2** weather that is grey is dull and cloudy: *a grey day in February*

grey² *BrE*, **gray** *AmE noun* the colour you get when you mix black with white: *Do you have these skirts in grey?*

grid /grɪd/ *noun* a pattern of straight lines that cross each other and form squares: *The teacher told us to draw a grid on a piece of paper.*

grief /griːf/ *noun* (no plural) great sadness, especially because someone you love has died

griev·ance /ˈgriːvəns/ *noun* (formal) something that you think is unfair and that you complain about, especially to someone in authority: *The manager called a meeting to try and deal with our grievances.*

grieve /griːv/ *verb* to feel very sad because someone you love has died SYNONYM **mourn**: *It's ten years since her husband died, but she's still grieving for him.*

grill¹ /grɪl/ *verb* to cook meat, fish etc by putting it close to strong heat: *Grill the steak for about four minutes each side.*

grill² *noun BrE* the part of a COOKER which cooks food on a metal shelf, using strong heat: *Put the sandwich under the grill until the cheese melts.*

grim /grɪm/ *adjective* (**grimmer**, **grimmest**) **1** making you feel worried or unhappy: *The situation here is extremely grim – hundreds of people have lost their homes.* **2** a grim place is unattractive, dirty etc: *a grim area of the city*

gri·mace /grɪˈmeɪs $ ˈgrɪməs/ *verb* (written) to twist your face in an ugly way because something is hurting you or because you do not like something: *Trevor was grimacing with pain.* —**grimace** *noun*: *She gave a grimace as she tasted the food.*

grime /graɪm/ *noun* (no plural) thick black dirt: *The factory walls were covered in grime.*

grim·y /ˈgraɪmi/ *adjective* (**grimier**, **grimiest**) covered in thick black dirt: *a row of grimy houses near the railway*

grin¹ /grɪn/ *verb* (**grinned**, **grinning**) to smile a big smile: *"I've got good news," Sally said, grinning.* ➔ see Thesaurus at SMILE¹

grin² *noun* a big smile: *Simon had a great big grin on his face as he came out of the exam room.*

grind /graɪnd/ *verb* (past tense and past participle **ground** /graʊnd/) to crush something such as coffee beans into small pieces or powder: *This machine is for grinding wheat into flour.* → see Thesaurus at PRESS[1]

grip /grɪp/ *verb* (**gripped**, **gripping**) **1** to hold something very tightly: *I gripped the steering wheel of the car.* **2** to keep your attention completely: *The audience was gripped.* • *a gripping film* —**grip** *noun*: *He kept a tight grip on my arm.*

gris·ly /ˈgrɪzli/ *adjective* (**grislier**, **grisliest**) involving very unpleasant violence and death: *a grisly murder*

grit[1] /grɪt/ *noun* (no plural) very small pieces of stone: *I had a piece of grit stuck in my shoe.*

grit[2] *verb* (**gritted**, **gritting**) **grit your teeth** to decide to keep going in a difficult or painful situation: *He gritted his teeth against the pain.*

groan /grəʊn $ groʊn/ *verb* to make a long low sound when you are unhappy or in pain SYNONYM **moan**: *Kim groaned with pain as she got up.* —**groan** *noun*: *The students let out a groan when the teacher announced a test.*

gro·cer /ˈgrəʊsə $ ˈgroʊsɚ/ also **grocer's** *BrE noun* **1** a small shop that sells food and other small things you need in your home: *Do you want anything from the grocer's?* **2** someone who owns a grocer's shop

gro·cer·ies /ˈgrəʊsəriz $ ˈgroʊsəriz/ *plural noun* food and other things that you buy to use in your home: *We can deliver your groceries to your house.*

grog·gy /ˈgrɒgi $ ˈgrɑgi/ *adjective* (**groggier**, **groggiest**) feeling weak and ill: *The injection made him feel groggy.* —**groggily** *adverb*

groin /grɔɪn/ *noun* the place where your legs join at the front of your body: *a groin injury*

groom[1] /gruːm/ *verb* to clean and brush an animal: *The first task is to groom the horses.*

groom[2] *noun* **1** also **bridegroom** a man who is getting married, or has just got married: *a happy bride and groom* **2** someone whose job is to care for horses

groove /gruːv/ *noun* a line cut into a surface: *a pattern of deep grooves*

grope /grəʊp $ groʊp/ *verb* to try to find something or go somewhere using your hands, because you cannot see: *I groped in my handbag for the key.* • *Bob groped his way downstairs in the dark.*

gross /grəʊs $ groʊs/ *adjective* **1** (spoken) very unpleasant to look at or think about SYNONYM **disgusting**: *His jokes are really gross.* **2** (formal) very serious: *He was fired for gross incompetence.* —**grossly** *adverb*: *He is grossly overweight.*

gro·tesque /grəʊˈtesk $ groʊˈtesk/ *adjective* ugly in a strange frightening way: *a grotesque monster* —**grotesquely** *adverb*

grouch·y /ˈgraʊtʃi/ *adjective* (informal) (**grouchier**, **grouchiest**) someone who is grouchy is cross and complains a lot SYNONYM **bad-tempered**: *Dad's always grouchy in the morning.*

ground[1] /graʊnd/ *noun* **1 the ground** the surface of the Earth: *Moira was lying asleep* ***on the ground***. • *The* ***ground*** *was frozen.* **2** an area of earth or grass, especially one that is used for a special purpose: *They built all their houses on high ground.* • *The school has its own* ***sports ground***.

PHRASES

above ground, below ground: *The miners are working 1,000 feet below ground* (=1,000 feet under the ground).

> **WORD CHOICE**
> **ground** or **floor**?
> • The **ground** is the surface of the earth: *The* ***ground*** *was muddy after the rain.*
> • The **floor** is the surface that you walk on inside a building: *There weren't enough beds, so some people had to sleep on the* ***floor***.

ground[2] *verb* to stop an aircraft or pilot from flying: *All flights are grounded owing to the storms.*

ground[3] the past tense and past participle of GRIND

ˌground ˈbeef an American word for MINCE

ˈ**ground floor** *noun* the part of a building that is on the same level as the ground SYNONYM **first floor** *AmE*: *The men's clothing department is on the ground floor.*

group¹ /gruːp/ *noun*

KEY PATTERNS
a group of people/things

1 several people or things that are together in the same place: *a **group of** islands off the coast* • *A fight started between two **groups of** men.* • *Please can the class get into **groups of three*** (=groups of three people).
2 several musicians who play and sing popular music together SYNONYM **band**: *He used to be a guitarist in a **rock group**.*

THESAURUS
crowd: *A crowd was waiting outside the theatre to watch the stars arrive* (=a large group of people).
team: *Our **team** was the best and we won the competition* (=group of people who play a game together against other people). • *a **team** of researchers* (=a group of people who work together)
party (formal): *A representative will meet your **party** at the airport* (=group of people who are going somewhere together).
gang: *The **gang** surrounded me and asked me for my wallet* (=group of young people who often cause trouble).

group² *verb* (written) to arrange things in a group: *We grouped our results under two headings.*

grov•el /ˈgrɒvəl $ ˈgrʌvəl/ *verb* (**grovelled, grovelling** *BrE*, **groveled, groveling** *AmE*) to try very hard to please someone, because you are frightened of them or you have upset them: *I don't care how important she is, I'm not going to grovel to her.*

grow /grəʊ $ groʊ/ *verb* (**grew** /gruː/ **grown** /grəʊn $ groʊn/)
1 to get bigger in size or amount: *Babies grow quickly in their first year.* • *The number of overseas students is growing.*
2 if someone grows their hair or grows a beard, they let it get longer and do not cut it: *I think I'd like to grow a beard.* • *Are you growing your hair, or will you have it cut?*
3 if plants grow somewhere or if you grow them there, they are alive in that place: *There were weeds growing everywhere.* • *We grow our own vegetables.*

PHRASES
grow old, grow stronger etc to become old, stronger etc: *Grandad was growing old, and becoming forgetful.* • *We were lost, and it was growing dark.*
➔ see Thesaurus at BECOME

PHRASAL VERBS
grow up
to gradually change from being a child to being an adult: *Where did you live when you were growing up?*

growl /graʊl/ *verb* if a dog, bear etc growls, it makes a deep angry sound: *The dog started to growl and bark at us.* —**growl** *noun*: *I heard a low growl from behind the gate.*

growl

grown the past participle of GROW

ˌ**grown-ˈup¹** *noun* an adult; a word used by children

ˈ**grown-up²** *adjective* someone who is grown-up is an adult: *She has two grown-up daughters.*

growth /grəʊθ $ groʊθ/ *noun* (no plural) when something gets bigger or develops: *The nurse measured the children's growth.* • *The country is in a period of economic growth.*

grub /grʌb/ *noun* (no plural) (informal) food

grub•by /ˈgrʌbi/ *adjective* (**grubbier, grubbiest**) dirty: *grubby fingers*

grudge /grʌdʒ/ *noun* an unfriendly feeling towards someone because of something they did in the past: *She criticized him months ago, and he still has a grudge against her.*

gru•el•ling *BrE*, **grueling** *AmE* /ˈgruːəlɪŋ/ *adjective* very difficult and tiring: *a gruelling ten-mile run*

grue•some /ˈgruːsəm/ *adjective* connected with violence or death: *This castle has a gruesome history.*

grum·ble /ˈgrʌmbəl/ *verb* to complain: *All the hotel guests were grumbling about the food.*

grump·y /ˈgrʌmpi/ *adjective* (**grumpier**, **grumpiest**) if someone is grumpy, they show that they feel slightly angry or annoyed SYNONYM **bad-tempered**: *I'm feeling grumpy because I'm tired.* —**grumpily** *adverb*: *"Leave me alone," she said grumpily.*

grunt /grʌnt/ *verb* **1** to make a short, low sound to show that you are not interested in something: *I asked him several times, but he just grunted.* **2** if a pig grunts, it makes a low rough sound —**grunt** *noun*: *Alex answered with a grunt.*

guar·an·tee[1] /ˌgærənˈtiː/ *verb* to promise something: *We guarantee to repair your computer within 48 hours.* • *Of course, we can't guarantee that you'll pass the exam, but we'll help as much as we can.* ➔ see Thesaurus at PROMISE[1]

> **SPELLING**
> This word is often spelled wrongly. The correct spelling is: **guarantee**.

guarantee[2] *noun* a promise by a company to repair or replace something you have bought from them, for example if it breaks: *a two-year guarantee*

guard[1] /gɑːd $ gɑrd/ *noun*
1 someone whose job is to protect a person or a place, or to make sure that a person does not escape: *A **security guard** was sitting by the door.* • *Two **armed guards*** (=guards carrying guns) *walked behind the president.* • *a prison guard*
2 *BrE* someone whose job is to collect tickets on a train, help the passengers etc: *The guard asked to see our tickets.*
PHRASES
be on guard to be responsible for protecting a place or a person: *A policeman **is** always **on guard** outside the palace.*
be on your guard (against something) to be very careful because you may have to deal with a bad situation: *You have to **be on your guard against** thieves in this part of the city.*
catch someone off guard to surprise someone by doing something that they were not expecting: *His question **caught** me **off guard**.*

guard[2] *verb* to watch someone or something so that they do not escape, or get damaged or stolen: *Three men were sent to guard the prisoner.* • *We have two large dogs guarding the property at night.* ➔ see Thesaurus at PROTECT

guard·i·an /ˈgɑːdiən $ ˈgɑrdiən/ *noun* someone who is legally responsible for someone else's child

guer·ril·la /gəˈrɪlə/ *noun* a member of an unofficial army that is fighting for political reasons

> **SPELLING**
> Don't confuse the spelling of **guerrilla** and **gorilla** (=a large animal that looks like a monkey and is closely related to humans).

guess[1] /ges/ *verb*

> **KEY PATTERNS**
> **guess (that)**
> **guess how/what/whether/if etc**

to answer a question or decide something without being sure whether you are right: *The letter wasn't signed, but Louise **guessed that** Tom had sent it.* • ***Guess how much** this dress cost.* • *I could **guess what** Sandra was thinking.* • *I **guessed** her age **correctly**.*
PHRASES
I guess (so) (spoken) used to say that you think something is probably true: *"Is her dad very rich?" "**I guess so.**"* • *My car isn't running, so **I guess** we'll have to get the bus.*
guess what! (spoken) used before telling someone some surprising news: *Guess what! I've been picked for the basketball team!*

guess[2] *noun* (plural **guesses**)

> **KEY PATTERNS**
> **have/make/take a guess (at something)**

an attempt to guess something: *You were wrong the first time, but you can **have** another **guess**.* • *Listen to the tape and then **make a guess at** who is speaking.*

guest /gest/ *noun* **1** someone that you invite to stay in your home or invite to an event: *How many guests are coming to your party?* **2** someone who is staying in a hotel: *All the guests were given a free meal.*

guid·ance /ˈgaɪdns/ *noun* (no plural) helpful advice: *People taking the art course will receive expert guidance.*

guide¹ /gaɪd/ *noun* **1** someone whose job is to show a place to tourists: *The guide pointed out the cathedral on the left.* **2** also **guidebook** a book that has information and advice on a particular subject: *a guide for new students • I've bought you a book called 'The Idiot's Guide to the Internet'.* **3** something that helps you to make a decision: *As a rough guide, you need about 100 grams of meat per person.*

guide² *verb*

KEY PATTERNS
guide someone to/through/across etc a place

1 to help someone to go somewhere, for example by showing them the right direction: *He took the old lady's arm and **guided** her **across** the road.*
2 to help someone manage a difficult situation: *Your teacher can guide you when you make your college application.*

ˈguide dog *noun BrE* a specially trained dog that helps a blind person go to places SYNONYM **seeing eye dog** *AmE*

guide·lines /ˈgaɪdlaɪnz/ *plural noun* advice about how to do something: *The teacher gave the students some guidelines on writing essays.*

guilt /gɪlt/ *noun* (no plural) **1** a sad feeling you have when you have done something wrong: *a terrible sense of guilt and shame* **2** when someone has broken a law ANTONYM **innocence**: *We were sure he had done it, but could not prove his guilt.*

guilt·y /ˈgɪlti/ *adjective* (**guiltier**, **guiltiest**)

KEY PATTERNS
feel guilty about (doing) something

1 unhappy and ashamed because you have done something that you know is wrong: *Robyn **felt guilty about** stealing the pen. • The vase was broken, and Billy was looking guilty.*
2 find someone guilty (of something) if a court of law finds someone guilty of a crime, it decides that they committed that crime ANTONYM **innocent**: *Menzies was found guilty of murder.*

guin·ea pig /ˈgɪni ˌpɪg/ *noun* a small furry animal with no tail, that is often kept as a pet

guitars

acoustic guitar electric guitar

gui·tar /gɪˈtɑː $ gɪˈtɑr/ *noun* a wooden musical instrument with strings and a long neck, that you play by pulling the strings: *an electric guitar*

gui·tar·ist /gɪˈtɑːrɪst/ *noun* someone who plays the guitar

gulf /gʌlf/ *noun* **1** a large area of sea that is partly surrounded by land: *the Persian Gulf* **2** a very large difference between people or things

gull /gʌl/ a SEAGULL

gul·li·ble /ˈgʌləbəl/ *adjective* a gullible person is easy to trick because they always believe what people say: *I was angry with myself for being so gullible.*

gulp /gʌlp/ *verb* **1** also **gulp down** to swallow food or drink quickly: *Don't gulp your drink – it's rude.* → see Thesaurus at DRINK¹ **2** (written) to swallow suddenly because you are frightened or unhappy: *Nola gulped and tried not to cry.* —**gulp** *noun*: *He drank the whisky in a single gulp.*

gum /gʌm/ *noun* **1** your gums are the pink parts inside your mouth that your teeth grow out of **2** another word for CHEWING GUM

gun /gʌn/ *noun* a weapon that fires bullets: *The police here all carry guns.*

gun·fire /ˈgʌnfaɪə $ ˈgʌnfaɪɚ/ *noun* (no plural) shots fired from a gun: *the sound of gunfire*

gun·man /ˈgʌnmən/ *noun* (plural **gunmen**) /-mən/ a criminal who uses a gun: *The gunman was arrested at the airport.*

gun·point /ˈgʌnpɔɪnt/ *noun* **at gunpoint** if someone does something to you at gunpoint, they do it to you while threatening to shoot you: *He was robbed at gunpoint on his way to the bank.*

gun·shot /ˈgʌnʃɒt $ ˈgʌnʃɑt/ *noun* when a bullet is fired from a gun: *Neighbours said they heard gunshots.* • *a gunshot wound*

gur·gle /ˈgɜːgəl $ ˈgɚgəl/ *verb* to make a sound like flowing water: *The baby gurgled with pleasure.*

gu·ru /ˈgʊruː/ *noun* **1** (informal) someone that people respect because they are very wise or skilful in a particular subject: *a top management guru* **2** a Hindu religious teacher

gush /gʌʃ/ *verb* if liquid gushes somewhere, a large amount of it flows there SYNONYM **pour**: *Blood was gushing from his arm.*

gust /gʌst/ *noun* a sudden strong movement of the wind: *A gust of wind nearly knocked her over.*

gut¹ /gʌt/ *adjective* (informal) **gut feeling, gut reaction** a belief or reaction that you have in a situation, although it is not based on any facts: *My gut reaction was to refuse.*

gut² *noun* (informal) **1** also **guts** the tube in your body that food passes through after it leaves your stomach SYNONYM **intestine**: *I had a pain in my gut.* **2 guts** courage and determination to do something difficult: *Have you got the guts to ask for a pay rise?*

gut³ *verb* (**gutted**, **gutting**) **1** to destroy the inside of a building completely: *The house was gutted by fire.* **2** if you gut a dead fish or animal, you remove the parts that are inside it

gut·ted /ˈgʌtɪd/ *adjective BrE* (spoken) very disappointed: *The team were gutted when they lost.*

gut·ter /ˈgʌtə $ ˈgʌtɚ/ *noun* the low part at the edge of a road, or a pipe fixed to a roof, which carries away water: *The gutter was blocked by leaves.*

guy /gaɪ/ *noun* (informal) a man

guz·zle /ˈgʌzəl/ *verb* (informal) to drink or eat a lot very quickly: *The children were guzzling lemonade.*

gym /dʒɪm/ *noun* **1** a large room or a building containing equipment for doing physical exercise: *I go to the gym twice a week.* **2** (no plural) exercises done indoors, especially as a lesson at school: *Gym is on Friday afternoons.*

gym·na·si·um /dʒɪmˈneɪziəm/ *noun* (formal) a GYM

gym·nast /ˈdʒɪmnæst/ *noun* someone who performs gymnastics: *an Olympic gymnast*

gym·nas·tics /dʒɪmˈnæstɪks/ *noun* skilful physical exercises and movements: *a gymnastics display*

GRAMMAR
Gymnastics always has an 's' at the end, but has a singular verb after it: *Gymnastics is my favourite sport.*

gyp·sy also **gipsy** *BrE* /ˈdʒɪpsi/ *noun* (plural **gypsies**) a member of a group of people who travel around rather than living in one place

hab•it /ˈhæbɪt/ *noun*

KEY PATTERNS
a/the habit of doing something
be in the habit of doing something

something that you do often or regularly: *Smoking is a very* ***bad habit***. • *Changing your* ***eating habits*** *can be really difficult.* • *My teacher* ***has a habit of*** *forgetting people's names.* • *Irene* ***was in the habit of*** *visiting her uncle every weekend.* • *We* ***got into the habit of*** *staying up very late.*

THESAURUS
custom: *In many countries it is a* ***custom*** *to shake hands when you meet* (=something that people in a society do because they think it is polite or good).
tradition: *We have a family* ***tradition*** *that we all meet up once a year* (=something that people have done for a long time and continue to do).

hab•i•tat /ˈhæbətæt/ *noun* the habitat of a wild animal or a plant is the type of place in which it lives: *Pollution is damaging many wildlife habitats.*

ha•bit•u•al /həˈbɪtʃuəl/ *adjective* (formal) typical or happening often, as a habit: *I'm not happy about your habitual absences from work.* • *a habitual smoker*

hack /hæk/ *verb* **1** to cut something roughly or violently: *Tom hacked the branches from the tree.* **2 hack into something** to use a computer to enter someone else's computer system in order to damage it or get secret information: *They hacked into the bank's system and moved money into their accounts.*

hack•er /ˈhækə $ ˈhækɚ/ *noun* someone who uses computers a lot, especially in order to secretly use or change the information in another person's computer system

had /əd; strong hæd/ the past tense and past participle of HAVE

had•n't /ˈhædnt/ the short form of 'had not': *I hadn't got any money.*

hag /hæg/ *noun* an ugly unpleasant old woman

hag•gard /ˈhægəd $ ˈhægɚd/ *adjective* looking tired, thin, and ill: *His face looked haggard and pale.*

hag•gle /ˈhægəl/ *verb* to argue about the amount that you will pay for something before agreeing on a price SYNONYM **bargain**: *The owner of the shop and the tourist were haggling over the price of a rug.*

hail[1] /heɪl/ *verb* **1 hail a taxi, hail a cab** to wave at a taxi to make it stop **2** if it hails, frozen rain falls from the sky

hail[2] *noun* **1** (no plural) frozen rain that falls from the sky **2 a hail of bullets** a lot of bullets travelling through the air at the same time: *The two robbers died in a hail of bullets.*

hair /heə $ her/ *noun*
1 (no plural) the things like threads that grow on your head: *Both my sisters have fair hair.* • *Her hair is very long.* ➔ see picture on page A5
2 a thing like a thread that grows on the skin of a person or animal: *There are cat hairs all over this chair.*

GRAMMAR
Hair usually means 'all the hairs on someone's head': *He has brown hair.*
✘ Don't say 'he has brown hairs'.
Hair is also used to talk about a single piece of hair: *There's a hair in my soup!*

USAGE
You **have your hair cut** by a hairdresser (for women)/barber (for men): ***I have my hair cut*** *about twice a year.*
✘ Don't say 'I cut my hair' when you mean that another person cuts it.

hair•brush /ˈheəbrʌʃ $ ˈherbrʌʃ/ *noun* (plural **hairbrushes**) a brush you use to tidy your hair ➔ see picture at BRUSH[1]

hair•cut /ˈheəkʌt $ ˈherkʌt/ *noun* when someone cuts your hair, or the style in which your hair is cut: *I'm going to have a haircut this week.* • *a short, neat haircut*

hair·dress·er /'heəˌdresə $ 'herˌdresɚ/ *noun* someone whose job is to wash, cut, and arrange people's hair: *an appointment at the hairdresser's*

hair·dry·er /'heəˌdraɪə $ 'herˌdraɪɚ/ *noun* a machine you use to dry your hair that blows hot air onto it

hair·grip *BrE* /'heəgrɪp $ 'hergrɪp/ also **hair·pin** /'heəpɪn $ 'herpɪn/ *noun* a thin piece of metal, used to hold a woman's hair in place

'hair-ˌraising *adjective* (informal) frightening but exciting: *a hair-raising roller coaster ride*

hairstyles

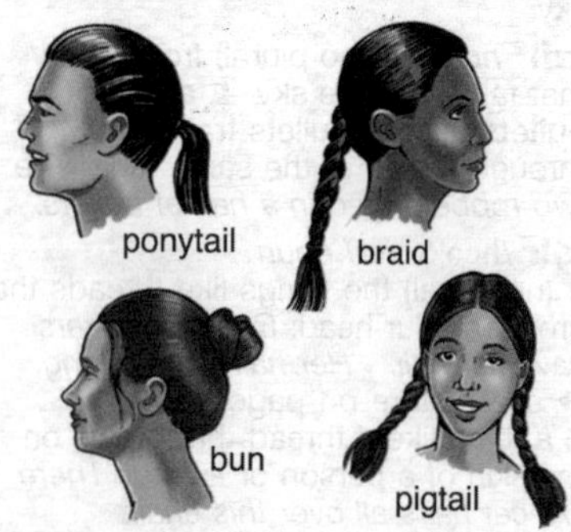

hair·style /'heəstaɪl $ 'herstaɪl/ *noun* the way in which your hair is cut and arranged: *I like her new hairstyle.*

hair·y /'heəri $ 'heri/ *adjective* (**hairier**, **hairiest**) a hairy person or animal has a lot of hair on their body: *hairy legs*

half

He cut the cake in half.

half¹ /hɑːf $ hæf/ *noun, determiner, pronoun* (plural **halves** /hɑːvz $ hævz/)

KEY PATTERNS
half (of) something
cut/break something in half

one of two equal parts: *The first half of the game was pretty dull.* • *Half the pupils in the school are ill.* • *I'll be ready in half an hour.* • *He decided to save* ***half of*** *the money and spend the rest.* • *Cut the grapes* ***in half*** (=into two equal pieces).

PHRASES

half past one, half past two etc: *It's* ***half past*** *two* (=it's half an hour after two o'clock).

half² *adverb* partly but not completely: *His eyes were half closed.* • *a half-empty glass*

'half-ˌbrother *noun* a brother who has either the same mother or the same father as you, but not both

ˌhalf-'hearted *adjective* (informal) a half-hearted attempt is one someone makes without any real effort or interest: *He made a half-hearted attempt to talk to me.*

'half-ˌsister *noun* a sister who has either the same mother or the same father as you, but not both

ˌhalf 'term *noun BrE* a short holiday in the middle of a school TERM

ˌhalf 'time *noun* (no plural) a short period of time between the two parts of a sports game: *The team discussed tactics at half time.*

half·way /ˌhɑːf'weɪ $ ˌhæf'weɪ/ *adjective, adverb* in the middle, between two places or between the beginning and the end of something SYNONYM **midway**: *I was at the halfway point when my car broke down.* • *Rosco dies halfway through the film.*

hall /hɔːl/ *noun* **1** also **hallway** the part of a house that you come into through the front door and that leads to the other rooms: *You can hang your coat in the hall.* **2** a large building or room, used for important events: *a concert hall*

hallo a British spelling of HELLO

ˌhall of 'residence *noun BrE* a college or university building where students live SYNONYM **dormitory** *AmE*

Hal·low·een /ˌhæləʊ'iːn $ ˌhælə'win/ *noun* the night of October 31, when children dress in strange clothes: *The children dressed up as ghosts and witches for our Halloween party.*

hal•lu•ci•nate /həˈluːsəneɪt/ *verb* to see, feel, or hear something that is not really there: *Jim started hallucinating after he took the drugs.*

hal•lu•ci•na•tion /həˌluːsəˈneɪʃən/ *noun* something you see, feel, or hear that is not really there: *They suffered from strange hallucinations.*

hall•way /ˈhɔːlweɪ/ another word for HALL (1)

ha•lo /ˈheɪləʊ $ ˈheɪloʊ/ *noun* in paintings, a golden circle above the head of a holy person: *The angel had wings and a halo.*

halt[1] /hɔːlt/ *verb* (formal) to stop or to make something stop: *The procession halted at the church gates. • Police halted traffic after the accident.*

halt[2] *noun* **come to a halt** to stop moving: *The car came to a halt in front of the house.*

halve /hɑːv $ hæv/ *verb* to reduce an amount by half: *Deaths from the disease have been halved.*

halves the plural of HALF

ham /hæm/ *noun* (no plural) meat from a pig's leg, that is usually eaten cold: *ham sandwiches*

ham•burg•er /ˈhæmbɜːgə $ ˈhæmˌbɚgɚ/ *noun* **1** a flat round piece of cooked BEEF (=meat from a cow), which you eat between two pieces of bread **2** an American word for MINCE

ham•mer[1] /ˈhæmə $ ˈhæmɚ/ *noun* a tool used for hitting nails into wood ➔ see picture at TOOL

hammer[2] *verb* to hit something with a hammer: *He hammered two nails into the door.*

ham•mock /ˈhæmək/ *noun* a long piece of material that you hang between two poles or trees and lie on

ham•per[1] /ˈhæmpə $ ˈhæmpɚ/ *verb* (written) to make it difficult for someone to do something: *Storms hampered their attempts to reach the crash victims.*

hamper[2] *noun* a large basket with a lid, used for carrying food somewhere: *a picnic hamper* ➔ see picture at BASKET

hamster

ham•ster /ˈhæmstə $ ˈhæmstɚ/ *noun* a small animal like a mouse with soft fur and no tail, often kept as a pet ➔ see picture on page A8

hand

They are holding hands.

hand[1] /hænd/ *noun*

1 the part of your body at the end of each of your arms that includes your fingers and thumb: *Polly put her hand on my shoulder. • He **held hands with** his daughter as they crossed the road. • She was carrying a bag in one hand.*

2 one of the parts of a clock that points to the numbers, telling you the time: *The big hand is pointing to three.* ➔ see picture at WATCH[2]

PHRASES

at hand, on hand, to hand near to you and ready to be used: *Keep the tools that you use most often **close at hand**. • Luckily, a doctor was **on hand** when Lucy collapsed.*

by hand something that is made or done by hand is made or done by a person, not by a machine: *These cushions were sewn **by hand**.*

shake hands to hold another person's right hand with your right hand and move it up and down as a sign of friendship: *The two men **shook hands**. • Marge felt so proud when she **shook hands with** the president.*

give someone a hand to help someone to do something: *Will you **give me a hand with** my homework? • Tom **gave us a hand** to clean the*

A B C D E F G H I J K L M N O P Q R S T U V W X Y Z

house. → see Thesaurus at HELP[1]

get out of hand to become impossible to control: *The party was starting to **get out of hand**.*

have your hands full to have a lot of things that you must do: *You'll have to make your own supper – I've **got my hands full** with the baby.*

in someone's hands, in the hands of someone if something is in your hands, you control it or are responsible for it: *I'll leave the decision **in your hands**.* • *Power was now **in the hands of** the terrorists.*

hand² *verb* **1** to give something to someone: *Could you hand me those scissors, please?* **2 hand something back** to give something back to the person who gave it to you: *Our teacher handed back our essays today.* **3 hand something in** to give something to someone in authority, usually a teacher: *Hand your test papers in now, please.* **4 hand something out** to give something to each person in a group: *I handed out the coursebooks to my classmates.*

hand·bag /ˈhændbæg/ *noun* a small bag that women use to carry money and personal things SYNONYM **purse** *AmE*: *There's a pen in my handbag.* → see picture at BAG[1]

hand·book /ˈhændbʊk/ *noun* a small book containing advice and information: *the student handbook*

hand·brake /ˈhændbreɪk/ *noun BrE* the BRAKE in a car that works when you pull a long handle inside the car SYNONYM **emergency brake** *AmE*

hand·cuffs /ˈhændkʌfs/ *plural noun* two metal rings joined by a chain, used to hold a prisoner's wrists together: *Each officer carries a pair of handcuffs.*

hand·ful /ˈhændfʊl/ *noun* **1** an amount that you can hold in your hand: *She scattered a handful of seed on the ground.* **2 a handful of something** a small number or amount SYNONYM **a few**: *We employ only a handful of people.*

hand·i·cap /ˈhændikæp/ *noun* a permanent problem with someone's body or mind that affects the way that they live SYNONYM **disability**

hand·i·capped /ˈhændikæpt/ *adjective* if someone is handicapped, they have a permanent problem with their body or mind that affects the way that they live SYNONYM **disabled**: *a charity for mentally handicapped children*

hand·ker·chief /ˈhæŋkətʃɪf $ ˈhæŋkɚtʃɪf/ *noun* a small piece of cloth or paper that you use for drying your nose or eyes

han·dle¹ /ˈhændl/ *verb* **1** to deal with or organize something: *I've handled some difficult situations in my career as a pilot.* • *Pat's agreed to handle the party invitations.* → see Thesaurus at DEAL[2] **2** to pick up or touch something: *The metal plate was too hot to handle.*

handles

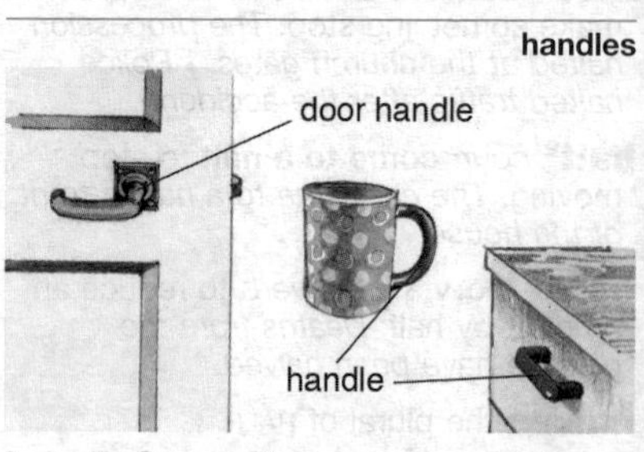

handle² *noun* the part of something that you hold when you use it or open it: *The handle of this mug has broken.* • *the door handle*

han·dle·bars /ˈhændlbɑːz $ ˈhændlˌbɑrz/ *plural noun* the bars at the front of a bicycle that you hold on to

han·dler /ˈhændlə $ ˈhændlɚ/ *noun* someone whose job is to work or deal with a particular thing: *airport baggage handlers* • *a police dog handler*

hand·made /ˌhændˈmeɪd/ *adjective* made by a person, not a machine: *handmade furniture*

hand·out /ˈhændaʊt/ *noun* a piece of paper with information on it that a speaker gives to the people in a class or a meeting: *Have you got a copy of the lecture handout?*

hand·set /ˈhændset/ *noun* the part of a telephone that you hold in your hand and speak into

A B C D E F G H I J K L M N O P Q R S T U V W X Y Z

ˌhands-ˈfree *adjective, adverb* a hands-free phone is one that you can use without using your hands: *Hands-free phones are much safer when you are driving.*

hand·shake /ˈhændʃeɪk/ *noun* an action in which two people hold each other's right hand and move it up and down when they make an agreement, meet each other, or leave: *The principal gave me a friendly handshake.*

hand·some /ˈhænsəm/ *adjective* a handsome man is attractive: *He was tall, dark and handsome.* ➔ see Thesaurus at ATTRACTIVE

hand·writ·ing /ˈhændˌraɪtɪŋ/ *noun* (no plural) your handwriting is your style of writing with a pen or a pencil: *I can't read your handwriting.*

hand·y /ˈhændi/ *adjective* (informal) (**handier**, **handiest**) useful: *handy tips on essay writing*

hang[1] /hæŋ/ *verb* (past tense and past participle **hung** /hʌŋ/)

KEY PATTERNS
hang something above/over etc something
hang something on a peg/hook etc
hang from something

1 also **hang up** if you hang something somewhere, you put it up somewhere so that its top part is supported or attached, but not the bottom part: *Peter **hung** the mirror **above** the bed.* • *You can **hang** your coat **on** the door.* • *Mom **hung up** the wet sheets in front of the fire.*
2 to have the top part supported or attached, but not the bottom part: *Flags **hung from** the windows of the house.*
3 (past tense and past participle **hanged**) to kill someone by putting a rope around their neck and then letting them fall, so that they are hanging in the air: *He tried to **hang himself** with his belt.* • *Some people said the killer should have been hanged for what he did.*

PHRASAL VERBS
hang around, hang about *BrE* (informal)
to stay in one place without doing very much, often because you are waiting for someone: *Some girls were **hanging around** outside the cafe.* • *We **hung about** waiting for Jack but he didn't arrive.*
hang on
1 (spoken): ***Hang on a minute*** (=wait) – *I want to talk to you!*
2 to hold something very firmly: *The dog bit the man's arm and **hung on**.*
hang onto
hang onto something (informal) to keep something that is important to you: *I'm surprised Gemma managed to **hang onto** her job after she was caught stealing.*
hang up
to finish a telephone conversation by putting the telephone down so that it is no longer connected: *Before you **hang up**, make sure you have written down all the details correctly.*

hang up

hang[2] *noun* **get the hang of something** (informal) to learn how to do something: *Once I got the hang of skiing, it was easy.* ➔ see Thesaurus at LEARN

hang·ar /ˈhæŋə $ ˈhæŋɚ/ *noun* a large building where aircraft are kept

hang·er /ˈhæŋə $ ˈhæŋɚ/ also **coathanger** *noun* a metal, plastic, or wooden object that you put a piece of clothing on to hang it up, for example in a cupboard

hang·o·ver /ˈhæŋəʊvə $ ˈhæŋˌoʊvɚ/ *noun* when someone feels ill because they drank too much alcohol the evening before: *He had a terrible hangover after the party.*

han·kie, hanky /ˈhæŋki/ *noun* (informal) (plural **hankies**) a HANDKERCHIEF

hap·haz·ard /ˌhæpˈhæzəd $ ˌhæpˈhæzɚd/ *adjective* not planned or organized: *We work in a very haphazard way.* —**haphazardly** *adverb*: *cars parked haphazardly*

hap·pen /ˈhæpən/ *verb*

KEY PATTERNS
happen to someone/something
happen to do something

1 to start and continue for a period of time: *Did anything interesting happen at school today?* • *I couldn't see what was happening on the stage.* • *Thomas was afraid that something terrible had happened.* • ***What happens if** you mix the two liquids?*
2 to affect someone or something: *What **happened to** you? Did you fall in the river?* • *When you didn't phone, I worried that something had **happened to** you.* • *The floods were the worst thing to **happen to** the country in years.*
3 to do something by chance: *Winchell **happened to** be a few minutes early.* • *I **happened to** have some tissues with me.*

THESAURUS
take place: *The wedding will **take place** in the local church* (=happen, especially after being planned).
occur (formal): *A robbery **occurred** around 9 p.m.* (=happened when people did not expect it).

hap·pen·ing /ˈhæpənɪŋ/ *noun* a strange or unusual event: *There have been some bizarre happenings in the old castle.*

hap·pi·ly /ˈhæpəli/ *adverb* in a happy way: *She laughed happily.*

hap·pi·ness /ˈhæpinəs/ *noun* (no plural) when someone is happy: *a feeling of great happiness*

hap·py /ˈhæpi/ *adjective* (**happier**, **happiest**)

KEY PATTERNS
happy to do something
happy with something

1 feeling pleased, satisfied, or in a good emotional state ANTONYM **unhappy**: *I was so **happy to** hear about the birth of your baby.* • *I'm very **happy with** the results.* • *Sam was **feeling happy** because it was his birthday.*
2 making you feel pleased or happy ANTONYM **sad**: *The story had a happy ending.* • *My wedding day was the **happiest day of my life**.*
3 Happy Birthday, Happy New Year used as a way of greeting someone on a special occasion

THESAURUS
glad: *I'm really **glad** you can come to the party* (=happy about the situation).
pleased: *Her parents were **pleased** that she had done so well* (=happy because something good had happened).
delighted (formal): *Everyone was **delighted** when they heard the news* (=very happy because something good had happened).
cheerful: *Tom's a very **cheerful** little boy* (=seeming happy and smiling a lot).

har·ass /ˈhærəs/ *verb* to deliberately annoy or threaten someone, usually over a period of time: *She was harassed by her neighbours for two years.*

har·ass·ment /ˈhærəsmənt/ *noun* (no plural) threatening or offensive behaviour towards someone: *racial harassment*

SPELLING
This word is often spelled wrongly. The correct spelling is: **harassment**.

harbour

har·bour¹ *BrE*, **harbor** *AmE* /ˈhɑːbə $ ˈhɑrbɚ/ *noun* an area of water next to the land where ships can stay safely

harbour² *BrE*, **harbor** *AmE* *verb* (written) if you harbour an unpleasant feeling or idea, it stays in your mind for a long time: *I began to harbour doubts about my boss.*

hard¹ /hɑːd $ hɑrd/ *adjective*

KEY PATTERNS
it is hard (for someone) to do something

1 very firm and difficult to cut, break, or bend ANTONYM **soft**: *The chairs were hard and uncomfortable to sit on.* • *This soil is too hard to dig.* • *a book with a hard cover*
2 difficult to do or understand ANTONYM **easy**: *That test was much harder than the one we had last week.* • *She finds* ***it hard to*** *get to sleep sometimes.* • *The government wants to* ***make it harder for*** *foreigners* ***to*** *work in this country.* • *That's a very* ***hard question*** *to answer.*
3 needing a lot of physical or mental effort: *Clearing the snow was* ***hard work.*** • *Mom's had a really* ***hard day*** *at the office.*

PHRASES

give someone a hard time (informal) to make life difficult or unpleasant for someone, for example by criticizing them or being unkind to them: *Suzie gave Tom* ***a hard time*** *when they were married.*

THESAURUS
firm: *Bake the cake until it is* ***firm*** *when you touch it* (=not soft to touch, but not completely hard).
solid: *The ice on the pond was frozen* ***solid*** (=completely hard, and not bending or moving).

hard² *adverb*
with a lot of effort or force: *Kay* ***worked hard*** *all year and came top of the class.* • *You can do anything if you* ***try hard enough.*** • *He pulled hard on the rope, but nothing happened, so he pulled harder.*

ˌhard-and-ˈfast *adjective* (informal) **hard-and-fast rule** a definite rule that is always the same: *There are no hard-and-fast rules for success.*

hard•back /ˈhɑːdbæk $ ˈhardbæk/ *noun* a book with a strong stiff cover —**hardback** *adjective*: *a hardback book*

ˌhard-ˈboiled *adjective* a hard-boiled egg has been boiled in its shell until the yellow part is firm

ˈhard ˌcopy *noun* information from a computer that is printed on paper: *Can I email the file or do you want hard copy?*

ˌhard ˈdisk *noun* a part fixed inside a computer that you use to store information: *I have no memory left on my hard disk.*

hard•en /ˈhɑːdn $ ˈhardn/ *verb* to become firm ANTONYM **soften**: *The plaster will harden in 24 hours.*

ˈhard hat *noun* a hard hat that protects your head, worn for example by a builder ➔ see picture at HAT

ˌhard-ˈheaded *adjective* practical and able to make difficult decisions: *A businessman needs to be hard-headed to succeed.*

ˌhard-ˈhearted *adjective* a hard-hearted person does not care about other people's feelings: *I don't know how you can be so hard-hearted.*

hard•ly /ˈhɑːdli $ ˈhardli/ *adverb*

KEY PATTERNS
can/could hardly do something
hardly any/anyone/anything
hardly ever

1 almost not, none etc SYNONYM **scarcely**: *Jean was so excited she* ***could hardly*** *speak.* • *Jill smiled at Jack, but he hardly noticed.* • ***Hardly anyone*** *could remember seeing Bill at the party.* • *He owns a big house, but he's* ***hardly ever*** (=almost never) *there.* ➔ see Thesaurus at RARELY
2 definitely not: *He was driving very fast, so it was* ***hardly surprising*** *that the police stopped him.*

ˌhard-ˈnosed *adjective* a hard-nosed person is determined to get what they want and is not affected by their feelings: *a hard-nosed businessman*

hard•ship /ˈhɑːdʃɪp $ ˈhardˌʃɪp/ *noun* something that makes your life unpleasant: *The family suffered years of poverty and hardship.* • *the hardships of war*

ˌhard ˈshoulder *noun BrE* the area at the side of a big road where you are allowed to stop if you have a problem with your car SYNONYM **shoulder** *AmE*

ˌhard ˈup *adjective* (informal) someone who is hard up does not have enough money: *We were very hard up when I was young.*

hard•ware /ˈhɑːdweə $ ˈhardwer/ *noun* (no plural) computer machinery and equipment: *The problem is with the hardware, not the program.*

ˌhard-ˈworking *adjective* working with a lot of effort ANTONYM **lazy**: *hard-working pupils*

har·dy /ˈhɑːdi $ ˈhɑrdi/ *adjective* (**hardier**, **hardiest**) strong and able to live in difficult conditions: *a hardy little horse*

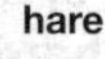

hare /heə $ her/ *noun* an animal like a rabbit with long ears, which can run very fast

harm¹ /hɑːm $ hɑrm/ *noun* **1** (no plural) damage, injury, or making a situation worse: *We have to protect old people from harm.* • *Staying out late once in a while* ***does you no harm*** (=does not hurt you). • *This new law could* ***do more harm than good*** (=make the situation worse rather than better).
2 there's no harm in doing something (spoken) used to say that doing something might help a situation, and that it cannot make the situation any worse: *Even if Dad refuses to lend you the car,* ***there's no harm in*** *asking.*

harm² *verb* to damage or hurt something or someone: *Luckily, he wasn't harmed by his experiences.*

harm·ful /ˈhɑːmfəl $ ˈhɑrmfəl/ *adjective* something that is harmful causes harm SYNONYM **damaging**: *products that are harmful to the environment*

harm·less /ˈhɑːmləs $ ˈhɑrmləs/ *adjective* something that is harmless does not cause any harm: *a harmless fly*

har·mon·i·ca /hɑːˈmɒnɪkə $ hɑrˈmɑnɪkə/ *noun* a small musical instrument with holes along the side that you blow into

har·mo·ny /ˈhɑːməni $ ˈhɑrməni/ *noun* **1** (no plural) when people are not arguing or fighting: *Why can't people live in harmony?* **2** (plural **harmonies**) musical notes that sound good together

har·ness¹ /ˈhɑːnɪs $ ˈhɑrnɪs/ *noun* (plural **harnesses**) **1** a set of bands that you put round a horse so that it can pull a vehicle **2** a set of bands that hold someone or stop them from falling: *The climbers used safety harnesses.*

harness² *verb* (written) to use the energy from something: *ways of harnessing the sun's energy*

harp /hɑːp $ hɑrp/ *noun* a large musical instrument with strings stretched on a frame with three corners

harsh /hɑːʃ $ hɑrʃ/ *adjective* (**harsher**, **harshest**) **1** unpleasant and extreme or rough: *a harsh winter* • *the harsh cries of the seabirds* **2** unkind or strict: *harsh laws* • *harsh criticism* —**harshly** *adverb*: *We should not judge him too harshly.*

har·vest¹ /ˈhɑːvɪst $ ˈhɑrvɪst/ *noun* when grain, vegetables etc are collected from the fields, or the amount that you collect: *Harvest is a busy time.* • *The harvest was good this year.*

harvest² *verb* to collect grain, vegetables etc from the fields

has the third person singular of the present tense of HAVE

ˈhas-been *noun* (informal) someone who is no longer important or popular

hash /hæʃ/ *noun* **make a hash of something** (informal) to do something very badly

has·n't /ˈhæzənt/ the short form of 'has not': *Peter hasn't come home yet.*

has·sle¹ /ˈhæsəl/ *noun* (informal) something that is annoying because it takes a lot of time or effort SYNONYM **bother**: *I didn't want the hassle of moving house again.*

hassle² *verb* (informal) to continuously ask someone to do something, in a way that is annoying: *He keeps hassling me about the money I owe him.*

haste /heɪst/ *noun* (no plural) (formal) when you do something very quickly, because you do not have enough time: *In her haste to leave, she forgot to lock the door.*

has·ten /ˈheɪsən/ *verb* (written) to make something happen sooner: *The accident hastened his death.*

PRONUNCIATION
In this word you do not pronounce the **t**.

hast·y /ˈheɪsti/ *adjective* (**hastier**, **hastiest**) done too quickly, without thinking carefully SYNONYM **hurried**: *He soon regretted his hasty decision.*

hats

hat /hæt/ *noun* something that you wear on your head

hatch¹ /hætʃ/ *verb* if an egg hatches, it breaks and a baby bird, fish, or insect comes out

hatch

chicks hatching

hatch² *noun* (plural **hatches**) a small door in a ship, plane, or wall

hatch·et /ˈhætʃɪt/ *noun* a small AXE

hate¹ /heɪt/ *verb*

KEY PATTERNS
hate (doing) something
hate to do something

to have a very strong feeling that you do not like someone or something ANTONYM **love**: *I hate poetry – it's so boring.* • *I hate my boss.* • *Anne hates cleaning the car.* • *We all* **hated to** *see the Red Sox lose a game.* • *If you eat all those biscuits, you'll hate yourself.*

THESAURUS
can't stand (spoken): *I can't stand chemistry lessons* (=hate them).
loathe (formal): *Dad loathes shopping at the weekend* (=hates it very much).
detest (formal): *Some children detest green vegetables* (=hate them very much).

hate² *noun* (no plural) a very strong feeling of not liking someone ANTONYM **love**

ha·tred /ˈheɪtrəd/ *noun* (no plural) (formal) a very strong feeling of not liking someone or something ANTONYM **love**: *her hatred of spiders*

ˈhat trick *noun* if a player scores a hat trick in a game of football or HOCKEY, they score three GOALS in one game

haul /hɔːl/ (formal) *noun* a large amount of things that someone has stolen, or that the police have found: *The robbers got away with their haul of jewellery.* • *a drugs haul*

haunt·ed /ˈhɔːntɪd/ *adjective* if people think a place is haunted, they think there are GHOSTS there: *The old church is haunted.*

haunt·ing /ˈhɔːntɪŋ/ *adjective* something that is haunting is so beautiful or sad that you remember it: *a haunting picture of a girl in a forest*

have → see box on pages 308 and 309

have·n't /ˈhævənt/ the short form of 'have not': *I haven't forgotten.*

hav·oc /ˈhævək/ *noun* (no plural) a situation in which there is a lot of CONFUSION: *The failure of the airport's computer system caused havoc.*

hawk /hɔːk/ *noun* a wild bird that eats small birds and animals

hay /heɪ/ *noun* (no plural) dried grass that is used to feed farm animals

ˈhay ˌfever *noun* (no plural) a medical condition like a bad cold that some people get from breathing in dust from plants

haz·ard /ˈhæzəd $ ˈhæzərd/ *noun* something that may be dangerous: *Those piles of boxes are a fire hazard.*

have /hæv/ *verb* (past tense and past participle **had** /hæd/, present participle **having**, third person singular **has**)

1 used to form the perfect tense: ***Have** you **met** Laura?* • *He**'s seen** the film six times.* • *I**'ve been** so worried!* • *I **haven't written** to her since Christmas.* • *Eric **hadn't told** the teacher about it.*

2 also **have got** used when describing someone or something: *He **has** short dark hair.* • *The school **has** over 1,500 students.* • *I **don't have** a lot of patience!* • *The car **has** only **got** two doors.*

The car **has** only **got** two doors.

3 also **have got** to own, possess, or be carrying something: *Everyone **has** a computer these days.* • *Do you **have** any money with you?* • *We **have got** plenty of time.*

Everyone **has** a computer these days.

4 also **have got** used when talking about your family or your friends: *I **have** two brothers.* • *She**'s got** three children.* • *He **had** lots of friends at school.*

5 to eat or drink something: ***Have** you **had** your breakfast?* • *I usually **have** a sandwich for lunch.* • *I**'ll have** a glass of orange juice.*

6 also **have got** to be affected by something bad such as an illness, a type of pain, or a problem: *She **has** a bad cold.* • *I**'ve got** a slight headache.* • *I**'ve got** problems with the car.*

I've got problems with the car.

7 to experience something: *I **had** a surprise when I opened the door.* • ***Did** you **have** a good trip?* • *We all **had** a great time.*

We all **had** a great time.

GRAMMAR

Questions and negative sentences with **have**

• You use **do** to form questions with **have**: *Do you have any more questions? • What kind of car does she have?*

• You use **do not** to form negative sentences: *I don't have any money. • She doesn't have any brothers or sisters.*

Using **have got**

• **Have got** is more commonly used than **have** in spoken British English. It is only used in the present tense, usually in the short forms **I've got**, **she's got**, **they've got** etc: *I've got lots of money. • He's got a big house. • We've got very little time.*

• In questions you say: *Have you got a car? • Has he got any money? • What have we got for dinner?*

• In negative sentences you say: *I haven't got any more time. • She hasn't got any more milk.*

PHRASES

have (got) to do something
if you have to do something, you must do it: ***I have to** go to work now. • You've **got to** talk to him. • You don't **have to** answer all the questions. • She's **got to** be at the airport by seven.*

GRAMMAR

The negative of **have to** is **don't have to**: *I don't have to get up early.*

had better do something (spoken)
say this when telling someone what is the best thing to do: *You'**d better** put your shoes on – it's almost time to go. • I'**d better** check that the doors are locked.*

GRAMMAR

• You say **You had better see a doctor**.

✗ Don't say 'You had better to see a doctor.'

may I have ...?, **could I have ...?**, **I'll have ...** (spoken)
say this to ask someone politely for something: *Dad, **may I have** a chocolate bar? • **I'll have** a cheese sandwich, please.*

Have is also used in these phrases:

have breakfast/lunch/dinner **have a coffee/a drink** **have something to eat/drink**
have a party **have a rest/a break/a holiday**
have a meeting/a discussion/an argument
have a good time/a good trip **have fun** **have problems/trouble**
have a bath/shower (American people usually say **take a bath/shower**)

VERB FORMS

Present tense

Singular	**Plural**
I **have** (I'**ve**)	we **have** (we'**ve**)
you **have** (you'**ve**)	you **have** (you'**ve**)
he, she, it **has** (he'**s**, she'**s**, it'**s**)	they **have** (they'**ve**)

Past tense

Singular	**Plural**
I **had** (I'**d**)	we **had** (we'**d**)
you **had** (you'**d**)	you **had** (you'**d**)
he, she, it **had** (he'**d**, she'**d**, it'**d**)	they **had** (they'**d**)

present participle: **having** past participle: **had**
negative short forms: **haven't**, **hasn't**, **hadn't**

A B C D E F G H I J K L M N O P Q R S T U V W X Y Z

haz·ard·ous /ˈhæzədəs $ ˈhæzərdəs/ *adjective* dangerous: *a hazardous journey through the mountains*

haze /heɪz/ *noun* (no plural) smoke, dust, or mist in the air

haz·y /ˈheɪzi/ *adjective* (**hazier**, **haziest**) if something is hazy, you cannot see or remember it clearly: *I only have a hazy memory of my first day at school.*

he /i; strong hiː/ *pronoun* used when talking about a man or boy: *David said he would see us later.* • *He didn't look very happy, did he?*

head¹ /hed/ *noun*

KEY PATTERNS
the head of an organization

1 the top part of your body that has your eyes, mouth, brain etc in it: *She rested her head on my shoulder.* • *"No," replied John, shaking his head.*
→ see picture on page A5
2 the most important person in a group or organization: *the head of the Engineering Department*
3 the head in Britain, the teacher who is in charge of a school SYNONYM **principal** *AmE*: *The head wants to see the student who broke the window.*
4 heads the side of a coin that has a picture of someone's head on it ANTONYM **tails**

PHRASES
a head, per head for each person: *The bus to Calais will cost £15 a head* (=each person will have to pay £15).
do something in your head to do a calculation in your mind, rather than writing it down: *I didn't have a pen, so I added it up in my head.*
laugh your head off, scream your head off (informal) to laugh or scream a lot: *When I told him what had happened, he laughed his head off.*

head² *verb* **1** if you head somewhere, you go towards that place: *I headed back to the house.* • *They headed for the beach.* **2 be heading for something, be headed for something** if you are heading for a situation, it is likely to happen: *Our team was heading for defeat.*

head·ache /ˈhedeɪk/ *noun* a pain in your head: *I've got a terrible headache.*

GRAMMAR
You say **She has a headache.**
✘ Don't say 'She has headache.'

head·ing /ˈhedɪŋ/ *noun* the title at the top of a piece of writing

head·light /ˈhedlaɪt/ also **head·lamp** /ˈhedlæmp/ *BrE noun* one of the large lights at the front of a vehicle

head·line /ˈhedlaɪn/ *noun* **1** the title of a newspaper report **2 the headlines** a sentence about each main piece of news on a television or radio news programme: *Here are today's headlines.*

head·long /ˈhedlɒŋ $ ˈhedlɔːŋ/ *adverb* if you fall or jump headlong, you do it with your head going first: *He fell headlong down the stairs.*

head·mas·ter /ˌhedˈmɑːstə $ ˈhedˌmæstər/ *noun BrE* a male teacher who is in charge of a school SYNONYM **principal** *AmE*

head·mis·tress /ˌhedˈmɪstrəs $ ˈhedˌmɪstrəs/ *noun* (plural **headmistresses**) *BrE* a female teacher who is in charge of a school SYNONYM **principal** *AmE*

ˌhead-ˈon *adverb* if two vehicles meet head-on, the front part of one vehicle hits the front part of the other —**head-on** *adjective*: *a head-on crash*

head·phones /ˈhedfəʊnz $ ˈhedfoʊnz/ *plural noun* a piece of equipment that you wear over your ears to listen to a radio, recorded music etc: *a pair of headphones*

head·quar·ters /ˈhedˌkwɔːtəz $ ˈhedˌkwɔrtərz/ (abbreviation **HQ**) *plural noun* the place where the people controlling an organization or military action work

ˌhead ˈstart *noun* an advantage that helps you to succeed: *With Tony on our team, we had a head start.*

ˌhead ˈteacher *noun BrE* a HEADMASTER or HEADMISTRESS SYNONYM **principal** *AmE*

head·way /ˈhedweɪ/ *noun* **make headway** to make progress

heal /hiːl/ *verb* if a wound or broken bone heals, it becomes healthy again: *The cut healed quickly.*

health /helθ/ *noun* (no plural)
your health is how well or ill you are: *Exercise is **good for your health**. • Do you have any **health problems**?*

PHRASES

in good health, in poor health if you are in good health, you are healthy: *He had been in poor health for some time.*

'health club *noun* a place where you pay to use equipment to do physical exercises

'health food *noun* food that contains only natural substances

health·y /'helθi/ *adjective* (**healthier, healthiest**)
1 not ill, or not likely to become ill
ANTONYM **unhealthy**: *I feel healthier since I stopped smoking. • The puppies looked healthy and strong.*
2 healthy food, activities etc are good for you and will help you stay well
ANTONYM **unhealthy**: *a healthy diet • It's healthier to live near the sea.*

> **THESAURUS**
> **well**: *I thought Anna looked very **well*** (=healthy and happy).
> **fine** (spoken): *"Hi, how are you?" "Fine, thanks* (=healthy)*."*
> **better**: *Jason's had a cold, but he's feeling **better** now* (=less ill than he was).
> **fit**: *I run every day to keep **fit*** (=healthy, with a strong body).

heap¹ /hiːp/ *noun* a large untidy pile of things: *a heap of stones* ➔ see Thesaurus at PILE¹

heap² *verb* to put a lot of things on top of each other in an untidy way

hear /hɪə $ hɪr/ *verb* (past tense and past participle **heard** /hɜːd $ hɝd/)

> **KEY PATTERNS**
> **hear a sound/noise**
> **hear someone**
> **hear someone singing/laughing/arguing**
> **hear someone say/do something**
> **hear about something**
> **hear (that)**

1 to notice a sound with your ears: *I **heard** footsteps in the kitchen. • You'll have to speak louder. I can't **hear** you. • I could **hear** the girls laughing. • I **heard** him go down the stairs.*
2 to get information about something: *Have you **heard the news** about Terry? • I had **heard** a lot **about** the Greek islands, but I was surprised how beautiful they were. • I **heard that** he was going too. • Have you **heard who** is going to be the new headteacher?*

> **WORD CHOICE**
> **hear** or **listen**?
> • **Hear** means "to notice a sound with your ears": *I **heard** the doorbell.*
> • **Listen** means "to pay attention to what someone is saying, or to music or other sounds": *He was **listening to** music in his bedroom.*

PHRASAL VERBS

hear from
to get news from someone, in a letter or by telephone: *I **heard from** Barbara at Christmas. • She went for a job interview, but she hasn't **heard from** them yet. • I look forward to hearing from you soon* (=you write this near the end of a letter).

hear of
to know about someone or something: *"Do you know Jerry Tonelli?" "No, I've never **heard of** him." • I've **heard of** the book, but I've never read it.*

hear·ing /'hɪərɪŋ $ 'hɪrɪŋ/ *noun* **1** (no plural) the sense that you use to hear sounds: *My Grandpa's hearing is getting worse.* **2** an official meeting to find out the facts about something

'hearing aid *noun* a small object that someone can put in their ear so that they can hear better

hearse /hɜːs $ hɝs/ *noun* a large car for carrying a dead body in a COFFIN at a funeral

heart /hɑːt $ hɑrt/ *noun*

> **KEY PATTERNS**
> **know/believe something in your heart**
> **wish/hope etc something with all your heart**

1 the part of your body inside your chest that pushes blood around your body: *I could feel her heart beating. • Tom had an operation on his heart last year.*
2 your strongest and most true feelings, especially feelings of love and caring: *Her sad story touched the hearts of people around the world. • I*

A B C D E F G H I J K L M N O P Q R S T U V W X Y Z

*knew **in my heart** that we could not win.* • *Penny believed **with all** her **heart** that Sam was a good man.*
3 the central or most important part of something: *We sat down to rest in **the heart of** the forest.* • *These different beliefs are **at the heart of** the dispute.*
4 a shape that is used to mean love: *The card had a big red heart on it.*
5 hearts a group of playing cards with the shape of a red heart printed on them: *the ace of hearts*
PHRASES
learn something by heart, know something by heart if you learn a piece of writing or music by heart, you can remember all of it correctly without having to look at it: *I **learned** the song **by heart** and sang it for the rest of the class.* • *I think I **know** my speech **by heart** now.*

ˈheart atˌtack *noun* when a person's heart suddenly stops beating normally, sometimes causing death: *He had a heart attack.*

heart·beat /ˈhɑːtbiːt $ ˈhɑrtbit/ *noun* the movement of your heart: *The baby's heartbeat is irregular.*

heart·break·ing /ˈhɑːtˌbreɪkɪŋ $ ˈhɑrtˌbreɪkɪŋ/ *adjective* something that is heartbreaking makes you feel very sad: *It's heartbreaking to lose a pet.*

heart·brok·en /ˈhɑːtˌbrəʊkən $ ˈhɑrtˌbroʊkən/ *adjective* very sad because of something that has happened SYNONYM **devastated**: *When he had to sell his car, he was heartbroken.*

heart·felt /ˈhɑːtfelt $ ˈhɑrtfelt/ *adjective* (written) honest and sincere: *a heartfelt apology*

hearth /hɑːθ $ hɑrθ/ *noun* the area of floor in front of the fire in a house

heart·i·ly /ˈhɑːtəli $ ˈhɑrtl-i/ *adverb* (written) **1** in a very CHEERFUL or friendly way: *He laughed heartily.*
2 very much or completely: *I heartily agree.*

heart·less /ˈhɑːtləs $ ˈhɑrtləs/ *adjective* cruel: *How can you be so heartless?*

heart·warm·ing /ˈhɑːtˌwɔːmɪŋ $ ˈhɑrtˌwɔrmɪŋ/ *adjective* a heartwarming story makes you feel happy because something nice happens in it

heart·y /ˈhɑːti $ ˈhɑrti/ *adjective* (**heartier, heartiest**) **1** very CHEERFUL or friendly: *hearty laughter* **2** a hearty meal is very large

heat¹ /hiːt/ *noun*
1 (no plural) when something is warm or hot: *The heat of the fire will soon make the room warmer.* • *I could feel the heat from the oven.*
2 the heat very hot weather: *We went into the house to escape from **the heat** outside.*
3 the American word for HEATING
4 one of the first races or games in a big competition. The winners of each heat compete against each other in the next race or game until someone wins the final one
PHRASES
in the heat of the moment if you do something in the heat of the moment, you do it without thinking, because you are very excited or angry: *She said some very cruel things **in the heat of the moment**.*

heat² *verb* **1** to make something warmer: *They use gas to heat the house.* **2 heat something up** if you heat up food, you make it warmer: *I'll heat up some soup for you.*

heat·ed /ˈhiːtɪd/ *adjective* a heated argument, discussion etc is one in which people become very angry

heat·er /ˈhiːtə $ ˈhitɚ/ *noun* a piece of equipment in a building, used to heat air or water

heath·er /ˈheðə $ ˈheðɚ/ *noun* a small bush with purple or white flowers that grows on hills

heat·ing /ˈhiːtɪŋ/ *noun* (no plural) *BrE* the system in a building that keeps it warm SYNONYM **heat** *AmE*: *I'll turn the heating up.*

heat·wave /ˈhiːtˌweɪv/ *noun* a period of unusually hot weather

heave /hiːv/ *verb* to pull, throw, or lift something heavy with a lot of effort: *He heaved the suitcase out of the car.*
➔ see Thesaurus at PULL¹

heav·en /ˈhevən/ *noun* (no plural)
1 also **Heaven** the place where many people believe God lives and good

people go after they die **2** (informal) a very pleasant situation or experience ANTONYM **hell**: *After standing up all day, it was heaven to sit down.* **3 for heaven's sake** (spoken) used when you are annoyed: *For heaven's sake, why didn't you phone me to say you'd be late?*

heav·ily /ˈhevəli/ *adverb* very much or a lot: *It was still raining heavily.*

heavy

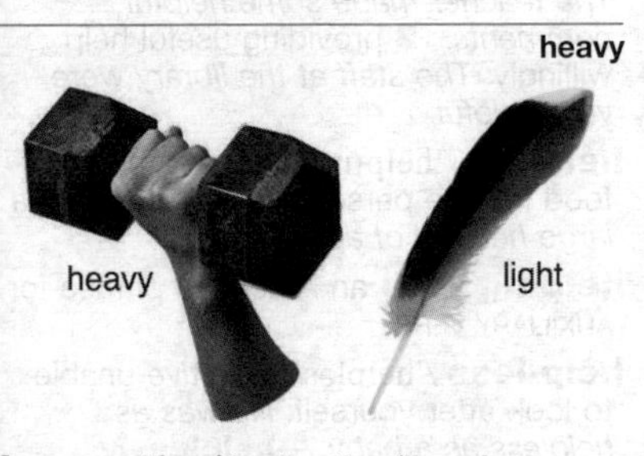

heav·y /ˈhevi/ *adjective* (**heavier**, **heaviest**)
1 something that is heavy weighs a lot ANTONYM **light**: *The women struggled along carrying their heavy bags.* • *How heavy is the parcel?*
2 if traffic is heavy, there are a lot of cars and other vehicles on the road ANTONYM **light**
3 very thick or warm ANTONYM **light**: *She pulled the heavy blanket tightly over us both.*
PHRASES
a heavy drinker, a heavy smoker someone who drinks a lot of alcohol or smokes a lot of cigarettes
heavy rain, heavy snow a lot of rain or snow that falls at once ANTONYM **light**: *There was* ***heavy rain*** *in the night, and in the morning some roads were flooded.*

ˌheavy-ˈhanded *adjective* too severe or using too much force: *He dealt with the problem in a heavy-handed way.*

heav·y·weight /ˈheviweɪt/ *adjective* a heavyweight BOXER is in the heaviest weight group —**heavyweight** *noun*

hec·tare /ˈhektɑː $ ˈhekter/ *noun* a unit for measuring the area of a piece of land, equal to 10,000 square metres

hec·tic /ˈhektɪk/ *adjective* very busy or full of activity: *I've had a really hectic week and I'm exhausted.*

he'd /id; strong hiːd/ the short form of 'he would' or 'he had': *I knew he'd understand.* • *He'd made a terrible mess.*

hedge /hedʒ/ *noun* a row of bushes along the edge of a field or garden ➔ see picture at FENCE[1]

hedgehog

hedge·hog /ˈhedʒhɒg $ ˈhedʒhɑg/ *noun* a small animal whose body is covered in sharp points

heel /hiːl/ *noun*
1 the back part of your foot ➔ see picture on page A5
2 the part of a shoe that is under your heel: *I can't walk in shoes with high heels.* ➔ see picture at SHOE

hef·ty /ˈhefti/ *adjective* (informal) (**heftier**, **heftiest**) large, heavy, or strong: *He had to pay a hefty fine for stealing.*

height /haɪt/ *noun*
1 how tall or high someone or something is: *We measured* ***the height of*** *the building.* • *My sister is about the same height as me.*
2 the height of something is the time when it is busiest or most successful SYNONYM **peak**: *I would never go to Paris* ***at the height of*** *the tourist season.*

PRONUNCIATION
You pronounce **height** like 'bite'.

height·en /ˈhaɪtn/ *verb* (written) to make a feeling stronger SYNONYM **increase**: *The rumours heightened people's worries.*

heir /eə $ er/ *noun* your heir is the person who will receive your money and property when you die

heir·ess /ˈeərəs $ ˈerəs/ *noun* (plural **heiresses**) a woman who will receive a lot of money or property when someone dies

heir·loom /ˈeəluːm $ ˈerlum/ *noun* a valuable object that the same family has owned for many years

held the past tense and past participle of HOLD

hel·i·cop·ter /ˈhelɪkɒptə $ ˈhelɪˌkɑptɚ/ *noun* an aircraft with long metal parts on top that go round very fast to make it fly ➔ see picture on page A11

he·li·um /ˈhiːliəm/ *noun* (no plural) a gas that is lighter than air

he'll /il; strong hiːl/ the short form of 'he will': *He'll be so surprised!*

hell, Hell /hel/ *noun* the place where some people believe bad people are punished after they die

hel·lo also **hallo** *BrE* /həˈləʊ $ həˈloʊ/ used when you meet someone or start talking to them on the telephone: *Hello, can I help you?* • *Hello, my name is Jessica.*

hel·met /ˈhelmət/ *noun* a hard hat that protects your head: *You have to wear a helmet when you ride a motorbike.*

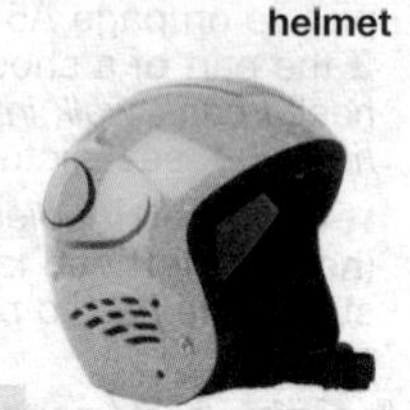
helmet

help¹ /help/ *verb*

KEY PATTERNS
help someone
help someone (to) do something
help someone with something

1 if you help someone, you do some of their work for them: *Thanks for helping me.* • *Shall I help you clean the car?* • *Sarah* ***helped*** *me* ***to*** *carry the boxes upstairs.* • *Will you* ***help*** *me* ***with*** *the washing up?*
2 to make it easier for someone to do something: *The extra money will help me pay for a new car.*
3 if something helps, it makes a situation better: *Would it help if you had someone to talk to?*
4 cannot help doing something, could not help doing something if you cannot help doing something, you cannot stop yourself from doing it: *I* ***couldn't help*** *laughing when I saw him in his costume.*
5 Help! (spoken) used to call someone when you are in danger

PHRASES
help yourself to take something that you want, without asking: *Please* ***help yourself*** *to a drink.*

THESAURUS
give someone a hand: *Can you give me a hand with the dinner* (=help me with it)*?*
assist (formal): *It's a nurse's job to assist the doctor* (=help him or her).

help² *noun* **1** (no plural) when you help someone SYNONYM **assistance**: *Thanks for all your help.* **2 be a help, be a lot of help** (spoken) to be useful: *"Shall I put these plates away?" "That would be a help."*

help·ful /ˈhelpfəl/ *adjective* **1** useful: *The teacher made some helpful comments.* **2** providing useful help willingly: *The staff at the library were very helpful.*

help·ing /ˈhelpɪŋ/ *noun* an amount of food for one person SYNONYM **serving**: *a large helping of apple pie*

ˈhelping verb an American phrase for AUXILIARY VERB

help·less /ˈhelpləs/ *adjective* unable to look after yourself: *He was as helpless as a baby.* —**helplessly** *adverb*: *She lay helplessly on the ground.*

hem /hem/ *noun* the edge of a piece of clothing that is turned under and stitched down

hem·i·sphere /ˈheməsfɪə $ ˈheməˌsfɪr/ *noun* one of the two halves of the Earth: *the northern hemisphere*

hen /hen/ *noun* a female chicken

hence /hens/ *adverb* (formal) for this reason: *The school is short of money; hence the need to reduce spending.*

hen·na /ˈhenə/ *noun* a reddish-brown substance used to change the colour of hair or to DYE the skin

her /ə $ ɚ; strong hɜː $ hɚ/ *pronoun, determiner*
1 used when talking about a woman or girl: *My mum loves flowers, so I bought these for her.* • *I really like her.*
2 belonging to a woman or girl: *She put her purse in her pocket.* • *Her name's Caroline.*

herb /hɜːb $ ɚb/ *noun* a plant used to improve the taste of food or to make medicine

PRONUNCIATION
British people pronounce the 'h' and say **herb.**
American people do not pronounce the 'h' and say **erb.**

her·bal /ˈhɜːbəl $ ˈɚbəl/ *adjective* made from herbs: *herbal medicine*

herd

a herd of deer

herd¹ /hɜːd $ hɚd/ *noun* a group of animals such as COWS, ELEPHANTS, or DEER: *a herd of cattle*

herd² *verb* to make people or animals move somewhere in a large group: *We were herded into a small room.*

here /hɪə $ hɪr/ *adverb* in or to the place where you are now: *I've lived here all my life.* • *Ben! Come here!* • *It's nice here* (=this is a nice place).

PHRASES

here's, here you are (spoken) used when you give or show something to someone: ***Here's** the magazine I was telling you about.* • ***Here you are** – you can borrow it for a few days.*

here it is, here he is etc (spoken) used when you find something or see someone: *I've got a pen in my bag somewhere – **here it is**.* • *"Is John coming too?" "Yes, **here he is**."*

GRAMMAR
You say **come here**.
✘ Don't say 'come to here'.

he·red·i·ta·ry /həˈredətəri $ həˈredəˌteri/ *adjective* a hereditary quality or disease is passed to a child by its parents

her·e·sy /ˈherəsi/ *noun* (formal) (plural **heresies**) a belief that a religious or political group thinks is wrong

her·i·tage /ˈherətɪdʒ/ *noun* things from a society's past that people think are valuable: *We must protect our musical heritage.*

he·ro /ˈhɪərəʊ $ ˈhɪroʊ/ *noun* (plural **heroes**) **1** someone who people admire because they have done something very brave or good: *When the soldiers returned, they were treated as heroes.* **2** the man who is the main character in a book, film, or play

he·ro·ic /hɪˈrəʊɪk $ hɪˈroʊɪk/ *adjective* very brave or determined to succeed: *The firefighters made heroic efforts to stop the fire from spreading.*

her·o·in /ˈherəʊɪn $ ˈheroʊɪn/ *noun* (no plural) a very strong illegal drug

her·o·ine /ˈherəʊɪn $ ˈheroʊɪn/ *noun* **1** the woman who is the main character in a book, film, or play **2** a woman who people admire because she has done something very brave or good

her·o·is·m /ˈherəʊɪzəm $ ˈheroʊˌɪzəm/ *noun* (no plural) great courage

hers /hɜːz $ hɚz/ *pronoun* a thing belonging to a woman or girl: *My hair is different from hers.* • *Sarah was here earlier, so I think this coat must be hers.*

her·self /ɜːˈself $ ɚˈself; strong hɜːˈself $ hɚˈself/ *pronoun* **1** used when the same woman or girl does an action and receives the action: *Jenny's mother introduced herself to the teacher.* • *Sophie bought some flowers for herself.* **2** used to emphasize that you are talking about one particular woman or girl: *Zoe arranged the trip for everyone, but she herself had to stay at home.*

PHRASES

by herself alone, or with no one helping: *She lives **by herself**.* • *She decorated the whole house **by herself**.*

he's /iz; strong hiːz/ the short form of 'he is' or 'he has': *He's my brother.* • *He's lost his keys.*

hes·i·tant /ˈhezətənt/ *adjective* (formal) if you are hesitant, you do not do something immediately, because you are nervous or not sure —**hesitantly** *adverb*: *"I'm not sure," she said hesitantly.*

hes·i·tate /ˈhezəteɪt/ *verb* **1** to stop for a moment before doing or saying something: *She hesitated a moment and then said "Yes".* **2 don't hesitate to do something** (written) used to tell someone that you are very willing for them to do something: *Please do not hesitate to contact me if you need any help.*

hes·i·ta·tion /ˌhezəˈteɪʃən/ *noun* when you hesitate: *He answered without hesitation.*

het·e·ro·sex·u·al /ˌhetərəˈsekʃuəl/ *adjective* (formal) sexually attracted to people of the opposite sex ANTONYM **homosexual**, **gay** —**heterosexual** *noun*

hex·a·gon /ˈheksəgən $ ˈheksəˌgɑn/ *noun* a flat shape with six sides

hey /heɪ/ (spoken, informal) used to get someone's attention or when you are surprised or interested: *Hey, that's amazing!*

hi /haɪ/ (spoken, informal) HELLO

hi·ber·nate /ˈhaɪbəneɪt $ ˈhaɪbɚˌneɪt/ *verb* if an animal hibernates, it sleeps during all of the winter and wakes up in spring

hic·cup[1], **hiccough** /ˈhɪkʌp/ *noun*
1 hiccups when your throat makes many short sounds that you cannot control: *I ate too fast and got hiccups.*
2 a small problem: *There were a few small hiccups before the concert began.*

hiccup[2] *verb* (**hiccupped, hiccupping**) if you hiccup, your throat makes many short sounds that you cannot control

hid the past tense of HIDE

hid·den[1] /ˈhɪdn/ *adjective* if something is hidden, you cannot see or find it easily: *They were filmed with hidden cameras.*

hidden[2] the past participle of HIDE

hide /haɪd/ *verb* (**hid** /hɪd/ **hidden** /ˈhɪdn/)

KEY PATTERNS
hide something in/behind/under etc something
hide in/behind/under etc something

1 if you hide something, you put it in a place where no one can find it SYNONYM **conceal**: *Mary **hid** the money **in** a cupboard.* • *He **hid** the papers **under** his bed.*
2 if you hide, you go to a place where no one can find you: *I **hid behind** the fence.*
3 if you hide your feelings, you do not show them SYNONYM **conceal**: *Steven tried to hide his disappointment.*

hid·e·ous /ˈhɪdiəs/ *adjective* very ugly or unpleasant: *a hideous yellow and purple dress*

hid·ing /ˈhaɪdɪŋ/ *noun* **be in hiding** to be hiding somewhere because you are in danger or you have done something wrong

hi-fi /ˈhaɪ faɪ/ *noun* a piece of electronic equipment that you use to play recorded music SYNONYM **stereo**

high

a high shelf

a tall building

high[1] /haɪ/ *adjective* (**higher, highest**)
1 measuring a lot from the bottom to the top ANTONYM **low**: *a high mountain*
2 a long way above the ground ANTONYM **low**: *The shelf is quite high and difficult to reach.*
3 used to talk about the height of something: *How high is Mount Everest?* • *The fence was about four feet high.*
4 above the usual level, amount, or standard ANTONYM **low**: *Student fees are quite high at some universities.* • *The temperature is highest at lunchtime.*
5 a high sound is near the top of the set of sounds that humans can hear ANTONYM **low**: *I can't sing the high notes.*

PHRASES

be high on something to feel happy or excited after taking an illegal drug: *Police said the driver must **have been high on drugs**.*

high in fat, high in salt etc a food that is high in fat, salt etc contains a lot of fat, salt etc: *Try to avoid foods that are high in fat.*

> **WORD CHOICE**
> **high** or **tall**?
> • You use **tall** about people, plants, and trees: *He's much **taller** than me.*
> • You use **high** about mountains and walls: *the world's **highest** mountain*
> • You can use either **high** or **tall** about buildings: *What is the name of the world's **highest/tallest** building?*

high² *adverb* a long way above the ground: *The balloon rose higher in the sky.* • *These birds build their nests **high up** on cliffs.*

ˌhigh-ˈclass *adjective* of good quality: *a high-class hotel*

ˌhigh-defiˈnition *adjective* high-definition television uses a system that shows images very clearly

ˌhigher eduˈcation *noun* (no plural) education at a college or university rather than a school

ˈhigh jump *noun* **the high jump** a sport in which you try to jump over a bar that is raised higher after each attempt

high·lands /ˈhaɪləndz/ *plural noun* an area with a lot of mountains: *the Scottish highlands*

high·light¹ /ˈhaɪlaɪt/ *verb* if you highlight something, you say it is very important: *In his speech, the president highlighted the issue of crime.*

highlight² *noun* the best part of something: *One of the highlights of the holiday was the boat trip.*

high·ly /ˈhaɪli/ *adverb* **1** very: *a highly intelligent girl* **2** if you think highly of someone, you respect and admire them a lot: *His employees think very highly of him.* • *a highly respected musician*

ˌhigh-ˈpitched *adjective* a high-pitched sound is high and sharp, and unpleasant to hear: *a high-pitched scream*

ˌhigh-ˈpowered *adjective* **1** a high-powered machine is very powerful **2** a high-powered job is important and difficult, with a lot of responsibility

high-rise

high-rise buildings

ˈhigh-rise *adjective* a high-rise building is a very tall modern building: *high-rise apartment blocks* —**high-rise** *noun*: *We live on the 17th floor of a high-rise.*

ˈhigh school *noun* **1** a school in the US or Canada for students between 14 and 18 years old **2** used in the names of some schools in Britain for students between 11 and 18 years old

ˈhigh street *noun BrE* the main street in a town, where shops and businesses are: *a busy high street*

high-tech, hi-tech /ˌhaɪ ˈtek/ *adjective* high-tech equipment is very modern, and uses the most advanced electronic parts

high·way /ˈhaɪweɪ/ *noun AmE* a wide main road that joins one city to another

hi·jack /ˈhaɪdʒæk/ *verb* to take control of a plane or vehicle by force —**hijacker** *noun*: *The hijackers told the pilot to fly to Rome.*

hike

hike /haɪk/ *verb* to walk a long way in the countryside for pleasure: *We hiked to the nearest pub.* —**hike** *noun*

A B C D E F G H I J K L M N O P Q R S T U V W X Y Z

hi·lar·i·ous /hɪˈleəriəs $ hɪˈleriəs/ *adjective* very funny: *a hilarious film* → see Thesaurus at FUNNY

hill /hɪl/ *noun* an area of high land, like a small mountain

hill·side /ˈhɪlsaɪd/ *noun* the sloping side of a hill

hill·y /ˈhɪli/ *adjective* (**hillier**, **hilliest**) a hilly area has a lot of hills

him /ɪm; strong hɪm/ *pronoun* used when talking about a man or boy: *Simon's parents gave him a skateboard for his birthday.* • *He seems friendly, but I don't trust him.* • *What did you say to him?*

him·self /ɪmˈself; strong hɪmˈself/ *pronoun*
1 used when the same man or boy does an action and receives the action: *Paul cut himself when he was slicing the bread.* • *He poured himself a glass of orange.*
2 used to emphasize that you are talking about one particular man or boy: *Roger loves dogs, but he doesn't own one himself.* • *I spoke to the owner of the shop himself.*

PHRASES

by himself alone, or with no one helping: *He spent the afternoon **by himself**.* • *He moved all the furniture **by himself**.*

hin·der /ˈhɪndə $ ˈhɪndɚ/ *verb* (formal) to make it difficult to do something SYNONYM **hamper**: *The lack of information is hindering the police investigation.*

hind·sight /ˈhaɪndsaɪt/ *noun* (no plural) the ability to understand or judge an event after it has happened: *With hindsight, I should never have let her use my car.*

Hin·du /ˈhɪnduː/ *noun* someone whose religion is Hinduism

Hin·du·is·m /ˈhɪndu-ɪzəm/ *noun* (no plural) the main religion in India, which has many gods and teaches that people live another life on Earth after they die

hinge¹ /hɪndʒ/ *noun* a piece of metal that is used to fix a door to a frame or a lid to a box, so that it can open and close

hinge² *verb* **hinge on something, hinge upon something** to depend on something: *My whole future hinges on my results this term.*

hint¹ /hɪnt/ *noun* **1** something you say in an indirect way, but not plainly: *She had given a few hints that she was going to leave.* **2** a small amount of something: *There was a hint of panic in his voice.* **3** a piece of advice on how to do something SYNONYM **tip**: *helpful hints on passing exams*

hint² *verb* to say something in an indirect way: *Ben had been hinting that he'd like a telescope for his birthday.*

hip¹ /hɪp/ *noun* your hips are the sides of your body between your legs and your waist: *She was standing with her hands on her hips, looking very angry.* → see picture on page A5

hip² *adjective* (informal) modern and fashionable

ˈhip-hop *noun* a kind of popular dance music with a regular beat, with words that are spoken rather than sung

hip·pie, **hippy** /ˈhɪpi/ *noun* (plural **hippies**) someone who deliberately does not live or dress like ordinary people and who believes in love and peace

hire¹ /haɪə $ haɪɚ/ *verb* **1** *BrE* to pay money to borrow something for a short time SYNONYM **rent** *AmE*: *They hired a car for three days.* **2** to pay someone to work for you: *They hired the best lawyer they could afford.*

hire² *noun* (no plural) *BrE* an arrangement in which you pay to borrow something for a short time: *Is this car for hire?*

his /ɪz; strong hɪz/ *determiner, pronoun*
1 belonging to a man or boy: *He wiped his hands on his shirt.* • *His sister was waiting for him.*
2 a thing belonging to a man or boy: *My eyesight is better than his.*

Hi·span·ic /hɪˈspænɪk/ *adjective* connected with people in the US whose families came originally from Latin America

hiss /hɪs/ *verb* **1** to make a noise that sounds like 'ssss': *The snake hissed at them.* → see picture on page A1

A B C D E F G H I J K L M N O P Q R S T U V W X Y Z

2 (written) to say something quietly, but in an angry way: *"I hate you!" she hissed.*

his·to·ri·an /hɪˈstɔːriən/ *noun* someone who studies or writes about history

his·tor·ic /hɪˈstɒrɪk $ hɪˈstɔrɪk/ *adjective* important in history: *the historic moment when man landed on the moon*

his·tor·i·cal /hɪˈstɒrɪkəl $ hɪˈstɔrɪkəl/ *adjective* in or related to history: *The film is based on a historical event.* • *historical records from the 18th century* —**historically** /-kli/ *adverb*: *Is the book historically accurate?*

his·to·ry /ˈhɪstəri/ *noun* (no plural)

KEY PATTERNS
the history of something
a history of something

1 all the things that happened in the past: *She's studying history at university.*
2 the history of something is how it has developed and changed since it started: *the history of pop music*
3 if someone has a history of an illness, they have had that illness in the past: *Do not take this drug if you have a history of heart problems.*

hit¹ /hɪt/ *verb* (past tense and past participle **hit**, **hitting**)

KEY PATTERNS
hit someone/something
hit someone on the head/nose etc
hit someone/something with a stick/bat/hammer etc
hit your head on something

1 to touch someone or something with a lot of force: *Simon swung his bat and hit the ball as hard as he could.* • *One of the bullets hit their car.* • *He **hit** me **on the head with** his tennis racket!* ➔ see picture on page A3
2 to crash into something: *The car came off the road and hit a tree.* • *She fell and **hit** her head **on** the pavement.*
3 (written) to reach a particular number or level: *The number of people who are unemployed has hit one million.*
4 to affect someone or something very badly: *The increase in fees will hit students from poorer families.*
5 if a thought hits you, you suddenly realize that it is true: *It suddenly **hit** me that I might fail the exam.*

THESAURUS
punch: *Steve **punched** the man in the stomach* (=hit him hard with his closed hand).
slap: *He was so rude that she **slapped** his face* (=hit his face with the flat part of her hand).
smack: *I don't agree with **smacking** children* (=hitting them as a punishment).
beat: *My brother saw the man **beating** his dog* (=hitting it hard many times).
strike (formal): *The dead man had been **struck** on the head* (=hit very hard, possibly with an object).
knock: *There's someone **knocking** at the door* (=hitting the door with a closed hand to get the attention of the people inside).
tap: *The man **tapped** on the car window* (=hit it gently with his fingers).
bang: *He **banged** his fist on the table* (=hit the table hard with his fist and made a loud noise).

hit² *noun*
1 a film, song, play etc that is very successful SYNONYM **success** ANTONYM **flop**: *The group's first album was a **big hit**.*
2 when something that you throw reaches the place that you are aiming at: *Of the five missiles, three were **direct hits** on their targets* (=three missiles hit the target exactly).

ˌhit-and-ˈrun *adjective* a hit-and-run accident is one in which a car driver hits someone but does not stop

hitch¹ /hɪtʃ/ (informal) another word for HITCHHIKE

hitch² *noun* (plural **hitches**) a small problem that causes a delay ➔ see Thesaurus at PROBLEM

hitch·hike /ˈhɪtʃhaɪk/ *verb* to travel by getting free rides in other people's cars: *He had hitchhiked down from Glasgow.* —**hitchhiker** *noun*: *We picked up three hitchhikers on the way to Glastonbury.* ➔ see picture on page 320

hi-tech another spelling of HIGH-TECH

hitchhike

HIV /ˌeɪtʃ aɪ ˈviː/ *noun* (no plural) a VIRUS that can cause the disease AIDS

hive /haɪv/ *noun* **1** also **beehive** a box that BEES are kept in **2 be a hive of activity** if a place is a hive of activity, everyone there is very busy

h'm or **hmm** /m, hm/ a sound that you make when you are thinking what to say or do

hoard¹ /hɔːd $ hɔrd/ *noun* a number of things hidden somewhere: *a secret hoard of biscuits*

hoard² *verb* to get and keep a large amount of food, money etc, and not use it: *People have been hoarding food in case snow blocks the roads.*

hoarse /hɔːs $ hɔrs/ *adjective* a hoarse voice sounds rough, as if the person speaking has a sore throat

hoax /həʊks $ hoʊks/ *noun* (plural **hoaxes**) an attempt to make people believe something that is not true: *He got a phone call saying he'd won $10,000, but it was just a hoax.*

hob /hɒb $ hɑb/ *noun BrE* the flat surface on the top of a COOKER where you cook food in pans

hob·by /ˈhɒbi $ ˈhɑbi/ *noun* (plural **hobbies**) an activity that you enjoy doing in your free time: *My hobbies are playing the guitar and reading.*

hock·ey /ˈhɒki $ ˈhɑki/ *noun* (no plural) *BrE* a game that you play on grass, in which two teams of players use long curved sticks to hit a ball SYNONYM **field hockey** *AmE*

hog /hɒg $ hɔg/ *verb* (informal) (**hogged, hogging**) to use too much or all of something yourself, instead of sharing it: *Lisa was there, hogging the whole sofa as usual.*

hoist /hɔɪst/ *verb* to raise something to a higher position, especially using ropes: *We hoisted the sail and then the boat was ready.*

hold¹ → see box on page 321 → see picture on page A3

hold² *noun*
if you take or keep hold of something, you hold it: *Sarah **took hold of** his hand and led him down the corridor.* • *Remember to **keep hold of** your bags as we leave the ship.*

PHRASES

get hold of someone/something to find someone or something when you need them: *I'll be at home later if you need to **get hold of** me.* • *Do you know where we can **get hold of** a map of the town centre?*

have a hold over someone to have power or control over someone

put someone on hold to make someone wait on the telephone: *He **put** me **on hold** while he went to look for the papers.*

hold·all /ˈhəʊld-ɔːl $ ˈhoʊld-ɔl/ *noun BrE* a bag used for carrying clothes, tools etc → see picture at BAG¹

hold·er /ˈhəʊldə $ ˈhoʊldɚ/ *noun* **1** someone who owns or controls something: *the world 400-metre record holder* **2** something that holds or contains something else: *a test tube holder*

hold·up, hold-up *BrE* /ˈhəʊldʌp $ ˈhoʊldʌp/ *noun* **1** a delay, especially one caused by traffic: *There are long hold-ups on the M25 due to an accident.* **2** when someone steals money from a bank, shop etc, by threatening them with a gun SYNONYM **robbery**: *Two people were injured during the holdup.*

hole /həʊl $ hoʊl/ *noun*

KEY PATTERNS
a hole in something

an empty space or opening in something: *We **dug a hole in the** garden.* • ***Cut a small hole in the** centre of the paper.* • *The dogs escaped **through a hole in the** fence.*

A B C D E F G H I J K L M N O P Q R S T U V W X Y Z

hold /həʊld $ hoʊld/ *verb* (past tense and past participle **held** /held/)

hold

1 to have something in your hands or arms: *He* ***was holding*** *a bunch of flowers.* • *I put my arms around her and* ***held*** *her* ***tight****.* • *She* ***held*** *the little boy* ***in her arms****.*

2 to keep something in a particular position: *Can you* ***hold*** *the wood for me while I'm cutting it?* • *He* ***held out*** *his hand and I shook it.* • *Ian* ***held*** *the door* ***open*** *for her.*

KEY PATTERNS
hold out your hand/ hold your hand out
hold up a sign/hold a sign up

He **held out his hand** and I shook it.

3 to have a meeting, party, election etc: *The meeting* ***was held*** *at the city hall.* • *The school* ***holds*** *a dance for the students each year.*

4 to have enough space for something: *I don't think my suitcase will* ***hold*** *all this stuff.* • *The hall* ***can hold*** *up to 500 people.*

I don't think my suitcase will ***hold*** *all this stuff.*

5 to keep information somewhere: *The patients' details* ***are held on*** *computer.*

PHRASES

hold hands, hold someone's hand
to hold someone's hand because you love them or because you want to keep them safe: *They walked along,* ***holding hands*** *and laughing.*

Hold it!
used when telling someone to stop moving or stop doing something: ***Hold it!*** *Now smile for the camera!*

PHRASAL VERBS

hold on (spoken)
used when telling someone to wait or stop doing something SYNONYM **hang on**: ***Hold on a minute*** *– let me just put my bags in the car.*

hold out
to hold something in your hand and give it to someone: *She held the glass out to him.* • *He held out the papers, and I took them.*

hold up
1 to make someone or something late SYNONYM **delay**: *The accident* ***held up*** *traffic for hours.* • *I don't want to* ***hold you up****.*
2 to try to steal money from a shop, bank etc using a gun: *A group of men wearing masks* ***held up*** *the bank.*

hol•i•day /ˈhɒlədi $ ˈhɑlədeɪ/ *noun*

KEY PATTERNS
be on holiday
go somewhere on holiday

1 *BrE* a period of time when you go to another place for enjoyment SYNONYM **vacation** *AmE*: *Did you have a nice holiday?* • *Sam isn't here this week – he's* ***on holiday in*** *Italy.* • *It's only three weeks until I* ***go on holiday****.*
2 a day when you do not have to go to work or school: *Next Monday is a holiday.*
3 **bank holiday** *BrE* a day when everyone in the country has a holiday and does not have to go to work or school

SPELLING
This word is often spelled wrongly. The correct spelling is: **holiday**.

hol•ler /ˈhɒlə $ ˈhɑlɚ/ *verb AmE* (informal) to shout loudly SYNONYM **yell**: *"Hurry up," Mom hollered up the stairs.*
→ see Thesaurus at SHOUT[1]

hol•low /ˈhɒləʊ $ ˈhɑloʊ/ *adjective* something that is hollow has an empty space inside ANTONYM **solid**: *an old hollow tree trunk*

hol•ly /ˈhɒli $ ˈhɑli/ *noun* (no plural) the green leaves of a tree with red berries that people use as a decoration at Christmas: *We decorated the walls with holly and ivy.*

holly

hol•o•gram /ˈhɒləgræm $ ˈhoʊləˌgræm/ *noun* a picture made in a special way so that it does not look flat, and looks more like the real object

ho•ly /ˈhəʊli $ ˈhoʊli/ *adjective* (**holier**, **holiest**) **1** connected with God or religion: *Jerusalem is a holy city for Muslims, Christians and Jews.*
2 someone who is holy is very religious and good

home¹ /həʊm $ hoʊm/ *noun*

KEY PATTERNS
be/stay/do something at home

1 the house or building where you usually live: *I wasn't feeling very well, so I* ***stayed at home****.* • *When are you moving into your new home?* • *Sally* ***left home*** (=stopped living with her parents) *as soon as she was 18.*
2 a place where old people or children with no parents are cared for: *She was brought up in a* ***children's home****.*

PHRASES
feel at home to feel comfortable, relaxed, and confident: *I felt quite* ***at home*** *with my friend's family.*
make yourself at home (spoken) used to tell someone to relax when they are visiting your home: *Come in and sit down –* ***make yourselves at home****.*
play at home, be at home if a sports team plays at home, it plays at its own sports field: *Manchester United are* ***playing at home*** *this Saturday.*

home² *adverb* if you go home, you go to the place where you live: *It's getting late – I think we ought to* ***go home****.* • *We* ***got home*** *at seven o'clock.* • *When he* ***arrived home****, Lucy had some news for him.* • *When will Dad* ***be home*** (=have come home)*?*

GRAMMAR
You say **go home** or **go back home**.
✘ Don't say 'go back to home' or 'go back my home'.

home³ *adjective* **1** connected with or belonging to your home or family: *the importance of a happy home life*
2 playing on your own sports field rather than an opponent's: *Newcastle lost their home match against Sunderland.* **3** connected with your own country, not other countries ANTONYM **foreign**: *the minister responsible for Home Affairs*

home•land /ˈhəʊmlænd $ ˈhoʊmlænd/ *noun* the country where you were born: *She returned to her homeland, Somalia.*

home•less /ˈhəʊmləs $ ˈhoʊmləs/ *adjective* someone who is homeless has no place to live: *Every large city has homeless people sleeping on the streets.*

home•ly /ˈhəʊmli $ ˈhoʊmli/ *adjective* **1** *BrE* ordinary and comfortable in a way that makes you feel relaxed: *a small family hotel with a homely atmosphere* **2** *AmE* a homely person is not very attractive

home·made /ˌhəʊmˈmeɪd $ ˌhoʊmˈmeɪd/ *adjective* made at home rather than bought from a shop: *Is this cake homemade?*

ho·me·op·a·thy /ˌhəʊmiˈɒpəθi $ ˌhoʊmiˈɑpəθi/ *noun* (no plural) a method of treating illness that involves using very small amounts of natural substances

home page *noun* the first part of a website, which contains basic information about a person or organization

home·sick /ˈhəʊmˌsɪk $ ˈhoʊmˌsɪk/ *adjective* feeling sad because you are a long way from your home: *Children often feel homesick when they arrive at summer camp.* → see Thesaurus at SAD

home·ward /ˈhəʊmwəd $ ˈhoʊmwərd/ *adjective, adverb* going towards home: *The homeward journey took three hours.*

home·work /ˈhəʊmwɜːk $ ˈhoʊmwərk/ *noun* school work that a student is given to do at home: *Have you finished your homework?*

GRAMMAR
Homework is not used in the plural.
✘ Don't say 'homeworks'.
You say **do your homework**.
✘ Don't say 'make your homework'.

hom·i·cide /ˈhɒmɪsaɪd $ ˈhɑməˌsaɪd/ *noun AmE* the crime of murder

ho·mo·sex·u·al /ˌhəʊməˈsekʃuəl $ ˌhoʊməˈsekʃuəl/ *noun* (formal) someone who has sexual relationships with people of the same sex SYNONYM **gay** ANTONYM **heterosexual**
—**homosexual** *adjective*

hon·est /ˈɒnɪst $ ˈɑnɪst/ *adjective*

KEY PATTERNS
honest with someone
honest about something

someone who is honest does not lie, cheat, or steal ANTONYM **dishonest**: *My father was a very honest man.* • *He wouldn't give me an honest answer to my question.* • *Please* **be honest with** *me* (=tell me the truth). • *She was very* **honest about** *her weaknesses.*

hon·est·ly /ˈɒnɪstli $ ˈɑnɪstli/ *adverb* **1** in an honest way ANTONYM **dishonestly**: *I've earned my money honestly, through hard work.* **2** (spoken) used to emphasize that you are telling the truth: *I've honestly never met him before.* **3** (spoken) used when you are annoyed: *Honestly! Why can't he get here on time?*

hon·es·ty /ˈɒnɪsti $ ˈɑnɪsti/ *noun* (no plural) the quality of being honest ANTONYM **dishonesty**: *I was impressed by his honesty.*

hon·ey /ˈhʌni/ *noun* (no plural) a sweet substance made by BEES, which people eat

hon·ey·moon /ˈhʌnimuːn/ *noun* a holiday that people have after their wedding: *We're going to Greece for our honeymoon.*

honk /hɒŋk $ hɑŋk/ another word for HOOT (1)

honor the American spelling of HONOUR

honorable the American spelling of HONOURABLE

hon·our[1] *BrE*, **honor** *AmE* /ˈɒnə $ ˈɑnər/ *noun* **1** (no plural) something that makes you feel proud and happy: *To represent your country, in any sport, is a great honour.* **2 in honour of someone, in someone's honour** if you do something in someone's honour, you do it to show special respect for them: *a formal dinner in honour of the Queen* **3** (no plural) the respect that people have for you, or behaviour that makes you deserve respect: *We are determined to protect our country's honour.*

honour[2] *BrE*, **honor** *AmE verb* **1 be honoured, feel honoured** (formal) to feel very proud and happy, especially because you have been asked to do something important: *I am deeply honoured to be invited here tonight.* **2** to give someone a special title, prize etc, or to treat them with great respect: *He was honoured with the Nobel Peace Prize.*

hon·our·a·ble *BrE*, **honorable** *AmE* /ˈɒnərəbəl $ ˈɑnərəbəl/ *adjective formal* an honourable person behaves in a way that people think is right: *It was not the honorable way to win an election.*

hood /hʊd/ *noun* **1** a part of a coat or other piece of clothing that you can

A B C D E F G H I J K L M N O P Q R S T U V W X Y Z

A B C D E F G H I J K L M N O P Q R S T U V W X Y Z

pull up to cover your head: *a warm jacket with a hood* **2** the American word for a car BONNET

hoof /huːf $ hʊf/ *noun* (plural **hoofs** or **hooves** /huːvz $ hʊvz/) the foot of an animal such as a horse → see picture at HORSE

hooks

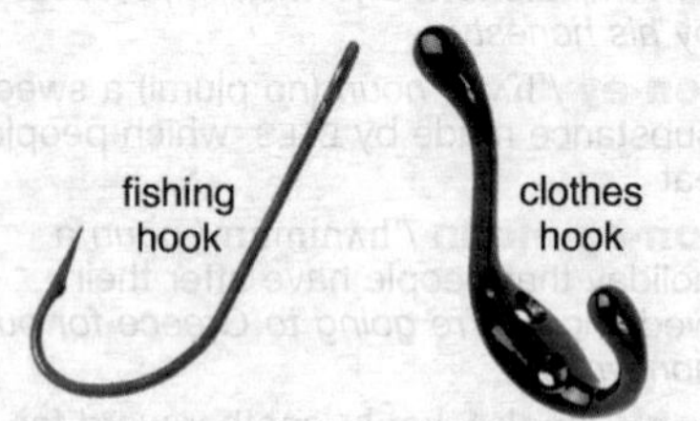

hook /hʊk/ *noun* a curved piece of metal or plastic that you use for hanging things on, or for catching fish: *Hang your coat on the hook over there.*

hooked /hʊkt/ *adjective* (informal) if you are hooked on something, you like it a lot and you do not want to stop doing it or using it SYNONYM **addicted**: *Thousands of children are hooked on computer games.*

hoo·li·gan /'huːlɪgən/ *noun* a noisy person who causes trouble by fighting or damaging things in public places: *a gang of football hooligans*

hoop /huːp/ *noun* a large ring made of metal, plastic, or wood: *Try and throw the hoops over the post.*

hooray another spelling of HURRAY

hoot /huːt/ *verb* **1** *BrE* if a car hoots its horn, the horn makes a loud noise SYNONYM **honk**: *All the cars behind me were hooting their horns.* **2** if an OWL hoots, it makes a loud noise —**hoot** *noun*

Hoo·ver /'huːvə $ 'huvɚ/ *BrE* (trademark) a VACUUM CLEANER

hoo·ver /'huːvə $ 'huvɚ/ *verb BrE* to clean the floor using a VACUUM CLEANER → see Thesaurus at CLEAN[2]

hooves a plural of HOOF

hop /hɒp $ hɑp/ *verb* (**hopped**, **hopping**) **1** to jump on one foot → see picture on page A2 **2** if birds and animals hop, they move by jumping with both feet together: *Two frogs hopped into the water with a splash.* → see Thesaurus at JUMP[1] —**hop** *noun*

hope[1] /həʊp $ hoʊp/ *verb*

KEY PATTERNS
hope (that)
hope to do something

to want something to happen: *I hope that Tom will come to the party.* • *I hope you feel better soon.* • *I* **hope to** *go to college next year.*

PHRASES

I hope so (spoken): *"Is Tom coming to the party?"* *"***I hope so** (=I hope he is coming to the party).*"*

I hope not (spoken): *"Are we going to be late?"* *"***I hope not** (=I hope we are not going to be late).*"*

hope[2] *noun*

KEY PATTERNS
hope that
hope of (doing) something
in the hope that/of doing something

1 when you hope for something and believe that it is possible: *He expressed the* **hope that** *we would meet again soon.* • *He* **has hopes of** *studying in the US.* • *I went to Laura's* **in the hope that** *Julie would be there* (=because I hoped Julie might be there).

2 a possibility that something will happen in the way that you want: *There is no* **hope of** *getting your money back now.* • *Is there any* **hope** *that the police will find your car?*

PHRASES

lose hope: *You mustn't* **lose hope** (=you must not stop believing that something good will happen).

someone's only hope, someone's last hope: *He's our* **only hope of** *winning the contest* (=he is the only person who can make us win the contest).

hope·ful /'həʊpfəl $ 'hoʊpfəl/ *adjective* feeling fairly confident that what you want to happen will happen SYNONYM **optimistic**: *Maria is quite hopeful that she'll pass her exams.*

hope·ful·ly /'həʊpfəli $ 'hoʊpfəli/ *adverb* **1** used to say what you hope will happen: *Hopefully, the weather will be better tomorrow.* **2** in a hopeful way: *"Can I come with you?" Alec asked hopefully.*

hope·less /ˈhəʊpləs $ ˈhoʊpləs/ *adjective* **1** a situation that is hopeless is very bad and not likely to improve: *Our relationship was getting worse, and the situation seemed hopeless.* **2** someone who is hopeless at doing something is very bad at it SYNONYM **terrible**: *I was hopeless at sport at school.*

horde /hɔːd $ hɔrd/ *noun* a very large crowd: *Hordes of reporters were waiting at the airport.*

ho·ri·zon /həˈraɪzən/ *noun* **1 the horizon** the line where the land or sea seems to meet the sky: *The sun slowly sank below the horizon.* **2 be on the horizon** (written) if something is on the horizon, it will happen soon: *Changes in the law are on the horizon.*

hor·i·zon·tal /ˌhɒrəˈzɒntl $ ˌhɔrəˈzɑntl/ *adjective* going from side to side, or parallel to the ground ANTONYM **vertical**: *a shirt with horizontal stripes*

hor·mone /ˈhɔːməʊn $ ˈhɔrmoʊn/ *noun* a chemical substance that your body produces naturally, which makes it develop in a particular way: *male hormones*

horn /hɔːn $ hɔrn/ *noun* **1** one of the hard pointed things that some animals, for example cows, have on their heads **2** the thing in a car, bus etc that makes a loud sound when you push a button: *The driver behind me kept hooting his horn.* **3** a metal musical instrument with a wide end, which you play by blowing into it: *the French horn*

hor·o·scope /ˈhɒrəskəʊp $ ˈhɔrəˌskoʊp/ *noun* a description of what might happen to you in the future, based on the position of the stars and PLANETS when you were born

hor·ren·dous /həˈrendəs/ *adjective* very bad or unpleasant SYNONYM **appalling**: *The smell from the drain was absolutely horrendous.*

hor·ri·ble /ˈhɒrəbəl $ ˈhɔrəbəl/ *adjective* very unpleasant or unkind: *That was a horrible thing to say.* • *That dress is horrible.* → see Thesaurus at BAD UNKIND

USAGE
✘ Don't say 'It's very horrible'.
Just say **It's horrible**, or **It's really horrible**.

hor·rid /ˈhɒrɪd $ ˈhɔrɪd/ *adjective* (informal) unpleasant or unkind SYNONYM **nasty**: *The carpet was a horrid brown colour.* • *Don't be so horrid, Brett!*

hor·rif·ic /həˈrɪfɪk/ *adjective* (formal) very shocking and unpleasant: *a horrific crime* → see Thesaurus at BAD

hor·ri·fy /ˈhɒrɪfaɪ $ ˈhɔrəˌfaɪ/ *verb* (**horrified, horrifies**) to shock someone very much in an unpleasant way: *Everyone was horrified by the news.* —**horrifying** *adjective*: *a horrifying accident*

hor·ror /ˈhɒrə $ ˈhɔrɚ/ *noun* **1** a strong feeling of shock and fear: *I listened in horror as he described what he had done.* **2 horror film, horror story** a film or story which deliberately tries to shock or frighten people in order to entertain them

horse

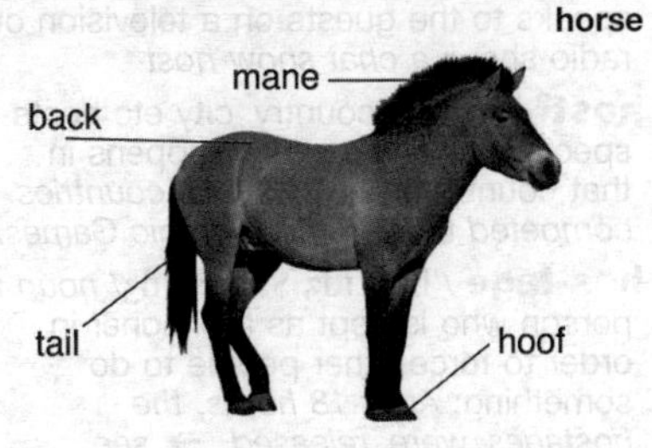

horse /hɔːs $ hɔrs/ *noun* a large animal that people ride on or use for pulling heavy things: *I learned to ride a horse when I was four.* → see picture on page A8

horse·back /ˈhɔːsbæk $ ˈhɔrsbæk/ *noun* **1 on horseback** riding a horse: *They did the journey on horseback.* **2 horseback riding** the American word for HORSE-RIDING

ˈhorse-ˌriding *noun* (no plural) *BrE* the activity of riding a horse SYNONYM **horseback riding** *AmE*

horse·shoe /ˈhɔːʃ-ʃuː $ ˈhɔrʃ-ʃu/ *noun* a curved piece of iron that is fixed to the bottom of a horse's foot

hose /həʊz $ hoʊz/ also **ˈhose-pipe** *noun* a long rubber tube that water can flow through and that you use in the garden, or to wash a car, stop a fire etc → see picture at GARDENING

hos·pi·ta·ble /ˈhɒspɪtəbəl $ hɑˈspɪtəbəl/ *adjective* friendly to visitors and ready to welcome them: *Greek people are very hospitable.* ➔ see Thesaurus at FRIENDLY

hos·pi·tal /ˈhɒspɪtl $ ˈhɑspɪtl/ *noun*

KEY PATTERNS
in/to/out of hospital *BrE*
in/to/out of the hospital *AmE*

a building where doctors help and treat people who are sick or injured: *My mother is* ***in hospital*** *at the moment.* • *We thought Sam had broken his arm, so we took him* ***to the hospital****.* • *She should be* ***out of hospital*** *next week.*

hos·pi·tal·i·ty /ˌhɒspəˈtæləti $ ˌhɑspəˈtæləti/ *noun* (no plural) when you behave in a friendly way towards visitors and make them feel welcome

host¹ /həʊst $ hoʊst/ *noun* **1** the person at a party who organized it and invited the guests **2** the person who speaks to the guests on a television or radio show: *a chat show host*

host² *verb* if a country, city etc hosts a special event, the event happens in that country or city: *Several countries competed to host the Olympic Games.*

hos·tage /ˈhɒstɪdʒ $ ˈhɑstɪdʒ/ *noun* a person who is kept as a prisoner in order to force other people to do something: *After 18 hours, the hostages were released.* ➔ see Thesaurus at PRISONER

hos·tel /ˈhɒstl $ ˈhɑstl/ *noun* a place where people can sleep and eat cheaply for a short time: *a hostel for the homeless*

host·ess /ˈhəʊstɪs $ ˈhoʊstɪs/ *noun* (plural **hostesses**) the woman at a party who organized it and invited the guests

hos·tile /ˈhɒstaɪl $ ˈhɑstl/ *adjective* **1** very unfriendly: *In some mountain villages, the people can be hostile to strangers.* **2** not agreeing with a particular idea or plan: *Most people are hostile towards the plan.*

hos·til·i·ty /hɒˈstɪləti $ hɑˈstɪləti/ *noun* unfriendly feelings or behaviour: *There has always been some hostility between the two countries.*

hot¹ /hɒt $ hɑt/ *adjective* (**hotter**, **hottest**)
1 something that is hot has a high temperature ANTONYM **cold**: *It was a very hot day.* • *You'll feel better after a hot bath.* • *My coffee is still too hot to drink.*
2 hot food has a burning taste because it has a lot of spice in it: *a hot curry*

THESAURUS
warm: *The sun was shining and it was warm outside* (=fairly hot).
boiling (hot): *It's boiling hot – let's go for a swim* (=extremely hot).

hot² *verb* (**hotted**, **hotting**) **hot up** (informal) if a situation hots up, it becomes more active or exciting: *The competition is hotting up.*

hot-air balloon // *noun* a large BALLOON filled with hot air, used esepcially for carrying people into the sky ➔ see picture on page A11

ˌhot ˈdog / $ ˈ. ./ *noun* a long SAUSAGE that people eat in a piece of bread

ho·tel /həʊˈtel $ hoʊˈtel/ *noun* a building where you pay to sleep and eat: *We stayed in a small hotel in the centre of Paris.*

hot·line /ˈhɒtlaɪn $ ˈhɑtlaɪn/ *noun* a special telephone number that people can call in order to get or give information: *Anyone with information should call the police hotline immediately.*

hound /haʊnd/ *verb* to follow someone or ask them questions all the time in an annoying or threatening way SYNONYM **harass**: *The press were criticized for hounding the Royal Family.*

hour /aʊə $ aʊɚ/ *noun*
1 a measure of time that is equal to 60 minutes: *We spent three hours in the museum.* • *I'll see you* ***in about an hour****.* • *James was* ***half an hour*** *late.* • *The test should only take* ***a quarter of an hour****.* • *The store is now open 24* ***hours a day*** (=all day and all night). • *I often go swimming in my* ***lunch hour*** (=the time when I stop working and have my lunch). • *All classes begin* ***on the hour*** (=at 1 o'clock, 2 o'clock etc).
2 hours (informal) a very long time: *We wandered around the shops* ***for hours****!* • *He* ***takes hours*** *getting ready to go out.*

hour·ly /ˈaʊəli $ ˈaʊɚli/ *adjective* **1** happening every hour: *There are hourly trains to London.* **2** an hourly

A B C D E F G H I J K L M N O P Q R S T U V W X Y Z

amount of money is the amount you are paid or have to pay each hour: *the minimum hourly wage*

house /haʊs/ *noun* (plural **houses** /ˈhaʊzɪz/)
1 a building that you live in: *We spent the evening at Harriet's house.* • *They are buying a new house.*
2 a building that is used for a particular purpose: *the court house*
3 a group of people who make the laws of a country: *He made an important speech to the House of Representatives.*
PHRASES
on the house (spoken) if drinks or food in a restaurant are on the house, they are free

house·bound /ˈhaʊsbaʊnd/ *adjective* unable to leave your house, because you are ill or cannot walk far

house·hold[1] /ˈhaʊshəʊld $ ˈhaʊshoʊld/ *adjective* used in or connected with your home SYNONYM **domestic**: *household appliances such as washing machines and dishwashers*

household[2] *noun* (written) all the people living together in a house or apartment: *Every member of the household helps with the cleaning.*

house·keep·er /ˈhaʊsˌkiːpə $ ˈhaʊsˌkipɚ/ *noun* someone whose job is to cook and clean for another person in their house

house·proud /ˈhaʊspraʊd/ *adjective BrE* someone who is houseproud spends a lot of time cleaning their home

ˌhouse-to-ˈhouse *adjective* house-to-house COLLECTIONS, searches etc involve going to every house in an area: *The police are making house-to-house enquiries.*

house·warm·ing /ˈhaʊsˌwɔːmɪŋ $ ˈhaʊsˌwɔrmɪŋ/ *noun* a party you have to celebrate when you move into a different house

house·wife /ˈhaʊs-waɪf/ *noun* (plural **housewives** /-waɪvz/) a woman who works at home doing the cooking, cleaning etc for her family

house·work /ˈhaʊswɜːk $ ˈhaʊswɚk/ *noun* (no plural) work that you do at home such as cleaning, washing clothes etc: *I usually do the housework at weekends.*

hous·ing /ˈhaʊzɪŋ/ *noun* (no plural) (formal) houses for people to live in: *More money is needed for housing, education and health.*

hov·er /ˈhɒvə $ ˈhʌvɚ/ *verb* to stay in one place in the air while flying: *A helicopter was hovering overhead.*

hov·er·craft /ˈhɒvəkrɑːft $ ˈhʌvɚˌkræft/ *noun* a type of boat that travels over land and water by pushing air down and backwards

how /haʊ/ *adverb*
1 used to ask or talk about the way something is done or happens: *How* (=in what way) *did you get my phone number?* • *How are we going to explain this to Mum?* • *He explained to us how the machine worked.* • *She showed me **how to** fill in the form.*
2 used to ask or talk about an amount: *How tall are you?* • *How often do you see her?* • *How many people do you think will come?* • *I don't know how much it will cost.*
3 used to ask about someone's health: *How are you?*
4 used to ask about someone's experience or opinion of something: *How was your trip to Italy?* • *"Well, how do I look?" "You look great!"*
PHRASES
how come? (spoken, informal) why?: *How come I'm always the one who has to clean the bathroom?*

> WORD CHOICE
> **how** or **what is ... like**?
> • You use **how** especially when asking about someone's health: *How is your grandmother?*
> • You also use it when asking someone to describe an experience: *How was your trip?*
> • You usually use **what is ... like?** when asking someone to describe a person or place to you: *"What is your new teacher like?" "She's very kind and helpful."*

how·ev·er /haʊˈevə $ haʊˈevɚ/ *adverb* used when you are adding something which is surprising or different from what you have just said: *Sarah is a very* *able student. However, she does need to work a bit harder if she wants to get good exam results.*

PHRASES

however long, however big, however careful etc used to say that it makes no difference how long, big etc something is: *I'm determined to get a ticket, **however long** I have to wait here!* • *Everyone makes mistakes, **however careful** they are.*

howl /haʊl/ *verb* to make a long loud crying sound, like a wild dog or a strong wind: *The wind howled around the house.* —**howl** *noun*

HQ /ˌeɪtʃ ˈkjuː/ the abbreviation of HEADQUARTERS

hr the written abbreviation of HOUR

hud·dle /ˈhʌdl/ also **huddle together, huddle up** *verb* to stand or sit closely together: *It was freezing cold so we huddled together to try and keep warm.*

huff /hʌf/ *noun* **in a huff** (informal) angry because someone has offended you: *She's in a huff and won't speak to me at the moment.*

hug /hʌg/ *verb* (**hugged, hugging**) to put your arms around someone and hold them, because you like or love them SYNONYM **embrace** —**hug** *noun*: *Come over here and give me a hug.*

huge /hjuːdʒ/ *adjective* very large SYNONYM **enormous**: *They have a huge house in the country.* → see Thesaurus at BIG → see picture at TINY

huge·ly /ˈhjuːdʒli/ *adverb* (informal) very: *The band is hugely popular at the moment.*

hull /hʌl/ *noun* the main body of a ship

hul·lo /hʌˈləʊ $ hʌˈloʊ/ a British spelling of HELLO

hum /hʌm/ *verb* (**hummed, humming**) **1** to sing a tune with your lips closed: *I didn't know the words, so I just hummed the tune.* **2** to make a low steady noise: *Everything was silent except for a computer humming in the corner.* —**hum** *noun* (no plural) (written): *Outside I could hear the hum of traffic.*

hu·man¹ /ˈhjuːmən/ *adjective* related to people rather than to machines or animals: *After two years alone, he longed for human company.* • *The accident was caused by **human error*** (=a mistake made by a person).

human² also ˌ**human ˈbeing** *noun* a man, woman, or child SYNONYM **person**

hu·mane /hjuːˈmeɪn/ *adjective* kind rather than cruel ANTONYM **inhumane**: *the humane treatment of animals*

hu·man·i·tar·i·an /hjuːˌmænəˈteəriən $ hjuˌmænəˈteriən/ *adjective* concerned with trying to help people who are ill, hungry etc: *The UN has sent humanitarian aid to help the refugees.*

hu·man·i·ty /hjuːˈmænəti/ *noun* (no plural) (formal) **1** all the people in the world, as a group SYNONYM **mankind**: *They think they are different from the rest of humanity.* **2** when you act in a kind and respectful way to other people: *We should treat prisoners with humanity and fairness.*

ˌ**human ˈrace** *noun* **the human race** all people, rather than animals or other types of life SYNONYM **mankind**: *There are many things that threaten the survival of the human race.* → see Thesaurus at PEOPLE

ˌ**human ˈrights** *plural noun* the basic rights that everyone has to be free and to be treated fairly, especially by their government: *The government has been accused of human rights abuses* (=treating people unfairly or badly).

hum·ble /ˈhʌmbəl/ *adjective* **1** someone who is humble is not proud and does not think that they are better than other people: *Although he was famous, he was a humble man.* **2** not important or special: *He was the son of a humble farm labourer.*

hu·mid /ˈhjuːmɪd/ *adjective* a place or weather that is humid is very warm and wet in an unpleasant way: *Florida is extremely humid in the summer.*

hu·mil·i·ate /hjuːˈmɪlieɪt/ *verb* to make someone feel stupid or weak: *He often humiliated other people in meetings.* —**humiliating** *adjective*: *Being arrested was a humiliating experience.*

A B C D E F G H I J K L M N O P Q R S T U V W X Y Z

hu·mor·ous /ˈhjuːmərəs/ *adjective* funny SYNONYM **amusing**: *She made a humorous speech.*

SPELLING
This word is often spelled wrongly. The correct spelling is: **humorous**.

hu·mour¹ *BrE*, **humor** *AmE* /ˈhjuːmə $ ˈhjumɚ/ *noun* **1 sense of humour** the ability to see that things are funny and laugh at them: *I really like Sam – he's got a great sense of humour.* **2** (no plural) the quality in something that makes it funny: *Carol can find the humor in almost any situation.*

humour² *BrE*, **humor** *AmE verb* to do what someone wants in order to stop them becoming upset: *I humoured Liz rather than getting into an argument with her.*

humps

hump /hʌmp/ *noun* **1** a large lump on a CAMEL's back **2** a raised part on a road, especially one that is put there in order to make cars go more slowly: *Go slowly – there are humps all along the road.*

hunch¹ /hʌntʃ/ *noun* **have a hunch** (informal) to have a feeling that something will happen or is true, although you have no definite information about it: *I had a hunch that something would go wrong.*

hunch² *verb* **be hunched** to be sitting or standing with your back and shoulders bent forwards: *He was sitting in his study, hunched over his books.*

hun·dred /ˈhʌndrəd/ *number* (plural **hundred** or **hundreds**) **1** 100: *There were at least a hundred people at the party.* • *The journey is about five hundred kilometres.* **2 hundreds of people/things** a very large number of people or things: *I have hundreds of CDs.* —**hundredth** *number*

GRAMMAR
You use the plural form **hundred** after a number: *two hundred years*
You use the plural form **hundreds** before **of**: *hundreds of years ago*

hung the past tense and past participle of HANG¹

hun·ger /ˈhʌŋgə $ ˈhʌŋgɚ/ *noun* (no plural) **1** the feeling you have when you want or need to eat: *By one o'clock the kids were complaining of hunger.* **2** when people do not have enough food, especially for a long period of time: *These refugees are dying of hunger and thirst.*

USAGE
You say **I'm hungry**.
✘ Don't say 'I have hunger.'

hun·gry /ˈhʌŋgri/ *adjective* (**hungrier**, **hungriest**)
1 if you are hungry, you need or want to eat: *I'm hungry. What time is lunch?* • *hungry children begging for food*
2 go hungry if you go hungry, you do not have enough food to eat: *We didn't have much money, but we never **went** hungry.*

hunk /hʌŋk/ *noun* **1** (informal) an attractive man who has a strong body **2** a thick piece of something, especially food SYNONYM **chunk**: *Dave passed me a hunk of bread.*

hunt /hʌnt/ *verb* **1** to chase wild animals in order to catch and kill them: *They still hunt deer in this forest.* **2** to try to find something or someone by looking carefully SYNONYM **look**, **search**: *I've hunted everywhere for my keys but I can't find them.* —**hunt** *noun*: *Chief Inspector Edwards is leading the hunt for the killer.*

hunt·er /ˈhʌntə $ ˈhʌntɚ/ *noun* someone who hunts wild animals

hunt·ing /ˈhʌntɪŋ/ *noun* (no plural) the activity of chasing wild animals in order to catch and kill them

hur·dle /ˈhɜːdl $ ˈhɚdl/ *noun* **1** a small fence that a person or a horse jumps over during a race **2** something difficult that you have to do before you can do something else: *Exams are a hurdle that everyone has to face.*

hurl /hɜːl $ hɚl/ *verb* to throw something using a lot of force SYNONYM **fling**: *The boys were hurling stones into the lake.* ➔ see Thesaurus at THROW[1]

hur·ray, **hooray** /hʊˈreɪ/ something you shout when you are very pleased about something: *Hurray! We've won!*

hur·ri·cane /ˈhʌrɪkən $ ˈhɚɪˌkeɪn/ *noun* a violent storm with very strong fast winds ➔ see Thesaurus at WIND[1]

hur·ried /ˈhʌrid $ ˈhɚid/ *adjective* (written) done more quickly than usual, especially because there is not much time SYNONYM **hasty**: *He said a hurried goodbye and ran for the bus.*
—**hurriedly** *adverb*: *I got dressed hurriedly.*

hur·ry[1] /ˈhʌri $ ˈhɚi/ *verb* (**hurried**, **hurries**)

KEY PATTERNS
hurry off/out/along etc

to go somewhere or do something quickly SYNONYM **rush**: *The party doesn't start till eight, so you don't need to hurry.* • *He picked up his bag and hurried out of the house.*

PHRASES
hurry up! (spoken) used to tell someone to do something more quickly

hurry[2] *noun*
1 be in a hurry if you are in a hurry, you need or want to do something very quickly SYNONYM **be in a rush**: *She was in a hurry to get to class.* • *Can I talk to you now, or are you in a hurry?*
2 there's no hurry (spoken) used to tell someone that they do not have to do something immediately: *"When do you need these books back?" "Oh, there's no hurry."*
3 not be in any hurry, be in no hurry (spoken) if you are not in any hurry, you are able to wait because you have a lot of time in which to do something: *"I'll wait for you. I'm **in no hurry**."*

hurt[1] /hɜːt $ hɚt/ *verb* (past tense and past participle **hurt**)
1 to injure someone or make them feel pain: *Let go, you're hurting me!* • *Ian, sit down before you hurt yourself.* • *I hurt my back playing basketball.* • *Four people were hurt in the accident.*
2 if part of your body hurts, it is painful: *It was so cold my hands started to hurt.*

PHRASES
hurt someone's feelings to make someone feel upset: *I don't want to **hurt** her **feelings** by telling her that I don't like the food.*

THESAURUS
be painful: *My back's still **painful** when I bend down* (=it hurts because of a problem or injury).
be sore: *Kylie says her throat **is sore*** (=hurts, possibly because of an infection or small injury).
ache: *After walking all day, my legs were **aching*** (=hurting a little all the time).
sting: *The smoke made our eyes **sting*** (=hurt with a sudden short sharp pain).

hurt[2] *adjective*
1 if you are hurt, you have been injured: *Fortunately, he wasn't badly hurt.*
2 unhappy because of what someone has said or done to you SYNONYM **upset**: *When her boyfriend suddenly left her, she felt very hurt.*

hurt·ful /ˈhɜːtfəl $ ˈhɚtfəl/ *adjective* a remark or action that is hurtful makes you feel upset or unhappy SYNONYM **upsetting**: *Some of the things he said were very hurtful.*

hur·tle /ˈhɜːtl $ ˈhɚtl/ *verb* to move very fast SYNONYM **speed**: *We hurtled down the road at 100 km an hour.*

hus·band /ˈhʌzbənd/ *noun* the man that a woman is married to

hus·ky /ˈhʌski/ *adjective* (**huskier**, **huskiest**) a husky voice is deep and sounds rough but attractive

hus·tle /ˈhʌsəl/ *verb* to make someone move somewhere quickly, often by pushing them: *Steve hustled his son into the house and shut the door.*

hut /hʌt/ *noun* a small building, often made of wood: *They live in huts in the forest.*

hutch /hʌtʃ/ *noun* (plural **hutches**) a wooden box that people keep rabbits in

hy·draul·ic /haɪˈdrɒlɪk $ haɪˈdrɔlɪk/ *adjective* moved or operated by the pressure of water or other liquids: *a hydraulic pump*

hy·dro·e·lec·tric /ˌhaɪdrəʊ-ɪˈlektrɪk $ ˌhaɪdroʊ-ɪˈlektrɪk/ *adjective* using water power to produce electricity: *The hydroelectric plant provides the town with energy.*

hy·dro·gen /ˈhaɪdrədʒən/ *noun* (no plural) a gas that is lighter than air

hy·e·na /haɪˈiːnə/ *noun* a wild animal like a dog that makes a loud laughing sound

hy·giene /ˈhaɪdʒiːn/ *noun* (no plural) when you keep yourself and the things around you clean in order to avoid diseases SYNONYM **cleanliness**: *The children are taught the importance of personal hygiene.*

hy·gien·ic /haɪˈdʒiːnɪk $ haɪˈdʒenɪk/ *adjective* something that is hygienic is clean and likely to stop diseases spreading: *Conditions in the camps were not very hygienic.*

hymn /hɪm/ *noun* a religious song that people sing in Christian churches

hype /haɪp/ *noun* (no plural) when something is talked about too much on television, in the newspapers etc and is made to seem important when it is not: *There's been a lot of media hype about the book.* —**hype** *verb*

hy·per·mar·ket /ˈhaɪpəˌmɑːkɪt $ ˈhaɪpɚˌmɑrkɪt/ *noun BrE* a very large shop outside a town that sells many different kinds of food and other things

hy·phen /ˈhaɪfən/ *noun* a short line (-) that joins words or parts of words

hyp·no·sis /hɪpˈnəʊsɪs $ hɪpˈnoʊsɪs/ *noun* (no plural) when someone is put into a state like sleep, so that another person can influence what they think or do: *Under hypnosis, Jean was able to remember exactly what had happened that day.*

hyp·no·tize also **hypnotise** *BrE* /ˈhɪpnətaɪz/ *verb* to make someone go into a state like sleep, so that you can influence what they think or do

hy·poc·ri·sy /hɪˈpɒkrəsi $ hɪˈpɑkrəsi/ *noun* (no plural) when someone pretends to have particular feelings or opinions, but then behaves in a way that shows that they do not really have them: *The government was accused of hypocrisy.*

hyp·o·crite /ˈhɪpəkrɪt/ *noun* someone who says that they have particular feelings or opinions, but then behaves in a way that shows that they do not really have them: *He's such a hypocrite! He tells us to be good, but he behaves badly himself!*

hys·ter·i·cal /hɪˈsterəkəl/ *adjective*
1 very upset or excited, and not able to control yourself: *She was hysterical and I couldn't stop her screaming*
2 (informal) very funny SYNONYM **hilarious**: *The movie was hysterical!*

I /aɪ/ *pronoun*
the person who is speaking or writing: *I don't understand.* • *I was surprised to see him.* • *Have I come to the right room?*

ice /aɪs/ *noun* (no plural) water that has frozen and become solid: *Would you like some ice in your drink?*

ice·berg /ˈaɪsbɜːg $ ˈaɪsbɚg/ *noun* a very large piece of ice floating in the sea

ˌice-ˈcold *adjective* very cold: *an ice-cold lemonade*

ˌice ˈcream / $ ˈ. ./ *noun* a sweet frozen food that is made from milk and sugar ➔ see picture at CONE

ˈice cube *noun* a small block of ice that you put in a drink

ˈice ˌhockey *noun* (no plural) a game played on ice in which two teams of players use sticks to hit a hard flat object into a GOAL ➔ see picture on page A14

ˈice skate¹ *verb* to slide on ice wearing boots with a metal part on the bottom SYNONYM **skate**

ice skate² *noun* a boot with a metal part on the bottom, used for ice skating SYNONYM **skate**

i·ci·cle /ˈaɪsɪkəl/ *noun* a thin pointed piece of ice that hangs down

ic·ing /ˈaɪsɪŋ/ *noun* (no plural) a sweet mixture made from sugar, water, and butter that you put on a cake to decorate it SYNONYM **frosting** *AmE*

i·con /ˈaɪkɒn $ ˈaɪkɑn/ *noun* **1** a small picture on a computer screen that you choose in order to make the computer do something: *Select the print icon, using the right mouse button.* **2** a famous person who many people admire and think is important: *Marilyn Monroe is an American film icon.*

ic·y /ˈaɪsi/ *adjective* (**icier**, **iciest**)
1 very cold: *an icy winter morning*
2 covered in ice: *an icy highway*

I'd /aɪd/ the short form of 'I had' or 'I would': *I wish I'd been there.* • *I'd like to go, but I can't.*

ID /ˌaɪ ˈdiː/ *noun* a document that shows your name, address etc, usually with a photograph SYNONYM **identification**: *Do you have any ID?*

i·dea /aɪˈdɪə/ *noun*

KEY PATTERNS
have an idea
an idea for something
the idea of (doing) something

a plan, thought, or suggestion that you have: *She* ***has*** *a lot of* ***good ideas***. • *Who came up with* ***the idea for*** *the show?* • *He liked the* ***idea of*** *starting a band.*

PHRASES

have an idea (of something) to have some knowledge of something: *By the time you've finished school, you'll* ***have*** *more of* ***an idea*** *of what you want to do.* • *I* ***have no idea*** *where David went* (=I do not know at all).

give someone an idea (of something) to give someone information about something: *Can you* ***give*** *me some* ***idea*** *of the size of the rooms?*

i·deal¹ /ˌaɪˈdɪəl/ *adjective* the best that something can be SYNONYM **perfect**: *This hotel is ideal for families.*

ideal² *noun* a standard or a way of behaving that you would like to achieve: *the ideals of democracy and freedom*

i·deal·is·tic /aɪˌdɪəˈlɪstɪk/ *adjective* believing in ideals that are difficult to achieve in real life

i·deal·ly /aɪˈdɪəli/ *adverb* **1** used to say how you would like things to be, even if it is not possible: *Ideally, we would like an extra month to finish this project.* **2** perfectly: *The hotel is ideally located.*

i·den·ti·cal /aɪˈdentɪkəl/ *adjective* exactly the same: *The two signatures looked identical.* • *identical twins*

i·den·ti·fi·ca·tion
/aɪˌdentəfəˈkeɪʃən/ *noun* (no plural)

1 an official document that shows your name, address etc, usually with a photograph SYNONYM **ID**: *You need some identification to travel across the border.* **2** when you say who someone is or what something is

i·den·ti·fy /aɪˈdentəfaɪ/ *verb* (**identified**, **identifies**)

KEY PATTERNS
identify someone/something (as something)

to say who someone is or what something is: *Police **identified** the victim of the accident as John Shelley.* • *I couldn't identify the flower.*

i·den·ti·ty /aɪˈdentəti/ *noun* **1** (plural **identities**) who someone is: *Police have discovered the identity of the murderer.* **2** (no plural) the qualities that a person or a group of people have that make them different from other people: *Joanna moved to England, but she still has a strong sense of her Polish identity.*

i·de·ol·o·gy /ˌaɪdiˈɒlədʒi $ ˌaɪdiˈɑlədʒi/ *noun* (plural **ideologies**) a set of beliefs or ideas, especially political beliefs: *the socialist ideology of Cuba*

id·i·om /ˈɪdiəm/ *noun* a group of words that have a special meaning when they are used together: *'On top of the world' is an idiom meaning 'extremely happy'.* → see Thesaurus at PHRASE

id·i·o·mat·ic /ˌɪdiəˈmætɪk/ *adjective* idiomatic language contains idioms and is typical of the way people usually talk and write

id·i·ot /ˈɪdiət/ *noun* (informal) a stupid person SYNONYM **fool**: *He's an idiot.*

id·i·ot·ic /ˌɪdiˈɒtɪk $ ˌɪdiˈɑtɪk/ *adjective* very stupid: *Don't ask idiotic questions.*

i·dle /ˈaɪdl/ *adjective* **1** someone who is idle is lazy and does not do what they should do: *They are rich idle women.* **2** (written) not working or being used: *The computers sit idle after school.* —**idly** *adverb*

i·dol /ˈaɪdl/ *noun* someone who is admired greatly by a large number of people

i·dol·ize also **idolise** *BrE* /ˈaɪdl-aɪz/ *verb* to admire someone so much that you think they are perfect: *Herman idolized his father.*

if /ɪf/ *conjunction*
1 used to mention an event that might happen or could have happened: *If you feel hungry, I can get you something to eat.* • *You'll be sick if you eat all that cake.* • *If you had worked harder, you could have passed your exams.*
2 whenever: *If I don't get enough sleep, I can't concentrate.* • *I buy a CD every week, if I can afford it.*
3 used to talk about a question, or say that you do not know about something SYNONYM **whether**: *I asked her if she was all right.* • *I wonder if I've upset him somehow.* • *I don't know if Sally still lives there.*

GRAMMAR
You say **if it rains, we'll have the party inside the house.**
✘ Don't say 'if it will rain ...'
✘ Don't use the future tense with 'will' in this type of clause with **if**.

ig·nite /ɪgˈnaɪt/ *verb* (formal) to start burning, or to make something start burning

ig·ni·tion /ɪgˈnɪʃən/ *noun* the part of a car engine that makes it start working: *He put the key in the ignition.*

ig·no·rance /ˈɪgnərəns/ *noun* (no plural) lack of knowledge or information about something: *Ignorance of the law is not an acceptable excuse.*

ig·no·rant /ˈɪgnərənt/ *adjective* not knowing facts or information that you should know: *Many older people are ignorant about computers.*

ig·nore /ɪgˈnɔː $ ɪgˈnɔr/ *verb* to know that someone or something is there, but to deliberately not do anything to show that you know: *I said hello, but he just ignored me.* • *Mike ignored the pain in his ankle and played football.*

WORD CHOICE
ignore or **ignorant**?
• **Ignore** means "to not pay attention to someone or something": *The other people on the train **ignored** him.*
• **Ignorant** means "not knowing about something, especially something that

you should know": *Many people are ignorant about computers.*

I'll /aɪl/ the short form of 'I will' or 'I shall'

ill /ɪl/ *adjective*
if you are ill, you do not feel well and are not healthy SYNONYM **sick**: *Mrs Jackson has been very ill for a long time.* • *After the meal, he **felt ill**.*

THESAURUS
sick: *He has to look after his **sick** mother* (=ill).
not very well: *You don't look very well. Have you got a fever* (=you look slightly ill)?
feel terrible: *There was something wrong with the food, and the next day I **felt terrible*** (=felt very ill).

il·le·gal /ɪˈliːɡəl/ *adjective* not allowed by law ANTONYM **legal**: *It is illegal to sell cigarettes to children.* —**illegally** *adverb*

il·le·gi·ble /ɪˈledʒəbəl/ *adjective* difficult or impossible to read ANTONYM **legible**: *Her writing is illegible.*

il·le·git·i·mate /ˌɪləˈdʒɪtəmət/ *adjective* an illegitimate child has parents who are not married

il·lit·e·rate /ɪˈlɪtərət/ *adjective* not able to read or write

ill·ness /ˈɪlnəs/ *noun* (plural **illnesses**) the state of being ill, or a particular kind of unhealthy state that affects someone or something: *a serious **mental illness*** • *Our grandmother died after **a long illness**.* • *Illnesses such as mumps are not very serious.*

THESAURUS
disease: *This **disease** is spread by a type of insect* (=this type of illness).
sickness: *I've had two days off work because of **sickness*** (=the state of being ill).

il·lo·gi·cal /ɪˈlɒdʒɪkəl $ ɪˈlɑdʒɪkəl/ *adjective* not reasonable ANTONYM **logical**: *I have an illogical fear of the dark.*

il·lu·sion /ɪˈluːʒən/ *noun* something that seems to be true or real but is not: *In expensive cars you get the illusion that you are floating on air.*

il·lus·trate /ˈɪləstreɪt/ *verb* **1** to give or be an example that makes something clearer: *This story illustrates how important it is to tell the truth.*
2 to draw or paint pictures for a book: *This book is beautifully illustrated.*

il·lus·tra·tion /ˌɪləˈstreɪʃən/ *noun*
1 a picture in a book → see Thesaurus at PICTURE[1] **2** an example that helps you understand something: *The best illustration of Jackson's coaching ability came in Game 2.*

I'm /aɪm/ the short form of 'I am': *I'm hungry.*

im·age /ˈɪmɪdʒ/ *noun*
1 the way that someone or something seems to the public: *The Football Association is trying to improve the image of the sport.*
2 a picture, for example in a newspaper or on television: *The Hubble telescope sends images of space back to Earth.*

i·ma·gi·na·ry /ɪˈmædʒənəri $ ɪˈmædʒəˌneri/ *adjective* not real, and only existing in your thoughts: *Many children have imaginary friends.*

i·ma·gi·na·tion /ɪˌmædʒəˈneɪʃən/ *noun*
your imagination is your ability to form new ideas, and to make pictures in your mind, even of things that do not exist or that you have never seen: *Toys and games should encourage a child to **use their imagination**.* • *Anna **has a very vivid*** (=strong) ***imagination**.*

i·ma·gi·na·tive /ɪˈmædʒənətɪv/ *adjective* having or showing imagination: *an imaginative writer*

i·ma·gine /ɪˈmædʒɪn/ *verb*

KEY PATTERNS
imagine (doing) something
imagine what
imagine (that)

1 to think about what something would or could be like: *Close your eyes, and imagine travelling through space.* • *She tried to **imagine what** the room **would be like**.*
2 to think that something is true or may happen: *No one **imagined that** Thomas would become a successful writer.*

im·i·tate /ˈɪmɪteɪt/ *verb* to deliberately do something in exactly the same way as someone else SYNONYM **copy**: *He can imitate people's voices really well.*

im·i·ta·tion¹ /ˌɪmə'teɪʃən/ *noun* when you deliberately do something in exactly the same way as someone else: *Harry can do an excellent imitation of Elvis.*

imitation² *adjective* imitation leather, wood etc looks like leather, wood etc, but is not SYNONYM **fake** → see Thesaurus at ARTIFICIAL

im·ma·ture /ˌɪmə'tʃʊə $ ˌɪmə'tʃʊr/ *adjective* **1** behaving in a way that is not correct or sensible enough for your age ANTONYM **mature**: *Many students are very immature when they first arrive.* **2** not fully developed ANTONYM **mature**: *Fishermen must return immature fish back to the lake.*

im·me·di·ate /ɪ'miːdiət/ *adjective* **1** happening or done now, without waiting: *The president called for an immediate end to the war.* **2 immediate family** your parents, children, brothers, and sisters → see Thesaurus at FAMILY

im·me·di·ate·ly /ɪ'miːdiətli/ *adverb* now or without waiting: *I need to see you in my office immediately.* • *A restaurant worker immediately came over to clean up the mess.*

THESAURUS
at once: *I sent her an email and she replied at once* (=immediately).
right away: *Janey decided to go right away* (=immediately).
right now (spoken): *I'll do it right now* (=immediately).
instantly: *Click on this button, and the webpage will appear instantly* (=immediately after you do something).

im·mense /ɪ'mens/ *adjective* (formal) very big SYNONYM **enormous**: *The problems are immense.*

im·mense·ly /ɪ'mensli/ *adverb* (formal) to a very great degree: *The movie was immensely popular.*

im·merse /ɪ'mɜːs $ ɪ'mɚs/ *verb* **1** if you immerse yourself in something, or you are immersed in it, you are completely involved in it and do not notice anything else: *Dad always immerses himself in the newspaper when he gets home.* • *Kay missed class because she was immersed in the Internet.* **2** (formal) to put something in a liquid so that the liquid covers it completely

im·mi·grant /'ɪməgrənt/ *noun* someone who comes to live in a country from another country: *My father came to England as an immigrant.* • *The US has a lot of illegal immigrants* (=people living in a country without permission).

im·mi·grate /'ɪməgreɪt/ *verb* to come to live in another country: *Juan immigrated to the US last year.*

im·mi·gra·tion /ˌɪmə'greɪʃən/ *noun* (no plural) **1** when people come to a country in order to live there **2** the place at an airport, border etc where your PASSPORT and other documents are checked

im·mor·al /ɪ'mɒrəl $ ɪ'mɔrəl/ *adjective* bad or evil ANTONYM **moral**: *Stealing is stupid, not to mention immoral.* → see Thesaurus at BAD —**immorally** *adverb*: *Do you think Ruth behaved immorally when she left her husband?*

im·mor·tal /ɪ'mɔːtl $ ɪ'mɔrtl/ *adjective* living or continuing for ever: *The ancient Greeks believed their gods were immortal.* • *Her beauty is immortal.*

im·mune /ɪ'mjuːn/ *adjective* not able to be affected by a disease: *Only a few people are immune to this disease.*

im·mu·ni·za·tion also **immunisation** *BrE* /ˌɪmjənaɪ'zeɪʃən $ ˌɪmjənə'zeɪʃən/ *noun* the act of immunizing someone: *immunization against polio*

im·mu·nize also **immunise** *BrE* /'ɪmjənaɪz/ *verb* to give someone a drug to stop them getting a disease SYNONYM **vaccinate**: *Children in the US must be immunized before attending school.*

im·pact /'ɪmpækt/ *noun* the effect that something or someone has: *The program had a positive impact on the children's reading ability.*

A B C D E F G H I J K L M N O P Q R S T U V W X Y Z

im·paired /ɪmˈpeəd $ ɪmˈperd/ *adjective* damaged or made worse: *His vision is impaired, and he needs very strong glasses.*

im·par·tial /ɪmˈpɑːʃəl $ ɪmˈpɑrʃəl/ *adjective* (formal) not supporting or preferring one person, group, or opinion more than another ANTONYM **biased**: *A judge must be impartial and fair.*

im·pas·sive /ɪmˈpæsɪv/ *adjective* (formal) not showing any feelings —**impassively** *adverb*: *He sat there impassively as the judge read out the verdict.*

im·pa·tience /ɪmˈpeɪʃəns/ *noun* (no plural) when someone becomes angry because they have to wait

im·pa·tient /ɪmˈpeɪʃənt/ *adjective*

KEY PATTERNS
impatient with someone

someone who is impatient becomes angry because they have to wait ANTONYM **patient**: *The officer was rude and impatient when I didn't understand.* • *My husband* ***is*** *sometimes* ***impatient with*** *the kids.* • *Don't* ***be*** *so* ***impatient*** *– it's your turn next!*

im·pec·ca·ble /ɪmˈpekəbəl/ *adjective* (formal) perfect and without any mistakes: *She speaks impeccable English.* —**impeccably** *adverb*: *She was impeccably dressed.*

im·ped·i·ment /ɪmˈpedəmənt/ *noun* **speech impediment, hearing impediment** a problem that makes speaking or hearing difficult

im·pend·ing /ɪmˈpendɪŋ/ *adjective* (formal) an impending event or situation, especially an unpleasant one, will happen very soon: *He sensed the impending danger.*

im·per·a·tive /ɪmˈperətɪv/ *noun* the form of a verb that you use to tell someone to do something. In 'Do it now!' the verb 'do' is an imperative.

im·per·fect¹ /ɪmˈpɜːfɪkt $ ɪmˈpɚfɪkt/ *adjective* not completely perfect: *We're all imperfect.*

imperfect² *noun* the form of a verb that shows an incomplete action in the past. In 'We were walking down the road' the verb 'were walking' is in the imperfect.

im·per·son·al /ɪmˈpɜːsənəl $ ɪmˈpɚsənəl/ *adjective* not showing any feelings of kindness, friendliness etc: *Sue complained about the doctor's impersonal manner.*

im·per·so·nate /ɪmˈpɜːsəneɪt $ ɪmˈpɚsəˌneɪt/ *verb* to copy the way someone talks, behaves etc in order to pretend that you are that person, or to make people laugh: *Rick can impersonate many different actors.*

im·per·ti·nent /ɪmˈpɜːtɪnənt $ ɪmˈpɚtn-ənt/ *adjective* (formal) rude and not showing respect SYNONYM **cheeky**: *She did not answer the maid's impertinent question.*

im·pet·u·ous /ɪmˈpetʃuəs/ *adjective* (formal) doing things quickly, without thinking: *I was young and impetuous, and did several things I shouldn't have.*

im·plau·si·ble /ɪmˈplɔːzəbəl/ *adjective* not likely to be true ANTONYM **plausible**: *His excuse is totally implausible.*

im·ple·ment /ˈɪmpləment/ *verb* to begin to use a plan or system: *The school will be implementing changes next year.*

im·pli·cate /ˈɪmpləkeɪt/ *verb* (formal) to show that someone is involved in something bad or illegal: *Howard was implicated in the crime.*

im·pli·ca·tion /ˌɪmpləˈkeɪʃən/ *noun* (formal) a possible result of a plan, action etc: *This research has many important implications.*

im·ply /ɪmˈplaɪ/ *verb* (**implied**, **implies**) to suggest that something is true without saying or showing it directly: *What exactly are you implying?*

im·po·lite /ˌɪmpəˈlaɪt/ *adjective* (formal) not polite: *It is impolite to leave in the middle of the lecture.* → see Thesaurus at RUDE

im·port¹ /ɪmˈpɔːt $ ɪmˈpɔrt/ *verb* to bring something into a country from abroad in order to sell it ANTONYM **export**: *The store imports Italian cheeses and meats.* —**importer** *noun*: *Germany is Europe's biggest importer of organic food.*

im•port² /ˈɪmpɔːt $ ˈɪmpɔrt/ *noun* the business of bringing things into another country to be sold, or something that is sold ANTONYM **export**: *The import of wild birds from Africa is restricted.*

im•por•tance /ɪmˈpɔːtəns $ ɪmˈpɔrtns/ *noun* (no plural) how important something is: *Good teams understand **the importance of** working together.*

im•por•tant /ɪmˈpɔːtənt $ ɪmˈpɔrtnt/ *adjective*

KEY PATTERNS
it is important to do something

1 something important has a big effect or influence: *Love and respect are more important than a big car and lots of money.* • ***It is important to** exercise regularly.* • *There is an important difference between the two experiments we carried out.*
2 someone who is important has a lot of power or influence: *an important businesswoman*

THESAURUS
major: *Boston, Washington, and other **major** cities* (=important and big)
serious: *This is a **serious** problem now* (=important and bad).
crucial: *Doctors have to make **crucial** decisions every day* (=very important in their effects).

im•pose /ɪmˈpəʊz $ ɪmˈpoʊz/ *verb* (formal) to force people to accept a rule, a tax, beliefs etc: *The king imposed his authority on the whole country.*

im•pos•ing /ɪmˈpəʊzɪŋ $ ɪmˈpoʊzɪŋ/ *adjective* large and impressive: *a grand, imposing hotel*

im•pos•si•ble /ɪmˈpɒsəbəl $ ɪmˈpɑsəbəl/ *adjective*

KEY PATTERNS
it is impossible to do something

if something is impossible, it cannot happen or you cannot do it ANTONYM **possible**: *an impossible task* • ***It was impossible to** get tickets for the game.*

im•pos•tor, **imposter** /ɪmˈpɒstə $ ɪmˈpɑstɚ/ *noun* someone who pretends to be someone else in order to trick people

im•po•tent /ˈɪmpətənt/ *adjective* a man who is impotent is not able to have sex

im•prac•ti•cal /ɪmˈpræktɪkəl/ *adjective* not sensible ANTONYM **practical**

im•pre•cise /ˌɪmprɪˈsaɪs/ *adjective* not exact ANTONYM **precise**: *Our measurements were imprecise.*

im•press /ɪmˈpres/ *verb* to make someone feel admiration and respect: *He spent a lot of money just to try and impress his girlfriend.*

im•pressed /ɪmˈprest/ *adjective* if you are impressed by something, you admire it: *I was really impressed by how well the team played in its first game.*

im•pres•sion /ɪmˈpreʃən/ *noun*

KEY PATTERNS
your impression of someone/something
get/give the impression that
make an impression

1 the feeling you have about something or someone because of the way they seem: *I don't know what your **impression of** him was, but I didn't like him.* • *I **got the impression that** they weren't expecting us.* • *Sam **gave the impression that*** (=made people think that) *he didn't care about his school work.* • *The article is about **making a good impression** on your first date.*
2 when someone copies the way a famous person talks or behaves, in order to make people laugh SYNONYM **impersonation**: *Dawn **does a** good **impression of** Marilyn Monroe.*

im•pres•sion•a•ble /ɪmˈpreʃənəbəl/ *adjective* (formal) someone who is impressionable is easy to influence: *This TV show isn't appropriate for impressionable young children.*

im•pres•sive /ɪmˈpresɪv/ *adjective* if something is impressive, it is very good and you admire it: *Their victory over Toronto was very impressive.* • *Winning five gold medals is an impressive achievement.*

im•print /ˈɪmprɪnt/ *noun* (formal) the mark left by an object that has been pressed onto something: *We could still see the imprint of their feet in the sand.*

A B C D E F G H I J K L M N O P Q R S T U V W X Y Z

im·pris·on /ɪm'prɪzən/ *verb* to put someone in prison or to keep them in a place they cannot escape from: *He was arrested and imprisoned.*

im·prop·er /ɪm'prɒpə $ ɪm'prɑpɚ/ *adjective* (written) not correct according to moral, social, or professional rules —**improperly** *adverb*: *You will not be allowed in the nightclub if you are improperly dressed.*

im·prove /ɪm'pruːv/ *verb*
1 to make something better: *I'm staying in London to improve my English.*
2 to become better ANTONYM **worsen**: *The team is improving with every game.* • *The doctor says my mother's health has improved.*

im·prove·ment /ɪm'pruːvmənt/ *noun*

KEY PATTERNS
a/some improvement in something
an improvement on something else

1 when something becomes better than it was: *There has been **a** great **improvement in** her work recently.*
2 something that is better than a previous thing: *The new house is **a big improvement on** that tiny flat we used to live in.*

im·pro·vise /'ɪmprəvaɪz/ *verb* to do or make something without preparing first, using whatever you have got: *If you do not have a screwdriver, you will have to improvise and use the end of a knife.*

im·pulse /'ɪmpʌls/ *noun* a sudden desire to do something: *My first impulse was to hit him.*

in¹ /ɪn/ *preposition*
1 inside a container, building, car etc: *He had a pencil in his pocket.* • *I've left my coat in the car.*
2 showing the town or city where someone or something is: *The competition will take place in Manchester.*
3 being part of a group: *Joe's in the army now.* • *She's the smartest girl in our class.*
4 showing the month, year, or time when something happens: *My birthday is in June.* • *They got married in 1968.* • *It is very cold here in the winter.* • *We went out in the evening.*
5 after a period of time: *I'll be back in ten minutes.* • ***In a year's time*** (=a year from now) *I'll be going to university.*
6 showing the book, letter etc where something is written: *She says in her letter that she'll see us at Christmas.* • *There's a great description of London in the book.*
7 showing the picture or film where something is shown: *You can see in this picture that she looks ill.* • *In the film, he is left alone on a desert island.*
8 wearing something: *a woman in a smart suit*
9 showing how something is said or written: *I think they were speaking in Chinese.* • *Write your name in large letters at the top of the page.*

PHRASES

in his twenties, in her thirties etc used when saying how old someone is: *The police are looking for a dark-haired man **in his twenties*** (=aged between 20 and 29).

WORD CHOICE
in, **on**, or **at**?
• You use **in** with months, years, seasons, and parts of the day: *See you in September.* • *She was born in 1998.* • *They're getting married **in** the summer.* • *I do my homework **in** the evening.*
• You use **on** with days of the week: *The class is on Monday.*
• You use **at** with times of the day, or with names of holidays: *The meeting starts **at** 9.30.* • *I see my parents **at** Christmas.*
• If you use **next**, **last**, or **this**, you do not use **in**, **on**, or **at**: *See you **next** week.* • *The term ended **last** Friday.* • *The test is **this** morning.*
✘ Don't say 'on last Friday' or 'in next week'.

in² *adverb, adjective*
1 into a place ANTONYM **out**: *He opened the door and walked in.* • *Hello, come in.*
2 at the place where you live or work ANTONYM **out**: *Mr Hibbs isn't in today* (=is not at work today). • *I'll be in tomorrow morning.* • *I'm staying in* (=staying at home) *tonight.*
3 given to a teacher: *This homework has to be in by Friday.* • *Have you handed your essay in yet?*

4 (informal) fashionable: *Long skirts are in this winter.* ➔ see Thesaurus at FASHIONABLE

PHRASES

be in for something (informal) to be going to experience something very good, bad, or surprising: *He's **in for** a surprise when he opens that door!*

have it in for someone (informal) if someone has it in for you, they do not like you and try to cause problems for you: *My boss really **has it in for** me!*

in·a·bil·i·ty /ˌɪnəˈbɪləti/ *noun* when you are not able to do something ANTONYM **ability**: *They were worried about their child's inability to speak.*

in·ac·cu·rate /ɪnˈækjərət/ *adjective* not correct ANTONYM **accurate**: *The newspaper article about the high school was inaccurate.* —**inaccurately** *adverb*

in·ac·tive /ɪnˈæktɪv/ *adjective* (formal) not doing anything or not working ANTONYM **active**: *Many children are inactive because they watch too much TV.*

in·ad·e·quate /ɪnˈædəkwət/ *adjective* not enough or not good enough for a particular purpose ANTONYM **adequate**: *The supply of food was inadequate.* —**inadequately** *adverb*: *He was inadequately prepared for college.*

in·ad·ver·tent·ly /ˌɪnədˈvɜːtəntli $ ˌɪnədˈvɚtntli/ *adverb* if you do something inadvertently, you do it even though you did not intend to SYNONYM **accidentally**: *Sam inadvertently pressed on the car's brake.*

in·ap·pro·pri·ate /ˌɪnəˈprəʊpri-ət $ ˌɪnəˈproʊpri-ət/ *adjective* not suitable or correct ANTONYM **appropriate**: *It is inappropriate to wear a T-shirt to a wedding.* —**inappropriately** *adverb*

in·au·gu·rate /ɪˈnɔːgjəreɪt/ *verb* (formal) to have a formal ceremony when someone new starts an important job: *American presidents are always inaugurated in January.*

Inc. the written abbreviation of INCORPORATED, used after names of companies in the US: *Apple Computer Inc.*

in·ca·pa·ble /ɪnˈkeɪpəbəl/ *adjective* not able to do or feel something ANTONYM **capable**: *The team seem to be incapable of scoring goals.*

in·car·ce·rate /ɪnˈkɑːsəreɪt $ ɪnˈkɑrsəˌreɪt/ *verb* (formal) to put someone in prison SYNONYM **imprison**

in·cense /ˈɪnsens/ *noun* (no plural) a substance that you burn because it has a nice smell

in·cen·tive /ɪnˈsentɪv/ *noun* something that makes you want to work hard or do something new: *Money is a good incentive for hard work.*

in·ces·sant /ɪnˈsesənt/ *adjective* (written) never stopping SYNONYM **constant**: *a week of incessant rain* —**incessantly** *adverb*: *He talks incessantly.*

inch¹ /ɪntʃ/ *noun* (plural **inches**) a unit for measuring length, equal to 2.54 centimetres

inch² *verb* (written) to move very slowly or carefully: *Prices have inched upwards this year.*

in·ci·dent /ˈɪnsədənt/ *noun* (written) something unusual, serious, or violent that happens: *The police are investigating the incident.*

in·ci·den·tal·ly /ˌɪnsəˈdentli/ *adverb* used when giving more information or starting to talk about something new: *He's an excellent player. Incidentally, he's also my cousin.*

in·cite /ɪnˈsaɪt/ *verb* (formal) to deliberately make someone feel so angry or excited that they do something bad: *The opposition leader incited a riot.*

in·cli·na·tion /ˌɪnkləˈneɪʃən/ *noun* (formal) the desire to do something: *His first inclination was to laugh at Jean's mistake.*

in·cline /ˈɪnklaɪn/ *noun* (formal) a slope: *The car was parked on an incline.*

in·clined /ɪnˈklaɪnd/ *adjective* likely or wanting to do something: *Families with children are less inclined to move house.*

in·clude /ɪnˈkluːd/ *verb*

KEY PATTERNS
include someone/something

A B C D E F G H I J K L M N O P Q R S T U V W X Y Z

include someone/something in a group/book etc
include someone/something in/on a list

1 if something includes a person or thing, it has that person or thing as one of its parts: *The film festival includes several Chinese movies.* • *Does the price of a hotel room include breakfast?* **2** to make or consider a person or thing part of something: *She has included several of her mother's recipes in the book.* • *I noticed that my name was not included on the list.* • *The team has 20 people in it, if you include all the managers.*

in·clud·ing /ɪn'kluːdɪŋ/ *preposition* used to show that the thing or person you are talking about is part of a larger thing or group ANTONYM **except**: *He was wearing a full army uniform, including the hat.* • *There will be six people in the car, including the driver.*

in·clu·sion /ɪn'kluːʒən/ *noun* (no plural) when you include someone or something in a larger group: *Here's the list of books we're considering for inclusion on the reading list.*

in·clu·sive /ɪn'kluːsɪv/ *adjective* **1** including a particular thing, especially the price of something: *The all-inclusive charge covers meals, rooms, and entertainment.* **2** *BrE* the first and last number or date you say, and all those in between: *He will be on holiday from 22 to 24 March inclusive.*

in·come /'ɪŋkʌm/ *noun* money that you receive, for example from your job: *Her annual income is £20,000.* → see Thesaurus at PAY[2]

in·com·pat·i·ble /ˌɪnkəm'pætəbəl/ *adjective* **1** two people who are incompatible have different ideas or interests, and are not able to have a good relationship ANTONYM **compatible** **2** two things that are incompatible cannot exist or be used together ANTONYM **compatible**: *Some software may be incompatible with your computer.*

in·com·pe·tence /ɪn'kɒmpətəns $ ɪn'kɑmpətəns/ *noun* (no plural) when someone is not able to do their job correctly ANTONYM **competence**

in·com·pe·tent /ɪn'kɒmpətənt $ ɪn'kɑmpətənt/ *adjective* not having the ability or skill to do your job correctly ANTONYM **competent**: *Airlines need to get rid of incompetent pilots.*

incomplete

in·com·plete /ˌɪnkəm'pliːt/ *adjective* not finished, or not having all its parts ANTONYM **complete**: *The drawings of the building were incomplete.*

in·com·pre·hen·si·ble /ɪnˌkɒmprɪ'hensəbəl $ ˌɪnkɑmprɪ'hensəbəl/ *adjective* (formal) impossible to understand: *The instructions were incomprehensible.*

in·con·clu·sive /ˌɪnkən'kluːsɪv/ *adjective* (formal) not leading to any decision or result: *The medical tests were inconclusive.*

in·con·sid·er·ate /ˌɪnkən'sɪdərət/ *adjective* not caring about other people's needs or feelings ANTONYM **considerate**: *Some inconsiderate person had parked in front of our driveway.*

in·con·sis·ten·cy /ˌɪnkən'sɪstənsi/ *noun* (no plural) when something changes or happens differently each time ANTONYM **consistency**: *The team's inconsistency disappointed fans.*

in·con·sis·tent /ˌɪnkən'sɪstənt/ *adjective* always changing and being of different quality ANTONYM **consistent**: *Pam's school work has been really inconsistent this term.*
—**inconsistently** *adverb*: *The team plays inconsistently.*

in·con·ve·ni·ence /ˌɪnkən'viːniəns/ *noun* when someone has small problems or difficulties: *We're sorry for any inconvenience to our customers.*
—**inconvenience** *verb*: *The work on the roads has inconvenienced drivers.*

in·con·ve·ni·ent /ˌɪnkən'viːniənt/ *adjective* causing small problems or difficulties ANTONYM **convenient**: *The plane leaves at a very inconvenient time.*

in·cor·po·rate /ɪn'kɔːpəreɪt $ ɪn'kɔrpəˌreɪt/ *verb* (formal) to include something as part of a group, system etc: *The building incorporates many energy-saving features.*

in·cor·po·rat·ed /ɪnˈkɔːpəreɪtɪd $ ɪnˈkɔrpəˌreɪtɪd/ (written abbreviation **Inc.**) *adjective* used after the name of a company in the US to show that it is a CORPORATION

in·cor·rect /ˌɪnkəˈrekt/ *adjective* wrong or not true ANTONYM **correct**: *The address on the letter was incorrect.*
→ see Thesaurus at WRONG[1]
—**incorrectly** *adverb*: *She spelled his name incorrectly.*

in·crease[1] /ɪnˈkriːs/ *verb*

KEY PATTERNS
increase by an amount
increase (from one amount) to another amount
increase in size/value etc
increase something
increase something (from one amount) to another amount

1 to become larger in number, amount, size etc ANTONYM **decrease**: *The price of fuel **has increased by** 5%.* • *Last year, the company's profits **increased to** £56 million.* • *Our house **has increased in** value.* • *The number of women who work has increased dramatically* (=a lot).
2 to make something larger in number, amount, size etc ANTONYM **decrease**, **reduce**: *The government has promised not to increase taxes.* • *His salary **was increased from** £40,000 **to** £50,000.*
—**increasing** *adjective*: *an increasing population* —**increased** *adjective*: *an increased risk of cancer*

THESAURUS
go up: *The cost of travelling by train has **gone up** again* (=increased).
rise: *Car crime in the city has **risen*** (=increased).
double: *In a short time, the population almost **doubled*** (=increased to twice the original amount).

in·crease[2] /ˈɪŋkriːs/ *noun*

KEY PATTERNS
an increase in something

when an amount or level becomes larger SYNONYM **rise** ANTONYM **decrease**: *a tax increase* • *an **increase in** crime in the area*

PRONUNCIATION
You pronounce the verb **inCREASE**, with the stress on the second syllable.
You pronounce the noun **INcrease**, with the stress on the first syllable.

in·creas·ing·ly /ɪnˈkriːsɪŋli/ *adverb* (formal) more and more: *Our society is becoming increasingly violent.*

in·cred·i·ble /ɪnˈkredəbəl/ *adjective*
1 very good or large: *Winning the game gave me an incredible feeling.*
2 strange and difficult to believe: *It's incredible that no one checked her statement.*

USAGE
✘ Don't say 'It's very incredible'. Just say **It's incredible**, or **It's absolutely incredible**.

in·cred·i·bly /ɪnˈkredəbli/ *adverb*
1 very: *The show is incredibly popular among teenagers.* **2** in a way that is difficult to believe: *Incredibly, no one was hurt in the crash.*

in·cu·ba·tor /ˈɪŋkjəbeɪtə $ ˈɪŋkjəˌbeɪtɚ/ *noun* a machine used in hospitals to keep weak babies alive

in·cur /ɪnˈkɜː $ ɪnˈkɚ/ *verb* (formal) (**incurred**, **incurring**) to be punished in some way because of something bad you have done: *If the amount is not paid in seven days, you will incur a charge of £15.*

in·cur·a·ble /ɪnˈkjʊərəbəl $ ɪnˈkjʊrəbəl/ *adjective* impossible to cure: *an incurable disease*

in·de·cent /ɪnˈdiːsənt/ *adjective* if something is indecent, it is likely to offend or shock people because it is related to sex: *indecent photographs*

in·de·ci·sive /ˌɪndɪˈsaɪsɪv/ *adjective* not able to make decisions ANTONYM **decisive**: *a weak, indecisive leader*

in·deed /ɪnˈdiːd/ *adverb* used when you want to say something very strongly: *The team has done very well indeed this year.* • *They enjoyed the trip very much indeed.*

in·def·i·nite /ɪnˈdefənət/ *adjective* an indefinite period of time is not fixed and you do not know when it will end: *The flood victims will live at the camp for an indefinite period.* —**indefinitely**

adverb: *This period of economic growth could continue indefinitely.*

in,definite 'article *noun* the word 'a' or 'an' in the English language

in·de·pen·dence /ˌɪndəˈpendəns/ *noun* (no plural) **1** the freedom to make your own decisions and be responsible for yourself: *Women want to keep their independence after they get married.* • *The children are starting to show some independence.*
2 political freedom from control by another country: *When did India gain independence from Britain?* • *the American War of Independence*

> SPELLING
> This word is often spelled wrongly. The correct spelling is: **independence**.

in·de·pen·dent /ˌɪndəˈpendənt/ *adjective*
1 responsible for yourself, making your own decisions, and not needing help from other people ANTONYM **dependent**: *My grandmother is still very independent.* • *I'd like to be financially independent instead of relying on my parents.*
2 an independent country or organization is not controlled by another country or organization: *Senegal **became independent** in 1960.* —**independently** *adverb*

> SPELLING
> This word is often spelled wrongly. The correct spelling is: **independent**.

'in-depth *adjective* considering all the details: *an in-depth interview with the Prime Minister*

in·dex /ˈɪndeks/ *noun* (plural **indexes** or **indices** /-dɪsiːz/) an alphabetical list at the end of a book that tells you where things are mentioned in the book: *I looked up 'meat dishes' in the index.*

'index ,finger *noun* the finger next to your thumb

In·di·an /ˈɪndiən/ *noun* someone from India —**Indian** *adjective*: *Do you like Indian food?*

in·di·cate /ˈɪndəkeɪt/ *verb* **1** (formal) to show that something is likely: *Studies indicate that children from poorer areas are less likely to go to university.* **2** (formal) to say or show what you intend to do: *More than 100 women have indicated they will run for Congress.* **3** *BrE* to show which way you are going to turn when you are driving SYNONYM **signal**: *I indicated left.*

in·di·ca·tion /ˌɪndəˈkeɪʃən/ *noun* (formal) a sign that something is likely: *There were indications that the fire had been started deliberately.*

in·dic·a·tive /ɪnˈdɪkətɪv/ *adjective* (formal) **1 be indicative of something** to show that something exists or is likely to be true: *They've lost a few games, but this is not really indicative of the team's ability.* **2** in grammar, an indicative verb expresses a fact or action

in·di·ca·tor /ˈɪndəkeɪtə $ ˈɪndəˌkeɪtɚ/ *noun BrE* one of the lights on a car which show which way it is going to turn SYNONYM **turn signal** *AmE*

indices a plural of INDEX

in·dif·fer·ence /ɪnˈdɪfərəns/ *noun* (no plural) when someone is not interested in or does not care about something or someone: *The factory's indifference to safety rules led to several injuries.*

in·dif·fer·ent /ɪnˈdɪfərənt/ *adjective* not interested and not caring: *How could a father be so indifferent to his own children?*

in·di·ges·tion /ˌɪndɪˈdʒestʃən/ *noun* (no plural) pain in your stomach that you get when you eat too much or too fast

in·dig·nant /ɪnˈdɪgnənt/ *adjective* (formal) angry because you feel someone has insulted you or treated you unfairly: *Mother was indignant that we didn't believe her.* —**indignantly** *adverb*: *"I'm not too fat!" she shouted indignantly.*

in·dig·ni·ty /ɪnˈdɪgnəti/ *noun* (formal) (plural **indignities**) a situation that makes you feel ashamed, not important, and not respected: *I hated the indignity of the medical examination.*

in·di·rect /ˌɪndəˈrekt/ *adjective* **1** not directly caused by something ANTONYM **direct**: *Political decisions made in the US can have direct and indirect effects in Europe.* **2** not following the straightest way between two places ANTONYM **direct**: *an indirect route* —**indirectly** *adverb*: *He had indirectly caused the accident.*

ˌindirect 'object *noun* the person or thing that receives something as a result of the action mentioned in a sentence. In the sentence 'Joe gave her a sandwich', 'her' is the indirect object.

ˌindirect 'speech REPORTED SPEECH

in·dis·crim·i·nate /ˌɪndɪ'skrɪmənət/ *adjective* (formal) indiscriminate actions are done without thinking about who or what will be affected or hurt by them: *The government should prevent the indiscriminate cutting down of rain forests.* —**indiscriminately** *adverb*

in·di·spens·a·ble /ˌɪndɪ'spensəbəl/ *adjective* (formal) someone or something that is indispensable is so important or useful that you cannot manage without them SYNONYM **essential**: *The book is indispensable to anyone using a computer for the first time.*

in·dis·tin·guish·a·ble /ˌɪndɪ'stɪŋgwɪʃəbəl/ *adjective* so similar that you cannot see any difference: *The copy was almost indistinguishable from the original.*

in·di·vid·u·al¹ /ˌɪndə'vɪdʒuəl/ *adjective* related to one person or thing, rather than to a whole group: *Individual schools can make their own rules about what students can wear.*

individual² *noun* a person: *Many individuals who develop this disease need special treatment.* • *Jack is a strange individual.*

in·di·vid·u·al·i·ty /ˌɪndəvɪdʒu'æləti/ *noun* (no plural) the quality that makes someone different from everyone else: *Your clothes can help show your individuality.*

in·di·vid·u·al·ly /ˌɪndə'vɪdʒuəli/ *adverb* separately, not together in a group: *We paid for our meals individually.*

in·door /'ɪndɔː $ 'ɪndɔr/ *adjective* inside a building ANTONYM **outdoor**: *an indoor tennis court*

indoor

an indoor tennis court

in·doors /ˌɪn'dɔːz $ ˌɪn'dɔrz/ *adverb* into or inside a building ANTONYM **outdoors**: *Keep the plant indoors during the winter.*

in·duce /ɪn'djuːs $ ɪn'dus/ *verb* (formal) to cause someone to do something or cause something to happen: *Can too much exercise induce illness?*

in·dulge /ɪn'dʌldʒ/ *verb* to let yourself do something that you enjoy, especially something that you should not do: *I often indulge myself with chocolates.*

in·dul·gent /ɪn'dʌldʒənt/ *adjective* willing to let someone have whatever they want, even if it is bad for them: *an indulgent grandparent*

in·dus·tri·al /ɪn'dʌstriəl/ *adjective* related to industry or to the people working in industry: *He is meeting industrial leaders and government officials.* —**industrially** *adverb*

in·dus·tri·al·ized also **industrialised** *BrE* /ɪn'dʌstriəlaɪzd/ *adjective* an industrialized country or area has a lot of industry

in·dus·try /'ɪndəstri/ *noun* **1** (plural **industries**) all the companies that make or sell the same kind of thing: *the airline industry* • *the steel industry* → see Thesaurus at BUSINESS **2** (no plural) the work people do to make things in factories: *This type of software is widely used in industry.*

in·ef·fec·tive /ˌɪnə'fektɪv/ *adjective* not producing the result you want ANTONYM **effective**: *Older drugs were ineffective against this disease.* —**ineffectively** *adverb*

in·ef·fi·cient /ˌɪnə'fɪʃənt/ *adjective* a system, organization, or person that is inefficient does not work well and wastes time, money, or energy ANTONYM **efficient**: *We have an inefficient railway system.*

in•e•qual•i•ty /ˌɪnɪˈkwɒləti $ ˌɪnɪˈkwɑləti/ *noun* (plural **inequalities**) when some groups in society have less money, fewer opportunities etc than others, in a way that seems unfair ANTONYM **equality**: *Inequality between men and women still exists today.*

in•ev•i•ta•ble /ɪˈnevətəbəl/ *adjective* something that is inevitable will definitely happen and you cannot avoid it: *Getting older is inevitable.*

in•ex•cus•a•ble /ˌɪnɪkˈskjuːzəbəl/ *adjective* (formal) inexcusable behaviour is so bad or rude that it is difficult to forgive: *The way you spoke to her was completely inexcusable.*

in•ex•pen•sive /ˌɪnɪkˈspensɪv/ *adjective* something that is inexpensive does not cost a lot to buy or use ANTONYM **expensive**: *You can make a tasty meal from inexpensive ingredients.*

in•ex•pe•ri•enced /ˌɪnɪkˈspɪəriənst $ ˌɪnɪkˈspɪriənst/ *adjective* without much experience of doing something ANTONYM **experienced**: *The team had a number of inexperienced young players.*

in•ex•plic•a•ble /ˌɪnɪkˈsplɪkəbəl/ *adjective* very strange and impossible to explain or understand: *For some inexplicable reason, he started to laugh.*

in•fal•li•ble /ɪnˈfæləbəl/ *adjective* never wrong: *Scientists are not infallible.*

in•fan•cy /ˈɪnfənsi/ *noun* (no plural) the period when you are a baby or a young child

in•fant /ˈɪnfənt/ *noun* (formal) a baby or very young child

in•fan•try /ˈɪnfəntri/ *noun* (no plural) soldiers who fight on foot, not on horses or in vehicles

in•fat•u•at•ed /ɪnˈfætʃueɪtɪd/ *adjective* someone who is infatuated with another person feels very strongly that they love that person, but the feeling does not usually last long

in•fect /ɪnˈfekt/ *verb* to give someone an illness: *The local people were infected with the disease through the water supply.*

in•fect•ed /ɪnˈfektɪd/ *adjective* a wound that is infected has become dirty and painful and takes longer to get better: *This cut has become infected.* • *an infected wound*

in•fec•tion /ɪnˈfekʃən/ *noun* an illness which you get from BACTERIA, and which often passes from one person to another: *Infections spread quickly in a school.* • *a chest infection*

in•fec•tious /ɪnˈfekʃəs/ *adjective* an infectious illness can pass from one person to another SYNONYM **catching**

in•fe•ri•or /ɪnˈfɪəriə $ ɪnˈfɪriɚ/ *adjective* not as good as someone or something else ANTONYM **superior**: *Luke had a way of looking at me that always made me feel inferior.*

in•fer•tile /ɪnˈfɜːtaɪl $ ɪnˈfɚtl/ *adjective* **1** infertile land is not good enough for growing plants ANTONYM **fertile**: *infertile stony soil* **2** someone who is infertile is not able to have babies ANTONYM **fertile**

in•fi•del•i•ty /ˌɪnfəˈdeləti/ *noun* when someone who is married has sex with someone who is not their husband or wife

in•fil•trate /ˈɪnfɪltreɪt $ ɪnˈfɪlˌtreɪt/ *verb* to become part of a group, organization etc, especially a criminal one, in order to get information about it: *Trent was ordered to try and infiltrate the terrorists' group.*

in•fi•nite /ˈɪnfənət/ *adjective* something that is infinite has no end or limit: *Is the universe infinite?*

in•fin•i•tive /ɪnˈfɪnətɪv/ *noun* the basic form of a verb, used with 'to'. In the sentence 'I forgot to buy milk', 'to buy' is an infinitive

in•fin•i•ty /ɪnˈfɪnəti/ *noun* (no plural) **1** space or time that has no end or limit **2** a number that is larger than all others

in•flamed /ɪnˈfleɪmd/ *adjective* a part of your body that is inflamed is red and painful SYNONYM **sore**: *an inflamed throat*

in•flam•ma•ble /ɪnˈflæməbəl/ *adjective* materials or substances that are inflammable burn very easily ANTONYM **nonflammable**: *inflammable gases*

in·flam·ma·tion /ˌɪnfləˈmeɪʃən/ *noun* pain and swelling on or in a part of the body: *inflammation of the knee*

in·flat·a·ble /ɪnˈfleɪtəbəl/ *adjective* an inflatable object is one that you fill with air before you use it: *an inflatable boat*

in·flate /ɪnˈfleɪt/ *verb* to fill something such as a BALLOON or a tyre with air SYNONYM **blow up**: *Nick inflated the tires of his bike.*

in·flat·ed /ɪnˈfleɪtɪd/ *adjective*
1 inflated prices, figures etc are higher than is usual or reasonable: *Fans are prepared to pay hugely inflated prices for the tickets.* **2** filled with air or gas: *an inflated life jacket*

in·fla·tion /ɪnˈfleɪʃən/ *noun* (no plural) a continuing increase in prices: *the government's attempts to control inflation*

in·flec·tion, **inflexion** /ɪnˈflekʃən/ *noun* the way the ending of a word changes to show that it is plural, in the past tense etc

in·flex·i·ble /ɪnˈfleksəbəl/ *adjective* not able to change or be changed ANTONYM **flexible**: *As we get older, our attitudes become more inflexible.*

in·flict /ɪnˈflɪkt/ *verb* (written) to make a person, place etc suffer something unpleasant: *The earthquake inflicted an enormous amount of damage on the whole area.*

in·flu·ence¹ /ˈɪnfluəns/ *noun*

KEY PATTERNS
influence on/over someone/something

the ability to change how people or things develop, behave, or think: *Kate used her influence to get her friend a job.* • *How much political influence does the Japanese emperor have?* • *The food that you eat **has** an important **influence on** your health.* • *Keith still **has a great deal of influence over** his daughter, even though she is 24.*

influence² *verb*
to change how someone or something develops, behaves, or thinks: *Several things influenced my decision to leave.* • *Her music influenced me greatly when I was younger.*

in·flu·en·tial /ˌɪnfluˈenʃəl/ *adjective* able to influence what happens or what people think: *John is an influential man in the community.* • *influential journalists and critics*

in·flu·en·za /ˌɪnfluˈenzə/ *noun* (formal) FLU

in·fo /ˈɪnfəʊ $ ˈɪnfoʊ/ *noun* (informal) information

in·form /ɪnˈfɔːm $ ɪnˈfɔrm/ *verb* (formal)

KEY PATTERNS
inform someone about/of something
inform someone that

to formally tell someone about something: *No one **informed** me **about** the change of plan.* • *She was **informed of** the accident by the police.* • *The college **informed me that** I had been accepted.*

in·for·mal /ɪnˈfɔːməl $ ɪnˈfɔrməl/ *adjective* **1** relaxed and friendly ANTONYM **formal**: *an informal party* **2** suitable for ordinary situations, rather than special ones ANTONYM **formal**: *Everyone was told to wear informal clothes.* —**informally** *adverb*

in·for·ma·tion /ˌɪnfəˈmeɪʃən $ ˌɪnfəˈmeɪʃən/ *noun* (no plural)

KEY PATTERNS
information on/about something

facts or details about something: *The website provides **information about** the organization's activities.* • *I need more **information on** the course before I decide whether or not to do it.*

GRAMMAR
Information is not used in the plural.
✘ Don't say 'informations'.
When talking about a single fact, you say **a piece of information**: *She told me an interesting **piece of** information.*
You often use **information** with **some** or **any**: *I need some information about flights to New York.* • *Do you have **any information** about hotels?*
You use **information** with a singular verb: *Are you sure this information is correct?*

A B C D E F G H I J K L M N O P Q R S T U V W X Y Z

infor'mation tech,nology (abbreviation **IT**) *noun* (no plural) the use of computers to store and manage information

in·form·a·tive /ɪn'fɔːmətɪv $ ɪn'fɔrmətɪv/ *adjective* an informative book, talk etc provides useful information: *The lecture was very informative.*

in·formed /ɪn'fɔːmd $ ɪn'fɔrmd/ *adjective* having plenty of knowledge and information about something: *It is important for everyone to keep well informed about what's going on in the world.*

in·form·er /ɪn'fɔːmə $ ɪn'fɔrmɚ/ *noun* someone who helps the police by secretly giving them information about crimes and criminals

in·fre·quent /ɪn'friːkwənt/ *adjective* not happening often ANTONYM **frequent**: *The buses from here into town are pretty infrequent.*

in·fu·ri·ate /ɪn'fjʊərieɪt $ ɪn'fjʊri,eɪt/ *verb* to make someone very angry: *It infuriates me when she behaves so badly.* —**infuriating** *adjective*: *The noise from next door was infuriating.*

in·ge·ni·ous /ɪn'dʒiːniəs/ *adjective* very clever: *What an ingenious idea!*

in·grat·i·tude /ɪn'grætətjuːd $ ɪn'grætə,tud/ *noun* (no plural) when someone is not grateful for something, although they should be

in·gre·di·ent /ɪn'griːdiənt/ *noun* one of the things that you use to make a particular type of food: *Mix all the ingredients together in a bowl.*

in·hab·it /ɪn'hæbɪt/ *verb* (formal) to live in a particular place: *the people who inhabit the rain forests*

in·hab·i·tant /ɪn'hæbətənt/ *noun* (formal) the inhabitants of a place are the people who live there: *France has about 60 million inhabitants.*

in·hale /ɪn'heɪl/ *verb* to breathe air, smoke, or gas into your lungs: *Andrew lit a cigarette and inhaled deeply.*

in·her·it /ɪn'herɪt/ *verb* to receive money, a house etc from someone when they die: *He inherited £100,000 from his aunt.*

in·her·i·tance /ɪn'herɪtəns/ *noun* money, property etc that you receive from someone when they die: *When his father died, Peter received a large inheritance.*

in·hos·pi·ta·ble /,ɪnhɒ'spɪtəbəl $,ɪnhɑ'spɪtəbəl/ *adjective* a place that is inhospitable is difficult to live in because it is very hot, cold etc: *Siberia is one of the most inhospitable regions on earth.*

in·hu·man /ɪn'hjuːmən/ *adjective* very cruel and bad: *inhuman acts of violence and terrorism*

in·hu·mane /,ɪnhjuː'meɪn/ *adjective* inhumane conditions, treatment etc are cruel and not acceptable ANTONYM **humane**: *The animals are kept in inhumane conditions, without enough space or light.*

i·ni·tial[1] /ɪ'nɪʃəl/ *adjective* happening at the beginning: *There will be an initial period of training when you start the job.* —**initially** *adverb*: *Initially, I didn't like him at all.*

initial[2] *noun* the first letter of a name: *His initials are EW, for Ed Williams.*

i·ni·tia·tive /ɪ'nɪʃətɪv/ *noun* (no plural) when you make decisions and do things without waiting for someone to tell you what to do: *We are looking for someone with imagination and initiative to join our sales team.*

in·ject /ɪn'dʒekt/ *verb* to put a drug into someone's body, using a special needle: *The vaccine is injected into your upper arm.*

in·jec·tion /ɪn'dʒekʃən/ *noun* when a drug is put into your body, using a special needle: *The nurse gave me an injection against tetanus.*

in·jure /'ɪndʒə $ 'ɪndʒɚ/ *verb* to damage part of someone's body: *Eight people were injured in the crash.*
→ see Thesaurus at DAMAGE[2]
—**injured** *adjective*: *The injured passengers were taken to a nearby hospital.*

in·jur·y /'ɪndʒəri/ *noun* (plural **injuries**) damage to someone's body caused by an accident or attack: *He was lucky to survive with only **minor injuries**.* • *Laura had **internal injuries*** (=injuries inside her body) *after the car accident.* • *Matt can't play basketball this season because of a knee injury.*

THESAURUS
wound: *The woman died from knife **wounds*** (=injuries caused by a weapon).
cut: *The **cut** on his finger was bleeding* (=a small injury made by something sharp cutting his skin).
sprain: *He couldn't play football because of a knee **sprain*** (=an injury caused by suddenly twisting it).

in·jus·tice /ɪnˈdʒʌstɪs/ *noun* when people are treated in a bad and unfair way ANTONYM **justice**: *The organization fights against injustice all over the world.*

ink /ɪŋk/ *noun* a coloured liquid used for writing, printing, or drawing

in·land /ˈɪnlənd/ *adjective, adverb* away from the coast: *We visited some inland villages.* • *Lake Sabaya lies about six miles inland.*

ˈin-laws *plural noun* (informal) the parents of your husband or your wife: *We're spending Christmas with my in-laws this year.*

in·ner /ˈɪnə $ ˈɪnɚ/ *adjective* on the inside or near the centre of something ANTONYM **outer**: *the castle's inner walls* • *inner London*

ˌinner ˈcity *noun* (plural **inner cities**) the part of a city that is near the centre, especially the part where the buildings are in a bad condition and the people are poor: *the problem of crime in our inner cities*

in·ning /ˈɪnɪŋ/ *noun* one of the nine periods of play in a game of baseball

in·nings /ˈɪnɪŋz/ *noun* (plural **innings**) one of the periods of play in a game of CRICKET

in·no·cence /ˈɪnəsəns/ *noun* **1** the fact that someone is not guilty of a crime ANTONYM **guilt**: *Her husband is the only one who believes in her innocence.* **2** when someone has not had much experience of life: *the innocence of a child*

in·no·cent /ˈɪnəsənt/ *adjective*

KEY PATTERNS
innocent of a crime

1 someone who is innocent has not done anything wrong ANTONYM **guilty**: *He says he is **innocent of** the murder.* • *the innocent victims of war*
2 someone who is innocent does not know about the bad things in life: *an innocent child* —**innocently** *adverb*

in·noc·u·ous /ɪˈnɒkjuəs $ ɪˈnɑkjuəs/ *adjective* (formal) not likely to harm anyone or cause trouble: *It seemed like a fairly innocuous thing to say.*

in·no·va·tion /ˌɪnəˈveɪʃən/ *noun* a new idea or method: *scientific and technological innovations*

in·put /ˈɪnpʊt/ *noun* (no plural) ideas that you have or things that you do to help make something succeed: *Thanks for coming to the meeting, Julie – we value your input.*

in·quest /ˈɪŋkwest/ *noun* an official process to try and discover why someone has died suddenly

in·quire also **enquire** *BrE* /ɪnˈkwaɪə $ ɪnˈkwaɪɚ/ *verb* (formal)

KEY PATTERNS
inquire about something

to ask someone for information: *I called to **inquire about** changes to the train schedules.* → see Thesaurus at ASK

in·quir·ing also **enquiring** *BrE* /ɪnˈkwaɪərɪŋ/ *adjective* someone who has an inquiring mind wants to learn new things: *a lively boy with a very inquiring mind*

in·quir·y also **enquiry** *BrE* /ɪnˈkwaɪəri/ *noun* (plural **inquiries**) **1** a question you ask in order to get information: *I made some further enquiries and found out that he had been dismissed from his previous job.* **2** an official process to try and discover why something bad happened: *There will be a government inquiry into the causes of the disaster.*

in·quis·i·tive /ɪnˈkwɪzətɪv/ *adjective* an inquisitive person or animal is very interested in everything: *Cats are very inquisitive animals.*

in·sane /ɪnˈseɪn/ *adjective* **1** (informal) very stupid, often in a way that is dangerous ANTONYM **sane**: *Don't be insane! You can't possibly jump down from here!* **2** seriously mentally ill ANTONYM **sane**

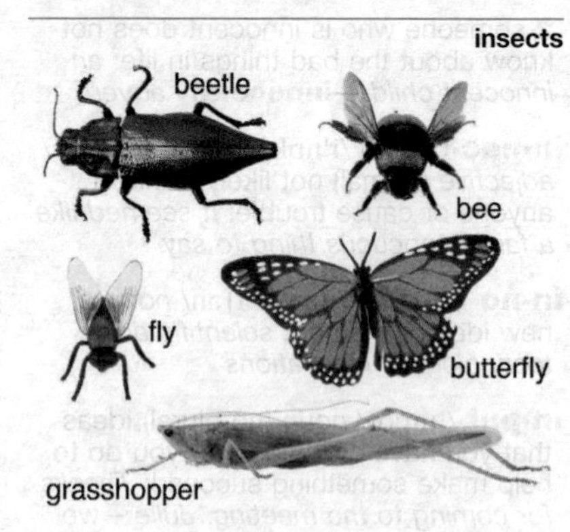

in•sect /ˈɪnsekt/ *noun* any small creature that has six legs, for example a fly

in•se•cure /ˌɪnsɪˈkjʊə $ ˌɪnsɪˈkjʊr/ *adjective* someone who is insecure does not feel confident that other people like them, or confident about their ability to do something: *She was only 17 and very insecure.*

in•sen•si•tive /ɪnˈsensətɪv/ *adjective* someone who is insensitive does not notice other people's feelings and often does or says things that upset them ANTONYM **sensitive**: *He can be rude and insensitive.* • *insensitive remarks about religion*

in•sep•a•ra•ble /ɪnˈsepərəbəl/ *adjective* people who are inseparable are always together and are very friendly with each other: *As children, my brother and I were inseparable.*

in•sert /ɪnˈsɜːt $ ɪnˈsɜrt/ *verb* (written) to put something inside or into something else: *Insert the coins in the machine.*

insert

in•side¹ /ɪnˈsaɪd/ *preposition, adverb* in or into a container or building ANTONYM **outside**: *Is there anything inside the box?* • *Let's go inside – it's cold.*

inside² *noun* **the inside** the part of something that is surrounded by the rest of it ANTONYM **the outside**: *The inside of the house was much bigger than I'd thought.* • *I bit the inside of my mouth.*

in•side³ /ˈɪnsaɪd/ *adjective* on the inside of something: *My new jacket has three inside pockets.*

in•sight /ˈɪnsaɪt/ *noun* an ability to understand something clearly, especially because you have done it, studied it etc: *The museum gave us a real insight into how people used to live.*

in•sig•nif•i•cant /ˌɪnsɪɡˈnɪfɪkənt/ *adjective* too small or unimportant to think or worry about ANTONYM **significant**: *I felt small and insignificant beside all these important people.*

in•sin•cere /ˌɪnsɪnˈsɪə $ ˌɪnsɪnˈsɪr/ *adjective* someone who is insincere pretends to feel or think something that they do not really feel or think ANTONYM **sincere**: *What a horrible man, thought Maisie, giving him an insincere smile.*

in•sist /ɪnˈsɪst/ *verb*

KEY PATTERNS
insist that
insist on (doing) something

1 to say firmly that something is true: *Don **insisted that** he hadn't gone out of the house at all.*
2 to say very strongly that you must do something, or that something must happen: *She **insisted on** paying for the meal herself.* • *I **insist that** you leave the theatre immediately.*

GRAMMAR
You **insist on doing something**.
✘ Don't say 'insist to do something'.

in•sis•tence /ɪnˈsɪstəns/ *noun* (no plural) when you say very firmly that something must happen or be done: *My parents' insistence on good manners was a very good thing.*

in•sis•tent /ɪnˈsɪstənt/ *adjective* saying very firmly that something must happen or be done: *The teachers are all insistent that our homework is done on time.*

in•so•lent /ˈɪnsələnt/ *adjective* rude and not showing someone respect: *Don't be so insolent!*

in•sol•u•ble /ɪnˈsɒljəbəl $ ɪnˈsɑljəbəl/ *adjective* an insoluble substance does not disappear when you mix it with water: *Sand is insoluble.*

in·som·ni·a /ɪn'sɒmniə $ ɪn'sɑmniə/ *noun* (no plural) the problem you have when you often cannot sleep: *Dad's suffered from insomnia for years.*

in·spect /ɪn'spekt/ *verb* to examine something carefully, especially as an official activity: *The city regularly inspects restaurants for health and safety reasons.*

in·spec·tion /ɪn'spekʃən/ *noun* when you examine something carefully, especially as an official activity: *Officials completed their inspection of the new building.*

in·spec·tor /ɪn'spektə $ ɪn'spektɚ/ *noun* **1** someone whose job is to discover whether something is being done in the correct way: *a school inspector* **2** a police officer of middle rank

in·spi·ra·tion /ˌɪnspə'reɪʃən/ *noun* new ideas about what to do: *The landscape is a source of inspiration for many artists.*

in·spire /ɪn'spaɪə $ ɪn'spaɪɚ/ *verb* to make someone feel that they want to do or achieve something: *What exactly inspired you to go back to university at the age of 40?*

in·spired /ɪn'spaɪəd $ ɪn'spaɪɚd/ *adjective* very skilful and special: *It was an inspired piece of football.*

in·stall /ɪn'stɔːl/ *verb* to put a piece of equipment somewhere and connect it so that you can use it: *A plumber is coming to install the new washing machine today.*

in·stal·ment *BrE*, **installment** *AmE* /ɪn'stɔːlmənt/ *noun* **1** a payment that you make every week, month etc in order to pay for something: *Would you like to pay for your sofa now or in instalments?* **2** one part of a long story that you can watch or read over a period of time on television, in a magazine etc: *Wait for next week's exciting instalment!*

in·stance /'ɪnstəns/ *noun* **for instance** for example: *In many countries, for instance Japan, fish is a very important part of the diet.*

in·stant[1] /'ɪnstənt/ *adjective*
1 something that is instant happens immediately and very quickly: *When she used the cream, she saw an instant improvement in her skin.*
2 instant food can be prepared very quickly, for example because you just mix it with hot water: *instant coffee*
—**instantly** *adverb*: *The doorbell rang, and Joe jumped instantly out of his chair.* ➔ see Thesaurus at IMMEDIATELY

instant[2] *noun* a very short period of time SYNONYM **moment**: *An instant later, the telephone rang.*

in·stan·ta·ne·ous /ˌɪnstən'teɪniəs/ *adjective* happening immediately and very quickly: *The effect of the drug was instantaneous.* —**instantaneously** *adverb*

in·stead /ɪn'sted/ *adverb*

KEY PATTERNS
instead of something

in the place of someone or something else: *You can use yogurt **instead of** cream in this recipe.* • *I decided to go in May instead.*

in·stil *BrE*, **instill** *AmE* /ɪn'stɪl/ *verb* (**instilled**, **instilling**) to make someone think, feel, or behave in a particular way: *It's my job to instil confidence into the whole team.*

in·stinct /'ɪnstɪŋkt/ *noun* a natural force that makes people or animals do something, without thinking or having to learn it: *All people and animals have a basic instinct to survive.* • *a woman's maternal instinct*

in·sti·tute /'ɪnstɪtjuːt $ 'ɪnstəˌtut/ *noun* an organization where people are studying a particular thing, especially in science or education

in·sti·tu·tion /ˌɪnstɪ'tjuːʃən $ ˌɪnstə'tuʃən/ *noun* a large important organization such as a university or bank: *financial institutions* (=banks and other organizations that invest money)

in·struct /ɪn'strʌkt/ *verb* **1** to officially tell someone to do something: *The government instructed farmers to stop using the chemicals on their crops.* **2** to teach someone how to do something

in·struc·tion /ɪn'strʌkʃən/ *noun*

KEY PATTERNS
instructions on how to do something
instruction in something

information that tells you what to do: *Instructions on how to put the toy together are printed on the box.* • ***Follow the instructions** carefully.* • *The air stewardess **gave** us some **instruction in** using the oxygen masks.*

in·struc·tor /ɪn'strʌktə $ ɪn'strʌktɚ/ *noun* someone who teaches a particular activity or sport: *a driving instructor*

in·stru·ment /'ɪnstrəmənt/ *noun* **1** something such as a piano, GUITAR etc that you play in order to make music: *Do you **play** any **musical instruments**?* **2** a special piece of equipment that you use to do a particular thing: *An airline pilot must learn how to use all these instruments.* • *medical instruments*

in·stru·men·tal /ˌɪnstrə'mentl/ *adjective* instrumental music is played on instruments, rather than sung —**instrumental** *noun*: *The next number the band played was an instrumental.*

in·suf·fi·cient /ˌɪnsə'fɪʃənt/ *adjective* (formal) not enough ANTONYM **sufficient**: *The people here have insufficient food and water.*

in·su·late /'ɪnsjəleɪt $ 'ɪnsəˌleɪt/ *verb* to cover or protect something with a material that stops electricity, sound, heat etc getting in or out: *Make sure you've insulated the pipes before the cold weather.*

in·su·lin /'ɪnsjəlɪn $ 'ɪnsələn/ *noun* (no plural) a substance that your body makes so that it can use sugar for energy

in·sult¹ /ɪn'sʌlt/ *verb* to say or do something rude to someone and offend them: *Sometimes he drinks too much wine, and then insults people.* —**insulting** *adjective*: *an insulting remark* → see Thesaurus at RUDE

in·sult² /'ɪnsʌlt/ *noun* something rude that you say that offends someone: *Rival supporters shouted insults at each other.*

in·sur·ance /ɪn'ʃʊərəns $ ɪn'ʃʊrəns/ *noun* (no plural) an arrangement in which you pay a company money and they pay the costs if you get ill, have an accident in your car etc: *How much does your car insurance cost each year?*

in·sure /ɪn'ʃʊə $ ɪn'ʃʊr/ *verb* **1** to buy or provide insurance for something: *Have you insured your house and its contents?* • *We can insure your car for less.* **2** an American spelling of ENSURE

in·tact /ɪn'tækt/ *adjective* (formal) something that is intact is not broken or damaged: *Most of the houses were destroyed, but the church remained intact.*

in·take /'ɪnteɪk/ *noun* **1** (formal) the amount of food, liquid etc that you eat or drink: *If you're on a diet, you should reduce your sugar intake.* **2** the number of people that join a school, profession etc at a particular time: *The school has an intake of about 100 children each year.*

in·te·gral /'ɪntəgrəl/ *adjective* an integral part of something is an important and necessary part of it: *Music is an integral part of my life.*

in·te·grate /'ɪntəgreɪt/ *verb* to become part of a group or a society, or to help someone do this: *Our neighbours have never really integrated into the local community.*

in·teg·ri·ty /ɪn'tegrəti/ *noun* (no plural) the quality of being honest and doing what you believe is right: *No one doubts your integrity.*

in·tel·lect /'ɪntəlekt/ *noun* a person's mind and their ability to understand things: *He has a brilliant intellect.*

in·tel·lec·tual /ˌɪntə'lektʃuəl/ *adjective* related to your ability to think, learn, and understand ideas and information: *Mary's intellectual ability is very advanced for her age.*

in·tel·li·gence /ɪn'telədʒəns/ *noun* (no plural) the ability to understand things: *a person of above-average intelligence*

in·tel·li·gent /ɪn'telədʒənt/ *adjective* someone who is intelligent is able to understand things quickly: *Lisa is highly intelligent.* • *That's an intelligent question.*

THESAURUS
clever: *Are you **clever** enough to be able to solve the problem* (=able to understand and learn things quickly or to think of good ideas)?
smart (informal): *Craig's a really smart guy* (=intelligent).
bright: *She's a bright student* (=intelligent).
brilliant: *a brilliant scientist* (=extremely intelligent)

in·tel·li·gi·ble /ɪnˈtelədʒəbəl/ *adjective* if something you read or hear is intelligible, you can understand it ANTONYM **incomprehensible**: *He tries to make his astronomy books intelligible to the general public.*

in·tend /ɪnˈtend/ *verb*

KEY PATTERNS
intend to do something
intend that
be intended for something/someone

1 to plan to do something SYNONYM **mean**: *We **intend to** install a lift for disabled people.* • *I didn't **intend to** upset her.* • *Pete had **intended that** I would see him with his new girlfriend.*
2 if something is intended for a particular purpose or person, it has been made especially for that purpose or person: *The film **is intended for** older children.*

in·tense /ɪnˈtens/ *adjective* a feeling, reaction etc that is intense is very strong: *He had an intense love of music.* • *The pain in my leg was intense.*

in·ten·si·fy /ɪnˈtensəfaɪ/ *verb* (**intensified**, **intensifies**) to increase in strength, size, or amount, or to make something do this: *The pressure at work had slowly intensified.*

in·ten·sive /ɪnˈtensɪv/ *adjective* an intensive course, activity etc involves a lot of work or effort in a short time: *an intensive advertising campaign*

in·tent /ɪnˈtent/ *adjective* if you are intent on doing something, you are determined to do it: *The team has been training hard and they're intent on winning.*

in·ten·tion /ɪnˈtenʃən/ *noun* something that you plan to do: *My original intention was to study in America.* ➔ see Thesaurus at PLAN[1]

in·ten·tion·al /ɪnˈtenʃənəl/ *adjective* done deliberately SYNONYM **deliberate**: *Yes, I broke the window, but it wasn't intentional.* —**intentionally** *adverb*
➔ see Thesaurus at DELIBERATELY

in·ter·act /ˌɪntəˈrækt/ *verb* to talk to people and make friends with them: *Children need to learn to interact with each other at an early age.*

in·ter·act·ive /ˌɪntəˈræktɪv/ *adjective* involving communication between a computer, television etc and the person who is using it: *interactive CD-ROMs*

in·ter·cept /ˌɪntəˈsept $ ˌɪntɚˈsept/ *verb* to stop someone or something that is moving from one place to another: *The aircraft was intercepted and shot down.*

in·ter·com /ˈɪntəkɒm $ ˈɪntɚˌkɑm/ *noun* a system that people in a large building use to speak to people in other parts of the building: *They made the announcement over the intercom.*

in·terest[1] /ˈɪntrəst/ *noun*

KEY PATTERNS
(an) interest in something

1 (no plural) the feeling that you want to know more about a subject or activity: *She has **shown a lot of interest in** learning ballet.* • *I **have no interest in** sport.* • *When Paul realized how much work was involved, he **lost interest*** (=stopped being interested).
2 interests your interests are the things that you enjoy doing: *We have similar interests.*
3 (no plural) money that you pay a bank when you borrow money from it, or that the bank pays you when you save money: *Banks **charge interest** on their loans.* • *The account **pays** six per cent **interest**.* • ***Interest rates** have gone up again.*

interest[2] *verb* if a subject, activity etc interests you, you want to know more about it: *Cooking doesn't interest me at all.*

in·terest·ed /ˈɪntrəstɪd/ *adjective*

KEY PATTERNS
interested in (doing) something

if you are interested in something, you want to know more about it or do it: *Jo*

A B C D E F G H I J K L M N O P Q R S T U V W X Y Z

has been ***interested in*** *animals all her life.* • *Would you* ***be interested in*** *going to India this summer?* • *I can show you some other books, if you're interested.* • *I'd be* ***interested to know*** *whether she passes the exam.*

WORD CHOICE
interested or **interesting**?
• **Interested** means "enjoying something or wanting to know more about it": *Are you* ***interested in*** *computer games?*
• **Interesting** means "making you want to know more about something": *I saw an* ***interesting*** *article in the paper.*

in·terest·ing /'ɪntrəstɪŋ/ *adjective* unusual or exciting in a way that makes you think and want to know more ANTONYM **boring**: *A good teacher can make any subject interesting.* • *There's a really interesting article about foxes in this month's 'Nature' magazine.*

in·ter·fere /ˌɪntə'fɪə $ ˌɪntɚ'fɪr/ *verb*

KEY PATTERNS
interfere in something
interfere with something

1 if someone interferes in a situation, they do something when other people do not want them to SYNONYM **meddle**: *Her mother has* ***interfered in*** *our marriage from the beginning.*
2 if something interferes with something, it stops it continuing or developing properly: *Playing football must not* ***interfere with*** *your education.*

in·ter·fer·ence /ˌɪntə'fɪərəns $ ˌɪntɚ'fɪrəns/ *noun* (no plural) **1** when someone interferes in something: *We want to handle this situation ourselves, without interference from other countries.* **2** when bad weather makes it difficult to hear a radio signal or see a television programme

in·te·ri·or /ɪn'tɪəriə $ ɪn'tɪriɚ/ *noun* the inside part of something ANTONYM **exterior**: *I loved the outside of the house, but the interior was disappointing.*

in·ter·jec·tion /ˌɪntə'dʒekʃən $ ˌɪntɚ'dʒekʃən/ *noun* a word or phrase that is used to express surprise, shock, pain etc. In the sentence 'Ouch! That hurts!', 'ouch' is an interjection.

in·ter·me·di·ate /ˌɪntə'miːdiət $ ˌɪntɚ'midiət/ *adjective* an intermediate student has learned about a subject but is not very advanced: *classes for intermediate English students*

in·ter·mis·sion /ˌɪntə'mɪʃən $ ˌɪntɚ'mɪʃən/ *noun* a short period of time when a play, film, game etc stops for a short time before starting again SYNONYM **interval**: *We had an ice cream during the intermission.*

in·tern /'ɪntɜːn $ 'ɪntɚn/ *noun AmE* **1** someone who works without pay, so that they can learn how to do a job: *Kelly is working this summer as an intern for the senator.* **2** someone who has almost finished training as a doctor and is working in a hospital

in·ter·nal /ɪn'tɜːnl $ ɪn'tɚnl/ *adjective* on the inside or related to the inside of something ANTONYM **external**: *internal injuries*

in·ter·na·tion·al /ˌɪntə'næʃənəl $ ˌɪntɚ'næʃənəl/ *adjective* involving or existing in many countries: *international football matches* • *an international bank*

In·ter·net /'ɪntənet $ 'ɪntɚˌnet/ *noun* **the Internet** a system that allows people using computers around the world to send and receive information: *You can find all the latest information on the Internet.*

GRAMMAR
You look at something **on the Internet.**
✘ Don't say 'by Internet'.

in·ter·pret /ɪn'tɜːprɪt $ ɪn'tɚprɪt/ *verb* to say what someone has just said in one language in another language: *As Mr Bates doesn't speak Polish, I interpreted for him.*

in·ter·pret·er /ɪn'tɜːprɪtə $ ɪn'tɚprɪtɚ/ *noun* a person whose job is to say what someone has said in one language in another language: *Cairns, a fluent Japanese speaker, acted as interpreter.*

in·ter·ro·gate /ɪn'terəgeɪt/ *verb* to ask someone a lot of questions, often in an unpleasant way: *Forty people were arrested and interrogated by military police.*

in·ter·rog·a·tive /ˌɪntəˈrɒɡətɪv $ ˌɪntəˈrɑɡətɪv/ *noun* a word or sentence that asks a question —**interrogative** *adjective*

in·ter·ro·ga·tor /ɪnˈterəɡeɪtə $ ɪnˈterəˌɡeɪtɚ/ *noun* someone who tries to get information by asking lots of questions, often in an unpleasant way: *She managed to trick her interrogators and escape.*

in·ter·rupt /ˌɪntəˈrʌpt/ *verb*
1 to say something at the same time as someone else is speaking: *I tried to explain, but people kept interrupting me.* • *"I think you're wrong," interrupted Angela angrily.*
2 to stop something happening for a short time: *The war interrupted his studies.*

in·ter·rup·tion /ˌɪntəˈrʌpʃən/ *noun*
1 when someone says something while someone else is speaking: *She ignored my interruption, and carried on speaking.*
2 when something is stopped for a short time: *I need a place where I can work without interruption.*

in·ter·sec·tion /ˌɪntəˈsekʃən/ *noun* a place where two roads, lines etc meet, especially where they cross each other SYNONYM **junction**: *Meet me at the intersection of Main Street and Queen Street.*

in·ter·val /ˈɪntəvəl $ ˈɪntɚvəl/ *noun*
1 a period of time between one thing happening and another: *The buses come at ten-minute intervals.* **2** *BrE* an INTERMISSION

in·ter·vene /ˌɪntəˈviːn $ ˌɪntɚˈvin/ *verb* to do something to try to stop an argument, problem, war etc: *I could hear them arguing, but decided not to intervene.*

in·ter·view¹ /ˈɪntəvjuː $ ˈɪntɚvju/ *noun*

KEY PATTERNS
an interview with someone
give an interview

1 a meeting in which one or more people ask you questions to discover whether you are suitable for something: *I've got a* ***job interview*** *this afternoon.* • *Do some research about the company before you* ***go to the interview****.* • *Could you* ***come for an interview*** *on Tuesday?* • *Admission to the university is by interview.*
2 an occasion when someone asks a famous person lots of questions, and the famous person talks about their life, work etc: *In an* ***interview with*** *the newspaper, he discussed his marriage problems.* • *Bob Dylan says he hates* ***giving interviews*** (=being asked to talk a lot about himself).

interview² *verb*
to ask someone questions during an interview: *Later in the programme I will be interviewing the prime minister.* • *Fifteen people* ***were interviewed for*** *the job.*

in·ter·view·er /ˈɪntəvjuːə $ ˈɪntɚˌvjuɚ/ *noun* someone whose job is to interview famous people, especially on television or radio

in·tes·tine /ɪnˈtestɪn/ *noun* the long tube in your body that carries food away from your stomach SYNONYM **gut**

in·ti·mate /ˈɪntəmət/ *adjective* very private or personal: *She wrote all her most intimate thoughts in her diary.*

in·tim·i·date /ɪnˈtɪmədeɪt/ *verb* to frighten someone, especially so that they do what you want them to: *Some of the older boys were trying to intimidate him into giving them money.*

in·to /ˈɪntə; before vowels ˈɪntʊ; strong ˈɪntuː/ *preposition*
1 to the inside of a place or container: *Teresa ran into the house.* • *She poured some more orange juice into her glass.*
2 used to talk about hitting something by accident: *He drove into another car.* • *He bumped into her desk.*
3 used to say that something becomes a different shape or a different thing: *Can everyone please get into a straight line?* • *Caterpillars turn into butterflies.*
4 (informal) if you are into something, you like it a lot: *Ben's really into football.*

in·tol·e·ra·ble /ɪnˈtɒlərəbəl $ ɪnˈtɑlərəbəl/ *adjective* very unpleasant or painful SYNONYM **unbearable**: *In the middle of the day, the heat was intolerable.*

in·tol·e·rant /ɪnˈtɒlərənt $ ɪnˈtɑlərənt/ *adjective* if someone is intolerant, they are not willing to accept ways of thinking and behaving that are different from their own ANTONYM **tolerant**: *People in this small village are intolerant of progress.*

in·tra·net /ˈɪntrənet/ *noun* a system for sending computer messages between people who work for the same company or organization, which is similar to the Internet but smaller

in·tran·si·tive /ɪnˈtrænsətɪv/ *adjective* an intransitive verb does not have an object. In the sentence, 'She was crying,' 'cry' is an intransitive verb. ANTONYM **transitive**

in·tri·cate /ˈɪntrɪkət/ *adjective* an intricate pattern or design has a lot of details or different parts: *intricate carvings*

in·trigue /ɪnˈtriːg/ *verb* to interest someone a lot, especially by being strange or mysterious: *The story of the young girl who used to live in the house intrigued me.*

introduce

Dan introduced me to his mother.

in·tro·duce /ˌɪntrəˈdjuːs $ ˌɪntrəˈdus/ *verb*

KEY PATTERNS
introduce someone to someone else
introduce someone to something new

1 if you introduce people who are meeting for the first time, you tell them each other's names. If you introduce yourself to someone, you tell them your name: *Eric **introduced** me **to** his mother.* • *Please **introduce yourself to** the person sitting next to you.*
2 to make something happen or start to be used for the first time: *The store has introduced a new range of food for children.*
3 to tell someone about something or show them something for the first time: *I wanted to **introduce** the kids **to** jazz.*

in·tro·duc·tion /ˌɪntrəˈdʌkʃən/ *noun*

KEY PATTERNS
the introduction to a book
an introduction to chemistry/philosophy etc
the introduction of something new

1 a short explanation at the beginning of a book or speech: *The author's wife wrote the **introduction to** the book.*
2 something that helps you understand the basic or easiest parts of a subject: *The course provides an **introduction to** computing.*
3 when you tell people who are meeting for the first time each other's names: *There was no time for formal introductions.*
4 when people start using something new for the first time: *What effects will the **introduction of** the new tax have?*

in·tro·duc·to·ry /ˌɪntrəˈdʌktəri/ *adjective* **1** an introductory remark, CHAPTER etc comes at the beginning of something and introduces the subject: *Write an introductory paragraph to your essay.* **2** an introductory price, offer etc is a cheap price that is available for a short time when something new is being sold: *The software is available at an introductory price of $175.*

in·tro·vert /ˈɪntrəvɜːt $ ˈɪntrəˌvɚt/ *noun* someone who is quiet and shy ANTONYM **extrovert**

in·tro·vert·ed /ˈɪntrəvɜːtɪd $ ˈɪntrəˌvɚtɪd/ *adjective* quiet and shy

in·trude /ɪnˈtruːd/ *verb* to enter a place or become involved in a situation when you should not, because people do not want you to: *"I hope I'm not intruding," Mum said as she opened my bedroom door.*

in·trud·er /ɪnˈtruːdə $ ɪnˈtrudɚ/ *noun* someone who enters a building or area without permission or illegally: *The alarm will go off if there's an intruder.*

in·tu·i·tion /ˌɪntjuˈɪʃən $ ˌɪntuˈɪʃən/ *noun* the feeling that you know something is correct or true, although you do not have any definite facts: *My intuition told me not to trust him.*

in•vade /ɪn'veɪd/ *verb* to enter a country with an army in order to take control of it: *Hitler invaded Poland in 1939.* —**invader** *noun*

in•val•id¹ /ɪn'vælɪd/ *adjective* not acceptable because of a law or rule ANTONYM **valid**: *This visa is invalid in this country.*

in•va•lid² /'ɪnvəliːd $ 'ɪnvələd/ *noun* someone who is ill, injured, or weak and needs other people to help them do things

PRONUNCIATION
You pronounce the adjective **inVAlid**, with the stress on the second syllable.
You pronounce the noun **INvalid**, with the stress on the first syllable.

in•val•u•a•ble /ɪn'væljuəbəl $ ɪn'væljəbəl/ *adjective* very useful: *I gained invaluable experience while I was working abroad.*

in•var•i•a•bly /ɪn'veəriəbli $ ɪn'veriəbli/ *adverb* always: *The trains are invariably late in the morning.*

in•va•sion /ɪn'veɪʒən/ *noun* when a country's army enters another country in order to take control of it: *the Roman invasion of Britain*

in•vent /ɪn'vent/ *verb* to think of or make something completely new: *Who invented the first computer?*

THESAURUS
make up: *Lisa loves* ***making up*** *stories about animals* (=inventing them).
create: *The gardens around the palace were* ***created*** *in the 18th century* (=made for the first time, in an artistic way).

WORD CHOICE
invent or **discover**?
• You **invent** a new machine or a new way of doing something: *The telephone was* ***invented*** *by Alexander Graham Bell.*
• You **discover** a new place or substance, or a new type of animal or plant: *Scientists have* ***discovered*** *a new planet.* • *Marie Curie* ***discovered*** *radium.*

in•ven•tion /ɪn'venʃən/ *noun* **1** a completely new thing that someone invents: *The iPod is a wonderful invention.* **2** (no plural) when someone invents something: *the invention of the telephone in the 1870s*

in•ven•tive /ɪn'ventɪv/ *adjective* good at thinking of new and interesting ideas: *an inventive solution to an old problem*

in•ven•tor /ɪn'ventə $ ɪn'ventɚ/ *noun* someone who thinks of or makes something completely new: *the inventor of the telephone, Alexander Graham Bell*

in•vert•ed com•mas /ɪnˌvɜːtɪd 'kɒməz $ ɪnˌvɚtɪd 'kɑməz/ *plural noun BrE* another word for QUOTATION MARKS

in•vest /ɪn'vest/ *verb* to put money in a bank or buy something in order to get more money back later when you sell it: *He invested all his money in property.* —**investor** *noun*: *Large investors such as banks have invested millions in the project.*

in•ves•ti•gate /ɪn'vestəgeɪt/ *verb* to try to discover the truth about something, especially a crime or accident: *Police are investigating the robbery.*

in•ves•ti•ga•tion /ɪnˌvestə'geɪʃən/ *noun* an official attempt to discover the truth about something, especially a crime or accident: *There will be an investigation into the train crash.* • *The accident is still under investigation* (=being investigated).

in•vest•ment /ɪn'vestmənt/ *noun* when you put money in a bank or buy something in order to get more money back later: *We need more investment in small businesses.*

in•vis•i•ble /ɪn'vɪzəbəl/ *adjective* if something is invisible, you cannot see it ANTONYM **visible**: *Germs are invisible.*

in•vi•ta•tion /ˌɪnvə'teɪʃən/ *noun*

KEY PATTERNS
an invitation to dinner/a party
an invitation to do something

if you get an invitation, someone asks you if you would like to do something nice with them: *We got an invitation to their New Year's party.* • *I did receive an*

A B C D E F G H I J K L M N O P Q R S T U V W X Y Z

invitation to go, but I will be on holiday. • *Have you* ***sent the party invitations*** *yet?*

in·vite¹ /ɪnˈvaɪt/ *verb*

KEY PATTERNS
invite someone to dinner/a party/a place
invite someone to do something

to ask someone to go somewhere, or to do something with you: *Are you going to* ***invite*** *your ex-boyfriend* ***to*** *your birthday party?* • *We* ***were invited over to*** *the Smiths' house for supper.* • *Parents are* ***invited to*** *come to the school and meet the teachers.*

PHRASAL VERBS
invite in
invite someone in to ask someone to come into your house: *I didn't* ***invite*** *him* ***in*** *because the place was such a mess.*

in·vit·ing /ɪnˈvaɪtɪŋ/ *adjective* something that is inviting looks nice and makes you want to enjoy it: *The swimming pool looked very inviting.*

in·voice /ˈɪnvɔɪs/ *noun* a list showing how much money you must pay for things you have received or work that has been done: *You haven't paid these invoices.*

in·volve /ɪnˈvɒlv $ ɪnˈvɑlv/ *verb*

KEY PATTERNS
an activity involves someone
involve someone in an activity
involve (doing) something

1 if something involves you, it includes or affects you: *The celebrations will involve thousands of people across the country.*
2 to ask or allow someone to take part in something: *The band like to* ***involve*** *the audience* ***in*** *their performances.*
3 if one thing involves another thing, it includes that thing as a necessary part of it: *Success always involves hard work.* • *Her job involves helping students with their problems.*

in·volved /ɪnˈvɒlvd $ ɪnˈvɑlvd/ *adjective* if you are involved in an activity or event, you take part in it: *Were you involved in the fight?*

in·volve·ment /ɪnˈvɒlvmənt $ ɪnˈvɑlvmənt/ *noun* (no plural) when someone takes part in an activity or event: *They thanked us for our involvement in the project.*

in·wards /ˈɪnwədz $ ˈɪnwɚdz/ *BrE*, **in·ward** /ˈɪnwəd $ ˈɪnwɚd/ *AmE* *adverb* towards the inside of something ANTONYM **outwards**: *The windows open inwards.*

IPA /ˌaɪ piː ˈeɪ/ (International Phonetic Alphabet) a system of signs showing the sounds made in speech

iPod /ˈaɪ pɒd $ ˈaɪ pɑd/ *noun* (trademark) an MP3 PLAYER that can store a lot of music, pictures, and film

i·rate /ˌaɪˈreɪt/ *adjective* (formal) very angry: *An irate customer complained to the manager.*

irk /ɜːk $ ɚk/ *verb* (written) to annoy someone: *It irks me how he never helps his mother.*

i·ron¹ /ˈaɪən $ ˈaɪɚn/ *noun* **1** a common heavy strong metal that is used to make steel: *an iron gate* • *They used tools made of iron.* **2** a piece of electrical equipment that you heat and press onto your clothes to make them smooth: *Be careful with that hot iron.*
→ see picture at BOARD

iron² *verb* to make clothes smooth using an iron: *Did you iron my shirt?*

PRONUNCIATION
In this word you do not pronounce the **r**.

i·ron·ic /aɪˈrɒnɪk $ aɪˈrɑnɪk/ *adjective* if you are ironic, you mean the opposite of what you say, in order to be amusing or show that you are annoyed: *I think when he said "Thanks a lot" he was being ironic.*

i·ron·ing /ˈaɪənɪŋ $ ˈaɪɚnɪŋ/ *noun* (no plural) the activity of using an iron to make clothes smooth: *I've done the ironing.*

i·ron·y /ˈaɪrəni/ *noun* **1** (no plural) a way of saying something that shows that you mean the opposite of what you say: *There was a note of irony in his voice.* **2** an unusual or surprising part of a situation that seems strange or amusing because it is not what you expected: *The irony was that the more the media criticized the film, the more people went to see it.*

ir·ra·tion·al /ɪˈræʃənəl/ *adjective* irrational feelings and behaviour are not sensible or reasonable ANTONYM **rational**: *She has an irrational fear of mice.* —**irrationally** *adverb*

ir·reg·u·lar /ɪ'regjələ $ ɪ'regjələ˞/ *adjective* **1** not happening at regular times ANTONYM **regular**: *They have their meals at irregular times.* **2** not following the usual rules in grammar ANTONYM **regular**: *an irregular verb*

ir·rel·e·vant /ɪ'reləvənt/ *adjective* something that is irrelevant is not important because it has no effect in a particular situation ANTONYM **relevant**: *She thinks my opinion is irrelevant.*

ir·re·sist·i·ble /ˌɪrɪ'zɪstəbəl/ *adjective* impossible not to want, like, enjoy etc: *The chocolate cake was irresistible.*

ir·re·spon·si·ble /ˌɪrɪ'spɒnsəbəl $ ˌɪrɪ'spɑnsəbəl/ *adjective* behaving in a careless way, without thinking of the bad results you might cause: *It's irresponsible to leave small children alone.*

ir·re·vers·i·ble /ˌɪrɪ'vɜːsəbəl $ ˌɪrɪ'vɚsəbəl/ *adjective* if something that has been done is irreversible, it is impossible to change it back to the way it was before ANTONYM **reversible**: *The power cut caused irreversible damage to our computer system.*

ir·ri·ta·ble /'ɪrətəbəl/ *adjective* an irritable person gets annoyed quickly: *She gets irritable when she's tired.*

ir·ri·tate /'ɪrəteɪt/ *verb* to annoy someone: *Her little sister really irritates me.* —**irritating** *adjective*: *What's that irritating noise?*

is /z, s, əz; strong ɪz/ the third person singular of the present tense of BE

Is·lam /'ɪslɑːm/ *noun* (no plural) the religion that was started by Mohammed and whose holy book is the Koran

Is·lam·ic /ɪz'læmɪk/ *adjective* related to Islam: *the Islamic faith*

is·land /'aɪlənd/ *noun* a piece of land that is completely surrounded by water: *Britain is an island.*

island

isle /aɪl/ *noun* used in the names of some islands: *Jersey is one of the Channel Isles.*

is·n't /'ɪzənt/ the short form of 'is not': *The hotel isn't far.*

i·so·late /'aɪsəleɪt/ *verb* to keep one person or thing separate from others: *We isolate dangerous prisoners in another part of the prison.*

i·so·lat·ed /'aɪsəleɪtɪd/ *adjective* far away from other places or people: *He lives in an isolated village.* • *Working away from your home and family makes you feel isolated.*

i·so·la·tion /ˌaɪsə'leɪʃən/ *noun* (no plural) a feeling of being lonely: *Moving to a new town can lead to a sense of isolation.*

is·sue¹ /'ɪʃuː/ *noun*
1 an important subject or problem that people discuss SYNONYM **matter**: *The environment is an issue which is very important to young people.*
2 a magazine or newspaper printed for a particular day, week, or month: *Have you seen this month's issue of 'Vogue'?*

issue² *verb* **1** to make an official statement or give an order or warning: *The authorities issued a warning about the level of air pollution in the city.* **2** to officially give people something they need to do a particular job: *All staff are issued with a special uniform.*

it /ɪt/ *pronoun*
1 used when talking about a thing: *Where's my mobile phone? I left it here a minute ago.* • *If you've lost your homework, you'll have to do it all again.*
2 used when talking about the weather, time, or date: *It's raining.* • *I hope it stays sunny.* • *It's nearly ten o'clock.* • *It's the 21st of June today.*
3 used when talking about an action or situation: *It was nice seeing her again* (=seeing her again was nice). • *It seemed unkind to tell her the truth.* • *It would be awful if she died.* • *It's nice and warm in here.* • *I hated it at school* (=I hated being at school).
4 used when asking or saying which person has done something: *It was Emily who told them.* • *"Who was that on the phone?" "It was Lauren."*

IT /ˌaɪ 'tiː/ the abbreviation of INFORMATION TECHNOLOGY

i·tal·ics /ɪˈtælɪks/ *plural noun* a style of printed letters that slope to the right: *The examples in this dictionary are written in italics.*

itch¹ /ɪtʃ/ *verb* if your skin itches, it feels slightly unpleasant in a way that makes you want to scratch it with your hand: *These woollen socks make my feet itch.*

itch² *noun* (plural **itches**) a slightly unpleasant feeling on your skin that makes you want to scratch it with your hand: *I've got an itch on my nose.*

itch·y /ˈɪtʃi/ *adjective* (**itchier**, **itchiest**) if your skin is itchy, it feels slightly unpleasant and you want to rub it with your hand

it'd /ˈɪtəd/ the short form of 'it would' or 'it had': *You said it'd be a short film.* • *I didn't know it'd been sold.*

i·tem /ˈaɪtəm/ *noun* one thing in a set, group, or list: *What's the first item on the shopping list?*

i·tin·e·ra·ry /aɪˈtɪnərəri $ aɪˈtɪnəˌreri/ *noun* (plural **itineraries**) a plan or list of the places you will visit on a trip: *The first stop on our itinerary is Rome.*

it'll /ˈɪtl/ the short form of 'it will': *It'll be a great party.*

it's /ɪts/ the short form of 'it is' or 'it has': *It's time to go.* • *It's fallen down again.*

SPELLING

it's or **its**?

It's means 'it is': ***It's** cold today,* or 'it has': ***It's** been raining all morning.*

Its means 'relating to or belonging to something': *The company has changed **its** name* (=the name of the company has changed).

its /ɪts/ *determiner*
belonging to a thing or animal: *He put the game back in its box.* • *The dog wagged its tail.*

it·self /ɪtˈself/ *pronoun*
1 used when the same thing or animal does an action and receives the action: *The machine switches itself off when it is not being used.*
2 used to emphasize that you are talking about one particular thing: *The lesson itself was quite boring, but I enjoyed the discussion afterwards.*

PHRASES

by itself alone, or with no one helping or doing anything: *Did the radio go on by itself?*

I've /aɪv/ the short form of 'I have': *I've got an idea.*

i·vo·ry /ˈaɪvəri/ *noun* the hard smooth white substance that the TUSKS (=the two large front teeth) of an ELEPHANT are made of

i·vy /ˈaɪvi/ *noun* a plant with dark green shiny leaves that grows on the walls of buildings: *The cottage was covered in ivy.*

A B C D E F G H I J K L M N O P Q R S T U V W X Y Z

Jj

jab¹ /dʒæb/ *verb* (**jabbed**, **jabbing**) to push something pointed into or towards something else with a short quick movement: *She jabbed her fork into the pizza.*

jab² *noun* **1** a sudden hard push, especially with a pointed object: *I felt a jab in my arm.* **2** *BrE* (informal) an INJECTION: *I have to have a yellow fever jab.*

jack /dʒæk/ *noun* a playing card with a picture of a young man on it: *Do you have the jack of diamonds?*

jack·et /ˈdʒækɪt/ *noun* a short light coat: *a leather jacket* ➔ see picture at CLOTHES

jack·pot /ˈdʒækpɒt $ ˈdʒækpɑt/ *noun* a large amount of money that you can win: *The lottery jackpot is £3 million.*

ja·ded /ˈdʒeɪdɪd/ *adjective* if you feel jaded, you are no longer excited about something because you are tired of it or it no longer interests you: *After years in the music business, she was beginning to feel jaded.*

jag·ged /ˈdʒægɪd/ *adjective* something that is jagged has a rough edge with sharp points: *The sea near the shore is full of jagged rocks.*

jail¹ also **gaol** *BrE* /dʒeɪl/ *noun* a place where criminals are kept as a punishment SYNONYM **prison**: *The murderer is still in jail.*

jail² also **gaol** *BrE* *verb* to put someone in prison: *He was jailed for six years for robbery.*

jam¹ /dʒæm/ *noun* a thick sticky sweet food made from fruit: *strawberry jam*

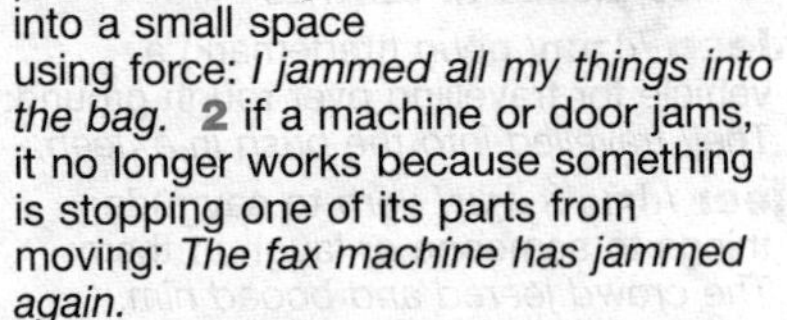

jam² *verb* (**jammed**, **jamming**) **1** to push something into a small space using force: *I jammed all my things into the bag.* **2** if a machine or door jams, it no longer works because something is stopping one of its parts from moving: *The fax machine has jammed again.*

jan·gle /ˈdʒæŋgəl/ *verb* if metal objects jangle, they make sounds as they hit each other: *I could hear his keys jangling.* —**jangle** *noun*: *the jangle of heavy jewellery*

jan·i·tor /ˈdʒænətə $ ˈdʒænətɚ/ the American word for CARETAKER

Jan·u·a·ry /ˈdʒænjuəri $ ˈdʒænjuˌeri/ (written abbreviation **Jan**) *noun* the first month of the year: *It's very cold here in January.* • *His birthday is on January 11th.*

jar /dʒɑː $ dʒɑr/ *noun* a round glass container with a lid, used for storing food: *a jar of marmalade* ➔ see picture at CONTAINER

jar·gon /ˈdʒɑːgən $ ˈdʒɑrgən/ *noun* (no plural) words and phrases that people doing the same type of work use and that other people find difficult to understand: *I can't understand these documents – they're written in legal jargon.*

jav·e·lin /ˈdʒævəlɪn/ *noun* (no plural) a sport in which you throw a long pointed stick as far as you can

jaw /dʒɔː/ *noun* the bottom part of your face that contains the two bones that your teeth grow in: *My jaw hurts when I eat.* ➔ see picture on page A5

jazz /dʒæz/ *noun* (no plural) a type of music that started in the early 1900s

jeal·ous /ˈdʒeləs/ *adjective* **1** angry or unhappy because you want something that someone else has: *She gets jealous when her sister gets new clothes.* **2** angry or unhappy because you think that someone you love likes or loves another person: *She went out with Paul to make Steve jealous.*

jeal·ous·y /ˈdʒeləsi/ *noun* the feeling of being jealous: *Jealousy can ruin a relationship.*

jeans /dʒiːnz/ *plural noun* a popular type of trousers made from DENIM: *He was wearing an old pair of jeans.*
→ see picture at CLOTHES

Jeep /dʒiːp/ *noun* (trademark) a vehicle for travelling over rough ground: *They travelled into the bush in a Jeep.*

jeer /dʒɪə $ dʒɪr/ *verb* to say rude things to someone or laugh at them: *The crowd jeered and booed him.* —**jeer** *noun*: *the angry jeers of demonstrators*

Jell-O /ˈdʒeləʊ $ ˈdʒeloʊ/ (trademark) the American word for JELLY

jel·ly /ˈdʒeli/ *noun* **1** *BrE* a sweet food made with fruit juice that shakes when you move it SYNONYM **Jell-O** *AmE*: *Kids love jelly and ice cream.* **2** (no plural) *AmE* the American word for JAM: *a peanut butter and jelly sandwich*

jerk /dʒɜːk $ dʒɝk/ *verb* to move with a sudden quick movement: *I jerked the child out of the way.* —**jerk** *noun*: *He woke up with a jerk.*

jerk·y /ˈdʒɜːki $ ˈdʒɝki/ *adjective* (**jerkier**, **jerkiest**) jerky movements are rough and sudden, not smooth: *We had a very jerky ride in his car.*

jer·sey /ˈdʒɜːzi $ ˈdʒɝzi/ *noun* a shirt made of soft material: *I need a new football jersey.*

jet /dʒet/ *noun* **1** a very fast plane: *He has his own private jet.* **2** a thin stream of gas or liquid that is forced out of a small hole: *A jet of water came from the hosepipe.*

ˈjet lag *noun* (no plural) the feeling of being very tired after a long journey in a plane: *Sue was suffering from jet lag after her flight from Australia.*

jet·ty /ˈdʒeti/ *noun* (plural **jetties**) a wide stone or wooden structure used for getting on and off boats: *He got off the boat onto a little wooden jetty.*

Jew /dʒuː/ *noun* someone whose religion is JUDAISM

jew·el /ˈdʒuːəl/ *noun* a valuable stone, such as a DIAMOND SYNONYM **gem**: *The crown is covered in precious jewels.*

jew·el·ler *BrE*, **jeweler** *AmE* /ˈdʒuːələ $ ˈdʒuələr/ *noun* someone who sells or makes jewellery: *The jeweller fixed my watch.*

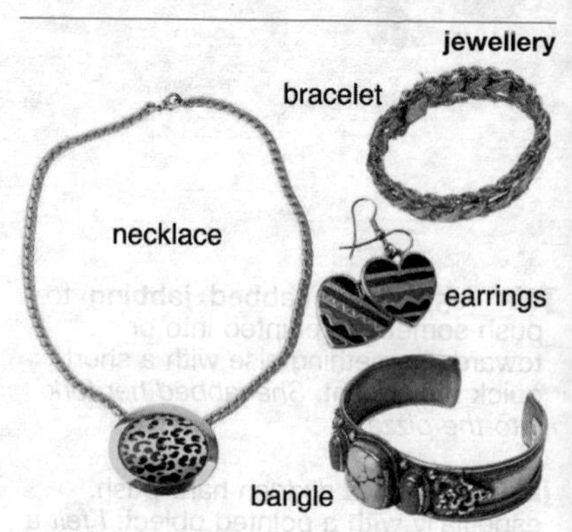

jew·el·lery *BrE*, **jewelry** *AmE* /ˈdʒuːəlri/ *noun* (no plural) things that you wear for decoration, such as rings and NECKLACES: *She wears a lot of gold jewellery.*

Jew·ish /ˈdʒuːɪʃ/ *adjective* related to Judaism

jibe, gibe /dʒaɪb/ *noun* something that you say that criticizes someone or makes them seem silly: *She's always making jibes about my weight.*

jig·saw /ˈdʒɪgsɔː/ also **ˈjigsaw ˌpuzzle** *noun* a game consisting of a picture that has been cut up into many small pieces that you try to fit together again: *Let's do a jigsaw.*

jigsaw

jilt /dʒɪlt/ *verb* to suddenly end a romantic relationship with someone: *She jilted him the day before their wedding.*

jin·gle /ˈdʒɪŋgəl/ *verb* if metal objects jingle, they hit each other, making a noise like small bells: *The coins jingled in his pockets.* —**jingle** *noun*: *I heard the jingle of bells.*

jit·ter·y /ˈdʒɪtəri/ *adjective* worried and nervous: *I get very jittery about going to the dentist.*

A B C D E F G H I J K L M N O P Q R S T U V W X Y Z

job /dʒɒb $ dʒɑb/ *noun*

KEY PATTERNS
do a job
it is someone's job to do something

1 your job is work that you do regularly in order to earn money: *Teaching is an interesting job.* • *I had to* ***get a job*** *to pay the rent.* • *I started* ***applying for jobs*** (=writing to companies, businesses etc to ask for a job) *as soon as I left college.* • *Graham* ***found a job*** (=got a job) *at a local farm.* • *Mark* ***lost his job*** (=did not have a job any more) *when the factory closed.* • *a well-paid job*
2 a piece of work that you must do SYNONYM **task**: *Dad asked me to* ***do*** *a few* ***jobs*** *around the house.* • ***It's not my job to*** *clean your bedroom.*

PHRASES
out of a job not having a job, although you want one: *How long have you been* ***out of a job****?*
do a good job, do a great job etc to do something very well: *The people who organized the party* ***did a fantastic job****.*
make a good job of something *BrE* to do something well: *She* ***made a good job of*** *painting the house.*
it's a good job *BrE* (spoken) used to say that a situation is fortunate: ***It's a good job*** *I'm not vegetarian because all there was to eat was burgers.*

THESAURUS
work: *I started* ***work*** *when I was 18* (=activities done to earn money).
position/post (formal): *How long have you been in your present* ***position*** (=job in an organization)?
occupation (formal): *Please give your name, age, and* ***occupation*** (=job).
profession: *the teaching* ***profession*** (=a job that needs education and special training)
career: *The university can help you decide on a* ***career*** (=a type of work, which you do for a long time).

jock·ey /ˈdʒɒki $ ˈdʒɑki/ *noun* someone who rides horses in races: *The jockey was injured when he fell off his horse.*

jog /dʒɒg $ dʒɑg/ *verb* (**jogged, jogging**) **1** to run slowly, especially for exercise: *Two girls were jogging around the park.* → see picture on page A2

USAGE
When talking about jogging as an activity that you do, you say **go jogging**: *She* ***goes jogging*** *to help her stay fit.*

2 jog someone's memory to make someone remember something that they had forgotten: *A photo might jog your memory about the man.*

jog·ging /ˈdʒɒgɪŋ $ ˈdʒɑgɪŋ/ *noun* (no plural) when you run for exercise

join[1] /dʒɔɪn/ *verb*

KEY PATTERNS
join things together

1 to become a member of an organization or group: *Helen has joined a running club to try and get fit.* • *Pete's thinking of joining the army.*
2 if two things join, they come together or are connected at a particular place: *This is where the pipe joins the tank.* • *The road joins the motorway at Bridge Lane.*
3 if you join two things, you connect them or fasten them together: ***Join*** *the two pieces of string* ***together****.* → see Thesaurus at FASTEN
4 to go somewhere to do something with someone else: *Trevor will join his older brother at university in September.* • *Will you join me in a glass of wine* (=I'm having a glass of wine – would you like one too)?

PHRASAL VERBS
join in
join in, join in something to begin to do an activity with other people: *Everyone started singing, but I didn't feel like* ***joining in****.* • *Are you going to* ***join in*** *the dancing?*
join together
if two organizations join together, they start working together or become one organization

join[2] *noun* a place where two parts of an object join: *the join between the main part of the boot and the sole*

joint[1] /dʒɔɪnt/ *adjective* shared by, owned by, or involving two or more people: *This was a joint decision*

A B C D E F G H I J K L M N O P Q R S T U V W X Y Z

between me and Jo. • *"Who made the cake?" "It was a joint effort* (=we all helped to make it)*."* —**jointly** *adverb*: *Sam and I own the house jointly.*

joint² *noun* a part of your body where two bones meet: *I've damaged my knee joint.*

joke¹ /dʒəʊk $ dʒoʊk/ *noun*

KEY PATTERNS
make/tell a joke
a joke about something

something funny that you say to make people laugh: *He keeps* ***making jokes about*** *my hair.* • *I heard a* ***funny joke*** *the other day.* • *He* ***told a joke about*** *a man who lost his dog.*

PHRASES

get the joke, see the joke: *Sorry, but I just don't* ***get the joke*** (=understand why the joke is funny).

play a joke on someone to trick someone to make people laugh: *He bought a plastic spider to* ***play a joke on*** *his sister.*

joke² *verb*

KEY PATTERNS
joke about something

1 to say funny things to make people laugh: *They all* ***joke about*** *the way he speaks.*
2 to say something without meaning it: *I didn't mean to upset you – I was* ***only joking.***

jol·ly /ˈdʒɒli $ ˈdʒɑli/ *adjective* (**jollier**, **jolliest**) happy and CHEERFUL: *It's Christmas so everyone's very jolly.*

jolt /dʒəʊlt $ dʒoʊlt/ *verb* to move suddenly and roughly: *The car jolted forward.* —**jolt** *noun*: *He sat up with a jolt.*

jos·tle /ˈdʒɒsəl $ ˈdʒɑsəl/ *verb* to push against other people in a crowd: *We all jostled towards the front of the stage.*

jot /dʒɒt $ dʒɑt/ *verb* (**jotted**, **jotting**) **jot something down** to write something quickly on a piece of paper: *Can you jot down your address?* → see Thesaurus at WRITE

jour·nal /ˈdʒɜːnl $ ˈdʒɚnl/ *noun* a serious magazine about a particular subject: *I read about the disease in a medical journal.*

jour·nal·is·m /ˈdʒɜːnəlɪzəm $ ˈdʒɚnlˌɪzəm/ *noun* (no plural) the job of writing reports for newspapers, magazines, television, or radio: *I'm interested in a career in journalism.*

jour·nal·ist /ˈdʒɜːnəlɪst $ ˈdʒɚnl-ɪst/ *noun* someone who writes reports for newspapers, magazines, television, or radio: *There's a journalist on the phone – he wants to interview you.*

jour·ney /ˈdʒɜːni $ ˈdʒɚni/ *noun* a trip from one place to another, especially a long one: *How long does your journey to school take?* • *I've made several journeys to Ireland already this year.* • *I met him on a train journey.* → see Thesaurus at TRAVEL²

joy /dʒɔɪ/ *noun* a feeling of great happiness and pleasure: *My heart filled with joy when I heard the news.*

joy·ful /ˈdʒɔɪfəl/ *adjective* (formal) very happy: *The wedding was a joyful occasion.*

joy·rid·er /ˈdʒɔɪˌraɪdə $ ˈdʒɔɪˌraɪdɚ/ *noun* someone who steals a car and drives it in a fast and dangerous way

joy·rid·ing /ˈdʒɔɪˌraɪdɪŋ/ *noun* (no plural) when someone steals a car and drives it in a fast and dangerous way: *He was arrested for joyriding.*

joy·stick /ˈdʒɔɪˌstɪk/ *noun* a handle used to control a computer game

Ju·da·is·m /ˈdʒuːdeɪ-ɪzəm $ ˈdʒudiˌɪzəm/ *noun* (no plural) the religion that was started in Israel in ancient times, and that is based on a group of writings and laws. People who believe in Judaism are JEWS.

judge¹ /dʒʌdʒ/ *noun*
1 the person in a law court who decides what punishment a criminal should get: *The judge sentenced him to one year in prison.*
2 someone who decides who has won a competition: *The judges decided that Mary's painting was the best.*

judge² *verb*

KEY PATTERNS
judge someone by/on something

1 to decide something or form an opinion about someone or something: *Never* ***judge*** *someone* ***by*** *the way they look.* • *It's not fair to* ***judge*** *him* ***on*** *his performance today – he was ill.* • *Here*

are the two pictures – ***judge for yourself*** (=you decide) *which one you prefer.*
2 to decide who has won a competition: *Mrs Taylor will judge the poetry competition.*

PHRASES

judging by something, judging from something used when you are giving a reason for something that you are saying: ***Judging by*** *his reaction, he still loves Sara.*

judg•ment, judgement /ˈdʒʌdʒmənt/ *noun* **1** (no plural) the ability to make sensible decisions: *Tracy has very good judgment.* **2** a legal decision made by a judge in a court of law: *The judge will give his judgment tomorrow.*

ju•do /ˈdʒuːdəʊ $ ˈdʒudoʊ/ *noun* (no plural) a sport from Japan in which you try to throw your opponent onto the ground

jug /dʒʌg/ *noun* a container used for pouring liquids: *a jug of water*

jug•gle /ˈdʒʌgəl/ *verb* to keep objects moving through the air by throwing and catching them very quickly: *He juggled three oranges.*

juggle

juice /dʒuːs/ *noun* the liquid from fruit or vegetables: *a glass of* ***orange juice*** • *I'd like a* ***tomato juice*** (=a glass of tomato juice)*, please.*

juic•y /ˈdʒuːsi/ *adjective* (**juicier, juiciest**) food that is juicy contains a lot of juice: *a nice, crisp, juicy apple*

Ju•ly /dʒʊˈlaɪ/ (written abbreviation **Jul**) *noun* the seventh month of the year: *We got married last July.* • *It's Saturday 3rd July.*

jum•ble¹ /ˈdʒʌmbəl/ *noun* an untidy group of things: *The clothes lay in a jumble on her bed.*

jumble² also **jumble up** *verb* to mix things together so that they become untidy: *You've jumbled all my CDs up.*

ˈjumble sale *noun BrE* an event at which old clothes, toys etc are sold to get money for a school, church etc SYNONYM **rummage sale** *AmE*

jum•bo /ˈdʒʌmbəʊ $ ˈdʒʌmboʊ/ *adjective* (informal) larger than other things of the same type SYNONYM **giant**: *jumbo sausages*

ˈjumbo jet *noun* a very big plane that carries many passengers: *I went to New York on a jumbo jet.*

jump¹ /dʒʌmp/ *verb*

> KEY PATTERNS
> **jump off/into/out of something**
> **jump over something**

1 to push yourself off the ground using your legs: *Jordan jumped but the ball flew over his head.* • *A man* ***jumped off*** *the bridge into the river.* ➔ see picture on page A2
2 to get over something by jumping SYNONYM **leap**: *He* ***jumped over*** *the gate and ran off.* • *None of the horses managed to jump the fence.*
3 to move somewhere quickly and suddenly SYNONYM **leap**: *When the police arrived, the two men* ***jumped in*** *the car and drove off.* • *She* ***jumped out of*** *bed.*

PHRASES

make someone jump if something makes you jump, it makes you feel suddenly afraid: *A loud bang in the street* ***made me jump.***

jump at the chance, jump at the opportunity to accept an opportunity as soon as you get it: *I would* ***jump at the chance of*** *going out with Peter.*

> THESAURUS
> **leap**: *The boy* ***leapt*** *over the fence and ran off* (=jumped over it).
> **dive**: *I* ***dived*** *off the rock into the sea* (=jumped into water with my head first).
> **hop**: *A bird* ***hopped*** *onto the table* (=made small jumps).

jump² *noun* when you push yourself off the ground using your legs SYNONYM **leap**

jump•er /ˈdʒʌmpə $ ˈdʒʌmpɚ/ *noun BrE* a piece of clothing made of wool that covers the upper part of your body and your arms SYNONYM **sweater**

junc•tion /ˈdʒʌŋkʃən/ *noun* a place where roads or railway lines join: *a very busy motorway junction*

A B C D E F G H I J K L M N O P Q R S T U V W X Y Z

June /dʒuːn/ (written abbreviation **Jun**) *noun* the sixth month of the year: *We're going on holiday in June.* • *On the 7th of June, I'll be 15.*

jun·gle /ˈdʒʌŋɡəl/ *noun* a large tropical forest with trees and large plants growing very close together ➔ see Thesaurus at FOREST

ju·ni·or[1] /ˈdʒuːniə $ ˈdʒunjɚ/ *adjective* a junior person has a low rank in an organization or profession ANTONYM **senior**: *a junior doctor*

junior[2] *noun* **1** *AmE* a student in the third year of HIGH SCHOOL or college **2** *BrE* a child who goes to a junior school

ˌjunior ˈcollege *noun* a college in the US or Canada where students do a course for two years

ˌjunior ˈhigh school also **ˌjunior ˈhigh** *noun* a school in the US or Canada for students who are between 12 and 15 years old

ˈjunior ˌschool *noun* a school in Britain for children between the ages of seven and 11: *I learnt all this stuff in junior school.*

junk /dʒʌŋk/ *noun* (no plural) (informal) old things that have no use or value: *Let's get rid of some of this junk.*

ˈjunk food *noun* (no plural) (informal) food that is not healthy because it contains a lot of fat or sugar: *You eat too much junk food.*

ˈjunk mail *noun* (informal) letters that companies send to your house to tell you about the things they sell: *I get far too much junk mail, and most of goes in the bin.* ➔ see Thesaurus at ADVERTISEMENT

ju·ror /ˈdʒʊərə $ ˈdʒʊrɚ/ *noun* a member of a jury: *The jurors must decide whether or not he is guilty.*

ju·ry /ˈdʒʊəri $ ˈdʒʊri/ *noun* (plural **juries**) **1** a group of people in a court who decide whether someone is guilty of a crime: *Has the jury reached its verdict?* **2** a group of people who choose the winner of a competition: *Here are the votes of the French jury.*

just[1] /dʒəst; strong dʒʌst/ *adverb* **1** only: *It's not serious – it's just a scratch.* • *Calls cost just five pence a minute.* • *I just wanted to say I'm sorry.* **2** only a short time ago: *I've just had a very odd experience.* • *She had just driven off when I realized she'd left her purse behind.* ➔ see Thesaurus at RECENTLY **3** doing something now: *"Have you done all your packing?" "I'm just doing it."* • *I'm just on my way there now.* **4** used to show that you achieve something, but almost do not manage it: *I just managed to catch the bottle before it hit the ground.* • *I just passed the test.* **5** (spoken) used for emphasizing something you are saying: *It just doesn't seem possible.* • *I just knew that was going to happen!*

PHRASES

just before, just after a short time before or after: *I got home* ***just after*** *12 o'clock.*

just behind, just in front of etc a short way behind, in front of etc: *Emma was sitting* ***just behind*** *me.*

just like exactly like: *Jo looks* ***just like*** *her sister.*

just as good, just as big etc equally as good, big etc: *This computer is* ***just as good*** *as the other one.*

just as at the very time you are doing something: ***Just as*** *I was leaving, the phone rang.*

just about to, just going to going to do something very soon: *I was* ***just about to*** *have a bath when Steve called round.*

just a second, just a minute (spoken) used to ask someone to wait for a short time: ***Just a minute*** *– you forgot your receipt.*

just now **a)** a very short time ago: *When I saw him* ***just now*** *he seemed a bit upset.* **b)** now: *Things are a bit complicated* ***just now.***

it's just as well (spoken) used to say that something is lucky: ***It's just as well*** *you didn't give him any money.*

just[2] /dʒʌst/ *adjective* (formal) morally right and fair: *Is this a just war?*

jus·tice /ˈdʒʌstəs/ *noun* (no plural) **1** when people are treated in a way that is fair and right ANTONYM **injustice**: *We are fighting for justice for everyone.*

2 the laws of a country and how they are used: *the criminal justice system* • *His conviction is a **miscarriage of justice*** (=a legal decision that is wrong).

jus•ti•fi•a•ble /ˈdʒʌstəˌfaɪəbəl $ ˌdʒʌstəˈfaɪəbəl/ *adjective* if a feeling or action is justifiable, you feel it or do it for a good reason: *She has justifiable pride in her son.*

jus•ti•fi•ca•tion /ˌdʒʌstəfəˈkeɪʃən/ *noun* a good reason for doing something: *There's no justification for violence.*

jus•ti•fied /ˈdʒʌstəfaɪd/ *adjective* if something is justified, there are good reasons for it: *Her criticism is justified.*

jus•ti•fy /ˈdʒʌstəfaɪ/ *verb* (**justified, justifies**) to give a good reason for doing something that other people think is unreasonable: *He keeps trying to justify his bad behaviour.*

ju•ve•nile /ˈdʒuːvənaɪl $ ˈdʒuvənl/ *adjective* (formal) related to young people: *There has been an increase in juvenile crime.*

Kk

kan•ga•roo /ˌkæŋɡəˈruː/ *noun* a large Australian animal that moves by jumping and carries its babies in a special place on its stomach ➔ see picture on page A9

kangaroo

ka•ra•te /kəˈrɑːti/ *noun* (no plural) a sport from Japan in which you fight using your hands and feet

keen /kiːn/ *adjective*

> KEY PATTERNS
> **keen to do something**
> **keen on (doing) something**

1 if you are keen to do something, you want to do it very much SYNONYM **eager**: *She seemed **keen to** meet my brother.*
2 If you are keen on doing something, or keen on it, you like doing it: *She's not very **keen on** going out to clubs.* • *a keen gardener*

keep ➔ see box on pages 368 and 369

ken•nel /ˈkenl/ *noun* a small outdoor house for a dog to sleep in

kept the past tense and past participle of KEEP

kerb *BrE*, **curb** *AmE* /kɜːb $ kɚb/ *noun* the edge of the PAVEMENT, where it joins the road: *You're driving too close to the kerb.* ➔ see picture at ZEBRA CROSSING

ketch•up /ˈketʃəp/ *noun* (no plural) a thick liquid made from tomatoes that you put on food: *Do you want ketchup on your burger?*

ket•tle /ˈketl/ *noun* a container with a lid that you use to boil water in: *I'll put the kettle on* (=make it start boiling water, usually to make a hot drink).

key¹ /kiː/ *noun*

key

1 a small object with a special shape that you use to open or close a lock or to start a car: *This is the key for the front door.* • *I can't find my **house keys*** (=the keys to lock or unlock the door on my house). • *I **turned the key** but the car wouldn't start.*
2 one of the parts of a computer or piano that you press to make it work: *She had pressed the **'Shift' key** by mistake.*
3 the answers to an exercise, usually found at the back of a school book: *The answer key is on page 92.*
4 the key to something the most important thing that helps you to do something: *Hard work is **the key to** doing well in exams.*

key² *adjective* very important and necessary: *Research is a key part of our work.*

key³ *verb* **key something in** to type information into a computer SYNONYM **enter**: *Now key in your name.*

keyboards

piano keyboard

computer keyboard

key•board /ˈkiːbɔːd $ ˈkibɔrd/ *noun*
1 all the keys on a computer or piano

A B C D E F G H I J K L M N O P Q R S T U V W X Y Z

that you press to make it work **2** also **keyboards** a musical instrument like a small electric piano

key·hole /ˈkiːhəʊl $ ˈkihoʊl/ *noun* the hole where you put a key into a lock

ˈkey ring *noun* a metal ring that you keep keys on

kg the written abbreviation of KILOGRAM

kick¹ /kɪk/ *verb*

KEY PATTERNS
kick something/someone
kick something around
kick something into/over something

to hit something or someone with your foot: *Tom just kicked me.* • *A group of boys were kicking a stone around outside.* • *He **kicked the ball into** the back of the net.* • *The police had to **kick the door down*** (=kick it until it opened) *to get in the flat.* ➔ see picture on page A3

PHRASES
kick a habit to stop doing something bad such as smoking

PHRASAL VERBS
kick out
kick someone out to make someone leave a place because they have done something wrong: *He **was kicked out** of school for fighting.*

kick² *noun* the action of hitting something or someone with your foot: *Gaye gave him a sharp kick on his ankle.*

kick·off /ˈkɪk-ɒf $ ˈkɪk-ɔf/ *noun* when a game of football begins: *Kickoff is at 3 pm.*

kid¹ /kɪd/ *noun* (informal) a child or young person: *Do you want to have kids?* • *She's just a kid.* ➔ see Thesaurus at CHILD

kid² *verb* (informal) (**kidded**, **kidding**) to say something that is not true as a joke SYNONYM **joke**: *I was only kidding when I said you were ugly.*

kid·nap /ˈkɪdnæp/ *verb* (**kidnapped**, **kidnapping**) to take someone and keep them as your prisoner until people give you money or things you want SYNONYM **abduct**: *They kidnapped the bank manager's wife.* —**kidnapper** *noun*: *The kidnappers are demanding £50,000 for the release of Mr Emmery.*

kid·ney /ˈkɪdni/ *noun* one of the two things inside in your body that remove waste liquid from your blood

kill¹ /kɪl/ *verb*
to cause someone to die: *They accused him of killing his wife.* • *Hundreds of people were killed in the earthquake.* • *Smoking kills.*

PHRASES
I'll kill you, she'll kill him etc (spoken) used to say that someone will be very angry with another person: *Mum will **kill us** if we're late again.*
be killing you (spoken) if a part of your body is killing you, it is very painful: *I need to sit down for a minute – my feet **are killing me**.*
kill time, have time to kill to spend time doing something while you wait for something more important to happen: *We've **got** an hour **to kill** before the train leaves, so let's have some lunch.*

THESAURUS
murder: *He was jailed for **murdering** his wife* (=deliberately killing her).
assassinate: *They had planned to **assassinate** the president* (=kill him – used about deliberately killing an important person).
execute: *The murderer will be **executed** tomorrow* (=killed as an official punishment).
massacre: *Hundreds of innocent people were **massacred*** (=killed together).

kill² *noun* when an animal is killed: *The lion moved in for the kill.*

kill·er /ˈkɪlə $ ˈkɪlɚ/ *noun* (written) someone who has killed a person: *Police are looking for the man's killer.*

kill·ing /ˈkɪlɪŋ/ *noun* (written) a murder: *The killing took place outside a nightclub.*

ki·lo /ˈkiːləʊ $ ˈkiloʊ/ *noun* a KILOGRAM: *The package weighs 30 kilos.*

kil·o·byte /ˈkɪləbaɪt/ *noun* a unit for measuring computer information, equal to 1,024 BYTES

keep /kiːp/ *verb* (past tense and past participle **kept** /kept/)

1 to continue to be in the same condition, or to make something do this: ***Keep calm** and try not to worry.* • *I **kept** my eyes **closed** while the doctor gave me the injection.* • *We sat around the fire in order to **keep warm**.*

KEY PATTERNS
keep calm/still/warm
keep something closed/open/still

We sat around the fire in order to keep warm.

keep

2 keep (on) doing something to continue to do something, or to do something very often: *I **keep** losing my keys.* • *He **keeps** interrupting me.* • ***Keep on** driving until you come to the next set of traffic lights.*

3 to continue to have something and not throw it away or give it to another person: *"Do you want your book back?" "No, you can **keep** it."* • ***Keep** a copy of the form for your records.* • *I **kept** all the letters he sent me.*

4 to have something always in the same place, so that you can find it easily: *Where do you **keep** the sugar?* • ***Keep** your passport in a safe place.*

5 to make someone stay in a place: *They're **keeping** her in hospital until tomorrow.* • *Her son wasn't feeling well, so she **kept** him home from school.*

6 to own and look after animals such as cows, sheep, or chickens: *His grandparents had a small farm where they **kept** some cows and a few chickens.*

PHRASES

keep a diary/a record etc
to regularly write down information in a book, on a computer etc: *Many students* ***keep a*** *vocabulary* ***diary.***

keep an eye on someone/something
to watch someone or something carefully, so that nothing bad happens: *Will you* ***keep an eye on*** *the baby for me while I'm upstairs?*

keep in mind
to remember something because it might be important or useful later: ***Keep in mind*** *that it will get dark soon.* • *Thanks for the advice. I'll* ***keep it in mind.***

keep in touch (with someone)
to continue to talk to someone you do not see very often any more: *We* ***keep in touch*** *by email.* • *I've* ***kept in touch with*** *a lot of people from school.*

keep a promise
to do what you have promised to do: *He* ***kept*** *his* ***promise,*** *and a letter arrived the following day.*

keep a secret
to not tell anyone about something: *Can you* ***keep a secret?***

PHRASAL VERBS

keep away
1 to not go near someone or something: ***Keep away*** *from the edge of the cliff.*

Keep away *from the edge of the cliff.*

2 to prevent someone or something from coming near you or attacking you: *The smoke helps* ***keep away*** *the mosquitoes.*

keep from
to stop someone from doing something, or to stop something happening: *Suzy covered her mouth to* ***keep from*** *laughing.* • *His friends* ***kept*** *him* ***from*** *feeling lonely.*

keep off
to stop something or someone from doing something, going somewhere etc: *Try to* ***keep*** *the cat* ***off*** *the sofa.* • ***Keep off*** *the grass.*

keep out
1 **Keep out!** used on signs to tell people they are not allowed in a place: *Danger!* ***Keep out!***
2 to stop someone or something from going into a place or doing something: *The heavy curtains* ***kept out*** *the light.* • *Smith's injury* ***kept*** *him* ***out*** *of the game.*

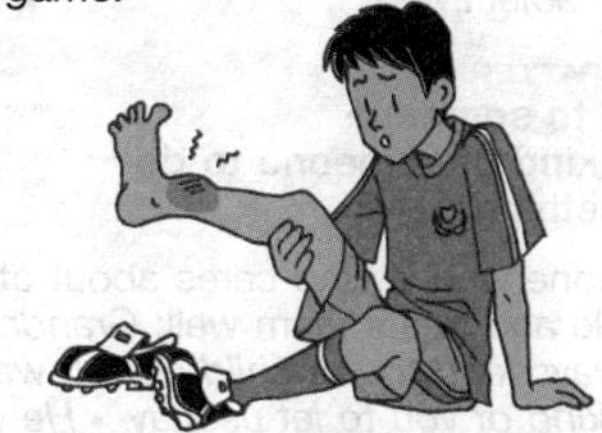

Smith's injury ***kept*** *him* ***out*** *of the game.*

keep up
1 to continue to do something that is good: *They* ***kept up*** *their friendship with phone calls and letters.* • *That's good work –* ***keep it up!***
2 to do something as well or as quickly as other people: *Paul had to run to* ***keep up.*** • *I don't know if I'll be able to* ***keep up with*** *all the reading in the course.*

A B C D E F G H I J K L M N O P Q R S T U V W X Y Z

kil·o·me·tre *BrE*, **kilometer** *AmE* /ˈkɪləˌmiːtə $ kɪˈlɑmətɚ/ (written abbreviation **km**) *noun* a unit for measuring length, equal to 1,000 metres: *The town is 3 kilometres from the hotel.*

kil·o·watt /ˈkɪləwɒt $ kɪləwɑt/ *noun* a unit for measuring electrical power, equal to 1,000 WATTS

kilt /kɪlt/ *noun* a skirt traditionally worn by Scottish men

kin /kɪn/ *noun* **next of kin** (formal) the person in your family that you are most closely related to: *We should inform his next of kin of his death.* ➔ see Thesaurus at FAMILY

kind¹ /kaɪnd/ *noun*

KEY PATTERNS
a kind of person/thing

a type of person or thing SYNONYM **sort**: *What **kind of** music do you like?* • *It's a great place, and **all kinds of** people go there.* • *"I'm buying a dog." "What kind?"* ➔ see Thesaurus at TYPE¹

kind² *adjective*

KEY PATTERNS
kind to someone
it is kind of someone to do something

someone who is kind cares about other people and treats them well: *Grandma is always **kind to** the children.* • *It was very **kind of** you **to** let us stay.* • *He was a very kind man.*

THESAURUS
nice: *He is always **nice** to his little sister* (=kind).
considerate: *I have **considerate** neighbours who try not to make a noise when I'm working* (=neighbours who think about other people's feelings and needs).
thoughtful: *It was **thoughtful** of her to invite the new girl to the party* (=it was kind of her to think of doing this).

kin·der·gar·ten /ˈkɪndəgɑːtn $ ˈkɪndɚˌgɑrtn/ *noun* **1** *BrE* a school for children aged between two and five **2** *AmE* a class for young children, usually aged around five, that prepares them for school

ˌkind-ˈhearted *adjective* kind and generous: *A kind-hearted neighbour did her shopping.*

kind·ly /ˈkaɪndli/ *adverb* used when someone has done something kind or generous: *Mr Smith kindly offered to lend us his car.*

kind·ness /ˈkaɪndnəs/ *noun* (no plural) behaviour that is kind and generous: *How can I thank you for your kindness?*

king /kɪŋ/ *noun* **1** a man who belongs to a royal family and who rules a country: *The King of Spain is visiting England.* • *King George IV* **2** a playing card with a picture of a king on it: *the king of diamonds*

king·dom /ˈkɪŋdəm/ *noun* a country that has a king or queen: *The queen ruled a vast kingdom.*

kiosk

ki·osk /ˈkiːɒsk $ ˈkiɑsk/ *noun* a small shop where you can buy things such as newspapers or tickets through a window

kiss /kɪs/ *verb* to touch someone with your lips, to show that you love them or when you are saying hello or goodbye: *She kissed the children goodnight.* —**kiss** *noun*: *Give me a kiss.*

kit

tool kit

kit /kɪt/ *noun* a set of clothes or equipment that you use for a particular purpose or activity: *His sports kit needed washing.* • *a tool kit*

kitch·en /ˈkɪtʃən/ *noun* the room where you prepare and cook food: *Jo is in the kitchen making a sandwich.*

kite /kaɪt/ *noun* a toy that you fly in the air on the end of a long string: *Children love flying kites.*

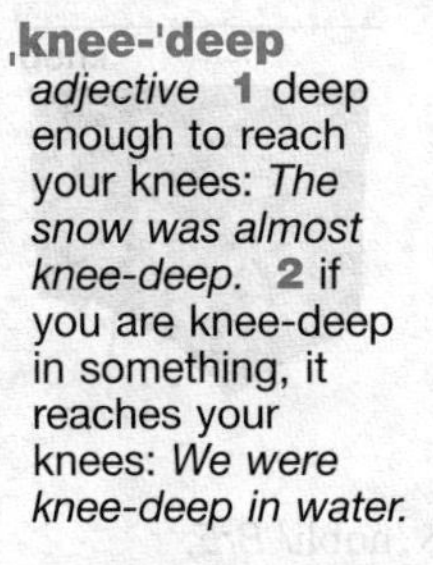
kite

kit·ten /ˈkɪtn/ *noun* a young cat

kit·ty /ˈkɪti/ *noun* (plural **kitties**) money that a group of people have collected for a particular purpose: *We only had £3 in the kitty.*

ki·wi fruit /ˈkiːwi ˌfruːt/ *noun,* (plural **kiwi fruit** or **kiwi fruits**) a small round green fruit with a hairy brown skin ➔ see picture on page A7

Kleen·ex /ˈkliːneks/ *noun* (trademark) a TISSUE

km the written abbreviation of KILOMETRE

knack /næk/ *noun* (informal) the ability to do something well: *He has a knack for writing memorable songs.*

knead /niːd/ *verb* to press and stretch a mixture of flour and water with your hands, in order to make bread: *Knead the dough and then leave it to rise.* ➔ see picture on page A4

knee /niː/ *noun* **1** the middle part of your leg, where it bends: *I have very weak knees.* ➔ see picture on page A5 **2** the part of your trousers that covers your knee: *The knees of his jeans were torn.* **3 bring something to its knees** if something brings a country or organization to its knees, it almost destroys it: *The economic crisis brought the country to its knees.*

> **PRONUNCIATION**
> In this word you do not pronounce the **k**.

knee·cap /ˈniːkæp/ *noun* the bone at the front of your knee ➔ see picture on page A5

ˌknee-ˈdeep *adjective* **1** deep enough to reach your knees: *The snow was almost knee-deep.* **2** if you are knee-deep in something, it reaches your knees: *We were knee-deep in water.*

knee-deep

knee-deep in water

ˈknee-high *adjective* something that is knee-high is tall enough to reach your knees: *a pair of knee-high boots*

kneel /niːl/ *verb* (past tense and past participle **knelt** /nelt/ or **kneeled**) also **kneel down** to bend your legs so that your knees are on the ground and supporting the weight of your body: *I knelt down to stroke the cat.* ➔ see picture on page A3

knelt a past tense and past participle of KNEEL

knew the past tense of KNOW

knick·ers /ˈnɪkəz $ ˈnɪkərz/ *plural noun BrE* a piece of clothing that women wear under their clothes, which covers the area between their waist and the top of their legs SYNONYM **panties** *AmE*: *a pair of silk knickers*

knife /naɪf/ *noun* (plural **knives** /naɪvz/) a tool used for cutting or as a weapon: *This knife is very sharp.* • *He picked up his knife and fork and began to eat.* ➔ see picture at CUTLERY

knight /naɪt/ *noun* a soldier with a high rank in the Middle Ages

knight·hood /ˈnaɪthʊd/ *noun* in Britain, a special title that the King or Queen gives to a man: *Cliff Richard received a knighthood in 1995, making him 'Sir Cliff Richard'.*

knit /nɪt/ *verb* (past tense and past participle **knitted** or **knit**, **knitting**) to make clothes by twisting wool together, using long sticks: *My mom's knitting me a hat.*

knives the plural of KNIFE

knob /nɒb $ nɑb/ *noun* **1** a round handle on a door or drawer, which you pull to open it **2** a round control button on a piece of electrical equipment: *the volume knob*

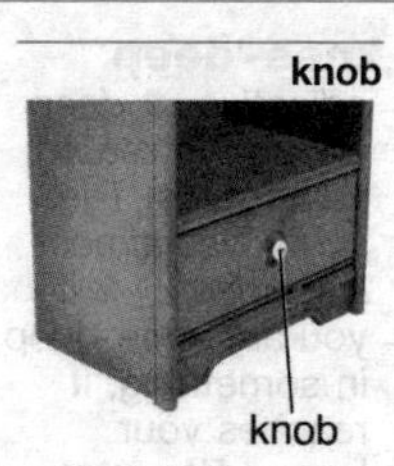

knob·bly /ˈnɒbli $ ˈnɑbli/ *BrE*, **knob·by** /ˈnɒbi $ ˈnɑbi/ *AmE adjective* (**knobblier, knobbliest**) something that is knobbly is not smooth, but has hard parts that stick out: *knobbly knees*

knock¹ /nɒk $ nɑk/ *verb*

KEY PATTERNS
knock at/on a door/window
knock something off a table/shelf
knock something over

1 to make a noise by hitting a door or window with your hand, usually in order to ask someone to open it: *Who's that* ***knocking at*** *the door?* • *A policeman* ***knocked on*** *the car window.* • *The sign read 'Please knock and enter'.* → see Thesaurus at HIT¹

2 to hit someone or something so that they move or fall down: *Someone knocked my arm and I spilled my drink.* • *I accidentally* ***knocked*** *the bowl* ***off*** *the shelf.* • *I slipped and* ***knocked over*** *a jug of water.*

PHRASAL VERBS

knock down

1 knock something down to destroy a building or wall by hitting it SYNONYM **demolish**: *They are going to* ***knock down*** *this apartment block.*

2 knock someone down to hit and injure someone with a car: *Jack* ***was knocked down*** *while he was crossing the road.*

knock out

knock someone out a) to hit someone very hard so that they cannot get up: *The punch* ***knocked out*** *his opponent.* **b)** to defeat a person or team so that they cannot stay in a competition: *England* ***were knocked out*** *of the World Cup in the semi-final.*

knock² *noun* the sound that you make when you hit a door with your hand or something with something hard: *Did you hear a knock at the door?*

knock·out /ˈnɒk-aʊt $ ˈnɑk-aʊt/ *noun* when a BOXER hits another boxer so that he falls on the ground and cannot get up: *He won the fight by a knockout.*

knot¹ /nɒt $ nɑt/ *noun* a part where one or more pieces of string, rope etc have been tied or twisted together: *There's a knot in my shoelace.*

knot² *verb* (**knotted, knotting**) to join two pieces of string, rope etc together by tying them: *Amy knotted the rope firmly to the boat.*

know¹ /nəʊ $ noʊ/ *verb* (**knew** /njuː $ nuː/ **known** /nəʊn $ noʊn/)

KEY PATTERNS
know about something
know who/what/where etc
know (that)
know how to do something
know a person/place/book etc

1 to have facts or information in your mind: *My brother* ***knows*** *a lot* ***about*** *cars.* • *I don't* ***know where*** *she's gone.* • *I* ***knew that*** *it would be a long journey.* • *Do you* ***know how to*** *switch this machine off?* • ***As you know,*** *we're thinking of going to Canada.*

2 to be familiar with someone or something, because you have met them, read their books, visited them etc before: *Do you two* ***know*** *each other?* • ***I've known*** *him* ***since*** *I was in high school.* • *I don't really* ***know*** *Barcelona.* • *She* ***knew*** *your father* ***very well.*** • *I* ***know his face*** *from somewhere – has he been in the news recently?*

GRAMMAR
Use **know** in simple tenses, not progressive tenses.
✘ Don't say 'I am knowing.'

PHRASES

as far as I know (spoken) say this when you think something is true, but you are not sure: *He lives in Liverpool, as far as I know.*

get to know someone to meet someone and find out about them: *It takes time to* ***get to know*** *people when you start at a new school.*

I know (spoken) say this to show that you agree with or understand what

someone is saying: *"Sam was so nice to us when we visited." "I know."*
let someone know (informal) to tell someone about something: *If you need any help, just **let me know**.*
you know (spoken) **a)** people say this when they cannot quickly think of exactly which words they are going to say next: *I think it's time to, **you know**, get things tidied up.* **b)** say this when you want to start talking about something: ***You know** that girl in my English class? She's asked me out to dinner.*

know² /nəʊ $ noʊ/ *noun* **be in the know** if you are in the know, you have information that most people do not have: *Those in the know say that in private he is very different.*

'know-all *BrE*, **'know-it-all** *AmE noun* (informal) an annoying person who thinks they know more than everyone else

'know-how *noun* (no plural) (informal) knowledge that you need to do something: *We don't have the know-how to build our own house.*

know·ing·ly /ˈnəʊɪŋli $ ˈnoʊɪŋli/ *adverb* (formal) if you knowingly do something wrong, you do it even though you know that it is wrong: *He claimed he had never knowingly sold alcohol to teenagers.*

knowl·edge /ˈnɒlɪdʒ $ ˈnɑlɪdʒ/ *noun* (no plural)

KEY PATTERNS
knowledge of/about something

things that you know about a particular subject: *Her **knowledge of** music is amazing.* • *advances in scientific knowledge* • *Our **knowledge about** this disease is quite limited* (=we do not know very much about it).

PHRASES
have no knowledge: ***I had no knowledge of*** (=I did not know about) *their plan.*

knowl·edge·a·ble /ˈnɒlɪdʒəbəl $ ˈnɑlɪdʒəbəl/ *adjective* a knowledgeable person knows a lot about a particular subject: *Sal's very knowledgeable about computers.*

known the past participle of KNOW

knuck·le /ˈnʌkəl/ *noun* one of the joints of your fingers, including where your fingers join your hand

ko·a·la /kəʊˈɑːlə $ koʊˈɑlə/ also **koˌala 'bear** *noun* an Australian animal like a small bear that climbs trees

Ko·ran, **Qur'an** /kɔːˈrɑːn $ kəˈræn/ *noun* **the Koran** the holy book of the Islamic religion

ko·sher /ˈkəʊʃə $ ˈkoʊʃɚ/ *adjective* kosher food is prepared according to Jewish law

kung fu /ˌkʌŋ ˈfuː/ *noun* (no plural) a sport from China in which you fight using your hands and feet

kW the written abbreviation of KILOWATT

l the written abbreviation of LITRE

lab /læb/ *noun* (informal) a LABORATORY

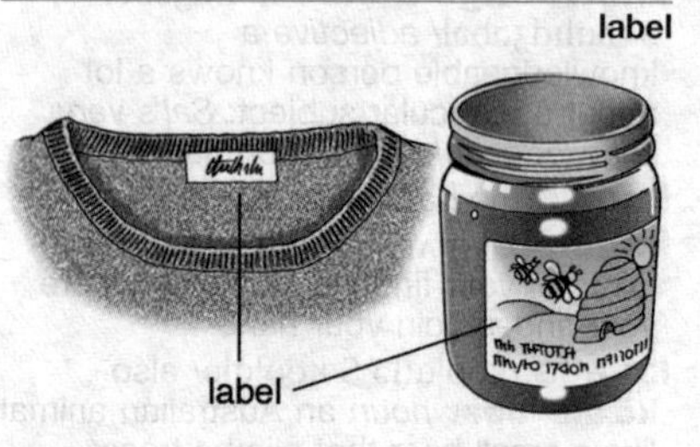

la·bel¹ /ˈleɪbəl/ *noun*
1 a piece of paper or cloth with information on it that is fixed to an object: *The label tells you how the dress should be washed.* • *There's no price label on this book.*
2 a record company: *The band was offered a contract by a major label.*

label² *verb* (**labelled**, **labelling** *BrE*, **labeled**, **labeling** *AmE*) to fix a label to something to show what it is: *We labelled the boxes so we would know what was in them.*

labor the American spelling of LABOUR

la·bor·a·tory /ləˈbɒrətri $ ˈlæbrəˌtɔri/ *noun* (plural **laboratories**) also **lab** /læb/ **1** a room or building in which people do scientific work **2 language laboratory** a room in a school or college where students can listen to tapes of a foreign language and practise speaking it

PRONUNCIATION
British people pronounce this word **laBOratory**.
American people pronounce this word **LAboratory**.

laborer the American spelling of LABOURER

lab·or·i·ous /ləˈbɔːriəs/ *adjective* taking a lot of time and effort to do: *the laborious task of repairing the bridge*

ˈlabor ˌunion the American word for UNION

la·bour *BrE*, **labor** *AmE* /ˈleɪbə $ ˈleɪbɚ/ *noun* (no plural) **1** hard work, usually physical work: *This garden is the result of years of labour.*
2 workers: *We need additional labour to complete the building.*

la·bour·er *BrE*, **laborer** *AmE* /ˈleɪbərə $ ˈleɪbərɚ/ *noun* someone who does a lot of physical work in their job: *farm labourers*

lace /leɪs/ *noun* (no plural) a type of cloth with a pattern of small holes that is often used to make clothes look attractive: *a lace collar*

lac·es /ˈleɪsɪz/ *plural noun* strings that you tie to fasten your shoes: *a pair of black laces*

lack /læk/ *noun* (no plural) when you do not have enough of something: *She was suffering from lack of sleep.*
—**lack** *verb*: *The school lacks modern equipment.*

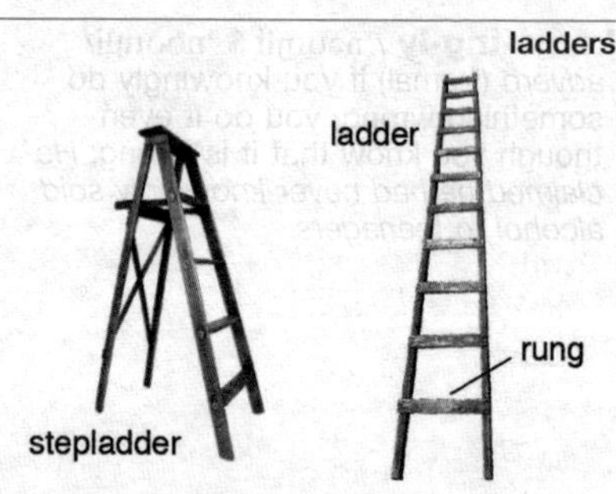

lad·der /ˈlædə $ ˈlædɚ/ *noun* a piece of equipment for climbing up to high places. A ladder has two long bars that are connected by short bars that you use as steps

la·den /ˈleɪdn/ *adjective* (written) carrying a lot of heavy things: *a truck laden with supplies*

la·dies /ˈleɪdiz/ *noun* **the ladies** *BrE* a room in a public building where there are toilets for women SYNONYM **ladies room** *AmE*

la·dle /ˈleɪdl/ *noun* a big deep spoon with a long handle that you use for putting soup into bowls

la·dy /ˈleɪdi/ *noun* (plural **ladies**) **1** a polite word for a woman: *Ask that lady if you can help.* • *Good evening, ladies and gentlemen.* **2 Lady** in Britain, a title for a woman of a high social rank: *Lady Katherine Dugdale*

> WORD CHOICE
> **lady** or **woman**?
> • The usual word is **woman**: *Who is that woman in the red dress?*
> • **Lady** sounds rather old-fashioned, and is often used about older women: *Her grandmother was an elderly **lady** in her late 70s.*
> • You also use **lady** in the phrase **Ladies and gentlemen**, when you are talking to a large group of people.

la·dy·bird /ˈleɪdibɜː $ ˈleɪdiˌbɚd/ *BrE*, **la·dy·bug** /ˈleɪdibʌg/ *AmE noun* a small round insect that is red with black spots

lag¹ /læg/ *verb* (**lagged**, **lagging**) **lag behind** (informal) to move or develop more slowly than other people: *Gina lagged behind, waiting for Rob.* • *My daughter is lagging behind in her studies.*

lag² also **time lag** *noun* the period of time between one event and another event that is connected with it

la·ger /ˈlɑːgə $ ˈlɑgɚ/ *noun BrE* a type of light yellow beer: *a pint of lager*

la·goon /ləˈguːn/ *noun* an area of sea water that is separated from the sea by sand

laid the past tense and past participle of LAY¹

ˌlaid-ˈback *adjective* (informal) relaxed and not worried about anything: *She seems very laid-back about her exams.*

lain the past participle of LIE¹

lake /leɪk/ *noun* a large area of water that is surrounded by land

lamb /læm/ *noun* **1** a young sheep **2** (no plural) the meat from a lamb

> PRONUNCIATION
> In this word you do not pronounce the **b**.

lame /leɪm/ *adjective* if a person or animal is lame, they cannot walk properly because they have hurt their leg: *His horse was lame because a stone had injured its foot.*

lamp /læmp/ *noun* a thing that produces light using electricity, oil, or gas: *a table lamp*

ˈlamp-post *noun* a tall pole in the street with a lamp on top → see picture at LIGHT¹

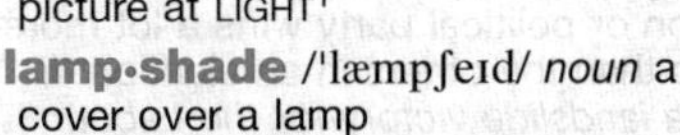
lamp·shade /ˈlæmpʃeɪd/ *noun* a cover over a lamp

land¹ /lænd/ *noun*
1 (no plural) an area of ground: *His family own a lot of land.* • *They have bought a piece of land.*
2 (no plural) the solid dry part of the Earth's surface, rather than the water or the air: *This is the fastest that anyone has ever travelled **on land**.*
3 (literary) a country: *He was one of the best actors **in the land**.*

land² *verb*

> KEY PATTERNS
> **land in/at a place**
> **land on/in something**

1 if a plane lands, or if a pilot lands a plane, the plane moves down until it is safely on the ground: *Our flight **landed at** Heathrow airport at 9.30.*
2 to fall onto something after moving through the air: *I slipped and **landed on** something sharp.* • *She dropped the cake and it **landed in** a puddle.*
3 to arrive somewhere by boat or plane: *We **landed in** Southampton on Friday.*

land·ing /ˈlændɪŋ/ *noun* **1** the area at the top of a set of stairs in a house **2** when a plane comes down from the air onto the ground ANTONYM **take-off**: *The pilot made an emergency landing.*

land·la·dy /ˈlændˌleɪdi/ *noun* (plural **landladies**) a woman that you rent a room or house from

land·lord /ˈlændlɔːd $ ˈlændlɔrd/ *noun* a man that you rent a room or house from

land·mark /ˈlændmɑːk $ ˈlændmɑrk/ *noun* something that helps you

A B C D E F G H I J K L M N O P Q R S T U V W X Y Z

recognize where you are, such as a famous building: *The Eiffel Tower is a well-known landmark in Paris.*

land·own·er /ˈlændˌəʊnə $ ˈlændˌoʊnɚ/ *noun* someone who owns a lot of land

land·scape /ˈlændskeɪp/ *noun* a large area of land that you can see: *the beauty of the landscape*

land·slide /ˈlændslaɪd/ *noun* **1** when soil and rocks fall down the side of a hill or mountain: *The village was destroyed in a landslide.* **2** when a person or political party wins a lot more votes than the others in an election: *It was a landslide victory for the Labour Party.*

lane /leɪn/ *noun* **1** a narrow country road ➔ see Thesaurus at ROAD **2** one of the parts that a road, sports track, or swimming pool is divided into: *You need to change lanes here to turn right.*

lan·guage /ˈlæŋgwɪdʒ/ *noun*
1 the words that are used by the people who live in a particular country: *She **speaks** three **languages**, including Japanese.*
2 (no plural) words, especially words of a particular kind: *the kind of technical language that scientists use*

lan·tern /ˈlæntən $ ˈlæntɚn/ *noun* a lamp in a glass or metal container that you can carry ➔ see picture at LIGHT[1]

lap

A cat sat on my lap.

The cat lapped up all the milk.

lap¹ /læp/ *noun* **1** the flat area at the top of your legs when you sit down: *A black cat sat on her lap.* **2** one trip around a race track during a long race: *The runners are on the last lap.*

lap² *verb* (**lapped**, **lapping**) **1** if water laps against something, it keeps hitting it gently: *Waves lapped against the side of the boat.* **2** also **lap up** if an animal laps up a drink, it drinks it with quick movements of its tongue: *The cat lapped up all the milk.*

la·pel /ləˈpel/ *noun* one of the parts at the front of a coat that join the collar and fold back on each side

lapse /læps/ *noun* when someone makes a mistake or forgets something, for only a short time or only once or twice: *a memory lapse • I've had a few lapses in my diet.*

lap·top /ˈlæptɒp $ ˈlæptɑp/ *noun* a small computer that you can carry: *I use a laptop if I'm travelling by train.*

large /lɑːdʒ $ lɑrdʒ/ *adjective* big in size, number, or amount ANTONYM **small**: *a large house with 15 rooms • Have you got this coat in a larger size? • They offered him a large amount of money for the information.* ➔ see Thesaurus at BIG

large·ly /ˈlɑːdʒli $ ˈlɑrdʒli/ *adverb* mostly or mainly: *The film was made largely in Mexico.* ➔ see Thesaurus at MAINLY

ˌlarge-ˈscale *adjective* large-scale situations or activities happen over a large area or involve a lot of people: *modern large-scale industry*

la·ser /ˈleɪzə $ ˈleɪzɚ/ *noun* a narrow line of powerful light, or the equipment that produces it

lash /læʃ/ *verb* (written) if rain, wind, or waves lash against something, they hit it hard: *Storms lashed the coast.*

lash·es /ˈlæʃɪz/ EYELASHES

last¹ /lɑːst $ læst/ *adjective, adverb, pronoun*
1 most recent or most recently: *Her spelling has improved over the last few months. • When did you last wash your hair?*
2 after all the other things or people: *How are you going to celebrate your last day at school? • He dies in the last chapter of the book. • Hilary **was the last to** arrive. • He **came last** in every race. • This part of the building was built last.*
3 the last one is the only remaining one: *Who ate the last biscuit? • That's **the last of** the boxes we have to move.*

PHRASES

last night, last week etc during the most recent night, week etc: *Did you*

last

He came last in the race.

*go out **last** night?* • *I saw James **last week**.* • *I went swimming **last Tuesday**.*
the week before last, the year before last etc during the week, year etc before the most recent one: *I got a letter from Yvonne **the week before last*** (=two weeks ago).
at last after a long time: *Good – you've finished **at last**.* • ***At last** the bus arrived.* → see Thesaurus at EVENTUALLY
the last person, the last thing etc a person or thing that you really do not expect or want: *He's **the last person** I'd invite!* • ***The last thing** I expected her to do was run away.*

GRAMMAR
You say **I saw him last week**.
✘ Don't say 'on last week'.

THESAURUS
previous: *Sales in 2006 were higher than in the **previous** year* (=the year before).
former: *the house's **former** owner* (=the person who used to own it)

WORD CHOICE
last or **latest**?
• **Last** means "the one before this one": *Her **last** book wasn't very good.*
• **Latest** means "the newest and most recent one": *His **latest** movie is about a boy who loves animals.*

last² *verb*

KEY PATTERNS
last (for) an hour/three days etc

1 to continue to happen or exist: *His first marriage lasted ten years.* • *The pain **lasted for** only a few seconds.*
2 to continue to be in good condition and suitable for use: *A good carpet will **last for** years.* • *Vegetables **last longer** if they are kept in the fridge.*

last·ing /ˈlɑːstɪŋ $ ˈlæstɪŋ/ *adjective* continuing for a long time: *a lasting friendship*

last·ly /ˈlɑːstli $ ˈlæstli/ *adverb* used before saying the last thing you want to say SYNONYM **finally**: *Lastly, I'd like to thank all my tutors.*

WORD CHOICE
lastly or **in the end**?
• You use **lastly** when mentioning the last one of a series of things: *Lastly I'd like to wish you good luck.*
• You use **in the end** when saying what happens at the end of a situation, after a lot of other things have happened: ***In the end**, our team won the game 4:3.*

ˈlast-minute *adjective* a last-minute action is done very near to the end of a period of time: *His last-minute goal saved the match.*

ˈlast name SURNAME

late /leɪt/ *adjective, adverb*

KEY PATTERNS
late for something

1 after the usual or expected time ANTONYM **early**: *I got up late.* • *Jack **was late for** school again today.* • *The train was 20 minutes late.*
2 near the end of a period of time ANTONYM **early**: *The school was built in the late 1970s.*
3 near the end of the day ANTONYM **early**: *It's getting late and I'm tired.*
4 (formal) used to talk about someone who died fairly recently: *the late Pope John Paul II*

PHRASES
too late if it is too late to do something, it is after the time when it should or could have been done: ***It's too late to** change your mind.*

late·ly /ˈleɪtli/ *adverb* recently: *I haven't seen her lately.* → see Thesaurus at RECENTLY

lat·er¹ /ˈleɪtə $ ˈleɪtɚ/ *adverb* after the present time or after a time that you are talking about: *You'll have to finish that later.* • *A couple of months later, I met her again at a party.* → see Thesaurus at AFTERWARDS

PHRASES
later on at some time in the future, or at some time after something else: *He*

A B C D E F G H I J K L M N O P Q R S T U V W X Y Z

kept things he thought might be useful ***later on.*** • ***Later on,*** *we can go shopping, if you like.*

later² *adjective* happening or coming after something else ANTONYM **earlier**: *Her later books weren't so popular.*

lat·est¹ /ˈleɪtəst/ *adjective* the most recent: *the latest news* ➔ see Thesaurus at NEW

latest² *noun* **at the latest** used to tell someone that something will or must happen before a particular time: *Applications must get here by tomorrow at the latest.*

Lat·in¹ /ˈlætɪn $ ˈlætn/ *noun* the language that was used in ancient Rome

Latin² *adjective* **1** written in Latin: *a Latin poem* **2** connected with a nation that speaks a language such as Italian or Spanish: *Latin music*

ˌLatin Aˈmerican *adjective* related to South or Central America: *Latin American countries*

laugh¹ /lɑːf $ læf/ *verb*

KEY PATTERNS
laugh at something funny
laugh at someone

1 to make a sound with your voice when you think that something is funny: *We couldn't stop laughing.* • *The audience* ***laughed at*** *all the jokes.*
2 if people laugh at someone, they laugh or make jokes about that person in an unkind way: *It's not kind to* ***laugh at*** *people who make mistakes.*

THESAURUS
chuckle: *He* ***chuckled*** *as he remembered how silly his brother had looked* (=laughed quietly).
giggle: *The children* ***giggled*** *at their teacher's bad joke* (=laughed in a silly or nervous way).
snigger *BrE*, **snicker** *AmE*: *The others* ***sniggered*** *when he gave the wrong answer* (=laughed quietly in an unpleasant way).
be in stitches: *The film was so funny we were all* ***in stitches*** (=laughing a lot)!

laugh² *noun* the sound you make when you laugh: *He* ***gave a short laugh.***

PHRASES
be a laugh *BrE* (informal) to be fun: *Come on – it'll* ***be a laugh!***

laugh·ter /ˈlɑːftə $ ˈlæftɚ/ *noun* (no plural) when you laugh, or the sound of people laughing: *We heard laughter outside.* • *The audience roared with laughter.*

PRONUNCIATION
laughter/daughter
You pronounce **laughter** like 'after'.
You pronounce **daughter** like 'water'.

launch /lɔːntʃ/ *verb* **1** to start a big important series of actions: *The government has launched an anti-racism campaign.* **2** to make a new product available: *The book will be launched next week.* **3** to send a spacecraft into the sky or to put a boat into the water —**launch** *noun*: *the launch of a new women's magazine*

laun·der·ette /ˌlɔːndəˈret/ *BrE*, **laun·dro·mat** /ˈlɔːndrəmæt/ *AmE* *noun* a public place where you pay to wash your clothes in a machine

laun·dry /ˈlɔːndri / *noun* (no plural) clothes, sheets etc that need to be washed, or that have just been washed: *Do you have any dirty laundry?*

la·va /ˈlɑːvə/ *noun* (no plural) hot liquid rock that comes out of a VOLCANO

lav·a·to·ry /ˈlævətəri $ ˈlævəˌtori/ *noun* (formal) (plural **lavatories**) a toilet

lav·en·der /ˈlævəndə $ ˈlævəndɚ/ *noun* a plant with small purple flowers, which has a beautiful smell and is used for making PERFUME

law /lɔː/ *noun*

KEY PATTERNS
a law against something

1 (no plural) the system of rules that people in a country must obey: ***The law*** *says that you must not sell alcohol to people under the age of 18.* • *according to international law*
2 a rule that people in a country must obey: *tough new anti-drug laws* • *There should be a* ***law against*** *it!* ➔ see Thesaurus at RULE¹
3 (no plural) the study of laws: *He did law at university.*
4 a scientific rule that explains why something happens: *the* ***law of*** *gravity*

PHRASES

be against the law: *Driving without a licence **is against the law*** (=is illegal).

break the law to do something illegal: *I didn't know I was **breaking the law**.*

law and order when people obey the law and do not act violently: *The local police are trying to keep **law and order**.*

lawn /lɔːn/ *noun* an area of grass that is cut short: *The children were playing on the lawn.*

'lawn ˌmower *noun* a machine that you use to cut grass

law•yer /ˈlɔːjə $ ˈlɔjɚ/ *noun* someone whose job is to advise people about the law and speak for them in court

lay

Jane is laying the table. Eric is laying bricks.

lay¹ /leɪ/ *verb* (past tense and past participle **laid** /leɪd/)

KEY PATTERNS
lay something on the table/ground
lay something down

1 to put something on a surface in a careful way so that it is lying flat: *She **laid** her gloves **on the table**. • He **laid down** his knife and fork.*
2 if you lay bricks, CARPETS, electrical wires etc, you put them down in the place where they will stay: *Men are digging up the road to **lay** television cables.*
3 if a bird, insect etc lays eggs, it produces them from its body

PHRASES

lay the table to put knives, forks etc on a table before a meal SYNONYM **set the table**

PHRASAL VERBS

lay down

lay down something to say officially what people should do: *The school **laid down** strict rules about appearance.*

lay² the past tense of LIE¹

'lay-by *noun BrE* an area at the side of a road where vehicles can stop: *We pulled into a lay-by for a rest.*

lay•er /ˈleɪə $ ˈleɪɚ/ *noun* a flat amount or piece of something that is covering a surface or between other things: *a layer of dust • Wear several layers of clothing.*

lay•out /ˈleɪaʊt/ *noun* the arrangement of the rooms or objects somewhere: *a picture showing the layout of Buckingham Palace*

laze /leɪz/ also **laze around** *verb* to relax and not do very much: *two cats lazing in the sun*

la•zy /ˈleɪzi/ *adjective* (**lazier**, **laziest**) a lazy person does not like working or doing things that need effort: *Don't be so lazy – come and help me clean up.*
—**laziness** *noun*

lb. the written abbreviation of POUND¹

lead¹ /liːd/ *verb* (past tense and past participle **led** /led/)

KEY PATTERNS
lead someone to/into etc a place
a door/road leads to/into a place

1 to take someone somewhere by going with them or in front of them: *She **led** me **into** the kitchen. • The man was **led away** by the police.*
2 if a door, road etc leads somewhere, you can get there by using it: *He walked down the corridor that **led to** the exit. • the door **leading into** the sitting room*
3 to be in charge of an activity or organization: *She led the campaign to save the school from being closed.*
4 if you are leading, you are winning a game or competition ANTONYM **trail**: *At half time, Manchester United were leading 2–0.*

PHRASES

lead a busy life, lead a normal life etc to have a particular kind of life: *He **had led an interesting life**.*

lead the way a) to go in front so that someone can follow you somewhere: *She **led the way** up a flight of stairs.* **b)** to be the first to do something: *American doctors **led the way** in using this new treatment.*

A B C D E F G H I J K L M N O P Q R S T U V W X Y Z

lead someone to do something to be the reason why someone does something: *What **led you to** make this decision?*

PHRASAL VERBS

lead to

lead to something to cause something to happen: *His laziness **led to** arguments with his parents.*

lead up to

lead up to something if events lead up to something, they come before it and may be a cause of it: *The police are investigating the events **leading up to** the murder.*

lead² *noun*

1 the distance, number of points etc by which one team or person is ahead of another: *Germany had an early two-goal lead.* • *The team managed to increase their lead.*

2 *BrE* a long piece of leather that you fasten to a dog's collar to keep it near you SYNONYM **leash**

3 *BrE* an electric wire that you use to connect a piece of equipment to a supply of electricity SYNONYM **cord** *AmE*

PHRASES

in the lead, into the lead if someone in a race, game, or competition is in the lead, they are winning at that time: *The Kenyan **was in the lead** at the first bend.* • *John's team raced **into the lead** by scoring 10 points in the first round.*

take the lead to start winning a race, game, or competition: *France **took the lead** when they scored a goal after ten minutes.*

lead³ /led/ *noun* **1** (no plural) a heavy soft grey metal **2** the grey substance in the middle of a pencil

PRONUNCIATION

Be careful how you pronounce this word:
lead¹ (*verb*) is pronounced like 'feed'
lead² (*noun*) is pronounced like 'feed'
lead³ (*noun*) is pronounced like 'said'

lead·er /ˈliːdə $ ˈlidɚ/ *noun* the person who is in charge of a country or group: *a meeting of world leaders*

lead·er·ship /ˈliːdəʃɪp $ ˈlidɚˌʃɪp/ *noun* the position of being in charge of a country or group, or the people who are in charge: *He took over the leadership of the party in 2003.*

lead·ing /ˈliːdɪŋ/ *adjective* best or most important: *one of Britain's leading sportsmen*

leaf /liːf/ *noun* (plural **leaves** /liːvz/) one of the flat green things that grow on a plant: *The leaves on the trees fall off in autumn.* ➔ see picture at FLOWER ➔ see picture on page A10

leaf·let /ˈliːflət/ *noun* a piece of paper with information printed on it: *We handed out leaflets about the meeting.*

league /liːg/ *noun* **1** a group of sports teams or players who compete against each other: *the football league* **2** a group of people or countries that work together because they have similar aims: *the League of Nations*

leak /liːk/ *verb* **1** if something leaks, there is a hole in it that lets liquid or gas come out or in: *My shoes are leaking.* • *The tank was leaking petrol.* **2** if liquid or gas leaks from something, it comes out of it through a hole: *Water was leaking out of the pipes.* ➔ see Thesaurus at FLOW² —**leak** *noun*: *a gas leak*

leak

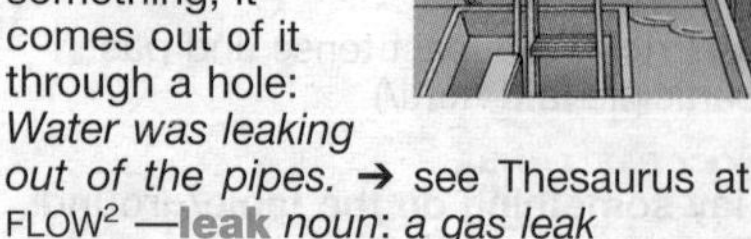

lean

Jane is leaning forward.

Billy is leaning against the wall.

lean¹ /liːn/ *verb* (past tense and past participle **leaned** or **leant** /lent/ *BrE*)

KEY PATTERNS

lean forwards/back/over
lean against/on something
lean something against/on something

1 to bend your body forwards, backwards, or to the side: *Jane **leaned forwards** to look out of the train window.* • *He **leaned back** in his chair.* • *Antony **leaned over** and kissed her.*
2 to stand or sit with part of your body resting against something: *He stood **leaning against** the wall.* • *He **leaned** his elbows **on** the table.*
3 to put an object in a sloping position against something else so that it will stay there: *He **leaned** his bicycle **against** the wall.*

lean² *adjective* thin, in an attractive healthy way: *a lean, muscular runner*
→ see Thesaurus at THIN

leant a past tense and past participle of LEAN¹

leap /liːp/ *verb* (past tense and past participle **leaped** or **leapt** /lept/) to jump somewhere: *The dog leapt the fence.* • *Joe leapt out of bed.* → see Thesaurus at JUMP¹ —**leap** *noun*: *With one leap, he was on the horse's back.*

leapt a past tense and past participle of LEAP

'leap year *noun* a year when February has 29 days instead of 28

learn /lɜːn $ lɚn/ *verb* (past tense and past participle **learned** or **learnt** /lɜːnt $ lɚnt/ *BrE*)

KEY PATTERNS
learn a subject/skill
learn (how) to do something
learn about something
learn from a person/experience
learn (that)
learn of an event

1 to get knowledge or a skill by studying or training: *How long have you been learning English?* • *I want to **learn to** drive when I'm 17.* • *They **learned how to** ski when they lived in Switzerland.* • *Today we **learned all about** dinosaurs.* • *I **have learned from** my mistakes.*
2 (formal) to hear some news or information SYNONYM **find out**: *The next day, I **learned that** I had passed the exam.* • *I only **learned of** the change of plan yesterday.*
3 if you learn a poem, part of a play etc, you read it many times so that you can remember it all exactly

THESAURUS
study: *She is **studying** geography at university* (=learning it).
master: *He had already **mastered** the language and could speak it fluently* (=learned it very well).
pick up: *I picked up gardening skills by watching my mother* (=learned them gradually).
get the hang of (informal): *Don't worry – you'll soon **get the hang of it*** (=learn how to do it).

learn·er /'lɜːnə $ 'lɚnɚ/ *noun* someone who is learning a language, skill etc: *a course for advanced learners of English* • *Teresa's a slow learner.*

learn·ing /'lɜːnɪŋ $ 'lɚnɪŋ/ *noun* (no plural) knowledge that you get by reading and studying, or the activity of reading and studying: *Learning should be fun.*

learnt a past tense and past participle of LEARN

leash /liːʃ/ *noun* (plural **leashes**) a long piece of leather that you fasten to a dog's collar to keep it near you SYNONYM **lead**: *I have to keep my dog on a leash.*

least /liːst/ *adverb, determiner, pronoun*
the smallest amount ANTONYM **most**: *It's the part of the world I know least about.* • *He answered the least difficult questions.* • *He always did the thing that required the least effort.* • *Let me pay for the meal – **it's the least I can do** after you've helped me so much.*
PHRASES
at least a) not less than a particular number or amount: *The bridge will take **at least** two years to build.* • *Her dress must have cost **at least** $2,000.* **b)** (spoken) used when mentioning a good part of a bad situation: ***At least** we now know what the problem is.* **c)** (spoken) used before correcting or changing what you have said: *He said he'd been swimming – **at least** I think that's what he said.* **d)** used to say what someone should do, even if they do nothing more: *If you can't stay for lunch, **at least** stay for a cup of coffee.*

leath·er /'leðə $ 'leðɚ/ *noun* (no plural) animal skin that is used to make shoes, coats etc: *a leather bag*

leave¹ → see box on page 383

leave² /liːv/ *noun* (no plural) time that you are allowed to spend away from your job: *Our tutor is on leave.* • *The maximum maternity leave* (=leave that a woman can have when she has a new baby) *is 12 months.*

leaves the plural of LEAF

lec·ture¹ /ˈlektʃə $ ˈlektʃɚ/ *noun* a talk to a group of people that teaches them about a subject: *a lecture on Beethoven*

lecture² *verb* to teach a group of people about a subject: *Dr Marks lectures in biology.* —**lecturer** *noun*: *Miss Jones is a university lecturer.*

led the past tense and past participle of LEAD¹

ledge /ledʒ/ *noun* a narrow flat surface sticking out from the side of a building or a mountain

leek /liːk/ *noun* a long white and green vegetable that tastes like an onion → see picture on page A6

left¹ /left/ *adjective* on or nearer the side of your body that contains your heart ANTONYM **right**: *She wore a gold bracelet on her left wrist.*

left² *adverb* **turn left, look left etc** to turn, look etc towards the left side ANTONYM **right**: *Turn left at the traffic lights and then the school is straight ahead of you.*

left³ *noun*
1 on the left, to your left etc nearer the left side of your body ANTONYM **right**: *The Taylors' house is* ***on the left.*** • *To your* ***left*** *you can see the church tower.*
2 the Left political groups that believe that money should be shared out more equally, for example Socialists

left⁴ the past tense and past participle of LEAVE

ˌleft-ˈhand *adjective* on the left ANTONYM **right-hand**: *The house is on the left-hand side of the street.*

ˌleft-ˈhanded *adjective* a left-handed person uses their left hand to do things such as writing or throwing a ball ANTONYM **right-handed**

left·o·vers /ˈleftəʊvəz $ ˈleftˌoʊvɚz/ *plural noun* food that has not been eaten during a meal: *We gave the leftovers to the dog.*

ˌleft-ˈwing *adjective* supporting the political ideas of groups such as Socialists and Communists: *left-wing politicians*

leg /leg/ *noun*
1 one of the long parts of your body that you use for walking and standing: *Can you touch your toes while keeping your legs straight?* → see picture on page A5
2 one of the parts that support a table, chair etc
3 one of the parts of a pair of trousers that cover your legs: *My jeans have a hole in the left leg.*

le·gal /ˈliːgəl/ *adjective*
1 allowed by the law or done correctly according to the law ANTONYM **illegal**: *Is the contract legal?*
2 related to the law: *the legal system* • *You should go to a lawyer for legal advice.* —**legally** *adverb*: *The school is legally responsible for the safety of its students.*

le·gal·ize also **legalise** *BrE* /ˈliːgəlaɪz/ *verb* to change the law so that something is made legal: *They want the government to legalize the drug.*

le·gend /ˈledʒənd/ *noun* **1** an old well-known story about people who lived in the past, which may not be true: *ancient Greek legends*
2 someone who is famous for being very good at something: *rock 'n' roll legend, Elvis Presley*

le·gen·da·ry /ˈledʒəndəri $ ˈledʒənˌderi/ *adjective* very famous and admired: *the legendary singer, Frank Sinatra*

leg·gings /ˈlegɪŋz/ *plural noun* a piece of women's clothing that fits closely around the legs: *She wore a pair of red leggings.*

le·gi·ble /ˈledʒəbəl/ *adjective* writing that is legible is clear enough for you to read ANTONYM **illegible**

le·git·i·mate /ləˈdʒɪtəmət/ *adjective* (formal) not illegal: *This is a legitimate business.*

lei·sure /ˈleʒə $ ˈliʒɚ/ *noun* (no plural) time when you are not working and can do things that you enjoy: *How do you spend your leisure time?*

leave /liːv/ *verb* (past tense and past participle **left** /left/, present participle **leaving**)

1 to go away from a place: *We **left** the party at about midnight.* • *Bruce **left** on Monday morning.* • *Harvard is a good school, but Mark doesn't really want to **leave** California.* • *I have to **leave for** the airport at seven.* • *The ferry **leaves** from Dover.*

GRAMMAR
leave or **leave from**?
• You say **She left her house at 8.30**.
✗ Don't say 'She left from her house.'
• You say that a train, plane, or bus leaves from a particular part of a station, airport, or town: *The next train for Cambridge will leave from platform 2.*

leave

2 to stop doing a job, going to school etc: *What are you going to do when you **leave school**?* • *Why **did** you **leave** your last **job**?*

3 to let something stay the same as it is now: *Who **left** the door **open**?* • ***Leave** your shoes **on** – we're going out again soon.*

KEY PATTERNS
leave the light on/off
leave the door open/closed
leave your coat/shoes on

4 to put something somewhere: *You can **leave** your coats in the bedroom.* • *I **left** a copy of the report on your desk.*

5 to not take something with you: *Oh no! I **left** my keys in the car!* • *I'll **leave** my stuff here until we get back.*

6 to end your relationship with your husband, girlfriend etc: *She **left** her husband after five years of marriage.*

PHRASES

leave something alone
to stop touching something: *Bad dog! **Leave** the plants **alone**!*

leave someone alone
to stop annoying someone: *I wish you would **leave** me **alone** – I'm trying to do my homework.*

leave a message
to give information to one person so that they can give it to another person: *"He isn't home right now." "Oh, can I **leave a message** for him, then?"*

leave out
to not include someone or something: *They **left** him **out** of the team.* • *My name had been **left out**.*

be left, be left over
if something is left or left over, it is still there after other things have been eaten or used: *Is there any cake **left**?* • *If there's any pasta **left over**, put it in the fridge.*

lei·sure·ly /ˈleʒəli $ ˈliʒəli/ *adjective* done in a fairly slow relaxed way: *a leisurely walk*

lem·on /ˈlemən/ *noun* a yellow fruit that tastes sour → see picture on page A7

lem·on·ade /ˌleməˈneɪd/ *noun* (no plural) **1** *BrE* a clear sweet drink with lots of bubbles: *a glass of lemonade* **2** a drink made from lemons, water, and sugar

lend

I lent him my book.

lend /lend/ *verb* (past tense and past participle **lent** /lent/)

KEY PATTERNS
lend someone something
lend something to someone

to let someone borrow something that you own: *I can lend you £10.* • *I had lent my best jacket to a friend.*

WORD CHOICE
lend or **borrow**?
• You **lend** something that you own to another person: *I lent him my car.*
• You **borrow** something that another person owns, so that you can use it for a short time: *Can I borrow your pen?*

length /leŋθ/ *noun*
1 how long something is: *They measured* ***the length of*** *the garden.* • *The snake was 2 metres* ***in length.***
2 the amount of time that something continues for: ***The length of*** *the course is ten weeks.* • *The* ***length of time*** *that people have to wait varies.*
3 a long piece of something: *She cut off* ***a length of*** *thread.*
PHRASES
go to any lengths to do something, go to great lengths to do something to do everything you can to achieve something: *She* ***went to great lengths to*** *hide the fact that she couldn't read.*

length·en /ˈleŋθən/ *verb* to make something longer or to become longer ANTONYM **shorten**: *I need to lengthen these trousers.* • *In the summer, the days lengthen and everyone seems happier.*

length·ways /ˈleŋθweɪz/ also **length·wise** /ˈleŋθwaɪz/ *adverb* in the direction of the longest side: *Cut the carrots lengthways.*

length·y /ˈleŋθi/ *adjective* (**lengthier, lengthiest**) continuing for a long time ANTONYM **brief**: *a lengthy performance*

lens

lens /lenz/ *noun* (plural **lenses**) **1** a piece of curved glass or plastic that makes things look bigger or smaller: *a camera with a zoom lens* • *glasses with tinted lenses* **2** the part of your eye that bends the light coming in

Lent /lent/ *noun* the 40 days before Easter, when some Christians stop doing something that they enjoy

lent the past tense and past participle of LEND

leop·ard /ˈlepəd $ ˈlepərd/ *noun* a large wild cat with yellow fur and black spots → see picture on page A9

le·o·tard /ˈliːətɑːd $ ˈliəˌtɑrd/ *noun* a piece of clothing that covers the main part of the body, which women wear when dancing or exercising

les·bi·an /ˈlezbiən/ *noun* a woman who is sexually attracted to other women: *lesbian and gay rights*

less /les/ *adverb, determiner, pronoun* a smaller amount ANTONYM **more**: *I wish it was less cold!* • *Catching the train is less effort than driving.* • *You should try to worry less.* • *Could you put less milk in my tea next time?* • *It cost* ***less than*** *£10.*
PHRASES
less and less: *Computers are becoming* ***less and less*** *expensive* (=they are continuing to become less expensive).
no less than used to emphasize that an amount is large: ***No less than*** *70% of this forest has been destroyed.*

WORD CHOICE
less or **fewer**?
• You use **less** before a noun that is not used in the plural: *I earn less money than she does.*
• You use **fewer** before a plural noun: *There were fewer cars on the street.*

less•en /ˈlesən/ *verb* (formal) to become smaller in amount, or to make something become smaller SYNONYM **decrease**: *The pain had lessened slightly.* • *Exercise lessens the risk of heart disease.* ➔ see Thesaurus at REDUCE

les•son /ˈlesən/ *noun*

KEY PATTERNS
have/take lessons

1 a period of time in which someone is taught a subject or skill: *I've only **had** two driving **lessons**.*
2 an experience from which you can learn something useful, or the thing that you learn: *This experience taught me an important lesson: don't judge people too quickly.*

let /let/ *verb* (past tense and past participle **let**, **letting**)

KEY PATTERNS
let someone/something do something
let someone/something in/out/through
let a room/house to someone

1 to allow someone to do something, or to allow something to happen: *Will your parents let you go to America alone?* • *We wanted to go outside but our teacher wouldn't let us.* • *Don't let yourself be hurt by their attitude.* • *They've let the garden become very untidy.* ➔ see Thesaurus at ALLOW
2 to make it possible for someone or something to go in, out, or through somewhere, for example by opening a door: *Open the door and **let** me **in**!* • *Don't forget to **let** the cat **out of** the house at night.* • *The crowds stood back to **let** the doctor **through**.*
3 if you let a room or house, you allow someone to use it and they pay you SYNONYM **rent**: *We went to France, and **let** our house **to** some students.*

PHRASES
let's, let's not (spoken) used to suggest doing something or not doing something: *"**Let's** go to the cinema tonight." "Oh, **let's not**."*
let someone know (informal) to tell someone something that they need or want to know: *Let me **know** if you need any help.* • *Will you **let** us **know** what time your plane's arriving?*
let someone/something go, let go to stop holding someone or something: ***Let** me **go**! You're hurting me!* • *Hold onto the rope and don't **let go**.* • *Jamie accidentally **let go of** the dog's lead.*
let me do something (spoken) used to offer to help someone: ***Let me** open that bottle for you.*

PHRASAL VERBS
let down
let someone down to not do what you promised you would do or what you were expected to do: *You can trust Jim – he'd never **let** you **down**.*
let in on
let someone in on something (spoken) to tell someone something that is a secret: *Shall we **let** Liz **in on** the plan?*
let off
let someone off to not punish someone when they have done something wrong: *"I'll **let** you **off** this time," the policeman said.*
let on
(spoken) if you do not let on that something is true, you do not tell anyone, because it is a secret: *He didn't **let on that** he'd met her before.*

let•down /ˈletdaʊn/ *noun* (informal) something that disappoints you SYNONYM **disappointment**: *The film was rather a letdown – I expected it to be more exciting.*

le•thal /ˈliːθəl/ *adjective* something that is lethal can kill you SYNONYM **deadly**: *a lethal weapon*

let's /lets/ the short form of 'let us', which is used to suggest doing something

let•ter /ˈletə $ ˈletər/ *noun*
1 a written message that you put in an envelope and send to someone: *I **got** a **letter from** my friend Anne yesterday.* • *I'll **post** the **letter to** him today.*
2 one of the signs that you use to write words: *the letter A*

let•ter•box /ˈletəbɒks $ ˈletərˌbɑːks/ *noun BrE* (plural **letterboxes**) **1** a hole in a door through which letters are put when they are delivered **2** a box in a post office or in the street, where you post letters SYNONYM **mailbox** *AmE* SYNONYM **postbox** *BrE*

let·tuce /'letɪs/ *noun* a round green vegetable whose leaves you eat without cooking them: *lettuce and tomato salad* ➔ see picture on page A6

lev·el¹ /'levəl/ *noun*
1 the amount of something: *The noise level in the building has increased.* • *the high* ***level of*** *crime* • *students with the same* ***level of*** *ability*
2 the height of a liquid: *Changes in sea levels may result in flooding.*
3 one of the ranks or layers in a system or structure: *This decision can only be taken at a higher level.*

PHRASES
at eye level, at ground level at the same height as your eyes or the ground: *All the controls are* ***at eye level.***

level² *adjective*

KEY PATTERNS
level with something

1 flat, with no part higher than any other part: *Make sure that the ground is level before sowing the grass seed.* ➔ see Thesaurus at FLAT¹
2 at the same height or as far forward as something else: *The top of her head* ***was level with*** *his chin.* • *The two cars were almost level.*

level³ *verb* (**levelled, levelling** *BrE*, **leveled, leveling** *AmE*) **1** (written) if something such as a storm levels buildings, it destroys them completely: *The earthquake has levelled this area of the city.* **2 level off, level out** to become steady after rising quickly: *House prices are beginning to level off.*

ˌlevel 'crossing *noun BrE* a place where a road and a railway cross

ˌlevel-'headed *adjective* calm and sensible: *He's a firm and level-headed leader.*

le·ver /'liːvə $ 'levɚ/ *noun* **1** a bar that you use to lift a heavy object by putting one end under the object and pushing the other end of the bar down **2** a handle on a machine that you move to make the machine work

li·a·bil·i·ty /ˌlaɪə'bɪləti/ *noun* (no plural) (formal) legal responsibility for something: *We accept no liability for cars that are left here overnight.*

li·a·ble /'laɪəbəl/ *adjective* **be liable to do something** to be likely to do something: *This film is liable to upset some viewers.*

li·ar /'laɪə $ 'laɪɚ/ *noun* someone who tells lies: *Are you calling me a liar?*

lib·e·ral /'lɪbərəl/ *adjective* someone who is liberal thinks that people should be allowed to do what they want SYNONYM **tolerant**: *a liberal attitude towards drugs*

lib·e·rate /'lɪbəreɪt/ *verb* (written) to free someone from a situation or place that they cannot get out of: *US soldiers liberated the prisoners.*

lib·e·ra·tion /ˌlɪbə'reɪʃən/ *noun* (no plural) when people are freed from a situation or place that they could not get out of: *the black liberation movement*

lib·er·ty /'lɪbəti $ 'lɪbɚti/ *noun* (formal) (plural **liberties**) when you are free to live how you want without being told what to do SYNONYM **freedom**: *This new law is a threat to our liberty.*

li·brar·i·an /laɪ'breəriən $ laɪ'breriən/ *noun* someone who works in a library

li·bra·ry /'laɪbrəri $ 'laɪˌbreri/ *noun* (plural **libraries**) a room or building containing books that you can borrow, and computers that you can use to get information

SPELLING
This word is often spelled wrongly. The correct spelling is: **library**.

WORD CHOICE
library or **bookshop**?
• A **library** is a place where you can borrow books for a short time.
• A **bookshop** or **bookstore** is a place where you can buy books.

li·cence *BrE*, **license** *AmE* /'laɪsəns/ *noun* an official document that gives you permission to do something: *Can I see your driving licence?*

'license plate the American word for NUMBER PLATE

lick /lɪk/ *verb* to move your tongue across something: *The dog licked my face.*

lid /lɪd/ *noun* a cover for the top of a container: *Put the lid on the paint tin.* → see picture at PAN → see Thesaurus at COVER²

lie¹ /laɪ/ *verb* (**lay** /leɪ/ **lain** /leɪn/ **lying**)

KEY PATTERNS
lie on something

1 also **lie down** to have or put your body flat on a surface, for example the floor or a bed: *She **was lying on** the grass.* • *I feel a bit ill – I think I'll go and **lie down**.* • *I lay awake for ages.*
2 if something is lying somewhere, it is on something in a flat position: *She picked up the parcel **lying on** the table.*

PHRASES
lie ahead to be going to happen in the future: *Who knows what **lies ahead**?*
lie in wait (written) to remain hidden in order to attack someone: *The robbers had been **lying in wait for** him.*

PHRASAL VERBS
lie around, lie about *BrE*
1 lie around, lie around something if things are lying around, they have been left in the wrong place, in an untidy way: *He always left letters and papers **lying around**.* • *It's not sensible to have that amount of money **lying around** the house!*
2 lie around, lie around something to spend time sitting or lying in a relaxed way: *He just **lies around** doing nothing all day.*
lie behind
lie behind something to be the true reason for an action: *What **lay behind** Keith's criticism of Tony?*

GRAMMAR
The past tense of **lie** (=to say something untrue) is **lied**: *You **lied** to me!*
The past tense of **lie** (=to rest your body somewhere) is **lay**: *She **lay** down on her bed.*

lie² *verb* (past tense and past participle **lied**, **lying**) to tell someone something that you know is not true: *He says he's rich but I think he's lying.* • *You lied to me!*

THESAURUS
mislead: *Advertisements should not **mislead** the public* (=give them incorrect information).
deceive: *He **deceived** her when he said he wasn't married* (=made her believe something that wasn't true).

lie³ *noun* something that you say that you know is not true: *We found out that she'd been telling lies.*

USAGE
You say **tell lies**.
✘ Don't say 'say lies'.

lieu·ten·ant /lef'tenənt $ lu'tenənt/ *noun* an officer who has a middle rank in the army, navy, or AIR FORCE

PRONUNCIATION
British people pronounce the first syllable of **lieutenant** like 'left'.
American people pronounce the first syllable of **lieutenant** like 'loot'.

life /laɪf/ *noun* (plural **lives** /laɪvz/)
1 the period of time during which someone is alive: *I have lived in England **all my life**.* • *Do you want to spend **the rest of your life** being unhappy?* • *My father had a very **hard life**.*
2 the state of being alive: *They filmed the baby's first moments of life.* • *The animal showed no **signs of life*** (=it looked dead).
3 the activities of someone, especially someone who is in a particular place or situation: *Life in the city is very busy.* • *Are you enjoying married life?* • *He doesn't like questions about his **private life**.*
4 (no plural) living things such as people, animals, or plants: *Is there life on Mars?* • *the sea life of the Great Barrier Reef*
5 (no plural) activity or movement: *Young children are always so **full of life**.*

PHRASES
save someone's life to stop someone from being killed: *The fireman **saved her life** by carrying her from the burning building.*
be for life if something is for life, it continues until you are dead: *Marriage is supposed to be **for life**.*

A B C D E F G H I J K L M N O P Q R S T U V W X Y Z

way of life the typical or usual things that someone does: *They enjoy a simple **way of life** in the country.*

real life what really happens, rather than what happens in stories or in your imagination: ***In real life** there is not always a happy ending.*

life·boat /ˈlaɪfbəʊt $ ˈlaɪfboʊt/ *noun* a boat that is used to save people who are in danger at sea: *They sent the lifeboat to search for the missing sailors.*

ˈlife guard *noun* someone whose job is to help swimmers who are in danger at the beach or at a swimming pool

ˈlife ˌjacket *noun* a piece of clothing that you wear around your chest so that you float if you fall into water

life·like /ˈlaɪflaɪk/ *adjective* a picture or model that is lifelike looks very much like a real person or thing: *The statue is quite lifelike.*

life·long /ˈlaɪflɒŋ $ ˈlaɪflɔŋ/ *adjective* continuing all through your life: *She was my mother's lifelong friend.*

ˈlife-size *adjective* a life-size picture or model is the same size as the real thing: *She painted a life-size picture of her dog.*

life·style /ˈlaɪfstaɪl/ *noun* the way that someone lives, including the things they do and the things they own: *the glamorous lifestyle of a rock star*

life·time /ˈlaɪftaɪm/ *noun* the period of time during which someone is alive: *There may not be a cure for cancer in my lifetime.*

lift¹ /lɪft/ *verb*
1 also **lift up** to move something or someone to a higher position: *I can't lift this table on my own.* • *Paul **lifted** the lid **off** the box.* • *My father **lifted** me **up** on his shoulders.*
2 to end a rule or law that stops people from doing something: *We hope they will **lift** the **ban** and allow us to play in the competition.* → see picture on page A2

lift² *noun* **1** *BrE* a machine that takes you up and down in a building SYNONYM **elevator** *AmE*: *I took the lift to the tenth floor.* **2** *BrE* a ride in a car SYNONYM **ride** *AmE*: *I'll give you a lift to the station.*

light¹ /laɪt/ *noun*
1 (no plural) the brightness that comes from the sun or from a lamp, which allows you to see things: *There isn't much light in this room because the window is small.*
2 an electric lamp that gives light. You switch on or turn on a light to make it work, and you switch off or turn off a light to make it stop working: *Remember to **turn the lights off** before you go to bed.* • *the bright lights of Las Vegas*
3 lights a set of red, green, and yellow lights that tell drivers when to stop and when to go: *Turn right at **the lights**.*

PHRASES

see something in a new light, see something in a different light to have a different idea about something because of something that happens: *After talking to my mother, I **saw** things **in a different light**.*

shed light on something, throw light on something to explain something or make it easier to understand: *They got some new information that **shed light** on the accident.*

light² *adjective*
1 if it is light, it is daytime and there is enough light to see ANTONYM **dark**: *We need to finish the game while **it is** still **light**.*
2 a light colour is not very strong or not very dark: *a light grey shirt*
3 a light room is full of light from the sun ANTONYM **dark**: *The living room is very light because it has a large window.*
4 not heavy: *These small computers are light and easy to carry.* → see picture at HEAVY

5 not very thick or warm: *Just bring a light jacket.*
6 if traffic is light, there are not many cars and other vehicles on the road ANTONYM **heavy**
7 gentle or without much force ANTONYM **heavy**: *A light rain began to fall.* • *I gave him a light tap on the shoulder.*

THESAURUS
pale: *This plant has* ***pale*** *pink flowers* (=light).
pastel: *You look good in* ***pastel*** *colours* (=light).
faded: *She wore* ***faded*** *jeans* (=having gradually lost their colour).

light³ *verb* (past tense and past participle **lit** /lɪt/ or **lighted**)
1 to start burning, or to make something start burning: *I can't get this wood to light.* • *He lit his pipe and began to smoke.*
2 also **light up** to make a place become light or bright: *Orange lights lit the stage.* • *A sudden flash of lightning lit up the whole sky.*
3 someone's face lights up, someone's eyes light up used to say that someone suddenly looks happy or excited: *Paula's eyes lit up when she saw all the presents.*

'light bulb *noun* a round glass and metal object that produces light from electricity: *Sue changed the light bulb* (=put in a new one).

light·er /ˈlaɪtə $ ˈlaɪtɚ/ *noun* a small object that produces a flame to light a cigarette

light·house /ˈlaɪthaʊs/ *noun* a tower with a bright light that warns ships of danger

light·ing /ˈlaɪtɪŋ/ *noun* the lights in a place, or the way a place is lit: *Soft lighting creates a romantic mood.*

light·ly /ˈlaɪtli/ *adverb* without using a lot of force SYNONYM **gently**: *I tapped him lightly on the shoulder.*

light·ning /ˈlaɪtnɪŋ/ *noun* (no plural) a bright flash of electrical light in the sky during a storm: *There was thunder and lightning.* → see picture on page A13

SPELLING
This word is often spelled wrongly. The correct spelling is: **lightning**.

likable *adjective* another spelling of LIKEABLE

like¹ /laɪk/ *verb*

KEY PATTERNS
like someone/something
like doing something
like to do something
like something about someone/something
like it when something happens

to think that someone or something is nice or good ANTONYM **dislike**: *Katie likes John a lot.* • *I think you would* ***really like*** *this movie.* • *Katherine likes playing basketball.* • *I* ***like to*** *go jogging at weekends.* • *What* ***do you like*** *best about teaching?* • *I* ***don't like it when*** *Dave doesn't come home on time.*

PHRASES
I would like, I'd like ... (spoken) say this to tell someone politely what you want or what you want to do: *I'd like a glass of milk, please.* • *I'd* ***like to*** *talk to Jim first.* • *I* ***would*** *really* ***like to*** *get some sleep.* • *Mr Robbins* ***would like*** *you* ***to*** *come to the meeting.*
would you like ...? (spoken) say this to ask someone politely if they want something: ***Would you like*** *a cup of tea?* • ***Would*** *Dana* ***like to*** *come with us?* • *What* ***would you like*** *for dinner?*

GRAMMAR
Like is not used in the progressive.
✘ Don't say 'I'm liking'.

THESAURUS
love: *She loves chocolate* (=likes it very much).
prefer: *I prefer the blue dress* (=like it more than the other ones).

like² *preposition*
1 if one thing or person is like another, it is almost the same as the other person or thing: *I'd love to have a car like Diane's.* • *His new film is a lot like his last one.* • *It* ***tastes*** *a little* ***like*** *chicken.* • *Harry* ***looks like*** *his dad.*
→ see Thesaurus at SIMILAR
2 used to give examples of something you are talking about SYNONYM **such as**: *Vegetables like broccoli and carrots are very good for you.* • *Games like chess take a long time to learn.*
3 what is someone/something like? say this to ask someone to describe a person, place, or thing: ***What was the***

A B C D E F G H I J K L M N O P Q R S T U V W X Y Z

movie **like**? • **What does** *Robbie* **look like**? *Is he tall?* • *They asked* **what it was like** *to work for an MP.*

like³ *noun* **someone's likes and dislikes** the things someone likes and the things they do not like: *What are your girlfriend's likes and dislikes?*

like⁴ *conjunction* (spoken) **1** as if: *He talks like he's American.* **2** in the same way as: *Do it just like I said.*

like·a·ble, **likable** /ˈlaɪkəbəl/ *adjective* likeable people are nice and easy to like: *Jo's a very likeable girl.*

like·li·hood /ˈlaɪklihʊd/ *noun* (no plural) how likely something is to happen SYNONYM **probability**: *What's the likelihood of you passing your exams?*

like·ly /ˈlaɪkli/ *adjective* (**likelier, likeliest**)

> KEY PATTERNS
> **likely to do something**
> **it is likely (that)**

1 if something is likely to happen, it will probably happen: *Rain is likely this afternoon.* • *Ruth* **is not likely to** *make many mistakes.* • **It's likely that** *he will have to miss Tuesday's game.*
2 if something is likely, it is probably true: *She thinks he has stolen her purse, but that's not very likely.* • **Is it likely that** *John is lying?*

like·ness /ˈlaɪknəs/ *noun* (no plural) if there is a likeness between two people, they look similar to each other SYNONYM **resemblance**: *The likeness between Sara and her mother is incredible.*

lil·y /ˈlɪli/ *noun* a large white or coloured flower: *He gave me a beautiful bunch of lilies.* ➔ see picture on page A10

limb /lɪm/ *noun* an arm or leg: *Have you ever broken a limb?*

> PRONUNCIATION
> In this word you do not pronounce the **b**.

lime /laɪm/ *noun* a bright green fruit with a sour taste ➔ see picture on page A7

lime·light /ˈlaɪmlaɪt/ *noun* **be in the limelight** (informal) if you are in the limelight, you have the attention of a lot of people: *Geri loves being in the limelight.*

lim·it¹ /ˈlɪmɪt/ *noun*

> KEY PATTERNS
> **a limit on/to something**

the greatest amount, number, or speed that is allowed or possible: *Is there a* **limit on** *the amount of money you can borrow?* • *The* **speed limit** *is 30 miles per hour on this road.*

limit² *verb*

> KEY PATTERNS
> **limit something (to a particular amount)**
> **limit someone to a particular amount**
> **be limited to a place**

1 to keep something at or below a particular amount or number: *Try to limit the amount of salt you eat.* • *We* **are limiting** *the working week* **to** *35 hours.*
2 to allow someone to have or use only a particular amount of something SYNONYM **restrict**: *She* **has limited** *us* **to** *only one piece of cake each.* • *Fans will* **be limited to** *two tickets each.*
3 if something is limited to a place, it only exists or happens there SYNONYM **restrict**: *Her injuries* **were limited to** *her back.*

lim·i·ta·tions /ˌlɪməˈteɪʃənz/ *plural noun* the limits of what someone or something is able to do: *You have to understand the limitations of the software.*

lim·it·ed /ˈlɪmətɪd/ *adjective* small in amount or number: *There are only a limited number of tickets.*

lim·ou·sine /ˈlɪməziːn/ *noun* a big expensive car in which someone is driven somewhere: *He arrived at the party in a black limousine.*

limp /lɪmp/ *verb* to walk with difficulty because one leg is hurt: *He had hurt his leg and was limping badly.* —**limp** *noun*: *Sue walks with a limp.*

line¹ /laɪn/ *noun*
1 a long thin mark on a surface: *Draw a line under the title.* • *Someone had put a line through* (=crossed out) *my name.* • *Which runner crossed the finishing line first?*
2 a number of people or things behind or next to each other: *Ian went straight*

to the front of the line. • *The line of cars moved slowly forward.*
3 a long piece of rope, string, or wire that is used for a particular purpose: *Sally hung the wet clothes on the line.*
4 the connection between two telephones: *Stay* ***on the line*** *while I try and find Maxine.* • *I have been* ***holding the line*** (=waiting to speak to someone) *for twenty minutes.*
5 a track for trains to travel along: *the main line between London and Edinburgh*
6 a group of words in a poem, play, or song: *Actors spend a long time* ***learning their lines.***

PHRASES
on line using a computer that is connected to other computers: *You can book tickets* ***on line.***

> **THESAURUS**
> **stripe**: *a tie with blue and white* ***stripes*** (=neat lines of colour)
> **streak**: *There was a* ***streak*** *of dirt across his forehead* (=a rough line).

line² *verb* **1** to cover the inside of something with a material: *Line the drawers with paper.* **2** if people or things line something, they are in rows along the edges: *Cheering children lined the streets.* **3 line up** if people line up, they move to form a line: *The children lined up at the door.*

lined /laɪnd/ *adjective* lined paper has straight lines printed on it

lin·en /ˈlɪnən/ *noun* (no plural) a high quality cloth like thick strong cotton: *a blue linen jacket*

lin·ger /ˈlɪŋgə $ ˈlɪŋgɚ/ *verb* to stay somewhere for a long time: *The smell of cigarettes lingered in the room.*

lin·guis·tic /lɪŋˈgwɪstɪk/ *adjective* related to language, or to people's use of language: *The children had different linguistic abilities.*

lin·ing /ˈlaɪnɪŋ/ *noun* a piece of material that covers the inside of a piece of clothing: *The lining of her coat was torn.*

link¹ /lɪŋk/ *verb* **1** to join one place or thing to another SYNONYM **connect**: *The bridge links the two sides of the town.* **2** to decide that there is a connection between different situations, events, or people: *Scientists have linked cancer with smoking.*

link² *noun* **1** a relationship or connection between different situations, events, or people: *There is a link between crime and unemployment.*
2 one of the rings in a chain

li·on /ˈlaɪən/ *noun* a large African and Asian wild cat: *The male lion has long thick hair around his neck.* → see picture on page A9

lip /lɪp/ *noun* one of the two edges of your mouth where the skin is redder or darker: *Her lips curved into a smile.* → see picture on page A5

lip·stick /ˈlɪpˌstɪk/ *noun* a coloured substance that some women wear on their lips: *She put on some red lipstick.*

liq·uid /ˈlɪkwɪd/ *noun* a substance such as water which flows and is not solid or a gas: *The nurse cleaned the wound with a clear liquid.*

liq·uor /ˈlɪkə $ ˈlɪkɚ/ *noun AmE* a strong alcoholic drink such as WHISKY: *I could smell liquor on his breath.*

list¹ /lɪst/ *noun*

> **KEY PATTERNS**
> **a list of things**
> **be on a list**
> **make/write a list**

a number of different things that you write one below the other: *I need a* ***list of*** *the people coming to the party.* • *What is the first item* ***on your list****?* • *Why don't you* ***make a shopping list****?*

list² *verb* to write a list: *List all the subjects you are studying.*

lis·ten /ˈlɪsən/ *verb*
1 to pay attention to what someone is saying, or to music or other sounds: *He kept talking but she wasn't listening.* • *I like* ***listening to*** *all kinds of music.* • *She was* ***listening to*** *the news on the car radio.*
2 Listen! (spoken) used when telling someone to listen carefully to what you are saying, especially because it is important, or you feel annoyed: *Listen, all of you! It's time to go home!* • *Listen! I'm not going to give you any more money!*

A B C D E F G H I J K L M N O P Q R S T U V W X Y Z

PHRASAL VERBS
listen for
to try to hear a particular sound: *He stopped by the door and* ***listened for*** *the sound of footsteps.* • *The dog was* ***listening for*** *his master.*
listen up (spoken)
used when you want everyone in a room to pay attention to what you are going to say: *Hey everybody,* ***listen up!*** *I have an announcement to make.*

WORD CHOICE
listen or **hear**?
• **Listen** means "to pay attention to what someone is saying, or to music or other sounds": *He was* ***listening to*** *music in his bedroom.*
• **Hear** means "to notice a sound with your ears": *I* ***heard*** *the doorbell.*

GRAMMAR
You say **listen to music** or **listen to someone**.
✗ Don't say 'listen music' or 'listen someone'.

PRONUNCIATION
In this word you do not pronounce the **t**.

lis·ten·er /ˈlɪsənə $ ˈlɪsənɚ/ *noun* someone who listens to something or someone: *Most of the radio station's listeners are young people.* • *Mary's a good listener.*

lit a past tense and past participle of LIGHT[3]

liter the American spelling of LITRE

lit·e·ral·ly /ˈlɪtərəli/ *adverb*
1 according to the basic or first meaning of a word: *'Television' literally means 'seeing at a distance'.* **2** used to emphasize that what you are saying is true even if it seems unlikely: *I was literally weak with hunger.*

lit·e·ra·ry /ˈlɪtərəri $ ˈlɪtəˌreri/ *adjective* related to literature: *She won a literary prize for her first book.*

lit·e·ra·ture /ˈlɪtərətʃə $ ˈlɪtərətʃɚ/ *noun* (no plural) books, poems, and plays that are well written and considered to be good and important: *I'm interested in French literature.*

li·tre *BrE*, **liter** *AmE* /ˈliːtə $ ˈliːtɚ/ *noun* a unit for measuring liquid: *a litre of water*

lit·ter[1] /ˈlɪtə $ ˈlɪtɚ/ *noun* (no plural) waste paper, cans etc that people leave on the ground: *The streets were covered in litter.* ➔ see Thesaurus at RUBBISH

litter

litter[2] *verb* if a lot of things litter a place, they are spread all over it in an untidy way: *The desk was littered with old letters.*

lit·tle[1] /ˈlɪtl/ *adjective*
1 small in size ANTONYM **large**: *Look at that little baby.* • *a* ***tiny little*** *insect*
➔ see Thesaurus at SMALL
2 continuing for a short time: *There might be a little wait before you can see the doctor.* • *We'll be back in a* ***little while*** (=a short time).
3 not very far: *Let's go for a little walk.*
4 not important: *We only had one little problem.*

little[2] *determiner, pronoun* (**less** /les/ **least** /liːst/)
(formal) not much: *Little has been done to improve the situation.* • *There's* ***very little*** *work to do.*
PHRASES
a little, a little bit a) a small amount of something: *Can I have* ***a little bit*** *of cheese?* • *"Would you like some cake?" "Just* ***a little****."* **b)** slightly: *My back still hurts* ***a little****.*

WORD CHOICE
a little or **a few**?
• You use **a little** about a small amount of something: *I only want a little sugar.*
• You use **a few** about a small number of things or people: *Only a few people came to the party.*

live[1] /lɪv/ *verb*

KEY PATTERNS
live in/at a place

1 if you live in a place, that place is your home: *Where do you live?* • *I* ***live at*** *12 Queen Street.* • *She* ***lives in*** *London.*
2 to continue to be alive: *He doesn't seem to care if I live or die.* • *My grandfather lived until he was 90.*

3 to have a particular kind of life: *Rock stars live exciting lives.*

PHRASAL VERBS

live on, live off

1 live on/off something if you live on or off a small amount of money, you only have that amount to buy all the things that you need: *How can I **live on** £30 a week?*

2 live on/off something to eat only a particular kind of food: *These animals **live on** leaves and fruit.* • *She **lives on** pizza.*

live together

if two people live together, they live in the same house and have a sexual relationship, but they are not married: *We **lived together** for two years before getting married.*

live with

1 live with someone to live in the same house as someone: *How long have you **lived with** your brother?*

2 live with someone to live in the same house as someone and have a sexual relationship with them, without being married: *He's my boyfriend, but I don't want to **live with** him yet.*

> **WORD CHOICE**
> **live** or **stay**?
> • You use **live** when talking about being in a place permanently or for a long time: *I've **lived** in Spain all my life.*
> • You use **stay** when talking about being in a place for a short time: *I'm **staying** with my sister for a few weeks while I find an apartment.*

live² /laɪv/ *adjective*

1 live animals are alive ANTONYM **dead**: *I've never seen a live snake.*

2 if a television or radio programme is live, you see it or hear it at the same time as it happens: *Many things can go wrong in a live broadcast.*

3 live music is performed for people who are watching and listening in the same place: *You can see the band live tomorrow night.*

> **PRONUNCIATION**
> Be careful how you pronounce this word:
> **live¹** (*verb*) is pronounced like 'give'
> **live²** (*adjective*) is pronounced like 'dive'

live•li•hood /ˈlaɪvlihʊd/ *noun* the job that you do to earn money in order to live: *Painting is my livelihood.*

live•ly /ˈlaɪvli/ *adjective* (**livelier, liveliest**) full of activity: *a group of lively six-year-olds* • *The town becomes livelier at night when people go out to clubs.*

liv•en /ˈlaɪvən/ *verb* **liven something up** to make something more interesting or exciting: *We need some music to liven the party up.*

liv•er /ˈlɪvə $ ˈlɪvɚ/ *noun* **1** a large part inside your body that cleans your blood **2** (no plural) the liver of an animal that people eat as food: *lamb's liver*

lives the plural of LIFE

liv•id /ˈlɪvɪd/ *adjective* extremely angry SYNONYM **furious**: *My mother was livid when she saw the mess.*

liv•ing¹ /ˈlɪvɪŋ/ *adjective* **1** alive now ANTONYM **dead**: *Who is your favourite living author?* **2 living things** things that are alive, such as animals and plants

living² *noun* the way that you earn money in order to live, or the money that you earn: *She earns a living by giving music lessons.*

ˈliving room *noun* the main room in a house, where you relax by watching television, listening to music, reading etc SYNONYM **lounge** *BrE*

liz•ard /ˈlɪzəd $ ˈlɪzɚd/ *noun* a type of REPTILE that has four short legs, a long tail, and skin like a snake

load¹ /ləʊd $ loʊd/ *noun*

an amount of something that a vehicle carries: *a train carrying a **load of** coal* • *A lorry has **shed its load** on the motorway* (=its load has fallen off).

PHRASES

a load of something

(spoken) a lot of something: *We have a **load of** prizes to give away.*

load

We loaded the boxes into the van.

A B C D E F G H I J K L M N O P Q R S T U V W X Y Z

loads (of something) (spoken) a lot of something: *His father earns* ***loads of*** *money.* • *You can have one of my pens – I've got* ***loads****.*
a load of rubbish, a load of nonsense (spoken) used to say that something is completely wrong or very stupid: *Don't listen to what she says – it's* ***a load of nonsense****.*

load[2] *verb*

KEY PATTERNS
load something onto/into a car/truck etc
load software onto a computer

1 also **load up** to put a lot of things into a vehicle ANTONYM **unload**: *Will you help me load the car?* • *We* ***loaded*** *the wood* ***onto*** *the back of the truck.* • *The boxes* ***are*** *then* ***loaded into*** *vans.* • *It took us ages to* ***load up*** *the van.*
2 to put a program into a computer: *You need to* ***load*** *the software* ***onto*** *your computer.*
3 to put a film into a camera: *I just need to load a new film and then I'll be ready to take the pictures.*
4 to put bullets into a gun

load•ed /ˈləʊdɪd $ ˈloʊdɪd/ *adjective*
1 a loaded weapon is one that contains bullets: *Is the gun loaded?*
2 if something is loaded with things, it has a lot of them on it or in it: *The shelves were loaded with books.*

loaf /ləʊf $ loʊf/ *noun* (plural **loaves** /ləʊvz $ loʊvz/) bread that has been baked in one large piece: *I bought a loaf of bread.*

loan[1] /ləʊn $ loʊn/ *noun*
an amount of money that you borrow: *We* ***took out a loan*** *to buy our new car.* • *We're never going to be able to* ***pay back*** *this* ***loan****.*
PHRASES
be on loan if something is on loan, you have borrowed it from somewhere: *This book* ***is on loan from*** *the library.*

loan[2] *verb* to lend someone something, especially money: *I'll loan you the money.*

loathe /ləʊð $ loʊð/ *verb* to hate someone or something very much SYNONYM **detest**: *I loathe shopping.* ➔ see Thesaurus at HATE[1]

loaves the plural of LOAF

lob•by /ˈlɒbi $ ˈlɑbi/ *noun* (plural **lobbies**) a large area inside the entrance of a building SYNONYM **foyer**: *I'll meet you in the theatre lobby.*

lo•cal[1] /ˈləʊkəl $ ˈloʊkəl/ *adjective*
1 a local place is one near to the place where you live: *You can now get these fruits in your local supermarket.* **2** a local person lives in a particular area or in the same area as you: *The local residents do not want the factory built near them.* —**locally** *adverb*: *People who live locally can also attend the college.* ➔ see Thesaurus at NEARBY

local[2] *noun* someone who lives in a place: *It's a lovely village and the locals are very friendly.*

lo•cate /ləʊˈkeɪt $ ˈloʊkeɪt/ *verb* (formal) **1** to find the exact position of something: *We need to locate the gas pipe.* ➔ see Thesaurus at FIND **2 be located** to be in a particular place or position SYNONYM **be situated**: *The engine is located in the front of the car.*

lo•ca•tion /ləʊˈkeɪʃən $ loʊˈkeɪʃən/ *noun* (formal) the place or position where someone or something is: *What is your exact location?*

lock[1] /lɒk $ lɑk/ *verb*

KEY PATTERNS
lock someone in/out of a place

1 to fasten something with a lock ANTONYM **unlock**: *He closed the door and then locked it.* • *I accidentally* ***locked*** *myself* ***in*** *the bathroom* (=I locked the door and was unable to get out). • *She* ***locked*** *me* ***out of*** *the house* (=she locked the door so I could not get in).
2 if a part of a machine locks, it becomes fixed in one position and unable to move: *The brakes locked, causing him to crash.*
PHRASAL VERBS
lock up
1 lock up, lock something up to make a building safe by locking all the doors: *Don't forget to* ***lock up*** *before you go home.* • *They* ***had locked*** *the house* ***up*** *and gone away.*
2 lock someone up to put someone in prison: *They should* ***lock*** *him* ***up*** *for what he did.*

lock² *noun*
1 a metal part of a door that you use to keep the door closed. You usually open a lock with a key: *Was there a lock on the door?*
2 (formal) a small number of hairs that are growing together on your head: *She sat twisting **a lock of hair** around her finger.*

lock·er /ˈlɒkə $ ˈlɑkɚ/ *noun* a small cupboard where you leave books, clothes etc, for example at school: *I've left my pen in my locker.*

lodg·er /ˈlɒdʒə $ ˈlɑdʒɚ/ *noun BrE* someone who lives in someone else's house and pays rent

loft /lɒft $ lɔft/ *noun BrE* a room or space under the roof of a house SYNONYM **attic**: *Our old photographs are in the loft.*

log¹ /lɒg $ lɔg/ *noun* a thick piece of wood that has been cut from a tree: *Put another log on the fire.* → see picture on page A10

log² *verb* (**logged**, **logging**) **1** to make an official record of events or facts: *We log all our telephone calls.* **2 log off, log out** to stop using a computer **3 log on, log in** to start using a computer: *I logged on and read my emails.*

lo·gic /ˈlɒdʒɪk $ ˈlɑdʒɪk/ *noun* (no plural) a sensible way of thinking: *There does not seem to be any logic in what they are planning to do.*

lo·gic·al /ˈlɒdʒɪkəl $ ˈlɑdʒɪkəl/ *adjective* reasonable and sensible ANTONYM **illogical**: *There's no logical reason for you to be jealous.*
—**logically** /-kli/ *adverb*: *Let's think about this logically.*

lo·go /ˈləʊgəʊ $ ˈloʊgoʊ/ *noun* a design that is the official sign of a company or organization and goes on their products, letters etc

lone·ly /ˈləʊnli $ ˈloʊnli/ *adjective* (**lonelier**, **loneliest**)
1 unhappy because you are alone: *I felt really **lonely** while my parents were away. • Don't you ever **get lonely** living by yourself?*
2 (written) a lonely place is somewhere that very few people visit: *They arranged to meet on a lonely road near the beach.*

lon·er /ˈləʊnə $ ˈloʊnɚ/ *noun* someone who likes being alone

long¹ /lɒŋ $ lɔŋ/ *adjective* (**longer** /ˈlɒŋgə $ ˈlɔŋgɚ/, **longest** /ˈlɒŋgəst $ ˈlɔŋgəst/)
1 something that is long measures a large distance from one end to the other ANTONYM **short**: *She's tall and slim, with long legs. • a long piece of string • It's **a long way** from here to the beach.*
2 continuing for a great amount of time ANTONYM **short**: *The chemistry lesson seemed very long. • We had to wait quite **a long time**.*
3 used to talk about the length of something: *Our garden is about 50 metres long. • **How long** is the film?*

long² *adverb*
a great amount of time: *Have you lived here long? • They hadn't been married **for long**. • Where have you been? I've been waiting so long! • I'm going to the shops but I'll try not to be long.*

PHRASES
as long as if: *We're going to the beach tomorrow, **as long as** the weather's nice.*
no longer, not any longer used to say that something has stopped happening or cannot continue: *My brother **no longer** goes to the same school as me. • We can't wait **any longer**.*

long³ *verb* (formal) to want something very much: *I longed to go to America.*

ˈlong-ˌdistance *adjective* travelling or happening between places that are a long distance apart: *She made a long-distance phone call.*

long·ing /ˈlɒŋɪŋ $ ˈlɔŋɪŋ/ *noun* (written) a feeling of wanting something very much SYNONYM **desire**: *Her longing to see her mother increased.*
—**longingly** *adverb*: *She looked longingly at the ice cream.*

ˈlong jump *noun* a sport in which you jump as far as possible: *She's quite good at the long jump.*

long·sight·ed /ˌlɒŋˈsaɪtɪd $ ˌlɔŋˈsaɪtɪd/ *adjective BrE* someone who is longsighted can only see things clearly when they are far away SYNONYM **farsighted** *AmE* ANTONYM **shortsighted** *BrE*, ANTONYM **nearsighted** *AmE*

ˌlong-ˈstanding *adjective* a long-standing problem or situation has

A B C D E F G H I J K L M N O P Q R S T U V W X Y Z

existed for a long time: *The two companies have a long-standing business relationship.*

ˈ**long-term** *adjective* a long-term plan or situation is connected with a time that is a long time in the future ANTONYM **short-term**: *We don't know about the long-term effects of using drugs.*

loo /luː/ *noun BrE* (informal) a toilet

look¹ → see box on pages 398 and 399

look² *noun*

KEY PATTERNS
take/have a look (at something)
have a look for something
give someone a look

1 when you look at something: *Take a look at this photo.* • *What's in the box – can I have a look?*
2 when you search for something: *Will you **have a look for** my keys?*
3 when you look at someone in a way that shows how you feel: *He **gave her** a surprised **look**.*
4 an expression on someone's face: *She had a puzzled look on her face.*
5 a particular fashion or type of appearance: *How do you like my new look?*
6 looks someone's appearance and how attractive they are: *You shouldn't judge a person by their looks.* • *a young man with charm and good looks*

look·out /ˈlʊk-aʊt/ *noun* **be on the lookout for something** to pay attention to things around you because you hope to see or find something: *I'm always on the lookout for good, cheap clothes.*

loom /luːm/ *verb* **1** (written) to appear as a large unclear shape: *The church loomed ahead of us.* **2** if a difficult situation looms, it is likely to happen soon: *Exams are looming.*

loop¹ /luːp/ *noun* a shape like a circle in a piece of string, wire etc: *Make a loop with the wire.*

loop² *verb* to make a loop or to tie something with a loop: *He looped the rope over the cow's head.*

loop

loop·hole /ˈluːphəʊl $ ˈluphoʊl/ *noun* a small mistake in a law that makes it possible to legally avoid doing what the law says: *Because of a loophole in the law, he pays no tax.*

loose /luːs/ *adjective*
1 clothes that are loose are big and do not fit you tightly SYNONYM **baggy** ANTONYM **tight**: *These jeans are a bit loose. Have you got a smaller size?* • *She was wearing trousers and a loose sweater.*
2 not firmly fixed in place: *There's a loose button on my jacket that needs sewing on.* • *Some of the screws **had come loose**.*
3 not fastened together or kept together in a container: *His desk was covered with loose pieces of paper.*
—**loosely** *adverb*

loos·en /ˈluːsən/ *verb* to make something less tight ANTONYM **tighten**: *I loosened my belt.*

loot /luːt/ *verb* to steal things during a war or another time of violence: *They looted shops and burned cars.*

lop·sid·ed /ˌlɒpˈsaɪdɪd $ ˌlɑpˈsaɪdɪd/ *adjective* something that is lopsided has one side that is heavier or lower than the other

Lord /lɔːd $ lɔrd/ *noun* a title for God or Jesus Christ: *Praise the Lord.*

lord /lɔːd $ lɔrd/ *noun* a man who has a high social rank in Britain

lor·ry /ˈlɒri $ ˈlɔri/ *noun BrE* (plural **lorries**) a large heavy vehicle for carrying things SYNONYM **truck** *AmE*: *The lorry was carrying bricks.* → see picture on page A11

lose /luːz/ *verb* (past tense and past participle **lost** /lɒst $ lɔst/)

KEY PATTERNS
lose to an opponent

1 if you lose something, you stop knowing where it is and cannot find it: *I was worried I might lose my camera if I took it on the trip.* • *I've lost my pen – have you seen it anywhere?*
2 if you lose something, you stop having it: *When the factory closed, 500 people **lost** their **jobs**.* • *He **lost** a lot of **money** by making bad business decisions.*
3 to not win a game, competition, or fight ANTONYM **win**: *The government lost*

lose

I have lost weight.

Dad lost his temper.

*the **election**. • We've only **lost** three **games** all season. • Manchester United **lost to** Leeds.*

PHRASES

lose weight: *You **lose weight*** (=become lighter) *by eating less and exercising more.*

lose your temper: *Dad **lost** his **temper*** (=became angry) *and started to shout.*

lose interest: *Kate's 16 now and she's **lost interest in** horses* (=is not interested in horses any more).

lose touch with someone to gradually stop meeting or talking to someone: *I **lost touch with** my old friends when I moved to a new school.*

> **SPELLING**
> Don't confuse the spelling of **lose** and **loose** (=not tight).

los·er /ˈluːzə $ ˈluzɚ/ *noun*
1 someone who loses a competition or game ANTONYM **winner**: *The loser has to buy everyone a drink.* **2** (informal) someone who is never successful in life, work, or relationships

loss /lɒs $ lɔs/ *noun* (plural **losses**)

> **KEY PATTERNS**
> **the loss of something/someone**
> **a company makes a loss**

1 when you stop having something: *There have been many **job losses** in banking. • How will he cope with **the loss of** his sight?*
2 (no plural) the death of someone: *They couldn't bear to talk about **the loss of** their son.*
3 if a business makes a loss, it spends more money than it gets ANTONYM **profit**: *The company **made a loss** of about $43,000 last year.*

lost¹ /lɒst $ lɔst/ *adjective*
1 if you are lost, or get lost, you do not know where you are: *After walking for several hours, we realized that we were lost. • It was such a big building that I **got lost** in it!*
2 if something is lost, or gets lost, you cannot find it: *My suitcase **got lost** and I had no more money or clothes.*

PHRASES

Get lost! (spoken) used to rudely tell someone to go away

lost² the past tense and past participle of LOSE

lot /lɒt $ lɑt/ *noun*
1 a lot also **lots** (informal) **a)** a large amount or number: *A million dollars is **a lot of** money. • **Lots of** my friends have pets. • I've learned **a lot** in the last few months.* **b)** very much: *He's **a lot** nicer than he used to be. • I like Kelly **a lot**.* **c)** often: *That kind of thing happens **a lot**.* → see Thesaurus at OFTEN
2 the lot (informal) the whole of an amount: *If I don't put these crisps away, I'll eat **the lot**!*

lo·tion /ˈləʊʃən $ ˈloʊʃən/ *noun* a liquid that you put on your skin in order to make it soft or to protect it: *a bottle of suntan lotion*

lot·te·ry /ˈlɒtəri $ ˈlɑtəri/ *noun* (plural **lotteries**) a competition in which people choose a set of numbers and win money if they have chosen the winning numbers: *What would you do if you won the lottery?*

loud¹ /laʊd/ *adjective*
something that is loud makes a lot of noise ANTONYM **quiet**: *Turn that music down! It's too loud! • I could hear loud voices arguing.* —**loudly** *adverb*: *"Stop!" she shouted loudly.*

loud² *adverb* **1** loudly: *Can you speak louder?* **2 out loud** if you read or say something out loud, you say it so that people can hear you: *I asked her to read the poem out loud.*

loud·speak·er /ˌlaʊdˈspiːkə $ ˈlaʊdˌspikɚ/ *noun* a piece of equipment that makes sound louder: *the loudspeakers of his stereo system*

lounge¹ /laʊndʒ/ *noun* **1** a room in a hotel or airport, where people can sit and relax: *He's in the TV lounge.*
2 *BrE* a LIVING ROOM

lounge² *verb* **1** to stand or sit somewhere in a relaxed way: *I was just*

look /lʊk/ *verb*

1 to turn your eyes towards someone or something in order to see them: *"You're late!" he said,* ***looking at*** *his watch. •* ***Look,*** *there's Mark and the kids. • Mrs Mitchell stood* ***looking through*** *the window. • Zack* ***looked up*** (=turned his head upwards) *in surprise as she walked in. • Tina came into the restaurant and* ***looked around*** (=turned her head and looked in all directions).

KEY PATTERNS

look at someone/something
look out of/through a window
look up/down/around

GRAMMAR

• You **look at someone.**
✗ Don't say 'look someone'.

look

2 to use your eyes to try to find someone or something: *Stella was here a few minutes ago – she was* ***looking for*** *Max. •* ***Look in*** *the red box – I think it's in there. • I spent a long time* ***looking****, but I couldn't find anything I really liked.*

KEY PATTERNS

look for something/someone
look in a place

3 to have a particular appearance: *You* ***look*** *tired! Have you had a hard day? • The rooms* ***looked*** *really dirty. • David* ***looks*** *a lot like his grandfather. • He's over 60 years old, but he only* ***looks*** *50. • They* ***look*** *like bananas, but they're not.*

KEY PATTERNS

look happy/sad/good/clean
look like someone/something

GRAMMAR

• You say **She looks like her mother.**
✗ Don't say 'She is looking like her mother.'

WORD CHOICE

look at, **see**, or **watch**?

• You **look at** a picture, person, or thing deliberately, because you want to. You usually look at things that are not moving: *We **looked at** the map.* • *The man was **looking at** me.* • ***Look at** the view!*

• You **see** something or someone accidentally, or because you are trying to find them: *We **saw** some beautiful flowers.* • *I can't **see** her anywhere.*

• You **watch** television, a film, an event, or a person. You usually watch things that are moving: *I like **watching** baseball.* • *I **watched** him get out of the car.* • *We spent the evening **watching** TV.* • *We **watched** television for a couple of hours.*

✗ Don't say 'We looked at the television.'
Say **We watched television**.

*Jane can't **see** anything.*

*They are **looking at** the pictures.*

*Richard is **watching** TV.*

PHRASAL VERBS

look after
to do things to make sure that someone or something is safe and well SYNONYM **take care of**: *She **looks after** her sister's children during the week.* • *Their son is **looking after** the farm while they're away.*

look around
to look at different things in a place, in order to find out more about it: *We spent a few hours **looking around** the museum.* • *Kelly and Maria went to the mall to **look around**.*

look back (on/over something)
to think about something that happened in the past: ***Looking back**, I think I made the wrong decision.* • *In his book, he **looks back over** his political career.*

look forward to (doing) something
to be happy because you know that you are going to do something soon: *I'm **looking forward to** seeing my family again.*

GRAMMAR

• You **look forward to doing something**.

✗ Don't say 'look forward to do something'.

look out
to be careful: ***Look out**! People drive very quickly here.*

look out for
to pay attention and try to see someone or something: *I'll **look out for** him when I'm at the station.*

look up
to find information in a book, on a computer etc: *Frances **looked up** some information about him on the web.* • *If you don't know the meaning of a word, **look it up** in a dictionary.*

lounging on the sofa. **2 lounge about, lounge around** *BrE* to be lazy and waste your time doing nothing: *Stop lounging around and do some work!*

lou•sy /ˈlaʊzi/ *adjective* (informal) (**lousier**, **lousiest**) very bad SYNONYM **terrible**: *The food was lousy.*

lov•a•ble, **loveable** /ˈlʌvəbəl/ *adjective* a lovable person or animal is very nice and easy to love

love¹ /lʌv/ *verb*

KEY PATTERNS
love doing something
love to do something

1 to like someone and care about them a lot ANTONYM **hate**: *Anna says she loves Steve and wants to marry him.* • *I really love my mum and dad.*
2 to like something a lot ANTONYM **hate**: *I love that dress you're wearing!*
➔ see Thesaurus at LIKE¹
3 to enjoy doing something very much ANTONYM **hate**: *Adam loves playing computer games.* • *I'd* **love to** *go clubbing.*

love² *noun*

KEY PATTERNS
someone's love for someone
a love of something

1 (no plural) a very strong feeling that you have for someone you like and care about a lot ANTONYM **hate**, **hatred**: *Her* **love for** *her children was obvious.*
2 when you like or enjoy doing something very much ANTONYM **hatred**: *Tom has a great* **love of** *travel.*

PHRASES
be in love, fall in love if you are in love with someone, you love them in a romantic way: *Everyone could see that she* **was in love with** *Nick.* • *Simon realized that he* **was falling in love with** *Maria* (=starting to love Maria).
make love to have sex with someone
love from, love you use this at the end of a letter to a friend or a member of your family: *I'll write again soon.* **Love** *from Mum.*

love•ly /ˈlʌvli/ *adjective* very nice, attractive, or pleasant: *She has a lovely face.* • *I've had a lovely day.*

lov•er /ˈlʌvə $ ˈlʌvɚ/ *noun*
1 someone who has a sexual relationship with another person: *She had secret meetings with her lover.*
2 someone who enjoys something very much: *Rick is a film lover.*

lov•ing /ˈlʌvɪŋ/ *adjective* behaving in a gentle kind way that shows you love someone: *His loving wife looked after him while he was ill.* —**lovingly** *adverb*: *He looked lovingly into her face.*

low

a low wall

shallow water

low /ləʊ $ loʊ/ *adjective*
1 something that is low is not high, or not far above the ground: *The house was surrounded by a low wall.* • *There was a low branch that I could climb onto.*
2 below the usual level, amount, or standard ANTONYM **high**: *It was an unpleasant job and the pay was low.* • *My exam results were lower than usual.*
3 a low voice or sound is quiet or deep ANTONYM **high**: *They were in the kitchen, talking in low voices.* ➔ see Thesaurus at QUIET¹

low•er¹ /ˈləʊə $ ˈloʊɚ/ *adjective* below a higher part ANTONYM **upper**: *The lower half of the building was made of stone.* • *She had pains in her lower back.*

lower² *verb* **1** to make an amount less: *I wish they'd lower the price.* ➔ see Thesaurus at REDUCE **2** to move something down ANTONYM **raise**: *The men lowered the ship's lifeboats into the water.*

ˌ**lower case** *noun* (no plural) letters written in their small form, for example

A B C D E F G H I J K L M N O P Q R S T U V W X Y Z

a, b, c ANTONYM **upper case**, **capitals**: *Her email address is written in lower case.*

ˌlower ˈclass *noun* **the lower class, the lower classes** the people in society who have less money or power than anyone else —**lower class** *adjective*

loy·al /ˈlɔɪəl/ *adjective* always supporting someone or something ANTONYM **disloyal**: *She's very loyal to her friends.*

loy·al·ty /ˈlɔɪəlti/ *noun* (no plural) when someone is loyal ANTONYM **disloyalty**: *I expect loyalty from my family.*

Ltd the written abbreviation of LIMITED, used after the names of companies

luck /lʌk/ *noun* (no plural) something good that happens by chance: *We won, but I think it was luck, not skill!* • *You* ***haven't had much luck*** *this year, have you?*

PHRASES

good luck, bad luck the good or bad things that happen to you by chance: *The whole family* ***has had a lot of bad luck*** *recently.*

with any luck, with a bit of luck (spoken) used to say that you think something good will probably happen: ***With any luck*** *we should be home before it gets dark.*

good luck, best of luck (spoken) used to say to someone that you hope they will be successful: ***Good luck with*** *your exams tomorrow.*

wish someone luck to tell someone that you hope they will be successful: *Sarah* ***wished*** *me* ***luck with*** *my exams.*

bad luck, hard luck (spoken) used to tell someone that you are sorry something bad has happened to them: *"I've got to stay late at school tonight." "Oh, bad luck!"*

luck·i·ly /ˈlʌkəli/ *adverb* used to say that you are glad that something happened or did not happen SYNONYM **fortunately**: *Luckily, it didn't rain all day.*

luck·y /ˈlʌki/ *adjective* (**luckier**, **luckiest**)

KEY PATTERNS
lucky to do something
lucky (that)
it is lucky (that)

1 if you are lucky, something good happens to you by chance ANTONYM **unlucky**: *"I'm going to Florida this summer." "Oh, you are lucky!"* • *He's* ***lucky to*** *have such a good job.* • *You're lucky you weren't killed.* • *I look at you and think I'm the luckiest man in the world.*
2 something that is lucky is good and happens by chance ANTONYM **unlucky**: ***It was lucky that*** *we had brought some extra food.*
3 if something is lucky, some people think it causes good luck ANTONYM **unlucky**: *Six is my lucky number.*

lu·di·crous /ˈluːdəkrəs/ *adjective* stupid, wrong, and unreasonable SYNONYM **ridiculous**: *That's a ludicrous idea.*

lug·gage /ˈlʌgɪdʒ/ *noun* (no plural) the bags that you carry when you are travelling SYNONYM **baggage**: *Our luggage was searched at the airport.*

luggage

GRAMMAR
Luggage is not used in the plural.
✘ Don't say 'luggages'.
When talking about a single bag or case, you say **a piece of luggage**.

luke·warm /ˌluːkˈwɔːm $ ˌlukˈwɔrm/ *adjective* slightly warm: *a cup of lukewarm tea*

lull /lʌl/ *noun* a short period when there is less activity or noise than usual: *There has been a slight lull in the fighting.*

lul·la·by /ˈlʌləbaɪ/ *noun* (plural **lullabies**) a song that you sing to babies to make them sleep

lum·ber¹ /ˈlʌmbə $ ˈlʌmbɚ/ *noun AmE* wood that is used for building or making things SYNONYM **timber** *BrE*

lumber² *verb* (informal) if you lumber someone with a job, you give it to them when they do not want it: *They lumbered me with the job of cleaning the floor.*

lu·mi·nous /ˈluːmənəs/ *adjective* able to shine in the dark: *The clock has luminous hands.*

A B C D E F G H I J K L M N O P Q R S T U V W X Y Z

lump /lʌmp/ *noun* **1** a small piece of something solid: *I put two lumps of sugar in my tea.* → see Thesaurus at PIECE **2** an unusual raised area on someone's body: *She discovered a lump in her neck.*

lump·y /ˈlʌmpi/ *adjective* (**lumpier**, **lumpiest**) something that is lumpy has lumps or raised areas: *I sat on the lumpy sofa.*

lu·nar /ˈluːnə $ ˈlunɚ/ *adjective* (formal) related to the moon: *the lunar surface*

lu·na·tic /ˈluːnətɪk/ *noun* someone who behaves in a stupid or very strange way that can be dangerous: *He drives like a lunatic.*

lunch /lʌntʃ/ *noun* (plural **lunches**)

KEY PATTERNS
have lunch
have something for lunch

a meal that you eat in the middle of the day: *We **had** a light **lunch** at the bar.* • *I'm going to **have** soup **for lunch**.* • *She bought me lunch.*

lunch·time /ˈlʌntʃtaɪm/ *noun* the time in the middle of the day when people usually eat lunch: *I usually just have a sandwich at lunchtime.*

lung /lʌŋ/ *noun* your lungs are the two parts in your body that you use for breathing

lurch /lɜːtʃ $ lɚtʃ/ *verb* to move in an unsteady or uncontrolled way: *The car lurched forward.*

lure /lʊə $ lʊr/ *verb* to persuade someone to do something by making it seem attractive or exciting SYNONYM **entice**: *He lured her into his home by pretending to be an artist.*

lurk /lɜːk $ lɚk/ *verb* (written) to wait somewhere secretly, usually before doing something bad: *He lurked by the house, waiting to attack his enemy.*

lust /lʌst/ *noun* (no plural) a very strong sexual feeling towards someone

lux·u·ri·ous /lʌgˈzjʊəriəs $ lʌgˈʒʊriəs/ *adjective* very comfortable, beautiful, and expensive: *He has a luxurious apartment in the south of France.*

lux·u·ry /ˈlʌkʃəri/ *noun* (plural **luxuries**) **1** (no plural) great comfort and pleasure that you get from having beautiful or expensive things: *She married a rich man and lived in luxury.* **2** something that you do not really need but that you buy because you will enjoy it ANTONYM **necessity**: *We don't have as much money now, so we can't afford as many luxuries.*

lying the present participle of LIE

lyr·ics /ˈlɪrɪks/ *plural noun* the words of a song: *I write the music and Max writes the lyrics.*

m the written abbreviation of METRE

MA, **M.A.** /ˌem ˈeɪ/ *noun* (Master of Arts) a higher university degree: *She is studying for an MA in music.*

ma·chine /məˈʃiːn/ *noun* a piece of equipment that uses electricity to do a job: *We've just bought a new washing machine.* • *I wanted to buy a cola from the drinks machine.* • *Letters and parcels are sorted* ***by machine.***

THESAURUS
piece of equipment: *A vital* ***piece of equipment*** *on the spacecraft has stopped operating* (=a machine or part of a machine that is used to do something).
device: *an electronic* ***device*** *for locating wires and pipes when digging* (=a machine, usually a complicated one)
appliance (formal): *household* ***appliances*** *such as washing machines* (=electrical machines that people use in their homes)
gadget: *He buys lots of kitchen* ***gadgets*** (=small machines or tools).

maˈchine gun *noun* a gun that fires a lot of bullets very quickly: *We heard the sound of machine-gun fire.*

ma·chin·e·ry /məˈʃiːnəri/ *noun* (no plural) large machines: *On the farm, I had to learn how to use heavy machinery.*

mach·o /ˈmætʃəʊ $ ˈmɑːtʃoʊ/ *adjective* (informal) a man who is macho likes to show people that he is strong and brave: *You think you're so macho!*

mad /mæd/ *adjective* (**madder**, **maddest**)

KEY PATTERNS
mad to do something
mad at/with someone

1 stupid or silly SYNONYM **crazy**, **insane**: *You'd be* ***mad to*** *give up a good job like that.* • *That's a mad idea!* • *You* ***must be mad*** *if you think I'm going to do the work for you!*
2 mentally ill SYNONYM **insane**: *He's always talking to himself – I think he's a bit mad.*
3 (informal) angry: *My teacher will be* ***mad at*** *me if I don't do this work.* • *My dad's* ***mad with*** *me because I spent so much money.* → see Thesaurus at ANGRY

PHRASES
go mad (spoken) to become very angry or excited: *Dad* ***went mad*** *when I got home so late.* • *At last the band walked on and the audience* ***went mad.***
be mad about someone/something *BrE* (informal) to like someone or something very much: *Jack's always* ***been mad about*** *football.*

mad·am /ˈmædəm/ *noun* used to show respect when talking or writing to a woman who you do not know: *Yes, madam, what would you like?* • *Dear Madam, I am writing to you about my son.*

mad·den·ing /ˈmædn-ɪŋ/ *adjective* extremely annoying: *It's maddening when you can't find a pen.*

made¹ the past tense and past participle of MAKE

made² /meɪd/ *adjective* **be made of something, be made from something** to be built from something: *The shelves* ***are made of*** *wood.* • *The blankets are* ***made from*** *bits of old clothes.*

mad·ly /ˈmædli/ *adverb* **1** in a wild, excited way: *The dogs ran madly around him.* **2 madly in love** very much in love: *I'm madly in love with Tim.*

mad·man /ˈmædmən/ *noun* (plural **madmen**) /-mən/ a man who behaves in a very dangerous or stupid way SYNONYM **maniac**: *He was driving like a madman.*

mad·ness /ˈmædnəs/ *noun* very stupid and dangerous behaviour: *It would be madness to try to cross the desert on your own.*

mag·a·zine /ˌmægəˈziːn $ ˈmægəˌzin/ *noun* a large thin book with a paper cover, which is sold every week or every month: *I bought a magazine to read on the train.*

ma·gic /ˈmædʒɪk/ *noun* (no plural) a special power that makes strange or impossible things happen: *By magic, she turned the frog into a prince.* • *I can do magic tricks.*

ma·gic·al /ˈmædʒɪkəl/ *adjective* very enjoyable and exciting, in a strange or special way: *There's something magical about his music.*

ma·gi·cian /məˈdʒɪʃən/ *noun* someone who entertains people by doing magic tricks SYNONYM **conjurer**

ma·gis·trate /ˈmædʒəstreɪt/ *noun* someone who decides if people are guilty in a court of law that deals with less serious crimes

mag·net /ˈmægnət/ *noun* a piece of iron that makes other metal objects move towards it

mag·net·ic /mægˈnetɪk/ *adjective* having the power of a magnet

mag·net·is·m /ˈmægnətɪzəm/ *noun* (no plural) the power that a magnet has to make metal things move towards it

mag·ni·fi·ca·tion /ˌmægnəfəˈkeɪʃən/ *noun* when something is magnified

mag·nif·i·cent /mægˈnɪfəsənt/ *adjective* very impressive: *a magnificent palace* • *What a magnificent performance!*

mag·ni·fy /ˈmægnəfaɪ/ *verb* (**magnified, magnifies**) to make something look bigger by putting it under a piece of special glass: *a microscope that can magnify an image 100 times*

magnifying glass

maid /meɪd/ *noun* a female servant

maid·en /ˈmeɪdn/ *adjective* **maiden flight, maiden voyage** the first trip that a plane or ship makes

ˈ**maiden name** *noun* the family name that a woman has before she marries

mail¹ /meɪl/ *noun* (no plural)

KEY PATTERNS
in the mail
by mail

1 the letters and packages that are delivered to your house or office SYNONYM **post** *BrE*: *Was there any mail for me this morning?* • *I'm expecting a letter **in the mail** today.*
2 the system of delivering letters and packages to people's houses and offices SYNONYM **post** *BrE*: *The invitation arrived **by mail** this morning.*
3 messages that you receive by email: *I'm just logging on to read my mail.*

mail² *verb* to send a letter or package to someone SYNONYM **post** *BrE*: *Will you mail this letter for me?*

mail·box /ˈmeɪlbɒks $ ˈmeɪlbɑks/ *noun* (plural **mailboxes**) **1** a box where letters are put when they are delivered to your house or office **2** a file on a computer where you store email messages

mail·man /ˈmeɪlmæn/ the American word for POSTMAN

maim /meɪm/ *verb* to injure someone very badly: *The bomb killed and maimed many innocent people.*

main /meɪn/ *adjective* biggest or most important: *Maths is the main subject I am studying.* • *The main problem is lack of money.*

main·land /ˈmeɪnlənd/ *noun* **the mainland** the main part of a country, not the islands near it: *People on the islands come to the mainland at least once a month to do shopping.*
—**mainland** *adjective*: *mainland China*

main·ly /ˈmeɪnli/ *adverb* mostly: *Our students are mainly from Europe.* • *Tomorrow will be mainly cloudy but dry.*

THESAURUS
largely/chiefly: *His success was **largely** due to his persistence* (=mainly).
primarily/principally (formal): *Women are still **primarily** responsible for buying food* (=mainly).

ˌ**main ˈroad** *noun* a large important road

main·tain /meɪnˈteɪn/ *verb* **1** to continue to have or do something as much as you did in the past: *The*

website provides an easy way to ***maintain contact with*** your old friends. • The college must maintain its very high standards.
2 to keep a building, road, or machine in good condition: *The government is responsible for maintaining our roads.*

main·te·nance /ˈmeɪntənəns/ *noun* (no plural) work that is done to keep something working properly: *Who will pay for all the computer maintenance?*

maize /meɪz/ *noun* (no plural) *BrE* a tall plant with yellow seeds that can be cooked and eaten SYNONYM **corn** *AmE*

maj·es·ty /ˈmædʒəsti/ *noun* **Your Majesty** a formal title that is used to talk to a king or queen

ma·jor¹ /ˈmeɪdʒə $ ˈmeɪdʒɚ/ *adjective* large and important ANTONYM **minor**: *There has been a major earthquake in the south of the country. • This is one of our major problems.* → see Thesaurus at IMPORTANT

major² *noun* **1** an officer in the army
2 *AmE* the main subject that you study at college or university: *His major is science.*

major³ *verb* **major in something** *AmE* to study something as your main subject at college or university: *She majored in history.*

ma·jor·i·ty /məˈdʒɒrəti $ məˈdʒɔrəti/ *noun*

KEY PATTERNS
a/the majority of people or things

most of the people or things in a group ANTONYM **minority**: *The* ***majority of*** *our students come from Europe and Asia. •* ***A majority of*** *countries still support the idea.*

make¹ → see box on page 406

make² *noun* a type of product made by a company: *"What make is your laptop?" "It's a Dell."*

mak·er /ˈmeɪkə $ ˈmeɪkɚ/ *noun* a person or company that makes something: *Honda is a Japanese car maker. • a furniture maker*

make·shift /ˈmeɪkʃɪft/ *adjective* made quickly from things that you have available: *They slept in a makeshift tent made from a sheet.*

make-up, make·up /ˈmeɪkʌp/ *noun* (no plural) coloured creams and powders that a woman puts on her face to make herself look more attractive: *Do you ever wear make-up?*

ma·lar·i·a /məˈleəriə $ məˈleriə/ *noun* (no plural) a serious disease that is spread by MOSQUITOes

male¹ /meɪl/ *adjective*
1 someone who is male is a man or a boy ANTONYM **female**: *Most of my teachers were male. • There is an increasing number of male nurses.*
2 male animals belong to the sex which cannot have babies or lay eggs ANTONYM **female**: *The male bird is bigger than the female.*

male² *noun*
a male person or animal ANTONYM **female**: *Is your dog a male or a female?*

mal·ice /ˈmælɪs/ *noun* (no plural) a feeling of wanting to hurt someone: *Her eyes were full of malice.*

ma·li·cious /məˈlɪʃəs/ *adjective* intended to hurt or upset someone: *a malicious lie*

ma·lig·nant /məˈlɪgnənt/ *adjective* containing CANCER cells: *They are doing tests to see if the growth is malignant.*

mall /mɔːl/ *noun* a covered area that contains a lot of shops: *a huge shopping mall*

mam·mal /ˈmæməl/ *noun* a type of animal that gives birth to live babies rather than eggs. Humans and cows are examples of mammals.

mam·moth /ˈmæməθ/ *adjective* very big SYNONYM **huge**: *We had the mammoth task of organizing the concert.*

man¹ /mæn/ *noun* (plural **men** /men/)
1 an adult male person: *Two men were standing at the door. • My father was a very kind man.*
2 (no plural) all people, including men, women, and children: *This is one of the most deadly poisons known to man.*

man² *verb* (**manned, manning**) to be in charge of a machine or a place: *The boat was manned by volunteers.*

make /meɪk/ *verb* (past tense and past participle **made** /meɪd/)

make

1 to produce something: *The company **makes** cars.* • *She **makes** all her own clothes.* • *They're **making** a film about his life story.*

2 to cook a meal or prepare something to drink: *I usually **make** dinner as soon as I get home from work.* • *Sammy **made** me a cup of tea.* • *He expects his wife to **make** all his **meals for** him.*

KEY PATTERNS
make a meal/drink
make someone a meal/drink
make a meal/drink for someone

3 to cause something or someone to have a feeling: *The heat **made** her feel sleepy.* • *I'm sorry I **made** you cry.* • *The disease **makes** it **difficult** for him to walk.*

KEY PATTERNS
make someone happy/sad/angry etc
make someone laugh/cry etc
make it difficult/easy to do something

4 to force someone to do something: *They **made** us work really hard.*

GRAMMAR
• You **make someone do something.**
✗ Don't say 'make someone to do something'.

5 to earn money: *She **makes** about £30,000 a year.* • *The main goal of any business is to **make money**.*

WORD CHOICE
make or **do**?
• You use **make** about producing things: *The company makes cars.*
• You use **do** about doing an action or an activity: *We did some stretching exercises.*
• Be careful that you don't use **make** when you should be using a different verb:
You do the shopping. • **You go for a walk.** • **You do your homework.**
✗ Don't say 'make the shopping', 'make a walk', or 'make your homework'.

PHRASES

make sure
to do whatever you need to do in order to be certain about something: ***Make sure** that you understand the test question before you begin answering it.*

make up your mind
to make a decision after you have spent time thinking about it: *I **made up my mind** to go to the party after all.*

PHRASAL VERBS

make into
to change something so that it becomes something else: *They're **making** the book **into** a movie.* • *The corn is **made into** a type of bread.*

make up
to think of a story, explanation, excuse etc that is not true: *The children **made up** stories and drew pictures to go with them.* • *I couldn't think of an answer, so I just **made** something **up**.*

man•age /ˈmænɪdʒ/ *verb*

KEY PATTERNS
manage to do something
manage a business/shop etc

1 to succeed in doing something: *Nobody knows how the prisoners* ***managed to*** *escape.* • *I thought we would never get the door open, but in the end we managed.*
2 if you can manage, you can do a job or deal with a situation without help: *"Would you like some help?" "No, it's all right, I* ***can manage****."*
3 to be in charge of a company or shop, and the people who work there: *His son now manages the restaurant.*

man•age•ment /ˈmænɪdʒmənt/ *noun* the job of organizing the work of a company or shop, and the people who work there: *He is responsible for the day-to-day management of the company.* • *The banks blamed the situation on bad management.*

man•ag•er /ˈmænɪdʒə $ ˈmænɪdʒɚ/ *noun* someone who is in charge of an organization, sports team, shop etc: *The hotel manager asked if we were happy with the service.* • *a bank manager*

mane /meɪn/ *noun* the long hair on the neck of a horse or a male lion → see picture at HORSE

maneuver the American spelling of MANOEUVRE

man•gled /ˈmæŋɡəld/ *adjective* if something is mangled, it is badly damaged by something crushing or twisting it: *Rescuers managed to reach the mangled car and help the driver.*

man•go /ˈmæŋɡəʊ $ ˈmæŋɡoʊ/ *noun* (plural **mangoes**) a sweet tropical fruit with red or green skin and yellow flesh → see picture on page A7

man•han•dle /ˈmænˌhændl/ *verb* to move or push someone roughly: *He claimed the police manhandled him.*

ma•ni•ac /ˈmeɪniæk/ *noun* (informal) someone who behaves in a stupid or dangerous way SYNONYM **madman**: *You drive like a maniac.*

man•i•cure /ˈmænɪkjʊə $ ˈmænɪˌkjʊr/ *noun* a treatment for the hands and nails that includes cutting and polishing the nails —**manicure** *verb*: *She spends hours manicuring her nails.*

ma•nip•u•late /məˈnɪpjəleɪt/ *verb* to make someone do what you want, often by deceiving them: *She's ambitious and good at manipulating people.*

man•kind /ˌmænˈkaɪnd/ *noun* (no plural) all humans, considered as a group SYNONYM **man**: *the history of mankind* → see Thesaurus at PEOPLE

ˌman-ˈmade *adjective* man-made materials are made by people and do not exist naturally SYNONYM **artificial**: *All these clothes are made of man-made fibres.*

man•ner /ˈmænə $ ˈmænɚ/ *noun*
1 your manner is the way in which you behave towards other people: *His manner was cold and unfriendly.*
2 the way in which something is done: *He reacted to the news* ***in a*** *very strange* ***manner****.*
3 manners ways of behaving, eating, and speaking that people consider to be polite or not polite: *It's* ***bad manners*** (=not polite) *to speak with your mouth full.* • *Her children have very* ***good manners****.* • *It's important to teach children good* ***table manners*** (=polite ways of behaving when eating).

ma•noeu•vre *BrE*, **maneuver** *AmE* /məˈnuːvə $ məˈnuvɚ/ *verb* to move something skilfully into a different position: *I manoeuvred the car into a parking space.* —**manoeuvre** *noun*: *She performed a difficult manoeuvre on her skis.*

man•sion /ˈmænʃən/ *noun* a very big house

man•tel•piece /ˈmæntlpiːs/ also **man•tel** /ˈmæntl/ *AmE noun* the shelf above a fire in someone's house: *A clock was ticking on the mantelpiece.*

man•u•al¹ /ˈmænjuəl/ *adjective* done with your hands: *He has always worked on the farm, doing manual work.* —**manually** *adverb*: *Adjust the controls manually.*

manual² *noun* a book that explains how to use a machine: *Consult your computer's user manual.*

man•u•fac•ture /ˌmænjəˈfæktʃə $ ˌmænjəˈfæktʃɚ/ *verb* to make large quantities of goods, using machines:

The factory manufactures plastic goods. —**manufacture** *noun* (no plural): *the manufacture of textiles*

man·u·fac·tur·er /ˌmænjəˈfæktʃərə $ ˌmænjəˈfæktʃərə/ *noun* a company that makes large quantities of goods, using machines: *an aircraft manufacturer*

man·u·script /ˈmænjəskrɪpt/ *noun* a piece of writing that has been written, not printed: *a medieval manuscript*

man·y /ˈmeni/ *determiner, pronoun* a large number of people or things. Use **many** about things that you can count, such as people, things, cars, books etc, especially in questions and negative sentences: *Were there* ***many*** *people at Jill's party?* • *There aren't* ***many*** *tickets left.* • ***Many of*** *the houses were very old.* • *Some people came, but* ***not many***. • *She has worked there* ***for many years***. • *You can use this tool in many ways.*

PHRASES

how many? use this to ask what number of people or things there are: *How many people are in your class?* • *How many eggs do you need?*

too many, so many use these when the number of something is larger than you want or need: *You've eaten* ***too many*** *sweets already.* • *We've had* ***so many*** *problems with our neighbours.*

as many use this to talk about a number of people or things, especially when you are comparing two numbers: *The older students don't study as many subjects as the younger ones.* • *I've downloaded as many tunes onto my mobile as I can.*

WORD CHOICE

many or **a lot of**?

• **Many** is usually used in questions and negative sentences: ***How many*** *people were there at the concert?* • *There* ***weren't many*** *songs that I liked.*

• In positive statements, people usually use **a lot of**: *He has* ***a lot of*** *old jazz records.*

• **Many** is used in positive statements in formal written English: *There are* ***many*** *reasons why the law needs to be changed.*

map /mæp/ *noun* a drawing of an area or country, showing rivers, roads, cities etc: *a map of the US*

mar·a·thon /ˈmærəθən $ ˈmærəˌθɑn/ *noun* a race in which people run 26 miles 385 YARDS along roads: *He's going to run the New York marathon.*

mar·ble /ˈmɑːbəl $ ˈmɑrbəl/ *noun* **1** (no plural) a hard rock that can be polished and used to make floors, STATUES etc **2** a small coloured glass ball that children play with: *Who wants to play marbles?*

March /mɑːtʃ $ mɑrtʃ/ (written abbreviation **Mar**) *noun* the third month of the year

march[1] /mɑːtʃ $ mɑrtʃ/ *verb*

KEY PATTERNS

march past/along etc

march into/through etc a place

1 when soldiers march, they walk together with regular steps: *We watched the soldiers* ***marching past***. • *The king's armies* ***marched into*** *the capital.* → see Thesaurus at WALK[1] → see picture on page A2

2 to walk somewhere quickly, often because you are angry: *"I hate you," she shouted, and she* ***marched out of*** *the room.* → see Thesaurus at WALK[1]

3 if people march, they walk together in a large group in order to protest about something: *The students* ***marched through*** *the city centre and called for the president to resign.* → see Thesaurus at PROTEST[2]

march[2] *noun* (plural **marches**) **1** an event in which people walk together to protest about something: *Thousands of people went on a march to protest about the war.* **2** when soldiers walk together with regular steps

mar·ga·rine /ˌmɑːdʒəˈriːn $ ˈmɑrdʒərɪn/ *noun* (no plural) a food similar to butter, made from animal or vegetable fat

SPELLING

This word is often spelled wrongly. The correct spelling is **margarine**.

mar·gin /ˈmɑːdʒɪn $ ˈmɑrdʒɪn/ *noun* the empty space at the side of a printed page: *The teacher wrote 'Good' in the margin.*

mar·i·jua·na /ˌmærəˈwɑːnə/ *noun* (no plural) an illegal drug that people smoke SYNONYM **cannabis**

ma·ri·na /məˈriːnə/ *noun* a small area of water near the sea where people keep boats

ma·rine /məˈriːn/ *adjective* related to the sea: *marine life*

mark¹ /mɑːk $ mɑrk/ *verb*
1 when a teacher marks a student's work, he or she decides how good it is and gives it a number or letter showing this SYNONYM **grade** *AmE*: *Haven't they finished marking the exam papers yet?*
2 to put a word or sign on something to give information: *The door was marked 'Private'.*
3 to show where something is: *A white post marked the turning in the road.*
4 to be a sign of an important event: *This fight* ***marked the end of*** *his boxing career.* • *There will be a festival to* ***mark the anniversary of*** *the writer's birth.*

mark² *noun*
1 a spot or cut on something, which spoils its appearance: *The pen has* ***left a mark on*** *your shirt.* • *There were* ***dirty marks*** *all over the floor.*
2 *BrE* a letter or number given by a teacher to show how good a student's work is SYNONYM **grade** *AmE*: *If I get* ***good marks*** *in my exams, my dad will buy me a computer game.* • *She was the only student who got* ***full marks*** *in the test.*
3 a sign that is written or printed on something: *The customs official put a mark on the case to show it had been checked.*
4 a mark of something a sign of something: *The crowd was silent for two minutes as* ***a mark of*** *respect.*

THESAURUS
stain: *There was a coffee* ***stain*** *on her skirt* (=a mark that is difficult to remove).
spot: *This disease causes black* ***spots*** *on the leaves* (=small round areas of dirt or colour).
smear: *The plates had* ***smears*** *of grease on them* (=dirty marks).
blemish (formal): *Make sure you choose fruit without* ***blemishes*** (=small marks that spoil their appearance).
scar: *He had a* ***scar*** *above his left eye* (=a permanent mark on someone's skin, caused by a cut or burn).

mar·ket¹ /ˈmɑːkɪt $ ˈmɑrkɪt/ *noun*
1 an area where people bring food and other things to sell: *I usually buy fruit and vegetables* ***at the market.*** • *I bought some fish* ***from the market.*** • *Are you* ***going to the market*** *tomorrow?*
2 all the people who buy goods: *The market for mobile phones is increasing all the time.* • *Our company is always looking for new markets.*

PHRASES
on the market available for people to buy: *There are thousands of computer games* ***on the market.*** • *A new drink has just* ***come onto the market.*** • *They have decided to* ***put*** *their house* ***on the market.***

market² *verb* to try to persuade people to buy something by advertising it: *They are marketing the drink as a health product.*

mar·ket·ing /ˈmɑːkɪtɪŋ $ ˈmɑrkɪtɪŋ/ *noun* (no plural) the job of deciding how to advertise and sell a product: *Stella works in marketing.*

mark·ing /ˈmɑːkɪŋ $ ˈmɑrkɪŋ/ *noun*
1 the work a teacher does when he or she reads a student's work and gives it a mark: *I've got some marking to do tonight.* **2 markings** coloured shapes or patterns on something: *The road markings aren't very clear.* • *The young birds have paler markings on their wings.*

mar·ma·lade /ˈmɑːməleɪd $ ˈmɑrməˌleɪd/ *noun* (no plural) a sweet food made from oranges, lemons etc and sugar, that you spread on bread

ma·roon /məˈruːn/ *noun, adjective* a dark red colour

mar·quee /mɑːˈkiː $ mɑrˈki/ *noun* *BrE* a very big tent used for shows and parties: *We hired a marquee for the wedding.* → see picture on page 410

mar·riage /ˈmærɪdʒ/ *noun* **1** the relationship between a husband and wife: *We have a happy marriage.* **2** a wedding ceremony: *Their marriage took place in Los Angeles.*

marquee

mar·ried /ˈmærid/ *adjective* someone who is married has a husband or a wife: *She is* ***married to*** *a famous footballer.* • *a married couple*

mar·ry /ˈmæri/ *verb* (**married**, **marries**) if a man and a woman marry, they become husband and wife: *I asked her to marry me.* • *John and I are* ***getting married*** *in May.*

> **USAGE**
> You usually say that two people **get married**: *They got married in 2006.*
> ✘ Don't say 'marry with someone' or 'marry to someone'.

marsh /mɑːʃ $ mɑrʃ/ *noun* (plural **marshes**) an area of soft wet land

mar·tial art /ˌmɑːʃəl ˈɑːt $ ˌmɑrʃəl ˈɑrt/ *noun* a sport in which you fight using your hands and feet: *Kung Fu is a popular martial art.*

mar·vel /ˈmɑːvəl $ ˈmɑrvəl/ *verb* (**marvelled**, **marvelling** *BrE*, **marveled**, **marveling** *AmE*) if you marvel at something, you find it very good and surprising: *I marvel at his ability to learn.*

mar·vel·lous *BrE*, **marvelous** *AmE* /ˈmɑːvələs $ ˈmɑrvələs/ *adjective* very good or enjoyable SYNONYM **wonderful**: *I thought it was a marvellous film.*

mas·ca·ra /mæˈskɑːrə $ mæˈskærə/ *noun* (no plural) a dark substance that women use to colour their EYELASHes: *She was wearing mascara.*

mas·cot /ˈmæskət $ ˈmæskɑt/ *noun* an animal or toy that a team has, which they think will bring them good luck

mas·cu·line /ˈmæskjələn/ *adjective* **1** like a man or typical of a man ANTONYM **feminine**: *a deep masculine voice* **2** belonging to a group of nouns and adjectives in some languages that is different from the FEMININE and the NEUTER groups

mash /mæʃ/ *verb* to crush food until it is soft → see Thesaurus at PRESS[1] —**mashed** *adjective*: *mashed potatoes* → see picture on page A4

masks

gas mask

mask

mask /mɑːsk $ mæsk/ *noun* something you wear over your face to hide or protect it: *The thief wore a mask to hide his face.*

Mass /mæs/ *noun* the main religious ceremony in some Christian churches: *a Roman Catholic Mass*

mass[1] /mæs/ *noun* (plural **masses**) **1** a large amount of something all in a group: *There was a mass of letters and reports on my desk.* **2 masses** *BrE* (informal) a large number or amount of something: *There were* ***masses of*** *people there.* • *We've got* ***masses of*** *time.*

mass[2] *adjective* involving a large number of people: *The bomb caused mass panic.*

mas·sa·cre /ˈmæsəkə $ ˈmæsəkɚ/ *noun* when a lot of people who cannot defend themselves are killed: *a massacre of innocent women and children* —**massacre** *verb*: *The whole village was massacred.* → see Thesaurus at KILL[1]

mas·sage /ˈmæsɑːʒ $ məˈsɑʒ/ *verb* to press and rub someone's body to stop their muscles hurting or to help them relax: *He gently massaged my neck.* —**massage** *noun*: *Will you give me a massage?*

mas·sive /ˈmæsɪv/ *adjective* very big SYNONYM **huge**: *Their house is massive.* • *a massive earthquake*

A B C D E F G H I J K L M N O P Q R S T U V W X Y Z

Sounds

click
rustle
ring
splash
buzz
rattle
tick
crackle
crunch
snap
sizzle
squeak
creak
bang
smash
hiss
slam

Verbs of movement (body)

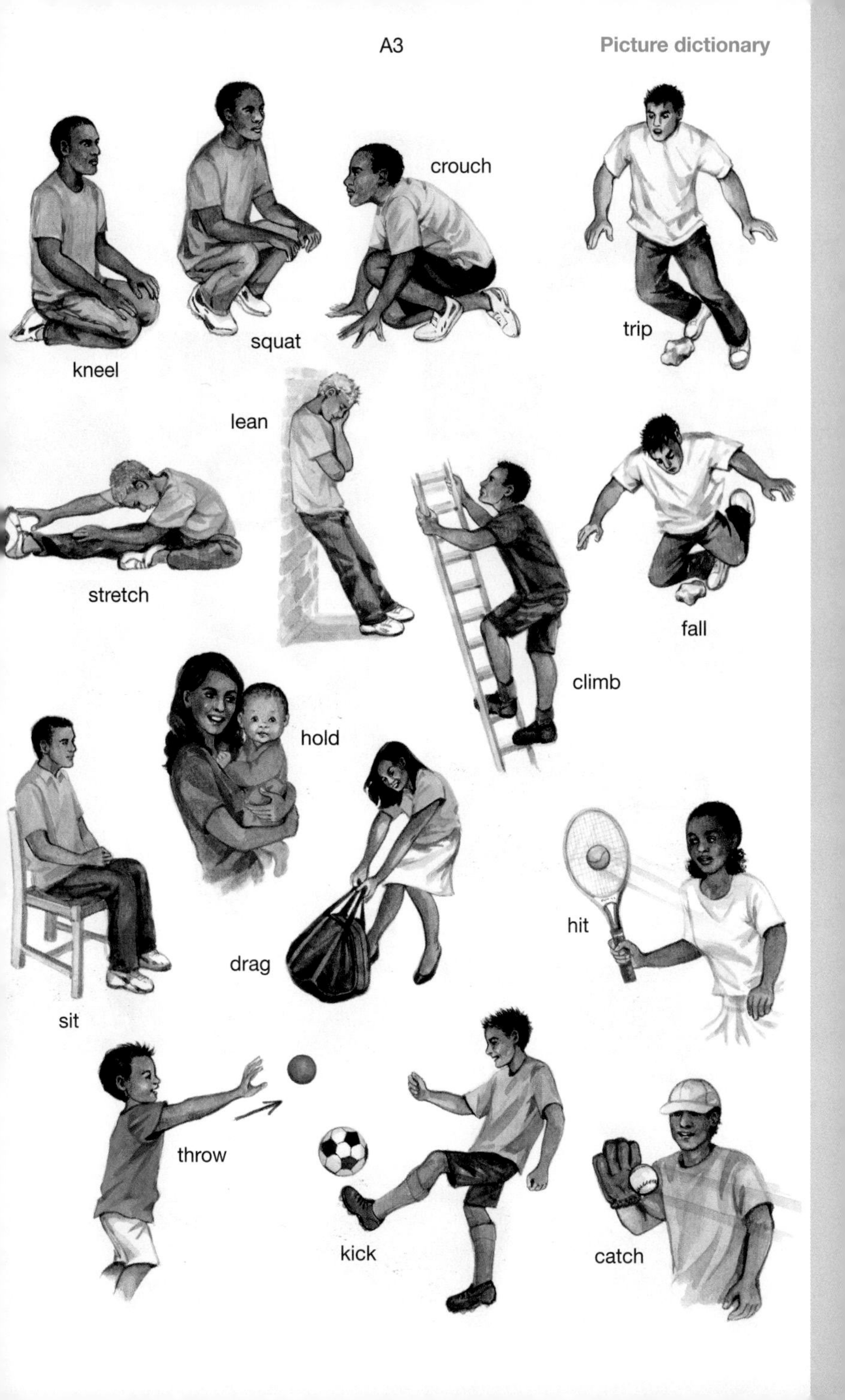
kneel
squat
crouch
trip
lean
stretch
climb
fall
hold
sit
drag
hit
throw
kick
catch

Verbs in the kitchen

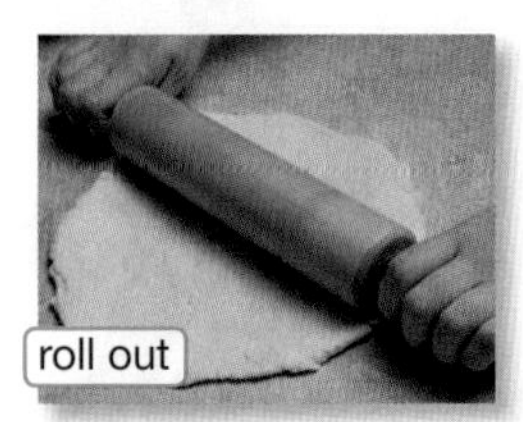

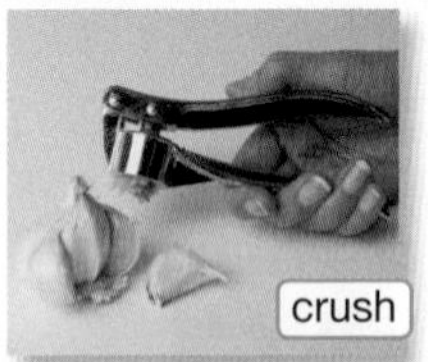

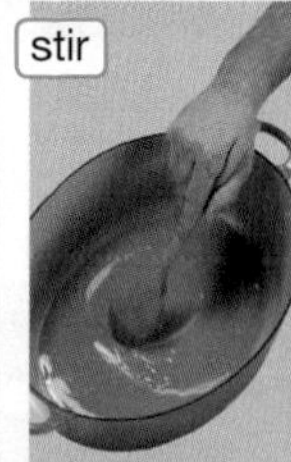

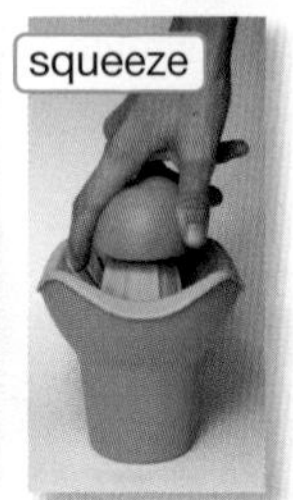

dip

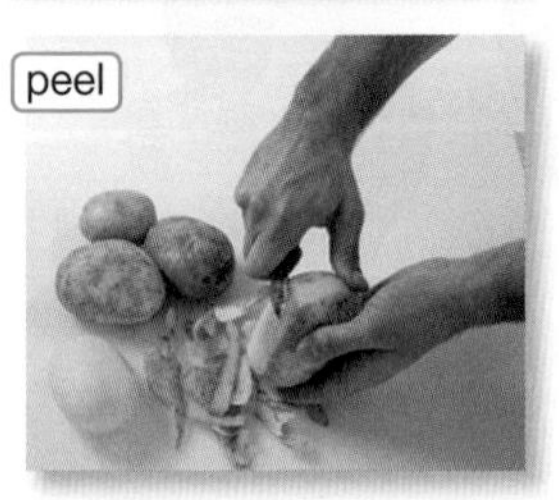

Human body

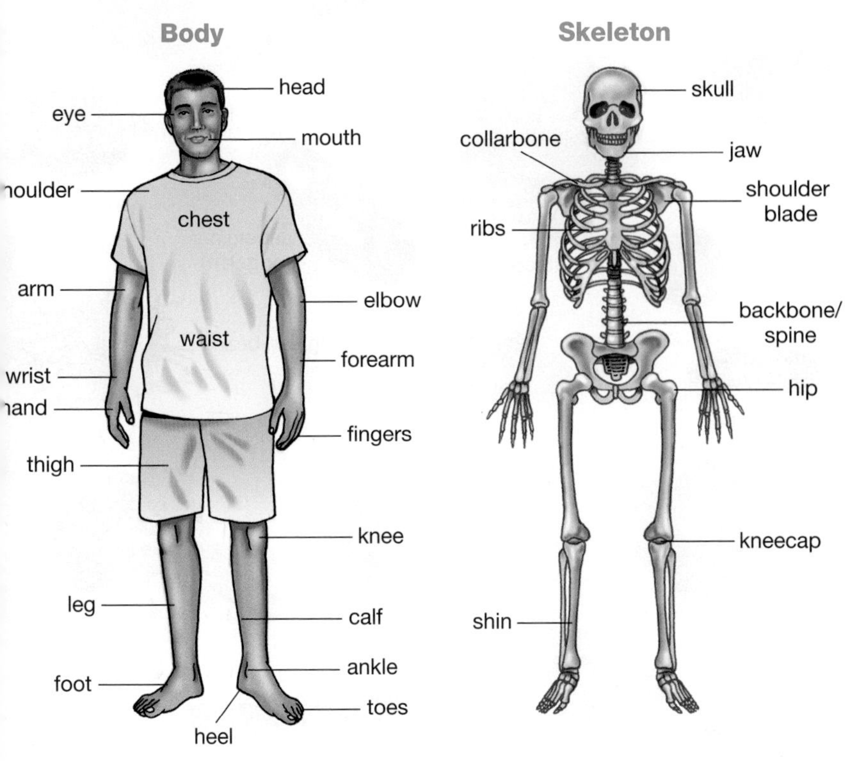
Body
head
eye
mouth
houlder
chest
arm
elbow
waist
forearm
wrist
hand
fingers
thigh
knee
leg
calf
ankle
foot
toes
heel
Skeleton
skull
collarbone
jaw
shoulder blade
ribs
backbone/ spine
hip
kneecap
shin

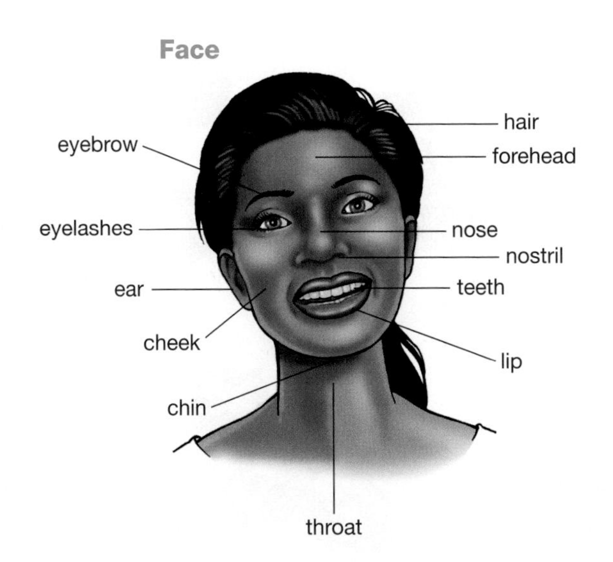
Face
hair
eyebrow
forehead
eyelashes
nose
nostril
ear
teeth
cheek
lip
chin
throat

Fruit and vegetables

apple
pear
tangerine
lemon
lime
grapes
melon
pineapple
kiwi
plum
peach
nectarine
cherries
banana
apricot
figs
orange
grapefruit
watermelon
rhubarb
mango
strawberries
raspberries
blackberries
avocado
prunes
apricots
figs
raisins
peanuts
coconut
dates
walnuts
almonds

Animals

Birds

Farm animals

Pets

Wild animals

Plants and flowers

Transport

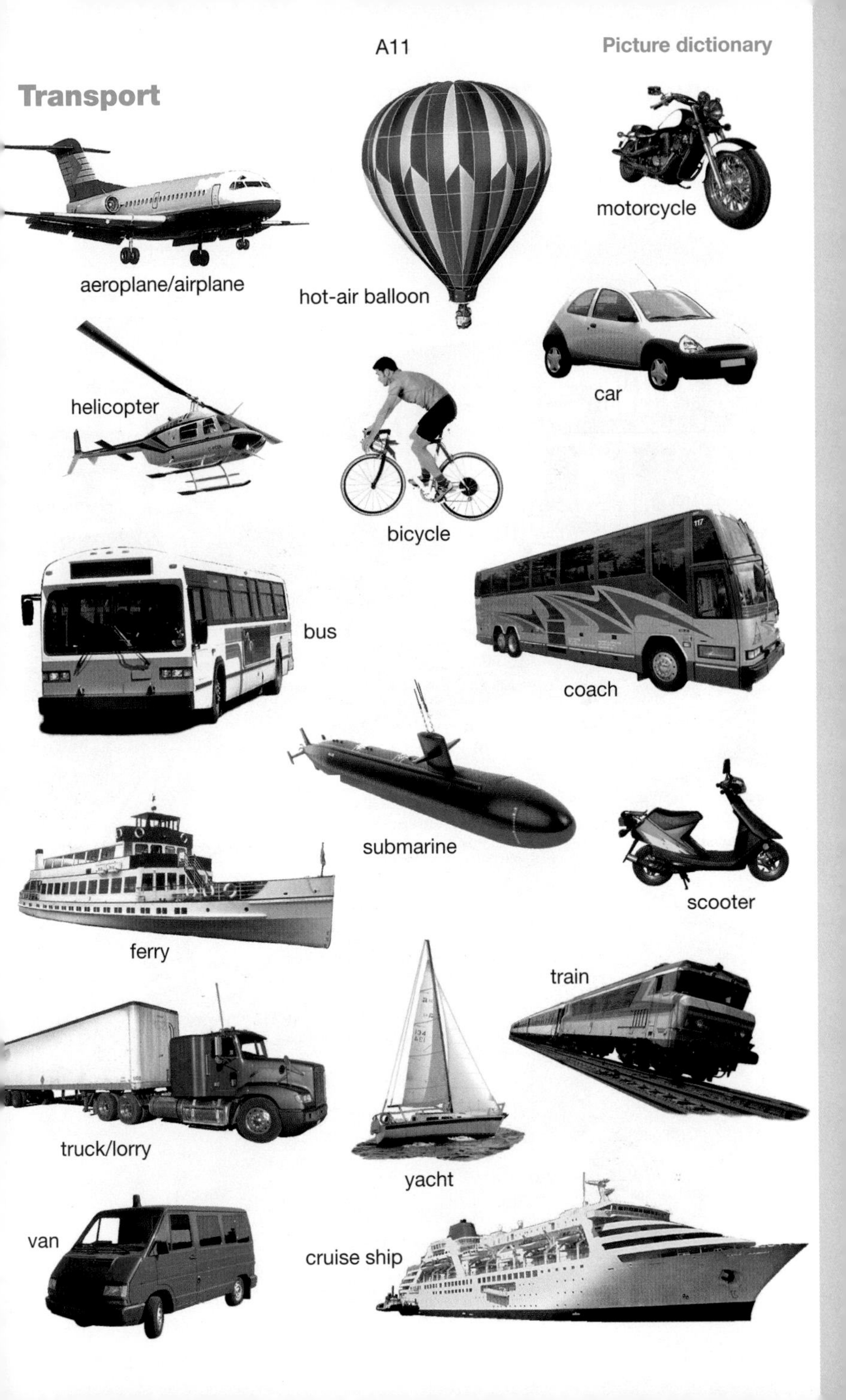
aeroplane/airplane
hot-air balloon
motorcycle
car
helicopter
bicycle
bus
coach
submarine
scooter
ferry
train
truck/lorry
yacht
van
cruise ship

Computers and technology

Weather

It's foggy.

It's snowing.

It's cloudy.

It's windy.

rainbow

lightning

winter

spring

summer

autumn

Sports

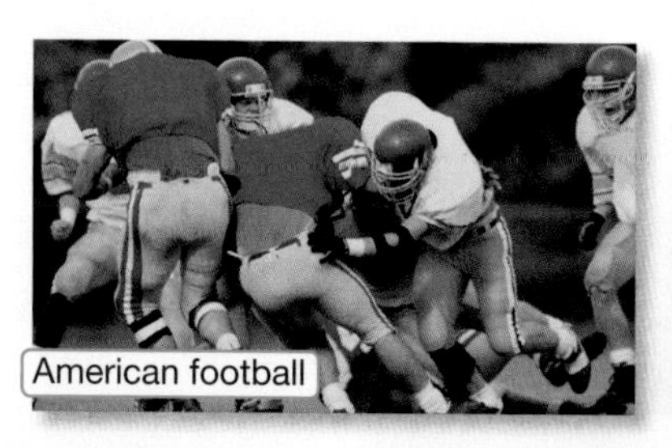
American football

cycling

windsurfing

ice hockey

karate

rowing

surfing

skiing

swimming

climbing

basketball

sailing

Map of the UK

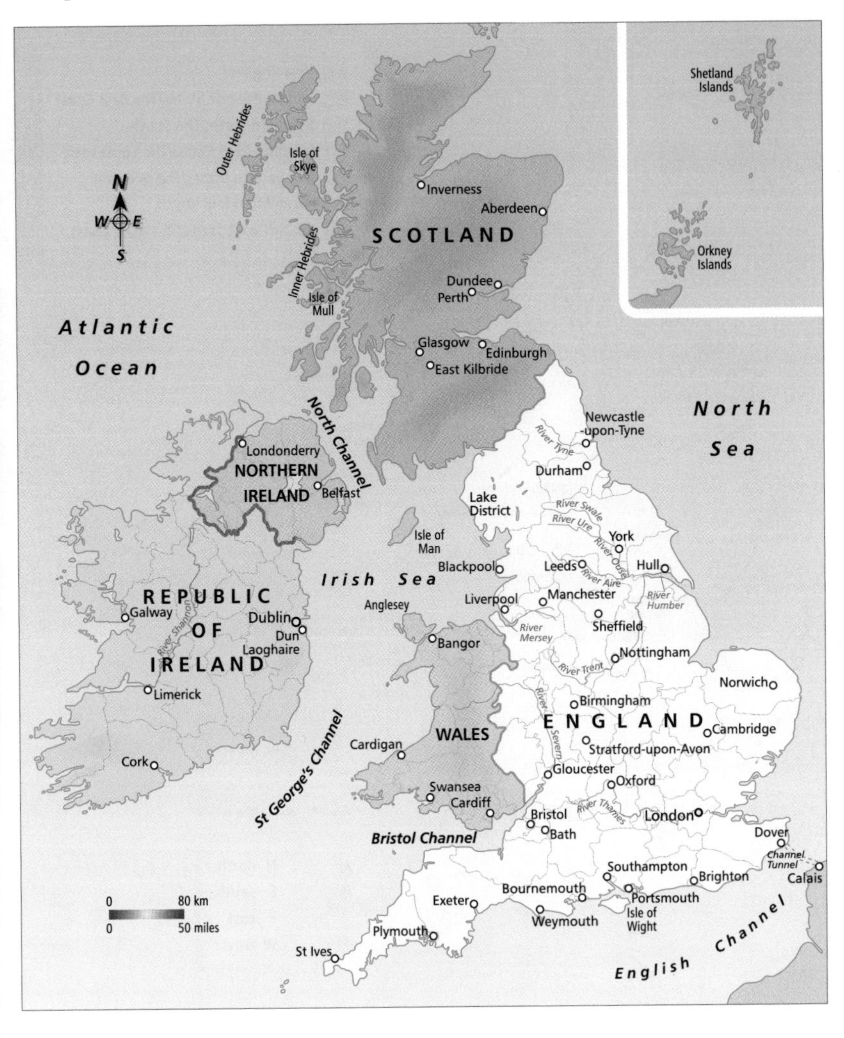

Shetland Islands
Orkney Islands
Outer Hebrides
Isle of Skye
Inverness
Aberdeen
SCOTLAND
Inner Hebrides
Isle of Mull
Dundee
Perth
Atlantic Ocean
Glasgow
Edinburgh
East Kilbride
North Channel
North Sea
Newcastle-upon-Tyne
River Tyne
Londonderry
NORTHERN IRELAND
Belfast
Durham
Lake District
River Swale
River Ure
Isle of Man
York
River Ouse
Blackpool
Leeds
River Aire
Hull
Irish Sea
REPUBLIC OF IRELAND
Galway
River Shannon
Dublin
Dun Laoghaire
Anglesey
Liverpool
Manchester
River Humber
River Mersey
Sheffield
Bangor
Nottingham
River Trent
Limerick
Norwich
Birmingham
ENGLAND
Cambridge
River Severn
Cardigan
WALES
Stratford-upon-Avon
Cork
St George's Channel
Gloucester
Oxford
Swansea
Cardiff
Bristol
River Thames
London
Bath
Bristol Channel
Dover
Channel Tunnel
Calais
Southampton
Brighton
Bournemouth
Portsmouth
Exeter
Weymouth
Isle of Wight
Plymouth
St Ives
English Channel
0 80 km
0 50 miles
N
W
E
S

Map of the US

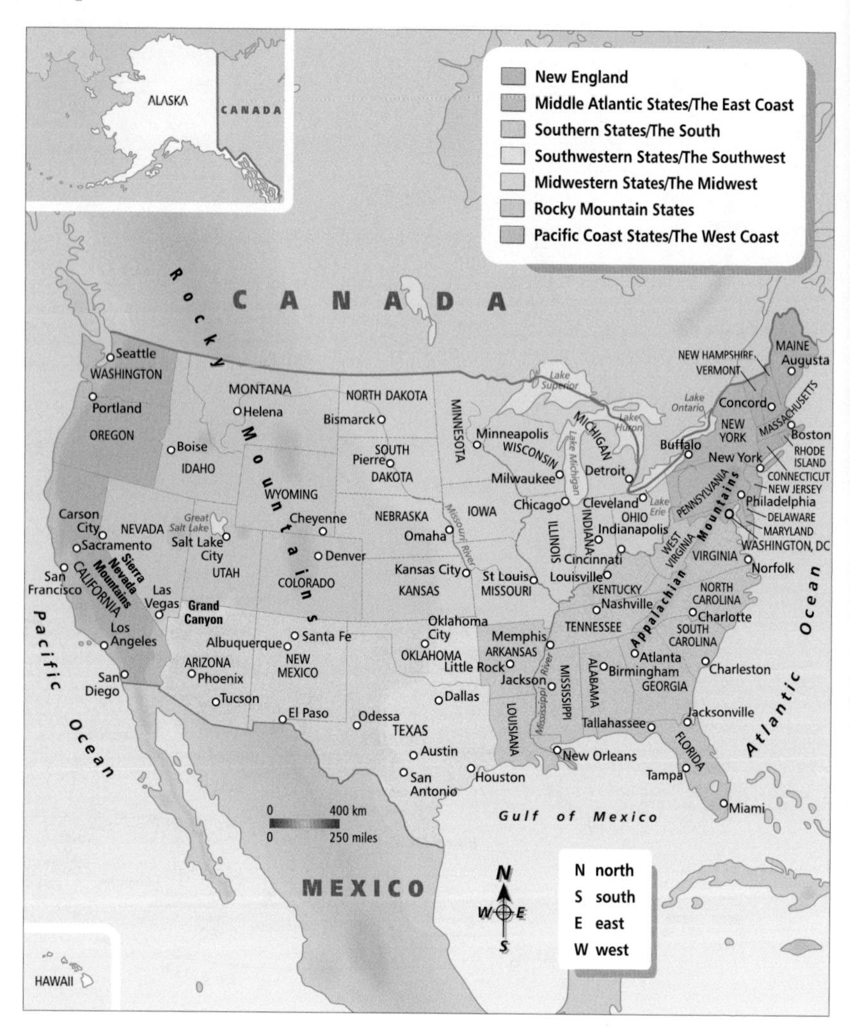
New England
Middle Atlantic States/The East Coast
Southern States/The South
Southwestern States/The Southwest
Midwestern States/The Midwest
Rocky Mountain States
Pacific Coast States/The West Coast
ALASKA
CANADA
HAWAII
MEXICO
Pacific Ocean
Atlantic Ocean
Gulf of Mexico
Rocky Mountains
Sierra Nevada Mountains
Appalachian Mountains
Grand Canyon
Great Salt Lake
Lake Superior
Lake Michigan
Lake Huron
Lake Erie
Lake Ontario
Missouri River
Mississippi River
WASHINGTON
Seattle
OREGON
Portland
CALIFORNIA
San Francisco
Sacramento
Los Angeles
San Diego
IDAHO
Boise
NEVADA
Carson City
Las Vegas
UTAH
Salt Lake City
ARIZONA
Phoenix
Tucson
MONTANA
Helena
WYOMING
Cheyenne
COLORADO
Denver
NEW MEXICO
Albuquerque
Santa Fe
NORTH DAKOTA
Bismarck
SOUTH DAKOTA
Pierre
NEBRASKA
Omaha
KANSAS
Kansas City
OKLAHOMA
Oklahoma City
TEXAS
El Paso
Odessa
Dallas
Austin
San Antonio
Houston
MINNESOTA
Minneapolis
IOWA
MISSOURI
St Louis
ARKANSAS
Little Rock
LOUISIANA
New Orleans
WISCONSIN
Milwaukee
ILLINOIS
Chicago
MICHIGAN
Detroit
INDIANA
Indianapolis
OHIO
Cleveland
Cincinnati
KENTUCKY
Louisville
TENNESSEE
Memphis
Nashville
MISSISSIPPI
Jackson
ALABAMA
Birmingham
GEORGIA
Atlanta
FLORIDA
Tallahassee
Jacksonville
Tampa
Miami
SOUTH CAROLINA
Charleston
NORTH CAROLINA
Charlotte
VIRGINIA
Norfolk
WEST VIRGINIA
WASHINGTON, DC
MARYLAND
DELAWARE
PENNSYLVANIA
Philadelphia
NEW JERSEY
NEW YORK
New York
Buffalo
CONNECTICUT
RHODE ISLAND
MASSACHUSETTS
Boston
VERMONT
NEW HAMPSHIRE
Concord
MAINE
Augusta
0 400 km
0 250 miles
N north
S south
E east
W west

Spelling

English words are often spelled differently from the way they are pronounced. Also similar words are often spelled differently. *Full* has two *l*'s, but *beautiful* only has one. *Four* is spelled *our*, but *forty* is spelled *or*.

Students often make the same spelling mistakes. The *Longman WordWise Dictionary* has notes to warn you about common problems, for example at **accommodation**:

ac•com•mo•da•tion /əˌkɒmə ˈdeɪʃən $ əˌkɑməˈdeɪʃən/ noun, also *plural* **accommodations** *AmE*
a place that you can live or stay in: *I need to find some cheap accommodation.* • *The price includes flights and hotel accommodation.*

SPELLING
This word is often spelled wrongly. The correct spelling is: **accommodation**.

Exercises

A Spelling

Look at the following pairs of words. Underline the word that is spelled correctly (you can check the spellings in your *Longman WordWise Dictionary* if you aren't sure):

For example: beautifull beautiful

1	accomodation	accommodation	**5**	until	untill
2	goverment	government	**6**	polution	pollution
3	beginning	begining	**7**	accustomed	acustomed
4	adress	address	**8**	successful	successfull

B Choosing the right spelling

Underline the correct spelling:

1	recieve	receive	**5**	mystery	mistery
2	vegeteble	vegetable	**6**	grammer	grammar
3	guarantee	garantee	**7**	friend	freind
4	potatos	potatoes	**8**	seperate	separate

C Separate or together?

Write the correct spelling on the line provided:

1	grand mother	grandmother	______________
2	thank you	thankyou	______________
3	girl friend	girlfriend	______________
4	in spite of	inspite of	______________

Focus on grammar

Choosing the right pattern

You need to know which patterns you can use with a particular verb. For example with the verb **enjoy**, do you say 'I enjoy to play tennis', or 'I enjoy playing tennis'?

Look up **enjoy** in the *Longman WordWise Dictionary*:

> **en•joy** /ɪnˈdʒɔɪ/ *verb*
> **1** to get pleasure from something: *The park was lovely, and I enjoyed the walk.* • *I enjoy cooking when I have time.*
> **2 enjoy yourself, enjoy myself etc** to be happy and have fun: *Did you **enjoy yourself** at the party?*
>
> GRAMMAR
> You **enjoy doing something**.
> ✘ Don't say 'enjoy to do something'.

Some verbs have a lot of patterns. The *Longman WordWise Dictionary* will show you the most important patterns that you need to know for each verb, for example at **suggest**:

> **sug•gest** /səˈdʒest $ səgˈdʒest/ *verb*
>
> KEY PATTERNS
> **suggest that someone does something**
> **suggest doing something**
> **suggest someone/something**
>
> **1** to say what you think someone should do: *I **suggest that** you make a list of things you will need on your trip.* • *Most airlines suggest arriving a couple of hours before the flight.*
> **2** to mention someone or something that would be suitable for a particular purpose: *They were looking for a new goalkeeper, so I suggested Callum.*
> **3** to say or show that something might be true: *Are you **suggesting that** she cheated in the test?* • *The evidence **suggests that** red wine may be good for your health.*

Choosing the right preposition

It is sometimes difficult to be sure which preposition is the right one to use with a word. For example, do you say 'I arrived in New York', or 'I arrived at New York'?

Look up **arrive** in the *Longman WordWise Dictionary*:

> **ar•rive** /əˈraɪv/ *verb*
>
> KEY PATTERNS
> **arrive at the station/airport/hotel**
> **arrive in a city/country**
> **arrive home**
>
> **1** to get to a place after a journey: *We **arrived at** the party just as Lee was leaving.* • *The next train to **arrive at** platform 2 is the 10:10 to London.* • *If the train is on time, we will **arrive in** Frankfurt by eight.* • ***Arriving home** was really great after three months abroad.* • *The parcel took two weeks to arrive.*

Countable or uncountable?

Do you say 'I need some informations', or 'I need some information'? The answer to this question depends on whether this noun is countable or uncountable. This is a common problem because words that are countable in other languages are not always countable in English. When you learn a new noun, you need to know if it is countable in order to use it correctly.

Look up **information** in the *Longman WordWise Dictionary*:

> **in•for•ma•tion** /ˌɪnfəˈmeɪʃən $ ˌɪnfɚˈmeɪʃən/ *noun* (no plural)
>
> KEY PATTERNS
> **information on/about something**
>
> facts or details about something: *The website provides **information about** the organization's activities.* • *I need more **information on** the course before I decide whether or not to do it.*
>
> GRAMMAR
> **Information** is not used in the plural.
> ✘ Don't say 'informations'.
> When talking about a single fact, you say **a piece of information**: *She told me an interesting **piece of information**.*
> You often use **information** with **some** or **any**: *I need some information about flights to New York.* • *Do you have **any information** about hotels?*

Exercises

A Choosing the right pattern

Look at the following sentences. Choose the right pattern or preposition that you should use, and underline the correct word. You can look up the word in the *Longman WordWise Dictionary* if you are not sure.

For example: *I've arranged <u>to meet</u>/meeting Kate in town.*

1 Have you finished reading/to read that book?
2 Oh no! I forgot locking/to lock the door.
3 I didn't expect failing/to fail the exam.
4 She's learning to speak/speaking Spanish.
5 He refused doing/to do what I asked.

B Choosing the right preposition

Choose the right preposition, and underline the correct word.

For example: *She got married with/<u>to</u> an American.*

1 She's very good at/in maths.
2 Who's that waving for/at you?
3 Can I have a ticket to/towards Boston?
4 I read the story on/in the newspaper.
5 I felt tired in/at the end of the day.

C Choosing to use a preposition or not

Decide if each sentence is right or wrong. If it is right, put a tick (✓). If it is wrong, write the sentence correctly.

For example: *He's watching TV.* (✓)
I'm waiting Mum to phone. (✗) *I'm waiting for Mum to phone.*

1 He still hasn't answered to my letter. ____________________
2 I don't agree his opinion. ____________________
3 It's time to go home. ____________________
4 I love listening music. ____________________
5 I'll call to him when I get home. ____________________

D Countable or uncountable?

In the following sentences, cross out the wrong words. The first one has been done for you.

1 Can you give me some advice/~~some advices~~?
2 I'd like some banana/some bananas, please.
3 We need to buy some furniture/some furnitures.
4 I need some informations/some information about train times.
5 Do you have a lot of homework/homeworks to do?

Choosing the right combination of words

If you want to use a word in a sentence, it is important to know which other words are normally used with it.

Choosing the right verb

For example, if you want to talk about a party, you need to know which verb to use. Do you 'make a party', or 'have a party'?

Look up party in the *Longman WordWise Dictionary*:

par·ty[1] /'pɑːti $ 'pɑrti/ *noun* (plural **parties**)
1 a social event when people meet to talk, drink, dance etc: *We're* ***having a party*** *next Saturday.* • *Fiona invited 25 people to her* ***birthday party****.*
2 an organization of people who have the same political ideas: *Which party did you vote for in the election?*
3 (formal) a group of people who go somewhere together: ***a party of*** *tourists that was visiting the museum* → see Thesaurus at GROUP[1]

USAGE
You say **have a party**.
✗ Don't say 'make a party'.

Similarly, if you want to talk about crime, which verb do you use? Look up crime in the *Longman WordWise Dictionary*:

crime /kraɪm/ *noun*
an illegal action: *Anyone who* ***commits a crime*** *must be punished.* • *Crime in our cities is increasing.*

USAGE
You say **commit a crime**.
✗ Don't say 'do a crime'.

Whenever you learn a new noun, it's important to also learn the verbs that normally go with it.

Choosing the right adjective

You also need to know which adjective you can use with a noun. If you want to talk about the rain, do you say 'strong rain' or 'heavy rain'?

Look up rain in the *Longman WordWise Dictionary*:

rain[1] /reɪn/ *noun* (no plural)
water that falls in small drops from the sky: *The* ***rain*** *continued to* ***fall*** *overnight.* • *If the* ***rain stops****, we'll go out.* • *There was* ***heavy rain*** (=a lot of rain) *last night.*

Whenever you learn a noun, it is important to know which adjectives you can use with it.

Choosing the right adverb

You also need to know which adverbs you can use with a verb or an adjective. For example, instead of saying 'very disappointed', you can also say 'bitterly disappointed'. If you can vary your language like this, your English will sound much more natural.

Look up disappointed in the *Longman WordWise Dictionary*:

dis·ap·point·ed /ˌdɪsə'pɔɪntɪd/ *adjective*
unhappy because something good that you expected did not happen: *Julie* ***was disappointed that*** *her friends couldn't come.* • *I'm very* ***disappointed in*** *you, Mark – I thought you could do better.* • *The coach* ***was bitterly disappointed with*** (=very disappointed with) *our performance.*
→ see Thesaurus at SAD

Exercises

A Choosing the right verb

Complete the chart below by looking in the *Longman WordWise Dictionary* and ticking (✓) the verbs that you can use with the nouns:

1

	a mistake	the shopping	a bath	some medicine	your homework
make	✓				
do					
take					
have					

2

	a shower	a walk	a party	a (telephone) call	a meeting
make					
do					
take					
have					

B Choosing the right adjective

Match the adjectives on the top row with the nouns on the bottom row by drawing a line between them. The first one has been done for you:

strong deep rotten strict heavy hard stale

work traffic coffee voice bread rules apples

C Choosing the right adverb

Complete the sentences with the right adverb from the lists below:

highly, strongly, bitterly, heavily

1 I was ________________ disappointed.
2 She's ________________ intelligent.
3 It rained ________________ last night.
4 The kitchen smelled ________________ of fish.
5 It was ________________ cold outside.
6 She is a ________________ skilled artist.

deeply, seriously, absolutely, completely

7 The food was ________________ delicious.
8 She was ________________ ill.
9 Make sure that the paint is ________________ dry.
10 The view was ________________ incredible.
11 The names are ________________ different.
12 I was ________________ upset by what had happened.

Times, dates, and numbers

Time

When saying the time when something happens, you need to choose the right preposition. Usually the choice is between at, in, or on:

at
at 9 o'clock
at 5:30
at Christmas
at night
at the weekend (*BrE*)

in
in the afternoon
in (the) winter
in 2010
in the 1980s
in June
in the 21st century

on
on Monday
on Monday morning
on 30 June/June 30th
on the weekend (*AmE*)

no preposition
today
tomorrow
this morning
next week

What time is it?

It's eight o'clock.

It's eight fifteen.
It's quarter past eight.
also *It's quarter after eight.* (*AmE*)

It's eight forty-five.
It's quarter to nine.
also *It's quarter of nine.* (*AmE*)

Dates

You write:

BrE	*AmE*
20th June (or 20 June)	June 20th (or June 20)
20/6/09	6/20/09

You say:
"What's the date today?"
"It's the twentieth of June." (*BrE*)
"It's June twentieth." (*AmE*)

Also:
"two thousand and nine" (2009)
"nineteen ninety-four" (1994)
"sixteen hundred" (1600)
"twenty twenty" (2020)

Numbers

100 = a/one hundred
1,000 = a/one thousand
1,000,000 = a/one million

You usually say *and* for numbers after a hundred.

152 one hundred and fifty-two
2,240 two thousand, two hundred and forty

USAGE
Don't use 'and' between thousands and hundreds.
✗ Don't say 'two thousand and two hundred'.

In telephone numbers, if the same number is repeated twice, you say 'double' and then the number. For example, 44 = 'double four'. If the same number appears together three times, you say 'treble' or 'triple'. For example, 777 = treble seven.

How to say the number '0'

	BrE	*AmE*
Telephone numbers	Oh/zero	Zero
Temperature	Zero	Zero
Decimal numbers (0.5)	Nought ('nought point five')	Zero
Scores in games	Nil (2–0 = 'two nil')	Nothing/ zero

Exercises

A Which preposition?

Fill in the spaces with the right preposition of time (in, on, or at):

1 I'll see you ______________ Thursday.
2 I saw him ______________ the morning.
3 We went there ______________ (the) spring.
4 My birthday is ______________ March.
5 The next train will leave ______________ 7:20.
6 What are you doing ______________ the weekend?
7 She was born ______________ 1998.
8 Where are you going ______________ Easter?
9 My birthday is ______________ 15th November.
10 The town was built ______________ the 19th century.
11 We're meeting ______________ Saturday evening.
12 The band was famous ______________ the 1960s.

B What time is it?

Write how you say the time in two different ways beside these clocks:

____
____
____

____
____
____

____
____
____

C Saying dates

Write how you say these dates:

1 the first day of the year ______________________
2 1066 ______________________
3 the year after 2008 ______________________

D Saying numbers

Write how you say these numbers:

1 178 ______________________
2 5,620 ______________________
3 Her telephone number is 033779. ______________________
4 My team lost 3–0. ______________________
5 The answer is 0.8. ______________________

Choosing between similar words

Word sets

Some sets of words are very similar in meaning, and so you need to be sure that you have chosen the right one.

For example, if you want to say that someone is 'angry', there is a wide range of words you can choose from – **angry**, **furious**, **mad**, **annoyed**, or **bad-tempered**. The *Longman WordWise Dictionary* gives the following information at **angry**:

an•gry /ˈæŋgri/ *adjective* (**angrier**, **angriest**)

KEY PATTERNS
angry about something
angry with someone
angry that

if you are angry, you feel anger towards someone who has done something bad: *My father was* ***angry about*** *the broken window.* • *I was* ***angry with*** *him for laughing at me.* • *Will Simon be* ***angry that*** *I forgot his birthday?*
—**angrily** *adverb*: *"It's not funny," my mother said angrily.*

THESAURUS
furious: *He was* ***furious*** *when he saw the damage to his car* (=very angry).
mad (spoken): *My parents will be* ***mad*** *with me when they see what's happened to their car* (=very angry).
annoyed: *I was* ***annoyed*** *with him for being late* (=slightly angry).
bad-tempered: *The taxi driver was a* ***bad-tempered*** *old man* (=he often behaved in an unfriendly and angry way).

This shows you that in everyday conversation, people often use **mad**. If you are very angry, you say **furious**, and if you feel rather angry about something that is not very important, you say **annoyed**. If you can use a wider range of words, instead of using the same basic words all the time, your English will sound much more natural.

Confusable words

Do not confuse some words that sound similar but have a different meaning. For example, when do you use **cooker**, and when do you use **cook**? Look up the word **cooker**:

cook•er /ˈkʊkə $ ˈkʊkɚ/ *noun BrE* a large piece of kitchen equipment that you use for cooking food SYNONYM **stove** *AmE*

WORD CHOICE
cooker or **cook**?
• A **cook** is a person who prepares food for people to eat: *My Dad is a very good* ***cook*** (=he is very good at cooking).
• A **cooker** is the equipment that you use for cooking: *I left the pan on the* ***cooker*** (=stove).

This shows that you use **cook** about a person, and you use **cooker** about the equipment you use for cooking.

Do not confuse **sensible** and **sensitive** because they sound very similar. Look up the word **sensible**:

sen•si•ble /ˈsensəbəl/ *adjective*
1 someone who is sensible is able to make good decisions: *You can trust Julia. She's a very sensible girl.*
2 something that is sensible is a good idea: *My friend gave me some sensible advice.* • ***It seemed sensible to*** *move to London.* —**sensibly** *adverb*: *If you won't behave sensibly, you must leave.*

WORD CHOICE
sensible or **sensitive**?
• **Sensible** means "making good decisions and not doing anything stupid": *He seems a very* ***sensible*** *young man.*
• **Sensitive** means "always considering other people's feelings": *She is very* ***sensitive*** *to other people's needs.*
• **Sensitive** also means "easily offended by what other people say": *He's very* ***sensitive*** *about his nose.*

This shows that **sensitive** is the word to use when talking about people's feelings, and **sensible** is used when talking about making the right decision.

Exercises

A Word sets

Look at the following sentences. Find another word that has the same meaning as the word(s) that has (have) been underlined. The first one has been done for you:

1. He was very angry when he found out what had happened. *furious*
2. I was happy that I had passed my exam. ________
3. She's feeling sad because she's just had a big argument with her boyfriend. ________
4. We had to walk for 20 kilometres, and I felt very tired. ________
5. Cut the onions into small pieces. ________
6. She looked very healthy when she came back from her holiday. ________
7. Have you read his newest book? ________
8. The Sahara desert covers a very big area of land. ________
9. Where did you buy those shoes? ________
10. The food tasted really bad. ________
11. How much money does she earn? ________

B Confusable words

Look at the following sentences. Underline the correct word to use in the sentence. The first one has been done for you:

1. She is very kind and she is always *sensible/sensitive* to other people's feelings.
2. Do you mind if I *lend/borrow* your pen?
3. I felt *alone/lonely* when I first came to live in England.
4. Small cars are much more *economical/economic* to drive.
5. She wrote about the meeting in her *dairy/diary*.
6. The thieves *robbed/stole* all his money.
7. He has been living here *for/since* five years.
8. I have been studying English *for/during* two years.
9. I didn't enjoy the film, and I was very *boring/bored*.
10. The teacher sent him to the *principal's/principle's* office.
11. The company has changed *it's/its* name.

Understanding signs and notices

In everyday life, we are surrounded by signs telling us what we can or must do. It is important to be able to understand what they mean.

For example:

This sign means: *You must not smoke.*

This sign means: *You must be careful because there is a guard dog.*

This sign means: *You can rent an apartment here.*

Exercises

A Understanding signs

Here are some more signs. Write underneath what the sign means:

1

PLEASE KEEP
OFF THE GRASS

You must not ______________________________ .

2

You can ______________________________ .

3

NO PARKING
7–9 AM
4–6 PM
MON – FRI

You must not ______________________________ .

4

You must not ____ .

B Matching signs to their meanings

Look at these signs and notices. Match the signs to the correct meaning:

A

Sell by: 21/03/09
Use by: 23/03/09

B

NO
THROUGH
ROAD

C

BOX OFFICE ENTRANCE
→

D

SALE
STARTS
28 JUNE
50% OFF

E

SLOW!
ROADWORKS
AHEAD

F

ADULTS £7.00
CHILDREN/SENIOR CITIZENS £4.50

1 You can soon buy things at half the usual price. D
2 Drive carefully because the road is being repaired here. ___
3 If you buy this food, you must use it before March 23rd. ___
4 Go this way if you want to buy theatre tickets. ___
5 Older people and children can pay less. ___
6 You can drive along this road but you cannot get out at the other end. ___

Writing letters and filling in forms

Style for informal letters

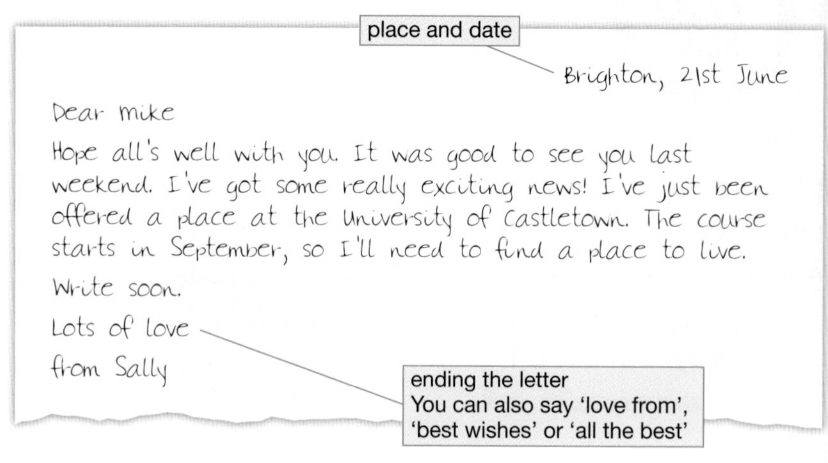
place and date

Brighton, 21st June

Dear Mike

Hope all's well with you. It was good to see you last weekend. I've got some really exciting news! I've just been offered a place at the University of Castletown. The course starts in September, so I'll need to find a place to live.

Write soon.

Lots of love

from Sally

ending the letter
You can also say 'love from', 'best wishes' or 'all the best'

Style for formal letters

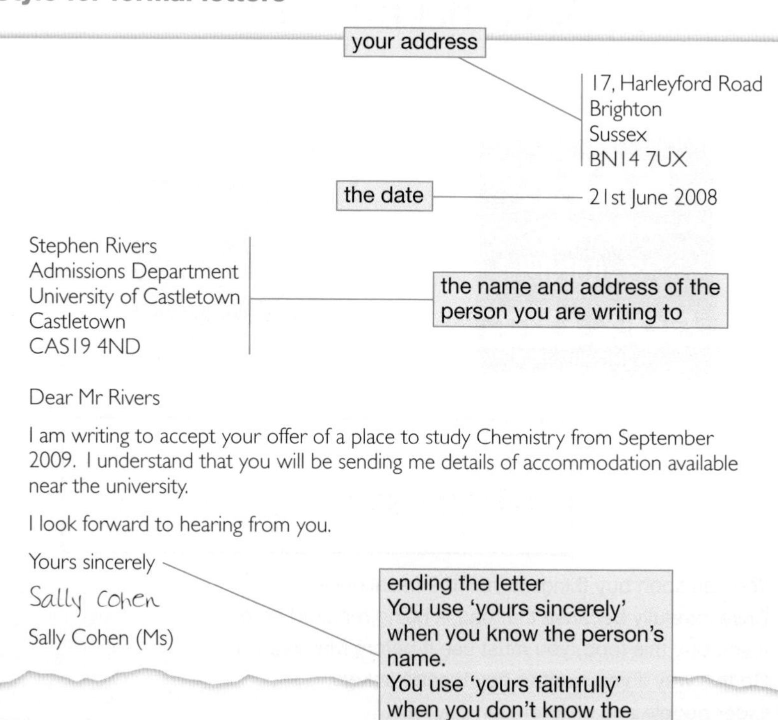
your address

17, Harleyford Road
Brighton
Sussex
BN14 7UX

the date — 21st June 2008

Stephen Rivers
Admissions Department
University of Castletown
Castletown
CAS19 4ND

the name and address of the person you are writing to

Dear Mr Rivers

I am writing to accept your offer of a place to study Chemistry from September 2009. I understand that you will be sending me details of accommodation available near the university.

I look forward to hearing from you.

Yours sincerely

Sally Cohen

Sally Cohen (Ms)

ending the letter
You use 'yours sincerely' when you know the person's name.
You use 'yours faithfully' when you don't know the person's name.

Emails

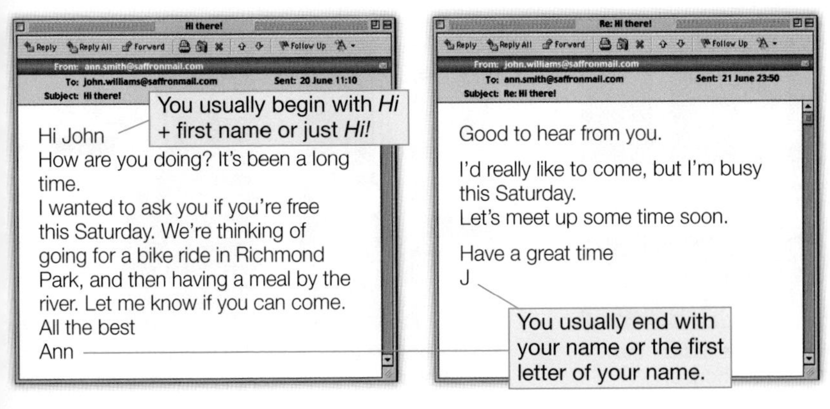

Hi there!

From: ann.smith@saffronmail.com
To: john.williams@saffronmail.com Sent: 20 June 11:10
Subject: Hi there!

Hi John
How are you doing? It's been a long time.
I wanted to ask you if you're free this Saturday. We're thinking of going for a bike ride in Richmond Park, and then having a meal by the river. Let me know if you can come.
All the best
Ann

Re: Hi there!

From: john.williams@saffronmail.com
To: ann.smith@saffronmail.com Sent: 21 June 23:50
Subject: Re: Hi there!

Good to hear from you.

I'd really like to come, but I'm busy this Saturday.
Let's meet up some time soon.

Have a great time
J

Filling in forms

LONDON ENGLISH SCHOOL **Application form**

Please complete clearly in CAPITAL LETTERS

Family name ...TANAKA... First name ...KEN...
Mr/Mrs/Miss/Ms ...MR...
Date of birth ...5/12/91... Nationality ...JAPANESE...
Email address ...ken.tanaka@hotmail.com... Daytime telephone number ...0207 005055...
What kind of course do you want? Elementary (Intermediate) Advanced
When would you like to start your course? ...AS SOON AS POSSIBLE...

Exercise

You are standing at the reception desk of the school, next to a Turkish girl called Asli. She's from Istanbul, and she wants to take an elementary course, starting next week. She was born on 5th May 1991. Her family name is Coskun. She is single. Her phone number is 020 855005 and her email address is coskun.asli@hotmail.com.

Can you help her to fill in her application form?

LONDON ENGLISH SCHOOL **Application form**

Please complete clearly in CAPITAL LETTERS

Family name .... First name ....
Mr/Mrs/Miss/Ms ....
Date of birth .... Nationality ....
Email address .... Daytime telephone number ....
What kind of course do you want? Elementary Intermediate Advanced
When would you like to start your course? ....

Prepositions of place and direction

She is **inside** the house.

He is **outside** the house.

He is waiting **in front of** the door.

The man is standing **behind** the woman.

The cat is **under** the table.

The books are **on** the shelf.

There is a vase of flowers **next to** the clock.

The men are sitting **opposite** each other.

The motorcycle is parked **between** the cars.

There is a picture **above** the mantlepiece.

There is a bridge **over** the river.

The man is getting **into** the car.

The man is getting **out of** the car.

The cat is jumping **onto** the table.

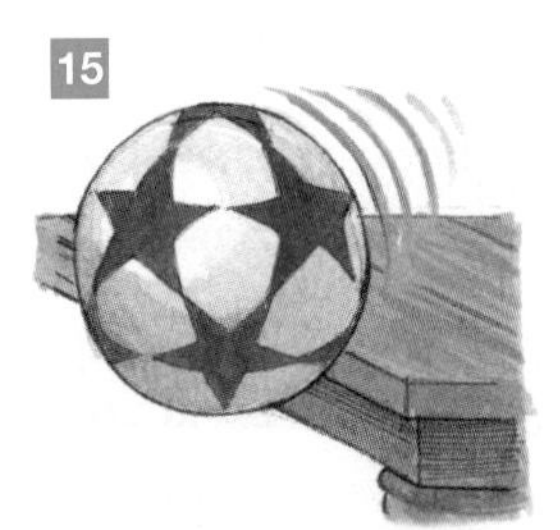

The ball is rolling **off** the table.

The boy is walking **up** the stairs.

She is coming **down** the stairs.

The ball is rolling **towards** the goal.

The train is going **through** the tunnel.

He is walking **away from** his car.

The car is going **round** the roundabout.

He is climbing **over** the wall.

The car is going **under** the bridge.

Exercise

Saying where things are in a room

Choose the correct preposition from the list below and write it in the space provided. The first one has been done for you.

on the left of on the right of in the corner of under above
in front of next to on

There is a picture of some flowers **1** ___*above*___ the fireplace.
2 ____________ the fireplace there is a small table with a lamp
3 ____________ it. **4** ____________ the fireplace there is a big television set. **5** ____________ the television set there is a wooden unit. There is a big sofa **6** ____________ the small table. **7** ____________ the sofa there is a low coffee table. There is a plant **8** ____________ the room.

mast /mɑːst $ mæst/ *noun* a tall pole that supports the sails on a ship

mas·ter¹ /ˈmɑːstə $ ˈmæstɚ/ *verb* to learn a skill or language very thoroughly so that you can use it well: *It takes years to master a game like chess.*
→ see Thesaurus at LEARN

master² *noun* **1** a male school teacher **2** someone who is very good at doing something: *He is one of the best known masters of the sport.* **3** a document from which people can make copies

mas·ter·piece /ˈmɑːstəpiːs $ ˈmæstɚˌpis/ *noun* a work of art or piece of writing that is the best that someone has produced: *The 'Mona Lisa' is Leonardo's masterpiece.*

mats

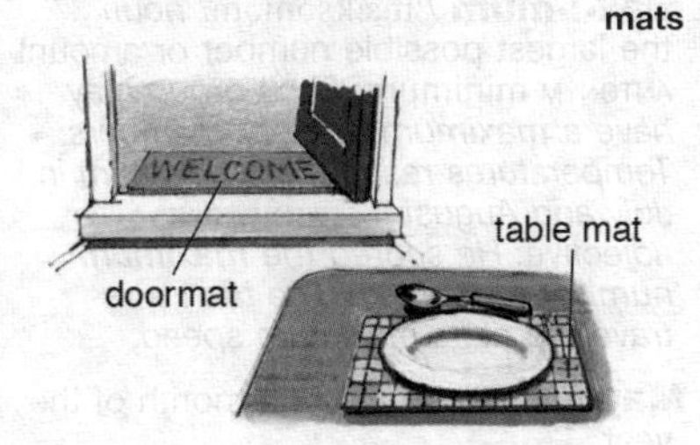

mat /mæt/ *noun* **1** a piece of thick material that covers part of a floor **2** a piece of material that you put under a plate or glass to protect a table

match¹ /mætʃ/ *noun* (plural **matches**)

KEY PATTERNS
a match against/with someone

1 a small wooden stick that produces a flame when you rub it against something. You light or strike a match: *He* ***struck a match*** *to find his way through the dark room.* • *a* ***box of matches***
2 *BrE* a game between two people or teams: *John* ***played*** *his first* ***football match*** *on Saturday.* • *We need to* ***win*** *this match.* • *England could* ***lose the match against*** *Kenya.* • *They've got a* ***match with*** *Manchester United next week.*

match² *verb*

KEY PATTERNS
match your eyes/hair/shirt etc
match something to/with something

1 if one thing matches another, the two things look attractive together because

match

These socks don't match.

they are similar: *Her blue dress matched her eyes.* • *Pink and orange don't match.*
2 also **match up** to find something that is similar to another thing or that belongs with another thing: *See if you can* ***match*** *the names* ***to*** *the voices you will hear.* • ***Match up*** *each sentence* ***with*** *the right picture.*

PHRASAL VERBS
match up to
match up to something to be as good as something: *The experience of flying certainly* ***matched up to*** *his expectations.*

match·ing /ˈmætʃɪŋ/ *adjective* matching things have the same colour, style, or pattern and so look attractive together: *black shoes and a matching handbag*

mate¹ /meɪt/ *noun* **1** *BrE* (informal) a friend: *This is my mate Jim.* **2** the sexual partner of an animal

mate² *verb* if animals mate, they have sex: *Birds mate in the spring.*

ma·te·ri·al /məˈtɪəriəl $ məˈtɪriəl/ *noun*
1 cloth: *She sewed the pieces of material together.*
2 any solid substance: *Plastic is a very easy material to work with.* • *All our products are made from recycled materials.*
3 (no plural) information that you can use when you are writing about something: *I think I've got enough material for my essay now.*
4 materials the things you use in order to do a job or an activity: *teaching materials*

ma·ter·ni·ty /məˈtɜːnəti $ məˈtɚnəti/ *adjective* used by or given to a woman who is going to have a baby or who has recently had a baby: *a maternity dress* • *She didn't get any maternity pay.*

math /mæθ/ the American word for MATHS

math·e·mat·i·cal /ˌmæθəˈmætɪkəl/ *adjective* related to mathematics

math·e·ma·ti·cian /ˌmæθəməˈtɪʃən/ *noun* someone who studies or teaches mathematics

math·e·mat·ics /ˌmæθəˈmætɪks/ *noun* (no plural) the study of numbers and shapes

maths /mæθs/ *BrE* mathematics SYNONYM **math** *AmE*

mat·ter¹ /ˈmætə $ ˈmætər/ *noun*
1 a subject or situation: *Your education is an important matter.* • *We can discuss this matter at the next meeting.* • *I'm no good at dealing with financial matters.*
2 matters the situation you are talking about SYNONYM **things**: *Matters became complicated when he fell in love with his brother's girlfriend.* • *That would only* ***make matters worse.***
3 the matter (spoken) if something is the matter, something is making a person feel upset or worried: *You look upset.* ***What's the matter?*** • *Is there something* ***the matter with*** *Jane?*
4 no matter how/where/what etc used to say that a situation remains the same whatever happens or whatever someone does: ***No matter how*** *hard he worked, he always failed his exams.*
5 as a matter of fact (spoken) used when you are telling someone something that is surprising: *"Will you be here in August?" "Well,* ***as a matter of fact*** *I'm thinking of spending the whole summer here."*
6 be a matter of opinion used to say that not everyone agrees that something is true: *"He's a great singer." "That's a matter of opinion."*

matter² *verb*

KEY PATTERNS
matter what/how etc
it matters/doesn't matter (to someone)

to be important: *"You've put the wrong date." "Does it matter?"* • ***It doesn't matter what*** *the score is as long as you've done your best.* • *Nothing* ***matters to*** *her except music.*

mat·tress /ˈmætrəs/ *noun* (plural **mattresses**) the soft part of a bed, which you lie on

ma·ture /məˈtʃʊə $ məˈtʃʊr/ *adjective*
1 someone who is mature behaves sensibly and like an adult ANTONYM **immature**: *She's very mature for her age.* **2** fully grown or developed ANTONYM **immature**: *mature trees* —**mature** *verb*: *It takes seven years for the wine to mature.*

maˌture ˈstudent *noun BrE* a student at college or university who starts studying after they are 21 years old

max·i·mum /ˈmæksəməm/ *noun* the largest possible number or amount ANTONYM **minimum**: *Each group may* ***have a maximum of*** *eight members.* • *Temperatures reach their maximum in July and August.* —**maximum** *adjective*: *He scored* ***the maximum number of*** *points.* • *The train was travelling at its maximum speed.*

May /meɪ/ *noun* the fifth month of the year

may /meɪ/ *modal verb*
1 if something may happen, it is possible that it will happen SYNONYM **might**: *If I stand on this box, I may be able to reach the shelf.*
2 used to say that it is possible that something is true or that something happened SYNONYM **might**: *You may be right.* • *Ring the door bell again – they* ***may not have*** *heard us the first time.*
3 (formal) used when giving someone permission to do something: *You may leave at 5.00 pm.* • *Students may not* (=are not allowed to) *remove CDs from the library.*
4 used when asking very politely to do something: *May I see your passport, sir?*

may·be /ˈmeɪbi/ *adverb*
1 used when saying what might be true or what might happen SYNONYM **perhaps**: *Maybe they haven't got your letter yet.* • *Maybe the switch is broken.* • *"Can we go to the beach tomorrow?" "Maybe* (=we might go, or we might not)."

2 used when making a suggestion SYNONYM **perhaps**: *Maybe we could meet up some time.*

may·on·naise /ˌmeɪəˈneɪz $ ˈmeɪəˌneɪz/ *noun* (no plural) a thick white sauce that you put on cold food

mayor /meə $ ˈmeɪɚ/ *noun* someone who is the head of the local government in a town or city

maze /meɪz/ *noun* a set of small roads or passages where you have difficulty finding where to get out: *I was lost in a maze of long dark corridors.*

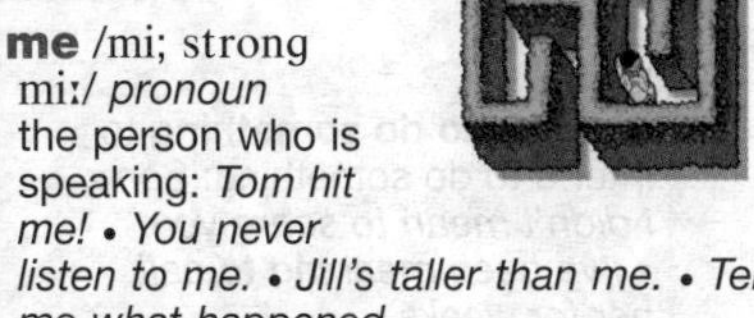
maze

me /mi; strong miː/ *pronoun* the person who is speaking: *Tom hit me! • You never listen to me. • Jill's taller than me. • Tell me what happened.*

mead·ow /ˈmedəʊ $ ˈmedoʊ/ *noun* a field with wild grass and flowers

mea·gre *BrE*, **meager** *AmE* /ˈmiːgə $ ˈmigɚ/ *adjective* very small in amount: *They paid him a meagre salary.*

meal /miːl/ *noun*

KEY PATTERNS
have a meal

a time when you eat food, or the food that you eat then: *Would you like to come to our place on Sunday for a meal? • Let's* ***go out for a meal*** *tonight. • We usually* ***have*** *our evening* ***meal*** *at around 7 o'clock. • What a delicious meal!*

mean¹ → see box on page 414

mean² *adjective*

KEY PATTERNS
be mean to someone
a mean thing to do

1 unkind: *Why are you always so* ***mean to*** *him? • That was* ***a very mean thing to do.*** → see Thesaurus at UNKIND
2 *BrE* not willing to spend money ANTONYM **generous**: *He was so mean that he didn't buy his girlfriend a birthday present.*

mean·ing /ˈmiːnɪŋ/ *noun*
1 the idea or message that something gives you: *This word has several meanings. • I couldn't understand the meaning of his remark.*
2 (no plural) the purpose of something: *He had lost everything that gave meaning to his life.*

mean·ing·ful /ˈmiːnɪŋfəl/ *adjective* serious and important: *a meaningful discussion about religion*

mean·ing·less /ˈmiːnɪŋləs/ *adjective* without any purpose or meaning: *Most song lyrics are practically meaningless.*

means /miːnz/ *noun* (plural **means**)

KEY PATTERNS
a means of something
a means of doing something

a way of doing something: *Art is a* ***means of*** *expressing your ideas and feelings. • The police had* ***no means of*** *proving that Harris was guilty.*

PHRASES
by means of something using something: *Their movements were recorded* ***by means of*** *a hidden camera.*
by all means used to emphasize that you are willing for someone to do something: ***By all means*** *check the measurements for yourself.*

meant the past tense and past participle of MEAN¹

mean·time /ˈmiːntaɪm/ *noun* **in the meantime** until something happens: *The film starts in ten minutes. In the meantime, here's some music.*

mean·while /ˈmiːnwaɪl/ *adverb* in the period while something is happening or before something happens: *William took the dog for a walk. Meanwhile Jack fed the rabbits. • Jill will be here soon. Meanwhile you can tell me about your holiday.*

mea·sles /ˈmiːzəlz/ also **the measles** *noun* (no plural) an illness which makes you feel very hot and gives you small red spots on your face and body: *Did you have measles as a child?*

mea·sure¹ /ˈmeʒə $ ˈmeʒɚ/ *verb*
1 to find out the size or amount of something, using a piece of equipment:

mean /miːn/ *verb* (past tense and past participle **meant** /ment/)

mean

1 to have a particular meaning: *'Start' and 'begin' **mean** the same thing.* • *"What does 'arigatou' **mean** in English?" "It **means** 'thank you'."* • *The red light **means** that you should stop.*

2 to intend to express a particular thing by what you say: *I'm sorry. I don't understand what you **mean**.* • *He said "this Saturday", but he **meant** next Saturday.* • *What do you think the writer **means**?*

3 **mean to do something** to intend to do something: *Sorry, I didn't **mean to scare** you.* • *I've been **meaning to call** her for weeks.*

*I've been **meaning** to call her for weeks.*

4 used when saying what the result of something is: *If I change schools, it **will mean** leaving the house 20 minutes earlier.* • *He wants to be a doctor, which **means that** he'll have at least six years of training after university.*

*If I change schools, it **will mean** leaving the house 20 minutes earlier.*

5 **be meant to be something, be meant for something** to be for a particular purpose: *It **was meant to be** a joke, but no one laughed.* • *These books **are meant for** children who are learning to read.*

PHRASES

I mean (spoken)
a) used when you are explaining or adding something to what you have just said: *The piano will be hard to move – **I mean** it's really heavy.* • *I like Tony a lot – **I mean** he's a really nice person.*
b) used when you want to correct what you have just said: *I think the papers are in the red folder – **I mean** the yellow one.*

Do you mean ...?, You mean ...? (spoken)
used when you want to check that you understand something: *"I'm looking for a tall guy, with red hair." "Oh, **do you mean** Dave?"* • *"I really miss this." "Walking in the woods, **you mean**?"*

What do you mean? (spoken)
used when you want someone to explain what they have said, especially when you are annoyed: *"Sorry, you can't go in there." "**What do you mean?** Why not?"* • ***What do you mean**, "they won't accept my credit card"? Why not?*

I ***measured*** *the window* ***with*** *a ruler.* • *How can we measure the temperature of the water?*
2 (formal) to be a particular size or amount: *His feet measure over 45 cm in length.*

PHRASAL VERBS

measure up
to be as good as you expected or wanted: *Did New York* ***measure up to*** *your idea of it?*

measure² *noun*

KEY PATTERNS
take measures to change/improve etc something

an official action that someone takes to deal with a problem: *The government must* ***take measures to*** *reduce the number of young people who are homeless.*

mea·sure·ment /ˈmeʒəmənt $ ˈmeʒɚmənt/ *noun* the length, height etc of something: *What are the exact measurements of the room?*

meat /miːt/ *noun* (no plural) the flesh of animals and birds that you eat: *I don't eat very much meat.*

me·chan·ic /mɪˈkænɪk/ *noun* someone whose job is to repair vehicles and machinery

me·chan·i·cal /mɪˈkænɪkəl/ *adjective* related to machines, or using power from a machine: *His car developed mechanical problems.* • *a mechanical toy*

mech·a·nis·m /ˈmekənɪzəm/ *noun* the part of a machine that does a particular job: *The door has a special locking mechanism.*

med·al /ˈmedl/ *noun* a round flat piece of metal that is given to someone as a prize or reward: *He received a medal for bravery.*

med·al·list *BrE*, **medalist** *AmE* /ˈmedl-ɪst/ *noun* someone who has won a medal in a competition: *She's an Olympic medalist.*

med·dle /ˈmedl/ *verb* to try to change or influence a situation, even though you should not because it does not involve you SYNONYM **interfere**: *Stop meddling in my affairs.*

me·di·a /ˈmiːdiə/ *noun* **1 the media** television, radio, and newspapers: *The crime was reported by the media.*
2 the plural of MEDIUM

mediaeval a British spelling of MEDIEVAL

med·i·cal¹ /ˈmedɪkəl/ *adjective* relating to medicine and treating diseases or injuries: *medical qualifications* • *She needs medical care.*
—**medically** /-kli/ *adverb*

medical² *noun BrE* an examination of your body by a doctor to find out whether you are healthy SYNONYM **physical** *AmE*: *You must have a medical before you join the army.*

med·i·ca·tion /ˌmedəˈkeɪʃən/ *noun* (formal) medicine: *"Are you taking any medication at present?" asked the nurse.*

medi·cine /ˈmedsən $ ˈmedəsən/ *noun* **1** a substance for treating an illness, especially one that you drink: *cough medicine* • *Keep medicines away from children.* **2** (no plural) the treatment and study of illnesses and injuries: *Sue wants to study medicine.*

USAGE
You say **take some medicine.**
✘ Don't say 'drink some medicine'.

THESAURUS
drug: *This condition can be treated with* ***drugs*** (=medicines).
pill/tablet: *He took a* ***pill*** *to help him sleep* (=a small solid piece of medicine that can be swallowed).

med·i·e·val also **mediaeval** *BrE* /ˌmediˈiːvəl $ ˌmɪdˈivəl/ *adjective* related to the MIDDLE AGES, the period of European history from about 100 to 1500 AD: *a medieval castle*

me·di·o·cre /ˌmiːdiˈəʊkə $ ˌmidiˈoʊkɚ/ *adjective* (formal) not very good in quality: *Tim got mediocre grades in his exams.*

med·i·tate /ˈmedəteɪt/ *verb* to stay silent and calm for a period of time as part of your religion or to help you relax: *I meditate for 20 minutes every morning.*

med·i·ta·tion /ˌmedəˈteɪʃən/ *noun* (no plural) when you stay silent and calm for a period of time as part of your religion or to help you relax: *We spent 15 minutes in meditation.*

me·di·um[1] /ˈmiːdiəm/ *adjective*

KEY PATTERNS
of medium height/size/length etc

something that is medium in size or amount is not very big and not very small, but in the middle: *He's of medium height, with brown eyes.*

medium[2] *noun* (plural **media** /-diə/) something that is used to communicate information or ideas: *Advertising is a powerful medium for communication.*

ˌmedium-ˈsized also **ˌmedium-ˈsize** *adjective* not very small and not very large: *a medium-sized bed*

meet /miːt/ *verb* (past tense and past participle **met** /met/)

KEY PATTERNS
meet someone
meet someone's needs/standards

1 to see and talk to someone for the first time: *Have you ever met her husband?* • *They first met at university.* • *Pleased to meet you* (=used to say hello to someone when you meet them). • *It was nice meeting you* (=used when you say goodbye to someone you have just met).
2 to come to the same place as someone else because you have arranged it: *We'll meet at eight o'clock outside the theatre.* • *Her mother came to the airport to meet her.*
3 to see someone by chance when you are out somewhere: *She was walking to the library when she met Vicky.*
4 (formal) if something meets someone's standards or needs, it is good enough: *The rooms are designed to* ***meet the needs*** *of older people.*
5 (written) if two things meet, they join or touch: *the point where the two roads meet*

PHRASAL VERBS
meet with (formal)
meet with someone to have a meeting with someone: *The tutor* ***met with*** *students to discuss the problem.*

meet·ing /ˈmiːtɪŋ/ *noun*

KEY PATTERNS
be in a meeting
have a meeting

an organized event where people discuss something. You organize, arrange, or call a meeting. Then you have or hold it somewhere. You cancel a meeting if you decide not to have it: *Mr Thompson is* ***in a meeting.*** • *We're* ***having a meeting*** *next week to talk about this problem.* • *She* ***called a meeting*** *to discuss the future of the company.*

meg·a·byte /ˈmegəbaɪt/ (written abbreviation **MB**) *noun* a unit for measuring computer information, equal to one million BYTEs

mel·low /ˈmeləʊ $ ˈmeloʊ/ *adjective* relaxed, gentle, and calm: *After my bath, I felt really mellow.* • *The club has a lovely mellow atmosphere.*

mel·o·dy /ˈmelədi/ *noun* (plural **melodies**) a tune: *She sang to a series of traditional melodies.*

mel·on /ˈmelən/ *noun* a large round fruit with yellow, orange, or green skin and a lot of flat seeds → see picture on page A7

melt /melt/ *verb* to change from solid to liquid, or to make something do this by heating it: *The sun had melted the snow.* • *The candle started to melt.*

melt

mem·ber /ˈmembə $ ˈmembɚ/ *noun* someone who has joined a club, group, or organization: *We want our members to feel involved in our work.* • *a member of the college staff*

ˌMember of ˈParliament (abbreviation **MP**) *noun* in the UK, someone whom the people elect to speak and act for them in parliament

mem·ber·ship /ˈmembəʃɪp $ ˈmembɚˌʃɪp/ *noun* (no plural)
1 when you are a member of a group or organization: *Your membership of the Student Union will last for three years.* • *How much is the membership fee?* **2** all the people who belong to a club or organization: *There has been a fall in membership* (=fewer members) *this year.*

me·men·to /məˈmentəʊ $ məˈmentoʊ/ *noun* (plural **mementos**) a small object that you keep to remind you of someone or something: *The photograph is a memento of my schooldays.*

mem·o /ˈmeməʊ $ ˈmemoʊ/ *noun* (plural **memos**) a short official note that you write to another person working in the same organization as you

mem·oirs /ˈmemwɑːz $ ˈmemwɑrz/ *plural noun* a book that someone writes about their life and experiences: *The ex-prime minister has published his memoirs.*

mem·o·ra·ble /ˈmemərəbəl/ *adjective* very good and likely to be remembered: *a memorable film*

me·mo·ri·al¹ /məˈmɔːriəl/ *adjective* done to remind people of someone who has died: *Each year there is a memorial ceremony for people who died in the war.*

memorial² *noun* a building or other structure that is built to remind people of someone who has died: *a war memorial*

mem·o·rize also **memorise** *BrE* /ˈmeməraɪz/ *verb* to learn and remember words, music, or other information: *She memorized her speech.*

mem·o·ry /ˈeməri/ *noun* (plural **memories**)

KEY PATTERNS
have a memory of something

1 the ability to remember things: *She's got a good memory.*
2 something that you remember from the past: *She **had** very happy **memories of** her time at college.* • *She **has no memory of** the accident* (=she cannot remember it at all).
3 the part of a computer where information is stored: *How much memory does your computer have?*

PHRASES
from memory if you can do something from memory, you can do it without needing to read anything or look at anything: *She can play the whole piece of music **from memory**.*
in memory of someone if you do something in memory of someone who has died, you do it in order to remember them: *This statue was put up **in memory of** the soldiers who died.*

WORD CHOICE
memory or **souvenir**?
• A **memory** is a thought which you have when you remember something that happened a long time ago: *I have lots of happy **memories** of my schooldays.*
• A **souvenir** is an object that you keep to remember a place that you visited: *The vase is a **souvenir** from a holiday in Spain.*

men the plural of MAN

men·ace /ˈmenɪs/ *noun* something or someone that is dangerous: *Leaking gas ovens are a menace to old people.*

mend /mend/ *verb*
to repair something that is broken or damaged: *If they can't mend the TV, we'll have to get a new one.* • *We'll have to **get** the roof **mended*** (=ask someone to mend it). ➔ see Thesaurus at REPAIR¹

ˈmen's room the American word for the GENTS

men·tal /ˈmentl/ *adjective* related to the mind, or happening in the mind: *mental health* • *I did a quick mental calculation.* —**mentally** *adverb*: *a mentally ill patient*

men·tion /ˈmenʃən/ *verb*

KEY PATTERNS
mention that
mention something to someone
mention what/how/whether etc
mention something

if you mention something, you say something about it, but you do not give a lot of information: *She **mentioned that** she'd just got back from the US.* • *I'll **mention** it **to** Rob.* • *Did Phil **mention whether** he'd come to the party?* • *He never mentioned his illness.*

PHRASES
not to mention used when you are adding something better, bigger, or more surprising: *He stole my money, **not to mention** my girlfriend.*
—**mention** *noun*: *There was no mention of the president in the article about the palace.*

GRAMMAR
You **mention something**.
✘ Don't say 'mention about something'.

men•u /ˈmenjuː/ *noun* **1** a list of all the food that is available to eat in a restaurant: *The waiter brought us the menu to look at.* **2** a list of things that is shown on a computer screen: *Select 'Programs' from the menu.*

mer•cu•ry /ˈmɜːkjəri $ ˈmɚkjəri/ *noun* (no plural) a silver-coloured liquid metal

mer•cy /ˈmɜːsi $ ˈmɚsi/ *noun* (no plural) **1** kindness and willingness to forgive people: *The hostages pleaded for mercy.* **2 be at the mercy of someone/something** to be unable to protect yourself from someone or something: *We were at the mercy of the killers.*

mere /mɪə $ mɪr/ *adjective* only, or not more than; used to emphasize how small or unimportant something is: *We had a mere ten minutes to do the test.* • *He won by a mere 3 points.*

mere•ly /ˈmɪəli $ ˈmɪrli/ *adverb* (formal) only: *Smoking is not merely unpleasant, it's unhealthy.*

merge /mɜːdʒ $ mɚdʒ/ *verb* to join together to form one thing: *Havering College is merging with the university.*

mer•it /ˈmerɪt/ *noun* a good quality or feature: *The plan had the merit of being simple.* • *Job applicants are chosen on merit.*

mer•maid /ˈmɜːmeɪd $ ˈmɚmeɪd/ *noun* an imaginary creature with a woman's body and a fish's tail instead of legs

mer•ry /ˈmeri/ *adjective* **Merry Christmas!** used to greet someone at Christmas

mesh /meʃ/ *noun* (no plural) material made of threads or wires that have been fastened together like a net: *The windows were protected by metal mesh.*

mess¹ /mes/ *noun*
1 (no plural) if a place is a mess, it is very untidy: *I'm afraid my room's a bit of a mess.*
2 a situation in which there are a lot of problems: *I've got to sort out this mess.*

PHRASES

in a mess if a place is in a mess, it is very untidy: *The house was **in a** terrible mess.*

make a mess of something (spoken, informal) to spoil something or do something badly: *I knew you'd **make a mess of** things!*

mess² *verb*

PHRASAL VERBS

mess around, mess about *BrE* (informal)
1 mess around to do things that are silly or not useful: *We were just **messing around** on the computer.* • *Don't **mess around with** my books.*
2 mess someone around to treat someone badly, for example by not doing what you promised to do: *Sorry to **mess you around**, but could I come over tomorrow instead of tonight?*

mess up (informal)
mess something up to do something badly or make a mistake: *I **messed up** the exam.*

mes•sage /ˈmesɪdʒ/ *noun*

KEY PATTERNS
a message for someone
a message from someone

1 a piece of information that you send or give to another person: *I've got a message **for** you **from** Sammy.* • *I'm afraid Mr Jacobs isn't here at the moment. Would you like to **leave a message** for him?* • *I had 19 **email messages** this morning.*
2 the main idea in a film, speech, book etc that the writer is trying to make people understand: *The message is clear: don't drink and drive.*

mes•sen•ger /ˈmesəndʒə $ ˈmesəndʒɚ/ *noun* someone who takes messages to other people, especially as a job: *a motorbike messenger service*

mess•y /ˈmesi/ *adjective* (**messier, messiest**) dirty or untidy: *Your bedroom is very messy.*

met the past tense and past participle of MEET

met•al /ˈmetl/ *noun* a substance such as iron, gold, or steel: *a metal gate*

me•te•or /ˈmiːtiə $ ˈmitiɚ/ *noun* a small piece of rock or metal that is moving through space

me•te•o•rite /ˈmiːtiəraɪt/ *noun* a small meteor that has landed on the Earth's surface

messy

a messy room

a tidy room

me·ter /ˈmiːtə $ ˈmitɚ/ *noun* **1** the American spelling of METRE **2** a machine that measures the amount of power such as gas or electricity you have used

meth·od /ˈmeθəd/ *noun*

KEY PATTERNS
a method of doing something

a way of doing something: *What is the best* ***method of*** *teaching children to read?* • *There are many different methods of payment* (=ways of paying).

me·thod·i·cal /məˈθɒdɪkəl $ məˈθɑdɪkəl/ *adjective* done carefully and in the right order, or doing things in this way: *a well-planned, methodical piece of writing* • *My father's very methodical when he's working.*

me·tre *BrE*, **meter** *AmE* /ˈmiːtə $ ˈmitɚ/ (written abbreviation **m**) *noun* a unit for measuring length, equal to 100 centimetres CENTIMETRES

met·ric /ˈmetrɪk/ *adjective* using the system of weighing and measuring that is based on the kilogram and the metre

mg the written abbreviation of MILLIGRAM

mice the plural of MOUSE (1)

mi·cro·chip /ˈmaɪkrəʊˌtʃɪp $ ˈmaɪkroʊˌtʃɪp/ *noun* a small part of a computer or a machine, containing the electronic parts that control what the machine does

mi·cro·phone /ˈmaɪkrəfəʊn $ ˈmaɪkrəˌfoʊn/ *noun* a piece of equipment that you use to record sounds or to make a sound louder

mi·cro·pro·ces·sor /ˈmaɪkrəʊˌprəʊsesə $ ˌmaɪkroʊˈprɑsesɚ/ *noun* the main microchip in a computer

mi·cro·scope /ˈmaɪkrəskəʊp $ ˈmaɪkrəˌskoʊp/ *noun* a scientific instrument that makes it possible to see very small things: *I examined the virus under a microscope.*

microscope

mi·cro·wave /ˈmaɪkrəweɪv/ also **ˌmicrowave ˈoven** *noun* a machine that cooks food very quickly, using electric waves instead of heat —**microwave** *verb*: *It takes only three minutes to microwave a potato.*

mid- /mɪd/ in the middle of a time or place: *They went to Boston in mid-June.* • *She was born in the mid-1980s.*

mid·air /ˌmɪdˈeə $ ˌmɪdˈer/ *noun* **in midair** in the sky or in the air: *The ball seemed to stop in midair.* —**midair** *adjective*: *The planes were involved in a midair collision.*

mid·day /ˌmɪdˈdeɪ $ ˈmɪd-deɪ/ *noun* (no plural) 12 o'clock in the middle of the day SYNONYM **noon**

middle

Sam was sitting in the middle.

mid·dle¹ /ˈmɪdl/ *noun*

KEY PATTERNS
the middle of something
in the middle

1 the middle the part of something that is in the centre, furthest from the edges: *The middle of the cake is still not cooked.* • *There was an island in the middle of the lake.*

A B C D E F G H I J K L M N O P Q R S T U V W X Y Z

2 the part that is between the beginning and the end of a period of time: *We're going on holiday **in the middle of** June.* • *It was **the middle of** the night by the time we got home.*

PHRASES

in the middle between other people or things: *The three boys sat on the bench, with Sam in the middle.*

be in the middle of doing something to be busy doing something: *I can't talk now – I'm **in the middle of** doing my homework.*

middle² *adjective*

1 the middle one of a number of things is the one between the others: *The scissors are in the middle drawer.*

2 half of the way between the beginning and the end of an event or period of time: *The middle part of the film was a bit boring.*

ˌmiddle-ˈaged *adjective* a middle-aged person is between about 40 and 60 years old

ˌMiddle ˈAges *noun* **the Middle Ages** the period in European history between about 1100 and 1400 AD

ˌmiddle ˈclass *noun* **the middle class, the middle classes** people such as teachers, doctors, and managers, who are neither very rich nor very poor —**middle-class** *adjective*: *a middle-class family*

ˌMiddle ˈEast *noun* **the Middle East** the part of Asia that includes Iran and Egypt and the countries between them

ˌmiddle ˈname *noun* the name that comes between your first name and your SURNAME (=your family name)

ˈmiddle school *noun* in Britain, a school for children between the ages of nine and 13, and in the US for children between 11 and 14

mid·night /ˈmɪdnaɪt/ *noun* (no plural) 12 o'clock at night: *We stayed up until midnight.*

WORD CHOICE

midnight or **middle of the night**?

• **Midnight** is 12 o'clock at night: *I went to bed at midnight.*

• **The middle of the night** is the period between 12 and 4 o'clock at night: *We were woken up by a strange noise in the middle of the night.*

mid·way /ˌmɪdˈweɪ/ *adjective, adverb* at the middle point between two places, or in the middle of a period of time SYNONYM **halfway**: *We scored at the midway stage of the game.* • *The Comoro Islands lie midway between Madagascar and the coast of Tanzania.*

mid·week /ˌmɪdˈwiːk/ *adjective, adverb* in the middle of the week: *I never go to parties midweek.* • *a midweek match*

mid·wife /ˈmɪdwaɪf/ *noun* (plural **midwives** /-waɪvz/) a nurse who has been trained to help women when they are having a baby

might /maɪt/ *modal verb*

1 if something might happen, it is possible that it will happen SYNONYM **may**: *Be careful! You might hurt yourself!* • *I might not be back until much later.*

2 used to say that it is possible that something is true SYNONYM **may**: *You might be right.* • *He might not be living there any more.*

3 if something might have happened, it is possible that it happened, or it was possible but did not happen: *He **might have** got lost* (=it is possible). • *We **might have** been killed* (=but we weren't)*!*

4 used when making a polite suggestion: *You might try ringing her at home.*

GRAMMAR

The negative of **might** is **might not** or **mightn't**.

might've /ˈmaɪtəv/ the short form of 'might have': *This might've been a bad idea.*

mi·graine /ˈmiːgreɪn $ ˈmaɪgreɪn/ *noun* a very bad HEADACHE

mi·grant /ˈmaɪgrənt/ *noun* a person, bird, or animal that regularly moves from one place to another —**migrant** *adjective*: *The farm employs a large number of migrant workers.*

mi·grate /maɪˈgreɪt $ ˈmaɪgreɪt/ *verb* **1** if birds or animals migrate, they travel to a warmer part of the world in winter and return in the spring **2** to go to live in another place, usually in order to find work: *Thousands of workers migrated west.*

mi·gra·tion /maɪˈɡreɪʃən/ *noun* when a large group of birds, animals, or people move from one place to another

mike /maɪk/ (informal) a MICROPHONE

mild /maɪld/ *adjective* **1** not too severe, strong, or serious: *Dean had a mild case of the flu.* • *a mild punishment* **2** not having a strong taste: *The sauce is very mild.* **3** mild weather is not too cold: *It's very mild for January.*

mile /maɪl/ *noun* a unit for measuring distance, equal to 1,760 yards or 1,609 metres: *Our school is about three miles away.*

mile·age, milage /ˈmaɪlɪdʒ/ *noun* (no plural) **1** the total number of miles a vehicle has travelled: *The mileage is very low for the age of the vehicle.* **2** the distance a car or other vehicle can travel using a particular amount of FUEL: *Diesel engines get better mileage but they are noisier.*

mil·i·ta·ry¹ /ˈmɪlətəri $ ˈmɪləˌteri/ *adjective* related to the army, navy etc: *military vehicles* • *military conflicts*

military² *noun* **the military** the army, navy etc: *Jeff decided to join the military.*

mi·li·tia /məˈlɪʃə/ *noun* an organized group of soldiers who are not members of an official army

milk¹ /mɪlk/ *noun* (no plural) a whitish liquid produced by female animals and humans to feed their babies: *a glass of milk*

milk² *verb* to take milk from a cow or goat

milk·man /ˈmɪlkmən/ *noun* (plural **milkmen** /-mən/) someone who delivers milk to people's houses

milk·shake /ˌmɪlkˈʃeɪk $ ˈmɪlkʃeɪk/ *noun* a cold drink made from milk mixed with fruit or chocolate

mill /mɪl/ *noun* **1** a building containing a large machine for crushing grain **2** a factory that produces paper, steel, or cloth: *a paper mill*

mil·len·ni·um /mɪˈleniəm/ *noun* (plural **millennia** /-niə/) a period of 1,000 years: *The year 2000 was the start of a new millennium.*

mil·li·gram /ˈmɪləɡræm/ (written abbreviation **mg**) *noun* a unit for measuring weight, equal to 1/1,000th of one GRAM

mil·li·li·tre *BrE*, **milliliter** *AmE* /ˈmɪləˌliːtə $ ˈmɪləˌlitɚ/ (written abbreviation **ml**) *noun* a unit for measuring liquids, equal to 1/1,000th of one LITRE

mil·li·me·tre *BrE*, **millimeter** *AmE* /ˈmɪləˌmiːtə $ ˈmɪləˌmitɚ/ (written abbreviation **mm**) *noun* a unit for measuring length, equal to 1/1,000th of one METRE

mil·lion /ˈmɪljən/ *noun* (plural **million** or **millions**) **1** 1,000,000: *$75 million* • *ten million people* **2** also **millions** (spoken, informal) a very large number of people or things: *I have millions of things to do today.* —**millionth** *number*

> **GRAMMAR**
> You use the plural form **million** after a number: *two million pounds*
> You use the plural form **millions** before **of**: *millions of years ago*

mil·lion·aire /ˌmɪljəˈneə $ ˌmɪljəˈner/ *noun* someone who is very rich and has a million pounds or a million dollars

mime /maɪm/ *verb* to show something using movements, but no words: *Dana mimed pouring a glass of water.* —**mime** *noun*

mim·ic /ˈmɪmɪk/ *verb* (**mimicked**, **mimicking**) to copy someone's speech or actions: *Jodie mimicked the teacher's voice.*

mince /mɪns/ *noun* (no plural) *BrE* meat that has been cut or ground into very small pieces SYNONYM **ground beef** *AmE*

mind¹ /maɪnd/ *verb*
1 Do you mind ...?, Would you mind ...? *BrE* (spoken) **a)** say this to politely ask if you can do something: *Do you mind if I call my mom?* • *Would you mind if I borrowed your blue dress?* • *I have to ask you a couple of questions – do you mind?* **b)** say this to politely ask if someone can do something for you: *Do you mind signing these forms?* • *Would you mind turning up the heat a little?* • *I hate to ask you to wait, but* ***would you mind****? I'm not ready.*

2 never mind (spoken) say this to tell someone that something does not matter: *"Do you want the big box or the little one?" "**Never mind**, I'll get it myself."* • *"What did you say?" "Oh, **never mind**. It's not important."* • ***Never mind**, that mud will wash off.*
3 I wouldn't mind ... (spoken) say this when you would like to do something: ***I wouldn't mind** another cup of coffee. Do you want one too?* • *It's supposed to be a good movie. **I wouldn't mind** seeing it.*
4 I don't mind (spoken) say this when you will be happy with whatever happens or with whatever someone decides: *"Do you want pasta or chicken tonight?" "**I don't mind**."* • *I just need a drink – **I don't mind what** it is.* • *You can put it in the box or over there, **I don't mind which**.*
5 mind your own business (spoken) say this when you are annoyed and want to tell someone not to ask questions. This is not a polite expression: *"Can't you keep that baby quiet?" "Why don't you **mind your own business**?"* • *"So, are you married?" "**Mind your own business**."*
6 mind something (spoken) used to tell someone to be careful, so that they do not hit something or fall: ***Mind** your head; the ceiling is very low.* • ***Mind** the step! Everyone trips over it.*

GRAMMAR
You say that you **don't mind doing something**.
✘ Don't say that you 'don't mind to do something'.

mind² *noun*
the part of your brain that you use to think and imagine things: *I kept picturing what would happen **in my mind**.* • *New ideas were always **coming into her mind**.* • *He tried to push these worries **out of his mind*** (=he tried not to think about them).
PHRASES
change your mind to change your opinion or decision about something: ***I changed** my **mind** about going to college.*
make up your mind to decide about something: *The desserts all looked so good I couldn't **make up** my **mind** which one to have.* • *He still **has** not **made his mind up** which club he will play for next season.*
have something in mind to be thinking about something and have a plan about it: *Most of the students did not **have** a particular career **in mind**.*
be on your mind if something is on your mind, you are thinking or worrying about it a lot: *You look worried. What's **on your mind**?*
have something on your mind to be thinking or worrying about something a lot: *I don't want to bother him. He **has** a lot **on his mind** right now.*
keep something in mind, bear something in mind if you tell someone to bear something in mind, you tell them to remember an important piece of information: *You must **keep in mind** that the weather changes quickly in the mountains.* • ***Bear in mind** that young children will not sit still during a long plane flight.*
come to mind, spring to mind if something comes to mind, you begin to think of it or remember it: *As I read, two questions kept **coming to mind**.* • *"Do you have any ideas?" "Nothing that **springs to mind**, I'm afraid."*

mine¹ /maɪn/ *pronoun*
a thing belonging to the person who is speaking: *Could I borrow your pen? I've lost mine.* • *Hey, that's mine! Give it back!* • *A friend **of mine*** (=one of my friends) *gave it to me.*

mine² *noun*
1 a place where people take coal, gold etc out of the ground, usually by digging a deep hole
2 a type of bomb that someone hides under the ground or in water, that explodes when something touches it: *The ship hit a mine and sank.* • *Many children have been killed by **land mines**.*

mine³ *verb* to dig into the ground to find gold, coal etc: *People came to mine for gold.*

mine·field /ˈmaɪnfiːld/ *noun* **1** an area of land or sea where bombs have been hidden **2** a situation in which there are many hidden difficulties and dangers: *The whole process is a legal minefield.*

min·er /ˈmaɪnə $ ˈmaɪnɚ/ *noun*
someone who works in a mine: *a coal miner*

min·e·ral /ˈmɪnərəl/ *noun* a natural substance such as iron or salt that is in the earth and some foods

ˈmineral ˌwater *noun* water that comes from the ground naturally and that you can buy in bottles

min·gle /ˈmɪŋgəl/ *verb* if sounds or smells mingle, they mix together: *The smells of flowers and spices mingled in the hot air.*

min·ia·ture /ˈmɪnətʃə $ ˈmɪniətʃɚ/ *adjective* much smaller than normal: *a miniature camera*

min·i·mal /ˈmɪnəməl/ *adjective* very small, and therefore not something you should worry about: *The accident caused only minimal damage to the car.* —**minimally** *adverb*

min·i·mize also **minimise** *BrE* /ˈmɪnəmaɪz/ *verb* to make something as small as possible: *We hope to minimize the effects of pollution.*

min·i·mum /ˈmɪnəməm/ *noun* the smallest number or amount that is possible ANTONYM **maximum**: *Most people need a minimum of seven hours' sleep.* • *Quickly, and with* ***the minimum of*** *noise, the police surrounded the house.* • *The airline tried to* ***keep*** *delays* ***to a minimum.*** —**minimum** *adjective*: *The government wants to increase the* ***minimum wage*** *for workers.*

min·ing /ˈmaɪnɪŋ/ *noun* (no plural) the job or process of digging gold, coal etc out of the ground

min·is·ter /ˈmɪnəstə $ ˈmɪnəstɚ/ *noun* **1** a religious leader in some Christian churches **2** a politician who is the head of a government department in some countries: *the Minister of Agriculture*

min·is·try /ˈmɪnəstri/ *noun* **1** (plural **ministries**) a government department in some countries: *the Ministry of Defence* **2 the ministry** some parts of the Christian church, or the work done by those parts: *Sam planned to join the ministry.*

SPELLING
This word is often spelled wrongly. The correct spelling is: **ministry**.

mi·nor /ˈmaɪnə $ ˈmaɪnɚ/ *adjective* not very important or serious ANTONYM **major**: *You have made only a few* ***minor mistakes.*** • *The driver suffered* ***minor injuries*** *in the accident.*

mi·nor·i·ty /maɪˈnɒrəti $ məˈnɔrəti/ *noun*

KEY PATTERNS
a minority of people or things

1 a small part of a larger group of people or things ANTONYM **majority**: *Only* ***a minority of*** *students passed the exam.* • *The changes in the law were supported by only* ***a small minority.***
2 (plural **minorities**) a group of people whose race or religion is different from the race or religion of most people in a country: *The school has several children from* ***ethnic minorities.***

PHRASES
be in the minority, be in a minority: *Smokers* ***are in the minority*** *in our office* (=there are fewer people who do smoke cigarettes than people who do not).

mint /mɪnt/ *noun* **1** a type of sweet that tastes of PEPPERMINT **2** a place where the official coins of a country are made

mi·nus¹ /ˈmaɪnəs/ *preposition* used in mathematics when you take one number away from another ANTONYM **plus**: *12 minus 7 equals 5 (12 – 7 = 5)*

minus² *noun* (plural **minuses**) also **ˈminus ˌsign** a sign (–) showing that a number is less than zero, or that you must take one number away from another

min·ute¹ /ˈmɪnɪt/ *noun*
1 a measure of time that is equal to 60 seconds. There are 60 minutes in an hour: *I waited 20 minutes for the bus.* • *Sharon was a few minutes late for the meeting.* • *The goal was scored in the 89th minute of the game.* • *It's a two-minute walk to the train station.*
2 minutes an official written record of the things that people say during a meeting

PHRASES
a minute a very short period of time SYNONYM **a moment**: *Wait there a minute.* • *Leave me alone* ***for a minute.*** • *Mum will be back* ***in a minute.*** • *I'm going to the shop – I*

won't be a minute (=I won't be away for very long at all). ➔ see Thesaurus at SOON

any minute (now) very soon: *Hurry up, the play starts **any minute**.* • *Don't worry, the doctor will be here **any minute now**.* ➔ see Thesaurus at SOON

this minute immediately: *Stop that **this minute** and come here!* • *You don't have to decide **this minute** – you can tell me tomorrow.*

the last minute the latest possible time: *I was planning to go to the party, but I changed my mind **at the last minute**.* • *Diane never leaves for work **until the last minute**.*

mi·nute² /maɪˈnjuːt $ maɪˈnut/ *adjective* (formal) very small SYNONYM **tiny**: *I made a few minute changes to my essay.* ➔ see Thesaurus at SMALL

> **PRONUNCIATION**
> Be careful how you pronounce this word:
> **minute¹** (*noun*) is pronounced like 'minit'
> **minute²** (*adjective*) is pronounced like 'my nyoot'

mir·a·cle /ˈmɪrəkəl/ *noun*
1 something good that you did not expect to happen or did not think was possible: *It's a miracle she wasn't killed in the accident.* **2** an action or event that seems impossible and that people think has been done by God

mi·rac·u·lous /mɪˈrækjələs/ *adjective* very good and surprising
—**miraculously** *adverb*: *He has recovered miraculously from his illness.*

mir·ror /ˈmɪrə $ ˈmɪrɚ/ *noun* an object made of special glass in which you can see yourself when you look in it: *Anna looked at her reflection in the mirror.*

mis·be·have /ˌmɪsbɪˈheɪv/ *verb* to behave badly: *Anyone who misbehaves will have to leave the room.*

mis·cel·la·ne·ous /ˌmɪsəˈleɪniəs/ *adjective* (formal) of many different kinds: *There were a few miscellaneous books on the shelf.*

mis·chief /ˈmɪstʃɪf/ *noun* (no plural) (formal) bad behaviour, especially by children, that is annoying but causes no serious harm: *The girls always caused a lot of mischief on the farm.*

mis·chie·vous /ˈmɪstʃəvəs/ *adjective* (formal) a mischievous child behaves badly, but in a way that makes people laugh

> **SPELLING**
> This word is often spelled wrongly. The correct spelling is: **mischievous**.

mis·e·ra·ble /ˈmɪzərəbəl/ *adjective*
1 very unhappy: *Paula looked miserable yesterday.* ➔ see Thesaurus at SAD **2** very bad: *miserable weather*
—**miserably** *adverb*: *Our team played miserably.*

mis·e·ry /ˈmɪzəri/ *noun* (no plural) when someone is very unhappy: *Andy remembered the misery of his childhood.*

mis·judge /ˌmɪsˈdʒʌdʒ/ *verb* (formal) to make a wrong decision about what someone or something is like: *We seriously misjudged the students' views.*

mis·lead /mɪsˈliːd/ *verb* (past tense and past participle **misled** /-ˈled/) to deliberately give someone incorrect information: *The company misled people about the real cost of its products.* ➔ see Thesaurus at LIE²
—**misleading** *adjective*: *a misleading advertisement*

misled the past tense and past participle of MISLEAD

mis·print /ˈmɪs-prɪnt/ *noun* a mistake in the way a word is spelled in a book, magazine etc

Miss /mɪs/ *noun* used in front of the name of a girl or unmarried woman when you are speaking or writing to her: *Our teacher is Miss Rogers.*

miss¹ /mɪs/ *verb*

> **KEY PATTERNS**
> **miss school/a match/a concert**
> **miss your friends/family**
> **miss doing something**
> **miss a train/bus**

1 to not be able to go to something or do something: *I had to miss the first day of school.* • *Graham will miss the next match because he has hurt his leg.*
2 to not hit or catch something: *He missed a really easy goal.* • *The bullet missed and hit the wall.*

miss

John missed the bus. Andy missed the goal.

3 to feel sad because someone that you like is not with you, or because you can no longer have something you enjoyed in the past: *I really miss Mum and Dad now I'm at university.* • *She missed going for walks in the countryside.*
4 to be too late for something: *We **missed** the **train**, so we had to catch the next one.* • *If you don't hurry, we'll miss the start of the movie.*
5 to not notice something: *I think we must have missed the road for the airport.*

PHRASAL VERBS

miss out
1 (spoken) to not have the chance to do something that you would enjoy: *I saw other students going to parties and felt that I was **missing out**.* • *Don't **miss out on** the fun – join the sports club!*
2 miss something out to not include something: *When he sang the song, he **missed out** one verse.*

miss² *noun*
1 give something a miss *BrE* (spoken) to decide not to do something: *I'm not feeling very well, so I think I'll **give** the party **a miss**.*
2 when you do not hit or catch something: *That was his second penalty miss this year.* • *The plane was involved in a **near miss*** (=when one plane nearly hits another plane in the air).

mis•sile /ˈmɪsaɪl $ ˈmɪsəl/ *noun* a weapon that can fly over long distances and that explodes when it hits the thing it is aiming at: *The army has been firing missiles across the border.*

miss•ing /ˈmɪsɪŋ/ *adjective*
1 someone or something that is missing is not in the place where you expect it to be: *The missing child has been found safe and well.* • *My keys have gone missing.* **2** not included: *Jane's name was missing from the list.*

mis•sion /ˈmɪʃən/ *noun* an important job that someone has been sent to do: *The men were on an important mission from their government.* • *The soldiers' mission was to destroy the bridge.*

mis•sion•a•ry /ˈmɪʃənəri $ ˈmɪʃəˌneri/ *noun* (plural **missionaries**) someone who goes to a foreign country in order to teach people about a religion

mis•spell /ˌmɪsˈspel/ *verb* (past tense and past participle **misspelled** or **misspelt** /-ˈspelt/ *BrE*) to spell a word wrongly: *They misspelled my name on the list.* —**misspelling** *noun*

misspelt a past tense and past participle of MISSPELL

mist /mɪst/ *noun* very small drops of rain in the air, which make it difficult for you to see very far

mis•take¹ /mɪˈsteɪk/ *noun*

> **KEY PATTERNS**
> **make a mistake**
> **it is a mistake to do something**
> **do something by mistake**

1 if you make a mistake, you do, say, or write something that is not correct: *You **made** two **mistakes** in the spelling test.* • *It **was a mistake to** invite Tom to the party because he always argues with the other guests.* • *This computer program **corrects** your **mistakes** automatically.*
2 by mistake if you do something by mistake, you do something wrong without meaning to: *I took another student's bag **by mistake**.*

> **THESAURUS**
> **error** (formal): *There seems to be an error in your calculations* (=a mistake).
> **slip**: *That one **slip** caused him to lose the game* (=one small mistake).

mistake² *verb* (**mistook** /-ˈstʊk/ **mistaken** /-ˈsteɪkən/)

> **KEY PATTERNS**
> **mistake someone for another person**

if you mistake one person for another, you think wrongly that one person is someone else: *She **mistook** the man **for** a policeman and asked him for help.*

mis·tak·en¹ /mɪˈsteɪkən/ *adjective* (formal) someone who is mistaken is wrong about something: *No, I think you must be mistaken.* —**mistakenly** *adverb*

mistaken² the past participle of MISTAKE²

Mis·ter /ˈmɪstə $ ˈmɪstɚ/ MR

mistook the past tense of MISTAKE²

mis·trust¹ /mɪsˈtrʌst/ *noun* (no plural) the feeling that you cannot trust someone SYNONYM **distrust**: *Susan has a mistrust of strangers.*

mistrust² *verb* to not trust someone: *Jenny mistrusts salesmen.*

mist·y /ˈmɪsti/ *adjective* (**mistier**, **mistiest**) covered by mist or having a lot of mist: *a cold, misty day*

mis·un·der·stand /ˌmɪsʌndəˈstænd $ ˌmɪsʌndɚˈstænd/ *verb* (past tense and past participle **misunderstood** /-ˈstʊd/) to not understand something correctly: *He must have misunderstood my instructions.*

mis·un·der·stand·ing /ˌmɪsʌndəˈstændɪŋ $ ˌmɪsʌndɚˈstændɪŋ/ *noun* **1** when someone does not understand something correctly: *We need to be clear in order to avoid any misunderstanding.* **2** an argument that is not very serious: *It was just a small misunderstanding.*

mit·ten /ˈmɪtn/ *noun* a type of GLOVE that does not have separate parts for each finger → see picture at GLOVE

mix¹ /mɪks/ *verb*

KEY PATTERNS
mix one substance with another
mix one substance and another substance (together)

1 also **mix in** if you mix two different substances, you put them together so that they combine and become a single substance: *Mix the eggs **with** the milk.* • ***Mix** the powder **and** the water **together**.* • *She **mixed in** (=added) some sugar to make the sauce taste better.* → see picture on page A4

2 if two substances mix, they combine and become a single substance: *Oil and water will not mix.*

3 to put different activities, ideas, or styles together: *Jude likes to **mix** her studies **with** her interest in sport.*

4 if a DJ mixes two records, he or she plays one record after another with no stops between them, or plays them both at the same time

PHRASAL VERBS

mix up

1 mix people/things up to think wrongly that a person or thing is someone or something else SYNONYM **confuse**: *I **mixed** Alan **up with** his brother, Pete.* • *I got the days **mixed up** and went on Tuesday instead of Thursday.*

2 mix things up if you mix things up, you put them in the wrong order: *I arranged these books, and now you've **mixed** them **up**!*

THESAURUS
combine: *Combine all the ingredients* (=mix them).
blend: *You can **blend** cosmetics to create new colours* (=mix them thoroughly together).
beat: *Beat the butter and sugar with a wooden spoon* (=mix them together quickly).

mix² *noun* **1** (no plural) all the different people or things that are in a place: *There was a good mix of people at the party.* **2** (plural **mixes**) a powder that is added to liquid to make something: *Put the cake mix into a bowl and add water.*

mixed /mɪkst/ *adjective* **1** consisting of a lot of different types of things, people, ideas etc: *a package of mixed nuts* • *Kelly had mixed feelings about going to college.* **2** *BrE* for both girls and boys: *Simon goes to a mixed school.*

ˌmixed ˈup *adjective* confused: *Tony got mixed up and went to the wrong house.*

mix·er /ˈmɪksə $ ˈmɪksɚ/ *noun* **1** a piece of kitchen equipment that you use for mixing food **2** a piece of electronic equipment that a DJ uses to mix different pieces of music together

mix•ing /ˈmɪksɪŋ/ *noun* when a DJ plays one record after another without any stops between them, or plays two records at the same time

mix•ture /ˈmɪkstʃə $ ˈmɪkstʃɚ/ *noun*

KEY PATTERNS
mixture of different things/feelings

1 a substance that is made of several different substances that are mixed together: *Stir the mixture with a spoon until it is smooth.* • *a bottle of cough mixture*
2 a mixture of things is several different ones that exist together SYNONYM **combination**: *Singapore has **an** exciting **mixture of** Chinese, Malay, and Indian cultures.* • *Noah felt **a mixture of** fear and disgust.*

ˈmix-up *noun* (informal) a mistake or problem that happens when people get confused or do not understand each other: *There was a mix-up with our bags at the airport.*

ml the written abbreviation of MILLILITRE

mm the written abbreviation of MILLIMETRE

moan /məʊn $ moʊn/ *verb* **1** to make a long low sound, especially because a part of your body hurts SYNONYM **groan**
2 *BrE* to complain about something in an annoying way: *I wish she'd stop moaning.* —**moan** *noun*

mob /mɒb $ mɑb/ *noun* a large noisy crowd of angry violent people: *a mob of demonstrators*

mo•bile /ˈməʊbaɪl $ ˈmoʊbəl/ *adjective* able to move quickly and easily: *A mobile health clinic travels to all the towns in the area.*

ˌmobile ˈphone also **mobile** *BrE* *noun* a telephone that you can carry with you and use anywhere SYNONYM **cell phone** *AmE*: *Call me on my mobile.* ➔ see picture on page A12

mock¹ /mɒk $ mɑk/ *verb* (formal) to laugh at someone or say unkind things about them in order to make them seem stupid: *Farley's ideas were mocked by many scientists.*

mock² *adjective* not real, but intended to look real: *They're mock fights and the actors never get hurt.* • *They expressed mock horror at Sara's costume.*

mo•dal verb /ˌməʊdl ˈvɜːb $ ˌmoʊdl ˈvɚb/ also **modal** *noun* in grammar, a verb such as 'can', 'might', or 'must', that you use to show ideas such as possibility, permission, or intention

mod•el¹ /ˈmɒdl $ ˈmɑdl/ *noun*

KEY PATTERNS
a model of something

1 a small copy of a large object such as a car, plane, or building: *He had a **model of** the Eiffel Tower on his desk.* • *My brother **made** these aircraft **models**.*
2 one type of car or machine that a company makes: *The Golf is the most popular model in the VW range.*
3 someone who wears new clothes at special shows so that people will see them and want to buy the clothes: *a top fashion model*
4 someone who sits or stands so that an artist can paint or draw them, or a photographer can take a photograph of them

model² *adjective* **1** a model plane, train, car etc is a small copy of a real one **2** a model student, worker etc does everything perfectly: *She has been a model student.*

model³ *verb* (**modelled, modelling** *BrE*, **modeled, modeling** *AmE*) **1** to wear new clothes at special shows so people will see them and want to buy them: *Claudia was modelling a long blue dress.* **2 model something on something** to make one thing similar to another thing: *Luis modeled the characters in his story on real people.*

mod•el•ling *BrE*, **modeling** *AmE* /ˈmɒdl-ɪŋ $ ˈmɑdl-ɪŋ/ *noun* (no plural) the work of wearing new clothes to show them to people: *She moved from modelling into acting.*

mo•dem /ˈməʊdem $ ˈmoʊdəm/ *noun* a piece of electronic equipment used for sending information such as emails from one computer to another

mod•e•rate /ˈmɒdərət $ ˈmɑdərət/ *adjective* **1** neither very big nor very small, very fast nor very slow etc: *Cook the mixture over moderate heat.*
2 having political opinions or beliefs that are not extreme: *Moderate Republicans support his ideas.*

mod•e•ra•tion /ˌmɒdəˈreɪʃən $ ˌmɑdəˈreɪʃən/ *noun* if you do

A B C D E F G H I J K L M N O P Q R S T U V W X Y Z

something in moderation, you do not do it too much: *Eat fatty foods only in moderation.*

mod•ern /ˈmɒdn $ ˈmɑdərn/ *adjective* **1** using new methods, new equipment, or new ideas: *modern farming methods • a modern hotel • an exhibition of modern art* → see Thesaurus at NEW **2** about recent or present times, rather than the past: *a degree in modern history • modern Britain*

mod•ern•ize also **modernise** *BrE* /ˈmɒdənaɪz $ ˈmɑdərˌnaɪz/ *verb* to change something so that it uses new methods, new equipment, or new ideas: *The airline has modernized its airplanes. • The new president hopes to modernize society.*

mod•est /ˈmɒdɪst $ ˈmɑdɪst/ *adjective* **1** not talking too proudly about your own skills or the things you have done ANTONYM **boastful**: *He's always very modest about his achievements.* **2** (formal) not very big in size, amount, value etc: *The economy is growing at a modest rate.* **3** shy and embarrassed about showing your body —**modestly** *adverb*

mod•es•ty /ˈmɒdəsti $ ˈmɑdəsti/ *noun* (no plural) **1** not talking too proudly about your own skills or the things you have done **2** when someone is shy and embarrassed about showing their body

mod•i•fy /ˈmɒdəfaɪ $ ˈmɑdəˌfaɪ/ *verb* (**modified**, **modifies**) **1** to make small changes to something: *They decided to modify the original design.* **2** in grammar, if one word modifies another, it gives more information about it: *The adjective modifies the noun.*

moist /mɔɪst/ *adjective* slightly wet, in a pleasant way: *Keep the soil around the plant moist. • a moist chocolate cake*

moist•en /ˈmɔɪsən/ *verb* to make something slightly wet: *Add milk to moisten the mixture.*

mois•ture /ˈmɔɪstʃə $ ˈmɔɪstʃər/ *noun* (no plural) small amounts of water in the air, on a surface etc: *Moisture in the wood will make the paint come off.*

mois•tur•iz•er also **moisturiser** *BrE* /ˈmɔɪstʃəraɪzə $ ˈmɔɪstʃəˌraɪzər/ *noun* a cream you put on your skin to keep it soft and stop it from being too dry

mo•lar /ˈməʊlə $ ˈmoʊlər/ *noun* one of the large teeth at the back of your mouth

mold the American spelling of MOULD

moldy the American spelling of MOULDY

mole /məʊl $ moʊl/ *noun* **1** a small dark brown mark on your skin **2** a small animal with black fur that cannot see well and lives under the ground

mol•e•cule /ˈmɒlɪkjuːl $ ˈmɑləˌkjul/ *noun* the smallest amount of a substance that can exist: *a molecule of water*

mo•lest /məˈlest/ *verb* to sexually attack or harm someone, especially a woman or a child —**molester** *noun*: *a child molester*

molt the American spelling of MOULT

mom /mɒm $ mɑm/ the American word for MUM

mo•ment /ˈməʊmənt $ ˈmoʊmənt/ *noun*
1 a very short time: ***After a moment**, Lou returned. • We waited **for a few moments** before going into the house.*
2 a particular point in time: ***At that moment**, the teacher walked in. • Winning the school prize was an emotional moment for me.*

PHRASES

at the moment now: ***At the moment**, the hospital is caring for 17 patients. • What are you reading **at the moment**?* → see Thesaurus at NOW[1]

in a moment very soon: ***In a moment**, I will explain how the machine works.* → see Thesaurus at SOON

moments later a short time later: ***Moments later**, we saw Sally getting on the bus.*

mo•men•tar•i•ly /ˈməʊməntərəli $ ˌmoʊmənˈterəli/ *adverb* (written) for a very short time: *He paused momentarily, then began speaking again.*

mo•men•ta•ry /ˈməʊməntəri $ ˈmoʊmənˌteri/ *adjective* (formal) continuing for a very short time: *The class was surprised into a momentary silence.*

mo·men·tous /məʊ'mentəs $ moʊ'mentəs/ *adjective* a momentous event, decision etc is very important: *The birth of my first child was a momentous occasion.*

mo·men·tum /məʊ'mentəm $ moʊ'mentəm/ *noun* (no plural) **1** the force that makes a moving object continue to move: *The ball lost momentum and stopped rolling.*
2 when something keeps increasing, developing, or becoming more successful: *We've won three games in a row now, so we need to keep up the momentum.*

mom·my /'mɒmi $ 'mɑmi/ the American word for MUMMY

mon·arch /'mɒnək $ 'mɑnɚk/ *noun* a king or queen

mon·ar·chy /'mɒnəki $ 'mɑnɚki/ *noun* (plural **monarchies**) **1** (no plural) the system of government in which a country is ruled by a king or queen
2 a country that is ruled by a king or queen: *In spite of many changes, the UK remains a monarchy.*

mon·as·tery /'mɒnəstri $ 'mɑnəsˌteri/ *noun* (plural **monasteries**) a building where MONKS live

Mon·day /'mʌndi/ (written abbreviation **Mon**) *noun* the day of the week between SUNDAY and TUESDAY

mon·ey /'mʌni/ *noun* (no plural) the coins and paper notes that you use to buy things: *Billy* ***spent*** *lots of* ***money*** *in town today.* • ***How much money*** *have you got in the bank?* • *He wants to become a footballer and* ***earn*** *lots of* ***money***. • *I'm going to* ***save money*** (=not spend money) *by going out less often.*

THESAURUS
cash: *I need to get some* ***cash*** *from the bank* (=money in the form of notes and coins).
change: *I've only got 76p in* ***change*** (=money in the form of coins). • *I gave the shop assistant a ten pound note and she gave me four pounds* ***change*** (=money you are given back when you pay for something with too much money).
currency: *Shops there only accept the local* ***currency*** (=the money of that country).

mon·i·tor¹ /'mɒnɪtə $ 'mɑnətɚ/ *noun* a piece of computer equipment with a screen that shows information or pictures

monitor² *verb* (written) to watch or measure something carefully for a period of time to see how it changes: *The study monitored the health of 87,000 women for many years.*

monk /mʌŋk/ *noun* a man who is a member of a religious group that live in a MONASTERY

mon·key /'mʌŋki/ *noun* an animal that lives in hot countries and uses its long tail, feet, and hands to climb trees

mo·nop·o·ly /mə'nɒpəli $ mə'nɑpəli/ *noun* (plural **monopolies**) a situation in which one person or organization controls all of a particular business or industry and there is no competition: *AT&T once had a monopoly on telephone services in the US.*

mo·not·o·nous /mə'nɒtənəs $ mə'nɑtn-əs/ *adjective* boring and not changing very often: *a low-paid, monotonous job* → see Thesaurus at BORING

mon·soon /ˌmɒn'suːn $ ˌmɑn'sun/ *noun* the time of year in southern Asia and India when it rains a lot

mon·ster /'mɒnstə $ 'mɑnstɚ/ *noun* a large ugly frightening creature in stories

mon·strous /'mɒnstrəs $ 'mɑnstrəs/ *adjective* very wrong, bad, or unfair: *a monstrous lie*

month /mʌnθ/ *noun* one of the 12 periods of time that a year is divided into, for example February or December: *I'm visiting the States* ***next month***. • *We stayed in Thailand* ***for*** *nearly two* ***months***.

GRAMMAR
You usually use **in** with months of the year: *I saw him* ***in*** *May.*
✘ Don't use 'on' before **next**, **last**, or **this**.
✘ Don't say 'on next July'. Just say **next July**.

month·ly /ˈmʌnθli/ *adjective, adverb* happening or done every month: *a monthly magazine • The club meets monthly.*

mon·u·ment /ˈmɒnjəmənt $ ˈmɑnjəmənt/ *noun* a building or other structure that is built to remind people of an important event or famous person: *an ancient monument*

mood /muːd/ *noun*

KEY PATTERNS
in a good/bad mood

your feelings and emotions at a particular time: *Dad's* ***in a bad mood*** (=cross and bad-tempered) *today. • Sam* ***seems in a very good mood****. • A good actor can always sense* ***the mood*** *of his audience. • Mina's sudden changes of mood annoyed Joe.*

PHRASES

be in the mood for doing something to feel that you want to do something: *I'm* ***in the mood for*** *dancing.*

be in no mood for doing something, be in no mood to do something to feel strongly that you do not want to do something: *Selena* ***was in no mood for*** *joking. • Taki* ***was in no mood to*** *listen to my advice.*

mood·y /ˈmuːdi/ *adjective* (**moodier, moodiest**) a moody person becomes angry or unhappy quickly and without any warning: *After his divorce, he became moody and began drinking too much.*

moon /muːn/ *noun* **the moon** the large white object that you can see shining in the sky at night

moon·light /ˈmuːnlaɪt/ *noun* (no plural) the light of the moon

moon·lit /ˈmuːnˌlɪt/ *adjective* a moonlit place or night is made bright by the light of the moon

moor /mʊə $ mʊr/ *noun BrE* an area of high land covered with rough grass or low bushes

mop¹ /mɒp $ mɑp/ *noun* a stick with a soft end that you use for cleaning floors

mop

sweep mop

mop² *verb* (**mopped, mopping**) **1** to clean a floor with a mop **2 mop something up** to use a piece of soft material to clean liquid from a surface SYNONYM **wipe up**: *Sara used some paper towels to mop up the milk she spilled.*

mope /məʊp $ moʊp/ also **mope around** *verb* to feel unhappy and not try to become happy again

mo·ped /ˈməʊped $ ˈmoʊped/ *noun* a vehicle like a bicycle with a small engine

mor·al¹ /ˈmɒrəl $ ˈmɔrəl/ *adjective* right and good, or relating to ideas about actions that are right ANTONYM **immoral**: *We have a* ***moral duty*** *to protect our planet. • a society with* ***high moral standards*** (=strict ideas of good behaviour) —**morally** *adverb*: *I think killing animals is* ***morally wrong****.*

moral² *noun* **1 morals** standards of good behaviour, such as honesty and kindness: *Parents want to teach their children good morals.* **2** an idea that a story teaches you about life or how you should behave: *The moral of the story is that you can't believe everything people tell you.*

mo·rale /məˈrɑːl $ məˈræl/ *noun* (no plural) the confidence and hope that a person or group feels: *The team's morale is low after losing several games.*

mo·ral·i·ty /məˈræləti/ *noun* (no plural) whether something is right: *Some people questioned the morality of the war.*

more /mɔː $ mɔr/ *adverb, determiner, pronoun*
1 a larger amount or number: *You look much more attractive with long hair. •*

We ought to meet more often. • *I think physics is* ***much more*** *interesting than history.* • *It's not fair – you've got more people in your team than we have!* • *You should spend more time checking your spelling.* • *We want* ***more of*** *our students to go to university.* • ***More than*** *50 people died in the fire.*
2 an additional amount or number: *Can I have some more cake?* • *I have 15 more cards to write.*

PHRASES
more and more: *As the storm got worse, he became* ***more and more*** *anxious* (=he continued to become more anxious).
more or less nearly, but not exactly: *We've* ***more or less*** *finished now.* • *That's* ***more or less*** *what she said.*

> **GRAMMAR**
> **More** is used to form the comparative of adjectives with more than two syllables: *more attractive* • *more intelligent*
> **More** is also the opposite of both **less** and **fewer**: *more wine* • *more people.*

> **THESAURUS**
> **another**: *Can I have* ***another*** *biscuit* (=one more)?
> **further**: *Further research is needed* (=additional).

more·o·ver /mɔːrˈəʊvə $ mɔrˈoʊvɚ/ *adverb* (formal) used when you give more information to support something that you have just said: *I have always lived here, and moreover, I do not plan to move.*

morn·ing /ˈmɔːnɪŋ $ ˈmɔrnɪŋ/ *noun*

> **KEY PATTERNS**
> **in the morning**
> **on Monday/Tuesday etc morning**
> **this morning**

1 the time from when the sun rises to the middle of the day: *I'm busy* ***in the morning****, but I could meet you after lunch.* • *Ruth and I are going into town* ***on*** *Saturday* ***morning****.* • *Have you seen Steve* ***this morning****?* • *I get up at 7.00 most mornings.*
2 the part of the night from 12 at night until the sun rises: *I heard a loud bang at 2 o'clock* ***in the morning****.*

PHRASES
(Good) Morning (spoken) used when you meet someone in the morning: *Good morning, Class 5.*

mort·gage /ˈmɔːɡɪdʒ $ ˈmɔrɡɪdʒ/ *noun* money you borrow from a bank in order to buy a house

mor·ti·cian /mɔːˈtɪʃən $ mɔrˈtɪʃən/ an American word for UNDERTAKER

mo·sa·ic /məʊˈzeɪ-ɪk $ moʊˈzeɪ-ɪk/ *noun* a design made from small pieces of coloured stone and glass that is fixed to a surface

mosaic

Mos·lem /ˈmɒzləm $ ˈmɑzləm/ another word for MUSLIM

mosque /mɒsk $ mɑsk/ *noun* a building where MUSLIMS go to pray

mos·qui·to /məˈskiːtəʊ $ məˈskitoʊ/ (plural **mosquitoes**) *noun* a small flying insect that bites and sucks blood

mosquito

moss /mɒs $ mɔs/ *noun* (no plural) a small flat green plant that looks like fur and grows on trees and rocks

most /məʊst $ moʊst/ *adverb, determiner, pronoun*
1 more than any other person or thing ANTONYM **least**: *This is the most expensive perfume in the world.* • *The most important thing is to stay calm.* • *What scares me* ***the most*** *is the thought of being injured.* • *Who's got* ***the most*** *money?* • ***The most*** *I ever scored was 100.*
2 nearly all: *I like most kinds of food.* • *Most people have heard of him.* • ***Most of*** *my friends live nearby.* • *Gary did* ***most of*** *the hard work.*

PHRASES
at most, at the most: *This test won't take long – half an hour* ***at the most*** (=the largest amount of time it will take is half an hour).
make the most of something to use or enjoy something as much as

possible: *This good weather won't last, so we'd better* **make the most of it**.

GRAMMAR
You use **the most** to form the superlative of adjectives with two or more syllables: *the most beautiful place in the world* • *the most attractive man I've ever met*
You also use **most** before a noun, to mean 'nearly all': *Most people think she's right.*
You use **most of** before **the**, **this**, **my**, **his** etc: *I do most of the housework.* • *He spends most of his money on computer games.*

most·ly /ˈməʊstli $ ˈmoʊstli/ *adverb* in most cases or most of the time: *The players were mostly men.*

mo·tel /məʊˈtel $ moʊˈtel/ *noun* a hotel where people who are travelling by car can stay

moth /mɒθ $ mɔθ/ *noun* an insect with wings that flies around lights at night

moth·er /ˈmʌðə $ ˈmʌðɚ/ *noun* your female parent: *My mother taught me how to cook.*

moth·er·hood /ˈmʌðəhʊd $ ˈmʌðɚhʊd/ *noun* (no plural) the state of being a mother

ˈmother-in-ˌlaw *noun* (plural **mothers-in-law**) the mother of your husband or wife

mo·tion /ˈməʊʃən $ ˈmoʊʃən/ *noun*

KEY PATTERNS
in motion
the motion of a planet/the sea etc

when something moves SYNONYM **movement**: *He photographs animals while they are* **in motion** (=moving). • ***the motion of the Earth** around the sun* • *The slightest motion could have sent him tumbling over the edge of the cliff.*

mo·tion·less /ˈməʊʃənləs $ ˈmoʊʃənləs/ *adjective* (written) not moving at all SYNONYM **still**: *Rick lay motionless on the ground.*

mo·ti·vate /ˈməʊtəveɪt $ ˈmoʊtəˌveɪt/ *verb* to make someone want to do something: *Teachers should motivate students to stay in school.* —**motivated** *adjective*: *a group of highly motivated students*

mo·ti·va·tion /ˌməʊtəˈveɪʃən $ ˌmoʊtəˈveɪʃən/ *noun* **1** (no plural) when you want to achieve something: *Pam's intelligent, but her teachers say she lacks motivation.* **2** the reason why you want to do something: *The motivation for the change is money.*

mo·tive /ˈməʊtɪv $ ˈmoʊtɪv/ *noun* (formal) the reason why you do something: *I wonder what his motives really are?*

mo·tor¹ /ˈməʊtə $ ˈmoʊtɚ/ *noun* the part of a machine that uses electricity, petrol etc to make it move

motor² *adjective* **1** a motor vehicle uses an engine to make it move **2** related to cars: *the motor industry*

mo·tor·cy·cle /ˈməʊtəˌsaɪkəl $ ˈmoʊtɚˌsaɪkəl/ also **mo·tor·bike** /ˈməʊtəˌbaɪk $ ˈmoʊtɚˌbaɪk/ *BrE noun* a vehicle with two wheels and an engine, that you sit on SYNONYM **bike**

mo·tor·cy·clist /ˈməʊtəˌsaɪklɪst $ ˈmoʊtɚˌsaɪklɪst/ *noun* someone who rides a motorcycle

mo·tor·ist /ˈməʊtərɪst $ ˈmoʊtərɪst/ *noun* (formal) someone who drives a car SYNONYM **driver**

mo·tor·way /ˈməʊtəweɪ $ ˈmoʊtɚˌweɪ/ *noun BrE* a wide road on which you can drive fast for long distances SYNONYM **freeway** *AmE*
→ see Thesaurus at ROAD

mot·to /ˈmɒtəʊ $ ˈmɑtoʊ/ *noun* (plural **mottoes** or **mottos**) a short statement that says what the aims or principles of a person or organization are: *The school's motto is 'Reach for the Sun'.*

mould¹ *BrE*, **mold** *AmE* /məʊld $ moʊld/ *noun* **1** an unpleasant green or black substance that grows on old food or on wet things: *Mold was growing on the walls of the bathroom.* **2** a container with a special shape that you pour liquid into, so that when the liquid becomes solid it will have that shape: *a teddy bear mould for cakes*

mould² *BrE*, **mold** *AmE verb* to make a substance have a particular shape by pressing it or by putting it in a mould: *chocolate molded into heart shapes*

mould·y *BrE*, **moldy** *AmE* /ˈməʊldi $ ˈmoʊldi/ *adjective* covered with mould: *The bread was mouldy.*

A B C D E F G H I J K L M N O P Q R S T U V W X Y Z

moult *BrE*, **molt** *AmE* /məʊlt $ moʊlt/ *verb* when an animal or bird moults, it loses hair or feathers so that new ones can grow

mound /maʊnd/ *noun* a large pile of something: *a mound of stones*

Mount /maʊnt/ *noun* used in the names of mountains: *Mount Everest*

mount /maʊnt/ *verb* **1** (written) to organize and begin an event: *The museum mounted a show of Egyptian art.* • *We want to mount a campaign against racism.* **2** also **mount up** (written) to gradually increase: *Concern for the girl's safety is mounting.* **3** to get on a horse or bicycle

moun·tain /ˈmaʊntən/ *noun* a very high hill: *We spent a weekend climbing in the mountains.* ➔ see picture at ABOVE

moun·tain·eer /ˌmaʊntəˈnɪə $ ˌmaʊntəˈnɪr/ *noun* someone who climbs mountains

moun·tain·eer·ing /ˌmaʊntəˈnɪərɪŋ $ ˌmaʊntəˈnɪrɪŋ/ *noun* (no plural) the sport of climbing mountains

moun·tain·ous /ˈmaʊntənəs/ *adjective* having a lot of mountains: *a mountainous region*

mourn /mɔːn $ mɔrn/ *verb* to feel very sad because someone has died: *The family were still mourning the death of two of their sons.*

mourn·er /ˈmɔːnə $ ˈmɔrnɚ/ *noun* someone who is at a funeral

mourn·ing /ˈmɔːnɪŋ $ ˈmɔrnɪŋ/ *noun* (no plural) when you feel very sad because someone has died: *Everyone was in mourning for the people who had died in the earthquake.*

mouse /maʊs/ *noun* **1** (plural **mice** /maɪs/) a small animal with smooth fur, a long tail, and a pointed nose
2 (plural **mice**, **mouses**) a small object connected to a computer, that you move with your hand and press to make the computer do things

ˈmouse mat *BrE*, **ˈmouse pad** *AmE* *noun* a small piece of material that you use with a computer mouse

mousse /muːs/ *noun* **1** a substance that you put in your hair to hold it in position **2** a cold sweet food made from cream, eggs, and fruit or chocolate

mous·tache *BrE*, **mustache** *AmE* /məˈstɑːʃ $ ˈmʌstæʃ/ *noun* hair that a man grows on his upper lip

mouth /maʊθ/ *noun* (plural **mouths** /maʊðz/)
the part of your face, including your lips, teeth, and tongue, that you use for speaking and eating ➔ see picture on page A5

mouth·ful /ˈmaʊθfʊl/ *noun* the amount of food or drink that you put into your mouth at one time: *Steve took another mouthful of fish.*

mouth·wash /ˈmaʊθwɒʃ $ ˈmaʊθwɑʃ/ *noun* (plural **mouthwashes**) a liquid that you use to make your mouth clean and your breath smell fresh

move[1] /muːv/ *verb*

KEY PATTERNS
move around
move towards someone
move to a place
move away from a place

1 to go from one position or place to another: *Just then, the shape behind the curtain moved.* • *Tony* ***was moving around*** *slowly.* • *The dog* ***moved*** *slowly* ***towards us.***
2 to take something and put it in a different place or position: *I can't move my arm – I think it's broken.*
3 to go to live in a different place: *She* ***moved to*** *France in 2006.* • *Teenagers need to* ***move away from home*** *and be independent.* • *When are you* ***moving house*** (=going to live in a different house)?

PHRASAL VERBS

move in
to start living in a different house: *The day after we* ***moved in,*** *the roof started to leak.* • *I* ***moved in with*** *my cousin.*

move off
if a vehicle moves off, it starts its journey by going forward: *Our friends waved as the train started* ***moving off.***

move out
to leave the house where you are living to go and live somewhere else: *Dad sold the house and we* ***moved out.***

move[2] *noun*
something that you do in order to achieve something: *Accepting the job* ***was a good move.***

move•ment /ˈmuːvmənt/ *noun* when someone or something moves: *With an awkward movement, Nick turned his head.* • *We could hear movement in the room above us.*
→ see pictures on pages A3 and A3

mov•ie /ˈmuːvi/ *noun* **1** a film[1] **2 the movies** the American word for the CINEMA

ˈmovie ˌtheater the American word for a CINEMA

mov•ing /ˈmuːvɪŋ/ *adjective* making you feel strong emotions, especially sadness or sympathy: *a moving story*

mow /məʊ $ moʊ/ *verb* (**mown** /məʊn $ moʊn/ or **mowed**) to cut grass with a machine: *Our son mows the lawn for us.*

MP /ˌem ˈpiː/ the abbreviation of MEMBER OF PARLIAMENT

MP3 play•er /ˌem piː ˈθriː ˌpleɪə $ ˌem pi ˈθri ˌpleɪə/ *noun* a piece of equipment that plays music or films that you have DOWNLOADed from the Internet

mph the written abbreviation of 'miles per hour'; used to say how fast a vehicle goes: *The car was travelling at 85 mph when it crashed.*

Mr /ˈmɪstə $ ˈmɪstɚ/ *noun* used in front of a man's family name when you are speaking or writing to him

Mrs /ˈmɪsɪz/ *noun* used in front of a married woman's family name when you are speaking or writing to her

PRONUNCIATION
You pronounce **Mrs** like 'misses'.

Ms /məz/ *noun* used in front of a woman's family name when you are speaking or writing to her

PRONUNCIATION
You pronounce **Ms** like 'muzz'.

MSc /ˌem es ˈsiː/ *BrE noun*, **M.S.** /ˌem ˈes/ *AmE* (Master of Science) a higher university degree in science

Mt. the written abbreviation of MOUNT

much /mʌtʃ/ *determiner, pronoun, adverb*
a large amount of something. Use **much** about things that you cannot count, such as work, time, food, information etc, or after a verb, especially in questions and negative sentences: *I don't have much time. Can I call you back later?* • *Was there much traffic?* • *There wasn't much difference between the two pictures.* • *I didn't have **much of** a chance to talk to her.* • *Has Bobby grown much since you last saw him?* • *"Did you enjoy the film?" "Not much."*

PHRASES

how much? use this to ask about the amount or cost of something: ***How much** was your new computer?* • ***How much** ice cream do you want?*

too much, so much use these when an amount of something is larger than you want or need: *He ate **too much** last night.* • *There was **so much** noise I couldn't hear her at all.*

too much, so much, very much use these to show how much someone does something or how much something happens: *Thank you **very much**!* • *His maths has improved **so much** this year.* • *I can't walk on this leg – it hurts **too much**.*

as much as use this to talk about an amount of something, especially when you are comparing two amounts: *I don't like this book **as much as** his other novels.* • *Abby earns **as much** money **as** her husband.*

much better, much bigger, much more expensive etc better, worse, more expensive etc by a large amount: *I'm feeling much better today.* • *Lamb is much more expensive than chicken.*

much too fast, much too cold etc too fast, cold etc by a large amount: *Sara was driving much too fast.* • *It was much too cold to stay outside.*

WORD CHOICE
much or **a lot of**?
• **Much** is usually used in questions and negative sentences: *How much did the ring cost?* • *There **wasn't much** food left.*
• In positive statements, you use **a lot of**: *That man caused **a lot of** trouble.*
✘ Don't say 'That man caused much trouble.'

muck[1] /mʌk/ *noun* (no plural) (informal) dirt or mud: *There's some muck on the carpet.*

muck[2] *verb* **muck about, muck around** *BrE* (spoken, informal) to behave in a silly way and waste time SYNONYM **mess around**: *Don't muck about while I'm working.*

mud /mʌd/ *noun* (no plural) wet earth: *Joe got mud on his shoes.*

mud·dle¹ /ˈmʌdl/ *noun* a situation in which things are badly organized or confusing: *My notes are in a bit of a muddle.*

muddle² *verb* **1** also **muddle up** to put things in the wrong order: *Someone's muddled up my socks.* **2 get someone/something muddled up** (informal) to wrongly think that one person or thing is someone or something else: *I always get their names muddled up.*

mud·dy /ˈmʌdi/ *adjective* (**muddier**, **muddiest**) covered with mud: *Take your muddy boots off!* ➔ see Thesaurus at DIRTY

muddy

muddy boots

muf·fle /ˈmʌfəl/ *verb* (written) to make a sound less loud or less clear: *The falling snow muffled all sounds.* —**muffled** *adjective*: *I heard muffled laughter behind the door.*

mug¹ /mʌg/ *noun* a large cup with straight sides: *a mug of coffee* ➔ see picture at CUP¹

mug² *verb* (**mugged**, **mugging**) to attack someone in a public place and steal their money: *He was mugged by two boys in the city centre.* ➔ see Thesaurus at STEAL —**mugger** *noun*: *The mugger ran off when the police arrived.*

mug·gy /ˈmʌgi/ *adjective* (**muggier**, **muggiest**) muggy weather is unpleasantly wet and warm

Mu·ham·med /mʊˈhæməd/ also **Mo·ham·med** /məʊˈhæməd $ moʊˈhæməd/ a PROPHET who taught the ideas that the Islamic religion is based on

mule /mjuːl/ *noun* an animal that has a DONKEY and a horse as parents

mull /mʌl/ *verb* **mull over** to think about something carefully: *He wanted to be left alone to mull things over.*

mul·ti·cul·tur·al /ˌmʌltiˈkʌltʃərəl/ *adjective* involving people and ideas from many different countries: *America is a multicultural society.*

mul·ti·me·di·a /ˌmʌltɪˈmiːdiə/ *adjective* multimedia computer products use sound, pictures, films, and writing: *multimedia software*

mul·ti·ple /ˈmʌltəpəl/ *adjective* involving many parts, people, events etc: *The driver died from multiple injuries.*

ˌmultiple ˈchoice *adjective* a multiple choice test or question shows several possible answers and you must choose the correct one

mul·ti·pli·ca·tion /ˌmʌltəpləˈkeɪʃən/ *noun* (no plural) a calculation in which you add a number to itself a particular number of times

mul·ti·ply /ˈmʌltəplaɪ/ *verb* (**multiplied**, **multiplies**) **1** to do a calculation in which you add a number to itself a particular number of times: *6 multiplied by 2 equals 12 (6 x 2 = 12).* ➔ see Thesaurus at CALCULATE **2** to increase greatly in number: *The number of TV channels has multiplied over the last 15 years.*

mul·ti-ra·cial /ˌmʌlti ˈreɪʃəl/ *adjective* involving people from many different races

mul·ti-task·ing /ˈmʌlti ˌtɑːskɪŋ $ ˈmʌlti ˌtæskɪŋ/ *noun* **1** doing several different things at the same time: *Women are much better at multi-tasking than men.* **2** operating several different computer programs at the same time: *The software has multi-tasking capabilities.*

mul·ti·tude /ˈmʌltətjuːd $ ˈmʌltəˌtud/ *noun* (written) a very large number of things or people: *The changes in the law created a multitude of problems.*

mum /mʌm $ mɑːm/ *BrE noun* (informal) a word for mother SYNONYM **mom** *AmE*: *How old is your mom?* • *Mum, can you drive me to college?*

mum·ble /ˈmʌmbəl/ *verb* to speak in a quiet way that is difficult to understand: *He mumbled an excuse.*

A B C D E F G H I J K L M N O P Q R S T U V W X Y Z

A B C D E F G H I J K L M N O P Q R S T U V W X Y Z

mum·my /ˈmʌmi $ ˈmɑmi/ *BrE noun* a word for mother, used by children SYNONYM **mommy** *AmE*: *Mummy, can I have some sweets?*

mumps /mʌmps/ also **the mumps** *noun* (no plural) an illness that makes your throat and neck hurt

munch /mʌntʃ/ *verb* to eat food that is hard and makes a noise as you eat it: *He was munching an apple.*

mu·ni·ci·pal /mjuːˈnɪsəpəl/ *adjective* related to the government of a city: *municipal elections*

mu·ral /ˈmjʊərəl $ ˈmjʊrəl/ *noun* a picture that is painted onto a wall

mur·der¹ /ˈmɜːdə $ ˈmɚdɚ/ *noun* the crime of deliberately killing someone: *There were four murders here last year.* • *Her jealousy led her to* ***commit murder****.*

murder² *verb* to deliberately kill someone: *I was frightened he might murder me.* • *She was murdered by terrorists.* → see Thesaurus at KILL¹

murk·y /ˈmɜːki $ ˈmɚki/ *adjective* (**murkier**, **murkiest**) dark and difficult to see through: *a murky river*

mur·mur¹ /ˈmɜːmə $ ˈmɚmɚ/ *noun* (written) a soft low continuous sound: *the murmur of distant traffic*

murmur² *verb* to speak in a quiet soft way: *Miguel murmured goodbye.*

mus·cle /ˈmʌsəl/ *noun* your muscles are the pieces of flesh inside your body that you use to move your body: *Running gives you strong leg muscles.*

mus·cu·lar /ˈmʌskjələ $ ˈmʌskjəlɚ/ *adjective* having a lot of big muscles: *muscular legs*

mu·se·um /mjuːˈziːəm/ *noun* a building where people can go and see objects connected with art, history, science etc: *She is planning a class trip to the museum.*

mush·room /ˈmʌʃruːm/ *noun* a grey or white plant with a short stem and a round top. You can eat certain mushrooms: *pizza with pepperoni and mushrooms* → see picture on page A6

mushroom

mu·sic /ˈmjuːzɪk/ *noun* (no plural)

> **KEY PATTERNS**
> **play music**
> **listen to music**

an attractive pattern of sounds that people make by singing or playing musical instruments: *Do you like this music?* • *They were* ***playing*** *very loud music.* • *Would you like to* ***listen to*** *some music?* • *a music teacher*

> **GRAMMAR**
> **Music** is not used in the plural.
> ✘ Don't say 'musics'.
> Say **a piece of music** or **several pieces of music**.

mu·sic·al¹ /ˈmjuːzɪkəl/ *adjective* related to music: *Do you play a musical instrument?*

musical² *noun* a play or film that uses songs to tell a story

musicians

mu·si·cian /mjuːˈzɪʃən/ *noun* someone who plays a musical instrument, especially as their job

Mus·lim /ˈmʊzləm/ also **Moslem** *noun* someone whose religion is ISLAM

must /məst; strong mʌst/ *modal verb*
1 used to say that something is necessary, or that it is important for it to happen: *You must be careful.* • *You mustn't forget to finish your essay.* • *I must leave or I'll miss the bus.* • *Students must pass the exam to continue on the course.*
2 must not used to say strongly that someone is not allowed to do something: *You must not smoke in the house.* • *This telephone must not be used by members of the public.*

3 used to say that something is probably true or probably happened: *Her eldest child must be about 12 now.* • *I suppose he must know what he's doing.* • *I* ***must have*** *left my essay at home.*
4 used when giving advice strongly: *You must try this soup – it's delicious.*

> **GRAMMAR**
> The negative of **must** is **must not** or **mustn't**: *You mustn't tell him.*

mustache the American spelling of MOUSTACHE

mus•tard /ˈmʌstəd $ ˈmʌstərd/ *noun* (no plural) a yellow or brown sauce with a strong taste that people eat with meat: *a hamburger with ketchup and mustard*

must•n't /ˈmʌsənt/ the short form of 'must not': *You mustn't be late for school.*

must've /ˈmʌstəv/ (spoken) the short form of 'must have': *She must've left already.*

mu•ti•lat•ed /ˈmjuːtəleɪtɪd/ *adjective* a mutilated body has been very badly damaged, for example by having pieces cut off

mut•ter /ˈmʌtə $ ˈmʌtər/ *verb* to say something quietly in a way that is difficult to understand, especially when you are annoyed: *"Leave me alone," Jay muttered.*

mut•ton /ˈmʌtn/ *noun* the meat from an adult sheep

mu•tu•al /ˈmjuːtʃuəl/ *adjective*
1 used to say that people have the same feelings about each other: *Mutual trust is important in any marriage.*
2 shared by two or more people: *We have a mutual friend.*

my /maɪ/ *determiner*
belonging to the person who is speaking: *My bedroom is quite large.* • *I'd better phone my mother.* • *My feet are cold.*

my•self /maɪˈself/ *pronoun*
1 used when the same person who is speaking does an action and receives an action: *I've cut myself!* • *I can look after myself.* • *I'm making myself a sandwich.*
2 used to emphasize the person speaking: *People tell me it's a lovely place, but I haven't been there myself.*
PHRASES
by myself alone, or with no one helping: *I'm quite happy to be* ***by myself.*** • *I had to do all the packing* ***by myself.***

mys•te•ri•ous /mɪˈstɪəriəs $ mɪˈstɪriəs/ *adjective*
something that is mysterious seems strange and is difficult to understand or explain: *Police are puzzled by his mysterious disappearance.*
—**mysteriously** *adverb*: *She left as mysteriously as she had arrived.*

> **SPELLING**
> This word is often spelled wrongly. The correct spelling is: **mysterious**.

mys•te•ry /ˈmɪstəri/ *noun* (plural **mysteries**)
something that seems very strange and is difficult to explain or understand: *The cause of her illness is a mystery.* • *The* ***mystery was solved*** *when we found the bike behind a tree.*

> **SPELLING**
> This word is often spelled wrongly. The correct spelling is: **mystery**.

mys•tic•al /ˈmɪstɪkəl/ *adjective*
something that is mystical is connected with religions or magical powers that people cannot understand: *Many saints had mystical experiences.*

mys•ti•fy /ˈmɪstəfaɪ/ *verb* (formal) (**mystified**, **mystifies**) if you are mystified by something, you do not understand it or you are confused by it SYNONYM **baffle**: *His parents are mystified by his behaviour.*

myth /mɪθ/ *noun* **1** something that is not true, although many people believe it: *It's a myth that men are better drivers than women.* **2** an old story about gods and people: *Greek myths about the creation of the world*

myth•i•cal /ˈmɪθɪkəl/ also **mythological** *adjective* existing in stories, but not real: *mythical monsters and dragons*

myth•o•log•i•cal /ˌmɪθəˈlɒdʒɪkəl $ ˌmɪθəˈlɑdʒɪkəl/ another word for MYTHICAL

N the written abbreviation of NORTH or NORTHERN

nag /næg/ *verb* (**nagged**, **nagging**) to keep asking someone to do something in an annoying way: *Mum keeps nagging me to tidy my bedroom.*

nag·ging /ˈnægɪŋ/ *adjective* making you worry or feel pain all the time: *a nagging headache*

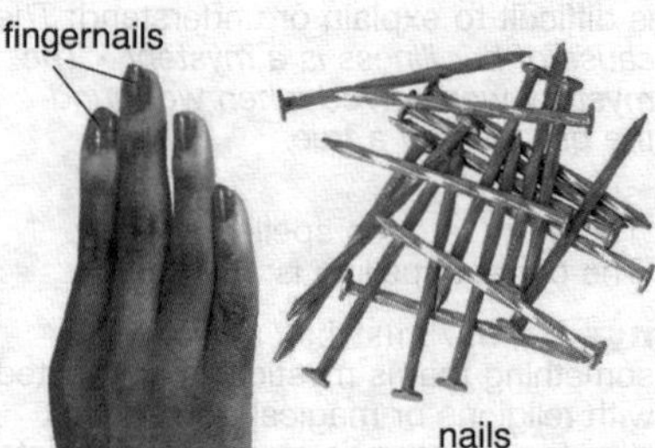

nail¹ /neɪl/ *noun* **1** a thin pointed piece of metal with a flat end that you hit with a hammer: *I hammered a nail into the wall.* **2** the thin hard parts that grow at the end of your fingers and toes: *She had long nails.*

nail² *verb* to fasten something to something else with a nail: *The windows were nailed shut.*

ˈnail-ˌbiting *adjective* very exciting: *The crowd cheered as the race came to a nail-biting finish.*

nail·brush /ˈneɪlbrʌʃ/ *noun* (plural **nailbrushes**) a small brush for cleaning your nails

ˈnail ˌvarnish *BrE* also **ˈnail ˌpolish** *noun* (no plural) paint for women's nails: *She wore pink nail varnish.*

na·ive /naɪˈiːv $ nɑˈiv/ *adjective* if someone is naive, they believe that people are nicer and things are easier than they really are, because they have not had much experience of life: *I was young and naive then.* —**naively** *adverb*: *Naively, I trusted him.*

na·ked /ˈneɪkɪd/ *adjective* not wearing any clothes SYNONYM **nude**: *The baby was crawling around in the sand naked.*

name¹ /neɪm/ *noun*
what someone or something is called: *What's his brother's name?* • *Hello, my name's Clare.* • *I've forgotten **the name of** the school he goes to.*

PHRASES

first name, Christian name: *Mrs Lee's first name is Sara.*

last name, family name the name that all the people in your family have SYNONYM **surname**: *Smith is a very common **last name** in England.*

a good name, a bad name the good or bad opinion that people have about a person, school, company etc: *This kind of behaviour gives the school **a bad name**.*

name² *verb*

KEY PATTERNS
name a baby Jason/Sally etc
name someone/something after someone
name someone/something for someone *AmE*
name someone as chairman/principal etc

1 to give someone or something a name: *They named their new baby Thomas.* • *Their daughter was **named** Rose **after** her grandmother.* • *The college was **named for** Edward Kennedy.*
2 to say what the name of someone or something is: *Can you name three American presidents?*
3 (written) to officially choose someone for a job: *Miss Taylor **was named as** the new school principal.*

name·ly /ˈneɪmli/ *adverb* (written) used to add more information about the people or things that you have just mentioned: *He was arrested for possessing a weapon, namely a knife.*

name·sake /ˈneɪmseɪk/ *noun* your namesake is someone who has the same name as you: *Daniel Craig is a builder, unlike his famous namesake, the actor.*

nan·ny /ˈnæni/ *noun* (plural **nannies**) a woman whose job is to take care of a family's children: *The young princes are looked after by a nanny.*

nap /næp/ *noun* a short sleep during the day: *I had a quick nap before work.*

nap·kin /ˈnæpkɪn/ *noun* a square of cloth or paper that you use at meals to keep your clothes, hands, and mouth clean

nap·py /ˈnæpi/ *noun BrE* (plural **nappies**) a piece of cloth or paper that a baby wears on its bottom SYNONYM **diaper** *AmE*: *Who's going to change the baby's nappy?*

nar·cot·ic /nɑːˈkɒtɪk $ nɑrˈkɑtɪk/ *noun* a drug that stops pain and makes people want to sleep: *Morphine is a powerful narcotic.*

nar·ra·tive /ˈnærətɪv/ *noun* the narrative of a film or book is its story: *The narrative is hard to follow.*

nar·ra·tor /nəˈreɪtə $ ˈnæˌreɪtɚ/ *noun* someone who tells a story or explains what is happening in a book or a film: *At the start of the film you hear the voice of the narrator.*

narrow

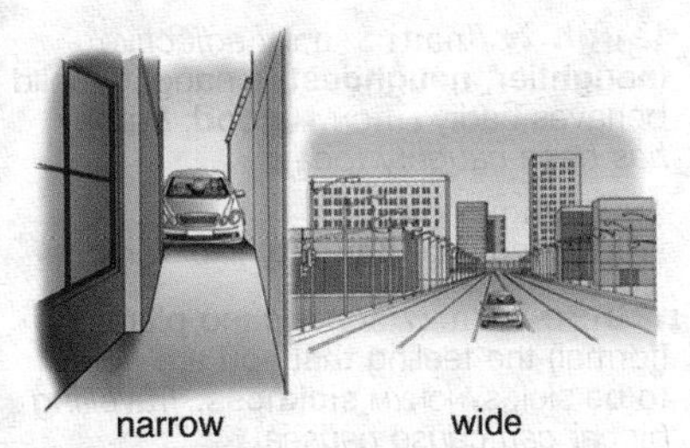

narrow wide

nar·row¹ /ˈnærəʊ $ ˈnæroʊ/ *adjective* something that is narrow measures a short distance from one side to the other ANTONYM **wide**: *the narrow streets of the old town*

PHRASES

a narrow escape when you just manage to avoid danger or trouble: *We had a narrow escape when a bus hit the car.*

narrow² *verb* **1** to become more narrow ANTONYM **widen**: *The river narrows as we go under the bridge.* **2 narrow something down** to reduce the number of people or things that you can choose from: *I've narrowed down the choice of courses to three.*

nar·row·ly /ˈnærəʊli $ ˈnæroʊli/ *adverb* only by a small amount: *They narrowly avoided being killed.*

ˌnarrow-ˈminded / $ ˈ.. ˌ../ *adjective* someone who is narrow-minded is not willing to accept ideas that are new and different from their own ANTONYM **broad-minded**

na·sal /ˈneɪzəl/ *adjective* **1** a nasal sound or voice comes mostly through your nose: *She had a high nasal voice.* **2** for your nose: *a nasal spray*

nas·ty /ˈnɑːsti $ ˈnæsti/ *adjective* (**nastier**, **nastiest**) unpleasant or unkind: *The letter gave me a nasty shock.* • *Stop being so nasty to your sister.* ➔ see Thesaurus at UNKIND

na·tion /ˈneɪʃən/ *noun* a country and its people: *America is the richest nation in the world.*

na·tion·al¹ /ˈnæʃənəl/ *adjective* relating to all of a country, not just one part of it: *the national flag of the US*

national² *noun* (formal) a British national, French national etc is a British person, French person etc: *Only Japanese nationals are employed by the firm.*

ˌnational ˈanthem *noun* a country's official song: *The crowd sang their national anthem before the match started.*

na·tion·al·is·m /ˈnæʃənəlɪzəm/ *noun* (no plural) the feeling that you are proud of your own country and believe that it is better than other countries: *We are worried about the growth of nationalism.*

na·tion·al·ist /ˈnæʃənəlɪst/ *noun* someone who is very proud of their country and believes that it is better than other countries

na·tion·al·i·ty /ˌnæʃəˈnæləti/ *noun* (plural **nationalities**) your nationality is the country that you belong to: *Students of many different nationalities come to study here.*

na·tion·al·ize also **nationalise** *BrE* /ˈnæʃənəlaɪz/ *verb* if a government nationalizes an organization, it takes control of it ANTONYM **privatize**: *Bolivia nationalized its oil and gas industry in 2006.*

na·tion·al·ly /ˈnæʃənəli/ *adverb* in all of a country: *a TV show that is broadcast nationally*

na·tion·wide /ˌneɪʃənˈwaɪd/ *adjective, adverb* happening in every part of a country SYNONYM **countrywide**: *There was a nationwide search for the missing girl.* • *adverts that appear nationwide*

na·tive¹ /ˈneɪtɪv/ *adjective* of the country where you were born: *Her native language is Spanish.*

native² *noun* someone who was born in a particular country: *a native of Brazil*

ˌNative Aˈmerican *noun* a member of the group of people who were living in North America before the Europeans arrived

ˌnative ˈspeaker *noun* someone who learned to speak a language when they were a baby, as their first language: *Laurence is not a native speaker of English.*

nat·ter /ˈnætə $ ˈnætɚ/ *verb BrE* (informal) to talk a lot about unimportant things SYNONYM **chat**: *What are you two nattering about?* —**natter** *noun*: *I stopped and had a natter with Jo.*

nat·u·ral /ˈnætʃərəl/ *adjective*

KEY PATTERNS
it's natural (for someone) to be/feel/think etc something
it's natural that

1 normal and usual: ***It's natural for** parents **to** feel proud of their children.* • ***It's only natural that** you feel shy if you don't know anyone.* • *Anger is a natural reaction when someone criticizes you.*
2 natural things are found in nature rather than being made by humans: *Water is a natural resource.* • *She doesn't wear make-up because she prefers to look natural.*

nat·u·ral·ist /ˈnætʃərəlɪst/ *noun* someone who studies plants and animals

nat·u·ral·ize also **naturalise** *BrE* /ˈnætʃərəlaɪz/ *verb* **be naturalized** to be given the official right to live in a country where you were not born —**naturalized** *adjective*: *a naturalized Australian*

nat·u·ral·ly /ˈnætʃərəli/ *adverb*
1 used to say that something is what you would expect SYNONYM **of course**: *Naturally, we wanted to win.*
2 if something happens naturally, it happens on its own, without people doing anything to make it happen: *The tomatoes are left to dry naturally in the sun.* • *Is your hair naturally blonde?*

SPELLING
This word is often spelled wrongly. The correct spelling is: **natura<u>l</u>ly**.

ˌnatural reˈsources / $ ˌ... ˈ.../ *plural noun* the oil, coal, metals etc in a place that are available for the people who live there to use: *Japan has few natural resources of its own.*

na·ture /ˈneɪtʃə $ ˈneɪtʃɚ/ *noun*
1 (no plural) everything in the world that is not made or caused by humans, for example animals, plants, and the weather: *Storms remind us of the power of nature.* • *I love watching nature programmes on television.*
2 someone's character: *Terry has a kind nature.*

naugh·ty /ˈnɔːti $ ˈnɒti/ *adjective* (**naughtier**, **naughtiest**) a naughty child behaves badly ANTONYM **good**: *Barney has been naughty today.*

PRONUNCIATION
You pronounce **naughty** like 'forty'.

nau·se·a /ˈnɔːziə/ *noun* (no plural) (formal) the feeling that you are going to be sick SYNONYM **sickness**: *Travelling by car can cause nausea.*

nau·se·a·ting /ˈnɔːzieɪtɪŋ/ *adjective* very unpleasant, and making you feel like you are going to be sick SYNONYM **sickening**: *the nauseating smell of rotting fish*

nau·ti·cal /ˈnɔːtɪkəl/ *adjective* related to ships and sailing: *England's nautical history*

na·val /ˈneɪvəl/ *adjective* related to a country's navy: *a naval battle*

na·vel /ˈneɪvəl/ *noun* the small hole in your stomach SYNONYM **belly button**

nav·i·gate /ˈnævəgeɪt/ *verb* to decide which way a car or ship should go,

A B C D E F G H I J K L M N O P Q R S T U V W X Y Z

using maps: *I'll drive and you can navigate.* —**navigator** *noun*

nav·i·ga·tion /ˌnævəˈɡeɪʃən/ *noun* (no plural) when you decide which direction your car or ship should go: *Navigation is difficult without a compass.*

na·vy /ˈneɪvi/ *noun* (plural **navies**) the people and ships that a country has for fighting a war at sea: *At 18 he joined the navy.*

navy 'blue also **navy** *adjective* very dark blue: *a navy blue car* —**navy blue** *noun* (no plural): *a woman dressed in navy blue*

NB, N.B. /ˌen ˈbiː/ used in writing to tell someone to pay attention to something important you have written: *NB: switch off the electricity before cleaning the machine.*

near

near¹ /nɪə $ nɪr/ *preposition, adverb* a short distance away from something: *He lives near Bristol.* • *Don't stand too near the fire.* • *I watched as the car came nearer.*

> **GRAMMAR**
> You say *My hotel is* ***near*** *the airport.*
> ✘ Don't say 'My hotel is near from the airport.'

near² *adjective*
a short distance away: *The nearest beach is only a mile away.*

PHRASES
in the near future (formal) soon: *The school hopes to teach Chinese* ***in the near future.***

near·by /ˈnɪəbaɪ $ ˈnɪrbaɪ/ *adjective, adverb* not far away: *Her cousins live in a nearby village.* • *My mother stood nearby.*

> **THESAURUS**
> **locally**: *He couldn't get a job* ***locally*** (=in the nearby area).
> **around here** (spoken): *Is there a baker's* ***around here*** (=nearby)?

near·ly /ˈnɪəli $ ˈnɪrli/ *adverb*
almost: *I could answer nearly all the questions.* • *I've nearly finished.* • *Dinner is nearly ready.* • *It's nearly time to go home.*

near·sight·ed /ˌnɪəˈsaɪtɪd $ ˈnɪrˌsaɪtɪd/ *adjective* unable to see things clearly unless they are close to you SYNONYM **shortsighted** *BrE*

neat /niːt/ *adjective*
1 arranged in a tidy and careful way ANTONYM **untidy**: *Ros has a very neat handwriting.* • *His bedroom is always neat and tidy.*
2 *AmE* (spoken informal) very good SYNONYM **cool**: *The concert was really neat!*

neat·ly /ˈniːtli/ *adverb* in a tidy and careful way: *Her clothes were neatly folded.*

ne·ces·sar·i·ly /ˈnesəsərəli $ ˌnesəˈserəli/ *adverb* **not necessarily** used to say that something may not be true, or may not always happen: *Expensive restaurants do not necessarily have the best food.*

ne·ces·sa·ry /ˈnesəsəri $ ˈnesəˌseri/ *adjective*

> **KEY PATTERNS**
> **it is necessary to do something**
> **it is necessary for someone to do something**

if something is necessary, you need it: ***Is it necessary to*** *get a visa to go to China?* • ***It is not necessary for*** *you to spend the whole day there.* • *"Do I need to bring some money with me?" "No, that won't be necessary."* • *You can take the test again* ***if necessary.*** • *Her parents made all the necessary arrangements* (=did everything that needed to be done) *for the wedding.*

> **SPELLING**
> This word is often spelled wrongly. The correct spelling is: **necessary**.

> **THESAURUS**
> **essential**: *In the mountains, warm clothes are* ***essential*** (=completely necessary).
> **vital**: *A* ***vital*** *piece of equipment was missing* (=completely necessary).

ne·ces·si·ty /nəˈsesəti/ *noun*
1 (plural **necessities**) something that you need ANTONYM **luxury**: *A car is a*

necessity for this job. **2** (no plural) when you must do something: *They did it out of necessity* (=because they had to).

neck /nek/ *noun*
1 the part of your body that joins your head to your shoulders: *She wore a gold chain around her neck.*
2 the part of a piece of clothing that goes around your neck
3 the narrow part near the top of a bottle

neck·lace /'nek-ləs/ *noun* a piece of jewellery that you wear around your neck: *a diamond necklace* → see picture at JEWELLERY

neck·tie /'nektaɪ/ a formal American word for TIE²

need¹ /niːd/ *verb*

KEY PATTERNS
need to do something
needn't do something
something needs cleaning/tidying

1 if you need something, you must have it SYNONYM **require**: *These plants need plenty of light and water.* • *I live in the city, so I don't really need a car.* • *How much money do you need?*
2 if you need to do something, it is necessary for you to do it: *I **need to** speak to Mike urgently.* • *Do you think he **needs to** see a doctor?* • *We don't **need to** get up early tomorrow.* • *You needn't worry* (=don't worry) – *everything will be fine.*
3 if something needs doing, you should do it because it is necessary SYNONYM **require**: *Does this shirt need washing?* • *The house needs painting this year.*

GRAMMAR
The usual negative form of **need** is **do not need** or **don't need**: *These plants **don't need** any more water.*
When saying that someone does not have to do something, you can say either 'do not need to do something' or 'needn't do something': *You don't need to worry, You needn't worry.*

WORD CHOICE
need or **necessary**?
• **Need** is a verb: *You don't need to stay.*
• **Necessary** is an adjective: *It is not necessary for you to stay.*
✘ Don't say 'It is not need.'

need² *noun* **1** (no plural) something that is necessary: *There is an urgent need for more qualified nurses.*
2 needs your needs are the things that you need: *We try to meet the needs of all the children here.*

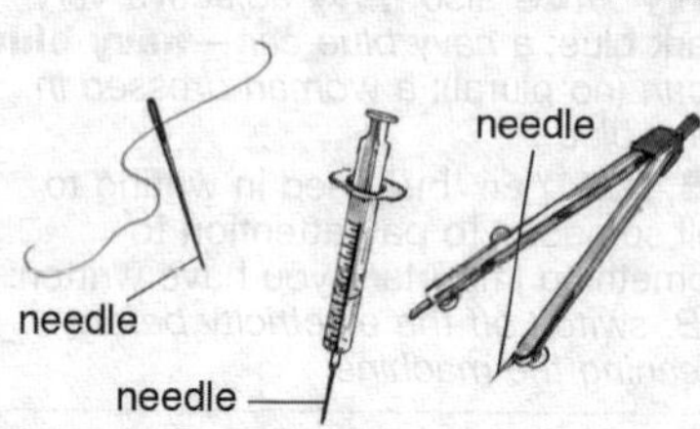

nee·dle /'niːdl/ *noun*
1 a small thin piece of steel that you use for sewing: *Have you got a needle and thread? I need to mend my trousers.*
2 a very thin metal tube that a doctor uses to put medicine into your body through your skin
3 a thin pointed object that points to a number or sign on an instrument for measuring something: *a compass needle*

need·less /'niːdləs/ *adjective*
1 needless to say used when you are telling someone about something that they probably already know: *Needless to say, Jon loved his new bike.* **2** not necessary SYNONYM **unnecessary**: *We must stop this needless suffering.*
—**needlessly** *adverb*: *Children are dying needlessly.*

need·n't /'niːdnt/ (spoken) the short form of 'do/does not need to': *You needn't call me back.*

need·y /'niːdi/ *adjective* (**needier**, **neediest**) having very little food or money: *a needy family*

neg·a·tive¹ /'negətɪv/ *adjective*

KEY PATTERNS
be negative about someone/something

1 if something has a negative effect, it has a bad or harmful effect ANTONYM **positive**: *Smoking has a very negative effect on health.*

2 considering only the bad things about a situation or person ANTONYM **positive**: *My mother is always so negative about my friends.*
3 if you give a negative answer, you say no ANTONYM **affirmative**: *When people were asked if they liked the ad, the response was negative.*
4 a scientific or medical test that is negative shows that someone does not have a disease or chemical in their body ANTONYM **positive**
5 less than zero ANTONYM **positive**: *Do you know how to multiply negative numbers?*
6 a negative sentence contains a word such as 'not' or 'never' ANTONYM **positive**

negative[2] *noun* **1** the film from which a photograph is printed, which shows dark areas as light, and light areas as dark: *Do you have the negatives for these photos?* **2** a word or phrase that is used to say that something is not true

ne·glect[1] /nɪ'glekt/ *verb* to fail to look after someone or something as well as you should: *You mustn't neglect your family.* —**neglected** *adjective*: *a neglected house*

neglect[2] *noun* (no plural) when someone or something does not get enough care or attention: *children suffering from neglect*

neg·li·gence /'neglɪdʒəns/ *noun* (no plural) when someone does not do their job properly, causing a mistake or accident: *They have accused the doctor of negligence.*

neg·li·gent /'neglɪdʒənt/ *adjective* not doing your job properly, causing a mistake or accident: *Was the pilot negligent?*

neg·li·gi·ble /'neglɪdʒəbəl/ *adjective* very small and unimportant: *The damage was negligible.*

ne·go·ti·ate /nɪ'gəʊʃieɪt $ nɪ'goʊʃiˌeɪt/ *verb* to discuss something in order to reach an agreement: *He is in Japan negotiating an important business deal.*

> SPELLING
> This word is often spelled wrongly. The correct spelling is: **negotiate**.

ne·go·ti·a·tion /nɪˌgəʊʃi'eɪʃən $ nɪˌgoʊʃi'eɪʃən/ *noun* discussion between groups of people who are trying to reach an agreement: *After months of negotiation, the two sides agreed to a treaty.*

neigh /neɪ/ *verb* if a horse neighs, it makes a loud noise

neigh·bour *BrE*, **neighbor** *AmE* /'neɪbə $ 'neɪbɚ/ *noun* **1** someone who lives in a house very near you: *All our friends and neighbours are coming to the party.* **2** a person or country that is next to another one: *Write your name on the list and then pass it to your neighbor.* • *Poland's neighbours*

> SPELLING
> This word is often spelled wrongly. The correct spelling is: **neighbour** or **neighbor**.

neigh·bour·hood *BrE*, **neighborhood** *AmE* /'neɪbəhʊd $ 'neɪbɚˌhʊd/ *noun* a small area of a town: *This is a poor neighbourhood.*
➔ see Thesaurus at AREA

> SPELLING
> This word is often spelled wrongly. The correct spelling is: **neighbourhood** or **neighborhood.**

neigh·bour·ing *BrE*, **neighboring** *AmE* /'neɪbərɪŋ/ *adjective* near the place you are talking about SYNONYM **nearby**: *people who live in London and neighbouring towns*

nei·ther[1] /'naɪðə $ 'niðɚ/ *determiner, pronoun*
not one of two things or people: *Neither team played well* (=both teams played badly). • ***Neither of us** could drive.* • *I tried on two pairs of shoes, but neither fitted.*

> WORD CHOICE
> **neither** or **neither of**?
> • **Neither** is always used with a singular noun and verb: *Neither answer is right.*
> • **Neither of** is used with a plural noun or pronoun, and the verb can be singular or plural: *Neither of us has/have ever been to America before.*

neither[2] *adverb*
used in negative statements, when adding something else: *"I'm not tired."*

A B C D E F G H I J K L M **N** O P Q R S T U V W X Y Z

"Neither am I (=and I'm not tired)." • *I can't swim, and neither can my brother.*

neither³ *conjunction* **neither ... nor ...** used to emphasize that something is not true about two people or things: *Neither Sue nor Colin were clever.*

ne·on /ˈniːɒn $ ˈniɑn/ *noun* (no plural) a gas that is used in tubes in electric lights and signs —**neon** *adjective*: *flashing neon lights*

neph·ew /ˈnefjuː/ *noun* the son of your brother or sister

nerd /nɜːd $ nɚd/ *noun* (informal) a boring or unfashionable man SYNONYM **geek**

nerve /nɜːv $ nɚv/ *noun*
1 your nerves are the parts of your body that send information to your brain from different parts of your body. If your nerves are damaged, you cannot feel pain or move part of your body properly
2 nerves the feeling of being nervous: *Most people suffer from* ***nerves*** *before an exam.*

PHRASES
get on someone's nerves to annoy someone: *His singing* ***is getting on*** *my* ***nerves.***
have the nerve to do something to be brave enough to do something dangerous or difficult
lose your nerve to no longer feel brave enough to do something dangerous or difficult: *She* ***lost*** *her* ***nerve*** *and decided not to jump.*

nerve-rack·ing, nerve-wrack·ing /ˈnɜːv ˌrækɪŋ $ ˈnɚv ˌrækɪŋ/ *adjective* very worrying or frightening: *Appearing on TV was a nerve-racking experience.*

ner·vous /ˈnɜːvəs $ ˈnɚvəs/ *adjective*

KEY PATTERNS
nervous about something

if you are nervous, you feel worried and frightened, and cannot relax: *Julie looked nervous before the test.* • *I get very* ***nervous about*** *speaking in public.* • *His driving makes me nervous.*
→ see Thesaurus at WORRIED
—**nervously** *adverb*: *"Are you Tim Kelly?" she asked nervously.*

ˌnervous ˈbreakdown *noun* when someone becomes so worried and unhappy that they are unable to live a normal life for a while: *He had a nervous breakdown last year.*

ˈnervous ˌsystem *noun* the system of nerves in your body: *The human nervous system is very complex.*

nest /nest/ *noun* a place made by a bird to lay its eggs in: *The young birds are still in their nest.*

nes·tle /ˈnesəl/ *verb* to be in a safe place among a group of hills, trees, buildings etc: *I could see our house far below, nestling in the valley.*

nets

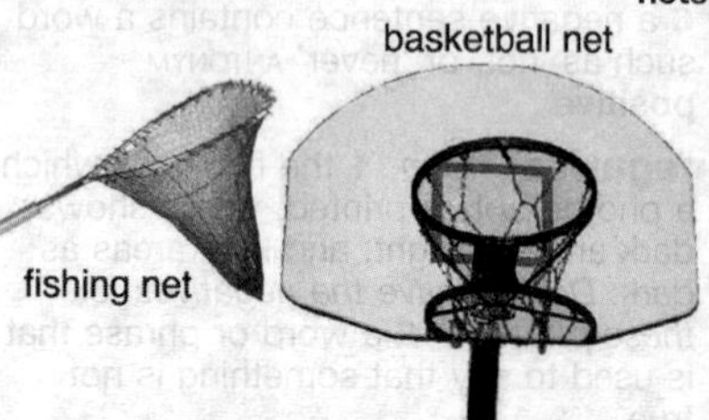

net¹ /net/ *noun* **1** a piece of material with large spaces between the threads, which you use in some sports: *The ball went into the back of the net.* • *a volleyball net* **2** a piece of material with spaces between the threads, which you use for catching fish **3** a type of light thin cloth: *The dancers' skirts were made of pink net.* **4 the Net** the Internet SYNONYM **the Web**: *He's been on the Net all afternoon.*

net² also **nett** *BrE* /net/ *adjective* a net amount of money is the amount that remains after you have paid taxes and other amounts have been taken away ANTONYM **gross**: *Our net profit for that year was £200,000.*

net·work /ˈnetwɜːk $ ˈnetwɚk/ *noun* **1** a system of things that are connected with each other: *a network of computers* • *the railway network* **2** a group of companies that broadcast the same television or radio programmes

neu·rot·ic /njʊˈrɒtɪk $ nʊˈrɑtɪk/ *adjective* very worried or frightened about something in a way that does not seem normal: *My mother's neurotic about her health.*

neu·ter /ˈnjuːtə $ ˈnuːtər/ *adjective* belonging to a group of nouns, adjectives etc in some languages that is different from the MASCULINE and FEMININE groups

neu·tral /ˈnjuːtrəl $ ˈnutrəl/ *adjective* someone who is neutral does not support any of the sides in a competition or war: *Switzerland was a neutral country during the war.*

nev·er /ˈnevə $ ˈnevɚ/ *adverb* not at any time: *I've never flown in a plane before.* • *He'll never be successful.* • *I never sign anything without reading it through first.*

GRAMMAR
Use **never** before the main verb in a sentence unless it is the verb 'to be': *We **never go** on holiday in August.* • *I **have never lived** in this town.* • *Jeff is **never** late for school.*

nev·er·the·less /ˌnevəðəˈles $ ˌnevɚðəˈles/ *adverb* in spite of what has just been said SYNONYM **nonetheless**: *He was unreliable, but I loved him nevertheless.*

new /njuː $ nu/ *adjective*

KEY PATTERNS
new to someone

1 something that is new has been made, built, or developed recently: *Have you heard the band's new album?* • *New technology is changing our lives.* • *He bought a **brand new** (=very new) motorbike.*
2 different or changed ANTONYM **old**: *Her new boyfriend is a policeman.* • *Do you like their new apartment?*
3 not used or owned by anyone before ANTONYM **used**, **secondhand**: *Did you get a second-hand computer or a new one?*
4 if something is new to you, you did not know it before or have never used it before: *Some of the food in Japan was completely **new to me**.*

PRONUNCIATION
British people pronounce the **-ew** like 'you'.
American people pronounce the **-ew** like 'do'.

THESAURUS
modern: *Modern technology has made communication very easy* (=of a new kind).
latest: *Have you read her latest book* (=most recent)?

new·born /ˈnjuːbɔːn $ ˈnubɔrn/ *adjective* a newborn baby has just been born: *newborn lambs*

new·com·er /ˈnjuːkʌmə $ ˈnuˌkʌmɚ/ *noun* someone who has recently arrived in a place: *We're newcomers to this town.*

new·ly /ˈnjuːli $ ˈnuli/ *adverb* very recently: *a newly married couple*

news /njuːz $ nuz/ *noun* (no plural)

KEY PATTERNS
news about someone/something
news of an attack/accident/defeat
the news that

1 information about something that has happened recently: *I **heard** some interesting **news about** Charlie.* • ***News of** the disaster spread quickly.* • *The teacher gave the class a surprising **piece of news**.* • *I've got some **good news** for you – you've passed all your exams.* • *We were told the **bad news** that grandma had died.*
2 the news a regular television or radio programme that gives you reports of recent events: *I usually watch **the news**.* • *The president was interviewed **on the news** this morning.*

PHRASES
in the news if someone is in the news, they are mentioned in newspapers and on the television because they have done something important recently

GRAMMAR
You say **some news** or **a piece of news**.
✘ Don't say 'a news'.
You use **news** with a singular verb: *The news isn't very good.*

news·a·gent /ˈnjuːzˌeɪdʒənt $ ˈnuzˌeɪdʒənt/ *noun BrE*
1 newsagent's a shop that sells newspapers and magazines: *There's a newsagent's at the end of our street.*
2 someone who owns or works in a shop selling newspapers and magazines

ˈnews ˌbulletin *noun* **1** *BrE* a short news programme **2** the American word for NEWSFLASH

news·cast·er /ˈnjuːzˌkɑːstə $ ˈnuzˌkæstɚ/ *noun* someone who reads the news on television or radio SYNONYM **newsreader** *BrE*

news·flash /ˈnjuːzflæʃ $ ˈnuzflæʃ/ *noun* (plural **newsflashes**) a special short news programme about something important that has just happened SYNONYM **news bulletin** *AmE*: *There was a newsflash about her death.*

news·let·ter /ˈnjuːzˌletə $ ˈnuzˌletɚ/ *noun* a sheet of printed news about an organization, that is sent regularly to its members: *The school newsletter comes out each month.*

news·pa·per /ˈnjuːsˌpeɪpə $ ˈnuzˌpeɪpɚ/ also **paper** *noun* a set of folded sheets of paper containing news and advertisements: *I read about it in the newspaper.*

> **USAGE**
> You read something **in a newspaper**.
> ✘ Don't say 'read something on a newspaper'.

news·read·er /ˈnjuːzˌriːdə $ ˈnuzˌridɚ/ *noun BrE* someone who reads the news on television or radio SYNONYM **anchor** *AmE* SYNONYM **newscaster**

ˌNew ˈYear *noun* the time when you celebrate the beginning of the year: *Happy New Year!*

ˌNew Year's ˈDay *noun* 1st January

ˌNew Year's ˈEve *noun* 31st December: *a New Year's Eve party*

next /nekst/ *adjective, adverb, pronoun*
1 after this thing or person: *What time is the next train to York?* • *I hope the next head teacher we have is less strict than this one!* • *What's next on the list?* • *The first house they looked at was too small, and* ***the next*** *was on a busy road.* • *I'll clean the bathroom next, after I've finished cleaning the kitchen.* • *He couldn't decide what to do next.* ➔ see Thesaurus at AFTERWARDS

next

Max is sitting next to the window.

2 nearest to the place or thing mentioned: *There's a pharmacy in the next village.* • *Turn left at the next traffic lights.*

PHRASES

next to someone/something very close to someone or something: *Come and sit* ***next to*** *me.* • *At the restaurant, they were given a table* ***next to*** *the window.*

next week, next Tuesday etc: *We're having a day in London* ***next week*** (=during the week after this one). • *We'll see you* ***next Saturday***.

the next day the day after: *I didn't feel very well the next day.*

the week after next, the year after next etc during the week, year etc after the one that will come after this one: *I'm going to apply to college* ***the year after next*** (=in two years' time).

next time on the next occasion that something happens: *Never mind, I'm sure you'll pass the test* ***next time***. • *I'll ask him* ***next time*** *I see him.*

> **GRAMMAR**
> You say **See you next Friday**.
> ✘ Don't say 'on next Friday'.

ˈnext door *adverb, adjective* in the building that is next to another building: *We live next door to a police station.* • *my next-door neighbour*

ˌnext of ˈkin *noun* (formal) (plural **next of kin**) your closest relative who is still alive: *His next of kin was informed about the accident.*

nib·ble /ˈnɪbəl/ *verb* to take small bites from a piece of food: *Cindy was sitting at the table, nibbling a sandwich.*

nice /naɪs/ *adjective*

> **KEY PATTERNS**
> **it's nice to do something**
> **it's/that's nice of someone**
> **be nice to someone**

1 pleasant or enjoyable: *We had a really nice time at the party.* • *She's got a nice car.* • *You* ***look nice*** *in that hat.* • ***It is nice to*** *see old friends.*
2 friendly and kind: *He's a really nice man.* • ***It was nice of*** *you* ***to*** *help Ken with his homework.* • *Please* ***be nice to*** *your cousin.* ➔ see Thesaurus at KIND[2]

PHRASES

nice to meet you, nice meeting you (spoken) used when you meet someone for the first time

> **THESAURUS**
> **enjoyable**: *A good teacher tries to make learning **enjoyable*** (=fun and making you feel happy).
> **pleasant**: *a **pleasant** walk in the sunshine* (=good to experience)
> **great/fantastic**: *We had a **great** holiday in Florida* (=very nice).

ˌnice-ˈlooking *adjective* attractive: *Your brother's really nice-looking.*

nice·ly /ˈnaɪsli/ *adverb* in a pleasant or attractive way: *Ask me nicely!* • *a nicely decorated house*

nick¹ /nɪk/ *noun* a small cut on the surface of something: *a tiny nick on her hand*

nick² *verb* **1** to accidentally cut the surface of something: *I nicked my chin when I was shaving.* **2** *BrE* (spoken informal) to steal something SYNONYM **pinch**: *Someone's nicked my purse!*

nick·el /ˈnɪkəl/ *noun* a coin used in the US and Canada, worth 5 cents: *I put a nickel in the slot.*

nick·name /ˈnɪkneɪm/ *noun* a funny name your friends or family give you: *My nickname at school was 'Spike'.* —**nickname** *verb*: *His teammates nicknamed him 'Ginger'.*

nic·o·tine /ˈnɪkətiːn/ *noun* (no plural) a substance contained in tobacco

niece /niːs/ *noun* the daughter of your brother or sister

> **SPELLING**
> This word is often spelled wrongly. The correct spelling is: **niece**.

nig·gle /ˈnɪgəl/ *verb* to annoy or worry you slightly: *This pain has been niggling me for days.* —**niggle** *noun*: *I began to feel a niggle of doubt.*

night /naɪt/ *noun*

> **KEY PATTERNS**
> **in the night**
> **at night**
> **last/tomorrow night**
> **on Monday/Tuesday etc night**

1 the time when it is dark, when people usually sleep ANTONYM **day**: *It snowed **in the night**.* • *She doesn't like being alone in the house **at night**.* • *The party went on **all night**.*
2 the evening: *We went out for a meal **last night**.* • *Shall we go out **tomorrow night**?* • *There's a good film on TV **on** Friday **night**.*

PHRASES

a late night, an early night when you go to bed later or earlier than usual: *You shouldn't have so many **late nights** during the school week.*

a night out when you go out for the evening, to the cinema, for a meal etc: *You need **a night out**.*

Good night (spoken) used to say goodbye to someone when it is late in the evening or when they are going to bed: *Good night. See you in the morning!*

night·club /ˈnaɪtklʌb/ *noun* a place where people go late in the evening to drink and dance SYNONYM **club**: *London has some great nightclubs.*

night·dress /ˈnaɪtdres/ *noun* (plural **nightdresses**) also **nightgown** /ˈnaɪtgaʊn/ a loose dress that a woman wears in bed

night·ie /ˈnaɪti/ *noun* (informal) a NIGHTDRESS

night·life /ˈnaɪtlaɪf/ *noun* (no plural) all the entertainment that is available in the evening in a town: *The big attraction in Berlin is the nightlife.*

night·ly /ˈnaɪtli/ *adjective, adverb* happening every night: *The bar is open nightly from 9.30.*

night·mare /ˈnaɪtmeə $ ˈnaɪtmer/ *noun* a very frightening dream: *I had a nightmare about nuclear war.*

ˈnight school *noun* (no plural) classes that you go to in the evening: *I'm studying Spanish at night school.*

night·time /ˈnaɪt-taɪm/ *noun* (no plural) the time during the night when it is dark ANTONYM **daytime**: *It was nighttime when we arrived.*

nil /nɪl/ *noun* (no plural) zero: *Brazil won the match two-nil* (=2–0).

nim·ble /ˈnɪmbəl/ *adjective* able to move quickly and easily SYNONYM **agile**: *She sewed with nimble fingers.* —**nimbly** *adverb*: *She landed nimbly on her toes.*

A B C D E F G H I J K L M N O P Q R S T U V W X Y Z

nine /naɪn/ *number* 9

nine·teen /ˌnaɪnˈtiːn/ *number* 19 —**nineteenth** *number*: *the nineteenth century*

SPELLING
This word is often spelled wrongly. The correct spelling is: **nineteen**.

ˌnine-to-ˈfive *adverb* **work nine-to-five** to work every day from nine o'clock in the morning until five o'clock in the evening

nine·ty /ˈnaɪnti/ *number* (plural **nineties**) **1** 90 **2 the nineties** the years between 1990 and 1999: *They met in the early nineties.* **3 be in your nineties** to be aged between 90 and 99 —**ninetieth** *number*

SPELLING
This word is often spelled wrongly. The correct spelling is: **ninety**.

ninth /naɪnθ/ *number* **1** 9th **2** one of nine equal parts of something; 1/9

nip /nɪp/ *verb* (**nipped, nipping**) **1** if an animal or person nips you, they bite you, using the teeth at the front of their mouth: *The dog nipped her on the ankle.* **2** *BrE* (informal) to go somewhere for a short time SYNONYM **pop**: *I need to nip out to the shops.*

nip·ple /ˈnɪpəl/ *noun* **1** one of the two small dark circles on your chest. Babies suck milk through their mothers' nipples **2** the American word for TEAT (2)

ni·tro·gen /ˈnaɪtrədʒən/ *noun* (no plural) a gas that is the main part of the Earth's air

no[1] /nəʊ $ noʊ/ *adverb* a word you say when you do not agree with something or do not think that something is true ANTONYM **yes**: *"Is that your bag?" "No." • "Do you need any help?" "No thanks."*

no[2] *determiner* not any: *I have no brothers or sisters. • There had been no rain for three months.*

no[3] *noun* (plural **noes**) a negative answer or decision ANTONYM **yes**: *I need a yes or no before the end of the day.*

no. (plural **nos.**) the written abbreviation of NUMBER: *page nos. 12 to 16*

no·bil·i·ty /nəʊˈbɪləti $ noʊˈbɪləti/ *noun* **the nobility** the group of people with the highest social rank SYNONYM **the aristocracy**

no·ble /ˈnəʊbəl $ ˈnoʊbəl/ *adjective* (written) morally good or generous: *It was noble of you to share your prize.* —**nobly** *adverb*: *"Keep the money," Jay said nobly.*

no·bo·dy /ˈnəʊbədi $ ˈnoʊˌbɑdi/ *pronoun* not anyone

GRAMMAR
Nobody is followed by a singular verb.
You say **Nobody is happy**.
✘ Don't say 'Nobody are happy.'

nod /nɒd $ nɑd/ *verb* (**nodded, nodding**) **1** to move your head up and down, to show that you understand something or agree with someone ANTONYM **shake**: *"Good," said Laura, nodding. • Ben nodded his head.* **2 nod off** to begin to sleep: *I nodded off during the lecture.*

noise /nɔɪz/ *noun* a loud or annoying sound: *The children were **making** too much **noise**. • I heard a strange noise.*

WORD CHOICE
noise or **sound**?
• A **sound** is something that you hear: *We listened to the sound of the waves.*
• You use **noise** especially about a loud or unpleasant sound: *The children are making too much noise.*

nois·y /ˈnɔɪzi/ *adjective* (**noisier, noisiest**) **1** noisy people make a lot of noise ANTONYM **quiet**: *You're being too noisy.* **2** a noisy place is full of noise ANTONYM **quiet**: *a noisy city street* —**noisily** *adverb*

nom·i·nate /ˈnɒməneɪt $ ˈnɑməˌneɪt/ *verb* to officially suggest that someone should be given a job or prize: *The team nominated Harry as captain.*

nom·i·na·tion /ˌnɒməˈneɪʃən $ ˌnɑməˈneɪʃən/ *noun* when people officially suggest that someone should be given a job or prize: *the Oscar nominations*

ˌnon-alcoˈholic *adjective* a non-alcoholic drink has no alcohol in it ANTONYM **alcoholic**

none /nʌn/ *pronoun*
not any: ***None of*** *the other children could speak Italian.* • ***None of*** *the information they gave us was correct.* • *By the time I phoned for tickets, there were none left.*

WORD CHOICE
• When you use **none of** with a plural noun, the verb is plural: *None of my friends* ***were*** *there.*
• When you use **none of** with a noun that you cannot count, the verb is singular: *None of the food* ***was*** *left.*

none·the·less /ˌnʌnðəˈles/ *adverb* (formal) in spite of what you have just said SYNONYM **nevertheless**: *Martin was not well, but nonetheless he came to school.*

non·ex·ist·ent /ˌnɒnɪgˈzɪstənt $ ˌnɑnɪgˈzɪstənt/ *adjective* (formal) not existing at all: *The boyfriend she talked about was nonexistent.*

non·fic·tion /ˌnɒnˈfɪkʃən $ ˌnɑnˈfɪkʃən/ *noun* (no plural) books about real facts or events ANTONYM **fiction**: *I read a lot of nonfiction.*

non·flam·ma·ble /ˌnɒnˈflæməbəl $ ˌnɑnˈflæməbəl/ *adjective* (formal) something that is nonflammable is very difficult to burn ANTONYM **inflammable**

ˌno-ˈnonsense *adjective* working in a practical way, making decisions quickly and not spending too much time discussing things: *a no-nonsense approach to teaching*

non·sense /ˈnɒnsəns $ ˈnɑnsens/ *noun* (no plural)
1 things that someone says that are stupid and not true SYNONYM **rubbish** *BrE*: *You're talking nonsense.*
2 speech or writing that you cannot understand because it has no meaning: *Computer programs look like nonsense.*

non·smok·ing /ˌnɒnˈsməʊkɪŋ $ ˌnɑnˈsmoʊkɪŋ/ *adjective* a nonsmoking area is one where people are not allowed to smoke ANTONYM **smoking**

non·stan·dard /ˌnɒnˈstændəd $ ˌnɑnˈstændərd/ *adjective* not the usual size or type: *Dialects are a form of nonstandard English.*

non·start·er /ˌnɒnˈstɑːtə $ ˌnɑnˈstɑrtər/ *noun* (informal) an idea or plan that is very unlikely to succeed: *The whole idea sounds like a nonstarter.*

non·stop /ˌnɒnˈstɒp $ ˌnɑnˈstɑp/ *adverb, adjective* without stopping: *Over dinner, we talked nonstop.* • *a nonstop flight to Bangkok*

noo·dles /ˈnuːdlz/ *plural noun* food made from flour, eggs, and water, cut into long thin pieces and cooked in boiling water: *chicken with noodles*

noon /nuːn/ *noun* (no plural) 12 o'clock in the middle of the day SYNONYM **midday**: *Lunch will be served at noon.*

ˈno one *pronoun*
not anyone SYNONYM **nobody**: *The telephone rang but no one answered.*

noose /nuːs/ *noun* a circle at the end of a long piece of rope that can be pulled tight to catch animals or hang people

nor /nɔː $ nɔr/ *adverb, conjunction*
1 used in negative statements, when adding something else: *"I don't want to go." "Nor do I* (=and I don't want to go)*."* • *I didn't tell Mum, and nor did John.*
2 neither ... nor (written) used to say that two things are not true: *He was* ***neither*** *handsome* ***nor*** *ugly.* • *The government has* ***neither*** *confirmed* ***nor*** *denied the report.*

norm /nɔːm $ nɔrm/ *noun* **the norm** what is usual or normal: *Going to university is becoming the norm.*

nor·mal /ˈnɔːməl $ ˈnɔrməl/ *adjective*

KEY PATTERNS
it's normal to do something
it's normal for someone to do something

something that is normal is how you would usually expect it to be: *It started out as a normal day.* • *She's just a normal 15-year-old girl.* • *The library will be open at the normal times next week.* • *It's quite* ***normal to*** *feel nervous before you go into hospital.* • ***It is normal for*** *women in this country to work.*

A B C D E F G H I J K L M N O P Q R S T U V W X Y Z

THESAURUS
ordinary: *He thinks politicians are out of touch with* ***ordinary*** *people* (=not different or special).
standard: *a* ***standard*** *computer keyboard* (=normal or usual)
average: *The* ***average*** *person doesn't know much about science* (=normal or typical).
routine: *a* ***routine*** *safety check on the aircraft* (=done because that is what is normally done)

nor·mal·i·ty /nɔːˈmæləti $ nɔrˈmæləti/ *noun* (no plural) (formal) when things happen in the usual or normal way: *After the war, normality gradually returned.*

nor·mal·ly /ˈnɔːməli $ ˈnɔrməli/ *adverb* usually: *I normally cycle to college.*

north /nɔːθ $ nɔrθ/ *noun* **1** (no plural) the direction towards the top of a map **2 the north** the northern part of a country: *It will be windy in the north.* —**north** *adverb, adjective*: *The army was marching north.* • *We climbed the north face of the mountain.*

north·bound /ˈnɔːθbaʊnd $ ˈnɔrθbaʊnd/ *adjective* travelling towards the north: *I took the northbound train to Chicago.*

north·east /ˌnɔːθˈiːst $ ˌnɔrθˈist/ *noun* (no plural) the direction that is between north and east: *Towns in the northeast have been badly affected by the storms.* —**northeast** *adverb, adjective*

north·er·ly /ˈnɔːðəli $ ˈnɔrðəli/ *adjective* towards the north: *The wind is blowing in a northerly direction.*

nor·thern /ˈnɔːðən $ ˈnɔrðən/ *adjective* in or from the north: *northern California*

nor·thern·er /ˈnɔːðənə $ ˈnɔrðənə/ *noun* someone who comes from the north of a country

ˌNorth ˈPole *noun* the place on Earth that is farthest north → see picture at GLOBE

north·ward /ˈnɔːθwəd $ ˈnɔrθwəd/ also **northwards** /ˈnɔːθwədz $ ˈnɔrθwədz/ *adverb, adjective* towards the north: *We headed northwards.*

north·west /ˌnɔːθˈwest $ ˌnɔrθˈwest/ *noun* (no plural) the direction that is between north and west —**northwest** *adverb, adjective*

nose /nəʊz $ noʊz/ *noun* the part of your face that you use for smelling things and for breathing: *She had a spot on her nose.* → see picture on page A5

nose·bleed /ˈnəʊzbliːd $ ˈnoʊzblid/ *noun* if you have a nosebleed, blood comes out of your nose

nose·dive /ˈnəʊzdaɪv $ ˈnoʊzdaɪv/ *verb* if an aircraft nosedives, it flies fast towards the ground with its front end pointing down, usually before crashing —**nosedive** *noun*: *The plane did a sudden nosedive.*

nosey another spelling of NOSY

nos·tal·gia /nɒˈstældʒə $ nɑˈstældʒə/ *noun* (no plural) the slightly sad feeling you have when you think about nice things that happened in the past: *He was looking at the photo of his old home with nostalgia.*

nos·tril /ˈnɒstrəl $ ˈnɑstrəl/ *noun* one of the two holes in your nose, which you breathe through → see picture on page A5

nos·y, nosey /ˈnəʊzi $ ˈnoʊzi/ *adjective* (**nosier, nosiest**) a nosy person is always trying to find out about things that other people want to keep secret: *Don't be so nosy!*

not /nɒt $ nɑt/ *adverb* used to give a negative meaning: *That would not be a good idea* (=that would be a bad idea). • *They had not been there before.* • *There were not many people there.* • *I read a lot because I want to, not because I have to.* • *"Have the others gone?" "I hope not."*

no·ta·ble /ˈnəʊtəbəl $ ˈnoʊtəbəl/ *adjective* important, interesting, or unusual: *This area is notable for its forests.*

no·ta·bly /ˈnəʊtəbli $ ˈnoʊtəbli/ *adverb* used when you are giving an especially important or interesting example: *She failed in several subjects, notably English.*

notch /nɒtʃ $ nɑtʃ/ *noun* (plural **notches**) a cut in a surface that is in the shape of a V: *The arrow has a notch in the end for the bowstring.*

note[1] /nəʊt $ noʊt/ *noun*

KEY PATTERNS
write a note to someone
play a note on the violin/trumpet

1 a short letter: *Mum **wrote a note to** my teacher saying that I was sick.*
2 a musical sound, or the sign in written music that means this: *He **played** a few **notes** on the piano.*
3 *BrE* a piece of paper money SYNONYM **bill** *AmE*: *Milly paid with a five-pound note.*
4 notes information that you write down during a lesson or from a book so that you will remember it: *While the teacher talked, the students **took notes**.*

PHRASES
make a note of something to write something down so that you remember it: *She **made a note of** his birthday.*
→ see Thesaurus at WRITE
take note (of something) to pay careful attention to something: *You should **take note of** what your grandmother says.*

note[2] *verb* **1** to notice or pay careful attention to something: *Please note that visiting time is 2 until 3.* **2** also **note down** to write something down so that you will remember it: *I noted down the time of the train.*

note·book /ˈnəʊtbʊk $ ˈnoʊtbʊk/ *noun* a small book in which you can write things that you need to remember

note·pa·per /ˈnəʊtˌpeɪpə $ ˈnoʊtˌpeɪpɚ/ *noun* (no plural) paper that you use for writing letters

noth·ing[1] /ˈnʌθɪŋ/ *pronoun*
1 not anything: *Nothing surprises me any more.* • *"What did Tessa say on the phone?" "Nothing important."* • *There's nothing we can do.*
2 no money: *We got into the concert for nothing!* • *She likes buying people presents but spends nothing on herself.*

PHRASES
for nothing without achieving or getting anything: *I did all that work **for nothing!***
have nothing to do with someone/something a) to not be related to someone or something: *Their argument **had nothing to do with** work.* **b)** if something has nothing to do with someone, they do not have a right to know about it or get involved with it: *Go away – this **has nothing to do with** you.*
there's nothing to it (spoken) it's very easy: *I'll show you how to download some music – **there's nothing to it** really.*

nothing[2] *adverb* **be nothing like someone/something** (informal) to have no qualities that are similar to someone or something: *My brother is nothing like me.*

no·tice[1] /ˈnəʊtɪs $ ˈnoʊtɪs/ *verb* to see, feel, or hear someone or something: *I didn't notice you come in.*

notice

notice poster

notice[2] *noun*
a piece of writing that you put on a wall to give information to people: *We'll **put a notice on** the board with your test results.* • *They **put up** a notice saying 'No Smoking'.*

PHRASES
not take any notice, take no notice to not give any attention to someone or something because you do not think that they are important: *He shouted something at me, but **I took no notice** of him.*
a day's notice, a week's notice etc a warning about something that is going to happen, that you receive only a day, a week etc before it happens: *We only had **two days' notice** about the exam.*
at short notice if something happens at short notice, it happens without very much warning, so that you have only a short time to prepare for it: *I can't get time off work **at such short notice**.*

hand in your notice, give in your notice to tell your employer that you are leaving your job

no·tice·a·ble /ˈnəʊtɪsəbəl $ ˈnoʊtɪsəbəl/ *adjective* easy to notice: *There's been a noticeable improvement in your work.* —**noticeably** *adverb*: *He was noticeably thinner.*

> THESAURUS
> **clear/obvious**: *It was **clear** that she was unhappy* (=easy to see or notice).
> **conspicuous**: *The bird has a **conspicuous** white patch on its head* (=very easy to notice).
> **striking**: *The most **striking** feature of the house is its very high ceilings* (=unusual or noticeable).

no·tice·board /ˈnəʊtɪsˌbɔːd $ ˈnoʊtɪsˌbɔrd/ *noun BrE* a board on a wall, where you can put information or pictures SYNONYM **bulletin board** *AmE*: *The exam results will be put up on the noticeboard.* → see Thesaurus at BOARD[1]

no·ti·fy /ˈnəʊtəfaɪ $ ˈnoʊtəˌfaɪ/ *verb* (formal) (**notified**, **notifies**) to tell someone something officially SYNONYM **inform**: *She immediately notified the police.*

no·tion /ˈnəʊʃən $ ˈnoʊʃən/ *noun* an idea or belief about something: *I had a notion that you were looking for a new job.*

no·to·ri·ous /nəʊˈtɔːriəs $ noʊˈtɔriəs/ *adjective* famous for something bad: *This stretch of road is notorious for accidents.* —**notoriously** *adverb*: *Phrasal verbs are notoriously difficult for students.*

nought /nɔːt/ *noun BrE* the number 0 SYNONYM **zero**

> PRONUNCIATION
> You pronounce **nought** like 'sort'.

noun /naʊn/ *noun* a word that is the name of a person, place, thing, or idea. 'Money' and 'table' are nouns.

nour·ish /ˈnʌrɪʃ $ ˈnɜːɪʃ/ *verb* (formal) to give a person or living thing the substances they need to live and be healthy: *The cream contains vitamins A and E to nourish the skin.* —**nourishing** *adjective*: *good nourishing food*

nov·el /ˈnɒvəl $ ˈnɑvəl/ *noun* a book that tells a story: *He is writing a novel about a boy's life.*

nov·el·ist /ˈnɒvəlɪst $ ˈnɑvəlɪst/ *noun* someone who writes novels: *the American novelist Dan Brown*

nov·el·ty /ˈnɒvəlti $ ˈnɑvəlti/ *noun* (plural **novelties**) when something is new and unusual: *I've just passed my test so driving is still a novelty for me.*

No·vem·ber /nəʊˈvembə $ noʊˈvembɚ/ (written abbreviation **Nov**) *noun* the eleventh month of the year

nov·ice /ˈnɒvɪs $ ˈnɑvɪs/ *noun* someone who has just begun learning how to do something SYNONYM **beginner**: *I am a novice at chess.*

now[1] /naʊ/ *adverb*

1 at the present time: *They now live in Yorkshire. • He was ill, but he's better now. • I'll do it later – I'm busy **right now**. • Sam's late. I thought he'd be back **by now**. • If you wanted to get there by noon, you should have left **before now**.*

2 immediately: *We'd better go now, before the weather gets any worse.*

3 used when starting to talk to someone: *Now, be quiet everyone! • Now, what did you want to ask me?*

PHRASES

now and then, now and again (spoken) sometimes, not regularly: *I still see him **now and then**.*

from now on starting at this time and continuing: ***From now on** I'm going to work really hard!*

> THESAURUS
> **at the moment**: *I'm a bit busy **at the moment** – can I call you back* (=now)?
> **at present**: *At present, these phones are very expensive* (=now).
> **currently**: *She is **currently** working on her next book* (=at the present time).

now[2] also ˈ**now that** *conjunction* used to mention a new situation, when talking about its result: *Now he's got a car, he'll be able to take us everywhere. • **Now that** you've seen the town, do you think you'll be happy there?*

now·a·days /ˈnaʊədeɪz/ *adverb* (informal) used to talk about what happens now, compared to the past SYNONYM **today**: *More people work at home nowadays.*

SPELLING
This word is often spelled wrongly. The correct spelling is: **nowadays**.

no•where /ˈnəʊweə $ ˈnoʊwer/ *adverb* not in any place: *He **has nowhere to** sleep tonight.* • *There **is nowhere to** put the computer in here, so it will have to go in my bedroom.*

PHRASES
get nowhere to have no success or make no progress: *I'm **getting nowhere** with this work – it's too difficult.*
nowhere near **a)** not nearly: *She is **nowhere near** as tall as her sister.* **b)** not near at all: *You can't walk to the cinema. It's **nowhere near** your house.*

nu•cle•ar /ˈnjuːkliə $ ˈnukliɚ/ *adjective* **1** using the energy that is produced when an atom is split or joined to another atom: *nuclear power* • *nuclear weapons* **2** related to the nucleus of an atom: *nuclear physics*

nuclear re•ac•tor /ˌnjuːkliə riˈæktə $ ˌnukliɚ riˈæktɚ/ *noun* a large machine that produces energy by splitting or joining atoms

nu•cle•us /ˈnjuːkliəs $ ˈnukliəs/ *noun* (plural **nuclei** /-kliaɪ/) **1** the central part of an atom **2** the central part of a cell

nude /njuːd $ nud/ *adjective* not wearing any clothes SYNONYM **naked**: *a painting of a nude man*

nudge

nudge /nʌdʒ/ *verb* to push someone or something gently with your elbow: *Ken nudged me and said, "Look!"* → see Thesaurus at PUSH[1] —**nudge** *noun*: *She gave me a nudge when it was my turn.*

nu•di•ty /ˈnjuːdəti $ ˈnudəti/ *noun* (no plural) when people are not wearing any clothes: *Nudity is allowed on some beaches.*

nui•sance /ˈnjuːsəns $ ˈnusəns/ *noun* something or someone that annoys you or causes problems: *What a nuisance! I forgot to buy milk.*

numb /nʌm/ *adjective* not able to feel anything: *It was so cold that my fingers went numb.* —**numbness** *noun* (no plural): *The disease causes numbness in the legs.*

PRONUNCIATION
In this word you do not pronounce the **b**.

num•ber[1] /ˈnʌmbə $ ˈnʌmbɚ/ *noun*

KEY PATTERNS
a number of people/things

1 a word or written sign that shows a quantity: *2, 4, 6 — what number comes next?* • ***even numbers*** (=2, 4, 6, 8 etc) • ***odd numbers*** (=1, 3, 5, 7 etc)
2 the set of numbers that you use to telephone someone: *She gave me her number and asked me to call her.*
3 an amount of something that you can count: *A large **number of** tickets were still unsold.* • ***The number of** girls at the school has increased.*

PRONUNCIATION
You write **105**. You say **a hundred and five**.
You write **1965**. You say **nineteen sixty-five** if it is a date, or **one thousand nine hundred and sixty-five** if it is a number.
You write **0.5**. You say **zero point five** or **nought point five**.

number[2] *verb* to give a number to something that is part of a set or list: *I numbered all the photographs.*

ˈnumber ˌplate *noun BrE* the sign on the front and back of a vehicle that shows its official number SYNONYM **license plate** *AmE*

nu•me•rous /ˈnjuːmərəs $ ˈnumərəs/ *adjective* (formal) many: *He has visited Japan on numerous occasions.*

nun /nʌn/ *noun* a woman who lives as part of a group of religious women, away from other people

nurse¹ /nɜːs $ nɚs/ *noun* someone whose job is to look after people who are ill or injured, usually in a hospital

nurse² *verb* to look after someone who is ill or injured: *His wife nursed him at home.*

nur•se•ry /ˈnɜːsəri $ ˈnɚsəri/ *noun* (plural **nurseries**) **1** *BrE* a place where people look after young children during the day: *Does your son go to nursery?* **2** a place where plants and trees are grown and sold

ˈnursery ˌschool *noun* a school for children between three and five years old SYNONYM **kindergarten**

nurs•ing /ˈnɜːsɪŋ $ ˈnɚsɪŋ/ *noun* (no plural) the job of looking after people who are ill, injured, or very old: *Nursing is a tough job.*

nut /nʌt/ *noun* **1** a large seed that you can eat, that usually grows in a hard brown shell: *a cashew nut* → see picture on page A7 **2** a small piece of metal with a hole in the middle, that is used with a BOLT for fastening things together

nu•tri•ent /ˈnjuːtriənt $ ˈnutriənt/ *noun* (formal) a chemical that helps plants, animals, or people to live and grow: *Plants take nutrients from the soil.*

nu•tri•tious /njuːˈtrɪʃəs $ nuˈtrɪʃəs/ *adjective* food that is nutritious contains a lot of things that your body needs to be healthy: *Bananas are very nutritious.* • *a nutritious diet*

ny•lon /ˈnaɪlɒn $ ˈnaɪlɑn/ *noun* (no plural) a strong material that is used for making clothes, rope etc: *nylon stockings* • *a carpet made of wool and nylon*

A B C D E F G H I J K L M N O P Q R S T U V W X Y Z

oak /əʊk $ oʊk/ *noun* a type of large tree, or the wood that comes from it: *an oak table*

oar /ɔː $ ɔr/ *noun* a long pole that is wide at one end, that you use for moving a boat through water

o·a·sis /əʊˈeɪsɪs $ oʊˈeɪsɪs/ *noun* (plural **oases** /-siːz/) a place in a desert where there is water and plants

oath /əʊθ $ oʊθ/ (plural **oaths** /əʊðz $ oʊðz/) *noun* an official promise: *You must swear an oath to tell the truth in court.*

oats /əʊts $ oʊts/ *plural noun* a grain that is used in cooking: *Porridge is made with oats and milk.*

o·be·di·ence /əˈbiːdiəns/ *noun* (no plural) when someone does what a person or rule tells them to do ANTONYM **disobedience**: *Her father expects complete obedience.*

o·be·di·ent /əˈbiːdiənt/ *adjective* someone who is obedient does what a person or rule tells them to do ANTONYM **disobedient**: *She expects children to be quiet and obedient.* • *a very obedient dog* —**obediently** *adverb*: *"Yes, father," he said obediently.*

o·bese /əʊˈbiːs $ oʊˈbis/ *adjective* (formal) much too fat, in a way that is dangerous to your health: *More and more children are becoming obese.* ➔ see Thesaurus at FAT[1]

o·bey /əʊˈbeɪ $ əˈbeɪ/ *verb* to do what a person or rule tells you to do ANTONYM **disobey**: *Students must obey the school rules.*

ob·ject¹ /ˈɒbdʒɪkt $ ˈɑbdʒɪkt/ *noun*
1 a thing that you can see and hold: *She had several strange-looking objects in her bag.*
2 the noun that says which person or thing is affected by a verb: *In the sentence 'He kissed the girl', the object of the verb is 'the girl'.*
3 the thing that you are trying to do SYNONYM **aim**: *The object of the game is to throw the ball into the basket.*

ob·ject² /əbˈdʒekt/ *verb*

> KEY PATTERNS
> **object to something**
> **object to someone doing something**

to say that you do not like something or do not want it to happen: *A lot of people* ***objected to*** *the violence in the film.* • *My father* ***objects to*** *me staying out so late.* • *I said we should share the cost, and no one objected.*

> PRONUNCIATION
> You pronounce the noun **OBject**, with the stress on the first syllable.
> You pronounce the verb **obJECT**, with the stress on the second syllable.

ob·jec·tion /əbˈdʒekʃən/ *noun*

> KEY PATTERNS
> **have an objection to something**
> **make an objection**

if you make an objection to something, you say that you do not like it or do not want it to happen: *Do you* ***have any objection to*** *smoking?* • *If the local people do not* ***make an objection***, *we can start building the new houses.*

ob·jec·tive /əbˈdʒektɪv/ *noun* something that you are trying to achieve SYNONYM **goal**: *Our main objective is to raise money.* ➔ see Thesaurus at PURPOSE

ob·li·ga·tion /ˌɒbləˈɡeɪʃən $ ˌɑbləˈɡeɪʃən/ *noun* (formal) something that you must do because it is the law or it is your duty: *You have an obligation to inform the police of any accident on the road.*

ob·lig·a·to·ry /ə'blɪgətəri $ ə'blɪgə,tɔri/ *adjective* (formal) if something is obligatory, you must do it because of a law or rule SYNONYM **compulsory**: *Attending school is obligatory.*

o·blige /ə'blaɪdʒ/ *verb* **1** (formal) if you are obliged to do something, you must do it because it is the law or it is your duty: *Doctors are obliged to offer the best possible treatment to their patients.* **2** to do something that someone has asked you to do: *We asked for her help, and she was happy to oblige.*

o·blit·er·ate /ə'blɪtəreɪt/ *verb* (formal) to destroy something completely SYNONYM **wipe out**: *The earthquake had obliterated the cathedral.*

o·bliv·i·ous /ə'blɪviəs/ *adjective* (formal) not noticing what is happening around you SYNONYM **unaware**: *The children were fast asleep, oblivious to the noise.*

ob·long /'ɒblɒŋ $ 'ɑblɔŋ/ *noun* a shape with four corners that has two long sides and two shorter sides SYNONYM **rectangle** —**oblong** *adjective*: *an oblong table*

ob·nox·ious /əb'nɒkʃəs $ əb'nɑkʃəs/ *adjective* extremely unpleasant or rude: *What an obnoxious man!*

o·boe /'əubəu $ 'oubou/ *noun* a long thin wooden musical instrument that you play by blowing and pressing holes with your fingers

ob·scene /əb'siːn/ *adjective* showing or talking about sex in an offensive and shocking way: *obscene photographs* • *obscene language*

ob·scure /əb'skjuə $ əb'skjur/ *adjective* not familiar or well known: *The play was written in the 16th century and is full of obscure words*

ob·ser·vant /əb'zɜːvənt $ əb'zɚvənt/ *adjective* good at noticing things: *A good police officer needs to be observant.*

ob·ser·va·tion /,ɒbzə'veɪʃən $,ɑbzɚ'veɪʃən/ *noun* **1** (no plural) when you watch someone or something carefully: *You can learn a lot about animals just by observation.* **2** (formal) a spoken or written remark: *She made some interesting observations in her article.*

ob·serve /əb'zɜːv $ əb'zɚv/ *verb* **1** to watch someone or something carefully: *An inspector came to observe the lesson.* **2** to obey a law, agreement, or religious custom: *Both sides are observing the ceasefire.*

ob·sessed /əb'sest/ *adjective* if you are obsessed with something, you think about it too much, in a way that is not normal: *Julie is obsessed with losing weight.*

ob·ses·sion /əb'seʃən/ *noun* something that you think about too much, in a way that is not normal: *He has an obsession with money.*

ob·so·lete /'ɒbsəliːt $,ɑbsə'lit/ *adjective* old, and no longer used: *Technology changes quickly, and machines become obsolete.*

ob·sta·cle /'ɒbstɪkəl $ 'ɑbstɪkəl/ *noun* **1** something that makes it difficult to do something: *She's intelligent, so there should be no obstacle to her going to university.* **2** something that blocks a road or path: *The entrance was blocked by a chair and other obstacles.*

ob·sti·nate /'ɒbstənət $ 'ɑbstənət/ *adjective* (formal) refusing to change your opinions or behaviour SYNONYM **stubborn**: *Lucy can be very obstinate.*

ob·struct /əb'strʌkt/ *verb* (formal) to block a road or path SYNONYM **block**: *A van was obstructing the entrance.*

ob·struc·tion /əb'strʌkʃən/ *noun* (formal) something that blocks a road or path SYNONYM **blockage**: *The accident caused an obstruction.*

ob·tain /əb'teɪn/ *verb* (formal) to get something: *You can obtain more information by phoning our main office.*

ob·tain·a·ble /əb'teɪnəbəl/ *adjective* (formal) if something is obtainable, you can get it SYNONYM **available**: *Fresh fish is easily obtainable.*

ob·vi·ous *adjective* /'ɒbviəs $ 'ɑbviəs/

KEY PATTERNS
it is obvious to someone (that)

if something is obvious, you can see it or understand it easily: ***It was obvious** that Joe was unhappy.* • *It was **obvious to** me that she was lying.* • *There is an obvious reason why Sam wanted to leave.* ➔ see Thesaurus at NOTICEABLE
—**obviously** *adverb*: *He was obviously upset.*

oc•ca•sion /əˈkeɪʒən/ *noun*
1 (formal) a time when something happens: *I have been there **on many occasions**.*
2 an important event or ceremony: *An 18th birthday is a **special occasion**.*

oc•ca•sion•al /əˈkeɪʒənəl/ *adjective* happening sometimes but not very often: *We have occasional arguments.*
—**occasionally** *adverb*: *I still see my ex-boyfriend occasionally.*

oc•cu•pant /ˈɒkjəpənt $ ˈɑkjəpənt/ *noun* (formal) someone who lives in or is using a building or room: *The occupants of the house were away.*

oc•cu•pa•tion /ˌɒkjəˈpeɪʃən $ ˌɑkjəˈpeɪʃən/ *noun* (formal) a job or profession: *Please state your name and occupation.* ➔ see Thesaurus at JOB

occupied

All the seats in the front row were occupied.

oc•cu•pied /ˈɒkjəpaɪd $ ˈɑkjəˌpaɪd/ *adjective* **1** if a room, bed, or seat is occupied, someone is using it ANTONYM **free**, **vacant**: *All the seats in the row were occupied.* **2** busy doing or thinking about something: *The game kept us occupied all afternoon.*

oc•cu•py /ˈɒkjəpaɪ $ ˈɑkjəˌpaɪ/ *verb* (**occupied**, **occupies**) **1** to be using a building or room: *Three companies now occupy this building.* **2** to go into a place and take control of it by force: *Enemy soldiers occupied the city.*
3 occupy yourself (spoken) to find things to do and not become bored: *It's hard for young kids to occupy themselves when it is raining.*

oc•cur /əˈkɜː $ əˈkɚ/ *verb* (formal) (**occurred**, **occurring**) to happen, without being planned: *When did the accident occur?* ➔ see Thesaurus at HAPPEN

PHRASAL VERBS

occur to
occur to someone if an idea occurs to you, you think of it: *It didn't **occur to me** that she could be lying.*

> **SPELLING**
> This word is often spelled wrongly. The correct spelling is: **occur**.

oc•cur•rence /əˈkʌrəns $ əˈkɚəns/ *noun* (formal) something that happens: *Earthquakes are a common occurrence in this part of the world.*

o•cean /ˈəʊʃən $ ˈoʊʃən/ *noun* **the ocean** the sea: *the Pacific Ocean* • *Our house is right beside the ocean.*

o'clock /əˈklɒk $ əˈklɑk/ *adverb* **one o'clock, two o'clock etc** used to say what time of day it is: *Dinner will be ready at 8 o'clock, but get here by 7.30.*

> **USAGE**
> You only use **o'clock** with exact hours: *It's seven o'clock.*
> Don't use **o'clock** when talking about times between exact hours.
> You say **It's half past five.**
> ✘ Don't say 'It's half past five o'clock.'

oc•ta•gon /ˈɒktəgən $ ˈɑktəˌgɑn/ *noun* a flat shape with eight sides

Oc•to•ber /ɒkˈtəʊbə $ ɑkˈtoʊbɚ/ (written abbreviation **Oct**) *noun* the tenth month of the year: *The arts festival will be in October.*

oc•to•pus /ˈɒktəpəs $ ˈɑktəpəs/ *noun* (plural **octopuses** or **octopi** /-paɪ/) a sea creature with a soft body and eight long arms

octopus

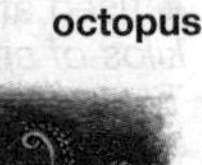

A B C D E F G H I J K L M N O P Q R S T U V W X Y Z

odd /ɒd $ ɑd/ *adjective*

KEY PATTERNS
it's odd that

strange or unusual: *Her behaviour seemed a bit odd.* • ***It's odd that** he still hasn't come home.* • *What an odd name!* → see Thesaurus at STRANGE

PHRASES

odd number an odd number is a number that you cannot divide exactly by two. For example, 1, 3, 5, and 7 are all odd numbers ANTONYM **even number**

odd jobs small jobs that need to be done in the house and garden: *I earn a bit of money doing **odd jobs** for people.*

odd·ly /ˈɒdli $ ˈɑdli/ *adverb* in a strange or unusual way SYNONYM **strangely**: *He's been behaving very oddly recently.*

odds /ɒdz $ ɑdz/ *plural noun* how likely it is that something will happen, often expressed using numbers: *The odds of winning the lottery are about 14 million to 1.*

ˌodds and ˈends *plural noun* (informal) small things that are not important or valuable: *She made a doll out of a few odds and ends.*

o·dour *BrE*, **odor** *AmE* /ˈəʊdə $ ˈoʊdɚ/ *noun* (formal) a smell, especially an unpleasant one: *Inside, there was the unpleasant odour of cigarette smoke and beer.* → see Thesaurus at SMELL²

of /əv; strong ɒv $ ʌv/ *preposition*
1 used when talking about a part, feature, quality etc that something has: *The door of the car was open.* • *I didn't notice the colour of her eyes.*
2 belonging to someone: *She is the daughter of a famous actor.* • *A friend of my brother's offered to lend me his car.*
3 containing something: *There was a vase of flowers on the table.* • *a packet of sweets* • *a cup of coffee*
4 used after an amount: *I bought two kilos of apples.* • *a group of people* • *Two of the plates were broken.*
5 used to say what a picture shows: *a photograph of my mother* • *a picture of the cathedral*
6 used to say who or what is involved in an action: *the arrival of a visitor* (=the visitor arrived) • *the cancellation of the meeting* (=the meeting was cancelled)
7 used to show how old someone is: *an old man of 70*

PHRASES

it is nice of someone to do something, that is brave of someone etc used to say that someone's action is nice, brave etc: ***It was nice of her to** phone.* • ***That was kind of** him.*

off¹ /ɒf $ ɔf/ *adverb, preposition*
1 used to show that something is removed from a place: *He brushed the crumbs off the table.* • *She took her coat off.* • *He knocked a glass off the table.*
2 used to say that someone leaves a place: *The boy rang the doorbell and then ran off.* • *He got into his car and drove off.*
3 if a machine or electrical equipment is off, it is not being used or not working: *All the lights in the house were off.* • ***Switch** the television **off**.*
4 not at school or at work: *Robert's been off school for a week because he's ill.* • *Can I have a day off?*

PHRASES

off and on, on and off sometimes stopping and then starting again, in an irregular way: *It had been raining **off and on** for a week.*

off² *adjective*
1 food or drink that is off is not fresh any more: *Don't use that milk – it's off.*
2 an event that is off is not going to happen any more: *The picnic's off because of the rain.* • *We had to **call** the game **off** because so many of our players were ill.*

ˈoff-chance *noun* **on the off-chance** (informal) because you hope that something will happen, although it is unlikely: *I went to the library on the off-chance that I might see Harry.*

of·fence *BrE*, **offense** *AmE* /əˈfens/ *noun*
(formal) a crime: *Driving too fast is an offence.* • *If he has **committed** an **offence**, we will arrest him.*

PHRASES

take offence to feel upset or annoyed by something someone does or says to you: *She **took offence** when I refused her invitation.*

of·fend /ə'fend/ *verb*
to make someone feel upset or annoyed: *I hope I haven't offended you.* • *His remarks offended many Scottish people.*

of·fend·er /ə'fendə $ ə'fendɚ/ *noun*
(formal) someone who is guilty of a crime: *a prison for young offenders*

offense¹ the American spelling of OFFENCE

of·fense² /'ɔfens/ *noun AmE* the players in a game such as American football who try to get points ANTONYM **defense**

of·fen·sive¹ /ə'fensɪv/ *adjective*
1 likely to make people feel upset or annoyed ANTONYM **inoffensive**: *She said some very offensive things.* ➔ see Thesaurus at RUDE **2** (formal) used for attacking people ANTONYM **defensive**: *an offensive weapon*

offensive² *noun* **1** an attack on a place by an army: *a military offensive*
2 go on the offensive to attack or criticize people: *We have to go on the offensive if we are going to win this election.*

of·fer¹ /'ɒfə $ 'ɔfɚ/ *verb*

KEY PATTERNS
offer someone a biscuit/drink/lift
offer a biscuit/drink/lift etc to someone
offer to do something
offer someone a job

1 to ask someone if they would like something: *He came over and **offered** me a drink.* • *She **offered** some chocolates **to** the children.*
2 to say that you will do something for someone if they want you to: *Simon **offered to** take me to the station.*
3 to say that you will give something to someone, if they want it: *They've offered me a job!* • *I'll offer him £5,000 for the car.*

offer² *noun*

KEY PATTERNS
an offer of help
an offer of £30/$2 million etc
make someone an offer
an offer to do something
accept someone's offer

when you say that you will do something for someone or give them something if they want it: *Thanks for your kind **offer of help**.* • *I'm willing to **make you an offer** of $300.* • *I accepted his **offer to** clean the house for me.*

PHRASES
a good offer, a special offer a lower price than usual in the shops: *If you buy in January, there are usually some **good offers**.*

off·hand /ɒf'hænd $ ɔf'hænd/ *adverb*
if you do not know something offhand, you do not know it immediately, but need time to think or check it: *I don't know his address offhand.*

of·fice /'ɒfɪs $ 'ɔfɪs/ *noun*

KEY PATTERNS
in an office
at the office

1 a room where someone works at a desk, or where people work together: *The manager's office is on the second floor.* • *I'm afraid Mr Stokes isn't **in his office** at the moment.*
2 a building that belongs to a company, with rooms where people work: *Did you have a good day **at the office**?*

of·fi·cer /'ɒfəsə $ 'ɔfəsɚ/ *noun*
1 someone who has a position of authority in the army, navy etc: *an army officer* **2** a policeman or policewoman SYNONYM **police officer**

of·fi·cial¹ /ə'fɪʃəl/ *adjective*
done or given by someone in authority: *The official report will be published next month.* • *The chairman has given his official support to the idea.*

official² *noun*
a person who has an important job in an organization or a government: *Senior government officials were waiting to greet the president.*

of·fi·cial·ly /ə'fɪʃəli/ *adverb* in an official or formal way: *We will announce the results officially next week.*

'off-ˌlicence *noun BrE* a shop that sells alcoholic drinks

off·line /ɒf'laɪn $ ɔf'laɪn/ *adverb, adjective* **1** with your computer not connected to the Internet: *You can download whole books and read them* *offline.* **2** not connected to a computer: *The printer is offline.*

ˈoff-peak *adjective, adverb BrE* off-peak services are cheaper because they are used at less busy times ANTONYM **peak**: *an off-peak bus ticket for evenings and weekends • It only costs £24.99 if you travel off-peak.*

off•side /ˌɒfˈsaɪd $ ˌɔfˈsaɪd/ *adjective, adverb* in games such as football, a player who is offside is in a position that is not allowed by the rules when the ball is passed to them

of•ten /ˈɒfən $ ˈɔfən/ *adverb* many times ANTONYM **rarely**: *I often go through the park on my way home from school. • I don't watch television very often. • Quite often there is no obvious cause for the pain. •* ***How often*** *do you wash your hair?*

USAGE
Often usually comes before the main verb, and after words like 'is', 'have', 'don't' etc: *Dad often gets home late. • I don't often go to the cinema.*
Very often is used at the end of a negative sentence: *He doesn't telephone very often.*

THESAURUS
a lot: *I play tennis a lot in the summer* (=often).
frequently (formal): *Trains are frequently cancelled* (=often).
again and again: *He read the letter again and again* (=very many times).
repeatedly (formal): *I have repeatedly complained about the noise* (=many times).
regularly: *You should have your eyes tested regularly* (=often, at regular times).

oh /əʊ $ oʊ/ (spoken) **1** used before replying: *"How was the film?" "Oh, it was OK."* **2** used to express strong emotions: *Oh, isn't she cute!*

oil¹ /ɔɪl/ *noun* (no plural)
1 a thick liquid used for making petrol, or for making machines work smoothly: *Kuwait is one of the countries that export oil. • The engine needs some more oil.*
2 a liquid used for cooking, made from plants or animal fat: *Heat a little oil in a pan.*

oil² *verb* to put oil onto part of a machine: *He needs to oil the wheels of his bike.*

ˈoil ˌpainting *noun* a picture painted with paint that contains oil

ˈoil rig *noun* a large structure with equipment for getting oil out of the ground

ˈoil slick *noun* a layer of oil on the sea or a river, which has come out of a ship carrying oil

ˈoil well *noun* a deep hole made to get oil out of the ground

oil•y /ˈɔɪli/ *adjective* (**oilier, oiliest**) covered with oil, or containing a lot of oil: *He wiped his oily hands on a rag.*

oint•ment /ˈɔɪntmənt/ *noun* a soft substance that you rub into your skin as a medical treatment

OK, okay /əʊˈkeɪ $ oʊˈkeɪ/ *adjective, adverb* (informal)
1 satisfactory or acceptable SYNONYM **all right**: *Is it OK if I phone you tonight? • Does this dress look OK?* → see Thesaurus at SATISFACTORY
2 safe and not ill, hurt, or upset SYNONYM **all right**: *Are you feeling OK?*
3 used to say that you agree with something or are willing to do something SYNONYM **all right**: *"Can you come round at about eight o'clock?" "Okay."*

old

old /əʊld $ oʊld/ *adjective*
1 someone who is old has lived a long time ANTONYM **young**: *an old woman • He was very old when he died.*

THESAURUS
elderly: *an elderly man with white hair* (=a polite way of saying that someone is old)
aged: *She looks after her aged parents* (=very old).

A B C D E F G H I J K L M N **O** P Q R S T U V W X Y Z

senior citizen: *There are special prices for **senior citizens*** (=people over the age of 60 or 65).

2 used when talking or asking about the age of a person or thing: *My sister's three years old.* • ***How old** are you?* • *Do you know **how old** the building is?*
3 not modern or new ANTONYM **new**: *We lived in an old house in the country.* • *This is an old dress – I've had it for years.*

THESAURUS
ancient: *They dug up some **ancient** coins* (=many hundreds of years old).
antique: *an **antique** clock* (=old and usually valuable – used about objects such as furniture and jewellery)
secondhand: *I buy a lot of **secondhand** books* (=previously owned by someone else).

4 used when talking about something that you used to have but do not have any more ANTONYM **new**: *I liked my old school better than this one.*

PHRASES
an old friend a friend that you have known for a long time: *Laura's **an old friend** of mine.*
older brother, older sister a brother or sister who is older than you

ˌold 'age *noun* (no plural) the time in your life when you are old: *You should save some money for your old age.*

ˌold-'fashioned *adjective* not modern or fashionable ANTONYM **fashionable**: *Her clothes are a bit old-fashioned.*

ol•ive /ˈɒlɪv $ ˈɑlɪv/ *noun* a small bitter black or green fruit, often used for making oil

O•lym•pic /əˈlɪmpɪk/ *adjective* related to the Olympic Games: *She won two Olympic gold medals.*

Oˌlympic 'Games also **Olympics** *plural noun* **the Olympic Games, the Olympics** an international sports event held every four years

ome•lette *BrE*, **omelet** *AmE* /ˈɒmlət $ ˈɑmlət/ *noun* eggs mixed together and cooked in a pan, often with other foods added: *a cheese omelette*

om•i•nous /ˈɒmənəs $ ˈɑmənəs/ *adjective* making you feel that something bad is going to happen: *My car's engine was making an ominous noise.* **—ominously** *adverb*: *The sky looked ominously dark.*

o•mit /əʊˈmɪt $ oʊˈmɪt/ *verb* (formal) (**omitted, omitting**) to not include something: *They had omitted his name from the list.*

om•ni•bus /ˈɒmnɪbəs $ ˈɑmnɪbəs/ *noun* a book or television programme that consists of several previous books or programmes put together: *I missed an episode so I'll have to watch the omnibus.*

on[1] /ɒn $ ɔn/ *preposition*
1 used to talk about the surface where something is resting or where it is put: *Gloria was lying on the grass.* • *He put his mug of coffee down on the table.* • *There was a mirror on the wall.*
2 used to show where something is written or drawn: *Look at the picture on page 23.*
3 used to show which part of your body or of a thing is touching the ground, floor etc: *She was lying on her back.* • *He was on his hands and knees, looking for the missing button.*
4 next to a road, river, or sea: *The hotel is on the main road into Oxford.* • *a small town on the River Thames*
5 used to talk about the day or date when something happens: *I'll see you on Saturday.* • *I was born on 17th June 1986.* • *I called her on Tuesday afternoon.*
6 used to talk about the subject of a book, talk etc: *She loves reading books on animals.* • *a talk on the history of the cinema* → see Thesaurus at ABOUT[1]
7 travelling by bus, train, boat, or plane: *I've never been on a ship before.* • *A woman with two dogs got on the bus.*
8 using a machine or instrument: *I've added up the figures on my calculator.* • *Rosie was playing a tune on the piano.*

PHRASES
on television, on the radio being broadcast by television or radio: *Did you see that film **on television** last night?*
on holiday, on vacation: *We went **on holiday** to Jamaica last year* (=Jamaica was the place we went to for a holiday last year).

have something on you (informal) to have something in your pocket or bag: *I have his address **on** me somewhere.*

on² *adverb, adjective*
1 if a machine or piece of equipment is on, it is working and someone is using it ANTONYM **off**: *The washing machine's still on.* • *Do you want the TV on?*
2 if a television programme or film is on, it is possible to watch it: *There's a good programme on tonight.* • ***What's on** at the cinema?*
3 an event that is on is going to happen ANTONYM **off**: *There's an outdoor concert on at the weekend.* • *Is the football match still on this Saturday?*
PHRASES
have something on, put something on to be wearing something or start wearing something: *She **had on** jeans and a T-shirt.* • ***Put** your coat **on**.*
from now on, from then on after this or that time: ***From now on** I'm going to be more careful.* • ***From then on** I never saw him again.*

once¹ /wʌns/ *adverb*
1 one time: *I've only been there once.* • *Press the switch once.* • *She goes out clubbing **once a week*** (=one night every week).
2 at a time in the past: *The house was once owned by a famous film star.* • *She must have been beautiful once.* • *He once gave a party for 2,000 people.*
PHRASES
at once a) at the same time: *It will save time if we make several copies **at once**.* • *I can't understand you if you all talk **at once**!* **b)** immediately: *If he starts causing trouble, you must tell me **at once**.* • *I could see **at once** that something was wrong.* → see Thesaurus at IMMEDIATELY

once² *conjunction*
from the time when something happens: *Once someone lies to you, you can never trust them again.*

one /wʌn/ *number, pronoun*
1 the number 1: *I have one brother and two sisters.* • *Only **one of** them can be right.* • ***One of** the children was crying.*
2 used when talking about a thing that is the same as something you have already mentioned: *Jim's got a puppy – can I have one too* (=can I have a puppy too)? • *My shoes are totally worn out – I'll have to get some new ones* (=some new shoes). • *All my presents were good, but I liked the one from my granddad best.* • *That one's too expensive.*
3 only: *This is my one chance to become famous!* • *That's the one thing I forgot.*
4 (formal) people in general: *One doesn't often* (=people don't often) *get the chance to talk to a president.*
PHRASES
one day, one afternoon etc at a time in the past or future: ***One day** last week the bus was 40 minutes late!* • *Why don't you come round **one evening**?*
one after the other, one after another if things happen one after the other, there is not much time between them: *He ate ten biscuits, **one after the other**.*
one another: *They try to help **one another** when they can* (=they each try to help the other person).
one or two (spoken) a few: *I've got **one or two** things to sort out.*

ˈone-off *adjective* one-off things only happen once: *a one-off payment*

ˌone-to-ˈone *adjective* a one-to-one talk or lesson involves only two people: *You will be given one-to-one training.*

ˌone-ˈway *adjective* **1** in a one-way street, cars can travel in only one direction **2** a one-way ticket is for travelling to a place, but not for coming back SYNONYM **single** ANTONYM **return** *BrE* ANTONYM **round-trip** *AmE*

on•ion /ˈʌnjən/ *noun* a round white vegetable that has a thin brown skin and a very strong smell → see picture on page A6

on•line, on-line /ˌɒnˈlaɪn $ ˌɔnˈlaɪn/ *adjective, adverb* connected to the Internet, or available through the Internet ANTONYM **offline**: *We do most of our work online.* • *an online teaching programme*

on•look•er /ˈɒnˌlʊkə $ ˈɔnˌlʊkɚ/ *noun* someone who watches something happening but is not involved in it: *A crowd of onlookers had gathered.*

on•ly¹ /ˈəʊnli $ ˈoʊnli/ *adverb*
1 showing that an amount is very small: *William lived only half a mile away from the school.* • *She got married when she was only 17.*

2 showing that something is not important: *Don't get upset – it's only a game.*
3 not anyone or anything else: *Only Richard knew the answer.* • *She only likes cornflakes for breakfast.* • *There's only one thing we can do: say we're sorry.* • *You can only get there by car.*
4 showing that something happened a very short time ago: *He only bought that computer on Monday.* • *I saw her only last week.*

PHRASES

only just **a)** a very short time ago: *Martin's **only just** left.* **b)** used to show that you do something, but with difficulty: *I could **only just** reach the top shelf.*

if only (spoken): ***If only** I'd kept a copy of the letter* (=I wish I'd kept a copy, but I didn't).

only² *adjective*
one single person or thing: *You're the only person I can trust.* • *It was the only ticket they had left.* • *It was the only vegetarian meal on the menu.* • *His only problem is his lack of confidence.*

PHRASES

an only child someone who has no brothers or sisters

only³ *conjunction* (spoken) but; used especially to talk about a problem that makes it difficult for you to do something: *I want to go the party, only I don't have anything to wear.*

on•to /ˈɒntə $ ˈɔntə; before vowels ˈɒntʊ $ ˈɔntʊ; strong ˈɒntuː $ ˈɔntu/ *preposition*
1 to a position on the surface of something: *He dropped two coins onto the table.*
2 to a position with a particular part touching the ground, floor etc: *Mark woke up and rolled onto his back.*

on•wards /ˈɒnwədz $ ˈɔnwərdz/ also **onward** *adverb* forward in space or time: *The army marched onwards.* • *I'll be free from two o'clock onward.*

ooze /uːz/ *verb* (**oozing**) if a liquid oozes, it flows slowly: *Fat oozed out of the cooked chicken.*

o•pal /ˈəʊpəl $ ˈoʊpəl/ *noun* a white stone used in jewellery

open

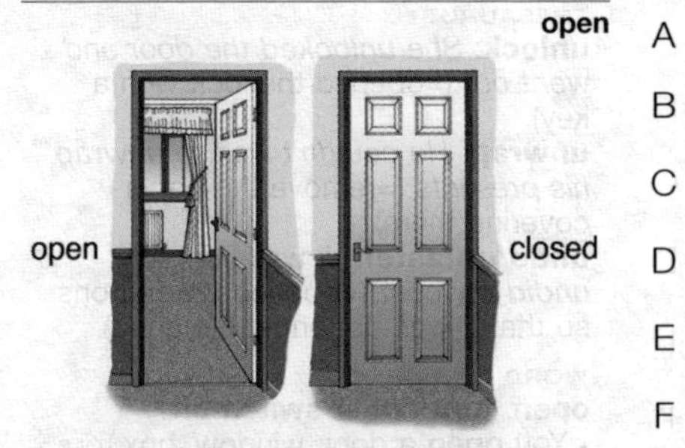

open¹ /ˈəʊpən $ ˈoʊpən/ *adjective*

KEY PATTERNS
open to people/the public/visitors
be open with someone

1 not closed ANTONYM **shut**: *The door was open, so I went in.* • *An open book lay on the desk.* • *Please could you **leave** the window **open**?*
2 if a shop, restaurant etc is open, people can come into it and use it ANTONYM **closed**: *The Indian restaurant is only open in the evening.* • *Is the new swimming pool open yet?* • *The library is not **open to** the public this week.*
3 an open person is honest and willing to talk about things: *Parents should try to be **open with** their children.*
4 if something is open to people, it is available for them to do: *A lot of interesting jobs are **open to** people with science qualifications.*

PHRASES

in the open air outside: *In summer, we often eat **in the open air**.*

open² *verb*
1 to move something so that it is open ANTONYM **close**, **shut**: *She opened her bag and took out some money.*
2 to become open ANTONYM **close**, **shut**: *At that moment the door opened.*
3 when a shop, bank etc opens, people can go in and use it ANTONYM **close**, **shut**: *Most shops open at 9.30 on Saturday.* • *The new hospital will open in September.*

PHRASES

open fire to start shooting at someone: *The soldiers were ordered to **open fire**.*

open an account, open a bank account if you open a bank account, you put money into the bank and start to use the bank's services

A B C D E F G H I J K L M N O P Q R S T U V W X Y Z

THESAURUS
unlock: *She unlocked the door and went out* (=opened the lock with a key).
unwrap: *He couldn't wait to unwrap his presents* (=remove the paper covering them).
undo/unfasten: *It was hot, so I undid my coat* (=opened the buttons so that it was no longer fastened).

WORD CHOICE
open, **turn on**, or **switch on**?
• You **open** a door, window, box, or book.
• You **turn on** a tap.
• You **switch on** or **turn on** a light, engine, television, computer etc.
✗ Don't say 'I opened the television.'

open[3] *noun* **1 (out) in the open** outside, not in a building: *We slept out in the open last night.* **2 be out in the open** to be no longer a secret: *I want the truth to be out in the open.*

ˌopen-ˈair *adjective* outside, not in a building SYNONYM **outdoor**: *an open-air concert • an open-air swimming pool*

ˈopen day *noun BrE* a day when people can visit a school or company and see what is done there SYNONYM **open house** *AmE*

o•pen•ing[1] /ˈəʊpənɪŋ $ ˈoʊpənɪŋ/ *noun* **1** when the public can start using a new place: *He invited them to the opening of his new restaurant.* **2** the beginning of something SYNONYM **start**: *The opening of the book is very exciting.* **3** a hole or space that something can go through: *The dog managed to get through an opening in the fence.*

opening[2] *adjective* happening first or coming at the beginning: *Dixon scored in the opening minutes of the game.*

o•pen•ly /ˈəʊpənli $ ˈoʊpənli/ *adverb* without keeping anything secret: *She spoke openly about her feelings.*

o•pen•ness /ˈəʊpnən-nəs $ ˈoʊpən-nəs/ *noun* (no plural) when someone does not keep things secret: *I liked his honesty and openness.*

ˌopen-ˈplan *adjective* an open-plan building does not have walls dividing it into separate rooms: *an open-plan office*

op•e•ra /ˈɒpərə $ ˈɑprə/ *noun* a play in which all the words are sung

op•e•rate /ˈɒpəreɪt $ ˈɑpəˌreɪt/ *verb*

KEY PATTERNS
operate a machine or piece of equipment
operate on someone

1 if you operate a machine or piece of equipment, you make it work: *How do you operate this machine? • My job was to operate the lighting for the concert.*
2 (formal) if a machine or piece of equipment operates, it works: *The computers weren't operating properly.*
3 if a doctor operates on someone, he or she cuts open their body to remove or repair a part that is damaged: *Doctors **operated on** him and removed one of his kidneys.*

op•e•ra•tion /ˌɒpəˈreɪʃən $ ˌɑpəˈreɪʃən/ *noun*

KEY PATTERNS
have an operation on your knee/hip etc

1 if someone has an operation, doctors cut open their body in order to remove or repair a part that is damaged: *Doug's got to **have an operation on** his back. • The surgeon **performed** an emergency **operation**.*
2 an organized activity in which people work together in order to do something: *The police organized a big search operation.*

op•e•ra•tor /ˈɒpəreɪtə $ ˈɑpəˌreɪtɚ/ *noun* **1** (formal) someone whose job is to use a machine or piece of equipment: *a computer operator*
2 someone whose job is to connect telephone calls

o•pin•ion /əˈpɪnjən/ *noun*

KEY PATTERNS
an opinion of someone/something
an opinion about a problem/subject/issue etc

your opinion of someone or something is what you think about them: *What's your **opinion of** the new head teacher? • George has strong **opinions about** divorce.*

PHRASES
in my opinion used to tell someone what you think about something: ***In my***

***opinion**, you should go to America if you have the chance.*

have a high opinion of something/someone to think that something or someone is very good: *I have a very **high opinion of** Sarah's work.*

have a low opinion of something/someone to think that something or someone is not very good: *He **has a rather low opinion of** Jenny.*

SPELLING
This word is often spelled wrongly. The correct spelling is: **opinion**.

THESAURUS
view: *She has strong **views** on children's education* (=opinions).
point of view: *You will have the opportunity to express your **point of view*** (=your opinion).
position: *the government's **position** on nuclear weapons* (=its official opinion)

o'pinion ˌpoll *noun* when a lot of people are asked what they think about something, done in order to find out how popular someone or something is: *The opinion polls show that the Labour party is the most popular in this area.*

op·po·nent /ə'pəunənt $ ə'pounənt/ *noun* someone who is competing against you in a sport or competition: *Our opponents seemed to be much bigger and stronger than us.*

op·por·tun·ist /ˌɒpə'tjuːnɪst $ ˌɑpɚ'tunɪst/ *noun* someone who uses every opportunity to get things they want, without caring whether their actions are right or wrong

op·por·tu·ni·ty /ˌɒpə'tjuːnəti $ ˌɑpɚ'tunəti/ *noun* (plural **opportunities**)

KEY PATTERNS
have an/the opportunity to do something
an opportunity for someone

if you have an opportunity to do something, you get a chance to do it: *I'd love to **have the opportunity to** study abroad. • A job in Paris? What a wonderful **opportunity for** you!*

PHRASES
take the opportunity (to do something) to do something when you get the chance to do it: *He was alone, so I **took the opportunity to** ask him some questions.*

op·pose /ə'pəuz $ ə'pouz/ *verb* to disagree with something and try to stop it happening ANTONYM **support**: *Many local people oppose the plan.*

op·posed /ə'pəuzd $ ə'pouzd/ *adjective* if you are opposed to something, you believe that it is wrong and should not be allowed: *He is strongly opposed to scientific tests on animals.*

opposite

The bank is opposite the library.

op·po·site¹ /'ɒpəzɪt $ 'ɑpəzɪt/ *adjective*

KEY PATTERNS
in the opposite direction/order
on the opposite side/page

1 completely different: *They were travelling in opposite directions.*
2 on the other side of something, or directly across from something: ***On the opposite side** of the road was the hospital. • We rowed across to the opposite bank of the river.*

SPELLING
This word is often spelled wrongly. The correct spelling is: **opposite**.

opposite² *preposition, adverb* facing someone or something: *She sat next to her sister, opposite her parents. • The school is opposite the church.*

GRAMMAR
You say **The bank is opposite the station**.
✘ Don't say 'The bank is opposite to the station.'

A B C D E F G H I J K L M N O P Q R S T U V W X Y Z

opposite[3] *noun* something that is completely different from something else: *They think I hit Bill but the opposite is true – he hit me.*

op·po·si·tion /ˌɒpəˈzɪʃən $ ˌɑpəˈzɪʃən/ *noun* **1** (no plural) when people disagree strongly with something ANTONYM **support**: *There was a lot of opposition to the plan.* **2 the opposition** the person or team that you are trying to defeat in a game or competition **3 the Opposition** *BrE* the second biggest political party in parliament, which is not in government

op·press /əˈpres/ *verb* if a government oppresses people, it treats them in an unfair and cruel way: *We have been oppressed for too long.* —**oppressor** *noun*

op·pres·sion /əˈpreʃən/ *noun* (no plural) when a government treats people in an unfair and cruel way: *They suffered years of oppression.*

op·pres·sive /əˈpresɪv/ *adjective* cruel and unfair: *an oppressive military government*

opt /ɒpt $ ɑpt/ *verb* **1** to choose something or choose to do something: *I opted for the cheaper car.* • *You can opt to do two extra subjects.* **2 opt out** to choose not to be involved in something: *Several students opted out of this class.*

ˌ**optical ilˈlusion** *noun* something that you think you are seeing, because your eyes are being tricked

op·ti·cian /ɒpˈtɪʃən $ ɑpˈtɪʃən/ *noun BrE* someone who tests people's eyes and sells glasses SYNONYM **optometrist** *AmE*

op·ti·mis·m /ˈɒptəmɪzəm $ ˈɑptəˌmɪzəm/ *noun* (no plural) the belief that good things will happen ANTONYM **pessimism**

op·ti·mist /ˈɒptəmɪst $ ˈɑptəˌmɪst/ *noun* someone who believes that good things will happen ANTONYM **pessimist**

op·ti·mis·tic /ˌɒptəˈmɪstɪk $ ˌɑptəˈmɪstɪk/ *adjective* believing that good things will happen ANTONYM **pessimistic**: *She was optimistic about her chances of passing the exam.*

op·tion /ˈɒpʃən $ ˈɑpʃən/ *noun* **1** something that you can choose to do: *We have three options.* **2 keep your options open, leave your options open** to not make a definite decision yet, so that you can still choose what to do: *I'm keeping my options open until I hear what Helen's decided to do.*

op·tion·al /ˈɒpʃənəl $ ˈɑpʃənəl/ *adjective* if something is optional, you can choose to do it but you do not have to ANTONYM **compulsory**: *All children have to study maths and English, but French is optional.*

op·tom·e·trist /ɒpˈtɒmətrɪst $ ɑpˈtɑmətrɪst/ the American word for OPTICIAN

or /ə $ ɚ; strong ɔː $ ɔr/ *conjunction* **1** used to mention another possible thing or another choice: *Do you like this one or the blue one best?* • *You can work on your own or in teams.* • *You must take French or German, or both.*
2 used in negative sentences, when you are adding something: *He hasn't invited Kevin or Mark.* • *She can't read or write.* • *I'm not angry or upset about it.*
3 used when giving a warning or threat: *Be careful, or you might get hurt.* • *Stop that or I'll tell Mom!*

PHRASES

two or three, 30 or 40 etc used when giving a number that is not exact: *You made **two or three** spelling mistakes.* • *We're expecting 30 or 40 people to come to the party.*

o·ral[1] /ˈɔːrəl/ *adjective* an oral examination, report etc is spoken, not written: *an oral test*

oral[2] *noun* an examination in which questions and answers are spoken, not written

or·ange[1] /ˈɒrɪndʒ $ ˈɔrɪndʒ/ *noun* **1** a round fruit that is a colour between red and yellow and has a thick skin: *a sweet, juicy orange* → see picture on page A7 **2** a colour that is between red and yellow

orange[2] *adjective* something that is orange is the colour that is between red and yellow

or·bit[1] /ˈɔːbɪt $ ˈɔrbɪt/ *noun* the curved line that a PLANET or space vehicle moves in as it travels around another object in space: *the Earth's orbit of the sun*

orbit² *verb* to travel around an object in space: *The moon orbits the Earth.*

or•chard /ˈɔːtʃəd $ ˈɔrtʃərd/ *noun* an area of land where fruit trees grow

or•ches•tra /ˈɔːkɪstrə $ ˈɔrkɪstrə/ *noun* a large group of people who play musical instruments together: *She plays violin in the school orchestra.*

or•chid /ˈɔːkɪd $ ˈɔrkɪd/ *noun* a very rare and expensive plant that has beautiful flowers → see picture on page A10

or•deal /ɔːˈdiːl $ ɔrˈdil/ *noun* a very difficult and unpleasant experience: *The journey took 12 hours and it was a real ordeal.*

or•der¹ /ˈɔːdə $ ˈɔrdər/ *noun*

KEY PATTERNS
in the right/wrong order
in alphabetical order
give the order to do something
an order for a book/CD etc

1 the way in which you arrange things so that they follow each other in a particular way: *Please put the books back on the shelf* ***in the right order.*** • *The pieces of paper were all* ***in the wrong order.*** • *This list should be* ***in alphabetical order.***
2 something that a person in authority tells you to do: *The general* ***gave the order to fire.*** • *Soldiers must* ***obey orders*** *at all times.*
3 something that a customer asks a company to make or send them: *I've* ***put in an order for*** *the DVD.*
4 the food and drink that you ask for in a restaurant: *A waitress came and* ***took our order*** (=asked us what we would like to eat and drink).

PHRASES
in order to do something so that you can do something: *I went to the shop* ***in order to*** *buy some stamps.*
be out of order if a machine is out of order, it is not working because something is wrong with it: *The telephone* ***is out of order*** *again.*

order² *verb*

KEY PATTERNS
order a meal or drink
order someone to do something

1 to ask for food or drink in a restaurant: *"Are you ready to order?" the waiter asked.* • *We ordered a bottle of red wine with our meal.* → see Thesaurus at ASK
2 to ask a company to send you something that you want to buy: *To order one of our computers, just telephone the number below.*
3 if someone orders you to do something, they say that you must do it: *The police officer* ***ordered*** *the man* ***to*** *stay where he was.*

or•der•ly /ˈɔːdəli $ ˈɔrdərli/ *adjective* arranged or organized in a neat way ANTONYM **disorderly** SYNONYM **tidy**: *Her wardrobe is very neat and orderly.*

or•di•na•ri•ly /ˈɔːdənərəli $ ˌɔrdnˈerəli/ *adverb* (spoken) usually: *Ordinarily, I don't like listening to classical music.*

or•di•na•ry /ˈɔːdənəri $ ˈɔrdnˌeri/ *adjective*
normal or usual, and not different from other people or things: *Nothing much has happened – it's been a very ordinary day.* → see Thesaurus at NORMAL

ore /ɔː $ ɔr/ *noun* rock or earth from which you can get metal: *iron ore*

or•gan /ˈɔːgən $ ˈɔrgən/ *noun* **1** a part inside your body that has a particular purpose, for example your heart: *the stomach and other internal organs* **2** a musical instrument like a piano that is often played in churches: *Mr Reed will play the organ.*

organ

or•gan•ic /ɔːˈgænɪk $ ɔrˈgænɪk/ *adjective* organic food is grown or produced without using artificial chemicals: *organic carrots*
—**organically** /-kli/ *adverb*: *organically grown fruit*

organisation a British spelling of ORGANIZATION

organise a British spelling of ORGANIZE

or·gan·is·m /'ɔːgənɪzəm $ 'ɔrgəˌnɪzəm/ *noun* (formal) a living thing: *fish, plants, and other living organisms*

or·gan·i·za·tion also **organisation** *BrE* /ˌɔːgənaɪ'zeɪʃən $ ˌɔrgənə'zeɪʃən/ *noun*
1 a group of people, companies, or countries that meet and work together in order to do something: *a political organization • The United Nations is an organization of many countries.*
2 when you plan and arrange how something happens: *Who was responsible for the organization of the party?*

or·gan·ize also **organise** *BrE* /'ɔːgənaɪz $ 'ɔrgəˌnaɪz/ *verb* to plan and arrange an event or activity: *The school has organized a trip to the sea.*

or·gan·i·zed also **organised** *BrE* /'ɔːgənaɪzd $ 'ɔrgəˌnaɪzd/ *adjective*
1 well organized, badly organized planned and arranged well or badly: *a well-organized party, with plenty of food and drink* **2** good at planning and doing the things that you have to do ANTONYM **disorganized**: *Lucy's very organized and always does her homework on time.*

or·gan·i·zer also **organiser** *BrE* /'ɔːgənaɪzə $ 'ɔrgəˌnaɪzɚ/ *noun* someone who plans and arranges an event: *the organizers of the race*

o·ri·en·tal, Oriental /ˌɔːri'entl/ *adjective* relating to Asia, or coming from Asia: *an oriental rug*

or·i·gin /'ɒrədʒɪn $ 'ɔrədʒɪn/ *noun*
1 the beginning or cause of something: *the origin of Christianity* **2** (formal) the country or type of family that someone comes from: *children of Asian origin*

o·rig·i·nal¹ /ə'rɪdʒɪnəl/ *adjective*
1 an original thing or idea is the one that existed first, before any changes were made: *The original price that he wanted for the car was too high. • The castle still had some of its original doors.*
2 new, different, and interesting: *He's a great teacher, full of original ideas. • Her music is very original.*
3 an original painting or document is the real one, not a copy of it: *an original Van Gogh*

original² *noun* a painting or document that is the real one, not a copy: *This painting is an original.*

o·rig·i·nal·i·ty /əˌrɪdʒə'næləti/ *noun* (no plural) when something is new, different, and interesting: *His movies were famous for their originality and style.*

o·rig·i·nal·ly /ə'rɪdʒɪnəli/ *adverb* in the beginning: *My family are originally from Ireland.*

o·rig·i·nate /ə'rɪdʒəneɪt/ *verb* (formal) to start to exist in a particular place or at a particular time: *This type of music originated in the 15th century.*

or·na·ment /'ɔːnəmənt $ 'ɔrnəmənt/ *noun* an attractive object that you put on a table, shelf etc in your house

or·phan /'ɔːfən $ 'ɔrfən/ *noun* a child whose parents are dead

or·phan·age /'ɔːfənɪdʒ $ 'ɔrfənɪdʒ/ *noun* a home for children whose parents are dead

or·tho·dox /'ɔːθədɒks $ 'ɔrθədɑks/ *adjective* orthodox ideas or methods are the ones that most people accept as right and normal SYNONYM **conventional**: *Mr Bristow's teaching methods were not very orthodox.*

oth·er /'ʌðə $ 'ʌðɚ/ *determiner, pronoun*
1 the rest of a group, or the second person or thing of two: *He's cleverer than the other kids in his class. • Why don't you go to the cinema with* ***the others****? • John's at university, but my other brother's still at school. • Here's one sock, but where's* ***the other****?*
2 different or additional people or things of the same kind: *I like carrots and peas, but I don't like other vegetables much. • We play against teams from other schools. • Are there any other questions? • Some mistakes are easier to correct than others.*

PHRASES

other than something except for something: *I've got a cold.* ***Other than*** *that, I'm fine.*

the other day, the other week etc (informal) recently: *I saw her **the other day** and she seemed OK.*
every other day, every other week etc every second day, week etc: *I wash my hair **every other day**.*
someone or other, something or other, somehow or other (spoken, informal) used when you are not certain about something: *He wanted to ask me about **something or other*** (=something, but I don't know what). • ***Somehow or other** her parents found out what she'd done.*

oth•er•wise /ˈʌðəwaɪz $ ˈʌðɚˌwaɪz/ *adverb*
1 used when saying that something bad will happen if someone does not do what you have said they should do: *Hurry up! Otherwise we'll miss the bus.*
2 in all other ways: *The weather was bad but otherwise we enjoyed ourselves.*

ought /ɔːt/ *modal verb*
1 used when saying that something is or was the right or sensible thing to do SYNONYM **should**: *You ought to work harder at school.* • *Something ought to be done about car pollution.* • ***I ought to have** bought a return ticket, not a single* (=but I didn't).
2 used when saying that you expect something to happen or be true SYNONYM **should**: *When I press this button, the computer ought to start.* • *Rowena's party ought to be good.* • *Class 2 **ought to have** finished their exam by now.*
3 used when making a suggestion or giving advice strongly SYNONYM **should**: *You ought to play chess – you'd like it.* • *This is an opportunity you ought not to miss.*

PRONUNCIATION
You pronounce **ought** like 'short'.

GRAMMAR
The negative of **ought** is **ought not** or **oughtn't**: *You oughtn't to say things like that.*

ounce /aʊns/ (written abbreviation **oz**) *noun* a measure of weight, equal to 28.35 grams or 1/16 of a pound

our /aʊə $ aʊɚ/ *determiner* belonging to the person who is speaking and others: *Our house is not far from the river.* • *Our work is very important.*

ours /aʊəz $ aʊɚz/ *pronoun* a thing belonging to the person who is speaking and others: *His house is bigger than ours.* • *Their car is like ours.*

our•selves /aʊəˈselvz $ aʊɚˈselvz/ *pronoun*
1 used to show that you do something that affects both you and the person or people you are talking to or writing to: *Shall we make ourselves some spaghetti?*
2 used to emphasize the person speaking and others: *We ourselves must find a solution.*

PHRASES
by ourselves with no one else there, or with no one helping: *We're spending Christmas **by ourselves**.*

out /aʊt/ *adverb, adjective*
1 from the inside of a room, place, container etc ANTONYM **in**: *She turned and walked out.* • *George got **out of** the car.* • *Smoke was coming **out of** the chimney.* • *She opened her suitcase and took out a pair of shoes.* • *He took all his books **out of** his bag.*
2 not in your home ANTONYM **in**: *Mum and Dad are out, so we can turn the music up really loud.*
3 no longer burning or shining: *The fire was out.* • *Suddenly all the lights went out.*

PHRASES
be out of something to have none of something left: *We seem to **be out of** milk.*

out•break /ˈaʊtbreɪk/ *noun* when something bad suddenly starts: *We were living in Austria at the outbreak of the war.*

out•come /ˈaʊtkʌm/ *noun* the final result of an event or situation: *What was the outcome of the meeting?*

out•dat•ed /ˌaʊtˈdeɪtɪd/ *adjective* not modern or useful any more SYNONYM **old-fashioned**, **out-of-date**: *outdated equipment.*

outdid the past tense of OUTDO

out•do /aʊtˈduː/ *verb* (**outdid** /-ˈdɪd/ **outdone** /-ˈdʌn/) to be better or more

A B C D E F G H I J K L M N O P Q R S T U V W X Y Z

successful than someone else: *The two brothers were always trying to outdo each other.*

outdone the past participle of OUTDO

out·door /ˈaʊtdɔː $ ˈaʊtdɔr/ *adjective* happening or used outside, not inside a building ANTONYM **indoor**: *outdoor sports*

out·doors /ˌaʊtˈdɔːz $ ˌaʊtˈdɔrz/ *adverb* outside, not inside a building ANTONYM **indoors**: *In the summer we often eat outdoors.*

out·er /ˈaʊtə $ ˈaʊtɚ/ *adjective* on or near the outside of something, away from the middle ANTONYM **inner**: *We live on the outer edge of the town.*

ˌouter ˈspace *noun* (no plural) the area outside the Earth's air, where the stars are

out·fit /ˈaʊtfɪt/ *noun* a set of clothes that you wear together: *I'll have to buy myself a new outfit for their wedding.*

out·go·ing /ˌaʊtˈgəʊɪŋ $ ˈaʊtˌgoʊɪŋ/ *adjective* someone who is outgoing enjoys meeting and talking to people: *a girl with a very outgoing personality*
→ see Thesaurus at SOCIABLE

outgrew the past tense of OUTGROW

out·grow /aʊtˈgrəʊ $ aʊtˈgroʊ/ *verb* (**outgrew** /-ˈgruː/ **outgrown** /-ˈgrəʊn $ -ˈgroʊn/) if children outgrow their clothes, they grow too big for them: *John's outgrown all the trousers he wore last year.*

outgrown the past participle of OUTGROW

out·ing /ˈaʊtɪŋ/ *noun* a day trip to a place, for you to enjoy yourself: *We're going on a school outing to the seaside.*

out·law /ˈaʊtlɔː/ *verb* to officially say that something is illegal: *The new law has outlawed smoking in public places.*

out·line /ˈaʊtlaɪn/ *noun* a line around the edge of something that shows its shape: *In the distance I could just see the outline of a ship.*

outline

out·live /aʊtˈlɪv/ *verb* to live longer than someone: *Women usually outlive men.*

out·look /ˈaʊtlʊk/ *noun* your attitude to life and the world: *I think I have a positive outlook on life.*

out·num·ber /aʊtˈnʌmbə $ aʊtˈnʌmbɚ/ *verb* if the people or things in one group outnumber those in another group, there are more of them: *Girls greatly outnumber boys in our class.*

ˌout of ˈbounds *adjective* if a place is out of bounds, people are not allowed to go there: *Some parts of the school are out of bounds to the children.*

ˌout of ˈdate *adjective* not new, and no longer useful or correct: *The map was out of date, and did not show the new road.*

ˌout of ˈwork *adjective* someone who is out of work does not have a job SYNONYM **unemployed**: *Mark's been out of work since he lost his job last year.*

out·pa·tient /ˈaʊtˌpeɪʃənt/ *noun* someone who goes to a hospital for treatment and then goes home on the same day

out·put /ˈaʊtpʊt/ *noun* the amount of goods that a country, company etc produces: *Britain's industrial output fell by 2% in January.*

out·ra·geous /aʊtˈreɪdʒəs/ *adjective* something that is outrageous makes you feel very angry or shocked: *His drunken behaviour was completely outrageous.* • *That's an outrageous price to pay.*

out·side¹ /aʊtˈsaɪd/ *preposition, adverb*

1 not in a building or room ANTONYM **inside**, **in** SYNONYM **outdoors**: *I'll wait for you outside the cinema* (=not in it, but near it). • *It was a nice sunny day, so we had lunch outside.* • *I ran outside to see what was going on.*

2 not in a city or country: *My grandparents live just outside Oxford.* • *people from outside the United Kingdom*

3 not in a particular group or organization: *She didn't want to discuss the problem with anyone outside the family.*

outside² *noun* **the outside** the part of something that surrounds the rest of it ANTONYM **the inside**: *The outside of the box is covered with gold.*

A B C D E F G H I J K L M N O P Q R S T U V W X Y Z

out·side³ /ˈaʊtsaɪd/ *adjective* an outside wall, light etc is not inside a building ANTONYM **inside**, **internal**

out·sid·er /aʊtˈsaɪdə $ aʊtˈsaɪdɚ/ *noun* someone who does not belong to a group, organization etc: *I felt like an outsider when I first started at the college.*

out·skirts /ˈaʊtskɜːts $ ˈaʊtskɝts/ *plural noun* **the outskirts** the parts of a town that are furthest from the centre: *My parents have an apartment on the outskirts of Paris.*

out·spo·ken /aʊtˈspəʊkən $ aʊtˈspoʊkən/ *adjective* an outspoken person says what they think even though it may shock or offend people ANTONYM **reticent**: *She has been very outspoken in her opposition to the plan.*

out·stand·ing /aʊtˈstændɪŋ/ *adjective* very good SYNONYM **excellent**: *Eddie got outstanding results in his exams.*

out·stretched /ˌaʊtˈstretʃt/ *adjective* (written) outstretched arms or hands are stretched towards someone: *She ran into her father's outstretched arms.*

out·ward /ˈaʊtwəd $ ˈaʊtwɚd/ *adjective* an outward journey takes you away from the place where you live ANTONYM **inward**: *The outward flight took five hours.*

out·wards /ˈaʊtwədz $ ˈaʊtwɚdz/ also **outward** *AmE adverb* towards the outside of something or away from its centre ANTONYM **inwards**: *The town had grown and spread outwards since I left home.*

o·val /ˈəʊvəl $ ˈoʊvəl/ *noun* a shape like an egg —**oval** *adjective*: *She had a pretty, oval face.* ➔ see picture at SHAPE¹

o·va·ry /ˈəʊvəri $ ˈoʊvəri/ *noun* (plural **ovaries**) the part of a woman or a female animal that produces eggs

ov·en /ˈʌvən/ *noun* a piece of cooking equipment with a door that you open when you want to cook food in it. An oven is a square shape like a large box and is part of a COOKER: *Heat the oven to 200 degrees Celsius.*

o·ver¹ /ˈəʊvə $ ˈoʊvɚ/ *preposition*
1 from one side of something to the other SYNONYM **across**: *He jumped over the fence.* • *the bridge over the river*
2 above something ANTONYM **under**: *There was a large mirror over the fireplace.*
3 on the other side of a road SYNONYM **across**: *There's a supermarket just over the road.*
4 covering something: *She quickly put a scarf over her head.* • *Spread the glue over the top of the box* (=so that it covers the top of the box).
5 more than ANTONYM **under**: *There were over 5,000 people at the concert.* • *This book is over 200 years old.*
6 during a period of time: *I'll think about it over the weekend.*
7 used to show what people are arguing about SYNONYM **about**: *They were arguing over who should pay for the tickets.*

PHRASES

all over a place everywhere in a place: *The disease could spread **all over** the world.*

over² *adverb*
1 more than the amount or age mentioned ANTONYM **under**: *This film is for people aged 18 and over* (=people aged 18 or more than 18).
2 to or in a place: *Can I go over to Scott's house?* • *Come over here!* • *"Where's Oliver?" "Over there."*

PHRASES

over and over again very many times: *I've told you **over and over again** – I don't know where the money is.*

over³ *adjective* if something is over or all over, it is finished: *We were sad when the holiday was over.* ➔ see Thesaurus at FINISHED

o·ver·all /ˌəʊvərˈɔːl $ ˌoʊvɚˈɔl/ *adjective* considering or including everything: *The overall price of the holiday is $700.*

o·ver·alls /ˈəʊvərɔːlz $ ˈoʊvɚˌɔlz/ *plural noun* **1** *BrE* a piece of clothing covering your legs and body that you wear over your usual clothes in order to keep them clean: *a clean pair of overalls* **2** the American word for DUNGAREES

o·ver·board /ˌəʊvəˈbɔːd $ ˈoʊvɚˌbɔrd/ *adverb* over the side of a boat or ship into the water: *The little boy had fallen overboard and nearly drowned.*

overcame the past tense of OVERCOME

o·ver·cast /ˌəʊvəˈkɑːst $ ˈoʊvɚˌkæst/ *adjective* if it is overcast, the sky is dark and cloudy: *an overcast November day*

o·ver·coat /ˈəʊvəkəʊt $ ˈoʊvɚˌkoʊt/ *noun* a long warm coat that you wear when it is cold

o·ver·come /ˌəʊvəˈkʌm $ ˌoʊvɚˈkʌm/ *verb* (**overcame** /-ˈkeɪm/ **overcome**) to succeed in controlling a feeling or solving a problem: *Ally was struggling to overcome her disappointment.*

o·ver·crowd·ed /ˌəʊvəˈkraʊdɪd $ ˌoʊvɚˈkraʊdɪd/ *adjective* a place that is overcrowded has too many people in it: *Britain's overcrowded cities*

overdid the past tense of OVERDO

o·ver·do /ˌəʊvəˈduː $ ˌoʊvɚˈdu/ *verb* (**overdid** /-ˈdɪd/ **overdone** /-ˈdʌn/) to do or use too much of something: *It's good to take some exercise, but don't overdo it.*

overdone the past participle of OVERDO

o·ver·draft /ˈəʊvədrɑːft $ ˈoʊvɚˌdræft/ *noun* an arrangement with your bank, that allows you to spend more money than you have in your account: *The bank have agreed to give me a £1,000 overdraft.*

o·ver·drawn /ˌəʊvəˈdrɔːn $ ˌoʊvɚˈdrɔn/ *adjective* if you are overdrawn, you have spent more money than you have in your bank account: *If I go overdrawn again, the bank will charge me twice.*

o·ver·due /ˌəʊvəˈdjuː $ ˌoʊvɚˈdu/ *adjective* late in arriving or being done: *I must finish this essay – it's already overdue.*

o·ver·es·ti·mate /ˌəʊvərˈestəmeɪt $ ˌoʊvɚˈestəˌmeɪt/ *verb* to think that something is bigger, longer etc than it really is: *I overestimated how long the journey would take.*

overflow

o·ver·flow /ˌəʊvəˈfləʊ $ ˌoʊvɚˈfloʊ/ *verb* if a liquid overflows, it goes over the edges of its container: *I forgot to turn the tap off and the water overflowed.*

o·ver·head¹ /ˌəʊvəˈhed $ ˌoʊvɚˈhed/ *adverb, adjective* high up in the air, above your head: *Several planes flew overhead.* • *overhead electricity wires*

o·ver·head² /ˈəʊvəhed $ ˈoʊvɚˌhed/ *AmE noun* (no plural) **overheads** *BrE plural noun* the money that a business has to spend regularly on rent, electricity, salaries etc: *The company will have to reduce its overheads.*

o·ver·hear /ˌəʊvəˈhɪə $ ˌoʊvɚˈhɪr/ *verb* (past tense and past participle **overheard** /-ˈhɜːd $ ˈhɚd/) to hear what someone is saying when they are talking to another person and do not know you are listening: *I overheard what you were saying on the phone.*

o·ver·lap /ˌəʊvəˈlæp $ ˌoʊvɚˈlæp/ *verb* (**overlapped**, **overlapping**) if two things overlap, part of one thing covers part of the other: *I want you to draw two circles that overlap each other at the edge.*

o·ver·load /ˌəʊvəˈləʊd $ ˌoʊvɚˈloʊd/ *verb* to put too many people or things into a vehicle: *It's dangerous to overload your car.*

o·ver·look /ˌəʊvəˈlʊk $ ˌoʊvɚˈlʊk/ *verb* **1** if a building or room overlooks something, you can see that thing from the building or room: *Our hotel overlooked the sea.* **2** to not notice something or to not realize how important it is: *I overlooked the fact that prices have gone up since last year.*

o·ver·night /ˌəʊvəˈnaɪt $ ˌoʊvɚˈnaɪt/ *adverb, adjective* **1** for or during the night: *Is it all right if I stay overnight at Tom's house?* **2** if something happens overnight, it happens very quickly: *He became a star overnight.* • *The play was an overnight success.*

o•ver•pop•u•lat•ed /ˌəʊvəˈpɒpjəleɪtɪd $ ˌoʊvɚˈpɑpjəˌleɪtɪd/ *adjective* a place that is overpopulated has too many people living in it

o•ver•pow•er•ing /ˌəʊvəˈpaʊərɪŋ $ ˌoʊvɚˈpaʊərɪŋ/ *adjective* (formal) a feeling or smell that is overpowering is very strong: *Sam woke up with a feeling of overpowering excitement.*

o•ver•priced /ˌəʊvəˈpraɪst $ ˌoʊvɚˈpraɪst/ *adjective* something that is overpriced is more expensive than it should be: *It's a nice restaurant, but it's a little overpriced.* ➔ see Thesaurus at EXPENSIVE

o•ver•rat•ed /ˌəʊvəˈreɪtɪd $ˌoʊvɚˈreɪtɪd/ *adjective* something that is overrated is not as good as some people think: *I think their music is overrated.*

o•ver•seas /ˌəʊvəˈsiːz $ ˌoʊvɚˈsiːz/ *adverb, adjective* (formal) from or in a foreign country that is across the sea: *My father had to travel overseas several times each year.* • *overseas students*

o•ver•sight /ˈəʊvəsaɪt $ ˈoʊvɚˌsaɪt/ *noun* a small mistake made because you did not notice something or forgot to do something

o•ver•sleep /ˌəʊvəˈsliːp $ ˌoʊvɚˈslip/ *verb* (past tense and past participle **overslept** /-ˈslept/) to sleep for longer than you intended to, especially so that you are late for something: *Matt overslept this morning and missed the bus.*

overslept the past tense and past participle of OVERSLEEP

overtake

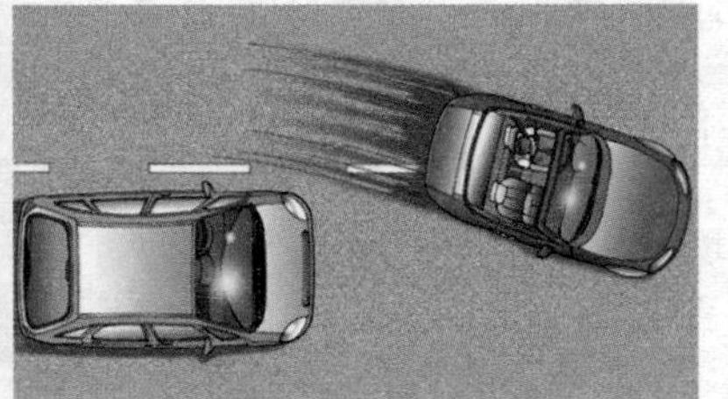

o•ver•take /ˌəʊvəˈteɪk $ ˌoʊvɚˈteɪk/ *verb* (**overtook** /-ˈtʊk/ **overtaken** /-ˈteɪkən/) to pass another vehicle or person because you are moving faster than them: *A police car overtook us.*

overtaken the past participle of OVERTAKE

overthrew the past tense of OVERTHROW

o•ver•throw /ˌəʊvəˈθrəʊ $ ˌoʊvɚˈθroʊ/ *verb* (**overthrew** /-ˈθruː/ **overthrown** /-ˈθrəʊn $ -ˈθroʊn/) to remove a leader or government from power, by using force: *The country's military leaders planned to overthrow the government.*

overthrown the past participle of OVERTHROW

o•ver•time /ˈəʊvətaɪm $ ˈoʊvɚˌtaɪm/ *noun* (no plural) hours that you work in addition to your usual working hours: *How much do you get paid for overtime?*

overtook the past tense of OVERTAKE

o•ver•turn /ˌəʊvəˈtɜːn $ ˌoʊvɚˈtɚn/ *verb* if something overturns, it turns over completely or falls onto its side: *A truck carrying wood had overturned on the freeway.*

o•ver•weight /ˌəʊvəˈweɪt $ ˌoʊvɚˈweɪt/ *adjective* a person who is overweight is too fat and heavy: *an overweight businessman* ➔ see Thesaurus at FAT[1]

o•ver•whelm /ˌəʊvəˈwelm $ ˌoʊvɚˈwelm/ *verb* if a feeling overwhelms you, you feel it very strongly

o•ver•whelm•ing /ˌəʊvəˈwelmɪŋ $ ˌoʊvɚˈwelmɪŋ/ *adjective* **1** if a feeling is overwhelming, you feel it very strongly: *He felt an overwhelming desire to leave.* **2** big in number or amount: *An overwhelming majority voted against the government.*

o•ver•worked /ˌəʊvəˈwɜːkt $ ˌoʊvɚˈwɚkt/ *adjective* someone who is overworked works too much

owe /əʊ $ oʊ/ *verb*

KEY PATTERNS
owe someone money
owe money to someone
owe someone an apology
owe your success to someone

1 if you owe money to someone, you need to give it back to them because you borrowed it from them: *I owe James £5.* • *They* ***owe money to*** *the bank.*

A B C D E F G H I J K L M N O P Q R S T U V W X Y Z

2 if you owe someone something, you feel that you should give it to them or do it for them: *I owe you an apology.* **3** if you owe your success to someone or something, you were successful because of someone or something: *I owe my success to my parents.*

ˈowing to *preposition* (formal) because of SYNONYM **due to**: *He could not play in the match, owing to an injury.*

owl /aʊl/ *noun* a bird that hunts at night and has large eyes and a loud call ➔ see picture on page A8

own¹ /əʊn $ oʊn/ *adjective, pronoun*

KEY PATTERNS
a house/car etc of your own

belonging to a particular person: *He has his own way of doing things.* • *She borrowed a friend's car because her own was being repaired.* • *I'm going to start looking for a place* ***of my own.***

PHRASES

on your own without anyone with you or helping you: *She was quite happy living* ***on her own.*** • *Do you think you'll be able to carry it* ***on your own****?*

own² *verb* **1** if you own something, it belongs to you SYNONYM **possess**: *He was the only person I knew who owned a van.* **2 own up** to admit that you did something wrong: *She didn't want to own up to her mistake.*

own·er /ˈəʊnə $ ˈoʊnɚ/ *noun* someone who owns something: *Who is the owner of this car?*

ox·y·gen /ˈɒksɪdʒən $ ˈɑːksɪdʒən/ *noun* (no plural) a gas in the air that all living things need

oy·ster /ˈɔɪstə $ ˈɔɪstɚ/ *noun* a small sea animal that has a shell and makes a jewel called a PEARL

oyster

oz the written abbreviation of OUNCE or ounces

o·zone lay·er /ˈəʊzəʊn ˌleɪə $ ˈoʊzoʊn ˌleɪɚ/ *noun* (no plural) a layer of gases around the Earth that stops harmful heat from the sun reaching the Earth

A B C D E F G H I J K L M N O P Q R S T U V W X Y Z

p /piː/ *BrE* the abbreviation of PENNY or PENCE

PA /ˌpiː ˈeɪ/ *noun BrE* (personal assistant) someone in an office who writes letters, answers the telephone, and arranges meetings for one other person

pace¹ /peɪs/ *noun* **1** (no plural) how quickly you do something, or how quickly something happens: *Technology is changing at a very fast pace.* **2 keep pace with something/someone** to move or change as fast as something or someone: *He walked so quickly that she found it difficult to keep pace with him.*

pace² *verb* (written) to walk around a lot when you are waiting or when you are worried about something: *She paced up and down the corridor, waiting for news.*

pac·i·fi·er /ˈpæsəfaɪə $ ˈpæsəˌfaɪər/ the American word for DUMMY

pac·i·fist /ˈpæsəfɪst/ *noun* someone who believes that all wars are wrong

pack

Louise is packing her suitcase.

pack¹ /pæk/ *verb* **1** also **pack up** to put things into bags or boxes so that you can take them somewhere: *Did you remember to pack your swimming costume? • She went upstairs to pack. • He helped Kelly pack up all her books.* **2 pack up** (informal) **a)** *BrE* if a machine packs up, it stops working **b)** to finish doing something: *We packed up and went home.*

pack² *noun* **1 a pack of things** a number of things that are kept together in a container: *a pack of envelopes • an information pack* **2** a group of animals that hunt together: *a pack of dogs* **3** a set of playing cards SYNONYM **deck** *AmE*

pack·age¹ /ˈpækɪdʒ/ *noun* **1** something that has been put in a box or wrapped in paper and sent somewhere by post SYNONYM **parcel** **2** *AmE* the box or bag that food is put in so that it can be sold SYNONYM **packet**: *a package of butter*

package² *verb* to put something in a box or bag so that it can be sold: *They packaged the biscuits in cardboard boxes.*

pack·ag·ing /ˈpækɪdʒɪŋ/ *noun* (no plural) the bag or box that a product is in when you buy it

packed /pækt/ also **ˌpacked ˈout** *adjective* (informal) full of people: *The hall was absolutely packed.* → see Thesaurus at FULL

pack·et /ˈpækɪt/ *noun* a bag or box of things that you can buy: *a packet of crisps*

pack·ing /ˈpækɪŋ/ *noun* (no plural) when you put things into bags or boxes so that you can take them somewhere: *I'll help you do the packing.*

pad /pæd/ *noun* **1** a book of sheets of paper, that you use for writing or drawing: *She wrote something down on her pad.* **2** a thick piece of material that you use to protect something: *The boy on the skateboard was wearing elbow pads.*

pad·ded /ˈpædɪd/ *adjective* something that is padded has soft material inside it, to make it thicker and bigger or more comfortable: *a padded chair*

pad·dle¹ /ˈpædl/ *noun* a short pole with a flat end, that you use for moving a small boat along

paddle² *verb* **1** to move a small boat through water, using a paddle **2** *BrE* to walk around in water that is not very deep SYNONYM **wade** *AmE*

padlock

pad·lock¹ /ˈpædlɒk $ ˈpædlɑk/ *noun* a strong lock that you put on a bicycle or a door

padlock² *verb* to fasten something, using a padlock: *I padlocked my bike to the fence.*

page /peɪdʒ/ *noun* a sheet of paper in a book, newspaper etc: *I tore a page out of my notebook.* • *What's on the next page?*

pag·er /ˈpeɪdʒə $ ˈpeɪdʒɚ/ *noun* a small machine you carry with you that makes a noise when it receives a message, for example when someone telephones you

paid the past tense and past participle of PAY¹

pain /peɪn/ *noun*

KEY PATTERNS
have a pain in your stomach/back
be in pain

1 the unpleasant feeling you have when part of your body hurts: *She had a pain in her chest.* • *Do you feel any pain?* • *He was in terrible pain.*
2 a feeling of sadness: *the pain of seeing someone you love die*

PHRASES
be a pain, be a pain in the neck (spoken informal) to be very annoying: *It's a pain having to look after my little brother.* • *My boss is a pain in the neck.*

pain·ful /ˈpeɪnfəl/ *adjective*
1 something that is painful causes you physical pain ANTONYM **painless**: *Her sore throat was very painful.* • *a painful injury* → see Thesaurus at HURT¹
2 something that is painful makes you feel very unhappy: *Breaking up with her boyfriend had been a painful experience.*

pain·kill·er /ˈpeɪnˌkɪlə $ ˈpeɪnˌkɪlɚ/ *noun* a drug that makes you feel less pain

pain·less /ˈpeɪnləs/ *adjective* not making you feel any pain ANTONYM **painful**: *Having my tooth pulled out was quite painless.*

pains·tak·ing /ˈpeɪnzˌteɪkɪŋ/ *adjective* done very carefully: *She had checked every detail with painstaking care.*

paint¹ /peɪnt/ *noun* (no plural) a coloured liquid that you use to cover surfaces or make pictures: *Be careful – the paint on the door is still wet.*

paint² *verb* **1** to put paint on a surface: *They painted the walls green.* **2** to make a picture of someone or something using paint: *She was painting a picture of some flowers.*

paint·brush /ˈpeɪntbrʌʃ/ *noun* (plural **paintbrushes**) a brush that you use to paint pictures or to paint walls → see picture at BRUSH¹

paint·er /ˈpeɪntə $ ˈpeɪntɚ/ *noun* **1** someone who paints pictures SYNONYM **artist**: *My favourite painter is Monet.* **2** someone whose job is painting houses SYNONYM **decorator** *BrE*

paint·ing /ˈpeɪntɪŋ/ *noun* a painted picture: *a painting of a horse* → see Thesaurus at PICTURE¹

pairs

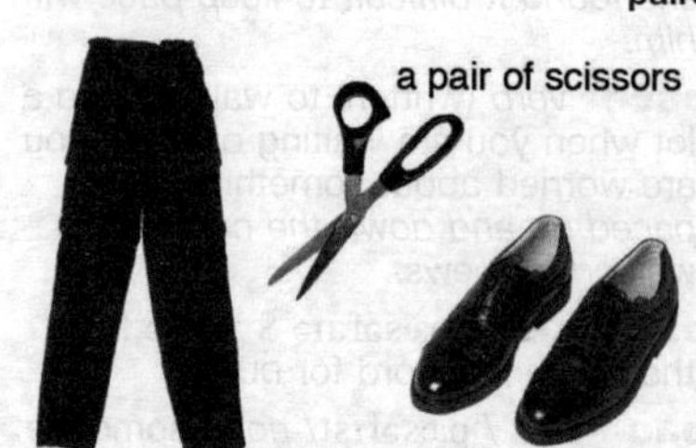

pair /peə $ per/ *noun*

KEY PATTERNS
a pair of jeans/glasses
a pair of shoes/gloves etc
work/walk in pairs

1 something that is made of two similar parts that are joined together: *a pair of trousers* • *a sharp pair of scissors*
2 two similar things that you use together: *a pair of socks* → see Thesaurus at TWO
3 two people who do something together: *We all had to work in pairs.*

pajamas the American spelling of PYJAMAS

pal /pæl/ *noun* (informal) a friend

pal·ace /ˈpælɪs/ *noun* a very large house where a king or queen lives: *Buckingham Palace*

pale /peɪl/ *adjective* **1** light in colour ANTONYM **dark**: *a pale blue shirt* → see Thesaurus at LIGHT[2] **2** someone who is pale has skin that looks white, for example because they are ill or frightened: *You look pale – are you all right?*

palm /pɑːm/ *noun* the surface of the inside of your hand: *The palms of her hands were sweaty.*

ˈpalm tree *noun* a tall tree that grows in hot dry places → see picture on page A10

pal·try /ˈpɔːltri/ *adjective* a paltry amount is too small: *We work long hours for paltry pay.*

pam·per /ˈpæmpə $ ˈpæmpɚ/ *verb* to treat someone too kindly, by giving them everything they want SYNONYM **spoil**: *Some people pamper their children too much.*

pam·phlet /ˈpæmflɪt/ *noun* a thin book that contains information about something

pans

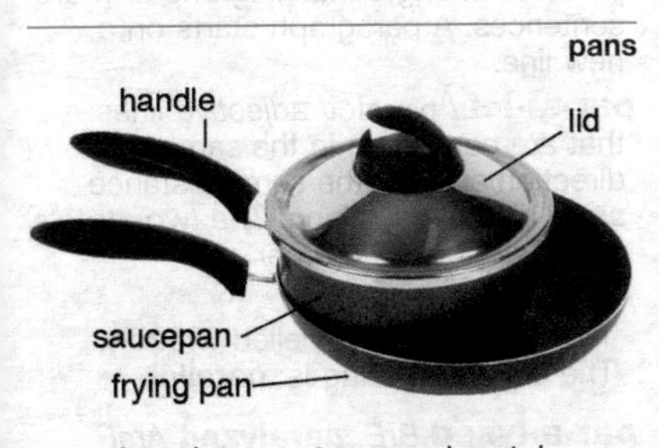

pan /pæn/ *noun* **1** a round metal container with a long handle that you cook things in SYNONYM **saucepan**: *There was a pan of soup on the cooker.* **2** *AmE* a metal container for baking things SYNONYM **tin** *BrE*: *a pie pan*

pan·cake /ˈpænkeɪk/ *noun* a thin round food that you make by mixing flour, milk, and eggs and cooking the mixture in a pan

panda

pan·da /ˈpændə/ *noun* a large black and white bear that lives in China

pan·de·mo·ni·um /ˌpændəˈməʊniəm $ ˌpændəˈmoʊniəm/ *noun* (no plural) (formal) when there is a lot of noise and excitement SYNONYM **chaos**

pan·der /ˈpændə $ ˈpændɚ/ *verb* to give someone what they want, even though you know it is not good for them: *You shouldn't pander to the children when they ask you for sweets.*

pane /peɪn/ *noun* a piece of glass in a window or door

pan·el /ˈpænl/ *noun* **1** a group of people who are chosen to discuss something: *A panel of teachers will choose the best story.* **2 instrument panel, control panel** the part inside a plane, boat etc where the controls are fixed

pang /pæŋ/ *noun* a sudden strong feeling of pain, sadness etc: *I had a pang of guilt about leaving Sally alone.*

pan·ic[1] /ˈpænɪk/ *noun* (no plural) a sudden very strong feeling of fear or worry: *The bomb warning caused panic.* • *In a panic, he searched all his pockets for the keys.*

panic[2] *verb* (**panicked**, **panicking**) to feel so frightened or worried that you cannot think clearly: *When I saw him lying on the ground, I just panicked.*

pant /pænt/ *verb* to breathe quickly because you have been running

pan·ties /ˈpæntiz/ *plural noun* underwear for women that covers the area between the waist and the top of the legs SYNONYM **knickers** *BrE* → see picture at UNDERWEAR

pan·to·mime /ˈpæntəmaɪm/ *noun* a funny play for children that is performed at Christmas in Britain

pants /pænts/ *plural noun* **1** *BrE* a piece of underwear that covers the area between your waist and your legs SYNONYM **underpants** *AmE* **2** the American word for TROUSERS: *I need to buy a new pair of pants.*

A B C D E F G H I J K L M N O P Q R S T U V W X Y Z

pan·ty·hose /ˈpæntihəʊz $ ˈpæntiˌhoʊz/ the American word for TIGHTS

pa·per /ˈpeɪpə $ ˈpeɪpɚ/ *noun*
1 (no plural) a thin material that you use for writing on or for wrapping things in: *She wrote the address on a piece of paper.* • *a paper bag*
2 a newspaper: *The story was in all the papers.*
3 papers documents: *He was sorting through the papers on his desk.*
4 a piece of writing or a talk about a particular subject: *She is **giving a paper on** the Spanish civil war.*
5 an examination: *He found the maths paper very hard.*

GRAMMAR
You say **a sheet of paper**.
✘ Don't say 'a paper'.

pa·per·back /ˈpeɪpəbæk $ ˈpeɪpɚˌbæk/ *noun* a book with a soft paper cover ANTONYM **hardback**

ˈpaper clip *noun* a small piece of curved wire that you use for holding pieces of paper together

pa·per·work /ˈpeɪpəwɜːk $ ˈpeɪpɚˌwɚk/ *noun* (no plural) work such as writing letters or reports: *I have to do a lot of paperwork in my job.*

par /pɑː $ pɑr/ *noun* **be on a par with something** to be of the same standard as something: *This qualification is on a par with a degree.*

parachute

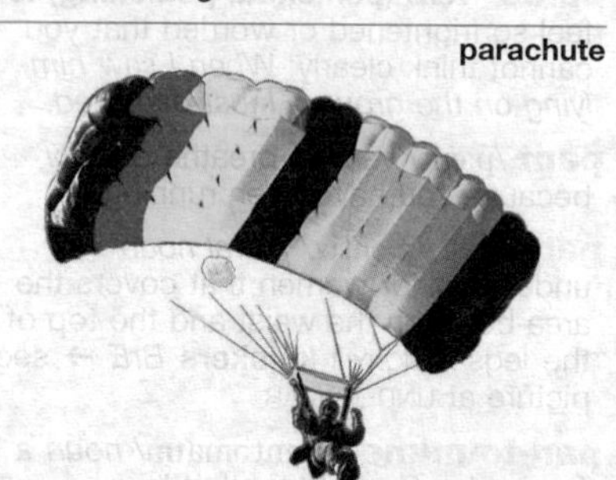

par·a·chute¹ /ˈpærəʃuːt/ *noun* a large piece of cloth that people use when they jump out of a plane, to make them fall through the air slowly and come to the ground safely

parachute² *verb* to jump from a plane, using a parachute

parade

The children paraded through the town.

pa·rade¹ /pəˈreɪd/ *noun* an event in which people walk through the streets and play music to celebrate something

parade² *verb* to walk through the streets in a large group in order to celebrate something: *The children paraded through the town.*

par·a·dise /ˈpærədaɪs/ *noun* a perfect place where some people think good people go after they die

par·a·dox /ˈpærədɒks $ ˈpærəˌdɑks/ *noun* (plural **paradoxes**) something that seems strange because it contains two very different ideas: *It is a paradox that when you do more exercise, you feel less tired.*

par·af·fin /ˈpærəfɪn/ *noun BrE* a kind of oil that you use for heating and in lamps SYNONYM **kerosene** *AmE*

par·a·graph /ˈpærəgrɑːf $ ˈpærəˌgræf/ *noun* one part of a long piece of writing containing one or more sentences. A paragraph starts on a new line.

par·al·lel /ˈpærəlel/ *adjective* lines that are parallel go in the same direction and are the same distance apart all the way along: *The two streets are parallel to each other.*

SPELLING
This word is often spelled wrongly. The correct spelling is: **parallel**.

par·a·lysed *BrE*, **paralyzed** *AmE* /ˈpærəlaɪzd/ *adjective* if you are paralysed, you cannot move part of your body, for example because you have injured it

pa·ral·y·sis /pəˈræləsɪs/ *noun* (no plural) when you cannot move part of your body, for example because you have injured it

par·a·med·ic /ˌpærəˈmedɪk/ *noun* someone who is not a doctor or nurse but is trained to help people who are ill or injured until they get to hospital

par·a·mil·i·ta·ry /ˌpærəˈmɪlətəri $ ˌpærəˈmɪləˌteri/ *adjective* a paramilitary organization is organized like an army, but is not part of a country's official army: *a paramilitary terrorist group*

par·a·mount /ˈpærəmaʊnt/ *adjective* (formal) more important than anything else: *The safety of the children is paramount.*

par·a·noi·a /ˌpærəˈnɔɪə/ *noun* (no plural) when you wrongly think that everyone is against you or wants to hurt you

par·a·phrase /ˈpærəfreɪz/ *verb* to write or say in different words what someone else has written or said: *We had to paraphrase what the teacher said.*

par·a·site /ˈpærəsaɪt/ *noun* a plant or animal that lives on another plant or animal and gets food from it

par·a·troop·er /ˈpærəˌtruːpə $ ˈpærəˌtrupɚ/ *noun* a soldier who is trained to jump out of planes, using a PARACHUTE

par·cel /ˈpɑːsəl $ ˈpɑrsəl/ *noun* something that has been wrapped in paper so that it can be sent somewhere SYNONYM **package**

parcel

par·don¹ /ˈpɑːdn $ ˈpɑrdn/ *verb* to officially decide not to punish someone for a crime —**pardon** *noun*

pardon² (spoken) **1** used to ask someone to repeat something SYNONYM **excuse me** *AmE* **2 pardon me, I beg your pardon** used to say sorry politely SYNONYM **excuse me**: *She burped and said, "Pardon me."*

par·ent /ˈpeərənt $ ˈperənt/ *noun* your parents are your father and mother: *I didn't want to disappoint my parents.*

pa·ren·the·ses /pəˈrenθəsiːz/ *plural noun* the curved lines ( ) that are used in writing when adding more information after something: *Put the dates in parentheses.*

par·ent·hood /ˈpeərənthʊd $ ˈperəntˌhʊd/ *noun* (no plural) when you are a parent: *They were really enjoying parenthood.*

par·ish /ˈpærɪʃ/ *noun* an area that has its own church

park¹ /pɑːk $ pɑrk/ *noun* an area with grass and trees, where people can walk, play games etc

park² *verb* to leave your car somewhere: *We parked behind the school.*

park·ing /ˈpɑːkɪŋ $ ˈpɑrkɪŋ/ *noun* (no plural) when you park your car: *Parking is not allowed in front of the gates.*

ˈparking lot the American word for a CAR PARK

ˈparking ˌmeter *noun* a machine that you put money into when you park your car

ˈparking ˌticket *noun* a piece of paper that is put on your car to tell you that you must pay an amount of money because you have parked your car in an illegal place

par·lia·ment /ˈpɑːləmənt $ ˈpɑrləmənt/ *noun* a group of people who make or change a country's laws. A parliament is chosen by all the people in a country who are able to vote: *Laws are made by parliament.*

par·lia·men·ta·ry /ˌpɑːləˈmentəri $ ˌpɑrləˈmentri/ *adjective* related to parliament: *a parliamentary committee*

par·o·dy¹ /ˈpærədi/ *noun* (plural **parodies**) a piece of writing, a performance etc that copies someone else's style in a funny way: *His performance was a parody of Elvis Presley.*

parody² *verb* (**parodied, parodies**) to copy someone's style or behaviour in a funny way: *He can parody Gary's voice very well.*

par·rot /ˈpærət/ *noun* a brightly coloured bird that you can teach to speak → see picture on page A8

parrot

pars·ley /ˈpɑːsli $ ˈpɑrsli/ *noun* (no

plural) a plant with small curled leaves that you eat

pars·nip /ˈpɑːsnɪp $ ˈpɑrsnɪp/ *noun* a white or yellow vegetable that is the root of a plant

part[1] /pɑːt $ pɑrt/ *noun*

KEY PATTERNS
(a) part of something
in the first/last etc part of something
someone's part in something

1 one piece or amount of something: *Part of the roof was missing.* • *The best* ***part of*** *the job is meeting lots of different people.* • *in the early* ***part of*** *the 19th century*

2 your part in an action or event is what you do in it SYNONYM **role**: *She was given a medal for her* ***part in*** *the rescue.*

3 if an actor plays a part in a play or film, they pretend to be a particular person in it: *I've always wanted to* ***play the part of*** *Juliet.*

PHRASES

take part to be involved in an event or activity: *Hundreds of children* ***took part in*** *the festival.*

play a part in something to be one of several things that makes something happen: *The death of his wife* ***played a part in*** *his decision to leave London.*

on someone's part, on the part of someone (formal) by someone: *Organizing the concert will mean a lot of work* ***on my part.***

THESAURUS
section: *The book is divided into three sections* (=parts).
component: *The factory makes components for cars* (=parts that can be put together to make cars).
piece: *Do you want a piece of this pizza* (=a part that is taken from it)?

part[2] *verb*

KEY PATTERNS
be parted from someone

to be separated from someone or something that you love: *She didn't want to* ***be parted from*** *her family.*

PHRASAL VERBS

part with

part with something to give away or sell something that you like very much: *He refused to* ***part with*** *his collection of old records.*

part[3] *adverb* **part ... part ...** partly one thing and partly another: *Tanya is part Russian and part English.*

par·tial /ˈpɑːʃəl $ ˈpɑrʃəl/ *adjective* not complete: *She suffers from partial blindness.*

par·tial·ly /ˈpɑːʃəli $ ˈpɑrʃəli/ *adverb* partly, but not completely: *The window was partially covered by a curtain.*

par·tic·i·pant /pɑːˈtɪsəpənt $ pɑrˈtɪsəpənt/ *noun* (formal) someone who is involved in an activity with other people: *Mark was a willing participant in the study.*

par·tic·i·pate /pɑːˈtɪsəpeɪt $ pɑrˈtɪsəˌpeɪt/ *verb* (formal) to do an activity with other people: *The whole class participated in the play.*

GRAMMAR
You **participate in** something.
✘ Don't say 'participate to something'.

par·ti·ci·pa·tion /pɑːˌtɪsəˈpeɪʃən $ pɑrˌtɪsəˈpeɪʃən/ *noun* (no plural) (formal) when you do an activity with other people: *A good teacher encourages student participation in discussions.*

par·ti·ci·ple /ˈpɑːtəsɪpəl $ ˈpɑrtəˌsɪpəl/ *noun* the form of a verb that is used to form some verb tenses

par·ti·cle /ˈpɑːtɪkəl $ ˈpɑrtɪkəl/ *noun* a very small piece of something: *particles of dust*

par·tic·u·lar[1] /pəˈtɪkjələ $ pɚˈtɪkjəlɚ/ *adjective* **1** used to talk about one thing and not any other: *If a particular food makes you ill, avoid it.*
2 special: *You need to pay particular attention to your spelling.*

particular[2] *noun* **in particular** especially: *I like all subjects, but maths in particular.*

par·tic·u·lar·ly /pəˈtɪkjələli $ pɚˈtɪkjəlɚli/ *adverb* especially: *Crime is increasing, particularly in the cities.* • *We are particularly concerned about the effect on the young children.*

PHRASES

not particularly (spoken) not very much: *"Are you hungry?" "Not particularly."*

part·ing /ˈpɑːtɪŋ $ ˈpɑrtɪŋ/ *BrE*, **part** *AmE noun* the line on your head that you make when you separate your hair with a comb: *She has a centre parting.*

par·ti·tion /pɑːˈtɪʃən $ pɑrˈtɪʃən/ *noun* a thin wall that separates one part of a room from another: *There's a partition between the two offices.*

part·ly /ˈpɑːtli $ ˈpɑrtli/ *adverb* to some degree, but not completely ANTONYM **wholly**: *The accident was partly my fault.* • *The door was partly open.*

part·ner /ˈpɑːtnə $ ˈpɑrtnɚ/ *noun*
1 the person who you are married to or are having a relationship with: *She invited all her colleagues and their partners to the party.*
2 someone that you do something with: *her tennis partner* • *his business partner*

part·ner·ship /ˈpɑːtnəʃɪp $ ˈpɑrtnɚˌʃɪp/ *noun* a situation in which two people or organizations work together: *Helping a child to learn is a partnership between teachers and parents.*

ˌpart of ˈspeech *noun* one of the groups that you can divide words into, for example 'noun', 'verb', or 'adjective'

ˌpart-ˈtime *adjective, adverb* working or studying for less than the usual number of hours ANTONYM **full-time**: *a part-time job* • *I can only work part-time.*

par·ty¹ /ˈpɑːti $ ˈpɑrti/ *noun* (plural **parties**)
1 a social event when people meet to talk, drink, dance etc: *We're **having a party** next Saturday.* • *Fiona invited 25 people to her **birthday party**.*
2 an organization of people who have the same political ideas: *Which party did you vote for in the election?*
3 (formal) a group of people who go somewhere together: ***a party of** tourists who were visiting the museum* → see Thesaurus at GROUP¹

USAGE
You say **have a party**.
✘ Don't say 'make a party'.

THESAURUS
get-together: *We usually have a family **get-together** at Christmas* (=an informal party).
reception: *A hundred people have been invited to the **reception*** (=a big formal party for a wedding or an important visitor).

party² *verb* (informal) (**partied, parties**) to enjoy yourself with other people, especially by dancing and drinking: *Jo loves to party.*

pass

Andy passed the ball.

Could you pass me the salt, please?

pass¹ /pɑːs $ pæs/ *verb*

KEY PATTERNS
pass (by) someone/something
pass through/under/around etc something
pass someone the salt/a pen etc
pass the salt/a pen etc to someone
pass someone the ball
pass the ball to someone

1 also **pass by** to move past someone or something without stopping: *A police car passed him as he walked down the road.* • *We **passed by** a large white house.*
2 to go through, under, or around something: *The road **passes through** a tunnel.*
3 to give something to someone by putting it in their hand: *Could you pass me the butter, please?* • *He **passed** the letter **to** his father.*
4 to kick or throw a ball to another player in your team during a game: *Latimer **passed** the ball **to** Geller.*
5 to succeed in a test or examination ANTONYM **fail**: *Heather was sure she would **pass** the history **exam**.* • *If you don't pass, you have to do the course again.*
6 (written) if time passes, it ends: *An hour passed, and then another hour.*

A B C D E F G H I J K L M N O P Q R S T U V W X Y Z

PHRASES
pass the time to do something during a period of time so that you are not bored: *They **passed the time** playing word games.*

PHRASAL VERBS
pass around, pass round *BrE*
pass something around to give something to each person in a group: *She **passed around** the plate of cookies.*

pass away
a phrase meaning 'to die', used in order to avoid saying this directly: *My grandmother **passed away** last year.*

pass down
pass something down to give or teach something to people who are born after you: *The skill **was passed down** from father to son.*

pass on
pass something on to give something that you have received to someone else: *I'll **pass** the information **on**.*

pass out
to suddenly become unconscious: *It was so hot I nearly **passed out**.*

pass² (plural **passes**) **1** when you kick or throw a ball to another member of your team during a game: *That was a very clever pass!* **2** an official document that proves you are allowed to enter a place or do something: *I showed my bus pass to the driver.*

pas·sage /ˈpæsɪdʒ/ *noun*
1 also **pas·sage·way** /ˈpæsɪdʒweɪ/ a narrow area that connects one room or building with another: *He led me down the **passage to** the back of the house.*
2 a short part of a longer piece of writing or music: *She read a **passage from** 'Macbeth'.*

pas·sen·ger /ˈpæsəndʒə $ ˈpæsəndʒɚ/ *noun*
someone who is travelling in a vehicle but is not driving it: *The boat sank, but all the passengers and crew were rescued.*

pass·er·by /ˌpɑːsəˈbaɪ $ ˌpæsɚˈbaɪ/ *noun* (plural **passersby**) someone who is walking past a place when something happens: *Several passersby saw the robbery.*

pass·ing /ˈpɑːsɪŋ $ ˈpæsɪŋ/ *noun* **in passing** if you say something in passing, you mention it while you are mainly talking or writing about something else: *She mentioned in passing that she knew Dan.*

pas·sion /ˈpæʃən/ *noun* a very strong feeling, especially of love, desire, or anger: *She loved Africa, and she spoke with passion about it.*

pas·sion·ate /ˈpæʃənət/ *adjective* showing strong feelings, especially of love, desire, or anger: *a passionate speech* —**passionately** *adverb*: *He kissed her passionately.*

pas·sive¹ /ˈpæsɪv/ *adjective* **1** if you are passive, you let things happen to you rather than doing things yourself: *She's a quiet, passive child.* **2** if a verb is passive, the subject of the verb is affected by the action of the verb. For example, in the sentence 'The house was built ten years ago', the verb 'was built' is passive.

passive² *noun* **the passive (voice)** the passive form of a verb

pass·port /ˈpɑːspɔːt $ ˈpæspɔrt/ *noun* a small official book with your photograph inside that you need when you travel to a foreign country

pass·word /ˈpɑːswɜːd $ ˈpæswɚd/ *noun* a secret word that allows you to use a computer system or enter a place: *I've forgotten my password.*

past¹ /pɑːst $ pæst/ *adjective*
1 used to talk about a period of time that has just finished: *He's been pretty miserable over the past few weeks.*
2 used to talk about something that happened some time ago: *She regrets her past actions.*

PHRASES
the past tense the form of a verb that is used to talk about things that happened in the time before now: *'Saw' is **the past tense** of 'see'.*

past² *preposition, adverb*
1 if you go past someone or something, you move towards them and keep moving until they are behind you: *He walked right past me as if he hadn't seen me.* • *He watched the cars going past.*
2 further on than something SYNONYM **beyond**: *The hotel is just past the church.*
3 later than a particular hour: *It's half past three* (=half an hour after three

o'clock). • *I've got to leave at ten past* (=ten minutes past the hour).

PHRASES

be past it *BrE* (informal) to be too old to do something: *My car's completely past it now.*

past³ *noun*

> **KEY PATTERNS**
> **in the past**

1 the past the time that existed before now: *I've worked with Julia in the past.* **2** someone's past is all the things that have happened in their life: *The newspaper revealed secrets about his past.*

pas·ta /'pæstə $ 'pɑstə/ *noun* (no plural) an Italian food that is made by mixing flour, eggs, and water and then cooking the mixture in hot water. Pasta is usually eaten with a sauce.

paste¹ /peɪst/ *noun* thick glue: *wallpaper paste*

paste² *verb* to stick one thing to another using paste: *Cut the pictures out and paste them on the chart.*

pas·tel /'pæstl $ pæ'stel/ *adjective* a pastel colour is pale and light, not dark or bright: *a pastel blue dress* ➔ see Thesaurus at LIGHT²

pas·time /'pɑːstaɪm $ 'pæstaɪm/ *noun* something that you enjoy doing when you are not working: *His favourite pastimes are football and computer games.*

ˌpast ˈparticiple *noun* a form of a verb that you use in PERFECT tenses or as an adjective. You usually form it by adding '-ed' to a REGULAR verb.

ˌpast ˈperfect *noun* **the past perfect** the tense of a verb that shows that an action was completed before another event or time in the past. In the sentence 'I had finished my breakfast before Rick phoned', 'had finished' is in the past perfect.

pas·try /'peɪstri/ *noun* **1** (no plural) a mixture of flour, fat, and water that you fill with other food and bake **2** (plural **pastries**) a small sweet cake

pas·ture /'pɑːstʃə $ 'pæstʃɚ/ *noun* land that is covered with grass which cows and sheep can eat

pat /pæt/ *verb* (**patted**, **patting**) to touch someone or something lightly with your hand flat in a friendly way: *"Good dog," she said, patting it on the head.* ➔ see Thesaurus at TOUCH¹ —**pat** *noun*: *She gave me a pat on the shoulder.*

pat

patch /pætʃ/ *noun* (plural **patches**) **1** a small area of something that looks different from the rest: *a wet patch on the carpet* **2** a piece of material that you use for covering a hole in your clothes: *a pair of jeans with a patch on one knee*

patch

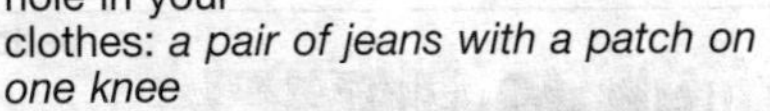

patch·work /'pætʃwɜːk $ 'pætʃwɝk/ *noun* (no plural) when you sew many different coloured pieces of cloth together to make a larger piece of cloth: *a patchwork quilt*

pa·tent·ly /'peɪtntli $ 'pætntli/ *adverb* **patently obvious, patently false etc** completely obvious, false etc, in a way that anyone can notice: *That's patently untrue!*

path /pɑːθ $ pæθ/ *noun* (plural **paths** /pɑːðz, pɑːθs $ pæðz, pæθs/) a track for people to walk along: *He walked along a narrow path leading down to the sea.*

pa·thet·ic /pə'θetɪk/ *adjective* very bad, useless, or weak: *Stop crying – you're being pathetic!* • *That's a pathetic excuse.* —**pathetically** /-kli/ *adverb*

pa·tience /'peɪʃəns/ *noun* (no plural)

> **KEY PATTERNS**
> **have the patience to do something**

the ability to stay calm and not get angry when you have to wait for a long time or when someone is behaving badly ANTONYM **impatience**: *I don't have* *the **patience** to look after young children. • You need a lot of **patience** to be a teacher.*

PHRASES

lose your patience, run out of patience to no longer be patient: *People have been queueing up for hours and are beginning to **lose their patience**. • I'm **running out of patience** with you, Lance.*

patient¹ /ˈpeɪʃənt/ *adjective*

KEY PATTERNS
be patient with someone

able to stay calm and not get angry when you have to wait for a long time or when someone is behaving badly ANTONYM **impatient**: *My father is a kind and patient man. • You'll have to be **patient with** him – he's always late.*
—**patiently** *adverb*: *David waited patiently in the corridor.*

patient² *noun* someone who is getting medical treatment

patio

pat·i·o /ˈpætiəʊ $ ˈpætiˌoʊ/ *noun* an area of a garden next to a house, that has a surface of flat stones SYNONYM **terrace**

pat·ri·ot /ˈpætriət $ ˈpeɪtriət/ *noun* someone who is very proud of their country

pat·ri·ot·ic /ˌpætriˈɒtɪk $ ˌpeɪtriˈɑtɪk/ *adjective* very proud of your country: *I'm not very patriotic.*

pat·ri·o·tis·m /ˈpætriətɪzəm $ ˈpeɪtriəˌtɪzəm/ *noun* (no plural) when someone is very proud of their country

pa·trol¹ /pəˈtrəʊl $ pəˈtroʊl/ *noun*
1 when police or soldiers go regularly around a place in order to protect it: *There were two policemen **on patrol** in the High Street.* **2** a group of police officers or soldiers who go regularly around an area to protect it: *the California Highway Patrol*

patrol² *verb* (**patrolled**, **patrolling** *BrE*, **patroled**, **patroling** *AmE*) if police or soldiers patrol a place, they go regularly around it in order to protect it: *Soldiers patrol the prison camp every hour.*

pa·trol·man /pəˈtrəʊlmən $ pəˈtroʊlmən/ *noun AmE* (plural **patrolmen** /-mən/) a police officer who goes regularly around an area in order to protect it

pat·ron·ize also **patronise** *BrE* /ˈpætrənaɪz $ ˈpeɪtrəˌnaɪz/ *verb* to speak to someone in a way that shows you think they are less important or intelligent than you: *I don't like the way Ray patronizes me.*

pat·ro·niz·ing also **patronising** *BrE* /ˈpætrənaɪzɪŋ $ ˈpeɪtrəˌnaɪzɪŋ/ *adjective* talking to someone in a way that shows you think they are less important or intelligent than you: *patronizing behaviour*

pat·ter /ˈpætə $ ˈpætɚ/ *verb* (written) to make a light knocking noise: *A child's feet pattered along the hallway.*
—**patter** *noun* (no plural): *the patter of rain on the windows*

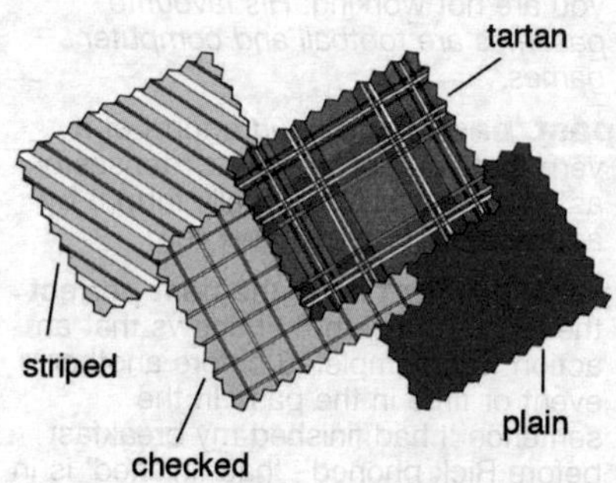

patterns

pat·tern /ˈpætn $ ˈpætɚn/ *noun*
1 a design made from shapes or lines that are arranged in a regular way: *The wallpaper has a very modern pattern. • a flag with a **pattern of** stars and stripes*
2 the regular way in which something happens: ***Is there any pattern to his***

bad behaviour? • *We are studying people's sleeping patterns.*

pat·terned /ˈpætnd $ ˈpætərnd/ *adjective* decorated with a pattern: *a patterned skirt*

pause¹ /pɔːz/ *verb*

KEY PATTERNS
pause to do something

(written) to stop doing something for a short time before you start again: *He paused a moment and then added, "I meant what I said yesterday."* • *Sue **paused to** check her watch.*

pause² *noun*

KEY PATTERNS
a pause in something

a short time when you stop doing something: *There was **a pause in** the conversation, and then it continued again.*

pave /peɪv/ *verb* to cover a path or road with a surface of flat stones

pave·ment /ˈpeɪvmənt/ *noun* **1** *BrE* the path you walk on at the side of a road SYNONYM **sidewalk** *AmE* → see picture at ZEBRA CROSSING **2** (no plural) *AmE* the hard surface of a road

ˈpaving stone *noun* a flat piece of stone that you use to make a surface for walking on

paw /pɔː/ *noun* an animal's foot: *The cat licked its paws.*

pawn /pɔːn/ *noun* a weak person who is controlled by other people

pay¹ /peɪ/ *verb* (past tense and past participle **paid** /peɪd/)

KEY PATTERNS
pay for your shopping/a ticket etc
pay £5/$8 etc for something
pay by cash/cheque/credit card
pay someone for something
pay the rent/bill
pay someone £10/$80 etc
pay someone to do something

1 to give someone money for something that you are buying from them: *You pay over there.* • *Have you **paid for** that CD?* • *I **paid** ten pounds **for** this book.* • *Are you **paying by** cash or credit card?* • *You haven't **paid** me **for** your ticket yet.*

2 to give someone money that you owe them: *I don't have enough money to pay the rent.*

3 to give someone money for doing work for you: *They pay me £6 an hour to work in the shop.* • *When do you **get paid**?* • *I had to **pay** them **to** take my old car away.* • *Waiters aren't very **well paid**.* • *a **highly paid** businessman*
→ see Thesaurus at EARN

4 if you pay for something bad you have done, someone punishes you for it: *You're going to **pay for** ruining our concert!*

PHRASES

pay attention to listen or watch carefully: *You must **pay** more **attention** in class.*

pay someone a visit, pay a visit to someone to visit a person or place: *Why don't you **pay** me **a visit** while you're in Chicago?*

pay someone a compliment to tell someone that you think they are nice, attractive, or intelligent

PHRASAL VERBS

pay someone/something back
to give someone the money that you borrowed from them: *Can I borrow $10? I'll **pay** you **back** tomorrow.* • *When will you **pay back** that money you borrowed?*

pay off
if something that you do pays off, it has a good result: *All her hard work **paid off**.*

pay² *noun* (no plural)
money that you get for working SYNONYM **salary**: *They are always asking for more pay.* • *I asked for a **pay rise**.*

THESAURUS
salary: *At that time, I was a teacher with a **salary** of £25,000 a year* (=the pay that professional or office workers get every month).
wages: *Many farm workers have low **wages*** (=the pay that a worker gets every week).
earnings: *a tax on **earnings*** (=money from working)
income: *help for people on low **incomes*** (=money from working, from the government, or from investments)

pay·a·ble /ˈpeɪəbəl/ *adjective* (formal)
1 an amount of money that is payable must be paid: *A deposit of £50 is*

payable when you order the goods. **2 make a cheque payable to someone** to write someone's name on a cheque etc to show that the money must be paid to them: *Please make the cheque payable to Mr Richard Walter.*

pay·day /ˈpeɪdeɪ/ *noun* (no plural) the day on which you receive your wages

pay·ment /ˈpeɪmənt/ *noun* an amount of money that you pay to someone, especially one of several amounts: *Did you **make the payments** by credit card? • Your first payment will be £50.*

ˈpay phone *noun* a public telephone that you pay to use

pay·roll /ˈpeɪrəʊl $ ˈpeɪroʊl/ *noun* **the payroll** a list of the people who work in an organization: *They have over 500 staff on the payroll.*

PC¹ /ˌpiː ˈsiː/ *noun* a computer that you can use in your home → see picture at KEYBOARD

PC² POLITICALLY CORRECT

PDA /ˌpiː diː ˈeɪ/ *noun* a very small light computer that you can carry with you and use for storing information, sending emails etc

PE /ˌpiː ˈiː/ *noun* (no plural) (physical education) sports and exercises that you do as a school subject

pea /piː/ *noun* peas are small round green vegetables → see picture on page A6

peace /piːs/ *noun* (no plural)
1 when there is no war: *When will there be peace in Northern Ireland? • Both sides are at the peace talks.*
2 when everything is very calm and quiet: *I'm going out to **get some peace**. • If you want **peace and quiet**, go to your room.*

PHRASES

leave someone in peace to not interrupt someone, and allow them to rest or do something quietly: ***Leave** your mother **in peace** – she's tired.*

peace of mind the feeling you have when you are not worried: *Insurance gives you **peace of mind** when you are on holiday.*

peace·ful /ˈpiːsfəl/ *adjective*
1 calm and quiet: *I just want a peaceful weekend with my family.*
2 not violent: *This is a peaceful protest.* —**peacefully** *adverb*: *The children were all sleeping peacefully.*

peace·keep·ing /ˈpiːsˌkiːpɪŋ/ *adjective* **peacekeeping forces, peacekeeping operations etc** soldiers or military activities that are in a place where there is a war, to try to stop the fighting

peace·time /ˈpiːstaɪm/ *noun* (no plural) when a country is not fighting a war ANTONYM **wartime**

peach /piːtʃ/ *noun* (plural **peaches**) a round fruit with soft yellow and red skin and a large seed inside → see picture on page A7

pea·cock /ˈpiːkɒk $ ˈpikɑk/ *noun* a large male bird with long blue and green tail feathers that it can spread out

peak¹ /piːk/ *noun* **1** the peak of something is the time when it is biggest or most successful: *She is now at the peak of her career.* **2** the pointed top of a mountain

peak² *adjective* peak times are when the largest number of people are travelling somewhere, using something etc: *July and August are the peak holiday periods.*

peak³ *verb* (written) if something peaks, it reaches its highest or most successful level: *The song peaked at number 2 in the UK charts.*

pea·nut /ˈpiːnʌt/ *noun* **1** a small nut with a soft light brown shell → see picture on page A7 **2 peanuts** (informal) a very small amount of money: *$2 an hour is peanuts!*

ˌpeanut ˈbutter / $ ˈ.. ˌ../ *noun* (no plural) a soft food made from crushed peanuts that you spread on bread

pear /peə $ per/ *noun* a sweet juicy yellow or green fruit that is round at the bottom and becomes thinner at the top → see picture on page A7

pearl /pɜːl $ pərl/ *noun* a valuable small white round object that is used in jewellery: *pearl earrings*

ˈpear-shaped *adjective* **go pear-shaped** *BrE* (informal) if something you try to do goes pear-shaped, it fails because things do not happen in the way you planned:

Our trip to the beach went pear-shaped when the car broke down.

peas·ant /ˈpezənt/ *noun* someone who lives in the country and works on the land, used especially about people in a poor country or people who lived a long time ago

peb·ble /ˈpebəl/ *noun* a small smooth stone

peck¹ /pek/ *verb* if a bird pecks something, it hits or bites it with its beak: *A bird was pecking at some breadcrumbs.*

peck² *noun* **a peck on the cheek** a quick light kiss on someone's cheek

pe·cu·li·ar /pɪˈkjuːliə $ pɪˈkjuljər/ *adjective* strange and surprising: *The car was making a peculiar noise.* → see Thesaurus at STRANGE —**peculiarly** *adverb*: *She's been behaving peculiarly for weeks.*

pe·cu·li·ar·i·ty /pɪˌkjuːliˈærəti/ *noun* (formal) (plural **peculiarities**) an unusual habit that only one person has: *One of her peculiarities is sleeping on the floor.*

ped·al¹ /ˈpedl/ *noun* **1** the part of a bicycle that you push with your foot in order to make it move forward: *I'll have to lower the seat so my feet can reach the pedals.* **2** the part of a car or machine that you press with your foot to control its movements: *the brake pedal*

pedal² *verb* (**pedalled**, **pedalling** *BrE*, **pedaled**, **pedaling** *AmE*) to ride a bicycle by pushing the pedals with your feet: *Pedal harder!*

ped·dle /ˈpedl/ *verb* to sell something, especially something illegal: *He was found guilty of peddling drugs.*

ped·es·tal /ˈpedəstəl/ *noun* a base for something such as a STATUE → see picture at STATUE

pe·des·tri·an /pəˈdestriən/ *noun* someone who is walking in the streets, rather than driving a car or riding a bicycle: *Two pedestrians were injured when the car ran off the road.* → see picture at ZEBRA CROSSING

peˌdestrian ˈcrossing *noun BrE* a place where people who are walking can safely cross a road SYNONYM **crosswalk** *AmE*

ped·i·gree /ˈpedəgriː/ *noun* an animal's pedigree is its parents and its family —**pedigree** *adjective*: *pedigree puppies* (=puppies whose parents are dogs of the same special breed)

peek

peek /piːk/ *verb* to look at something quickly and secretly SYNONYM **peep**: *He peeked in her bag to see what she had bought.* —**peek** *noun* (informal): *I took a peek at my present when he wasn't looking.*

peel¹ /piːl/ *verb* **1** to remove the skin of a fruit or vegetable: *Will you peel the potatoes, please?* → see Thesaurus at CUT¹ → see picture on page A4 **2 peel something off** to remove something that is stuck to a surface: *Peel the label off carefully.*

peel² *noun* the skin of a fruit or vegetable that you remove before eating it: *orange peel*

peep¹ /piːp/ *verb* to look at something quickly and secretly SYNONYM **peek**: *I peeped through the keyhole to see what was happening.*

peep² *noun* **1** a quick or secret look at something SYNONYM **peek**: *She took a peep at the answers in the back of the book.* **2 not hear a peep out of someone** if you do not hear a peep out of someone, they do not make any noise: *I didn't hear a peep out of the kids all afternoon.*

peer /pɪə $ pɪr/ *verb* to look at something very carefully and for a long time, especially because you cannot see it well: *Someone was peering at us through the window.*

peers /pɪəz $ pɪrz/ *plural noun* also **ˈpeer group** **1** your peers or your peer group are the people who are the same age as you or who have the same type of job or social position: *Teenagers prefer to spend their time with their peers.* **2 peer (group) pressure** the feeling that you should do the same things as other people who are the same age as you: *There is a lot of peer group pressure to wear fashionable clothes.*

peeved /piːvd/ *adjective* (informal) slightly annoyed: *He'll be peeved if you don't call around and see him.*

peg¹ /peg/ *noun* **1** a piece of wood or metal on a wall that you hang coats on **2** also **clothes peg** *BrE* a small object that you use for fastening wet clothes to a line where they can dry SYNONYM **clothes pin** *AmE*

peg² *verb* (**pegged**, **pegging**) to fasten something with pegs: *Peg the clothes on the washing line.*

pel·i·can cross·ing /ˌpelɪkən ˈkrɒsɪŋ $ ˌpelɪkən ˈkrɔsɪŋ/ *noun BrE* a place on the road where you can push a button that makes TRAFFIC LIGHTS turn red, so you can cross the road safely

pel·let /ˈpelɪt/ *noun* a small hard ball made from something such as paper or metal: *a gun that fires plastic pellets*

pelt¹ /pelt/ *verb* (informal) if someone pelts you with things, they attack you by throwing a lot of things at you: *They pelted us with snowballs.*

pelt² *noun* **at full pelt** (informal) running as fast as you can SYNONYM **at top speed**: *She came running down the road at full pelt.*

pen /pen/ *noun* a thing you use for writing and drawing in ink: *I need a pen and some paper.* • *Could you* ***write in pen*** *please, not pencil.*

pe·nal·ize also **penalise** *BrE* /ˈpiːnl-aɪz/ *verb* to punish a player or sports team by giving an advantage to their opponent: *The referee penalized our team for wasting time.*

pen·al·ty /ˈpenlti/ *noun* (plural **penalties**) **1** a punishment for not obeying a law or rule: *There will be a penalty of £50 for anyone who does not pay their bill.* **2** in SOCCER, an occasion when a player from one team can place the ball directly in front of the other team's GOAL and kick the ball towards the goal. A penalty is taken when the other team has broken the rules.

pence /pens/ (abbreviation **p** *BrE*) *noun* the plural of PENNY: *Can I borrow 10 pence for the phone?*

pen·cil /ˈpensəl/ *noun* a wooden stick with a black or coloured substance inside, which you use for writing and drawing: *Can I borrow your pencil?* • *Sally sharpened her* ***pencil***. • *First, he drew the picture* ***in pencil*** (=using a pencil).

pen·dant /ˈpendənt/ *noun* a jewel or small decoration that hangs from a chain around your neck

pen·du·lum /ˈpendjələm/ *noun* a long object with a weight at the bottom that moves from side to side inside a large clock

pen·e·trate /ˈpenətreɪt/ *verb* to enter something or pass through it: *bullets that can penetrate metal*

pen·e·trat·ing /ˈpenətreɪtɪŋ/ *adjective* **a penetrating look, a penetrating stare** a look that makes you feel uncomfortable because the other person seems to know what you are thinking

ˈpen friend *BrE noun* a PEN PAL

pen·guin /ˈpeŋgwɪn/ *noun* a large black and white bird that lives in Antarctica. Penguins cannot fly and use their wings for swimming. → see picture on page A8

pen·i·cil·lin /ˌpenəˈsɪlən/ *noun* (no plural) a medicine that destroys BACTERIA that are in your body and make you ill

pe·nin·su·la /pəˈnɪnsjələ $ pəˈnɪnsələ/ *noun* a long thin piece of land that is almost completely surrounded by water but is joined to a larger area of land

pe·nis /ˈpiːnɪs/ *noun* the male sex organ

pen·i·ten·tia·ry /ˌpenəˈtenʃəri/ *noun* (plural **penitentiaries**) a prison in the US: *He was sent to the state penitentiary.*

pen·knife /ˈpen-naɪf/ *noun* (plural **penknives** /-naɪvz/) a small knife with a blade or blades that you can fold into its handle

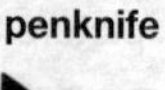
penknife

ˈpen name *noun* a name used by a writer instead of their real name SYNONYM **pseudonym**

pen·ni·less /ˈpenɪləs/ *adjective* (informal) someone who is penniless has no money: *I'll be penniless if I keep giving you money.*

pen·ny /ˈpeni/ *noun* (plural **pennies** or **pence**) (abbreviation **p**) **1** a coin worth 1/100 of a pound: *I found a penny on the floor.* **2** a cent

ˈpen pal *noun* someone living in another country who you write friendly letters to, but who you have never met SYNONYM **pen friend** *BrE*

pen·sion /ˈpenʃən/ *noun* money that a company or the government pays regularly to someone after they have stopped working because they are old or ill

pen·sion·er /ˈpenʃənə $ ˈpenʃənɚ/ *noun BrE* someone who is receiving a pension because they are old and have stopped working SYNONYM **senior citizen**

pen·sive /ˈpensɪv/ *adjective* (formal) thinking about something a lot and seeming slightly worried or sad: *He sat by the river, looking pensive.*

pen·ta·gon /ˈpentəgən $ ˈpentəˌgɑn/ *noun* a flat shape with five straight sides and five angles

peo·ple /ˈpiːpəl/ *plural noun* men, women, or children. 'People' is the plural of 'person': *There are too many people in this room.* • *I don't like people who smoke.*

THESAURUS
the public: *The gardens are open to the public* (=all the people in a country).
the human race/mankind: *the future of the human race* (=all human beings)
population: *Half the population of the country have mobile phones* (=the people who live in a country or area).

pep·per /ˈpepə $ ˈpepɚ/ *noun* **1** (no plural) a hot-tasting powder made from the seeds of a plant: *The soup needs a little more salt and pepper* **2** a red, yellow, or green vegetable with a hot taste: *chilli peppers* ➔ see picture on page A6

pep·per·mint /ˈpepəmɪnt $ pepɚˌmɪnt/ *noun* a plant with a strong fresh taste, or a sweet that tastes of this

per /pɜː $ pɚ/ *preposition* for each: *There will be one book per child.* • *He charges £20 per lesson.*

per·ceive /pəˈsiːv $ pɚˈsiv/ *verb* (formal) **1** to understand or think about something in a particular way: *They perceive us as being troublemakers.* **2** to notice something that is not easy to notice: *It is difficult to perceive the difference between the two sounds.*

per·cent also **per cent** *BrE* /pəˈsent $ pɚˈsent/ *adjective, adverb, noun* **5 percent, 10 percent etc** used after a number to show how many in every hundred. 'Percent' is often written as %: *Thirty percent of people think that taxes should be reduced.* • *Sales are up 30%.* • *He needs 70% of the vote to win.*

per·cen·tage /pəˈsentɪdʒ $ pɚˈsentɪdʒ/ *noun* an amount that is part of a larger amount: *A high percentage of teenagers* (=a large number of teenagers) *play computer games.*

per·cep·tion /pəˈsepʃən $ pɚˈsepʃən/ *noun* (formal) your opinion of what something is like: *You have a strange perception of marriage.*

per·cep·tive /pəˈseptɪv $ pɚˈseptɪv/ *adjective* good at noticing and understanding things: *She is very perceptive for a young girl.*

perch¹ /pɜːtʃ $ pɚtʃ/ *noun* a branch or stick where a bird sits

perch² *verb* (written) to be on the top or edge of something, or to put something there: *The hotel was perched high on a cliff.* • *She perched herself on the stool.*

per·cus·sion /pəˈkʌʃən $ pɚˈkʌʃən/ *noun* (no plural) drums and other musical instruments that you hit

per·fect¹ /ˈpɜːfɪkt $ ˈpɚfɪkt/ *adjective*

KEY PATTERNS
perfect for something

1 something that is perfect is so good that it could not be any better ANTONYM

A B C D E F G H I J K L M N O P Q R S T U V W X Y Z

imperfect: *She speaks perfect English.* • *The car is in perfect condition.*
2 exactly right for a particular purpose SYNONYM **ideal**: *The conditions were perfect for sailing.*
PHRASES
the perfect tenses the perfect tenses in English are the PRESENT PERFECT, the PAST PERFECT, and the FUTURE PERFECT

per·fect² /pəˈfekt $ pɚˈfekt/ *verb* to make something perfect: *I'm always trying to perfect my skills.*

per·fect³ /ˈpɜːfɪkt $ ˈpɚfɪkt/ *noun* **the perfect** the PRESENT PERFECT

per·fec·tion /pəˈfekʃən $ pɚˈfekʃən/ *noun* (no plural) when something is so good that it cannot be any better: *She tries to achieve perfection in her work.*

per·fec·tion·ist /pəˈfekʃənɪst $ pɚˈfekʃənɪst/ *noun* someone who likes to do things so well that they cannot be any better: *Jo is a perfectionist and her work is always beautifully presented.*

per·fect·ly /ˈpɜːfɪktli $ ˈpɚfɪktli/ *adverb* **1** in a perfect way: *She speaks English perfectly.* **2** used to emphasize what you are saying, especially when you are annoyed: *You know perfectly well what I'm talking about!*

per·fo·rat·ed /ˈpɜːfəreɪtɪd $ ˈpɚfəˌreɪtɪd/ *adjective* perforated paper has a line of small holes in it so that you can tear part of it off easily

per·form /pəˈfɔːm $ pɚˈfɔrm/ *verb*

KEY PATTERNS
perform in a play/show
perform an operation/task

1 to entertain people, for example by being in a play, singing, or dancing: *Many students **performed in** the school play.* • *I have never performed in public before.*
2 (formal) to do a job or a piece of work SYNONYM **carry out**: *Surgeons had never **performed** this **operation** before.* • *Computers can **perform tasks** that used to take a very long time.*
3 if something or someone performs well, they work well. If they perform badly, they work badly: *In tests, the car **performed** very **well**.* • *She began to **perform badly** at school.*

per·form·ance /pəˈfɔːməns $ pɚˈfɔrməns/ *noun*

KEY PATTERNS
a performance of a play/song/dance
give a performance

1 an event when one person or a group entertains people, for example by acting or singing: *We watched a **performance of** Hamlet.* • *Robbie Williams **gave** a brilliant **performance** at the concert.*
2 how successful someone has been or how well a person or machine does a job: *The company's performance has been very good this year.* • *I'm quite pleased with the car's performance.*

per·form·er /pəˈfɔːmə $ pɚˈfɔrmɚ/ *noun* someone such as an actor or musician who does things to entertain people: *a circus performer*

per·fume /ˈpɜːfjuːm $ ˈpɚfjum/ *noun* a liquid with a strong pleasant smell that you put on your skin SYNONYM **scent**: *She never wears perfume.*

per·haps /pəˈhæps $ pɚˈhæps/ *adverb* **1** used when saying what might be true or what might happen SYNONYM **maybe**: *Perhaps you'll win next time.* • *I can't find Jessica. Perhaps she's upstairs.*
2 used when making a suggestion: *Perhaps we could go to a club.*

per·il /ˈperəl/ *noun* (formal) great danger: *Our soldiers are in great peril.*

per·il·ous /ˈperələs/ *adjective* (written) very dangerous: *a perilous journey*

pe·ri·od /ˈpɪəriəd $ ˈpɪriəd/ *noun*

KEY PATTERNS
for a short/long period
a period of time/ten years etc

1 an amount of time: *Do not sit at a computer **for long periods**.* • *She has only been at the school for a short **period of time**.*
2 one of the parts of a schoolday in which you have a particular class SYNONYM **lesson** *BrE*: *We have history last period on Friday.*
3 the American word for a FULL STOP
4 a woman's period is the flow of blood from her body every month

pe·ri·od·ic /ˌpɪəriˈɒdɪk $ ˌpɪriˈɑdɪk/ also **pe·ri·od·ic·al** /ˌpɪəriˈɒdɪkəl $ ˌpɪriˈɑdɪkəl/ *adjective* regular but not very frequent: *one of her periodic visits* *to the dentist* —**periodically** /-kli/ *adverb*: *The river floods the valley periodically.*

pe·riph·e·ral /pəˈrɪfərəl/ *adjective* a peripheral idea or activity is less important than the main one

per·ju·ry /ˈpɜːdʒəri $ ˈpɚdʒəri/ *noun* (no plural) the crime of telling a lie in a law court: *He was found guilty of perjury.*

perk /pɜːk $ pɚk/ *noun* something such as a car or free meals that you get from your work in addition to your pay: *Free travel is one of the perks of the job.*

perm /pɜːm $ pɚm/ *verb* to put special chemicals on straight hair so that it will have curls: *Debbie's had her hair permed.* —**perm** *noun*: *I've decided to have a perm.*

per·ma·nent /ˈpɜːmənənt $ ˈpɚmənənt/ *adjective* something that is permanent continues for a long time or for all time ANTONYM **temporary**: *His injury left a permanent scar.* • *Will the job be permanent?*

per·ma·nent·ly /ˈpɜːmənəntli $ ˈpɚmənəntli/ *adverb* for all time ANTONYM **temporarily**: *Why don't you come and live with us permanently?*

per·mis·sion /pəˈmɪʃən $ pɚˈmɪʃən/ *noun* (no plural)

KEY PATTERNS
have permission to do something
give someone permission to do something
without (someone's) permission
with someone's permission
ask (someone's) permission

if you have permission to do something, someone allows you to do it: *Do you* ***have permission to*** *park your car here?* • *Who* ***gave*** *you* ***permission to*** *work in this room?* • *She went home* ***without*** *the teacher's* ***permission.*** • *Do not use the telephone before* ***asking permission.***

per·mit¹ /pəˈmɪt $ pɚˈmɪt/ *verb* (formal) (**permitted**, **permitting**) to allow something to happen: *Smoking is not permitted inside the hospital.* • *The visa permits you to stay for three weeks.* ➔ see Thesaurus at ALLOW

per·mit² /ˈpɜːmɪt $ ˈpɚmɪt/ *noun* an official document that allows you to do something: *You can't park here without a permit.* • *Do you have a work permit?*

per·pe·trate /ˈpɜːpətreɪt $ ˈpɚpəˌtreɪt/ *verb* (formal) to do something that is wrong: *people who perpetrate crimes*

per·plexed /pəˈplekst $ pɚˈplekst/ *adjective* (formal) very confused SYNONYM **puzzled**: *He looked totally perplexed.*

per·se·cute /ˈpɜːsɪkjuːt $ ˈpɚsɪˌkjut/ *verb* to treat someone cruelly and unfairly: *These people are persecuted because of their beliefs.*

per·se·ver·ance /ˌpɜːsəˈvɪərəns $ ˌpɚsəˈvɪrəns/ *noun* (no plural) when you keep trying to do something difficult because you want to succeed: *She achieved her ambition through hard work and perseverance.*

per·se·vere /ˌpɜːsəˈvɪə $ ˌpɚsəˈvɪr/ *verb* to keep trying to do something difficult in order to achieve something: *My father wants me to persevere with my studies.*

per·sist /pəˈsɪst $ pɚˈsɪst/ *verb* (formal) to continue to do something or to happen in an annoying way: *Why do you persist in disobeying me?* • *If the rain persists, we'll cancel the game.*

per·sis·tent /pəˈsɪstənt $ pɚˈsɪstənt/ *adjective* **1** continuing for a long time: *There have been persistent rumours that he is leaving.* **2** a persistent person keeps trying to do something even when it is annoying for other people: *He's called me four times today – he's very persistent.*

per·son /ˈpɜːsən $ ˈpɚsən/ *noun* (plural **people** /ˈpiːpəl/) a man, woman, or child: *Diana is a very kind person.* • *How many people live in England?*

PHRASES
in person if you do something in person, you go there yourself and do it: *I wanted to come and thank you* ***in person.***

per·son·al /ˈpɜːsənəl $ ˈpɚsənəl/ *adjective*
1 your personal things are things that belong to you and no one else: *The students have lockers to keep their*

personal belongings in. • *Each child has their own personal bank account.*
2 your personal experiences or views are your own and are not heard or copied from someone else: *The story is based on her* ***personal experience*** *of life in Argentina.* • *My personal opinion is that it is a bad idea.*
3 involving your health, relationships, or feelings: *The doctor will ask you a lot of personal questions.* • *Does he have any* ***personal problems****?*
4 involving rude criticism: *They kept making personal remarks about my age.*

ˌpersonal comˈputer a PC[1]

per·son·al·i·ty /ˌpɜːsəˈnæləti $ ˌpɚsəˈnæləti/ *noun* (plural **personalities**) **1** the type of person someone is, and the way they behave towards other people: *He's not good-looking but he has a great personality.* **2** a famous person, especially in sport or television: *a TV personality*

per·son·a·lized also **personalised** *BrE* /ˈpɜːsənəlaɪzd $ ˈpɚsənəˌlaɪzd/ *adjective* personalized objects have the name or INITIALS of the owner on them: *a car with personalized number plates*

per·son·al·ly /ˈpɜːsənəli $ ˈpɚsənəli/ *adverb* **1** (spoken) used to emphasize that you are only giving your own opinion: *Personally, I don't like war movies.* **2** if you know someone personally, you have met them: *I know who she is, but I don't know her personally.* **3** if you do something personally, you do it yourself instead of letting someone else do it SYNONYM **in person**: *The teacher thanked us personally.*

personal organizer

ˌpersonal ˈorganizer *noun* a small book or a very small computer for recording addresses, times of meetings etc

ˌpersonal ˈpronoun *noun* in grammar, a PRONOUN, such as 'I', 'you', and 'they'

ˌpersonal ˈstereo *noun* a small machine that plays CASSETTES or CDS. You carry it with you and listen through EARPHONES.

per·son·nel /ˌpɜːsəˈnel $ ˌpɚsəˈnel/ *plural noun* the people who work in an organization: *military personnel*

per·spec·tive /pəˈspektɪv $ pɚˈspektɪv/ *noun* a way of thinking about something: *Travel to other countries gives you a whole new perspective on life.*

per·spi·ra·tion /ˌpɜːspəˈreɪʃən $ ˌpɚspəˈreɪʃən/ *noun* (no plural) (formal) liquid that comes from your skin when you are very hot SYNONYM **sweat**

per·suade /pəˈsweɪd $ pɚˈsweɪd/ *verb*

> **KEY PATTERNS**
> **persuade someone to do something**
> **persuade someone that**

1 to make someone do something by explaining to them why it is a good idea: *I managed to* ***persuade*** *Tom* ***to*** *come to the party.*
2 to make someone believe something: *Can you* ***persuade*** *Sue* ***that*** *this is a good idea?*

> **THESAURUS**
> **talk someone into something**: *She didn't really want to lend me the money, but I* ***talked*** *her* ***into*** *it* (=persuaded her to do it).
> **get someone to do something** (informal): *I've been trying to* ***get*** *him* ***to*** *stop smoking* (=persuade him to stop).
> **coax**: *The nurse coaxed her to eat* (=persuaded her by talking gently and kindly).

per·sua·sion /pəˈsweɪʒən $ pɚˈsweɪʒən/ *noun* (no plural) when you persuade someone to do something: *With a little persuasion, I'm sure she'll agree.*

per·sua·sive /pəˈsweɪsɪv $ pɚˈsweɪsɪv/ *adjective* good at persuading people to do things: *Salesmen can be very persuasive.*

per·vert /ˈpɜːvɜːt $ ˈpɚvɚt/ *noun* someone whose sexual behaviour is not natural and not acceptable

pes·si·mis·m /ˈpesəmɪzəm/ *noun* (no plural) the belief that bad things will happen ANTONYM **optimism**

pes·si·mist /ˈpesəmɪst/ *noun* someone who always expects that bad things will happen ANTONYM **optimist**: *Don't be such a pessimist – you're sure to pass your exam.*

pes·si·mis·tic /ˌpesəˈmɪstɪk/ *adjective* someone who is pessimistic always expects that bad things will happen ANTONYM **optimistic**: *I am pessimistic about my chances of winning.*

pest /pest/ *noun* **1** a small animal or insect that destroys crops **2** (informal) an annoying person: *Stop being a pest.*

pes·ter /ˈpestə $ ˈpestɚ/ *verb* if you pester someone, you ask them for something so often that they get annoyed: *I'm busy – stop pestering me.*

pes·ti·cide /ˈpestəsaɪd/ *noun* a chemical substance that you put on plants to kill insects that cause damage to the plants

pet /pet/ *noun* an animal that you keep at home: *Do you have any pets?* ➔ see picture on page A8

pet·al /ˈpetl/ *noun* one of the coloured parts of a flower: *rose petals* ➔ see picture at FLOWER ➔ see picture on page A10

pet·er /ˈpiːtə $ ˈpitɚ/ **peter out** *verb* if something peters out, it gradually becomes smaller or less and finally disappears: *After a few days our food supplies petered out.*

pe·ti·tion /pəˈtɪʃən/ *noun* a piece of paper that a lot of people sign, which asks someone in authority to do something: *Will you sign a petition to save the library from closing?*

pet·ri·fied /ˈpetrəfaɪd/ *adjective* very frightened SYNONYM **terrified**: *I'm petrified of spiders.*

pet·rol /ˈpetrəl/ *noun* (no plural) *BrE* a liquid that you put in a car or other vehicle to make the engine work SYNONYM **gas** *AmE* SYNONYM **gasoline** *AmE*: *I had to stop to fill the car up with petrol.*

pe·tro·le·um /pəˈtrəʊliəm $ pəˈtroʊliəm/ *noun* (no plural) oil from under the ground that is used to make petrol and other chemical substances

ˈpetrol ˌstation *noun BrE* a place where you can buy petrol to put in your car SYNONYM **gas station** *AmE* SYNONYM **filling station**

pet·ti·coat /ˈpetikəʊt $ ˈpetiˌkoʊt/ *noun* a piece of clothing like a thin dress or skirt that a woman wears under a dress or skirt

pet·ty /ˈpeti/ *adjective* **1** petty things are not important SYNONYM **trivial**: *a petty argument* **2** if someone is petty, they care too much about small unimportant things: *She can be very petty about money.*

pew /pjuː/ *noun* a long wooden seat in a church

pha·raoh /ˈfeərəʊ $ ˈferoʊ/ *noun* a ruler of ancient Egypt

phar·ma·cist /ˈfɑːməsɪst $ ˈfɑrməsɪst/ *noun* someone whose job is to prepare drugs and medicines SYNONYM **chemist**

phar·ma·cy /ˈfɑːməsi $ ˈfɑrməsi/ *noun* **1** (plural **pharmacies**) a store where you can buy medicine SYNONYM **chemist**, **drugstore** **2** the study of drugs and medicines

phase¹ /feɪz/ *noun* one part of a process: *Phase 1 of the project will start next week.*

phase² *verb* **1 phase something in** to gradually start using something or doing something: *They are phasing in the new exams over the next two years.* **2 phase something out** to gradually stop using something or doing something: *The old car design will be gradually phased out.*

PhD, Ph.D. /ˌpiː eɪtʃ ˈdiː/ *noun* Doctor of Philosophy; the highest university degree

phe·nom·e·nal /fɪˈnɒmənəl $ fɪˈnɑmənl/ *adjective* very unusual and impressive: *This was a phenomenal success for our team.* —**phenomenally** *adverb*: *a phenomenally successful film*

phe·nom·e·non /fɪˈnɒmənən $ fɪˈnɑmənən/ *noun* (plural **phenomena** /-nə/) something that happens or exists, especially something unusual: *Earthquakes and hurricanes are natural phenomena.*

phi·los·o·pher /fɪˈlɒsəfə $ fɪˈlɑsəfɚ/ *noun* someone who studies philosophy: *ancient Greek philosophers*

phil·o·soph·i·cal /ˌfɪləˈsɒfɪkəl $ ˌfɪləˈsɑfɪkəl/ *adjective* related to philosophy

phi·los·o·phy /fɪˈlɒsəfi $ fɪˈlɑsəfi/ *noun* (no plural) the study of ideas about life and how people should live: *Eastern philosophy*

pho·bi·a /ˈfəʊbiə $ ˈfoʊbiə/ *noun* a strong fear of something: *She had a phobia about spiders.*

phone[1] /fəʊn $ foʊn/ *noun* a telephone: *A woman **answered the phone**. • I wish someone would **pick up** (=answer) the phone. • I wrote down her **phone number**. • You can contact me **by phone** or email.*

PHRASES

be on the phone to be talking to someone, using a telephone: *Could you be a little quieter? I'm **on the phone**.*

put the phone down on someone *BrE* to end a telephone conversation immediately because you are angry with the person you are talking to: *When I mentioned the money she **put the phone down on me**.*

USAGE
You say **phone someone**.
✘ Don't say 'phone to someone'.

phone[2] also **phone up** *verb* to speak to someone, using a telephone SYNONYM **telephone**, **call**, **ring** *BrE*: *Steve phoned me seven times last week. • I **phoned up** to book tickets.*

ˈphone booth also **ˈphone box** *BrE noun* a small covered area containing a public telephone

ˈphone-in *noun* a radio or television programme in which people telephone the PRESENTER to give their opinions or ask questions: *Call our phone-in now and give us your views.*

pho·ney *BrE*, **phony** *AmE* /ˈfəʊni $ ˈfoʊni/ *adjective* (informal) false and not real SYNONYM **fake**: *a phoney American accent*

pho·to /ˈfəʊtəʊ $ ˈfoʊtoʊ/ *noun* (plural **photos**) (informal) a photograph: *I took some photos of the wedding.*

pho·to·cop·i·er /ˈfəʊtəʊˌkɒpiə $ ˈfoʊtəˌkɑpiɚ/ *noun* a machine that makes copies of documents SYNONYM **copier** *AmE*

pho·to·cop·y[1] /ˈfəʊtəʊˌkɒpi $ ˈfoʊtəˌkɑpi/ *noun* (plural **photocopies**) a copy of a document that you make using a photocopier: *Send a photocopy of your certificate to the college.*

photocopy[2] *verb* (**photocopied**, **photocopies**) to make a copy of a document using a photocopier: *Could you photocopy this article, please?*

pho·to·graph[1] /ˈfəʊtəgrɑːf $ ˈfoʊtəˌgræf/ also **photo** (informal) *noun* a picture that you make using a camera: *I took a photograph of the beach.*

photograph[2] *verb* to make a picture of someone or something using a camera: *Jill hates being photographed.* —**photographer** *noun*: *a fashion photographer*

pho·to·graph·ic /ˌfəʊtəˈgræfɪk $ ˌfoʊtəˈgræfɪk/ *adjective* relating to photographs and photography: *expensive photographic equipment*

pho·tog·ra·phy /fəˈtɒgrəfi $ fəˈtɑgrəfi/ *noun* (no plural) taking photographs: *He developed an interest in photography.*

ˌphrasal ˈverb *noun* a verb that is used with an adverb or preposition, which has a different meaning from the verb used alone. 'Set off' and 'put up with' are examples of phrasal verbs.

phrase /freɪz/ *noun* a group of words that are used together: *What does the phrase 'in good time' mean?*

THESAURUS
expression: *What does the expression 'by yourself' mean* (=the phrase)?
idiom: *'On top of the world' is an idiom meaning 'extremely happy'* (=a group of words that have a special meaning when they are used together).
cliché: *the cliché that the kitchen is the heart of the home* (=a group of words that is used too often)

phys·i·cal¹ /ˈfɪzɪkəl/ *adjective*
1 relating to someone's body, not their mind: *Do you do much physical exercise?* • *Their child has a physical disability.*
2 physical things are objects that you can touch and see: *We need some physical evidence to prove our case.*
—**physically** *adverb*: *He was physically attractive.*

physical² the American word for MEDICAL²

phys·ics /ˈfɪzɪks/ *noun* (no plural) the study of things that happen naturally in the world, such as heat, light, and movement

> SPELLING
> This word is often spelled wrongly. The correct spelling is: **physics**.

phys·i·o·ther·a·pist /ˌfɪziəʊˈθerəpɪst $ ˌfɪzioʊˈθerəpɪst/ *noun* someone whose job is doing physiotherapy

phys·i·o·ther·a·py /ˌfɪziəʊˈθerəpi $ ˌfɪzioʊˈθerəpi/ *noun* (no plural) medical treatment, especially exercises, for people who cannot move a part of their body

phy·sique /fəˈziːk/ *noun* the shape and size of your body: *a tall man with a powerful physique* (=a strong body with big muscles)

pi·a·nist /ˈpiːənɪst $ piˈænɪst/ *noun* someone who plays the piano

pi·an·o /piˈænəʊ $ piˈænoʊ/ *noun* a large musical instrument that you play by pressing small black and white keys → see picture at KEYBOARD

pick¹ /pɪk/ *verb*

> KEY PATTERNS
> **pick a number/chocolate etc**
> **pick someone to come/help etc**
> **pick someone for a team/job**
> **pick something from/off something**

1 to choose something or someone: *Pick which jumper you want to wear.* • *I picked Sara to be my partner.* → see Thesaurus at CHOOSE
2 to take a flower or fruit from a plant: *Let's go to the farm and pick strawberries.*
3 to pull small pieces from something: *Stop picking bits off the cake!*

pick

Lisa picked up the book.

John picked up his wife.

PHRASES
pick a fight, pick an argument to behave in an unpleasant way towards someone so that they will fight you or argue with you: *It is always the older children who* ***pick fights****.*

PHRASAL VERBS
pick on
pick on someone to keep criticizing or upsetting someone unfairly: *Why do you always* ***pick on*** *me?*

pick up
1 pick something/someone up to lift something or someone: *I* ***picked up*** *a stick that was lying on the path.* • *You are too heavy for me to* ***pick you up****.* → see picture on page A2
2 pick someone/something up to collect someone or something: *Could you* ***pick up*** *my clothes from the cleaner's?* • *Can you* ***pick me up*** *from school today?*
3 pick something up (informal) to learn something by watching or listening to other people: *She* ***picked up*** *a bit of German from her Swiss cousins.* → see Thesaurus at LEARN
4 pick someone up (informal) to talk to someone and try to start a sexual relationship with them

pick² *noun* something that you choose: *What would you like to drink? Take your pick.*

pick·axe *BrE*, **pickax** *AmE* /ˈpɪk-æks/ *noun* a large metal tool with a long handle, used to break up hard ground

pick·et /ˈpɪkɪt/ also **ˈpicket ˌline** *noun* a group of people who stand in front of a factory or other building to protest about something or to stop people from going in during a STRIKE: *They've been on the picket line for two* months. —**picket** *verb*: *About 200 people picketed outside the courthouse.*

pick·le /ˈpɪkəl/ *noun* **1** *BrE* a cold sauce made with vegetables that have been preserved in VINEGAR or salt **2** *AmE* a CUCUMBER preserved in VINEGAR and salt or sugar: *Could I have pickles on my hamburger?*

pick·pock·et /ˈpɪkˌpɒkɪt $ ˈpɪkˌpɑkɪt/ *noun* someone who steals from people's pockets in public places

pick·y /ˈpɪki/ *adjective* (informal) (**pickier**, **pickiest**) a picky person only likes a few things and is difficult to please SYNONYM **fussy**: *Jeremy's a very picky eater.*

pic·nic /ˈpɪknɪk/ *noun* a meal that you eat outside, away from home: *Let's have a picnic on the beach.*

pic·ture¹ /ˈpɪktʃə $ ˈpɪktʃɚ/ *noun*

KEY PATTERNS
a picture of something/someone
go to the pictures

1 a painting, drawing, or photograph: *That's a nice **picture of** Oscar.* • *I drew **a picture of** a vase of flowers.*
2 the pictures *BrE* the cinema: *Do you want to **go to the pictures** on Saturday?*

PHRASES
take a picture of someone/something, take someone's picture to take a photograph of someone or something: *Will you **take a picture of** us?*

THESAURUS
drawing: *She did a beautiful **drawing** of a cat* (=a picture done with a pencil or pen).
painting: *an exhibition of early Dutch **paintings*** (=painted pictures)
sketch: *I did a **sketch** of the house to show Dan* (=a quick drawing without details).
diagram: *a **diagram** of the heating system* (=a simple drawing showing its structure)
illustration: *He both wrote the book and did the **illustrations*** (=the pictures in the book).

picture² *verb* (written) **1** to imagine something: *I pictured myself swimming in the warm ocean.* **2** to show something or someone in a photograph in a newspaper: *Tom Parker, pictured above, plays the part of a doctor in the play.*

pic·tur·esque /ˌpɪktʃəˈresk/ *adjective* a picturesque place is very attractive: *the picturesque villages of southern Spain*

pie /paɪ/ *noun* a food made with fruit, meat, or vegetables baked inside PASTRY: *apple pie*

piece /piːs/ *noun*

KEY PATTERNS
a piece of paper/glass/cake etc
be/lie in pieces
tear/smash/blow something to pieces

1 a part of something that has been separated or broken off from the rest of it: *a **piece of** cheese* • *I need a new **piece of** paper.* • *The broken glass **lay in pieces** on the floor.* • *It had been smashed **to pieces**.* → see Thesaurus at PART¹
2 a piece of music, poetry, or work is a song, poem etc that someone has written or produced: *What is your favourite **piece of music**?* • *Choose your three best pieces of work.*
3 a piece of furniture, clothing, equipment etc is an object of that kind: *The table in the dining room is my favourite **piece of furniture**.*

PHRASES
a piece of advice, a piece of evidence etc some advice, evidence etc: *The most important piece of advice of all is to trust your own instincts.*
a piece of land a small area of land: *We want to buy a piece of land and build a house.*

SPELLING
This word is often spelled wrongly. The correct spelling is **pie̲ce**.

THESAURUS
scrap: *He wrote something on a **scrap** of paper* (=a small piece).
chunk: *The stew had big **chunks** of meat in it* (=large pieces).
lump: *a **lump** of clay* (=a piece with a shape that is not regular)
slice: *a **slice** of cheese* (=a thin piece that is cut from something)

pier /pɪə $ pɪr/ *noun* a structure that is built out into the sea so that people can walk along it

pierce /pɪəs $ pɪrs/ *verb* to make a hole in something, using a sharp object: *The blade of the knife pierced his arm.* • *pierced ears*

pierc·ing /ˈpɪəsɪŋ $ ˈpɪrsɪŋ/ *adjective* a piercing sound is high, loud, and unpleasant: *a piercing scream*

pig /pɪg/ *noun* a farm animal with short legs, a fat, usually pink body, and a curled tail SYNONYM **hog** *AmE*

pi·geon /ˈpɪdʒən/ *noun* a grey bird that is common in cities

pig·head·ed /ˌpɪgˈhedɪd/ *adjective* (informal) a pigheaded person refuses to change their opinion about something, even when they are wrong SYNONYM **stubborn**: *I've never met a woman so obstinate and pigheaded.*

pig·let /ˈpɪglət/ *noun* a young pig

pig·sty /ˈpɪgstaɪ/ also **pig·pen** /ˈpɪgpen/ *AmE noun* a place where pigs are kept

pig·tail /ˈpɪgteɪl/ *noun* hair that has been twisted together and tied SYNONYM **braid**, **plait**: *a fat child with hair in pigtails* → see picture at HAIRSTYLE

pile¹ /paɪl/ *noun*

KEY PATTERNS
a pile of books/papers/stones etc
put something in a pile

a lot of similar things put one on top of the other: *There was a huge pile of dirty washing.* • *Put those books in a pile on my desk.*

THESAURUS
heap: *The building is now just a heap of rubble* (=a large untidy pile).
stack: *a stack of books* (=a pile with each thing on top of another)

pile² *verb* to put things together in a pile, or to be in a pile: *Clothes were piled up on Lily's bed.* • *My plate was piled with food.*

ˈpile-up *noun* (informal) a road accident involving several vehicles: *a 16-car pile-up* → see Thesaurus at ACCIDENT

pil·grim /ˈpɪlgrəm/ *noun* someone who travels to a holy place for religious reasons

pil·grim·age /ˈpɪlgrəmɪdʒ/ *noun* a trip to a holy place for religious reasons

pill /pɪl/ *noun* **1** a small solid piece of medicine that you swallow SYNONYM **tablet** → see Thesaurus at MEDICINE **2 the pill** a pill that women can take to stop them becoming PREGNANT

pil·lar /ˈpɪlə $ ˈpɪlɚ/ *noun* a tall solid piece of stone, wood, or metal used to support part of a building

pil·low /ˈpɪləʊ $ ˈpɪloʊ/ *noun* the soft object you put your head on when you sleep → see picture at BED

pi·lot /ˈpaɪlət/ *noun* someone who flies a plane

pin¹ /pɪn/ *noun*
a short thin piece of metal with a sharp point, used especially for holding pieces of cloth together

pin² *verb* (**pinned**, **pinning**) **1** to fasten something or join things together with a pin: *Karen pinned a flower to her hat.* **2** to press someone against something, stopping them from moving: *He grabbed me and pinned me to the wall.*

PIN also **PIN number** /ˈpɪn ˌnʌmbə $ ˈpɪn ˌnʌmbɚ/ *noun* (Personal Identification Number) a number that you use when you put a plastic card in a machine to get money or pay for something

pinch¹ /pɪntʃ/ *verb*
1 to press a part of someone's skin tightly between your finger and thumb: *I pinched his arm.*
2 *BrE* (informal) to steal something that is not valuable: *Who's pinched my pencil?*

pinch² *noun* **1** an act of pressing someone's flesh between your finger and thumb **2** a very small amount: *Add a pinch of salt to the sauce.* **3 at a pinch** *BrE*, **in a pinch** *AmE* (spoken, informal) only with difficulty or only if really necessary: *At a pinch, I could fit six people in the car.*

pine¹ /paɪn/ *noun* a tall tree with very thin leaves, or the wood from this tree: *a pine table* → see picture on page 498

pine² also **pine away** *verb* to become ill because you are sad or lonely: *I found myself pining for home.*

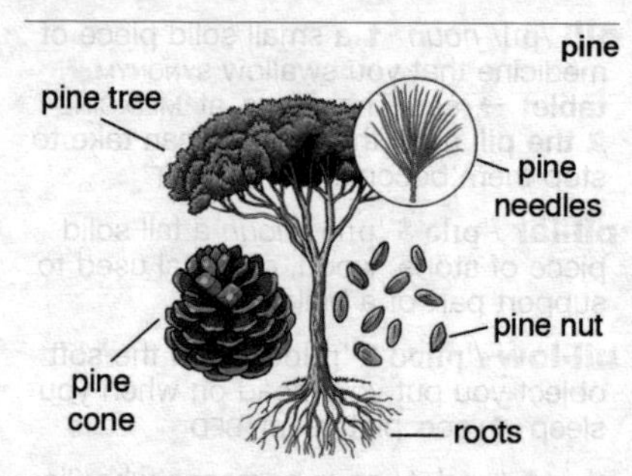

pine·ap·ple /ˈpaɪnæpəl/ *noun* a large tropical fruit with pointed leaves and sweet yellow flesh → see picture on page A7

pink /pɪŋk/ *adjective, noun* pale red

ˌpins and ˈneedles *plural noun* the sharp, slightly uncomfortable pain you get in your arms or legs after you have been sitting in an awkward position: *I woke up with pins and needles in my foot.*

pint /paɪnt/ *noun* a unit for measuring liquid, equal to 0.473 litres in the US or 0.568 litres in Britain

pin·up /ˈpɪnʌp/ *noun* a large picture of someone famous or attractive, that is put up on a wall

pi·o·neer /ˌpaɪəˈnɪə $ ˌpaɪəˈnɪr/ *noun* one of the first people or companies to do something that other people then develop: *The bank was one of the pioneers of online banking.* —**pioneer** *verb*: *They pioneered genetic fingerprinting.*

pi·ous /ˈpaɪəs/ *adjective* a pious person has strong religious beliefs: *He grew up to be a quiet, pious man.*

pip /pɪp/ *noun BrE* a small seed of a fruit such as an apple or orange

pipe¹ /paɪp/ *noun*
1 a tube that liquid or gas flows through: *There is something blocking the water pipe.* • *Water was coming out of a* ***hole in the pipe***.
2 an object shaped like a tube with a round container on the end, which is used for smoking tobacco: *My father smokes a pipe.*

pipe² *verb* to send a liquid or gas through a pipe to another place: *Our water is piped from the Colorado River.*

pipe·line /ˈpaɪp-laɪn/ *noun* **1** pipes used for carrying a liquid or gas over long distances **2 be in the pipeline** (informal) if something is in the pipeline, it will happen soon: *The band's third album is in the pipeline.*

pi·ping /ˈpaɪpɪŋ/ *adjective* **piping hot** very hot: *piping hot soup*

pi·rate¹ /ˈpaɪərət $ ˈpaɪrət/ *noun*
1 someone who illegally copies a computer game, DVD etc and sells it: *software pirates* **2** someone who attacks other boats and steals things from them

pirate² *verb* to illegally copy a computer game, DVD etc in order to sell it

pis·tol /ˈpɪstl/ *noun* a small gun

pit /pɪt/ *noun* **1** a coal mine **2** a deep hole in the ground **3 be the pits** (spoken, informal) to be very bad: *Isn't work the pits?* **4** *AmE* the large hard seed in some fruits SYNONYM **stone** *BrE*: *a cherry pit*

pitch¹ /pɪtʃ/ *verb* **1** to throw the ball to the BATTER in a game of baseball: *Who's pitching in tonight's game?* **2** to present something so that it is suitable for a particular group of people: *This English course is pitched at Japanese learners.*

pitch² *noun* (plural **pitches**) **1** *BrE* an area of ground used for playing a sport SYNONYM **field**: *a football pitch* **2** the pitch of a sound is how high or low it is: *Jean's voice rose to a higher pitch.* **3** a throw of the ball in a game of baseball

ˌpitch ˈblack also **ˌpitch ˈdark** *adjective* completely black or dark: *It's pitch dark outside.*

pitch·er /ˈpɪtʃə $ ˈpɪtʃɚ/ *noun* **1** a container used for pouring liquids SYNONYM **jug** *BrE*: *a pitcher of beer* **2** the baseball player who throws the ball to the BATTER

pit·i·ful /ˈpɪtɪfəl/ *adjective* making you feel very sorry for someone: *the pitiful sight of homeless children*

pit·y¹ /ˈpɪti/ *noun*

KEY PATTERNS
feel pity for someone

sadness that you feel for someone who is suffering or sad: *I **felt pity for** the family of the dead man.* • *Ali listened to her story **with pity**.*

PHRASES

it's a pity (that), that's a pity used when you are disappointed about a situation and wish it was different: ***It's a pity that** we don't live nearer to each other.* • *"I'll have to miss your party." "**That's a pity**."*

out of pity (spoken) if you do something out of pity, you do it because you feel sorry for someone: *I don't want you to stay with me **out of pity**.*

take pity on someone, have pity on someone to try to help someone who is suffering or in trouble because you feel sorry for them: *The people are starving and we must have pity on them.*

pity² *verb* (**pitied**, **pities**) to feel sympathy for someone who is suffering or in a bad situation: *These poor children should be pitied.*

piv·ot /ˈpɪvət/ *noun* a central point that something balances or turns on

pix·el /ˈpɪksəl/ *noun* the smallest unit of an image on a computer screen

pix·ie /ˈpɪksi/ *noun* a small imaginary person who has magic powers

piz·za /ˈpiːtsə/ *noun* a thin flat round bread, baked with cheese, meat, vegetables etc on top

plac·ard /ˈplækɑːd $ ˈplækərd/ *noun* a large sign that is carried by a person: *Protestors were carrying placards.*

placard

placard

place¹ → see box on page 500

place² /pleɪs/ *verb* to put something carefully somewhere SYNONYM **put**: *Kevin placed his books on the shelf.*

plac·id /ˈplæsɪd/ *adjective* calm and peaceful: *He is a very placid baby.* • *The woman had a round placid face.* —**placidly** *adverb*: *She smiled placidly.*

pla·gia·ris·m /ˈpleɪdʒərɪzəm/ *noun* when someone uses another person's words or ideas in their writing and pretends that they are their own: *Students need to understand that plagiarism is a serious offence.*

plague /pleɪg/ *noun* a disease that spreads quickly, killing a lot of people

plaice /pleɪs/ *noun* a flat sea fish that people eat

plaid /plæd/ the American word for TARTAN

plain¹ /pleɪn/ *adjective*

1 all one colour, with no pattern or design: *Do you have any plain white envelopes?*

2 without a lot of decoration; simple: *Mark likes good plain cooking* • *Their house is neat and plain.*

3 easy to see or understand SYNONYM **clear**: *The facts were plain.* • *She **made her feelings plain** (=she told everyone how she felt).*

4 a plain woman is not very attractive SYNONYM **homely** *AmE*

plain² *noun* a large area of flat land: *the plains of North America*

plain·ly /ˈpleɪnli/ *adverb* **1** easily seen or recognized SYNONYM **clearly**: *He's plainly unhappy.* **2** simply or without decoration: *a plainly dressed young girl*

plait /plæt/ *verb BrE* to twist three long pieces of hair, rope etc together to make one long piece SYNONYM **braid** *AmE*: *I combed and plaited my hair.* —**plait** *noun*

plan¹ /plæn/ *noun*

KEY PATTERNS
a plan to do something
a plan for something
have a plan

an idea or arrangement for doing something in the future: *Their **plan is to** travel around Europe by train.* • *Do you **have any plans for** your future?*

PHRASES

make plans to arrange to do something: *I can't come on Saturday night – I've already **made plans**.*

THESAURUS
intention: *My **intention** is to make money* (=what I am planning to do).
scheme: *a **scheme** to increase children's fitness* (=a plan)

A B C D E F G H I J K L M N O P Q R S T U V W X Y Z

place /pleɪs/ *noun*

1 a particular area or town, or a particular building, shop, restaurant etc: *I like this* ***place*** *a lot – they have really good food. • She's looking for* ***a place to live****. • The town is a really* ***good place for*** *a holiday. • It's* ***a great place for*** *the kids to play. • I know a* ***place*** *where they sell bikes.*

KEY PATTERNS
a place to live/sleep/play
a good place for a holiday/picnic
a place where ...

2 the position where you put, keep, or write something: *Is this a good* ***place*** *to put the TV? • Always keep your passport in a* ***safe place****. • Please sign the form in these two* ***places****.*

3 the position where you stand or sit: *When I got back, someone had* ***taken my place****. • Please* ***stay in your places*** *while I call your names. • Save me a* ***place*** *next to you, okay?*

4 (spoken) someone's house or apartment: *I'm going over to Bill's* ***place*** *later. • You've got a nice* ***place*** *here.*

5 *BrE* if you have a place on a course, you are able to study on that course. If you have a place on a team, you are a member of that team: *She got a* ***place on*** *the swimming team. • He has applied for a* ***place at*** *the university. • There are no* ***places*** *left* ***at*** *the school.*

KEY PATTERNS
a place on a course/team
a place at a school/university

PHRASES

all over the place (informal)
if things or people are all over the place, there are a lot of them in many different parts of an area: *There were cans and bottles* ***all over the place****.*

first place, second place etc
the person who finishes a race, competition etc in first place is the winner; the person who finishes in second place finishes next etc: *Dan won* ***third place****. • Last year, the team finished in* ***second place****.*

in someone's place, in something's place
instead of someone or something: *He was ill, so I went* ***in his place****.*

in the first place (spoken)
used when saying what someone should do, or should have done, especially when you are annoyed with them: *If you'd done it right* ***in the first place****, we wouldn't have to do it again.*

take place
to happen, especially after being planned to happen: *The wedding* ***took place*** *outside, in the gardens of the hotel.*

take someone's place, take something's place
to do something instead of someone or something else: *When he left, I* ***took his place*** *as team captain.*

plot/conspiracy: *a plot to kidnap a millionaire's son* (=a secret plan by several people to do something bad)

plan² *verb* (**planned, planning**)

KEY PATTERNS
plan a trip/party etc
plan what/who/when etc
plan to do something
plan on doing something

1 to think about something you want to do, and how you will do it: *Kathy is already planning her wedding.* • *Have you* ***planned what*** *you're going to do at the weekend?* • *I've* ***planned where*** *we will go to eat.*
2 to intend to do something: *She* ***plans to*** *get a part-time job.* • *Julia* ***plans on*** *being a lawyer.* • *I didn't* ***plan on*** *telling you that.*

plane /pleɪn/ *noun*
a vehicle that flies SYNONYM **aeroplane, airplane** ➔ see picture on page A11

USAGE
You **get on a plane** or **get off a plane.**
You go somewhere **by plane.**

plan·et /'plænət/ *noun* **1** a large round object in space that moves around a star: *Mercury is the planet nearest to the sun.* **2 the planet** the world: *Is the climate of the planet really changing?* ➔ see Thesaurus at EARTH

plank /plæŋk/ *noun* a long flat piece of wood

plant¹ /plɑːnt $ plænt/ *noun*
1 a living thing that has leaves and roots and is usually smaller than a tree: *She likes to have lots of plants in the house.* ➔ see picture on page A10
2 a factory and all its equipment: *a nuclear plant*

plant² *verb* **1** to put plants or seeds in the ground to grow: *We planted an apple tree in the yard.* **2** to hide something, especially a bomb, somewhere: *Terrorists planted a bomb in the city centre.*

plan·ta·tion /plæn'teɪʃən/ *noun* a large farm, especially in a hot country, where a single crop is grown: *a tobacco plantation*

plas·ter¹ /'plɑːstə $ 'plæstɚ/ *noun*
1 (no plural) a smooth substance used for covering walls and ceilings **2** *BrE* a piece of sticky material used to cover small wounds SYNONYM **band-aid** *AmE*
3 be in plaster *BrE* if someone's leg, arm etc is in plaster, it is covered with a hard white substance to protect a broken bone: *Greg returned from his skiing holiday with his leg in plaster.*

plaster² *verb* (informal) to spread or stick something all over a surface: *Her bedroom walls were plastered with posters.*

ˌplaster 'cast *noun* a hard cover made from a special type of plaster, used to protect a broken bone

plas·tic¹ /'plæstɪk/ *noun*
a light material made from chemicals, which is used for making many different objects: *garden furniture* ***made of plastic***

plastic² *adjective* made of plastic: *a plastic cup*

ˌplastic 'surgery *noun* (no plural) medical operations to improve the way someone looks: *She needed plastic surgery after she was badly burnt in a fire.*

plate /pleɪt/ *noun*

KEY PATTERNS
a plate of biscuits/spaghetti etc

1 a flat dish that you use for eating or serving food
2 also **plate·ful** /'pleɪtfʊl/ the amount of food that a plate will hold: *Lunch was* ***a plate of*** *sandwiches.*

plat·form /'plætfɔːm $ 'plætfɔrm/ *noun*
1 the part of a station where you get on and off trains: *The train for Brighton leaves from platform four.* • *I was standing* ***on platform 11*** *at Liverpool Street station.*
2 a raised structure for people to stand or work on: *The speaker stood on a platform at the front of the hall.*
3 the type of computer system or software that someone uses: *You can run the program on a wide range of different platforms.*

plat·i·num /'plætənəm/ *noun* (no plural) an expensive white metal, used for making jewellery

pla·ton·ic /plə'tɒnɪk $ plə'tɑnɪk/ *adjective* if you have a platonic

A B C D E F G H I J K L M N O P Q R S T U V W X Y Z

relationship with someone, it is friendly but not sexual: *Their friendship was purely platonic.*

plau·si·ble /ˈplɔːzəbəl/ *adjective* likely to be true ANTONYM **implausible**: *The story he told the police was not very plausible.*

play

play¹ /pleɪ/ *verb*

KEY PATTERNS
play football/tennis/chess etc
play (against) Spain/the champion
play for the school team/Manchester United etc
play the guitar/violin etc
play with a toy
play with a friend
play a part in a film/play

1 to take part in a sport or game: *Do you know how to play tennis?* • *The boys were playing computer games.* • *England* ***played against*** *France in the final.* • *The US will play Norway.* • *He* ***plays for*** *the Chicago Bulls* (=he is on their team).
2 if you play a musical instrument, you use it to produce music: *I'm learning to* ***play the*** *piano.* • *He played me a tune on his guitar.*
3 if children play, they have fun doing things with toys or with their friends: *Henry loves* ***playing with*** *his toy cars.* • *When you've finished your lunch, you can go and play.*
4 if you play a record, radio etc, or it plays, it produces music or sounds: *The DJ played some great records.* • *My favourite song was playing on the radio.*
5 to take part in a film, programme, or play as one of the characters in it: *Brad Pitt* ***played*** *the hero* ***in the film.***

PHRASES
play a part, play a role if something plays a part or role in something, it is one of several causes that makes it happen: *Alcohol* ***played a part in*** *the accident.*
play a trick, play a joke to do something to surprise or trick someone: *They* ***played a stupid trick on*** *me.*

PHRASAL VERBS
play around
1 to do silly things when you should be serious: *Stop* ***playing around*** *there at the back!*
2 play around with something to try different ways of doing something: *You can* ***play around with*** *the picture on the computer screen.*
play at
play at something a) to not do something seriously or properly: *They're just* ***playing at*** *running a business.* **b)** *BrE* to pretend to be something as part of a game: *The kids are* ***playing at*** *soldiers.*
play back
play something back to play part of a programme, song etc that you have recorded, in order to watch or listen to it again: *When they* ***played back*** *the goal again, you could see it was offside.*
play down
play something down to try to make something seem less important than it really is: *He tried to* ***play down*** *the fact that there had been a fight.*
play up *BrE* (informal)
if children play up, they behave badly SYNONYM **act up** *AmE*

play² *noun*
1 a story that is written to be performed by actors: *'Murder in the Cathedral' is a play by TS Eliot.* • *Are you* ***in*** *the school* ***play****?* • *My class is going to* ***put on a play*** (=perform a play).
2 the activity of doing things you enjoy for fun, especially when you are a child: *We all need time for work and play.*

play·er /ˈpleɪə $ ˈpleɪər/ *noun*
1 someone who plays a game or sport: *one of the top tennis players*

A B C D E F G H I J K L M N O **P** Q R S T U V W X Y Z

2 someone who plays a musical instrument: *a horn player*

play·ful /ˈpleɪfəl/ *adjective* very active and happy: *a playful little kitten*

play·ground /ˈpleɪgraʊnd/ *noun* an outdoor area connected to a school where children play

play·group /ˈpleɪgruːp/ *noun BrE* a place where children can go to play and learn in the years before they go to school SYNONYM **pre-school** *AmE*

ˈplaying ˌfield *noun* an area used for playing sports SYNONYM **pitch** *BrE*

play·time /ˈpleɪtaɪm/ *noun* the time when children at school can play SYNONYM **recess** *AmE*

play·wright /ˈpleɪraɪt/ *noun* someone who writes plays SYNONYM **dramatist**

plea /pliː/ *noun* **1** an urgent request for something: *Neighbours ignored her desperate pleas for help.* **2** (formal) in a law court, the answer someone gives when they are asked whether they are guilty or not guilty of a crime: *a plea of not guilty*

plead /pliːd/ *verb* (past tense and past participle **pleaded** or **pled** /pled/) **1** to ask for something in a very strong way, with a lot of emotion SYNONYM **beg**: *Sarah pleaded with him to stay.*
2 (formal) to say officially in a law court whether or not you are guilty of a crime: *"How do you plead?" "Not guilty."*

pleas·ant /ˈplezənt/ *adjective*
1 enjoyable or nice ANTONYM **unpleasant**: *The village is a pleasant place to live.* • *The weather in June is very pleasant.* → see Thesaurus at NICE
2 polite and friendly ANTONYM **unpleasant**: *Our boss is always very pleasant to us.* —**pleasantly** *adverb*: *I was pleasantly surprised to see Max.*

please¹ /pliːz/
used when you are politely asking for something: *Please don't be late.* • *Can I have a drink of water, please?*
PHRASES
yes, please (spoken) used to politely say that you want something that someone offers you: *"Another cookie?" "Yes, please!"*

GRAMMAR
You say **Please sit down.**
✘ Don't say 'Please to sit down.'

please² *verb*
to make someone feel happy or satisfied ANTONYM **displease**: *She tries hard to please her parents.*
PHRASES
whatever you please, as you please, as she pleases etc used to say that someone can do anything they want: *When you've finished your work, you can do **whatever you please**.* • *Women should be able to dress **as they please**.*

pleased /pliːzd/ *adjective*

KEY PATTERNS
pleased with someone (for doing something)
pleased with progress/the result
pleased to hear/see something
pleased that
pleased about something

happy or satisfied: *Mom **was pleased with** me **for** cleaning my room.* • *I'm really **pleased with** my new haircut.* • *I'm so **pleased to** hear that you're coming.* • *Are you **pleased that** Joe got the job?* • *He wasn't very **pleased about** what happened.* → see Thesaurus at HAPPY
PHRASES
(I'm) pleased to meet you (spoken) something that you say to be polite when you meet someone for the first time

plea·sur·a·ble /ˈpleʒərəbəl/ *adjective* (formal) enjoyable ANTONYM **unpleasant**: *Preparing a meal should be a pleasurable experience.*

plea·sure /ˈpleʒə $ ˈpleʒər/ *noun* (no plural)
a feeling of happiness, satisfaction, or enjoyment that something gives you: *Seeing her grandchildren **gives** her a lot of **pleasure**.* • *He draws and paints **for pleasure**.*
PHRASES
it's a pleasure, it's my pleasure (spoken) used to reply politely to someone who has thanked you: *"Thanks for your help." "**It's a pleasure.**"*

pleat /pliːt/ *noun* a narrow flat fold in a piece of clothing

pleat·ed /ˈpliːtɪd/ *adjective* a pleated skirt, dress etc has lots of pleats

pled a past tense and past participle of PLEAD

pledge /pledʒ/ *verb* (formal) to make a formal promise to do something: *The mayor is pledging to reduce crime.* • *European nations pledged $1 billion to help the earthquake victims.*

plen·ti·ful /ˈplentɪfəl/ *adjective* if something is plentiful, there is a large amount of it: *plentiful supplies of fresh water* —**plentifully** *adverb*: *The bar was plentifully stocked with wine.*

plen·ty¹ /ˈplenti/ *noun* (no plural)

KEY PATTERNS
have plenty of time/money/energy

quite a lot or more than enough: *We've got* ***plenty of*** *time left.* • *She has* ***plenty*** *of confidence.* • *You'll have* ***plenty to*** *talk about.* • *They've got* ***plenty more*** *work to keep them busy.*

plenty² *adverb*
plenty more (spoken, informal) a lot more, so that there is enough or more than enough: *There's* ***plenty more*** *pizza if anyone's still hungry.*

pli·ers /ˈplaɪəz $ ˈplaɪərz/ *plural noun* a tool for cutting wire or pulling nails out of wood: *a pair of pliers*

plight /plaɪt/ *noun* when someone is in a difficult or dangerous situation: *the plight of homeless young people*

plod /plɒd $ plɑd/ *verb* (**plodded**, **plodding**) to move or do something slowly, because you are tired or bored: *Neil plodded through the snow.*

plot¹ /plɒt $ plɑt/ *noun* **1** a secret plan to do something bad: *a plot to kill the king* ➔ see Thesaurus at PLAN¹ **2** the main events in a book, film, or play: *The plot is difficult to follow.*

plot² *verb* (**plotted**, **plotting**) to plan secretly to do something bad: *The three men had plotted to rob a bank.*

plough¹ *BrE*, **plow** *AmE* /plaʊ/ *noun* a large machine that is used on farms to turn over the soil before crops are planted

plough² *BrE*, **plow** *AmE verb* **1** to turn over the soil with a plough so that seeds can be planted: *They ploughed the field near the river this morning.* **2** to hit something with a lot of force: *The plane ploughed into electricity lines.* **3 plough on** to continue doing something, even though it is difficult: *We were tired but ploughed on anyway.*

ploy /plɔɪ/ *noun* a dishonest but clever way of getting what you want: *He's not really ill – it's just a ploy to avoid going to school.*

pluck /plʌk/ *verb* **1** (written) to pull something quickly to remove it from its place: *She plucked a rose from her garden.* **2 pluck up the courage** to decide to do something difficult or unpleasant, which you were not brave enough to do before: *I finally plucked up the courage to audition for the play.*

plug¹ /plʌg/ *noun* **1** the thing that you use to connect a piece of electrical equipment to the electricity supply **2** a round flat piece of rubber used for blocking the hole in a bath or SINK

plug² *verb* (**plugged**, **plugging**) **1** also **plug up** to fill or block a hole: *I managed to plug most of the leaks round the bath.* **2 plug something in, plug something into something** to connect a piece of equipment to the electricity supply, or to another piece of equipment ANTONYM **unplug**: *Plug the printer into the back of your laptop.*

ˌplug-and-ˈplay *noun* a system in which a computer and a new piece of equipment can be used together as soon as they are connected —**plug-and-play** *adjective*: *the development of plug-and-play technology*

plug·hole /ˈplʌghəʊl $ ˈplʌghoʊl/ *noun BrE* a hole in a bath or SINK, where the water can flow out SYNONYM **drain** *AmE*

ˈplug-in¹ *adjective* able to be connected to the electricity supply, or to another piece of electrical equipment: *a plug-in microphone*

plug-in² *noun* a piece of software that you can add to software that you already have, so that your computer system can do more things: *This*

A B C D E F G H I J K L M N O P Q R S T U V W X Y Z

plug-in allows you to correct the colour balance of your photos.

plum /plʌm/ *noun* a soft round fruit, which is purple, red, or yellow, and has a large seed in the middle ➔ see picture on page A7

plumb·er /ˈplʌmə $ ˈplʌmɚ/ *noun* someone whose job is to repair water pipes, toilets etc

plumb·ing /ˈplʌmɪŋ/ *noun* (no plural) the system of water pipes in a building

plume /pluːm/ *noun* **1** a small cloud of smoke or dust that is moving upwards: *a plume of smoke* **2** a large feather: *ostrich plumes*

plump /plʌmp/ *adjective* slightly fat: *Dora's not fat, she's just a little plump.* ➔ see Thesaurus at FAT[1]

plun·der /ˈplʌndə $ ˈplʌndɚ/ *verb* (written) to steal or take large amounts of money or things from somewhere: *Foreign armies plundered and burned the city.*

plunge[1] /plʌndʒ/ *verb* to fall or move quickly down with a lot of force, especially into water: *The workman plunged 200 feet from the bridge.*

plunge[2] *noun* when something suddenly becomes much lower in value: *a plunge in the price of shares in some companies*

plu·per·fect /pluːˈpɜːfɪkt $ pluˈpɚfɪkt/ *noun* **the pluperfect** the PAST PERFECT

plu·ral /ˈplʊərəl $ ˈplʊrəl/ *noun* the form of a word that shows you are talking about more than one person, thing, etc, which is usually formed by adding 's'. For example, 'dogs' is the plural of 'dog', and 'children' is the plural of 'child' ANTONYM **singular**

plus[1] /plʌs/ *preposition* used to show that one number or amount is added to another. In calculations, plus is written as + ANTONYM **minus**: *Three plus 6 equals 9.*

plus[2] *adjective* **1** more than the number or amount you have mentioned: *Donna makes £30,000 a year plus.* **2 plus or minus** used to say how much more or less an amount can be: *The price may vary by plus or minus 5%.*

plus[3] *noun* something that is an advantage, or a quality that you think is good: *Politeness is always a plus when you first meet someone.*

plu·to·ni·um /pluːˈtəʊniəm $ pluˈtoʊniəm/ *noun* (no plural) a metal used for producing NUCLEAR power

ply·wood /ˈplaɪwʊd/ *noun* (no plural) a board made from several layers of thin wood

pm, p.m. /ˌpiː ˈem/ **2 pm, 11 pm etc** 2 or 11 o'clock in the afternoon or evening, not in the morning: *We should get back by 8:30 pm.*

pneu·mo·ni·a /njuːˈməʊniə $ nʊˈmoʊnjə/ *noun* (no plural) a serious lung disease

pock·et[1] /ˈpɒkɪt $ ˈpɑkɪt/ *noun*

> KEY PATTERNS
> **have/put something in your pocket**
> **take something out of your pocket**

part of a piece of clothing that is like a small flat bag, for keeping small things in: *He* ***took*** *some money* ***out of the pocket*** *of his jeans.* • *I* ***put*** *my hands* ***in*** *my coat* ***pockets****.*

pocket[2] also **ˈpocket-ˌsized** *adjective* small enough to fit into a pocket: *a pocket knife*

ˈpocket ˌmoney *noun BrE* money given to children by their parents to spend on things such as sweets SYNONYM **allowance** *AmE*

pod /pɒd $ pɑd/ *noun* the long thin object containing seeds that grows on some plants: *a pea pod*

pod·cast /ˈpɒdkɑːst $ ˈpɑdˌkæst/ *noun* a file that you can DOWNLOAD from the Internet, which contains words, music, film etc that you can listen to or watch on your computer, MP3 PLAYER, phone etc: *The show is available as a podcast.* —**podcaster** *noun* —**podcasting** *noun*

po·di·um /ˈpəʊdiəm $ ˈpoʊdiəm/ *noun* a small raised area on which a performer or speaker stands: *The orchestra's conductor stepped up to the podium.*

po·em /ˈpəʊɪm $ ˈpoʊəm/ *noun* a piece of writing in which the words are chosen for their sound or beauty, and arranged in short lines: *a poem by John Keats*

po•et /ˈpəʊɪt $ ˈpoʊɪt/ *noun* someone who writes poems

po•et•ic /pəʊˈetɪk $ poʊˈetɪk/ *adjective* relating to or typical of poetry: *poetic language*

po•et•ry /ˈpəʊətri $ ˈpoʊətri/ *noun* (no plural) poems in general: *I like modern poetry best.*

poi•gnant /ˈpɔɪnjənt/ *adjective* (formal) making you have strong feelings of sadness: *a poignant farewell*

point[1] /pɔɪnt/ *noun*

KEY PATTERNS
at this/that/one point
a point in the future/story/ conversation etc
reach a point where/when
the point of doing something

1 a fact or idea that someone talks or writes about: *What were the main points in the article? • That's a very **good point**.*
2 the point what is really important in a situation: ***The point is**, we can't go because we weren't invited. • I don't want to marry him – **that's the point**.*
3 a time in a process or series of events when something happens: ***At that point**, I decided to leave. • I fell asleep **at one point in the film**. • Things have **reached the point where** they won't even talk to each other.*
4 an exact position or place: *You can cross the river easily **at this point**.*
5 the purpose or reason for doing something: ***The point of** going to college is to learn.*
6 the sharp end of something: ***The point of** a needle*
7 a unit used for showing the score in a game or competition: *You **get a point** for each correct answer.*
8 (spoken) the sign (.) used for separating a whole number from the DECIMALS that follow it: *He weighs 65 point 5 (=65.5) kilos.*

PHRASES

there's no point, what's the point used to say that an action will not succeed or will not achieve anything useful: ***There's no point** asking him – he doesn't know. • **What's the point** in talking to you when you don't listen?*
miss the point to not understand what is really important in a situation: *You're **missing the point** – the whole plan was wrong from the beginning.*
the high point, the low point the best or worst part of something: *Getting divorced was **the low point** of my life.*
good points, bad points, weak points etc things about a person or thing that are good, bad etc: *The movie did **have** some **good points**.*
boiling point, freezing point the temperature at which something boils or freezes: *The water has reached **boiling point**.*
make a point (about something) to show that your idea or opinion is right: *I was exaggerating to **make a point**.*
make a point of doing something to do something deliberately or carefully: *She **made a point of** telling everyone that I had failed my driving test.*
to the point mentioning only the most important thing, and not anything else: *His speech was short and **to the point**.*

point[2] *verb*

KEY PATTERNS
point at someone/something
point a finger/gun etc at someone
point to a sign/picture/door etc
point towards south/north/downtown etc

1 to move your finger in the direction of something in order to show it to someone: *He **pointed to** a blonde girl and said, "That's my girlfriend." • Everyone **pointed at** the car and laughed. • The teacher **pointed** her pen **at** me and said, "Stand up."*
2 to be facing a particular direction, or to move something so that it faces a particular direction: *He saw a sign **pointing towards** the motorway.*

PHRASAL VERBS

point out
1 point something out to tell someone about a mistake that they had not noticed or a fact they had not thought about: *She **pointed out that** I had made a mistake.*
2 point something/someone out to point at a person or thing so that people will know who they are or where they are: *Geoff **pointed out** his sister on the dance floor.*

ˌpoint-ˈblank *adverb* **1** if you say something point-blank, you do it directly without trying to explain your reasons: *I asked him point-blank where he'd been.* **2** a gun fired point-blank is fired very close to the person or thing it is aimed at —**point-blank** *adjective*: *Ken was shot at point-blank range.*

point·ed /ˈpɔɪntɪd/ *adjective* having a point at the end: *a dog with pointed ears*

point·er /ˈpɔɪntə $ ˈpɔɪntɚ/ *noun* a helpful piece of advice SYNONYM **tip**: *Sharon may be able to give you some pointers on where to find information.*

point·less /ˈpɔɪntləs/ *adjective* without any sense or purpose: *There is too much pointless violence on TV.*

ˌpoint of ˈview *noun* your personal opinion about something: *We share the same point of view on music.* • *The story is told from a 14-year-old's point of view.* ➔ see Thesaurus at OPINION

poised /pɔɪzd/ *adjective* ready to move or do something: *The army was poised to attack.*

poi·son¹ /ˈpɔɪzən/ *noun* a substance that can kill or harm you if you eat it, drink it etc: *The plant's leaves contain a poison.* • *rat poison* (=a substance used to kill rats)

poison² *verb* **1** to kill or harm someone by giving them poison: *Nobody knows who poisoned him.* **2** to damage or harm water, land, air etc by adding dangerous chemicals to it: *Toxic waste has poisoned many rivers in the area.*

poi·son·ing /ˈpɔɪzənɪŋ/ *noun* when someone swallows, touches, or breathes a substance that contains poison and it makes them ill: *lead poisoning*

poi·son·ous /ˈpɔɪzənəs/ *adjective* containing poison: *poisonous chemicals*

poke /pəʊk $ poʊk/ *verb* **1** to press something quickly, using your finger or a pointed object: *He poked at his food with his knife.* **2** to appear, or make something appear, through an opening: *Her toe poked through a hole in her sock.* • *David poked his head around the door.* —**poke** *noun*: *He gave me a poke in the shoulder.*

pok·er /ˈpəʊkə $ ˈpoʊkɚ/ *noun* **1** (no plural) a card game that people usually play for money **2** a metal stick that you use for moving wood or coal in a fire

pok·y, pokey /ˈpəʊki $ ˈpoʊki/ *adjective* (informal) too small: *a poky apartment*

po·lar /ˈpəʊlə $ ˈpoʊlɚ/ *adjective* related to the North or South Pole: *the polar ice caps*

ˌpolar ˈbear / $ ˈ.. ˌ./ *noun* a large white bear that lives near the North Pole ➔ see picture on page A9

pole /pəʊl $ poʊl/ *noun* **1** a long round piece of wood or metal: *tent poles* **2 North Pole, South Pole** the most northern or southern point on Earth

ˈpole vault *noun* (no plural) a sport in which you jump over a high bar using a special long pole

po·lice¹ /pəˈliːs/ *noun* **the police** the official organization whose job is to catch criminals and make sure that people obey the law: *Have the police caught the person who stole your car?* • *a police car*

police² *verb* if the police or the army police an area or an event, they make sure that people obey the law: *A United Nations force is policing the area.*

poˈlice force *noun* the official police organization in a country or area: *The city is proud of its police force.*

po·lice·man /pəˈliːsmən/ *noun* (plural **policemen** /-mən/) a man who is a member of the police

poˈlice ˌofficer *noun* a member of the police

poˈlice ˌstation *noun* the building used by police who work in an area

po·lice·wom·an /pəˈliːsˌwʊmən/ *noun* (plural **policewomen** /-ˌwɪmɪn/) a woman who is a member of the police

po·li·o /ˈpəʊliəʊ $ ˈpoʊliˌoʊ/ *noun* (no plural) a serious disease that makes you unable to move your muscles

pol·ish¹ /ˈpɒlɪʃ $ ˈpɑlɪʃ/ *noun* a substance used for polishing things: *shoe polish*

polish² *verb* **1** to make something clean and shiny by rubbing polish into it with a cloth or brush: *Dad polished his shoes.* **2 polish something off** (informal) to quickly eat or finish all of something: *Jim polished off the rest of the cake.*

po·lite /pəˈlaɪt/ *adjective*

KEY PATTERNS
be polite to someone
it is polite to do something

someone who is polite speaks or behaves in a way that is not rude and shows respect for other people ANTONYM **impolite**, **rude**: *Kevin is a very polite young man.* • *You should be more polite to our neighbours.* • ***It is polite to*** *stand up so that older people can sit down.* —**politely** *adverb*: *"Excuse me," she said politely.*

po·lit·i·cal /pəˈlɪtɪkəl/ *adjective* **1** related to politics and the government: *The US has two main political parties.* **2** interested in or involved in politics: *I'm not a political person.* —**politically** /-kli/ *adverb*

poˌlitical aˈsylum *noun* (no plural) the right to stay in another country because your political activities make it dangerous for you to live in your own country

poˌlitically corˈrect (abbreviation **PC**) *adjective* very careful not to offend people who belong to a particular group

pol·i·ti·cian /ˌpɒləˈtɪʃən $ ˌpɑləˈtɪʃən/ *noun* someone who works in politics, especially a member of a parliament (=the group of people elected to make a country's laws): *The idea is supported by politicians of all parties.*

pol·i·tics /ˈpɒlətɪks $ ˈpɑlətɪks/ *noun* (no plural)
ideas and activities that are concerned with government and power in a country or area: *She wanted a career in politics.*

poll /pəʊl $ poʊl/ also **opinion poll** *noun* when a lot of people are asked a question in order to find out what they think about something SYNONYM **survey**: *Recent polls show that the mayor is still popular.*

pol·len /ˈpɒlən $ ˈpɑlən/ *noun* (no plural) a powder produced by flowers, which is carried by the wind or insects to make other flowers produce seeds

pol·li·nate /ˈpɒləneɪt $ ˈpɑləˌneɪt/ *verb* to make a flower or plant produce seeds by giving it pollen

ˈpolling ˌday *noun* the day when people vote in an election

pol·lute /pəˈluːt/ *verb* to make the air, water, or land dirty or dangerous: *The oil has polluted many beaches.*

pol·lut·ed /pəˈluːtɪd/ *adjective* polluted air, water, or land is dirty and dangerous because harmful chemicals are in it: *polluted rivers*

pollution

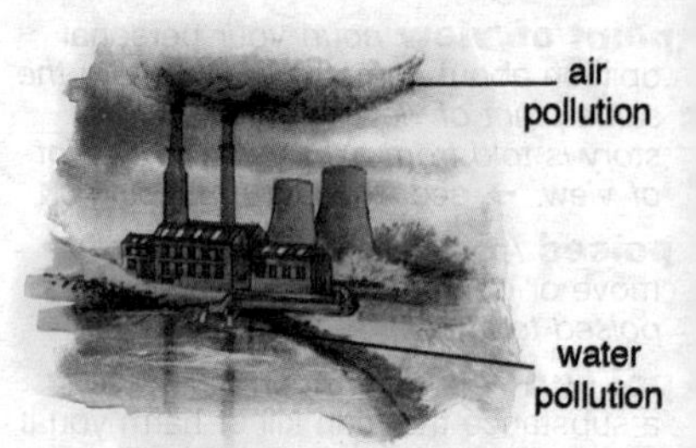

pol·lu·tion /pəˈluːʃən/ *noun* (no plural) harmful chemicals and waste, and the damage they cause to the environment: *Plants and fish are dying because of pollution.* • ***Air pollution*** *is worst in big cities.*

SPELLING
This word is often spelled wrongly. The correct spelling is: **pollution**.

po·lo neck /ˈpəʊləʊ ˌnek $ ˈpoʊloʊ ˌnek/ *noun BrE* a SWEATER with a high band at the top that covers most of your neck SYNONYM **turtleneck** *AmE*

pol·y·sty·rene /ˌpɒlɪˈstaɪriːn $ ˌpɑliˈstaɪrin/ *noun* (no plural) a very light plastic material, used especially to make containers or to pack things safely

pom·pous /ˈpɒmpəs $ ˈpɑmpəs/ *adjective* someone who is pompous behaves or speaks in a formal way so that people think they are more important than they really are: *a pompous politician* —**pompously** *adverb*

pond /pɒnd $ pɑnd/ *noun* a small area of water in a garden, field, or wood

pon•der /'pɒndə $ 'pɑndɚ/ *verb* (formal) to think carefully and seriously about something SYNONYM **consider**: *He pondered the problem for a long time.*

po•ny /'pəʊni $ 'poʊni/ *noun* (plural **ponies**) a small horse

po•ny•tail /'pəʊniteɪl $ 'poʊniˌteɪl/ *noun* long hair tied at the back of your head so that it hangs down: *Kim's hair was pulled back in a ponytail.* ➔ see picture at HAIRSTYLE

poo•dle /'puːdl/ *noun* a type of dog with thick curly hair

pool¹ /puːl/ *noun*
1 a place that has been made for people to swim in SYNONYM **swimming pool**: *They have a pool in their back garden.*
2 a pool of water, blood etc is a small area of it somewhere: *There was **a pool of oil** under the motorbike.*
3 (no plural) a game in which you use a long stick to hit numbered balls into holes at the edge of a table. You play or shoot pool

pool² *verb* if people pool their money, knowledge etc, they put it all together in order to share it: *We pooled our money and bought a new TV.*

poor /pʊə $ pʊr/ *adjective*
1 someone who is poor has very little money and does not own many things ANTONYM **rich**, **wealthy**: *We were so poor we couldn't afford to heat the house properly.* • *He came from a poor background* (=from a family that had very little money).
2 something that is poor is not as good as it should be: *His schoolwork has been poor recently.*
3 (spoken) used to show that you feel sorry for someone: *Poor Ted had no idea what was happening.*

poor•ly¹ /'pʊəli $ 'pʊrli/ *adverb* badly: *a poorly paid job*

poorly² *adjective BrE* (informal) ill: *Are you feeling poorly?*

pop¹ /pɒp $ pɑp/ *verb* (**popped**, **popping**) **1** to make a sound like a small explosion: *The balloon popped.* **2 pop out, pop up** to suddenly appear from somewhere: *I saw Sergio's head pop out of the water.* **3** (spoken) to go somewhere for a short time: *I'm just popping out to my friend's house.*

pop² *noun* **1** (no plural) modern music that is popular with young people: *a pop singer* **2** a sound like a small explosion: *The cork came out of the bottle with a loud pop.* **3** (no plural) a sweet FIZZY drink such as LEMONADE

pop•corn /'pɒpkɔːn $ 'pɑpkɔrn/ *noun* (no plural) corn that is heated until it swells and bursts open and then is eaten

Pope /pəʊp $ poʊp/ *noun* **the Pope** the leader of the Roman Catholic Church

pop•py /'pɒpi $ 'pɑpi/ *noun* (plural **poppies**) a bright red flower with small black seeds ➔ see picture at FLOWER

pop•u•lar /'pɒpjələ $ 'pɑpjəlɚ/ *adjective*

KEY PATTERNS
popular with people

liked by a lot of people ANTONYM **unpopular**: *He's one of the most popular boys in the school.* • *The cafe is popular with young people.*

pop•u•lar•i•ty /ˌpɒpjə'lærəti $ ˌpɑpjə'lærəti/ *noun* (no plural) when a lot of people like someone or something: *Skiing has increased in popularity.*

pop•u•lar•ly /'pɒpjələli $ 'pɑpjəlɚli/ *adverb* **popularly believed, popularly known as etc** believed to be the case or called a particular name by many people: *Crime in this part of town is much more common than is popularly believed.*

pop•u•lat•ed /'pɒpjəleɪtɪd $ 'pɑpjəˌleɪtɪd/ *adjective* used to describe the type of people or the

A B C D E F G H I J K L M N O P Q R S T U V W X Y Z

A B C D E F G H I J K L M N O P Q R S T U V W X Y Z

number of people that live in an area: *England is a densely populated country.*

pop·u·la·tion /ˌpɒpjəˈleɪʃən $ ˌpɑpjəˈleɪʃən/ *noun* the people who live in a country or area, or the number of people there: *What's the population of Tokyo?* ➔ see Thesaurus at PEOPLE

ˈ**pop-up** *noun* a notice, often containing an advertisement, that suddenly appears on your computer screen when you are looking at a website

porce·lain /ˈpɔːslən $ ˈpɔrsəlɪn/ *noun* (no plural) a hard shiny white material that is used to make plates, cups etc: *a porcelain vase*

porch /pɔːtʃ $ pɔrtʃ/ *noun* an entrance to a building, which has a roof and walls

por·cu·pine /ˈpɔːkjəpaɪn $ ˈpɔrkjəˌpaɪn/ *noun* an animal with long sharp parts on its back and sides

pore[1] /pɔː $ pɔr/ *noun* one of the small holes in your skin that SWEAT can pass through

pore[2] *verb* **pore over something** to read or look at something very carefully for a long time: *He spent hours poring over the photographs.* ➔ see Thesaurus at READ

pork /pɔːk $ pɔrk/ *noun* (no plural) meat from a pig: *roast pork*

po·rous /ˈpɔːrəs/ *adjective* with small holes that allow liquid, air etc to pass through slowly: *It's best to keep your plants in pots made of a porous material such as clay.*

port /pɔːt $ pɔrt/ *noun* an area or town where ships arrive and leave from: *Liverpool is a large port.*

por·ta·ble /ˈpɔːtəbəl $ ˈpɔrtəbəl/ *adjective* portable televisions etc are small and easy to carry: *a portable stereo*

por·ter /ˈpɔːtə $ ˈpɔrtɚ/ *noun* someone whose job is to carry bags at an airport, station, or hotel

port·hole /ˈpɔːthəʊl $ ˈpɔrthoʊl/ *noun* a small round window in the side of a ship

por·tion /ˈpɔːʃən $ ˈpɔrʃən/ *noun* an amount of food for one person: *Two portions of fries, please.*

por·trait /ˈpɔːtrɪt $ ˈpɔrtrɪt/ *noun* a painting, drawing, or photograph of a person: *a portrait of the queen*

por·tray /pɔːˈtreɪ $ pɔrˈtreɪ/ *verb* (written) to describe or show something or someone in a story, film etc: *The film portrayed him as evil.*

pose /pəʊz $ poʊz/ *verb* **1 pose a problem, pose a danger etc** to cause a problem or danger: *The chemicals pose a risk to people.* **2** to sit or stand in a particular position in order to be photographed or painted: *In the photograph, a woman poses with her sleeping child.*

posh /pɒʃ $ pɑʃ/ *adjective* (informal) **1** expensive and used by rich people: *a posh hotel* **2** typical of people from a high social class: *a posh voice*

po·si·tion /pəˈzɪʃən/ *noun*

KEY PATTERNS
be in a strong/difficult etc position
someone's position on a matter

1 a good or bad situation that someone is in: *She is **in a** strong **position** because many people agree with her.* • *It's your fault that we are **in this position**.*
2 the way someone stands or sits: *Her back hurt because she was sitting in an uncomfortable position.*
3 the place that someone or something is in relation to other things: *If you get a stiff neck, try changing the position of your computer.*
4 the official opinion or attitude of a person or group about something: *What is the school's **position on** students wearing make-up?* ➔ see Thesaurus at OPINION
5 (formal) a job in an organization SYNONYM **post**: *We would like to offer you the position.* ➔ see Thesaurus at JOB

PHRASES
be in a position to do something (formal) to be able to do something: *We **are** not **in a position to** give you financial help.*
be in position if something or someone is in position, they are in the place where they should be: *Troops were **in position** on the border.*

pos·i·tive /ˈpɒzətɪv $ ˈpɑzətɪv/ *adjective*

KEY PATTERNS
positive (that)

1 very sure that something is true SYNONYM **certain**: *I'm* ***positive that*** *this is the right way home.* • *"Are you sure you saw Tim and Suzy together?" "Yes, positive."*
2 considering the good qualities of a situation or person and expecting success ANTONYM **negative**: *It's important to have a positive attitude towards your work.* • *His reaction to our suggestion was very positive.*
3 having a good or useful effect, especially on someone's character ANTONYM **negative**: *Living abroad has been a positive experience for Jim.*
4 a scientific or medical test that is positive shows signs that something is present or has happened ANTONYM **negative**: *She had a pregnancy test and the result was positive.*
5 greater than zero ANTONYM **negative**
6 a positive sentence does not contain a word such as 'not' or 'never'. For example, 'I saw Simon yesterday' is a positive sentence. ANTONYM **negative**

pos·i·tive·ly /ˈpɒzətɪvli $ ˈpɑzətɪvli/ *adverb* (spoken) used to emphasize what you are saying: *This is positively the worst party I've ever been to.*

pos·sess /pəˈzes/ *verb* (formal) to own or have something: *We lost everything we possessed in the fire.*

pos·ses·sion /pəˈzeʃən/ *noun* something that belongs to you: *Don't bring any valuable possessions with you on holiday.* • *His car is his favourite possession.* → see Thesaurus at PROPERTY

SPELLING
This word is often spelled wrongly. The correct spelling is: **possession**.

pos·ses·sive[1] /pəˈzesɪv/ *adjective*
1 not wanting to share someone's love or attention with other people: *He is very possessive about his wife.* **2** not wanting to share the things you own with other people

possessive[2] *noun* a word such as 'my', 'mine', 'your', or 'their', used to show who something belongs to

pos·si·bil·i·ty /ˌpɒsəˈbɪləti $ ˌpɑsəˈbɪləti/ *noun* (plural **possibilities**)

KEY PATTERNS
a possibility (that)
a possibility of (doing) something

1 something that may happen: ***There's a possibility that*** *we might go to America in the summer.* • *Do you think there's* ***any possibility of*** *another world war?*
2 something that may be true: *I think* ***there's a possibility that*** *George is lying to you.*
3 one of the things that you might try or choose to do: *I'm not sure what I want to study, but medicine is one possibility.*

pos·si·ble /ˈpɒsəbəl $ ˈpɑsəbəl/ *adjective*

KEY PATTERNS
it is possible to do something
it is possible (that)

1 if something is possible, people can do it ANTONYM **impossible**: ***Is it possible*** *to get a train to Bristol from here?*
2 something that is possible may happen ANTONYM **impossible**: ***It's possible that*** *Rod will be at the party too.*
3 something that is possible may be true ANTONYM **impossible**: *So you think Fiona is in London? Well,* ***it's certainly possible.***

PHRASES
if possible: ***If possible*** (=if you can), *could you phone me later today?*
as quickly as possible, as soon as possible etc: *You should see a doctor* ***as soon as possible*** (=as soon as you can).

pos·si·bly /ˈpɒsəbli $ ˈpɑsəbli/ *adverb* perhaps SYNONYM **maybe**: *"Are you going to the beach tomorrow?" "Possibly. It depends on the weather."*

PHRASES
can't possibly do something used to emphasize that someone cannot do something: *I* ***can't possibly*** *get there before six o'clock.*
as quickly as you possibly can, as much as you possibly can etc used to emphasize that you do something as quickly as you can etc: *I ran* ***as fast as I possibly could.***

A B C D E F G H I J K L M N O P Q R S T U V W X Y Z

post¹ /pəʊst $ poʊst/ *noun*
1 (no plural) *BrE* letters or packages that are delivered to your house, office etc SYNONYM **mail** *AmE*: *What time does the post come?* • *There's no post for you today.*
2 (no plural) *BrE* the system of sending and delivering letters, packages etc SYNONYM **mail** *AmE*: *A big parcel arrived* ***by post.*** • *I'll put these photographs* ***in the post.***
3 a narrow upright piece of wood or metal that is fixed in the ground: *Wooden posts supported the roof.*
4 (formal) a job in an organization SYNONYM **position**: *Simon has applied for a teaching post.* → see Thesaurus at JOB

post² *verb*

KEY PATTERNS
post a letter/package to someone
post someone a letter/package

BrE to send a letter or package to someone by post SYNONYM **mail** *AmE*: *Don't forget to* ***post*** *that letter* ***to*** *Mum.* • *I've* ***posted*** *Sally a birthday card.*

post·age /ˈpəʊstɪdʒ $ ˈpoʊstɪdʒ/ *noun* (no plural) the money you pay to send a letter or package by post

post·al /ˈpəʊstl $ ˈpoʊstl/ *adjective* related to sending letters or packages by post: *postal charges*

post·box /ˈpəʊstbɒks $ ˈpoʊstbɑks/ *noun BrE* (plural **postboxes**) a box in a public place where you put letters that you want to send SYNONYM **mailbox** *AmE* SYNONYM **letter box** *BrE*

post·card /ˈpəʊstkɑːd $ ˈpoʊstkɑrd/ *noun* a card with a picture on the front that you send without an envelope: *Mary sent us a postcard from Spain.*

post·code /ˈpəʊstkəʊd $ ˈpoʊstkoʊd/ *noun BrE* a group of letters and numbers that you put at the end of someone's address SYNONYM **zip code** *AmE*

post·er /ˈpəʊstə $ ˈpoʊstɚ/ *noun* a large notice or picture used to advertise something or as a decoration
→ see Thesaurus at ADVERTISEMENT
→ see picture at NOTICE²

pos·ter·i·ty /pɒˈsterəti $ pɑˈsterəti/ *noun* (no plural) (formal) the people who will live after you are dead: *I photographed the scene for posterity.*

post·grad·u·ate /ˌpəʊstˈgrædjuət $ ˌpoʊstˈgrædʒuət/ *noun BrE* someone who is studying at a university who has already done a degree SYNONYM **graduate student** *AmE*

post·man /ˈpəʊstmən $ ˈpoʊstmən/ *noun BrE* (plural **postmen** /-mən/) someone whose job is to collect and deliver letters SYNONYM **mailman** *AmE*

post·mark /ˈpəʊstmɑːk $ ˈpoʊstmɑrk/ *noun* a mark on an envelope that shows the place and time it was sent

post-mor·tem /ˌpəʊst ˈmɔːtəm $ ˌpoʊst ˈmɔrtəm/ *noun* an official medical examination of a dead body to discover why the person died

ˈpost ˌoffice *noun* a place where you can buy stamps and send letters and packages

post·pone /pəʊsˈpəʊn $ poʊsˈpoʊn/ *verb* to change an event to a later time or date: *The concert was postponed because of rain.* → see Thesaurus at DELAY¹

pos·ture /ˈpɒstʃə $ ˈpɑstʃɚ/ *noun* the way that you sit or stand: *Good posture is important if you want to avoid backache.*

pots

pot /pɒt $ pɑt/ *noun*
a round container, especially one for storing food or growing plants: *a pot of jam* • *a plant pot*

PHRASES
a pot of tea, a pot of coffee a container with hot tea or coffee in it: *I sat down and ordered* ***a pot of tea.***

po·ta·to /pəˈteɪtəʊ $ pəˈteɪtoʊ/ *noun* (plural **potatoes**) a round vegetable with a pale brown or yellow skin that grows under the ground ➔ see picture on page A6

SPELLING
The plural of this word is often spelled wrongly. The correct spelling is: **potatoes**.

po'tato chip the American word for CRISP[2]

po·tent /'pəʊtnt $ 'poʊtnt/ *adjective* (formal) strong or powerful: *This home-made wine is very potent.* • *Advertising has a potent influence on what we buy.*

po·ten·tial[1] /pə'tenʃəl/ *adjective* possible but not yet achieved: *We believe that Rob is a potential tennis champion.* —**potentially** *adverb*: *a potentially dangerous situation*

potential[2] *noun* (no plural) **1** natural qualities which could make someone very successful in the future: *She has great potential as a dancer.* **2** the possibility that something will develop or happen in a particular way: *There is always a potential for trouble at football games.*

pot·ter /'pɒtə $ 'pɑtɚ/ also **potter around/about** *verb BrE* to spend time doing unimportant but pleasant things: *I like just pottering around at home.*

pot·ter·y /'pɒtəri $ 'pɑtəri/ *noun* (no plural) pots, dishes etc made out of baked earth, or the art of making these

pot·ty /'pɒti $ 'pɑti/ *noun* (informal) (plural **potties**) a plastic pot that a very young child uses as a toilet

pouch /paʊtʃ/ *noun* (plural **pouches**) **1** a small bag **2** a pocket of skin that animals such as KANGAROOS carry their babies in

poul·try /'pəʊltri $ 'poʊltri/ *noun* (no plural) birds such as chickens and ducks that are kept on farms, or their meat

pounce /paʊns/ *verb* to suddenly jump towards a person or animal in order to catch them: *The cat pounced on a mouse.*

pound[1] /paʊnd/ *noun* **1** (written abbreviation **lb**) a unit for measuring weight, equal to 16 OUNCES or 453.6 grams: *a pound of apples* **2** (written sign **£**) the standard unit of money in Britain and some other countries: *The ticket cost me ten pounds.*

pound[2] *verb* **1** to hit something hard many times, making a lot of noise: *The police were pounding on the door.* **2** if your heart pounds, it beats very quickly: *My heart was pounding as I walked towards her.*

pour /pɔː $ pɔr/ *verb*

KEY PATTERNS
pour water/coffee etc into/onto/over something
pour someone a drink
water/blood etc pours from/out of something

1 to make a liquid flow out of a container, often into another container: *Jane* ***poured*** *some more coffee* ***into*** *our mugs.* • *Shall I pour you a glass of wine?* • *Simon poured drinks for everyone.* ➔ see picture on page A4
2 if liquid pours somewhere, it flows very quickly: *Blood was* ***pouring from*** *a cut on his head.* • *Water was* ***pouring out of*** *the tank.* ➔ see Thesaurus at FLOW[2]

PHRASES
it's pouring, it's pouring with rain *BrE* it's raining a lot

pov·er·ty /'pɒvəti $ 'pɑvɚti/ *noun* (no plural) when people do not have enough money: *Millions of people are living in poverty.*

pow·der /'paʊdə $ 'paʊdɚ/ *noun* a dry substance in the form of very small grains: *washing powder*

pow·er[1] /'paʊə $ 'paʊɚ/ *noun*

KEY PATTERNS
have the power to do something

1 someone who has power is important and is able to control people and events: *All his life he'd wanted power and money.* • *a position of power* • *Parliament* ***has the power to*** *make new laws.*
2 (no plural) energy that is used to make a machine work, or to give light, heat etc: *We use solar power* (=energy from the sun) *to heat the house.*

PHRASES
be in power: *Which political party is in power* (=has political control) *in the US?*

A B C D E F G H I J K L M N O P Q R S T U V W X Y Z

power² *verb* to supply power to a machine: *The camera is powered by a small battery.*

pow•er•ful /ˈpaʊəfəl $ ˈpaʊɚfəl/ *adjective*
1 a powerful person is important and has a lot of control over people or situations: *The king was the most powerful person in the country.*
2 something that is powerful is very strong or has a strong effect: *a powerful engine • It's a very powerful poem.*

pow•er•less /ˈpaʊələs $ ˈpaʊɚləs/ *adjective* unable to stop or control something: *I was powerless to stop the car as it rolled down the hill.*

ˈpower ˌstation also **ˈpower ˌplant** *noun* a building where electricity is made

pp the written abbreviation of 'pages': *Read pp 20–35.*

PR /ˌpiː ˈɑː $ ˌpi ˈɑr/ PUBLIC RELATIONS

prac•ti•cal¹ /ˈpræktɪkəl/ *adjective*
1 work that is practical involves doing things rather than thinking or talking about them ANTONYM **theoretical**: *Science involves a lot of practical work in the laboratory. • practical skills such as carpentry*
2 sensible and likely to be effective ANTONYM **impractical**: *Don't ask Peter to help – he's not very practical! • We need a practical solution.*
3 useful and suitable for a particular purpose ANTONYM **impractical**: *You'll need plenty of clothes that are practical for cold wet weather.*

practical² *noun BrE* a lesson or test where you do or make something, rather than reading, writing, or answering questions: *a physics practical*

ˌpractical ˈjoke *noun* a trick to surprise someone and make other people laugh at them

prac•ti•cally /ˈpræktɪkli/ *adverb*
1 (spoken) almost: *These shoes are practically new.* **2** in a sensible way: *You need to think about this more practically.*

prac•tice /ˈpræktɪs/ *noun* (no plural) when you do something regularly in order to improve your skill at it: *Learning a musical instrument takes a lot of practice. • We go to football practice every week.*

PHRASES
be out of practice to have not done something for a long time, so that you cannot do it well or easily now: *I'm not sure that I can run ten kilometres now – I'm very **out of practice**.*

prac•tise *BrE*, **practice** *AmE* /ˈpræktɪs/ *verb*

> **KEY PATTERNS**
> **practise (doing) something**
> **practise for something**

to do something in order to improve your skill at it: *I have to practice playing the trumpet every day. • The students are busy **practising for** the Christmas play.*

prac•tis•ing *BrE*, **practicing** *AmE* /ˈpræktəsɪŋ/ *adjective* **practising Catholic, practising Jew etc** someone who obeys the rules of a particular religion

prai•rie /ˈpreəri $ ˈpreri/ *noun* a large area of flat land in North America that is covered in grass

praise¹ /preɪz/ *verb*

> **KEY PATTERNS**
> **praise someone/something**
> **praise someone for (doing) something**

to say that someone has done something well, or that something is good ANTONYM **criticize**: *Everyone praised her cooking. • General Simms **praised** the men **for** their bravery. • Mrs Watts **praised** all the children **for** working so hard.*

praise² *noun* (no plural) things you say to praise someone or something ANTONYM **criticism**: *Her novel has won the praise of critics.*

pram /præm/ *noun BrE* a thing that a small baby lies in, with wheels so you can push it around SYNONYM **baby carriage** *AmE*

prawn /prɔːn/ *noun* a small sea animal with ten legs whose body you can eat SYNONYM **shrimp** *AmE*

pray /preɪ/ *verb* **1** to ask or thank God for something: *Let us pray for peace.* **2** to hope for something very strongly: *We're praying for good weather for the wedding.*

pray·er /preə $ prer/ *noun* words that you say to God: *We used to say our prayers every night.*

preach /priːtʃ/ *verb* to give a religious speech, usually in a church: *He preached about love.* —**preacher** *noun*: *The preacher spoke out against war.*

pre·cau·tion /prɪˈkɔːʃən/ *noun* something that you do to prevent something bad or dangerous from happening: *I took the precaution of locking the door before I left.*

pre·cede /prɪˈsiːd/ *verb* (formal) to happen or exist before something else: *Mr Clark preceded Miss Lee as head teacher.* —**preceding** *adjective* (formal): *Her new album was number one the preceding week.*

pre·ce·dence /ˈpresədəns/ *noun* **take precedence over something** (formal) to be more important than something else SYNONYM **take priority**: *For me, education takes precedence over everything else.*

pre·ce·dent /ˈpresədənt/ *noun* (formal) an action or decision that can be used as an example when saying that similar actions or decisions that happen later are correct: *The result of his trial set a precedent for similar cases.*

pre·cinct /ˈpriːsɪŋkt/ *noun* **1 shopping precinct, pedestrian precinct** *BrE* an area of a town where there are shops and cars are not allowed **2** *AmE* a part of a city that has its own police force, local government etc: *the 12th precinct*

pre·cious /ˈpreʃəs/ *adjective* extremely valuable: *Gold and silver are precious metals.* • *Your time is precious.*

pre·ci·pice /ˈpresəpɪs/ *noun* a very steep side of a mountain or cliff

pre·cise /prɪˈsaɪs/ *adjective* exact and correct: *He gave us precise details of how to get there.* • *I think it was nine or ten o'clock – I'm sorry I can't be more precise.*

pre·cise·ly /prɪˈsaɪsli/ *adverb* exactly: *That's precisely what I mean.* • *The judge came into the courtroom at precisely 8:55 am.*

pre·ci·sion /prɪˈsɪʒən/ *noun* (no plural) when something is measured or described very exactly: *This watch keeps time with incredible precision.*

pre·con·ceived /ˌpriːkənˈsiːvd/ *adjective* if you have preconceived ideas about something, you have ideas about it before you know what it is really like: *People often arrive in India with preconceived ideas about the country.*

pred·a·tor /ˈpredətə $ ˈpredətɚ/ *noun* an animal that kills and eats other animals

pre·de·ces·sor /ˈpriːdəsesə $ ˈpredəˌsesɚ/ *noun* your predecessor is the person who had your job before you ANTONYM **successor**: *My predecessor worked here for ten years.*

pre·dic·a·ment /prɪˈdɪkəmənt/ *noun* if you are in a predicament, you are in a difficult situation and you do not know what to do

pre·dict /prɪˈdɪkt/ *verb* to say that something will happen: *His teachers predicted that he would get high grades.*

pre·dict·a·ble /prɪˈdɪktəbəl/ *adjective* behaving or happening in the way that you expect, and not at all interesting: *The ending of the film was so predictable.* —**predictably** *adverb*: *Predictably, a crowd gathered to watch the fire.*

pre·dic·tion /prɪˈdɪkʃən/ *noun* when you say what you think will happen in the future: *Here are our predictions for next year's fashions.*

pre·dom·i·nant·ly /prɪˈdɒmənəntli $ prɪˈdɑmənəntli/ *adverb* (formal) mostly or mainly: *The students here are predominantly boys.*

pref·ace /ˈprefəs/ *noun* an introduction at the beginning of a book

pre·fect /ˈpriːfekt/ *noun BrE* an older student who has special powers and duties in a school

pre·fer /prɪˈfɜː $ prɪˈfɚ/ *verb* (**preferred, preferring**)

KEY PATTERNS
prefer something (to something else)
prefer doing something
prefer to do something

A B C D E F G H I J K L M N O **P** Q R S T U V W X Y Z

to like one thing or person more than another: *I **prefer** football **to** cricket.* • *Do you prefer travelling by train or car?* • *I'd **prefer to** stay at home today.*
→ see Thesaurus at LIKE[1]

pref·e·ra·ble /'prefərəbəl/ *adjective* better or more suitable: *Even a short walk is preferable to no exercise.*

pref·e·ra·bly /'prefərəbli/ *adverb* used to say what would be the best or most suitable: *The form needs to be signed by an adult, preferably your teacher.*

pref·e·rence /'prefərəns/ *noun* (formal) when someone likes one thing more than other things: *There are several movies we could see tonight – do you have a preference?*

pre·fix /'priːfɪks/ *noun* (plural **prefixes**) a group of letters added to the beginning of a word to make a new word

preg·nan·cy /'pregnənsi/ *noun* (plural **pregnancies**) when someone is pregnant: *The study shows that most teenage pregnancies are accidents.*

preg·nant /'pregnənt/ *adjective* if a woman or female animal is pregnant, she has a baby growing in her body: *She got pregnant soon after they were married.*

pre·his·tor·ic /ˌpriːhɪ'stɒrɪk $ ˌprihɪ'stɔrɪk/ *adjective* related to the time a long way in the past before anything was written down: *prehistoric cave paintings*

prej·u·dice /'predʒədɪs/ *noun* an unfair opinion about someone that is not based on facts or reason: *There's still a lot of prejudice against disabled people.*

prej·u·diced /'predʒədɪst/ *adjective* having an unfair attitude towards someone or something, so that you dislike them without any good reason: *She is prejudiced against me just because I am young.*

pre·lim·i·na·ry /prɪ'lɪmənəri $ prɪ'lɪməˌneri/ *adjective* (formal) happening or done at the beginning of a process, usually to prepare for what will come later: *Joe made some preliminary drawings before starting to paint.*

pre·ma·ture /'premətʃə $ ˌprimə'tʃʊr/ *adjective* happening too early: *Smoking causes premature death.* —**prematurely** *adverb*: *The baby was born prematurely.*

pre·med·i·tat·ed /priː'medəteɪtɪd/ *adjective* a premeditated crime has been planned before it happens

prem·i·er /'premiə $ prɪ'mɪr/ *noun* (written) the leader of a government

prem·i·ere /'premieə $ prɪ'mɪr/ *noun* the first public performance of a film or play: *All the stars were at the premiere.*

prem·is·es /'preməsɪz/ *plural noun* the buildings and land that a shop or company uses: *No children are allowed on the premises.*

prem·o·ni·tion /ˌpremə'nɪʃən/ *noun* a feeling that something bad is going to happen: *I had a premonition that the plane was going to crash.*

pre·oc·cu·pied /pri'ɒkjəpaɪd $ pri'ɑkjəˌpaɪd/ *adjective* thinking or worrying about something a lot, so that you do not pay attention to other things: *I was so preoccupied with my work that I didn't hear him.*

prep·a·ra·tion /ˌprepə'reɪʃən/ *noun*

KEY PATTERNS
the preparation of something
preparation for an event
make preparations (for an event)

1 (no plural) getting something ready, or getting yourself ready for something: *He sometimes spends hours on the **preparation of** one meal.* • *You need to do plenty of **preparation for** your exams.*
2 preparations the things that you do in order to get ready for something: *Our **preparations for** the party took several days.* • *We are **making preparations for** the king's visit.*

pre·pare /prɪ'peə $ prɪ'per/ *verb*

KEY PATTERNS
prepare for something
prepare to do something
prepare something (for someone/ something)
prepare someone for something

1 to make yourself ready for something SYNONYM **get ready**: *I went home early to **prepare for** my holiday.* • *Craig stood up and **prepared to** go.*

2 to make something ready, so that it can be used: *At the moment we're busy **preparing** some new courses **for** our students. • It took us several hours to **prepare** the room **for** the party.*
3 to make another person ready for something: *As a teacher it's your job to **prepare** the children **for** their exams.*

pre·pared /prɪˈpeəd $ prɪˈperd/ *adjective* **1** ready to deal with a situation: *I wasn't prepared for his questions.* **2 be prepared to do sth** to be willing to do something: *She is not prepared to discuss her personal life.*

prep·o·si·tion /ˌprepəˈzɪʃən/ *noun* a word such as 'at' or 'into' that is used before a noun to show the place or position of something, or to talk about time

pre·pos·ter·ous /prɪˈpɒstərəs $ prɪˈpɑstərəs/ *adjective* (formal) completely unreasonable or silly: *What a preposterous idea!*

prep school /ˈprep skuːl/ *noun* **1** a private school in Britain for children aged between eight and 13 **2** a private school in the US that prepares students for college

pre·school /ˈpriːskuːl/ *noun* a school for children aged between two and five SYNONYM **playgroup** *BrE* SYNONYM **kindergarten** *BrE*

pre-school /ˈpriː skuːl/ *adjective* related to children who are not old enough to go to school: *people who look after pre-school children*

pre·scribe /prɪˈskraɪb/ *verb* to say what medicine or treatment someone should have: *The doctor prescribed an antibiotic.*

pre·scrip·tion /prɪˈskrɪpʃən/ *noun* a piece of paper on which a doctor writes what medicine someone should have

pres·ence /ˈprezəns/ *noun* (no plural)
1 when someone or something is in a particular place at a particular time ANTONYM **absence**: *His presence in the classroom upset the students.*
2 presence of mind the ability to deal with a dangerous or difficult situation quickly and calmly: *She had the presence of mind to jump out of the way of the bus.*

pres·ent¹ /ˈprezənt/ *adjective* existing now, rather than being in the past or the future: *Prices have increased a lot during the present year. • Our present situation is very difficult.*

PHRASES

be present (at something) to be in a particular place, or at a particular event: *Only half the class **was present at** the talk.*
the present tense the form of a verb which shows what is happening now

pre·sent² /prɪˈzent/ *verb*

KEY PATTERNS
present someone with a gift/prize
present a gift/prize to someone

1 to give something to someone at a formal ceremony: *The children **presented** their teacher **with** some flowers. • When he retired, Professor Fletcher **was presented with** a gold watch. • She **presented** the trophy **to** the winning team.*
2 if something presents a problem, a new opportunity etc, it causes or provides it: *If it rains, it will **present** a serious **problem**.*
3 to introduce a television or radio programme SYNONYM **host** *AmE*: *He has presented many wildlife programmes.*

PRONUNCIATION
You pronounce the noun **PREsent**, with the stress on the first syllable. You pronounce the verb **preSENT**, with the stress on the second syllable.

WORD CHOICE
present or **give**?
• You **present** someone **with** something such as a prize at an official ceremony.
• You **give** someone a present, for example on their birthday or at Christmas.

pres·ent³ /ˈprezənt/ *noun* something that you give to someone SYNONYM **gift**: *I went into town to **buy** a **present for** my dad. • They gave me a lovely **present for** my birthday. • He got a very expensive **Christmas present** from his wife.*

PHRASES

the present the time that we live in now: ***The present** is more important than the past.*

at present: *Debbie's working in London **at present*** (=at this time).
➔ see Thesaurus at NOW[1]

pres·en·ta·tion /ˌprezənˈteɪʃən $ ˌprizənˈteɪʃən/ *noun* **1** an event at which someone explains an idea to a group of people: *I gave a presentation to the class about my history project.* **2** when someone is given a prize or present at a formal ceremony: *the presentation of the medal* **3** (no plural) the way something looks because of how it has been arranged: *Your essay contains some good ideas, but the presentation is poor.*

pre·sent·er /prɪˈzentə $ prɪˈzentɚ/ *noun* someone who introduces a television or radio programme SYNONYM **host** *AmE*

pres·ent·ly /ˈprezəntli/ *adverb* (formal) **1** now: *They are presently on holiday.* **2** after a short time: *Presently, he became aware he was being watched.*

ˌpresent ˈparticiple *noun* the form of a verb that ends in '-ing'

ˌpresent ˈperfect *noun* **the present perfect** the verb tense that you use to talk about a time up to and including the present, which is formed with 'have' and the PAST PARTICIPLE, as in 'he has gone'

pre·ser·va·tive /prɪˈzɜːvətɪv $ prɪˈzɚvətɪv/ *noun* a chemical that is added to food to keep it in good condition

pre·serve /prɪˈzɜːv $ prɪˈzɚv/ *verb* to keep something safe or in good condition: *It is important to preserve your culture.* • *The group is working to preserve rain forests.* ➔ see Thesaurus at PROTECT

pres·i·den·cy /ˈprezədənsi/ *noun* (plural **presidencies**) the job or time of being president: *towards the end of his presidency*

pres·i·dent /ˈprezədənt/ *noun* **1** the leader of a country that does not have a king or queen: *President Kennedy* • *the president of France* **2** someone who is in charge of an organization: *the president of the chess club*

pres·i·den·tial /ˌprezəˈdenʃəl/ *adjective* related to the president of a country: *the presidential election*

press[1] /pres/ *verb*

KEY PATTERNS
press a button/switch
press something against/into something

1 if you press a button or switch, you push it in order to make something work: *You press this button to turn the TV on.*
2 to push something firmly against a surface: *Kate **pressed** her shoulder **against** the door and it opened.* • *She **pressed** the money **into** his hand.*

THESAURUS
squash: *I'm afraid these tomatoes have been **squashed*** (=pressed flat and damaged).
crush: *Crush the biscuits into crumbs* (=press them hard so that they break).
mash: *Mash the potatoes* (=press them to make a soft substance. You mash soft fruit and cooked vegetables).
grind: *The wheat is **ground** to make flour* (=pressed into powder using a machine or tool).
squeeze: *She **squeezed** the tube of toothpaste* (=pressed it firmly from both sides with her fingers).

press[2] *noun*
the press newspapers and magazines: *The accident was reported **in the local press**.* • *The press has a lot of influence over what people think.*

ˈpress ˌconference *noun* a meeting at which someone answers questions asked by people who work for newspapers, radio, and television: *The police dealing with the murder held a press conference today.*

ˈpress reˌlease *noun* an official statement giving information to newspapers, radio, and television

ˈpress-up *noun BrE* an exercise in which you lie facing the ground and push your body up using your arms SYNONYM **push-up**: *He does 20 press-ups every day before breakfast.*

pres·sure[1] /ˈpreʃə $ ˈpreʃɚ/ *noun*

KEY PATTERNS
pressure on someone (to do something)
pressure from someone

A B C D E F G H I J K L M N O P Q R S T U V W X Y Z

pressure for a change/an action
the pressure(s) of life/work

1 (no plural) when other people try to make someone do something: *There's a lot of* ***pressure on*** *her* ***to*** *get married now.* • *His family* ***put pressure on*** *him* ***to*** *go to university.* • *I get a lot of* ***pressure from*** *my family* ***to*** *do well in exams.* • *There's* ***pressure for*** *a change in the law.*
2 when something makes you feel anxious or unhappy, for example because you have too much to do: *John eventually became ill because of* ***the pressure of*** *his work.*
3 (no plural) the force of something pushing on another thing: ***The pressure of*** *his hand on her shoulder was annoying her.*

PHRASES
be under pressure to be in a difficult situation: *A lot of small businesses* ***are under pressure*** *at the moment.*
be under pressure to do something to feel that you must try hard to do something, because of the situation you are in: *The minister* ***is under pressure to*** *resign.* • *I* ***felt under pressure to*** *earn more and more money.*

pressure² *verb AmE* to make someone feel that they must do something SYNONYM **pressurize** *BrE*: *Carrie's friends pressured her into going to the dance.*

ˈpressure group *noun* a group of people who try to make the government, a company etc do a particular thing: *an environmental pressure group*

pres•sur•ize also **pressurise** *BrE* /ˈpreʃəraɪz/ *verb* to try to make someone do something by threatening them, arguing with them etc SYNONYM **pressure** *AmE*: *Her parents tried to pressurize her into going to college.*

pres•tige /preˈstiːʒ/ *noun* (no plural) the respect and admiration that someone has when they are very successful or have an important position in society

pres•ti•gious /preˈstɪdʒəs $ preˈstidʒəs/ *adjective* a prestigious job, school etc makes you respected and admired

pre•su•ma•bly /prɪˈzjuːməbli $ prɪˈzuməbli/ *adverb* used when you think that something is probably true: *The burglars presumably knew he was out.*

pre•sume /prɪˈzjuːm $ prɪˈzum/ *verb* to think that something is probably true SYNONYM **assume**: *I presume we'll be finished by two o'clock.*

pre•tence *BrE*, **pretense** *AmE* /prɪˈtens $ ˈpritens/ *noun* when you pretend that something is true: *He seemed confident, but I knew it was just a pretence.*

pre•tend /prɪˈtend/ *verb*

KEY PATTERNS
pretend to do something
pretend (that)

to behave in a particular way in order to make people believe something is true, although it is not: *Helen* ***pretended to*** *be ill so that she could stay at home.* • *The kids lay on the floor* ***pretending that*** *they were dead.*

pre•ten•tious /prɪˈtenʃəs/ *adjective* trying to seem more important or clever than you really are

pre•text /ˈpriːtekst/ *noun* a false reason that you give for doing something: *He stayed at home on the pretext of having some homework to do.*

pret•ty¹ /ˈprɪti/ *adverb* (spoken) fairly or quite: *Their house is pretty big.* • *It was a pretty quick journey, really.* → see Thesaurus at FAIRLY

pretty² *adjective* (**prettier, prettiest**) pleasant and attractive to look at: *Alison was sixteen, and very pretty.* • *a pretty garden* → see Thesaurus at ATTRACTIVE

pre•vent /prɪˈvent/ *verb*

KEY PATTERNS
prevent something (from happening)
prevent someone from doing something

to stop something from happening, or to stop someone from doing something: *There was nothing we could do to prevent the war.* • *She tried to* ***prevent*** *me* ***from*** *leaving.*

pre·ven·ta·tive /prɪˈventətɪv/ *adjective* PREVENTIVE

pre·ven·tion /prɪˈvenʃən/ *noun* (no plural) when something is prevented: *the prevention of tooth decay*

pre·ven·tive /prɪˈventɪv/ also **preventative** *adjective* intended to prevent something bad from happening: *preventive medicine* (=actions that prevent people from becoming ill)

pre·view /ˈpriːvjuː/ *noun* **1** an occasion when you see a film or show before the rest of the public **2** an advertisement for a film or television programme, which consists of short parts from it SYNONYM **trailer**

pre·vi·ous /ˈpriːviəs/ *adjective* a previous time or event happened in the past: *We've already discussed that idea at a previous meeting.* • *Last year we went to Italy on holiday. The previous year, we went to Majorca.* ➔ see Thesaurus at LAST[1]

pre·vi·ous·ly /ˈpriːviəsli/ *adverb* before a particular time in the past: *The car had previously belonged to his dad.*

prey /preɪ/ *noun* (no plural) an animal that is hunted and eaten by another animal: *The cat pounced on its prey.*

price /praɪs/ *noun*

KEY PATTERNS
the price of something
sell/buy something at a particular price

the amount of money that you must pay in order to buy something: ***The price of*** *petrol has increased a lot.* • *It's a lovely shop but their* ***prices*** *are quite* ***high.*** • *You can get meals there at quite* ***low prices.*** • *Everything in the shop is being sold* ***at half price.*** ➔ see Thesaurus at COST[1]

PHRASES

at any price even if there are a lot of problems or difficulties: *I was determined to get into the team* ***at any price.***

price·less /ˈpraɪsləs/ *adjective* worth a very large amount of money: *a priceless diamond necklace*

pric·ey /ˈpraɪsi/ *adjective* (informal) expensive ➔ see Thesaurus at EXPENSIVE

prick /prɪk/ *verb* to make a small hole in the surface of something

prick·ly /ˈprɪkli/ *adjective* covered with sharp points: *a prickly cactus*

prickly

a prickly cactus

pride[1] /praɪd/ *noun* (no plural)

KEY PATTERNS
pride in someone/something

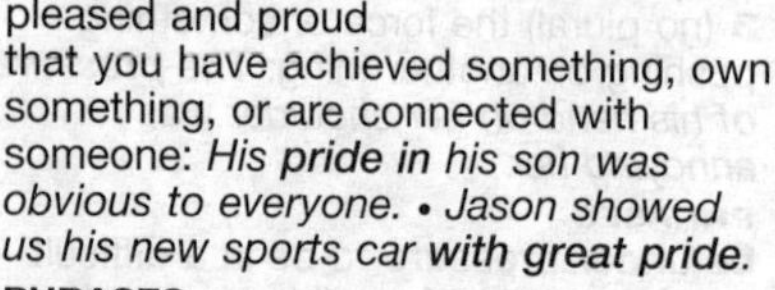

the feeling you have when you are pleased and proud that you have achieved something, own something, or are connected with someone: *His* ***pride in*** *his son was obvious to everyone.* • *Jason showed us his new sports car* ***with great pride.***

PHRASES

take pride in something to get pleasure from doing something well: *Richard* ***took pride in*** *his tennis, and practised every day.*

pride[2] *verb* **pride yourself on something** to be very proud of something that you do well: *Allen prides himself on being the fastest swimmer on the team.*

priest /priːst/ *noun* someone who performs religious duties and ceremonies, especially in the Christian church

pri·ma·ri·ly /ˈpraɪmərəli $ praɪˈmerəli/ *adverb* mainly: *The club is used primarily by teenagers.* ➔ see Thesaurus at MAINLY

pri·ma·ry /ˈpraɪməri $ ˈpraɪˌmeri/ *adjective* first or most important SYNONYM **main**: *The police's primary goal is to prevent crime.*

ˈprimary ˌschool *noun* a school for children between the ages of five and 11 SYNONYM **elementary school** *AmE*

prime[1] /praɪm/ *adjective* **1** main or most important: *Vincent is the prime suspect in the murder case.* **2** of the very best quality or kind: *The office is in a prime location on the river.*

prime[2] *noun* **be in your prime, be in the prime of life** to be at the time in your life when you are strongest and most active

ˌprime ˈminister *noun* the leader of the government in some countries with a parliament

prim·i·tive /ˈprɪmətɪv/ *adjective* **1** primitive people have a simple way of life, without modern machines ANTONYM **advanced** **2** very simple or old-fashioned, and therefore not very good: *The washing facilities were a bit primitive.*

prince /prɪns/ *noun* the son of a king or queen, or one of their male relations: *Prince Charles*

prin·cess /ˌprɪnˈses $ ˈprɪnsɪs/ *noun* (plural **princesses**) the daughter of a king or queen, one of their female relations, or the wife of a prince: *Princess Margaret*

prin·ci·pal¹ /ˈprɪnsəpəl/ *adjective* most important SYNONYM **main**: *Coffee is Brazil's principal export.*

principal² *noun* the person in charge of a school or college

prin·ci·pally /ˈprɪnsəpli/ *adverb* mainly: *The money will be spent principally on new books for the school.* → see Thesaurus at MAINLY

prin·ci·ple /ˈprɪnsəpəl/ *noun* an idea that you believe is right, and that you use to guide the way you behave: *The old lady* ***had very strong*** *principles.*

PHRASES

be against someone's principles: *We do not test our products on animals because it* ***is against our principles*** (=we believe it is wrong).

on principle: *I don't work on Sundays,* ***on principle*** (=because I believe it is wrong).

SPELLING

Don't confuse the spelling of **principle** (=an idea that you believe is right) and **principal** (=most important).

print¹ /prɪnt/ *verb*
1 to produce words or pictures on paper, using a machine: *They had to print more copies of the book.*
2 to write words without joining the letters: *Print your name at the top of your entry form.*

PHRASAL VERBS

print off, print out
print something off/out to print information from a computer onto paper: *She* ***printed off*** *the list of names.*

print² *noun* **1** (no plural) writing that has been printed in books, newspapers etc: *We bought Grandma a book in large print.* **2** a picture or photograph that has been printed: *She has a Renoir print on her wall.* **3 be in print, be out of print** if a book is in print, it is available to buy; if a book is out of print, it is not available to buy **4** a mark made on a surface when you press something onto it: *The dog left paw prints in the sand.*

print·er /ˈprɪntə $ ˈprɪntɚ/ *noun* **1** a machine that prints a document from a computer onto paper → see picture on page A12 **2** someone who works for a company that prints books, newspapers etc

print·out /ˈprɪntˌaʊt/ *noun* paper with information from a computer printed on it

pri·or /ˈpraɪə $ ˈpraɪɚ/ *adjective* (formal) **1 prior to something** before something: *Prior to this, we had never had any trouble.* **2** existing or happening before something else SYNONYM **previous**: *You do not need any prior knowledge of the subject.*

pri·or·i·ty /praɪˈɒrəti $ praɪˈɔrəti/ *noun* (plural **priorities**) the thing that you think is most important and should be dealt with first: *The government's priority is education.*

PHRASES

take priority, have priority to be treated as more important than other people or things: *His family* ***took priority over*** *everything else.*

give priority to someone/something to treat one person or thing as more important than others: *Hospitals must* ***give priority to*** *people who are seriously ill.*

prise /praɪz/ *verb BrE* to force something open or away from something else SYNONYM **pry** *AmE*: *I tried to prise open the door.*

pris·on /ˈprɪzən/ *noun* a building where criminals are kept SYNONYM **jail**: *He's been in prison for two years.*

pris·on·er /ˈprɪzənə $ ˈprɪzənɚ/ *noun*
1 someone who is in prison
2 someone who is kept somewhere by force: *The rebels have released their prisoners.* • *Her father was taken prisoner* (=made a prisoner) *in the war.*

THESAURUS
captive: *He treated his* **captives** *well* (=prisoners).
hostage: *The rebels demanded a ransom for the release of the hostages* (=prisoners being held in order to force other people to do something).

priv·a·cy /ˈprɪvəsi $ ˈpraɪvəsi/ *noun* (no plural) when other people cannot see or hear you, or know what you are doing: *You must respect your father's privacy.*

pri·vate¹ /ˈpraɪvət/ *adjective*
1 owned by one person or group and not available for others to use ANTONYM **public**: *This is private land.*
2 not owned or paid for by the government ANTONYM **state**: *a private school* • *a private hospital*
3 if something is private, you do not want other people to know about it: *I can't tell you – that information is private.* → see Thesaurus at SECRET¹
4 a private place is one where you can be alone ANTONYM **public**: *Can we talk about this somewhere more private?*

private² *noun* **1 in private** without other people listening or watching: *Kevin waited after class, so he could speak to the teacher in private.* **2** a soldier who has the lowest rank in the army

pri·vat·ize also **privatise** *BrE* /ˈpraɪvətaɪz/ *verb* if a government privatizes an organization that it owns, it sells it ANTONYM **nationalize**: *The railways have been privatized.*

priv·i·lege /ˈprɪvəlɪdʒ/ *noun* a special advantage or right that only a small number of people are given: *The older students were given special privileges.*

prize /praɪz/ *noun*

KEY PATTERNS
a prize for (doing) something

something that is given to someone who is successful in a competition, race etc: *She* **won first prize** *in a poetry competition.* • *There will be a* **prize for** *the best picture.*

prob·a·bil·i·ty /ˌprɒbəˈbɪləti $ ˌprɑbəˈbɪləti/ *noun* (no plural) how likely it is that something will happen SYNONYM **likelihood**: *What's the probability of the disease coming back?*

prob·a·ble /ˈprɒbəbəl $ ˈprɑbəbəl/ *adjective* very likely to happen, exist, or be true: *A gas leak was the probable cause of the explosion.*

prob·a·bly /ˈprɒbəbli $ ˈprɑbəbli/ *adverb*
used when saying what is likely to be true or what is likely to happen: *They've probably got lost.* • *I haven't been working very hard, so I'll probably fail all my exams.*

pro·ba·tion /prəˈbeɪʃən $ proʊˈbeɪʃən/ *noun* (no plural) a system of keeping an official check on criminals, instead of keeping them in prison: *He has to go to the police station every week while he's on probation.*

probe /prəʊb $ proʊb/ *verb* (written) to ask a lot of questions in order to find out information: *I don't want people probing into my private life!* —**probing** *adjective*: *My boss always asks the most probing questions.*

prob·lem /ˈprɒbləm $ ˈprɑbləm/ *noun*

KEY PATTERNS
have a problem
a problem with something
the problem of pollution/poverty

something bad or difficult that you have to deal with: *She's* **had** *a lot of personal* **problems** *recently.* • *I've been* **having problems with** *my car.* • *There's* **a problem with** *the computer.* • **the problem of** *how to deal with crime* • *We must try to* **solve** *this* **problem**. • *This is a very* **serious problem**.

THESAURUS
hitch: *The wedding went without a* **hitch** (=a small problem causing a delay).
snag (informal): *There was one* **snag**: *the cost* (=one small problem).
setback: *The team has had a few*

A B C D E F G H I J K L M N O P Q R S T U V W X Y Z

setbacks recently (=problems that stopped it from being successful for a while).

pro·ce·dure /prəˈsiːdʒə $ prəˈsidʒɚ/ *noun* the correct or normal way of doing something: *What's the procedure for getting a driver's licence?*

pro·ceed /prəˈsiːd/ *verb* (formal) to continue: *The police have decided not to proceed with the case.*

pro·ceed·ings /prəˈsiːdɪŋz/ *plural noun* (formal) a series of events: *She sat down and took no further part in the proceedings.*

pro·ceeds /ˈprəʊsiːdz $ ˈproʊsidz/ *plural noun* the money that you get from selling something or holding an event: *They sold their car and spent the proceeds on a boat.*

pro·cess¹ /ˈprəʊses $ ˈprɑses/ *noun* (plural **processes**)
something that happens over a period of time: *Learning a new language is a long process.*

PHRASES

be in the process of doing something to have started doing something and not finished doing it: *I'm in the process of choosing which universities to apply to.*

process² *verb* **1** to deal with information by putting it through a system or computer: *Your application has not yet been processed.* **2** to do things to food or a substance before it is used or sold: *The meat is processed in huge factories.*

pro·ces·sion /prəˈseʃən/ *noun* a line of people or vehicles moving slowly along as part of a ceremony

pro·claim /prəˈkleɪm $ proʊˈkleɪm/ *verb* (formal) to formally tell people something: *The country proclaimed its independence in 1956.*

prod /prɒd $ prɑd/ *verb* (**prodded, prodding**) to push someone or something with your finger or a long object SYNONYM **poke**: *She prodded the girl next to her and asked what was going on.* ➔ see Thesaurus at PUSH¹
—**prod** *noun*: *He gave the meat a prod.*

prod·i·gy /ˈprɒdɪdʒi $ ˈprɑdədʒi/ *noun* (plural **prodigies**) a young person who is unusually good at doing something

pro·duce¹ /prəˈdjuːs $ prəˈdus/ *verb*
1 to grow or make something: *The tree produces red berries in the autumn.* • *The company produced 30,000 cars last year.*
2 to make something happen: *Which method will produce the results we want?*
3 to bring something out so that someone can see it: *He put his hand in his pocket and produced his ticket.*
4 to be in charge of the making of a film, show, or record: *The film was produced by Nick Staines.*

prod·uce² /ˈprɒdjuːs $ ˈprɑdus/ *noun* (no plural) food that is grown on a farm and sold

PRONUNCIATION
You pronounce the verb **proDUCE**, with the stress on the second syllable.
You pronounce the noun **PROduce**, with the stress on the first syllable.

pro·duc·er /prəˈdjuːsə $ prəˈdusɚ/ *noun* someone who is in charge of making a film, record etc: *a film producer*

prod·uct /ˈprɒdʌkt $ ˈprɑdʌkt/ *noun* something that is made and sold by a company: *The company produces a range of household products.*

pro·duc·tion /prəˈdʌkʃən/ *noun* (no plural)
the process of making or growing things, or the amount that you make or grow: *How can we increase our production?*

pro·duc·tive /prəˈdʌktɪv/ *adjective* producing a lot or producing a good result: *That was a very productive meeting.*

pro·duc·tiv·i·ty /ˌprɒdʌkˈtɪvəti $ ˌproʊdəkˈtɪvəti/ *noun* (no plural) the amount that is produced by each worker at a factory in a particular time: *Productivity at the factory has increased by 5% over the last year.*

Prof. the written abbreviation of PROFESSOR

pro·fes·sion /prəˈfeʃən/ *noun* a job for which you need special education

A B C D E F G H I J K L M N O **P** Q R S T U V W X Y Z

and training, such as being a doctor or a teacher: *the legal profession* → see Thesaurus at JOB

pro·fes·sion·al¹ /prəˈfeʃənəl/ *adjective*
1 a professional football player, artist etc does a sport or activity as their job: *a professional photographer*
2 made or done well: *The magazine produced by the students looked very professional.*

professional² *noun* someone who earns money by doing a sport that other people do for enjoyment ANTONYM **amateur**

pro·fes·sor /prəˈfesə $ prəˈfesɚ/ *noun* **1** *BrE* a teacher with the highest job in a university department: *Professor Sinclair* **2** *AmE* a teacher at a university or college who has a PHD

SPELLING
This word is often spelled wrongly. The correct spelling is: **professor**.

pro·fi·cien·cy /prəˈfɪʃənsi/ *noun* (no plural) (formal) the ability to do something well: *her proficiency in French*

pro·file /ˈprəʊfaɪl $ ˈproʊfaɪl/ *noun* a side view of someone's head: *She looked at the handsome profile of the man sitting next to her.*

prof·it¹ /ˈprɒfɪt $ ˈprɑfɪt/ *noun*

KEY PATTERNS
make a profit

if you make a profit when you sell something, you get more money for it than you spent on it ANTONYM **loss**: *The company made a good profit this year.*

profit² *verb* (formal) to get money or something useful from a situation: *Some groups profited from the war.*

prof·it·a·ble /ˈprɒfɪtəbəl $ ˈprɑfɪtəbəl/ *adjective* producing a profit: *a profitable business*

pro·found /prəˈfaʊnd/ *adjective* a profound shock, effect etc is a very great one: *a profound disappointment*

pro·gram¹ /ˈprəʊgræm $ ˈproʊgræm/ *noun* **1** the American spelling of PROGRAMME **2** a set of instructions given to a computer or other machine: *a computer program*

program² *verb* (**programmed**, **programming**) the American spelling of PROGRAMME

pro·gramme¹ *BrE*, **program** *AmE* /ˈprəʊgræm $ ˈproʊgræm/ *noun*

KEY PATTERNS
a programme about/on something

1 a show on television or radio: *Did you see that TV programme about earthquakes?* • *Do you want to* **watch** *this programme?*
2 a set of planned actions or activities: *a four-year research programme*
3 a small book that you get at a concert or play, which gives information about it

programme² *BrE*, **program** *AmE* *verb* to set controls so that a machine will work a particular way: *The satellite has been programmed to take photographs of particular areas.*

pro·gram·mer /ˈprəʊgræmə $ ˈproʊˌgræmɚ/ *noun* someone whose job is to write sets of instructions for computers: *a computer programmer*

pro·gram·ming /ˈprəʊgræmɪŋ $ ˈproʊˌgræmɪŋ/ *noun* the activity of writing sets of instructions for computers

pro·gress¹ /ˈprəʊgres $ ˈprɑgrəs/ *noun* (no plural)

KEY PATTERNS
make progress

if you make progress, you get better or get closer to achieving something: *Parents want to be told about their child's progress at school.* • *The patient is* **making good progress** *after the operation.*

pro·gress² /prəˈgres/ *verb* **1** to develop and become better or more complete: *She was told that her baby was progressing well.* **2** to continue or move forward: *I got more and more bored as the meeting progressed.*

pro·gres·sive¹ /prəˈgresɪv/ *adjective* a progressive change is gradual and continuous

progressive² *noun* **the progressive** a verb form that consists of 'be' and the PRESENT PARTICIPLE, as in 'She was reading'

pro·hib·it /prəˈhɪbət $ proʊˈhɪbɪt/ *verb* (formal) if people in authority prohibit something, they do not allow it SYNONYM **ban**: *Skateboarding is prohibited in the town centre.* → see Thesaurus at FORBID

proj·ect /ˈprɒdʒekt $ ˈprɑdʒekt/ *noun* **1** a piece of planned work that is done over a period of time: *This is part of a project to make this area of the city more attractive.*
2 a piece of school work in which students have to collect information about a subject: *Cindy's in the library working on her history project.* • *We're doing a project on global warming.*

pro·jec·tor /prəˈdʒektə $ prəˈdʒektɚ/ *noun* a piece of equipment for showing film or pictures on a screen

pro·lif·ic /prəˈlɪfɪk/ *adjective* producing a lot of things: *a prolific writer*

pro·long /prəˈlɒŋ $ prəˈlɔŋ/ *verb* to make something continue for longer: *Heart transplants have prolonged many people's lives.*

pro·longed /prəˈlɒŋd $ prəˈlɔŋd/ *adjective* continuing for a long time: *a prolonged period of silence*

prom·i·nent /ˈprɒmənənt $ ˈprɑmənənt/ *adjective* well known or important: *a prominent supporter of animal rights*

prom·ise¹ /ˈprɒmɪs $ ˈprɑmɪs/ *verb*

KEY PATTERNS
promise to do something
promise (that)
promise someone (that)
promise someone a present/some money etc

to say that you will definitely do or give something: *She* ***promised to*** *write to me.* • *I* ***promise that*** *I'll be there.* • *He* ***promised*** *me* ***that*** *he wouldn't be late.* • *His parents had promised him a camera for his birthday.*

THESAURUS
swear: *He swore not to tell anyone my secret* (=promised seriously).
vow (formal): *She has* ***vowed*** *to continue the fight for justice* (=made a serious promise to herself or other people).
guarantee: *I guarantee you'll enjoy this book* (=promise).

promise² *noun*

KEY PATTERNS
the promise of something
a promise to do something
make a promise

if you make a promise, you say that you will definitely do or give something: *He came to England last year with* ***the promise of*** *a good job.* • *I reminded my aunt of her* ***promise to*** *take us to the zoo.* • *He* ***made*** *all sorts of* ***promises*** *before he left.* • *I knew she would* ***keep her promise*** (=do what she said she would do). • *He said he would wait for me, but he* ***broke his promise*** (=did not do what he said he would do).

prom·is·ing /ˈprɒmɪsɪŋ $ ˈprɑmɪsɪŋ/ *adjective* likely to be successful in the future: *a very promising student*

pro·mo /ˈprəʊməʊ $ ˈproʊmoʊ/ *noun* (informal) a short film or public appearance to advertise a film, record, book etc: *She's filming a promo for her new album.*

pro·mote /prəˈməʊt $ prəˈmoʊt/ *verb* **1** to give someone who works for you a higher job: *He is hoping to be promoted to manager soon.* **2** to try to make something happen or help something be successful: *a campaign promoting the use of cycle helmets* • *She's been on lots of talk shows, promoting her latest film.*

pro·mo·tion /prəˈməʊʃən $ prəˈmoʊʃən/ *noun* **1** when you are given a higher job: *She felt she deserved promotion.* **2** an advertisement or special attempt to sell something: *a big promotion campaign on national television*

prompt¹ /prɒmpt $ prɑmpt/ *verb* to make someone decide to do something, especially something they were already thinking about doing: *John's leaving prompted me to look for a new job.*

prompt² *adjective* **1** done quickly or immediately: *I expect a prompt reply to my letter.* **2** arriving at the right time: *The meeting starts at 11, so please be prompt.* —**promptly** *adverb*

prone /prəʊn $ proʊn/ *adjective* likely to do something bad, or likely to suffer from something: *He was prone to* *jealousy.* • *Young drivers are more accident-prone than older ones.*

pro·noun /'prəʊnaʊn $ 'proʊnaʊn/ *noun* a word such as 'he' or 'themselves' that is used instead of using a noun

pro·nounce /prə'naʊns/ *verb* **1** to say a word using particular sounds: *He always pronounces my name wrong.* **2** (formal) to state something officially: *The doctor pronounced him dead at 11 p.m.*

pro·nun·ci·a·tion /prəˌnʌnsi'eɪʃən/ *noun* the way in which you say a word: *Is that the correct pronunciation?*

SPELLING
This word is often spelled wrongly. The correct spelling is: **pronunciation**.

proof /pru:f/ *noun*

KEY PATTERNS
proof of something
proof that

something that proves something is true: *She needed **proof of** her theory.* • *This letter is **proof that** Higson knew about the robbery.*

prop¹ /prɒp $ prɑp/ *verb* (**propped**, **propping**) **1** to lean or rest something on something: *He propped his feet on the table.* **2 prop something up** to support something so that it does not fall or hang down: *We propped the fence up with some old bits of wood.*

prop

We propped the fence up.

prop² *noun* an object that is used in a play or film

prop·a·gan·da /ˌprɒpə'gændə $ ˌprɑpə'gændə/ *noun* (no plural) false information that a political organization gives to the public to influence them: *This is just government propaganda.*

pro·pel·ler /prə'pelə $ prə'pelɚ/ *noun* the part of a boat or aircraft that spins round and makes it move along

prop·er /'prɒpə $ 'prɑpɚ/ *adjective* **1** correct for a particular situation: *Have you filled in the proper form?* **2** *BrE* real, with every necessary feature: *I wanted a proper job where I got paid.* • *I always try to eat a proper meal in the evenings.*

prop·er·ly /'prɒpəli $ 'prɑpɚli/ *adverb* in a correct or satisfactory way: *The printer isn't working properly.*

ˌproper 'noun *noun* a noun such as 'Mike' or 'Paris' that is the name of a person, place, or thing and is spelled with a capital letter

prop·er·ty /'prɒpəti $ 'prɑpɚti/ *noun* (formal) **1** (no plural) something that you own: *Make sure you take all your property with you when you leave the train.* **2** (plural **properties**) a building: *We have quite a lot of properties for sale.* • *Is this a good time to buy property?* **3** (plural **properties**) a natural quality that a substance has: *What are the properties of mercury?* → see Thesaurus at QUALITY

THESAURUS
possessions: *He sold most of his possessions* (=things that he owned).
things/belongings: *Go and pack your things* (=things that you own or have with you).
stuff (informal): *He's taken all his stuff* (=things that he owns or had with him).

proph·e·cy /'prɒfəsi $ 'prɑfəsi/ *noun* (plural **prophecies**) a statement in which you say what you believe will happen in the future

proph·et /'prɒfɪt $ 'prɑfɪt/ *noun* someone who people believe God has chosen to be a religious leader or teacher

pro·por·tion /prə'pɔ:ʃən $ prə'pɔrʃən/ *noun* **1** part of an amount or group: *A large proportion of the students go on to college after leaving school.* **2** the relationship between two amounts: *What is the proportion of girls to boys in the class?* **3 proportions** the size of something: *a problem of huge proportions*

pro·pos·al /prə'pəʊzəl $ prə'poʊzəl/ *noun* **1** a suggested plan: *I have a proposal to make.* **2** when you ask someone to marry you

pro·pose /prəˈpəʊz $ prəˈpoʊz/ *verb* **1** to officially suggest a plan: *The president proposed a five per cent cut in income tax.* • *I propose we discuss this at a later meeting.* **2** to ask someone to marry you: *Tom proposed to me last night.* **3** (formal) to intend to do something: *Where do you propose to put the television?*

prop·o·si·tion /ˌprɒpəˈzɪʃən $ ˌprɑpəˈzɪʃən/ *noun* **1** an offer or suggestion, especially in business or politics: *They came to me with a business proposition.* **2** *AmE* a suggestion for a new law that people in a state vote on

pros /prəʊz $ proʊz/ *plural noun* **the pros and cons** the ways that something is good and the ways it is bad: *I spent some time considering the pros and cons, but eventually decided to accept the job.*

prose /prəʊz $ proʊz/ *noun* (no plural) ordinary written language, not poetry: *a great prose writer*

pros·e·cute /ˈprɒsəkjuːt $ ˈprɑsəˌkjut/ *verb* to say officially that you think someone is guilty of a crime and must be judged by a court of law: *The police decided to prosecute him for dangerous driving.*

pros·e·cu·tion /ˌprɒsəˈkjuːʃən $ ˌprɑsəˈkjuʃən/ *noun* **the prosecution** the lawyers who are trying to prove that someone is guilty of a crime in a court of law ANTONYM **defence**: *The prosecution told the jury that Henson was seen stealing the car.*

pros·pect /ˈprɒspekt $ ˈprɑspekt/ *noun* something that will probably or definitely happen: *Laura was dreading the prospect of Christmas without her family.*

pro·spec·tive /prəˈspektɪv/ *adjective* (formal) likely to do or be something in the future: *Find out as much as you can about your prospective employer before the interview.*

pro·spec·tus /prəˈspektəs/ *noun* (plural **prospectuses**) a small book in which a university, school, or company gives information about itself

pro·sper·i·ty /prɒˈsperəti $ prɑˈsperəti/ *noun* (no plural) when people have a lot of money: *years of prosperity*

pros·per·ous /ˈprɒspərəs $ ˈprɑspərəs/ *adjective* rich and successful: *a prosperous businessman* ➔ see Thesaurus at RICH

pros·ti·tute /ˈprɒstətjuːt $ ˈprɑstəˌtut/ *noun* someone who earns money by having sex with people

pros·ti·tu·tion /ˌprɒstəˈtjuːʃən $ ˌprɑstəˈtuʃən/ *noun* (no plural) when someone earns money by having sex with people

pro·tect /prəˈtekt/ *verb*

KEY PATTERNS
protect someone/something (from someone/something bad)
protect someone/something against something bad

to prevent someone or something from being harmed or damaged: *The police should **protect** people **from** dangerous men like him.* • *Wear a hat to **protect** yourself **against** the sun.*

THESAURUS
guard: *The building is **guarded** by soldiers* (=watched and protected).
shield: *He wanted to **shield** her from publicity* (=protect her against it).
shelter: *They **sheltered** some of the refugees* (=gave them a safe place to stay).
preserve: *The group wants to **preserve** the countryside* (=keep it safe and in good condition).

pro·tec·tion /prəˈtekʃən/ *noun* (no plural)

KEY PATTERNS
protection from/against something bad

if something gives protection, it prevents someone or something from being harmed or damaged: *The trees gave them some **protection against** the rain.*

pro·tec·tive /prəˈtektɪv/ *adjective* **1** intended to protect someone or something from damage: *The players wear protective helmets.* **2** wanting to protect someone from harm: *She was very protective towards her children.*

pro·tein /ˈprəʊtiːn $ ˈproʊtin/ *noun* a substance in food such as meat and eggs, which helps your body to grow and be healthy

pro·test¹ /ˈprəʊtest $ ˈproʊtest/ *noun*

KEY PATTERNS
a protest against something
in protest at something

an action by which a group of people show publicly that they think something is wrong: *He took part in a **protest against** the government's treatment of refugees.* • *The workers went on strike **in protest at** not being paid.*

pro·test² /prəˈtest/ *verb*

KEY PATTERNS
protest against/about something
protest something *AmE*

if people protest against something, they show publicly that they think it is wrong: *Thousands of people gathered to **protest against** the new law.* • *The students were protesting the war.*

THESAURUS
demonstrate: *A group of his supporters are **demonstrating** outside the prison* (=protesting).
march: *Thousands of protesters **marched** on the capital* (=walked to the capital to protest).
riot: *When the election was cancelled, people **rioted** in the streets* (=protested by behaving violently).

Prot·es·tant /ˈprɒtəstənt $ ˈprɑtəstənt/ *noun* a Christian who is not a Roman Catholic —**Protestant** *adjective*: *a Protestant church*

pro·test·er /prəˈtestə $ ˈproʊtestə/ *noun* someone who shows publicly that they think something is wrong, for example by being in a DEMONSTRATION: *a demonstration by anti-war protesters*

pro·trac·tor /prəˈtræktə $ proʊˈtræktə/ *noun* a flat object shaped like a half circle, used for measuring and drawing angles

proud /praʊd/ *adjective*

KEY PATTERNS
proud of something/someone
proud to do something
proud that

if you feel proud, you feel pleased because you think that something you have achieved or are connected with is very good ANTONYM **ashamed**: *He is **proud of** his son's achievement.* • *A success like this makes you **proud to** be British.* • *She was **proud that** her work was chosen for the exhibition.*

PHRASES
be too proud to do something to not do something because you feel that it would make you look weak or bad in some way: *She **was too proud to** ask her family for money.* —**proudly** *adverb*

THESAURUS
conceited/bigheaded: *I didn't want to appear **conceited*** (=too proud of my abilities or achievements).
vain: *She was too **vain** to wear glasses, even though she needed them* (=too proud of her appearance).

prove /pruːv/ *verb* (**proved**, **proved** or **proven** /ˈpruːvən/)

KEY PATTERNS
prove (that)
prove a theory/claim etc
prove useful/difficult etc
prove to be something

1 to show that something is definitely true: *You can't **prove that** I took the money.* • *The scientists are trying to prove the theory by doing an experiment.* → see Thesaurus at SHOW¹

2 if something proves useful, difficult etc, it is found to be useful, difficult etc: *Getting a job proved difficult.* • *This information **proved to be** extremely useful.*

PHRASES
prove someone right, prove someone wrong to show that what someone said was true or not true: *I said he would be successful, and I **was proved right**.*

proven a past participle of PROVE

prov·erb /ˈprɒvɜːb $ ˈprɑvəb/ *noun* an old, well-known sentence that tells you something about life, such as 'Many hands make light work.'

pro·vide /prəˈvaɪd/ *verb*

KEY PATTERNS
provide something (for someone)
provide someone with something

to give someone something they need: *This book will provide all the information you need.* • *I can **provide you with** a place to stay.* • *We provide financial help **for** students.*

pro·vid·ed /prəˈvaɪdɪd/ also **pro·vid·ing** /prəˈvaɪdɪŋ/ used to say that something will only happen if another thing happens: *You'll get good marks, provided you do the work.*

prov·ince /ˈprɒvɪns $ ˈprɑvɪns/ *noun* one of the large areas into which some countries are divided: *the Canadian province of Ontario*

pro·vi·sion /prəˈvɪʒən/ *noun* **1** when people provide something: *the provision of health care* **2 provisions** supplies of food: *After a week they were running short of provisions.*

pro·vi·sion·al /prəˈvɪʒənəl/ *adjective* likely to be changed: *A provisional date for the meeting has been agreed.*

prov·o·ca·tion /ˌprɒvəˈkeɪʃən $ ˌprɑvəˈkeɪʃən/ *noun* an action that is likely to make someone attack you: *He attacked me totally without provocation.*

pro·voke /prəˈvəʊk $ prəˈvoʊk/ *verb* **1** to deliberately make someone attack you: *Ignore him – he's just trying to provoke you.* **2** to cause a feeling: *Her comments provoked a lot of anger.*

prowl /praʊl/ *verb* to move around an area quietly: *A cat prowled the streets.*

pru·dent /ˈpruːdənt/ *adjective* sensible and careful

prune /pruːn/ *noun* a dried PLUM → see picture on page A7

prune /pruːn/ *verb* to cut some of the branches of a tree or bush

pry /praɪ/ *verb* (**pried**, **pries**) **1** to try to find out about someone's private life, when the person does not want you to: *I don't mean to pry, but are you still seeing Tom?* **2** to force something open or away from something else SYNONYM **prise**: *He pried off the lid.*

PS /ˌpiː ˈes/ used at the end of a letter when you want to add something after you have signed your name: *PS Don't forget Jane's birthday.*

pseu·do·nym /ˈsjuːdənɪm $ ˈsudn̩ɪm/ *noun* a false name used by a writer SYNONYM **pen name**: *She wrote under a pseudonym.*

psy·chi·at·ric /ˌsaɪkiˈætrɪk/ *adjective* related to mental illness: *a psychiatric hospital*

psy·chi·a·trist /saɪˈkaɪətrɪst/ *noun* a doctor for people who have a mental illness: *She needs to see a psychiatrist.*

psy·chi·a·try /saɪˈkaɪətri/ *noun* (no plural) the treatment of mental illness

psy·chic /ˈsaɪkɪk/ *adjective* related to strange events or things such as GHOSTS that cannot be explained by science: *She claimed to have psychic powers and be able to predict the future.*

psy·cho·an·a·lyst /ˌsaɪkəʊˈænl-ɪst $ ˌsaɪkoʊˈænl-ɪst/ *noun* someone who treats people with problems by helping them talk about their lives, feelings etc

psy·cho·log·i·cal /ˌsaɪkəˈlɒdʒɪkəl $ ˌsaɪkəˈlɑdʒɪkəl/ *adjective* related to people's minds: *Some soldiers came back from the war with psychological problems.* —**psychologically** /-kli/ *adverb*: *The crash affected her psychologically.*

psy·chol·o·gist /saɪˈkɒlədʒɪst $ saɪˈkɑlədʒɪst/ *noun* someone who studies the way people's minds work

psy·chol·o·gy /saɪˈkɒlədʒi $ saɪˈkɑlədʒi/ *noun* (no plural) the study of the mind

> PRONUNCIATION
> In this word you do not pronounce the **p**.

psy·cho·path /ˈsaɪkəpæθ/ *noun* someone who is very violent because of mental illness

pub /pʌb/ *noun* a place where you can buy and drink alcohol: *I'll meet you at the pub for a drink.*

pu·ber·ty /ˈpjuːbəti $ ˈpjubəˑti/ *noun* (no plural) the time when your body changes from a child's to an adult's: *Has she reached puberty yet?*

pub·lic¹ /ˈpʌblɪk/ *adjective* **1** available for anyone to use or take part in ANTONYM **private**: *public transport • a public meeting* **2** related to the government and the services that it provides for people ANTONYM **private**: *The government wants to reduce public spending.* **3** related to all the people in a country: *Car theft is a matter of great public concern.* **4** done in a place where anyone can see or hear you ANTONYM **private**: *a*

A B C D E F G H I J K L M N O P Q R S T U V W X Y Z

series of public arguments —**publicly** *adverb*: *He had to apologise publicly.*

PHRASES

become public if a piece of information becomes public, it becomes known to everyone: *News of their wedding soon **became public**.*

make something public to give people information that was not known before: *We don't want this information to **be made public**.*

public² *noun*

the public, the general public all the people in a country: *The public have a right to know what the government is doing.* → see Thesaurus at PEOPLE

PHRASES

in public in a place where anyone can see or hear you ANTONYM **in private**: *It was the first time she had sung **in public**.*

pub·li·ca·tion /ˌpʌbləˈkeɪʃən/ *noun* **1** (no plural) when a book becomes available to the public: *The date of publication is May 1st.* **2** (formal) a book or magazine: *scientific publications*

ˌpublic ˈholiday the American word for BANK HOLIDAY

pub·lic·i·ty /pʌˈblɪsəti/ *noun* (no plural) attention from newspapers and television: *The protesters got a lot of publicity.*

pub·li·cize also **publicise** *BrE* /ˈpʌbləsaɪz/ *verb* to tell people about an event or a new film, book etc, especially in the newspapers and on television: *She appeared on TV to publicize her new film.*

ˌpublic reˈlations (abbreviation **PR**) *noun* (no plural) the work of keeping a good relationship between a company and the public: *Giving money to local schools is good for the company's public relations.*

ˌpublic ˈschool *noun* **1** *BrE* a school that parents pay to send their children to **2** *AmE* a free school that is paid for by the government

pub·lish /ˈpʌblɪʃ/ *verb* to print a book or information and make it available for people to read: *a company that publishes children's books*

pub·lish·er /ˈpʌblɪʃə $ ˈpʌblɪʃɚ/ *noun* a company that produces books or magazines: *a publisher of scientific journals*

pub·lish·ing /ˈpʌblɪʃɪŋ/ *noun* (no plural) the business of producing books: *a career in publishing*

pud·ding /ˈpʊdɪŋ/ *noun* a sweet food that you eat as the last part of a meal: *Christmas pudding*

pud·dle /ˈpʌdl/ *noun* a small pool of rain

puddle

puff¹ /pʌf/ *verb* **1** to breathe quickly and with difficulty: *Max was puffing after running for the bus.* **2** to breathe smoke from a cigarette or pipe: *an old man puffing on his pipe*

puff² *noun* a small amount of air, smoke, or wind: *Puffs of smoke came from the chimney.*

pull

pull

push

pull¹ /pʊl/ *verb*

KEY PATTERNS
pull something (towards/over etc something)
pull a door open/closed/shut

to move something towards you ANTONYM **push**: *She pulled the chair forward.* • *He **pulled** a small table **towards** him.* • *He **pulled** the door **closed** behind him.* • *Pull harder!*

PHRASES

pull a gun, pull a knife to take out a gun or knife and threaten someone with it: *He suddenly **pulled a gun on** me.*

pull a face to make your face have a funny or ugly expression

pull your weight to do your share of the work: *The others said he wasn't **pulling** his **weight**.*
pull someone's leg to tell someone something that is not true, as a joke: *He must have been **pulling your leg**!*

PHRASAL VERBS

pull down
pull something down to destroy a building that is no longer needed: *The old factory **was pulled down** in 1995.*

pull in
to drive to the side of the road and stop: *I **pulled in** just past the school.*

pull out
1 to not take part in something that you have agreed to do: *He **pulled out** of the competition because he was ill.* **2** if a car pulls out, it moves towards the middle of the road: *A van **pulled out** in front of me.*

pull over
to drive to the side of the road and stop: *I saw Jenny on the pavement, so I **pulled over**.*

pull through (informal)
to stay alive after a serious injury or illness: *The doctors thought he might not **pull through**.*

pull up
if a car pulls up, it stops: *A taxi **pulled up** outside the house.*

THESAURUS
tug: *I **tugged** at the man's sleeve to get his attention* (=suddenly pulled at it hard).
drag: *She **dragged** a chair closer to the fire* (=pulled it along).
tow: *The car was **towing** a trailer* (=pulling it along behind it. One vehicle tows another).
heave: *They **heaved** the huge fish into the boat* (=pulled it with a lot of effort).

pull² *noun* when you pull something towards you ANTONYM **push**: *He gave the rope a good pull, but it wouldn't move.*

pul·ley /ˈpʊli/ *noun* a piece of equipment for lifting things, which has a wheel and a rope

pull·o·ver /ˈpʊlˌəʊvə $ ˈpʊlˌoʊvɚ/ *noun* a SWEATER

pulp /pʌlp/ *noun* (no plural) a soft substance, especially one made by crushing something: *Mash the bananas to a pulp.*

pul·pit /ˈpʊlpɪt/ *noun* a high place where a priest stands to speak to people in a church

pulse /pʌls/ *noun* the regular beat made by your heart when it is moving blood around your body: *A nurse took my pulse* (=measured how fast it was).

pump¹ /pʌmp/ *noun* **1** a machine that forces liquid or gas into or out of something: *a fuel pump* **2** a type of plain light shoe for women

pump² *verb*

KEY PATTERNS
pump a liquid/gas into/out of something

to make liquid or gas flow somewhere using a machine: *They **pumped** the water out of the boat.*

pump

pump up

PHRASAL VERBS

pump up
pump something up to fill a tyre, ball etc with air: *I **pumped up** some balloons for the party.*

pump·kin /ˈpʌmpkɪn/ *noun* a large round orange vegetable → see picture on page A6

pun /pʌn/ *noun* a joke that is based on two words that sound the same but have different meanings

punch¹ /pʌntʃ/ *verb* to hit something hard with your closed hand: *I'll punch you on the nose!* → see Thesaurus at HIT¹

punch² *noun* **1** (plural **punches**) when someone hits something with their closed hand: *a punch in the stomach* **2** (no plural) a drink that contains fruit juice, water, and often alcohol: *a glass of fruit punch*

punch·line /ˈpʌntʃlaɪn/ *noun* the last few words of a joke or story, which make it funny or clever: *I've forgotten the punchline.*

punc·tu·al /ˈpʌŋktʃuəl/ *adjective* arriving at exactly the right time SYNONYM **on time**: *She's usually so*

A B C D E F G H I J K L M N O P Q R S T U V W X Y Z

punctual. —**punctually** *adverb*: *We expect you to arrive punctually for school.*

punc·tu·a·tion /ˌpʌŋktʃuˈeɪʃən/ *noun* (no plural) the use of marks such as COMMAS and FULL STOPS in a piece of writing: *Make sure your essay has the correct punctuation.*

punc·ture[1] /ˈpʌŋktʃə $ ˈpʌŋktʃɚ/ *noun* a small hole made by a sharp point: *The glass made a puncture in my tyre.*

puncture[2] *verb* to make a small hole in something: *A piece of broken bone had punctured his lung.*

pun·ish /ˈpʌnɪʃ/ *verb*

KEY PATTERNS
punish someone
punish someone for (doing) something

to do something unpleasant to someone because they have done something wrong or illegal: *His dad* ***punished*** *him* ***for*** *lying by not letting him go out for two weeks.* • *He must* ***be punished for*** *this terrible crime.* • *The people who did this will be* ***severely punished.***

pun·ish·ment /ˈpʌnɪʃmənt/ *noun* an action taken to punish someone: *He was made to clear up rubbish as a punishment.*

punk /pʌŋk/ *noun* (no plural) a type of loud violent music popular in the late 1970s and early 1980s

pu·ny /ˈpjuːni/ *adjective* (**punier, puniest**) small, thin, and weak: *a puny little kid*

pu·pil /ˈpjuːpəl/ *noun* a child in a school: *There are 30 pupils in my class.*

pup·pet /ˈpʌpɪt/ *noun* a model of a person or animal that you can move by pulling wires, or by putting your hand inside it

pup·py /ˈpʌpi/ *noun* (plural **puppies**) a young dog

pur·chase[1] /ˈpɜːtʃəs $ ˈpɚtʃəs/ *verb* (formal) to buy something: *You can purchase tickets by phone.* → see Thesaurus at BUY

purchase[2] *noun* (formal) **1** when you buy something: *the purchase of new computers* **2** something you have bought: *This car is my most expensive purchase.*

puppets

glove puppet

puppet

pure /pjʊə $ pjʊr/ *adjective*
1 not mixed with anything else: *This shirt is made of pure silk.*
2 pure water or air does not contain anything harmful: *The air is very pure in the mountains.*

PHRASES
pure chance, pure luck if something happens by pure chance, it happens completely by chance: *We found the right place by* ***pure luck.***

pu·ree /ˈpjʊəreɪ $ pjʊˈreɪ/ *noun* a soft wet food made by crushing something or cutting it up: *tomato puree*

pur·ple /ˈpɜːpəl $ ˈpɚpəl/ *adjective, noun* a colour made by mixing red with blue: *They were both dressed in purple.* • *purple flowers*

pur·pose /ˈpɜːpəs $ ˈpɚpəs/ *noun*

KEY PATTERNS
the purpose of something
do something for a particular purpose

1 the thing that you want to achieve when you do or use something: *My purpose today is to explain how the Internet works.* • *What is* ***the purpose of*** *this meeting?* • *When was this structure built, and* ***for what purpose?*** • *Exercises from this book can be used* ***for teaching purposes.***
2 on purpose if you do something bad on purpose, you intend to do it and do not do it by accident ANTONYM **accidentally**: *Geoff went the wrong way* ***on purpose.*** → see Thesaurus at DELIBERATELY

THESAURUS
aim: *The aim of science is to explain events (=purpose).*
goal: *the best way to achieve this*

A B C D E F G H I J K L M N O P Q R S T U V W X Y Z

goal (=what we want to achieve)
objective (formal): *The government's objective was to make the industry more efficient* (=what it wanted to achieve).

purr /pɜː $ pɚ/ *verb* if a cat purrs, it makes a low soft sound —**purr** *noun*

purse /pɜːs $ pɚs/ *noun* **1** *BrE* a small container that women use to carry money SYNONYM **wallet** *AmE*: *I had very little money in my purse.* **2** the American word for HANDBAG

pur·sue /pəˈsjuː $ pɚˈsu/ *verb* (formal) to chase someone: *A police car pursued them for five miles.* ➔ see Thesaurus at FOLLOW

pur·suit /pəˈsjuːt $ pɚˈsut/ *noun*
1 (no plural) when you chase someone: *The pursuit lasted 20 minutes.*
2 pursuits things that you spend time doing: *outdoor pursuits such as climbing and sailing*

push¹ /pʊʃ/ *verb*

KEY PATTERNS
push something along/over/open
push past someone

1 to put your hand on something and make it move away from you ANTONYM **pull**: *He* ***pushed*** *the wheelchair* ***along****.* • *He* ***pushed*** *her* ***into*** *the car.* • *Joey* ***pushed*** *me* ***over*** *in the playground.* • *Push this button to turn the computer on.* • *Gary* ***pushed*** *the door* ***open****.* ➔ see picture at PULL¹
2 to move forward by pushing people away from you: *Rod* ***pushed past*** *Sal very rudely.* • *Joe* ***pushed his way to*** *the front of the queue.*
3 push someone into doing something to make someone do something that they do not really want to do: *Phil* ***was pushed into*** *joining the Marines by his dad.*

THESAURUS
prod: *He prodded the snake with a stick* (=pushed it. You prod things with your finger or with a long object).
nudge: *I nudged the girl sitting next to me* (=pushed her gently with my elbow, to get her attention or wake her).
shove: *He shoved her aside* (=pushed her roughly).
elbow: *She elbowed her way to the front of the crowd* (=pushed people so that they got out of her way).

push² *noun* (plural **pushes**) **1** when you push someone or something ANTONYM **pull**: *Give the gate a push.*
2 when people try very hard to achieve something: *a push to get more money for schools*

push·chair /ˈpʊʃ-tʃeə $ ˈpʊʃˌtʃer/ *noun BrE* a chair on wheels that is used for pushing a child somewhere SYNONYM **stroller** *AmE*

ˈ**push-up** *noun* an exercise in which you lie on the floor and push yourself up with your arms SYNONYM **press-up**

push·y /ˈpʊʃi/ *adjective* (**pushier**, **pushiest**) determined to get what you want, in a way that seems rude: *a pushy salesman*

put ➔ see box on page 534

puz·zle¹ /ˈpʌzəl/ *noun* **1** a game or toy that is difficult to do: *a crossword puzzle* • *a jigsaw puzzle* **2** something that is difficult to understand: *The meaning of the poem has always been a puzzle.*

puzzle² *verb* if something puzzles you, it confuses you because you cannot understand it: *It puzzles me why you don't like him.*

puz·zled /ˈpʌzəld/ *adjective* confused and unable to understand something: *You look puzzled.*

puz·zling /ˈpʌzlɪŋ/ *adjective* difficult to understand: *I find his reaction puzzling.*

py·ja·mas *BrE*, **pajamas** *AmE* /pəˈdʒɑːməz/ *plural noun* light trousers and a shirt that you wear in bed: *a pair of pyjamas*

pyr·a·mid /ˈpɪrəmɪd/ *noun* a solid shape which is square at the base and pointed at the top: *a paperweight in the shape of a pyramid* ➔ see picture at SHAPE¹

pyramid

py·thon /ˈpaɪθən $ ˈpaɪθɑn/ *noun* a large snake that kills the animals it eats by crushing them

A B C D E F G H I J K L M N O P Q R S T U V W X Y Z

put /pʊt/ *verb* (past tense and past participle **put**, present participle **putting**)

to move something to a place and leave it there: *Where did I **put** my keys?* • *Harry **put** the pen **in** his pocket.* • *I thought I **put** my purse **on** the table, but it's not there now.* • *Did you **put** the cat **outside**?*

PHRASAL VERBS

put away
put something away to put something in the place where you usually keep it: *The kids never **put** anything **away**!* • *Mom is upstairs, **putting away** the clothes.*

put back
put something back to put something in the place where it was before: *Sandy always forgets to **put** the milk **back** in the refrigerator.*

put down
put something down to put something you are holding onto a table or the floor: *Just **put** it **down** on the floor over there.* • *Brianna **put down** her glass.*

put off
put something off to not do something at the time when you should do it, and instead decide to do it later: *I had to **put off** the meeting until next week.*

put on
put something on to put clothes on your body ANTONYM **take off**: ***Put** your coat **on** – it's cold outside!* • *Let me **put on** my glasses – I can't read this.*

put together
put something together to make something by joining all the different parts together: *You can buy really nice furniture there, but you have to **put** it **together** yourself.*

*You can buy really nice furniture there, but you have to **put** it **together** yourself.*

put up
put something up to put something on a wall or in a high position: *The teachers had **put** the children's paintings **up** on the walls.*

put up with
put up with something to accept an annoying situation or someone's annoying behaviour, without trying to stop it or change it: *I don't get paid enough to **put up with** customers being rude to me.* • *How do you **put up with** all this noise?*

WORD CHOICE
put off or **take off**?
• **Put off** means 'to decide to do something later': *I think we should **put off** the meeting till next week.*
• **Take off** means 'to remove something': *He **took off** his coat.*
✗ Don't say 'put off your coat'.

quack /kwæk/ *verb* if a duck quacks, it makes a short loud noise —**quack** *noun*

quad·ru·ple /ˈkwɒdrʊpəl $ kwɑˈdrupəl/ *verb* to become four times as big: *The company's sales quadrupled last year.*

quaint /kweɪnt/ *adjective* attractive in an old-fashioned way: *a quaint little village*

quake /kweɪk/ (informal) an EARTHQUAKE

qual·i·fi·ca·tion /ˌkwɒləfəˈkeɪʃən $ ˌkwɑləfəˈkeɪʃən/ *noun* an official examination that you have passed, which shows what level of education you have reached or what training you have had: *What qualifications do you have?* • *You need to get a qualification in nursing.*

qual·i·fied /ˈkwɒləfaɪd $ ˈkwɑləˌfaɪd/ *adjective* someone who is qualified has passed an official examination that shows they are trained to do a particular job: *a qualified football trainer* • *Are you qualified to be a life guard?*

qual·i·fi·er /ˈkwɒləfaɪə $ ˈkwɑləˌfaɪɚ/ *noun* a person or team that has achieved the standard that is needed to enter a sports competition: *Johnson was the fastest qualifier.*

qual·i·fy /ˈkwɒləfaɪ $ ˈkwɑləˌfaɪ/ *verb* (**qualified**, **qualifies**) **1** to pass an official examination that shows you are trained to do a particular job: *It takes a long time to qualify as a doctor.* **2** to be successful at one stage of a sports competition so that you can continue to the next stage: *She's hoping to qualify for the Olympic Games.*

qual·i·ty /ˈkwɒləti $ ˈkwɑləti/ *noun*
1 (no plural) how good something is: *The quality of the food in that restaurant is very high* (=very good). • *a good quality bed* • *Some of the work was of very* ***poor quality***. • ***top quality*** (=highest quality) *products*
2 (plural **qualities**) something that a person or thing has as part of their character or nature, especially something good: *What qualities do you look for in a student?*

> **THESAURUS**
> **characteristic**: *His most striking characteristic is his modesty* (=quality).
> **property**: *the physical and chemical properties of silicon* (=natural qualities that a substance has)

quan·ti·fi·er /ˈkwɒntəfaɪə $ ˈkwɑntəˌfaɪɚ/ *noun* a word or phrase such as 'much', 'few', or 'a lot of', which is used with a noun to show an amount

quan·ti·ty /ˈkwɒntəti $ ˈkwɑntəti/ *noun* (plural **quantities**) an amount of something that you can measure or count: *We brought* ***a large quantity of*** *food with us.* • ***a small quantity of*** *butter* • *The police discovered huge* ***quantities of*** *drugs hidden in the old building.*

quar·an·tine /ˈkwɒrəntiːn $ ˈkwɔrənˌtin/ *noun* (no plural) when someone with a disease must stay apart from other people so that other people do not get the disease too: *The hospital kept her in quarantine for a week.*

quar·rel¹ /ˈkwɒrəl $ ˈkwɔrəl/ *noun* an angry argument SYNONYM **row** *BrE* SYNONYM **argument**: *I've had a quarrel with my father.*

quarrel² *verb* (**quarrelled**, **quarrelling** *BrE*, **quarreled**, **quarreling** *AmE*) to have an angry argument: *I'm always quarrelling with my sister.* → see Thesaurus at ARGUE

quar·ry /ˈkwɒri $ ˈkwɔri/ *noun* (plural **quarries**) a place where sand or stone is dug out of the ground

quart /kwɔːt $ kwɔrt/ (written abbreviation **qt**) *noun* a unit for measuring liquid, which is equal to two PINTS

quar·ter /ˈkwɔːtə $ ˈkwɔrtɚ/ *noun*

KEY PATTERNS
a quarter of something

1 one of four equal parts that you can divide something into: *She cut the cake into quarters.*
2 25 per cent: *About* **a quarter of** *the students here are Chinese.* • *Over* **three-quarters of** *the forest* (=75 per cent of it) *was destroyed in the fire.*

quarter

He cut the cake into quarters.

3 a coin in the US and Canada worth 25 cents: *Can you lend me a quarter?*
4 *AmE* one of the four periods of time into which the school year is divided

PHRASES
a quarter of an hour 15 minutes: *We waited* **a quarter of an hour** *for the bus.*
(a) quarter to two, quarter to three etc *BrE*, **(a) quarter of two, quarter of three etc** *AmE*: *We leave school at* **quarter to four** (=at 15 minutes before four o'clock).
(a) quarter past two, quarter past three etc *BrE*, **(a) quarter after two, quarter after three etc** *AmE*: *It's a* **quarter after eight** (=it's 15 minutes after eight o'clock).

quar·ter·back /ˈkwɔːtəbæk $ ˈkwɔrtɚˌbæk/ *noun* the most important player in an American football team, who makes the decisions about what the team should do

quar·ter·fi·nal /ˌkwɔːtəˈfaɪnl $ ˌkwɔrtɚˈfaɪnl/ *noun* one of the last four games at the end of a sports competition. The winners play in the two SEMIFINALS

quar·ter·ly /ˈkwɔːtəli $ ˈkwɔrtɚli/ *adjective, adverb* produced or happening four times a year: *a quarterly magazine* • *We pay our electricity bill quarterly.*

quartz /kwɔːts $ kwɔrts/ *noun* (no plural) a type of hard rock used for making electronic clocks

quash /kwɒʃ $ kwɑʃ/ *verb* (formal) **1** to officially say that a decision is not legal or correct any more: *The higher court quashed his conviction for murder.* **2** to use force to stop fighting or protests: *Troops were sent in to quash the rebellion.*

quay /kiː/ *noun* a place beside the sea or a big river for loading and unloading boats

quea·sy /ˈkwiːzi/ *adjective* (**queasier, queasiest**) if you feel queasy, you feel as if you are going to be sick: *The awful smell was making me feel queasy.*

queen /kwiːn/ *noun* **1** the female ruler of a country, or the wife of a king: *Queen Victoria* **2** a playing card with a picture of a queen on it: *the queen of hearts*

queer /kwɪə $ kwɪr/ *adjective* strange and not normal: *His behaviour seemed a bit queer.*

quench /kwentʃ/ *verb* **quench your thirst** to drink something so that you no longer feel thirsty: *I had a drink of water to quench my thirst.*

que·ry[1] /ˈkwɪəri $ ˈkwɪri/ *noun* (plural **queries**) a question asking for more information: *Does anyone have any queries?*

query[2] *verb* (formal) (**queried, queries**) to check that something is correct by asking questions about it: *My mother queried the bill.*

quest /kwest/ *noun* (formal) a long and difficult search: *the quest for life on Mars*

ques·tion[1] /ˈkwestʃən/ *noun*

KEY PATTERNS
ask a question
a question about something
do an exam question

1 something that you say or write when you are asking about something ANTONYM **answer**: *Does anyone want to* **ask** *any* **questions** *before we begin?* • *The police* **asked** *him a lot of* **questions about** *the car.* • *The teacher could not* **answer** *my* **question**.
2 a part of a test that asks you to give information ANTONYM **answer**: *I didn't understand some of the questions in the exam.* • *We had to do 30 questions in an hour.*

PHRASES

be out of the question: *Dad says that having the party here* ***is out of the question*** (=is definitely not allowed).

good question! (spoken) used to say in an amusing way that you do not know the answer to a question: *"How many paintings did Picasso actually do?" "Good question! I have no idea!"*

question² *verb*

> KEY PATTERNS
> **question someone about something**

to ask someone a lot of questions about something: *The police* ***questioned*** *him* ***about*** *the robbery.*

ques·tion·a·ble /ˈkwestʃənəbəl/ *adjective* something that is questionable does not seem to be completely true, correct, or honest: *It is questionable whether this is a good method of teaching.*

ˈquestion mark *noun* the sign (?) that you write at the end of a question

ques·tion·naire /ˌkwestʃəˈneə $ ˌkwestʃəˈner/ *noun* a set of written questions that people answer in order to give information about something: *Could you fill in this questionnaire?*

queue¹ /kjuː/ *noun BrE* a line of people or vehicles that are waiting for something SYNONYM **line** *AmE*: *I joined the back of the queue.* • *There's a long queue at the bank.*

queue

queue² also **queue up** *verb BrE* to wait in a line of people SYNONYM **line up** *AmE*: *How long have you been queueing for tickets?*

quib·ble /ˈkwɪbəl/ *verb* to argue about something that is not very important: *Let's not quibble about 10p.*

quick /kwɪk/ *adjective*

1 something that is quick does not take very much time to do: *Can I make a quick telephone call?* • *Do you know the quickest way to the station?* • *We need a quick decision on this.*

2 someone who is quick moves or does something fast ANTONYM **slow**: *He tried to stop me reaching the door, but I was too quick for him.* • *Children are very* ***quick to*** *learn.*

quick·ly /ˈkwɪkli/ *adverb*

1 with great speed SYNONYM **fast** ANTONYM **slowly**: *Rick ran quickly to the car.*

2 after only a short amount of time SYNONYM **soon**: *We must leave quickly or we'll miss the coach.*

quick·sand /ˈkwɪksænd/ *noun* (no plural) wet sand that is dangerous to walk on because you sink into it

quid /kwɪd/ *noun BrE* (informal) (plural **quid**) a pound in British money: *Will you lend me a quid?*

qui·et¹ /ˈkwaɪət/ *adjective*

1 something that is quiet does not make a lot of noise ANTONYM **loud**: *She spoke in a quiet voice.* • *The music became quieter.*

2 someone who is quiet does not talk very much: *Emily was a quiet, shy girl.* • *"****Be quiet*** (=stop talking)*!" said the teacher.*

3 if a place is quiet, there is not very much noise there and not many things happen there ANTONYM **busy**: *They live in a quiet little village.* • *a quiet country road* • *It was very quiet in town today.*

PHRASES

keep something quiet, keep quiet about something to not talk about something because you do not want other people to know about it: *I've found a job, but I want to* ***keep it quiet*** *for now.* • *It's typical of Roy to* ***keep quiet about*** *winning.*

> THESAURUS
> **low**: *She could just hear the* ***low*** *murmur of voices in the next room* (=quiet).
> **soft**: *the* ***soft*** *rustling of the leaves* (=quiet and pleasant to listen to)

quiet² *noun* (no plural) when there is not very much noise and not many things are happening: *We sat outside, enjoying the quiet of the night.*

qui·et·en /ˈkwaɪətn/ *BrE*, **quiet** *AmE* also **quieten down** *BrE*, **quiet down** *AmE verb* to become quiet after making a lot of noise: *After a while the children quietened down.*

A B C D E F G H I J K L M N O P Q R S T U V W X Y Z

qui•et•ly /ˈkwaɪətli/ *adverb* without making much noise ANTONYM **loudly**: *She quietly turned the key.* • *"I'm sorry," he said quietly.*

quilt /kwɪlt/ *noun* a bed cover filled with soft warm material

quirk•y /ˈkwɜːki $ ˈkwɚki/ *adjective* (**quirkier**, **quirkiest**) slightly strange: *a quirky sense of humour*

quit /kwɪt/ *verb* (informal) (past tense and past participle **quit**, **quitting**) **1** to leave a place or job permanently: *Dad was furious when he found out I'd quit college.* **2** to close a computer program: *If the program won't run, try quitting and restarting.* **3** to stop doing something: *My doctor told me I have to quit smoking.*

quite /kwaɪt/ *adverb*
1 fairly: *It can be quite cold at night.* • *I was quite surprised when Sandy turned up.* • *We had to wait for quite a long time.* • *I quite liked the book.* ➔ see Thesaurus at FAIRLY
2 completely: *I'm afraid that's quite impossible.* • *The special effects in the film were quite amazing!*

PHRASES

not quite almost, but not completely or not exactly: *I **haven't quite** finished.* • *I'm **not quite** sure where the sports centre is.* • *I **don't quite** understand.*

quiv•er /ˈkwɪvə $ ˈkwɪvɚ/ *verb* to shake slightly, especially because you are angry, upset, or nervous SYNONYM **tremble**: *He was quivering with rage.*

quiz /kwɪz/ *noun* (plural **quizzes**) a competition in which you have to answer questions: *Ten teams entered the quiz.*

quo•ta /ˈkwəʊtə $ ˈkwoʊtə/ *noun* an amount of something that someone is allowed to have: *They are not allowed to catch more than their quota of fish.*

quo•ta•tion /kwəʊˈteɪʃən $ kwoʊˈteɪʃən/ *noun* **1** words that come from a book, poem etc SYNONYM **quote**: *a quotation from one of Shakespeare's plays* **2** a statement showing how much money it will cost to do something: *You should obtain several quotations for the job.*

quoˈtation ˌmark *noun* a sign (" or ') that you write before and after someone's speech SYNONYM **inverted comma** *BrE*

quote[1] /kwəʊt $ kwoʊt/ *verb* **1** to say some of the words that are written in a book, poem etc, or that someone else has said: *He's always quoting from the Bible.* **2** to tell a customer the price you will charge them for something: *They quoted us £20 for delivering the bed.*

quote[2] *noun* a QUOTATION

rab·bi /ˈræbaɪ/ *noun* a Jewish religious leader

rab·bit /ˈræbɪt/ *noun* a small animal with long ears and soft fur that lives in holes in the ground → see picture at HARE → see picture on page A8

rab·ble /ˈræbəl/ *noun* (no plural) a noisy crowd of people who are behaving badly: *Get this rabble to be quiet.*

ra·bies /ˈreɪbiːz/ *noun* (no plural) a disease that kills animals and people that are bitten by an infected animal

race[1] /reɪs/ *noun*
1 a competition in which people try to run or drive faster than each other: *Twelve people* ***took part in the race.*** • *Very few of the British athletes* ***won*** *their* ***races.*** • *She came second in her race.*
2 one of the main groups that people can be divided into because they look similar and have the same colour skin: *We employ people of every race and religion.*

race[2] *verb* **1** to run or drive somewhere very quickly: *I raced to catch up with them.* • *A fire engine raced past.* **2** to compete in a race: *She will be racing against athletes from all over the world.*

race·course /ˈreɪs-kɔːs $ ˈreɪs-kɔrs/ *noun* a place where horses compete in races SYNONYM **racetrack** *AmE*

race·horse /ˈreɪshɔːs $ ˈreɪshɔrs/ *noun* a horse that competes in races

race·track /ˈreɪs-træk/ *noun* a special road or area where runners, cars, or horses race

ra·cial /ˈreɪʃəl/ *adjective* relating to the race that someone belongs to: *people from different racial groups* • *The company was accused of racial discrimination* (=treating people unfairly because of their race). —**racially** *adverb*: *a racially motivated attack*

rac·ing /ˈreɪsɪŋ/ *noun* (no plural) a sport in which horses or cars race: *horse racing*

ra·cis·m /ˈreɪsɪzəm/ *noun* (no plural) unfair treatment of someone because of the race that they belong to: *We will not tolerate racism in this school.*

rac·ist /ˈrɪsɪst/ *noun* someone who treats people of another race unfairly —**racist** *adjective*: *Some of the other children were unkind and made racist remarks.*

rack /ræk/ *noun* a shelf or frame for holding things: *a luggage rack* • *a wine rack*

rack·et /ˈrækɪt/ *noun* **1** also **racquet** the thing you use for hitting the ball in games such as tennis: *a tennis racket*
2 (informal) a lot of loud noise: *Who's making that racket?*

ra·dar /ˈreɪdɑː $ ˈreɪdɑr/ *noun* a piece of equipment that finds the position of things such as planes and ships by sending out radio signals

ra·di·ant /ˈreɪdiənt/ *adjective* happy and beautiful: *Sarah, you look radiant!*

ra·di·ate /ˈreɪdieɪt/ *verb* **1** to show a feeling very strongly in your appearance or behaviour: *She radiated confidence.* **2** to send out light or heat: *The electric fire was radiating a lot of heat.*

ra·di·a·tion /ˌreɪdiˈeɪʃən/ *noun* (no plural) dangerous energy that some substances send out: *The process produces high levels of radiation.*

ra·di·a·tor /ˈreɪdieɪtə $ ˈreɪdiˌeɪtɚ/ *noun* **1** an object full of hot water on a wall, which heats the room: *Hang your shirt on the radiator to dry.* **2** a piece of equipment that stops a vehicle's engine from getting too hot

rad·i·cal[1] /ˈrædɪkəl/ *adjective* a change that is radical is big and very noticeable: *They are planning radical changes in education.* —**radically** /-kli/ *adverb*: *It's not radically different.*

radical² *noun* someone who wants to change a political system completely ANTONYM **conservative**

ra·di·o¹ /ˈreɪdiəʊ $ ˈreɪdiˌoʊ/ *noun* **1** a piece of electronic equipment that you use to listen to programmes that are broadcast: *Al* ***switched the radio on*** *to hear his favourite music programme.* • *I listen to English programmes* ***on the radio*** *to improve my listening skills.*
2 (no plural) a system used to broadcast sounds or send messages by electrical waves: *In the early days of radio, equipment was much larger.*

> GRAMMAR
> You hear something **on the radio**.
> ✘ Don't say 'in the radio'.

radio² *verb* to send a message to someone by electrical waves: *The ship's captain radioed for help.*

ra·di·o·ac·tive /ˌreɪdiəʊˈæktɪv $ ˌreɪdioʊˈæktɪv/ *adjective* something that is radioactive sends out RADIATION: *Plutonium is highly radioactive.* • *radioactive nuclear waste*

ra·di·o·ac·tiv·i·ty /ˌreɪdiəʊækˈtɪvəti $ ˌreɪdioʊækˈtɪvəti/ *noun* (no plural) when a substance sends out RADIATION

ra·di·o·ther·a·py /ˌreɪdiəʊˈθerəpi $ ˌreɪdioʊˈθerəpi/ *noun* (no plural) the treatment of illnesses such as CANCER using RADIATION: *She may have to have radiotherapy.*

radish /ˈrædɪʃ/ *noun* a small vegetable whose root is eaten raw. It has a strong spicy taste ➔ see picture on page A6

ra·di·us /ˈreɪdiəs/ *noun* (plural **radii** /-diaɪ/) **1** the distance from the centre of a circle to the edge **2 within a two-mile radius, within a ten-mile radius etc** within a particular distance from a place in any direction: *Police searched houses within a two-mile radius of the crime.*

raf·fle /ˈræfəl/ *noun* a competition in which people buy tickets with numbers on them and win a prize if one of their numbers is chosen: *Would you like to buy some raffle tickets?*

raft /rɑːft $ ræft/ *noun* a flat boat made from long pieces of wood tied together

rag /ræg/ *noun* a piece of old cloth: *Clean the lamp with a rag.*

rage¹ /reɪdʒ/ *noun* extreme anger: *She went wild with rage.*

rage² *verb* if fighting, a storm etc rages, it continues with a lot of force or violence: *The war raged for five years.*

rag·ged /ˈrægɪd/ *adjective* clothes that are ragged are old and torn: *an old pair of ragged jeans.*

raid /reɪd/ *noun* **1** a sudden military attack on a place: *Several buildings were destroyed in the air raid.* **2** a sudden visit by police who are looking for something: *Police found a large number of stolen guns during a raid on the house.* **3** a crime in which thieves enter a bank, shop etc and steal something: *a daring bank raid* —**raid** *verb*: *Thieves broke in and raided the post office.*

rail /reɪl/ *noun* **1** a metal bar that prevents you from moving forward or falling: *She held onto the rail as the boat rocked.* **2** a metal bar that you hang things on: *a towel rail* **3 the rails** the two long metal tracks that trains move along **4 by rail** by train: *It would be quicker to go by rail.*

rail·ings /ˈreɪlɪŋz/ *plural noun* a fence that is made of metal bars: *The gates were shut, so we climbed over the railings.* ➔ see picture at FENCE¹

rail·way /ˈreɪlweɪ/ *BrE*, **rail-road** /ˈreɪlrəʊd $ ˈreɪlroʊd/ *AmE noun* a track for trains to travel along

rain¹ /reɪn/ *noun* (no plural) water that falls in small drops from the sky: *The* ***rain*** *continued to* ***fall*** *overnight.* • *If the* ***rain stops,*** *we'll go out.* • *There was* ***heavy rain*** (=a lot of rain) *last night.*

rain² *verb* when it rains, small drops of water fall from the sky: *If* ***it's raining,*** *we'll have to do something indoors.* • *Take an umbrella in case* ***it rains.*** • ***It started to rain*** *just as we were leaving.*

rain·bow /ˈreɪnbəʊ $ ˈreɪnboʊ/ *noun* a curve of different colours in the sky that

A B C D E F G H I J K L M N O P Q R S T U V W X Y Z

you see when there is sun and rain at the same time → see picture on page A13

rain·coat /ˈreɪnkəʊt $ ˈreɪnkoʊt/ *noun* a coat that you wear to protect you from the rain

raincoat

rain·drop /ˈreɪndrɒp $ ˈreɪndrɑp/ *noun* a single drop of rain

rain·fall /ˈreɪnfɔːl/ *noun* the total amount of rain that falls on an area in a period of time: *Sri Lanka has an annual rainfall of 200–510 cm.*

ˈrain ˌforest *noun* a tropical forest with tall trees that are very close together: *the Amazon rain forests* → see Thesaurus at FOREST

rain·y /ˈreɪni/ *adjective* (**rainier**, **rainiest**) a rainy day, afternoon etc is a day when it rains a lot

raise¹ /reɪz/ *verb*

KEY PATTERNS
raise something
raise money (for someone/something)

1 to move something so that it is higher ANTONYM **lower**: *She raised her head to look at him.* • *The batter raised his bat, ready to hit the ball.*
2 to increase the amount or level of something ANTONYM **lower**: *The company has raised its prices.* • *This drug will raise your temperature.* • *We are raising the standard of our housing.*
3 if you raise money, you collect money from other people so that you can help people who are hungry, ill, poor etc: *The class* ***raised*** *$500* ***for*** *cancer patients.* • *We are* ***raising funds*** (=money) ***for*** *children in Africa.*

PHRASES
raise your voice to speak more loudly than usual, often because you are annoyed with someone: *The teacher had to raise her voice to make the children listen.*
raise a question to mention something to someone because you want them to think about it: *When I* ***raised the question of*** *getting a new car, Rick got quite angry.*
raise fears, raise hopes: *The bomb has* ***raised fears*** (=made people feel afraid) *of more terrorist attacks.* • *I didn't want to* ***raise their hopes*** (=make them feel hopeful).

WORD CHOICE
raise or **rise**?
• **Raise** (=to increase something) is a verb: *The government plans to raise taxes.*
• **Rise** (=an increase) is a noun: *There has been a big* ***rise*** *in the price of oil.*

raise² the American word for RISE²

rai·sin /ˈreɪzən/ *noun* a dried GRAPE that is often used in cakes

rake¹ /reɪk/ *noun* a garden tool that you use for gathering dead leaves together or making the earth level

rake² *verb* **1** to pull a rake over the ground in order to gather dead leaves together or make the earth level: *Rake the soil thoroughly before planting the seeds.* → see picture at GARDENING
2 be raking it in (informal, spoken) to be earning a lot of money: *Hank's really raking it in with his new job!*

ral·ly¹ /ˈræli/ *noun* (plural **rallies**) **1** a very large public meeting that shows support for a political idea: *30,000 workers attended a rally in the capital.*
2 a race for cars or MOTORCYCLES

rally² *verb* (**rallied**, **rallies**) **1** to come together to support someone or something: *In the end, everyone rallied to the president's support.* **2 rally around** also **rally round** *BrE* to support someone when they are in a difficult situation: *My family always rallied round each other in a crisis.*

RAM /ræm/ *noun* (no plural) the part of a computer that keeps information for a short time so that you can use it immediately

ram¹ /ræm/ *verb* (**rammed**, **ramming**) also **ram into** to crash into something: *The driver lost control and rammed into the back of my car.*

ram² *noun* a male sheep

ram·ble¹ /ˈræmbəl/ also **ramble on** *verb* to talk in a boring or confused

A B C D E F G H I J K L M N O P Q R S T U V W X Y Z

way: *He rambled on about all the places he had visited.*

ramble² *noun* a long walk

ramp /ræmp/ *noun* a slope that is put somewhere so that you can get from one level to another: *They walked up the ramp and onto the ship.*

ram·page /ræm'peɪdʒ/ *verb* if people rampage, they behave in a noisy and violent way: *Football fans rampaged through the town.* —**rampage** /'ræmpeɪdʒ/ *noun*: *drunken tourists on the rampage*

ram·pant /'ræmpənt/ *adjective* something bad that is rampant is increasing quickly and is difficult to control: *The disease is rampant throughout the population.* • *rampant inflation*

ram·shack·le /'ræmʃækəl/ *adjective* a ramshackle building is in very bad condition: *a ramshackle old shed*

ran the past tense of RUN

ranch /rɑːntʃ $ ræntʃ/ *noun* (plural **ranches**) a big farm in the US where cows, horses, or sheep are kept

ran·cid /'rænsɪd/ *adjective* food that is rancid smells or tastes unpleasant because it is no longer fresh: *the smell of rancid butter*

ran·dom /'rændəm/ *adjective* **at random** if you choose something or someone at random, you choose them for no particular reason: *Ten people were chosen at random from the audience.*

rang the past tense of RING²

range¹ /reɪndʒ/ *noun*

KEY PATTERNS
a range of things
in the range of 20% to 25% etc

1 a number of different things that are all the same type of thing: *Mitsubishi has brought out **a new range of** small cars.* • *People have **a wide range of** views on this issue.* • *If you want to buy a tent, there's **a huge range** to choose from.*
2 the amounts or numbers between two limits: *The water temperature should be **in the range of** 76 to 89 degrees.* • *The school has children in the five to 11 **age range**.*

range² *verb* **range from something to something** to be between two limits: *The children ranged in age from five to 14.* • *Prices range from about £100 to £500.*

rang·er /'reɪndʒə $ 'reɪndʒɚ/ *noun* someone whose job is to look after a large area of public land: *She works as a park ranger at Yellowstone National Park.*

rank¹ /ræŋk/ *noun*
1 the position that someone has in the army, the police etc, that shows how important they are: *He **held the rank of** colonel in the British army.*
2 the ranks the ordinary soldiers in an army: *Morale in **the ranks** was low after the defeat.*
3 a line of people or things: *a taxi rank* • *Ranks of people lined the streets.*

rank² *verb* to have a particular position in a list that shows how good someone or something is: *The team ranks third in the nation.*

ran·sack /'rænsæk/ *verb* to damage a place and make it very untidy, often because you are looking for something: *The thieves ransacked the house and stole jewellery worth £2,000.*

ran·som /'rænsəm/ *noun* the money that criminals ask you to pay before they will free a prisoner: *The kidnappers demanded a ransom of £175,000 for the child.*

rant /rænt/ also **rant on** *verb* to talk for a long time in an angry way: *My father was ranting on about me coming home too late.*

rap¹ /ræp/ *noun* **1** a quick light knock on a door or window **2** a type of popular music in which the words are spoken, not sung

rap² *verb* (**rapped**, **rapping**) **1** to hit something quickly and lightly: *A policeman came and rapped on my car window.* **2** to speak the words of a song in the type of popular music called rap

rape¹ /reɪp/ *verb* to force someone to have sex when they do not want to

rape² *noun* the crime of raping someone

rap·id /ˈræpɪd/ *adjective* very quick: *I did some rapid calculations in my head.* —**rapidly** *adverb*: *He walked rapidly away.*

rap·ids /ˈræpɪdz/ *plural noun* a part of a river where the water is moving very fast over rocks

rap·ist /ˈreɪpɪst/ *noun* someone who forces someone else to have sex with them when they do not want to

rare /reə $ rer/ *adjective* if something is rare, it does not happen often or there are not many things of that type ANTONYM **common**: *Mary was born with a rare heart disease.* • *He was excited to see such a rare bird.*

rare·ly /ˈreəli $ ˈrerli/ *adverb* not very often ANTONYM **frequently**: *I rarely see my parents now.*

> **THESAURUS**
> **seldom** (formal): *He **seldom** goes to bed before midnight* (=rarely).
> **hardly ever**: *It **hardly ever** rains here* (=very rarely).

rar·ing /ˈreərɪŋ $ ˈrerɪŋ/ *adjective* **be raring to go** (informal) to be eager to start doing something: *Come on! We're all raring to go!*

ras·cal /ˈrɑːskəl $ ˈræskəl/ *noun* a child who behaves badly, but not in a very serious way

rash¹ /ræʃ/ *adjective* done too quickly, without enough thought: *Giving up my job was a rash decision.*

rash² *noun* (plural **rashes**) a lot of small red spots on someone's skin that is often a sign of illness: *Tom had a temperature, and a rash all over his chest.*

rasp·ber·ry /ˈrɑːzbəri $ ˈræzˌberi/ *noun* (plural **raspberries**) a small soft sweet red fruit that grows on bushes → see picture on page A7

rat /ræt/ *noun* an animal like a large mouse with a long tail

rate¹ /reɪt/ *noun*
1 the number of times that something happens over a period of time: *The exam has a very **high** failure **rate*** (=a lot of people fail it). • *The crime **rate rose*** (=increased) *by 3% last year.*
2 the speed at which something happens: ***the rapid rate of** change in technology*
3 the amount of money that you earn or pay for something: *What is the **rate of pay** for the job?* • *The government has increased the tax rate.*
4 at any rate (spoken): *Tom brought a torch, so **at any rate*** (=whatever else happens) *we'll be able to see where we are.*

rate² *verb* to say how good or bad you think someone or something is: *Each game is rated on a scale of 1 to 4, with 4 being best.*

ra·ther /ˈrɑːðə $ ˈræðɚ/ *adverb*
1 fairly: *I think you're being rather unfair.* • *It's rather cloudy – do you think it's going to rain?* • *That's rather an odd thing to do.* → see Thesaurus at FAIRLY
2 or rather used to give different information to what you have just said: *She's at university, or rather she was until last week.*

PHRASES
rather than something/someone not something or someone else: *The pupils wear their ordinary clothes **rather than** a school uniform.* • *We could walk to the station **rather than** waiting for a taxi.*
would rather if you would rather do something, you would prefer to do it: *I'd **rather** be outside on a lovely sunny day like this.* • *He said he **would rather** not talk about his problems.*

rat·ing /ˈreɪtɪŋ/ *noun* a measurement of how good or popular something or someone is: *The hotel had a five-star rating, and was very expensive.*

ra·ti·o /ˈreɪʃiəʊ $ ˈreɪʃiˌoʊ/ *noun* the difference in size between two numbers or amounts that you are comparing: *In our school, the ratio of boys to girls is about 2:1.*

ra·tion¹ /ˈræʃən/ *noun* the amount of food, petrol etc that you are allowed to have when there is not very much available: *During the war the weekly meat ration was very small.*

ration² *verb* to limit the amount of something that people are allowed to have because there is not very much available: *On the ship, water had to be strictly rationed.*

ra·tion·al /ˈræʃənəl/ *adjective*
1 rational decisions are based on facts

or knowledge, not on your feelings ANTONYM **irrational**: *You should be fully informed so that you can make a rational decision.* **2** someone who is rational is able to think clearly about things ANTONYM **irrational**: *Lucy was upset, and was not being very rational.*

'rat race *noun* **the rat race** (informal) the way people live when they are always competing against each other in order to be richer or more successful: *I was tired of the rat race so I gave up my job and went to live in the country.*

rat·tle¹ /'rætl/ *verb* if something rattles, or if it is rattled, it shakes and makes a noise: *The earthquake only lasted a few seconds, but it rattled all the doors and windows.* → see picture on page A1

rattle² *noun* **1** a baby's toy that makes a noise when you shake it **2** the noise something makes when it rattles: *the rattle of cups and plates*

rattlesnake

rat·tle·snake /'rætlsneɪk/ *noun* a poisonous American snake that makes a noise with its tail

rav·age /'rævɪdʒ/ *verb* to destroy or badly damage a town or an area: *The enemy soldiers attacked, ravaging villages and towns.*

rave¹ /reɪv/ *noun* a large party where young people dance to electronic music

rave² also **rave on** *verb* (spoken) **1** to talk in an excited way about something because you think it is very good: *Sam's always raving about this music, but I don't like it much.* **2** to talk for a long time in an angry way: *Mum raved on at me about the state of my bedroom.*

rave³ *adjective* **rave reviews** if a new film, book, or play gets rave reviews, people praise it a lot in newspapers, on the television etc

rav·e·nous /'rævənəs/ *adjective* extremely hungry SYNONYM **starving**

ra·vine /rə'viːn/ *noun* a deep narrow valley with steep sides SYNONYM **gorge**

rav·ing /'reɪvɪŋ/ *adjective* (informal) crazy: *He was acting like a raving lunatic.*

raw /rɔː/ *adjective*
1 raw food has not been cooked SYNONYM **uncooked**: *a salad of raw vegetables • You can cook apples, or eat them raw.*
2 raw materials or substances are still in their natural state and have not been changed or used for making anything yet: *France imports **raw materials** such as coal and steel. • raw cotton*

> **PRONUNCIATION**
> You pronounce **raw** like 'more'.

ray /reɪ/ *noun* a narrow line of light from the sun: *A ray of light came through a gap in the curtains.*

ra·zor /'reɪzə $ 'reɪzɚ/ *noun* a sharp tool that you use for removing hair from your face or body

Rd. *noun* the written abbreviation of ROAD, used in addresses: *46 Cranberry Rd.*

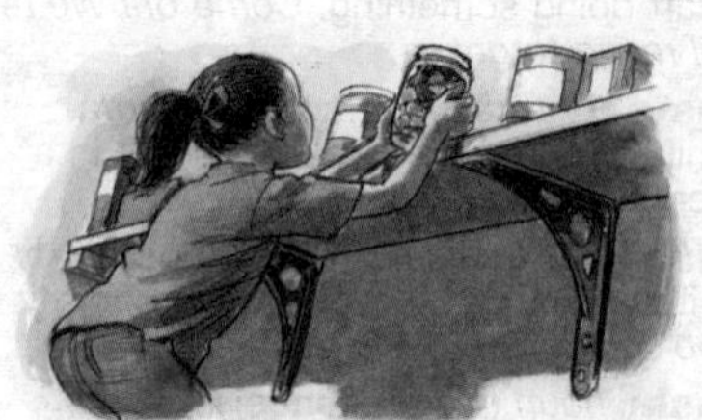
reach

reach¹ /riːtʃ/ *verb*

> **KEY PATTERNS**
> **reach a place/person/thing**
> **reach for something**

1 to arrive at a place: *We reached the village just after lunchtime. • Your email took three hours to reach me.* → see Thesaurus at ARRIVE
2 to move your hand in order to touch something or pick it up: *The man **reached for** his gun. • She had to **reach up** to close the window. • Ann **reached out her hand** and caught the ball.*
3 if you can reach something, you are able to touch it or pick it up by stretching towards it: ***Can you reach** that book on the top shelf?*

A B C D E F G H I J K L M N O P Q R S T U V W X Y Z

4 to get to a particular level or amount: *We reached the quarterfinal of the competition.* • *The number of deaths from the disease has reached 700.*
5 to speak to someone, especially by telephone SYNONYM **contact**: *You can reach me on my mobile.*

GRAMMAR
You **reach a place**.
✘ Don't say 'reach to a place'.

reach² *noun* **1 out of reach, out of someone's reach** too far away for someone to pick up or touch by stretching out their hand: *Keep the medicine out of children's reach.*
2 within reach, within someone's reach near enough for someone to pick up or touch when they stretch out their hand: *The key was just within my reach.*

re·act /ri'ækt/ *verb*

KEY PATTERNS
react to an event
react by doing something

if you react to something that has happened, you behave in a particular way because of it: *I didn't know how you would* ***react to*** *my news.* • *After the new rules were announced, the staff* ***reacted by*** *refusing to teach any more classes.* • *The workers reacted angrily when smoking was banned in the factory.*

PHRASAL VERBS
react against something/someone to show that you do not accept something that someone is telling you to do by deliberately doing the opposite: *My parents were very strict, and I* ***reacted against*** *them.*

re·ac·tion /ri'ækʃən/ *noun*

KEY PATTERNS
a reaction to an event

1 what you do, feel, or say because of something that happens or something you see: *What was her reaction when you told her the school was going to close?* • *I was very surprised by John's* ***reaction to*** *the news.* • *What was the reaction of the audience when she came onto the stage?*
2 reactions your ability to move quickly when something happens suddenly: *This computer game tests your reactions.*

read /riːd/ *verb* (past tense and past participle **read** /red/)

KEY PATTERNS
read a book/newspaper/letter etc
read about a subject/event
read (a story/letter etc) to someone
read someone a story/letter etc

1 to look at something that is written down, and understand what it means: *Dad sat in his chair, reading the paper.* • *My little brother is learning to read.* • *I like* ***reading about*** *space travel.*
2 to say words that are written down in a book, letter etc so that other people can hear: *Fathers now have more time to* ***read to*** *their kids.* • *Mum, will you read me a story?*

PHRASAL VERBS
read out
read something out to say the words that are written in a message, list etc so that other people can hear them: *I will now* ***read out*** *the names of the winners.*
read through, read over
read something through, read something over to read something carefully from the beginning to the end, especially in order to check it: *Would you mind* ***reading through*** *my essay?* • *I* ***read over*** *my notes the night before the exam.*
read up on
read up on something to read a lot about something so that you can learn about it: *Catherine* ***read up on*** *the company before her job interview.*

THESAURUS
look through: *I've* ***looked through*** *the guide book to get an idea of what the city is like* (=read it quickly).
flip through/flick through (informal) *BrE: While I waited, I* ***flipped through*** *a magazine* (=looked at the pages quickly).
pore over: *He spent hours* ***poring over*** *books on architecture* (=reading or looking at them carefully).

read·a·ble /'riːdəbəl/ *adjective* interesting and enjoyable to read: *His second book is more readable than his first.*

read·er /ˈriːdə $ ˈridɚ/ *noun* someone who reads books, magazines etc: *These books are aimed at adult readers.*

read·er·ship /ˈriːdəʃɪp $ ˈridɚˌʃɪp/ *noun* the number or type of people who read a newspaper, magazine etc: *The newspaper has a readership of 460,000.*

read·i·ly /ˈredəli/ *adverb* quickly and easily: *Jack readily agreed.*

read·i·ness /ˈredinəs/ *noun* (no plural) willingness to do something: *Small children have a natural readiness to learn.*

read·ing /ˈriːdɪŋ/ *noun* (no plural) when you read books, magazines etc: *Did you enjoy the reading?*

read·y /ˈredi/ *adjective*

KEY PATTERNS
get ready
ready to do something
ready for something
ready to use/eat

1 if you are ready, you have done everything that you need to do in order to prepare for something: *Are you* ***ready to*** *go yet?* • *I need to go home and* ***get ready for*** *the party.*
2 something that is ready is prepared and available for someone to use, eat, have etc: *Your dinner will be ready soon.* • *When will my shoes be* ***ready for*** *collection?* • *The mixture is now* ***ready to*** *use.*
3 if you are ready for something, you are old enough or sensible enough to do it: *I don't think I'm* ***ready for*** *a full-time job yet.* • *He doesn't* ***feel ready to*** *get married.*

ˌready-ˈmade *adjective* ready-made meals, clothes etc have been prepared or made before you buy them and are ready for you to use: *ready-made pasta dishes*

real /rɪəl/ *adjective*
1 something that is real is not imagined, because it actually happens or exists: *The story is based on real events.*
2 true and not pretended: *Joe Brown is not his real name.* • *What's the real reason you were late?*
3 not false or artificial ANTONYM **fake**: *The necklace was made of real gold.*
4 used to emphasize what you are saying: *At this price, the tickets are a real bargain.*

ˈreal esˌtate *noun* (no plural) property such as houses or land

ˈreal estate ˌagent the American word for ESTATE AGENT

rea·lis·tic /rɪəˈlɪstɪk/ *adjective* someone who is realistic accepts the facts about a situation and realizes what is possible and what is not possible: *Be realistic! We can't possibly afford to buy that car!*

re·al·i·ty /riˈæləti/ *noun* (no plural) what is true or what actually happens: *You must accept the reality of the situation.* • *He said he was a pilot but in reality he was a salesman.*

reˈality ˌshow *noun* a television programme that shows real people in real situations, and does not use actors. The people are filmed continuously over a period of time.

reˈality TˌV *noun* television programmes that show real people being filmed continuously over a period of time

rea·li·za·tion also **realisation** *BrE* /ˌrɪəlaɪˈzeɪʃən $ ˌrɪələˈzeɪʃən/ *noun* (no plural) when you realize something that you did not know before: *the realization that Dan had lied to me*

rea·lize also **realise** *BrE* /ˈrɪəlaɪz/ *verb*

KEY PATTERNS
realize (that)
realize how/what/who etc

to notice or understand something that you did not notice or understand before: *I suddenly realized it was getting late.* • *The school acted quickly once it* ***realized that*** *the problem was serious.* • *Nobody* ***realized how*** *unhappy she was.* • *I finally* ***realized what*** *I had done.*

real·ly /ˈrɪəli/ *adverb*
1 very or very much: *She's been really ill.* • *I really enjoyed our holiday there.*
2 if something really happens or is really true, it does happen or is true and is not imagined: *You're not really sleeping – you're just pretending.* • *Are you really going to America for your holidays?*

3 **Really?** (spoken) used when you are surprised about what someone has said: *"Sandra's having a party on Friday night." "Really?"*

re·ap·pear /ˌriːəˈpɪə $ ˌriəˈpɪr/ *verb* to appear again: *At that moment the door opened and Anna reappeared.*

rear¹ /rɪə $ rɪr/ *noun* **the rear** the back part of a vehicle, building etc ANTONYM **the front**: *I went round to the rear of the house but there was no one there.* —**rear** *adjective*: *the car's rear window*

rear² *verb* to look after a person or animal until they grow up SYNONYM **raise**

re·ar·range /ˌriːəˈreɪndʒ/ *verb* **1** to change the position or order of things: *We could rearrange these chairs to make a little more space.* **2** to change the time of a planned event: *The match has been rearranged for April 28th.*

rear·ward /ˈrɪəwəd $ ˈrɪrwərd/ *adverb* *AmE* towards the back of something: *I'd prefer a seat facing rearward on the train.*

rea·son¹ /ˈriːzən/ *noun*

KEY PATTERNS
the reason for something
the reason (that)
the/any reason why
a reason to do something

1 why someone does something, or why something happens: *What was **the reason for** the delay?* • *One reason the team played so badly was that Malcolm was injured.* • *Did he give you **any reason why** he called?*
2 a fact that makes it sensible or fair for you to do something or think something: *I **had no reason to** think he was lying.* • *You **have every reason to** feel angry.*

GRAMMAR
You say the **reason for** something.
✗ Don't say 'the reason of something'.

reason² *verb* **1** to decide that something is true by thinking carefully about the facts: *I reasoned that I had at least half an hour before the others got back.* **2 reason with someone** to talk to someone in order to persuade them to be more sensible: *I've tried reasoning with him, but he won't listen.*

rea·son·a·ble /ˈriːzənəbəl/ *adjective*
1 a reasonable amount or number is not too much or too big: *The hotel has good food, and the prices are reasonable.*
2 fair and sensible: *It seems like a reasonable idea to me.*

rea·son·a·bly /ˈriːzənəbli/ *adverb*
1 fairly: *I felt reasonably sure that I knew the way.* **2** in a way that is fair or acceptable: *He could not have reasonably asked you to do more.*

rea·son·ing /ˈriːzənɪŋ/ *noun* (no plural) the reasons that make you decide or think something: *What was the reasoning behind the decision?*

re·as·sure /ˌriːəˈʃʊə $ ˌriəˈʃʊr/ *verb* to make someone feel less worried: *"It'll be all right," Tim said, reassuring her.* —**reassuring** *adjective*: *New students should make a reassuring phone call home.*

reb·el¹ /ˈrebəl/ *noun* someone who fights against the government or opposes a person in authority: *There has been further fighting between the army and the rebels in the south.*

re·bel² /rɪˈbel/ *verb* (**rebelled**, **rebelling**) to fight against the government or oppose a person in authority: *Jim hated school and rebelled against his teachers.*

re·bel·lion /rɪˈbeljən/ *noun* fighting against the government or opposing a person in authority: *There was widespread rebellion and eventually civil war.*

re·bel·lious /rɪˈbeljəs/ *adjective* deliberately disobeying someone in authority: *At 15, Karl began to get very rebellious.*

re·build /ˌriːˈbɪld/ *verb* (past tense and past participle **rebuilt** /-ˈbɪlt/) to build something again, after it has been damaged or destroyed: *The cathedral had to be rebuilt after the war.*

rebuilt the past tense and past participle of REBUILD

re·buke /rɪˈbjuːk/ *verb* (formal) to tell someone that something they have done is wrong: *My mother rebuked me for being unkind.*

re·call /rɪˈkɔːl/ *verb* to remember something: *I'm afraid I don't recall his name.*

re·cap /ˈriːkæp/ *noun* when you repeat the main points of something you have already said: *It's time for a quick recap of tonight's main news.*

re·cede /rɪˈsiːd/ *verb* (formal) if something you can hear or see recedes, it gets further away from you: *The sound of his footsteps receded down the stairs.*

re·ceipt /rɪˈsiːt/ *noun* a piece of paper which shows how much you have paid for something: *I paid the bill and the waiter brought me a receipt.*

re·ceive /rɪˈsiːv/ *verb*

> KEY PATTERNS
> **receive something (from someone)**

to get something that is given or sent to you: *You should receive the package by Saturday.* • *I* **received** *a letter from my aunt.*

> SPELLING
> This word is often spelled wrongly. The correct spelling is: **receive**.

re·ceiv·er /rɪˈsiːvə $ rɪˈsivɚ/ *noun* the part of a telephone that you hold to your ear

re·cent /ˈriːsənt/ *adjective* something recent happened or was done only a short time ago: *This is John Irving's most recent book.*

re·cent·ly /ˈriːsəntli/ *adverb* not very long ago: *I saw James quite recently.* • *Have you talked to Anna recently?* • *James recently changed schools.*

> THESAURUS
> **lately**: *The team hasn't been doing well* ***lately*** (=recently).
> **just**: *I've* ***just*** *spoken to him on the phone* (=only a short time ago).

re·cep·tion /rɪˈsepʃən/ *noun* **1** (no plural) a desk near the entrance of a hotel or other organization where you go when you first arrive: *Please sign your name at reception when you arrive.* **2** a big formal party to celebrate a wedding or welcome an important visitor ➔ see Thesaurus at PARTY[1]

re·cep·tion·ist /rɪˈsepʃənɪst/ *noun* someone who works at a desk near the entrance of a hotel or other organization, and helps people when they arrive

re·cep·tive /rɪˈseptɪv/ *adjective* willing to listen to new ideas or opinions: *The other members of staff were quite receptive to my ideas.*

re·cess /rɪˈses $ ˈrises/ *noun* **1** (plural **recesses**) a period of time when a parliament is not working: *The bill will not be passed before Congress begins its autumn recess.* **2** (no plural) *AmE* a short period of time between classes at school SYNONYM **break** *BrE*

re·ces·sion /rɪˈseʃən/ *noun* a time when businesses in a country are not successful: *During the recession there were more than three million people unemployed.*

re·charge /ˌriːˈtʃɑːdʒ $ ˌriˈtʃɑrdʒ/ *verb* to put more electricity into a BATTERY (=an object that provides the electrical power for a toy, machine, car etc): *I need to recharge the car's battery.*

re·charge·a·ble /ˌriːˈtʃɑːdʒəbəl $ ˌriˈtʃɑrdʒəbəl/ *adjective* able to be recharged: *rechargeable batteries*

re·ci·pe /ˈresəpi/ *noun* a list of the things you need in order to cook something, and instructions on how to cook it: *a recipe for strawberry ice cream*

re·cip·ro·cal /rɪˈsɪprəkəl/ *adjective* a reciprocal arrangement or relationship involves two people, groups, or countries who each do something for the other: *It's a reciprocal arrangement – our students visit their school, and their students visit ours.*

re·cite /rɪˈsaɪt/ *verb* to repeat the words of something you have learned, such as a poem, in front of an AUDIENCE: *Susan recited the whole poem without a single mistake.*

reck·less /ˈrekləs/ *adjective* doing something in a dangerous way, without thinking about the risks: *Hazlett was fined £80 for reckless driving.*

reck·on /ˈrekən/ *verb* (informal) to think or guess something: *I reckon you have a very good chance of winning.*

re•claim /rɪˈkleɪm/ *verb* (formal) to ask for something that is yours to be given back to you SYNONYM **claim back**: *If you pay now, you can reclaim the money later.*

re•cline /rɪˈklaɪn/ *verb* (formal) to lie or sit back in a relaxed way: *Alice was reclining on the sofa, reading a magazine.*

re•clin•ing /rɪˈklaɪnɪŋ/ *adjective* a reclining chair has a back that you can move, so that it slopes backwards

rec•og•ni•tion /ˌrekəgˈnɪʃən/ *noun* (no plural) **1** when a lot of people admire or respect someone or something: *These examinations have worldwide recognition.* **2** being recognized by people: *It's impossible for someone like Madonna to avoid recognition.*

rec•og•nize also **recognise** *BrE* /ˈrekəgnaɪz/ *verb*

KEY PATTERNS
recognize someone/something
recognize that

1 to know someone or something because you have seen them before and remember them: *I recognized quite a few people in the crowd.* • *I hadn't seen her for years – I hardly recognized her.*
2 (formal) to accept that something is true: *The school has recognized the need for improvement.* • *I **recognize that** this will be difficult.*

re•coil /rɪˈkɔɪl/ *verb* to move back suddenly, away from something that is unpleasant or that you are afraid of: *Lisa recoiled from the spider, and screamed.*

rec•ol•lect /ˌrekəˈlekt/ *verb* (formal) to remember something: *I don't recollect the name of the hotel.*

rec•ol•lec•tion /ˌrekəˈlekʃən/ *noun* (formal) when you are able to remember something, or something that you remember: *I woke up in the morning with no recollection of where I was.* • *We listened to his recollections of life during the war.*

rec•om•mend /ˌrekəˈmend/ *verb*

KEY PATTERNS
recommend something (to someone)
recommend (that)

1 to tell someone that something is good or enjoyable: *I've **recommended** the book **to** all my friends.*
2 to tell someone that they should do something: *Doctors **recommend that** people eat more fresh fruit and vegetables.*

SPELLING
This word is often spelled wrongly. The correct spelling is: **recommend**.

rec•om•men•da•tion /ˌrekəmenˈdeɪʃən/ *noun* (formal) a suggestion about what someone should do: *The report made several recommendations for action.*

rec•on•cile /ˈrekənsaɪl/ *verb* (formal) **be reconciled** to become friendly with someone again after you have had a serious argument: *They were finally reconciled with each other, after two years of not speaking.*

re•con•sid•er /ˌriːkənˈsɪdə $ ˌrikənˈsɪdɚ/ *verb* (formal) to think about something again so that you can decide whether you should change your opinion: *Do you think you might reconsider your decision in the future?*

re•con•struct /ˌriːkənˈstrʌkt/ *verb* (formal) to build something again after it has been destroyed SYNONYM **rebuild**: *There are plans to reconstruct the old bridge.*

rec•ord¹ /ˈrekɔːd $ ˈrekɚd/ *noun*

KEY PATTERNS
a record of events
keep a record
the record for (doing) something
hold/set/break a record

1 information that you write down and keep so that you can look at it later: ***Keep a record of** all the money you spend.* • *The police **keep records of** all crimes, even minor ones.*
2 the best that anyone has ever achieved, especially in a sport: *She **holds** the current **world record for** downhill skiing.* • *Powell **broke the record** in the long jump* (=he got a better result than the last record).

3 a round flat black piece of plastic that music is stored on: *He's got a wonderful collection of old Beatles records.*

PHRASES

on record information that is on record has been written down and kept: *This winter was the warmest **on record*** (=the warmest since temperatures have been written down).

re·cord² /rɪˈkɔːd $ rɪˈkɔrd/ *verb*

1 to store music, words, television programmes etc on tape or DISCS so that people can listen to them or watch them again: *The band has just recorded a new album.*

2 to write down information and keep it so that you can look at it later: *We have been recording information about the weather for many years.*

PRONUNCIATION

You pronounce the verb **reCORD**, with the stress on the second syllable. You pronounce the noun **REcord**, with the stress on the first syllable.

re·cord·er /rɪˈkɔːdə $ rɪˈkɔrdɚ/ *noun* a simple musical instrument, which you play by blowing into it and covering the holes with your fingers

re·cord·ing /rɪˈkɔːdɪŋ $ rɪˈkɔrdɪŋ/ *noun* a piece of music, speech etc that has been recorded: *a new recording of Beethoven's Fifth Symphony*

ˈrecord ˌplayer *noun* a piece of equipment that you use for playing records

re·count /rɪˈkaʊnt/ *verb* (formal) to describe an event or to tell a story: *Jeremy was in the kitchen, recounting the events of the day.*

re·cov·er /rɪˈkʌvə $ rɪˈkʌvɚ/ *verb*

KEY PATTERNS

recover from an illness/injury etc

1 to become healthy again after you have been ill or hurt: *Gordon is **recovering from** a knee injury.*

2 to become strong again: *It will be years before the country **recovers from** the war.*

re·cov·er·y /rɪˈkʌvəri/ *noun* (no plural)

1 when someone becomes healthy again after being ill or hurt: *She will make a full recovery after the operation.*

2 when something becomes strong again after it has been weak: *Creating more jobs should help the country's economic recovery.*

re·cre·ate /ˌriːkriˈeɪt/ *verb* to make something like it was in the past, or like something in another place: *The zoo aims to recreate the animals' natural habitats as closely as possible.*

rec·re·a·tion /ˌrekriˈeɪʃən/ *noun* (formal) the things you do for pleasure when you are not working: *The town has excellent facilities for recreation and leisure.*

recruit¹ /rɪˈkruːt/ *verb* to find new people to work in a company or join an organization: *Many companies are keen to recruit young people during their last year at university.*

recruit² *noun* someone who has recently joined an organization, especially the army: *New recruits are sent on a training course.*

rec·tan·gle /ˈrektæŋgəl/ *noun* a shape such as a square, with four straight sides and four right angles → see picture at SHAPE¹

rec·tan·gu·lar /rekˈtæŋgjələ $ rekˈtæŋgjəlɚ/ *adjective* shaped like a rectangle: *a rectangular room*

rec·ti·fy /ˈrektəfaɪ/ *verb* (formal) (**rectified**, **rectifies**) to change something that is wrong and make it right SYNONYM **put right**: *We need to rectify all the problems with the system.*

re·cu·pe·rate /rɪˈkjuːpəreɪt/ *verb* (formal) to spend time resting after an illness or injury until you feel better again SYNONYM **recover**: *He spent the summer recuperating after a back operation.*

re·cur /rɪˈkɜː $ rɪˈkɚ/ *verb* (formal) (**recurred**, **recurring**) to happen again: *The doctor told me to come back if the problem recurred.*

re·cy·cle /ˌriːˈsaɪkəl/ *verb* if people recycle things that have been used, they use them again, after putting them through a special process: *Things like used bottles, paper, and cans are collected for recycling.*

red¹ /red/ *adjective* (**redder**, **reddest**)

1 something that is red is the colour of

blood: *a red car* **2** red hair is an orange-brown colour

red² *noun* the colour of blood: *the reds and yellows of the autumn leaves*

ˌred-ˈhanded *adjective* **catch someone red-handed** (informal) to catch someone at the moment when they are doing something wrong: *The police caught the burglars red-handed, climbing through the window.*

red·head /ˈredhed/ *noun* someone who has red hair, especially a woman

ˌred-ˈhot *adjective* something that is red-hot has become so hot that it is red in colour: *red-hot coals*

redid the past tense of REDO

re·do /riːˈduː/ *verb* (**redid** /-ˈdɪd/, **redone** /-ˈdʌn/) to do something again: *I've just cleaned this room, and I don't want to have to redo it.*

redone the past participle of REDO

ˌred ˈtape *noun* (no plural) official rules that seem unnecessary and prevent people from doing things quickly and easily: *There's so much red tape it took me ages to get my visa.*

re·duce /rɪˈdjuːs $ rɪˈdus/ *verb*

KEY PATTERNS
reduce something (by an amount)
reduce something (from one amount to another amount)

to make the amount or size of something less than it was before ANTONYM **increase**: *We had to reduce the price of our house in order to sell it.* • *We have* **reduced** *our heating bills* **by** *ten per cent.* • *The number of employees has been* **reduced from** *30* **to** *only 22.*

THESAURUS
lower: *They keep* **lowering** *their prices* (=reducing them).
decrease (formal): *How can you* **decrease** *your risk of heart disease* (=reduce it)?
lessen: *ways to* **lessen** *the effects of pollution* (=reduce them)
cut: *They want to* **cut** *the number of deaths on the roads* (=reduce them).

re·duc·tion /rɪˈdʌkʃən/ *noun*

KEY PATTERNS
a reduction in something

when the amount or size of something becomes less than it was before ANTONYM **increase**: *There's been* **a reduction in** *the number of deaths from car accidents.*

re·dun·dant /rɪˈdʌndənt/ *adjective* **make someone redundant** *BrE* to stop employing someone because there is not enough work for them any more: *Part of the factory was closed, and 100 workers were made redundant.*

reed /riːd/ *noun* a plant like tall grass that grows in or near water → see picture on page A10

reef /riːf/ *noun* a long line of rocks or CORAL (=a hard substance formed from dead sea animals) near the surface of the sea: *a coral reef*

reek /riːk/ *verb* to smell strongly of something unpleasant SYNONYM **stink**: *He came in reeking of cigarettes and beer.*

reel¹ /riːl/ *noun* a round object that you wind something long onto, for example thread or film: *a cotton reel*

reel² *verb* **1** to walk in an unsteady way: *The man was reeling a little, as if he was drunk.* **2 reel something off** to say a list of things quickly and easily, using your memory: *Sally reeled off the names of everyone who she had invited to the party.*

re·fer /rɪˈfɜː $ rɪˈfɚ/ *verb* (**referred**, **referring**)

PHRASAL VERBS
refer to
refer to someone/something to talk about a person or thing without giving very many details: *Moran* **referred to** *her parents several times.* • *I talked to him all evening, but he never* **referred to** *his fight with Henry.*

ref·e·ree /ˌrefəˈriː/ *noun* someone who makes people obey the rules when they are playing a game such as football: *Just at that moment the referee blew his whistle.* —**referee** *verb*: *He refereed last year's World Cup final.*

ref·er·ence /ˈrefərəns/ *noun* **1** when you mention another person or thing: *There was no reference to his family in his letter.* **2 for reference** so that you can find information when you need it: *You should keep all your old letters, for* *reference.* **3** a letter that says whether someone is suitable for a new job or course: *Your employer will normally give you a reference.*

ˈreference book *noun* a book that you use for finding information, for example a dictionary

ref·e·ren·dum /ˌrefəˈrendəm/ *noun* an occasion when the people of a country vote on one particular political subject, not on who will govern the country: *The government has promised a referendum on independence for the region.*

re·fill /ˌriːˈfɪl/ *verb* to fill something again: *Waitresses kept coming round to refill our glasses.*

re·fine /rɪˈfaɪn/ *verb* to make a natural substance pure by using a special process: *methods of refining oil*

re·fined /rɪˈfaɪnd/ *adjective* **1** made pure by using a special process: *refined sugar* **2** (old-fashioned) polite and educated: *a very refined young lady*

re·fin·e·ry /rɪˈfaɪnəri/ *noun* (plural **refineries**) a factory where something such as oil, sugar, or metal is made pure by using a special process: *an oil refinery*

re·flect /rɪˈflekt/ *verb* **1 be reflected in something** if something is reflected in a mirror or in water, you can see an image of it in the mirror or the water: *The mountains around us were reflected in the lake.* **2** if a surface reflects heat, light, or sound, it sends it back: *Snow reflects a lot of light because it is white.* **3 reflect on something** (formal) to think carefully about something: *I went home and reflected on what Sally had just told me.*

re·flec·tion /rɪˈflekʃən/ *noun* **1** the picture that you see when you look in water or a mirror: *She stared at her own reflection in the mirror.* **2** careful and serious thinking: *After days of reflection, she decided to leave.*

re·flec·tive /rɪˈflektɪv/ *adjective* a reflective object is made of material that reflects light, so that it looks very bright when light shines on it: *If you're cycling at night you should wear a reflective belt.*

re·flex /ˈriːfleks/ *noun* (plural **reflexes**) a quick physical reaction that your body makes without you thinking about it: *Goalkeepers need to have good reflexes.*

re·flex·ive /rɪˈfleksɪv/ *adjective* a reflexive verb or pronoun shows that an action affects the person or thing that does the action. In the sentence 'He hated himself', 'himself' is a reflexive pronoun.

re·form¹ /rɪˈfɔːm $ rɪˈfɔrm/ *verb* (formal) to change a system or an organization in order to make it better: *We need to reform the education system.* ➔ see Thesaurus at CHANGE¹

reform² *noun* (formal) a change that is made to a system or organization in order to make it better: *government reforms*

re·frain /rɪˈfreɪn/ *verb* (formal) to not do something that you want to do: *She politely refrained from saying what she really thought.*

re·fresh /rɪˈfreʃ/ *verb* to make someone feel less tired or hot: *We went to refresh ourselves in the swimming pool.*

re·fresh·ing /rɪˈfreʃɪŋ/ *adjective* **1** making you feel less tired or less hot: *a long cool refreshing drink* **2** interesting and different in a pleasant way: *It was refreshing to be working on something completely new.*

re·fresh·ments /rɪˈfreʃmənts/ *plural noun* food and drinks that are provided at a cinema, theatre, or public event: *Refreshments are available in the coffee shop downstairs.*

re·fri·ge·rate /rɪˈfrɪdʒəreɪt/ *verb* to put food or drinks in a refrigerator in order to keep them cold

re·fri·ge·ra·tor /rɪˈfrɪdʒəreɪtə $ rɪˈfrɪdʒəˌreɪtɚ/ also **fridge** /frɪdʒ/ *noun* a metal kitchen cupboard that is kept cold by electricity, and that you put food into to keep it cool

ref·uge /ˈrefjuːdʒ/ *noun* a safe place that people can go to, for example to escape from violence: *a refuge for homeless people*

ref·u·gee /ˌrefjʊˈdʒiː/ *noun* someone who has had to leave their country to escape from danger or war: *The refugees fled across the border.*

re·fund /ˈriːfʌnd/ *noun* money that is given back to you in a shop, restaurant etc, for example because you are not satisfied with what you bought: *The shop assistant gave me a refund.* —**refund** /rɪˈfʌnd/ *verb*: *Your money will be refunded if you are not entirely satisfied.*

re·fur·bish /ˌriːˈfɜːbɪʃ $ rɪˈfɚbɪʃ/ *verb* (formal) to improve a building by decorating it and buying new equipment for it: *The old cinema has been completely refurbished.*

re·fus·al /rɪˈfjuːzəl/ *noun* when someone refuses to do, allow, or accept something: *I was disappointed by her refusal to come.*

re·fuse[1] /rɪˈfjuːz/ *verb*

KEY PATTERNS
refuse to do something
refuse someone something

1 to say firmly that you will not do something: *I asked Steve to help me, but he refused.* • *Carl absolutely **refuses to** eat vegetables.*
2 to say that you will not allow someone to do something: *The chairman refused him permission to speak.* • *He tried to get into the club, but the owner refused him entry.*

ref·use[2] /ˈrefjuːs/ *noun* (no plural) (formal) waste material such as old food or paper → see Thesaurus at RUBBISH

PRONUNCIATION
Be careful how you pronounce this word:
refuse[1] (*verb*) is pronounced with the stress on the second syllable, and with a 'z' sound at the end
refuse[2] (*noun*) is pronounced with the stress on the first syllable, and with an 's' sound at the end

re·gain /rɪˈgeɪn/ *verb* (formal) to get something back after you have lost it: *It took me a few minutes to regain my self-control.*

re·gal /ˈriːgəl/ *adjective* suitable for a king or queen: *He looked at her with a very regal expression.*

re·gard[1] /rɪˈgɑːd $ rɪˈgɑrd/ *noun*
1 (no plural) (formal) if you have regard for other people, you respect them and care about how they feel: *He always does exactly what he wants, with **no regard for** anyone else.*
2 regards used when ending a letter, or when passing on a greeting from someone: *Hope to see you soon. Regards, Chris.* • *Andrew **sends** his **regards**.*

PHRASES
with regard to something (formal) used to say what subject you are talking about: ***With regard to** the cost, it will be a little more expensive than we first thought.*

regard[2] *verb* (formal) **1 regard someone/something as something** to think about someone or something in a particular way SYNONYM **consider**: *I've always regarded science as a fascinating subject.* **2** to look at someone or something, especially in a particular way: *"What do you think?" she asked, regarding him carefully.*

re·gard·ing /rɪˈgɑːdɪŋ $ rɪˈgɑrdɪŋ/ *preposition* (formal) about a particular subject SYNONYM **with regard to**: *I would like more information regarding the course.* → see Thesaurus at ABOUT[1]

reg·gae /ˈregeɪ/ *noun* (no plural) a type of music from Jamaica with a strong regular beat

re·gime /reɪˈʒiːm/ *noun* **1** a government of a particular type: *They did not want to live under such a brutal regime.* **2** a system or way of doing something: *my new exercise regime*

reg·i·ment /ˈredʒəmənt/ *noun* a group of soldiers in an army

reg·i·ment·ed /ˈredʒəmentɪd/ *adjective* strictly controlled: *Her lessons are always highly regimented.*

re·gion /ˈriːdʒən/ *noun* a fairly large area within a country: *We don't get very much snow in this region.* → see Thesaurus at AREA

re·gion·al /ˈriːdʒənəl/ *adjective* related to a particular region: *the regional government*

reg·is·ter[1] /ˈredʒəstə $ ˈredʒəstɚ/ *noun* an official list: *Our classroom register contains the names of all the students.*

A B C D E F G H I J K L M N O P Q R S T U V W X Y Z

A B C D E F G H I J K L M N O P Q R S T U V W X Y Z

register² *verb* **1** to put a name on an official list: *I need to register with a doctor.* **2** if an instrument registers an amount, it shows it: *The thermometer registered 84°F.*

reg·is·tra·tion /ˌredʒəˈstreɪʃən/ *noun* (no plural) when names are put on an official list

regisˈtration ˌnumber *noun BrE* the numbers and letters on a car's NUMBER PLATE SYNONYM **license number** *AmE*

re·gret¹ /rɪˈɡret/ *verb* (**regretted**, **regretting**)

KEY PATTERNS
regret (doing) something
regret that
regret to say/inform you

1 if you regret something, you feel sorry that you did it and wish you had not done it: *I really regret leaving school so young.* • *I now* ***regret that*** *I didn't travel more when I was younger.* **2** (formal) used in formal situations when giving information that will disappoint someone or make them unhappy: *I regret to say that I cannot help you with your enquiry.*

GRAMMAR
You **regret doing something** or **regret that you did something**.

regret² *noun* sadness that you feel when you wish you had not done something: *I don't have any regrets about the choices I've made in life.*

re·gret·ta·ble /rɪˈɡretəbəl/ *adjective* a regrettable thing is something you wish had never happened SYNONYM **unfortunate**: *This was a regrettable mistake.*

reg·u·lar¹ /ˈreɡjələ $ ˈreɡjələr/ *adjective*
1 happening with the same amount of time between events ANTONYM **irregular**: *We have regular meetings.* • *The patient's breathing was slow and regular.* • *We check all the babies* ***at regular intervals***.
2 happening often: *Regular exercise is good for you.*
3 doing something or going somewhere often: *She's a* ***regular customer*** *at the coffee shop* (=she uses the coffee shop often).
4 normal, usual, or ordinary: *He has returned to his regular duties.*
5 a regular verb or noun changes its forms in the same way as most verbs or nouns. The verb 'walk' is regular, but 'be' is not. ANTONYM **irregular**

regular² *noun* (informal) someone who goes to the same shop, restaurant etc very often

reg·u·lar·ly /ˈreɡjələli $ ˈreɡjələrli/ *adverb*
1 every day, every week, every month etc: *They meet regularly, once a month.*
2 often: *Delete your old emails regularly.* → see Thesaurus at OFTEN

reg·u·late /ˈreɡjəleɪt/ *verb* **1** to control an activity or process with rules: *the organization that regulates the sport* **2** to keep a speed, temperature etc at a particular level: *Special equipment regulates the temperature of the swimming pool.*

reg·u·la·tion /ˌreɡjəˈleɪʃən/ *noun* an official rule: *There are too many rules and regulations.* • *safety regulations* → see Thesaurus at RULE¹

re·hab /ˈriːhæb/ *noun* (no plural) treatment to help someone stop taking drugs or drinking alcohol

re·hears·al /rɪˈhɜːsəl $ rɪˈhɜrsəl/ *noun* a practice for a performance: *Please don't be late for the rehearsal.*

re·hearse /rɪˈhɜːs $ rɪˈhɜrs/ *verb* to practise a song, play etc for a performance: *We need to rehearse a couple of songs.*

reign /reɪn/ *noun* a period of time during which a king or queen rules a country: *the reign of Queen Victoria* —**reign** *verb*: *King Henry VIII reigned from 1509 to 1547.*

re·in·car·na·tion /ˌriːɪnkɑːˈneɪʃən $ ˌriɪnkɑrˈneɪʃən/ *noun* (no plural) the belief that people are born again in another body after they have died

re·in·force /ˌriːɪnˈfɔːs $ ˌriɪnˈfɔrs/ *verb* to make something stronger: *They used concrete to reinforce the walls.* • *reinforced glass*

re·in·force·ments /ˌriːɪnˈfɔːsmənts $ ˌriɪnˈfɔrsmənts/ *plural noun* more soldiers or police that go to help other soldiers or police: *It's time to send in reinforcements.*

reins /reɪnz/ *plural noun* long narrow bands of leather that you use to control a horse

re•in•state /ˌriːɪnˈsteɪt/ *verb* to give a job back to someone: *They lost their jobs but the company later reinstated them.*

re•it•e•rate /riːˈɪtəreɪt/ *verb* (formal) to say something again: *Let me reiterate that smoking is not allowed anywhere on the school premises.*

re•ject /rɪˈdʒekt/ *verb*
to say that you will not accept something or someone ANTONYM **accept**: *The committee rejected the plan.* • *She applied to the college, but they rejected her.*

re•jec•tion /rɪˈdʒekʃən/ *noun* **1** when someone refuses to accept something ANTONYM **acceptance**: *He felt disappointed by the publisher's rejection of his first novel.* **2** (no plural) when someone stops giving you love or attention: *I can't take any more rejection.*

re•joice /rɪˈdʒɔɪs/ *verb* (formal) to be very happy because something good has happened

re•lapse /rɪˈlæps $ ˈrilæps/ *noun* when someone becomes ill again after they were getting better: *Unfortunately, he had a relapse and had to return to the hospital.*

re•late /rɪˈleɪt/ *verb* **1** if you relate one thing to another, you show that they are similar or connected in some way SYNONYM **connect**: *Police have tried to relate this murder to others in the area.* **2** (formal) to tell a story or talk about something that happened: *She couldn't wait to relate the day's events to her friends.* **3** **relate to something** to be about something or connected with it: *I collect anything that relates to baseball.*

re•lat•ed /rɪˈleɪtɪd/ *adjective*

> KEY PATTERNS
> **related to something/someone**

1 if two things are related, there is a connection between them: *Norwegian and Danish are **closely related** languages.* • *Today's traffic problems are **related to** the heavy rain we had last night.*
2 if two people are related, they are members of the same family: *Are you **related to** Jean Benson?* • *We look alike, but we're not related.*

re•la•tion /rɪˈleɪʃən/ *noun*

> KEY PATTERNS
> **a relation between things**

1 a connection between events or facts: *Is there a **relation between** drinking coffee and health problems?*
2 a member of your family SYNONYM **relative**: *She is staying with some relations in Canada.* ➔ see Thesaurus at FAMILY
3 **relations** the way in which two countries or groups behave towards each other, for example whether they are friendly or not: *Relations between the two countries have got better recently.*

PHRASES
in relation to something used when comparing two things: *The picture shows the size of the whale **in relation to** a person.*

re•la•tion•ship /rɪˈleɪʃənʃɪp/ *noun*

> KEY PATTERNS
> **a relationship with someone/something**
> **a relationship between people/things**

1 the way in which two people or groups feel and behave towards each other, for example whether they like each other or not: *Her **relationship with** her father has always been difficult.* • *I had a very **good relationship with** my mother.* • *The **relationship between** the two countries is friendly.*
2 the way in which two things are connected: *The **relationship between** health and exercise is clear.*

rel•a•tive¹ /ˈrelətɪv/ *noun*
a member of your family SYNONYM **relation**: *We'll be visiting relatives at Christmas.* ➔ see Thesaurus at FAMILY

relative² *adjective* true to some degree, especially when compared with other things: *The park is a place where the children can play in relative safety.*

ˌrelative ˈclause *noun* a part of a sentence that has a verb in it and gives information about something mentioned in the sentence. It is joined to the rest of the sentence by a relative pronoun.

rel·a·tive·ly /ˈrelətɪvli/ *adverb* fairly: *Our house is relatively small.*

ˌrelative ˈpronoun *noun* a PRONOUN such as 'who', 'which', or 'that' which connects a relative clause to the rest of the sentence

re·lax /rɪˈlæks/ *verb*
to feel more calm and less worried, by resting or doing something you enjoy: *I decided to just stay home and relax.* • *A hot bath should help to relax you* (=make you relax) *after a day's work.*

re·lax·a·tion /ˌriːlækˈseɪʃən/ *noun* (no plural) when you relax: *It's a great place to go for relaxation.*

re·laxed /rɪˈlækst/ *adjective* calm and not worried about anything: *She looked happy and relaxed on her wedding day.*

re·lax·ing /rɪˈlæksɪŋ/ *adjective*
something that is relaxing makes you feel calm and comfortable: *a relaxing bath* • *relaxing music*

re·lay /ˈriːleɪ/ also **ˈrelay ˌrace** *noun* a race in which each member of a team runs or swims part of the distance: *the 100 metres relay*

release

re·lease¹ /rɪˈliːs/ *verb*

KEY PATTERNS
release someone (from somewhere)

1 to allow someone to be free again after keeping them as a prisoner: *When will he be* ***released from*** *prison?*
2 to stop holding something: *He grabbed her arm and refused to release it.*
3 to make a CD, film etc available for people to buy or see: *We're just about to release our second album.*
4 to give information to people after keeping it secret: *The names of the victims were not released.*

release² *noun* **1** when someone is allowed to be free and no longer a prisoner: *They have demanded the release of political prisoners.* **2** a new CD, film etc that is available for people to buy or see: *a review of the new film releases*

rel·e·gate /ˈreləgeɪt/ *verb* if a sports team is relegated, it has to play in a lower group of teams because it has finished at the bottom of the higher group

re·lent /rɪˈlent/ *verb* (formal) to let someone do something that you would not let them do before: *His parents relented, and allowed his friends to stay.*

re·lent·less /rɪˈlentləs/ *adjective* never stopping: *the relentless pressure on children to achieve*

rel·e·vance /ˈreləvəns/ *noun* (no plural) how relevant something is: *That is of no relevance to what we're talking about.*

rel·e·vant /ˈreləvənt/ *adjective* directly related to the subject or problem that you are discussing ANTONYM **irrelevant**: *Is that information really relevant?*

SPELLING
This word is often spelled wrongly. The correct spelling is: **relevant**.

re·li·a·ble /rɪˈlaɪəbəl/ *adjective* if someone or something is reliable, you can trust them to do what you want them to do ANTONYM **unreliable**: *Rick is a good, reliable worker.* • *We need a computer system that is reliable and fast.*

re·li·ance /rɪˈlaɪəns/ *noun* (no plural) when you depend on something SYNONYM **dependence**: *our reliance on the car*

re·li·ant /rɪˈlaɪənt/ *adjective* (formal) if you are reliant on someone or something, you depend on them SYNONYM **dependent**: *I'm still reliant on my family for money.*

rel·ic /ˈrelɪk/ *noun* something from the past that still exists

re•lief /rɪ'liːf/ *noun* (no plural) the feeling you have when you are no longer worried that something bad might happen: *It **was a great relief** when Ben finally called to tell me where he was.* • *This news will **come as a great relief to** his family.* • *I **breathed a sigh of relief** (=felt great relief) when I saw the little boat enter the harbour.*

re•lieve /rɪ'liːv/ *verb* to make something bad seem better: *drugs for relieving pain* • *We sang songs to relieve the boredom.*

re•lieved /rɪ'liːvd/ *adjective* happy because something bad did not happen: *We were all relieved when she returned home safely.*

re•li•gion /rɪ'lɪdʒən/ *noun* belief in one or more gods, and actions related to this: *Christianity and other religions*

re•li•gious /rɪ'lɪdʒəs/ *adjective* **1** related to religion: *a religious ceremony* **2** believing strongly in your religion: *a very religious man*

re•li•gious•ly /rɪ'lɪdʒəsli/ *adverb* if you do something religiously, you always do it: *I clean my teeth religiously every night.*

rel•ish /'relɪʃ/ *verb* if you relish the thought that something is going to happen, you are very happy that it is going to happen: *I don't relish the thought of another argument.*

re•live /ˌriː'lɪv/ *verb* to remember something so well that you seem to experience it again: *I relived that first kiss over and over in my mind.*

re•lo•cate /ˌriːləʊ'keɪt $ ri'loʊˌkeɪt/ *verb* (formal) to move to a new place: *The company is relocating to London.*

re•luc•tant /rɪ'lʌktənt/ *adjective* if you are reluctant to do something, you do not want to do it: *He was reluctant to talk about his problems.*

re•ly /rɪ'laɪ/ *verb* (**relied, relies**)

PHRASAL VERBS

rely on

1 rely on someone/something if you rely on someone or something, you need them and always use them: *She **relies on** relatives **to** drive her to the store.* • *He **relies on** his parents **for** money.* • *We **rely** very **heavily on** our car.*

2 can rely on someone/something if you can rely on someone or something, you know they will do what you want or expect them to do: *You **can rely on** Toby **to** do the work well.*

re•main /rɪ'meɪn/ *verb* (formal)

KEY PATTERNS
remain in/at a place

1 to stay in the same place or position: *Harris **remained in** jail for ten years.* • *I decided to **remain at** home.*
2 to continue to be something or to be in the same state: *Children can't remain quiet* (=continue to be quiet) *for long.* • *He remained in power for over 40 years.*

re•main•der /rɪ'meɪndə $ rɪ'meɪndɚ/ *noun* the part of something that is left after everything else has gone SYNONYM **the rest**: *Most of us took the train and the remainder went by bus.*

re•main•ing /rɪ'meɪnɪŋ/ *adjective* left when others have gone or the rest has been used: *Add the remaining ingredients and fry for two minutes.*

re•mains /rɪ'meɪnz/ *plural noun* the parts of something that are left after the rest has disappeared: *the remains of an ancient theatre*

re•mand /rɪ'mɑːnd $ rɪ'mænd/ *verb* *BrE* **be remanded in custody** to be kept in prison until your TRIAL

re•mark¹ /rɪ'mɑːk $ rɪ'mɑrk/ *noun*

KEY PATTERNS
a remark about someone/something
make a remark

something that you say SYNONYM **comment**: *Several of the men **made** rude **remarks about** the way she was dressed.*

remark² *verb* **1** to say something SYNONYM **comment**: *My sister remarked that she thought Celia looked unhappy.*
2 remark on/upon something to say something about a thing that you have noticed: *Several people remarked on the horrible smell.*

re•mark•a•ble /rɪ'mɑːkəbəl $ rɪ'mɑrkəbəl/ *adjective* very unusual and good: *That's a remarkable achievement.*

re·mark·a·bly /rɪˈmɑːkəbli $ rɪˈmɑrkəbli/ *adverb* extremely: *You boys look remarkably similar.*

re·mar·ry /ˌriːˈmæri/ *verb* (**remarried, remarries**) to marry again: *He said he would never remarry after his wife died.*

rem·e·dy¹ /ˈremədi/ *noun* (plural **remedies**) something that ends an illness or a bad situation: *an effective remedy for headaches* • *What is the remedy for rising crime?*

remedy² *verb* (**remedied, remedies**) to make a bad situation better SYNONYM **put right**: *Engineers are trying to remedy the problem now.*

re·mem·ber /rɪˈmembə $ rɪˈmembɚ/ *verb*

> KEY PATTERNS
> **remember (doing) something**
> **remember that**
> **remember to do something**

1 if you remember something, it comes back into your mind ANTONYM **forget**: *I **couldn't remember** her name.* • *I don't remember seeing John at the party.* • *Do you remember going to the fair with her when we were little?* • *I suddenly **remembered that** I had promised to meet my mother for lunch.*
2 if you remember to do something, you do not forget to do it: ***Remember to** buy Anne a card when you go to town.*

re·mind /rɪˈmaɪnd/ *verb* **1** to make someone remember something that they must do: *Remind me to take the cake out of the oven.* **2 remind someone of someone** if someone reminds you of another person, they make you think of that person because they are similar to them: *You remind me of my sister.*

re·mind·er /rɪˈmaɪndə $ rɪˈmaɪndɚ/ *noun* something that makes you remember something

rem·i·nisce /ˌreməˈnɪs/ *verb* to talk about pleasant events in your past: *They sat reminiscing about the old days.*

rem·i·nis·cent /ˌreməˈnɪsənt/ *adjective* (formal) making you think of something similar: *The garden was reminiscent of a jungle.*

rem·nant /ˈremnənt/ *noun* a small part of something that remains after the rest is gone

re·morse /rɪˈmɔːs $ rɪˈmɔrs/ *noun* (no plural) (formal) a feeling that you are sorry for doing something very bad: *He showed no remorse for his crime.*

re·mote /rɪˈməʊt $ rɪˈmoʊt/ *adjective* **1** far away SYNONYM **isolated**: *His brother lived on a remote farm.* **2** very small SYNONYM **slight**: *There's a remote possibility that we'll finish early.*
—**remotely** *adverb*: *I'm not remotely interested in computer games.*

reˌmote conˈtrol *noun* a piece of equipment that you use for controlling a television, DVD PLAYER etc → see picture on page A12

remote control

re·mov·al /rɪˈmuːvəl/ *noun* (no plural) (formal) when you take something away: *A lot of people protested about the removal of so many trees.*

re·move /rɪˈmuːv/ *verb* (formal)

> KEY PATTERNS
> **remove something (from somewhere)**

1 to take something away from a place: *Please do not **remove** these books **from** the library.*
2 to take a piece of clothing from your body: *He removed his hat and sat down.*

> THESAURUS
> **take off**: *She **took off** her coat* (=removed it).
> **tear off**: *The wind **tore** the roof **off*** (=violently removed it).
> **cut off**: *She **cut** all the fat **off** the meat* (=removed it by cutting it).
> **break off**: *They **broke** a branch **off** the tree* (=removed it by breaking it).
> **scrape off**: ***Scrape** the remains of the food **off** the plates* (=remove the food by scraping the plates).
> **wipe off**: *He **wiped** the blood **off** his face with a handkerchief* (=removed it by wiping his face).

re·name /riːˈneɪm/ *verb* to give something a new name: *The new owners renamed the company.*

ren·dez·vous /ˈrɒndɪvuː $ ˈrɑndeɪˌvu/ *noun* (plural **rendezvous**) an arrangement to meet someone: *He had arranged a secret rendezvous with his girlfriend.*

re·new /rɪˈnjuː $ rɪˈnu/ *verb* **1** to arrange for an official document or agreement to continue: *I need to renew my passport.* **2** (formal) to begin to do something again: *They will renew their search in the morning.*

re·nounce /rɪˈnaʊns/ *verb* to say publicly that you no longer support or want something: *Why will you not renounce violence?*

ren·o·vate /ˈrenəveɪt/ *verb* to repair a building so that it looks new ➔ see Thesaurus at REPAIR[1]

re·nowned /rɪˈnaʊnd/ *adjective* (formal) famous for something: *The restaurant is renowned for its excellent food.*

rent[1] /rent/ *verb*

> KEY PATTERNS
> **rent a house/car etc (from someone)**
> **rent a house/room to someone**

1 to pay money to live in a place or to use something such as a car: *We **rent** the flat **from** my uncle.* • *We rented bicycles and rode along the beach.*
2 also **rent out** if you rent a house, room etc to someone, you allow them to use it, and they pay you money SYNONYM **let** *BrE*: *Some people don't like to **rent** rooms **to** students.* • *They **rent** the house **out to** tourists in the summer.*

rent[2] *noun* money that you pay to use a house, car etc that belongs to someone else: *I pay the rent at the beginning of the month.*

rent·al /ˈrentl/ *noun* an arrangement to use something that belongs to someone else in return for money: *a car rental agreement* • *Bike rental is £8.00.*

re·or·gan·ize also **reorganise** *BrE* /riːˈɔːgənaɪz $ riˈɔrgəˌnaɪz/ *verb* to organize something in a new way: *They are reorganizing the company.*

rep /rep/ *noun* (informal) someone who sells products for a company: *a sales rep*

re·pair[1] /rɪˈpeə $ rɪˈper/ *verb* to make something in good condition again after it has been damaged or has not been working properly: *How much will it cost to repair the washing machine?* • *We need to **get** the car **repaired*** (=arrange for someone to repair it).

> THESAURUS
> **fix**: *He's trying to **fix** the car* (=repair it).
> **mend**: *I'll have to **mend** his shirt – there's a tear in it* (=repair a hole in it. In British English, you can mend anything that is broken, not just things with holes in them).
> **renovate**: *They're **renovating** an old house* (=repairing a building so that it looks new).
> **restore**: *The painting has been **restored*** (=repaired so that it is in its original condition).

repair[2] *noun* something that you do to repair something that is damaged or not working properly: *He's just doing a few repairs on my car.* • *The school buildings are badly in need of repair.*

re·pay /rɪˈpeɪ/ *verb* (past tense and past participle **repaid** /-ˈpeɪd/) **1** to give money back to someone after you have borrowed it from them: *You can repay the loan over two years.* **2** to reward someone for helping you: *How can I ever repay you?*

re·pay·ment /rɪˈpeɪmənt/ *noun* an amount of money that you pay to someone whom you have borrowed money from: *Your first repayment is due next week.*

re·peal /rɪˈpiːl/ *verb* to officially end a law

re·peat[1] /rɪˈpiːt/ *verb*
1 to say or do something again: *Could you repeat what you just said?* • *If the operation is not successful the first time, we may have to repeat it.*
2 if a television or radio programme is repeated, it is broadcast again: *The programme will be repeated on Saturday afternoon.*

repeat[2] *noun* **1** a situation or event that has happened before: *We don't*

A B C D E F G H I J K L M N O P Q R S T U V W X Y Z

A B C D E F G H I J K L M N O P Q R S T U V W X Y Z

want a repeat of last year's train disaster. **2** a television or radio programme that is broadcast again

re·peat·ed /rɪˈpiːtɪd/ *adjective* done several times: *Despite repeated efforts, they failed to capture the animal.* —**repeatedly** *adverb*: *I asked him repeatedly to leave.* → see Thesaurus at OFTEN

re·pel /rɪˈpel/ *verb* (**repelled, repelling**) to force someone or something away: *sprays that repel insects*

re·pel·lent /rɪˈpelənt/ *noun* a substance that keeps insects away: *mosquito repellent*

re·pent /rɪˈpent/ *verb* (formal) to be sorry for something bad that you have done: *If you repent, you will be forgiven.*

re·per·cus·sions /ˌriːpəˈkʌʃənz $ ˌripɚˈkʌʃənz/ *plural noun* bad things that happen as a result of something that you do: *Children are afraid of repercussions if they report bullies.*

rep·e·ti·tion /ˌrepəˈtɪʃən/ *noun* when something happens again or is done again many times: *Avoid repetition by using different words.*

re·pet·i·tive /rɪˈpetətɪv/ *adjective* something that is repetitive is boring because the same thing is repeated many times: *Typing is a very repetitive job.*

re·phrase /ˌriːˈfreɪz/ *verb* to say or write something using different words: *Can you rephrase the question?*

re·place /rɪˈpleɪs/ *verb* (formal)

> KEY PATTERNS
> **replace a person/thing (with another)**

to get a new person or thing to use instead of the one you use now: *When the TV broke, we didn't replace it.* • *He left in June, and they still haven't* ***replaced*** *him* ***with*** *anyone* (=employed someone else to do his job).

re·place·ment /rɪˈpleɪsmənt/ *noun* a new person or thing that you can use instead of the one you used before: *If the battery is dead, you need to get a replacement.*

re·play /ˈriːpleɪ/ *noun* **1** a piece of action in a sports game on television that is shown again immediately after it happens: *The replay clearly shows that it was a foul.* **2** *BrE* a sports game that is played again because there was not a winner in the first game

rep·li·ca /ˈreplɪkə/ *noun* an exact copy of something

re·ply¹ /rɪˈplaɪ/ *verb* (**replied, replies**)

> KEY PATTERNS
> **reply to a question/letter/person**
> **reply that**

to answer: *"Yes, that's true," she replied.* • *He didn't* ***reply to*** *my question.* • *I asked George whether he enjoyed the film, and he* ***replied that*** *he found it disappointing.*

> GRAMMAR
> You **reply to someone** or **reply to a question/letter**.
> ✘ Don't say 'reply someone' or 'reply someone's question/letter'.

reply² *noun* (plural **replies**)

> KEY PATTERNS
> **a reply to a question/letter**
> **make no reply**
> **in reply (to a question/letter)**

something that you say or write as an answer SYNONYM **answer**: *I am still waiting for a* ***reply to*** *my letter.* • *I asked Helen if she was all right, but she* ***made no reply*** (=did not answer). • *Jeff said very little* ***in reply to*** *my questions.*

re·port¹ /rɪˈpɔːt $ rɪˈpɔrt/ *noun*

> KEY PATTERNS
> **a report on a situation/event**
> **a report of an event**

something that gives facts about a situation or event: *Each child wrote a* ***report on*** *their visit to the museum.* • *a weather report* • *There have been* ***reports of*** *more fighting on the streets of the capital.*

report² *verb*

> KEY PATTERNS
> **report that**
> **report on a situation/event**
> **report something/someone bad to someone**

1 to tell people about something that has happened: *The pilot* ***reported that*** *he had trouble with one engine.* • *I've been asked to* ***report on*** *how the meeting goes.*

2 to tell someone that a crime or accident has happened: *Have you **reported** the burglary **to** the police?* **3** to give someone's name to a person in authority because they have done something wrong: *One of the older children saw Jake smoking and **reported** him **to** the head teacher.*

re'port card *noun AmE* a written statement showing how well a student has worked

re,ported 'speech *noun* (no plural) the style of writing that is used for telling people what someone says, without repeating the actual words SYNONYM **indirect speech** ANTONYM **direct speech**

re·port·er /rɪˈpɔːtə $ rɪˈpɔrtə˞/ *noun* someone who writes or tells news stories: *a newspaper reporter*

rep·re·sent /ˌreprɪˈzent/ *verb* **1** if someone represents you, they officially speak for you or do a job for you because you cannot do it yourself: *You will need a good lawyer to represent you in court.* **2** to show or mean something: *This line on the graph represents temperature.*

rep·re·sen·ta·tive[1] /ˌreprɪˈzentətɪv/ *noun* someone who people have chosen to do things for them: *Jean Mason will be the student representative on the committee.*

representative[2] *adjective* typical of a group of people or things: *Sally isn't representative of teenagers as a whole.*

re·press /rɪˈpres/ *verb* **1** to stop yourself from saying something or showing your feelings: *It's not good to repress your feelings.* **2** to control people by force: *a brutal leader who repressed his people*

re·pres·sive /rɪˈpresɪv/ *adjective* cruel and very strict SYNONYM **oppressive**: *a repressive government*

re·prieve /rɪˈpriːv/ *noun* when something bad that was going to happen does not happen: *I got a last-minute reprieve.*

rep·ri·mand /ˈreprəmɑːnd $ ˈreprəˌmænd/ *verb* (formal) to tell someone officially that they have done something wrong: *His manager reprimanded him for being late.* —**reprimand** *noun*

re·pri·sal /rɪˈpraɪzəl/ *noun* something that is done to punish an enemy: *He's afraid to help the police for fear of reprisals against his family.*

re·proach /rɪˈprəʊtʃ $ rɪˈproʊtʃ/ *verb* (formal) to criticize someone for doing something bad or disappointing: *His daughter reproached him for not telling her the truth.*

re·pro·duce /ˌriːprəˈdjuːs $ ˌriprəˈdus/ *verb* to produce young animals, people, or plants

re·pro·duc·tion /ˌriːprəˈdʌkʃən/ *noun* **1** (no plural) when animals, people, or plants produce new ones **2** a copy of something such as a work of art

rep·tile /ˈreptaɪl/ *noun* an animal such as a snake or LIZARD

re·pub·lic /rɪˈpʌblɪk/ *noun* a country that elects its government and does not have a king or queen

re·pub·li·can /rɪˈpʌblɪkən/ *noun* someone who believes in having a republic

re·pul·sive /rɪˈpʌlsɪv/ *adjective* extremely unpleasant SYNONYM **disgusting**: *What a repulsive smell!*

rep·u·ta·ble /ˈrepjətəbəl/ *adjective* respected for being honest and doing good work: *a reputable builder*

rep·u·ta·tion /ˌrepjəˈteɪʃən/ *noun* the opinion that people have of someone or something: *This school has a very good reputation.*

re·quest[1] /rɪˈkwest/ *noun* when someone asks for something: *Can I make a request? • Send us your requests for your favourite songs.*

request[2] *verb* (formal) to ask for something: *They requested some drinks. • We request that you do not smoke.* ➔ see Thesaurus at ASK

re·quire /rɪˈkwaɪə $ rɪˈkwaɪə˞/ *verb* **1** to need something: *Pets require a lot of care.* **2** (formal) to officially say that someone must do something: *The law requires all drivers to wear seat belts.*

re·quire·ment /rɪˈkwaɪəmənt $ rɪˈkwaɪə˞mənt/ *noun* (formal) something that you need: *What are the university's entry requirements?*

re·run /ˈriːrʌn/ *noun* a television programme that is shown again

SYNONYM **repeat**: *endless reruns of old comedy programmes*

resat the past tense and past participle of RESIT

res•cue¹ /ˈreskjuː/ *verb*

KEY PATTERNS
rescue someone (from a fire/sinking ship etc)

to save someone when they are in danger: *Roberts* ***rescued*** *a two-year-old girl* ***from*** *the burning car.*

rescue² *noun* when someone is saved from danger: *The storm made the rescue difficult.*

re•search¹ /rɪˈsɜːtʃ $ ˈrisɚtʃ/ *noun* (no plural) detailed study of a subject in order to find out new information: *research into the causes of cancer • She's doing research on tropical diseases.*

research² *verb* to study a subject in detail so you can discover new facts about it: *He spent several days researching the company.*
—**researcher** *noun*

re•sem•blance /rɪˈzembləns/ *noun* when two people or things look similar to each other: *We're brothers – can you see the resemblance?*

re•sem•ble /rɪˈzembəl/ *verb* to look similar to someone or something: *You don't resemble your father at all.*

re•sent /rɪˈzent/ *verb* to feel angry and upset about something that someone has done to you: *I always resented my mother for leaving us.*

re•sent•ful /rɪˈzentfəl/ *adjective* angry and upset about something that someone has done SYNONYM **bitter**: *He feels resentful about the way he was treated by the company.*

re•sent•ment /rɪˈzentmənt/ *noun* (no plural) a feeling of anger about something that someone has done to you SYNONYM **bitterness**

res•er•va•tion /ˌrezəˈveɪʃən $ ˌrezɚˈveɪʃən/ *noun* **1** an arrangement to have a seat on a plane, a table in a restaurant etc ready for you: *I'd like to make a reservation for dinner tonight.* **2** a feeling of doubt about something: *I still have reservations about leaving home.*

re•serve¹ /rɪˈzɜːv $ rɪˈzɚv/ *verb*

KEY PATTERNS
reserve a place/thing (for something/someone)

1 to arrange that a seat on a plane, a table in a restaurant etc will be available for you to use: *Tom reserved a table at the hotel restaurant. • It's best to reserve your seat in advance.* **2** to keep something for a particular purpose: *This parking area has been* ***reserved for*** *buses.*

reserve² *noun* a supply of something that is kept to be used when it is needed: *The country has huge reserves of grain.*

re•served /rɪˈzɜːvd $ rɪˈzɚvd/ *adjective* unwilling to show or talk about your thoughts and feelings

res•er•voir /ˈrezəvwɑː $ ˈrezɚˌvwɑr/ *noun* an artificial lake used for storing water

res•i•dence /ˈrezədəns/ *noun* (formal) **1** a house where someone lives: *the Prime Minister's official residence* **2** (no plural) when someone lives in a particular place: *They have applied to* ***take up residence*** (=start living) *in the US.*

res•i•dent /ˈrezədənt/ *noun* someone who lives in a particular place: *a park for local residents*

res•i•den•tial /ˌrezəˈdenʃəl/ *adjective* consisting of houses, not offices or factories: *a residential area of the city*

res•i•due /ˈrezədjuː $ ˈrezəˌdu/ *noun* a substance that remains after something else has disappeared

re•sign /rɪˈzaɪn/ *verb* **1** to officially say that you are going to leave your job: *I've decided to resign from the bank.* **2** if you resign yourself to something, you accept it because you cannot change it: *He's resigned himself to a few more years studying.*

res•ig•na•tion /ˌrezɪgˈneɪʃən/ *noun* when someone officially says they are going to leave their job: *Her resignation was a big surprise.*

re•sil•i•ent /rɪˈzɪliənt/ *adjective* strong enough to be able to deal with problems

re•sist /rɪˈzɪst/ *verb* **1** to refuse to accept something and try to prevent it:

He resists any kind of change. **2** to stop yourself doing something you would like to do but should not: *I managed to resist looking in the bag.*

GRAMMAR
You **resist something.**
✘ Don't say 'resist to something'.

re·sist·ance /rɪˈzɪstəns/ *noun* (no plural) when someone refuses to accept something and tries to prevent it: *There is strong resistance to the scheme.*

re·sis·tant /rɪˈzɪstənt/ *adjective* **1** not harmed or damaged by something: *Some bacteria are resistant to antibiotics.* **2** unwilling to accept new ideas or changes: *Old people can be very resistant to change.*

re·sit /ˌriːˈsɪt/ *verb BrE* (past tense and past participle **resat** /-ˈsæt/ **resitting**) to take an examination again —**resit** /ˈriːsɪt/ *noun*: *He failed some of his exams, so he's doing resits.*

res·o·lu·tion /ˌrezəˈluːʃən/ *noun* **1** an official decision, especially after a vote: *The United Nations passed a resolution calling for an end to the fighting.* **2** a promise that you make to yourself to do something: *I made a New Year resolution to stop smoking.*

re·solve¹ /rɪˈzɒlv $ rɪˈzɑlv/ *verb* **1** to deal with a problem or end a disagreement SYNONYM **solve**: *Everyone wants to resolve this matter as soon as possible.* **2** (formal) to make a definite decision to do something: *He resolved to work harder.*

resolve² *noun* (no plural) (formal) strong determination to do something: *I admire your resolve.*

re·sort¹ /rɪˈzɔːt $ rɪˈzɔrt/ *noun* **1** a place where a lot of people go for a holiday: *a popular tourist resort* **2 as a last resort** if everything else fails: *I could borrow the money, but only as a last resort.*

resort² *verb* **resort to something** to do something that you do not want to do, in order to achieve something: *In the end he resorted to borrowing money from his parents.* • *We will not resort to violence.*

re·sound·ing /rɪˈzaʊndɪŋ/ *adjective* **1** used for emphasizing that something is very successful: *a resounding victory* **2** very loud: *a resounding crash*

re·source /rɪˈzɔːs $ ˈrisɔrs/ *noun* something that is available for people to use: *The library is a useful resource.* • *the country's natural resources* (=oil, coal, gold etc)

PRONUNCIATION
British people put the stress on the second syllable: 'reSOURCE'.
American people put the stress on the first syllable: 'REsource'.

re·source·ful /rɪˈzɔːsfəl $ rɪˈsɔrsfəl/ *adjective* good at finding ways to deal with problems

re·spect¹ /rɪˈspekt/ *noun* (no plural)

KEY PATTERNS
have respect for someone/something
show respect (for someone)

1 if you have respect for someone, you admire them and have a very good opinion of them: *He was a very good teacher – I* ***had great respect for*** *him.* • *I've got* ***a lot of respect for*** *Henry.*
2 a polite way of behaving towards other people: *We expect everyone at this school to treat each other* ***with respect.*** • *You must learn to* ***show respect for*** *other people* (=treat them in a polite way).
3 if you have respect for something, you believe that it is important: *Many people* ***have no respect for*** *religion any more.*

respect² *verb*

KEY PATTERNS
respect someone/something
respect someone for (doing) something

1 to admire someone and have a good opinion of them: *I respected him* ***for*** *saying exactly what he thought.*
2 if you respect other people's feelings or ideas, you show that you understand and care about them: *Parents should respect a teenager's need for privacy.*
3 if you respect a law or rule, you obey it

re·spec·ta·ble /rɪˈspektəbəl/ *adjective* **1** someone who is respectable is good and honest: *a* *respectable businessman* **2** neatly dressed and not dirty or untidy: *Do I look respectable?*

re·spect·ful /rɪˈspektfəl/ *adjective* showing respect for someone or something

re·spec·tive /rɪˈspektɪv/ *adjective* used to talk about each different person or thing in order: *I invited three friends and their respective boyfriends.* —**respectively** *adverb*: *For English and French, I got 58% and 59% respectively.*

re·spi·ra·to·ry /rɪˈspɪrətəri $ ˈresprəˌtɔri/ *adjective* (formal) related to breathing: *Smoking causes respiratory illnesses.*

res·pite /ˈrespaɪt $ ˈrespɪt/ *noun* (no plural) (formal) when something unpleasant stops happening for a short time: *There was no respite from the rain.*

re·spond /rɪˈspɒnd $ rɪˈspɑnd/ *verb* (formal) **1** to answer SYNONYM **reply**: *He hasn't responded to my email.* **2** to do something because of something that has happened SYNONYM **react**: *Some animals respond to danger by running away.*

re·sponse /rɪˈspɒns $ rɪˈspɑns/ *noun* (formal) a reply or reaction to something: *Every time I asked her a question I got no response.* • *I am writing in response to your advertisement.*

re·spon·si·bil·i·ty /rɪˌspɒnsəˈbɪləti $ rɪˌspɑnsəˈbɪləti/ *noun* (plural **responsibilities**)

KEY PATTERNS
it is someone's responsibility to do something
have responsibility for (doing) something

1 if something is your responsibility, it is your job to do it: *In the holidays it is Jim's* ***responsibility to*** *feed all the animals.* • *The manager explained what my responsibilities were.* • *Who* ***has responsibility for*** *training new staff?*
2 accept responsibility, take responsibility if you accept responsibility for something bad that has happened, you admit that you did it or caused it: *The hospital has accepted responsibility for the mistake.*

re·spon·si·ble /rɪˈspɒnsəbəl $ rɪˈspɑnsəbəl/ *adjective*

KEY PATTERNS
responsible for (doing) something

1 if you are responsible for something, it is your job to do it: *Mrs Hendrick is* ***responsible for*** *all the cooking.* • *I am* ***responsible for*** *putting the books away at the end of the lesson.*
2 a young person who is responsible always behaves in a sensible way ANTONYM **irresponsible**: *You can trust Mary – she's very responsible.*
3 if you are responsible for something bad that has happened, you did it or caused it: *The driver of the truck said that he was not* ***responsible for*** *the accident.*

re·spon·si·bly /rɪˈspɒnsəbli $ rɪˈspɑnsəbli/ *adverb* in a sensible way: *I don't trust them to behave responsibly.*

re·spon·sive /rɪˈspɒnsɪv $ rɪˈspɑnsɪv/ *adjective* paying attention to what people need, and doing something to help them: *The government needs to be responsive to people's needs.*

rest[1] /rest/ *noun*

KEY PATTERNS
the rest of something

1 the part of something that still remains: *I'll keep* ***the rest of*** *the cake until tomorrow.* • *What shall we do for* ***the rest of*** *the day?*
2 the other people or things: *Some people were in the house and* ***the rest*** *were in the garden.*
3 a period of time when you can relax or sleep: *I went upstairs to* ***have a rest*** *before dinner.* • *You've got a busy day tomorrow so you'd better* ***get some rest.***

rest[2] *verb*

KEY PATTERNS
rest something on/against something

1 to spend some time relaxing or sleeping: *Tessa lay down on the sofa to rest.* • *We spent the afternoon resting.*
2 to put something in a position where it is supported by something else: *Kyle was drinking a beer and*

A B C D E F G H I J K L M N O P Q **R** S T U V W X Y Z

resting his feet *on* the table. • She *rested* her bicycle *against* the wall.

res·tau·rant /ˈrestərɒnt $ ˈresˌtrɑnt/ *noun* a place where you can buy and eat a meal: *They had dinner in a Chinese restaurant.*

> **SPELLING**
> This word is often spelled wrongly. The correct spelling is: **restaurant**.

rest·ful /ˈrestfəl/ *adjective* peaceful and quiet

rest·less /ˈrestləs/ *adjective* unable to relax and keep still: *The children were getting restless.*

re·store /rɪˈstɔː $ rɪˈstɔr/ *verb* **1** to repair something so that it looks new → see Thesaurus at REPAIR[1] **2** to make something exist again: *How can we restore his confidence?*

restrain

The man is restraining the dog.

re·strain /rɪˈstreɪn/ *verb* to stop someone from doing something, usually by holding them: *I put my hand on Jim's arm to restrain him.*

re·straint /rɪˈstreɪnt/ *noun* **1** (no plural) when you act calmly even though a situation is very difficult: *The police showed great restraint.* **2** something that limits what you can do: *The government has introduced new restraints on free speech.*

re·strict /rɪˈstrɪkt/ *verb* to limit something: *laws that restrict people's freedom*

re·strict·ed /rɪˈstrɪktɪd/ *adjective* limited to a small group of people or things: *Cancer is not restricted to old people.*

re·stric·tion /rɪˈstrɪkʃən/ *noun* a rule that limits what you are allowed to do: *There are a lot of travel restrictions on people in some countries.* → see Thesaurus at RULE[1]

rest·room /ˈrestruːm/ *noun AmE* a room containing a toilet, in a public place such as a restaurant

re·sult[1] /rɪˈzʌlt/ *noun*

> **KEY PATTERNS**
> **a result of something**
> **as a result (of something)**

1 something that happens because of something else: *The whole situation was* **the result of** (=was caused by) *a silly mistake.* • *Bill died* **as a result of** (=because of) *the accident.*
2 the number of points or votes that each person or team has at the end of a game or competition: *A lot depends on* **the result of** *this match.* • *The election results will be announced today.*
3 the information you get from studying something carefully or doing a scientific test: *You will get* **the result of** *your blood test next week.* • *I decided to show* **the results of** *my survey by drawing a graph.*
4 a number or letter that shows how well you have done in an examination SYNONYM **score**, **grade** *AmE*: *Dave got excellent results in his exams this year.*

> **THESAURUS**
> **consequence**: *This mistake had disastrous* **consequences** (=results).
> **effect**: *the effect of pollution on people's health* (=a change that happens as a result of it)

result[2] *verb* **1 result in something** to make something happen: *The extremely cold weather resulted in the deaths of three people.* → see Thesaurus at CAUSE[1] **2 result from something** to happen because of something: *The flooding resulted from the heavy rain last week.*

re·sume /rɪˈzjuːm $ rɪˈzum/ *verb* (formal) to start again: *Normal service will resume soon.*

rés·u·mé /ˈrezjʊmeɪ $ ˌrezʊˈmeɪ/ the American word for CV

re·sus·ci·tate /rɪˈsʌsəteɪt/ *verb* to make someone start breathing again: *Doctors tried to resuscitate her but it was too late.*

re·tail /ˈriːteɪl/ *noun* (no plural) the activity of selling things to people in shops: *Retail sales are rising steadily.*

A B C D E F G H I J K L M N O P Q R S T U V W X Y Z

A B C D E F G H I J K L M N O P Q R S T U V W X Y Z

re·tail·er /ˈriːteɪlə $ ˈriˌteɪlɚ/ *noun* a person or company that sells things to people in shops

re·tain /rɪˈteɪn/ *verb* (formal) to keep something: *The village has retained its old charm.*

re·tal·i·ate /rɪˈtælieɪt/ *verb* to do something unpleasant to someone because they have done something unpleasant to you: *Don't retaliate if he hits you.*

re·tal·i·a·tion /rɪˌtæliˈeɪʃən/ *noun* (no plural) when someone retaliates

ret·i·cent /ˈretəsənt/ *adjective* (formal) not wanting to say what you know or think about something

re·tire /rɪˈtaɪə $ rɪˈtaɪɚ/ *verb* to stop working at the end of your working life: *I'm going to retire when I'm 60.*

re·tire·ment /rɪˈtaɪəmənt $ rɪˈtaɪɚmənt/ *noun* the time when or after you stop working at the end of your working life: *It's important to save money for your retirement.*

re·tir·ing /rɪˈtaɪərɪŋ/ *adjective* shy and nervous with other people

re·treat /rɪˈtriːt/ *verb* **1** to move away from someone or something that is unpleasant or frightening: *The shouting made her retreat into the house.* **2** if an army retreats, it moves back to avoid fighting ANTONYM **advance**
—**retreat** *noun*: *the army's retreat from the capital*

ret·ri·bu·tion /ˌretrəˈbjuːʃən/ *noun* (no plural) (formal) when someone is hurt or punished for doing something: *They would not give evidence against the men for fear of retribution.*

re·trieve /rɪˈtriːv/ *verb* to get something and bring it back from the place where you left it: *I retrieved my bags from the car.*

ret·ro·spect /ˈretrəspekt/ *noun* **in retrospect** used when you are thinking about something that happened in the past, and you know more about it now than you knew then: *In retrospect, I shouldn't have sold my computer.*

re·turn¹ /rɪˈtɜːn $ rɪˈtɚn/ *verb*

KEY PATTERNS
return to a place/job etc
return from a place
return something to someone

1 to come back or go back to a place: *At 11 o'clock I was still waiting for Simone to return.* • *Years later I* ***returned to*** *the house I used to live in.* • *He's been much happier since* ***returning from*** *the States.* • *He* ***returned home*** *just after midnight.*
2 to give or send something back to someone: *I decided to* ***return*** *the jeans* ***to*** *the shop where I had bought them.* • *The letter was* ***returned to*** *me without being opened.*
3 if something returns, it starts to happen again: *By the evening my headache had returned.*
4 if you return to something, you start to do it again: *The doctor said I was well enough to* ***return to*** *work.* • *Ten years later I decided to* ***return to*** *teaching.*

PHRASES
return to normal: *It was a long time before the situation at work* ***returned to normal*** (=became normal again).
return someone's call to telephone someone after they have tried to telephone you: *Lyn's not here at the moment. Shall I ask her to* ***return your call****?*

return² *noun* **1** (no plural) when someone comes back or goes back to a place: *After three years abroad he was looking forward to his return to England.* **2 in return** if you do something in return for what someone has done for you, you do it because they did that thing for you: *She offered to help, but wouldn't take anything in return.* **3** *BrE* also **return ticket** a ticket for a journey to a place and back again SYNONYM **round-trip ticket** *AmE*

re·u·nion /riːˈjuːnjən/ *noun* a meeting of people who have not met for a long time: *a college reunion*

re·u·nite /ˌriːjuːˈnaɪt/ *verb* to bring people together again: *He was at last reunited with his family.*

rev /rev/ *verb* (**revved, revving**) also **rev up** to make an engine work faster: *Rev the engine by pressing on the accelerator.*

re•veal /rɪˈviːl/ *verb* **1** to tell people information that was secret ANTONYM **conceal**: *He finally revealed the name of his partner.* **2** to show something that you could not see before: *The door opened to reveal a large hall.*

re•veal•ing /rɪˈviːlɪŋ/ *adjective* showing someone's true character or feelings: *a revealing interview*

rev•el /ˈrevəl/ *verb* (**revelled**, **revelling** *BrE*, **reveled**, **reveling** *AmE*) **revel in something** to enjoy something very much

rev•e•la•tion /ˌrevəˈleɪʃən/ *noun* a fact that people did not know before: *newspaper revelations about her private life*

re•venge /rɪˈvendʒ/ *noun* (no plural) when you hurt or punish someone because they have done something bad to you: *She was determined to get her revenge.*

rev•e•nue /ˈrevənjuː $ ˈrevəˌnu/ *noun* (no plural) money that a company or organization earns: *Most of the theatre's revenue comes from ticket sales.*

re•verse¹ /rɪˈvɜːs $ rɪˈvɚs/ *verb* **1** to drive a car backwards SYNONYM **back**: *I'll reverse the car into the garage.* **2** to make something the opposite of what it was: *We will never reverse our decision.* **3 reverse the charges** *BrE* to make the person you are telephoning pay for the call SYNONYM **call collect** *AmE*

reverse² *noun* (no plural) **1** if a car is in reverse, it is ready to drive backwards: *Put the car in reverse.* **2** the opposite: *In fact, the reverse is true.*

reverse³ *adjective* in the opposite way to usual: *I will read the winners' names in reverse order.*

re•vers•i•ble /rɪˈvɜːsəbəl $ rɪˈvɚsəbəl/ *adjective* **1** something that is reversible can be changed ANTONYM **irreversible**: *Any bad effects from the treatment are easily reversible.* **2** a reversible piece of clothing can be worn with the inside part on the outside

re•vert /rɪˈvɜːt $ rɪˈvɚt/ *verb* to go back to a previous state or thing: *Leningrad reverted to its former name, St Petersburg.*

re•view¹ /rɪˈvjuː/ *noun* **1** a report about a new book, film, or television show: *The film got very good reviews.* **2** when someone thinks about something again and decides how to change it: *We are having a review of all our safety procedures.*

review² *verb* **1** to write a report about a new book, film, or television show: *He reviews films for a Sunday newspaper.* **2** to think about something again and decide how to change it: *The school is reviewing its policy on homework.* **3** the American word for REVISE²

re•vise /rɪˈvaɪz/ *verb* **1** to change something to make it better: *We need to revise our plans.* **2** *BrE* to prepare for a test by learning work again SYNONYM **review** *AmE*: *I need to revise for my maths test.*

re•vi•sion /rɪˈvɪʒən/ *noun* (no plural) *BrE* when you learn work again before a test: *Have you done enough revision?*

re•vi•val /rɪˈvaɪvəl/ *noun* when something becomes popular or successful again: *the revival of 70s music*

re•vive /rɪˈvaɪv/ *verb* **1** to make something popular or strong again: *Attempts to revive the economy have failed.* **2** to make someone conscious again: *The doctors could not revive him.*

re•volt¹ /rɪˈvəʊlt $ rɪˈvoʊlt/ *verb* to refuse to obey a government and use violence in order to try to change it SYNONYM **rebel**: *The people revolted against the government.*

revolt² *noun* when people refuse to obey a government and use violence against it SYNONYM **rebellion**: *The riots turned into a full-scale revolt.*

re•volt•ing /rɪˈvəʊltɪŋ $ rɪˈvoʊltɪŋ/ *adjective* very unpleasant SYNONYM **disgusting**: *the revolting smell of dead fish* ➔ see Thesaurus at BAD

rev•o•lu•tion /ˌrevəˈluːʃən/ *noun* **1** when the people of a country change the political system completely, using force: *the French Revolution* **2** a complete change in the way people do something: *a revolution in scientific thinking*

A B C D E F G H I J K L M N O P Q R S T U V W X Y Z

rev•o•lu•tion•a•ry¹ /ˌrevəˈluːʃənəri $ ˌrevəˈluʃəˌneri/ *adjective* completely new and different: *a revolutionary new product*

revolutionary² *noun* (plural **revolutionaries**) someone who is involved in a political revolution

rev•o•lu•tion•ize also **revolutionise** *BrE* /ˌrevəˈluːʃənaɪz/ *verb* to completely change the way people do something: *Email has revolutionized the way we work.*

re•volve /rɪˈvɒlv $ rɪˈvɑlv/ *verb* **1** (formal) to move around in a circle: *The wheel revolved slowly.* **2 revolve around something** to have something as the most important part: *Our lives revolve around the school.*

re•volv•er /rɪˈvɒlvə $ rɪˈvɑlvɚ/ *noun* a type of small gun

re•ward¹ /rɪˈwɔːd $ rɪˈwɔrd/ *noun* something, especially money, that is given to someone to thank them for doing something: *She offered a reward to anyone who could find her cat.*

reward² *verb* if you are rewarded for what you have done, something good happens to you or is given to you: *The person who sells the most cars will be rewarded with a bonus.*

re•ward•ing /rɪˈwɔːdɪŋ $ rɪˈwɔrdɪŋ/ *adjective* a job that is rewarding makes you feel happy and satisfied: *Teaching can be rewarding work.*

re•wind /riːˈwaɪnd/ *verb* (past tense and past participle **rewound** /-ˈwaʊnd/) to make a tape go back towards the beginning ANTONYM **fast-forward**

rewound the past tense and past participle of REWIND

re•write /ˌriːˈraɪt/ *verb* (**rewrote** /-ˈrəʊt $ ˈroʊt/ **rewritten** /-ˈrɪtn/) to write something again in a different way: *They rewrote the ending of the film.*

rewritten the past participle of REWRITE

re•wrote the past tense of REWRITE

rhe•tor•i•cal ques•tion /rɪˌtɒrɪkəl ˈkwestʃən $ rɪˌtɔrɪkəl ˈkwestʃən/ *noun* a question that you ask in order to make a statement, without expecting an answer, such as "Why can't they leave me alone?"

rheu•ma•tis•m /ˈruːmətɪzəm/ *noun* (no plural) a disease that makes your muscles and joints painful and difficult to move

rhi•no•ce•ros /raɪˈnɒsərəs $ raɪˈnɑsərəs/ also **rhi•no** /ˈraɪnəʊ $ ˈraɪnoʊ/ *noun* a large heavy animal with a horn on its nose → see picture on page A9

rhubarb /ˈruːbɑːb $ -ɑːrb/ *noun* a plant with big leaves and long pink STEMS which you can cook and eat → see picture on page A7

rhyme¹ /raɪm/ *verb* if two words or phrases rhyme, they end with the same sound: *'Car' rhymes with 'far'.*

rhyme² *noun* **1** a short poem or song that uses words that rhyme **2** when someone uses words that rhyme: *a letter all in rhyme*

> **PRONUNCIATION**
> You pronounce **rhyme** like 'time'.

rhyth•m /ˈrɪðəm/ *noun* a regular repeated pattern of sounds or movements: *the rhythm of the music*

> **SPELLING**
> This word is often spelled wrongly. The correct spelling is: **rhythm**.

rib /rɪb/ *noun* one of the curved bones in your chest → see picture on page A5

rib•bon /ˈrɪbən/ *noun* a narrow piece of coloured cloth that you use to make your clothes or hair look attractive: *She wore ribbons in her hair.*

ribbon

ribbon

rice /raɪs/ *noun* (no plural) food that consists of small white or brown grains that are cooked in water: *We had chicken with boiled rice.*

rich /rɪtʃ/ *adjective* **1** someone who is rich has a lot of money or owns a lot of things ANTONYM **poor**: *He became rich and powerful.* • *She's one of the richest people in the world.* **2** rich food has a lot of fat or egg in it, so you cannot eat very much of it: *The food was delicious, but very rich.* • *a rich sauce*

3 a rich smell, taste, or colour is strong and pleasant: *I love the rich colours in that painting.* • *the rich smell of fresh coffee*

PHRASES

rich in something containing a lot of something good: *It's a beautiful country, **rich in** natural resources.*

> **THESAURUS**
> **well-off**: *Only **well-off** people could afford to live there* (=fairly rich).
> **wealthy**: *She married a **wealthy** landowner* (=rich).
> **prosperous** (formal): *a **prosperous** businessman* (=rich and successful)

rick·et·y /ˈrɪkəti/ *adjective* (informal) in bad condition and likely to break: *a rickety old chair*

ric·o·chet /ˈrɪkəʃeɪ/ *verb* if a bullet or stone ricochets off a surface, it hits the surface and moves away from it in a different direction

rid /rɪd/ *adjective*
1 get rid of something a) to throw away or sell something because you do not want it any more: *I'm going to **get rid of** this car and buy a new one.*
b) to make something that you do not want go away: *We couldn't **get rid of** the smell in the house.*
2 get rid of someone to make someone leave a place or job: *Most people were glad to **get rid of** the old president.* • *Andy stayed for hours – we couldn't **get rid of** him!*

rid·dle /ˈrɪdl/ *noun* **1** an event that people cannot understand or explain SYNONYM **mystery**: *The riddle of Len's death was never solved.* **2** a joke or question that you must guess the answer to

rid·dled /ˈrɪdld/ *adjective* **riddled with something** containing a lot of something bad: *His essay was riddled with mistakes.*

ride¹ /raɪd/ *verb* (**rode** /rəʊd $ roʊd/ **ridden** /ˈrɪdn/ **riding**)

> **KEY PATTERNS**
> **ride a horse/bicycle**
> **ride off/away/along etc**
> **ride (in/on) a bus/train etc** *AmE*

1 to move along on a horse or bicycle: *I learnt to ride a horse when I was five.* • *Can you ride a bicycle?* • *Paul jumped on his bike and **rode off**.* • *We decided to **ride through** the woods.*
2 *AmE* to travel in a bus, train, car etc: *This was the first time she had ridden in a train.*

ride

She is riding a horse. He is riding a bike.

ride² *noun* **1** a trip in a car or train, or on a bicycle or horse: *I went for a ride on my bike.* • *Dad took us for a ride in his new car.* **2** a large moving machine that people go on for fun: *We went on lots of rides at the amusement park.*

rid·er /ˈraɪdə $ ˈraɪdɚ/ *noun* someone who rides a horse, bicycle, or MOTORCYCLE

ridge /rɪdʒ/ *noun* a long narrow area of high land along the top of a mountain: *We could see climbers on the ridge.*

rid·i·cule /ˈrɪdəkjuːl/ *verb* (formal) to laugh and say unkind things about someone or something SYNONYM **mock**: *They ridiculed his appearance.*
—**ridicule** *noun* (no plural) (formal): *My idea was greeted with ridicule.*

ri·dic·u·lous /rɪˈdɪkjələs/ *adjective* very silly: *That's a ridiculous idea!*

ri·dic·u·lous·ly /rɪˈdɪkjələsli/ *adverb* extremely, in a way that seems silly: *Their clothes are ridiculously expensive.*

rid·ing /ˈraɪdɪŋ/ *noun* (no plural) the sport of riding horses

rife /raɪf/ *adjective* if something bad is rife, it is very common: *Burglary is rife in large cities.*

ri·fle /ˈraɪfəl/ *noun* a long gun that you hold against your shoulder to shoot

rift /rɪft/ *noun* a serious disagreement between people: *The argument created a rift between them.*

rig¹ /rɪg/ *verb* (**rigged**, **rigging**) to make an election or competition have the result that you want, by doing something dishonest: *They claim the election was rigged.*

rig² *noun* a large structure that is used for getting oil or gas from under the bottom of the sea

right¹ /raɪt/ *adjective*

KEY PATTERNS
right about something
it is right to do something
right for something/someone

1 correct ANTONYM **wrong**: *In the test, all my answers were right. • Are you sure this is the right way? • You* ***were right about*** *the weather – it's raining now.*
2 on or nearer the side nearest the hand that most people write with ANTONYM **left**: *Dan's broken his right leg.*
3 fair or morally good ANTONYM **wrong**: ***It's*** *never* ***right to*** *steal.*
4 suitable ANTONYM **wrong**: *Make sure you wear something that's* ***right for*** *the occasion.*
PHRASES
that's right (spoken) something you say when someone is correct about something: *"You live in London, don't you?" "Yes,* ***that's right.****"*

right² *adverb*
1 exactly in a particular position or at a particular stage: *A child was standing* ***right in the middle*** *of the road. • They arrived* ***right at the end*** *of the show.*
2 (spoken) used when you want to make someone listen or get ready to do something: *Right, everyone! It's time to go!*
3 correctly ANTONYM **wrong**: *Have I done this question right?*
PHRASES
turn right, look right etc to turn, look etc towards the right side ANTONYM **left**: ***Turn right*** *by the traffic lights.*
right now, right away (spoken) immediately: *I'll go and talk to him* ***right now.*** → see Thesaurus at IMMEDIATELY

right³ *noun*

KEY PATTERNS
the right to do something
the right to something

1 something that you are allowed to do or have by law: *In Britain everyone* ***has the right to*** *vote when they are 18. • All children* ***have the right to*** *free education. • Of course men and women should have* ***equal rights*** (=the same rights).
2 (no plural) behaviour that is good and fair ANTONYM **wrong**: *It's important to teach children the difference between right and wrong.*
PHRASES
on the right, to the right on or near your right side: *Walk straight on and you'll see a post office* ***on the right.***
the right political groups that believe that the government should not own any business or try to control business by making too many rules

ˈright ˌangle *noun* an angle of 90°, like the angles at the corners of a square

ˈright-ˌangled *adjective* a right-angled TRIANGLE has two sides that join each other at 90°

right·ful /ˈraɪtfəl/ *adjective* (formal) according to what is legally and morally right: *He is the rightful owner of the house.* —**rightfully** *adverb*: *The money should rightfully be hers.*

ˈright-hand *adjective* on or near your right side ANTONYM **left-hand**: *Their house is on the right-hand side of the road.*

ˌright-ˈhanded *adjective* someone who is right-handed uses their right hand rather than their left hand to do most things ANTONYM **left-handed**

right·ly /ˈraɪtli/ *adverb* correctly or for a good reason ANTONYM **wrongly**: *Her father quite rightly said that she was too young to drive.*

ˌright of ˈway *noun* (no plural) the right to drive into or across a road before other vehicles

ˌright-ˈwing *adjective* someone with right-wing views does not like changes in society, and supports CAPITALISM rather than SOCIALISM ANTONYM **left-wing**

ri·gid /ˈrɪdʒɪd/ *adjective* **1** rules or ideas that are rigid are strict and difficult to change: *a society with rigid traditions* **2** something that is rigid is stiff and does not move or bend easily ANTONYM **flexible**: *His body was rigid with fear.*

rig·or·ous /ˈrɪgərəs/ *adjective* done in a careful and thorough way: *Some people are demanding a more rigorous driving test.* —**rigorously** *adverb*: *The new rules will be rigorously enforced.*

rile /raɪl/ *verb* (informal) to make someone angry: *Don't let him rile you.*

rim /rɪm/ *noun* the outside edge of something round, such as a glass or a wheel ➔ see picture at CUP[1]

rind /raɪnd/ *noun* the thick skin on the outside of some foods or fruits: *lemon rind*

PRONUNCIATION
You pronounce **rind** like 'find'.

ring¹ /rɪŋ/ *noun*
1 a circle of silver, gold etc that you wear on your finger: *a gold* ***wedding ring*** ➔ see picture at GOLD[2]
2 a circle: *The kids sat* ***in a ring*** *in the middle of the room.* • *There was* ***a ring of*** *policemen around the building.*
➔ see picture on page A1

PHRASES
give someone a ring *BrE* (informal) to telephone someone: *I'll* ***give you a ring*** *at the weekend.*
a ring at the door the sound that a door bell makes: *At that moment there was* ***a ring at the door.***

ring

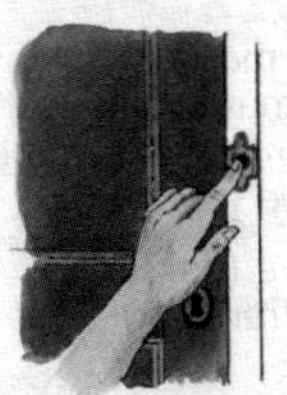

I rang the bell.

The telephone is ringing.

ring² *verb* (**rang** /ræŋ/ **rung** /rʌŋ/)
1 if a bell or telephone rings, it makes a sound: *I could hear the church bells ringing.* • *We were just going out when the telephone rang.*
2 if you ring a bell, you press it so that it makes a sound: *The postman rang the front door bell.*
3 *BrE* also **ring up** to telephone someone SYNONYM **phone**, **call**: *Jim* ***rang*** *me* ***up*** *and asked me to go to a party.*

PHRASAL VERBS
ring back
ring back, ring someone back *BrE* to telephone someone again, or telephone someone who telephoned you SYNONYM **call back** *AmE*: *Mr Todd's busy at the moment. Can he* ***ring you back****?*

ring·lead·er /ˈrɪŋˌliːdə $ ˈrɪŋˌlidɚ/ *noun* someone who leads a group that is doing something wrong: *He is the ringleader of the gang.*

rink /rɪŋk/ *noun* an area where you can ICE SKATE

rinse /rɪns/ *verb* to wash something in clean water in order to remove soap or dirt from it: *Rinse the shampoo out of your hair.* —**rinse** *noun*: *He gave the glass a quick rinse.*

ri·ot¹ /ˈraɪət/ *noun* when a crowd of people behave very violently in a public place: *The demonstration became a riot.*

riot² *verb* if a crowd of people riot, they behave violently in a public place: *People rioted against the new law.*
➔ see Thesaurus at PROTEST[2]
—**rioting** *noun* (no plural): *There was rioting in the streets of the city.*

ri·ot·ous /ˈraɪətəs/ *adjective* noisy and uncontrolled: *riotous New Year celebrations*

rip¹ /rɪp/ *verb* (**ripped**, **ripping**)
1 to tear something, or become torn: *He ripped the letter open.* • *My sleeve ripped.* **2 rip something up** to tear something into a lot of pieces: *I ripped up all his love letters.* **3 rip someone off** (informal) to charge someone too much money for something: *The taxi driver really ripped me off.*

rip

My sleeve ripped.

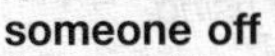

A B C D E F G H I J K L M N O P Q R S T U V W X Y Z

rip² *noun* a hole in a piece of clothing or material where it has torn SYNONYM **tear**: *There's a rip in your skirt.*

ripe /raɪp/ *adjective* fruit that is ripe is ready to pick and eat: *a ripe red apple • Those bananas aren't ripe yet.*

rip·en /ˈraɪpən/ *verb* (formal) to become ripe: *As the tomatoes ripen, they change from green to red.*

rip·off /ˈrɪpɒf $ ˈrɪpɔːf/ *noun* (informal) something that is much too expensive: *Some designer clothes are a ripoff.*

rip·ple¹ /ˈrɪpəl/ *verb* when water ripples, it moves in small waves: *The pond rippled in the breeze.*

ripple

ripple² *noun* a small wave: *I watched the ripples on the lake.*

rise¹ /raɪz/ *verb* (**rose** /rəʊz $ roʊz/ **risen** /ˈrɪzən/)

KEY PATTERNS
rise by an amount
rise (from one amount) to another amount

1 if an amount rises, it increases ANTONYM **fall**: *The amount of crime in our cities is rising all the time. • House prices have **risen by** ten per cent this year. • The cost has **risen from** £100 **to** £200. • Unemployment **rose to** 2 million.* → see Thesaurus at INCREASE¹
2 also **rise up** (formal) to move upwards: *Suddenly the bird **rose up** in the sky and disappeared.*
3 (formal) to stand up: *We all rose when the president entered. • Mr Millet **rose from** his chair and walked across the room.*
4 when the sun or moon rises, it appears in the sky ANTONYM **set**: *We got up early to watch the sun rising.*

rise² *noun* **1** an increase ANTONYM **fall**: *There has been a rise in food costs. • We haven't had a pay rise this year.*
2 when someone or something becomes more successful or more powerful ANTONYM **fall**: *Hitler's rise to power*

risen the past participle of RISE¹

risk¹ /rɪsk/ *noun*

KEY PATTERNS
the risk of injury/failure etc
the risk of getting caught/dying etc
the risk (that)
a risk to someone/something

1 a possibility that something bad may happen: *Most sports involve **the risk of** injury. • There is always **a risk of** dying during an operation. • Is there **a risk** that I will become ill too?* → see Thesaurus at DANGER
2 something that may be dangerous: *Smoking cigarettes is **a risk to** your health.*

PHRASES
take a risk to do something even though you know it is dangerous or you may not succeed: *It's best not to **take risks** with your money.*
at risk (from something) likely to be harmed or lost: *Children are most **at risk from** pollution. • Hundreds of jobs are **at risk** if we lose the contract.*

risk² *verb*

KEY PATTERNS
risk doing something
risk losing something/being caught
risk your life/money etc

1 to do something which may be dangerous or may cause something bad to happen: *He didn't want to risk travelling in such bad weather. • He risks losing everything.*
2 if you risk your life, money etc, you do something which may make you lose it: *Thousands of men and women **risked their lives** in the war.*

risk·y /ˈrɪski/ *adjective* (**riskier**, **riskiest**) dangerous: *Travelling alone can be risky.*

rit·u·al¹ /ˈrɪtʃuəl/ *noun* a ceremony or set of actions that is always done in the same way: *The priest began the ritual of lighting the candles.*

ritual² *adjective* done as part of a ritual: *a ritual sacrifice*

ri•val[1] /ˈraɪvəl/ *noun* a person or group that you compete with: *The two sisters have always been rivals.* —**rival** *adjective*: *rival gangs*

rival[2] *verb* (**rivalled, rivalling** *BrE*, **rivaled, rivaling** *AmE*) if one thing rivals another, it is as good as the other thing: *The city's nightlife rivals London's.*

ri•val•ry /ˈraɪvəlri/ *noun* (plural **rivalries**) when people or groups try to show that they are better than each other SYNONYM **competition**: *There's a lot of rivalry between our schools.*

riv•er /ˈrɪvə $ ˈrɪvɚ/ *noun* a long area of water that flows into a sea: *the River Ganges*

riv•et /ˈrɪvɪt/ *verb* **be riveted** if you are riveted by something, you cannot stop looking at it or listening to it because it is very interesting: *The film riveted the children's attention from the start.* —**riveting** *adjective*: *a riveting story*

roach /rəʊtʃ $ roʊtʃ/ *AmE* a COCKROACH

road /rəʊd $ roʊd/ *noun*

KEY PATTERNS
the road to a place

a hard surface that cars and other vehicles travel on: *Is this* ***the road to*** *Stratford?* • *You're too young to cycle* ***on the road.*** • *A police car was coming* ***along the road.*** • *We live just* ***down the road.*** • *I live at 73, Middle Road.*

PHRASES

by road in a car, bus etc: *If we go* ***by road*** *it will take at least seven hours.*

cross the road to walk across a road in order to get to the other side: *Look left and right before you* ***cross the road.***

THESAURUS

street: *There was a car parked on the other side of the* ***street*** (=a road in a town).

lane: *They cycled along the* ***lane*** *to the next village* (=a narrow country road).

avenue: *I walked down Winchester* ***Avenue*** (=a road in a town, especially one with trees on either side of it).

motorway *BrE*, **freeway** *AmE: We sped along the* ***motorway*** (=a wide road for travelling fast over long distances).

road•block /ˈrəʊdblɒk $ ˈroʊdblɑk/ *noun* a place where the police or army have blocked the road: *Police have set up roadblocks to stop the terrorists escaping.*

ˈroad rage *noun* (no plural) when a driver becomes angry and starts shouting at or attacking other drivers

road•side /ˈrəʊdsaɪd $ ˈroʊdsaɪd/ *noun* (no plural) the land at the edge of a road: *We stopped at the roadside to eat our picnic.*

road•works /ˈrəʊdwɜːks $ ˈroʊdwɚks/ *noun* work that is being done to repair a road

roam /rəʊm $ roʊm/ *verb* to walk around all over a place: *Gangs of thieves roam the city.*

roar /rɔː $ rɔr/ *verb* to make a very loud deep noise: *We heard a lion roar.* —**roar** *noun*: *a roar of laughter*

roar•ing /ˈrɔːrɪŋ/ *adjective* **roaring fire** a fire that burns with a lot of flames and heat

roast[1] /rəʊst $ roʊst/ *verb* to cook food such as meat or vegetables in an OVEN: *Shall I roast or boil the potatoes?* ➔ see picture at COOK[1] ➔ see picture on page A4

roast[2] *adjective* roast meat or vegetables have been cooked in an OVEN: *roast beef*

roast[3] *noun* a large piece of roasted meat: *We always have a roast on Sunday.*

rob /rɒb $ rɑb/ (**robbed, robbing**) *verb*

KEY PATTERNS
rob a bank/shop/person
rob someone of something

to steal money or other things from a bank, shop, or person: *They decided to rob a bank.* • *Two men broke into the house, and* ***robbed*** *the old lady* ***of*** *all her jewellery.* ➔ see Thesaurus at STEAL

WORD CHOICE
rob or **steal**?
• A thief **robs** a bank, a shop, or a person: *He was planning to use the gun to rob.* • *She was* ***robbed*** *on her way home from work.*
• A thief **steals** money or things from someone: *The men* ***stole*** *all his money.*

A B C D E F G H I J K L M N O P Q R S T U V W X Y Z

rob·ber /ˈrɒbə $ ˈrɑbɚ/ *noun* someone who steals money or other things from a bank, shop etc: *a gang of armed robbers*

rob·ber·y /ˈrɒbəri $ ˈrɑbəri/ *noun* (plural **robberies**) the crime of stealing money or other things from a bank, shop etc: *Barker spent two years in jail for robbery.*

robe /rəʊb $ roʊb/ *noun* **1** a long loose piece of clothing that people wear especially for formal ceremonies: *a judge's robe* **2** the American word for DRESSING GOWN

rob·in /ˈrɒbɪn $ ˈrɑbɪn/ *noun* a small brown bird with a red chest

ro·bot /ˈrəʊbɒt $ ˈroʊbɑt/ *noun* a machine that can move and do jobs like a person: *Most of the work in the factory is now done by robots.*

ro·bust /rəˈbʌst $ roʊˈbʌst/ *adjective* strong and not likely to become ill or be damaged: *She is 75, but still robust.*

rock¹ /rɒk $ rɑk/ *noun* **1** (no plural) the hard substance in the Earth's surface that cliffs and mountains are made of: *They had to drill through solid rock.* **2** a large piece of stone: *We sat on a large rock.* **3** (no plural) a type of loud popular music with a strong beat: *Their music is a mixture of rock and disco.*

rock² *verb* if something rocks, or if you rock it, it moves gently from side to side: *The boat rocked slowly.* • *I rocked the baby to sleep.*

ˌrock and ˈroll *noun* ROCK 'N' ROLL

ˌrock ˈbottom *noun* **hit rock bottom, reach rock bottom** (informal) to become as bad as it is possible to be: *His musical career has now hit rock bottom.*

ˈrock-bottom *adjective* (informal) rock-bottom prices are as low as they can be: *The houses are being sold for rock-bottom prices.*

rock·et¹ /ˈrɒkɪt $ ˈrɑkɪt/ *noun* **1** a long thin vehicle that carries people or scientific equipment into space **2** a long thin weapon that carries a bomb and is fired from a plane, ship etc **3** a FIREWORK that goes high into the air and explodes

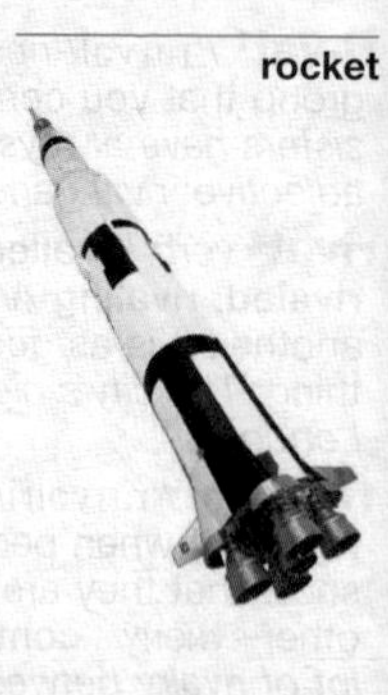
rocket

rocket² *verb* (informal) to increase very quickly SYNONYM **shoot up**: *Sales of MP3 players have rocketed.*

ˈrocking chair *noun* a chair with curved pieces of wood on the bottom that allow it to move backwards and forwards when you sit on it ➔ see picture at CHAIR¹

rock 'n' roll /ˌrɒk ən ˈrəʊl $ ˌrɑk ən ˈroʊl/ *noun* (no plural) a type of loud music with a strong beat that became popular in the 1950s

rock·y /ˈrɒki $ ˈrɑki/ *adjective* (**rockier**, **rockiest**) covered with rocks or made of rock: *a rocky coastline*

rod /rɒd $ rɑd/ *noun* a long thin pole or stick: *a fishing rod*

rod

rode the past tense of RIDE¹

ro·dent /ˈrəʊdənt $ ˈroʊdnt/ *noun* (formal) an animal such as a rat or a mouse that has long sharp front teeth

rogue /rəʊg $ roʊg/ *noun* a man or boy who is not honest or who behaves badly

role /rəʊl $ roʊl/ *noun* **1** what one person does in a group or situation: *The mother of the family has an important role.* **2** a character in a play or film SYNONYM **part**: *Rob played the role of the king.*

SPELLING
Don't confuse the spelling of **role** and **roll** (=a round piece of bread).

ˈrole ˌmodel *noun* someone you admire and try to copy: *A father should be a good role model for his sons.*

roll¹ /rəʊl $ roʊl/ *verb*

KEY PATTERNS
roll down/across/over etc something

1 to move somewhere smoothly, by turning over many times like a ball: *The coin fell out of my hands and **rolled across** the floor.*
2 if a vehicle rolls somewhere, it moves on its own, with no one driving it: *The car began to **roll down** the hill.*
3 also **roll over** to turn your body over when you are lying down: *Dan **rolled over** onto his back and fell asleep.*

PHRASAL VERBS
roll in
(informal) if people or things roll in, large amounts of them arrive: *Letters soon **rolled in** complaining about the show.*
roll out
roll something out to make something flat after it has been in the shape of a ball or a tube: ***Roll** the pastry **out** and make eight circles from it.* ➔ see picture on page A4
roll up
1 (informal) to arrive late: *We'd arranged to meet at eight, but he didn't **roll up** till nine o'clock!*
2 roll something up to bend something over many times so that it is in the shape of a tube, or is shorter: *He stood up and rolled up his newspaper.* • *She rolled up her sleeves and began washing the dishes.*

roll² *noun* **1** a piece of paper, plastic etc that has been rolled up into the shape of a tube: *I bought eight rolls of wallpaper.* **2** a small round amount of bread for one person

ˈroll call *noun* when someone reads out all the names on a list to check who is there: *We must take a roll call to make sure everyone is here.*

Rol•ler•blade /ˈrəʊləbleɪd $ ˈroʊlɚˌbleɪd/ *noun* (trademark) a boot with a single row of wheels fixed under it that you wear for SKATING

rol•ler•blad•ing /ˈrəʊləˌbleɪdɪŋ $ ˈroʊlɚˌbleɪdɪŋ/ *noun* (no plural) SKATING when you are wearing Rollerblades: *We went rollerblading in the park.*

roller coaster

ˈroller ˌcoaster *noun* a small railway which carries people up and down a steep track very fast for fun

ˈroller skate *noun* a boot with four wheels fixed under it that you wear for SKATING ➔ see picture at SKATE¹

ˈroller ˌskating *noun* (no plural) SKATING when you are wearing roller skates

roll•ing /ˈrəʊlɪŋ $ ˈroʊlɪŋ/ *adjective* **be rolling in it** (informal) to be very rich

Ro•man¹ /ˈrəʊmən $ ˈroʊmən/ *adjective* related to ancient Rome: *the Roman Empire*

Roman² *noun* the Romans were the people of ancient Rome

ˌRoman ˈCatholic CATHOLIC

ro•mance /rəʊˈmæns $ ˈroʊmæns/ *noun* **1** an exciting relationship between two people who love each other: *I don't think their relationship will last – it was just a summer romance.* **2** a story or film about two people who love each other

ro•man•tic /rəʊˈmæntɪk $ roʊˈmæntɪk/ *adjective* connected with or showing love: *I wish my boyfriend was more romantic.* • *a romantic novel*

roof /ruːf $ ruf/ *noun*
the top part of a building or vehicle: *The roof of the church had been damaged in a storm.*

PHRASES
the roof of your mouth the top part of the inside of your mouth: *The soup was hot and burnt **the roof of my mouth**.*
hit the roof *BrE* (informal) to become very angry: *Dad **hit the roof** when he saw the scratch on the car.*

A B C D E F G H I J K L M N O P Q R S T U V W X Y Z

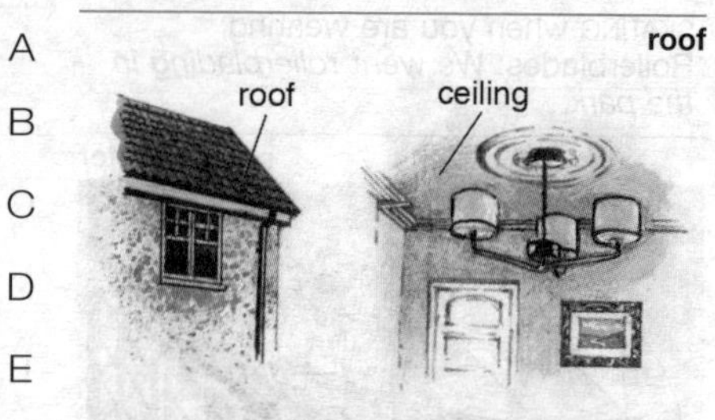

WORD CHOICE
roof or **ceiling**?
• The **roof** is the top part of a building, which protects it from the rain.
• The **ceiling** is the surface above your head inside a room.

roof·top /ˈruːftɒp $ ˈruftɑp/ *noun* the top surface of a roof

room¹ /ruːm/ *noun*

KEY PATTERNS
there is room for something somewhere

1 a part of a building that has its own walls, floor, and ceiling: *This is the room I work in.* • *My brother was sleeping in the next room.* • *the living room*
2 (no plural) space for something or someone: *Is there* ***room for*** *my camera in your bag?*
PHRASES
make room for someone/something to move so that there is enough space for someone or something: *Please move along and make room for Jerry.*
leg room, head room the amount of space in front of you or above you in a vehicle: *There's never much leg room in aeroplanes.*

room² *verb* **room with someone** *AmE* to live in the same room, apartment, or house as someone else

room·mate /ˈruːmˌmeɪt/ *noun* someone you share a room, apartment, or house with: *We were roommates at college.*

room·y /ˈruːmi/ *adjective* (**roomier**, **roomiest**) a roomy building has plenty of space inside SYNONYM **spacious** ANTONYM **cramped**: *a nice roomy apartment*

roost·er /ˈruːstə $ ˈrustə˞/ *noun* a male chicken

root¹ /ruːt/ *noun* **1** the part of a plant that grows under the ground and takes water from the soil → see picture on page A10 **2** the basic cause of a problem: *Family problems are at the root of his bad behaviour.* **3** the part of a tooth or hair that is under the skin **4 roots** where something first started or where someone was born: *She has never forgotten her roots in Ireland.*

root² *verb* **1** also **root around** to search for something by moving things around SYNONYM **rummage**: *I rooted around in my bag for my key.* **2 root something out** to find out where a problem exists and get rid of it: *We will root out drugs from our school.*

rope¹ /rəʊp $ roʊp/ *noun*
1 very strong thick string: *We tied the other end of the rope around a tree.*
2 know the ropes (informal) to know how a system works or how to do a job

rope

a coil of rope

rope² *verb* **1** to tie things or people together, using rope: *The climbers roped themselves together.* **2 rope someone in** (informal) to persuade someone to help you: *I was roped in to help organize the party.*

rose¹ /rəʊz $ roʊz/ *noun* a garden flower that smells sweet and has sharp parts called THORNS on its stem → see picture at FLOWER → see picture on page A10

rose² the past tense of RISE¹

ro·sé /ˈrəʊzeɪ $ roʊˈzeɪ/ *noun* (no plural) pink wine

ros·ter /ˈrɒstə $ ˈrɑstə˞/ *noun* a list showing the jobs people must do and when they must do them SYNONYM **rota** *BrE*

ros·trum /ˈrɒstrəm $ ˈrɑstrəm/ *noun* a small raised area that someone stands on, for example to make a speech

ros·y /ˈrəʊzi $ ˈroʊzi/ *adjective* (**rosier**, **rosiest**) pink: *a baby with rosy cheeks*

rot /rɒt $ rɑt/ (**rotted**, **rotting**) *verb* if something rots, it goes bad and soft because it is old or wet SYNONYM **decay**: *The apple had started to rot.*

ro·ta /ˈrəʊtə $ ˈroʊtə/ a British word for ROSTER

ro·tate /rəʊˈteɪt $ ˈroʊteɪt/ *verb* (formal) if something rotates, or if you rotate it, it turns round: *The Earth rotates once every 24 hours.*

rote /rəʊt $ roʊt/ *noun* **learn something by rote** to learn something by repeating it many times until you remember it

rot·ten /ˈrɒtn $ ˈrɑtn/ *adjective* **1** rotten food or wood has gone bad and soft: *rotten apples* **2** (informal) very bad, unpleasant, or unfair SYNONYM **awful**: *What a rotten thing to do!*

rough

rough /rʌf/ *adjective*
1 not smooth or even: *The road up the mountain was steep and rough.* • *She scratched the rough skin on her foot.*
2 using too much force, and not careful ANTONYM **gentle**: *Don't be so rough! Someone will get hurt.* • *Rugby can be a rough game.*
3 if the sea is rough, there are large waves because there are strong winds ANTONYM **calm**: *The little boat was tossed about on the rough seas.*
4 a rough description or idea is not exact and does not have very many details: *Can you give me a rough idea of where the station is?*
5 if your life is rough, it is unpleasant or difficult SYNONYM **tough**: *She's had a rough time recently.*
6 a rough place has a lot of violence and crime in it

PRONUNCIATION
You pronounce **rough** like 'stuff'.

rough·ly /ˈrʌfli/ *adverb* **1** not exactly SYNONYM **about**: *Roughly 100 people came.* → see Thesaurus at ABOUT[2]
2 not gently or carefully: *He pulled me along roughly.*

round[1] /raʊnd/ *adjective* something that is round is the same shape as a circle or ball: *a round table* • *The Earth is round.*

round[2] *noun* **1** a set of events that are connected: *the latest round of peace talks* **2** one of the parts of a sports competition that you have to finish before you go to the next part: *Dallas will play Atlanta in the first round of the competition.* **3** **a round of applause** when people hit their hands together to show that they enjoyed a performance: *Let's give tonight's performers a big round of applause.*
4 alcoholic drinks that one person buys for all the people in a group: *Joe bought us a round of drinks.*

round[3] *adverb, preposition BrE*
1 surrounding something: *There's a path round the lake.* • *He had a woollen scarf round his neck.*
2 in or to many parts of a place: *Come on – I'll show you round the office* (=I'll take you to every part of the office).
3 to someone's home: *We're going round to Bill's.*
4 (spoken) somewhere in a place: *Do you live round here?*
5 moving in a circle: *The cars raced round the track.* • *The dancers spun round and round.*

PHRASES
round about (spoken) used when mentioning an amount or time that is nearly right, but not exact SYNONYM **around**: *The school was built* ***round about*** *1930.*

round[4] *verb* **round people up** to find and bring together a group of people: *Will someone go and round up all the children?*

round·a·bout /ˈraʊndəbaʊt/ *noun BrE* a circle where several roads meet, which you have to drive around until you reach the road you want to go on SYNONYM **traffic circle** *AmE*

round·ed /ˈraʊndɪd/ *adjective* curved, not pointed: *We recommend rounded scissors for small children.*

A B C D E F G H I J K L M N O P Q **R** S T U V W X Y Z

'round trip *noun* a journey to a place and back again

round·up /ˈraʊndʌp/ *noun* **1** a short description of the most important pieces of news SYNONYM **summary**: *Here's a roundup of today's news.* **2** when a lot of people or animals are brought together, often by force: *a roundup of criminals by the FBI*

rous·ing /ˈraʊzɪŋ/ *adjective* making people feel excited and eager to do something: *The song has a rousing chorus.*

route /ruːt $ rut, raʊt/ *noun* the way from one place to another: *This is the shortest route to school.*

PRONUNCIATION
British people pronounce **route** like 'shoot'.
American people pronounce **route** like 'shout'.

rout·er /ˈruːtə $ ˈrutə˞, ˈraʊtə˞/ *noun* a piece of electronic equipment on a computer NETWORK that controls the movement of information around the network

rou·tine¹ /ruːˈtiːn/ *noun* **1** the usual way in which you do things: *My daily routine starts with breakfast at 7.* **2** a set of actions, songs, or jokes that someone performs to entertain people: *They're learning a new dance routine.*

routine² *adjective* ordinary and usual: *The interview began with a few routine questions.* ➔ see Thesaurus at NORMAL

row¹ /rəʊ $ roʊ/ *noun*

KEY PATTERNS
a row of people/things
stand/sit in a row

1 a line of people or things: *a* ***row of*** *shops* • *The children were all* ***standing in a row****, waiting for their parents.*
2 a line of seats in a cinema or theatre: *I always prefer to sit in* ***the back row****.*

PHRASES
three times in a row, four days in a row etc three times, one after the other, or four days, one after the other etc: *The bus was late four days* ***in a row****.*

row² /rəʊ $ roʊ/ *verb* to make a boat move through water using OARs: *We rowed over to the island.* ➔ see picture on page A14

a row of chairs — They were standing in a row.

row³ /raʊ/ *noun BrE* an angry argument SYNONYM **quarrel**: *The neighbours were having a row.*

PRONUNCIATION
Be careful how you pronounce this word:
row¹ (*noun*) is pronounced like 'go'
row² (*verb*) is pronounced like 'go'
row³ (*noun*) is pronounced like 'now'

row·dy /ˈraʊdi/ *adjective* (**rowdier, rowdiest**) behaving in a noisy and uncontrolled way: *a rowdy class*

roy·al /ˈrɔɪəl/ *adjective* connected with or belonging to a king or queen: *the royal family*

roy·al·ty /ˈrɔɪəlti/ *noun* (no plural) members of a royal family: *These seats are reserved for royalty.*

RSVP /ˌɑːr es viː ˈpiː/ an abbreviation that is written on invitations to ask someone to reply

rub /rʌb/ *verb* (**rubbed, rubbing**)

KEY PATTERNS
rub a surface
rub a substance into/onto/over something
rub against something

1 to move your hand or a cloth backwards and forwards on a surface: *You'll have to rub a bit harder if you want to get those shoes clean.* • *Andy got out his sunscreen and* ***rubbed*** *it* ***into*** *his skin.* ➔ see Thesaurus at TOUCH¹
2 if something rubs against your skin, it presses and moves against it in a way that is uncomfortable: *It was hot and my shirt collar was* ***rubbing against*** *my neck.*

PHRASES

rub it in (informal) to make someone remember something embarrassing or stupid that they have done: *I made a mistake, but you don't need to keep rubbing it in!*

PHRASAL VERBS

rub out

rub something out to remove something that you have written or drawn with a pencil SYNONYM **erase**: *I quickly **rubbed out** what I had written.*

rub·ber /ˈrʌbə $ ˈrʌbɚ/ *noun* **1** (no plural) a substance that is used for making tyres, boots etc: *His boots were made of rubber.* • *rubber gloves* **2** *BrE* a small piece of rubber that is used for removing pencil marks from paper SYNONYM **eraser** *AmE*

ˌrubber ˈband *noun* a thin circular piece of rubber used for holding things together

rub·bish /ˈrʌbɪʃ/ *noun* (no plural) *BrE* **1** things such as old food, empty bottles etc that you do not need any more and that you throw away: *Could you put this rubbish outside in the bin?* • *a pile of rubbish* **2** (informal) something that you think is silly or wrong SYNONYM **nonsense**, **garbage** *AmE*: *I don't agree with that – it's rubbish!*

THESAURUS

garbage/trash *AmE: Can somebody take out the **garbage*** (=rubbish)?

refuse (formal): *There is a **refuse** collection every week* (=rubbish).

litter: *You shouldn't drop **litter*** (=waste paper, cans etc that people leave on the ground).

waste: *the disposal of industrial **waste*** (=substances or things that are left and are not needed)

rub·ble /ˈrʌbəl/ *noun* (no plural) broken stones or bricks from a building that has been destroyed: *After the explosion, the house was just a pile of rubble.*

ru·by /ˈruːbi/ *noun* (plural **rubies**) a valuable dark red jewel

ruck·sack /ˈrʌksæk/ a British word for BACKPACK ➔ see picture at BAG[1]

rud·der /ˈrʌdə $ ˈrʌdɚ/ *noun* a part at the back of a boat or plane that helps it change direction

rude /ruːd/ *adjective* **1** not polite: *She was rude to the teacher.* **2** talking about things to do with sex, in a way that may offend people: *The boys were telling rude jokes.* —**rudely** *adverb*: *"Go away," she said rudely.* —**rudeness** *noun* (no plural): *I've had enough of your rudeness!*

THESAURUS

impolite (formal): *It would be **impolite** to refuse their invitation* (=rude).

offensive: *He made **offensive** remarks about her appearance* (=likely to make her feel upset or angry).

insulting: *It is **insulting** to suggest that they do not know how to care for their children* (=very rude or offensive).

ru·di·men·ta·ry /ˌruːdəˈmentəri/ *adjective* (formal) very simple and basic: *I have only a rudimentary knowledge of grammar.*

ruf·fle /ˈrʌfəl/ *verb* to make something that was smooth uneven or untidy: *He gently ruffled my hair.*

ruffle

ruffle

rug /rʌg/ *noun* a piece of thick material that you put on the floor: *a beautiful Turkish rug*

rug·by /ˈrʌgbi/ *noun* (no plural) a game played by two teams who carry and kick a ball that is the shape of a large egg

rug·ged /ˈrʌgɪd/ *adjective* **1** rugged land is rough and uneven, with large rocks: *the country's rugged coastline* **2** if a man has a rugged appearance, he is attractive and looks strong and quite rough

ru·in[1] /ˈruːɪn/ *verb* to spoil or destroy something completely: *Her behaviour ruined the party.* ➔ see Thesaurus at DAMAGE[2]

ruin[2] *noun* **1** also **ruins** part of a building that is left after the rest of it has been destroyed: *the ruins of an old castle* **2 be in ruins** to have been completely spoiled or destroyed: *His* *football career was in ruins after he broke his leg.* **3** (no plural) a situation in which someone loses all their money and possessions: *He faced ruin when his business failed.*

rule¹ /ruːl/ *noun* something that tells you what you are allowed to do or what you cannot do, for example at school or in a game: *Jamie explained the rules of the game to us.* • *We were given a long list of school rules.*

PHRASES

against the rules not allowed by the rules: *Smoking at school* ***is against the rules.***

break a rule, break the rules to do something that is not allowed by the rules: *You're* ***breaking the rules*** *if you touch the ball with your hands.*

as a rule (formal) usually: ***As a rule,*** *I go to the gym three times a week.*

THESAURUS

law: *There was no* ***law*** *against employing young children* (=a rule that people in a country must obey).

regulation: *new safety* ***regulations*** *relating to trains* (=official rules)

restriction: *restrictions on immigration* (=rules that limit what people are allowed to do)

ban: *a ban on cigarette advertising* (=an official order saying that people are not allowed to do something)

rule² *verb* **1** to control a country: *At that time, the Romans ruled Britain.* **2** to make an official decision about a legal problem: *The judge ruled that Thompson had been fired from his job illegally.* **3 rule something out** to decide that something is not possible: *Doctors have ruled out an operation at this time.*

ruled /ruːld/ *adjective* ruled paper has lines printed across it for writing on SYNONYM **lined**

rul·er /ˈruːlə $ ˈrulɚ/ *noun* **1** someone such as a king who controls a country **2** a flat narrow piece of plastic, wood, or metal that you use for measuring and drawing straight lines

rul·ing¹ /ˈruːlɪŋ/ *noun* an official decision that is made by a law court: *The company is refusing to accept the court's ruling.*

ruler

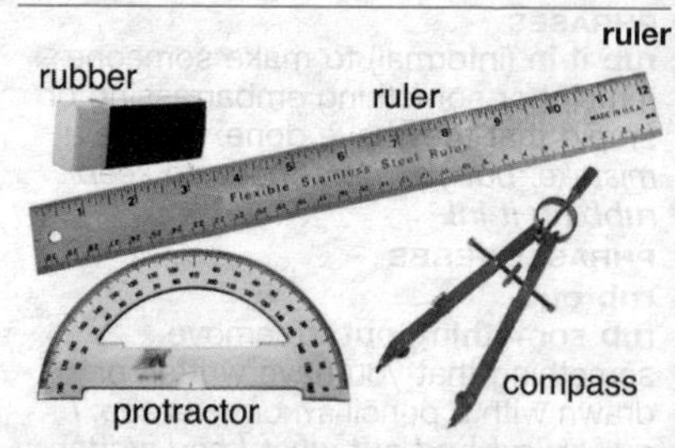

ruling² *adjective* having power in a country or organization: *The ruling class still get the best education.*

rum /rʌm/ *noun* a strong alcoholic drink made from sugar

rum·ble /ˈrʌmbəl/ *verb* to make a series of low sounds: *Traffic rumbled in the distance.* —**rumble** *noun* (no plural): *a rumble of thunder*

rum·mage /ˈrʌmɪdʒ/ *verb* (informal) to search for something by moving things around in an untidy way: *I rummaged through my bag for a pen.*

ˈrummage sale the American word for JUMBLE SALE

ru·mour *BrE*, **rumor** *AmE* /ˈruːmə $ ˈrumɚ/ *noun* information that one person tells another, which may not be true: *I heard a rumour that Joe and Liz were getting married.*

ru·moured *BrE*, **rumored** *AmE* /ˈruːməd $ ˈrumɚd/ *adjective* if something is rumoured to be true, people are saying that it may be true but no one is sure: *The band is rumoured to be splitting up.*

rump /rʌmp/ *noun* (formal) the part of an animal at the top of its back legs

run¹ → see box on page 581 → see picture on page A2

run² /rʌn/ *noun*
1 go for a run, do a run to run for pleasure or for exercise: *I try to* ***go for a run*** *at least twice a week.* • *We had to* ***do a*** *three-kilometre* ***run*** *at school.* **2 in the long run** not immediately, but after some time: *If you buy good quality clothes, it's cheaper* ***in the long run.*** **3** a point in the games of CRICKET and baseball: *New Zealand scored 278 runs on the first day of their match against Australia.*

run /rʌn/ *verb* (past tense **ran** /ræn/, past participle **run**, present participle **running**)

1 to move quickly, going faster than when you walk: *I can **run** faster than Tom.* • *A small boy grabbed my bag and **ran** out of the shop.* • *My dog loves to **run** after cats.* • *The girls came **running** towards me.*

GRAMMAR
When talking about running as an activity that you do for exercise, you say **go running**: *He goes running three times a week.*

2 to manage or control a business, organization etc: *The same family has been **running** the company for years.* • *They **run** a small restaurant in the centre of town.*

3 to go or flow somewhere – used when talking about roads, rivers etc: *Which river **runs** through Paris?* • *A high wall **ran along** the back of the house.* • *The road **runs right across** the country.*

4 if buses or trains run at particular times, they travel at those times: *How often do trains **run from** Oxford to Birmingham?*

5 to make a computer program work: *Every time I **run** that software on my computer, it crashes.*

6 if an engine is running, it is working: *He got out of the car and left the engine **running**.*

PHRASES

run into problems/trouble/difficulties
to start to have problems or trouble: *The business **ran into trouble,** and eventually had to close.*

be running late/be running on time
to be late or at the right time: *Are the trains **running on time**?* • *I'm afraid we're **running** a bit **late**.*

run for office/for president
to try to get elected or become president: *He plans to **run for office** in the next presidential election.*

PHRASAL VERBS

run away
to leave a place without telling anyone because you are unhappy there: *Danny had **run away from** home several times.*

run into
1 run into someone (informal) to meet someone by chance: *I **ran into** Miguel in town yesterday.*
2 run into something if a vehicle runs into something, it hits it: *Our car went off the road and **ran into** a tree.*

run on
to use a particular type of fuel: *The car **runs on** vegetable oil.* • *The air conditioning **runs on** solar power.*

run out
to have no more of something left because you have used it all: *Oh no! I've **run out of** coffee!* • *Hurry up! We're **running out of** time!*

run over
if a vehicle runs over someone or something, it hits them and drives over them: *Careful you don't get **run over** when you cross the road!*

A B C D E F G H I J K L M N O P Q R S T U V W X Y Z

run·a·way[1] /ˈrʌnəweɪ/ *adjective* **1** a runaway vehicle is moving fast and is out of control: *a runaway train*
2 happening quickly and in a way that is difficult to control: *Their first record was a runaway success.*

runaway[2] *noun* a young person or child who has left home without telling anyone

run·down /ˈrʌndaʊn/ *noun* (no plural) a quick description or explanation: *I gave him a rundown on what had happened.*

ˌrun-ˈdown *adjective* **1** in very bad condition: *run-down school buildings*
2 if you are run-down, you feel tired and ill

rung[1] the past participle of RING[2]

rung[2] /rʌŋ/ *noun* **1** one of the steps of a LADDER → see picture at LADDER
2 (informal) a level in an organization: *She started on the bottom rung in the company.*

run·ner /ˈrʌnə $ ˈrʌnɚ/ *noun* someone who runs as a sport: *He's a brilliant long-distance runner.*

ˌrunner-ˈup *noun* (plural **runners-up**) the person or team that finishes second in a competition: *The judge chose one winner and two runners-up.*

run·ning[1] /ˈrʌnɪŋ/ *noun* (no plural)
1 when you run for pleasure or as a sport: *Running keeps me fit.* **2 be in the running** to have a chance of winning: *We were never really in the running for the finals.*

running[2] *adjective* **1 running water** water that flows from a TAP: *Some people had no running water or electricity.* **2 a running total** a total that increases gradually as new amounts are added to it: *Keep a running total of the amount you have spent.*

running[3] *adverb* **three years running, five times running etc** for three years, five times etc without changing: *I was late for the third day running.*

run·ny /ˈrʌni/ *adjective* (**runnier, runniest**) a runny nose or runny eyes have liquid coming out of them: *I had a sore throat and a runny nose.*

run·way /ˈrʌnweɪ/ *noun* a long wide road that planes use when they are landing or taking off

ru·ral /ˈrʊərəl $ ˈrʊrəl/ *adjective* related to the country rather than the city ANTONYM **urban**: *Do you think you will enjoy rural life?*

rush[1] /rʌʃ/ *verb*

> KEY PATTERNS
> **rush to/from a place**
> **rush to do something**

1 to go somewhere or do something quickly: *Maria* ***rushed out of*** *the room, crying.* • *The telephone rang, and we all* ***rushed to*** *answer it.*
2 to do something too quickly, without taking enough care: *Don't rush your homework.* • *If you rush your dinner, you'll get a stomach ache.*
3 if you rush someone, you try to make them hurry SYNONYM **hurry**: *I'm sorry to rush you, but we're going to miss the bus.*

PHRASES

rush someone to hospital to take someone to hospital very quickly: *An ambulance arrived and* ***rushed*** *her* ***to hospital.***

PHRASAL VERBS

rush around
to be very busy going to different places or doing a lot of things: *Sally rushed around, making sure everyone had plenty to eat.*

rush into
rush into something to do something without thinking carefully about it first: *I don't think you should* ***rush into*** *buying a house.*

rush[2] *noun* (no plural)

> KEY PATTERNS
> **do something/be in a rush**
> **a rush to do something**
> **a rush for something**

1 a situation in which you need to hurry: *Can I phone you later? I'm* ***in a rush to*** *catch the bus.* • *Enjoy your meal. There's no rush.*
2 a situation in which a lot of people are trying to do something or get something: *There's always* ***a rush for*** *the bathroom in the morning.*

rushed /rʌʃt/ *adjective* **1** a piece of work that is rushed has been done too quickly and carelessly: *His essay was* *obviously rushed, and full of mistakes.* **2 be rushed off your feet** (informal) to be very busy

'rush hour *noun* the time of day when there is a lot of traffic because people are going to and from work: *If you leave by 7, you should miss the rush hour.*

rust¹ /rʌst/ *noun* (no plural) a brown substance that forms on metal when it gets wet: *Check your car each month for signs of rust.*

rust² *verb* if metal rusts, a brown substance forms on it: *The hinges on the box had rusted.*

rus•tle /'rʌsəl/ *verb* to make a soft light sound like the sound of paper moving: *leaves rustling in the wind*
→ see picture on page A1

rust•y /'rʌsti/ *adjective* (**rustier, rustiest**) **1** covered with rust: *a heap of rusty metal* **2** if a skill or knowledge that you have is rusty, it is not as good as it used to be because you have not used it for a long time: *My French is a bit rusty.*

rut /rʌt/ *noun* **1 be in a rut** (informal) to be living or working in a boring situation that you cannot easily change: *Many office workers feel they are in a rut after a few years.* **2** a deep narrow track made by a wheel

ruth•less /'ruːθləs/ *adjective* cruel and not caring about other people: *The judge described Marshall as a ruthless killer.* —**ruthlessly** *adverb*: *The soldiers ruthlessly destroyed anything in their way.*

rye /raɪ/ *noun* (no plural) a type of grain, used for making bread and WHISKY

Ss

's /z, s/ **1** is: *What's the time?* **2** has: *She's got a cold.* **3** used to show who owns something: *Peter's car*

S the written abbreviation of SOUTH or SOUTHERN

sab·o·tage /'sæbətɑːʒ/ *verb* to secretly damage or destroy something: *He tried to sabotage her plans.* —**sabotage** *noun*: *The bridge was destroyed in a deliberate act of sabotage.*

sach·et /'sæʃeɪ $ sæ'ʃeɪ/ *noun* a small packet containing a liquid or powder SYNONYM **packet** *AmE*: *a sachet of salt*

sack¹ /sæk/ *noun* **1** a large bag made of strong material: *We store the potatoes in sacks.* • *a sack of flour* **2 get the sack** *BrE* (informal) to be told that you must leave your job: *I worked for a while in a shop, but I got the sack.* **3 give someone the sack** *BrE* (informal) to tell someone that they must leave their job

sack² *verb BrE* (informal) if your employer sacks you, they tell you that you cannot work for them any longer SYNONYM **fire**: *If you continue to be late, the company will sack you.*

sa·cred /'seɪkrɪd/ *adjective* important and special according to a religion: *For Hindus, the River Ganges is sacred.*

sac·ri·fice¹ /'sækrəfaɪs/ *noun* **1** something important that you give up in order to help someone or get something that is more important: *Her parents made many sacrifices so that they could pay for their daughter's education.* **2** an animal or person that is killed in order to please a god

sacrifice² *verb* **1** to give up something important in order to help someone or get something that is more important: *I sacrificed my family for my career.* **2** to kill an animal or person in order to please a god

sad /sæd/ *adjective* (**sadder**, **saddest**)

KEY PATTERNS
sad to do something
sad (that)

1 not happy ANTONYM **happy**: *Why are you so sad?* • *I liked him and I* ***was sad to*** *say goodbye.* • *Of course the team* ***felt sad that*** *they had lost the match.* **2** making you feel sad: *The movie had a very sad ending.* **3** (informal) boring or not fashionable

THESAURUS
unhappy: *She had an* ***unhappy*** *childhood* (=she was often sad when she was a child).
miserable: *I was so* ***miserable*** *I couldn't eat* (=very sad).
depressed: *He felt* ***depressed*** *after losing his job* (=sad and not hopeful about the future).
upset: *She's* ***upset*** *because she's just had a big argument with her boyfriend* (=sad because something bad has happened).
disappointed: *I was* ***disappointed*** *that I had missed the party* (=sad because something I wanted to happen did not happen).
homesick: *I felt* ***homesick*** *and I phoned my Mum almost every day* (=sad because I was a long way from my home).

sad·den /'sædn/ *verb* (formal) if something saddens you, it makes you feel sad: *We are all very saddened by her death.*

saddle

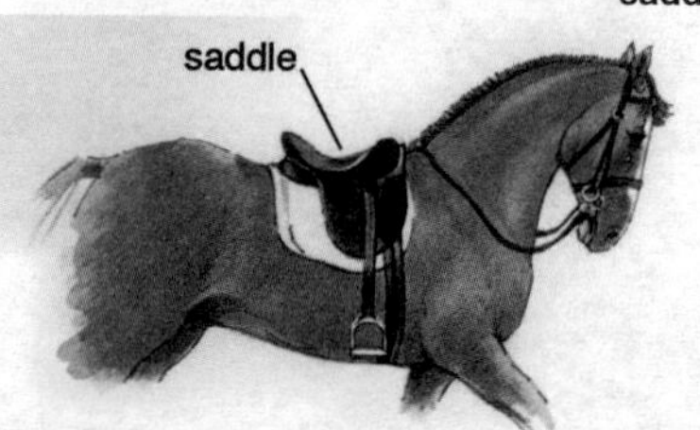

sad·dle¹ /'sædl/ *noun* a leather seat on a horse or bicycle

saddle² *verb* **saddle someone with something** (informal) to give someone a difficult or boring job: *I've been saddled with organizing the party.*

sad·ly /ˈsædli/ *adverb* **1** in a sad way SYNONYM **unhappily**: *She smiled sadly.* **2** used when you are saying something that you wish were not true: *Sadly, the museum will have to close next year.*

sa·fa·ri /səˈfɑːri/ *noun* a trip through wild areas of Africa to hunt or watch wild animals: *We spent three weeks on safari in Kenya.*

safe¹ /seɪf/ *adjective*

KEY PATTERNS
it is safe to do something
safe to use/drink etc
safe for someone
safe from something/someone dangerous

1 something that is safe will not hurt people: *You can walk on the bridge – it's perfectly safe.* • *Walking is the safest form of travel.* • ***Is it safe to** swim here?* • *Is the water here **safe to** drink?* • *We need more play areas that are **safe for** young children.*
2 if you are safe, you are not likely to be hurt: *I knew that when we got across the river we would be safe.* • *I didn't **feel safe** in the house on my own.* • *Stay indoors, where you will be **safe from** the fighting.*

PHRASES
a safe place a place where something is not likely to be stolen or lost: *You'd better put that money **in a safe place**.*
safe and sound, safe and well not harmed or damaged in any way: *The horse was returned to its owner, **safe and sound**.*
to be on the safe side, just to be safe in order to be very careful and avoid any problems: *We got to the airport very early, **just to be on the safe side**.*
in safe hands if something is in safe hands, it is with a person who will look after it carefully: *Don't worry – the kids **are in safe hands**.* —**safely** *adverb*: *Drive safely.* • *Make sure that medicines are safely locked away.*

safe² *noun* a strong metal box with a lock on it, where you keep money and valuable things

safe·ty /ˈseɪfti/ *noun* (no plural)

KEY PATTERNS
carry/lead/drag etc someone to safety
do something in safety

when people are safe and not likely to be hurt: *There are new laws to **improve safety** on aircraft.* • *She is concerned for **the safety of** her son.* • *The firefighters carried the children **to safety**.* • *We were able to watch the lions **in complete safety**.*

ˈ**safety belt** a SEAT BELT

ˈ**safety pin** *noun* a metal pin with a cover, used for fastening clothes together

sag /sæg/ *verb* (**sagged**, **sagging**) to hang down loosely: *The bed sags in the middle.*

sa·ga /ˈsɑːgə/ *noun* a long complicated story

sage /seɪdʒ/ *noun* (no plural) a plant with grey-green leaves that you use in cooking

said the past tense and past participle of SAY

sail¹ /seɪl/ *verb*

KEY PATTERNS
sail to/for/from a place
sail a boat

1 to travel across water in a ship or boat: *The next day we **sailed from** Malta **to** Cairo.* • *We **sail for** America next week.*
2 to make a boat with sails move across water, especially as a sport: *I spent the summer learning to sail.* • *Do you want to have a go at sailing the boat?*

USAGE
When talking about sailing as an activity that you do, you say **go sailing**: *We **went sailing** on the lake.*

sail² *noun* **1** a large piece of strong cloth used to catch the wind and make a boat move **2 set sail** to begin a trip on a boat: *They set sail for America.*

sail·ing /ˈseɪlɪŋ/ *noun* (no plural) when people sail boats as a sport → see picture on page A14

sail·or /ˈseɪlə $ ˈseɪlɚ/ *noun* someone who works on a ship or sails a ship

A B C D E F G H I J K L M N O P Q R S T U V W X Y Z

saint /seɪnt/ (written abbreviation **St**) *noun* someone who has been given the title 'Saint' by the Christian church because their life was very good and holy: *March 1 is Saint David's Day.*

sake /seɪk/ *noun* **1 for someone's sake** in order to help or please someone: *I did it for your sake, because I love you.* **2 for heaven's sake** (spoken) used when you are very annoyed about something: *For heaven's sake, switch that music off!*

sal·ad /ˈsæləd/ *noun* a mixture of vegetables, eaten cold: *a tomato salad* • *Meals are served with chips and salad.*

sa·la·mi /səˈlɑːmi/ *noun* a type of SAUSAGE that is eaten cold

sal·a·ry /ˈsæləri/ *noun* (plural **salaries**) the pay you receive from the organization you work for: *She gets a salary of at least £60,000 a year.*
➔ see Thesaurus at PAY²

sale /seɪl/ *noun*
1 when you sell something to someone: *He made a lot of money from **the sale of** his house.*
2 an event when a shop sells things for lower prices than usual: *The summer sales start next week.* • *I bought this shirt for £15 **in the sale**.*
PHRASES
for sale if something is for sale, someone is trying to sell it: *The house next door is **for sale**.*
on sale if something is on sale, you can buy it: *Tickets for the concert will be **on sale** next week.*

sales·man /ˈseɪlzmən/ *noun* (plural **salesmen** /-mən/) a man whose job is to sell things for a company

sales·per·son /ˈseɪlzˌpɜːsən $ ˈseɪlzˌpɚsən/ *noun* (plural **salespeople** /-ˌpiːpəl/) someone whose job is to sell things for a company

sales·wom·an /ˈseɪlzˌwʊmən/ *noun* (plural **saleswomen** /-ˌwɪmɪn/) a woman whose job is to sell things for a company

sa·li·va /səˈlaɪvə/ *noun* (no plural) the liquid that you produce naturally in your mouth

salm·on /ˈsæmən/ *noun* (plural **salmon**) a large silver fish with pink flesh that you can eat

sal·on /ˈsælɒn $ səˈlɑn/ *noun* a place where you can get your hair cut, have your nails cut etc: *a beauty salon*

PRONUNCIATION
British people put the stress on the first syllable: 'SAlon'.
American people put the stress on the second syllable: 'saLON'.

sa·loon /səˈluːn/ *noun* **1** a place where alcoholic drinks were served in the US in the past **2** *BrE* a car with a separate space at the back for bags, cases etc

salt /sɔːlt/ *noun* (no plural) **1** a white substance that is found naturally in sea water and that is used in cooking to make food taste better: *This sauce needs more salt.* **2 take something with a pinch of salt** (informal) to not completely believe what someone tells you: *You have to take some of Jill's stories with a pinch of salt.*

salt·y /ˈsɔːlti/ *adjective* (**saltier**, **saltiest**) containing salt or tasting of salt: *The meat is too salty.*

sa·lute /səˈluːt/ *verb* to hold your right hand to your head to show respect for someone: *The soldiers saluted General Fox as he approached.* —**salute** *noun*: *His arm was raised in a salute.*

sal·vage /ˈsælvɪdʒ/ *verb* to save something from a situation in which other things have been damaged or lost: *They managed to salvage a few of their things from the fire.*

same /seɪm/ *adjective, pronoun*

KEY PATTERNS
the same as something

1 exactly like something else ANTONYM **different**: *Your shoes are **the same as** mine!* • *All their songs sound the same.* • *The two girls have the same posters on their bedroom walls.* • *Yes, I had the same problem with my computer.*
2 the exact one, not a different one ANTONYM **different**: *They go to the same school.* • *He lives in **the same** street **as** me.* • *Her new car is **the same** colour **as** her old one.*

sam·ple¹ /ˈsɑːmpəl $ ˈsæmpəl/ *noun* a small amount of something that shows what the rest of it is like: *Take samples* *of your work to the interview. • A small sample of blood is tested for the virus.*

sample² *verb* to try something to see what it is like: *We decided to sample the food from the local market.*

sanc·tion /ˈsæŋkʃən/ *verb* (formal) to officially allow something to happen SYNONYM **approve**: *The college has sanctioned the use of dictionaries in examinations.*

sanc·tions /ˈsæŋkʃənz/ *plural noun* laws that stop trade with another country, as a punishment when the country has behaved badly: *Several countries voted to impose trade sanctions on Iran.*

sanc·tu·a·ry /ˈsæŋktʃuəri $ ˈsæŋktʃuˌeri/ *noun* (plural **sanctuaries**) a place where people or animals are protected from danger: *The refugees sought sanctuary in neighbouring countries. • a bird sanctuary*

sand¹ /sænd/ *noun* (no plural) the very small grains of rock that you find in deserts and on beaches: *The children played on the sand.*

sand² *verb* to make a wooden surface smooth by rubbing it with SANDPAPER

san·dal /ˈsændl/ *noun* a light open shoe that you wear in warm weather: *a pair of leather sandals* ➔ see picture at SHOE

sand·cas·tle /ˈsændˌkɑːsəl $ ˈsændˌkæsəl/ *noun* a pile of sand in the shape of a castle, that children make on the beach

sand·pa·per /ˈsændpeɪpə $ ˈsændˌpeɪpɚ/ *noun* (no plural) strong rough paper that you rub on a wooden surface in order to make it smooth

sand·trap /ˈsændtræp/ the American word for BUNKER

sand·wich¹ /ˈsænwɪdʒ/ *noun* (plural **sandwiches**) two pieces of bread with cheese, meat, egg etc between them: *We had chicken sandwiches for lunch.*

sandwich² *verb* **be sandwiched between things** to be in a very small space between two things: *The hairdresser's shop was sandwiched between two hotels.*

sand·y /ˈsændi/ *adjective* (**sandier**, **sandiest**) covered with sand: *a sandy beach*

sane /seɪn/ *adjective* **1** able to think in a normal, reasonable way ANTONYM **insane**: *They have to decide whether the murderer was sane when he committed his crimes.* **2** sensible and reasonable ANTONYM **insane**: *Leaving home seemed the only sane thing to do.*

sang the past tense of SING

san·i·ty /ˈsænəti/ *noun* (no plural) the ability to think normally and reasonably ANTONYM **insanity**: *Kate was having doubts about her own sanity.*

sank the past tense of SINK¹

San·ta Claus /ˈsæntə ˌklɔːz/ also **Santa** *noun* an old man with red clothes and a white beard. Children believe he brings presents at Christmas SYNONYM **Father Christmas** *BrE*

sar·cas·m /ˈsɑːkæzəm $ ˈsɑrˌkæzəm/ *noun* (no plural) when you clearly say the opposite of what you really mean, to be rude or when you are annoyed

sar·cas·tic /sɑːˈkæstɪk $ sɑrˈkæstɪk/ *adjective* using sarcasm: *I was really upset by his sarcastic comments.* —**sarcastically** /-kli/ *adverb*: *"Nice dress," he said sarcastically.*

sar·dine /sɑːˈdiːn $ sɑrˈdin/ *noun* a small silver fish that you can eat

sa·ri /ˈsɑːri/ *noun* a type of loose dress worn by Asian women

sash /sæʃ/ *noun* (plural **sashes**) a long piece of cloth that you wear around your waist or across one shoulder: *a red satin sash*

sas·sy /ˈsæsi/ *adjective* (informal) (**sassier**, **sassiest**) the American word for CHEEKY

sat the past tense and past participle of SIT

Sa·tan /ˈseɪtn/ *noun* the DEVIL

sat·el·lite /ˈsætəlaɪt/ *noun* a machine that has been sent into space to receive and send radio or television signals

ˈsatellite ˌdish *noun* (plural **satellite dishes**) a large circular piece of metal on a building, that receives television or radio signals from a satellite

sat·in /ˈsætɪn $ ˈsætn/ *noun* (no plural) a type of smooth shiny cloth: *a red satin dress*

sat·ire /ˈsætaɪə $ ˈsætaɪɚ/ *noun* amusing speech or writing that shows how silly or wrong something is: *The play is a satire on modern American life.*

sat·ir·i·cal /səˈtɪrɪkəl/ *adjective* using satire: *a satirical TV show*

sat·is·fac·tion /ˌsætɪsˈfækʃən/ *noun* the happiness you feel when you succeed or get what you want: *I get a lot of satisfaction from my job.*

sat·is·fac·to·ry /ˌsætɪsˈfæktəri/ *adjective*
quite good, or good enough: *Liam's work has been satisfactory this term.* • *The arrangement was not really very satisfactory.*

THESAURUS
acceptable (formal): *His work is of an* ***acceptable*** *standard* (=satisfactory).
adequate (formal): *They have not received* ***adequate*** *training* (=enough, or good enough).
all right/OK (informal): *The food was* ***all right*** (=satisfactory).

sat·is·fied /ˈsætɪsfaɪd/ *adjective*

KEY PATTERNS
satisfied with something

pleased with something that you have done or got ANTONYM **dissatisfied**: *I didn't* ***feel satisfied with*** *my exam results.* • *We try to keep our customers satisfied.*

sat·is·fy /ˈsætɪsfaɪ/ *verb* (**satisfied**, **satisfies**) to make someone happy by giving them what they want: *We always try to satisfy our guests.* • *I offered him £50, but that didn't satisfy him.*

sat·is·fy·ing /ˈsætɪsfaɪ-ɪŋ/ *adjective* something that is satisfying makes you feel pleased because you have achieved something or got what you want: *Photography is a satisfying hobby.*

sat·u·rate /ˈsætʃəreɪt/ *verb* (formal) to make something completely wet: *The back of his shirt was saturated with sweat.*

Sat·ur·day /ˈsætədi $ ˈsætɚdi/ (written abbreviation **Sat**) *noun* the day of the week between Friday and Sunday: *What are you doing on Saturday?*

sauce /sɔːs/ *noun* a thick liquid that you eat with food: *cheese sauce*

sauce·pan /ˈsɔːspən $ ˈsɔspæn/ *noun* a metal pot with a handle that you use for cooking SYNONYM **pan** → see picture at PAN

sau·cer /ˈsɔːsə $ ˈsɔsɚ/ *noun* a small round plate that you put a cup on → see picture at CUP[1]

sau·na /ˈsɔːnə/ *noun* if you have a sauna, you sit in a hot room that is filled with steam

saun·ter /ˈsɔːntə $ ˈsɔntɚ/ *verb* to walk slowly and confidently: *The door opened and Guy sauntered in.*

saus·age /ˈsɒsɪdʒ $ ˈsɔsɪdʒ/ *noun* a small tube of skin filled with a mixture of meat and spices

sav·age /ˈsævɪdʒ/ *adjective* very cruel and violent: *a savage war* —**savagely** *adverb*: *The woman was savagely beaten.*

save[1] /seɪv/ *verb*

KEY PATTERNS
save someone/something (from harm)
be saving (up) for a bicycle/holiday
save something (for someone)
save someone a journey/the trouble
save someone doing something

1 to prevent someone from being hurt or killed SYNONYM **rescue**: *Mark ran into the burning building to save the child.* • *She* ***saved*** *me* ***from*** *drowning.*
2 to prevent something from being damaged or destroyed: *Many people are fighting to* ***save*** *the rain forests* ***from*** *destruction.*
3 also **save up** to keep money instead of spending it, so that you can use it later: *You should try and save some money each month.* • *I'm* ***saving up for*** *a new computer game.* • *My brother's saving his money to buy a car.*
4 to keep something instead of using it or throwing it away: *We'd better* ***save*** *some of the cake* ***for*** *Dad.*
5 to kindly do something so that someone else does not have to do it: *If you could meet Tom from school, it*

A B C D E F G H I J K L M N O P Q R S T U V W X Y Z

would save me a journey. • I'll take the shopping home in the car to save you carrying it.
6 to make a computer store information that you want to keep: *Don't forget to save your work before you log off.*
7 to stop the ball from going into the GOAL in a game such as football or HOCKEY: *It was a great shot, but Jack saved it.*

PHRASES
save time, save energy etc to use less time, energy etc: *It'll* ***save time*** *if we both do some of the work. • In a small house, you need to find ways of* ***saving space.***

save² *noun* when a GOALKEEPER in football, HOCKEY etc stops the ball from going into their GOAL

sav·ings /ˈseɪvɪŋz/ *plural noun* all the money that you have saved: *My aunt withdrew all her savings from the bank.*

sa·vour·y *BrE*, **savory** *AmE* /ˈseɪvəri/ *adjective* salty, or not sweet: *savoury snacks such as crisps*

saw¹ the past tense of SEE

saw² /sɔː/ *noun* a flat metal blade with a series of sharp points on it, that you use for cutting wood ➔ see picture at TOOL

saw³ (**sawed, sawn** /sɔːn/) to cut something using a saw: *Cyril sawed some logs for the fire.*

sax·o·phone /ˈsæksəfəʊn $ ˈsæksəˌfoʊn/ *noun* a large metal musical instrument that you play by blowing into it and pressing buttons

saxophone

say¹ ➔ see box on page 590

say² /seɪ/ *noun* (no plural) if you have a say in something, you can give your opinion about it and help decide it: *The kids should have a say in where we go for our vacation.*

say·ing /ˈseɪ-ɪŋ/ *noun* a well-known statement that gives good advice about something SYNONYM **proverb**

scab /skæb/ *noun* a layer of dried blood that forms over a wound

scaf·fold·ing /ˈskæfəldɪŋ/ *noun* (no plural) a structure made from poles and boards that workers can stand on when they are working on the outside walls of a building

scald /skɔːld/ *verb* to burn someone with hot liquid: *The water was so hot that it scalded his hand.*

scales

scale¹ /skeɪl/ *noun*

KEY PATTERNS
the scale of a problem
measure 6/80 etc on a scale

1 the scale of something is how big, serious, or important it is: *We don't yet know* ***the scale of*** *her injuries. • This is a* ***large-scale*** *project.*
2 a set of numbers that you use to measure how big something is: *The earthquake measured 3.5* ***on the*** *Richter* ***scale.***
3 the scale of a map, drawing, or model is the relationship between its size and the actual size of the thing that it shows: *a map with a scale of 1 centimetre to 1 kilometre*
4 scales a piece of equipment that you use to weigh people or objects: *a set of kitchen scales • The doctor asked me to stand on the scales.*
5 a series of musical notes that you play or sing in a fixed order, getting higher or lower

scale² *verb* (formal) if you scale a mountain, you climb to the top of it

scalp /skælp/ *noun* the skin on the top of your head, where your hair grows

scal·y /ˈskeɪli/ *adjective* an animal that is scaly is covered with small flat pieces of hard dry skin: *Birds have tough, scaly skin on their legs.*

say /seɪ/ *verb* (past tense and past participle **said** /sed/, present participle **saying**)

1 to speak words in order to give information or to show your thoughts, feelings etc: *What did you **say**? • Sandra **said that** she wasn't feeling well. • Mrs Robbins came over and **said** something to her daughter. • Did she **say what** they were going to do? • "Just a minute," **said** Sharon. • "I'm very busy," he **said**.*

KEY PATTERNS
say (that)
say something to someone
say what/where/how etc

*Sandra **said that** she wasn't feeling well.*

say

2 to show information in numbers or pictures, or give information in writing: *My alarm clock **said** six o'clock. • The weather report **says** it's going to rain tomorrow. • The recipe **says** to mix the sugar and eggs.*

*My alarm clock **said** six o'clock.*

GRAMMAR
✗ Don't say 'say someone that'.
• Say **tell someone that**: *She told me that she wanted to go home.*
✗ Don't say 'say someone to do something'.
• Say **tell someone to do something**: *The doctor told me to get plenty of rest.*
✗ Don't say 'say someone about something'.
• Say **tell someone about something** or **talk about something**: *He told me about his family* or *He talked about his family.*
✗ Don't say 'say someone no/say someone hello'.
• Say **say no/say hello**: *I asked if he wanted to come to the party, but he said no. • Say hello to your sister for me.*

WORD CHOICE
say, tell, or **talk**?
• You **say** words to someone: *She **said** that she was tired.*
• You **tell** someone facts or information: *Someone **told** me that the class was cancelled.*
• You **talk** about a subject: *He **talked** about his home in Spain.*

scam•per /ˈskæmpə $ ˈskæmpɚ/ *verb* to run somewhere with short quick steps: *The children scampered back to bed.*

scan /skæn/ *verb* (**scanned**, **scanning**) **1** to read something very quickly SYNONYM **skim**: *She scanned the lists, looking for her name.* **2** if you scan a picture into a computer, you use a machine called a scanner to copy it into the computer: *Once the image has been scanned, you can make it bigger or smaller.* **3** if a machine scans an object or your body, it produces a picture of what is inside: *All luggage is scanned at the airport.* —**scan** *noun*: *The scan produces a picture of the baby inside its mother.*

scan•dal /ˈskændl/ *noun* when people are shocked because someone has done something very bad or wrong: *His behaviour caused a political scandal.*

scan•ner /ˈskænə $ ˈskænɚ/ *noun* a piece of equipment that copies a picture into a computer → see picture on page A12

scar¹ /skɑː $ skɑr/ *noun* a permanent mark on someone's skin, caused by a cut or burn → see Thesaurus at MARK²

scar² *verb* (**scarred**, **scarring**) if something such as a knife or fire scars you, it makes a permanent mark on your skin: *The fire scarred her quite badly.*

scarce /skeəs $ skers/ *adjective* if something is scarce, there is not enough of it ANTONYM **plentiful**: *Fresh water and food were scarce.*

scarce•ly /ˈskeəsli $ ˈskersli/ *adverb* hardly at all: *I scarcely go out these days.*

scare¹ /skeə $ sker/ *verb* (informal) to frighten someone: *The movie really scared the children.* • *Your dad **scares me to death*** (=makes me feel very frightened).

PHRASAL VERBS

scare away, scare off
scare someone away, scare someone off to frighten someone so that they go away: *A barking dog scared the attackers **away**.*

scare² *noun* **1** a sudden feeling of fear SYNONYM **fright**: *You gave me a terrible scare!* **2** a situation in which many people become frightened because it is possible that something bad might happen: *There was a bomb scare at the airport.*

scared /skeəd $ skerd/ *adjective*

> KEY PATTERNS
> **scared of someone/something**
> **scared to do something**
> **scared (that)**

frightened SYNONYM **afraid**: *My brother is **scared of** dogs.* • *Hazel was **scared to** tell Mum what had happened.* • *I'm **scared that** the car might break down.* • *I was **scared stiff*** (=very scared) *that someone would find us.* → see Thesaurus at FRIGHTENED

scarf /skɑːf $ skɑrf/ *noun* (plural **scarves** /skɑːvz $ skɑrvz/ or **scarfs**) a piece of material that you wear around your neck to keep you warm

scar•let /ˈskɑːlət $ ˈskɑrlət/ *adjective, noun* bright red

scar•y /ˈskeəri $ ˈskeri/ *adjective* (informal) (**scarier**, **scariest**) frightening: *It's a really scary movie.*

scat•ter /ˈskætə $ ˈskætɚ/ *verb* **1** to throw or drop things all over an area: *Scatter the seeds evenly over the ground.* **2** if people scatter, they go quickly in different directions: *The crowd scattered in terror.*

scene /siːn/ *noun*
1 one part of a play or film: *I loved the scene where the children arrived home.* • *The battle scenes were very exciting.*
2 a picture: *a Christmas card with a winter scene on the front*
3 the scene of an accident or crime is the place where it happens: *Police stayed at **the scene of** the crash for some hours.*
4 what can be seen happening in a place: *There were scenes of confusion and panic at the airport after the bomb exploded.*

sce•ne•ry /ˈsiːnəri/ *noun* (no plural) the natural things such as woods and rivers that you see around you in the countryside: *the spectacular scenery of the Alps*

sce•nic /ˈsiːnɪk/ *adjective* a scenic place has very beautiful scenery

A B C D E F G H I J K L M N O P Q R S T U V W X Y Z

scent /sent/ *noun* **1** a pleasant smell: *the scent of fresh flowers* → see Thesaurus at SMELL[2] **2** a liquid with a pleasant smell that you put on your skin SYNONYM **perfume**

scent·ed /ˈsentɪd/ *adjective* something that is scented has a pleasant smell: *scented soap*

scep·ti·cal *BrE*, **skeptical** *AmE* /ˈskeptɪkəl/ *adjective* if you are sceptical about something, you have doubts about whether it is true or right SYNONYM **doubtful**: *Many doctors are sceptical about this new treatment.*

PRONUNCIATION
You pronounce **sc-** as 'sk'.

sched·ule¹ /ˈʃedjuːl $ ˈskedʒəl/ *noun* **1** a list of things that people will do and when they will do them: ***Draw up*** (=write) ***a schedule*** *of all the things you need to do.*
2 the American word for TIMETABLE

PHRASES
have a busy schedule to have a lot of things to do
on schedule if something is on schedule, everything is happening at the right time: *The train is* ***on schedule.***
behind schedule if something is behind schedule, things are happening later than you had planned: *The building work is already eight months* ***behind schedule.***

schedule² *verb* to plan when something will happen: *We have scheduled the competition for March 8.*

PRONUNCIATION
British people pronounce the start of **schedule** like 'shed'.
American people pronounce the start of **schedule** like 'sked'.

scheme¹ /skiːm/ *noun* *BrE* a plan that you use to try to achieve something: *This new government scheme will help young people to find jobs.* • *Have you heard about Michael's latest money-making scheme?* → see Thesaurus at PLAN[1]

scheme² *verb* (formal) to secretly make plans to do something, especially something bad SYNONYM **plot**: *He had been scheming to get control of the company.*

schol·ar /ˈskɒlə $ ˈskɑːlɚ/ *noun* someone who has studied a subject and knows a lot about it: *Most scholars agree that the poem was written in the 14th century.*

schol·ar·ship /ˈskɒləʃɪp $ ˈskɑːlɚˌʃɪp/ *noun* money that is given to a student so that they can go to college: *Pat was awarded a scholarship to study in the US.*

school /skuːl/ *noun*
1 a place where children are taught, or the time they spend there every day: *Mr Mamood is a teacher* ***at*** *my school.* • *Are the children* ***at school*** *today?* • *Dad drives us to school in the morning.* • *I was late for school this morning.* • *When do the* ***school*** *holidays start?* • *I'll meet you* ***after*** *school.*
2 a place where one particular subject or skill is taught: *I'm going to a language school this summer.* • *He's at drama school.*
3 *AmE* a university

USAGE
You usually say **go to school**: *She* ***goes to school*** *by bus.*
You say **the school** when talking about a particular school: ***The school*** *has over 1,200 students.*

school·boy /ˈskuːlbɔɪ/ *noun* a boy who goes to school

school·child /ˈskuːltʃaɪld/ *noun* (plural **schoolchildren** /-ˌtʃɪldrən/) a child who goes to school

school·days /ˈskuːldeɪz/ *plural noun* the time during your life when you go to school

school·girl /ˈskuːlgɜːl $ ˈskulgɚl/ *noun* a girl who goes to school

school·teach·er /ˈskuːlˌtiːtʃə $ ˈskulˌtitʃɚ/ *noun* a teacher in a school

sci·ence /ˈsaɪəns/ *noun* (no plural) the study of natural things, especially by doing tests, and the knowledge we get from this: *We've been learning about electricity in our science lessons.* • *Science made great progress in the 17th century.*

ˌscience ˈfiction *noun* (no plural) books and films about imaginary things in the future or in other parts of the universe

sci·en·tif·ic /ˌsaɪənˈtɪfɪk/ *adjective* related to science or using the methods of science: *a scientific experiment*

sci·en·tist /ˈsaɪəntɪst/ *noun* someone who studies science

sci-fi /ˈsaɪ ˌfaɪ/ *noun* (informal) SCIENCE FICTION

scis·sors /ˈsɪzəz $ ˈsɪzɚz/ *plural noun* a small tool with two blades that you use for cutting paper, hair, or material: *a pair of sharp scissors* → see picture at PAIR

> GRAMMAR
> You say **a pair of scissors.**
> ✗ Don't say 'a scissors'.

scoff /skɒf $ skɔf/ *verb* to speak about a person or their ideas in a way that shows you do not respect them or think they are stupid: *Andy's friends scoffed at his plans to become famous.*

scold /skəʊld $ skoʊld/ *verb* to tell someone angrily that they have done something wrong: *Her father scolded her for staying out late.*

scoop¹ /skuːp/ *noun* **1** a deep spoon for picking up or serving food such as ICE CREAM **2** an important news story that appears in only one newspaper: *News of the prime minister's illness was a real scoop for the 'Daily Record'.*

scoop² *verb* to pick up or remove something by using a spoon or putting your hand under it: *Cut the melon in half and scoop out the seeds.*

scoot·er /ˈskuːtə $ ˈskutɚ/ *noun* a vehicle like a small MOTORCYCLE with a low seat → see picture on page A11

scooter

scope /skəʊp $ skoʊp/ *noun* the scope of a piece of work is the range of subjects it deals with or discusses: *Looking at the airline's safety records will be within the scope of this inquiry.*

scorch /skɔːtʃ $ skɔrtʃ/ *verb* to burn the surface of something, leaving a brown mark: *The ceiling and the walls were badly scorched by the fire.*

scorch·ing /ˈskɔːtʃɪŋ $ ˈskɔrtʃɪŋ/ *adjective* (informal) if the weather is scorching, it is very hot: *It's been a scorching summer.*

score¹ /skɔː $ skɔr/ *verb* to win points in a game or competition: *Jim scored two goals in yesterday's game.* • *Who scored the most points?*

score² *noun*
1 the number of points that a team or player gets in a game or competition: *The final score was 3–1.* • *I got a score of 700.*
2 the printed copy of a piece of music
3 scores a very large number of people or things: *Scores of people were injured in the crash.*

score·board /ˈskɔːbɔːd $ ˈskɔrbɔrd/ *noun* a large sign showing the score of a game

scor·er /ˈskɔːrə $ ˈskɔrɚ/ *noun* someone who scores a point in a game or competition: *the club's top goal scorer*

scorn /skɔːn $ skɔrn/ *noun* (no plural) (formal) if you treat something with scorn, you show that you think it is very stupid or unimportant ANTONYM **admiration**: *My ideas were treated with scorn.* —**scornful** *adjective*: *He made some very scornful remarks about my work.*

scor·pi·on /ˈskɔːpiən $ ˈskɔrpiən/ *noun* a small brown creature that uses its tail to sting

Scotch /skɒtʃ $ skɑtʃ/ *noun* (no plural) a strong alcoholic drink made in Scotland SYNONYM **whisky**: *a bottle of Scotch*

ˌScotch ˈtape (trademark) the American word for SELLOTAPE

scour /skaʊə $ skaʊɚ/ *verb* if you scour a place, you search everywhere in it very carefully and thoroughly: *I scoured the library for more information.*

scout /skaʊt/ *noun* **1** a soldier who is sent to search an area of land in front of an army to find out information **2** someone whose job is to find good sports players, musicians etc in order to employ them: *a football scout*

A B C D E F G H I J K L M N O P Q R S T U V W X Y Z

3 also **boy scout, girl scout** a member of an organization called the Scouts that teaches young people practical skills

scowl /skaʊl/ *verb* to look at someone in a way that shows you are angry: *She scowled and turned away.* —**scowl** *noun*: *He walked into the room with a scowl on his face.*

scram·ble[1] /ˈskræmbəl/ *verb* **1** to climb up or over something quickly, using your hands: *I scrambled up the steep hillside.* **2** to quickly try to get or do something, especially when competing with other people: *Fans scrambled to buy tickets for the concert.*

scramble[2] *noun* (informal) when people quickly try to get or do something, especially when competing with other people: *There was a scramble for the best seats.*

ˌ**scrambled ˈeggs** *plural noun* eggs mixed together and cooked in butter

scrap[1] /skræp/ *noun*
1 a small piece of something SYNONYM **bit**: *I wrote her phone number on a scrap of paper.* ➔ see Thesaurus at PIECE
2 (no plural) old objects, especially metal objects, that can be made into something else: *scrap metal*

scrap[2] *verb* (informal) (**scrapped, scrapping**) to decide not to do or use something: *We have now scrapped this idea.*

scrap·book /ˈskræpbʊk/ *noun* a book with empty pages in which you can stick pictures or newspaper articles

scrape[1] /skreɪp/ *verb*

KEY PATTERNS
scrape mud/food etc off/from a surface
scrape mud/food etc off/away
scrape a surface

1 to remove a substance from a surface by moving an edge across the surface: *She bent down and scraped away the soil.* • *Bill was scraping the mud* **from** *his boots.* • *They scraped their plates* **clean**. ➔ see Thesaurus at REMOVE
2 to damage something by rubbing against it: *A branch scraped her cheek.* • *You've scraped the floor with your shoe.*

scrape

scrape[2] *noun* **1** a small injury that you get when you rub a part of your body against a rough surface SYNONYM **graze**: *She had a few scrapes on her knees.*
2 (informal) a difficult or dangerous situation: *I knew that I was now in a bit of a scrape.*

scratch

scratch[1] /skrætʃ/ *verb* **1** to rub your skin with your nails: *He scratched his head thoughtfully.* **2** to make a long thin cut or mark on something with a sharp object: *Bill's dad was furious when he scratched the car door.*

scratch[2] *noun* (plural **scratches**) **1** a long thin cut on something: *Nicole had several scratches on her face.* **2 from scratch** if you do something from scratch, you do it without using anything that was done or made before: *My computer crashed, and I had to start my essay again from scratch.*

scrawl /skrɔːl/ *verb* to write something in a careless or untidy way: *She scrawled her phone number on the back of an envelope.* —**scrawl** *noun* (informal): *I can't read your scrawl.*

scream[1] /skriːm/ *verb*

KEY PATTERNS
scream at someone
scream for something/someone

to shout very loudly because you feel frightened, angry, or very excited

A B C D E F G H I J K L M N O P Q R S T U V W X Y Z

SYNONYM **shriek**: *Sally screamed when she saw the rat.* • *The children were screaming with excitement.* • *"Don't touch me!" she screamed.* • *Sometimes I* ***scream at*** *the kids.* • *I tried to* ***scream for*** *help.* • *I screamed out her name.* → see Thesaurus at SHOUT[1]

scream² *noun*
a loud shout that you give when you are frightened, angry, or very excited SYNONYM **shriek**: *We heard screams outside.*

screech /skriːtʃ/ *verb* to make a high loud unpleasant sound: *Our tyres screeched as we turned the corner.* —**screech** *noun*: *She gave a screech of alarm.*

screen¹ /skriːn/ *noun* **1** the glass part of a television or computer that you look at: *a television with a 26-inch screen* **2** the large, flat white surface that pictures are shown on in a cinema

screen² *verb* **1** to do medical tests on people to find out whether any of them have an illness: *People who are at risk of the disease should be screened.* **2** to show a film or programme at the cinema or on television: *Many new films will be screened at the festival.*

screw

screw¹ /skruː/ *noun* a pointed piece of metal that you use to fix things together by pushing it into a surface and turning it round

screw² *verb* **1** to fix something somewhere, using screws: *I screwed the mirror to the wall.* **2 screw up** (informal) to spoil a plan or arrangement SYNONYM **mess up**: *The car broke down, so that screwed up our holiday.*

screw·driv·er /ˈskruːˌdraɪvə $ ˈskruˌdraɪvɚ/ *noun* a tool that you use for turning screws → see picture at TOOL

scrib·ble /ˈskrɪbəl/ *verb* to write something in a quick and untidy way: *I scribbled down the number of the license plate.* → see Thesaurus at WRITE

script /skrɪpt/ *noun* **1** the words of a speech, play, film etc that have been written down: *He writes scripts for TV shows.* **2** (formal) the letters used to write a language: *Arabic script*

scrip·ture /ˈskrɪptʃə $ ˈskrɪptʃɚ/ *noun* the holy books of a religion, for example the Bible

scroll /skrəʊl $ skroʊl/ *verb* (**scrolled**, **scrolling**) to move information up or down a computer screen: *Scroll down until you reach the end of the file.*

scrounge /skraʊndʒ/ *verb* (informal) to get something you want by asking someone to give it to you, instead of buying it yourself: *I scrounged a cigarette off the girl sitting next to me.*

scrub¹ /skrʌb/ *verb* to rub something hard in order to clean it: *We scrubbed and polished the floors until they shone.* → see Thesaurus at CLEAN[2]

scrub² *noun* (no plural) plants that grow in a dry place

scruf·fy /ˈskrʌfi/ *adjective* (**scruffier**, **scruffiest**) dirty and untidy: *a scruffy old man*

scru·pu·lous /ˈskruːpjələs/ *adjective* (formal) trying very hard to behave in a fair and honest way —**scrupulously** *adverb*: *We try to be scrupulously fair.*

scru·ti·nize also **scrutinise** *BrE* /ˈskruːtənaɪz/ *verb* (formal) to examine something very carefully and thoroughly: *The customs official scrutinized his passport.*

scru·ti·ny /ˈskruːtəni/ *noun* (no plural) (formal) when something is very carefully watched or examined: *The police are keeping the men under close scrutiny.*

scu·ba div·ing /ˈskuːbə ˌdaɪvɪŋ/ *noun* (no plural) the sport of swimming under water using a container of air to help you breathe

sculp·tor /ˈskʌlptə $ ˈskʌlptɚ/ *noun* someone who makes sculptures

sculp·ture /ˈskʌlptʃə $ ˈskʌlptʃɚ/ *noun* a work of art made from stone, wood, or metal, or the art of making these: *a bronze sculpture* • *She studied sculpture at art college.*

scum /skʌm/ *noun* (no plural) **1** an unpleasant dirty layer on the surface of a liquid: *The pond was covered with scum.* **2** (informal) people you have a very low opinion of

scur·ry /ˈskʌri $ ˈskɚi/ *verb* (**scurried**, **scurries**) to move very quickly with small steps: *A mouse scurried across the floor.*

sea /siː/ *noun*

KEY PATTERNS
at sea

the salt water that covers large parts of the Earth SYNONYM **ocean** *AmE*: *We swam in **the sea**.* • *The ship was lost **at sea**.* • *The Red Sea lies between Arabia and North Africa.*

sea·bed, **sea bed** /ˈsiːbed/ *noun* the land at the bottom of the sea

sea·food /ˈsiːfuːd/ *noun* (no plural) fish and other creatures from the sea that you can eat

sea·front /ˈsiːfrʌnt/ *noun* (no plural) a part of a town that is next to the sea: *I went into a shop on the seafront.*

sea·gull /ˈsiːgʌl/ also **gull** *noun* a common grey and white bird that lives near the sea

seal¹ /siːl/ *noun* a large animal that lives in the sea in cold areas

seal

seal² *verb* **1** to close something very tightly or firmly: *He addressed the envelope and sealed it.* **2 seal something off** to stop people entering an area or building, especially because it is dangerous: *The police have sealed off the area.*

ˈ**sea** ˌ**lion** *noun* a large type of seal

seam /siːm/ *noun* the line where two pieces of cloth have been sewn together

search¹ /sɜːtʃ $ sɚtʃ/ *noun*

KEY PATTERNS
a search for something/someone

an attempt to find someone or something: *The police led the **search for** the missing boy.*

PHRASES

go in search of something to try to find something: *I **went in search of** a present for Grandma.*

search² *verb*

KEY PATTERNS
search for something/someone
search a place (for something)
search through a container/group of things

to try to find someone or something: *We **searched for** you everywhere!* • *The police searched his car and found the gun.* • *We **searched** the room **for** money.* • *He was **searching through** the drawers.*

ˈ**search** ˌ**engine** *noun* a computer program that helps people to find information on the Internet

sea·shore /ˈsiːʃɔː $ ˈsiʃɔr/ *noun* **the seashore** the land next to the sea
→ see Thesaurus at SHORE

sea·sick /ˈsiːˌsɪk/ *adjective* if you feel seasick, you feel ill because of the movement of a boat

sea·side /ˈsiːsaɪd/ *noun* **the seaside** a place or area next to the sea, especially where people go on holiday: *I love being at the seaside.* • *a seaside holiday*

sea·son¹ /ˈsiːzən/ *noun*
1 one of the four periods in the year that have different weather – spring, summer, autumn, and winter: *Spring is my favourite season.*
2 a period of time in a year when something usually happens: *The football season starts in August.*

PHRASES

the holiday season, high season the time of year when most people take their holiday: *Accommodation is more expensive in **high season**.*

in season vegetables and fruit that are in season are ready to pick and eat

season² *verb* to add salt, pepper etc to food to make it taste better: *She seasoned the chicken with a few herbs and spices.*

sea·son·ing /'siːzənɪŋ/ *noun* salt, pepper etc that you add to food to make it taste better

'season ˌticket / $ ˌ..'../ *noun* a ticket that you can use for a lot of journeys or events during a fixed period of time

seat¹ /siːt/ *noun*
a chair or something else that you can sit on: *I couldn't **get a seat** on the bus this morning.* • *I rang the theatre and booked two seats for tonight's show.* • *This isn't a very comfortable seat.*
PHRASES
take a seat to sit down: *Please **take a seat** and the doctor will see you soon.*

seat² *verb* **1 be seated a)** to be sitting down: *A nurse was seated behind the desk.* **b)** (spoken formal) used to ask someone politely to sit down: *Please be seated, Ms Williams.*
2 to have enough seats for a particular number of people: *The hall seats 500 people.*

'seat belt *noun* a strong belt that holds you in your seat in a car or plane SYNONYM **safety belt**

seat·ing /'siːtɪŋ/ *noun* (no plural) the seats in a public place

sea·weed /'siːwiːd/ *noun* (no plural) a plant that grows in the sea

se·clud·ed /sɪ'kluːdɪd/ *adjective* a secluded place is very quiet and private: *a secluded beach*

sec·ond¹ /'sekənd/ *number, adverb, adjective*
1 coming after the first thing or person: *his second wife* • *We only saw **the second half** of the match.* • *She won the first game but lost the second.* • *John **came second** in the race.*
2 have second thoughts to have doubts about whether you are making the right decision: *Mary was going to study physics, but now she's **having second thoughts**.*

second² *noun*
1 one of the 60 parts that a minute is divided into: *He ran the race in 2 minutes 35 seconds.*
2 a very short period of time: *Wait **a few seconds** for the computer to start.* • ***For a second**, I thought I'd broken my leg.* • *I'll be back **in a second**.*

second³ *verb* to say that you agree with a suggestion made by another person at a meeting: *Parker seconded the idea.*

sec·ond·a·ry /'sekəndəri $ 'sekənˌderi/ *adjective* secondary education is the education of children between the ages of 11 and 18: *a secondary school*

'secondary ˌschool *noun* a school for children between the ages of 11 and 18

ˌsecond 'best *adjective* not as good as the best thing: *He got the second best exam results in the school.*

ˌsecond-'class¹ *adjective* **1** cheaper than something that is FIRST-CLASS and with service that is not quite as good: *I only put a second-class stamp on the letter.* **2** less important than other people or things: *Old people should not be treated as second-class citizens.*

ˌsecond-'class² *adverb* if someone travels or sends something second-class, they do it using a service that is cheaper and less expensive than FIRST-CLASS service: *I sent the letter second-class.*

sec·ond·hand /ˌsekənd'hænd/ *adjective, adverb* previously owned by someone else: *a cheap, secondhand computer* • *I bought the car secondhand.* → see Thesaurus at OLD

ˌsecond 'language *noun* a language that you speak in addition to the language that you learned to speak as a child

sec·ond·ly /'sekəndli/ *adverb* used to introduce a second fact, reason etc: *And secondly, we must consider the cost.*

ˌsecond 'nature *noun* (no plural) something you have done so often that you do it almost without thinking: *Lying had become second nature to him.*

ˌsecond 'person *noun* **the second person** the form of a verb that you use with 'you'

se·cre·cy /'siːkrəsi/ *noun* (no plural) when you keep something secret

se·cret¹ /'siːkrət/ *adjective*
if something is secret, only a few people know about it and they deliberately do not tell anyone else: *We*

held a secret meeting after school. • *Keep your computer password secret* (=don't tell it to anyone). —**secretly** *adverb*: *She secretly wished that she had been invited to the party.*

THESAURUS
private: *She didn't want anyone to read her diary because it was* **private** (=she did not want other people to know about it).
confidential: *The bank's records are* **confidential** (=not meant to be seen by anyone outside the bank).

secret² *noun*
1 something that you do not tell other people about: *Don't tell anyone our secret.* • *Can you* **keep a secret**? • *The peace talks were held* **in secret** (=without other people knowing).
2 the secret of something (informal) the way to achieve something: *What's the secret of a happy marriage?*

ˌsecret ˈagent *noun* a SPY

sec·re·ta·ry /ˈsekrətəri $ ˈsekrəˌteri/ *noun* (plural **secretaries**) **1** someone whose job is to write letters, arrange meetings, answer telephone calls etc in an office **2** also **Secretary** someone who is in charge of a large government department: *the Defence Secretary*

se·cre·tive /ˈsiːkrətɪv/ *adjective* unwilling to tell people about something: *John was very secretive about his new girlfriend.*

sect /sekt/ *noun* a group of people with its own religious beliefs, that has separated from a larger religious group

sec·tion /ˈsekʃən/ *noun* one of the parts that something is divided into: *Does the library have a children's section?* • *Some* **sections of** *this road are very busy.* → see Thesaurus at PART[1]

sec·tor /ˈsektə $ ˈsektər/ *noun* part of an economic system, such as business, industry, or trade: *the nation's manufacturing sector* (=all the companies that make goods)

se·cure¹ /sɪˈkjʊə $ sɪˈkjʊr/ *adjective* **1** fixed and not likely to change: *The company now has a secure future.* **2** a secure place is one which people cannot get into or out of if you do not want them to: *Make sure the building is secure before you leave.* —**securely** *adverb*: *She kept the room securely locked.*

secure² *verb* (formal) **1** to get something important, especially after a lot of effort: *He managed to secure a job in a university.* **2** to fasten or tie something firmly: *They secured the bookcase to the wall.*

se·cu·ri·ty /sɪˈkjʊərəti $ sɪˈkjʊrəti/ *noun* (no plural) **1** the things that you do to protect a place: *He is in charge of security at the airport.* **2** if you have security, you are not likely to suffer or lose something: *The new contract will give you more security in your job.* **3** the feeling that you are safe and cannot be hurt: *Children need security.*

se·date /sɪˈdeɪt/ *verb* to give someone a drug to make them feel sleepy and calm

sed·a·tive /ˈsedətɪv/ *noun* a drug that makes someone sleepy or calm

se·duc·tive /sɪˈdʌktɪv/ *adjective* attractive, especially in a sexual way: *her soft, seductive voice*

see → see box on page 599

seed /siːd/ *noun* a small hard thing produced by a plant, from which a new plant will grow → see picture on page A10

seed·y /ˈsiːdi/ *adjective* (informal) (**seedier**, **seediest**) a seedy person or place looks dirty and poor: *a seedy nightclub*

ˌseeing ˈeye ˌdog the American word for GUIDE DOG

seek /siːk/ *verb* (formal) (past tense and past participle **sought** /sɔːt/) **1** to try to find or get something: *She sought the help of several organizations.* **2** to try to do something: *We are always seeking to improve our results.*

seem /siːm/ *verb*

KEY PATTERNS
seem happy/quiet etc
seem to be happy/quiet etc
seem like a nice place/a good idea
seem to someone
it seems (that)
seem as if

how something seems is how it appears to you: *The house seemed*

A B C D E F G H I J K L M N O P Q R S T U V W X Y Z

see /siː/ *verb* (past tense **saw** /sɔː/, past participle **seen** /siːn/)

1 to notice something using your eyes: *It was too dark to **see** anything.* • *Did you **see what** Patrick did?* • *I couldn't **see who** was at the door.* • *Did you **see** Jean leave?* • *I **saw** Steven running for the bus.*

KEY PATTERNS
see someone/something
see who/what/where etc
see someone doing something
see someone do something

see

5 to watch a film, programme, or play: *I've **seen** the film twice already.* • *Did you **see** that programme about polar bears?*

2 to know or understand something: *Do you **see how** it works?* • *"It's very heavy." "I **see what** you mean!"* • *"Then you just add these two numbers together." "Oh, **I see**."*

4 to find out something: *Can you **see who** is at the door?* • ***Let's see how** much it costs.* • *Plug in the TV and **see if** it's working.*

KEY PATTERNS
see how/who/why etc
see if/whether

3 to meet or visit someone: *I **see** her every Saturday.* • *Ken **hasn't seen** his daughters for a month.* • *You should **see** a doctor.*

WORD CHOICE
see, **watch**, or **look at**?
• You **see** something or someone accidentally, or because you are trying to find them: *We **saw** some beautiful flowers.* • *I **can't see** her anywhere.*
• You **watch** television, a film, an event, or a person. You usually watch things that are moving: *I like **watching** baseball.* • *I **watched** him get out of the car.* • *We spent the evening **watching** TV.* • *We **watched** television for a couple of hours.*
• You **look at** a picture, person, or thing deliberately, because you want to. You usually look at things that are not moving: *We **looked at** the map.* • *The man was **looking at** me.* • ***Look at** the view!*
✗ Don't say 'We looked at the television.' Say **We watched television.**

PHRASES

let me see (spoken)
used when you are trying to think of something: *"How many people were there?" "**Let me see** … I think there were about 50."*

see someone off
to go with someone to the airport or a station in order to say goodbye to them when they leave: *My parents **saw me off** at the airport.*

see you/see you later (spoken)
say this to friends when saying goodbye: *"Bye, Ben." "**See you**."* • *I'll **see you** later.* • ***See you** tomorrow, Cathy.*

very quiet after everyone had left. • *She* ***seemed to be*** *upset.* • *Toronto* ***seems like*** *such a nice place to live.* • ***It seems to me that*** *we're lost.* • ***It*** *seemed strange* ***that*** *she wasn't at home.* • *It* ***seemed as if*** *everything was going wrong.*

THESAURUS
appear (formal): *He* ***appeared*** *to be asleep* (=seemed to be asleep).
look: *You* ***look*** *tired* (=seem from your appearance to be tired).
sound: *It* ***sounded*** *like a good idea* (=seemed good when I heard about it).

seem·ing·ly /ˈsiːmɪŋli/ *adverb* used to say how something seems SYNONYM **apparently**: *a seemingly endless list of jobs*

seen the past participle of SEE

seep /siːp/ *verb* if a liquid seeps somewhere, it flows there slowly through small holes: *Water was seeping into the boat.*

see·saw /ˈsiːsɔː/ *noun* a long board on which children play outdoors, that is balanced in the middle so that when one end goes up the other end goes down

seethe /siːð/ *verb* to be very angry, but not show it SYNONYM **fume**: *By this time I was quietly seething.*

seg·ment /ˈsegmənt/ *noun* one of the parts that something is divided into: *a segment of orange*

seg·re·gate /ˈsegrɪgeɪt/ *verb* to separate one group of people from others ANTONYM **integrate**: *They were segregated from the rest of the prisoners.*

seize /siːz/ *verb* **1** to take something in your hand quickly and roughly SYNONYM **grab**: *She seized his arm excitedly.* **2** if someone seizes power or control, they take it using force: *The army seized power last September.*

sel·dom /ˈseldəm/ *adverb* (formal) not often: *He seldom goes out of the house.* → see Thesaurus at RARELY

se·lect[1] /sɪˈlekt/ *verb* to choose something or someone: *It wasn't easy to select a winner.* → see Thesaurus at CHOOSE

select[2] *adjective* (formal) a select group is a small group of special people: *a select group of students*

se·lec·tion /sɪˈlekʃən/ *noun* **1** (no plural) when something or someone is chosen: *Selection of the jury for the trial will begin tomorrow.* **2** a group of things that someone has chosen: *He read a selection of his favourite poems.* **3** a group of things that you can choose from SYNONYM **range**: *The shop has a wide selection of books for all ages.*

se·lec·tive /sɪˈlektɪv/ *adjective* careful about the things or people that you choose: *He is very selective about what he eats.*

self /self/ *noun* (plural **selves** /selvz/) your nature and character: *You'll soon be back to your old self.*

ˌself-ˈcentred *BrE*, **self-centered** *AmE adjective* only interested in yourself SYNONYM **selfish**

ˌself-ˈconfidence *noun* (no plural) the belief that you can do things successfully

ˌself-ˈconfident *adjective* feeling sure that you are able to do things successfully

ˌself-ˈconscious *adjective* uncomfortable and worried about how you seem to other people: *He felt self-conscious in his new suit.*

ˌself-defence *BrE*, **self-defense** *AmE noun* (no plural) the use of force to protect yourself when you are attacked: *He said he used the knife in self-defence.*

ˌself-emˈployed *adjective* someone who is self-employed has their own business rather than being employed by a company

ˌself-esˈteem *noun* (no plural) how you feel about yourself and whether, for example, you feel that you are a nice or successful person: *Many of our patients suffer from low self-esteem* (=feel that they are not nice or successful people).

ˌself-inˈdulgent *adjective* allowing yourself to have or do something that you do not need but which you enjoy having or doing

self·ish /ˈselfɪʃ/ *adjective* caring only about yourself and not about other people ANTONYM **unselfish**: *That was a very selfish thing to do.* • *She was a selfish, bad-tempered little girl.*

ˌself-ˈmade *adjective* a self-made person has become rich and successful by working hard: *He was proud of being a self-made man.*

ˌself-ˈpity *noun* (no plural) when you feel sorry for yourself and there is not a good reason

ˌself-ˈportrait *noun* a picture of yourself, painted by you

ˌself-reˈspect *noun* (no plural) a feeling of respect that you have for yourself

ˌself-ˈservice *adjective* a self-service restaurant is one where you get the food for yourself before paying for it

sell /sel/ *verb* (past tense and past participle **sold** /səʊld $ soʊld/)

KEY PATTERNS
sell someone something
sell something to someone
sell something for $10/£20 etc

1 to give something to someone and accept money from them in return ANTONYM **buy**: *I sold Joe my computer.* • *She **sold** her bike **for** £50.* • *I sold two tickets **to** Mary.*
2 to offer something for people to buy: *The shop sells computer games.*

PHRASAL VERBS
sell off
sell something off to sell goods quickly and cheaply: *The library is **selling off** some of its old books.*
sell out
if a shop sells out of something, or if something sells out, the shop sells all of it and there is none left: *I'm sorry we've **sold out of** bread.* • *All the tickets for the evening performance have **sold out**.*

ˈsell-by ˌdate *noun BrE* the date printed on a food product after which a shop should not sell it: *This yoghurt's past its sell-by date.*

Sel·lo·tape /ˈseləteɪp/ *noun* (no plural) *BrE* (trademark) tape that you use for sticking pieces of paper or card together SYNONYM **scotch tape** *AmE*

selves the plural of SELF

se·mes·ter /səˈmestə $ səˈmestɚ/ *noun AmE* one of two periods into which the school or college year is divided: *I'm taking three classes this semester.*

sem·i·cir·cle /ˈsemiˌsɜːkəl $ ˈsemiˌsɚkəl/ *noun* half a circle
→ see picture at SHAPE[1]

sem·i·co·lon /ˌsemiˈkəʊlən $ ˈsemiˌkoʊlən/ *noun* the mark (;) that you use in writing to separate different parts of a sentence or list

ˌsemi-deˈtached *adjective BrE* a semi-detached house is joined on one side to another house

sem·i·fi·nal /ˌsemiˈfaɪnl/ *noun* one of the two games that are played in a competition before the last game. The winners of the two semifinals play each other in the last game to find the final winner.

sem·i·nar /ˈsemənɑː $ ˈseməˌnɑr/ *noun* a meeting in which a group of people discuss a subject

sen·ate /ˈsenɪt/ *noun* the smaller of the two parts of government in countries such as the US and Australia

sen·a·tor /ˈsenətə $ ˈsenətɚ/ *noun* a member of a senate: *Senator Dole*

send

The referee sent him off.

send /send/ *verb* (past tense and past participle **sent** /sent/)

KEY PATTERNS
send someone something
send something to someone
send someone to a place
send someone to do something

1 to arrange for something to go to a place or a person: *I sent you an email yesterday.* • *He **sent** some money **to** his sister.* • *When did you send the parcel?*
2 to make someone go somewhere: *The judge **sent** him **to** prison.* • *I sent Jo to buy some food.*

PHRASAL VERBS
send for
send for someone/something to ask someone to come to you: *We must **send for** an ambulance.*
send off
1 send something off to send something somewhere by mail: *I **sent off** a job application.*
2 send someone off *BrE* to order a sports player to leave a game because they have behaved badly: *Vincent **was sent off** for fighting.*
send out
1 send something out to send things to several people so that they receive one each: *I **sent out** all the party invitations.* • *The school is **sending** a letter **out** to all the parents.*
2 if a machine sends out light, sound etc, it produces it: *The ship's radio **sends out** a powerful signal.*

'send-off *noun* (informal) when a group of people say goodbye to someone who is leaving: *They gave her a good send-off when she retired.*

se•nile /'siːnaɪl/ *adjective* mentally confused because of old age

se•ni•or¹ /'siːniə $ 'sinjɚ/ *adjective* a senior person has an important position or rank ANTONYM **junior**: *senior members of staff*

senior² *noun AmE* a student in the last year of HIGH SCHOOL or college

,senior 'citizen *noun* a person who is over the age of 65 → see Thesaurus at OLD

,senior 'high school HIGH SCHOOL

sen•sa•tion /sen'seɪʃən/ *noun* **1** a feeling or experience: *She felt a burning sensation in her throat.* • *Watching himself on TV was a strange sensation.* **2** (informal) extreme excitement or interest, or something that causes this: *The film caused a sensation when it was first shown.*

sen•sa•tion•al /sen'seɪʃənəl/ *adjective* very interesting, exciting, or good: *Her performance in that film was sensational.*

sense¹ /sens/ *noun*
1 one of the five physical abilities of sight, hearing, touch, taste, and smell: *Dogs have a good **sense of smell**.*
2 the meaning of a word, phrase, sentence etc: *The word 'bank' has two main senses.*
PHRASES
make sense if something makes sense, it has a clear meaning that you can understand: *This essay does not make sense.*
make sense of something if you can make sense of something, you can understand it: *Can you **make sense of** the instructions?*
it makes sense to do something if it makes sense to do something, it is a reasonable and sensible thing to do: *It would **make sense to** leave early, so that we miss the traffic.*
have some sense, have good sense to be able to make good decisions: *Come on, **have some sense**. We can't possibly have a picnic in this rain!*
not have any sense to be unable to make good decisions
have the sense to do something to do the thing that is most sensible: *She **had the sense to** call the police.*
sense of humour someone who has a sense of humour enjoys things that are funny: *I want to meet a boy with a **good sense of humour**.*

sense² *verb* to feel or know something without being told: *Rebecca sensed that something was wrong.*

sense•less /'sensləs/ *adjective* **1** a senseless action is bad and will not achieve anything: *senseless violence* • *The destruction of the rain forest is senseless.* **2** if someone is beaten senseless, they are hit until they are not conscious

sen•si•ble /'sensəbəl/ *adjective*
1 someone who is sensible is able to make good decisions: *You can trust Julia. She's a very sensible girl.*
2 something that is sensible is a good idea: *My friend gave me some sensible advice.* • ***It seemed sensible to** move to London.* —**sensibly** *adverb*: *If you won't behave sensibly, you must leave.*

WORD CHOICE
sensible or **sensitive**?
• **Sensible** means "making good decisions and not doing anything stupid": *He seems a very **sensible** young man.*
• **Sensitive** means "always considering other people's feelings":

*She is very **sensitive** to other people's needs.*
• **Sensitive** also means "easily offended by what other people say": *He's very **sensitive** about his nose.*

sen·si·tive /ˈsensətɪv/ *adjective*
1 thinking of how other people will feel about something ANTONYM **insensitive**: *He was very **sensitive to** other people's needs.*
2 easily offended or upset: *Billy is such a sensitive child.* • *She's **sensitive about** her big nose.*
3 if you have sensitive skin, it is easily affected by something such as water, wind, soap etc: *The skin around my eyes is very sensitive.*

sen·su·al /ˈsenʃuəl/ *adjective* related to physical pleasure: *sensual pleasures such as sunbathing*

sen·su·ous /ˈsenʃuəs/ *adjective* making you feel physical pleasure: *the sensuous feel of silk*

sent the past tense and past participle of SEND

sen·tence¹ /ˈsentəns/ *noun*
1 a group of words that are written with a capital letter at the beginning and a FULL STOP at the end
2 a punishment that a judge gives to someone who is guilty of a crime: *The judge gave him a six-month **prison sentence*** (=the judge sent him to prison for six months).

sentence² *verb* when a judge sentences someone, he or she gives them a punishment for a crime: *The judge sentenced Larsen to six years in prison.*

sen·ti·ment·al /ˌsentəˈmentl/ *adjective* showing emotions such as love, pity, and sadness too strongly or in a silly way: *an old-fashioned, sentimental story*

sen·try /ˈsentri/ *noun* (plural **sentries**) a soldier who stands outside a building, guarding it

sep·a·rate¹ /ˈsepərət/ *adjective*
1 separate things are different ones, not the same one: *Two drivers were injured in the race, in two separate accidents.*
2 if two things are separate, they are not touching or connected to each other: *Keep the wires separate.* • *The science building was **separate from** the main school building.* —**separately** *adverb*: *He spoke to each child separately.*

SPELLING
This word is often spelled wrongly. The correct spelling is **separate**.

sep·a·rate² /ˈsepəreɪt/ *verb*

KEY PATTERNS
separate people/things into groups
separate one group from another

1 to divide people or things into different groups: *The teacher **separated** the children **into** three groups.* • *Separate the male rabbits **from** the female ones.*
2 if something separates one thing from another, it is between the two things so they do not touch or are not connected: *A high fence separated the two gardens.*
3 if people who are married separate, they start living apart SYNONYM **split up**: *My parents separated when I was ten years old.* → see Thesaurus at DIVORCE²

sep·a·rat·ed /ˈsepəreɪtɪd/ *adjective* not living with your husband, wife, or partner any more: *My husband and I are separated.*

sep·a·ra·tion /ˌsepəˈreɪʃən/ *noun* when two people stop being together: *She found the separation from her boyfriend hard to bear.*

Sep·tem·ber /sepˈtembə $ sepˈtembɚ/ (written abbreviation **Sept**) *noun* the ninth month of the year: *Lisa's birthday is September 21st.*

sep·tic /ˈseptɪk/ *adjective BrE* if a cut or wound is septic, it is infected by disease

se·quel /ˈsiːkwəl/ *noun* a film, book etc that continues the story of an earlier one

se·quence /ˈsiːkwəns/ *noun* a series of events that are connected to each other: *A long sequence of events has led up to this crisis.*

ser·geant /ˈsɑːdʒənt $ ˈsɑrdʒənt/ *noun* an officer in the army or police

se·ri·al¹ /ˈsɪəriəl $ ˈsɪriəl/ *noun* a story that is shown on television, broadcast on radio, or printed in a magazine in several separate parts

serial² *adjective* a serial killer, RAPIST etc has attacked several people over a period of time

se·ries /ˈsɪəriːz $ ˈsɪriz/ *noun* (plural **series**) **1** several events of the same kind that happen one after the other: *The police are investigating a series of robberies.* **2** a set of television or radio programmes with the same characters or about the same subject

se·ri·ous /ˈsɪəriəs $ ˈsɪriəs/ *adjective*
1 a serious problem or situation is very bad ANTONYM **minor**: *a serious accident* • *Luckily there were no serious problems.*
→ see Thesaurus at IMPORTANT
2 if you are serious about something, you are sincere about what you are saying: ***Are** you **serious about** wanting to come with me?* • *I didn't know if it was a serious offer.*
3 a serious person thinks carefully about things and does not laugh very often: *Philip was a very serious child.*

se·ri·ous·ly /ˈsɪəriəsli $ ˈsɪriəsli/ *adverb*
1 very: *My mother is seriously ill.*
2 if you say or think about something seriously, you do it in a sincere way: *I am seriously thinking of leaving school.*
PHRASES
take something seriously to believe that something is important: *You're not **taking** our friendship **seriously**!*

ser·mon /ˈsɜːmən $ ˈsɚmən/ *noun* a religious talk that someone gives at a church

ser·pent /ˈsɜːpənt $ ˈsɚpənt/ *noun* (written) a snake

ser·vant /ˈsɜːvənt $ ˈsɚvənt/ *noun* someone who works for someone in a large house, doing jobs such as cleaning and cooking

serve¹ /sɜːv $ sɚv/ *verb*
1 if you serve food or drink, you give it to people: *Could you serve the vegetables?* • *This pie can be served hot or cold.*
2 if you serve people in a shop, you give them the things they want to buy and take the money they pay: *I couldn't find anyone to serve me.*
3 to work in the army or another public organization: *He served in the army for three years.*
4 if you serve in a game such as tennis, you start the game by throwing the ball in the air and hitting it to the other person
PHRASES
it serves someone right (spoken) used to say that someone deserves something unpleasant that happens to them: *"Sarah won't speak to me." "**It serves you right** for telling lies about her!"*

serve² *noun* when you serve in a game such as tennis: *That was a brilliant serve!*

serv·er /ˈsɜːvə $ ˈsɚvɚ/ *noun* the main computer in a network

ser·vice¹ /ˈsɜːvɪs $ ˈsɚvɪs/ *noun*
1 an organization that provides help for people or does a job for people: *The new government has promised to improve local services in all areas.* • *the **health service*** (=the government department that organizes hospitals, doctors etc for people)
2 (no plural) the help that people who work in a restaurant, hotel, shop etc give you: *It was a lovely meal, and the service was excellent.* • *The bill includes a 12% charge for service.*
3 a formal religious ceremony in a church: *Everyone stood around chatting after the service.* • *a funeral service* (=a ceremony for someone who has died)
4 a regular examination of a machine or vehicle to make sure it works correctly: *You should take your car for a service every six months.*
5 bus service, train service a bus or train that regularly travels to a particular place: *There's a very good train service between London and Peterborough.*

service² *verb* to examine a machine or vehicle and fix it if necessary: *Bill offered to service my car for me.*

ˈservice ˌstation *noun* a place beside a road that sells petrol, food etc SYNONYM **gas station** *AmE*

ser·vi·ette /ˌsɜːviˈet $ ˌsɚviˈet/ *noun BrE* a NAPKIN

serv·ing /ˈsɜːvɪŋ $ ˈsɚvɪŋ/ *noun* an amount of food that is enough for one person

A B C D E F G H I J K L M N O P Q R S T U V W X Y Z

ses•sion /ˈseʃən/ *noun* a period of time when people work or do an activity: *a football training session*

set¹ /set/ *verb* (past tense and past participle **set**, **setting**)
1 if you set a date, price, or amount, you decide what it will be: *Shall we **set a date** for the next meeting?* • *We've set a limit of £15,000 on the building costs.*
2 if you set a machine, you put the control on it in a particular position so that the machine will do something you want it to do: *I've **set** my alarm clock **for** six o'clock.* • *The heating **is set at** 18 degrees.* • *The oven was set to come on at four o'clock.*
3 if a story or film is set in a particular time or place, the events in it happen in that time or place: *The story is set in the future.*
4 to carefully put something down somewhere: *She set the tray down on the table next to his bed.*
5 to give someone some work to do: *The teacher set us an essay for homework.*
6 when the sun sets, it moves lower in the sky until you cannot see it any more ANTONYM **rise**: *The sun doesn't set until nine o'clock in the summer.*
PHRASES
set a record to do something better or faster than anyone has ever done it before: *He has **set a new record** for the high jump.*
set an example to behave in a good way that shows other people how they should behave: *You should always **set an example** by being polite.*
set fire to something, set light to something to make something start burning: *Someone had dropped a cigarette, which **set fire to** a piece of paper.*
set someone free to allow someone to leave a place after they have been a prisoner: *All the prisoners have now been **set free**.*
set a trap to make a clever plan to catch someone: *The police **set a trap** for the thieves.*
PHRASAL VERBS
set about
set about doing something to start doing something that will take a long time: *Tim **set about** raising money for his trip to Africa.*
set aside
set something aside if you set aside money or time, you keep it so that it is available for a particular purpose: *You should **set aside** an hour each evening for homework.*
set back
set something/someone back if something sets back a piece of work, it delays it: *This problem could **set** the project **back** by several months.* • *The bad weather **set** us **back** a bit.*
set off
to start a journey somewhere: *If we **set off** early, we should get there by five o'clock.*
set out
1 set out to start a journey: *In the autumn the two men **set out for** Egypt again.*
2 set out to do something to start trying to achieve something: *He **set out** to write a best-selling novel.*
3 set something out to say or write something in a clear and organized way: *The rules of the competition **are set out** below.*
set up
set something up to start a company or organization: *The government wants to encourage people to **set up** new businesses.*

set² *noun*
KEY PATTERNS
a set of things
a group of things that belong together: *She packed a spare **set of** clothes.* • *a **chess set***

set³ *adjective* **1** a set time, price, amount etc is fixed and does not change: *You can have a full meal for a set price of £10.* **2** (informal) if you are set to do something, you are ready to do it: *Are you all set to go?*

set•back /ˈsetbæk/ *noun* a bad event that stops you from being successful for a while: *Losing the head teacher was a big setback for the school.*
➔ see Thesaurus at PROBLEM

set•tee /seˈtiː/ *noun BrE* a SOFA

set•ting /ˈsetɪŋ/ *noun* **1** the place where something happens: *It was the perfect setting for a romantic meal.*

2 one of the positions that the controls on a machine can be turned to: *Use your hairdryer on its lowest setting.*

set·tle /'setl/ *verb*
1 to make a decision that ends an argument or disagreement: *How can we settle this argument?* • ***That's settled** then – we're going to France for our holiday.*
2 to start living in a place where you intend to live for a long time: *His parents came to America from Ireland and **settled in** Boston.*
3 if dust or snow settles on something, it falls onto it and stays there: *The snow had **settled on** the ground.*

PHRASES
settle a bill, settle a debt to pay money that you owe: *They **settled** the **bill** and left the restaurant.*

PHRASAL VERBS
settle down
1 to stop travelling around and start living in one place: *Isn't it time you got married and **settled down**?*
2 to sit down quietly: *They **settled down** to watch the match on TV.*
settle for
settle for something to accept something that is less than what you wanted: *I'd like to win, but I'll **settle for** second place.*
settle in
to start to feel happy after moving to a new house, job, or school: *It's difficult starting a new school, but you'll soon **settle in**.*

set·tled /'setld/ *adjective* **1** happy in your new house, job, or school: *I'm beginning to feel a bit more settled.*
2 if the weather is settled, it is dry and warm and not likely to change ANTONYM **unsettled**: *The weather should stay settled for the next few days.*

set·tle·ment /'setlmənt/ *noun* **1** an official agreement that ends fighting: *The two sides have agreed on a settlement.* **2** a place where a group of people live: *a small settlement high up in the mountains*

'set-up *noun* (informal) **1** the way that something is organized: *I didn't understand the set-up at the college.*
2 a trick or trap: *I should have realized it was a set-up.*

sev·en /'sevən/ *number* 7

sev·en·teen /ˌsevən'tiːn/ *number* 17 —**seventeenth** *number*

sev·enth /'sevənθ/ *number* **1** 7th **2** one of seven equal parts of something; 1/7

sev·en·ty /'sevənti/ *number* (plural **seventies**) **1** 70 **2 the seventies** the years between 1970 and 1979 **3 be in your seventies** to be aged between 70 and 79 —**seventieth** *number*

sev·er /'sevə $ 'sevɚ/ *verb* (formal) to cut through something completely: *His hand was completely severed in the accident.*

sev·er·al /'sevərəl/ *determiner, pronoun*
a few: *The journey took several days.* • *She applied to several different universities.* • ***Several of** the apples were rotten.*

se·vere /sə'vɪə $ sə'vɪr/ *adjective* a severe thing is very bad: *They suffered severe hardship.* • *a severe earthquake*

> **WORD CHOICE**
> **severe** or **strict**?
> • **Severe** means "very bad or extreme": ***severe** delays* • *a **severe** punishment*
> • **Strict** means "very careful to make sure that people obey rules": *a **strict** teacher*

se·vere·ly /sə'vɪəli $ sə'vɪrli/ *adverb* very badly: *Her mother was severely injured in the crash.*

se·ver·i·ty /sə'verəti/ *noun* (no plural) (formal) how bad something is: *We didn't understand the severity of the problem.*

sew /səʊ $ soʊ/ *verb* (**sewed, sewn** /səʊn $ soʊn/ or **sewed**) to use a needle and thread to join pieces of cloth together: *Next she sewed on the sleeves of the dress.* • *I need to sew a button on my shirt.*

> **PRONUNCIATION**
> You pronounce **sew** like 'so'.

sew·age /'sjuːɪdʒ $ 'suɪdʒ/ *noun* (no plural) dirty water that is carried away from buildings through pipes

sew·er /'sjuːə $ 'suɚ/ *noun* a pipe under the ground that carries away sewage

sew·ing /ˈsəʊɪŋ $ ˈsoʊɪŋ/ *noun* (no plural) making or mending clothes, using a needle and thread: *Are you any good at sewing?*

sewn a past participle of SEW

sex /seks/ *noun* **1** (no plural) the activity that a male and female do together to produce children or that two people do together for pleasure **2** (no plural) the sex of a person or animal is whether they are male or female: *What sex is your cat? • Write down your name, sex, age, and occupation on the form. • He is shy with the opposite sex* (=women).

sex·is·m /ˈseksɪzəm/ *noun* (no plural) when people, especially women, are treated unfairly because of their sex

sex·ist /ˈseksɪst/ *adjective* treating people unfairly because of what sex they are: *Her boss has a very sexist attitude.* —**sexist** *noun*

sex·u·al /ˈsekʃuəl/ *adjective* **1** related to sex: *I'm not ready for a sexual relationship.* **2** related to whether someone is male or female: *Sexual discrimination at work is illegal.* —**sexually** *adverb*: *I don't find him sexually attractive.*

ˌsexual ˈharassment *noun* (no plural) when someone you work with speaks to you or touches you in a sexual way when you do not want them to

sex·u·al·i·ty /ˌsekʃuˈæləti/ *noun* (no plural) someone's sexual feelings

sex·y /ˈseksi/ *adjective* (**sexier**, **sexiest**) sexually attractive: *He had sexy brown eyes.*

sh, **shh** /ʃ/ used to tell someone to be quiet

shab·by /ˈʃæbi/ *adjective* (**shabbier**, **shabbiest**) old and in bad condition: *shabby clothes* —**shabbily** *adverb*: *a shabbily dressed man*

shack /ʃæk/ *noun* a small building that has not been built very well

shade¹ /ʃeɪd/ *noun* **1** (no plural) a pleasant area that is away from the heat and light of the sun: *I'd rather sit in the* ***shade***. **2** one particular type of a colour: *They painted the ceiling a darker* ***shade of*** *blue.*

shade

Mark is sitting in the shade.

shade² *verb* to cover something so that the light from the sun cannot reach it: *The tables were shaded from the sun by a tree.*

shades /ʃeɪdz/ (informal) SUNGLASSES

shad·ow /ˈʃædəʊ $ ˈʃædoʊ/ *noun* **1** a dark shape that appears on a surface when the light cannot shine on it because something is in the way: *The leaves made shadows on the wall.* **2** (no plural) if something is in shadow, it is dark because light cannot reach it: *His face was* ***in shadow***.

shadow

shadow

shad·y /ˈʃeɪdi/ *adjective* (**shadier**, **shadiest**) a shady place is outside, but away from the direct heat and light of the sun: *a shady corner of the garden*

shaft /ʃɑːft $ ʃæft/ *noun* a deep straight hole: *an elevator shaft*

shake¹ /ʃeɪk/ *verb* (**shook** /ʃʊk/ **shaken** /ˈʃeɪkən/) **1** if something shakes, it moves quickly up and down or from side to side: *His hands were shaking.* **2** to move something about quickly and roughly: *She shook the bottle of medicine.*

shake

They shook hands.

A B C D E F G H I J K L M N O P Q R S T U V W X Y Z

A B C D E F G H I J K L M N O P Q R S T U V W X Y Z

3 also **shake up** if you are shaken by something, it makes you feel shocked and upset: *She was shaken by her parents' divorce.*

PHRASES

shake your head to move your head from side to side as a way of saying no: *When I asked her if she was all right, she just* ***shook** her **head**.*

shake hands if you shake hands with someone, you hold their hand and move it up and down, as a greeting or when you have made an agreement: *The two men* ***shook hands***. • *He refused to* ***shake hands with*** *me.*

THESAURUS

tremble: *His hands were* ***trembling*** *as he opened the letter* (=shaking slightly because he was afraid or excited).

shiver: *She stood* ***shivering*** *in the rain for hours* (=shaking because she was cold).

wobble: *My legs* ***wobbled*** *when I tried to stand up* (=moved unsteadily from side to side).

vibrate: *The loud music made the whole room* ***vibrate*** (=shake with small fast movements).

shake² *noun* when someone shakes something: *He held my hand and gave it a friendly shake.*

shaken the past participle of SHAKE¹

'shake-up *noun* when big changes are made to the way that something is organized: *There's going to be a big shake-up in the company where she works.*

shak·y /'ʃeɪki/ *adjective* (**shakier**, **shakiest**) upset and weak because something has shocked or hurt you: *I was still feeling a bit shaky after the accident.*

shall /ʃəl; strong ʃæl/ *modal verb*

1 used to offer to do something: *Shall I give you a lift home?* • *Shall we fetch the bags from the car while you make a drink?*

2 used to suggest doing something: *Shall we stop for a beer?* • *Come on – let's get on with it, shall we?*

3 used to ask about what to do: *What time shall I wake you?*

4 (formal) will: *I shall never forget his words.*

GRAMMAR

The negative of **shall** is **shall not** or **shan't**: *I shan't forget you.*

shallow

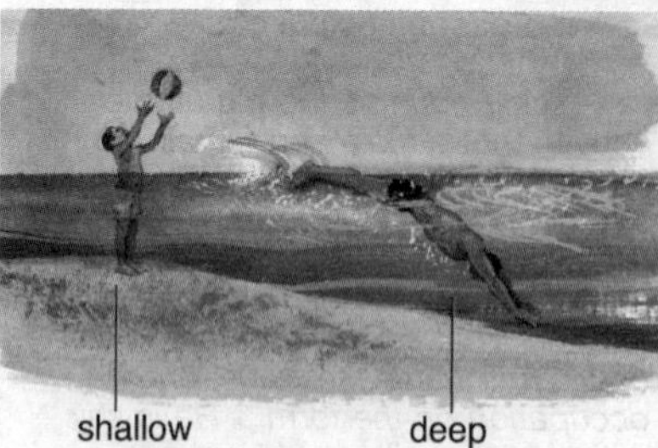

shal·low /'ʃæləʊ $ 'ʃæloʊ/ *adjective* not deep: *They paddled in the shallow water.* • *a shallow stream*

sham·bles /'ʃæmbəlz/ *noun* **be a shambles** (informal) to be very untidy or badly organized: *The place was a shambles.*

shame /ʃeɪm/ *noun* (no plural) the feeling that you have when you know that you have done something bad or embarrassing: *He felt* ***a great sense of shame*** *about leaving her.*

PHRASES

it's a shame, what a shame (spoken) used to say that something is disappointing: ***It's a shame*** *you can't come with us.* • *"He was too ill to play." "Oh,* ***what a shame!****"*

shame·ful /'ʃeɪmfəl/ *adjective* if something you do is shameful, you should be ashamed of it: *It's shameful the way he treats his wife!*

shame·less /'ʃeɪmləs/ *adjective* behaving badly and not caring that other people do not approve: *I was surprised by the shameless way in which he lied to people.*

sham·poo /ʃæm'puː/ *noun* a liquid that you use for washing your hair

shan't /ʃɑːnt $ ʃænt/ *BrE* the short form of 'shall not': *I shan't be long.*

shape¹ /ʃeɪp/ *noun* the shape of something is whether it is a circle, square etc: *What shape is the box?* • *a card* ***in the shape of*** *a heart*

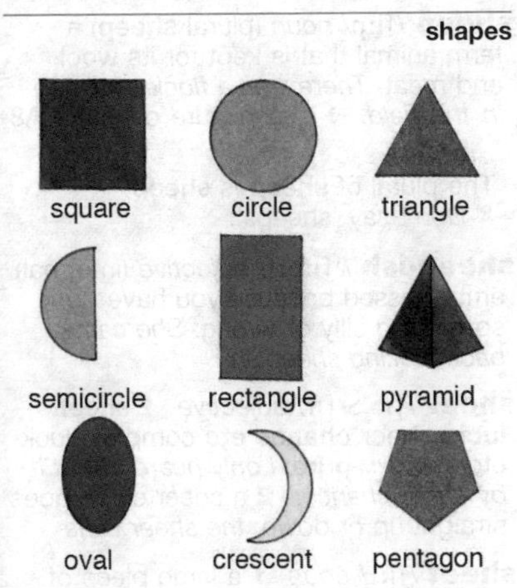

PHRASES

be in good shape, be in bad shape to be in good condition or in bad condition: *The boxer was obviously **in bad shape**.*

get in shape, keep in shape to become fit or stay fit by doing exercise: *What do you do to **keep in shape**?*

take shape if an idea takes shape, it develops and becomes clear and definite: *The plans for the show **are taking shape**.*

shape² *verb* if something is shaped like a particular thing, it has the same shape as that thing: *cookies shaped like snowmen*

share¹ /ʃeə $ ʃer/ *verb*

KEY PATTERNS
share something with someone
share something between two people/groups
share something among a group of people

1 if two people share something, they both have it or use it: *The two secretaries share an office.* • *He **shares** a room **with** his brother.*
2 also **share out** to give part of something to each person in a group: *We **shared** the work **between** us.* • *The children **shared out** the sweets.* • *The money will be **shared out among** all the members of the family.*
3 if you share something with someone, you tell them about it: *Would you like to **share** your thoughts **with** us?*

share² *noun*

KEY PATTERNS
someone's share of something
shares in a company

1 a part of something which each person in a group has received: *What will you do with your **share of the** money?*
2 one of the equal parts that a company is divided into and that people can buy: *A lot of people **are buying shares in** mobile phone companies.*

shark /ʃɑːk $ ʃɑrk/ *noun* a large sea fish with very sharp teeth

sharp¹ /ʃɑːp $ ʃɑrp/ *adjective*

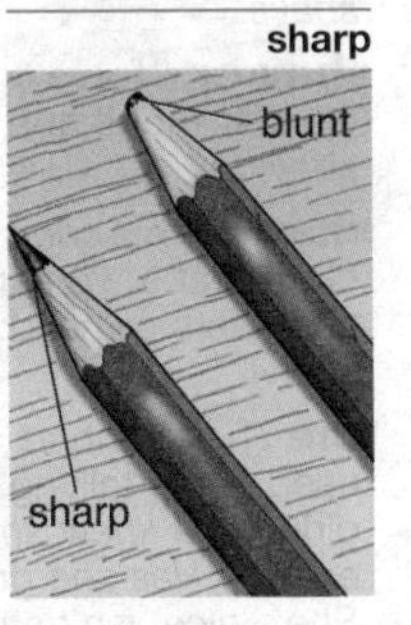

1 something that is sharp has a very thin edge or narrow point and can cut things easily
ANTONYM **blunt**: *Cut off the leaves with a sharp knife.* • *The dog's teeth were sharp.*
2 a sharp increase is large and sudden: *There has been a sharp increase in the price of oil.*
3 a sharp pain is bad and sudden
SYNONYM **acute**: *He felt a sharp pain in his stomach.*
4 good at noticing things or thinking quickly: *Her **sharp eyes** missed nothing.*
5 a sharp line or shape is very clear: *the sharp outline of the mountain*
6 a sharp taste is strong and slightly sour
7 A sharp, B sharp etc the musical note that is slightly higher than A, B etc
ANTONYM **flat**: *He played F sharp instead of F.*

sharp² *adverb* **at 8 o'clock sharp, at two-thirty sharp etc** at exactly 8:00, 2:30 etc: *Class starts at 9 a.m. sharp.*

sharp·en /ˈʃɑːpən $ ˈʃɑrpən/ *verb* to make something sharp: *I sharpened my pencil.*

shat·ter /ˈʃætə $ ˈʃætɚ/ *verb* **1** to break into very small pieces: *The glass hit the floor and shattered.* ➔ see Thesaurus at BREAK¹ **2** to break something into very small pieces: *The explosion shattered the window.*

shat·tered /ˈʃætəd $ ˈʃætərd/ *adjective* **1** very shocked and upset: *They were shattered when they heard the news.* **2** *BrE* (informal) very tired SYNONYM **exhausted**

shave¹ /ʃeɪv/ *verb* to cut off the hair on your face, legs etc: *He washed and shaved.*

shave² *noun* **1** (no plural) an act of shaving: *He needs a shave.* **2 a close shave** (informal) a situation in which you only just avoid something bad: *Nobody was injured, but it was a close shave.*

shav·er /ˈʃeɪvə $ ˈʃeɪvər/ *noun* an electric tool that a man uses for shaving

shawl /ʃɔːl/ *noun* a large piece of cloth that a woman wears around her shoulders or head: *She wore a red shawl.*

she /ʃiː/ *pronoun* used when talking about a woman or girl: *Fiona knew she would pass the exam.* • *Has she got any sisters?* • *She's nice, isn't she?*

shear /ʃɪə $ ʃɪr/ *verb* (**sheared, sheared** or **shorn** /ʃɔːn $ ʃɔrn/) to cut the wool off a sheep: *We watched him shearing sheep.*

shears /ʃɪəz $ ʃɪrz/ *plural noun* large scissors for cutting plants or grass: *a pair of garden shears*

shears

shed¹ /ʃed/ *noun* a small building that you use for storing things: *a tool shed*

shed² *verb* (past tense and past participle **shed, shedding**) **1** when a tree sheds its leaves, the leaves drop off **2 shed light on something** to explain something: *Can you shed any light on what he was doing there?* **3 shed tears** to cry: *Nobody shed any tears when she left.*

she'd /ʃiːd/ the short form of 'she had' or 'she would': *She'd already left.* • *I knew she'd like it.*

sheep /ʃiːp/ *noun* (plural **sheep**) a farm animal that is kept for its wool and meat: *There was a flock of sheep in the field.* ➔ see picture on page A8

GRAMMAR
The plural of **sheep** is **sheep**.
✘ Don't say 'sheeps'.

sheep·ish /ˈʃiːpɪʃ/ *adjective* (informal) embarrassed because you have done something silly or wrong: *She came back looking sheepish.*

sheer /ʃɪə $ ʃɪr/ *adjective* **1 sheer luck, sheer chance etc** complete luck etc SYNONYM **pure**: *I only heard about it by sheer chance.* **2** a sheer slope goes straight up or down: *the sheer cliffs*

sheet /ʃiːt/ *noun* **1** a large piece of thin cloth that you put on a bed: *I prefer cotton sheets.* **2** a flat piece of paper, metal, glass etc: *a sheet of paper*

shelf /ʃelf/ *noun* (plural **shelves** /ʃelvz/) a board to put things on, fixed to a wall or in a cupboard: *He put the jar back on the shelf.*

shell¹ /ʃel/ *noun* **1** the hard outside part of a nut or egg **2** the hard part that covers some animals, for example SNAILS and CRABS: *We took the shells off the shrimps.* **3** a bomb which is fired from a large gun: *Shells fell on the city all night.*

shell² *verb* **1** to fire bombs at something from a large gun: *The town was shelled during the war.* **2 shell out** (informal) to pay a lot of money for something: *I had to shell out 50 pounds to have my bike mended.*

she'll /ʃiːl/ the short form of 'she will': *She'll go crazy when she finds out!*

shell·fish /ˈʃelˌfɪʃ/ *noun* (plural **shellfish**) a small creature that lives in water and has a shell

shel·ter¹ /ˈʃeltə $ ˈʃeltər/ *noun* **1** a small building in which you are safe from bad weather or from attack: *They built themselves a shelter out of branches.* **2** (no plural) protection from bad weather or from danger: *These people need food and shelter.* • *The line of trees provides* ***shelter from*** *the wind.*

PHRASES
take shelter to go into or under something so that you are safe from bad weather or from danger: *The rain forced them to **take shelter** under a tree.*

shelter² *verb* **1** to give someone a safe place to stay: *Relatives offered to shelter the family until it was safe for them to go home.* ➔ see Thesaurus at PROTECT **2** to go into or under a place so that you are safe from bad weather or danger: *We sheltered from the sun under a tree.*

shelve /ʃelv/ *verb* if you shelve a plan, you decide not to continue with it immediately, although you might continue with it later: *They have shelved plans to expand the college.*

shelves the plural of SHELF

shep·herd /ˈʃepəd $ ˈʃepɚd/ *noun* someone whose job is to take care of sheep

sher·iff /ˈʃerɪf/ *noun* an elected police officer in the US

sher·ry /ˈʃeri/ *noun* (no plural) a strong Spanish wine: *a glass of sherry*

she's /ʃiːz/ the short form of 'she is' or 'she has': *She's very upset.* • *She's never been abroad.*

shh /ʃ/ another spelling of SH

shield¹ /ʃiːld/ *noun* a large flat object which a soldier or police officer holds in front of their body to protect themselves

shield

shield

sword

shield² *verb* to protect someone from something unpleasant: *I just wanted to shield her from the truth.* ➔ see Thesaurus at PROTECT

shift¹ /ʃɪft/ *noun* **1** a change in what people think or do: *There has been a shift in attitudes towards women at work.* **2** one of the periods of work in a factory, hospital etc: *She's on the night shift this week.*

shift² *verb* (informal) **1** to move something from one place to another: *I asked him to shift his car.* **2** to move slightly: *Could you shift up a bit, please?*

shim·mer /ˈʃɪmə $ ˈʃɪmɚ/ *verb* to shine with a soft unsteady light: *The moonlight shimmered on the water.*

shin /ʃɪn/ *noun* the front part of your leg between your knee and your foot: *He got kicked on the shin.* ➔ see picture on page A5

shine /ʃaɪn/ *verb* (past tense and past participle **shone** /ʃɒn $ ʃoʊn/)
1 to produce light or look bright: *The sun was shining.* • *The cat's eyes shone in the car's headlights.*
2 to point a light in a particular direction: *Can you shine your torch over here?*

THESAURUS
glow: *The logs in the fireplace were still **glowing*** (=producing a soft light).
flash: *the **flashing** lights of the police car* (=quickly going on and off, and shining brightly)
twinkle: *The stars **twinkled** in the sky* (=shone with a distant light that becomes stronger and then weaker).
gleam: *He polished his shoes until they **gleamed*** (=had a surface that shone in a bright and attractive way).
sparkle/glitter: *The sea **sparkled** in the sunshine* (=reflected a lot of small flashes of light).

shin·y /ˈʃaɪni/ *adjective* (**shinier, shiniest**) something that is shiny has a very bright surface: *a shiny new coin*

ship¹ /ʃɪp/ *noun* a large boat: *I was terrified that the ship might sink.* ➔ see Thesaurus at BOAT

ship² *verb* (**shipped, shipping**) to send goods a long distance, especially in a ship: *The coffee beans are dried and shipped to the United States.*

ship·ping /ˈʃɪpɪŋ/ *noun* (no plural) **1** ships in general: *The bad weather has caused delays to shipping.* **2** the activity of sending goods a long distance, or the cost of doing this: *The price does not include shipping.*

ship·wreck¹ /ˈʃɪp-rek/ *noun* an accident in which a ship is destroyed at sea: *Many sailors lost their lives in the shipwreck.*

shipwreck² *verb* **be shipwrecked** if people are shipwrecked, the ship they are travelling on is destroyed in an accident at sea, but they manage to reach land

shirk /ʃɜːk $ ʃɚk/ *verb* to avoid doing something you should do: *George worked hard and never shirked his responsibilities.*

shirt /ʃɜːt $ ʃɚt/ *noun* a piece of clothing that covers the top part of your body, and has buttons down the front: *He wore a shirt and tie.* → see picture at CLOTHES

shiv·er /ˈʃɪvə $ ˈʃɪvɚ/ *verb* if you shiver, your body shakes a little because you are cold or frightened: *I was cold and wet and I couldn't stop shivering.* → see Thesaurus at SHAKE[1] —**shiver** *noun*: *"I'm scared," she said with a shiver.*

shoal /ʃəʊl $ ʃoʊl/ *noun* a large group of fish that swim together

shoal

a shoal of fish

shock¹ /ʃɒk $ ʃɑk/ *noun* (no plural)
1 if you get a shock, something bad happens which you did not expect, and you feel very surprised and upset: *I got a terrible* ***shock*** *when I saw how ill Simon looked.* • *She's still* ***in a state of shock****.*
2 if someone is suffering from shock after an accident, their body is very weak because they have been frightened and upset: *The driver was taken to hospital and treated for shock.*

PHRASES

be a shock, come as a shock if something bad that happens is a shock or comes as a shock, it is very unexpected and upsets you a lot: *The news came as a terrible shock.*

shock² *verb* to make someone feel very surprised and upset: *The children's behaviour shocked me.* —**shocked** *adjective*: *I was deeply shocked by what I saw.* • *She was* ***shocked to*** *find out that her husband had been in prison.*

shock·ing /ˈʃɒkɪŋ $ ˈʃɑkɪŋ/ *adjective* something that is shocking is so bad that it makes you feel very upset or angry SYNONYM **appalling**: *It's shocking that so many young people are homeless in this country.*

shod·dy /ˈʃɒdi $ ˈʃɑdi/ *adjective* (**shoddier, shoddiest**) shoddy work is badly done, and shoddy goods are badly made: *markets selling cheap shoddy goods*

shoes

slippers
sandals
stilettos
trainers
boots
lace
sole

shoe /ʃuː/ *noun* **1** a piece of clothing that you wear on your feet, which is made of leather or some other strong material: *a pair of running shoes* **2 be in someone's shoes** to be in the situation that someone else is in: *I wouldn't want to be in her shoes.*

shoe·lace /ˈʃuːleɪs/ *noun* a thin piece of string or leather that you use to tie your shoes: *Your shoelace is undone.* → see picture at UNDO

shone the past tense and past participle of SHINE

shook the past tense of SHAKE

shoot¹ /ʃuːt/ *verb* (past tense and past participle **shot** /ʃɒt $ ʃɑt/)
1 to kill or injure someone with a gun: *He shot the man in the back.* • *Fifteen people* ***were shot dead****.*
2 to fire a gun: *Don't shoot!*
3 to make a film or take photographs SYNONYM **film**: *It takes several weeks to shoot a pop video.*

PHRASAL VERBS

shoot down

shoot something down to destroy an enemy plane while it is flying: *Three planes* ***were shot down****.*

shoot up
to increase very quickly SYNONYM **rocket**: *The number of car thefts has shot up.*

shoot² *noun* **1** a new part of a plant that is starting to grow: *A few green shoots appeared in the ground.* **2** a time when someone makes a film or takes photographs: *The film shoot lasted three months.*

shoot·ing /ˈʃuːtɪŋ/ *noun* **1** a situation in which someone is killed or injured by a gun: *Luckily, no one was hurt in the shooting.* **2** (no plural) the sport of killing animals and birds with guns

shop¹ /ʃɒp $ ʃɑp/ *noun*

KEY PATTERNS
buy something in/from a shop
go to the shops

a building where you can buy things SYNONYM **store** *AmE*: *The town has some good clothes shops.* • *I got these shoes* ***in a shop*** *near the town centre.* • *"Where's Sarah?" "She's gone to the shops."*

shop² *verb* (**shopped, shopping**)

KEY PATTERNS
go shopping
shop for clothes/food etc

to go to a shop or several shops to buy things: *I'm* ***going shopping*** *this afternoon.* • *Where do you* ***shop for*** *food?* • *We usually shop once a week.*

shop around
to compare the price and quality of things in different shops before you decide which to buy: ***Shop around*** *to find the best computer you can afford.*

ˈshop asˌsistant *noun BrE* someone who works in a shop selling things and helping customers

shop·keep·er /ˈʃɒpˌkiːpə $ ˈʃɑpˌkipɚ/ *noun* someone who owns or manages a small shop SYNONYM **storekeeper** *AmE*

shop·lift·ing /ˈʃɒpˌlɪftɪŋ $ ˈʃɑpˌlɪftɪŋ/ *noun* (no plural) the crime of stealing things from shops: *She was arrested for shoplifting.* —**shoplifter** *noun* —**shoplift** *verb* → see Thesaurus at STEAL

shop·ping /ˈʃɒpɪŋ $ ˈʃɑpɪŋ/ *noun* (no plural)
1 the activity of going to shops to buy things: *I'll* ***do the shopping*** *this week.*
2 things that you have just bought: *Maggie was carrying bags of shopping.*

USAGE
You say **do the shopping**.
✘ Don't say 'make the shopping'.

ˈshopping ˌcentre *BrE*, **shopping center** *AmE noun* a group of shops that are built together in one area, often inside one large building

shore /ʃɔː $ ʃɔr/ *noun* the land along the edge of the sea or a large lake: *the southern shore of Lake Geneva.*

THESAURUS
coast: *The rocky* ***coast*** *of Maine* (=the area next to the sea).
beach/the seashore: *We watched the children playing on the* ***beach*** (=an area of sand or small stones next to the sea).
bank: *the trees that grow on the* ***banks*** *of the river* (=the land along the sides of the river)

shorn the past participle of SHEAR

short¹ /ʃɔːt $ ʃɔrt/ *adjective*
1 happening for only a little time ANTONYM **long**: *It's quite a short film.* • *We made a short visit to his parents.*
2 a short distance or length is not long: *It's only a short walk to my school.* • *His hair is short and black.*
3 a short person is not tall: *Her father was a short fat man.* • *Louise is shorter than me.*

PHRASES
be short of something to not have enough of something that you need: *Ken is always* ***short of*** *money.*
be short for something to be a shorter way of saying a name: *Liz is* ***short for*** *Elizabeth.*

short² *noun* **in short** used to say something in only a few words: *In short, we're lost.*

short·age /ˈʃɔːtɪdʒ $ ˈʃɔrtɪdʒ/ *noun* when there is not enough of something that people need SYNONYM **lack**: *There is now a serious shortage of hospital beds.*

ˌshort ˈcut / $ ˈ. ./ *noun* a quicker more direct way of going somewhere or doing something: *We took a short cut over the fields to the station.*

short·hand /ˈʃɔːthænd $ ˈʃɔrthænd/ *noun* (no plural) a fast method of writing down what people say, using signs instead of words: *Candidates for the job must know shorthand.*

short·list /ˈʃɔːtlɪst $ ˈʃɔrtlɪst/ *noun BrE* a list of the most suitable people for a job or prize, chosen from a larger group: *Her first novel was on the shortlist for an important literary prize.*

ˈshort-list *verb* **be short-listed** *BrE* to be chosen for a shortlist: *No women were short-listed for the job.*

short·ly /ˈʃɔːtli $ ˈʃɔrtli/ *adverb* soon: *Liz left home shortly after 8 a.m.*
→ see Thesaurus at SOON

shorts /ʃɔːts $ ʃɔrts/ *plural noun* **1** short trousers that only reach to your knees: *Jack was wearing a pair of shorts and a T-shirt.* **2** the American word for UNDERPANTS

short·sight·ed /ˌʃɔːtˈsaɪtɪd $ ˌʃɔrtˈsaɪtɪd/ *adjective* **1** if you are shortsighted, you cannot see things very clearly if they are a long way away from you **2** thinking only about the effect that something will have immediately, rather than thinking about the effect it will have over a longer period of time: *The government's policy on the environment is shortsighted.*

ˌshort-ˈterm *adjective* continuing for only a short time ANTONYM **long-term**: *We have had some short-term financial problems.*

shot¹ /ʃɒt $ ʃɑt/ *noun* **1** when someone fires a gun, or the sound that this makes: *He fired two shots.* **2** when someone hits the ball in a game such as baseball, or kicks the ball towards the GOAL in a game of football: *The shot hit the goalpost.* **3** a photograph or piece of film: *The film opens with a shot of Central Park.*

shot² the past tense and past participle of SHOOT

shot·gun /ˈʃɒtɡʌn $ ˈʃɑtɡʌn/ *noun* a long gun that shoots small metal balls, and is used especially for shooting animals and birds

should /ʃəd; strong ʃʊd/ *modal verb* **1** used when saying that something is or was the right or sensible thing to do: *I think we should call a doctor.* • *Women should be paid the same as men.* • *People shouldn't use their cars so much.* • *I **shouldn't have** lost my temper with Tim* (=but I did).
2 used when saying that you expect something to happen or be true: *Tickets should be on sale next week.* • *You should be able to find vegetarian meals in most restaurants.*
3 used when giving or asking for advice: *You shouldn't worry about your exams.* • *Do you think I should change my shoes?*

> **GRAMMAR**
> The negative of **should** is **should not** or **shouldn't**.

shoul·der /ˈʃəʊldə $ ˈʃoʊldɚ/ *noun* your shoulders are the two parts of your body at the side of your neck where your arms join your body: *Sam patted me **on the shoulder**.* • *She carried her bag **over her shoulder**.*
→ see picture on page A5

PHRASES

shrug your shoulders to raise your shoulders to show that you do not know something or do not care about it: *I asked what happened and he just **shrugged his shoulders**.*

> **PRONUNCIATION**
> You pronounce **shoulder** like 'older'.

ˈshoulder bag *noun* a bag that you carry over your shoulder

ˈshoulder blade *noun* one of the two flat bones below your shoulders on your back → see picture on page A5

should·n't /ˈʃʊdnt/ *verb* the short form of 'should not': *You shouldn't leave your desk in such a mess.*

should've /ˈʃʊdəv/ *verb* the short form of 'should have': *I should've worn a coat.*

shout¹ /ʃaʊt/ *verb* to say something very loudly, sometimes in an angry way: *"Stop!" he shouted.* • *Mrs Keane is always **shouting at** us.*

> **USAGE**
> You **shout at someone** when you are angry.
> You **shout to someone** when you want to tell them something.

A B C D E F G H I J K L M N O P Q R S T U V W X Y Z

THESAURUS
scream: *After the explosion, he heard Anna* ***screaming*** *his name* (=shouting it in a very loud high voice because she was afraid).
cry (formal): *I cried for help* (=shouted).
yell also **holler** *AmE*: *When he saw what I'd done to his car, the man started* ***yelling*** *at me* (=shouting).

shout² *noun*
something that someone says very loudly: *I heard a shout outside my window.* • *There was a shout of "Hooray!"*

shove /ʃʌv/ *verb* (informal) to push someone or something in a rough or careless way: *People were shoving each other, trying to get on the bus.* • *He shoved the clothes into his bag.* → see Thesaurus at PUSH¹ —**shove** *noun*

shov•el¹ /ˈʃʌvəl/ *noun* a tool made of a wide piece of metal on a long handle, that you use for moving earth and stones

shovel

shovel² *verb* (**shovelled**, **shovelling** *BrE*, **shoveled**, **shoveling** *AmE*) to move earth, stones etc with a shovel

show¹ → see box on page 616

show² *noun*
1 a programme on television or radio: *What's your favourite show on TV?* • *He has his own* ***radio show***.
2 a performance involving singing, dancing etc in a theatre: *She is* ***in a show*** *on Broadway.*

PHRASES
be on show to be available for the public to look at: *His paintings* ***are on show*** *at the Museum of Modern Art.*

ˈshow ˌbusiness also **show biz** /ˈʃəʊ bɪz $ ˈʃoʊ bɪz/ *noun* (no plural) (informal) the industry that deals with providing entertainment for people: *a career in show business*

show•er¹ /ˈʃaʊə $ ˈʃaʊɚ/ *noun* **1** a flow of water that you stand under to wash your whole body: *a bedroom with a private shower* **2** when you wash your body in a shower: *I'm going to have a quick shower before dinner.* **3** a short period of rain: *It will be mainly sunny with a few showers.* **4** *AmE* a party at which people give presents to a woman who is going to get married or have a baby

shower² *verb* to wash your body by having a shower: *He showered and dressed quickly.*

show•er•y /ˈʃaʊəri/ *adjective* showery weather has a lot of short periods of rain: *Tomorrow will be brighter but showery.*

shown the past participle of SHOW¹

ˈshow-off *noun* someone who tries to show how clever, funny etc they are in order to make other people admire them

show•room /ˈʃəʊruːm $ ˈʃoʊrum/ *noun* a large room where you can look at large goods such as cars or electrical goods that are for sale: *Everything in the car showroom was too expensive for us.*

shrank the past tense of SHRINK

shred¹ /ʃred/ *noun* a small thin piece that has been torn from something: *She picked up his letter and tore it to shreds.*

shred² *verb* (**shredded**, **shredding**) to cut or tear something into small pieces: *Shred the cabbage leaves and cook them for two minutes.* —**shredded** *adjective*: *The burger comes with shredded lettuce.*

shrewd /ʃruːd/ *adjective* good at understanding people or situations and knowing how to get what you want from them SYNONYM **astute**: *a shrewd politician*

shriek /ʃriːk/ *verb* (written) to make a sudden high cry, especially because you are afraid or amused SYNONYM **scream**: *"Go away!" she shrieked.* —**shriek** *noun*: *We heard shrieks of laughter.*

shrill /ʃrɪl/ *adjective* a shrill sound or voice is very high and loud: *"That's not true!" she protested in a shrill voice.*

show /ʃəʊ $ ʃoʊ/ *verb* (past tense **showed**, past participle **shown** /ʃəʊn $ ʃoʊn/)

KEY PATTERNS
show someone something
show something to someone
show someone how to do something
show that something is true
show someone to their room/table

1 to let someone see something: *She **showed** me a picture of the hotel.* • *I **showed** the letter **to** my mother.* • *You have to **show** your ticket at the door.*

2 to tell someone how to do something: *Joan **showed** me **how to** use the computer.*

3 to provide facts or information that tells you that something is true: *The report **showed** an increase in sales of luxury goods.* • *His letter **showed that** he was still in love with her.* • *The statistics will **show whether** the advertising campaign is working.*

4 to take someone to a place: *The waiter **showed** us **to** our table.*

5 if you show a feeling or it shows, people can see it when they look at you: *He couldn't help **showing** his embarrassment.*

6 if a film or picture shows something, you can see it on the film or picture: *The photo **showed** surfers on a beach.*

7 if a film or programme is showing at a cinema or on television, people are able to see it: *They **are showing** 'Star Wars' **on TV** on Saturday.*

THESAURUS
prove: *You can't prove I killed him* (=show that something is definitely true, especially in law or science).
demonstrate: *She **demonstrated** how to use the new computer system* (=she showed people how to use it by using it herself).

PHRASAL VERBS

show around
show someone around to go with someone around a place and show them the important or interesting parts: *I offered to **show** the new boy **around** the school.*

show off
1 to do things to try to make people think you are clever, attractive, funny etc: *The boys all started **showing off** because Kate was there.*
2 show something off to show something to people because you are very proud of it: *I want to go out tonight and **show off** my new dress.*

shrimp /ʃrɪmp/ *noun* a small pink sea animal that you can eat, with ten legs and a shell

shrine /ʃraɪn/ *noun* a holy place that people visit: *People visit the shrine on the first day of the New Year.*

shrink /ʃrɪŋk/ *verb* (**shrank** /ʃræŋk/ **shrunk** /ʃrʌŋk/)
to become smaller: *My dress shrank when I washed it.*

shriv·el /ˈʃrɪvəl/ *verb* (**shrivelled**, **shrivelling** *BrE*, **shriveled**, **shriveling** *AmE*) also **shrivel up** if something shrivels, it gets smaller and its surface becomes covered with lines because it is dry or old: *A lot of the plants had shrivelled up in the heat.*

shroud¹ /ʃraʊd/ *noun* a cloth that is wrapped around a dead person's body before it is buried

shroud² *verb* **be shrouded in** (written) if something is shrouded in mist or smoke, it is covered and hidden by the mist or smoke: *It was early morning and the hills were shrouded in mist.*

shrub /ʃrʌb/ *noun* a plant that is smaller than a tree and has a lot of branches coming up from the ground

shrug /ʃrʌg/ *verb* (**shrugged**, **shrugging**) to raise your shoulders to show that you do not know something or do not care about it: *"Sorry, I don't know the answer," she said, and shrugged her shoulders.* —**shrug** *noun*: *Luke gave a casual shrug.*

shrug

shrunk the past participle of SHRINK

shud·der /ˈʃʌdə $ ˈʃʌdɚ/ *verb* to shake because you dislike something very much or are afraid of it: *The memory of that day makes me shudder.*

shuf·fle /ˈʃʌfəl/ *verb* **1** to walk in a slow or lazy way without lifting your feet off the ground: *Grandad got up and shuffled across the room.* **2** to mix playing cards into a different order before playing a game: *Shall I shuffle?*

shut¹ /ʃʌt/ *verb* (past tense and past participle **shut**, **shutting**)
1 to close something ANTONYM **open**: *Will you shut the door please? • I shut my eyes and went to sleep.*
2 to become closed ANTONYM **open**: *She let the gate shut behind her.*
3 if a shop, bank, or other public place shuts, it is not available for people to use SYNONYM **close** ANTONYM **open**: *What time do the shops shut? • The banks here shut for two hours at lunchtime.*

PHRASES

shut your mouth, shut your face! (spoken) used to tell someone rudely and angrily to stop talking

PHRASAL VERBS

shut down
1 if a company or factory shuts down, it stops doing any work: *The company **shuts down** for a week at Christmas.*
2 to make a computer stop working after you have finished using it, or to stop working: *I **shut down** my computer. • My computer sometimes **shuts down** for no reason.*

shut up (informal)
1 to stop talking: *Will you please **shut up** and listen!*
2 shut someone up to make someone stop talking: *We gave Joey some sweets to **shut** him **up**.*

shut² *adjective* closed ANTONYM **open**: *Is the gate shut? • His eyes were shut. • The shops are all shut.*

shut·ter /ˈʃʌtə $ ˈʃʌtɚ/ *noun* shutters are wooden or metal covers that you can close in front of a window

shutter

shut·tle /ˈʃʌtl/ *noun* **1** a plane, bus, or train that makes regular short trips between two places: *I arrived at Heathrow and caught the shuttle to Gatwick.* **2** a vehicle that can travel into space and return to Earth more than once: *They have had to delay the launch of the space shuttle.*

shut·tle·cock /ˈʃʌtlˌkɒk $ ˈʃʌtlˌkɑk/ *noun* a small object with feathers that you hit in the game of BADMINTON

shy /ʃaɪ/ *adjective* someone who is shy is nervous and finds it difficult to talk to other people: *a shy child* • *Come on, don't be shy.* —**shyly** *adverb*: *Shyly she told me her name.* —**shyness** *noun* (no plural): *He suffers from terrible shyness.*

sib·ling /ˈsɪblɪŋ/ *noun* (formal) your brother or sister

sick /sɪk/ *adjective*
1 someone who is sick is ill or has a disease: *I couldn't go to school because I was sick.* • *He looks after his sick mother.* → see Thesaurus at ILL
2 interested in things that are strange, cruel, and unpleasant: *a sick joke*

PHRASES
be sick *BrE* if you are sick, food comes up from your stomach through your mouth SYNONYM **throw up**, **vomit**: *The baby has **been sick** on me.*
feel sick to feel as if you are going to be sick: *She ate so much pizza she **felt sick**.*
be sick of something to be annoyed about a situation that has happened too often or for too long: *I **am absolutely sick of** you being late every day.*
make someone sick if something makes you sick, it makes you very angry: ***It makes me sick to** hear him lying like that.*

sick·ly /ˈsɪkli/ *adjective* (**sicklier**, **sickliest**) someone who is sickly is weak and often ill: *She was a pale sickly woman.*

sick·ness /ˈsɪknəs/ *noun* (no plural) when people are ill: *He misses a lot of school because of sickness.* → see Thesaurus at ILLNESS

side[1] /saɪd/ *noun*
1 one half of something: *She has a scar **on the left side of** her face.* • *I realized I was driving **on the wrong side of** the road.* • *He grew up on the city's west side.*
2 one surface of something: *Write **on both sides of** the paper.* • *A voice came from **the other side of** the fence.* • *A cube has six sides.*
3 a surface of something that is not the front, back, top, or bottom: *The company name is painted **on the side of** the truck.* • *I keep a glass of water **by the side of** my bed.*

side

They are sitting side by side.

4 the side of the road is the part at the edge, furthest from the middle: *She stopped her car **at the side of** the road.*
5 one part of a situation or argument, which may be different to other parts: *I need to hear her **side of** the story.* • *I saw **a different side to** his character that day.*
6 one person, group, or team in a fight or sports game: *They were **on the winning side** in the war.* • *England were the first side to score a goal.*
7 one side of your family is the grandparents and other people that are related to either your mother or your father: *I am half Irish **on my mother's side**.*

PHRASES
at someone's side, by someone's side with someone, especially when they need you to help them: *My boyfriend was **by my side** the whole time I was sick.*
side by side next to each other: *We sat **side by side**.*
from side to side from left to right and right to left many times: *The bird kept moving its head **from side to side**.*
be on someone's side to support someone in an argument, fight, or war: *Mom **is always on my side**.*
take sides to say that you support one person or group in an argument: *A teacher cannot **take sides** in a fight between students.*

side[2] *adjective*
1 on the side of something: *Students come into school by the side entrance.*
2 side street, side road a small street or road that is near a main street: *The restaurant is on a little **side road**.*

side[3] *verb* **side with someone** to support one person or group of people in an argument or fight: *Dad always sides with Mum when we argue.*

side•board /ˈsaɪdbɔːd $ ˈsaɪdbɔrd/ *noun* **1** a long low piece of furniture in which you keep plates and glasses **2 sideboards** *BrE* sideburns

side•burns /ˈsaɪdbɜːnz $ ˈsaɪdbɚnz/ also **sideboards** *BrE noun* hair that grows down the sides of a man's face

ˈside-efˌfect *noun* a bad effect that a drug has on your body, while you are using it to cure an illness: *Antibiotics can have serious side-effects.*

side•track /ˈsaɪdtræk/ *verb* if you are sidetracked, you become interested in something that is not important and stop doing or thinking about something that is important: *I was determined to get an answer and I refused to be sidetracked.*

side•walk /ˈsaɪdwɔːk/ the American word for PAVEMENT

side•ways /ˈsaɪdweɪz/ *adverb*, *adjective* towards one side: *a sideways step*

siege /siːdʒ/ *noun* when an army surrounds a place and stops any food, weapons etc from getting into it: *The city was under siege for six months.* • *the siege of Sarajevo*

sieve /sɪv/ *noun* a piece of kitchen equipment that looks like a net, and that you use for separating solid food from liquid or small pieces of food from larger pieces: *I put the soup through a sieve.*

sift /sɪft/ *verb* to put flour, sugar etc through a sieve in order to remove any large pieces

sigh /saɪ/ *verb* to breathe out loudly because you are tired, annoyed, or bored: *"I'll never finish this essay," she sighed.* —**sigh** *noun*: *He sat down with a sigh of relief.*

sight /saɪt/ *noun*
1 (no plural) when you see something: *I hate **the sight of** blood.* • *She turned pale **at the sight of** (=when she saw) Harry.*
2 (no plural) the ability to see: *He is 85 and losing his sight.*
3 sights places that are interesting to see, and which many people visit: *Will you have time to **see the sights** while you are in London?*

PHRASES

catch sight of someone/something to suddenly see someone or something: ***I caught sight of** Chris getting on a bus.*

in sight **a)** if something is in sight, you can see it: *I looked for Terry, but he was nowhere **in sight**.* **b)** going to happen soon: *The end of the exams is **in sight**.*

out of sight if something is out of sight, you cannot see it: *We parked the car behind the house, **out of sight**.*

SPELLING
Don't confuse the spelling of **sight** and **site** (=the place where something is).

sight•ing /ˈsaɪtɪŋ/ *noun* when someone sees something unusual or completely new: *This was the first sighting of this bird in Britain.*

sight•see•ing /ˈsaɪtˌsiːɪŋ/ *noun* (no plural) visiting famous or interesting places, especially as a tourist: *In the afternoon, we all went sightseeing round the town.*

sign¹ /saɪn/ *noun*
1 something with words or pictures on it that gives you information or tells you which way to go: *There was a 'No Entry' sign on the door.* • *We followed the signs for Birmingham.*
2 a fact that shows that something is true or is starting to happen SYNONYM **indication**: *Headaches can be **a sign** of stress.* • *She came out smiling, which was **a good sign**.*
3 a picture or shape that has a particular meaning: *a plus sign* • *dollar signs*

sign² *verb*
1 to write your name on a letter or document: *She signed the letter 'Dr Kay Hill'.* • *I showed them the contract and they all signed.*
2 to agree to give someone a job in a sports team or musical group: *Liverpool have signed a new player.*

PHRASAL VERBS

sign up
1 sign someone up to agree to give someone a job in a sports team or

A B C D E F G H I J K L M N O P Q R S T U V W X Y Z

sign

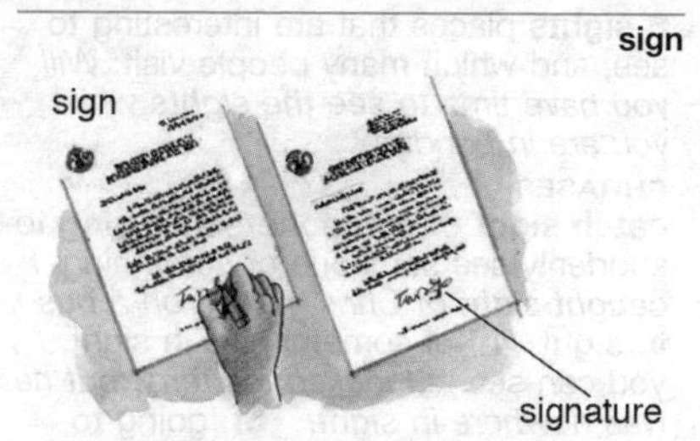

musical group: *He was **signed up** by the Bulls as soon as he finished college.*
2 sign up to put your name on a list because you want to do something SYNONYM **enrol**: *You should **sign up for** a computer course.*

> WORD CHOICE
> **sign** or **signature**?
> • **Sign** (=write your name) is a verb: *Can you sign this form?*
> • **Signature** (=the usual way of writing your name) is a noun: *His **signature** was at the bottom of the letter.*

sig·nal¹ /ˈsɪgnəl/ *noun* **1** a movement or sound which gives information or tells someone to do something: *Don't move until you hear the signal.* **2** a light that tells a train driver whether to go or stop: *The train stopped at a signal.*

signal² *verb* (**signalled**, **signalling** *BrE*, **signaled**, **signaling** *AmE*) **1** to move your hand or head as a way of telling someone something: *I put up my hand to signal that I knew the answer.* • *I looked at Dad, but he signalled to me to be quiet.* **2** the American word for INDICATE (3)

sig·na·ture /ˈsɪgnətʃə $ ˈsɪgnətʃɚ/ *noun* your usual way of writing your name, for example on a cheque: *His signature was on the letter.*

sig·nif·i·cance /sɪgˈnɪfɪkəns/ *noun* (no plural) the importance or meaning of something: *Could you explain the significance of this ceremony?*

sig·nif·i·cant /sɪgˈnɪfɪkənt/ *adjective* **1** important ANTONYM **insignificant**: *This is a very significant change.* **2** a significant amount is a large amount ANTONYM **insignificant**: *She received a significant pay increase.*
—**significantly** *adverb*: *Exam results were significantly better this year.*

sig·ni·fy /ˈsɪgnəfaɪ/ *verb* (formal) (**signified**, **signifies**) to be a sign of something: *Losing weight can signify a variety of health problems.*

ˈsign ˌlanguage *noun* a language for people who cannot hear, where you move your hands instead of using words

signpost

sign·post¹ /ˈsaɪnpəʊst $ ˈsaɪnpoʊst/ *noun* a sign at the side of the road that shows people which way to go and how far it is to a place

signpost² *verb* *BrE* **be signposted** if a place is signposted, there are signs that show you how to get there: *The castle is signposted off the main road.*

Sikh /siːk/ *noun* someone who belongs to an Indian religious group —**Sikh** *adjective*: *a Sikh temple*

si·lence /ˈsaɪləns/ *noun* **1** when there is no sound: *There was complete silence in the house.* **2 in silence** without talking or making a noise: *The class sat in silence.*

si·lent /ˈsaɪlənt/ *adjective* if a person is silent, they do not say anything or make any sound. If a place is silent, there is no sound there: *I asked her what happened but she was silent.* • *I came home to a silent, empty house.* • *The crowd **fell silent** (=became silent) as he began to speak.*
—**silently** *adverb*: *He walked silently across the grass.*

> WORD CHOICE
> **silent** or **quiet**?
> • **Silent** means "without any noise at all": *The room was **silent**.*
> • **Quiet** means "making no noise, or very little noise": *She spoke in a **quiet** voice.*

sil·hou·ette /ˌsɪluˈet/ *noun* a dark shape or shadow on a light background: *The silhouette of a man appeared on the wall.*

sil·i·con /ˈsɪlɪkən/ *noun* (no plural) a chemical substance that is used for making glass, bricks, and computer parts: *a silicon chip*

silk /sɪlk/ *noun* (no plural) very soft material that is made from the threads produced by an insect and used for making clothes: *a silk dress*

silk·y /ˈsɪlki/ *adjective* (**silkier**, **silkiest**) soft and smooth: *silky hair*

sil·ly /ˈsɪli/ *adjective* (**sillier**, **silliest**) stupid and not sensible: *That was a silly thing to do!*

sil·ver[1] /ˈsɪlvə $ ˈsɪlvɚ/ *noun* (no plural) a valuable shiny white metal that is used for making jewellery, coins etc

silver[2] *adjective* made of silver or the colour of silver: *a silver ring*

sim card /ˈsɪm kɑːd $ ˈsɪm kɑːrd/ also **sim** *noun* a plastic card in a MOBILE PHONE that stores your personal information and allows you to use the phone

sim·i·lar /ˈsɪmələ $ ˈsɪmələ˞/ *adjective*

KEY PATTERNS
similar to someone/something

things that are similar are almost the same: *Martine and her sister **look** very similar.* • *Your taste in music is **similar to** mine.*

THESAURUS
like: *Her hairstyle is **like** mine* (=similar to mine).
alike: *He and his brother are very **alike*** (=similar).

sim·i·lar·i·ty /ˌsɪməˈlærəti/ *noun* (plural **similarities**) if there is a similarity between two things, they are the same in some way ANTONYM **difference**: *There are some similarities between the two towns.*

sim·mer /ˈsɪmə $ ˈsɪmɚ/ *verb* if food that you are cooking simmers, it boils very gently: *Let the sauce simmer for about ten minutes.*

sim·ple /ˈsɪmpəl/ *adjective*
1 not difficult or complicated SYNONYM **straightforward**: *She explained her work in simple language.* • *Using the software is very simple.*
2 plain and ordinary, without a lot of special things: *I made a simple tomato soup.*
3 simple past, simple present, simple future a tense of a verb in English that is formed without using a participle that ends in '-ing': *'Went' is the simple past of 'go'.*

sim·pli·fy /ˈsɪmpləfaɪ/ *verb* (**simplified**, **simplifies**) to make something easier to do or understand: *The college hopes to simplify its procedure for admissions.*

sim·ply /ˈsɪmpli/ *adverb* **1** used to emphasize what you are saying: *We simply can't afford a holiday this year.* • *It was simply wonderful!* **2** in a way that is easy to understand: *I'll try to explain it more simply.* **3** in a plain way, without any decoration: *She was dressed simply, in a white blouse and black skirt.*

sim·u·late /ˈsɪmjəleɪt/ *verb* to do something that seems real, but is not: *The machine simulates conditions in space.*

sim·u·la·tion /ˌsɪmjəˈleɪʃən/ *noun* an activity that is not real, but looks or feels like it is: *a simulation of a nuclear attack*

sim·ul·ta·ne·ous /ˌsɪməlˈteɪniəs $ ˌsaɪməlˈteɪniəs/ *adjective* happening at exactly the same time as something else: *Two simultaneous explosions rocked the city centre.*
—**simultaneously** *adverb*: *They both spoke simultaneously.*

sin /sɪn/ *noun* something that breaks a religious law: *They believe that jealousy is a sin.*

since /sɪns/ *preposition, adverb, conjunction*
use **since** with a past date, time, or event to say how long something has been happening: *We've lived in London since 1992* (=we began living in London in 1992, and we still live there now). • *I haven't eaten anything since yesterday* (=yesterday is the last time I ate). • *Since he arrived in England, Philippe has been staying with friends.* • *Since leaving college, Rodrigo has worked in a burger bar.* • *"How long is it since you visited Spain?" "It's nearly ten years since I was here."*

WORD CHOICE
since or **for**?
• You use **for** to talk about a period of time. You can use it with the present

perfect or the simple past tense: *I have been living here **for** years.* • *He waited **for** a few minutes.*
• You use **since** to say that something has continued to happen from a point of time in the past until now. You use it with the present perfect: *She has lived in China **since** 2002.*

sin•cere /sɪnˈsɪə $ sɪnˈsɪr/ *adjective* someone who is sincere is honest and means what they say ANTONYM **insincere**: *He said he loved the painting, but he didn't seem sincere.* • *Please accept my sincere apologies.*

sin•cere•ly /sɪnˈsɪəli $ sɪnˈsɪrli/ *adverb* **1** used to emphasize that you really mean what you are saying: *I do sincerely hope that things improve for Sammy.* **2 Yours sincerely** *BrE* something you write at the end of a formal letter before you sign your name SYNONYM **Sincerely (yours)** *AmE*

SPELLING
This word is often spelled wrongly. The correct spelling is: **sincerely**.

sing /sɪŋ/ *verb* (**sang** /sæŋ/ **sung** /sʌŋ/) to produce musical sounds with your voice: *a mother singing to her baby* • *Kerry sings in a band.* • *Will you sing that song again?*

sing•er /ˈsɪŋə $ ˈsɪŋɚ/ *noun* someone who sings, especially as a job: *a pop singer*

sin•gle¹ /ˈsɪŋgəl/ *adjective*
1 only one: *Ten thousand people visited the exhibition in a single day.* • *Not one single person* (=no one at all) *offered to help me.*
2 not married or in a serious relationship: *Brad's gorgeous – is he single?*
3 intended to be used by only one person: *a single bed* → see picture at BED
4 *BrE* a single ticket is for a trip to a place but not back again SYNONYM **one-way**
PHRASES
every single used to emphasize that you are talking about every person or thing: *She phones him **every single** day.* • *I kept **every single** letter she sent me.*

single² *noun* **1** a musical record, CD etc with only one or two songs on it: *Have you heard the new Madonna single?* **2** *BrE* a ticket to travel to a place but not back again: *a single to London*

single³ *verb* **single someone/something out** to choose one person or thing from a group because they are different to the others: *One student was singled out for special praise.*

ˌsingle ˈfile *noun* (no plural) in a line with one person behind the other: *Please walk in single file.*

ˌsingle-ˈhandedly also **ˌsingle-ˈhanded** *adverb* if you do something difficult single-handedly, you do it alone, without any help: *He single-handedly saved the company.*

ˌsingle-ˈminded *adjective* very determined to achieve one particular thing: *Clare has always been very single-minded about her career.*

ˌsingle ˈparent *noun* a mother or father who looks after their children alone, without the other parent

sin•gly /ˈsɪŋgli/ *adverb* separately or one at a time: *You can buy stamps singly or in books of ten.*

sin•gu•lar¹ /ˈsɪŋgjələ $ ˈsɪŋgjəlɚ/ *adjective* the singular form of a word is the form you use when you are talking or writing about one person or thing

singular² *noun* **the singular** the form of a word that you use when you are talking or writing about one person or thing

sin•is•ter /ˈsɪnɪstə $ ˈsɪnɪstɚ/ *adjective* unpleasant or frightening in a way that seems bad or evil: *She moved toward me with a sinister laugh.*

sink¹ /sɪŋk/ *verb* (**sank** /sæŋk/ or **sunk** /sʌŋk/, **sunk**)
1 to go down below the surface of water: *His bike fell in the river and sank.* • *The boat **sank to the bottom** of the sea.* → see picture at FLOAT¹
2 to make something go down below the surface of water: *They sank 15 enemy ships.*
PHRASES
your heart sinks: ***My heart sank*** (=I felt suddenly sad, worried, or annoyed) *when I saw that Mum was waiting for me.*

PHRASAL VERBS

sink in
(informal) if information sinks in, you finally understand it and realize the effect it will have: *He paused for a moment in order to let the news sink in.*

sink² *noun*
the thing in a kitchen or bathroom that you fill with water to wash dishes or wash your hands: *He put the dirty dishes in the sink.*

sink·ing /ˈsɪŋkɪŋ/ *adjective* **a sinking feeling** a feeling you have when you realize that something bad is going to happen: *I opened the letter with a sinking feeling.*

sip /sɪp/ *verb* (**sipped**, **sipping**) to drink something slowly, taking only small amounts into your mouth: *Maria sat at the table, sipping her coffee.* ➔ see Thesaurus at DRINK¹ —**sip** *noun*: *Can I have a sip of your wine?*

si·phon¹, **syphon** /ˈsaɪfən/ *noun* a tube that you use to take liquid out of a container

siphon², **syphon** *verb* to remove liquid from a container using a siphon: *She caught him siphoning petrol out of her car.*

sir /sə; strong sɜː $ sɚ/ *noun*
1 (spoken) a polite way of speaking to a man, for example a customer in a shop: *Can I help you, sir?* **2 Dear Sir** used at the beginning of a formal letter to a man when you do not know his name

si·ren /ˈsaɪərən $ ˈsaɪrən/ *noun* a machine in police cars, fire engines etc which makes a very loud noise to warn people that they are coming: *We heard an ambulance siren.*

sis·ter /ˈsɪstə $ ˈsɪstɚ/ *noun*
1 a girl or woman who has the same parents as you: *I share a bedroom with my sister.* • *Do you get on well with your* ***big sister*** (=older sister)? • *He's always fighting with his* ***little sister*** (=younger sister).
2 *BrE* a nurse who is in charge of a group of patients in a hospital: *The sister told me to lie down.*

ˈsister-in-ˌlaw *noun* (plural **sisters-in-law**) **1** the sister of your husband or wife **2** the wife of your brother

sit /sɪt/ *verb* (past tense and past participle **sat** /sæt/ **sitting**)

KEY PATTERNS
sit on a chair/the floor
sit next to someone
sit down

1 if you are sitting somewhere, you are resting there with your weight on your bottom: *The children were all* ***sitting on*** *the floor.* • *Who is that* ***sitting next to*** *Mary?* • *He can't* ***sit still*** (=sit and not move) *for a minute.* ➔ see picture on page A3
2 also **sit down** to lower yourself down so that you are sitting: *She walked over and sat on my desk.* • *Come in, Mr Fox, and* ***sit down****.*
3 if something is sitting somewhere, it is in that place: *The letters were still* ***sitting on*** *the table.*
4 *BrE* to do an examination: *You will be ready to* ***sit the exam*** *in June.*

PHRASAL VERBS

sit around, sit about *BrE*
to sit and not do very much: *I spent the whole day* ***sitting around*** *reading magazines.*

sit in on
sit in on something to watch a meeting or activity but not get involved in it: *Sometimes the school principal* ***sits in on*** *lessons.*

sit through
sit through something to stay until the end of something that is long or boring: *I can't* ***sit through*** *that awful film again.*

sit up
to move to a sitting position after you have been lying down: *He* ***sat up*** *and got out of bed.*

sit·com /ˈsɪtkɒm $ ˈsɪtkɑm/ *noun* a funny television programme that is shown regularly and has the same characters but a different story each time

site /saɪt/ *noun* **1** a piece of land where buildings are being built: *Children must stay off the building site.*
2 a place where something important happened in the past: *the site of the battle*

ˈsitting room a British word for LIVING ROOM

A B C D E F G H I J K L M N O P Q R S T U V W X Y Z

sit·u·at·ed /ˈsɪtʃueɪtɪd/ *adjective* **be situated** (formal) to be in a particular place: *The house is situated on a cliff overlooking the sea.*

sit·u·a·tion /ˌsɪtʃuˈeɪʃən/ *noun* the things that are happening at a particular time and place: *We are **in a** very difficult **situation**. • I think the situation is improving.*

ˈsit-ups *plural noun* an exercise in which you lie down and then lift the top part of your body towards your feet while keeping your legs flat on the floor: *He does sit-ups every morning.*

six /sɪks/ *number* 6

six·teen /ˌsɪkˈstiːn/ *number* 16 —**sixteenth** *number*

sixth /sɪksθ/ *number* **1** 6th **2** one of six equal parts of something; 1/6

ˈsixth form *noun* the classes for young people at school in Britain between the ages of 16 and 18: *You don't have to wear school uniform when you are in the sixth form.*

six·ty /ˈsɪksti/ *number* (plural **sixties**) **1** 60 **2 the sixties** the years from 1960 to 1969 **3 be in your sixties** to be aged between 60 and 69 —**sixtieth** *number*

size /saɪz/ *noun*
1 how big or small something is: *Nigel and I are about **the same size**. • The animal was **the size of** a large cat. • People's bodies vary **in size** and shape.*
2 a number, letter etc that shows how big clothes and shoes are: *What size shoes do you **take**? • These shoes are size 6. • Do you have this shirt in a bigger size?*

siz·zle /ˈsɪzəl/ *verb* to make the sound of food cooking in oil: *The sausages were sizzling in the pan.* → see picture on page A1

skate¹ /skeɪt/ *noun* **1** an ICE SKATE **2** a ROLLER SKATE

skate² *verb* to move around on skates: *Can you skate? • She skated over to him.*

> **USAGE**
> When talking about skating as an activity that you do, you say **go skating**: *We went skating in the park.*

skate·board /ˈskeɪtbɔːd $ ˈskeɪtbɔrd/ *noun* a board on wheels, that you stand on and ride for fun or sport: *All the kids come here with their skateboards.*

skateboarding

skate·board·ing /ˈskeɪtˌbɔːdɪŋ $ ˈskeɪtˌbɔrdɪŋ/ *noun* (no plural) riding on a skateboard: *Skateboarding is very popular at my school.*

skat·ing /ˈskeɪtɪŋ/ *noun* (no plural) moving around on skates: *We all love skating.*

skel·e·ton /ˈskelətən/ *noun* the bones of a whole dead person or animal: *the skeleton of a sheep* → see picture on page A5

skeptical the American spelling of SCEPTICAL

sketch¹ /sketʃ/ *noun* (plural **sketches**) a drawing of something that is done quickly and without very many details: *He made a sketch of the building.*
→ see Thesaurus at PICTURE¹

sketch² *verb* to make a drawing of something quickly: *He sketched my face.*

sketch·y /ˈsketʃi/ *adjective* (**sketchier**, **sketchiest**) sketchy information does not include a lot of details SYNONYM **vague**: *The police could only give us some very sketchy information.*

ski¹ /skiː/ *noun* skis are long narrow pieces of wood or plastic that you fasten to boots so you can move easily on snow: *He put on his skis.*

ski² *verb* (past tense and past participle **skied**, **skiing**) to move over snow on skis: *I've never learnt to ski.*

> **USAGE**
> When talking about skiing as an activity that you do, you say **go skiing**: *In winter you can go skiing in the mountains.*

skid

skid /skɪd/ *verb* (**skidded**, **skidding**) if a vehicle skids, it suddenly slides sideways and you cannot control it: *The truck skidded on the ice and crashed.* —**skid** *noun*: *He fell off his bike after a skid.*

ski•ing /ˈskiː-ɪŋ/ *noun* (no plural) the sport of moving over snow on skis: *We went skiing in Switzerland.* ➔ see picture on page A14

skil•ful *BrE*, **skillful** *AmE* /ˈskɪlfəl/ *adjective* **1** someone who is skilful is able to do something very well: *a skilful player* **2** made or done very well: *It was a skilful speech.* —**skilfully** *adverb*

skill /skɪl/ *noun* an ability to do something well, especially because you have practised it: *She played the piano* ***with great skill.*** • *The game* ***takes a lot of skill.*** • *This is an opportunity for you to* ***learn*** *new* ***skills.*** ➔ see Thesaurus at ABILITY

skilled /skɪld/ *adjective* **1** a skilled person has the training and experience that is necessary to do a particular job: *skilled workers* **2** skilled work needs special training to do it

skillful the American spelling of SKILFUL

skim /skɪm/ *verb* (**skimmed**, **skimming**) to read something very quickly and not very carefully: *I only had time to skim through the newspaper.*

ˌ**skimmed ˈmilk** *BrE*, **ˈskim milk** *AmE* *noun* (no plural) milk with most of the fat removed from it

skin¹ /skɪn/ *noun* **1** the outside part of your body: *She had smooth dark skin.* • *Babies have such lovely soft skin.* • *I have sensitive skin.* **2** the outside part of a fruit, that you take off before you eat it: *a banana skin*

skin² *verb* (**skinned**, **skinning**) to remove the skin from an animal

skin•ny /ˈskɪni/ *adjective* (**skinnier**, **skinniest**) a skinny person is too thin ➔ see Thesaurus at THIN

skip¹ /skɪp/ *verb* (**skipped**, **skipping**) **1** to jump up and down over a rope that you keep turning over your head and under your feet **2** to run with a little jump on each step: *The children skipped along the path.* ➔ see picture on page A2

skip² *noun BrE* a large open metal container in which you can put large heavy things that you do not want any more

skirt /skɜːt $ skɚt/ *noun* a piece of clothing for girls and women that fits around the waist and hangs down like a dress: *She wore a white blouse and a blue skirt.* ➔ see picture at CLOTHES

skive /skaɪv/ also **skive off** *BrE verb* (informal) to not go to school or work when you should: *The boys skived off school and went down to the shops.*

skull /skʌl/ *noun* the bones which form a person's or animal's head ➔ see picture on page A5

sky /skaɪ/ *noun* (no plural) the space above the Earth, where the sun and clouds are: *The sky is blue and the sun is shining.* • *There wasn't a cloud* ***in the sky.***

sky•scrap•er /ˈskaɪˌskreɪpə $ ˈskaɪˌskreɪpɚ/ *noun* a very tall building in a city

slab /slæb/ *noun* a thick flat piece of something: *a big slab of chocolate*

slack /slæk/ *adjective* not pulled or fastened tightly: *These trousers are a bit slack at the waist.*

slam /slæm/ *verb* (**slammed**, **slamming**) to shut a door or gate quickly and loudly, usually because you are angry: *Milly ran up to her bedroom and slammed the door behind her.* —**slam** *noun*: *She shut the door with a slam.*

slang /slæŋ/ *noun* (no plural) very informal words and expressions that are not considered to be part of the ordinary language

slant /slɑːnt $ slænt/ *verb* to slope in a particular direction: *His handwriting slants backwards.*

slap /slæp/ *verb* (**slapped**, **slapping**) to hit someone with the flat part of your hand: *She was so angry that she slapped his face.* → see Thesaurus at HIT[1] —**slap** *noun*: *She gave the child a slap on the leg.*

ˈ**slap-up** *adjective* **a slap-up meal** *BrE* (informal) a big and good meal

slash /slæʃ/ *verb* to cut something in a violent way, making a long deep cut: *A gang of boys slashed our tyres.*

slate /sleɪt/ *noun* (no plural) a type of dark grey rock, or a thin piece of this rock that is used for covering roofs

slaugh·ter /ˈslɔːtə $ ˈslɔtɚ/ *verb* **1** to kill an animal for its meat **2** to kill a lot of people in a violent way SYNONYM **massacre** —**slaughter** *noun* (no plural): *the slaughter of innocent women and children*

> PRONUNCIATION
> You pronounce **slaughter** like 'water'.

slaugh·ter·house /ˈslɔːtəhaʊs $ ˈslɔtɚˌhaʊs/ *noun* a building where animals are killed for their meat

slave[1] /sleɪv/ *noun* someone who is owned by another person and must work for them without any pay: *Slaves were used to build the pyramids.*

slave[2] *verb* (informal) to work very hard: *I've been slaving away at this essay all morning.*

sla·ve·ry /ˈsleɪvəri/ *noun* (no plural) using people as slaves: *Slavery was abolished in the US after the Civil War.*

sledge /sledʒ/ also **sled** /sled/ *noun* a vehicle for travelling on snow, or sliding down snow for fun SYNONYM **toboggan**

ˈ**sledge** ˌ**hammer** *noun* a large heavy hammer

sleek /sliːk/ *adjective* sleek hair or fur is smooth and shiny

sleep[1] /sliːp/ *verb* (past tense and past participle **slept** /slept/)

> KEY PATTERNS
> **sleep on the floor/sofa**
> **sleep well/badly**

if you are sleeping, you are resting with your eyes closed and your mind and body are not active: *Did you* ***sleep well*** *last night?* • *I sometimes* ***sleep on the*** *floor.*

PHRASES

not sleep a wink (informal) to be unable to sleep at all: ***I didn't sleep a wink*** *last night with that party going on next door.*

sleep rough *BrE* to sleep outdoors because you have no home: *Many young people* ***sleep rough*** *in London.*

PHRASAL VERBS

sleep in
to sleep until later than your usual time in the morning: *I* ***slept in*** *and was late for school.*

> WORD CHOICE
> **sleeping** or **asleep**?
> • You usually use the adjective **asleep** to describe someone who is sleeping: *The children were already* ***asleep*** *when I got home.*
> **sleep** or **go to sleep/fall asleep**?
> • You say **go to sleep** or **fall asleep** when saying that someone starts sleeping: *I went to sleep soon after I got into bed.*

sleep[2] *noun* (no plural)
when you are sleeping: *Are you* ***getting*** *plenty of* ***sleep****?* • *I'm going to* ***have a*** *little* ***sleep****.* • *I closed my eyes and* ***fell into a deep sleep****.*

PHRASES

go to sleep to start sleeping: *I* ***went to sleep*** *in the chair.*

in your sleep if you do something in your sleep, you do it when you are sleeping: *Sometimes he talks* ***in his sleep****.*

ˈ**sleeping bag** *noun* a large warm bag that you sleep in when you are camping

sleep·less /ˈsliːpləs/ *adjective* **a sleepless night** a night when you cannot sleep, for example because you are worried

sleep·y /ˈsliːpi/ *adjective* (**sleepier**, **sleepiest**) tired and ready to sleep: *I*

felt so sleepy that I went straight to bed. ➔ see Thesaurus at TIRED
—**sleepily** *adverb*

sleet /sliːt/ *noun* (no plural) a mixture of rain and snow

sleeve /sliːv/ *noun* the part of a piece of clothing that covers your arm

sleeve·less /ˈsliːvləs/ *adjective* without sleeves: *a sleeveless shirt*

slen·der /ˈslendə $ ˈslendɚ/ *adjective* thin in an attractive way SYNONYM **slim**: *a tall slender girl* ➔ see Thesaurus at THIN

slept the past tense and past participle of SLEEP[1]

slice[1] /slaɪs/ *noun*

KEY PATTERNS
a slice of bread/pizza etc

a thin piece of bread, meat etc that you cut from a larger piece: *Would you like **a slice of** pizza? • Cut the bread **in thin slices**.* ➔ see Thesaurus at PIECE

slice[2] *verb*
1 also **slice up** to cut bread, cheese, meat etc into thin pieces: *Can you slice the bread for me?* ➔ see Thesaurus at CUT[1] ➔ see picture on page A4
2 to cut through something quickly and easily: *a knife that **slices through** metal*

slid the past tense and past participle of SLIDE[1]

slide

slide slip

slide[1] /slaɪd/ *verb* (past tense and past participle **slid** /slɪd/)
1 to move smoothly: *Ducks were **sliding about** on the frozen pond.*
2 to move something smoothly: *She **slid** my drink **along** the bar. • I **slid** the letter **into** my bag.*

slide[2] *noun* **1** a photograph in a frame. You shine light through it to show the photograph on a screen: *Mr Hall showed us some slides of his trip.*
2 a long metal slope with steps at one end, that children can climb up and slide down

slight /slaɪt/ *adjective* small and not very important ANTONYM **big**, **serious**: *There's a slight problem. • He had only slight wounds.*

slight·ly /ˈslaɪtli/ *adverb* a little, but not very much: *She sounded slightly annoyed. • "Does it hurt?" "Slightly."*

slim[1] /slɪm/ *adjective* (**slimmer**, **slimmest**) thin in an attractive way: *a slim pretty girl* ➔ see Thesaurus at THIN

slim[2] *verb* (**slimmed**, **slimming**) if you are slimming, you are trying to become thinner by eating less: *I'd better not have an ice cream – I'm slimming.*

slime /slaɪm/ *noun* (no plural) any thick sticky liquid that looks or smells unpleasant: *The sink was covered in slime.*

slim·y /ˈslaɪmi/ *adjective* (**slimier**, **slimiest**) covered with slime: *a slimy dead fish*

sling[1] /slɪŋ/ *verb* (informal) (past tense and past participle **slung** /slʌŋ/) to throw or put something somewhere carelessly: *Don't just sling your jacket on the sofa – hang it up!*

sling[2] *noun* a piece of cloth that you put under your arm and then tie around your neck in order to support your arm or hand when it is injured

slip[1] /slɪp/ *verb* (**slipped**, **slipping**)

KEY PATTERNS
slip on some ice
slip into/out of a place
slip something into a container

1 if you slip, your feet move accidentally and you fall: *She **slipped on** the icy path. • Careful that you don't slip – the floor is very wet.* ➔ see Thesaurus at FALL[1]
2 to go somewhere quickly and quietly: *She must have **slipped out through** the back door.*
3 to put something somewhere quietly or secretly: *He **slipped** a sleeping pill **into** her drink.*
4 if something slips, it drops out of your hand or it moves accidentally: *My cup slipped and dropped on the floor.*

A B C D E F G H I J K L M N O P Q R S T U V W X Y Z

A B C D E F G H I J K L M N O P Q R S T U V W X Y Z

PHRASES

slip your mind (spoken) if something slips your mind, you forget about it: *She asked me to phone you, but it **slipped** my **mind**.*

let something slip (informal) to say something that is supposed to be a secret without intending to: *Mary **let it slip** about John's surprise party.*

PHRASAL VERBS

slip into

slip into something (informal) to put on a piece of clothing quickly and easily: *She **slipped into** her pyjamas.*

slip off

slip something off (informal) to take off a piece of clothing quickly and easily: *Just **slip off** your jacket.*

slip on

slip something on (informal) to put on a piece of clothing, quickly and easily: *Jean got out of bed and **slipped on** her dressing gown.*

slip out

(informal) if something slips out, you say it without intending to: *Before she could stop herself, the words had **slipped out**.*

slip² *noun* **1** a small piece of paper: *She wrote the number on a slip of paper.* **2** a small mistake: *The team only made a couple of slips during the whole game.* → see Thesaurus at MISTAKE[1]

slip·per /ˈslɪpə $ ˈslɪpɚ/ *noun* a soft shoe that you wear indoors → see picture at SHOE

slip·per·y /ˈslɪpəri/ *adjective* something that is slippery is difficult to walk on or hold because it is wet, oily, or covered in ice: *It had snowed in the night and the roads were very slippery.*

slit¹ /slɪt/ *noun* a long narrow cut or opening: *a long dress with a slit up one side*

slit² *verb* (past tense and past participle **slit**, **slitting**) to make a long narrow cut in something: *I slit open the envelope with a knife.*

slob /slɒb $ slɑb/ *noun* (informal) someone who is lazy, dirty, or untidy

slo·gan /ˈsləʊgən $ ˈsloʊgən/ *noun* a short clever phrase that is used in advertising and politics

slope¹ /sləʊp $ sloʊp/ *noun* a piece of ground that gradually gets higher or lower: *Go up the slope till you get to the top of the hill.*

slope² *verb* if a road or path slopes down or up, it gradually gets lower or higher: *a garden that slopes down to the river*

slop·py /ˈslɒpi $ ˈslɑpi/ *adjective* (informal) (**sloppier**, **sloppiest**) not tidy or careful SYNONYM **careless**: *a sloppy piece of work*

slot /slɒt $ slɑt/ *noun* a long narrow hole in something, especially one for putting coins in: *Put the money in the slot.*

ˈslot maˌchine *noun* a machine that you put coins into to play a game and try to win money

slouch /slaʊtʃ/ *verb* to stand, sit, or walk in a lazy way, with your shoulders bent forward: *My mother's always telling me not to slouch.*

slow¹ /sləʊ $ sloʊ/ *adjective*
1 not moving or happening quickly ANTONYM **fast**: *This computer's very slow! • It was quite a slow journey because the roads were very busy. • Jamie's a very slow worker.*
2 a clock that is slow shows a time earlier than the true time ANTONYM **fast**: *My watch is two minutes slow.*
3 someone who is slow does not understand things very quickly or easily ANTONYM **bright**: *Some of the children in her class are a bit slow.*

slow² also **slow down** *verb* to become slower or make something slower: *The car slowed down and stopped. • It started to rain, which slowed down the rescue.*

slow·ly /ˈsləʊli $ ˈsloʊli/ *adverb* at a slow speed ANTONYM **quickly**: *I drove slowly into the drive. • Can you speak more slowly?*

ˌslow ˈmotion *noun* (no plural) if part of a film or television programme is shown in slow motion, it is shown at a slower speed than the real speed: *Let's look at the end of the race again in slow motion.*

slug /slʌg/ *noun* a small creature with a soft body that moves very slowly along the ground

slum /slʌm/ *noun* a house that is in very bad condition, where poor people live

slump /slʌmp/ *verb* if a price or value slumps, it suddenly becomes less ANTONYM **soar**: *House prices slumped last year.* —**slump** *noun*: *Many people are now expecting a slump in the economy.*

slung the past tense and past participle of SLING[1]

slurp /slɜːp $ slɚp/ *verb* (informal) to drink in a noisy way

slush /slʌʃ/ *noun* (no plural) snow that has partly melted and looks wet and dirty

sly /slaɪ/ *adjective* someone who is sly tries to get what they want by lying to people or not being completely honest: *He's sly and greedy.*

smack[1] /smæk/ *verb* to hit someone with the inside part of your hand as a punishment: *I don't agree with smacking children.* ➔ see Thesaurus at HIT[1] —**smack** *noun*: *When I was young, teachers were allowed to give you a smack.*

smack[2] *adverb* (informal) exactly in a place: *She was standing smack in the middle of the road.*

small /smɔːl/ *adjective*
1 not big: *There's a small hole in the roof.* • *A small number of students behaved badly.* • *My mom is smaller than me.*
2 not important ANTONYM **big**: *It's only a small problem.*

> THESAURUS
> **little**: *Can I have a little piece of cake* (=small)?
> **tiny**: *a tiny insect* (=very small)
> **minute**: *minute particles of dust* (=extremely small)

small·pox /ˈsmɔːlpɒks $ ˈsmɔlpɑks/ *noun* (no plural) a serious disease that killed a lot of people in the past

smart /smɑːt $ smɑrt/ *adjective*
1 (informal) intelligent SYNONYM **clever**: *John's much smarter than his brother.* • *Lucy is a smart kid.* ➔ see Thesaurus at INTELLIGENT
2 if you look smart, you are dressed in a neat and attractive way: *She looked very smart in her new uniform.* • *Alan was dressed in a smart suit.* —**smartly** *adverb*: *It's important to dress smartly for interviews.*

smart·phone /ˈsmɑːtfəʊn $ ˈsmɑrtfoʊn/ *noun* a MOBILE PHONE that you can also use as a PDA (=a very small computer that you can use for storing information, sending emails etc)

smash[1] /smæʃ/ *verb* to break into a lot of small pieces, or to make something break in this way: *When I dropped the cup, it smashed.* • *A stone smashed the car windscreen.* ➔ see Thesaurus at BREAK[1] ➔ see picture at BREAK[1]

smash[2] also **ˌsmash ˈhit** *noun* a very successful new song, film, or play: *The film is expected to be a smash hit at the box office.*

smear[1] /smɪə $ smɪr/ *verb* **1** to spread a soft substance on a surface: *Someone had smeared mud on the walls.* **2 be smeared with something** to be partly covered with a soft substance, especially in a way that looks unpleasant: *His hands were smeared with blood.*

smear[2] *noun* a dirty mark: *There were smears of paint on his face.* ➔ see Thesaurus at MARK[2]

smell[1] /smel/ *verb* (past tense and past participle **smelled** or **smelt** /smelt/)

> KEY PATTERNS
> **smell good/nice etc**
> **smell like something**
> **smell of something**

1 how something smells is what you notice about it, using your nose: *That soup smells delicious!* • *a perfume that smells like fresh flowers* • *The room smelled of cigarette smoke.*
2 if something smells, it has an unpleasant smell SYNONYM **stink**: *Your feet smell!*
3 if you can smell something, you can notice or recognize it with your nose: *I'm sure I can smell gas.*
4 if you smell something, you put your nose close to it to discover what kind of smell it has: *Smell this sauce – it's delicious.*

A B C D E F G H I J K L M N O P Q R S T U V W X Y Z

smell² *noun*

KEY PATTERNS
the smell of smoke/paint etc
have a nice/strong etc smell

1 the smell of something is what you notice about it, using your nose: *I love **the smell of** fresh coffee.* • *Some of the flowers have quite a **strong smell**.*
2 an unpleasant smell: *There's a **terrible smell** in the kitchen.* • *What's that **awful smell**?*
3 sense of smell your sense of smell is your ability to notice and recognize smells: *I've got a cold, so my **sense of smell** isn't very good.*

THESAURUS
scent/fragrance: *The roses had a lovely **scent*** (=a pleasant smell).
aroma: *the **aroma** of fresh coffee* (=a pleasant smell)
odour *BrE*, **odor** *AmE*: *The house had a strong **odour*** (=an unpleasant smell).
stench/stink: *the **stench** of rotting meat* (=a very strong unpleasant smell)

smell·y /'smeli/ *adjective* (**smellier**, **smelliest**) something that is smelly has a strong unpleasant smell: *This fish is a bit smelly.* • *smelly socks*

smelt a past tense and past participle of SMELL[1]

smile¹ /smaɪl/ *verb*

KEY PATTERNS
smile at someone

if you smile, the sides of your mouth curve upwards because you are happy: *Sue **smiled at** the children in a friendly way.* • *"It's lovely to see you again," she said smiling.* • *Come on – smile for the camera!*

THESAURUS
grin: *He **grinned** at her cheerfully* (=smiled widely).
beam: *She **beamed** with pleasure at the compliment* (=smiled very happily).
smirk: *He **smirked** at his defeated opponent* (=smiled in an unpleasant and annoying way).

smile² *noun*
when the sides of your mouth curve upwards because you are happy: *"Hello," she said, with a smile.* • *Dan **had a big smile on his face**.*

smirk /smɜːk $ smɜ˞k/ *verb* to smile in an unpleasant way, as though you are laughing at someone: *The other girls pointed at her and smirked.* ➔ see Thesaurus at SMILE[1]

smog /smɒg $ smɑg/ *noun* (no plural) unhealthy air in cities that is a mixture of smoke, gases, chemicals etc

smoke¹ /sməʊk $ smoʊk/ *noun* (no plural)
the white or grey gas that comes from something that is burning: *Smoke was coming from the chimney.* • *I could smell **cigarette smoke** on his clothes.*

smoke² *verb* to breathe in smoke from a cigarette or pipe: *Are you allowed to smoke at work?* • *a man who smokes 30 cigarettes a day* —**smoker** *noun*

smok·ing /'sməʊkɪŋ $ 'smoʊkɪŋ/ *noun* (no plural) the habit of smoking cigarettes or a pipe: *Smoking is very bad for you.*

smok·y /'sməʊki $ 'smoʊki/ *adjective* (**smokier**, **smokiest**) full of smoke: *The room was crowded and smoky.*

smol·der /'sməʊldə $ 'smoʊldə˞/ the American spelling of SMOULDER

smooth¹ /smuːð/ *adjective*
1 something that is smooth has an even surface ANTONYM **rough**: *Your skin feels so smooth.* • *What a beautiful cat – its fur is so lovely and smooth.* • *Make sure the walls are smooth before you paint them.* ➔ see Thesaurus at FLAT[1] ➔ see picture at ROUGH
2 a smooth substance has no big pieces in it: *Stir the mixture into a smooth paste.*
3 a smooth movement is graceful and has no sudden changes: *With a smooth turn, he caught the ball.*

smooth² *verb* to make something flat by moving your hands over it: *He carefully smoothed his hair.*

smooth·ie /'smuːði/ *noun* a thick drink made from fruit and sometimes milk or YOGHURT: *I'll have a strawberry smoothie.*

smooth·ly /'smuːðli/ *adverb* if something happens smoothly, it happens without any problems: *I hope everything goes smoothly when you move house.*

smoth·er /ˈsmʌðə $ ˈsmʌðɚ/ *verb* to kill someone by putting something over their face so that they cannot breathe

smoul·der *BrE*, **smolder** *AmE* /ˈsməʊldə $ ˈsmoʊldɚ/ *verb* if a fire is smouldering, it is burning slowly, with smoke but without flames: *The fire was still smouldering when I went to bed.*

SMS /ˌes em ˈes/ *noun* the abbreviation of 'Short Message Service'; a system that allows you to send or receive written messages by MOBILE PHONE: *She's always sending SMS messages to her friends.*

smudge¹ /smʌdʒ/ *noun* a dirty mark made by a pencil mark or ink: *The teacher complained that there were smudges all over my homework.*

smudge² *verb* if you smudge ink or paint, it makes a dirty mark

smug /smʌg/ *adjective* very pleased with yourself, in a way that is annoying to other people: *"I told you that would happen," she said with a smug smile.*

smug·gle /ˈsmʌgəl/ *verb* to secretly bring something or someone into a country, when it is illegal to do this: *She was accused of smuggling drugs.* • *Some friends smuggled him into the country.* —**smuggler** *noun*: *a drug smuggler*

snack /snæk/ *noun* a small quick meal

> **WORD CHOICE**
> **snack** or **snack bar**?
> • A **snack** is a quick small meal.
> • A **snack bar** is a place where you can buy quick meals and drinks.

ˈsnack bar *noun* a place where you can buy quick meals and drinks

snag /snæg/ *noun* (informal) a small difficulty or problem ➔ see Thesaurus at PROBLEM

snail /sneɪl/ *noun* a small garden creature that has a round shell on its back and moves very slowly

snake /sneɪk/ *noun* a long thin animal that slides across the ground and sometimes bites people ➔ see picture on page A9

snap¹ /snæp/ *verb* (**snapped**, **snapping**) **1** if something snaps, it breaks suddenly with a short loud noise: *Just at that moment the branch snapped.* ➔ see picture on page A1 **2** to speak suddenly in an angry way: *"I don't agree at all," she snapped.*

snap² *noun* **1** a sudden loud noise of something breaking: *The branch broke with a snap.* **2** also **snap·shot** /ˈsnæpʃɒt $ ˈsnæpʃɑt/ (informal) a photograph: *holiday snapshots*

snap³ *adjective* **snap decision, snap judgement** a decision or judgement that is made quickly and not very carefully

snarl /snɑːl $ snɑrl/ *verb* **1** to say something in an angry way: *"Go away!" he snarled.* **2** if an animal snarls, it makes a low angry sound and shows its teeth: *The dog started snarling at me.* —**snarl** *noun*

snarl

a snarling tiger

snatch¹ /snætʃ/ *verb* to take something from someone with a quick sudden movement SYNONYM **grab**: *I snatched the letter from him.*

snatch² *noun* (plural **snatches**) **a snatch of conversation** a short part of a conversation that you hear: *I could only hear snatches of their conversation.*

sneak /sniːk/ *verb* **1** to go somewhere quietly and secretly SYNONYM **creep**: *I managed to sneak into her bedroom.* **2 sneak up on someone** to move close to someone without them noticing you: *Stop sneaking up on me like that!*

sneak·er /ˈsniːkə $ ˈsnikɚ/ *noun AmE* a sports shoe

sneak·ing /ˈsniːkɪŋ/ *adjective* **have a sneaking suspicion, have a sneaking feeling** to think that something is true but not feel sure: *I have a sneaking suspicion that she's lying.*

sneak·y /ˈsniːki/ *adjective* (**sneakier**, **sneakiest**) doing things in a secret and clever but unfair way

sneer /snɪə $ snɪr/ *verb* to look at someone or speak to them in a way that shows you have no respect for them: *She sneers at people who are poor.*

sneeze /sniːz/ *verb* when you sneeze, air suddenly comes out of your nose and mouth in a noisy way: *Cats make me sneeze.* —**sneeze** *noun*: *He let out an enormous sneeze.*

sneeze

sniff /snɪf/ *verb* **1** to breathe in quickly through your nose: *She couldn't stop sniffing and coughing.* **2** to smell something: *I sniffed the milk to see if it was sour.* —**sniff** *noun*: *Take a sniff at these socks.*

snig·ger /ˈsnɪgə $ ˈsnɪgɚ/ *BrE*, **snick·er** /ˈsnɪkə $ ˈsnɪkɚ/ *AmE verb* to laugh quietly in an unpleasant way: *What are you sniggering at?* → see Thesaurus at LAUGH[1]

snip /snɪp/ *verb* (**snipped**, **snipping**) to cut something with quick small cuts, using scissors: *Snip the corner off the packet.*

snip·pet /ˈsnɪpɪt/ *noun* (informal) a small piece of information or news SYNONYM **bit**: *I heard snippets of the story from my sister.*

snob /snɒb $ snɑb/ *noun* someone who thinks they are better than other people

snoo·ker /ˈsnuːkə $ ˈsnʊkɚ/ *noun* (no plural) a game in which you hit coloured balls into holes around the edge of a green table, using a long stick called a CUE

snoop /snuːp/ *verb* to go into someone's room and look at their private things: *I caught Jo snooping around my room.*

snooze /snuːz/ *verb* (informal) to sleep for a short time SYNONYM **doze**: *Jack was snoozing by the fire.* —**snooze** *noun*: *I think I'll have a snooze.*

snore /snɔː $ snɔr/ *verb* to make a loud noise as you sleep: *Stop snoring!* —**snore** *noun*: *Loud snores were coming from the bedroom.*

snort /snɔːt $ snɔrt/ *verb* to make a loud noise by forcing air out through your nose because you think something is unpleasant or funny: *He read the letter and snorted in disgust.*

snot /snɒt $ snɑt/ *noun* (no plural) (informal) an impolite word for the thick liquid in your nose

snout /snaʊt/ *noun* an animal's long nose: *a pig's snout*

snow[1] /snəʊ $ snoʊ/ *noun* (no plural) soft white pieces of frozen water that fall like rain when the weather is very cold: *The fields were* ***covered with snow****.* • *Several roads were blocked by deep snow.*

snow[2] *verb*

KEY PATTERNS
it's snowing

when it snows, snow falls from the sky: *Mum, look,* ***it's snowing****!* • *Children love it when* ***it snows****.*

PHRASES

be snowed in, get snowed in to be unable to leave a place because so much snow has fallen: *Maybe we'll* ***get snowed in*** *and we won't be able to go to school.*

snow·ball /ˈsnəʊbɔːl $ ˈsnoʊbɔl/ *noun* a small ball made out of snow: *Who threw that snowball?*

snow·board·ing /ˈsnəʊˌbɔːdɪŋ $ ˈsnoʊˌbɔrdɪŋ/ *noun* (no plural) a sport in which you move over the snow on a long wide board

snow·flake /ˈsnəʊfleɪk $ ˈsnoʊfleɪk/ *noun* one small piece of snow that falls from the sky

snow·man /ˈsnəʊmæn $ ˈsnoʊmæn/ *noun* (plural **snowmen** /-men/) the shape of a person, made out of snow

snow·plough *BrE*, **snowplow** *AmE* /ˈsnəʊplaʊ $ ˈsnoʊplaʊ/ *noun* a vehicle for removing snow from roads

snow·y /ˈsnəʊi $ ˈsnoʊi/ *adjective* (**snowier**, **snowiest**) if it is snowy, there is a lot of snow: *a snowy day*

snub /snʌb/ *verb* (**snubbed**, **snubbing**) to deliberately not talk to someone or not be friendly towards them: *She always snubs me when she sees me.*

A B C D E F G H I J K L M N O P Q R S T U V W X Y Z

snug /snʌg/ *adjective* warm and comfortable SYNONYM **cosy**: *a snug little bed*

snug·gle /ˈsnʌgəl/ *verb* to get into a warm comfortable position: *Ed and Sara snuggled up on the sofa.*

so[1] /səʊ $ soʊ/ *conjunction*
1 because of something: *I had a headache, so I couldn't go to the party.* • *It was a lovely day, so we went to the beach.*
2 also **so that** in order to make something possible: *Can you draw a map so that I can find your house?* • *Mum gave me some money so I could buy Dad a present.*

so[2] *adverb*
1 use **so** in place of what someone has just asked you, to avoid repeating it: *"Has Jo got a dog?" "I think so* (=I think Jo has a dog)*."* • *Are you interested in films? If so* (=if you are interested in films)*, join our film club.* • *"Will you be going on holiday this year?" "Yes, I expect so."*
2 also SYNONYM **too**: *"I'm studying German." "So am I* (=I'm studying German too)*".* • *"I like living in Berlin." "So do I* (=I like living in Berlin too)*."* • *"I've spent too much money today." "So have I."* • *She's fair-haired, and so is her father.*
3 use **so** with an adjective or an adverb to make it stronger or to explain why something happened: *He's so good-looking!* • *You've been so kind to us during our stay.* • *I was **so** tired **that** I fell asleep immediately.* • *He was driving so fast I thought we'd crash.*
4 (spoken) use **so** to start a conversation or start talking about something different: *So, what did you do on your birthday?* • *So, after arguing for half an hour, we all agreed to go to Gino's Pizza.*

PHRASES

and so on used at the end of a list to show that you could add more things of the same type: *Bring a towel, sunglasses, suntan oil, **and so on**.*
so many, so much used to emphasize that a number or amount is very big: *You shouldn't worry **so much**.* • *She had **so many** things to do, she didn't know where to start.* • *I didn't realize **so many** people would turn up.* • *Carrie has changed **so much** since she went to college.*
or so used with an amount to show that it could be slightly bigger or slightly smaller: *Geoff is staying with us for a week **or so**.* • *There were 20 **or so** people in the room.*
so much for something (informal, spoken) used to say that something was not as good or successful as you had hoped: ***So much for** your map-reading! We're lost!*
so that in order to make something possible: *She's studying English so that she can get a better job.*
So what?, So? (informal, spoken) used to show that you do not care about what someone has just said: *"You've already bought a new computer game this week." "**So what?**"*

> **WORD CHOICE**
> **so** or **such**?
> • You use **so** before an adjective on its own: *I'm **so** tired!* • *He's **so** good-looking!*
> • You use **such a/an** before an adjective and a noun: *It's **such a** nice day!* • *It's **such an** ugly building!*

soak /səʊk $ soʊk/ *verb*

> **KEY PATTERNS**
> **soak clothes/fruit etc in water**
> **water soaks through/into something**

1 if you soak something, or let it soak, you cover it with water and leave it for a period of time: *It's best to soak very dirty clothes before you wash them.* • ***Soak** the beans **in** water overnight before you cook them.* • ***Leave** those dishes **to soak**.*
2 if a liquid soaks something, it makes it completely wet: *The rain has soaked her clothes.* • *The water had **soaked through** my shoes.* • *He was sweating a lot and it was **soaking into** his shirt.*

PHRASAL VERBS

soak up
soak something up if something soaks up a liquid, it takes the liquid into itself: *He used some paper to **soak up** the spilt drinks.*

soaked /səʊkt $ soʊkt/ *adjective* very wet SYNONYM **drenched**: *I'm completely soaked.*

soak·ing /ˈsəʊkɪŋ $ ˈsoʊkɪŋ/ also **ˌsoaking ˈwet** *adjective* completely wet: *The washing's still soaking wet.*

soap /səʊp $ soʊp/ *noun* **1** (no plural) a substance that you use to wash yourself: *a bar of soap* **2** (informal) a soap opera

ˈsoap ˌopera *noun* a television story about the ordinary lives of a group of people

soap·y /ˈsəʊpi $ ˈsoʊpi/ *adjective* soapy water has soap in it

soar /sɔː $ sɔr/ *verb* to increase quickly SYNONYM **shoot up**, **rocket**: *The price of houses has soared in recent months.*

sob /sɒb $ sɑb/ *verb* (**sobbed**, **sobbing**) to cry with quick noisy breaths: *She just wouldn't stop sobbing.* • *"I want him back," she sobbed.* —**sob** *noun*: *Melanie couldn't hide her sobs.*

so·ber[1] /ˈsəʊbə $ ˈsoʊbɚ/ *adjective* not drunk: *I can't tell if he's drunk or sober.*

sober[2] *verb* **sober up** to stop being drunk: *You need to sober up before you go home.*

ˈso-called *adjective* used when you think that a person or thing is not what people say they are: *That so-called expert has completely ruined my hair.*

soc·cer /ˈsɒkə $ ˈsɑkɚ/ *noun* (no plural) a game in which two teams try to kick a ball into a net at each end of a field; SYNONYM **football**

so·cia·ble /ˈsəʊʃəbəl $ ˈsoʊʃəbəl/ *adjective* someone who is sociable is friendly and enjoys being with people: *a very sociable child*

> **THESAURUS**
> **outgoing**: *She is more confident and outgoing than her sister* (=sociable).
> **extrovert**: *He was an* **extrovert** *who enjoyed going to parties* (=a sociable person).

so·cial /ˈsəʊʃəl $ ˈsoʊʃəl/ *adjective* **1** relating to the way people live in society: *Unemployment is a big social problem in this country.* **2** relating to things that you do with other people for enjoyment: *He works so hard that he doesn't have time for a social life.* —**socially** *adverb*: *We never go out socially.*

so·cial·is·m /ˈsəʊʃəlɪzəm $ ˈsoʊʃəˌlɪzəm/ *noun* (no plural) a political system that tries to give equal opportunities to all people, and in which many industries are owned by the state

so·cial·ist /ˈsəʊʃəlɪst $ ˈsoʊʃəlɪst/ *noun* someone who believes in socialism —**socialist** *adjective*: *a society built on socialist ideas*

so·cial·ize also **socialise** *BrE* /ˈsəʊʃəlaɪz $ ˈsoʊʃəlaɪz/ *verb* to go out with people for enjoyment: *I never socialize with people from work.*

ˈsocial work *noun* (no plural) the job of helping people who are poor or have problems with their families

ˈsocial ˌworker *noun* someone whose job is doing social work

so·ci·e·ty /səˈsaɪəti/ *noun* (plural **societies**) all the people who live in the same country and share the same way of life: *We live in a multi-racial society.*

so·ci·ol·o·gy /ˌsəʊsiˈɒlədʒi $ ˌsoʊsiˈɑlədʒi/ *noun* (no plural) the study of the relationships between different groups of people in society

sock /sɒk $ sɑk/ *noun* a piece of clothing that you wear on your foot: *a pair of woollen socks* ➔ see picture at UNDERWEAR

sock·et /ˈsɒkɪt $ ˈsɑkɪt/ *noun* **1** the place in a wall where you can connect electrical equipment to the supply of electricity **2** the place where one thing fits into another: *You nearly pulled my arm out of its socket!*

so·da /ˈsəʊdə $ ˈsoʊdə/ also **ˈsoda ˌwater** *noun* water containing bubbles that you mix with other drinks

so·fa /ˈsəʊfə $ ˈsoʊfə/ *noun* a comfortable seat that is wide enough for two or three people SYNONYM **settee** *BrE*

soft /sɒft $ sɔft/ *adjective* **1** if something is soft, you can press it easily because it is not hard or firm ANTONYM **hard**: *a soft chair* • *The ground was quite soft.* **2** something that feels soft feels smooth and pleasant when you touch

A B C D E F G H I J K L M N O P Q R S T U V W X Y Z

it: *the cat's soft fur* • *Your skin is lovely and soft.* • *I like silk – it's so soft to touch.* • *The wool felt soft against my skin.*
3 soft sounds are quiet: *She spoke in a soft voice.* → see Thesaurus at QUIET[1]
—**softly** *adverb*

'soft drink *noun* a cold drink that does not contain alcohol

soft·en /'sɒfən $ 'sɔfən/ *verb* to become softer ANTONYM **harden**: *Your shoes will soften as you wear them.*

> **PRONUNCIATION**
> In this word you do not pronounce the **t**.

soft·ware /'sɒftweə $ 'sɔft-wer/ *noun* (no plural)
the programs that a computer uses to do different jobs: *Have you* ***installed*** *the new* ***software****?* • *First you need to* ***load*** *the software* ***onto*** *your computer.*

sog·gy /'sɒgi $ 'sɑgi/ *adjective* wet and soft in an unpleasant way: *My sandwiches are all soggy.*

soil /sɔɪl/ *noun*
the earth in which plants grow: *Water the soil well when you plant out the young lettuces.* → see picture on page A10

so·lar /'səʊlə $ 'soʊlɚ/ *adjective* relating to or using the sun: *solar power*

'solar ˌsystem *noun* the sun and all the PLANETS that move around it: *Jupiter is the biggest planet in our solar system.*

sold the past tense and past participle of SELL

sol·dier /'səʊldʒə $ 'soʊldʒɚ/ *noun* someone who is in the army

ˌsold-'out *adjective* if a concert or other event is sold-out, all the tickets have been sold

sole[1] /səʊl $ soʊl/ *adjective* only: *He was the sole survivor of the accident.*

sole[2] *noun* the bottom surface of your foot or shoe: *I had a huge blister on the sole of my foot.* → see picture at SHOE

sole·ly /'səʊl-li $ 'soʊli/ *adverb* (formal) only: *This club is solely for students.*

sol·emn /'sɒləm $ 'sɑləm/ *adjective* serious and slightly sad: *I knew from the solemn expression on his face that something was wrong.*

sol·id[1] /'sɒlɪd $ 'sɑlɪd/ *adjective*
1 hard or firm, and not a liquid or gas: *He was too ill to eat solid food.* • *The lake was frozen solid.* → see Thesaurus at HARD[1] **2** having no space or holes inside: *a solid rubber ball*
3 solid gold, solid oak etc made only of gold, oak etc and not another metal or wood: *a solid gold chain*

solid[2] *noun* a substance that is not a liquid or a gas: *Wood is a solid.*

sol·i·ta·ry /'sɒlətəri $ 'sɑləˌteri/ *adjective* a solitary person or thing is the only one: *a solitary cottage on the side of the hill*

so·lo[1] /'səʊləʊ $ 'soʊloʊ/ *adjective, adverb* a solo activity is one that you do alone: *She did a wonderful solo dance.*

solo[2] *noun* a piece of music for one performer

so·lo·ist /'səʊləʊɪst $ 'soʊloʊɪst/ *noun* a musician who performs a solo

so·lu·tion /sə'luːʃən/ *noun* **1** the answer to a difficult question or problem: *Have you found the solution to that maths problem?* • *The only solution was to share the money.* **2** a liquid mixed with a solid or a gas: *a solution of salt and water*

solve /sɒlv $ sɑlv/ *verb*
1 to find a successful way to deal with a problem: *Students and teachers need to* ***solve*** *this* ***problem*** *by working together.*
2 to find the answer to something: *The police have been unable to* ***solve*** *the* ***murder****.*

som·bre *BrE*, **somber** *AmE* /'sɒmbə $ 'sɑmbɚ/ *adjective* sad and serious: *He was in a sombre mood.*

some[1] /səm; strong sʌm/ *determiner, pronoun*
1 an amount or number of something, but not a large amount or number. Use **some** when you are not saying exactly what the number or amount is: *"Would you like some cake?" "Yes, I'd love some."* • *Could I have* ***some more*** *tea?* • *There were some children*

A B C D E F G H I J K L M N O P Q R S T U V W X Y Z

playing in the street. • *He brought some pictures of his holiday to show us.*
2 a few people or things from a group, or part of an amount, but not all: *I've met* ***some of*** *Jack's friends.* • *Some babies start walking before they are a year old.* • *Anne has spent* ***some of*** *the money she got for her birthday.*
3 (spoken) use **some** to talk about a person or thing when you do not know their name or details about them, or when it is not important to say the name or details: *Some guy asked me for the time.* • *I read about it in some magazine.*

> WORD CHOICE
> **some** or **any**?
> • Use **some** in questions when you think the answer will be 'yes': *Would you like some coffee?*
> • Use **any** when you do not know what the answer will be: *Were there any letters for me?*

some² *adverb* a little more or less than a particular number: *Some 30 students have already completed the course.*

some·bod·y /ˈsʌmbɒdi $ ˈsʌmbɑdi/ *pronoun*
someone

some·day /ˈsʌmdeɪ/ *adverb* at an unknown time in the future: *Maybe someday I'll get married!*

some·how /ˈsʌmhaʊ/ *adverb* (informal)
in some way, although you do not know how: *We need to get the money back somehow.*

some·one /ˈsʌmwʌn/ also **somebody** *pronoun*
used to mention a person without saying who the person is: *Someone phoned you this morning.* • *She always tries to blame* ***someone else*** (=a different person) *when something goes wrong.*

> GRAMMAR
> In questions and negative sentences we usually use **anyone** and not **someone**.

some·place /ˈsʌmpleɪs/ *adverb AmE*
somewhere

som·er·sault /ˈsʌməsɔːlt $ ˈsʌmɚˌsɔlt/ *noun* a movement in which you roll forwards until your feet go over your head and touch the ground again: *She did a somersault in the air.*

some·thing /ˈsʌmθɪŋ/ *pronoun*
a thing: *I'm just going out to get something to eat.* • *There's something sticky on the bottom of my shoe.* • *Steven told me something very interesting.* • *Don't just stand there – do something!* • *Can't you use* ***something else*** (=some other thing) *instead?*
PHRASES
something like used when giving a number or amount that is not exact: *The journey will take* ***something like*** *four hours.*

some·time /ˈsʌmtaɪm/ *adverb* (spoken) at an unknown time in the past or future: *I'll call you sometime tomorrow.*

some·times /ˈsʌmtaɪmz/ *adverb*
on some occasions, but not always: *I go there for lunch sometimes.*

> GRAMMAR
> **Sometimes** usually comes before the main verb, and after words like 'is', 'have' etc: *Dad sometimes gets home late.*

some·what /ˈsʌwɒt $ ˈsʌmwʌt/ *adverb* (formal) a little, but not very much: *The weather improved somewhat in the second week.*

some·where /ˈsʌmweə $ ˈsʌmwer/ also **someplace** *AmE adverb*
in a place, although you do not know exactly where: *I put my keys down somewhere and now I can't find them.* • *Diane lives somewhere in London.* • *Let's sit* ***somewhere else*** (=somewhere different), *it's too noisy here.*
PHRASES
somewhere around, somewhere between a little more or a little less than a particular number: *There will be* ***somewhere between*** *40 and 50 people there.* • *It'll cost* ***somewhere around*** *£200.*

> GRAMMAR
> In questions and negative sentences we usually use **anywhere** and not **somewhere**.

son /sʌn/ *noun* your male child: *I have two sons and a daughter.*

song /sɒŋ $ sɔːŋ/ *noun*
a short piece of music with words that you can sing: *The kids were singing songs.*

'son-in-ˌlaw *noun* (plural **sons-in-law**) the husband of your daughter

soon /suːn/ *adverb*
after a short time: *We'll have to leave soon if we want to catch the bus.* • *We'll see you again soon!* • *I want the information* ***as soon as possible.*** • *He soon realized that he was in the wrong job.*

PHRASES
as soon as immediately after something has happened: *I'll call you* ***as soon as*** *I get any news from the hospital.* • ***As soon as*** *I saw him, I recognized his face.*
sooner or later (spoken) if something will happen sooner or later, it will definitely happen but you are not sure when: ***Sooner or later*** *he's going to find out the truth.*

THESAURUS
shortly (formal): *Please take your seats; the performance will begin* ***shortly*** (=soon).
before long: ***Before long,*** *the whole house was on fire* (=soon).
in a minute (spoken): *I'll be back* ***in a minute*** (=within a few minutes).
in a moment: *I'll get you a drink* ***in a moment*** (=very soon).
any minute now (spoken): *They should be here* ***any minute now*** (=very soon, but I do not know exactly when).

soot /sʊt/ *noun* (no plural) black powder that is produced when something burns

soothe /suːð/ *verb* to make someone feel better SYNONYM **calm**: *Music will often soothe a crying baby.*

so·phis·ti·cat·ed /səˈfɪstəkeɪtɪd/ *adjective* **1** someone who is sophisticated has a modern fashionable life: *a sophisticated city girl* **2** a sophisticated machine is designed in a very clever way and is more modern than similar machines: *a sophisticated computer*

sop·py /ˈsɒpi $ ˈsɑpi/ *adjective BrE* (informal) (**soppier, soppiest**) expressing sadness or love in a silly way: *a soppy film*

so·pra·no /səˈprɑːnəʊ $ səˈprænoʊ/ *noun* a female singer with a high voice

sor·did /ˈsɔːdɪd $ ˈsɔrdɪd/ *adjective* unpleasant and dishonest: *He told me all the sordid details of his love affair.*

sore[1] /sɔː $ sɔr/ *adjective*
painful: *I woke up with a* ***sore throat.*** • *Sophie was tired, and her arm still* ***felt sore.*** • *My legs are sore from running so far.* → see Thesaurus at HURT[1]

sore[2] *noun* a painful infected wound on your body: *His body was covered with sores.*

sor·row /ˈsɒrəʊ $ ˈsɑroʊ/ *noun* (formal) a feeling of great sadness

sor·ry /ˈsɒri $ ˈsɑri/ *adjective*

KEY PATTERNS
sorry about something
sorry for being late
sorry that
sorry to wake/interrupt etc you

1 if you are sorry, you feel bad about something that you have done and wish you had not done it: *I'm sorry, I didn't mean to scare you.* • *I'm* ***sorry about*** *the food being late.* • ***Sorry,*** *did I hurt you?* • ***I'm sorry for*** *calling you so late.* • *Sarah said she* ***was sorry that*** *she lost her temper.* • *Bill, I'm* ***sorry to*** *wake you, but Jennifer's on the phone.* • *I think you need to* ***say you're sorry*** (=apologize).
2 disappointed or sad about something: *I'm sorry now that I stopped taking piano lessons.* • *I am* ***sorry to*** *hear that your mother is ill.*

PHRASES
be sorry for someone, feel sorry for someone to feel sadness and sympathy for someone who has problems: *I* ***feel*** *really* ***sorry for*** *Chloe, but she won't let me help her.*
Sorry? used to ask someone to repeat something because you have not heard them properly SYNONYM **pardon?**: *Sorry? What did you say?*

sort[1] /sɔːt $ sɔrt/ *noun*
a type of thing SYNONYM **kind**: *What* ***sort of*** *car are you going to buy?* • *It's not the* ***sort of*** *thing you want to talk to your parents about.* • *The kids had* ***all***

sorts of (=many different types of) *interesting ideas.* ➔ see Thesaurus at TYPE[1]

PHRASES

sort of (spoken, informal) used when what you say is partly true but not exactly true: *It tasted really good,* ***sort of*** *sweet, but also spicy.* • *She's not really sick, just* ***sort of*** *tired.*

sort² *verb*

KEY PATTERNS
sort things into piles/groups/rows
be sorted by date/age etc

to put things in the right order or group: *She* ***sorted*** *the books* ***into*** *three piles.* • *The glass* ***is sorted by*** *colour for recycling.*

PHRASAL VERBS

sort out

sort something out (informal) if you sort something out, you deal with it or organize it: *We need to* ***sort*** *this problem* ***out*** *before the new term starts.* • *Have you* ***got*** *the food* ***sorted out*** *yet?*

sort through

sort through something to look at a lot of things in order to organize them: *Stella* ***sorted through*** *all the old letters.*

SOS /ˌes əʊ ˈes $ ˌes oʊ ˈes/ *noun* a message saying that someone is in danger: *The ship sent out an SOS.*

ˈso-so *adjective, adverb* (spoken, informal) not very good: *"How was the film?" "So-so."*

sought the past tense and past participle of SEEK

soul /səʊl $ soʊl/ *noun* your thoughts and feelings rather than your body, which some people believe continue to exist after your body dies

sound¹ /saʊnd/ *noun* something that you hear: *We could hear* ***the sound of*** *traffic outside.* • *The picture on the TV was okay, but there was no sound.* ➔ see picture on page A1

sound² *verb* the way something sounds is how it seems to you when you listen to it or hear about it: *The class sounded really interesting.* • *He sounds really depressed.* • *The band sounded really good tonight.* ➔ see Thesaurus at SEEM

sound³ *adjective* **1** sound advice is sensible and likely to produce good results: *The guide gives sound advice to young travellers.* **2** strong and in good condition: *The doors are old, but sound.* • *The doctors say his heart is basically sound.*

ˈsound efˌfects *plural noun* the sounds that someone makes for a film or radio show

sound·ly /ˈsaʊndli/ *adverb* **1** if you sleep soundly, you sleep well and peacefully **2** something that is soundly made is strong and unlikely to break: *The house is very soundly built.*

sound·proof /ˈsaʊndpruːf/ *adjective* a soundproof wall does not allow sound to get through it

sound·track /ˈsaʊndtræk/ *noun* the recorded music from a film

soup /suːp/ *noun* a hot liquid food: *chicken soup*

soup

sour /saʊə $ saʊɚ/ *adjective* **1** food that is sour is not sweet but has an unpleasant acid taste: *I don't like this apple. It's too sour.* **2** milk that is sour is not fresh and has an unpleasant taste

source /sɔːs $ sɔrs/ *noun* the place that something comes from: *An encyclopedia is a good source of information.*

south /saʊθ/ *noun* **1** (no plural) the direction towards the bottom of a map **2 the south** the southern part of a country: *It's warmer in the south* —**south** *adverb, adjective*: *The garden faces south.* • *the south coast of England*

south·bound /ˈsaʊθbaʊnd/ *adjective* going towards the south: *Southbound traffic is busy in summer.*

south·east /ˌsaʊθˈiːst/ *noun* (no plural) the direction that is between south and east: *a town to the southeast of Oxford* —**southeast** *adverb, adjective*: *We drove east and then headed southeast.*

south·er·ly /ˈsʌðəli $ ˈsʌðɚli/ *adjective* towards the south: *We drove in a southerly direction.*

south·ern /ˈsʌðən $ ˈsʌðɚn/ *adjective* in the south of a place: *southern Texas*

south·ern·er /ˈsʌðənə $ ˈsʌðɚnɚ/ *noun* someone who comes from the south of a country

ˌSouth ˈPole *noun* the place on Earth that is farthest south ➔ see picture at GLOBE

south·ward /ˈsaʊθwəd $ ˈsaʊθwɚd/ also **south·wards** /ˈsaʊθwədz $ ˈsaʊθwɚdz/ *adverb, adjective* towards the south: *We travelled southwards for three days.*

south·west /ˌsaʊθˈwest/ *noun* (no plural) the direction between south and west: *the southwest of China* —**southwest** *adverb, adjective*

sou·ve·nir /ˌsuːvəˈnɪə $ ˌsuvəˈnɪr/ *noun* something you keep to help you remember a place

sove·reign /ˈsɒvrən $ ˈsɑvrɪn/ *adjective* a sovereign country is independent and rules itself

sow /səʊ $ soʊ/ *verb* (**sowed, sown** /səʊn $ soʊn/ or **sowed**) to plant seeds in the ground: *Sow tomatoes in February or March.*

sowed the past tense and a past participle of SOW

sown a past participle of SOW

soy·a bean /ˈsɔɪə biːn/ also **soy·bean** /ˈsɔɪbiːn/ *noun* a bean that you can cook and eat or use to make other foods

space¹ /speɪs/ *noun*

KEY PATTERNS
there is space in a room/bag etc
have space for something
make space for something
in space

1 an area that is empty: *There isn't enough **space in** our house to have a big party.* • *We want a kitchen that **has space for** a table and chairs.* • *I moved the furniture around, trying to **make space for** the sofa.* • *Ron couldn't find a **parking space**.*
2 (no plural) the area around the Earth where the stars and PLANETs are: *The astronauts will spend two weeks **in space**.* • *I love the idea of travelling **through space**.* • *a creature from **outer space*** (=far away in space)

space² also **space out** *verb* to arrange things so that they have an equal amount of space between them: *Space the fence posts three feet apart.*

space·ship /ˈspeɪsˌʃɪp/ also **space·craft** /ˈspeɪskrɑːft $ ˈspeɪsˌkræft/ *noun* a vehicle that can travel into space

ˈspace ˌshuttle *noun* a vehicle that can travel into space and return to Earth more than once

spa·cious /ˈspeɪʃəs/ *adjective* a place that is spacious is large and has a lot of space ANTONYM **cramped**: *a spacious apartment*

spade /speɪd/ *noun* **1** a tool that you use for digging earth **2 spades** a group of playing cards with black shapes like pointed leaves on them: *the queen of spades*

spa·ghet·ti /spəˈgeti/ *noun* (no plural) long thin pieces of PASTA that look like pieces of string

spam /spæm/ *noun* unwanted emails, especially ones that contain advertisements: *Every day, my inbox is filled with spam from companies offering all kinds of things.*

span¹ /spæn/ *noun* **1 attention span, concentration span** the amount of time for which someone can CONCENTRATE on something: *Children have a short attention span.* **2 wing span** the distance from one side of a plane's or bird's wing to the other: *The plane has a wing span of 40 feet.*

span² *verb* (**spanned**, **spanning**) to include all of a period of time: *His career spanned 40 years.*

spank /spæŋk/ *verb* to hit a child on the bottom as a punishment

span·ner /ˈspænə $ ˈspænɚ/ *noun BrE* a tool that you use for making NUTs tighter SYNONYM **wrench** *AmE* ➔ see picture at TOOL

spare¹ /speə $ sper/ *adjective* a spare object is one that you do not usually use, but that you keep for when you might need it: *Have you got a*

A B C D E F G H I J K L M N O P Q R S T U V W X Y Z

spare key? • *Della can sleep in the* ***spare room.*** • *The* ***spare tyre*** *is in the boot of the car.*

PHRASES

spare time time when you are not working: *I have so much homework that I don't have much* ***spare time.***

spare² *verb* to be able to give someone something because you do not need it: *Can you spare a cigarette?*

spark¹ /spɑːk $ spɑrk/ *noun* a very small piece of brightly burning material from a fire: *Even a small spark from a fire can be very dangerous.*

spark² *verb* **spark something off** to make something start happening: *His speech sparked off a political crisis.*

spar·kle /ˈspɑːkəl $ ˈspɑrkəl/ *verb* to shine with small bright flashes: *Her eyes sparkled with delight.* ➔ see Thesaurus at SHINE

spar·row /ˈspærəʊ $ ˈspæroʊ/ *noun* a small brown or grey bird

sparse /spɑːs $ spɑrs/ *adjective* existing only in small amounts: *a rocky area with sparse vegetation* —**sparsely** *adverb*: *a sparsely populated area*

spas·m /ˈspæzəm/ *noun* when a muscle in your body becomes suddenly tight in a way you cannot control

spat the past tense and past participle of SPIT

spate /speɪt/ *noun* (no plural) a number of similar events that happen in a short time: *There has been a spate of burglaries in the town recently.*

speak ➔ see box on page 641

speak·er /ˈspiːkə $ ˈspikɚ/ *noun* **1** someone who speaks: *He asked the speaker's name.* **2** the part of a radio, computer etc where sound comes out

spear¹ /spɪə $ spɪr/ *noun* a long thin weapon with a blade at one end, for hunting or throwing at someone

spear² *verb* to push a pointed object into something: *I speared the steak with my fork.*

spear·head /ˈspɪəhed $ ˈspɪrhed/ *verb* to lead an attack or an organized action: *British soldiers spearheaded the attack.*

spe·cial¹ /ˈspeʃəl/ *adjective* **1** something that is special is slightly different to other things and better or more important: *We have a very special guest with us this evening.* • *I want to do something special for your birthday.* **2** a special thing is used by one particular person: *Winnie has her own special plate.*

special² *noun* **1** a television programme that is made for a particular purpose: *a two-hour rock music special* **2** a meal in a restaurant that has been made for that day only: *Today's special is roast lamb.*

ˌspecial eˈffects *plural noun* unusual pictures and sounds in a film or television programme that are not real, but that are made to look real: *a movie with brilliant special effects*

spe·cial·ist /ˈspeʃəlɪst/ *noun* someone who knows a lot about a subject: *a heart specialist* ➔ see Thesaurus at DOCTOR

spe·ci·al·i·ty /ˌspeʃiˈæləti/ *noun BrE* (plural **specialities**) **1** a subject that you know a lot about SYNONYM **specialty** *AmE*: *My speciality is European history.* **2** the speciality of a restaurant is the food that is cooked there in a special way and is always good SYNONYM **specialty** *AmE*: *Fish is the speciality of the restaurant.*

spe·cial·ize also **specialise** *BrE* /ˈspeʃəlaɪz/ *verb* to study only one subject or do only one activity: *a lawyer who specializes in divorce*

spe·cial·ly /ˈspeʃəli/ *adverb* for one particular purpose or person: *The dance costumes are specially made for the dancers.*

spe·cial·ty /ˈspeʃəlti/ *noun AmE* (plural **specialties**) a SPECIALITY

spe·cies /ˈspiːʃiːz/ *noun* (plural **species**) a type of animal or plant: *The forest is home to many species of birds.* ➔ see Thesaurus at TYPE¹

spe·cif·ic /spəˈsɪfɪk/ *adjective* **1** a specific thing is one particular thing: *The books are designed for this specific age group.* **2** detailed and exact: *Please be more specific.*

spe·cif·ic·ally /spəˈsɪfɪkli/ *adverb* **1** for a particular type of person or thing: *a book specifically for teenagers*

speak /spiːk/ *verb* (past tense **spoke** /spəʊk $ spoʊk/, past participle **spoken** /ˈspəʊkən $ ˈspoʊkən/)

1 to talk to someone or to a group of people: *He* ***spoke*** *for over an hour.* • *Can I* ***speak to*** *the manager, please?* • *Betty* ***spoke with*** *her friend after the concert.* • *She has never* ***spoken to*** *me* ***about*** *this before.* • *He* ***spoke of*** *his love for Rosemary.*

KEY PATTERNS
speak to someone (about something)
speak with someone *AmE*
speak of something (formal)

2 to be able to say and understand the words of a language: *Do you* ***speak*** *Russian?* • *She* ***speaks*** *perfect English.* • *My grandfather* ***spoke*** *four languages.* • *I* ***speak*** *a little Italian.*

GRAMMAR
Be careful how you use **speak**:
• *He speaks English* means 'he is able to speak this language'.
• *She is speaking English* means 'she is using English now'.
• *Could you speak in English, please?* means 'Could you speak using English, rather than another language?'

speak

3 to use your voice to say words: *She* ***spoke*** *in a quiet, tired voice.* • *No one* ***spoke*** *for about five minutes, then everyone started at once.*

WORD CHOICE
speak or **talk**?
• If one person is talking, you can use **speak** or **talk**: *He* ***spoke*** *for over an hour.* • *She* ***talked*** *about her trip to Berlin.*
• If two or more people are having a conversation, use only **talk**: *They* ***talked*** *about the old days.*

PHRASES

speak up (spoken)
a) used when telling someone to speak more loudly: *Could you* ***speak up****? I can't hear you very well.*
b) to say publicly what you think about something: *When I was younger, I was too shy to* ***speak up*** *in class.*

2 if you specifically say something, you say it clearly because it is important: *I specifically told you to be here by ten o'clock!*

spe·ci·fy /ˈspesəfaɪ/ *verb* (**specified**, **specifies**) to give exact details about something: *The doctor specified that you should take three pills a day.*

spe·ci·men /ˈspesəmən/ *noun* something from your body that is tested or examined: *a blood specimen*

speck /spek/ *noun* a very small piece of something: *a speck of dust*

spec·ta·cle /ˈspektəkəl/ *noun* an unusual or strange thing to see: *The man was leading an elephant along the street, which was an interesting spectacle.*

spec·ta·cles /ˈspektəkəlz/ *noun* (formal) glasses: *an expensive pair of spectacles*

spec·tac·u·lar /spekˈtækjələ $ spekˈtækjələ˞/ *adjective* very impressive or exciting: *We got a spectacular view of Niagara Falls.*

spec·ta·tor /spekˈteɪtə $ ˈspekteɪtə˞/ *noun* someone who watches an event

spec·u·late /ˈspekjəleɪt/ *verb* (formal) to guess the reason for something: *Everyone speculated about why he left.*

sped the past tense and past participle of SPEED

speech /spiːtʃ/ *noun* (plural **speeches**)

> KEY PATTERNS
> **make/give a speech**
> **a speech on/about a subject**
> **a speech to someone**

1 a talk about a subject that you give to a group of people: *The chairman **made a speech on** the environment.* • *He **gave a speech to** the conference.*
2 when someone speaks: *Only humans are capable of speech.* • *He was drunk, and his speech was unclear.*

PHRASES

freedom of speech, free speech the right to say or print whatever you want: *I believe strongly in the importance of **freedom of speech**.*

speech·less /ˈspiːtʃləs/ *adjective* (formal) unable to speak because you are too shocked: *She was speechless when I told her the news.*

ˈspeech marks *plural noun* the marks (“,”) or (‘,’) that you write to show when someone starts and stops speaking SYNONYM **inverted commas**, **quotation marks**

speed¹ /spiːd/ *noun*
1 how fast a person or thing moves: *What speed were you travelling at?* • *Try to **keep your speed down** (=not go too fast) on small roads.*
2 (no plural) how quickly something happens: *The speed of the changes has surprised many people.*

PHRASES

speed limit a limit on how fast you are allowed to drive: *The **speed limit** is 30 miles an hour.*

top speed the top speed of a vehicle is its fastest possible speed: *This car has a **top speed** of 80 miles an hour.*

at high speed very fast: *The police car drove away **at high speed**.*

speed² *verb* (past tense and past participle **sped** /sped/ or **speeded**)
1 to move very quickly: *We sped up the stairs.* • *The van sped along the motorway.* 2 **speed by** if time speeds by, it seems to pass very quickly: *The weeks sped by.* 3 **speed up** to move more quickly ANTONYM **slow down**: *The truck speeded up as it went down the hill.* 4 **speed something up** to make something happen more quickly ANTONYM **slow down**

speed·boat /ˈspiːdbəʊt $ ˈspidboʊt/ *noun* a small fast boat with a powerful engine → see picture at BOAT

speed·ing /ˈspiːdɪŋ/ *noun* (no plural) the crime of driving too fast: *The police stopped me for speeding.*

spell¹ /spel/ *verb* (past tense and past participle **spelled** or **spelt** /spelt/ *BrE*) to form a word by writing or saying the letters in the correct order: *Can you spell your name for me?*

spell² *noun* 1 a piece of magic: *They say that a witch cast a spell on her.*
2 a short period of time: *She had a short spell in hospital.*

spell·ing /ˈspelɪŋ/ *noun* 1 (no plural) the ability to spell words correctly: *My spelling is terrible.* 2 the way that you spell a word: *There are two different spellings for this word.*

spelt a past tense and past participle of SPELL[1]

spend /spend/ *verb* (past tense and past participle **spent** /spent/)

KEY PATTERNS
spend money/$50 etc (on something)
spend time on something
spend time doing something

1 to use your money to pay for something: *I've spent all my money.* • *Brendan* ***spent*** *over £600* ***on*** *his new mountain bike.*
2 to use time doing something: *After school, they* ***spend*** *about two hours* ***on*** *their homework.* • *We spent the afternoon playing football.*

spent the past tense and past participle of SPEND

sperm /spɜːm $ spɝm/ *noun* a cell produced inside a man, which, if it joins with an egg, produces new life

sphere /sfɪə $ sfɪr/ *noun* the shape of a ball

spher·i·cal /ˈsferɪkəl/ *adjective* (formal) round in shape like a ball

spice[1] /spaɪs/ *noun* a substance that you add to food to give it a special strong taste

spice[2] *verb* **spice something up** to make something more interesting or exciting: *I need a few jokes to spice up my speech.*

spic·y /ˈspaɪsi/ *adjective* (**spicier, spiciest**) spicy food has a strong taste because it contains a lot of spices

spi·der /ˈspaɪdə $ ˈspaɪdɚ/ *noun* a small creature with eight legs

spider

spike[1] /spaɪk/ *noun* a long thin object with a sharp point: *a fence with spikes along the top*

spike[2] *verb* to add alcohol or a drug to someone's drink without telling them: *She thinks that someone must have spiked her drink.*

spik·y /ˈspaɪki/ *adjective* (**spikier, spikiest**) something that is spiky has a lot of sharp points: *She had short spiky hair.*

spill[1] /spɪl/ *verb* (past tense and past participle **spilled** or **spilt** /spɪlt/)

KEY PATTERNS
spill a liquid on/over something/someone

1 if you spill a liquid, you let it fall out of a container by accident: *I've* ***spilt*** *some coffee* ***on*** *the carpet.* • *A waiter* ***spilled*** *water* ***all over*** *me.*
2 if a liquid spills, it pours out of a container by accident: *The paint* ***spilled all over*** *the floor.* • *Some beer had* ***spilt on*** *his shirt.*

spill[2] *noun* an amount of liquid that pours out of a container by accident: *An oil spill would kill all the fish in the area.*

spilt a past tense and past participle of SPILL[1]

spin[1] /spɪn/ *verb* (past tense and past participle **spun** /spʌn/, **spinning**)

KEY PATTERNS
spin around
spin round *BrE*
spin something/someone around
spin something/someone round *BrE*
spin a web

1 if something spins, or if you spin it, it turns around and around very quickly: *The dancers* ***spun round and round*** *on the ice.* • *He* ***spun*** *the rope* ***around*** *above his head.*
2 if a SPIDER spins a WEB, it produces the thread to make it

spin

spin[2] *noun* when something turns around and around very quickly: *The plane went into a spin.*

spin·ach /ˈspɪnɪdʒ $ ˈspɪnɪtʃ/ *noun* (no plural) a vegetable with large dark green leaves ➔ see picture on page A6

spin·al /ˈspaɪnl/ *adjective* related to your spine: *a spinal injury*

ˈspin ˌdoctor *noun* someone who gives advice to politicians and members of large organizations about what things they should say to make the public like and respect them

spine /spaɪn/ *noun* the row of bones down the centre of your back: *She fell and injured her spine.* → see picture on page A5

spine·less /ˈspaɪnləs/ *adjective* not brave: *He's too spineless to speak for himself.*

ˈspin-off *noun* a product, programme etc that is based on a successful book, film, or television series: *The film's spin-offs include toys, clothes, and a magazine.*

spin·ster /ˈspɪnstə $ ˈspɪnstɚ/ *noun* (old-fashioned) a woman who has never married

spi·ral /ˈspaɪərəl $ ˈspaɪrəl/ *noun* a shape that goes round and round as it goes up: *a spiral staircase*

spiral

a spiral staircase

spire /spaɪə $ spaɪɚ/ *noun* a tower on a church that rises steeply to a point

spir·it /ˈspɪrɪt/ *noun* **1** the part of you that many people think continues to live after you die: *He said he could talk to the spirit of his dead mother.* **2** an imaginary creature without an ordinary body and with special powers: *They performed a ceremony to make the evil spirits in the house go away.* **3** a strong alcoholic drink: *I never drink spirits.* **4 high spirits** if someone is in high spirits, they are happy and excited: *Why are the children in such high spirits?*

spir·i·tu·al /ˈspɪrətʃuəl/ *adjective* **1** relating to your thoughts and feelings, rather than to your body and the things you own **2** relating to religion SYNONYM **religious**: *spiritual songs*

spit¹ /spɪt/ *verb* (**spat** /spæt/ or **spit** *AmE*, **spat**, **spitting**) **1** to push liquid or food out of your mouth: *He tasted the meat, then spat it out.* • *One of the boys spat at me as I walked past.* **2** *BrE* if it is spitting, it is raining very lightly SYNONYM **drizzle**: *It's only spitting – you don't need an umbrella.*

spit² *noun* **1** SALIVA **2** a long thin stick for cooking meat over a fire

spite /spaɪt/ *noun* (no plural) the feeling of wanting to hurt or upset someone: *She only told Jim what had happened **out of spite*** (=because she wanted to upset him).

PHRASES

in spite of something although something else is also true SYNONYM **despite**: *We enjoyed the trip **in spite of** the bad weather.*

spite·ful /ˈspaɪtfəl/ *adjective* unkind or cruel to someone: *That was a spiteful thing to do.* —**spitefully** *adverb*: *"You can't come," Jane said spitefully.*

splash¹ /splæʃ/ *verb*

KEY PATTERNS
splash onto/into something
splash down
splash water onto/over something

1 if a liquid splashes, it moves through the air and falls on something: *Some wine had **splashed onto** his shirt.* • *Big drops of rain were **splashing down**.* **2** if you splash a liquid, you hit it or throw it so that it moves through the air and falls on something: *He splashed some cold water onto his face.* → see picture on page A1

splash² *noun* (plural **splashes**) **1** the sound that something makes when it hits water: *The stone fell in the water with a loud splash.* **2** a small amount of a liquid that falls onto a surface: *splashes of paint*

splat·ter /ˈsplætə $ ˈsplætɚ/ *verb* if a liquid splatters, it hits loudly against a surface: *Rain splattered against the window.*

splen·did /ˈsplendɪd/ *adjective* (old-fashioned) very good SYNONYM **brilliant**: *What a splendid idea!*

splint /splɪnt/ *noun* a flat piece of wood or plastic that stops a broken bone from moving: *I have to wear a splint until my leg gets better.*

splin·ter¹ /ˈsplɪntə $ ˈsplɪntɚ/ *noun* a small sharp piece of wood, glass, or metal

splinter² *verb* to break into thin sharp pieces: *The window frames had begun to splinter.*

split

They split the money between them.

split¹ /splɪt/ *verb* (past tense and past participle **split**, **splitting**)

KEY PATTERNS
split (something) open
split (something) in half/in two
split something between people
split something into groups/parts

1 to break something into two or more parts: *Meg dropped the box, which* ***split open*** *on the floor.* • *I got a knife and* ***split*** *the melon* ***open***. • *The wire had* ***split in half***. • *We* ***split*** *the pizza* ***in two*** *and ate it.*
2 to divide something into different parts and share it between people: *Nathan and I* ***split*** *the £25* ***between*** *us.*
3 to divide something into different groups or parts: *The teacher* ***split*** *the class* ***into*** *groups of four.* • *The book is* ***split into*** *three parts.*

PHRASAL VERBS

split up
if two people split up, their marriage or relationship ends SYNONYM **separate**: *Eve's parents* ***split up*** *when she was three.* ➔ see Thesaurus at DIVORCE²

split² *noun* **1** a long thin cut or hole in something: *He had a painful split in his lip.* **2** a serious disagreement that divides an organization or group of people: *Ministers are denying that there is any split in the party.*

ˌsplit ˈsecond *noun* a very short period of time: *For a split second, I thought I'd won.*

spoil /spɔɪl/ *verb* (past tense and past participle **spoiled** or **spoilt** /spɔɪlt/ *BrE*)
1 to make something less good or less enjoyable: *I didn't want to spoil the surprise.* • *Being ill spoiled the trip for me.*
2 to let a child have or do whatever they want, with the result that they behave badly: *Grandparents sometimes spoil their grandchildren.*
3 if food spoils, it becomes bad and you cannot eat it

spoiled /spɔɪld/ also **spoilt** /spɔɪlt/ *BrE adjective* a spoiled child behaves badly because they always get what they want

spoil·sport /ˈspɔɪlspɔːt $ ˈspɔɪlspɔrt/ *noun* (informal) someone who spoils other people's fun: *Don't be a spoilsport! Please let us go swimming.*

spoilt a past tense and past participle of SPOIL

spoke the past tense of SPEAK

spoken¹ the past participle of SPEAK

spok·en² /ˈspəʊkən $ ˈspoʊkən/ *adjective* **spoken English/Spanish etc** the form of language that you speak rather than write

spokes·man /ˈspəʊksmən $ ˈspoʊksmən/ *noun* (plural **spokesmen** /-mən/) someone who speaks for a group, especially a man

spokes·per·son /ˈspəʊksˌpɜːsən $ ˈspoʊksˌpɚsən/ *noun* (plural **spokespeople** /-ˌpiːpəl/) someone who speaks for a group

spokes·wo·man /ˈspəʊksˌwʊmən $ ˈspoʊksˌwʊmən/ *noun* (plural **spokeswomen** /-ˌwɪmɪn/) a woman who speaks for a group

sponge /spʌndʒ/ *noun* a soft object full of small holes that takes in and holds water and is used to wash things

spong·y /ˈspʌndʒi/ *adjective* (**spongier**, **spongiest**) soft and full of air or liquid, like a sponge: *The grass was wet and spongy.*

spon·sor¹ /ˈspɒnsə $ ˈspɑnsɚ/ *verb* **1** to provide the money to pay for an event: *Coca-Cola have offered to sponsor the tournament.* **2** to give someone money for a CHARITY if they manage to do something difficult: *I'm doing a walk for charity. Will you sponsor me?*

sponsor² *noun* a company that provides the money to pay for an event

spon·sor·ship /ˈspɒnsəʃɪp $ ˈspɑnsɚˌʃɪp/ *noun* (no plural) when someone sponsors an event or person: *We are still trying to get sponsorship for the competition.*

spon·tan·e·i·ty /ˌspɒntəˈneɪəti $ ˌspɑntəˈneɪəti/ *noun* (no plural) when you decide to do things very quickly, without thinking about them or planning them: *Greg's full of good ideas, and I really like his spontaneity.*

spon·ta·ne·ous /spɒnˈteɪniəs $ spɑnˈteɪniəs/ *adjective* if something is spontaneous, you do it without thinking about it or planning it: *The audience gave a spontaneous cheer.* —**spontaneously** *adverb*: *The crowd spontaneously started clapping.*

spook·y /ˈspuːki/ *adjective* (informal) (**spookier**, **spookiest**) strange and frightening: *a spooky old house*

spool /spuːl/ *noun* a small object that you wind something around: *a spool of thread*

spoon¹ /spuːn/ *noun* something that you use for eating food, shaped like a small bowl with a long handle ➔ see picture at CUTLERY

spoon² *verb* to lift food with a spoon: *Spoon the sauce over the meat.*

spoon·ful /ˈspuːnfʊl/ *noun* the amount that a spoon can hold: *a spoonful of medicine*

sport /spɔːt $ spɔrt/ *noun* a game or competition such as football or tennis, in which you use your body to play: *I like to **play** most **sports**, but basketball is my favourite.* • *I think children should **do** more **sport** at school.* ➔ see picture on page A14

sport·ing /ˈspɔːtɪŋ $ ˈspɔrtɪŋ/ *adjective* relating to sports: *sporting activities*

ˈsports car *noun* a fast car with only two seats

ˈsports ˌcentre *noun BrE* a place where you can do sports

sports·man /ˈspɔːtsmən $ ˈspɔrtsmən/ (plural **sportsmen** /-mən/) *noun* a man who plays sports

sports·wom·an /ˈspɔːtsˌwʊmən $ ˈspɔrtsˌwʊmən/ *noun* (plural **sportswomen** /-ˌwɪmɪn/) a woman who plays sports

sport·y /ˈspɔːti $ ˈspɔrti/ *adjective BrE* good at sport SYNONYM **athletic**: *I'm not very sporty.*

spot¹ /spɒt $ spɑt/ *noun*
1 a place: *This is a great spot for a holiday.*
2 a small round mark on a surface: *There were some **spots of** blood on the carpet.* ➔ see Thesaurus at MARK²
3 *BrE* a small red mark on someone's skin: *If you eat too much chocolate you'll get spots.*

PHRASES
on the spot **a)** at the place where something is happening: *One victim was taken to hospital; the other was treated **on the spot**.* **b)** immediately: *She gave him some money **on the spot**.*

spot² *verb* (**spotted**, **spotting**) to notice or see something: *I spotted my friend Anna in the audience.*

ˌspot ˈcheck / $ ˈ. ./ *noun* a check that is done without warning: *There are spot checks on goods before they leave the factory.*

spot·less /ˈspɒtləs $ ˈspɑtləs/ *adjective* completely clean: *a spotless kitchen* —**spotlessly** *adverb*: *Her house is always spotlessly clean.*

spot·light /ˈspɒtlaɪt $ ˈspɑtlaɪt/ *noun* **1** a very powerful light that you can point at different things **2 in the spotlight** receiving a lot of attention from newspapers or television

spot·ty /ˈspɒti $ ˈspɑti/ *adjective BrE* (**spottier**, **spottiest**) someone who is spotty has a lot of spots on their face: *a fat, spotty young boy*

spouse /spaʊs/ *noun* (formal) (plural **spouses**) someone's husband or wife

spout¹ /spaʊt/ *noun* a part on the side of a container that you use for pouring out liquid: *a teapot with a broken spout*

spout² *verb* if a liquid spouts, it comes out of something with a lot of force: *Water spouted from the burst pipe.*

sprain /spreɪn/ *verb* to injure your wrist, knee etc by suddenly twisting it SYNONYM **twist**: *I think I've sprained my* *ankle.* —**sprain** *noun*: *Your wrist isn't broken. It's just a bad sprain.* ➔ see Thesaurus at INJURY

sprang the past tense of SPRING[1]

sprawl /sprɔːl/ *verb* to lie or sit with your arms and legs stretched out: *Jo lay sprawled on the sofa.*

spray[1] /spreɪ/ *verb*

KEY PATTERNS
spray a liquid on/onto something
spray something/someone with a liquid

to force a lot of very small drops of liquid out of a container onto something: *Someone had* ***sprayed*** *paint* ***on*** *the walls.* • *She* ***sprayed*** *the children* ***with*** *cold water.*

spray[2] *noun* liquid in a special container that is forced out in very small drops: *a can of hair spray*

spread[1] /spred/ *verb* (past tense and past participle **spread**)

KEY PATTERNS
spread butter/cheese etc on something
spread something with butter/cheese etc
spread a map/cloth etc (out) on something
be spread across/over the floor
spread over/through an area

1 to put a layer of something over a surface so that the surface is covered: ***Spread*** *the icing* ***on*** *the top of the cake.* • *He* ***spread*** *the bread thickly* ***with*** *jam.* ➔ see picture on page A4
2 also **spread out** to open something so that it is flat: *She* ***spread*** *her towel* ***out on*** *the sand and lay down in the sun.*
3 if things are spread over an area, they cover that area, especially in an untidy way: *Dirty clothes were* ***spread across*** *the floor.* • *His papers were* ***spread all over*** *his desk.*
4 if something spreads, it affects a larger area or more people: *The fire* ***spread*** *quickly* ***through*** *the house.* • *This disease can spread very easily.*
5 if information spreads, a lot of people learn about it: *The rumours spread quickly.* • *You shouldn't spread gossip.*

PHRASAL VERBS
spread out
if a group of people spread out, they move apart from each other: *The children* ***spread out*** *across the playground.*

spread[2] *noun* when something affects a larger area or more people: *We must do more to stop the spread of this virus.*

spread·sheet /ˈspredʃiːt/ *noun* a computer program that you use for showing and calculating lists of numbers

spree /spriː/ *noun* when you spend a short time doing a lot of something you enjoy: *I went on a spending spree.*

spring[1] /sprɪŋ/ *verb* (**sprang** /spræŋ/ **sprung** /sprʌŋ/)

KEY PATTERNS
spring into/out of etc something
spring back/forward/up/down
spring to your feet

to jump suddenly and quickly SYNONYM **leap**: *Tim's cat* ***sprang into*** *my lap.* • *Josie* ***sprang out of*** *bed.* • *She* ***sprang back*** *in surprise.* • *He* ***sprang to his feet*** (=stood up quickly) *when I came in.*

PHRASAL VERBS
spring up
to suddenly appear: *New coffee shops are* ***springing up*** *all over town.*

spring[2] *noun*

KEY PATTERNS
in (the) spring

the season between winter and summer: ***In spring*** *all the plants start to grow again.* • *We're hoping to move house* ***this spring.*** • *I first met Simon* ***in the spring of*** *1998.* ➔ see picture on page A13

ˌ**spring-ˈclean** *verb* to clean a place thoroughly: *I'm going to spring-clean the bedrooms today.*
—**spring-cleaning** *noun* (no plural): *Do you need help with the spring-cleaning?*

ˌ**spring ˈonion** *noun BrE* a small white onion with a long green stem ➔ see picture on page A6

spring·time /ˈsprɪŋtaɪm/ *noun* (no plural) the time of year when it is spring

A B C D E F G H I J K L M N O P Q R S T U V W X Y Z

sprin·kle /ˈsprɪŋkəl/ *verb* to scatter small drops of liquid or small pieces of something onto something else: *Finally, sprinkle grated chocolate on top of the cake.* → see picture on page A4

sprint /sprɪnt/ *verb* to run very fast for a short distance: *She sprinted past the other runners.* —**sprint** *noun*: *Her jogging turned into a sprint.*

sprout[1] /spraʊt/ *verb* if a plant sprouts, it starts to grow new leaves

sprout[2] also **Brussels sprout** *noun* a round green vegetable like a very small CABBAGE

sprung the past participle of SPRING[1]

spun the past tense and past participle of SPIN[1]

spur[1] /spɜː $ spɚ/ *noun* **on the spur of the moment** if you do something on the spur of the moment, you do it suddenly without planning to do it: *On the spur of the moment, she booked a holiday in Thailand.*

spur[2] *verb* (**spurred**, **spurring**) **spur someone on** to encourage someone to try harder: *The fear of failure spurred him on.*

spurt[1] /spɜːt $ spɚt/ *verb* to flow out suddenly with a lot of force: *Juice spurted out over her fingers.*

spurt[2] *noun* a sudden short increase in effort, speed etc: *With one final spurt, she reached the top of the hill.*

spy[1] /spaɪ/ *verb* (**spied**, **spies**) **1** to secretly get information for a government: *He was found guilty of spying for the Americans.* **2 spy on** to secretly watch someone: *Have you been spying on me?*

spy[2] *noun* (plural **spies**) someone whose job is to find out secret information for a government

squab·ble /ˈskwɒbəl $ ˈskwɑbəl/ *verb* to argue about something unimportant SYNONYM **bicker**: *Sam and David are always squabbling with each other.* —**squabble** *noun*

squad /skwɒd $ skwɑd/ *noun* **1** a group of soldiers or police officers who work together: *the anti-terrorist squad* **2** *BrE* the group of players that a sports team is chosen from

squad·ron /ˈskwɒdrən $ ˈskwɑdrən/ *noun* a group of military planes or vehicles

squal·or /ˈskwɒlə $ ˈskwɑlɚ/ *noun* (no plural) (formal) extremely dirty conditions: *They lived in squalor.*

squan·der /ˈskwɒndə $ ˈskwɑndɚ/ *verb* (formal) to waste time or money in a stupid way: *He had squandered all his money on expensive clothes.*

square[1] /skweə $ skwer/ *adjective*
1 something that is square has four straight sides of equal length and four angles of 90 degrees: *a square table*
2 a square INCH, square metre etc is a measurement of an area which is a square with sides an inch long, a metre long etc: *The park covers two square miles of the city.*

square[2] *noun*
1 a shape with four straight sides of equal length and four angles of 90 degrees: *First, I want you to draw a square.* → see picture at SHAPE[1]
2 an open area with buildings around it in the middle of a town: *The police station is in the main* ***square.*** • *I live on Hanover Square.*

squash[1] /skwɒʃ $ skwɑʃ/ *verb*

KEY PATTERNS
squash something into somewhere

1 to damage something by pressing on it so that it becomes flat: *He sat on the bananas and squashed them.* → see Thesaurus at PRESS[1]
2 to push someone or something into a space that is too small: *Move over – you're squashing me!* • *I* ***squashed*** *a towel* ***into*** *my bag.*

squash[2] *noun* (no plural) a game that is played indoors by two people who hit a small rubber ball against the walls of a small room

squat[1] /skwɒt $ skwɑt/ *noun BrE* a building people live in without permission and without paying rent

squat² *verb* (**squatted, squatting**) to live in a building without permission and without paying rent: *In big cities, people without homes sometimes squat in empty buildings.*

squeak /skwiːk/ *verb* to make a very high sound: *As he crept up the stairs, a floorboard squeaked.* —**squeak** *noun*: *the squeak of a mouse* → see picture on page A1

squeak·y /ˈskwiːki/ *adjective* (**squeakier, squeakiest**) making a very high sound: *a squeaky voice*

squeal /skwiːl/ *verb* to make a long loud high sound: *The children squealed and giggled.* —**squeal** *noun*: *squeals of laughter*

squeam·ish /ˈskwiːmɪʃ/ *adjective* easily upset by seeing unpleasant things

squeeze

Tom squeezed through a gap in the hedge.

squeeze /skwiːz/ *verb*

KEY PATTERNS
squeeze an orange
squeeze someone's hand
squeeze the juice/water out of something
squeeze through/into a space

1 to press something firmly with your hand: *Mike squeezed my hand and said, "Don't worry."* • *She squeezed two oranges and drank the juice.* → see Thesaurus at PRESS¹
2 to push yourself into or through a small space: *You can't* ***squeeze*** *yourself* ***into*** *those jeans any more – they're too small!* • *Tom* ***squeezed through*** *a gap in the hedge.* • *There were already four people in the car but I managed to* ***squeeze in***.
3 to press or push something into a space that is small or full of things: *I don't think I can* ***squeeze*** *any more clothes* ***into*** *this suitcase.*
4 to remove something from a container by pressing it firmly: *Can you* ***squeeze*** *any more toothpaste* ***out*** *of this tube?*

squid /skwɪd/ *noun* (plural **squid**) a sea creature with a long soft body and ten soft arms

squint¹ /skwɪnt/ *verb* to look at something with your eyes partly closed so that you can see it better: *She squinted at the name on the envelope.*

squint² *noun* (no plural) a condition in which each eye looks in a different direction

squirm /skwɜːm $ skwɚm/ *verb* to twist your body from side to side: *Gary squirmed, trying to get free.*

squir·rel /ˈskwɪrəl $ ˈskwɚəl/ *noun* a small animal with a long furry tail that lives in trees and eats nuts

squirt

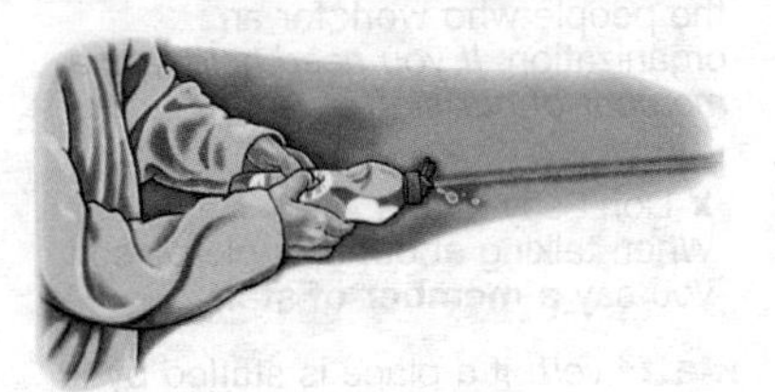

squirt /skwɜːt $ skwɚt/ *verb* if you squirt liquid, or if it squirts out, it is forced out of a narrow hole: *He squirted ketchup on his burger.*

St. **1** the written abbreviation of STREET: *Oxford St.* **2** the written abbreviation of SAINT: *St. Peter*

stab¹ /stæb/ *verb* (**stabbed, stabbing**) to push a knife into someone: *The boy stabbed him in the leg.*

stab² *noun* (no plural) (informal) an attempt to do something: *I wouldn't mind having another stab at playing the guitar.*

stab·bing /ˈstæbɪŋ/ *adjective* a stabbing pain is very sudden and strong

sta·bil·i·ty /stəˈbɪləti/ *noun* (no plural) when a situation does not change for a long time

sta·bil·ize also **stabilise** *BrE* /ˈsteɪbəlaɪz/ *verb* if something stabilizes, it stops changing: *There was a big increase in the population, but now it has stabilized.*

sta·ble¹ /ˈsteɪbəl/ *adjective* not likely to move or change ANTONYM **unstable**: *Make sure the ladder is stable before you go up it.*

stable² *noun* a building where horses are kept

stack¹ /stæk/ *noun* a pile of things one on top of the other: *a stack of dirty plates* → see Thesaurus at PILE¹

stack² also **stack up** *verb* to make a pile of things one on top of the other: *She stacked the old magazines on the floor.*

sta·di·um /ˈsteɪdiəm/ *noun* a large area for playing sports, surrounded by rows of seats: *a football stadium*

staff¹ /stɑːf $ stæf/ *noun* (no plural) the people who work for an organization: *If you need help, ask a member of our staff.*

> GRAMMAR
> ✘ Don't say 'staffs'.
> When talking about a single person, you say **a member of staff.**

staff² *verb* if a place is staffed by people, they work there: *The shop is staffed by volunteers.*

stag /stæg/ *noun* an adult male DEER

stage¹ /steɪdʒ/ *noun*

> KEY PATTERNS
> **a stage of/in a process**
> **on (the) stage**

1 one part of a long process: *Different books are suitable for different* ***stages*** *of your education.* • ***At this stage in*** *my life, I don't want a serious relationship.* **2** the raised part in a theatre where people perform: *I stood* ***on the stage*** *and sang.* • *The star of the show came* ***on stage****.*

stage² *verb* to organize an event or performance: *We were planning to stage an end-of-term show.*

stag·ger /ˈstægə $ ˈstægɚ/ *verb* to walk in a very unsteady way: *He staggered to the phone.*

stag·gered /ˈstægəd $ ˈstægɚd/ *adjective* extremely surprised SYNONYM **amazed**: *I was staggered to hear you're leaving.*

stag·ger·ing /ˈstægərɪŋ/ *adjective* extremely great or surprising SYNONYM **amazing**: *The car cost a staggering amount of money.*

ˈstag night *noun* an evening when a man goes out with his male friends just before his wedding

stain¹ /steɪn/ *verb* to make a mark on something that is difficult to remove: *The coffee had stained her skirt badly.*

stain² *noun* a mark that is difficult to remove: *The carpet was covered in wine stains.* → see Thesaurus at MARK²

stair /steə $ ster/ *noun* **1 stairs** a set of steps that you use to go from one level of a building to another: *I ran up the stairs to get my jacket.* • *The office is at the top of the stairs.* **2** one of the steps in a set of stairs: *Mia was sitting on the top stair.*

stair·case /ˈsteəkeɪs $ ˈsterkeɪs/ *noun* a set of stairs inside a building

staircase
banister
step

stair·way /ˈsteəweɪ $ ˈsterweɪ/ *noun* a wide set of stairs

stake /steɪk/ *noun* **1 be at stake** if something is at stake, you will lose it if an action is not successful: *People's jobs are at stake, so we have to finish the project on time.* **2 stakes** money that you risk losing as the result of a horse race, card game etc: *Gamblers in Las Vegas often play for high stakes.*

stale /steɪl/ *adjective* no longer fresh: *stale bread*

stalk¹ /stɔːk/ *noun* the main stem of a plant → see picture on page A10

stalk² *verb* to follow a person or animal in order to watch or attack them

stalk·er /ˈstɔːkə $ ˈstɔkɚ/ *noun* a person who keeps following someone in a way that upsets them or frightens them

stall¹ /stɔːl/ *noun* **1** a table that is used for selling things outdoors, or a small shop with an open front: *the fruit and vegetable stall in the market* **2** *AmE* a small enclosed area for washing or using the toilet **3 the stalls** the seats on the lowest level in a theatre or cinema

stall² *verb* **1** if an engine stalls, it suddenly stops **2** (informal) to deliberately delay doing something, especially answering a question: *He wanted me to say 'yes' but I kept stalling.* **3** (informal) to deliberately make someone wait or stop something from happening: *If she asks to see me, stall her.*

stal·lion /ˈstæljən/ *noun* an adult male horse

stam·i·na /ˈstæmənə/ *noun* (no plural) the physical or mental strength to continue doing something for a long time

stam·mer /ˈstæmə $ ˈstæmɚ/ *verb* to repeat the first sound of a word when you speak SYNONYM **stutter**: *"N-no," he stammered.* —**stammer** *noun*: *She speaks with a stammer.*

stamp¹ /stæmp/ *noun*

stamp

1 a small piece of paper that you stick on a letter before you post it to show that you have paid to send it: *Don't forget to **put** a stamp **on** that letter.* **2** an official mark that is printed on a document using a small block covered with ink: *They put a stamp in his passport.*

stamp² *verb*

KEY PATTERNS
stamp into/out of etc a place
stamp a document

1 to put your feet down very hard on the ground when you walk: *Andy got angry and **stamped out of** the room.* **2** to print an official mark on a document by pressing a small block covered with ink onto it: *Go to that office and they'll stamp your visa.* • *They **stamped** the date **on** my passport.* • *The letter was **stamped with** the word 'Urgent'.*

PHRASES

stamp your foot to put your foot down very hard on the ground: *Tess stamped her foot and shouted "No!"*

PHRASAL VERBS

stamp out
stamp something out to stop something bad from continuing SYNONYM **eradicate**: *The school has said that it will **stamp out** bullying.*

stam·pede /stæmˈpiːd/ *noun* when a large number of animals or people suddenly run somewhere: *There was a stampede for the door.*

stance /stɑːns $ stæns/ *noun* (formal) someone's public attitude towards something: *The Church will not change its stance on divorce.*

stand¹ /stænd/ *verb* (past tense and past participle **stood** /stʊd/)
1 if you are standing, you are on your feet in an upright position: *Miss Fell was standing in front of the class.* • *I stood and watched the rain coming down.* • ***Stand still** while I do your hair.*
2 also **stand up** to get up so that you are standing after you have been sitting or lying down: *He **stood up** when I came into the room.*
3 if something stands somewhere, it is there: *This is where the castle once stood.*

PHRASES

can't stand (spoken) to hate something or someone SYNONYM **can't bear**: *I can't stand that man!* • *She **can't stand** loud music.* → see Thesaurus at HATE¹

stand a chance to be likely to succeed: *I don't **stand a chance of** getting that job.*

PHRASAL VERBS

stand back
to move back so that you are standing a little further away: *Everyone **stood back** while Dad lit the fireworks.*

stand by
stand by someone to support someone when they are in trouble: *She **stood by** him when he went to jail.*

A B C D E F G H I J K L M N O P Q R S T U V W X Y Z

stand for
stand for something to be a short form of a word or phrase: *'PTO' **stands for** 'please turn over'.*
stand in
to do someone else's job for them while they are away: *He is **standing in for** Jenny while she has her baby.*
stand out
to be very easy to see or notice: *Wear something bright so that you **stand out**.*
stand up
to get up so that you are standing after you have been sitting or lying down: *Louise **stood up** and left the room.*
stand up for someone/something
to defend someone or something when people criticize them: *Pete always **stands up for** his younger brother.*

stand² *noun* **1** a piece of equipment that holds or supports something: *a music stand* **2** a table or small structure that you put things on in order to show them to people or to sell them: *Each class had a stand for displaying their work.* **3** a building at a sports ground where people sit or stand to watch a game

stan·dard¹ /ˈstændəd $ ˈstændərd/ *noun*
a level that measures how good something is or how well someone does something: *My maths teacher said she was not satisfied with the **standard of** my homework this term.* • *Most people here have well-paid jobs and a good **standard of living**.* • *The new hotel was built **to a very high standard**.* • *We must do more to **raise** academic **standards** in the college.* • *This restaurant used to be really good but the **standard** has **fallen** recently.* • *Students must **reach** this **standard** in order to pass the exam.*
PHRASES
by someone's standards compared to what a person normally does or achieves: *I stayed up until 11.00, which is late by my standards.*

standard² *adjective* normal or usual: *The doors are all a standard size.*
→ see Thesaurus at NORMAL

stan·dard·ize also **standardise** *BrE* /ˈstændədaɪz $ ˈstændərˌdaɪz/ *verb* to make things all the same as each other

stand·by /ˈstændbaɪ/ *noun* **on standby** ready to do something if needed: *There are medical staff on standby at the stadium.*

stand·ing /ˈstændɪŋ/ *noun* (no plural) people's opinion of someone: *The president's standing has never been higher.*

stand·point /ˈstændpɔɪnt/ *noun* a particular way of thinking about something SYNONYM **point of view**: *Obviously, from my standpoint it's a brilliant idea.*

stand·still /ˈstændˌstɪl/ *noun* (no plural) a situation in which things are not moving, or no one is doing anything: *All the traffic came to a standstill.* • *Work on the new bridge is at a standstill.*

stank the past tense of STINK

sta·ple¹ /ˈsteɪpəl/ *noun* a small U-shaped piece of metal wire that you push through pieces of paper to fasten them together

staple² *verb* to fasten pieces of paper together with staples: *She stapled the pages together.*

sta·pler /ˈsteɪplə $ ˈsteɪplər/ *noun* a machine for putting staples through paper

star¹ /stɑː $ stɑr/ *noun*
1 a point of light that you see in the sky at night: *Stars were shining above us.*
2 a shape with a lot of points sticking out of it: *The American flag has stars and stripes on it.*
3 a famous actor, singer, sports player etc: *She has posters of **pop stars** on her wall.* • *a **movie star***

star² *verb* (**starred**, **starring**) if a film or play stars someone, or if someone stars in it, they are the main character in it: *The film stars Drew Barrymore.* • *She has starred in more than 20 movies.*

star³ *adjective* a star PUPIL, player etc is the best in a group: *Liz is one of our star pupils.*

starch /stɑːtʃ $ stɑrtʃ/ *noun* (no plural) a substance in foods such as bread, rice, and potatoes

star·dom /ˈstɑːdəm $ ˈstɑrdəm/ *noun* (no plural) when someone is very famous as an actor, singer, sports player etc

stare /steə $ ster/ *verb*

KEY PATTERNS
stare at someone/something

to look at someone or something for a long time without moving your eyes: *Don't* ***stare at*** *people – it's rude.*
—**stare** *noun*: *She gave me a cold stare.*

stark¹ /stɑːk $ stɑrk/ *adjective* **1** a stark place is very plain and not attractive: *The building was stark and unwelcoming.* **2** very clear and unpleasant: *The government faces a stark choice.*

stark² *adverb* **stark naked** not wearing any clothes

ˈstar sign *noun* one of the twelve signs that show the part of the year when you were born, which some people believe influence your character: *"What star sign are you?" "Libra."*

start¹ /stɑːt $ stɑrt/ *verb*

KEY PATTERNS
start to do something
start doing something

1 to begin doing something: *Suddenly Sue* ***started to*** *cry.* • *I started writing my essay this morning.* • *My brother is* ***starting school*** *in September.*
2 to begin happening: *What time does the party start?*
3 to make something begin: *It was Kevin who started the argument.*
4 if a car or an engine starts, it begins to work: *Dad's car wouldn't start this morning.*
5 also **start up** to make a new company or organization: *My friends and I decided to start a band.*

PHRASES
to start with (spoken) **a)** used before you mention the first thing in a list: ***To start with****, you need a map.*
b) happening for a while at the beginning, and then stopping: *I didn't understand him* ***to start with.***

PHRASAL VERBS
start off
1 start off to begin something in a particular way: *Let's* ***start off*** *by introducing ourselves.*
2 start something off to make something start happening: *Linda read her report to* ***start off*** *the discussion.*
start on
start on something to begin doing something: *Have you* ***started on*** *your homework yet?*
start over *AmE*
to start doing something again from the beginning: *It's no good you'll have to* ***start over.***

start² *noun*

KEY PATTERNS
the start of something
from the start

the beginning of something: *He appears* ***at the start of*** *the movie.* • *I knew* ***from the start*** *that she was lying.*

PHRASES
get off to a good start, get off to a bad start to start with something good or something bad happening: *The party* ***got off to a bad start*** *when someone broke a chair.*
for a start (spoken) used when you mention the first in a list of things: *You're not going out – you've got too much homework* ***for a start.***

start·er /ˈstɑːtə $ ˈstɑrtɚ/ *noun BrE* the first part of a meal

start·le /ˈstɑːtl $ ˈstɑrtl/ *verb* to surprise someone by suddenly appearing in an unexpected way: *Oh, you startled me!* —**startled** *adjective*: *She looked up with a startled expression on her face.*

starv·a·tion /stɑːˈveɪʃən $ stɑrˈveɪʃən/ *noun* (no plural) when someone has little or no food to eat: *People there are dying of starvation.*

starve /stɑːv $ stɑrv/ *verb* to become ill or die because you do not have enough to eat: *He got lost in the desert and almost starved to death.*

starv·ing /ˈstɑːvɪŋ $ ˈstɑrvɪŋ/ *adjective* **1** someone who is starving is ill or dying because they have not had enough food for a long time
2 (informal) also **starved** /stɑːvd $ stɑrvd/ very hungry

stash /stæʃ/ *verb* (informal) to keep something in a secret place: *He stashed the money under his pillow.*

state[1] /steɪt/ *noun*

KEY PATTERNS
in a bad/terrible etc state
the state of the country/world etc

1 the condition that something is in, especially a bad condition: *Your bedroom is* ***in a terrible state.*** • *People worry a lot about* ***the state of*** *the environment.* • *Look at* ***the state of*** *your clothes! They're filthy!*
2 one of the parts that the US and some other countries are divided into: *the state of Texas*
3 (formal) a country that has its own government: *the former state of Yugoslavia*

PHRASES
be in a state to be very upset or nervous: *She* ***was in a real state*** *about her missing cat.* • *I always* ***get into a state*** *before an exam.*

state[2] *verb* (formal) to say something publicly or officially: *The president stated that he would introduce new laws to protect children.*

state·ment /ˈsteɪtmənt/ *noun*

KEY PATTERNS
a statement about/on something
make/issue a statement

something that a person says or writes publicly and officially: *The band* ***made a statement*** *to the press* ***about*** *their reasons for cancelling the concert.* • *The prime minister will* ***issue a statement on*** *the economy this afternoon.*

ˌstate-of-the-ˈart *adjective* something that is state-of-the-art is very good because it is made in the most modern way

States /steɪts/ *noun* **the States** (spoken) the United States

ˈstate ˌschool *noun BrE* a school which provides free education and is paid for by the government

states·man /ˈsteɪtsmən/ *noun* (plural **statesmen** /-mən/) an experienced and respected politician

stat·ic /ˈstætɪk/ also **ˌstatic elecˈtricity** *noun* (no plural) electricity produced when two surfaces rub together

sta·tion /ˈsteɪʃən/ *noun* **1** a place where trains or buses stop so that people can get on and off: *I'm getting off at the next station.* • *the railway station* **2** a company that broadcasts on radio or television: *your local radio station* **3** a building where the police or people who stop fires are based: *a police station* • *a fire station*

sta·tion·a·ry /ˈsteɪʃənəri $ ˈsteɪʃəˌneri/ *adjective* (formal) not moving: *The traffic was almost stationary.*

SPELLING
Don't confuse the spelling of **stationary** and **stationery** (=writing materials such as paper).

sta·tion·e·ry /ˈsteɪʃənəri $ ˈsteɪʃəˌneri/ *noun* (no plural) things such as paper and envelopes that you use for writing

ˈstation ˌwagon *noun AmE* a large car with space at the back for carrying things SYNONYM **estate car**

sta·tis·tics /stəˈtɪstɪks/ *plural noun* a set of numbers that give information about something: *These statistics show that the population is still increasing.*

stat·ue /ˈstætʃuː/ *noun* a stone or metal model of a person or animal: *the Statue of Liberty in New York*

statue

stat·ure /ˈstætʃə $ ˈstætʃɚ/ *noun* (no plural) (formal) the importance that someone has because of their work or achievements

sta·tus /ˈsteɪtəs $ ˈstætəs/ *noun* (no plural) **1** the position that someone has in a country or organization: *She fought to improve the status of women in society.* **2** special importance that someone has because of their job, achievements, or social position: *He wanted a job with status.*

staunch /stɔːntʃ/ *adjective* very loyal: *All you need is one staunch friend.*

stave /steɪv/ *verb* **stave off something** to prevent something bad from happening: *The team did their best to stave off defeat.*

A B C D E F G H I J K L M N O P Q R S T U V W X Y Z

stay[1] /steɪ/ *verb*

KEY PATTERNS
stay in a room/house/flat etc
stay at home/school/work
stay in Paris/France/Europe
stay at a hotel
stay with a friend/relative

1 to continue to be in the same place and not leave: *I'll* ***stay in*** *the car and wait for you.* • *Do you want to go over to Kathy's or* ***stay here****?* • *I've decided to* ***stay at*** *this school.* • *Do you think he will* ***stay with*** *his wife?*
2 if something stays the way it is, it continues to be the same and does not change SYNONYM **remain**: *The door won't* ***stay open****.* • *I* ***stayed awake*** *all night.*
3 to spend a short period of time in a place: *We are* ***staying in*** *London for a few days.* • *He* ***stayed at*** *the Ritz hotel.* • *They went to* ***stay with*** *Ed's parents.*

PHRASES
stay put (spoken) to remain in the same place and not move: ***Stay put*** *and I'll get someone who can help you.*

PHRASAL VERBS
stay away
to not go near someone or get involved with something: *You should* ***stay away from*** *drugs.*
stay behind
to stay in a place after other people have left: *Bob* ***stayed behind*** *after the party and helped me clear up.*
stay in
to stay in your home and not go out: *I hate* ***staying in*** *on Saturday night.*
stay on
to continue to study: *Are you* ***staying on*** *at school next year?*
stay out of
stay out of something to not become involved in something: *I try to* ***stay out of*** *their arguments.*
stay up
to not go to bed: *I* ***stayed up*** *late trying to finish my homework.*

stay[2] *noun* a period of time that you spend somewhere: *an overnight stay in New York*

stead·fast /ˈstedfɑːst $ ˈstedfæst/ *adjective* (written) refusing to change your beliefs: *his steadfast loyalty to his country*

stead·y[1] /ˈstedi/ *adjective* (**steadier**, **steadiest**)
1 something that is steady does not move or shake: *His hand was very steady as he signed his name.* • *It's important to* ***hold*** *the camera* ***steady****.*
2 something that is steady continues at the same speed or level: *We drove along at a steady 50 miles per hour.* —**steadily** *adverb*: *His work has improved steadily.*

PHRASES
a steady job a job that pays you regular money and is likely to continue for a long time: *My parents want me to find* ***a steady job****.*
a steady girlfriend, a steady boyfriend someone that you have a relationship with for a long time: *Rob was her first* ***steady boyfriend****.*

steady[2] *verb* (**steadied**, **steadies**) to stop something from moving: *He steadied the ladder against the wall.*

steak /steɪk/ *noun* a thick flat piece of meat or fish

steal /stiːl/ *verb* (**stole** /stəʊl $ stoʊl/ **stolen** /ˈstəʊlən $ ˈstoʊlən/)

KEY PATTERNS
steal something from someone/ somewhere

to take something that belongs to someone else: *Someone* ***stole*** *$5* ***from*** *her purse.* • *She* ***stole*** *money* ***from*** *her parents.* • *My bike was stolen.*

THESAURUS
rob: *They tried to rob a bank* (=steal money from it. You say that someone robs a person or a place, not that they rob things).
burgle *BrE*, **burglarize** *AmE*: *He admitted* ***burgling*** *three houses* (=going into them and stealing things. You can also say that a person has been burgled when things have been stolen from their home).
mug: *He* ***mugged*** *an old lady and ran off with her purse* (=attacked or threatened and robbed her).
shoplift: *She was accused of* ***shoplifting*** (=stealing things from shops).

stealth·y /ˈstelθi/ *adjective* (**stealthier**, **stealthiest**) a stealthy action is quiet and secret —**stealthily** *adverb*: *Andy crept stealthily up to the window.*

steam¹ /stiːm/ *noun* the gas that hot water produces: *The bathroom was full of steam.*

steam² *verb* to use steam to cook food: *It's healthier to steam vegetables rather than boil them.* → see picture at COOK¹

ˌsteamed ˈup *adjective* covered with very small drops of water: *The kitchen windows were all steamed up.*

steel /stiːl/ *noun* (no plural) a strong metal that is used for making knives, cars etc

steep /stiːp/ *adjective* a steep road or hill goes down or up very quickly: *I can't ride my bike here – it's too steep.* • *The garden is on quite a **steep slope**.* • *We had to climb up a **steep hill**.* —**steeply** *adverb*

steer /stɪə $ stɪr/ *verb*

KEY PATTERNS
steer a car/boat etc into a place
steer a car/boat etc out of a place

to control which way a vehicle goes: *He **steered** the truck **into** the driveway.* • *I steered my bike out of the garage.*

PHRASES

steer clear of someone/something to avoid someone or something: *I'm going to **steer clear of** Henry until he's in a better mood.*

ˈsteering wheel *noun* the wheel that you turn to make a vehicle go right or left

stem¹ /stem/ *noun* the long thin part of a plant, from which leaves or flowers grow SYNONYM **stalk** → see picture at FLOWER → see picture on page A10

stem² *verb* (**stemmed**, **stemming**) **stem from** to happen as a result of something: *All their problems stemmed from their lack of money.*

stench /stentʃ/ *noun* (no plural) a very strong unpleasant smell SYNONYM **stink** → see Thesaurus at SMELL²

sten·cil /ˈstensəl/ *noun* a piece of card or plastic with shapes cut out of it, which you can use to paint a design on something

step¹ /step/ *noun*

1 a movement in which you put one foot down in front of or behind the other: *She took a step backwards from the edge of the water.* • *The lion took another step towards us.*

2 one of a series of things that you do in order to achieve something: *The next step is to attach the wheels.*

3 a surface that you step onto so that you can go up or down to another level: *There were three steps leading up to the door.* • *She ran down the **flight of steps**.* → see picture at STAIRCASE

PHRASES

one step ahead to have done something or thought of something before someone else: *We've got to stay one step ahead of our competitors.*

step by step steadily, in stages: *Step by step, you will become more confident in using the language.*

take steps to do something in order to deal with a problem: *We must take steps to prevent any more accidents.*

step² *verb* (**stepped**, **stepping**) **1** to put one foot down in front of or behind the other: *He stepped forward to collect his prize.* • *She stepped carefully over the dog.* **2 step down** to leave an important job **3 step out of line** to break the rules **4 step something up** to increase something: *Security at the hospital is being stepped up.*

step·broth·er /ˈstepˌbrʌðə $ ˈstepˌbrʌðɚ/ *noun* someone who is not your brother but is the son of someone who is married to one of your parents

step·child /ˈsteptʃaɪld/ *noun* (plural **stepchildren** /-ˌtʃɪldrən/) a child that your husband or wife has from a previous relationship

step·daugh·ter /ˈstepˌdɔːtə $ ˈstepˌdɔtɚ/ *noun* a daughter that your husband or wife has from a previous relationship

step·fa·ther /ˈstepˌfɑːðə $ ˈstepˌfɑðɚ/ *noun* a man who is married to your mother but is not your father

A B C D E F G H I J K L M N O P Q R S T U V W X Y Z

step·lad·der /ˈstepˌlædə $ ˈstepˌlædɚ/ *noun* a LADDER with two sloping parts joined at the top → see picture at LADDER

step·moth·er /ˈstepˌmʌðə $ ˈstepˌmʌðɚ/ *noun* a woman who is married to your father but is not your mother

step·sis·ter /ˈstepˌsɪstə $ ˈstepˌsɪstɚ/ *noun* someone who is not your sister but is the daughter of someone who is married to one of your parents

step·son /ˈstepsʌn/ *noun* a son that your husband or wife has from a previous relationship

ster·e·o /ˈsteriəʊ $ ˈsteriˌoʊ/ *noun* a machine for playing music tapes, CDs etc that produces sound from two SPEAKERS → see picture on page A12

ster·e·o·type¹ /ˈsteriətaɪp/ *noun* the usual and well-known idea of what a type of person is like, which is probably not correct

stereotype² *verb* to think that someone is a particular type of person, especially when this is not correct: *The city is often stereotyped as being a dangerous place to live.*

ster·ile /ˈsteraɪl $ ˈsterəl/ *adjective* **1** completely clean and not containing any BACTERIA **2** unable to have children SYNONYM **infertile**

ster·il·ize also **sterilise** *BrE* /ˈsterəlaɪz/ *verb* **1** to make something completely clean and contain no BACTERIA: *a sterilized needle* **2** to perform a medical operation on someone so that they cannot have any children

ster·ling /ˈstɜːlɪŋ $ ˈstɚlɪŋ/ *noun* (no plural) the standard unit of money in the UK; the pound

stern¹ /stɜːn $ stɚn/ *adjective* very serious or strict: *The teacher gave me a stern look.*

stern² *noun* the back part of a ship

stew¹ /stjuː $ stu/ *noun* pieces of meat and vegetables that are cooked slowly in liquid

stew² *verb* to cook something slowly in liquid

stew·ard /ˈstjuːəd $ ˈstuɚd/ *noun* a man who serves food and drinks to people on a ship or plane

stew·ard·ess /ˈstjuːədes $ ˈstuɚdɪs/ *noun* (plural **stewardesses**) a woman who serves food and drinks to people on a ship or plane

stick¹ /stɪk/ *verb* (past tense and past participle **stuck** /stʌk/)

> KEY PATTERNS
> **stick a stamp/ticket etc on/to something**
> **stick on/to something**
> **stick a knife/pin/fork etc in/into something**

1 to join two things together using glue: *I stuck a label **on** the bottle.* • *Stick the ticket **to** the car windscreen.*
2 if something sticks to a surface, it stays on it, for example because it has glue on it: *These stamps won't **stick on** the envelope.* • *The leaves were **sticking to** my shoes.*
3 to push a pointed object into something: *She accidentally **stuck** the sewing needle **into** her finger.*
4 if something sticks, it becomes difficult to move: *The window sometimes sticks.*

PHRASAL VERBS

stick out
1 stick out if something sticks out, it comes out from a surface: *Michael's ears **stick out**.*
2 stick something out to deliberately make a part of your body come forward: *He **stuck** his leg **out** and I fell over it.* • *The boy **stuck** his tongue **out** at me.*

stick to
stick to something to continue doing something in the way you planned to do it: *I think we should **stick to** what we decided.*

stick together
if people stick together, they stay together and help each other: *The two sisters have always **stuck together**.*

stick up
if something sticks up, it is not flat but comes up above a surface: *Your hair is **sticking up**.*

stick² *noun* a long thin piece of wood: *a bundle of sticks*

stick·er /ˈstɪkə $ ˈstɪkɚ/ *noun* a small piece of paper or plastic with a picture or writing on it, which you can stick to something

stick·y /ˈstɪki/ *adjective* (**stickier**, **stickiest**)
covered with a substance like glue that sticks to surfaces: *Your hands are all sticky.*

sties the plural of STY

stiff /stɪf/ *adjective*
1 something that is stiff is hard and difficult to bend ANTONYM **flexible**: *a sheet of stiff paper*
2 if a part of your body is stiff, it is difficult to move because your muscles hurt: *I've got a stiff neck.*
3 stiff competition people or teams that are difficult to defeat: *The team will face **stiff competition** this season.*
4 a stiff sentence, a stiff punishment a severe punishment: *The judge gave him a **stiff sentence**.*

sti·fle /ˈstaɪfəl/ *verb* to stop something from happening or developing: *Living with my parents is stifling my social life.*

stif·ling /ˈstaɪflɪŋ/ *adjective* if it is stifling in a place, it is very hot, so that you feel uncomfortable: *It's stifling in here – can I open a window?*

sti·let·to /stɪˈletəʊ $ stɪˈletoʊ/ *noun* a woman's shoe with a high thin heel

still¹ /stɪl/ *adverb*
1 use 'still' to say that a situation has not changed: *Are there any sandwiches left? I'm still hungry. • Is Dad still asleep? • It's still raining. • I still think you should go back to college. • You still haven't given me the money you owe me.*
2 use 'still' to say that something continues to be possible: *We've still got time to catch that film, if we hurry. • You could still change your mind. • Can you still walk?*
3 use 'still' to say that there is a particular amount of something left: *It's still a week before we get paid. • I've still got some cigarettes from last night. • There are still three days to go before the final game.*
4 use 'still' with 'but' or 'although' to say that something did happen, even though something else might have stopped it: *Although Shelley hates cleaning, she still came and helped us. • Cliff had a bad cold, but he still went to work.*

still² *adjective*
not moving: ***Keep still** while I comb your hair. • He was **standing** perfectly **still**. • I wish those children would **sit still**.*

still·born /ˈstɪlbɔːn $ ˌstɪlˈbɔrn/ *adjective* a stillborn baby is born dead

stim·u·late /ˈstɪmjəleɪt/ *verb* **1** to make something grow, develop, or happen: *The light stimulates the plants to grow.* **2** to make someone interested and excited: *toys that stimulate children*

stim·u·lat·ing /ˈstɪmjəleɪtɪŋ/ *adjective* interesting and giving you new ideas ANTONYM **boring**: *a stimulating conversation*

stim·u·lus /ˈstɪmjələs/ *noun* (formal) (plural **stimuli** /-laɪ/) **1** (no plural) something that makes a thing develop or happen **2** something that makes you feel interested or excited: *Children need the visual stimulus of pictures in a book.*

sting¹ /stɪŋ/ *verb* (past tense and past participle **stung** /stʌŋ/)

KEY PATTERNS
sting someone on the arm/face etc

1 if an insect or plant stings you, it hurts you by putting poison into your skin: *A wasp **stung** me **on the leg**.*
2 if something stings, it gives you a sharp pain on your skin or eyes: ***It stung** when they cleaned the wound. • The salt from the sea **made my eyes sting**.* → see Thesaurus at HURT¹

sting² *noun* a wound on your skin where an insect or plant has stung you: *a wasp sting*

stin·gy /ˈstɪndʒi/ *adjective* (informal) (**stingier**, **stingiest**) not generous with your money SYNONYM **mean** *BrE*

stink /stɪŋk/ *verb* (informal) (**stank** /stæŋk/ or **stunk** /stʌŋk/ **stunk**) to have a very strong and unpleasant smell: *Ugh – you stink of smoke! • These socks stink!* —**stink** *noun*: *the stink of dead fish* → see Thesaurus at SMELL²

stir¹ /stɜː $ stɚ/ *verb* (**stirred**, **stirring**)

KEY PATTERNS
stir the mixture/paint etc
stir something with a spoon
stir in the eggs/liquid etc

stir the eggs/liquid etc into something
to mix something by moving a spoon around in it: *Kate* ***stirred*** *her tea* ***with*** *a spoon.* • *Next, stir in the milk.* • *Stir the grated cheese* ***into*** *the sauce.* → see picture on page A4

stir[2] *noun* **1 create a stir, cause a stir** to make people very excited, angry, or surprised: *Her first speech really caused a stir.* **2 give something a stir** to stir liquid or food: *Give the paint a good stir before using it.*

'stir-fry *verb* (**stir-fried, stir-fries**) to cook vegetables or meat quickly in a little hot oil —**stir-fry** *noun*: *Shall we have a stir-fry tonight?*

stir·ring /ˈstɜːrɪŋ/ *adjective* making people feel very excited, proud, or eager to do something SYNONYM **rousing**: *a stirring speech*

stir·rup /ˈstɪrəp $ ˈstɚəp/ *noun* one of the two metal things that you put your feet in when you are riding a horse

stitch[1] /stɪtʃ/ *noun* (plural **stitches**) **1** a single line of thread that has been sewn on material: *a black dress with white stitches around the collar* **2** one of the small circles of wool you make when you KNIT **3 in stitches** (informal) laughing a lot: *We were all in stitches!* → see Thesaurus at LAUGH[1]

stitch[2] *verb* to sew something: *Can you stitch this button on?*

stock[1] /stɒk $ stɑk/ *noun* **1** a supply of things that a shop has available to sell or that someone has ready to use: *The store now has a large stock of computer games.* **2 in stock** if a shop has something in stock, it has it available for people to buy there: *I'm afraid we haven't got that video in stock at the moment.* **3 stocks (and shares)** if you buy stocks in a company, you buy and own a small part of it, so that when the company's profits increase you make more money too: *A lot of people invest in stocks and shares.*

stock[2] *verb* **1** to have something available for people to buy: *We don't stock that brand of cereal any more.* **2 stock up** to buy a supply of things in order to have them ready to use later: *I need to stock up on tea and coffee.*

stock·brok·er /ˈstɒkˌbrəʊkə $ ˈstɑkˌbroʊkɚ/ *noun* someone whose job is to buy and sell company SHARES for other people

'stock exˌchange also **'stock ˌmarket** *noun* **1** a place where people buy and sell the SHARES of many different companies **2 the stock exchange, the stock market** the buying and selling of SHARES: *He made a lot of money on the stock exchange.*

stock·ing /ˈstɒkɪŋ $ ˈstɑkɪŋ/ *noun* a very thin piece of clothing that fits closely over a woman's foot and leg: *a pair of stockings*

'stock ˌmarket *noun* a STOCK EXCHANGE

stock·pile /ˈstɒkpaɪl $ ˈstɑkpaɪl/ *verb* to collect a large supply of something because you think that it may not be available later: *People have been stockpiling food in case there is a bad winter.*

stock·y /ˈstɒki $ ˈstɑki/ *adjective* (**stockier, stockiest**) someone who is stocky is short and has a heavy strong body

stole the past tense of STEAL

stolen the past participle of STEAL

stom·ach[1] /ˈstʌmək/ *noun* **1** the part inside your body where food is DIGESTED **2** the front part of your body, below your chest: *These exercises should help to keep your stomach flat.*

stomach[2] *verb* **can't stomach something** to be unable to watch or listen to something because it is so unpleasant or upsetting

stone /stəʊn $ stoʊn/ *noun*
1 a small piece of rock: *There's a stone in my shoe.* • *We were told off for throwing stones.*
2 (no plural) rock: *The fireplace is made of stone.* • *a stone wall*
3 (plural **stone**) a measurement of weight that is used in Britain and is equal to 14 pounds or 6.35 kilograms: *Sue weighs eight stone.*
4 *BrE* a large hard seed in the centre of a fruit SYNONYM **pit** *AmE*

stoned /stəʊnd $ stoʊnd/ *adjective* (informal) someone who is stoned is behaving in a strange way because they have used illegal drugs

A B C D E F G H I J K L M N O P Q R S T U V W X Y Z

ston·y /ˈstəʊni $ ˈstoʊni/ *adjective* (**stonier**, **stoniest**) covered with stones or containing a lot of stones: *the stony ground*

stood the past tense and past participle of STAND[1]

stool /stuːl/ *noun* a chair with no back

stool

stoop /stuːp/ *verb* to bend your head and shoulders down: *Try not to stoop when you walk.*

stop[1] /stɒp $ stɑp/ *verb* (**stopped**, **stopping**)

KEY PATTERNS
stop doing something
it stops raining/snowing
stop for coffee/lunch etc
stop to do something
stop someone from doing something

1 if you stop doing something, you do not continue to do it: *Suddenly she stopped laughing.* • *Stop making so much noise!* • *I stopped smoking several years ago.*
2 if something stops, it ends: *Suddenly the laughter stopped.* • *We all want the fighting to stop.* • ***It's stopped raining*** (=it is not raining any more).
3 if you stop something, you make it end: *The referee stopped the game.*
4 if a vehicle or machine stops, it does not continue to move or work: *The train stopped at the station.* • *Stop the car! I need to get out.* • *Has this clock stopped?*
5 to pause for a short time: *Shall we* ***stop for*** *a break?* • *Let's* ***stop to*** *get something to eat.*
6 to prevent someone from doing something: *I'm going out and you can't stop me!* • *I tried to* ***stop*** *her* ***from*** *leaving.*
7 if you stop someone, you ask them to stand still and talk to you: *A woman stopped me and asked me the way to the bank.*

PHRASES
stop it, stop that (spoken) used to tell someone not to do something: *I told him to* ***stop it*** *but he kept on hitting me.* • *Ian,* ***stop that*** *immediately!*

GRAMMAR
You **stop someone from doing something** or **stop something from happening**.
✘ Don't say 'stop someone to do something'.

stop[2] *noun*
1 a place where a bus or train regularly stops for its passengers: *She got off the bus* ***at the first stop***. • *This is my stop. Goodbye!*
2 a place that you visit during a trip: *Our first stop will be the Eiffel Tower.*

PHRASES
come to a stop to stop moving: *The plane finally* ***came to a stop*** *at the end of the runway.*
put a stop to something to prevent something from continuing to happen: *I'm going to* ***put a stop to*** *all this nonsense.*

stop·light /ˈstɒplaɪt $ ˈstɑplaɪt/ the American word for a TRAFFIC LIGHT

stop·watch /ˈstɒpwɒtʃ $ ˈstɑpwɑtʃ/ *noun* (plural **stopwatches**) a watch for measuring the exact time it takes to do something

stor·age /ˈstɔːrɪdʒ/ *noun* (no plural) when you keep things somewhere until you need them: *All our furniture is in storage.*

store[1] /stɔː $ stɔr/ *noun*
1 a building where you can buy things; shop *BrE*: *There's a big furniture store near here.* • *a new clothes store*
2 a supply of things that you can use later: *She has* ***a secret store of*** *sweets.*

store[2] *verb*

KEY PATTERNS
store something in a box/container
store information on a computer/ disk etc

1 also **store away** to put things somewhere and keep them there until you need them: *I* ***store*** *all my old books* ***in*** *the attic.* • *My summer clothes are all* ***stored away***.
2 to keep information in a computer: *The hard disk stores a large amount of information.* • *I* ***store*** *a lot of photos* ***on*** *my iPod.*

store·keep·er /ˈstɔːˌkiːpə $ ˈstɔrˌkipɚ/ the American word for a SHOPKEEPER

store·room /ˈstɔːruːm/ *noun* a room where you store things: *We use this bedroom as a storeroom.*

sto·rey (plural **storeys**) *BrE*, **story** (plural **stories** *AmE*) /ˈstɔːri/ *noun* one level of a tall building: *a building with 32 stories*

storm¹ /stɔːm $ stɔrm/ *noun* if there is a storm, there is a lot of wind and rain, and sometimes snow: *It looks like there's going to be a storm.* • *She got lost **in a snowstorm*** (=a storm with a lot of snow). • *We had a huge **thunderstorm*** (=a storm with THUNDER and LIGHTNING) *last night.*

storm² *verb* **1** if people storm a place, they attack it: *The army stormed the city last night.* **2** to walk somewhere in a way that shows you are very angry: *The tutor stormed in and asked why we weren't getting on with our work.*

storm·y /ˈstɔːmi $ ˈstɔrmi/ *adjective* (**stormier**, **stormiest**) if the weather is stormy, there is a lot of wind and rain or snow: *stormy weather* • *a stormy day*

sto·ry /ˈstɔːri/ *noun* (plural **stories**)

KEY PATTERNS
a story about something
the story of someone

1 a description of a set of events that can be real or imaginary: *For homework, we had to **write a story about** an exciting adventure.* • *The kids always love it if you **tell** them **a story**.* • *Dad, will you **read** me **a story**?* • *Do you know **the Greek story of** King Midas?*
2 a report of a real event in a newspaper or news programme: *I read an interesting story in the newspaper today.*
3 an explanation about something that happened, which may be untrue: *The police didn't believe his story.*

stout /staʊt/ *adjective* rather fat: *a stout 40-year-old man*

stove /stəʊv $ stoʊv/ *noun* a piece of kitchen equipment that you cook on SYNONYM **cooker**: *She heated a pan of milk on the stove.*

strad·dle /ˈstrædl/ *verb* to sit or stand with your legs on either side of something: *He sat straddling the gate.*

strag·gly /ˈstrægli/ *adjective* (**stragglier**, **straggliest**) growing or spreading out in an untidy way: *straggly hair*

straight¹ /streɪt/ *adjective*
1 not bent or curved: *Draw a straight line across the page.*
2 level or upright, and not leaning: *That picture isn't straight.* • *Try and keep your writing straight.*
3 straight hair does not have curls in it ANTONYM **curly**, **wavy**: *She had long straight hair.*
4 honest and direct: *I just want a **straight answer**.* • *Do you think he's **being straight with** us?*

PHRASES
get straight A's to get the highest possible mark in all your school subjects: *Elizabeth always **got straight A's** at school.*
get something straight (spoken) to make sure that people completely understand the true facts about a situation: *We need to **get this straight**. Do you want to live here or not?*
keep a straight face to not laugh or smile even though something is funny: *He looked so silly that I couldn't keep a straight face.*

PRONUNCIATION
You pronounce **straight** like 'gate'.

straight² *adverb*

KEY PATTERNS
straight ahead
go straight on
straight in front (of someone/something)

1 in a straight line: *Keep looking **straight ahead**.* • *Go **straight on*** (=continue in the same direction), *and turn left at the church.* • *Jon was sitting **straight in front of** me.*
2 immediately: *When I got home, I **went straight to** my room.* • *I've got French **straight after** lunch.*

PHRASES
straight away immediately: *I knew **straight away** that I had made a mistake.*
sit up straight, stand up straight to sit or stand with your body in an

upright position: *It's good for your back to* ***stand up straight***.

cannot think straight, could not think straight if you cannot think straight, you cannot think clearly because you are excited or upset

straight·en /ˈstreɪtn/ *verb* to make something straight: *Let me straighten your tie.*

straight·for·ward /ˌstreɪtˈfɔːwəd $ ˌstreɪtˈfɔrwərd/ *adjective* easy to do or understand SYNONYM **simple** ANTONYM **complicated**: *It's a straightforward question.*

straightjacket another spelling of STRAITJACKET

strain¹ /streɪn/ *noun* **1** worry and pressure caused by a difficult situation: *She found it hard to cope with the strain of being a teacher.* • *His work put a strain on our marriage.* **2** (no plural) when something is pulled too tightly or has to hold a lot of weight: *The cable broke under the strain* (=because of the strain). **3** an injury to part of your body, caused by using it too much: *Many nurses suffer from back strain.*

strain² *verb* **1** to use a lot of effort to do something: *I had to strain to hear the music.* **2** to separate solid things from a liquid by pouring the mixture through a strainer: *Will you strain the vegetables?* → see picture on page A4 **3** to injure part of your body by using it too much: *I've strained my neck.* **4** to make a relationship more difficult: *His job is straining our relationship.*

strain·er /ˈstreɪnə $ ˈstreɪnər/ *noun* a kitchen tool used for separating solid food from a liquid

strait·jack·et, straightjacket /ˈstreɪtˌdʒækɪt/ *noun* a very tight piece of clothing that is sometimes put on a violent or mentally ill person to stop them from moving their arms

strand /strænd/ *noun* a single thin piece of hair, wire, or thread

strand·ed /ˈstrændɪd/ *adjective* unable to get away from a place, for example because of bad weather: *I was stranded at the airport.*

strange /streɪndʒ/ *adjective* **1** unusual or surprising: *I could hear strange noises.* • *Kevin has some strange ideas.* • ***It's strange that*** *Sarah hasn't called.* **2** a strange place is a place where you have never been before: *She was all alone in a strange city.* —**strangely** *adverb*

> **THESAURUS**
> **funny/peculiar/odd**: *What's that funny noise* (=strange)?
> **weird**: *I had a weird dream last night* (=strange).

strang·er /ˈstreɪndʒə $ ˈstreɪndʒər/ *noun* someone whom you do not know: *A stranger approached him and asked for a cigarette.*

stran·gle /ˈstræŋɡəl/ *verb* to kill someone by tightly pressing their throat: *Her attacker had strangled her with a rope.*

strap¹ /stræp/ *noun* a band of cloth or leather for carrying or fastening something: *a bag with a leather strap* • *a watch strap* → see picture at WATCH²

strap² *verb* (**strapped, strapping**) to fasten something or someone, using straps: *They strapped the bags onto their bikes.* • *His two-year-old son was strapped in the back seat of the car.*

stra·te·gic /strəˈtiːdʒɪk/ *adjective* done as part of a military, business, or political plan: *The president made an important strategic decision.*

strat·e·gy /ˈstrætədʒi/ *noun* (plural **strategies**) a set of plans to achieve something: *What's your strategy going to be for winning the election?*

straw /strɔː/ *noun* **1** (no plural) dried stems of wheat: *We put down clean straw for the animals to sleep on.* **2** a thin tube of plastic used for drinking through **3 the last straw, the final straw** the last problem in a series of problems that finally makes you become angry or stop trying to do something: *It was the last straw when my car broke down.*

straw·ber·ry /ˈstrɔːbəri $ ˈstrɔˌberi/ *noun* (plural **strawberries**) a small red juicy fruit that grows on plants near the ground → see picture on page A7

stray[1] /streɪ/ *verb* to move away from a safe or familiar area: *The kitten had strayed from its mother.*

stray[2] *noun* an animal that is lost or has no home —**stray** *adjective*: *a stray dog*

streak /striːk/ *noun* a thin line of colour that is different to the colour around it: *He had streaks of grey in his hair.* → see Thesaurus at LINE[1]

stream[1] /striːm/ *noun* **1** a small river **2** a moving line of things: *There was a steady stream of traffic through the town centre.*

stream[2] *verb* to move somewhere quickly and continuously, in large amounts SYNONYM **pour**: *Tears were streaming down his face.* • *People streamed into the building.*

stream·line /ˈstriːmlaɪn/ *verb* **1** to make something work in a simpler and more effective way: *We are streamlining our business.* **2** if you streamline a vehicle, you improve its shape so that it moves more easily through air or water —**streamlined** *adjective*: *the streamlined shape of modern planes*

street /striːt/ *noun*
a road in a town or city with houses or shops on it: *Go to the end of the street and turn left.* • *The two boys live* **in** *the same* **street**. • *I live* **at** *75 Queen Street.* → see Thesaurus at ROAD

street·car /ˈstriːtkɑː $ ˈstritkɑr/ the American word for a TRAM

street·light, **street light** /ˈstriːtlaɪt/ *noun* a light on a long pole in a street

strength /streŋθ/ *noun*

KEY PATTERNS
have the strength to do something

1 (no plural) someone's strength is their ability to lift or carry heavy objects ANTONYM **weakness**: *She didn't* **have the strength to** *lift the box on her own.* • *You need a lot of* **strength to** *be a weightlifter.*
2 your strengths are the things that you are good at ANTONYM **weakness**: *Make a list of your strengths and weaknesses.*
3 (no plural) being brave and determined in difficult situations: *She has shown a lot of strength in dealing with her son's illness.* • *He didn't* **have the strength to** *carry on living.*

strength·en /ˈstreŋθən/ *verb* to make something stronger ANTONYM **weaken**: *an exercise to strengthen your legs*

stren·u·ous /ˈstrenjuəs/ *adjective* a strenuous activity needs a lot of effort or strength: *a strenuous exercise routine*

stress[1] /stres/ *noun* (plural **stresses**) **1** continuous feelings of worry that prevent you from relaxing: *I don't cope well with stress.* • *She's under a lot of stress at work.* **2** the force or loudness with which you say a part of a word: *The stress is on the first syllable.*

stress[2] *verb* **1** to say how important something is: *She stressed the importance of homework.* **2** to say a word or part of a word more loudly or with more force than other words: *He stressed the word 'everyone'.*

stressed /strest/ also **ˌstressed ˈout** *adjective* (informal) worried and unable to relax: *Don't get stressed about exams.*

stress·ful /ˈstresfəl/ *adjective* making you worried and unable to relax: *Pilots have a stressful job.*

stretch[1] /stretʃ/ *verb*

KEY PATTERNS
stretch something
stretch your arms over/above your head
stretch down to the river/sea/valley
stretch for a long way

1 to make something bigger by pulling it: *Don't pull my sweater – you'll stretch it.*
2 if something stretches, it becomes bigger when you pull it: *Tights stretch when you put them on.*
3 to push your arms or legs out as far as they can go: *He yawned and stretched.* • **Stretch** *your arms* **above** *your head.* → see picture on page A2
4 to spread over a large area: *The beach* **stretched down to** *the sea.* • *The traffic jam* **stretched for** *over two miles.*
5 to pull something so that it is straight and tight: *They* **stretched** *the net* **between** *the two posts.*

A B C D E F G H I J K L M N O P Q R S T U V W X Y Z

PHRASAL VERBS

stretch out

1 stretch out, stretch yourself out to lie down: *He* ***stretched out*** *on the bed and went to sleep.*

2 stretch your hand out, stretch your arm out to move your hand or arm forward so that you can reach something: *She* ***stretched out*** *her hand to touch his face.*

stretch² *noun* (plural **stretches**) an area of land or water: *a dangerous stretch of water*

stretch·er /ˈstretʃə $ ˈstretʃɚ/ *noun* a covered frame that you use for carrying an injured person: *He was carried off the pitch on a stretcher.*

strewn /struːn/ *adjective* if objects are strewn somewhere, they have been thrown or dropped there in an untidy way: *Toys were strewn all over the floor.*

strict /strɪkt/ *adjective*

KEY PATTERNS
strict with someone
strict about someone doing something

1 a strict person has a lot of rules and makes people obey them: *Most of the teachers here are quite strict.* • *Some parents are very* ***strict with*** *their children.* • *The school is very* ***strict about*** *students doing their homework on time.*

2 a strict rule or instruction must be obeyed: *There are strict rules about who is allowed in the country.* • *I have strict orders not to let you leave.*

3 always following your beliefs or religion very carefully: *Margaret is a strict Catholic who goes to mass every day.* • *a strict vegetarian*

strict·ly /ˈstrɪktli/ *adverb* **1** if something is not strictly true, it is not exactly true **2** in a strict way: *My father raised us very strictly.*

stridden the past participle of STRIDE¹

stride¹ /straɪd/ *verb* (**strode** /strəʊd $ stroʊd/ **stridden** /ˈstrɪdn/) to walk with quick long steps: *He strode down the hall.*

stride² *noun* **1** a long step: *He walks with great big strides.* **2 take something in your stride** to deal with a problem easily and calmly: *Kids seem to take everything in their stride.*

strike¹ /straɪk/ *verb* (past tense and past participle **struck** /strʌk/)

KEY PATTERNS
strike someone on the head/nose
be struck by lightning
it strikes me that
strike someone as strange/unusual etc

1 to hit something or someone: *A tile fell off the roof and* ***struck*** *Charlie* ***on the head.*** • *The church tower* ***was struck by lightning.*** → see Thesaurus at HIT¹

2 if an idea strikes you, you suddenly think of it: ***It struck me that*** *Peter was keeping very quiet.*

3 how something strikes you is how it seems to you: *Her attitude* ***struck*** *me* ***as*** *odd.*

4 if a clock strikes, its bell makes a number of sounds to show the time: *The clock struck four.*

strike² *noun*
when a group of workers stop working because they want better pay or working conditions: *Railway workers are planning a one-day strike next week.*

PHRASES

be on strike, go on strike if a group of workers are on strike, they have stopped working because they want better pay or working conditions: *The workers at the factory* ***went on strike.*** • *They've* ***been on strike*** *for three weeks now.*

strik·er /ˈstraɪkə $ ˈstraɪkɚ/ *noun* **1** someone who has stopped working in order to get better pay or working conditions: *Strikers stopped cars entering the factory.* **2** a football player whose main job is to try to get GOALS: *Our two strikers have scored over 30 goals this season.*

strik·ing /ˈstraɪkɪŋ/ *adjective*
1 unusual and noticeable: *There's a striking similarity between them.*
→ see Thesaurus at NOTICEABLE
2 very attractive, often in an unusual way: *She's a very striking woman.*

A B C D E F G H I J K L M N O P Q R S T U V W X Y Z

string /strɪŋ/ *noun*
1 a thin rope that you use for tying things: *He tied some string round the package.*
2 the strings on a GUITAR or other musical instrument are the long thin pieces of wire that are stretched across it
3 a number of similar things that happen one after the other SYNONYM **series**: *There's been **a string of** complaints about you.*

strip[1] /strɪp/ *verb* (**stripped**, **stripping**) also **strip off** **1** to take off your clothes: *He stripped and got into the shower.* **2** to remove something that is covering a surface: *We stripped the paint off the walls.*

strip[2] *noun* a long narrow piece of something: *a strip of paper*

stripe /straɪp/ *noun* a long narrow area of colour: *a shirt with red stripes*
→ see Thesaurus at LINE[1]

striped /straɪpt/ also **strip·y** /ˈstraɪpi/ *adjective* something that is striped has a pattern of stripes on it: *a striped dress*

strive /straɪv/ *verb* (formal) (**strove** /strəʊv $ stroʊv/ **striven** /ˈstrɪvən/) to try very hard to do something: *He always strives to do his best.*

striven the past participle of STRIVE

strode the past tense of STRIDE[1]

stroke[1] /strəʊk $ stroʊk/ *noun* **1** an illness in which a part of your brain becomes damaged, often with the result that you become unable to move a part of your body: *My grandad's had a stroke.* **2** a way of swimming: *back stroke*

stroke[2] *verb* to move your hand gently over something: *The cat likes it when you stroke her.* → see Thesaurus at TOUCH[1]

stroll /strəʊl $ stroʊl/ *verb* to walk in a slow relaxed way: *We strolled along the beach.* → see Thesaurus at WALK[1]
—**stroll** *noun*: *Are you coming for a stroll?*

stroll·er /ˈstrəʊlə $ ˈstroʊlɚ/ the American word for a PUSHCHAIR

strong /strɒŋ $ strɔŋ/ *adjective* (**stronger** /ˈstrɒŋgə $ ˈstrɔŋgɚ/, **strongest** /ˈstrɒŋgɪst $ ˈstrɔŋgɪst/)
1 someone who is strong has strength and energy ANTONYM **weak**: *At 19, Ricky was tall and strong.* • *He was not **strong enough to** lift the rock up.*
2 something that is strong cannot be broken or damaged easily ANTONYM **flimsy**, **fragile**: *She carried the bottles in a strong plastic bag.*
3 a strong wind is blowing with a lot of force ANTONYM **gentle**: *a strong wind*
4 a strong feeling or belief is one that you feel or believe a lot: *I had a strong desire to hit him.* • *There is strong evidence that smoking makes you ill.*
5 a strong drink contains a lot of a substance ANTONYM **weak**: *a cup of strong coffee*
6 if someone is strong, they are not made too upset by problems and are not easily persuaded by other people ANTONYM **weak**: *You have to be strong to cope with the death of a child.*

PHRASES
a strong chance, a strong possibility if there is a strong chance or possibility of something happening, it is very likely: *There's **a strong possibility that** he will be chosen for the school team.*

strong·ly /ˈstrɒŋli $ ˈstrɔŋli/ *adverb*
1 if you believe in something strongly, you think it is important or care a lot about it: *I believe strongly in the importance of education.* **2** tasting or smelling a lot of something: *The house smelled strongly of gas.*

strove the past tense of STRIVE

struck the past tense of STRIKE[1]

struc·tur·al /ˈstrʌktʃərəl/ *adjective* related to the structure of a building, bridge etc: *The storm caused structural damage.*

struc·ture[1] /ˈstrʌktʃə $ ˈstrʌktʃɚ/ *noun* **1** the way in which the parts of something are put together or organized: *the structure of society*
2 something that has been built, especially a building: *a huge wooden structure*

structure[2] *verb* to arrange something in a clear way: *The teacher taught us how to structure a piece of writing.*

strug·gle /ˈstrʌgəl/ *verb* **1** to try very hard to achieve something difficult: *Susie's really struggled to pass these exams.* **2** to fight someone who is

attacking or holding you: *She struggled but could not get away from him.*
—**struggle** *noun*: *He broke his glasses in the struggle.*

strut /strʌt/ *verb* (**strutted, strutting**) to walk in a very proud and annoying way: *He struts around the school as if he owns it.*

stub /stʌb/ *noun* the part of a cigarette that is left after the rest has been used

stub•ble /ˈstʌbəl/ *noun* (no plural) the very short hairs on a man's face when he has not SHAVEd for a few days

stub•born /ˈstʌbən $ ˈstʌbərn/ *adjective* someone who is stubborn refuses to change their opinions or beliefs in a way that seems unreasonable: *Stop being so stubborn.*

stuck[1] the past tense and past participle of STICK[1]

stuck[2] /stʌk/ *adjective* (spoken) **1** not able to move: *John's stuck up the tree!* • *The door's stuck!* **2** if you are stuck, you cannot continue with your work because it is too difficult: *Jane helps me when I get stuck with my homework.*

stud /stʌd/ *noun* a small round piece of metal that is stuck into the surface of something: *You need football shoes with studs in this wet weather.*

stu•dent /ˈstjuːdənt $ ˈstudnt/ *noun* someone who studies at a school or university

> WORD CHOICE
> **student** or **pupil**?
> • A **student** is someone who goes to a school, college, or university.
> • A **pupil** is someone who goes to a school.

stu•di•o /ˈstjuːdiəʊ $ ˈstudi,oʊ/ *noun* **1** a room where a painter or photographer works **2** a place where films, records, or television or radio programmes are made

stu•di•ous /ˈstjuːdiəs $ ˈstudiəs/ *adjective* someone who is studious spends a lot of time studying: *a studious young boy*

stud•y[1] /ˈstʌdi/ *noun* (plural **studies**)
1 a piece of work in which someone collects facts and information so that they can find out more about something: *They* ***carried out a study of*** *the types of food that children eat.*
2 (no plural) when you learn about a subject: *Biology is* ***the study of*** *living things.*
3 a room in your house where you write or study
4 your studies, his studies etc the work someone does at school or college: *You've got to continue with your studies.*

study[2] *verb* (**studied, studies**)
1 to learn about a subject: *She wants to study law at university.* ➔ see Thesaurus at LEARN
2 to look at something carefully: *He studied the map.*

stuff[1] /stʌf/ *noun* (no plural) (informal) **1** any substance or material: *What's that green stuff on the wall?* **2** things in general: *Do you need all this stuff on holiday?* • *It's the same old stuff on TV every night.* ➔ see Thesaurus at PROPERTY

stuff[2] *verb* to push something into a place quickly and carelessly: *I quickly stuffed some clothes into a bag.* • *He stuffed the letter into his pocket.*

stuff•ing /ˈstʌfɪŋ/ *noun* (no plural) material that is used to fill something: *All the stuffing's come out of the mattress.*

stuff•y /ˈstʌfi/ *adjective* (**stuffier, stuffiest**) places that are stuffy do not have enough fresh air: *It's very stuffy in here.*

stum•ble /ˈstʌmbəl/ *verb* to almost fall SYNONYM **trip**: *She stumbled over the rocks.* ➔ see Thesaurus at FALL[1]

stump /stʌmp/ *noun* the part of something that is left when the rest has been cut off: *a tree stump*

stun /stʌn/ *verb* (**stunned, stunning**) to surprise or shock someone very much: *Everyone was stunned by the news.*

stung the past tense and past participle of STING

stunk the past participle of STINK

stun•ning /ˈstʌnɪŋ/ *adjective* **1** very beautiful: *You look absolutely stunning.* **2** very surprising SYNONYM **staggering**: *stunning news*

stunt¹ /stʌnt/ *noun* **1** a dangerous thing that someone does to entertain people, especially in a film: *There's a great stunt in which his car has to jump across a 15 metre gap.* **2** something that people do to get attention: *The photograph was just a publicity stunt.*

stunt² *verb* to stop something from growing or developing properly: *a disease that stunts your growth*

stu•pid /ˈstjuːpɪd $ ˈstupɪd/ *adjective* **1** not intelligent or sensible: *You're so stupid you haven't switched the machine on!* • *I made a stupid mistake.* **2** (spoken) used to talk about something that annoys you: *The stupid machine's broken!*

stu•por /ˈstjuːpə $ ˈstupɚ/ *noun* a state in which you are almost unconscious: *He was lying on the bed in a drunken stupor.*

stur•dy /ˈstɜːdi $ ˈstɚdi/ *adjective* (**sturdier**, **sturdiest**) thick and strong: *sturdy shoes*

stut•ter /ˈstʌtə $ ˈstʌtɚ/ *verb* to have difficulty speaking so that you repeat the first sound of a word SYNONYM **stammer**: *"I w-w-want to g-g-go too," he stuttered.* —**stutter** *noun*: *I didn't always speak with a stutter.*

sty /staɪ/ *noun* (plural **sties**) a PIGSTY

style /staɪl/ *noun*

KEY PATTERNS
a style of writing/drawing/teaching
a style of life/living
in a similar/traditional etc style

1 a way of doing something: *He developed his own **style of** painting.* • *I just loved the Australian **style of** life.* • *The two poems are written **in** different **styles**.*
2 the shape or design of a piece of clothing: *Does this **style of** jacket suit me?*
3 the shape in which your hair is cut SYNONYM **hairstyle**: *I think a shorter style would suit you.*

styl•ish /ˈstaɪlɪʃ/ *adjective* attractive and fashionable: *Joe always wears very stylish clothes.* → see Thesaurus at FASHIONABLE —**stylishly** *adverb*: *She always dresses stylishly.*

sub /sʌb/ (informal) **1** a SUBMARINE **2** a SUBSTITUTE¹

sub•con•scious¹ /sʌbˈkɒnʃəs $ sʌbˈkɑnʃəs/ *adjective* subconscious feelings affect your behaviour although you do not realize that they exist —**subconsciously** *adverb*: *Our dreams often show us what we are feeling subconsciously.*

subconscious² *noun* (no plural) your subconscious is the part of you that has thoughts and feelings that you do not know about, but which influence your behaviour

sub•due /səbˈdjuː $ səbˈdu/ *verb* to stop someone from behaving violently: *Police were sent in to subdue the crowd.*

sub•dued /səbˈdjuːd $ səbˈdud/ *adjective* **1** quiet, especially because you are worried: *You seem a bit subdued.* **2** not as bright or loud as usual: *subdued lighting*

sub•ject /ˈsʌbdʒɪkt/ *noun*
1 one of the things such as literature or science that you study at school or university: *My favourite subject is English.*
2 the thing that you are talking or writing about: *I don't think we should talk about this subject in front of the children.* • *What was **the subject of** the student debate?* • *They discussed **the subject of** money.* • *I tried to **change the subject*** (=start talking about something else).
3 the word that usually comes before the verb in a sentence and shows who is doing the action. In the sentence 'Jean loves cats', 'Jean' is the subject.

sub•jec•tive /səbˈdʒektɪv/ *adjective* influenced by your own opinions and feelings rather than by facts ANTONYM **objective**: *Beauty is a very subjective thing.*

sub•junc•tive /səbˈdʒʌŋktɪv/ *noun* a verb form that you use to express a doubt, wish, or possibility. In the sentence 'He suggested we leave early', 'leave' is in the subjunctive.

submarine

sub·ma·rine /ˈsʌbməriːn/ *noun* a ship that can travel under water → see picture on page A11

sub·merge /səbˈmɜːdʒ $ səbˈmɚdʒ/ *verb* to put something below the surface of water: *The town was completely submerged by the floods.*

sub·mis·sion /səbˈmɪʃən/ *noun* (no plural) when you are forced to agree to do what someone tells you to: *The soldiers beat them into submission.*

sub·mit /səbˈmɪt/ *verb* (formal) (**submitted**, **submitting**) **1** to write something formal and give it to someone to look at or consider: *I've been asked to submit a report to the committee.* • *Have you submitted your job application yet?* **2** to agree to do something because someone is forcing you to do it

sub·or·di·nate /səˈbɔːdənət $ səˈbɔrdənət/ *noun* (formal) someone who has a less important job than another person in an organization: *It's important to get on well with both your colleagues and your subordinates.*

sub·scribe /səbˈskraɪb/ *verb* to pay money so that you receive a newspaper or magazine regularly: *I've always subscribed to the 'National Geographic' magazine.*

sub·scrip·tion /səbˈskrɪpʃən/ *noun* an amount of money that you pay to regularly get a newspaper or magazine

sub·se·quent /ˈsʌbsəkwənt/ *adjective* (formal) coming after something else ANTONYM **previous**: *His illness and subsequent death were a terrible shock to us all.*
—**subsequently** *adverb*: *We met on holiday and subsequently became good friends.*

sub·side /səbˈsaɪd/ *verb* (formal) if a feeling or noise subsides, it becomes less strong or loud SYNONYM **die down**: *Her grief eventually subsided.*

sub·sid·i·a·ry[1] /səbˈsɪdiəri $ səbˈsɪdiˌeri/ *noun* (plural **subsidiaries**) a company that another company owns or controls: *Ford has subsidiaries all over the world.*

subsidiary[2] *adjective* (formal) less important than something else: *We have to study two subsidiary subjects as well as our main subject.*

sub·si·dize also **subsidise** *BrE* /ˈsʌbsədaɪz/ *verb* to pay part of the cost of something: *The government subsidizes school meals.*

sub·si·dy /ˈsʌbsədi/ *noun* (plural **subsidies**) money a government pays to help with the cost of something: *The government gives subsidies to farmers.*

sub·stance /ˈsʌbstəns/ *noun* any type of solid or liquid: *Honey is a sweet substance made by bees.* • *There might be poisonous substances in the water.*

sub·stan·tial /səbˈstænʃəl/ *adjective* large in amount or size: *A substantial amount of money is missing.* • *We ate a substantial breakfast before setting off.*

sub·stan·tial·ly /səbˈstænʃəli/ *adverb* by a large amount SYNONYM **considerably**: *Costs have risen substantially.*

sub·sti·tute[1] /ˈsʌbstətjuːt $ ˈsʌbstəˌtut/ *noun* someone who takes the place of someone else: *a substitute goalkeeper*

substitute[2] *verb* to use something new or different instead of something else: *You can substitute olive oil for butter.*

sub·ti·tles /ˈsʌbˌtaɪtlz/ *plural noun* words on a film or television SCREEN that translate what the actors are saying: *a French film with English subtitles*

sub·tle /ˈsʌtl/ *adjective* not very noticeable, strong, or bright: *a subtle change* • *a subtle smell of roses*

sub·tract /səbˈtrækt/ *verb* to take one number away from another number: *If you subtract 10 from 45 you get 35.*
→ see Thesaurus at CALCULATE

sub·trac·tion /səbˈtrækʃən/ *noun* when you take one number away from another: *Subtraction is more difficult than addition.*

sub·urb /ˈsʌbɜːb $ ˈsʌbɚb/ *noun* an area on the edge of a big city where people live: *a suburb of New York*
→ see Thesaurus at AREA

sub·ur·ban /səˈbɜːbən $ səˈbɚbən/ *adjective* a suburban area is outside the main part of a big city: *suburban districts of London*

sub·way /ˈsʌbweɪ/ *noun* **1** *BrE* a path that goes under a road or railway SYNONYM **underpass**: *If you need to cross the road, use the subway.*
2 *AmE* a railway that runs under the ground SYNONYM **underground**: *I took the subway up to Ninth Avenue.*

suc·ceed /səkˈsiːd/ *verb* to achieve what you have been trying to do ANTONYM **fail**: *By pushing hard, he* ***succeeded in*** *opening the window.* • *I tried to light a fire, but didn't succeed.*

GRAMMAR
You **succeed in doing something**.
✘ Don't say 'succeed to do something'.

suc·cess /səkˈses/ *noun* (plural **successes**)

KEY PATTERNS
success in something
success in doing something
have some/no etc success

1 when you achieve what you have been trying to do ANTONYM **failure**: *They were pleased with their* ***success in*** *the tournament.* • *China has had a lot of* ***success in*** *raising living standards.* • *I tried to persuade Josh to come with us, but I didn't* ***have*** *much* ***success****.*
2 if a film, event, product etc is a success, many people like it ANTONYM **failure**: *The film was* ***a great success****.*

suc·cess·ful /səkˈsesfəl/ *adjective*

KEY PATTERNS
successful in doing something
successful at work/school

1 if you are successful in doing something, you achieve what you have been trying to do ANTONYM **unsuccessful**: *They were* ***successful in*** *persuading him to join their team.* • *I was never very* ***successful at*** *school.*
2 something that is successful achieves what you want it to achieve: *The treatment was successful, and she is able to walk again now.*
3 something that is successful is liked by many people and makes a lot of money: *He has written two successful books.* —**successfully** *adverb*: *She successfully applied for a place at university.*

SPELLING
This word is often spelled wrongly. The correct spelling is: **successful**.

suc·ces·sion /səkˈseʃən/ *noun* (no plural) a number of things that happen one after the other: *They finally managed to win a game after a succession of failures.*

suc·ces·sive /səkˈsesɪv/ *adjective* happening one after the other: *I had to go to London on three successive days.*

suc·ces·sor /səkˈsesə $ səkˈsesɚ/ *noun* the person who has someone's job after they leave: *Who will be his successor?*

suc·cinct /səkˈsɪŋkt/ *adjective* clear and not containing many words: *a succinct answer to the question*

suc·cu·lent /ˈsʌkjələnt/ *adjective* succulent food has a lot of juice and tastes very good: *a succulent steak*

suc·cumb /səˈkʌm/ *verb* (formal) to be unable to stop yourself from doing something: *She finally succumbed and had a chocolate biscuit.*

PRONUNCIATION
In this word you do not pronounce the **b**.

such /sʌtʃ/ *determiner*
1 use **such** with an adjective and noun to make the adjective stronger: *This is such a good computer game.* • *I didn't realize you worked in such a big building.* • *Italians are such nice people.*
2 (formal) also **such ... as** used to talk or write about something that has already been mentioned or seen: *There are a lot of violent shows on TV, and such shows are damaging our children.* • *Such behaviour as this is not acceptable at school.*

PHRASES

such as used to give an example of the type of thing you mean: *I enjoy sports **such as** swimming, football, and golf.* • *Pollution is a problem in big cities **such as** Tokyo.*

such ... that used with an adjective and noun that describes something to give a reason or result: *It was **such** a delicious cake **that** we ate all of it.*

there's no such thing used to say that something does not exist: *I don't believe in aliens – **there's no such thing**.*

suck /sʌk/ *verb* **1** to hold something in your mouth and pull on it with your tongue and lips: *Small children often suck their thumbs.* **2** if water or air sucks someone or something in a particular direction, the force of it pulls them there: *She tried to swim, but the water sucked her down.*

sud·den /ˈsʌdn/ *adjective* something that is sudden happens quickly, when you are not expecting it: *A sudden change in your life can cause stress.* • *His death was very sudden.*

sud·den·ly /ˈsʌdnli/ *adverb* if something happens suddenly, it happens quickly, when you are not expecting it: *Jim suddenly stopped the car.* • *I suddenly remembered that I had to phone Jane.*

suds /sʌdz/ *plural noun* the bubbles you get when you mix soap and water: *soap suds*

sue /sjuː $ su/ *verb* to start a legal process to get money from someone who has harmed you: *They're suing us for $10,000.*

suede /sweɪd/ *noun* (no plural) soft leather with a slightly rough surface: *a suede jacket*

suf·fer /ˈsʌfə $ ˈsʌfɚ/ *verb*
1 to experience pain: *It was a quick death – he didn't suffer much.*
2 to feel very upset: *Children often suffer a lot when their parents get divorced.*
3 (formal) to be harmed or made weaker by something: *A lot of small businesses suffered badly during the economic recession.*
4 to become worse because of something: *His school work is suffering because he goes out every evening.*

PHRASAL VERBS

suffer from
suffer from something to have an illness or health problem: *Do you suffer from headaches?*

suf·fi·cient /səˈfɪʃənt/ *adjective* as much as you need SYNONYM **enough** ANTONYM **insufficient**: *The police do not have sufficient evidence.*

suf·fix /ˈsʌfɪks/ *noun* (plural **suffixes**) letters that you add to the end of a word to make a new word, for example 'ness' at the end of 'kindness'

suf·fo·cate /ˈsʌfəkeɪt/ *verb* to kill someone by not allowing them to breathe air: *He suffocated her with a pillow.*

sug·ar /ˈʃʊgə $ ˈʃʊgɚ/ *noun* (no plural) a sweet substance that you add to food: *Do you take sugar in your tea?*

sug·gest /səˈdʒest $ səgˈdʒest/ *verb*

KEY PATTERNS
suggest that someone does something
suggest doing something
suggest someone/something

1 to say what you think someone should do: *I **suggest that** you make a list of things you will need on your trip.* • *Most airlines suggest arriving a couple of hours before the flight.*
2 to mention someone or something that would be suitable for a particular purpose: *They were looking for a new goalkeeper, so I suggested Callum.*
3 to say or show that something might be true: *Are you **suggesting that** she cheated in the test?* • *The evidence **suggests that** red wine may be good for your health.*

sug·ges·tion /səˈdʒestʃən $ səgˈdʒestʃən/ *noun*

KEY PATTERNS
make a suggestion about something
have a suggestion (to make)
a suggestion for doing something
a suggestion that
be a/no suggestion of something

1 an idea that someone suggests: *The teacher **made** some helpful **suggestions about** where to find the information.* • *I **have a suggestion to make**. Why don't we share the cost*

A B C D E F G H I J K L M N O P Q R S T U V W X Y Z

between us? • *Do you have any* **suggestions for** *raising the money?* • *There was a* **suggestion that** *we needed a new team captain.*
2 a sign or possibility that something might be true: *When was the first* **suggestion of** *a link between smoking and cancer?* • **One suggestion is that** *dinosaurs died out because of a change in the Earth's climate.*

su•i•cid•al /ˌsuːəˈsaɪdl/ *adjective* people who are suicidal feel so unhappy that they want to kill themselves: *I felt almost suicidal when my mother died.*

su•i•cide /ˈsuːəsaɪd/ *noun* when someone deliberately kills himself or herself: *More and more young men are committing suicide.*

suit¹ /suːt/ *noun*
1 a jacket and trousers or skirt that are made of the same material: *a businessman in a dark blue suit*
➔ see picture at CLOTHES
2 a set of clothes that you wear for a particular activity: *a ski suit*
3 one of the four types of playing card. The four suits are called CLUBS, DIAMONDS, HEARTS, and SPADES

> PRONUNCIATION
> You pronounce **suit** like 'root'.

suit² *verb*
1 if something suits you, it makes you look attractive: *That blue dress suits you.*
2 if something suits you, it is acceptable for you and does not cause any problems for you: *"I'd like to make an appointment." "Would Monday morning suit you?"*

suit•a•ble /ˈsuːtəbəl/ *adjective* right for a particular purpose or situation: *This movie's not suitable for children.*

suit•case /ˈsuːtkeɪs/ *noun* a case for carrying clothes and other things when you travel ➔ see picture at CASE

suite /swiːt/ *noun* **1** a set of expensive rooms in a hotel: *the honeymoon suite* **2** a set of furniture: *a dining room suite*

sulfur the American spelling of SULPHUR

sulk /sʌlk/ *verb* to show that you are annoyed by being silent and looking unhappy: *She'll sulk if you don't let her go to the party.* —**sulk** *noun* (no plural): *He's in a sulk again.*

sulk•y /ˈsʌlki/ *adjective* (**sulkier**, **sulkiest**) often sulking: *a sulky child*

sul•len /ˈsʌlən/ *adjective* quiet and looking angry: *Simon sat in the corner, looking sullen.*

sul•phur *BrE*, **sulfur** *AmE* /ˈsʌlfə $ ˈsʌlfɚ/ *noun* (no plural) a yellow chemical powder that smells unpleasant

sul•tan /ˈsʌltən/ *noun* a ruler in some Muslim countries

sul•ta•na /sʌlˈtɑːnə $ sʌlˈtænə/ *noun BrE* a dried white GRAPE

sum /sʌm/ *noun* **1** an amount of money: *They've spent huge sums of money on that house.* **2** *BrE* if you do a sum, you add, divide, multiply etc numbers: *I'm terrible at doing sums*
3 the total you get when you add two or more numbers together: *The sum of 3 and 7 is 10.*

sum•mar•ize also **summarise** *BrE* /ˈsʌməraɪz/ *verb* to give only the main information about something without all the details: *I'll summarize the main points of his speech.*

sum•ma•ry /ˈsʌməri/ *noun* (plural **summaries**) a short statement that gives the main information about something without all the details: *Write a summary of the article.*

sum•mer /ˈsʌmə $ ˈsʌmɚ/ *noun*

> KEY PATTERNS
> **in summer**
> **in the summer**

the season between spring and autumn, when the weather is hottest: *Last summer we went on vacation to Florida.* • *We often eat outside* **in summer**. • *We'll come and visit you* **in the summer**. ➔ see picture on page A13

sum•mer•time /ˈsʌmətaɪm $ ˈsʌmɚˌtaɪm/ *noun* (no plural) the time of year when it is summer: *It gets very hot in summertime.*

sum•mit /ˈsʌmɪt/ *noun* **1** a meeting between the leaders of several governments: *an economic summit*
2 the top of a mountain: *It took them three weeks to reach the summit.*

A B C D E F G H I J K L M N O P Q R S T U V W X Y Z

A B C D E F G H I J K L M N O P Q R S T U V W X Y Z

sum·mon /ˈsʌmən/ *verb* (formal) to officially order someone to come to a place: *The head teacher summoned me to his office.*

sun /sʌn/ *noun* the thing in the sky that gives us light and heat: *The sun's gone behind a cloud.* • *She lay in the sun reading.*

sun·bathe /ˈsʌnbeɪð/ *verb* to sit or lie outside in the sun so that your skin will become brown: *This is a good place to sunbathe.*

sun·burn /ˈsʌnbɜːn $ ˈsʌnbɚn/ *noun* (no plural) when your skin has become red and painful because you have stayed too long in the sun

sun·burnt /ˈsʌnbɜːnt $ ˈsʌnbɚnt/ also **sun·burned** /ˈsʌnbɜːnd $ ˈsʌnbɚnd/ *adjective* if you are sunburnt, your skin is red and painful because you have stayed too long in the sun: *Be careful not to get sunburnt.*

ˈsun cream SUNSCREEN

Sun·day /ˈsʌndi/ (written abbreviation **Sun**) *noun* the day of the week between Saturday and Monday: *I'll see you on Sunday.* • *Last Sunday it snowed.*

sun·flow·er /ˈsʌnflaʊə $ ˈsʌnˌflaʊɚ/ *noun* a tall plant with a large yellow flower ➔ see picture on page A10

sung the past participle of SING

sun·glass·es /ˈsʌnˌglɑːsɪz $ ˈsʌnˌglæsɪz/ *plural noun* dark glasses that protect your eyes from the sun: *She was wearing sunglasses.*

sunk the past participle of SINK[1]

sun·light /ˈsʌnlaɪt/ *noun* (no plural) light from the sun: *The room was full of sunlight.*

sun·ny /ˈsʌni/ *adjective* (**sunnier**, **sunniest**) a sunny day or place has a lot of sunlight ➔ see picture on page A13

sun·rise /ˈsʌnraɪz/ *noun* (no plural) the time when the sun appears in the morning ANTONYM **sunset**

sun·screen /ˈsʌnskriːn/ also **ˈsun cream** *BrE noun* a cream that you put on your skin to stop the sun from damaging your skin

sunrise

sunrise

sunset

sun·set /ˈsʌnset/ *noun* (no plural) the time when the sun disappears at night ANTONYM **sunrise**

sun·shine /ˈsʌnʃaɪn/ *noun* (no plural) light and heat from the sun: *We spent the afternoon sitting in the sunshine.*

sun·tan /ˈsʌntæn/ also **tan** *noun* if you have a suntan, your skin is brown because you have been in the sun: *She came back from Barbados with a wonderful suntan.*

su·per /ˈsuːpə $ ˈsupɚ/ *adverb* (spoken) extremely: *He's super fit.*

su·perb /sjuːˈpɜːb $ sʊˈpɚb/ *adjective* very good: *a superb four-course meal*

su·per·fi·cial /ˌsuːpəˈfɪʃəl $ ˌsupɚˈfɪʃəl/ *adjective* **1** done quickly, and not in a thorough or careful way: *Even after a superficial examination it was clear that the house was in a dangerous state.* **2** a superficial wound or superficial damage is not very deep or serious: *Our car escaped with only superficial damage.* **3** someone who is superficial does not think about serious or important things

su·per·in·tend·ent /ˌsuːpərɪnˈtendənt $ ˌsupɚɪnˈtendənt/ *noun* **1** someone who is officially responsible for looking after a building **2** a British police officer

su·pe·ri·or[1] /suːˈpɪəriə $ səˈpɪriɚ/ *adjective* better than something or someone else ANTONYM **inferior**: *He seems to think that he's superior to the rest of us.*

superior[2] *noun* someone who has a higher position than you at work: *You should never be rude to your superiors.*

su·per·la·tive /suːˈpɜːlətɪv $ sʊˈpɚlətɪv/ *noun* **the superlative** the form of an adjective or adverb that you use when saying that something is the biggest, best, most expensive etc

su·per·mar·ket /ˈsuːpəˌmɑːkɪt $ ˈsupɚˌmɑrkɪt/ *noun* a large shop that sells food, drink, cleaning products etc

su·per·mod·el /ˈsuːpəˌmɒdl $ ˈsupɚˌmɑdl/ *noun* a very famous fashion model

su·per·nat·u·ral /ˌsuːpəˈnætʃərəl $ ˌsupɚˈnætʃərəl/ *noun* **the supernatural** strange events that cannot be explained by science: *Do you believe in the supernatural?*
—**supernatural** *adjective*: *Some people believed that cats had supernatural powers.*

su·per·son·ic /ˌsuːpəˈsɒnɪk $ ˌsupɚˈsɑnɪk/ *adjective* supersonic aircraft travel faster than the speed of sound

su·per·star /ˈsuːpəstɑː $ ˈsupɚˌstɑr/ *noun* someone who is extremely famous and popular: *a footballing superstar*

su·per·sti·tion /ˌsuːpəˈstɪʃən $ ˌsupɚˈstɪʃən/ *noun* a belief that some things are lucky or unlucky

su·per·sti·tious /ˌsuːpəˈstɪʃəs $ ˌsupɚˈstɪʃəs/ *adjective* believing that some things are lucky or unlucky: *She's so superstitious she stays home every Friday 13th.*

su·per·store /ˈsuːpəstɔː $ ˈsupɚˌstɔr/ *noun BrE* a very large shop: *a computer superstore*

su·per·vise /ˈsuːpəvaɪz $ ˈsupɚˌvaɪz/ *verb* to make sure someone is doing their work or behaving correctly: *There is always someone there to supervise the children in the pool.*

su·per·vi·sion /ˌsuːpəˈvɪʒən $ ˌsupɚˈvɪʒən/ *noun* (no plural) when you supervise people

su·per·vis·or /ˈsuːpəvaɪzə $ ˈsupɚˌvaɪzɚ/ *noun* someone whose job is to supervise people who are doing a job

sup·per /ˈsʌpə $ ˈsʌpɚ/ *noun*

> KEY PATTERNS
> **have supper**
> **have something for supper**

a meal that you eat in the evening SYNONYM **dinner**: *Would you like to **have** supper with us?* • *We **had** baked potatoes **for supper**.*

sup·ple /ˈsʌpəl/ *adjective* able to bend or move your body easily: *You have to be quite supple in order to do these exercises.*

sup·ple·ment /ˈsʌpləmənt/ *noun*
1 an additional part of a newspaper or magazine: *This week's magazine contains a free fashion supplement.*
2 a special food or drink that contains substances that are good for your body: *He takes vitamin supplements every morning.*

sup·pli·er /səˈplaɪə $ səˈplaɪɚ/ *noun* a company that provides goods for shops and businesses: *an office equipment supplier*

sup·ply¹ /səˈplaɪ/ *noun* (plural **supplies**)
1 an amount of something that you have available to use: *While he was ill in bed, we made sure he had **a supply of** books and DVDs.*
2 supplies food, clothes, and other things that people need: *Emergency food supplies were flown out to the area.*

PHRASES
be in short supply if people or things are in short supply, there are not many of them available: *Good maths teachers **are in short supply**.*

supply² *verb* (formal) (**supplied, supplies**) to provide people with something that they need: *We were supplied with paper and pens for the test.*

sup·port¹ /səˈpɔːt $ səˈpɔrt/ *verb*
1 to like a particular team or person and want them to win in a game, election etc: *Which football team do you support?* • *Sixty-five per cent of voters still support the president.*
2 to help and encourage someone: *Whatever you decide to do, I will support you.*
3 to be under something, holding it up: *the pieces of wood that support the roof*
4 to provide someone with money for food, clothes, and other things they need: *You will have to support yourself one day.*

support² *noun* (no plural) help and encouragement: *I want to thank my* *teachers for all the support they gave me.* • *Poor families receive financial support from the government.*

sup·port·er /səˈpɔːtə $ səˈpɔrtɚ/ *noun* someone who supports a particular person, team, or plan: *loyal supporters of the president* • *a crowd of football supporters*

sup·por·tive /səˈpɔːtɪv $ səˈpɔrtɪv/ *adjective* giving help and encouragement: *My parents are usually very supportive.*

sup·pose /səˈpəʊz $ səˈpoʊz/ *verb* to think that something is probably true: *I suppose he's still in London.*

PHRASES

I suppose so, I suppose not (spoken) used to agree with someone in an uncertain or unwilling way: *"Can I come too?" "I suppose so."* • *"It's not a bad film, is it?" "I suppose not."*

be supposed to do something **a)** if something is supposed to happen, people expect it or have planned it, although it may not actually happen: *The fence **is supposed to** keep animals out.* • *He **was supposed to** meet me at the station, but he didn't arrive.* **b)** if you are supposed to do something, a rule or instruction says you should do it: *You're **supposed to** turn the computer off when you've finished.*

be supposed to be good/the first/the biggest etc used to show that many people say that something is good, the first etc: *This is supposed to be his best book.*

sup·pos·ed·ly /səˈpəʊzɪdli $ səˈpoʊzɪdli/ *adverb* if something is supposedly true, people say it is true but it may not be true: *These chemicals are supposedly harmless.*

sup·press /səˈpres/ *verb* **1** to stop people from opposing the government, especially by using force: *The police suppressed the riots.* **2** to not show a feeling

su·preme /suːˈpriːm $ səˈprim/ *adjective* (formal) the most important: *the Supreme Court*

sure¹ /ʃɔː $ ʃʊr/ *adjective*

> KEY PATTERNS
> **sure that**
> **sure about something**
> **not sure what/where/why etc**
> **sure of it/that**
> **sure to see/hear etc something**

1 certain about something: *I'm **sure that** everything will be all right.* • *Are you **sure about** the train times?* • *Monica will be late – I'm **sure of it**.* • *She's **not sure where** she put her keys.* **2** if something is sure to happen, it is certain to happen: *She's **sure to** find out.*

PHRASES

make sure **a)** to check that something has been done: *I'll just make sure the TV's switched off.* **b)** to be careful to do something: ***Make sure** you read the exam questions carefully.*

be sure to do something (spoken): ***Be sure to** lock the door* (=remember to lock the door)*!*

> WORD CHOICE
> **sure** or **certain**?
> • You say **I'm sure**, **I'm certain**, or **It is certain**.
> ✘ Don't say 'It is sure.'

sure² *adverb* (spoken) used to say yes or to agree with someone: *"Is it OK if I sit here?" "Sure."*

PHRASES

for sure (informal) if you know something for sure, you are certain about it: *Now I **know for sure** who stole my wallet.*

sure·ly /ˈʃɔːli $ ˈʃʊrli/ *adverb* used to show that you are very surprised about something: *Surely you're not going to invite Harry?* • *Surely you remember?*

surf¹ /sɜːf $ sɚf/ *verb* **1** to balance on ocean waves as they move towards the shore, standing on a SURFBOARD **2** **surf the net** to look for information on the INTERNET —**surfing** *noun* (no plural): *We went surfing every day when we were in Australia.* ➔ see picture on page A14

surf² *noun* the white water that forms when waves get near to the shore

sur·face¹ /ˈsɜːfɪs $ ˈsɚfɪs/ *noun*

> KEY PATTERNS
> **the surface of the earth/sea etc**
> **on the surface**
> **below/beneath/under the surface**

1 the top part of an area of land or water: *There were dead fish floating* ***on the surface of*** *the river.* • *I could see some tiny fish just* ***beneath the surface of*** *the water.* • *Two-thirds of the Earth's surface is covered by water.*
2 a flat area: *You need a nice smooth surface for skating.*

surface² *verb* to appear from under water after being hidden: *A shark surfaced from beneath the water.*

surf·board /ˈsɜːfbɔːd $ ˈsɚfbɔrd/ *noun* a long board that you stand on to SURF

surge¹ /sɜːdʒ $ sɚdʒ/ *verb* if people surge forward, they suddenly move forward

surge² *noun* a sudden large increase in something: *He felt a sudden surge of anger.*

sur·geon /ˈsɜːdʒən $ ˈsɚdʒən/ *noun* a doctor who cuts open people's bodies in order to repair or remove something inside → see Thesaurus at DOCTOR

sur·ge·ry /ˈsɜːdʒəri $ ˈsɚdʒəri/ *noun* **1** (no plural) medical treatment in which a doctor cuts open your body to repair or remove something inside: *She had surgery to remove a lump from her neck.* **2** (plural **surgeries**) *BrE* a place where you go to see a doctor or DENTIST SYNONYM **office** *AmE*

sur·gi·cal /ˈsɜːdʒɪkəl $ ˈsɚdʒɪkəl/ *adjective* relating to or used for medical operations: *surgical instruments*

sur·name /ˈsɜːneɪm $ ˈsɚneɪm/ *noun* the name you share with other people in your family SYNONYM **last name**

sur·plus /ˈsɜːpləs $ ˈsɚpləs/ (plural **surpluses**) *noun* more of something than you need: *We've got a surplus of milk.* —**surplus** *adjective*: *They sold their surplus books.*

sur·prise¹ /səˈpraɪz $ sɚˈpraɪz/ *noun*

KEY PATTERNS
a surprise for someone
to someone's surprise

1 something that you did not expect: *This is a surprise! I thought you weren't coming till tomorrow!* • *a surprise visit* • *I've* ***got a surprise for*** *you. I'm getting married!*
2 (no plural) the feeling you have when something you did not expect happens: *She expressed surprise when I told her my plans.* • ***To my surprise****, Dad wasn't angry.*

PHRASES
take someone by surprise, catch someone by surprise if something takes or catches you by surprise, you did not expect it: *His suggestion* ***took*** *us all* ***by surprise****.*
come as a surprise if something comes as a surprise, you did not expect it: *The news* ***came as a*** *complete* ***surprise to*** *me.*

surprise² *verb* if something surprises you, you did not expect it: *The result of the election surprised me.*

sur·prised /səˈpraɪzd $ sɚˈpraɪzd/ *adjective*

KEY PATTERNS
surprised that
surprised at/by something
surprised to see/hear/find etc something

if you are surprised by something, you did not expect it and it seems strange: *I'm surprised you haven't been there before.* • *Bill was* ***surprised that*** *we were leaving so early.* • *He seemed* ***surprised at*** *my question.* • *She was* ***surprised to find*** *Sally waiting for her.*

THESAURUS
amazed/astonished: *I'm amazed that no one was killed in the crash* (=very surprised).
astounded/flabbergasted: *They were* ***astounded*** *at his ignorance* (=extremely surprised).

sur·pris·ing /səˈpraɪzɪŋ $ sɚˈpraɪzɪŋ/ *adjective*

KEY PATTERNS
it is surprising that
it is surprising how/what

1 something that is surprising seems strange and makes you feel surprised: *This is a very surprising result.* • *A surprising number of adults cannot read.* • ***It's surprising that*** *so many people offered to help.* • ***It's surprising*** ***how*** *little a computer costs now.*
2 not surprising, hardly surprising if something is not surprising, it seems very normal and you expect it: *It's not*

A B C D E F G H I J K L M N O P Q R S T U V W X Y Z

surprising she was annoyed.
—**surprisingly** *adverb*: *The food was surprisingly good.*

THESAURUS
extraordinary/astonishing: *What an extraordinary decision* (=very surprising)*!*
astounding: *The young Australian player achieved an* ***astounding*** *victory* (=extremely surprising).

sur·ren·der /sə'rendə $ sə'rendɚ/ *verb* to stop fighting and put yourself under the control of your enemies: *The hijackers surrendered to the government forces.* —**surrender** *noun* (no plural)

sur·round /sə'raʊnd/ *verb* **1** if people surround someone or something, they go all around them: *Soldiers surrounded the building.* • *He was surrounded by his fans.* **2 be surrounded by something** to have something all around: *The house was surrounded by a tall fence.*

sur·round·ings /sə'raʊndɪŋz/ *plural noun* (formal) the place where you are and the things around you: *He will be more relaxed at home in familiar surroundings.*

sur·veil·lance /sə'veɪləns $ sɚ'veɪləns/ *noun* (no plural) when the police or the army carefully watch a person or place: *The police kept the group under surveillance.*

sur·vey /'sɜːveɪ $ 'sɚveɪ/ *noun* a set of questions that you ask a lot of people in order to find out about their opinions: *The company carried out a survey of people's attitudes to housework.*

sur·vey·or /sə'veɪə $ sɚ'veɪɚ/ *noun* someone whose job is to examine land or buildings

sur·viv·al /sə'vaɪvəl $ sɚ'vaɪvəl/ *noun* (no plural) when someone or something continues to live or exist after being in a dangerous situation: *Because of the cold, our chances of survival were low.*

sur·vive /sə'vaɪv $ sɚ'vaɪv/ *verb* **1** to continue to live after an accident or illness: *The driver survived the accident.* • *Only one of the children survived.* **2** to continue to exist: *Few of the town's old buildings survive.*

sur·vi·vor /sə'vaɪvə $ sɚ'vaɪvɚ/ *noun* someone who continues to live after an accident or illness: *The survivors of the crash are in hospital.*

sus·cep·ti·ble /sə'septəbəl/ *adjective* (formal) likely to be affected by an illness or problem: *Young children are susceptible to colds.*

sus·pect¹ /'sʌspekt/ *noun* someone that the police think may be guilty of a crime

sus·pect² /sə'spekt/ *verb* to think that someone may have done something bad: *I suspect that one of the boys took the money.* • *He is suspected of murder.*

sus·pend /sə'spend/ *verb* (formal) **1** to officially stop or delay something for a short time: *They had to suspend the rescue operation because of bad weather.* **2** to officially stop someone from working or going to school for a fixed time, because they have broken the rules

sus·pen·ders /sə'spendəz $ sə'spendɚz/ *plural noun* **1** *BrE* STRAPS that hold up a woman's STOCKINGS **2** the American word for BRACES

sus·pense /sə'spens/ *noun* (no plural) the feeling you have when you are waiting for something exciting to happen: *They all wanted to know if I'd passed the exam, but I kept them in suspense.*

sus·pen·sion /sə'spenʃən/ *noun* **1** when someone is not allowed to work or go to school for a fixed time because they have broken the rules: *The players received a three-match suspension for fighting.* **2** (no plural) the part of a vehicle that makes it move up and down more gently when the surface of the road is uneven, so that it is more comfortable to ride in

sus·pi·cion /sə'spɪʃən/ *noun* **1** the belief that someone may have done something wrong: *Until someone admits to stealing the money, everyone is under suspicion.* **2** a feeling that something may be true: *I've a suspicion she already knows about our relationship.*

sus·pi·cious /səˈspɪʃəs/ *adjective* **1** something that is suspicious appears to involve a crime: *She died in suspicious circumstances.* **2** if you are suspicious of someone, you do not trust them: *I'm suspicious of anyone who comes to the house selling things.* —**suspiciously** *adverb*: *"Who are you?" the old woman asked suspiciously.*

sus·tain /səˈsteɪn/ *verb* (formal) **1** to make something continue to exist SYNONYM **maintain**: *Can the team sustain their lead in the competition?* **2 sustain an injury, sustain damage** to be injured or damaged: *Mr Turner sustained serious head injuries in the attack.*

swag·ger /ˈswæɡə $ ˈswæɡɚ/ *verb* to walk in a way that annoys other people because it seems too proud and confident

swal·low /ˈswɒləʊ $ ˈswɑloʊ/ *verb* to make food or drink go down your throat and into your stomach: *Don't chew the pills, just swallow them.* • *My throat is sore and it's hard to swallow.* —**swallow** *noun*: *She took a swallow of tea.*

swam the past tense of SWIM

swamp /swɒmp $ swɑmp/ *noun* an area of land that is always very wet

swan

swan /swɒn $ swɑn/ *noun* a large white bird with a long neck that lives on lakes and rivers → see picture on page A8

swap, swop /swɒp $ swɑp/ *verb* (**swapped, swapping**) to exchange something you have for something that someone else has: *He swapped his torch for a CD.* • *We swapped places so that I could look out of the window.* —**swap** *noun*: *Let's do a swap.*

swarm¹ /swɔːm $ swɔrm/ *verb* **swarm with** to be full of a lot of people moving about: *The place was swarming with tourists.*

swarm² *noun* a large group of insects moving together: *a swarm of bees*

swarm

a swarm of bees

swat /swɒt $ swɑt/ *verb* (**swatted, swatting**) to hit a flying insect with your hand or a flat object

sway /sweɪ/ *verb* to move slowly from one side to another: *The wooden bridge swayed as they walked across it.*

swear /sweə $ swer/ *verb* (**swore** /swɔː $ swɔr/ **sworn** /swɔːn $ swɔrn/) **1** to use very rude words: *He was sent home for swearing at the teacher.* **2** to make a promise or statement very seriously: *I swear I didn't do it!* → see Thesaurus at PROMISE¹

ˈswear word *noun* a very rude word

sweat¹ /swet/ *verb* when you sweat, liquid comes out through your skin because you are hot or nervous: *I always sweat a lot when I exercise.*

sweat² *noun* (no plural) liquid that comes out through your skin when you are hot or nervous SYNONYM **perspiration**: *He wiped the sweat from his forehead.*

sweat·er /ˈswetə $ ˈswetɚ/ *noun* a piece of warm woollen clothing that you wear on the top half of your body

sweat·shirt /ˈswet-ʃɜːt $ ˈswet-ʃɚt/ *noun* a thick soft cotton shirt without buttons: *He was dressed casually, in a sweatshirt and jeans.*

sweat·y /ˈsweti/ *adjective* (**sweatier, sweatiest**) covered with sweat

sweep¹ /swiːp/ *verb* (past tense and past participle **swept** /swept/)

> KEY PATTERNS
> **sweep the floor/street**
> **sweep up the crumbs/leaves etc**
> **sweep something into a drawer/cupboard etc**
> **sweep something from/off somewhere**

1 to clean the dirt from a floor or the ground using a brush: *I swept the kitchen floor.* • *Could you sweep the*

leaves ***up****, please?* → see Thesaurus at CLEAN[2] → see picture at MOP[2]
2 to quickly move something into or away from a place with your hand: *I quickly* ***swept*** *his letters* ***into*** *a drawer. • Gina* ***swept*** *the hair* ***from*** *her eyes.*
3 sweep over/across/through somewhere if a fire, wind, or storm sweeps over an area, it moves or spreads over it quickly: *The fire* ***swept over*** *the dry hills.*
PHRASAL VERBS
sweep away
sweep something away to destroy or remove something by force: *The floods have* ***swept away*** *80 homes.*

sweep² *noun* a smooth swinging movement: *He knocked the glasses from the table with a sweep of his hand.*

sweet¹ /swiːt/ *adjective*
1 sweet food or drink contains sugar or tastes like sugar: *This chocolate sauce is very sweet.*
2 kind and friendly: *Jeff's a sweet boy.*
3 small and attractive: *Her baby is so sweet! • What a* ***sweet little*** *house!*

sweet² *noun BrE* **1** a small sweet thing that you eat SYNONYM **candy** *AmE*: *Don't let the kids eat too many sweets.*
2 something sweet that you eat at the end of a meal SYNONYM **dessert**: *What are you having as a sweet?*

sweetcorn /ˈswiːtkɔːn $ -kɔːrn/ *noun BrE* the sweet yellow seeds of the MAIZE plant, which are cooked and eaten → see picture on page A6

sweet·en /ˈswiːtn/ *verb* to make a food or drink taste sweeter

sweet·ener /ˈswiːtnə $ ˈswitnɚ/ *noun* a substance used instead of sugar to make food or drink taste sweeter

swell /swel/ *verb* (**swelled, swollen** /ˈswəʊlən $ ˈswoʊlən/) also **swell up** if a part of your body swells, it becomes bigger: *His ankle swelled to twice its normal size.*

swell·ing /ˈswelɪŋ/ *noun* an area on your body that has become bigger because of injury or illness

swept the past tense and past participle of SWEEP¹

swerve /swɜːv $ swɝv/ *verb* if a car swerves, it suddenly goes to the left or the right: *The car in front suddenly swerved across the road.*

swerve

swift /swɪft/ *adjective* happening or moving very quickly: *We had to make a swift decision.*

swim¹ /swɪm/ *verb* (**swam** /swæm/ **swum** /swʌm/)
to move through water using your arms and legs: *We swam in the lake. • George is just learning to swim. •* ***Can you swim*** *yet?* —**swimmer** *noun*: *I'm not a very good swimmer.*

USAGE
When talking about swimming as an activity that you do, you say **go swimming**: *I go swimming two or three times a week.*

swim² *noun* a time when you swim: *We're going for a swim after school.*

swim·ming /ˈswɪmɪŋ/ *noun* (no plural) when you swim: *Do you want to* ***go swimming****? • We* ***took*** *the children* ***swimming****.* → see picture on page A14

ˈswimming ˌcostume *noun BrE* a piece of clothing that girls and women wear for swimming SYNONYM **swimsuit**

ˈswimming pool also **pool** *noun* a large hole full of water that is built for swimming in

ˈswimming trunks also **trunks** *plural noun* a piece of clothing that boys and men wear for swimming: *He was wearing a pair of bright blue swimming trunks.*

swim·suit /ˈswɪmsuːt/ *noun* a piece of clothing that girls and women wear for swimming

swin·dle /ˈswɪndl/ *verb* to get money from someone by tricking them SYNONYM **cheat**: *The salesman had swindled the woman out of thousands of dollars.*
—**swindle** *noun*: *a tax swindle*
—**swindler** *noun*

swing[1] /swɪŋ/ *verb* (past tense and past participle **swung** /swʌŋ/)
1 to move something backwards and forwards or round and round: *Children sat on the bench, swinging their legs.* • *The rope hung down swinging backwards and forwards.* ➔ see picture on page A2
2 to move smoothly and easily: *The door swung shut behind him.*

PHRASAL VERBS

swing at
swing at someone to try to hit someone: *Dean **swung at** me and missed.*

swing[2] *noun* a seat that hangs from ropes or chains, for children to play on

swipe /swaɪp/ *verb* (informal) to steal something: *Who's swiped my pencil?*

swirl /swɜːl $ swɚl/ *verb* to turn around and around: *Leaves swirled to the ground.*

switch[1] /swɪtʃ/ *verb*

KEY PATTERNS
switch the day/time etc of something
switch to another/a different/a better etc something
switch from one thing to another
switch places/roles with someone

to change from one thing to a different one: *Dave switched the day of the meeting. It's on Monday now.* • ***Switch to** sugar-free drinks if you want to lose weight.* • *I've **switched from** using a PC **to** using a laptop.* • *Would you mind **switching places with** me?*

PHRASAL VERBS

switch off
switch something off to make a machine or light stop working by moving a button SYNONYM **turn off**: *Did you **switch off** the light in the kitchen?*

switch on
switch something on to make a machine or light start working by moving a button SYNONYM **turn on**: *Jen **switched on** the radio.*

switch over
to change from one television station to another: *Do you mind if I **switch over**?*

switch

switch on switch off

switch[2] *noun* (plural **switches**) a button that you move to make a machine or light start or stop working: *Where's the light switch?* • *I can't find **the switch for** the headlights.*

switch·board /ˈswɪtʃbɔːd $ ˈswɪtʃbɔrd/ *noun* the place in a large organization where telephone calls are answered and connected to the people who work there: *Hello, you're through to the switchboard.*

swiv·el /ˈswɪvəl/ *verb* (**swivelled, swivelling** *BrE*, **swiveled, swiveling** *AmE*) to turn around while staying in the same place: *You can swivel the computer screen to the right position.*

swollen[1] the past participle of SWELL

swol·len[2] /ˈswəʊlən $ ˈswoʊlən/ *adjective* a part of your body that is swollen is bigger than usual because of illness or injury: *Her lips are so swollen she can't eat.*

swollen

a swollen ankle

swoop /swuːp/ *verb* to move down through the air suddenly: *The bird swooped on the rabbit.*

swop /swɒp $ swɑːp/ another spelling of SWAP

sword /sɔːd $ sɔrd/ *noun* a weapon with a long sharp blade and a short handle ➔ see picture at SHIELD[1]

PRONUNCIATION
In this word you do not pronounce the **w**.

swore the past tense of SWEAR

sworn the past participle of SWEAR

swot¹ /swɒt $ swɑt/ *noun BrE* (informal) someone who studies too hard

swot² *verb BrE* (informal) (**swotted**, **swotting**) also **swot up** to study hard: *I need to swot up on my maths before the exam.*

swum the past participle of SWIM¹

swung the past tense and past participle of SWING¹

syl·la·ble /ˈsɪləbəl/ *noun* a part of a word that contains a single vowel sound. 'Dad' has one syllable and 'butter' has two syllables.

syl·la·bus /ˈsɪləbəs/ *noun* (plural **syllabuses**) a list of all the things that students will study on a course

sym·bol /ˈsɪmbəl/ *noun* **1** a simple shape or picture that has a meaning: *That symbol means the truck is carrying a dangerous chemical.* **2** something that shows or represents something else: *For some people, a big car is a symbol of how much money you have.*

sym·bol·ic /sɪmˈbɒlɪk $ sɪmˈbɑlɪk/ *adjective* (formal) if something is symbolic, it means more than its simple appearance because it shows or represents something else: *The new bridge is symbolic of the link between the two countries.*

sym·bol·ize also **symbolise** *BrE* /ˈsɪmbəlaɪz/ *verb* (formal) to be a symbol that shows or represents something

sym·met·ri·cal /sɪˈmetrɪkəl/ also **sym·met·ric** /sɪˈmetrɪk/ *adjective* if something is symmetrical, its two halves or sides are the same size and shape.

sym·me·try /ˈsɪmətri/ *noun* (no plural) when both halves or sides of something are the same size and shape

sym·pa·thet·ic /ˌsɪmpəˈθetɪk/ *adjective* kind and understanding to someone who is sad ANTONYM **unsympathetic**: *My parents weren't very sympathetic when I told them I had no money left.*

sym·pa·thize also **sympathise** *BrE* /ˈsɪmpəθaɪz/ *verb* **1** to be kind to someone who is sad by showing that you understand their problems **2** to support someone's ideas or actions: *On the whole, I sympathize with their aims.*

sym·pa·thy /ˈsɪmpəθi/ *noun* (no plural) **1** the feeling you have when you understand why someone is sad and want to help them feel better: *Rick was full of sympathy when I lost my job.* **2** support for someone's ideas or actions: *I have a lot of sympathy for the workers who are on strike.*

sym·pho·ny /ˈsɪmfəni/ *noun* (plural **symphonies**) a long piece of music that is written for an ORCHESTRA

symp·tom /ˈsɪmptəm/ *noun* a sign of a disease: *Sneezing is often the first symptom of a cold.*

syn·a·gogue /ˈsɪnəgɒg $ ˈsɪnəˌgɑg/ *noun* a building where Jewish people meet for religious services

sync /sɪŋk/ *noun* **be out of sync, be in sync** (informal) if two things are out of sync, they are not working together correctly. If they are in sync, they are working together correctly: *The sound was out of sync with the pictures.*

syn·di·cate /ˈsɪndəkət/ *noun* a group of people or companies that have joined together for business reasons

syn·drome /ˈsɪndrəum $ ˈsɪndroum/ *noun* (formal) a medical condition that produces a particular set of problems

syn·o·nym /ˈsɪnənɪm/ *noun* a word with the same meaning as another word in the same language: *'Enormous' is a synonym of 'huge'.*

syn·the·siz·er also **synthesiser** *BrE* /ˈsɪnθəsaɪzə $ ˈsɪnθəˌsaɪzɚ/ *noun* an electronic musical instrument that can produce many kinds of sound

syn·thet·ic /sɪnˈθetɪk/ *adjective* a synthetic material or substance is not natural but has been made in a factory ANTONYM **natural** → see Thesaurus at ARTIFICIAL

sy·ringe /səˈrɪndʒ/ *noun* a hollow tube and needle that a doctor uses for taking blood from people or for giving people medicine through their skin → see picture at NEEDLE

syr·up /ˈsɪrəp $ ˈsɚəp/ *noun* (no plural) a thick sticky liquid made from sugar

sys·tem /ˈsɪstəm/ *noun*

> KEY PATTERNS
> **a system for doing something**
> **a system of education/government etc**

1 a way of organizing something that is carefully planned according to a fixed set of rules: *We need a better* ***system for*** *dealing with complaints.* • *There is a very good education system in this country.* • *The school now has a new system for grading students.* • *Our present* ***system of*** *justice is not perfect.*
2 several pieces of equipment that are connected to each other and work together: *We're having a new computer system installed at college.* • *a central heating system* • *an expensive stereo system*

sys·te·mat·ic /ˌsɪstəˈmætɪk/ *adjective* (formal) using a planned and organized method: *a systematic search of the building* —**systematically** /-kli/ *adverb*

A B C D E F G H I J K L M N O P Q R S T U V W X Y Z

Tt

tab /tæb/ *noun* **1 pick up the tab** (informal) to pay for something, especially a meal in a restaurant
2 keep tabs on someone (informal) if you keep tabs on someone, you make sure you always know where they are and what they are doing

tables

coffee table

dining table

desk

ta•ble /ˈteɪbəl/ *noun*
1 a piece of furniture which has a flat top resting on legs: *A book lay open* ***on the table***. • *We eat breakfast* ***at the*** *kitchen* ***table***.
2 a table in a restaurant that you arrange to use at a particular time: *I'd like to* ***book a table*** *for two at 8.00 pm, please.*
3 a set of numbers or facts that are arranged in rows: *This table shows the city's monthly rainfall.*

PHRASES

set the table, lay the table *BrE* to put knives, forks, dishes etc on a table, ready for a meal: *John, will you* ***set the table****, please?*
the table of contents a list of the parts of a book and what page they are on: ***The table of contents*** *is on page iii.*

ta•ble•cloth /ˈteɪbəlklɒθ $ ˈteɪbəlˌklɔθ/ *noun* a cloth for covering a table

ta•ble•spoon /ˈteɪbəlspuːn/ *noun* a large spoon, or the amount it holds: *Add a tablespoon of flour.*

tab•let /ˈtæblət/ *noun* a small hard piece of medicine that you swallow SYNONYM **pill**: *She took two sleeping tablets.* → see Thesaurus at MEDICINE

ˈtable ˌtennis *noun* (no plural) a game in which people hit a ball to each other over a net that is stretched across a table

tab•loid /ˈtæblɔɪd/ *noun* a newspaper with small pages, short reports, and not very much serious news

ta•boo /təˈbuː/ *noun* something that you must not do or talk about because it offends or embarrasses people

tack /tæk/ *noun* a small nail with a sharp point and a flat top

tackle

tack•le[1] /ˈtækəl/ *verb* **1** to deal with a difficult problem: *How can we tackle the problem of pollution?* **2** to try to take the ball away from another player in a game such as football

tackle[2] *noun* an attempt to take the ball away from another player in a game such as football

tact /tækt/ *noun* (no plural) the quality that you show when you are careful not to say or do things that will upset people

tact•ful /ˈtæktfəl/ *adjective* careful not to say or do anything that will upset someone ANTONYM **tactless**

tac•tic /ˈtæktɪk/ *noun* an action that you plan carefully in order to achieve what you want: *The team have prepared their tactics for the game.*

tact•less /ˈtæktləs/ *adjective* carelessly saying or doing something that upsets someone ANTONYM **tactful**: *That was a rather tactless remark.*

tad•pole /ˈtædpəʊl $ ˈtædpoʊl/ *noun* a small creature that will become a FROG

tag[1] /tæg/ *noun* a small piece of paper, plastic etc that is fastened to something and gives information about it: *All the staff wore name tags.*

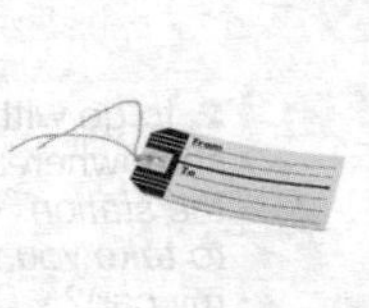

tag[2] *verb* (**tagged**, **tagging**) **tag along** (informal) to go somewhere with someone, although they have not asked you to: *The others were going to the cinema, so I decided to tag along.*

tail /teɪl/ *noun* **1** the long thin part on the back end of an animal's body: *The horse was brown with a black tail.* → see picture at HORSE **2** the back part of a plane → see picture at AEROPLANE **3 tails** the side of a coin that does not have a picture of someone's head on it ANTONYM **heads**

'tail-light, **tail light** *noun* one of the two red lights at the back of a car or plane

tai·lor /'teɪlə $ 'teɪlɚ/ *noun* someone whose job is to make men's clothes. Tailors usually measure their customers so that the clothes fit exactly

ˌtailor-'made *adjective* very suitable for someone or something: *The job seems tailor-made for him.*

tail·pipe /'teɪlpaɪp/ the American word for EXHAUST PIPE

take → see boxes on pages 684 and 685

take·a·way /'teɪkəweɪ/ *noun BrE* a meal that you buy from a restaurant to eat at home, or a restaurant that sells these meals SYNONYM **takeout** *AmE*: *a Chinese takeaway*

take-off, **take·off** /'teɪkɒf $ 'teɪkɔf/ *noun* when a plane moves off the ground and into the air

take·out /'teɪkaʊt/ the American word for TAKEAWAY

tale /teɪl/ *noun* an interesting story about things that happened in the past, or things that did not really happen: *We used to listen to his tales of life in the army.*

tal·ent /'tælənt/ *noun* a natural ability to do something well: *That boy has a lot of talent.* → see Thesaurus at ABILITY

tal·ent·ed /'tæləntɪd/ *adjective* having a natural ability to do something well: *a talented musician*

talk[1] → see box on page 686

talk[2] /tɔːk/ *noun*

KEY PATTERNS
have a talk with someone
have a talk about something
give a talk on a subject

1 when people talk to each other about a subject: *I **had a long talk with** Kelly today.* • *We've **had a talk about** the problem.*
2 a speech on a particular subject: *Davies **gave a talk on** his work at the university.*
3 talks formal discussions between different countries, organizations, leaders etc: *The peace talks are making good progress.*

talk·a·tive /'tɔːkətɪv/ *adjective* a talkative person talks a lot

tall /tɔːl/ *adjective*
1 a tall person, building, tree etc has great height: *a tall, beautiful woman* • *It is one of the tallest trees in the world.* → see picture at HIGH[1]
2 used to talk about the height of someone or something: *My mother's only five feet tall.* • ***How tall is** Ricky?*

tal·on /'tælən/ *noun* one of the sharp curved nails of a bird that hunts other animals

tame

tame[1] /teɪm/ *adjective* a tame animal is not afraid of people and does not attack people ANTONYM **wild**

tame[2] *verb* to train a wild animal to obey people and not be afraid of them

take /teɪk/ *verb* (past tense **took** /tʊk/, past participle **taken** /ˈteɪkən/, present participle **taking**)

take

1 to carry something with you when you go to another place: *I always* ***take*** *my camera* ***with*** *me when I go on holiday.* • *She* ***took*** *the books back* ***to*** *the library.* • *Don't forget to* ***take*** *your bag!*

KEY PATTERNS
take something with you
take something to a place

2 to go with someone somewhere: *I* ***took*** *Susan* ***to*** *the station.* • *Do you want me to* ***take*** *you* ***to*** *the airport* (=in my car)? • *Dad* ***took*** *me* ***with*** *him* ***to*** *the game.* • *I have to* ***take*** *my sister* ***to*** *the dentist.*

KEY PATTERNS
take someone to a place
take someone with you

3 to get hold of something with your hands: *I* ***took*** *his pen and wrote down my phone number.* • ***Take*** *my hand!* • *Jeff* ***took*** *Diana's bags from her and carried them to the car.*

Take *my hand!*

4 to need an amount of time: *The recipe only* ***takes*** *20 minutes to make.* • *It* ***takes*** *about ten hours on the plane to get from London to Los Angeles.* • *It* ***takes*** *me ten minutes to get to school.*

KEY PATTERNS
something takes 20 minutes/2 hours
it takes 20 minutes/2 hours to do something

5 to steal something: *The thieves* ***took*** *all her money.* • *I left my bag on the chair, and someone* ***took*** *it.*

6 to drink or eat some medicine: *If you've got a headache you should* ***take*** *some aspirin.* • *I have to* ***take*** *two tablets a day.*

You need to ***take*** *2 tablets a day.*

7 to travel in a car, bus, train etc: *I'll* ***take*** *the bus home.* • *Do you mind if we* ***take*** *your car* (=use your car)?

WORD CHOICE
take or **bring**?
• You **take** something with you when you go to another place: *I always* ***take*** *my camera with me when I go on holiday.*
• You **bring** something here, or to the place that you are going to with someone: *Did you remember to* ***bring*** *your passport?*

PHRASES

take care of someone
to watch and help someone, and make sure they stay safe and well: *Melanie has no idea what it's like to* ***take care of*** *a baby all day long.*

take care of something
to do things to keep something in good condition: *My brother usually* ***takes care of*** *the house when my parents are away.*

take a message
to write down information that someone gives you on the telephone, so that you can give the information to someone else: *Mrs Pattie isn't here – may I* ***take a message****?*

take milk, take sugar etc
to use milk, sugar etc in your coffee or tea: *Do you* ***take cream*** *in your coffee?*

take part
to be involved in something such as an activity or event with other people: *Teachers and students from six schools will* ***take part*** *in the competition.*

take place
to happen, especially after being planned to happen: *The wedding* ***took place*** *outside, in the gardens of the hotel.*

Take is also used in these phrases:
take a look (=look at something quickly)
take a walk (=have a walk)
take a bath/shower (=have a bath/shower)
take a rest/break/holiday (=have a rest or a holiday)
take a test/exam (=do a test/exam)
take a picture/photograph (=photograph something)
take notes (=write notes)
take a deep breath (=breathe deeply)
take a risk (=do something that may be dangerous)
take someone's advice (=do what someone has advised you to do)

PHRASAL VERBS

take away
to move something from a place: *The waitress* ***took*** *the plates* ***away****.* • *The police* ***took away*** *the gloves for examination.*

take back
to move something back to the place or person it came from SYNONYM **return**: *Shelley* ***took*** *the dress* ***back*** *to the store because it didn't fit.* • *We have to* ***take back*** *the library books today.*

take off
1 to move clothes off your body ANTONYM **put on**: *Jane* ***took off*** *her coat and hung it up.* • *I bent down and* ***took*** *my shoes* ***off****.*
2 if a plane takes off, it leaves the ground and goes into the air ANTONYM **land**: *The plane* ***took off*** *at 8.45.*
3 to not go to work for a period of time: *Emma* ***took*** *three days* ***off*** *school last week when she was ill.*

take out
1 to move something so that it is outside of the place where it was: *Lucy* ***took out*** *her books and started doing her homework.* • ***Take*** *the butter* ***out*** *of the refrigerator.* • *Can you* ***take*** *the cake* ***out*** *of the oven for me?*
2 to go with someone to a restaurant, film etc and pay for them: *He* ***took*** *Sabina* ***out*** *for dinner.*

take over
to do something that someone else did before: *Machines have* ***taken over*** *much of the work people used to do in factories.* • *Mrs Hudson* ***took over*** *as head teacher last term.*

talk /tɔːk/ *verb*

to speak, or to have a conversation with someone: *Sorry, I can't **talk** now – I have to go to a meeting.* • *Mr Samuels **talked** to the police for an hour.* • *Each student **talked about** a book they had read.* • *Lucy sat on the sofa, **talking with** Camille.*

*Each student **talked about** a book they had read.*

KEY PATTERNS

talk about something
talk to someone
talk with someone *AmE*

GRAMMAR

- You say **I want to talk to you.**
✗ Don't say 'talk you'.
- You say **He can speak English**.
✗ Don't say 'talk English'.

WORD CHOICE

talk, **speak**, or **tell**?

- If two or more people are having a conversation, you use **talk**: *They talked about the old days.*
- If one person is talking, you can use **talk** or **speak**: *He spoke for over an hour.* • *She **talked** about her trip to Berlin.*
- If you want someone to know about something, you **tell** them **about** it: *I told him **about** all the problems we've had.*

PHRASAL VERBS

talk back
if a child talks back to an adult, they answer the adult rudely: *He's been **talking back** to his teachers and getting into trouble.*

talk someone into (doing) something
to make someone agree to do something that they do not really want to: *I **talked** my mother **into** buying me the shoes.* • *Diane didn't really want to go, but Bill **talked** her **into** it.*

talk out of (doing) something
to make someone agree not to do something that they wanted to do: *I wanted to buy a car, but my dad **talked** me **out of** it.* • *His friends **talked** him **out of** trying drugs.*

tam·per /ˈtæmpə $ ˈtæmpɚ/ *verb* **tamper with** to change something without permission, especially in order to damage it: *Someone had tampered with the car's brakes.*

tan[1] /tæn/ *noun* brown skin that someone gets by spending time in the sun SYNONYM **suntan**: *She's come back from Spain with a great tan.*

tan[2] *adjective* pale yellow-brown in colour: *a tan bag*

tan[3] *verb* (**tanned**, **tanning**) to get brown skin by spending time in the sun: *I'm trying to tan my legs.* —**tanned** *adjective*: *He looked tanned and healthy.*

tan·ge·rine /ˌtændʒəˈriːn/ *noun* a small sweet orange ➔ see picture on page A7

tan·gle[1] /ˈtæŋɡəl/ *noun* a lot of hair, string, wires etc that are twisted together in an untidy way

tangle[2] *verb* to become twisted together in an untidy way: *My hair always tangles when I wash it.* —**tangled** *adjective*

tangle

tank /tæŋk/ *noun*
1 a large container for holding liquid or gas: *The tank's nearly empty – we'd better stop at the next petrol station.* **2** a heavy military vehicle with a large gun and a belt around the wheels on each side

tank·er /ˈtæŋkə $ ˈtæŋkɚ/ *noun* a ship or vehicle that carries liquid or gas: *an oil tanker*

tan·noy /ˈtænɔɪ/ *noun BrE* (trademark) a system of LOUDSPEAKERs that people use to announce things in public places: *I heard my name called over the tannoy.*

tan·trum /ˈtæntrəm/ *noun* when a young child suddenly becomes very angry: *She had a tantrum when I refused to buy her any sweets.*

tap[1] /tæp/ (**tapped**, **tapping**) *verb*

KEY PATTERNS
tap on a door/window
tap someone on the arm/back etc

1 to gently hit something with your hand or an object: *Someone **tapped on** the window.* • *Paul **tapped** her **on** the shoulder.* ➔ see Thesaurus at HIT[1]
2 if you tap your feet, you move them gently up and down in time to music

tap[2] *noun*

KEY PATTERNS
turn a tap on/off
a tap on the door/window

1 *BrE* something that you turn to make water come out of a pipe. You turn a tap on to make the water come out and turn it off to make the water stop coming out SYNONYM **faucet** *AmE*: *Water was dripping from the kitchen tap.* • *I **turned** the tap **on**.* • *Could you **turn off** the taps in the bathroom for me?*
2 the sound that someone makes by hitting something gently with their hand or an object: *I heard **a tap on** the window.*

tap

tape[1] /teɪp/ *noun*
1 a thin band of plastic inside a box, with sounds or pictures recorded on it SYNONYM **cassette**: *Keith has hundreds of old tapes and CDs.*
2 (no plural) a band of sticky material that you use to stick paper together: *You don't have enough tape to wrap all those presents.*

tape[2] *verb* **1** to record sounds or pictures on a tape: *Apparently, detectives had taped their conversation.*
2 to fasten something to a surface using tape: *He taped the poster above his desk.*

ˈtape deck *noun* the part of a STEREO which you use to play and record music on tapes

ˈtape ˌmeasure *noun* a very long piece of cloth or metal with inches or centimetres marked on it, which you use for measuring things

ˈtape reˌcorder *noun* a piece of equipment for recording and playing sounds on tapes

tap·es·try /ˈtæpəstri/ *noun* (plural **tapestries**) a piece of heavy cloth that is covered with a picture made of coloured threads

tar /tɑː $ tɑr/ *noun* a black sticky substance that is used to cover roads, roofs etc

tar·get¹ /ˈtɑːɡɪt $ ˈtɑrɡɪt/ *noun*

KEY PATTERNS
the target of attack/protest etc
a target for thieves/bullies etc
the target of an advertisement/campaign

1 a person or thing that people attack or criticize: *The exam system has been **the target of** a lot of criticism recently.* • *Military buildings are **an** obvious **target for** terrorists.*
2 a particular person or group of people that you are trying to affect or influence: *Young people are **the target of** these advertisements.*
3 an amount or level that you are trying to achieve: *The company has **reached** its sales **targets**.*
4 a board with circles on it that you try to hit when you are shooting: *The arrow hit the middle of the target.*

target² *verb* **1** to aim a weapon at a place: *They targeted their missiles on American cities.* **2** to choose a particular place to attack: *The bombers targeted popular tourist areas.* **3** to try to sell a product or give information about something to a particular group of people: *The company targets its clothing at teenagers.*

tar·mac /ˈtɑːmæk $ ˈtɑrmæk/ *noun* **1 Tarmac** (no plural) (trademark) a material made of tar and small stones that is used to cover the surface of a road **2 the tarmac** the part of an airport where the planes stand: *There were two planes on the tarmac.*

tart /tɑːt/ *noun* a small PIE without a top, usually containing fruit

tart

tar·tan /ˈtɑːtn $ ˈtɑrtn/ *noun* a traditional Scottish pattern with coloured lines and squares SYNONYM **plaid** *AmE* → see picture at PATTERN

task /tɑːsk $ tæsk/ *noun*

KEY PATTERNS
the task of doing something
set/give someone a task
do/perform a task

a piece of work that someone has to do: *I decided to begin **the task of** painting my bedroom.* • *The teacher **set** us some really difficult **tasks**.* • *Computers **do** many of the **tasks** that people used to do.*

taste¹ /teɪst/ *noun*

KEY PATTERNS
the taste of food/wine etc
have a taste of something
someone's taste in clothes/friends

1 your sense of taste is your ability to know what sort of food or drink you have in your mouth, and whether it is sweet, sour, bitter etc
2 the taste of a food or drink is the quality that you notice when you put it in your mouth SYNONYM **flavour**: *I don't like **the taste of** fish.* • *The coffee had a **strong, bitter taste**.*
3 a taste a small amount of a food or drink that you have in order to find out what it is like: *Do you want to **have a taste of** my curry?*
4 your taste in something is what kind of that thing you like: *What are your **tastes in** music?*

PHRASES
have taste, have good taste to be good at knowing what things are attractive or of good quality: *Kaufman **has good taste in** clothes.*
be in bad taste to be likely to upset people: *That joke **was in very bad taste**.*

taste² *verb*

KEY PATTERNS
something tastes of/like salt/garlic etc

1 to have a particular taste: *This coffee **tastes** great!* • *The sauce **tasted of** cheese.* • *Chillies **taste like** peppers, but they're much hotter.*
2 to eat or drink a small amount of something in order to find out what it is like: *Gabby tasted the soup and added a little salt.*

A B C D E F G H I J K L M N O P Q R S T U V W X Y Z

GRAMMAR
Taste is not usually used in the progressive:
You say **I can taste the spices.**
✘ Don't say 'I'm tasting'.

taste·ful /ˈteɪstfəl/ *adjective* attractive and of good quality: *He was wearing a tasteful blue tie.*

taste·less /ˈteɪstləs/ *adjective* **1** not attractive and not of good quality: *Some of her clothes are really tasteless!* **2** likely to offend people: *tasteless jokes* **3** tasteless food is not nice because it does not have a very strong taste

tast·y /ˈteɪsti/ *adjective* (**tastier, tastiest**) tasty food has a good strong taste: *This pizza is really tasty.*

tat·tered /ˈtætəd $ ˈtætərd/ *adjective* old and torn: *a tattered flag*

tat·too /təˈtuː/ *noun* a picture that is put onto someone's skin using a needle and ink: *She has a tattoo of a rose on her ankle.* —**tattoo** *verb*: *He had a lion tattooed on his chest.*

taught the past tense and past participle of TEACH

taunt /tɔːnt/ *verb* to say unkind things to someone in order to upset them SYNONYM **tease**: *The other kids taunted her about her clothes.* —**taunt** *noun*: *The taunts about his father upset him.*

taut /tɔːt/ *adjective* stretched tight: *They pulled the rope until it was taut.*

tax¹ /tæks/ *noun* (plural **taxes**)

KEY PATTERNS
a tax on petrol/cigarettes etc

money that you have to pay to the government: *There is no **tax on** food.* • *You have to **pay tax on** everything you earn.* • *Most people would like to see **lower taxes**.* • *People are protesting about the **high taxes**.*

tax² *verb* to make someone pay a particular amount of money to the government

ˌtax-ˈfree *adjective* if something is tax-free, you do not have to pay tax on it: *a tax-free savings account*

tax·i /ˈtæksi/ also **tax·i·cab** /ˈtæksiˌkæb/ *noun* a car with a driver that you pay to drive you somewhere SYNONYM **cab**: *We took a taxi to the station.*

USAGE
You **get in a taxi**.
✘ Don't say 'get on a taxi'.
You **get out of a taxi**.
✘ Don't say 'get off a taxi'.

tea /tiː/ *noun*

KEY PATTERNS
have tea
have something for tea

1 a drink that you make by pouring hot water onto dried leaves, or the leaves that you use to make this drink: *I'm going to make a cup of tea.*
2 *BrE* a meal that you eat in the afternoon or early evening: *What time are we **having tea**?* • *I had fish **for tea** yesterday.*

tea·bag /ˈtiːbæg/ *noun* a small paper bag containing dried leaves which you pour hot water on to make tea

teach /tiːtʃ/ *verb* (past tense and past participle **taught** /tɔːt/)

KEY PATTERNS
teach maths/geography etc to someone
teach someone maths/geography
teach someone how to do something
teach someone what to do

1 to give lessons in a subject: *She teaches history.* • *He teaches at a secondary school.* • *She **teaches** French **to** primary school children.* • *Mr Howard teaches me maths.*
2 to show someone how to do something: *My grandmother **taught** me **how to** bake cakes.* • *It's important to **teach** children to swim.* • *Will you **teach** me **what to** do?*

teach·er /ˈtiːtʃə $ ˈtitʃər/ *noun* someone whose job is to teach: *Miss Lind is my English teacher.*

teach·ing /ˈtiːtʃɪŋ/ *noun* (no plural) the work of being a teacher: *Teaching is not easy.*

team¹ /tiːm/ *noun*

KEY PATTERNS
a team of lawyers/engineers etc

A B C D E F G H I J K L M N O P Q R S T U V W X Y Z

1 a group of people who play a game together against another group: *a football team* ➔ see Thesaurus at GROUP[1]
2 a group of people who work together: ***a team of doctors*** ➔ see Thesaurus at GROUP[1]

team² *verb* **team up** to join another person or group in order to do something together: *Why don't we team up with class 5 for the school trip?*

team·mate /ˈtiːm-meɪt/ *noun* someone who is in the same team as you: *His teammates cheered as he scored.*

team·ster /ˈtiːmstə $ ˈtiːmstər/ the American word for TRUCK DRIVER

tea·pot /ˈtiːpɒt $ ˈtipɑt/ *noun* a container that you use for making and pouring tea ➔ see picture at POT

tear¹ /teə $ ter/ *verb* (**tore** /tɔː $ tɔr/ **torn** /tɔːn $ tɔrn/)

> KEY PATTERNS
> **tear your clothes**
> **tear open a letter/package**
> **tear something down/off**

1 if you tear cloth or paper, or if it tears, you make a hole in it or pull it into pieces SYNONYM **rip**: *I fell down and tore my trousers.* • *The bag tore on the way home.* • *The kids tore open their Christmas presents.*

tear

2 to remove something quickly by pulling it violently: *He* ***tore off*** *his shirt.* • *She* ***tore*** *the pictures* ***down.*** • *Strong winds* ***tore*** *the roofs* ***off*** *several houses.* ➔ see Thesaurus at REMOVE

PHRASAL VERBS
tear down
tear something down (informal) to deliberately destroy a building: *The old houses will* ***be torn down.***
tear up
tear something up to pull paper into lots of pieces: *I* ***tore up*** *Neil's letter.*

tear² /tɪə $ tɪr/ *noun* **1** one of the drops of water that come from your eyes when you cry: *She had tears in her eyes by the end of the movie.*
2 **be in tears** to be crying: *Sally was in tears when she heard the news.*
➔ see Thesaurus at CRY[1]

tear³ /teə $ ter/ *noun* a hole in paper or cloth where it has been torn SYNONYM **rip**: *There's a tear in your jacket.*

> PRONUNCIATION
> Be careful how you pronounce this word:
> **tear¹** (*verb*) is pronounced like 'fair'
> **tear²** (*noun*) is pronounced like 'here'
> **tear³** (*noun*) is pronounced like 'fair'

tear·ful /ˈtɪəfəl $ ˈtɪrfəl/ *adjective* crying or almost crying: *She looked very tearful.*

tease /tiːz/ *verb* to say amusing but unkind things about someone in order to embarrass or annoy them: *The other girls tease me because I haven't got a boyfriend.*

tea·spoon /ˈtiːspuːn/ *noun* a small spoon, or the amount it holds: *Add a teaspoon of salt.*

teat /tiːt/ *noun* **1** the part of a female animal that baby animals suck to get milk **2** *BrE* the soft rubber part of a baby's bottle that a baby sucks SYNONYM **nipple** *AmE*

ˈtea ˌtowel *noun BrE* a piece of cloth that you use for drying cups, plates etc after washing them

tech·ni·cal /ˈteknɪkəl/ *adjective* related to the knowledge and skills of people who know about science or know how to make something: *We had to learn all the technical words used in computing.*

tech·ni·cian /tekˈnɪʃən/ *noun* someone whose job is to do practical work connected with science or technology: *a laboratory technician*

tech·nique /tekˈniːk/ *noun* a special skill or way of doing something: *He showed us different guitar-playing techniques.*

tech·no·log·i·cal /ˌteknəˈlɒdʒɪkəl $ ˌteknəˈlɑdʒɪkəl/ *adjective* related to technology: *the latest technological developments*

tech·nol·o·gy /tekˈnɒlədʒi $ tekˈnɑlədʒi/ *noun* (plural **technologies**) the knowledge, equipment, and methods that are used in scientific or industrial work: *the development of modern computer* *technology* • *New technologies are appearing all the time.*

ted·dy bear /ˈtedi beə $ ˈtedi ˌber/ also **teddy** *BrE noun* (plural **teddies**) a soft toy that looks like a bear

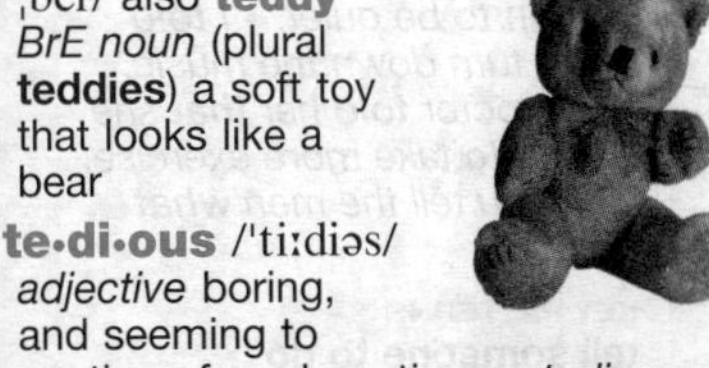
teddy bear

te·di·ous /ˈtiːdiəs/ *adjective* boring, and seeming to continue for a long time: *a tedious lesson*

teem /tiːm/ *verb* **teem with** to be full of people or animals that are moving around: *The ground was teeming with ants.*

teen·age /ˈtiːneɪdʒ/ *adjective* aged between 13 and 19, or suitable for people of this age: *She teaches teenage girls.* • *a teenage magazine*

teen·ag·er /ˈtiːneɪdʒə $ ˈtinˌeɪdʒɚ/ *noun* someone who is aged between 13 and 19 → see Thesaurus at CHILD

teens /tiːnz/ *plural noun* the time in your life when you are aged between 13 and 19: *The club is for people in their teens.* • *She was in her late teens* (=17, 18, or 19 years old).

ˈtee ˌshirt a T-SHIRT

teeth the plural of TOOTH

tee·to·tal /tiːˈtəutl $ tiˈtoutl/ *adjective* someone who is teetotal never drinks alcohol

tel·e·com·mu·ni·ca·tions /ˌtelɪkəmjuːnəˈkeɪʃənz/ *noun* the process of sending and receiving messages by telephone, radio, SATELLITE etc

tel·e·gram /ˈteləgræm/ *noun* a message sent by telegraph

tel·e·graph /ˈteləgrɑːf $ ˈteləˌgræf/ *noun* an old-fashioned way of sending messages along electrical wires

tel·e·phone¹ /ˈteləfəun $ ˈteləˌfoun/ *noun*
a piece of electrical equipment that you use to speak to someone who is in another place and has a similar piece of equipment SYNONYM **phone**: *Can I use your* ***telephone***? • *What's your* ***telephone number***? • *I've got to make a quick* ***telephone call***. • *The* ***telephone rang*** *and Vicky* ***answered*** *it.*

PHRASES

be on the telephone **a)** to be talking using the telephone: *I was on the telephone for 20 minutes.* **b)** to have a telephone at your house or office: *Are you on the telephone?*

telephone² *verb* (formal) to use a telephone to speak to someone SYNONYM **phone**, **call**, **ring** *BrE*: *I telephoned the shop several times.*

tel·e·sales /ˈtelɪseɪlz/ *noun* the activity of selling things to people by calling them on the telephone: *She works in telesales.*

tel·e·scope /ˈteləskəup/ *noun* a piece of equipment like a long tube that you use to look at things that are far away

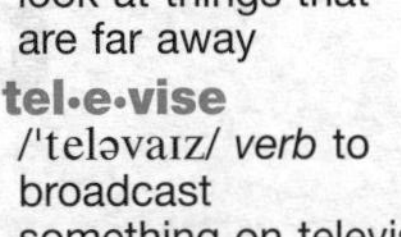
telescope

tel·e·vise /ˈteləvaɪz/ *verb* to broadcast something on television: *The concert will be televised.*

tel·e·vi·sion /ˈteləˌvɪʒən/ *noun* an object with a SCREEN which shows moving pictures and produces sounds. You turn on or switch on a television to watch it, and turn it off or switch it off when you have finished watching it SYNONYM **TV**: *Many children* ***watch*** *too much* ***television***. • *Is there anything good* ***on television*** *tonight?* • *It's time to* ***turn off the television***.

USAGE
You **watch television**.
✘ Don't say 'look at the television'.
You watch a programme **on television**.
✘ Don't say 'in (the) television'.

tell → see box on page 692

tel·ly /ˈteli/ *noun BrE* (informal) (plural **tellies**) a television: *What's on telly tonight?*

temp /temp/ *noun* a secretary who works for different companies for short periods of time: *We will need a temp while the secretary is away.*

tell /tel/ *verb* (past tense and past participle **told** /təʊld $ toʊld/)

1 to give someone facts or information by speaking to them: *Have you **told** him yet?* • ***Tell** me **about** your trip to New York.* • *She **told** us **that** she was planning to get married.* • *Can you **tell** me **what** is going on?* • *I **told** him **how** to get to the station.*

KEY PATTERNS
tell someone
tell someone something
tell someone about something
tell someone (that)
tell someone what/where/when etc

2 to say that someone must do something: *She **told** the children **to** be quiet.* • *I **told** him **to** turn down the music.* • *Her doctor **told** her **that** she needed to take more exercise.* • *Did you tell the men **what** to do?*

KEY PATTERNS
tell someone to do something
tell someone (that)
tell someone what to do

3 can/could tell (that) to know that something is true, because you can see something that shows you it is true: *I **could tell that** he hadn't had enough sleep.* • *You **can tell that** they're sisters – they look so much alike.* • *I **could tell** you didn't like him much.*

WORD CHOICE
tell, **talk**, or **say**?
• You **tell** someone facts or information: *Someone **told** me that the class was cancelled.*
• You **talk about** a subject: *He **talked about** his home in Spain.*
• You **say** words to someone: *She **said** that she was tired.*

PHRASES

tell the difference
to be able to know that two things are different: *It's easy to **tell the difference** between real coffee and instant coffee.*

tell someone off
to speak to someone in an angry way because they have done something wrong: *My dad **told me off** for coming home late.*

tell a story, tell a joke etc
to write or speak a story, joke etc: *Grandpa used to **tell us stories** about when he was little.*

tell the truth
to say what really happened: *I wasn't sure if Bobby was **telling the truth**.* • *I know Catherine **told** me the **truth** about what happened.*

tem·per /ˈtempə $ ˈtempɚ/ *noun*

KEY PATTERNS
be/get in a temper
have a temper

a sudden angry state, or a tendency to become angry suddenly: *Lucy* ***gets in a temper*** *if she can't have what she wants.* • *Julie's certainly* ***got a temper.***

PHRASES
in a bad temper: *Why are you* ***in a bad temper*** (=feeling annoyed or angry) *today?*
lose your temper to suddenly become very angry: *I* ***lose my temper*** *very quickly when I'm tired.*

tem·pera·ment /ˈtemprəmənt/ *noun* your basic character, which controls whether you are usually happy, sad, friendly etc: *a baby with a sweet temperament*

tem·pera·men·tal /ˌtemprəˈmentl/ *adjective* someone who is temperamental changes suddenly from being happy to being angry, sad etc: *She is so temperamental, I never know how she's going to act.*

tem·pe·rate /ˈtempərət/ *adjective* (formal) a temperate country has weather that is never very hot or very cold

tem·pera·ture /ˈtemprətʃə $ ˈtemprətʃɚ/ *noun*

KEY PATTERNS
the temperature of something
the temperature rises/drops

how hot or cold something is: *Check* ***the temperature of*** *the water before you get into the bath.* • *The* ***temperature drops*** *at night to 2°C.*

PHRASES
take someone's temperature to measure the temperature of someone's body, to find out whether they are ill: *The nurse* ***took*** *her* ***temperature*** *with a thermometer.*
have a temperature to be hot because you are ill: *Danny* ***had a temperature of*** *39°C.*

SPELLING
This word is often spelled wrongly. The correct spelling is: **temperature**.

tem·plate /ˈtempleɪt/ *noun* **1** a piece of paper, plastic etc in a particular shape that you use to help you cut other things in the same shape **2** a computer FILE that you use as a model for producing many similar documents: *a template for business letters*

tem·ple /ˈtempəl/ *noun* **1** a building where people in some religions go to pray: *a Hindu temple* **2** the area on the side of your head, between your eye and your ear

tem·po·ra·ri·ly /ˈtempərərəli $ ˌtempəˈrerəli/ *adverb* for a short limited period of time ANTONYM **permanently**: *The school has been closed temporarily.*

tem·po·ra·ry /ˈtempərəri $ ˈtempəˌreri/ *adjective* existing or happening for a short limited period of time ANTONYM **permanent**: *She got a temporary job.* • *This is only a temporary arrangement.*

tempt /tempt/ *verb* to make someone want something that they should not have: *She tried to tempt me to have a cigarette.*

temp·ta·tion /tempˈteɪʃən/ *noun* a strong feeling of wanting something that you should not have: *I resisted the temptation to have another cookie.*

tempt·ing /ˈtemptɪŋ/ *adjective* something that is tempting seems attractive because you would like to have it: *a tempting job offer*

ten /ten/ *noun* 10

ten·ant /ˈtenənt/ *noun* someone who pays rent to live in a room or house

tend /tend/ *verb*

KEY PATTERNS
tend to do something

to be likely to do a particular thing, or to often do it: *Older students* ***tend to*** *ask more questions in class.* • *I* ***tend to*** *wake up early.*

ten·den·cy /ˈtendənsi/ *noun* (plural **tendencies**) if you have a tendency to do something, you often do it: *He has a tendency to shout.*

ten·der /ˈtendə $ ˈtendɚ/ *adjective* **1** gentle and loving: *a tender kiss* **2** soft and easy to cut and eat ANTONYM **tough**: *a lovely tender piece of meat*

ten·ner /ˈtenə $ ˈtenɚ/ *noun BrE* (spoken, informal) £10 or a ten pound note

A B C D E F G H I J K L M N O P Q R S T U V W X Y Z

ten·nis /ˈtenɪs/ *noun* (no plural) a game in which two or four people use RACKETs to hit a ball to each other over a net

ten·or /ˈtenə $ ˈtenɚ/ *noun* a male singer with a fairly high voice

tense¹ /tens/ *adjective*
1 nervous and anxious: *John **looked** really **tense**. • I don't know why I **feel** so **tense**.*
2 a tense situation makes people feel anxious: *It was a tense game.*

tense² *noun* in grammar, one of the forms of a verb that shows whether you are talking about the past, the present, or the future. For example, 'he studied' is in the past tense and 'he studies' is in the present tense.

ten·sion /ˈtenʃən/ *noun* a nervous feeling that you have when you do not know what is going to happen: *You could feel the tension in the room as the teacher slowly read out the exam results.*

tent /tent/ *noun* a thing that you sleep in when you are camping, which is made of cloth and held up by poles and ropes: *We had to put up our tent in the dark.*

tent

ten·ta·cle /ˈtentəkəl/ *noun* one of the long soft arms of a sea creature such as an OCTOPUS → see picture at OCTOPUS

ten·ta·tive /ˈtentətɪv/ *adjective* not definite or certain: *We had tentative plans to meet for lunch.*

tenth /tenθ/ *number* **1** 10th **2** one of ten equal parts of something; 1/10

tep·id /ˈtepɪd/ *adjective* tepid liquid is slightly warm

term /tɜːm $ tɚm/ *noun*

KEY PATTERNS
the terms of an agreement/deal

1 *BrE* one of the parts of a school year: *We'll be learning about maps this term. • The exams are at the end of the summer term.*
2 terms the things that you accept or agree to do as part of a legal agreement: *Both sides have accepted **the terms of** the peace agreement.*
3 a scientific or technical word: *Doctors should explain difficult medical terms.*
4 a period of time during which someone does a job: *The president is hoping to win a second **term of office*** (=a second period of time as president).

PHRASES

in the long term, in the short term during a long or short period from now: *We're not sure what effect the changes will have **in the long term**. • **In the short term** I can borrow money from my parents, but **in the longer term** I'll have to get a job.*

in terms of something used to show what part of something you are talking about: ***In terms of** musical quality, his last album was better.*

be on good terms to have a good, friendly relationship with someone: *Joe and Jim **are on good terms** now that they sit together in class. • I'm afraid my uncle **is not on** very **good terms with** the rest of the family.*

come to terms with something to fully understand and accept a difficult situation: *He couldn't **come to terms with** losing his job.*

ter·mi·nal¹ /ˈtɜːmənəl $ ˈtɚmənəl/ *noun* **1** a building where people get onto planes, buses, or ships: *Our plane leaves from terminal 4.* **2** a SCREEN and KEYBOARD that are connected to a computer

terminal² *adjective* a terminal illness cannot be cured, and causes death —**terminally** *adverb*: *Her mother is terminally ill.*

ter·mi·nol·o·gy /ˌtɜːməˈnɒlədʒi $ ˌtɚməˈnɑlədʒi/ *noun* (formal) (plural **terminologies**) the technical words that are used in a subject: *a dictionary of medical terminology*

ter·mi·nus /ˈtɜːmənəs $ ˈtɚmənəs/ *noun* (plural **termini** /-naɪ/) the place at the end of a railway line or bus service where the trains and buses end their journeys

ter·race /ˈterɪs/ *noun* a flat area next to a building or on a roof, where you can sit SYNONYM **patio**: *We sat and had drinks on the terrace.*

terraced 'house also **,terrace 'house** *BrE noun* a house that is one of a long row of houses that are joined together

ter•ri•ble /'terəbəl/ *adjective* very bad: *I have a terrible headache.* • *a terrible accident* ➔ see Thesaurus at BAD, ILL

USAGE
✘ Don't say 'It's very terrible.' Just say **It's terrible.**

ter•ri•bly /'terəbli/ *adverb* **1** very badly: *She sang terribly.* **2** *BrE* very: *I'm terribly late.*

ter•ri•er /'teriə $ 'teriər/ *noun* a type of small dog

ter•rif•ic /tə'rɪfɪk/ *adjective* (informal) very good SYNONYM **great**: *I love your new hairstyle – it's terrific!*

ter•ri•fied /'terəfaɪd/ *adjective* very frightened: *I'm terrified of flying.* ➔ see Thesaurus at FRIGHTENED

WORD CHOICE
terrified or **terrifying**?
• **Terrified** means "very afraid": *When I first went on the stage I was terrified.*
• **Terrifying** means "making you feel very afraid": *Going to the dentist is a terrifying experience for some people.*

ter•ri•fy /'terəfaɪ/ *verb* (**terrified**, **terrifies**) to make someone very frightened: *That dog terrifies me.* —**terrifying** *adjective*: *a terrifying film*

ter•ri•to•ry /'terətəri $ 'terə,tɔri/ *noun* (plural **territories**) land that a country, person, or animal controls: *We knew that we were now in enemy territory.*

ter•ror /'terə $ 'terər/ *noun* a feeling of great fear: *He screamed in terror.*

ter•ror•is•m /'terərɪzəm/ *noun* (no plural) the use of violent actions, usually against ordinary people, to try to force a government to do something: *The government said the bombing was an evil act of terrorism.*

ter•ror•ist /'terərɪst/ *noun* someone who uses violent actions, usually against ordinary people, to try to force a government to do something

test[1] /test/ *noun*

KEY PATTERNS
pass a test
fail a test
take/do a test

1 a set of questions or activities that you do to show how much you know or how well you can do something. You take a test SYNONYM **exam**: *I passed my history test.* • *Michelle had to take her driving test three times before she passed.* • *I'm afraid I might fail my maths test.*
2 a short medical check on part of your body: *The children will be given eye tests.* • *a blood test*

USAGE
You say **do** or **take a test**.
✘ Don't say 'make a test'.

test[2] *verb*

KEY PATTERNS
test someone on a subject
test something
test someone for a disease/illness

1 to ask someone questions or make them do things to show how much they know or how well they can do something: *The teacher **tested** us **on** chapters 7 to 11.*
2 to use something to find out whether it works: *The school is testing some new educational software.*
3 to do a medical check on part of someone's body: *They **tested** him **for** malaria and other illnesses.*

tes•ti•fy /'testəfaɪ/ *verb* (**testified**, **testifies**) to formally say in a law court what you know about something: *She testified that she had seen the man leaving the bank.*

tes•ti•mo•ny /'testəməni $ 'testə,mouni/ *noun* (plural **testimonies**) a formal statement that someone makes in a law court

'test tube *noun* a small narrow glass container that is used in scientific tests

test tubes

test tubes

tet•a•nus /'tetənəs/ *noun* (no plural) a serious disease that you can get when you

A B C D E F G H I J K L M N O P Q R S T U V W X Y Z

are cut, which makes you unable to move the muscles in your body

text¹ /tekst/ *noun* **1** the writing in a book, magazine etc, rather than the pictures **2** also **text message** a written message sent to someone on their MOBILE PHONE

text² *verb* to send someone a text message on their MOBILE PHONE: *Text me when you get back home.*

text·book /ˈtekstbʊk/ *noun* a book about a subject which students use: *a history textbook*

tex·tile /ˈtekstaɪl/ *noun* (formal) any material that you make by crossing threads over and under each other

tex·ture /ˈtekstʃə $ ˈtekstʃɚ/ *noun* the way that something feels when you touch it: *I like the soft texture of this material.*

than /ðən; strong ðæn/ *preposition, conjunction*
used when comparing people or things: *These shoes are cheaper than the other ones. • My brother's older than me. • She's thinner than she used to be* (=she used to be fatter).

thank /θæŋk/ *verb*

KEY PATTERNS
thank someone for a present/their help
thank someone for doing something

to tell someone that you are grateful to them for something: *I must write and thank him* ***for*** *the flowers he sent. • She* ***thanked*** *the boy* ***for*** *helping her.*

thank·ful /ˈθæŋkfəl/ *adjective* glad about something: *We're thankful nobody was hurt in the accident.*
—**thankfully** *adverb*: *Thankfully, nobody lost their job* (=I'm glad nobody lost their job).

thanks¹ /θæŋks/ (informal)

KEY PATTERNS
thanks for your help/letter
thanks for coming/calling

thank you: *"Lunch is ready." "Thanks, Mom." •* ***Thanks for*** *the ride home. • Bye,* ***thanks for*** *coming. • "Do you want any help, Bob?" "No, thanks."*

PHRASES
thanks to something because of something: *Dealing with information is much easier now,* ***thanks to*** *modern computers.*

thanks² *plural noun* something that you say to thank someone: *I helped him a lot, but did I get any thanks? No.*

Thanks·giv·ing /ˌθæŋksˈgɪvɪŋ/ *noun* a holiday in the US and Canada in autumn, when families have a large meal together

thank you

KEY PATTERNS
thank you for something
thank you for doing something

1 used when someone does or says something kind to you: *"What a beautiful dress!" "Thank you." • Oh, this is just what I wanted.* ***Thank you very much.*** *•* ***Thank you for*** *dinner – it was really good. •* ***Thank you for*** *sending me those books.*
2 used to say yes or no to something that someone is offering you: *"Do you want a drink?"* ***"No, thank you."***

SPELLING
This word is often spelled wrongly. The correct spelling is: **thank you**.

ˈ**thank-you** *noun* something that you say or do to thank someone: *They gave her some flowers as a thank-you.*

that¹ *determiner, pronoun, conjunction*
1 /ðæt/ (plural **those** /ðəʊz $ ðoʊz/) used to talk about a thing or person which is farther away from you, often in a place you point at: *He lives in that house on the corner. • "Which piece would you like?" "I'd like that one, please." • Look at those cute little rabbits. • Can you park in that space over there?*
2 /ðæt/ (plural **those** /ðəʊz $ ðoʊz/) used to talk about a thing or person you are already talking about or know about: *Who told you that? • "She's pretty, isn't she?" "Yes, that's his sister." • We met for coffee later that day. • Those photographs you showed me were really good.*
3 /ðət/ who or which: *Is he the man that was shouting at you? • There are lots of things that I need to do before I leave.*

4 /ðət/ used to join two parts of a sentence together: *I hope that you get better soon.* • *I need to be sure that you're not lying.*

that² /ðæt/ *adverb* (spoken)
that long, that much, that big etc as long, much, big etc as you show, using your hands: *The car missed us by about that much.*

thatched /θætʃt/ *adjective* a thatched roof on a house is made of dried plant stems

thaw /θɔː/ also **thaw out** *verb* if something frozen thaws, it becomes warmer until all the ice is gone ANTONYM **freeze**: *The freezer broke and all the food thawed out.* • *In spring, the river thaws and sometimes floods the valleys.*

the /ðə; before vowels, and strong ðiː/ *determiner*
1 used before a noun to show that you are talking about a particular person or thing: *The boy was riding **the** blue bicycle.* • *That's **the** dress I want to buy.* • *He went to **the** shop to buy some milk.* • ***The** movie wasn't very good.*
2 used before the names of rivers, oceans, and seas and before the names of groups of mountains: ***the** Ganges* • ***the** Atlantic Ocean* • ***the** Mediterranean Sea*
3 used before the names of countries if they are plural or have the word 'state', 'union', 'republic', or 'kingdom' in them: ***the** Philippines* • ***the** United States* • ***the** People's Republic of China*
4 used to talk about all the people in a country: ***The** British like fish and chips.* • ***The** Japanese have a good school system.*
5 used to talk about all people who are blind, rich etc: *parking spaces for **the** disabled* • *a school for **the** deaf*
6 used to talk about a particular period of time: ***The** sixties* (=1960s) *were a time of great change.* • *In **the** 1800s, millions of people came to America.*

GRAMMAR
Don't use **the** when you are talking about something in general: *I like ice cream.* • *Cats often hunt at night.*
Use **the** when you are talking about a particular thing: *I like **the** ice cream I bought.* • ***The** cats on our street make a lot of noise.*
Don't use **the** before the names of airports, train stations, or streets: *We arrived at Gatwick Airport.* • *The train leaves from Euston Station.* • *She lives in Spencer Way.*
Use **the** when you are talking about an airport, station, or street without saying its name: *We arrived at **the** airport.* • *The train leaves from **the** new station.* • *She lives in **the** same street as me.*

thea·tre *BrE*, **theater** *AmE* /ˈθɪətə $ ˈθiətər/ *noun* **1** a building with a stage where plays are performed: *Would you like to go to the theater?* • *the Royal Gala Theatre* **2** also **movie theater** the American word for a CINEMA **3** the room in a hospital where doctors do operations

the·at·ri·cal /θiˈætrɪkəl/ *adjective* related to the theatre: *She makes theatrical costumes* (=clothes for actors to wear).

theft /θeft/ *noun* (formal) the crime of stealing something: *There is a lot of car theft around here.*

their /ðə $ ðər; strong ðeə $ ðer/ *determiner*
1 belonging to two or more people: *Someone stole their car.* • *Their plan was not successful.*
2 his or her: *Someone's left their coat behind.*

theirs /ðeəz $ ðerz/ *pronoun*
a thing belonging to a group of two or more people: *Our house is bigger than theirs.*

them /ðəm; strong ðem/ *pronoun*
1 used when talking about a group of people or things: *Some boys were talking, so the teacher told them to be quiet.* • *The magazines were old, so I threw them away.*
2 him or her: *If anyone calls, tell them I'll be back at 4 o'clock.*

theme /θiːm/ *noun* **1** the main subject or idea in a book, film etc: *Childhood was the main theme of the story.* **2 theme music, theme song** music that is always played with a particular television or radio programme

ˈtheme park *noun* a place where people pay to ride on machines that is based on one particular thing, such as space travel or animals

them·selves /ðəm'selvz/ *pronoun*
1 used when the same group does an action and receives an action: *The children might hurt themselves if they play on the rocks. • My parents are old and no longer able to look after themselves.*
2 used to emphasize that you are talking about a particular group: *Some of the students themselves said that the exam was too easy.*
3 himself or herself: *The person who did this should be ashamed of themselves.*
PHRASES
by themselves with no one else there, or with no one helping: *They spent the day* ***by themselves****. • Did they do all the work* ***by themselves****?*

then /ðen/ *adverb*
1 at a time in the past or future: *It happened in 1972, and things were different then. • "I'll come round at about 8." "OK, I'll see you then."*
2 after something else: *I'll get changed and then we can go out. • Fry the onions. Then add the mushrooms.*
→ see Thesaurus at AFTERWARDS
3 (spoken) used when saying something because of what has been said before: *"There are no seats here." "Then we'll have to go somewhere else." • "It's nearly ten." "Come on, then. We'd better go."*

the·ol·o·gy /θi'ɒlədʒi $ θi'ɑlədʒi/ *noun* (no plural) the study of religion

theo·ret·i·cal /ˌθɪə'retɪkəl/ *adjective* relating to or involving ideas rather than actions or reality: *Doctors should have both theoretical knowledge and practical skills.*

theo·ry /'θɪəri $ 'θiəri/ *noun* (plural **theories**) an idea that explains why something happens: *Can you prove your theory? • My theory is that he behaves badly because his parents are always arguing.*

ther·a·py /'θerəpi/ *noun* (plural **therapies**) the treatment of mental or physical illness without using drugs or operations: *She's having therapy to help with her fear of birds.*

there¹ /ðeə $ ðer/ *pronoun*
1 there is, there are used to say that something exists or happens: *There are some great photographs in the book. • At the beginning of the film, there's a robbery. • There has been a lot of rain recently.*
2 is there?, are there? used to ask whether something exists: *Is there a TV in your bedroom? • Are there any girls in the team?*

there² *adverb*
1 in another place, not the place where you are ANTONYM **here**: *You can sit over there. • I wish I had been there – it sounds so exciting! • If we leave home in the morning, we should get there by lunchtime.*
2 available or ready to help: *The offer's there if you want it. • We'll always be there for you when you need us.*
PHRASES
there's, there it is, there he is etc something you say when you are pointing at something or someone: *Look,* ***there's*** *our hotel! • We're still waiting for Jack. Look, there he is.*

GRAMMAR
You say **go there**.
✘ Don't say 'go to there'.

SPELLING
Don't confuse the spelling of **there** and **their** (=belonging to two or more people).

there·a·bouts /ˌðeərə'baʊts $ ˌðerə'baʊts/ *adverb* near the number, amount, time etc that you have just mentioned: *We should arrive at 9 o'clock or thereabouts.*

there·fore /'ðeəfɔː $ 'ðerfɔr/ *adverb* (formal) for the reason that you have just mentioned: *These shoes are made of fine leather, and are therefore very expensive.*

WORD CHOICE
therefore or **so**?
• **So** is used in both formal and informal English. It is usually used to join two parts of a sentence: *I wanted to find out more about his work,* ***so*** *I decided to look on the Internet.*
• **Therefore** is used especially in formal English: *The school was getting very cold in winter.* ***Therefore,*** *they decided to put in a new heating system.*

ther·mal /ˈθɜːməl $ ˈθɚməl/ *adjective* (formal) relating to or caused by heat: *thermal energy*

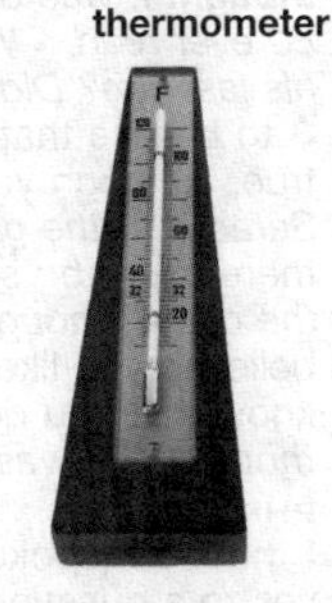
thermometer

ther·mom·e·ter /θəˈmɒmətə $ θɚˈmɑmətɚ/ *noun* a piece of equipment that measures the temperature of the air, your body etc

ther·mo·stat /ˈθɜːməstæt $ ˈθɚməˌstæt/ *noun* a piece of equipment that controls the temperature of a house

the·sau·rus /θɪˈsɔːrəs/ *noun* (plural **thesauruses**) a book containing lists of words that have similar meanings

these the plural form of THIS[1]

they /ðeɪ/ *pronoun*
1 used when talking about a group of people or things: *Her parents said they would be out that evening.* • *He had some paints but they were the wrong colour.*
2 he or she: *Anyone can learn to play the piano if they want to.*

they'd /ðeɪd/ **1** the short form of 'they had': *They'd seen him earlier.*
2 the short form of 'they would': *They said they'd love to come.*

they'll /ðeɪl/ the short form of 'they will': *They'll be late; they always are.*

they're /ðə $ ðɚ; strong ðeə $ ðer/ the short form of 'they are': *They're lovely earrings.*

they've /ðeɪv/ the short form of 'they have': *They've gone out.*

thick

thick /θɪk/ *adjective*
1 something that is thick has a wide distance between its two opposite sides ANTONYM **thin**: *a thick heavy book* • *I drew a thick line around the edge of the page.* • *a thick warm coat*
2 used to talk about the distance between the two opposite sides of something: *The castle walls are about one metre thick* (=the walls are one metre from front to back).
3 thick smoke or cloud is difficult to see through SYNONYM **dense**: *The ship could not sail because of thick fog.*
4 a thick liquid does not have much water in it ANTONYM **thin**: *Heat the mixture until it is quite thick.*
5 if you have thick hair, it grows closely together on your head ANTONYM **thin**
6 *BrE* (informal) stupid: *He's really thick!*

thick·ness /ˈθɪknəs/ *noun* how thick something is: *Cut the bread the same thickness as your finger.*

thief /θiːf/ *noun* (plural **thieves** /θiːvz/) someone who steals things: *a car thief*

> **SPELLING**
> This word is often spelled wrongly. The correct spelling is: **thief**.

thigh /θaɪ/ *noun* the top part of your leg above your knee: *She smiled and patted his thigh.* → see picture on page A5

thin /θɪn/ *adjective* (**thinner**, **thinnest**)
1 someone who is thin has very little fat on their body ANTONYM **fat**: *a tall thin man* • *Her face was thin and pale.*
2 something that is thin has very little distance between its opposite sides ANTONYM **thick**: *thin slices of ham* • *a thin layer of dust* → see picture at THICK
3 if someone's hair is thin, it does not grow closely together ANTONYM **thick**: *John looks older, and his hair is getting a bit thin.*

> **THESAURUS**
> **slim/slender**: *She was tall, slim, and beautiful* (=thin in an attractive way).
> **lean**: *his strong, lean body* (=thin in a healthy way)
> **skinny**: *She was so skinny you could see her ribs* (=too thin).

thing /θɪŋ/ *noun*
1 an object – used when you do not say its name, or do not know its name: *What's this little round thing for?* • *Just put all those things in a pile on the*

table. • *Turn that **thing** off! You've watched enough TV today.*

2 your/my/her things (spoken) books, clothes, or other objects that belong to you, or that you need in order to do something: *I can't find all **my things**.* • *Just put **your things** over there for now.* • *Have you brought **your** swimming **things**?*

3 something that happens, or something that you do or say: *A funny **thing** happened to me last night.* • *My brother says some strange **things** sometimes.* • *It was a stupid **thing** to do.*

4 things used when talking about the situation that you are in, and what is happening in your life: *"Hi, Jason, **how are things** with you?" "Fine thanks."* • *Dad's finally found another job, so **things are getting better**.* • *We've lived here for 15 years, and **things have changed a lot** in that time.*

PHRASES

all sorts/kinds of things a lot of different types of things: *We talked about **all kinds of things**.* • *They sell **all sorts of things** – everything from sweets to videos.*

for one thing used when giving a reason why you think something is true or will happen: *She's not a great basketball player. **For one thing**, she can't jump.* • ***For one thing**, smoking makes your breath smell horrible.*

the last thing I want/need, the last thing on my mind used when saying that someone does not want or need something at all, or that you are not thinking about something at all: ***The last thing I wanted** was to miss the class.* • *Marriage was **the last thing on her mind**.*

think /θɪŋk/ *verb* (past tense and past participle **thought** /θɔːt/)

> **KEY PATTERNS**
> **think about something**
> **think carefully**
> **think (that)**
> **what do you think of someone/something?**

1 to use your mind, for example to make a decision or to imagine what something is like: *Alison **thought about** what he had said.* • ***Think carefully** before you make any decisions.* • *I need some time to **think**.*

2 to have a particular opinion about someone or something: *Everyone **thought that** it was a good idea.* • *I **thought** it was one of the best books I'd ever read.* • ***What did you think of** his last film? Did you like it?*

3 to believe that something is probably true, although you are not sure: *I **think** Sarah is in the garden.* • *Jim **thinks that** there might be something wrong with the car.* • *I **thought** you liked carrots* (=I believed you liked carrots, but now I know that you do not). • *She's 16? I **thought** she was a lot older.*

PHRASES

I think so (spoken) used when saying yes to a question, when you are not completely sure: *"Is there any cake left?" "I think so."*

I don't think so (spoken) used when saying no to a question, when you are not completely sure: *"Will Ben be coming to the party?" "**I don't think so**."*

PHRASAL VERBS

think about/of
to consider doing something: *We're **thinking of** going to Florida this year.* • *Have you ever **thought about** marriage?* • ***I've been thinking about** joining the army.*

think of
1 to use your mind in order to produce an idea, plan, suggestion etc: *I couldn't **think of** anything I could do to help.*
2 to remember something or someone: *The flowers made Peter **think of** his mother's garden.*

think over
to think about something very carefully before you decide what to do: *I needed some time to **think** things **over**.* • *Take a few days to **think over** any job offers.*

think through
to think carefully about all the things that might happen if you do something: *Students need to **think through** their job and college decisions.* • *Make sure you **think** it **through** before you do it.*

think·ing /ˈθɪŋkɪŋ/ *noun* (no plural) someone's opinions and ideas about something: *What is your latest thinking on your choice of university?*

thin·ly /ˈθɪnli/ *adverb* **1 thinly sliced** cut into thin pieces ANTONYM **thickly sliced** **2 thinly populated** with few people in a large area ANTONYM **densely populated**: *a thinly populated mountain area*

third /θɜːd $ θɚd/ *number* **1** 3rd: *Josh came third in the race.* **2** one of three equal parts of something; 1/3: *One-third of the students are girls.*

ˌthird ˈperson *noun* **the third person** a form of a verb that you use with 'he', 'she', 'it', or 'they'

thirst /θɜːst $ θɚst/ *noun* (no plural) when you need a drink very much: *People are dying of thirst.*

> USAGE
> You say **I'm thirsty**.
> ✘ Don't say 'I have thirst.'

thirst·y /ˈθɜːsti $ ˈθɚsti/ *adjective* (**thirstier, thirstiest**) if you are thirsty, you want or need to drink something: *I'm really thirsty – let's get a drink.*

thir·teen /ˌθɜːˈtiːn $ ˌθɚˈtin/ *number* 13 —**thirteenth** *number*

thir·ty /ˈθɜːti $ ˈθɚti/ *number* (plural **thirties**) **1** 30 **2 the thirties** the years from 1930 to 1939 **3 be in your thirties** to be aged between 30 and 39 —**thirtieth** *number*

this¹ /ðɪs/ *determiner, pronoun* (plural **these** /ðiːz/)
1 used to talk about a thing or person that is near you: *This coffee's cold.* • *These trousers are a bit tight.* • *I've lived in this town all my life.* • *"What's this?" "A present."* • *This is Janet* (=used to introduce someone).
2 used to mention a period of time that is happening now or will happen very soon: *I've been pretty busy this week.* • *This year has been a difficult one.* • *Shall we go to the cinema this weekend* (=during the weekend that will come next)?
3 used to say something about the thing you are already talking about: *Barry was late. This didn't surprise her because he was often late.* • *This is very bad news.*

this² *adverb*
this late, this cold, this difficult etc as late, cold, difficult etc as something is at the present time: *It's never been this cold in October before.*

thistle

this·tle /ˈθɪsəl/ *noun* a wild plant with sharp points on its leaves

thorn /θɔːn $ θɔrn/ *noun* a sharp pointed part on a plant such as a rose

thor·ough /ˈθʌrə $ ˈθɚoʊ/ *adjective* if someone is thorough, they do things very carefully: *She's always very thorough in her school work.* • *The doctor gave me a thorough examination.* ➔ see Thesaurus at CAREFUL

thor·ough·ly /ˈθʌrəli $ ˈθɚoʊli/ *adverb* **1** very much: *He thoroughly enjoyed the meal.* **2** carefully and completely: *Check your work thoroughly.*

those the plural of THAT¹

though /ðəʊ $ ðoʊ/ *conjunction, adverb*
1 in spite of something SYNONYM **although**: *Though I was tired, I still decided to go out and meet the others.* • *I seem to be gaining weight **even though** I'm exercising regularly.*
2 but: *He's a nice dog, though he doesn't always obey me.* • *I don't know if I'll be able to fix it – I'll try though* (=but I'll try).

> PRONUNCIATION
> You pronounce **though** like 'low'.

thought¹ the past tense and past participle of THINK

thought² /θɔːt/ *noun*

> KEY PATTERNS
> **have a thought**
> **the thought that**
> **the thought of someone/something**
> **someone's thoughts on/about something**

something that you think, for example an idea or opinion: *I've just **had a thought**. Why don't we ask Steve to help?* • *I was upset by **the thought that** Mary might have been lying to me.* • *The **thought of** Simon made her want to scream.* • *Rachel, what are your **thoughts on** this?*

A B C D E F G H I J K L M N O P Q R S T U V W X Y Z

A B C D E F G H I J K L M N O P Q R S T U V W X Y Z

PHRASES
give something some thought, give some thought to something to think about something: *That's a good idea. I'll **give it some thought**.*

PRONUNCIATION
You pronounce **thought** like 'port'.

thought·ful /ˈθɔːtfəl/ *adjective*
1 serious and quiet because you are thinking: *She looked thoughtful.*
2 thinking of and doing kind things to make people happy: *It was thoughtful of you to remember my birthday.*
➔ see Thesaurus at KIND[2]
—**thoughtfully** *adverb*: *He thoughtfully offered to help.*

thought·less /ˈθɔːtləs/ *adjective* not thinking about how other people will feel about something: *How can you be so thoughtless?* —**thoughtlessly** *adverb*: *She thoughtlessly told everyone my secret.*

thou·sand /ˈθaʊzənd/ *noun* (plural **thousand** or **thousands**) 1,000: *It cost ten thousand dollars.* • *Thousands of people lost their homes.*

GRAMMAR
You use the plural form **thousand** after a number: *three thousand men*
You use the plural form **thousands** before **of**: *thousands of miles*

thrash /θræʃ/ *verb* **1** (informal) to easily win a game against someone: *We thrashed them 10–0.* **2** to hit someone violently, usually as a punishment

thread[1] /θred/ *noun* a long thin string of cotton, silk etc that you use to sew cloth: *a needle and thread*

PRONUNCIATION
You pronounce **thread** like 'bed'.

thread[2] *verb* to put thread, string etc through a small hole: *He threaded the wire carefully through the holes.*

threat /θret/ *noun* **1** when you tell someone that you will hurt them if they do not do what you want: *He sent her an email making threats against her family.* **2** someone or something that may cause harm or damage: *This method of farming is a threat to birds and animals.* ➔ see Thesaurus at DANGER

threat·en /ˈθretn/ *verb*

KEY PATTERNS
threaten someone
threaten to do something
be threatened with death/destruction

1 to tell someone that you will do something unpleasant to them if they do not do what you want: *The boys threatened him until he gave them all his money.* • *He **had threatened to kill** her if she didn't keep quiet.*
2 to be likely to harm or destroy something: *This new law threatens the rights of all of us.* • *Many of the animals in the area **are threatened with** extinction* (=are likely to stop existing).

three /θriː/ *number* 3

ˌthree-diˈmensional *adjective* a three-dimensional object has length, width, and height: *The computer game makes you feel you are in a three-dimensional space.*

threw the past tense of THROW[1]

thrill /θrɪl/ *noun* a strong feeling of excitement and pleasure: *I get such a thrill from scoring goals.*

thrilled /θrɪld/ *adjective* very excited, pleased, or happy: *I was thrilled when he told me he liked me.*

thrill·er /ˈθrɪlə $ ˈθrɪlɚ/ *noun* an exciting film or book about murder or crime

thril·ling /ˈθrɪlɪŋ/ *adjective* very exciting: *a thrilling game*

throat /θrəʊt $ θroʊt/ *noun* the back part of your mouth and the inside of your neck: *I have a sore throat.*

throb /θrɒb $ θrɑb/ *verb* (**throbbed, throbbing**) to hurt with a strong regular pain: *My finger was throbbing.*

throne /θrəʊn $ θroʊn/ *noun* **1** the large chair that a king or queen sits on **2 on the throne**: *This happened when Queen Victoria was on the throne* (=when she was queen).

throt·tle[1] /ˈθrɒtl $ ˈθrɑtl/ *verb* to hold someone's throat tightly, stopping them from breathing SYNONYM **strangle**: *He tried to throttle me.*

throttle[2] *noun* a part of a vehicle that controls the speed of the engine by controlling the amount of FUEL going into it

through

They drove through the tunnel under the mountain.

through[1] /θruː/ *preposition, adverb*
1 from one side of a thing or place to the other: *They drove through the tunnel under the mountain.* • *We went through Belgium on our way to Germany.* • *A man was looking at them through the window.* • *If we don't mend that hole in the roof, the rain will come through.*
2 from the beginning of something to the end: *She slept through the night without waking up.* • *The people in front of us talked all the way through the film.*
3 *AmE* until the end of a particular day or month: *I'm busy from Monday through Thursday.*

PRONUNCIATION
You pronounce **through** like 'you'.

through[2] *adjective*
be through with something (informal) to have finished using something or doing something: *Are you through with my lecture notes yet?*

through·out /θruːˈaʊt/ *preposition, adverb*
1 in every part of a place: *It's a large company, with offices throughout the world.* → see Thesaurus at EVERYWHERE
2 during all of a period of time: *The school runs language courses throughout the year.*

throw

throw[1] /θrəʊ $ θroʊ/ *verb* (**threw** /θruː/ **thrown** /θrəʊn $ θroʊn/)

KEY PATTERNS
throw a ball to someone
throw someone a pen/the keys
throw something into the air/a bin
throw a stone at someone/something

1 if you throw something you are holding, you make it go through the air: *Dad* ***threw*** *the ball* ***to*** *Alex* (=threw it so that Alex could catch it). • *He* ***threw*** *the empty bottle* ***into*** *the bin.* • *Could you throw me my sweater?* • *One of the boys* ***threw*** *a stone* ***at*** *the dog* (=threw it to try to hit the dog).
→ see picture at CATCH[1]
2 to suddenly move yourself or part of your body somewhere: *She* ***threw*** *herself* ***onto*** *the bed.* • *"Don't go," he said,* ***throwing*** *his arms* ***around*** *her.*

PHRASAL VERBS

throw away
throw something away if you throw away something that you do not want, you put it in a container where it will be removed: *This bread looks rather old – shall I* ***throw it away****?*

throw out
throw something out if you throw out something that you do not want, you get rid of it: *Are you* ***throwing out*** *those old clothes?*

throw up
(informal) if you throw up, the food you have eaten comes back out of your mouth SYNONYM **vomit**: *I'll* ***throw up*** *if I eat any more pizza!*

THESAURUS
chuck (informal): *I* ***chucked*** *a cushion at him* (=threw it).
toss: *He* ***tossed*** *the ball into the air* (=threw it in a careless way).

fling/hurl: *She flung the book across the room* (=threw it with a lot of force).

throw² *noun* when you throw something: *That was a good throw!*

thrown the past participle of THROW

thru /θruː/ another spelling of THROUGH that is sometimes used in notes, written signs etc

thrust /θrʌst/ *verb* (past tense and past participle **thrust**) to push something somewhere with quite a lot of force: *She thrust a letter into my hand.*

thud /θʌd/ *noun* the low sound of something heavy hitting something else: *He fell out of bed with a thud.*

thug /θʌg/ *noun* a rough violent person: *A gang of thugs attacked him.*

thumb¹ /θʌm/ *noun* the short thick finger at the side of your hand: *He broke his thumb playing rugby.*

thumb² *verb* **thumb through something** to quickly look at the pages in a book, magazine etc: *I thumbed through the guidebook, looking for a map.*

PRONUNCIATION
In this word you do not pronounce the **b**.

thumb·tack /ˈθʌmtæk/ the American word for a DRAWING PIN

thump /θʌmp/ *verb* **1** to hit someone or something hard with your hand closed: *I'll thump you if you say that again!* **2** if your heart is thumping, it is beating strongly and quickly because you are afraid or excited —**thump** *noun*: *Paul gave him a thump in the stomach.*

thun·der /ˈθʌndə $ ˈθʌndɚ/ *noun* (no plural) the loud noise that you hear during a storm: *Thunder roared and lightning flashed.*

thun·der·ous /ˈθʌndərəs/ *adjective* extremely loud: *thunderous applause*

Thurs·day /ˈθɜːzdi $ ˈθɝzdi/ (written abbreviation **Thurs**) *noun* the day of the week between Wednesday and Friday: *Claire goes to hospital on Thursday.*

tick¹ /tɪk/ *noun* **1** the sound that a clock makes every second: *The only sound was the tick of a clock.* → see picture on page A1 **2** *BrE* a mark that you write to show that something is correct SYNONYM **check** *AmE*: *She put a tick next to my answer to question 10.*

tick² *verb* **1** if a clock ticks, it makes a short sound every second: *His watch ticked loudly.* **2** *BrE* to mark something with a tick to show that it is correct SYNONYM **check** *AmE*: *Tick the box if you want to receive our magazine.*

tick·et /ˈtɪkɪt/ *noun*

KEY PATTERNS
a ticket to Oxford
a ticket for a film/match

a piece of paper that you buy in order to travel somewhere or go to an event: *How much is a* ***bus ticket*** *to London?* • ***Tickets for*** *the concert are £15.*

tick·le /ˈtɪkəl/ *verb* **1** to move your fingers over part of someone's body in order to make them laugh: *I tickled the baby's chin.* **2** if something tickles, it touches your body lightly in an uncomfortable way: *This sweater really tickles.*

tide

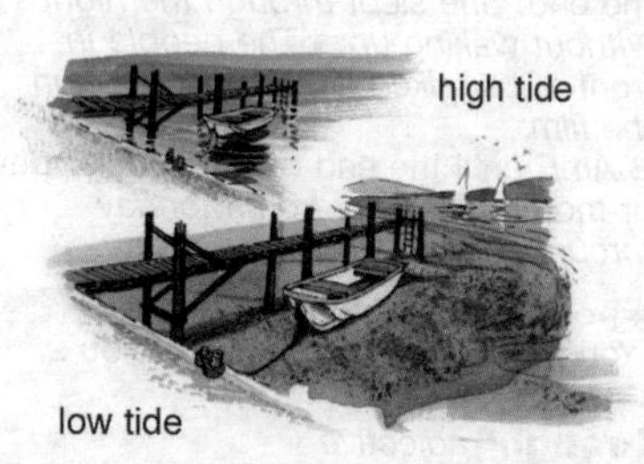

tide¹ /taɪd/ *noun* **1** the regular movement of the sea as it comes up to cover the land and goes down away from the land: *The tide is coming in* (=towards the land). **2 high tide, low tide** when the level of the sea is high or low: *You can walk to the island at low tide.*

tide² *verb* **tide someone over** to give someone money to help them while they are waiting to get money from somewhere else: *Mum lent me £20 to tide me over until I got paid.*

ti•dy[1] /ˈtaɪdi/ *adjective* (**tidier**, **tidiest**)
1 neat ANTONYM **untidy**: *Your grandmother's coming, so make sure your room is tidy!* • *Please leave the house tidy when you go.* ➔ see picture at MESSY
2 *BrE* someone who is tidy likes to keep things neat and in the right place SYNONYM **neat** *AmE*: *Sarah is very tidy.*
—**tidily** *adverb*

tidy[2] *verb BrE* (**tidied**, **tidies**)
also **tidy up** to make a place look tidy by picking things up and putting them in their correct place: *It took us two hours to* ***tidy up*** *after the party.* • *Don't forget to tidy your room.*

PHRASAL VERBS
tidy away *BrE*
tidy something away to put something back in its correct place or into a container: *Can you* ***tidy away*** *your papers please?*

tie[1] /taɪ/ *verb* (**tying**)

KEY PATTERNS
tie something to a tree/post
tie things together
tie something around something else
tie with someone
tie for first/second place

1 to fasten things together using rope, string etc: *George got out of the boat and* ***tied*** *it* ***to*** *a tree.* • *The soldier took some rope and* ***tied*** *Ken's hands* ***together****.* ➔ see Thesaurus at FASTEN
2 to fasten something in a particular position by making a knot in it: *Jack* ***tied*** *his sweater* ***around*** *his waist and went out.* • *He had forgotten to tie his shoelaces.*
3 if two people or teams tie with each other, they have the same number of points at the end of a competition: *Tom* ***tied for*** *first place* ***with*** *Craig.*

PHRASAL VERBS
tie up
1 tie someone up to tie someone's arms and legs with rope so that they cannot move: *They* ***tied*** *us* ***up*** *and left us in a dark room.*
2 tie something up to fasten something with rope, string etc: *a box of chocolates* ***tied up*** *with pink ribbon*

tie[2] *noun* **1** a long narrow piece of cloth that you wear around your neck with a shirt: *He has to wear a shirt and tie for work.* ➔ see picture at CLOTHES
2 when a competition ends with two people or teams getting the same number of points SYNONYM **draw** *BrE*: *The match ended in a tie.*

tier /tɪə $ tɪr/ *noun* a row of seats that has other rows above or below it: *We were in the first tier of seats.*

ti•ger /ˈtaɪɡə $ ˈtaɪɡɚ/ *noun* a large wild cat with yellow and black lines on its fur ➔ see picture on page A9

tight[1] /taɪt/ *adjective*
1 clothes that are tight fit your body very closely ANTONYM **loose**: *She was wearing a tight white T-shirt.* • *This skirt's a bit too tight.*
2 firmly fixed and difficult to move ANTONYM **loose**: *The lid's too tight. I can't get it off.* • *I fastened my hair up in a tight knot.*
3 tight laws or rules are very strict: *We need tighter controls on the burning of coal, gas and oil.*

tight[2] *adverb* if you hold something tight, you hold it with a lot of force: *I held on tight as the bus started to move.*

tight•en /ˈtaɪtn/ *verb* **1** to become tighter, or to make something tighter ANTONYM **loosen**: *How do I tighten my seat belt?* **2** also **tighten something up** to make a rule or law stricter: *They are tightening up the rules on smoking at school.*

tight•rope /ˈtaɪt-rəʊp $ ˈtaɪt-roʊp/ *noun* a wire high above the ground that a performer walks along in a CIRCUS

tights /taɪts/ *plural noun* a thin piece of clothing that fits around a woman's feet and legs, and up to her waist SYNONYM **pantyhose** *AmE*: *a pair of black tights* ➔ see picture at UNDERWEAR

tile /taɪl/ *noun* a thin square piece of a hard material that is used for covering roofs, walls, or floors: *Dad is fixing some new tiles in the bathroom.*

till[1] /tɪl/ *preposition* until: *Let's wait till later.*

till[2] *noun* a machine that is used in a shop to keep money in and show how much customers have to pay: *There was over £1,000 in the till.*

A B C D E F G H I J K L M N O P Q R S T U V W X Y Z

tilt /tɪlt/ *verb* if something tilts, or if you tilt it, it moves so that one side or edge is higher: *Jackie tilted the mirror slightly so that she could see herself better.*

tim·ber /ˈtɪmbə $ ˈtɪmbɚ/ *noun* (no plural) *BrE* wood that you use to build or make things SYNONYM **lumber** *AmE*

time[1] → see box on pages 708 and 709

time[2] /taɪm/ *verb* **1** to arrange for something to happen at a particular time: *The bomb was timed to explode at 6.00 pm.* **2** to measure how long it takes to do something: *The coach timed us as we ran around the track.*

time·less /ˈtaɪmləs/ *adjective* not affected by changes over time: *the timeless beauty of the sea*

ˌtime ˈoff *noun* (no plural) time when you do not have to be at work or school: *I'd like some time off this week.*

ˌtime ˈout *noun* a short break during a sports game to let the players rest or plan how they will play the rest of the game

tim·er /ˈtaɪmə $ ˈtaɪmɚ/ *noun* a part of a machine or system that you use to make it stop or start at a particular time: *You can set the timer to switch the cooker off.*

time·ta·ble /ˈtaɪmˌteɪbəl/ *noun* a list of times or dates, showing when things will happen: *the train timetable*

tim·id /ˈtɪmɪd/ *adjective* shy and nervous ANTONYM **confident**: *a timid girl who never spoke*

tin /tɪn/ *noun* **1** a metal container in which you can store food: *a biscuit tin* **2** *BrE* a small metal container in which food is sold SYNONYM **can** *AmE*: *a tin of baked beans* → see picture at CONTAINER

tin·gle /ˈtɪŋgəl/ *verb* if a part of your body tingles, the skin feels slightly uncomfortable: *Her lips tingled from the cold air.*

tin·ker /ˈtɪŋkə $ ˈtɪŋkɚ/ *verb* (informal) if you tinker with a machine, you make small changes to it: *He spends Sundays tinkering with his bike.*

tin·kle /ˈtɪŋkəl/ *verb* to make a sound like small bells: *A piano tinkled in the distance.*

tinned /tɪnd/ *adjective BrE* tinned food is sold in tins SYNONYM **canned** *AmE*: *tinned tomatoes*

ˈtin ˌopener *noun BrE* a tool that you use for opening tins of food SYNONYM **can opener** *AmE*

tin·sel /ˈtɪnsəl/ *noun* (no plural) Christmas decorations made of thin pieces of silver paper: *They hung tinsel on the Christmas tree.*

tint /tɪnt/ *noun* a small amount of a colour: *His eyes had a yellow tint.*

tint·ed /ˈtɪntɪd/ *adjective* tinted glass is slightly coloured

tiny

huge

tiny

ti·ny /ˈtaɪni/ *adjective* (**tinier**, **tiniest**) very small: *They live in a tiny house.* → see Thesaurus at SMALL

tip[1] /tɪp/ *noun*

> KEY PATTERNS
> **the tip of something**
> **a tip on how to do something**

1 the end of something long, narrow, and pointed: *He touched the flower with **the tip of** his finger.* • *the southern **tip of** the island*
2 a useful piece of advice: *Can you give me any **tips on how to** lose weight?* • *fashion tips*
3 an additional amount of money that you give to someone who has done a job for you as a way of thanking them: *Do you usually **leave a tip** in a restaurant?*
4 *BrE* (informal) a very dirty or untidy place SYNONYM **dump** *AmE*: *His flat is a complete tip!*

tip² *verb* (**tipped**, **tipping**)

KEY PATTERNS
tip your head/a chair back
tip a bottle/cup up
tip something onto the table/floor
tip something out of a bag/box

1 to move, or to move something, so that one side, end etc is higher: *"Could you just* ***tip*** *your head* ***back****?" the dentist said.* • ***Tip*** *the bottle* ***up*** *slightly.* • *The boat kept tipping to one side.*
2 to make something flow or fall out of a container, by moving the container: *I* ***tipped*** *all the shopping* ***onto*** *the table.* • *He* ***tipped*** *all his money* ***out of*** *his pocket.*
3 to give an additional amount of money to someone who has done a job for you as a way of thanking them

PHRASAL VERBS
tip over
tip over, tip something over if something tips over, or if you tip it over, it falls over: *I* ***tipped*** *the paint pot* ***over*** *by accident.*

tip·toe /ˈtɪptəʊ $ ˈtɪptoʊ/ *noun* **on tiptoe** if you stand or walk on tiptoe, you stand or walk just on your toes: *We couldn't see the stage, even when we stood on tiptoe.* → see picture on page A2

tire¹ the American spelling of TYRE

tire² /taɪə $ taɪɚ/ also **tire out** *verb* if something tires you, it makes you feel very tired: *All that dancing has tired me out.* —**tiring** *adjective*: *Teaching is a very tiring job.*

tired /taɪəd $ taɪɚd/ *adjective*

KEY PATTERNS
feel/get tired
tired of doing something
tired of something

1 someone who is tired feels that they want to sleep or rest: *By the end of the day, I* ***felt*** *so* ***tired*** *that I had to lie down.* • *Young children* ***get tired*** *very quickly.*
2 if you are tired of something, you have become bored with it, and you do not want to do or have that thing any more: *They soon* ***got tired of*** *playing that game.* • *He says he's* ***tired of*** *school and wants to get a job!* • *I'm* ***tired of*** *football now.*

PHRASES
tired out very tired: *I can't dance any more, I'm tired out.*

THESAURUS
exhausted/worn out: *They were* ***exhausted*** *after loading boxes all day* (=very tired because of what they had been doing).
sleepy: *I was* ***sleepy*** *so I went to bed early* (=I felt that I wanted to sleep).

WORD CHOICE
tired or **tiring**?
• **Tired** means "wanting to have a rest": *I always feel* ***tired*** *in the evenings after work.*
• **Tiring** means "making you feel that you want to have a rest": *It was a long and* ***tiring*** *journey.*

tire·some /ˈtaɪəsəm $ ˈtaɪɚsəm/ *adjective* (formal) annoying or boring: *I'm sick of hearing your tiresome excuses.*

tis·sue /ˈtɪʃuː/ *noun* a piece of soft thin paper that you use to blow your nose: *a box of tissues*

ti·tle /ˈtaɪtl/ *noun* **1** the name of a book, painting, play etc: *The title of his last book was 'Easy Computing'.* **2** a word such as Mr, Mrs, or Sir, that you use before someone's name

ˈtitle-ˌholder *noun* someone who has won an important sports competition that happens each year

T-junc·tion /ˈtiː ˌdʒʌŋkʃən/ *noun BrE* a place where two roads meet and form the shape of the letter T

to¹ /tə; before vowels, and strong tuː/
1 used before the basic form of a verb to make the INFINITIVE: *He decided to stay at home.* • *She asked the teacher to help her.* • *Sarah seems to be very happy.*
2 used to show the purpose of an action SYNONYM **in order to**: *I phoned her to say sorry.*

to² *preposition*
1 used to say where someone or something goes: *He ran to the door.* • *We're going on holiday to Iceland.* • *I went to a party last night.*
2 used to say who receives or is given something: *I gave my old jacket to my sister.* • *He sent presents to the children.*

time /taɪm/ *noun*

1 the hour or minute of the day: *"**What time is it?**" "It's half past four."* • *"**What time** does the meeting start?" "Nine o'clock."* • *I need to know **the time of** the next train to London.* • *"Excuse me, **have you got the time?**" "Yes, it's ten past four."*

2 a period of time: *I haven't seen him for **a long time**.* • *It all happened **a long time ago**.* • *"**How much time does it take** to get to New York?" "It takes about eight hours."* • *We had been waiting **for some time*** (=for quite a long time). • *I **don't have much time** right now* (=I'm busy).

3 an occasion when you do something or when something happens: *Your mother called you five **times** today.* • *I'll tell you about it the **next time** that I see you.* • *Do you remember **the time when** Dad lost his car keys?* • ***Every time** I see her, her hair is a different colour.* • *Okay, play the song louder **this time**.*

GRAMMAR
• You say **I have been there many times** or **I've been there lots of times**.
✗ Don't say 'I've been there many time.'

4 the thing that we measure in minutes, hours, years etc: *Do you think that one day people will be able to travel through **time**?* • *As you get older, **time** seems to **go by** more quickly.*

5 a period in history: *It was a **time of** great political change.*

WORD CHOICE
• Asking the time:
You can ask **What time is it?** or **Can you tell me the time?** In British English, people also say **Have you got the time?** In American English, people also say **Do you have the time?**
• Saying what time it is:
*It's **half past** seven./It's **four thirty**.*
*It's **quarter to** eight./It's **seven-forty five*** (also *It's **quarter of** eight. AmE*).
*It's **quarter past** seven./It's **seven fifteen*** (also *It's **quarter after** seven. AmE*).

*It's **half past** seven.*

*It's **seven forty-five**.*

*It's **quarter past** seven.*

• Times are often written as **4.30**, **9.45**, **11.15** etc

PHRASES

all the time
always or very often: *I used to play tennis* ***all the time.*** • *He just wears his glasses for reading – he doesn't have to wear them* ***all the time.***

at the time, at that time
if something happened at the time or at that time, it happened during a particular time in the past: ***At that time,*** *Paul was only five years old.* • *I was living in Detroit* ***at the time.***

by the time (=when)
use this to show that one thing happened later than another thing: ***By the time I*** *got home everyone else had finished dinner.*

from time to time
sometimes: *We still see each other* ***from time to time.***

have a good time, have a great time
to enjoy yourself: *We* ***had a*** *really* ***good time*** *on our holiday.*

have (the) time
to have enough time to do something: *You don't* ***have time*** *to change your clothes now!* • *I don't* ***have enough time*** *to do all the things I need to do.*

in 2 hours' time/in a month's time etc
after 2 hours, a month etc: *See you* ***in a month's time.***

in (good) time
at an early enough time, so that you are able to catch a train, watch a film etc: *Make sure you get back* ***in time for*** *dinner.* • *John wants to get home* ***in time to*** *watch the football.*

it's time
used when saying that something should happen now: ***It's time for*** *dinner.* • *I'll come get you when* ***it's time*** *to go.*

most of the time, some of the time
usually or sometimes: *Ken gets home by six o'clock* ***most of the time.*** • *Katie feeds the cats* ***some of the time,*** *and I do it other times.*

on time
if something happens on time, it happens at the correct time: *Most of the students finished their homework* ***on time.*** • *Is the train* ***on time?***

WORD CHOICE

on time or **in time**?

• Don't confuse **on time** (=at the right time) and **in time** (=early enough so that you are able to do something): *The train was* ***on time.*** • *We arrived* ***in time*** *to see the film.*

spend time
to use time to do something: *He wants to* ***spend*** *more* ***time*** *with his kids.* • *Jackie* ***spent*** *a lot of* ***time*** *on this report for school.*

take time
if something takes time, you need a long time to do it: *Learning a language well* ***takes time.***

take your time
to do something carefully, without hurrying: ***Take your time*** *during the exam, and check your answers.*

waste time, a waste of time
if you waste time, or if something is a waste of time, you do not do anything in the time you have, or you do something that is not successful or useful: *Studying Latin seems like a* ***waste of time.*** • *Why are you* ***wasting*** *your* ***time*** *just watching TV?*

3 used to say who is told something: *Mark is talking to Steve.* • *She whispered something to the girl beside her.*
4 used to say when something ends: *The museum is open from 10.30 to 5* (=it opens at 10.30 and closes at 5).
5 earlier than a particular hour: *It's ten to five* (=it's ten minutes before five). • *We left at a quarter to twelve.*
6 used to say who has an idea or opinion: *It looks OK to me* (=I think it's OK). • *The idea seemed ridiculous to Stan.*

PHRASES

be nice to someone, be cruel to someone etc to treat someone nicely, cruelly: *She's always **been nice to** me.*
have something to yourself, have someone to yourself to be alone in a place or with someone, and not sharing that place or person: *At last she **had** the house **to** herself.*

toad /təʊd $ toʊd/ *noun* a brown animal like a large FROG

to and fro /ˌtuː ənd ˈfrəʊ $ ˌtuː ənd ˈfroʊ/ *adverb* if someone or something moves to and fro, they move in one direction and then another

toast /təʊst $ toʊst/ *noun* (no plural) bread that has been heated until it is brown

> **GRAMMAR**
> You say **some toast** or **a piece of toast**.
> ✘ Don't say 'toasts'.

toast·er /ˈtəʊstə $ ˈtoʊstɚ/ *noun* a machine that you use to make toast: *I put some bread in the toaster.*

to·bac·co /təˈbækəʊ $ təˈbækoʊ/ *noun* (no plural) dried brown leaves that people smoke in cigarettes and pipes

> **SPELLING**
> This word is often spelled wrongly. The correct spelling is: **tobacco**.

to·bog·gan /təˈbɒgən $ təˈbɑgən/ *noun* a curved wooden board, used for going down hills that are covered in snow

to·bog·gan·ing /təˈbɒgənɪŋ $ təˈbɑgənɪŋ/ *noun* (no plural) the activity or sport of going down hills that are covered in snow while on a toboggan: *We went tobogganing in the park.*

to·day /təˈdeɪ/ *adverb, noun* (no plural)
1 this day: *It's Linda's birthday today.* • *What's today's date?*
2 the present period of time: *Today's teenagers have a lot more freedom than teenagers in the past.* • *A lot of the crime that happens today is in poor areas of the city.*

tod·dler /ˈtɒdlə $ ˈtɑdlɚ/ *noun* a young child who has just learned to walk

toe /təʊ $ toʊ/ *noun* one of the five parts at the end of your foot: *These shoes hurt my toes.* → see picture on page A5

toe·nail /ˈtəʊneɪl $ ˈtoʊneɪl/ *noun* the hard flat part at the end of your toe

tof·fee /ˈtɒfi $ ˈtɔfi/ *noun* a sticky brown sweet: *Would you like a piece of toffee?*

to·geth·er /təˈgeðə $ təˈgeðɚ/ *adverb*
1 when people do something with each other ANTONYM **alone**: *They wrote all the songs together.* • *We must all work together to solve this problem.*
2 when you join or mix things: *I stuck the pieces of wood together with glue.* • *Mix the eggs and the cream together.*
3 when people or things are next to each other: *The girls were all standing together in a group.* • *I put all the books together at one end of the table.*

toi·let /ˈtɔɪlɪt/ *noun* **1** a large bowl that you sit on when you get rid of waste substances from your body
2 *BrE* a small room with a toilet: *The toilet is upstairs, on the right.* **3 go to the toilet** *BrE* to use the toilet: *Mum, I want to go to the toilet!*

ˈtoilet ˌpaper *noun* (no plural) soft thin paper that you use to clean yourself after you have used the toilet

toi·let·ries /ˈtɔɪlətriz/ *plural noun* things such as soap that you use when you wash yourself

ˈtoilet roll *noun* toilet paper that is wound around a small tube: *We need some more toilet rolls.*

to·ken /ˈtəʊkən $ ˈtoʊkən/ *noun* a special piece of paper that you can use to buy certain things, instead of using money: *I gave her a record token for her birthday.*

told the past tense and past participle of TELL

tol•e•rant /ˈtɒlərənt $ ˈtɑlərənt/ *adjective* letting other people do or say what they want, even if you do not approve of it ANTONYM **intolerant**: *We should be tolerant of other people's beliefs.*

tol•e•rate /ˈtɒləreɪt $ ˈtɑləˌreɪt/ *verb* to accept behaviour or a situation that you do not like, and not do anything about it: *I will not tolerate this sort of behaviour.*

toll /təʊl $ toʊl/ *noun* **1** the number of people that have been killed by something: *The death toll from the crash has risen to 20.* **2** money that you pay so that you can use a road, bridge etc

to•ma•to /təˈmɑːtəʊ $ təˈmeɪtoʊ/ *noun* (plural **tomatoes**) a soft round red fruit eaten in salads or cooked like a vegetable: *tomato salad* → see picture on page A6

SPELLING
The plural of this word is often spelled wrongly. The correct spelling is: **tomatoes**.

PRONUNCIATION
British people pronounce the second syllable of **tomato** like 'art'. American people pronounce the second syllable of **tomato** like 'eight'.

tomb /tuːm/ *noun* a large GRAVE: *the tomb of an Egyptian king*

tom•boy /ˈtɒmbɔɪ $ ˈtɑmbɔɪ/ *noun* a young girl who likes to play or dress like a boy

tomb•stone /ˈtuːmstəʊn $ ˈtumstoʊn/ *noun* a stone on a GRAVE, showing the name of the dead person SYNONYM **gravestone**

to•mor•row /təˈmɒrəʊ $ təˈmɑroʊ/ *adverb, noun* (no plural)
the day after this day: *Shall we go shopping tomorrow?* • *Do you have any plans for tomorrow?*

ton /tʌn/ *noun* a unit for measuring weight, equal to 2,240 pounds or 1,016 kilograms in Britain, and 2,000 pounds in the US

tone /təʊn $ toʊn/ *noun*
1 the way that something sounds, especially a person's voice: *"Hi, Jane," Rod called out **in a** friendly **tone**.* • *Her **tone of voice** was definitely a bit angry.*
2 (no plural) the general feeling or quality that something has: *It's important to keep **the tone of** the meeting relaxed.*
3 one of the sounds that you hear on the telephone: *Please leave your name and number after the long tone.* • *Can you hear a **dialling tone*** (=the sound you hear when you pick a phone up and it is ready to use)?

tongs /tɒŋz $ tɑŋz/ *plural noun* a tool for picking things up, which has two thin pieces of metal joined together at the top: *She picked up the coal with a pair of tongs.*

tongs

tongue /tʌŋ/ *noun*
the soft part inside your mouth that moves when you eat and speak

PHRASES
stick your tongue out at someone to point your tongue at someone in order to be rude
mother tongue, native tongue the language that you learn as a baby: *Many Canadians have French as their **mother tongue**.*

PRONUNCIATION
You pronounce **tongue** like 'sung'.

ˈ**tongue-tied** *adjective* unable to speak because you are nervous: *I always feel tongue-tied when I have to answer in class.*

to•night /təˈnaɪt/ *adverb, noun* (no plural)
this evening or night: *What are you doing tonight?* • *Tonight's weather will be clear and cold.*

tonne /tʌn/ *noun* a unit for measuring weight, equal to 1,000 kilograms

too /tuː/ *adverb*
1 use **too** when you want to add a new fact or to show that something is true about two people or things: *Jan plays the guitar, and she plays the piano too.* • *I would like some water **too**.* •

A B C D E F G H I J K L M N O P Q R S T U V W X Y Z

*The sports centre has a large swimming pool, and it has a small pool for children, **too**.* • *"I'm really hungry." "Me **too**."*
2 use **too** to show that something is more than you need or more than you want: *It's **too** hot in here.* • *I'm **too** tired to go out tonight.* • *He was driving **much too** fast.* • *This house is **too** small for six people.*

PHRASES

too much use this before things you cannot count, such as amounts or costs: *I drank **too much** coffee.* • *She put **too much** salt in the soup.* • *He spent **too much** on that car.*
too many use this before things that you can count, such as numbers of people or things: *I drank **too many** cups of coffee.* • *There were **too many** people in the room.* • *Don't eat **too many** biscuits – it's nearly dinnertime.*

SPELLING
Don't confuse the spelling of **too** and to (=in the direction of something).

took the past tense of TAKE

tools

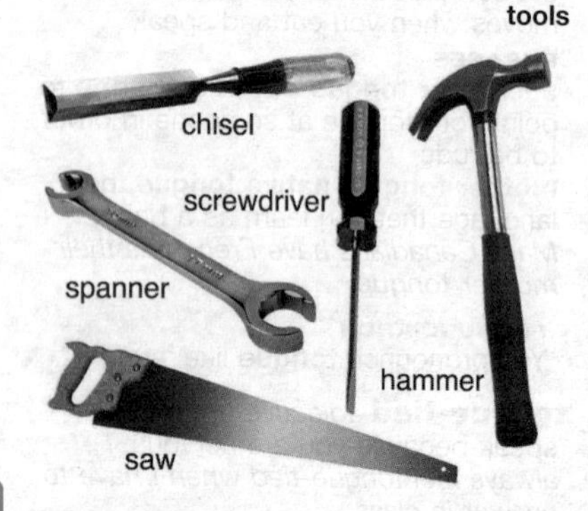

tool /tuːl/ *noun*
any object that you hold in your hand and use for doing a particular job: *I didn't have the right tools to fix the car.* • *gardening tools*

tool·bar /ˈtuːlbɑː $ ˈtulbɑr/ *noun* a row of symbols or words at the top of a computer screen that you can use to make things happen on the screen: *Click on the "Options" button on your toolbar.*

tooth /tuːθ/ *noun* (plural **teeth** /tiːθ/) one of the hard white things in your mouth that you use for biting food: *Don't forget to **brush your teeth**.* → see picture on page A5

tooth·ache /ˈtuːθ-eɪk/ *noun* a pain in a tooth: *I've got terrible toothache.*

tooth·brush /ˈtuːθbrʌʃ/ *noun* (plural **toothbrushes**) a small brush for cleaning your teeth → see picture at BRUSH[1]

tooth·paste /ˈtuːθpeɪst/ *noun* (no plural) a substance that you use for cleaning your teeth: *Use a small amount of toothpaste.*

top

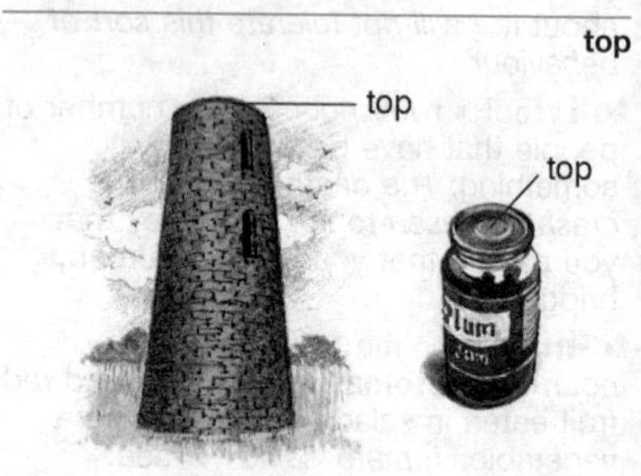

top[1] /tɒp $ tɑp/ *noun*

KEY PATTERNS
the top of something

1 the highest part of something ANTONYM **bottom**: *I'm going to try and climb to **the top of** that tree!* • *My name was at **the top of** the list.*
2 the lid or cover for a container, pen etc: *Can you get the top off this jar?* → see Thesaurus at COVER[2]
3 the top the best or most important position in a company etc: *He worked hard and got to **the top of** his profession.*
4 a piece of clothing that you wear on the top part of your body: *I've bought a blue top to wear with this skirt.*

PHRASES

on top on something, or on the highest part of something: *ice cream with chocolate sauce **on top*** • *They built the castle **on top of** a hill.*
on top of something as well as something else: ***On top of** all our other problems, my mother has been very ill.*
from top to bottom including every part of a place: *The police came in and searched the house **from top to bottom**.*

over the top (informal) too extreme: *I thought George's reaction was a bit over the top.*
get on top of someone (informal) if something gets on top of you, it makes you feel unhappy because it is too difficult for you to deal with: *My work's been getting on top of me recently.*

top[2] *adjective*
1 best or most successful: *Rick won the top prize of £500.* • *He's one of the top tennis players.*
2 highest ANTONYM **bottom**: *My family lived on the top floor of the building.*

top[3] *verb* (**topped**, **topping**) **1** to be more than a particular amount: *Audience figures topped 14 million last year.* **2** to be the best in a list of similar things: *The song topped the charts for five weeks* (=it was the most popular song). **3** if food is topped with something, it has that thing on top: *pizza topped with cheese*

top·ic /ˈtɒpɪk $ ˈtɑpɪk/ *noun* a subject that people talk or write about: *The main topic of conversation was the party.*

top·ic·al /ˈtɒpɪkəl $ ˈtɑpɪkəl/ *adjective* related to events that are happening now: *Racism is a very topical issue.*

top·less /ˈtɒpləs $ ˈtɑpləs/ *adjective* a woman who is topless is not wearing any clothes on the top part of her body

top·ping /ˈtɒpɪŋ $ ˈtɑpɪŋ/ *noun* food that you put on top of other food: *cake with a chocolate topping*

top·ple /ˈtɒpəl $ ˈtɑpəl/ *verb* to fall over: *The lamp toppled over and broke.*

ˌtop-ˈsecret *adjective* top-secret documents or information must be kept completely secret

torch /tɔːtʃ $ tɔrtʃ/ *noun* (plural **torches**) *BrE* a small electric lamp that you carry in your hand SYNONYM **flashlight** *AmE* ➔ see picture at LIGHT[1]

tore the past tense of TEAR

tor·ment /tɔːˈment $ tɔrˈment/ *verb* to deliberately hurt, upset, or annoy someone: *Stop tormenting your sister!*

torn the past participle of TEAR

tor·na·do /tɔːˈneɪdəʊ $ tɔrˈneɪdoʊ/ *noun* (plural **tornadoes**) a violent storm with strong winds that go round and round: *A tornado destroyed the building.* ➔ see Thesaurus at WIND[1]

tor·pe·do /tɔːˈpiːdəʊ $ tɔrˈpidoʊ/ *noun* (plural **torpedoes**) a weapon that is fired from a ship or SUBMARINE and travels under the sea: *The ship was sunk by a torpedo.*

tor·rent /ˈtɒrənt $ ˈtɔrənt/ *noun* a large amount of water moving very fast: *a torrent of cold water*

tor·so /ˈtɔːsəʊ $ ˈtɔrsoʊ/ *noun* (formal) the main part of your body, not including your arms, legs, or head: *He had injuries to his head and torso.*

tor·ture /ˈtɔːtʃə $ ˈtɔrtʃɚ/ *verb* to deliberately hurt someone a lot for a long time, especially in order to make them tell you something: *They tortured many of their prisoners.* —**torture** *noun* (no plural): *victims of torture*

toss /tɒs $ tɔs/ *verb* to throw something somewhere in a careless way: *He tossed the keys to me.* ➔ see Thesaurus at THROW[1]

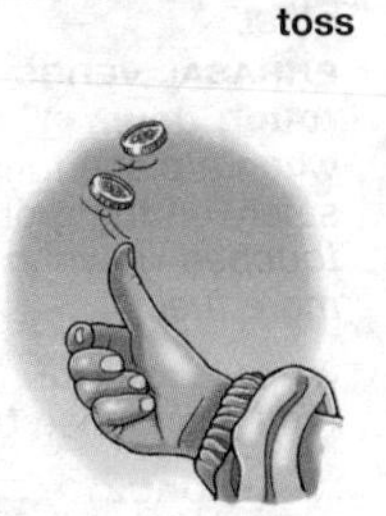
toss

to·tal[1] /ˈtəʊtl $ ˈtoʊtl/ *adjective*
1 (spoken) used to describe something as complete, in a strong way: *My date with John was a total disaster.* • *I have total confidence in the teachers.*
2 including everything: *What was the total cost of the holiday?*

total[2] *noun*
the number that you get when you have added everything together: *Our teacher gave us ten numbers and told us to find the total.* • *The team played a total of 36 matches.*
PHRASES
in total including everything: ***In total,*** *I spent at least £100.*

total[3] *verb* (**totalled**, **totalling** *BrE*, **totaled**, **totaling** *AmE*) to be a particular amount, when you have added everything together: *The bill for the meal totalled $45.*

tot·al·ly /ˈtəʊtl i $ ˈtoʊtl-i/ *adverb* completely: *The town was totally* *destroyed by the bombing.* • *a totally new approach to education*

tot·ter /ˈtɒtə $ ˈtɑtɚ/ *verb* to walk in an unsteady way: *Max tottered forward and fell over.*

touch¹ /tʌtʃ/ *verb*

KEY PATTERNS
touch something with your finger
two things are touching each other

1 to put your hand or finger on something: *Chantal **touched** his arm gently **with** her hand.* • *Don't touch that plate – it's very hot.*
2 if two things touch, or if they are touching each other, there is no space between them: *Their lips touched.* • *Lie on your back with your arms touching the floor.* • *The trees were close together, their leaves touching each other.*

PHRASAL VERBS

touch down
when a plane touches down, it lands safely on the ground: *The plane **touched down** in Dubai to take on more fuel.*

PRONUNCIATION
You pronounce **touch** like 'much'.

THESAURUS
feel: *His mother **felt** his forehead to see if it was hot* (=touched it in order to find out about it).
rub: *He **rubbed** his chin thoughtfully* (=moved his hand backwards and forwards across it).
pat: *He bent down to **pat** the dog* (=touch it lightly with his hand flat).
stroke: *She sat **stroking** the cat* (=moving her hand gently over it).

touch² *noun* (plural **touches**)
1 your ability to know what something is like when you feel it with your fingers: *The children were learning about the senses of taste and touch.*
2 when something or someone touches you: *At **the touch of** her hand he turned round.* • ***At** his **touch**, the horse began to move faster.*

PHRASES

get in touch, be in touch to write to someone or telephone them: *George decided to **get in touch with** an old friend of his.*
keep in touch, stay in touch to continue to speak or write to someone who does not live near you: *Jane and I have **kept in touch** since we left school.*
lose touch to stop speaking or writing to someone who does not live near you: *Sally moved to South Africa and I **lost touch with** her.*
out of touch if you are out of touch with something, it has changed and you no longer know about it or understand it: *I was **out of touch with** British pop music after living abroad for so long.*

touch·down /ˈtʌtʃdaʊn/ *noun*
1 when a plane lands safely on the ground **2** when a team playing RUGBY or American football gets points by taking the ball over the other team's line

touch·ing /ˈtʌtʃɪŋ/ *adjective* making you feel sad or sorry for someone: *The movie has some touching moments.*

touch·y /ˈtʌtʃi/ *adjective* (**touchier**, **touchiest**) easily annoyed or upset: *Are you always touchy about your work?*

tough /tʌf/ *adjective*
1 difficult and causing you a lot of problems ANTONYM **easy**: *Leaving home was a tough decision.* • *The match will be tough, but I'm sure we can win.* • *Life can be very tough sometimes.*
2 someone who is tough is strong, brave, or determined: *In business you have to be tough.* • *I like movies with **tough guys** and plenty of action.*
3 hard, and not easy to cut or bite ANTONYM **tender**: *This meat is tough.*
4 tough laws or rules are very strict: *We need tough new laws in order to fight crime.*

PRONUNCIATION
You pronounce **tough** like 'stuff'.

tough·en /ˈtʌfən/ also **toughen up** *verb* to make someone or something stronger: *The government wants to toughen up the law on drugs.*

tour¹ /tʊə $ tʊr/ *noun*

KEY PATTERNS
go on a tour (of a place)

1 a journey to several different places in a country, area etc: *In the summer we **went on a tour of** North America.*

2 a trip around the different parts of a building or city: *Would you like **a guided tour of** the castle?* • *Steve **took** us **on a tour of** Cambridge.*

PHRASES

be on tour to be travelling to different places in order to give concerts, perform plays etc: *The band **is on tour** in Europe at the moment.*

tour² *verb* to travel around an area, visiting different places: *The band will tour the States next year.*

tour·is·m /ˈtʊərɪzəm $ ˈtʊrɪzəm/ *noun* (no plural) the business of providing tourists with places to stay and things to do: *The island's main industry is tourism.*

tour·ist /ˈtʊərəst $ ˈtʊrɪst/ *noun* someone who visits a place for pleasure: *a group of Japanese tourists*

tour·na·ment /ˈtʊənəmənt $ ˈtʊrnəmənt/ *noun* a competition in which many players compete against each other until there is one winner: *a tennis tournament*

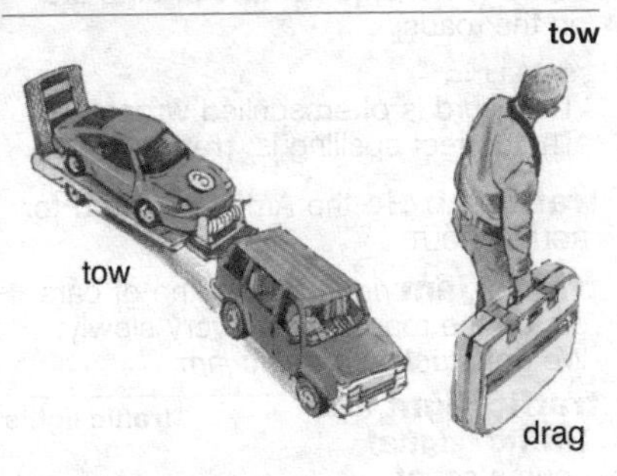

tow /təʊ $ toʊ/ *verb* if one vehicle tows another one, it pulls the other vehicle along behind it → see Thesaurus at PULL¹

to·wards /təˈwɔːdz $ tɔrdz/ also **to·ward** /təˈwɔːd $ tɔrd/ *preposition*
1 in the direction of someone or something: *Helen came running towards them.* • *Plants grow towards the light.*
2 just before a particular time: *The weather should get better towards the end of the week.*
3 used to show who someone's behaviour or attitude relates to: *He's always been quite friendly towards me.* • *her hostility towards her stepmother*

tow·el /ˈtaʊəl/ *noun* a large piece of thick soft cloth that you use to dry your body: *I went swimming and forgot my towel.*

tow·er /ˈtaʊə $ ˈtaʊɚ/ *noun* a tall narrow building or part of a building: *the bells at the top of the church tower*

town /taʊn/ *noun*

KEY PATTERNS
live in a town
go into town

a place with many buildings and streets, where people live and work: *We lived **in a** small **town** on the coast.* • *Oporto is a pretty town in Portugal.* • *I think I'll **go into town*** (=the main part of the town where the shops are) *this afternoon.*

tox·ic /ˈtɒksɪk $ ˈtɑksɪk/ *adjective* poisonous: *toxic chemicals*

toy /tɔɪ/ *noun* a thing for children to play with: *Polly was playing with her toys upstairs.*

trace¹ /treɪs/ *verb* **1** to find someone or something that is lost and may be far away: *Police are trying to trace her family.* **2** to copy a picture by drawing on a thin piece of paper that you put over it

trace² *noun* a sign that someone or something has been in a place: *There was no trace of the missing child.*

track¹ /træk/ *noun*
1 a small path or road, without a smooth surface: *The farm was at the end of a rough track.*
2 one of the songs or pieces of music on a CD etc: *This is my favourite track.*
3 the two metal lines that a train travels on SYNONYM **railway line** *BrE*: *The sign said 'Keep away from the track'.*
4 tracks marks on the ground that were made by an animal, person, or vehicle going over that ground: *It was easy to follow the lion's tracks.*

PHRASES

keep track of something to have all the most recent information about something: *I try to **keep track of** the situation by reading the newspapers.*

lose track of something to not have all the most recent information about something any more: *I've **lost track of** how many children he has.*

track² *verb* **track someone down** to find someone after searching for them in different places: *The police are determined to track down the robbers.*
→ see Thesaurus at FIND

track·suit /'træksuːt/ *noun BrE* loose trousers and a loose top, which you wear for sport

trac·tor /'træktə $ 'træktɚ/ *noun* a strong vehicle with large wheels that is used on farms

trade¹ /treɪd/ *noun*

KEY PATTERNS
trade with another country
trade between two countries
trade in cotton/sugar/oil

1 (no plural) the business of buying and selling things, especially between countries SYNONYM **commerce**: *Last year we increased our* ***trade with*** *Saudi Arabia. • There has been an increase in* ***trade between*** *the two countries. •* ***Trade in*** *agricultural goods has fallen.*
→ see Thesaurus at BUSINESS
2 the car trade, the tourist trade etc is the business of producing and selling a particular type of thing, or providing particular services: *It's been a very bad year for* ***the book trade.***

trade² *verb*

KEY PATTERNS
trade with another country
trade in oil/electronic goods

when people, companies, or countries trade, they do business by buying and selling things: *Britain continued to* ***trade with*** *Cuba. • The company* ***trades in*** *high quality children's clothing.*

PHRASAL VERBS
trade in
trade something in to give something that you own as part of the payment when you buy something similar: *You can* ***trade*** *your old computer games* ***in*** *for new ones.*

trade·mark /'treɪdmɑːk $ 'treɪdmɑrk/ *noun* a special word or picture on a product that shows it is made by a particular company: *'Coca-Cola' is a trademark.*

tra·di·tion /trə'dɪʃən/ *noun*

KEY PATTERNS
it's a tradition to do something
a/the tradition of doing something

something that people have done for a long time, and continue to do SYNONYM **custom**: *It's a* ***tradition to*** *celebrate the new year. • She wanted her daughter to carry on the family* ***tradition of*** *studying at Oxford.* → see Thesaurus at HABIT

tra·di·tion·al /trə'dɪʃənəl/ *adjective* traditional beliefs or activities are shared by a group of people and have existed for a long time: *traditional folk music • In America, it's traditional to hang candy on the Christmas tree.*
—**traditionally** *adverb*

traf·fic /'træfɪk/ *noun* (no plural) cars etc that are moving on the road: *There isn't as much traffic on the roads on Sunday. • The traffic's really bad* (=busy and slow) *in the morning. • I got to work late because of the* ***heavy traffic*** (=the large number of cars etc on the roads).

SPELLING
This word is often spelled wrongly. The correct spelling is: **traffic**.

'traffic ˌcircle the American word for ROUNDABOUT

'traffic ˌjam *noun* a long line of cars etc on the road. moving very slowly: *We got stuck in a traffic jam.*

'traffic ˌlight also **'traffic ˌsignal** *noun* a set of coloured lights at the side of the road, which show when cars etc are allowed to move: *Turn left at the traffic lights.*
→ see picture at ZEBRA CROSSING

traffic lights

'traffic ˌwarden *noun BrE* someone whose job is to check that cars are parked only where parking is allowed

tra·ge·dy /'trædʒədi/ *noun* (plural **tragedies**)
1 a very sad event: *The fishing trip* ***ended in tragedy*** *when one of the men drowned. • This is a* ***terrible tragedy.***

A B C D E F G H I J K L M N O P Q R S **T** U V W X Y Z

2 a play or book that ends very sadly: *We are studying Shakespeare's tragedies.*

tra•gic /'trædʒɪk/ *adjective* very sad: *a tragic accident* —**tragically** /-kli/ *adverb*: *Tragically, she died young.*

trail¹ /treɪl/ *noun* **1** something that shows the direction in which someone or something is moving: *a trail of muddy footprints* **2** a rough path: *a woodland trail*

trail² *verb* **1** to follow someone: *He hired a detective to trail his wife.* **2** if a player or team in a competition is trailing, they are losing: *By half-time, Germany was trailing by three goals.*

trail•er /'treɪlə $ 'treɪlɚ/ *noun* **1** a vehicle without an engine that can be pulled behind another vehicle **2** a short part of a film or television programme, which is shown to advertise it: *We saw a trailer for the new James Bond film.*

train¹ /treɪn/ *noun*
a line of vehicles that are connected together, which travels along a railway and carries people or things. You take, catch, or get a train when you want to travel in it: *I **caught** the nine o'clock **train to** Boston.* • *Shall we drive or **go by train**?* • *He was late and nearly **missed his train**.* • *You have to **change trains at** Cambridge* (=get on a different train there). ➔ see picture on page A11

USAGE
You **get on a train** or **get off a train**. You go somewhere **by train**.

train² *verb*

KEY PATTERNS
train someone to do something
train to be/become a doctor
train as a doctor
train for a race/competition

1 to teach someone the skills that they need to do something difficult: *We could **train** nurses **to** do these tests on patients.*
2 to learn how to do something that needs a particular skill: *I'd like to **train to become** a teacher.* • *Jeff **trained as** a pilot when he left school.* • *She was **trained as** a dancer.*
3 to prepare for a sports competition by exercising and practising, or to help someone to prepare: *The team have been **training for** the match every day.*

train•ee /ˌtreɪ'niː/ *noun* someone who is being trained for a job: *a trainee nurse*

train•er /'treɪnə $ 'treɪnɚ/ *noun* **1** someone whose job is to train people to do a job: *a teacher trainer* **2** *BrE* a kind of shoe that you wear for sports such as running SYNONYM **sneaker** *AmE*: *a pair of new trainers* ➔ see picture at SHOE

train•ing /'treɪnɪŋ/ *noun* (no plural) activities that help you learn how to do a job or play a sport: *a training programme for new employees* • *She was injured while in training for the Olympics.*

trait /treɪ $ treɪt/ *noun* a way of behaving or thinking that is typical of someone: *Honesty is one of his best traits.*

trai•tor /'treɪtə $ 'treɪtɚ/ *noun* someone who helps the enemies of their country or of a group that they belong to

tram /træm/ *noun* an electric vehicle which moves along the street on metal tracks SYNONYM **streetcar** *AmE*

tramp /træmp/ *noun* someone poor who has no home or job and moves from place to place

tram•ple /'træmpəl/ *verb* to step heavily on something, damaging it: *Don't trample on the flowers!*

trampoline

tram•po•line /'træmpəliːn $ ˌtræmpə'lin/ *noun* a flat piece of material that is fastened in a metal frame with springs, which you jump up and down on as exercise or as a sport

trance /trɑːns $ træns/ *noun* if you are in a trance, you seem to be asleep, but you are still able to hear and understand things: *The children watched TV as if they were in a trance.*

tran·quil /'træŋkwəl/ *adjective* calm and peaceful: *the tranquil waters of the lake*

tran·quil·liz·er also **tranquilliser** *BrE*, **tranquilizer** *AmE* /'træŋkwəlaɪzə $ 'træŋkwəˌlaɪzɚ/ *noun* a medicine that makes someone calm or sleepy: *Since his mother's death, he has been taking tranquillizers.*

trans·at·lan·tic /ˌtrænzət'læntɪk/ *adjective* on a transatlantic journey, you cross the Atlantic Ocean: *a transatlantic flight from London to New York*

trans·fer /træns'fɜː $ 'trænsfɚ/ *verb* (formal) (**transferred**, **transferring**) to move someone or something from one place to another: *They are transferring him to another hospital.* —**transfer** /'trænsfɜː $ 'trænsfɚ/ *noun*: *the transfer of money between bank accounts*

trans·form /træns'fɔːm $ træns'fɔrm/ *verb* to change something completely: *The new owners have transformed the building into a smart hotel.*

trans·fu·sion /træns'fjuːʒən/ *noun* (formal) if you are given a transfusion, doctors put blood into your body: *She needed to have a blood transfusion.*

tran·sis·tor /træn'zɪstə $ træn'zɪstɚ/ *noun* a small piece of electronic equipment that is used in radios, televisions etc

tran·si·tive /'trænsətɪv/ *adjective* a transitive verb can have a noun or a pronoun after it. In the sentence 'She makes her own clothes', 'makes' is a transitive verb.

trans·late /træns'leɪt/ *verb*

> KEY PATTERNS
> **translate something from French (into English)**
> **translate something into English (from French)**

if you translate something that someone has said or written, you change it from the language they used into another language: *It's easy to* ***translate*** *things* ***from*** *Spanish* ***into*** *English.* • *His books* ***have been translated into*** *ten different languages.*

trans·la·tion /træns'leɪʃən/ *noun* the process of translating something into a different language, or something that has been translated: *We study translation in the second half of the course.* • *a translation of a Spanish poem*

trans·la·tor /træns'leɪtə $ 'trænsˌleɪtɚ/ *noun* someone whose job is to translate things from one language into another: *She works as a translator at the UN.*

trans·mis·sion /trænz'mɪʃən $ træns'mɪʃən/ *noun* (no plural) (formal) the sending out of radio or television signals: *The announcer apologized for the break in transmission.*

trans·mit /trænz'mɪt $ træns'mɪt/ *verb* (formal) (**transmitted**, **transmitting**) to send out radio or television signals: *We will be transmitting live from the Opera House in Paris.*

trans·mit·ter /trænz'mɪtə $ træns'mɪtɚ/ *noun* equipment that sends out radio or television signals: *a radio transmitter*

trans·par·ent /træn'spærənt/ *adjective* if something is transparent, you can see through it: *The paper was so thin that it was transparent.* • *transparent plastic*

trans·plant /'trænsplɑːnt $ 'trænsplænt/ *noun* a medical operation in which doctors remove a part of someone's body and replace it with a part from another person's body: *a heart and lung transplant*

trans·port¹ /'trænspɔːt $ 'trænspɔrt/ *noun* (no plural) *BrE*

> KEY PATTERNS
> **a form/means of transport**
> **the transport of goods**

1 vehicles that people use to travel from one place to another SYNONYM **transportation** *AmE*: *Bicycles are the best* ***form of transport*** *in the city centre.* • *It's a poor country, with very little* ***public transport*** (=buses, trains etc that everyone can use). → see picture on page A10
2 moving things or people from one place to another in a vehicle SYNONYM **transportation** *AmE*: *the* ***transport of*** *grain by ship*

trans·port² /træn'spɔːt $ træns'pɔrt/ *verb* (formal) to move things or people from one place to another in a vehicle: *The coal is transported by train to all parts of the country.*

trans·por·ta·tion /ˌtrænspɔːˈteɪʃən $ ˌtrænspɚˈteɪʃən/ the American word for TRANSPORT[1]

trap¹ /træp/ *noun*
1 a piece of equipment that you use for catching animals or birds: *Farmers used to put down* ***traps for*** *rabbits.* • *a mouse trap*
2 something that you do in order to catch or trick someone: *She asked him to meet her, but it was a trap.*

trap² *verb* (**trapped**, **trapping**)

KEY PATTERNS
trap someone
be trapped in a place

1 to make it impossible for someone to escape from a place: *Water came up as far as the door, trapping us.* • *The boys* ***were trapped in*** *the bedroom after the door handle broke.*
2 to catch an animal or a person using a trap: *They trapped rabbits for food.* • *Police managed to trap the criminals.*

trash /træʃ/ an American word for RUBBISH → see Thesaurus at RUBBISH

trash·can /ˈtræʃkæn/ an American word for DUSTBIN

trau·ma /ˈtrɔːmə/ *noun* a very upsetting experience which has a strong effect on someone: *the trauma of seeing his dog run over by a car*

trau·mat·ic /trɔːˈmætɪk/ *adjective* very shocking and upsetting: *A death in the family is a traumatic event.*

trav·el¹ /ˈtrævəl/ *verb* (**travelled**, **travelling** *BrE*, **traveled**, **traveling** *AmE*)

KEY PATTERNS
travel by car/bus/train etc
travel from London to New York

if you travel, you go from one place to another, usually in a vehicle: *It's quicker if you* ***travel by*** *train.* • *We* ***travelled from*** *Birmingham* ***to*** *London in two hours.* • *My ambition is to* ***travel round the world.*** • *I've been traveling all day and I'm exhausted!*

travel² *noun* (no plural) when you travel: *Air travel is safe and cheap.*

USAGE
You say **take a trip** or **go on a trip**.
✘ Don't say 'make a travel'.

THESAURUS
trip: *He has just returned from a* ***trip*** *to New York* (=he has just been to New York and come back).
journey: *a two-hour train* ***journey*** (=a fairly long period of travelling somewhere)
voyage: *their* ***voyage*** *across the Atlantic* (=a long trip in a ship)

ˈtravel ˌagency *noun* a business that arranges holidays for people

ˈtravel ˌagent *noun* **1** also **travel agent's** a travel agency: *We went to a travel agent's on High Street.*
2 someone who works in a travel agency

trav·el·ler *BrE*, **traveler** *AmE* /ˈtrævələ $ ˈtrævəlɚ/ *noun* someone who is on a journey or who travels a lot: *She is an experienced traveller.*

ˈtraveller's ˌcheque *BrE*, **traveler's check** *AmE* *noun* a special cheque that can be exchanged in a foreign country for the money of that country: *Do you cash traveller's cheques?*

trawl·er /ˈtrɔːlə $ ˈtrɔlɚ/ *noun* a large boat that is used for fishing in the sea

tray /treɪ/ *noun* a flat piece of plastic, wood, or metal with raised edges, which you use to carry plates, food etc: *He brought in a tray of cakes.*

trea·cle /ˈtriːkəl/ *noun* (no plural) *BrE* a dark sweet sticky liquid that is made from sugar plants

tread¹ /tred/ *verb* (**trod** /trɒd $ trɑd/ **trodden** /ˈtrɒdn $ ˈtrɑdn/)

KEY PATTERNS
tread in something
tread on someone's foot/toes etc

to put your foot in or on something SYNONYM **step**: *Don't* ***tread in*** *that puddle!* • *I* ***trod on*** *the cat's tail by mistake.*

tread² *noun* the pattern of deep lines on the surface of a tyre: *This tyre has lost its tread.*

trea·son /ˈtriːzən/ *noun* (no plural) the crime of helping your country's enemies and putting your country in danger: *He had committed treason.*

trea·sure¹ /ˈtreʒə $ ˈtreʒɚ/ *noun* a quantity of valuable things such as gold or jewellery that has been hidden: *The map shows that the treasure is buried here.*

treasure² *verb* if you treasure something, you think it is very special or important: *I will always treasure the time we spent together.*

treat¹ /triːt/ *verb*

> KEY PATTERNS
> **treat someone well/badly**
> **treat something with care/respect**
> **treat someone like a child/an idiot**
> **treat someone as an adult/equal**
> **treat someone for an illness**

1 to behave towards a person or animal in a particular way: *He **treated** his wife and children really **badly**.* • *These animals need to **be treated with** care.* • *I wish you wouldn't **treat** me **like** a child* (=treat me as though I was a child). • *The teachers here **treat us as** equals.*
2 to deal with something in a way that shows what you think about it: *Police **are treating** the death **as** an accident.*
3 if a doctor treats someone, he or she gives them medical care or medicine in order to make them well again: *Mr Griffith is **being treated for** shock in hospital.* • *There are several drugs available for treating this condition.*
4 to buy something special for someone: *Come on! I'll **treat you to** burgers and chips.* • *You need to **treat yourself** occasionally.*

treat² *noun*

> KEY PATTERNS
> **as/for a treat**
> **a treat for someone**

something special that you buy or do in order to give someone pleasure: *We're taking all the kids to see a film **as a treat**.* • *I bought some sweets **as a treat for** the children.*

treat·ment /ˈtriːtmənt/ *noun*

> KEY PATTERNS
> **treatment for a disease/injury**
> **someone's treatment of a person or animal**

1 the medical care that you receive from doctors, nurses etc, or the medicine that they give you: *I was sent to hospital for immediate treatment.* • *There is no **treatment for** this type of snake bite.*
2 a way of behaving towards a person or animal: *We were shocked by his cruel **treatment of** the dog.*

treat·y /ˈtriːti/ *noun* (plural **treaties**) a formal written agreement between two or more countries: *a peace treaty*

treb·le /ˈtrebəl/ *verb* another word for TRIPLE

tree /triː/ *noun* a large plant with branches, leaves, and a TRUNK (=thick strong stem): *a cherry tree* ➔ see picture on page A10

trek /trek/ *verb* (**trekked, trekking**) to walk a very long way, especially across rough ground: *We trekked across the mountains.* —**trek** *noun*: *They went on a 22-day trek.*

trem·ble /ˈtrembəl/ *verb* to shake because you are afraid or excited: *The child trembled with fear.* ➔ see Thesaurus at SHAKE¹

tre·men·dous /trɪˈmendəs/ *adjective* **1** very great or very large: *There was a tremendous crash.* **2** very good: *You've done a tremendous job.*

trench /trentʃ/ *noun* (plural **trenches**) a long narrow hole that is dug along the ground, usually to put pipes or wires in

trend /trend/ *noun* the way that a situation is changing or developing: *the latest fashion trends*

trend·y /ˈtrendi/ *adjective* (informal) (**trendier**, **trendiest**) modern and fashionable: *a pair of trendy sunglasses* → see Thesaurus at FASHIONABLE

tres·pass /ˈtrespəs $ ˈtrespæs/ *verb* to go onto someone's land without permission: *Two men were arrested for trespassing on the railway line.* —**trespasser** *noun*

tri·al /ˈtraɪəl/ *noun*

KEY PATTERNS
on trial for murder/theft

when people in a court of law listen to information about a crime and then decide whether someone is guilty: *The trial ended, and he was sent to prison.* • *He **was on trial for** robbery with violence* (=a court of law was trying to decide whether he did the robbery).

tri·an·gle /ˈtraɪæŋgəl/ *noun* a shape with three straight sides and three angles

tri·an·gu·lar /traɪˈæŋgjələ $ traɪˈæŋgjələr/ *adjective* shaped like a triangle

trib·al /ˈtraɪbəl/ *adjective* connected with a tribe: *tribal dances*

tribe /traɪb/ *noun* a group of people with the same language and customs who live together in the same area, for example in the forests of South America or Africa: *The Masai are one of the largest tribes in Kenya.*

tri·bu·nal /traɪˈbjuːnl/ *noun* a special court of law whose purpose is to deal with a particular problem: *an employment tribunal*

trib·u·ta·ry /ˈtrɪbjətəri $ ˈtrɪbjəˌteri/ *noun* (plural **tributaries**) a river that flows into a larger river

trib·ute /ˈtrɪbjuːt/ *noun* something that people do to show how much they admire and respect someone: *The concert was arranged as a tribute to the queen on her birthday.*

trick¹ /trɪk/ *noun*
1 something that you do in order to deceive someone or as a joke: *It was a trick. He never intended to give me the money.* • *Let's **play a trick on** the girls* (=deceive them in a funny way as a joke).
2 a clever action that entertains people because they cannot see how you do it: *card tricks* • *Can you **do any magic tricks**?*

trick² *verb*

KEY PATTERNS
trick someone into doing something
trick someone out of their money

to make someone do something by deceiving them: *He **tricked** her **into** signing the letter.* • *They **tricked** the old lady **out of** all her money* (=they made her give them all her money).

trick·le /ˈtrɪkəl/ *verb* if liquid trickles somewhere, a small amount of it flows there slowly: *Water was trickling down the walls.* —**trickle** *noun*: *A trickle of sweat ran down his back.*

trick·y /ˈtrɪki/ (informal) (**trickier**, **trickiest**) *adjective* difficult: *That's a very tricky question.*

tried the past tense and past participle of TRY¹

trig·ger¹ /ˈtrɪgə $ ˈtrɪgər/ *noun* the part of a gun that you pull with your finger to fire it: *She raised the gun and pulled the trigger.*

trigger² also **trigger off** *verb* to make something start to happen: *His speech has triggered protests from some students.*

tril·o·gy /ˈtrɪlədʒi/ *noun* (plural **trilogies**) a set of three books, plays, films etc, which all have the same subject or characters

trim¹ /trɪm/ *verb* (**trimmed**, **trimming**) to cut a small amount off something to make it look neater: *Dad was outside, trimming the lawn.* —**trim** *noun*: *I'm going to the barber's for a trim* (=a haircut).

trim² *adjective* (**trimmer**, **trimmest**) thin and healthy looking SYNONYM **slim**: *You need exercise to keep trim.*

tri·mes·ter /trɪˈmestə $ ˈtraɪmestər/ *noun AmE* one of the three periods in a year at school or college: *I'm taking history this trimester.*

trin·ket /ˈtrɪŋkɪt/ *noun* a cheap pretty object or piece of jewellery

tri·o /ˈtriːəʊ $ ˈtrioʊ/ *noun* a group of three people, especially musicians

A B C D E F G H I J K L M N O P Q R S T U V W X Y Z

trip¹ /trɪp/ *noun*

KEY PATTERNS
a trip to London/the sea
go on a trip

a journey to a place and back again, especially when you only stay in the place for a short time: *Dad's promised us a **trip to** Disneyland.* • *The school **went on a day trip to** France* (=they went to France and back on the same day). ➔ see Thesaurus at TRAVEL²

trip² *verb* (**tripped**, **tripping**) also **trip up**

KEY PATTERNS
trip over/on something

1 to hit your foot against something while you are walking so that you fall or almost fall: *He **tripped up** and broke his ankle.* • *I **tripped over** the telephone wire and hit my head.* • *Be careful not to **trip on** that step.* ➔ see Thesaurus at FALL¹
2 to make someone fall by putting your foot in front of them as they are walking: *Mum! Jake **tripped** me **up**!* ➔ see picture on page A2

trip·le¹ /ˈtrɪpəl/ *adjective* consisting of three parts: *The prison has a triple barrier around it.*

triple² *verb* if something triples, it becomes three times as big as it was before SYNONYM **treble**: *The number of students getting the highest grade has tripled.*

trip·let /ˈtrɪplət/ *noun* one of three children who are born at the same time and have the same mother: *Di gave birth to triplets last year.*

tri·pod /ˈtraɪpɒd $ ˈtraɪpɑd/ *noun* a piece of equipment with three legs that you use to support something such as a camera

tripod

tri·umph /ˈtraɪəmf/ *noun* an important success or win: *The team were celebrating their triumph last night.* —**triumph** *verb*: *England triumphed yet again.*

tri·um·phant /traɪˈʌmfənt/ *adjective* very pleased because you have succeeded or won: *the triumphant team*

triv·i·al /ˈtrɪviəl/ *adjective* not important or serious: *a trivial mistake*

trod the past tense of TREAD¹

trodden the past participle of TREAD¹

trol·ley /ˈtrɒli $ ˈtrɑli/ *noun* **1** *BrE* a large metal container on wheels that you use for carrying things, for example in a SUPERMARKET SYNONYM **cart** *AmE*
2 the American word for TRAM

trom·bone /trɒmˈbəʊn $ trɑmˈboʊn/ *noun* a metal musical instrument that you play by blowing into it and moving a long tube backwards and forwards

troop /truːp/ *verb* if people troop somewhere, they walk in an organized group: *A group of tourists trooped out of the hotel.*

troops /truːps/ *plural noun* soldiers: *The US sent more troops to Iraq.*

tro·phy /ˈtrəʊfi $ ˈtroʊfi/ *noun* (plural **trophies**) an object such as a silver cup that you get as a prize when you win a race or competition: *Stella won the Rosebowl Trophy for best young female singer.*

trop·i·cal /ˈtrɒpɪkəl $ ˈtrɑpɪkəl/ *adjective* in or from the hottest and wettest parts of the world: *tropical rain forests*

trop·ics /ˈtrɒpɪks $ ˈtrɑpɪks/ *noun* **the tropics** the hottest and wettest parts of the world

trot /trɒt $ trɑt/ *verb* (**trotted**, **trotting**) if a horse trots, it runs with quick short steps

troub·le¹ /ˈtrʌbəl/ *noun*

KEY PATTERNS
have trouble doing something
trouble with something
cause trouble

1 problems or difficulties: *We **had** a lot **of trouble** parking the car.* • *There's often **trouble with** the computers at work.* • *He's had some trouble at school.* • *financial troubles*
2 a situation in which people fight or argue: *The police are ready to deal with any trouble at the football match.* • *If I complain, it will only **cause trouble**.*

3 (no plural) illness or pain in part of your body: *Mum's been **having** some **trouble with** her back.*

PHRASES

be in trouble, get into trouble if you are in trouble, you have done something wrong, so that someone in authority is likely to punish you: *I'll **be in trouble** at school if I'm late again.* • *As a teenager, Joey often **got into trouble with** the police.*

be in trouble to be in a difficult situation: *You should always try and help someone who **is in trouble**.*

trouble² *verb* to make you feel worried or upset: *We talked over some of the things that were troubling her.*

troub·led /ˈtrʌbəld/ *adjective* having a lot of problems or difficulties: *one of the most troubled areas of the world*

troub·le·mak·er /ˈtrʌbəlˌmeɪkə $ ˈtrʌbəlˌmeɪkɚ/ *noun* someone who deliberately causes trouble

troub·le·some /ˈtrʌbəlsəm/ *adjective* causing a lot of trouble: *a troublesome back injury*

trough /trɒf $ trɔːf/ *noun* a long container for animals to drink or eat from

trou·sers /ˈtraʊzəz $ ˈtraʊzɚz/ *plural noun* a piece of clothing that you wear on the lower part of your body, with a separate part for each leg SYNONYM **pants** *AmE*: *These trousers are too big.* • *I bought a new **pair of trousers** in the sale.* → see picture at CLOTHES

trout /traʊt/ *noun* (plural **trout**) a brown or silver fish that lives in rivers

trowel /ˈtraʊəl/ *noun* a small garden tool that you use for digging → see picture at GARDENING

tru·ant /ˈtruːənt/ *noun* **1** a student who stays away from school without permission **2 play truant** to stay away from school without permission: *His teachers found out that he had been playing truant.*

truce /truːs/ *noun* an agreement between two enemies to stop fighting or arguing for a short time: *The two countries have called a truce.*

truck /trʌk/ *noun* a large road vehicle that is used for carrying things SYNONYM **lorry** *BrE* → see picture on page A11

trudge /trʌdʒ/ *verb* to walk with slow heavy steps because you are tired: *An old man was trudging up the hill.* → see Thesaurus at WALK¹

true /truː/ *adjective*
1 correct and based on facts or things that really happened ANTONYM **false**: ***Is it true that** she's only 30 years old?* • *"There will be less traffic if we leave early." "That's true."* • *The film was based on a true story.*
2 real: *true love* • *a true friend*

PHRASES

come true if your dream or wish comes true, what you hope for actually happens: *She had hoped for a place at college, and now her dream had **come true**.*

tru·ly /ˈtruːli/ *adverb* (formal) used to emphasize that what you are saying is really true SYNONYM **really**: *He was a truly great man.*

trum·pet /ˈtrʌmpɪt/ *noun* a metal musical instrument that you play by blowing into it, and that plays quite high notes

trumpet

trun·cheon /ˈtrʌnʃən/ *noun* *BrE* a stick that police officers carry as a weapon

trunks

trunk /trʌŋk/ *noun* **1** the main part of a tree, which the branches grow from → see picture at TREE → see picture on page A10 **2** the American word for the BOOT of a car **3** the very long nose of an ELEPHANT **4** a strong box for carrying things in when you are travelling

trunks /trʌŋks/ *plural noun* a piece of clothing that boys and men wear when they go swimming: *a pair of swimming trunks*

trust¹ /trʌst/ *verb*

KEY PATTERNS
trust someone
trust someone to do what you want
trust someone with your money/ your car/a job

to believe that someone is good and will do what they say, or what is right ANTONYM **distrust**, **mistrust**: *Trust me. I'll look after you.* • *I'm afraid I don't trust politicians.* • *Can I* ***trust*** *you* ***to*** *lock the door when you go out?* • *Do you think I can* ***trust*** *David* ***with*** *my new car* (=believe that he will be careful with it)?

trust² *noun* (no plural)
when you believe that someone is good and will do what they say, or what is right ANTONYM **distrust**, **mistrust**: *Trust is very important in a marriage.*

trust·wor·thy /ˈtrʌstˌwɜːði $ ˈtrʌstˌwɚði/ *adjective* a trustworthy person can be trusted: *Don't tell Clare; she isn't very trustworthy.*

truth /truːθ/ *noun*
1 **the truth** the real facts about something: *Will we ever find out* ***the truth****?* • *I don't believe he's* ***telling*** *us* ***the truth****.*
2 (no plural) the quality of being correct and true: *There's* ***no truth in*** *what he said.*

truth·ful /ˈtruːθfəl/ *adjective* honest: *a truthful answer* • *He hasn't been very truthful about his past.* —**truthfully** *adverb*

try¹ /traɪ/ *verb* (**tried**, **tries**)

KEY PATTERNS
try to do something
try using a method
try a food or drink
be tried for a crime

1 if you try to do something, you make an effort to do it: *I've* ***been trying to*** *remember where I left my jacket.* • ***Try not to*** *worry.* • *The teacher told me that I had to* ***try harder*** (=make more effort) *in class.*
2 to do, use, or taste something in order to find out whether it is successful or good: *I'd tried eating less but I was still fat.* • *I tried turning the computer off and on again, but it still wouldn't work.* • *Would you like to try some of this soup?*
3 if someone is tried for a crime, people in a court of law listen to information about the crime and then decide whether the person is guilty: *The three men will* ***be tried for*** *robbery.*

PHRASAL VERBS
try on
try something on to put on a piece of clothing in order to find out whether you like it, especially before buying it: *I* ***tried on*** *three dresses but none of them fitted me.*

SPELLING
The past tense of this word is often spelled wrongly. The correct spelling is: **tried**.

THESAURUS
attempt: *Firefighters* ***attempted*** *to rescue the boy* (=tried).
do your best: *I did my best to reassure her* (=tried as hard as I could).
have a go (informal): *We all* ***had a go*** *at opening the tin* (=tried to do it).

try² *noun* (plural **tries**) **1** an attempt to do something: *I passed my driving test on my first try.* **2** when a team gets points in RUGBY by placing the ball behind the other team's GOAL line

tsar, **tzar**, **czar** /zɑː $ zɑr/ *noun* a ruler of Russia before 1917

T-shirt, **tee-shirt** /ˈtiː ʃɜːt $ ˈti ʃɚt/ *noun* an informal shirt with short sleeves and no buttons or collar

tub /tʌb/ *noun* **1** a deep round container: *The yard was full of tubs of brightly coloured flowers.* **2** a small plastic container for food: *a one-litre tub of ice cream*

tu·ba /ˈtjuːbə $ ˈtubə/ *noun* a large metal musical instrument that you play by blowing into it, and that has a wide opening that points upwards

tube /tjuːb $ tub/ *noun* **1** a long thin pipe made of plastic, glass, or metal that liquids or gases go through: *He was very ill, and had to be fed through a tube.* **2** a small narrow container that you press in order to make the substance inside come out of the end: *a tube of toothpaste* **3 the Tube** *BrE* (informal) another word for UNDERGROUND[2]

tuck /tʌk/ *verb* **tuck something in** to push the bottom of your shirt inside your trousers or the end of a sheet under a bed, so that it looks neat: *Keep still while I tuck your shirt in.*

tuck

He tucked his shirt in.

Tues•day /ˈtjuːzdi $ ˈtuzdi/ (written abbreviation **Tues**) *noun* the day of the week between MONDAY and WEDNESDAY: *Our next meeting is on Tuesday the 10th of March.*

tuft /tʌft/ *noun* a group of hairs, pieces of grass etc growing closely together

tug /tʌg/ *verb* (**tugged, tugging**) to pull something suddenly and hard: *I tugged at the door but it wouldn't open.* ➔ see Thesaurus at PULL[1] —**tug** *noun*: *John gave the rope a tug.*

tu•i•tion /tjuːˈɪʃən $ tuˈɪʃən/ *noun* (no plural) teaching, especially of small groups or only one person: *His parents have arranged for him to have extra tuition in the evenings to help him pass his exams.*

tu•lip /ˈtjuːlɪp $ ˈtulɪp/ *noun* a spring flower which is shaped like a cup and is often brightly coloured ➔ see picture on page A10

tum•ble /ˈtʌmbəl/ *verb* to suddenly fall: *He slipped and tumbled down the stairs.* —**tumble** *noun*: *She took a tumble on the ice.*

tum•bler /ˈtʌmblə $ ˈtʌmblɚ/ *noun* a drinking glass with straight sides and no handle

tum•my /ˈtʌmi/ *noun* (informal) (plural **tummies**) a word for stomach, used especially by children

tu•mour *BrE*, **tumor** *AmE* /ˈtjuːmə $ ˈtumɚ/ *noun* (formal) a group of cells in the body that grow more quickly than normal and that can cause serious illness or death: *a brain tumour*

tu•na /ˈtjuːnə $ ˈtunə/ *noun* a large fish that lives in the sea, or the meat from this fish: *tuna sandwiches*

tune[1] /tjuːn $ tun/ *noun* the series of musical notes in a song or piece of music: *He was whistling a cheerful tune.*

tune[2] *verb* **1** also **tune up** to make small changes to a musical instrument or a car engine so that it works better: *I need to tune my guitar before I start playing.* • *How much will it cost to tune up my car?* **2 tune to something** to change the controls of your radio so that you are listening to a particular radio STATION: *I tuned to the BBC for the news.* **3 tune in** to watch or listen to a particular television or radio programme: *14 million viewers tuned in for the big match.*

tun•nel /ˈtʌnl/ *noun* a long passage through a hill, under the ground, or under the sea for cars or trains to go through: *Trains go through the Channel Tunnel between Britain and France.*

tur•ban /ˈtɜːbən $ ˈtɚbən/ *noun* a type of head covering that is made from a long piece of cloth, which Sikh men and some Hindu and Muslim men wear

turf /tɜːf $ tɚf/ *noun* (no plural) short grass and the earth under it

tur•key /ˈtɜːki $ ˈtɚki/ *noun* **1** a bird that is like a chicken, but larger ➔ see picture on page A8 **2** (no plural) the meat from this bird. Many people eat turkey at Christmas in Britain and at Thanksgiving in the US

turn[1] ➔ see box on pages 726 and 727

turn[2] /tɜːn $ tɚn/ *noun*
1 the time when you can or should do something – used when different people do something at different times SYNONYM **go**: *It's your **turn to** wash the dishes.* • ***Whose turn** is it **to** do the shopping?* • *Sam, you have to **wait your turn*** (=wait until it is your turn).
2 a change in the direction you are moving in: *Go up to Lindley Avenue and **make a right turn**.*
3 a road that joins the road you are on: *Take the next turn on the right.*

PHRASES

take turns, take it in turns *BrE* if a group of people take turns doing

A B C D E F G H I J K L M N O P Q R S T U V W X Y Z

turn /tɜːn $ tɚn/ *verb*

1 to move your body so that you are looking in a different direction: *The man **turned** and looked at me.* • *He **turned around** and walked out of the room.* • *Joe **turned towards** us and started to walk back.* • *I **turned to** Steve and whispered, "Let's go!"*

2 to move something so that it is facing in a new direction: ***Turn** your chair **towards** the front of the class.* • *He **turned** his head **away** from her.*

3 to start going in a new direction: ***Turn right** on Baldwin Street, and then **turn left** onto Grissom Avenue.* • *He needs to **turn right** at the corner to go to the newsagent.*

*He needs to **turn right** at the corner to go to the newsagent.*

4 to move around in a circle, or to make something do this: *The wheels began to **turn** slowly.* • *She **turned** the key in the lock.*

5 also **turn over** to move a page of a book or magazine so that you can see the next one: *He sat in the waiting room, **turning over the pages** of a magazine.* • ***Turn to** page 31 in your books.*

6 to reach a particular age: *He **turned 60** on Thursday* (=it was his 60th birthday on Thursday).

*He **turned** 60 on Thursday.*

7 to change and become different: *In autumn, the weather **turns colder**.* • *The traffic lights **turned red**.* • *Be careful. He might **turn violent**.*

PHRASAL VERBS

turn away

1 turn away to move so that you are not facing someone: *When I tried to talk to her, she* ***turned away****.*

2 turn someone away to not allow someone to enter a place: *The soldiers at the border* ***turned away*** *some of the refugees.*

turn back

to go in the opposite direction to the one you were going in before: *He stopped and* ***turned back*** *toward the desk.*

turn down

1 turn something down to make a machine produce less sound, heat etc, using its controls ANTONYM **turn up**: *Could you* ***turn*** *the TV* ***down*** *a bit?*

2 turn someone/something down to say no when someone offers you something: *She was offered the job, but she* ***turned*** *it* ***down****.*

turn in

to give something to someone in authority, especially a teacher SYNONYM **hand in**: *We have to* ***turn in*** *our essays on Friday.*

turn into

1 turn into something to become something different: *The party* ***turned into*** *a complete disaster. • The rain* ***turned into*** *snow later that day* (=it stopped raining and started snowing).

The rain ***turned into*** *snow later that day.*

2 turn someone/something into something to change someone or something so that they become something different: *We* ***turned*** *this bedroom* ***into*** *an office. • His experiences in the war* ***turned*** *him* ***into*** *a violent man.*

turn off

1 turn off to leave the road you are on and to start going along a different road: *We need to* ***turn off*** *at the next road on the left.*

2 turn something off to make a machine, light etc stop working, using its controls ANTONYM **turn on**: *Sal* ***turned off*** *the tap when the bucket was full.*

turn on

to make a machine, light etc start working, using its controls ANTONYM **turn off**: *Paul* ***turned on*** *the TV to watch his favourite programme. • Can you* ***turn*** *the light* ***on****, please?*

turn out

1 turn out to happen in a particular way, so that there is a particular result: *You can make plans, but things don't always* ***turn out*** *the way you want. • The cake didn't* ***turn out*** *very well.*

2 turn something out to make a light stop working by pressing a button ANTONYM **turn on**: ***Turn out*** *the lights before you go to bed.*

turn over

1 if something turns over, or if you turn it over, it moves so that the top part faces down: *The car hit the bridge,* ***turned over*** *and burst into flames. • When the toast is cooked on one side,* ***turn*** *it* ***over****.*

2 turn over to press a button to change the television programme on your television: *Quick,* ***turn over****! The film's starting. • Shall I* ***turn over*** *to the news?*

turn up

1 turn something up to make a machine produce more sound, heat etc, using its controls ANTONYM **turn down**: ***Turn up*** *the heat – I'm freezing.*

2 turn up (informal) to arrive: *Her mother* ***turned up*** *about ten minutes later. • Did Joe* ***turn up*** *for classes today?*

3 turn up (informal) if something turns up after you have been looking for it, you suddenly find it: *I'd been looking for work for months when this job* ***turned up****.*

something, first one person does it, then another: *We **took turns** riding the skateboard.* • *Jill and Sandy will **take it in turns** to drive.*

the turn of the century (formal) the beginning of a century: *This house was built **at the turn of the century**.*

turn·ing /ˈtɜːnɪŋ $ ˈtɚnɪŋ/ *noun BrE* a road that joins the road you are on SYNONYM **turn**: *Go past the church and it's the next turning on your left.*

ˈturning point *noun* a time when an important change starts to happen: *Meeting Rick was a turning point in my life.*

tur·nip /ˈtɜːnɪp $ ˈtɚnɪp/ *noun* a round white vegetable that grows under the ground

turn·out /ˈtɜːnaʊt $ ˈtɚnaʊt/ *noun* (no plural) the number of people who go to an event such as a party, meeting, or election: *There was an excellent turnout at the meeting* (=a lot of people came).

tur·quoise /ˈtɜːkwɔɪz $ ˈtɚkwɔɪz/ *adjective, noun* a bright blue-green colour

tur·tle /ˈtɜːtl $ ˈtɚtl/ *noun* an animal with a hard shell that lives in the sea but lays its eggs on land

tur·tle·neck /ˈtɜːtlnek $ ˈtɚtlˌnek/ the American word for POLO NECK

tusk /tʌsk/ *noun* one of the two long pointed teeth that grow outside the mouth of some animals: *an elephant's tusks*

tu·tor /ˈtjuːtə $ ˈtutɚ/ *noun*
1 someone who teaches one person or a small group of people: *a private tutor*
2 a teacher at a British university
—**tutor** *verb*

tu·to·ri·al /tjuːˈtɔːriəl $ tuˈtɔriəl/ *noun* a class in which a small group of students discuss a subject with their tutor: *Most of the teaching is done in small tutorials.*

tux·e·do /tʌkˈsiːdəʊ $ tʌkˈsidoʊ/ the American word for DINNER JACKET

TV /ˌtiː ˈviː/ *noun* (informal) a TELEVISION → see picture on page A12

tweed /twiːd/ *noun* (no plural) a thick wool cloth that is used especially for making clothes such as coats and suits

twee·zers /ˈtwiːzəz $ ˈtwizɚz/ *plural noun* a small tool consisting of two thin pieces of metal joined at one end. You use tweezers for pulling out hairs or picking up small things: *a pair of tweezers*

twelfth /twelfθ/ *number* **1** 12th **2** one of twelve equal parts of something: 1/12

twelve /twelv/ *number* 12

twen·ty /ˈtwenti/ *number* (plural **twenties**) **1** 20 **2 the twenties** the years from 1920 to 1929 **3 be in your twenties** to be aged between 20 and 29 —**twentieth** *number*: *the twentieth of June*

ˌtwenty-four/ˈseven, 24/7 *adverb, adjective* (informal) all the time, every day: *Their offices are open 24/7.*

twice /twaɪs/ *adverb* two times: *I've been to America twice this year.*

twig /twɪg/ *noun* a very thin branch that grows on a larger branch of a tree

twin /twɪn/ *noun* one of two children who are born at the same time and have the same mother: *Denny and Daniel are identical twins* (=twins that look exactly the same as each other). • *my twin brother*

twinge /twɪndʒ/ *noun* a sudden slight pain

twin·kle /ˈtwɪŋkəl/ *verb* to shine very brightly but not continuously: *stars twinkling in the night sky* → see Thesaurus at SHINE

twist¹ /twɪst/ *verb*

KEY PATTERNS
twist the lid off a jar
twist a piece of rope/wire/hair around something
twist your ankle

1 to turn something around quickly when holding it with your hand: *I **twisted** the lid **off** the jar.*
2 to bend something around several times and change its shape: *He **twisted** the wire **around** the fence post.* • *Sharon **twisted** her hair **into** a rope and pinned it up.*
3 to hurt a part of your body by suddenly turning it SYNONYM **sprain**: *He **twisted** his **ankle** playing football.*

twist² *noun* **1** a shape that you make by twisting or bending something: *Decorate the cake with twists of lemon peel.* **2** a sudden change in a story or

twist

He is twisting the rope around the post.

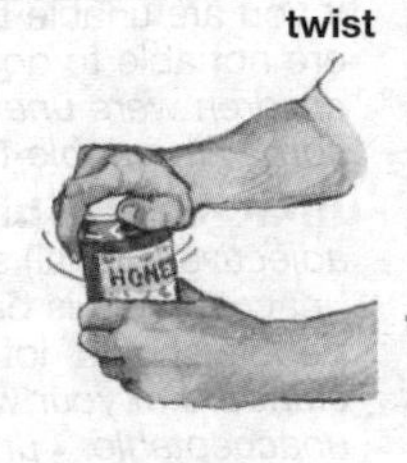

I twisted the lid off the jar.

situation that you did not expect: *There's an unusual twist at the end of the film.*

twitch /twɪtʃ/ *verb* if a part of your body twitches, it suddenly moves slightly and you cannot control it: *The muscles in his legs began to twitch.*

two /tuː/ *number* **1** 2 **2 in two, into two** if you break or cut something in two, it becomes two pieces instead of one: *She broke the cookie in two and gave the dog half.*

> THESAURUS
> **pair**: *a pair of shoes* (=two similar things that are used together)
> **couple**: *I saw him a **couple** of weeks ago* (=two, or about two). • *the **couple** who lived next door* (=two people who are married or having a romantic relationship)

ˌtwo-ˈway *adjective* moving in two directions: *two-way traffic*

ty·coon /taɪˈkuːn/ *noun* someone who is very successful in business and has a lot of money

tying the present participle of TIE[1]

type[1] /taɪp/ *noun*

> KEY PATTERNS
> **a type of person/thing**

a group of people or things that are similar to each other in some way: *I think you should try a **different type of** exercise.* • ***What type of** job are you looking for?* • *We grow **various types** of grass.*

> THESAURUS
> **kind/sort**: *What **kind** of music do you like* (=type)?
> **category**: *The books are divided up into different **categories*** (=groups into which something has been organized or arranged for a particular purpose).
> **species**: *Ninety species of birds live on the island* (=types – used about animals and plants).

type[2] *verb* **1** to write something using a computer or a typewriter: *Jill can type really fast.* **2 type into, type in** if you type information into a computer, or if you type it in, you press the keys so that the computer records the information: *Type in your name and password to log on.*

type·writ·er /ˈtaɪpˌraɪtə $ ˈtaɪpˌraɪtɚ/ *noun* a machine that prints letters, numbers etc on paper when you press keys

ty·phoon /ˌtaɪˈfuːn/ *noun* a tropical storm with very strong winds → see Thesaurus at WIND[1]

typ·i·cal /ˈtɪpɪkəl/ *adjective* something that is typical has the usual features or qualities of that type of thing: *a typical British school* • *On a typical day, I watch television for about three hours.* • *This painting **is typical of** his early work.*

typ·i·cally /ˈtɪpɪkli/ *adverb* used to say that something is typical: *The food was typically English.*

typ·ing /ˈtaɪpɪŋ/ *noun* (no plural) writing that you do using a TYPEWRITER: *Are you good at typing?*

typ·ist /ˈtaɪpɪst/ *noun* someone whose job is to type letters and other documents in an office

ty·rant /ˈtaɪərənt $ ˈtaɪrənt/ *noun* someone who uses their power in a cruel and unfair way: *My boss is a real tyrant!* • *The country was ruled by tyrants for many years.*

tyre *BrE*, **tire** *AmE* /taɪə $ taɪɚ/ *noun* the round piece of rubber that fits around a wheel of a car, bicycle etc and is filled with air: *My bicycle needs new tyres.* • *The car had a flat tyre* (=the air had gone out of one tyre). → see picture at TREAD[2]

A B C D E F G H I J K L M N O P Q R S T U V W X Y Z

Uu

UFO /ˈjuːfəʊ $ ˌju ef ˈoʊ/ *noun* (unidentified flying object) a moving object in the sky that some people believe could be carrying creatures from another world SYNONYM **flying saucer**

ug·ly /ˈʌgli/ *adjective* (**uglier, ugliest**) very unattractive or unpleasant to look at ANTONYM **beautiful**: *an ugly animal with a fat body and short legs*

ul·cer /ˈʌlsə $ ˈʌlsɚ/ *noun* a painful area on your skin or inside your body: *a mouth ulcer*

ul·ti·mate /ˈʌltəmət/ *adjective* (formal) **1** final and most important: *Our ultimate aim is to be the best team in the country.* **2** used to say that something is the best, greatest, or worst of its kind: *A Gucci bag is seen as the ultimate fashion accessory.*

ul·ti·mate·ly /ˈʌltəmətli/ *adverb* finally: *No one knows what will ultimately happen.*

ul·tra·vi·o·let /ˌʌltrəˈvaɪələt/ (abbreviation **UV**) *adjective* ultraviolet light makes your skin darker: *Ultraviolet light can be harmful to the skin.*

um·brel·la /ʌmˈbrelə/ *noun* a thing that you hold over your head to protect yourself from the rain

umbrella

um·pire /ˈʌmpaɪə $ ˈʌmpaɪɚ/ *noun* the person in a game such as tennis who makes sure that the players obey the rules

un·a·ble /ʌnˈeɪbəl/ *adjective* (formal)

KEY PATTERNS
be unable to do something

if you are unable to do something, you are not able to do it: *Some of the children were **unable to** read.* • *I'm sorry, I'm **unable to** help you.*

un·ac·cept·a·ble /ˌʌnəkˈseptəbəl/ *adjective* (formal) something that is unacceptable is bad or wrong and people should not do it or allow it: *The standard of your work is unacceptable.* • *unacceptable delays*

u·nan·i·mous /juːˈnænəməs/ *adjective* a unanimous decision or vote is one in which everyone agrees: *The vote was unanimous and Mr Edwards was re-elected.*

un·armed /ˌʌnˈɑːmd $ ˌʌnˈɑrmd/ *adjective* someone who is unarmed is not carrying any weapons: *The soldiers attacked unarmed civilians.*

un·at·tend·ed /ˌʌnəˈtendɪd/ *adjective* something that is unattended is not being watched, and so may be stolen, lost etc: *Please do not leave your suitcases unattended.* • *Unattended baggage will be removed.*

un·a·vail·a·ble /ˌʌnəˈveɪləbəl/ *adjective* **1** someone who is unavailable is not able to meet or speak to you because they are doing something else: *I'm afraid Mrs Brewer is unavailable this morning; she's in a meeting.* **2** if something is unavailable, you cannot buy it or get it: *Their website says that the book is currently unavailable.*

un·a·ware /ˌʌnəˈweə $ ˌʌnəˈwer/ *adjective* (formal) someone who is unaware of something does not know about it or does not see it: *Lucy seemed to be unaware of the dangers that we faced.* • *I was unaware that I was being watched.*

un·bear·a·ble /ʌnˈbeərəbəl $ ʌnˈberəbəl/ *adjective* very unpleasant, painful etc SYNONYM **intolerable**: *In summer, the heat was unbearable.*

un·beat·a·ble /ʌnˈbiːtəbəl/ *adjective* much better than other things: *Their prices are unbeatable!*

un·be·liev·a·ble /ˌʌnbəˈliːvəbəl/ *adjective* extreme or surprising, and therefore difficult to believe: *Jack's had some unbelievable bad luck in the last few years.*

un·cer·tain /ʌn'sɜːtn $ ʌn'sɚtn/ *adjective* (formal)

KEY PATTERNS
uncertain about/of something
uncertain what/where/how etc

not sure about something ANTONYM **certain**: *She was* ***uncertain about*** *how much money the trip would cost.* • *I'm* ***uncertain of*** *the date of the next meeting.* • *We were* ***uncertain what*** *to do next.*

un·cer·tain·ty /ʌn'sɜːtnti $ ʌn'sɚtnti/ *noun* (formal) (plural **uncertainties**) when something is not known or not definite: *There is uncertainty over the future of the project.*

un·cle /'ʌŋkəl/ *noun* the brother of your mother or father, or the husband of your aunt: *Uncle Mike always visits us at Christmas.*

un·clear /ˌʌn'klɪə $ ˌʌn'klɪr/ *adjective* (formal) difficult to understand or know: *It was unclear exactly what he meant.*

un·com·fort·a·ble /ʌn'kʌmftəbəl $ ʌn'kʌmftɚbəl/ *adjective*
1 if you are uncomfortable, you do not feel physically relaxed ANTONYM **comfortable**: *I'm always so uncomfortable on long plane journeys.*
2 something that is uncomfortable makes you unable to feel physically relaxed ANTONYM **comfortable**: *an uncomfortable chair* • *These shoes are terribly uncomfortable to wear.*
3 if you feel uncomfortable, you feel embarrassed or worried ANTONYM **comfortable**: *She felt really* ***uncomfortable*** *because the man was standing so close to her.* • *Alice is uncomfortable about being photographed.*

un·con·scious /ʌn'kɒnʃəs $ ʌn'kɑnʃəs/ *adjective* someone who is unconscious is not awake and cannot hear, feel, or see ANTONYM **conscious**: *The doctor said that she was still unconscious after the operation.*
—**unconsciousness** *noun* (no plural)

un·con·trol·lable /ˌʌnkən'trəʊləbəl $ ˌʌnkən'troʊləbəl/ *adjective* impossible to control or stop: *Everyone ran for the exits in uncontrollable panic.*

un·count·a·ble /ʌn'kaʊntəbəl/ *adjective* in grammar, an uncountable noun has no plural. 'Water', 'gold', and 'furniture' are examples of uncountable nouns ANTONYM **countable**

un·cov·er /ʌn'kʌvə $ ʌn'kʌvɚ/ *verb* to discover something secret or illegal: *The police uncovered evidence that the killer was living in Spain.*

un·de·cid·ed /ˌʌndɪ'saɪdɪd/ *adjective* (formal) if you are undecided about something, you have not made a decision about it yet SYNONYM **unsure**: *I'm still undecided which subjects I want to study.*

un·der[1] /'ʌndə $ 'ʌndɚ/ *preposition*
1 directly below something ANTONYM **over**: *Clare found the letter under a pile of papers.* • *She keeps her shoes under her bed.* • *He was sitting under a tree* (=below its branches).
2 below the surface of water: *She dived under the water.*
3 less than a number, amount, or age ANTONYM **over**: *Can you get a good camera for under $500?* • *Children under five* (=children less than five years old) *travel free.*
4 affected by something: *He's under a lot of pressure at work.* • *The country was under communist rule.*

WORD CHOICE
under or **below**?
• **Under** means "directly below something": *His feet were* ***under*** *the table.*
• **Below** means "at a lower level than another thing": *She looked down at the valley* ***below*** *her.*

under[2] *adverb*
1 below the surface of water: *He dived into the water and stayed under for over a minute.*
2 less than the number, amount, or age that is mentioned ANTONYM **over**: *You don't have to pay tax on goods worth £200 and under.*

'under-age *adjective* too young to legally buy alcohol, drive a car etc: *under-age smokers*

un·der·go /ˌʌndə'gəʊ $ ˌʌndɚ'goʊ/ *verb* (formal) (**underwent** /-'went/ **undergone** /-'gɒn $ -'gɔn/ **undergoes**) if you undergo something such as medical treatment, it is done to you or

A B C D E F G H I J K L M N O P Q R S T U V W X Y Z

it happens to you: *Mr Buckley underwent a five-hour emergency operation.*

undergone the past participle of UNDERGO

un·der·grad·u·ate /ˌʌndəˈɡrædʒuət $ ˌʌndɚˈɡrædʒuət/ *noun* a student who is at university, studying for his or her first degree

un·der·ground¹ /ˌʌndəˈɡraʊnd $ ˌʌndɚˈɡraʊnd/ *adjective, adverb* under the surface of the ground: *an underground tunnel • animals that stay underground during the day*

un·der·ground² /ˈʌndəɡraʊnd $ ˈʌndɚˌɡraʊnd/ *noun BrE* **the Underground** the railway system that runs under the city of London. Similar systems in American cities are called the SUBWAY SYNONYM **Tube**: *Shall we go by bus or use the Underground?*

un·der·growth /ˈʌndəɡrəʊθ $ ˈʌndɚˌɡroʊθ/ *noun* (no plural) low bushes and plants that grow around trees

un·der·line /ˌʌndəˈlaɪn $ ˈʌndɚˌlaɪn/ *verb* to draw a line under a word or sentence: *Underline the name of the book.*

un·der·neath¹ /ˌʌndəˈniːθ $ ˌʌndɚˈniθ/ *preposition, adverb*
1 directly below something: *She kept her diary in a box underneath her bed. • If we don't cut the trees back, the grass underneath will die.*
2 covered by something: *What's underneath that sheet? • They found their skis underneath a layer of snow.*

underneath² *noun* the bottom part of something: ***the underneath of the car***

un·der·pants /ˈʌndəpænts $ ˈʌndɚpænts/ *plural noun* **1** *BrE* a short piece of clothing that men or boys wear under their other clothes on the lower part of their body SYNONYM **pants**: *a pair of underpants* **2** *AmE* a short piece of clothing that both men and women wear under their clothes on the lower part of their body

un·der·pass /ˈʌndəpɑːs $ ˈʌndɚˌpæs/ *noun* (plural **underpasses**) a road or path that goes under another road or a railway SYNONYM **subway** *AmE*

un·der·stand /ˌʌndəˈstænd $ ˌʌndɚˈstænd/ *verb* (past tense and past participle **understood**) /-ˈstʊd/

KEY PATTERNS
understand what/how/why etc

1 if you understand something that is spoken or written, you know what it means: *Does Jim understand Spanish? • I couldn't **understand what** the men were saying. • Do you understand this computer manual?*
2 to know how something works or why something happens: *I don't **understand how** this machine works. • Scientists are beginning to **understand what** causes this phenomenon.*
3 to know what someone's feelings are and why they behave in a particular way: *Suddenly, I **understood how** Angela felt. • I don't understand my children any more.*

GRAMMAR
Understand is not used in the progressive.
✘ Don't say 'I'm understanding'.

un·der·stand·a·ble /ˌʌndəˈstændəbəl $ ˌʌndɚˈstændəbəl/ *adjective* understandable behaviour or feelings are normal and what you expect: *It is understandable for him to want to be with his parents at this time.*

un·der·stand·ing¹ /ˌʌndəˈstændɪŋ $ˌʌndɚˈstændɪŋ/ *noun* (no plural)
1 your understanding of something is how well you understand it: *My understanding of computers is very limited.* **2** sympathy and kindness that you show towards someone with problems or worries: *Teenagers need plenty of understanding and support.*

understanding² *adjective* an understanding person is kind and shows sympathy towards someone with problems or worries: *I'll talk to Alex – he's always very understanding.*

understood the past tense and past participle of UNDERSTAND

un·der·take /ˌʌndəˈteɪk $ ˌʌndɚˈteɪk/ *verb* (formal) (**undertook** /-ˈtʊk/ **undertaken** /-ˈteɪkən/) to start to do something that is difficult or will take a long time: *The university is undertaking a ten-year research programme.*

A B C D E F G H I J K L M N O P Q R S T U V W X Y Z

undertaken the past participle of UNDERTAKE

un·der·tak·er /ˈʌndəteɪkə $ ˈʌndɚˌteɪkɚ/ *noun BrE* someone whose job is to arrange funerals SYNONYM **mortician** *AmE* SYNONYM **funeral director**

undertook the past tense of UNDERTAKE

un·der·wa·ter /ˌʌndəˈwɔːtə $ ˌʌndɚˈwɔtɚ/ *adverb, adjective* below the surface of the water: *How long can you stay underwater?* • *the underwater explorer Jacques Cousteau*

un·der·wear /ˈʌndəweə $ ˈʌndɚˌwer/ *noun* (no plural) clothes that you wear next to your body, under your other clothes

underwent the past tense of UNDERGO

un·de·vel·oped /ˌʌndɪˈveləpt/ *adjective* undeveloped land has not been built on or used for anything: *undeveloped areas of the city*

undid the past tense of UNDO

un·do /ʌnˈduː/ *verb* (**undid** /-ˈdɪd/, **undone** /-ˈdʌn/) to make something looser, so that it is no longer tied or fastened ANTONYM **tie**, **do up**: *I can't undo this knot.* • *He undid the buttons on his shirt.* → see Thesaurus at OPEN[2]

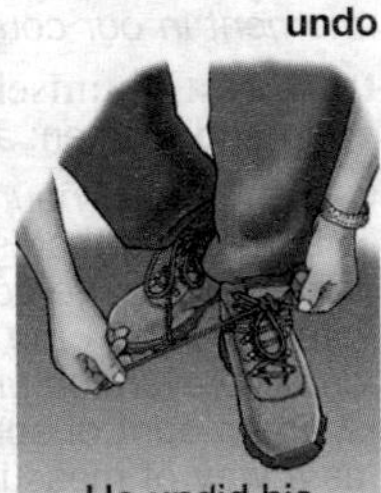
undo

He undid his shoelaces.

—**undone** *adjective*: *Your shoelaces are undone.*

undone the past participle of UNDO

un·dress /ʌnˈdres/ *verb* to remove your clothes —**undressed** *adjective*: *I got undressed and had a quick shower.*

un·eas·y /ʌnˈiːzi/ *adjective* (**uneasier**, **uneasiest**) worried or afraid about something: *I began to feel uneasy when he still wasn't home by ten.* → see Thesaurus at WORRIED

un·em·ployed /ˌʌnɪmˈplɔɪd/ *adjective* someone who is unemployed does not have a job SYNONYM **out of work**: *I'm unemployed at the moment, but I'm looking for work*

un·em·ploy·ment /ˌʌnɪmˈplɔɪmənt/ *noun* (no plural) when people do not have jobs, or the number of people who do not have jobs: *the problems of unemployment* • *the latest unemployment figures*

un·e·ven /ʌnˈiːvən/ *adjective* not flat, smooth, or level: *The surface of the road was very uneven.*

un·ex·pect·ed /ˌʌnɪkˈspektɪd/ *adjective* (formal) something that is unexpected is surprising because you did not expect it: *We had an unexpected visit from my parents.* —**unexpectedly** *adverb*

un·fair /ˌʌnˈfeə $ ˌʌnˈfer/ *adjective*

> KEY PATTERNS
> **it is unfair to do something**
> **it is unfair that**
> **be unfair to someone**

not treating people in a fair and equal way: ***It's unfair to** make him do all the work.* • *I think it's **unfair that** she got the job instead of me.* • *I didn't want to **be unfair to** anyone.* • *complaints about unfair treatment* —**unfairly** *adverb*: *He felt that he had been unfairly punished.*

un·faith·ful /ʌnˈfeɪθfəl/ *adjective* someone who is unfaithful has sex with someone who is not their wife, husband etc

un·fa·mil·i·ar /ˌʌnfəˈmɪliə $ ˌʌnfəˈmɪljɚ/ *adjective* (formal) if someone or something is unfamiliar, you do not recognize them: *The handwriting on the envelope was unfamiliar.* • *He felt like a stranger, lost in a crowd of unfamiliar faces.*

un·fash·ion·a·ble /ʌn'fæʃənəbəl/ *adjective* not popular or fashionable: *an unfashionable part of the city*

un·fas·ten /ʌn'fɑːsən $ ʌn'fæsən/ *verb* to undo a piece of clothing, rope etc so that it is not tied or fastened: *Can you unfasten my dress?* ➔ see Thesaurus at OPEN[2]

un·fit /ʌn'fɪt/ *adjective* **1** not healthy because you have not had enough exercise ANTONYM **fit**: *I'm so unfit I could only run half the race!* **2** not good enough or suitable for something: *The water here is unfit to drink.*

un·fold /ʌn'fəʊld $ ʌn'foʊld/ *verb* if you unfold something, or if it unfolds, it opens out and becomes bigger and flatter: *Jim carefully unfolded the piece of paper.* • *The buds of the flower had started to unfold.*

un·for·tu·nate /ʌn'fɔːtʃənət $ ʌn'fɔrtʃənət/ *adjective* (formal) unlucky ANTONYM **fortunate**: *It's* ***unfortunate that*** *she was hurt.* • *a very unfortunate accident*

un·for·tu·nate·ly /ʌn'fɔːtʃənətli $ ʌn'fɔrtʃənətli/ *adverb* used to say that you feel sad or disappointed about something: *Unfortunately, we had to go home early.*

un·friend·ly /ʌn'frendli/ *adjective* not friendly and often unkind: *Some of the kids in my class are really unfriendly towards me.*

un·grate·ful /ʌn'greɪtfəl/ *adjective* someone who is ungrateful does not thank someone who has been kind or helpful to them ANTONYM **grateful**: *You must write and thank her, or she'll think you're ungrateful.*

un·hap·py /ʌn'hæpi/ *adjective* (**unhappier**, **unhappiest**)

KEY PATTERNS
unhappy about something
unhappy with something

1 not happy: *Barbara had a very unhappy childhood.* • *The kids were really* ***unhappy about*** *moving away from their friends.* • *Sam, you seem terribly unhappy. Is something wrong?* • *It was the unhappiest year of my life.* ➔ see Thesaurus at SAD
2 if you are unhappy with something, you do not think it is good enough: *We* ***were unhappy with*** *the rooms in the hotel, which were small and dirty.* —**unhappiness** *noun* (no plural): *her unhappiness at school* —**unhappily** *adverb*: *His first marriage ended unhappily.*

un·health·y /ʌn'helθi/ *adjective* (**unhealthier**, **unhealthiest**) **1** not healthy: *Louise always looks so unhealthy.* **2** things that are unhealthy are likely to make you ill or less healthy: *unhealthy food such as burgers and chips*

un·help·ful /ʌn'helpfəl/ *adjective* not willing to help someone, in a way that seems rude and unfriendly: *The shop assistants were very unhelpful.*

u·ni·form /'juːnəfɔːm $ 'junəˌfɔrm/ *noun*
a set of clothes that people wear so that they all look the same: *the school uniform* • *The soldiers were* ***in uniform*** (=wearing their uniforms).

un·im·por·tant /ˌʌnɪm'pɔːtənt $ ˌʌnɪm'pɔrtnt/ *adjective* not important

un·in·hab·it·ed /ˌʌnɪn'hæbɪtɪd/ *adjective* (formal) an uninhabited place is one where no one lives: *an uninhabited island*

un·in·terest·ed /ʌn'ɪntrəstɪd/ *adjective* not interested: *The whole class seemed completely uninterested in the lesson.*

un·ion /'juːnjən/ *noun*
also **trade union** an organization that a group of workers form in order to protect their rights at work SYNONYM **labor union** *AmE*: *the National Union of Teachers* • *Employees have the right to* ***join a union***.

u·nique /juː'niːk/ *adjective* **1** different from any other person or thing: *Every person's fingerprints are unique.*
2 very unusual and special: *a unique moment in our country's history*

u·ni·sex /'juːnɪseks/ *adjective* for both men and women: *a unisex hairdresser's*

u·nit /'juːnɪt/ *noun*
1 something that is one whole part of a larger thing: *The coursebook is divided into six units.* • *the police department's crime prevention unit*
2 an amount of something that is used as a way of measuring how much there is: *The bill shows how many* ***units of*** *energy you have used.*

u•nite /juːˈnaɪt/ *verb* (formal)

KEY PATTERNS
unite with someone/something

1 if people unite, they join together as a group: *The workers united to demand better pay.* • *East Germany **united with** West Germany in 1990.*
2 if something unites people, it makes them join together or work together as a group: *The war united everyone in the country.*

u•nit•ed /juːˈnaɪtɪd/ *adjective* **1** if a group of people or countries is united, they all agree with each other about something: *The people in the town were united in their opposition to the plans.* **2** a united country is one that consists of two or more countries or states that have joined together: *hopes for a united Ireland*

u•ni•ver•sal /ˌjuːnəˈvɜːsəl $ ˌjunəˈvɚsəl/ *adjective* for or related to everyone: *the need for universal health care and education*

u•ni•verse /ˈjuːnəvɜːs $ ˈjunəˌvɚs/ *noun* **the universe** the whole of space and all the stars and PLANETS

u•ni•ver•si•ty /ˌjuːnəˈvɜːsəti $ ˌjunəˈvɚsəti/ *noun* (plural **universities**)
a place where students study for a degree in a subject at a high level: *"Did you go to university?" "Yes, I went to Oxford."*

SPELLING
This word is often spelled wrongly. The correct spelling is **university**.

USAGE
You **study at a university**.
✘ Don't say 'study in a university'.

un•just /ˌʌnˈdʒʌst/ *adjective* not fair or reasonable: *an unjust ruler* • *unjust laws*

un•kind /ˌʌnˈkaɪnd/ *adjective*

KEY PATTERNS
unkind to someone

if someone is unkind, they say or do things that are not pleasant or friendly: *She said some very unkind things.* • *Don't be so unkind!* • *Children are sometimes very **unkind to** each other.*

THESAURUS
mean (formal): *It was mean of you to tell him that everyone hates him* (=unkind).
horrible/nasty: *Why are you being so **horrible to** me* (=very unkind, especially in a way that upsets someone)?
cruel: *I can't stand people who are **cruel to** animals* (=extremely unkind).

un•known /ˌʌnˈnəʊn $ ˌʌnˈnoʊn/ *adjective* not known or not famous: *The number of people who died in the earthquake is still unknown.* • *an unknown singer*

un•lead•ed /ʌnˈledɪd/ *adjective* unleaded petrol does not contain any LEAD (=a harmful substance)

un•less /ʌnˈles, ən-/ *conjunction* used to say that one thing will happen or will not happen if another thing does not happen: *I'll meet you at 8 unless you phone me to say you can't go out* (=if you phone me, I won't meet you). • *I won't tell you unless you promise to keep it a secret.* • *You aren't allowed to drive a car unless you have a licence* (=you are only allowed to drive a car if you have a licence).

un•like /ˌʌnˈlaɪk/ *preposition* completely different from someone or something else: *Unlike beef, chicken has very little fat.* • *Our new house was quite unlike the old cottage.*

un•like•ly /ʌnˈlaɪkli/ *adjective*

KEY PATTERNS
unlikely that
unlikely to do something

something that is unlikely will probably not happen: ***It is unlikely that** you will get your money back.* • *Holt is **unlikely to** play in Saturday's game.* • *"Do you think they'll win?" "It's **highly unlikely*** (=very unlikely).*"*

un•lim•i•ted /ʌnˈlɪmətɪd/ *adjective* as much as you want: *The rail ticket allows students to have unlimited travel for a month.*

un•lit /ˌʌnˈlɪt/ *adjective* dark because there are no lights on: *a small unlit road*

unload

un·load /ʌn'ləʊd $ ʌn'loʊd/ *verb* to take things out of a car, off a ship etc, after bringing them from somewhere: *We arrived home late, and unloaded the car the next morning.*

un·lock /ʌn'lɒk $ ʌn'lɑk/ *verb* to open the lock on a door, car etc, using a key
→ see Thesaurus at OPEN[2]

un·luck·y /ʌn'lʌki/ *adjective* (**unluckier, unluckiest**)
1 if you are unlucky, bad things happen to you for no particular reason ANTONYM **lucky**: *He was* ***unlucky not to*** *score a goal.* • *They should have won the game, but they were unlucky.*
2 if something is unlucky, some people think it causes bad luck ANTONYM **lucky**: *It's* ***unlucky to*** *walk under a ladder.* • *Thirteen is an unlucky number.*

un·mar·ried /ˌʌn'mærid/ *adjective* not married SYNONYM **single**

un·ne·ces·sa·ry /ʌn'nesəsəri $ ʌn'nesəˌseri/ *adjective* if something is unnecessary, you do not need to have it or do it: *Having two cars is an unnecessary luxury.* • *Testing cosmetics on animals is unnecessary.*

SPELLING
This word is often spelled wrongly. The correct spelling is: **unnecessary**.

un·oc·cu·pied /ʌn'ɒkjəpaɪd $ ʌn'ɑkjəˌpaɪd/ *adjective* (formal) an unoccupied seat, house, room etc does not have anyone in it or using it: *The top floor of the house was completely unoccupied.*

un·of·fi·cial /ˌʌnə'fɪʃəl/ *adjective* not accepted or approved by anyone in authority: *There were unofficial reports that the president was seriously ill.* —**unofficially** *adverb*

un·pack /ʌn'pæk/ *verb* to take everything out of your cases, bags etc after travelling: *We arrived at the hotel, unpacked, and had dinner.*

un·paid /ˌʌn'peɪd/ *adjective*
1 someone who is unpaid works without receiving any money: *We have several unpaid helpers at the school.*
2 an unpaid bill or debt has not been paid

un·pleas·ant /ʌn'plezənt/ *adjective*
1 not pleasant or enjoyable: *an unpleasant smell* • *The weather was really unpleasant.*
2 someone who is unpleasant behaves in an unkind or rude way: *What an unpleasant man!* • *She was extremely* ***unpleasant to*** *me.* —**unpleasantly** *adverb*

un·plug /ʌn'plʌg/ *verb* (**unplugged, unplugging**) to take the PLUG on a piece of electrical equipment out of the SOCKET (=the place in a wall where you can connect electrical equipment to an electricity supply)

un·pop·u·lar /ʌn'pɒpjələ $ ʌn'pɑpjələ˞/ *adjective* not liked by many people ANTONYM **popular**: *Billy was unpopular at school and very unhappy.* • *She was the most unpopular politician in England.*

un·rea·lis·tic /ˌʌnrɪə'lɪstɪk/ *adjective* (formal) if you are unrealistic, you expect things to be better than they really are: *Teachers sometimes have unrealistic expectations of their students.*

un·rea·son·a·ble /ʌn'riːzənəbəl/ *adjective* unreasonable behaviour, ideas, prices etc are not fair, sensible, or acceptable: *I thought that what he said was very unreasonable.*

un·re·li·a·ble /ˌʌnrɪ'laɪəbəl/ *adjective* unreliable people or things cannot be trusted to do what they should do ANTONYM **reliable**: *an unreliable bus service* • *I wouldn't use him again – he's very unreliable.*

un·ru·ly /ʌn'ruːli/ *adjective* unruly people are difficult to control: *an unruly crowd*

un·safe /ˌʌn'seɪf/ *adjective* (formal) dangerous and likely to harm people: *The engineers said that the building was unsafe.*

un·sat·is·fac·to·ry /ˌʌnsætɪsˈfæktəri/ *adjective* not good enough and not acceptable: *an unsatisfactory explanation*

un·screw /ʌnˈskruː/ *verb* to open or undo something by twisting it: *I unscrewed the top of the jar.*

un·self·ish /ʌnˈselfɪʃ/ *adjective* an unselfish person is kind and cares more about other people than they do about themselves: *a mother's unselfish devotion to her children*

un·set·tle /ʌnˈsetl/ *verb* if something unsettles you, it makes you feel nervous or worried: *All the changes at work unsettled her.* —**unsettling** *adjective*: *an unsettling experience*

un·set·tled /ʌnˈsetld/ *adjective* **1** unsettled weather is wet and changes often ANTONYM **settled**: *The forecast is for more unsettled weather.* **2** feeling worried or unsure: *Children often feel unsettled by divorce.*

un·so·phis·ti·cat·ed /ˌʌnsəˈfɪstɪkeɪtɪd/ *adjective* simple and not modern: *Farmers were still using unsophisticated methods.*

un·sta·ble /ʌnˈsteɪbəl/ *adjective* likely to change suddenly and cause problems ANTONYM **stable**: *The country is unstable and tourists have been warned not to go there.*

un·suc·cess·ful /ˌʌnsəkˈsesfəl/ *adjective* not achieving what you wanted to achieve: *an unsuccessful attempt to break the world record* —**unsuccessfully** *adverb*: *She tried unsuccessfully to open the door.*

un·suit·able /ʌnˈsuːtəbəl/ *adjective* (formal) not acceptable or right for a particular purpose: *Her shoes were unsuitable for a long walk.*

un·sure /ˌʌnˈʃʊə $ ˌʌnˈʃʊr/ *adjective* not certain or confident about something: *Rob was unsure about passing the exam.*

un·sym·pa·thet·ic /ˌʌnsɪmpəˈθetɪk/ *adjective* not kind or helpful towards people who have problems ANTONYM **sympathetic**: *a stern, unsympathetic policeman*

un·ti·dy /ʌnˈtaɪdi/ *adjective* (**untidier**, **untidiest**) **1** not neat: *Why is your bedroom always so untidy?* • *Jim always left his clothes in an untidy heap on the floor.* **2** an untidy person does not care whether things are neat or arranged correctly: *You really are the untidiest person I have ever met!*

un·tie /ʌnˈtaɪ/ *verb* (**untying**) to undo something so that it is not tied or fastened ANTONYM **tie up**: *I untied the knot and opened the parcel.*

un·til /ʌnˈtɪl/ also **till** *preposition, conjunction*
used to say when something stops: *The football practice session will start at 4 o'clock and go on until 6.* • *We lived in Oxford until I was ten.* • *I'm allowed to stay out until 12 o'clock.*

PHRASES

not until **a)** only when something has been done: *You can't go out until you've done your homework* (=you can only go out when you've done your homework). **b)** at a particular time, after a long delay: *The next train is **not until** 4 o'clock.*

> **SPELLING**
> This word is often spelled wrongly. The correct spelling is: **until**.

un·true /ʌnˈtruː/ *adjective* not true

un·used /ˌʌnˈjuːzd/ *adjective* not being used, or never used: *an unused £20 note*

un·u·su·al /ʌnˈjuːʒuəl/ *adjective* something that is unusual does not happen often or is different from what you would normally expect: *He has an unusual name.* • ***It's very unusual for** Mandy **to** be ill.* —**unusually** *adverb*: *The train was unusually late this morning.*

un·veil /ʌnˈveɪl/ *verb* (formal) to officially let people know about something that was a secret: *BMW will unveil their latest car at the Paris Motor Show.*

un·well /ʌnˈwel/ *adjective* (formal) ill: *Judy left, saying she felt unwell.*

un·will·ing /ʌnˈwɪlɪŋ/ *adjective* if you are unwilling to do something, you do not want to do it: *Customers are unwilling to pay for poor service.*

un·wind /ʌnˈwaɪnd/ *verb* (past tense and past participle **unwound** /-ˈwaʊnd/) to relax and stop feeling worried: *Watching TV helps me unwind.*

unwound the past tense and past participle of UNWIND

un·wrap /ʌn'ræp/ *verb* (**unwrapped**, **unwrapping**) to remove the paper that is covering something ANTONYM **wrap**: *The children unwrapped their presents excitedly.*
→ see Thesaurus at OPEN²

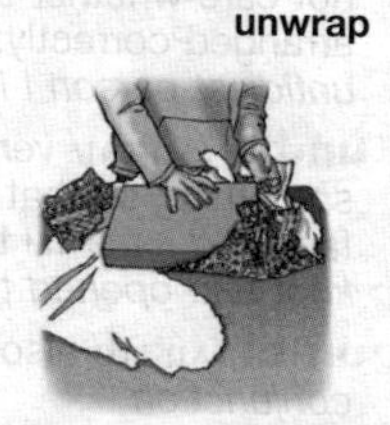
unwrap

un·zip /ʌn'zɪp/ *verb* (**unzipped**, **unzipping**) to unfasten something that is fastened with a zip: *He unzipped his jacket.*

up /ʌp/ *adverb, preposition*
1 towards or in a higher place ANTONYM **down**: *He climbed up the ladder.* • *The cups are up there on the top shelf.*
2 not in bed: *Is Martin up yet, or is he still in bed?* • *We **stayed up** to watch the late film.*
3 used to say that something becomes or has become higher in amount ANTONYM **down**: *Prices **are going up** quickly.* • *His temperature's up* (=it's higher than normal).
4 further along a road SYNONYM **down**: *I was going up Vine Street when I met Luke.* • *The school's just up the road.*
5 towards the north ANTONYM **down**: *She's going up to Scotland tomorrow.*
PHRASES
up to something **a)** used to mention the largest number or size that is possible: *The car can carry **up to** six people.* • *These fish can grow **up to** seven feet long.* **b)** if you go up to a person or place, you go towards them and stop when you are next to them: *A man came **up to** me in the street and asked where the police station was.* • *I walked **up to** the front door and rang the bell.*
be up to something (informal) if someone is up to something, they are secretly doing something bad: *I know he's **up to** something, and I'm going to find out what it is.*
be up to doing something (informal) to be strong enough and healthy enough to do something: *I'm not **up to** seeing anyone right now.*
be up to someone if something is up to you, you can choose what to do or have: *It's **up to** him whether he takes the exam or not.*

up·bring·ing /'ʌpˌbrɪŋɪŋ/ *noun* the way your parents treated you when you were a child, and the things they taught you: *I had a strict religious upbringing.*

up·date¹ /ʌp'deɪt/ *verb* to add new parts or the most recent information to something so that it stays modern: *We update our records every six months.*

up·date² /'ʌpdeɪt/ *noun* (formal) the most recent news about something: *a news update from the BBC*

up·front /ʌp'frʌnt/ *adjective* (informal) speaking honestly and openly: *It's best to be upfront about these things.*

up·grade /ʌp'greɪd/ *verb* to change something so that it is better or more modern: *We need to upgrade our computer system.* —**upgrade** /'ʌpgreɪd/ *noun*: *a software upgrade*

up·heav·al /ʌp'hiːvəl/ *noun* (formal) a very big change that causes problems: *the upheaval of moving house*

upheld the past tense and past participle of UPHOLD

uphill

He is walking downhill. He is walking uphill.

up·hill /ˌʌp'hɪl/ *adverb, adjective* towards the top of a hill ANTONYM **downhill**: *We walked uphill for over an hour.* • *an uphill slope*

up·hold /ˌʌp'həʊld $ ʌp'hoʊld/ *verb* (formal) (past tense and past participle **upheld** /-'held/) to support a law or decision and make sure it continues to exist: *The court upheld his decision.*

up·lift·ing /ʌp'lɪftɪŋ/ *adjective* (formal) making you feel happy: *an uplifting piece of music*

up·on /ə'pɒn $ ə'pɑn/ *preposition* (formal)
on: *They sat down upon the ground.*

up·per /'ʌpə $ 'ʌpɚ/ *adjective* in a higher position ANTONYM **lower**: *the upper parts of the body • a room on the upper floor*

up·per·case /ˌʌpə'keɪs $ ˌʌpɚ'keɪs/ *adjective* uppercase letters are CAPITALS, for example A, B, C etc

ˌupper 'class *noun* **the upper class, the upper classes** the people in society who belong to the highest social class —**'upper-class** *adjective*: *She spoke with an upper-class accent.*

up·right /'ʌp-raɪt/ *adjective, adverb* standing, sitting, or pointing up: *She sat upright in her bed. • Make sure that the bottle is in an upright position.*

up·ris·ing /'ʌpˌraɪzɪŋ/ *noun* a situation in which the people in a country try to get rid of their government, usually unsucessfully SYNONYM **rebellion**: *the Hungarian uprising of 1956*

up·roar /'ʌp-rɔː $ 'ʌp-rɔr/ *noun* (no plural) (formal) a lot of shouting and noise: *The school was in uproar.*

up·root /ʌp'ruːt/ *verb* to make someone leave their home: *The war has uprooted whole families.*

up·set¹ /ʌp'set/ *adjective*

KEY PATTERNS
upset about something
upset because
upset that

unhappy because something unpleasant has happened: *I know David was very upset about losing his job. • She **feels upset because** she wasn't invited to the party. • He **got** very **upset** when he found out she was leaving. • My parents were **upset that** I hadn't called to say that I would be late.* → see Thesaurus at SAD

upset² *verb* (past tense and past participle **upset, upsetting**) to make someone feel unhappy or worried: *Her remarks really upset me.* —**upsetting** *adjective*: *a very upsetting experience*

up·side·down, upside-down /ˌʌpsaɪd 'daʊn/ *adverb, adjective* if something is upsidedown, the part that should be at the top is at the bottom: *He turned the bag upsidedown and everything fell out. • The pattern is upside-down.*

up·stairs /ˌʌp'steəz $ ˌʌp'sterz/ *adverb, adjective*
on or going towards a higher floor of a building ANTONYM **downstairs**: *Julie is upstairs in her room. • Go upstairs and fetch my glasses. • We live in the upstairs flat.*

ˌup-to-'date *adjective* recent, modern, or fashionable ANTONYM **out-of-date**: *We try to keep the information up-to-date.*

up·town /ˌʌp'taʊn/ *adjective, adverb* *AmE* in or towards the northern part of a city and where rich people usually live

up·wards /'ʌpwədz $ 'ʌpwɚdz/ also **up·ward** /'ʌpwəd $ 'ʌpwɚd/ *adverb* towards a higher position or level ANTONYM **downwards**: *The balloon went slowly upwards into the air.*

u·ra·ni·um /jʊ'reɪniəm/ *noun* (no plural) a RADIOACTIVE metal used to produce NUCLEAR energy

ur·ban /'ɜːbən $ 'ɚbən/ *adjective* related to a town or city: *urban development*

urge¹ /ɜːdʒ $ ɚdʒ/ *verb* (formal) to advise someone very strongly to do something: *She urged him to think carefully before making a final decision.*

urge² *noun* (formal) a strong desire: *I felt a very strong urge to laugh.*

ur·gen·cy /'ɜːdʒənsi $ 'ɚdʒənsi/ *noun* (no plural) when something is urgent: *The minister stressed the urgency of the situation.*

ur·gent /'ɜːdʒənt $ 'ɚdʒənt/ *adjective* if something is urgent, it is important and someone must deal with it immediately: *I must speak to Mr Hill – it's very urgent. • an urgent message • John had to leave on urgent business.* —**urgently** *adverb*: *Food and medicine are urgently needed.*

u·ri·nate /'jʊərəneɪt $ 'jʊrəˌneɪt/ *verb* (formal) to let urine come out of your body

u·rine /ˈjʊərɪn $ ˈjʊrɪn/ *noun* the liquid that comes out of your body when you go to the toilet

us /əs; strong ʌs/ *pronoun* the person who is speaking and others: *Can you help us?*

us·a·ble /ˈjuːsəbəl/ *adjective* available or in a good enough condition for you to use: *Many of the clothes are still usable.*

us·age /ˈjuːsɪdʒ/ *noun* (no plural) (formal) **1** the way that words are used in a language: *modern English usage* **2** the amount of something that is used, or the way it is used: *We all need to reduce our energy usage.*

use¹ /juːz/ *verb*

KEY PATTERNS
use something to do something
use something for something
use something as something

1 if you use something, you do something with it: *Can I use your phone?* • *Neil* ***used*** *his cigarette lighter* ***to*** *start the fire.* • *The oranges are* ***used to*** *make marmalade.* • *I use the suit mainly* ***for*** *weddings and funerals.* • *We use this room* ***as*** *an office.* **2** also **use up** to finish all of something so that there is nothing left: *Sorry, I've* ***used up*** *all of the milk.* **3** if someone uses illegal drugs, they take them regularly **4** you can say that someone uses the toilet or bathroom as a polite way of saying that they go to the toilet: *Could I use the bathroom please?*

use² /juːs/ *noun* **1** (no plural) when people use something: ***The use of*** *sunscreens can help prevent skin cancer.* • *Our* ***use of*** *paper is increasing every year.* **2** the purpose that you use something for: *The new drug* ***has*** *many* ***uses.*** **3** (no plural) (formal) if you have the use of something, you are allowed to use it: *Students* ***have the use of*** *school computers on evenings and at weekends.*

PHRASES

make use of something to use something that is available: *These recipes* ***make use of*** *leftover turkey.*

be in use if something is in use, someone is using it: *I'm sorry, this room* ***is in use.*** • *These methods of making wine* ***have been in use*** *for hundreds of years.*

be of no use to someone if something is of no use to you, you do not need it: *You can have this old washing machine – it's of no use to me now.*

it's no use, what's the use (spoken) used to say that doing something will not have any effect, so you should not do it: ***It's no use.*** *The door won't open.* • ***What's the use*** *of arguing? It won't solve our problems.*

PRONUNCIATION
Be careful how you pronounce this word:
use¹ (*verb*) is pronounced with a 'z' sound at the end
use² (*noun*) is pronounced with an 's' sound at the end

used¹ /juːst/ *adjective* **be/get used to (doing) something** if you are used to something, it is not unusual or surprising for you, because you have done it many times or for a long time: *Sam* ***is used to*** *living in London.* • *You soon* ***get used to*** *the job.*

GRAMMAR
The negative of **be used to (doing) something** is **not used to (doing) something**: *She's* ***not used to*** *living in a big city.*

used² /juːzd/ *adjective* used cars or clothes are not new because someone else owned them before SYNONYM **secondhand**: *The garage sells used cars.*

used to /ˈjuːst tuː/ *modal verb* if something used to happen, it happened in the past but does not happen now: *The town used to be very quiet.* • *He used to be a very shy boy.*

GRAMMAR
The negative of **used to do something** is **didn't use to do something**: *I* ***didn't use to*** *like flying.*

WORD CHOICE
used to do something or **used to doing something**?
• You use **used to do something** to talk about things that happened in the past: *I* ***used to*** *live in Paris.*
• **Be used to doing something**

means "be accustomed to doing something": *She is used to living in a big city.*

use•ful /ˈjuːsfəl/ *adjective* helping you do or get what you want: *a useful map of the town centre*

use•less /ˈjuːsləs/ *adjective* not useful at all: *This knife is useless.*

us•er /ˈjuːzə $ ˈjuzɚ/ *noun* someone who uses something such as a product or service: *PC users*

ˌuser-ˈfriendly *adjective* something that is user-friendly is designed to be easy for people to use: *The website wasn't very user-friendly and I couldn't find the information I wanted.*

us•er•name /ˈjuːzəˌneɪm $ ˈjuzɚˌneɪm/ *noun* a name that you use when using a computer system: *Please enter your username and password.*

u•su•al /ˈjuːʒuəl/ *adjective* the same as happens most of the time: *I couldn't park my car **in the usual place*** (=the place where I park it most often). • *I'll see you **at the usual time*** (=the time that I most often see you). • *I ate more than usual* (=more than I would normally eat). • *Henry was late, **as usual*** (=Henry is often late).

u•su•al•ly /ˈjuːʒuəli/ *adverb* if something usually happens, it almost always happens: *I usually get up at about 8.* • *Saturday is usually our busiest day.*

u•ten•sil /juːˈtensəl/ *noun* (formal) a tool that you use for cooking: *kitchen utensils*

ut•most /ˈʌtməʊst $ ˈʌtmoʊst/ *adjective* (formal) the most that is possible: *He picked up the vase with the utmost care.*

ut•ter¹ /ˈʌtə $ ˈʌtɚ/ *adjective* (formal) complete or total: *a sense of utter helplessness* —**utterly** *adverb*: *The idea is utterly ridiculous.*

utter² *verb* to say something: *He looked at me without uttering a word.*

U-turn /ˈjuː tɜːn $ ˈju tɚn/ *noun* if the driver of a car does a U-turn, they turn the car round and go back in the direction they came from

Vv

v a written abbreviation of VERSUS

va·can·cy /ˈveɪkənsi/ *noun* (plural **vacancies**) **1** a room that is available in a hotel: *I'm sorry, we have no vacancies tonight.* **2** a job that is available for someone to do: *The company has a vacancy for a driver.*

va·cant /ˈveɪkənt/ *adjective* not being used SYNONYM **free** ANTONYM **occupied**: *We tried to find some vacant seats.*

va·ca·tion /vəˈkeɪʃən $ veɪˈkeɪʃən/ the American word for HOLIDAY

vac·cin·ate /ˈvæksəneɪt/ *verb* if you are vaccinated, a doctor gives you a vaccine to stop you getting a disease SYNONYM **immunize**: *Have you been vaccinated against measles?*

vac·cine /ˈvæksiːn $ vækˈsin/ *noun* a substance given to people to stop them getting a disease, which contains a very small amount of the GERM that causes the disease: *the measles vaccine*

vac·u·um¹ /ˈvækjuəm/ *noun* **1** a vacuum cleaner **2** a space that has no air in it

vacuum² *verb* to clean a place using a vacuum cleaner: *I need to vacuum the carpet.* ➔ see Thesaurus at CLEAN²

vacuum

ˈvacuum ˌcleaner *noun* a machine that cleans floors by sucking up dirt SYNONYM **Hoover™** *BrE*

vague /veɪɡ/ *adjective* not clear or definite: *His plans are rather vague at the moment.* —**vaguely** *adverb*: *I know vaguely where he lives.*

vain /veɪn/ *adjective* too proud of your appearance: *a vain, arrogant young man* ➔ see Thesaurus at PROUD

val·id /ˈvælɪd/ *adjective* **1** a valid ticket or document can be used and is officially correct ANTONYM **invalid**: *a valid passport* **2** a valid reason, argument, explanation etc seems reasonable and likely to be right: *a valid explanation for his behaviour*

val·ley /ˈvæli/ *noun* a low area of land between two hills or mountains

val·ua·ble /ˈvæljəbəl/ *adjective*
1 worth a lot of money: *a very valuable painting*
2 very useful SYNONYM **invaluable**: *She gave me some valuable advice.*

val·ua·bles /ˈvæljəbəlz/ *plural noun* small things that you own that are worth a lot of money

val·ue¹ /ˈvæljuː/ *noun*

KEY PATTERNS
the value of something

1 how much money something is worth: *What is **the total value of** the paintings in the collection?* • *Do you have anything **of value*** (=worth a lot of money) *in your bag?*
2 how important something is: *John **puts a high value on** honesty* (=he thinks honesty is very important).

value² *verb* to think that something is important: *I really value the time I spend with my friends.*

valve /vælv/ *noun* something that controls the flow of liquid or air passing through a tube: *There's a leak in the radiator valve in my bedroom.*

vam·pire /ˈvæmpaɪə $ ˈvæmpaɪə˞/ *noun* a person in stories who bites people's necks and sucks their blood

van /væn/ *noun* a large vehicle that is used for carrying goods ➔ see picture on page A11

van·dal /ˈvændl/ *noun* someone who deliberately damages public property

van·dal·is·m /ˈvændəlɪzəm/ *noun* (no plural) the crime of deliberately damaging public property

A B C D E F G H I J K L M N O P Q R S T U V W X Y Z

van·dal·ize also **vandalise** *BrE* /ˈvændəlaɪz/ *verb* to deliberately damage public property: *The train had been vandalized.*

va·nil·la /vəˈnɪlə/ *noun* (no plural) a substance with a slightly sweet taste, that you use to add taste to food: *vanilla ice cream*

van·ish /ˈvænɪʃ/ *verb*

KEY PATTERNS
vanish from somewhere

to disappear suddenly and in a way that people cannot explain: *My bike* ***vanished from*** *the shed overnight.* • *When I came outside again, the girl had vanished.*

van·i·ty /ˈvænəti/ *noun* (no plural) when someone is too proud of their appearance, their abilities etc: *Melony's friends respect her talent but dislike her vanity.*

va·pour *BrE*, **vapor** *AmE* /ˈveɪpə $ ˈveɪpɚ/ *noun* many small drops of liquid that float in the air: *a cloud of water vapour*

var·i·a·ble /ˈveəriəbəl $ ˈveriəbəl/ *adjective* likely to change often: *The weather is quite variable at this time of year.*

var·i·ant /ˈveəriənt $ ˈveriənt/ *noun* (formal) something that is slightly different from the usual form: *This tree is a variant of the English oak.* —**variant** *adjective*: *a variant spelling*

var·i·a·tion /ˌveəriˈeɪʃən $ ˌveriˈeɪʃən/ *noun* a change or difference: *We noticed huge price variations between different shops.* • *The variation in results might be due to a fault in the experiment.*

var·ied /ˈveərid $ ˈverid/ *adjective* consisting of many different types: *Try to eat a varied diet.*

va·ri·e·ty /vəˈraɪəti/ *noun* (plural **varieties**)

KEY PATTERNS
a variety of things

1 a type of something: *We tried three different* ***varieties of*** *cheese.* • *a new variety of apple*
2 (no plural) a lot of different kinds of things: *We sell* ***a wide variety of*** *books.*
3 (no plural) when things are different from each other and not all the same: *A good cinema should offer plenty of variety.*

var·i·ous /ˈveəriəs $ ˈveriəs/ *adjective* several different kinds: *There are various ways of sending money abroad.* • *I left my job for* ***various reasons.***

var·nish /ˈvɑːnɪʃ $ ˈvɑrnɪʃ/ *noun* a clear liquid that you paint onto wood to protect it and make it shine —**varnish** *verb*: *He varnished the front door.*

var·y /ˈveəri $ ˈveri/ *verb* (**varied**, **varies**) if things vary, they are all different from each other SYNONYM **differ**: *The rules vary from state to state.*

vase /vɑːz $ veɪs/ *noun* a container for flowers

PRONUNCIATION
British people pronounce **vase** like 'stars'.
American people pronounce **vase** like 'case'.

vast /vɑːst $ væst/ *adjective* very large SYNONYM **huge**: *a vast area of desert*
→ see Thesaurus at BIG

vat /væt/ *noun* a very large container for holding liquids: *a vat of wine*

vault¹ /vɔːlt/ *noun* a room in a bank with strong walls and doors, in which money, jewels etc can be kept safe

vault² *verb* to jump over something in one movement: *The thieves vaulted the wall and escaped.*

VCR /ˌviː siː ˈɑː $ ˌvi si ˈɑr/ *noun* a VIDEO CASSETTE RECORDER

VDU /ˌviː diː ˈjuː/ *noun* (visual display unit) a machine with a SCREEN that shows the information from a computer SYNONYM **monitor**

veal /viːl/ *noun* (no plural) meat from a young cow

veer /vɪə $ vɪr/ *verb* to change direction suddenly: *The car veered off the road and crashed.*

ve·gan /ˈviːgən/ *noun* someone who does not eat anything that is produced from animals —**vegan** *adj*

vege·ta·ble /ˈvedʒtəbəl/ *noun* a plant such as a potato or onion which is grown as food: *It's important to eat plenty of fresh vegetables.* → see picture on page A6

SPELLING
This word is often spelled wrongly. The correct spelling is **vegetable**.

veg·e·tar·i·an /ˌvedʒəˈteəriən $ ˌvedʒəˈteriən/ *noun* someone who does not eat meat or fish —**vegetarian** *adj*: *vegetarian food* (=food that does not contain meat)

veg·e·ta·tion /ˌvedʒəˈteɪʃən/ *noun* (no plural) the plants, flowers, and trees that grow in a particular area

ve·hi·cle /ˈviːɪkəl/ *noun* a thing such as a car or bus that is used for carrying people or things → see picture on page A11

veil /veɪl/ *noun* a piece of thin material that a woman wears to cover her face

vein /veɪn/ *noun* one of the tubes that carries blood around your body

Vel·cro /ˈvelkrəʊ $ ˈvelkroʊ/ *noun* (no plural) (trademark) a material you use for fastening things, made from two pieces of cloth that stick together → see picture at FASTENING

vel·vet /ˈvelvɪt/ *noun* (no plural) a type of material that is very thick and soft: *red velvet curtains*

ven·det·ta /venˈdetə/ *noun* (no plural) a serious argument between people which continues over a long time and often involves them trying to harm each other: *They were involved in a vendetta against their neighbours.*

ven·i·son /ˈvenɪsən/ *noun* (no plural) the meat of a DEER

ven·om /ˈvenəm/ *noun* (no plural) poison produced by snakes, insects etc

ven·o·mous /ˈvenəməs/ *adjective* a venomous snake or insect is poisonous: *a venomous spider*

vent /vent/ *noun* a hole in something that lets air in or lets smoke out

ven·ti·late /ˈventəleɪt $ ˈventlˌeɪt/ *verb* (formal) to allow air to come into and go out of a place —**ventilated** *adjective*: *a well-ventilated room*

ven·ture¹ /ˈventʃə $ ˈventʃɚ/ *noun* a new business activity that might earn money but involves taking risks: *an exciting new business venture*

venture² *verb* to go somewhere, especially when you are worried that something bad might happen: *Our cat rarely ventures outside the house.*

ven·ue /ˈvenjuː/ *noun* a place where a public event takes place: *a popular concert venue*

veranda

ve·ran·da, **verandah** /vəˈrændə/ *noun* a structure with a floor and a roof that is built outside a house's front or back door SYNONYM **porch** *AmE*

verb /vɜːb $ vɚb/ *noun* a word that describes an action, for example 'go', 'eat', or 'finish' → see pictures on pages A2, A3 & A4

verb·al /ˈvɜːbəl $ ˈvɚbəl/ *adjective* spoken rather than written: *He received a verbal warning.*

ver·dict /ˈvɜːdɪkt $ ˈvɚdɪkt/ *noun* an official decision in a court of law about whether someone is guilty

verge /vɜːdʒ $ vɚdʒ/ *noun* **be on the verge of (doing) something** to be about to do something: *Anita was on the verge of tears* (=she was almost crying).

ver·sa·tile /ˈvɜːsətaɪl $ ˈvɚsətl/ *adjective* having many different skills or uses: *a versatile actor*

verse /vɜːs $ vɚs/ *noun* a set of lines that form one part of a poem or song: *We will sing the first and third verses.*

ver·sion /ˈvɜːʃən $ ˈvɚʒən/ *noun* a form of something that is slightly different from others of the same type: *I prefer the original version of that song.*

ver·sus /ˈvɜːsəs $ ˈvɚsəs/ (written abbreviation **vs.** or **v**) *preposition* used to say that two teams or players are competing against each another: *Romania versus Hungary • England v Brazil*

ver·ti·cal /ˈvɜːtɪkəl $ ˈvɚtɪkəl/ *adjective* pointing straight upwards ANTONYM **horizontal**: *a vertical line*

ver·ti·go /ˈvɜːtɪɡəʊ $ ˈvɚtɪˌɡoʊ/ *noun* (no plural) a condition in which you feel dizzy and sick when you look down from a high place: *Do you suffer from vertigo?*

ve·ry /ˈveri/ *adverb* used to emphasize an adjective or adverb: *Joe looks very happy. • We finished the job very quickly. • I'm not very good at maths* (=not good at maths at all).

USAGE
Don't use **very** with these adjectives: **delicious, disgusting, horrible, terrible, incredible**, and **fantastic**.

ves·sel /ˈvesəl/ *noun* (formal) **1** a ship or large boat **2** a container for keeping liquids in

vest /vest/ *noun* **1** *BrE* a piece of underwear that you wear to keep the top part of your body warm → see picture at UNDERWEAR **2** the American word for WAISTCOAT

vet /vet/ *noun* someone who is trained to give medical treatment to sick animals SYNONYM **veterinarian** *AmE*

vet·e·ran /ˈvetərən/ *noun* someone who fought in a war: *a Vietnam veteran*

vet·e·ri·na·ri·an /ˌvetərəˈneəriən $ ˌvetərəˈneriən/ *noun* a vet

ve·to /ˈviːtəʊ $ ˈvitoʊ/ *verb* (**vetoes**) if someone in authority vetoes something, they refuse to allow it to happen: *The government has vetoed the proposals.* —**veto** *noun*: *France threatened to use its veto.*

vi·a /ˈvaɪə, ˈviːə/ *preposition* through a place: *The train goes via Washington.*

vi·a·duct /ˈvaɪədʌkt/ *noun* a long high bridge across a valley

vi·brant /ˈvaɪbrənt/ *adjective* full of excitement and energy SYNONYM **lively**: *New York is a very vibrant city.*

vi·brate /vaɪˈbreɪt $ ˈvaɪbreɪt/ *verb* to shake with small fast movements: *The windows vibrated in the wind.* → see Thesaurus at SHAKE[1]

vi·bra·tion /vaɪˈbreɪʃən/ *noun* a continuous shaking movement

vic·ar /ˈvɪkə $ ˈvɪkɚ/ *noun* a priest in the Church of England

vice /vaɪs/ *noun* a bad habit or a bad part of someone's character ANTONYM **virtue**: *Greed is not one of my vices.*

vice ver·sa /ˌvaɪs ˈvɜːsə $ ˌvaɪs ˈvɚsə/ *adverb* used to talk about the opposite of a situation you have just described: *Films that the boys like don't appeal to the girls, and vice versa.*

vi·cious /ˈvɪʃəs/ *adjective* violent and dangerous: *a vicious dog*

vic·tim /ˈvɪktɪm/ *noun* someone who has been hurt or killed: *the victims of the bomb attack*

vic·to·ri·ous /vɪkˈtɔːriəs/ *adjective* successful in a battle or competition: *The victorious team were celebrating a great win.*

vic·to·ry /ˈvɪktəri/ *noun* (plural **victories**) an occasion when someone wins a game, competition, or battle ANTONYM **defeat**: *Fans are celebrating the team's 7–1 victory over Roma. • The English troops won their first major victory.*

vid·e·o[1] /ˈvɪdiəʊ $ ˈvɪdioʊ/ *noun* **1** a tape on which a film or television programme has been recorded: *I watched the game **on video**.* **2** *BrE* a video cassette recorder

video[2] *verb* to record something, using a video cassette recorder or a camera SYNONYM **tape** *AmE*: *My father videoed the game so we could watch it later.*

ˌvideo casˈsette reˌcorder also **ˈvideo reˌcorder** (abbreviation **VCR**) *noun* a machine used for recording television programmes or playing videotapes

ˈvideo ˌgame *noun* a computer game you play by pressing buttons to move pictures on a SCREEN

vid·e·o·tape /ˈvɪdiəʊˌteɪp $ ˈvɪdioʊˌteɪp/ *noun* a long narrow band of material in a plastic container, on which you can record films, television programmes etc

A B C D E F G H I J K L M N O P Q R S T U V W X Y Z

view /vjuː/ *noun*

KEY PATTERNS
someone's views on/about a subject
somebody's view is that
in my/her/our view
a view of a place
the view from a building/mountain

1 an opinion or belief about something: *What are your* ***views on*** *animal rights? • John has very strong* ***views about*** *education. •* ***Their view was that*** *the problem could be solved using new technology. •* ***In my view****, the law needs to be changed. • The government should listen to the* ***views of*** *the people.* → see Thesaurus at OPINION **2** the things that you can see from a place, especially when this is very beautiful or interesting: *We bought a house with a* ***view of*** *the beach. • There are great* ***views from*** *the top of the mountain.*

view·er /ˈvjuːə $ ˈvjuɚ/ *noun* someone who watches television: *The programme attracted over 2 million viewers.*

vig·il /ˈvɪdʒəl/ *noun* when people stand or sit quietly somewhere as a way of showing their feelings of sadness: *Her family kept a vigil by her hospital bed.*

vig·i·lant /ˈvɪdʒələnt/ *adjective* (formal) watching what happens carefully, so that you notice anything dangerous or illegal: *The police have asked people to be vigilant and to report any suspicious-looking packages immediately.*

vig·o·rous /ˈvɪgərəs/ *adjective* using a lot of effort and energy: *a vigorous walk in the mountains*

vile /vaɪl/ *adjective* very unpleasant SYNONYM **horrible**: *That's a vile colour!*

vil·la /ˈvɪlə/ *noun* a large house in the countryside or near the sea, used especially for holidays

vil·lage /ˈvɪlɪdʒ/ *noun* a place in the countryside where people live, that is smaller than a town

vil·lain /ˈvɪlən/ *noun* a bad person in a book or film: *The villain gets caught at the end of the film.*

vin·dic·tive /vɪnˈdɪktɪv/ *adjective* deliberately cruel and unfair: *None of what she said was true – she was just being vindictive.*

vine /vaɪn/ *noun* a climbing plant, especially one that produces GRAPES

vin·e·gar /ˈvɪnɪgə $ ˈvɪnɪgɚ/ *noun* (no plural) a very sour liquid that you use to add FLAVOUR to food: *oil and vinegar salad dressing*

vine·yard /ˈvɪnjəd $ ˈvɪnjɚd/ *noun* an area of land where people grow GRAPES to make wine

vin·tage /ˈvɪntɪdʒ/ *adjective* **1** vintage wine is good quality wine: *a 1941 vintage wine* **2** a vintage car is one that was made a long time ago but is still in good condition and is still used today

vi·nyl /ˈvaɪnl/ *noun* (no plural) a type of strong plastic

vi·o·la /viˈəʊlə $ viˈoʊlə/ *noun* a wooden musical instrument, similar to a VIOLIN, but bigger

vi·o·lence /ˈvaɪələns/ *noun* (no plural) when people attack, hurt, or kill other people: *There is too much violence shown on television. • We always said that we would never* ***resort to violence*** (=use violence). *• The police deal with many cases of* ***domestic violence*** (=when one member of a family deliberately hurts another) *each week.*

vi·o·lent /ˈvaɪələnt/ *adjective* **1** a violent person attacks, hurts, or kills other people: *The man was* ***becoming violent****, so I called the police. • a* ***violent attack*** **2** a violent film or television programme shows people trying to hurt or kill each other: *The film contains some very violent scenes.* —**violently** *adverb*

vi·o·lin /ˌvaɪəˈlɪn/ *noun* a wooden musical instrument that you hold under your chin and play by pulling a special stick across four strings

violin

VIP /ˌviː aɪ ˈpiː/ *noun* (very important person) someone who receives special treatment because they are famous or powerful

vi·per /ˈvaɪpə $ ˈvaɪpɚ/ *noun* a small poisonous snake

vir·gin¹ /ˈvɜːdʒɪn $ ˈvɚdʒɪn/ *noun* someone who has never had sex

virgin² *adjective* virgin land has never been used or spoiled by people: *300 acres of virgin forest*

vir·ile /ˈvɪraɪl $ ˈvɪrəl/ *adjective* a virile man has a strong, sexually attractive body

vir·tu·al /ˈvɜːtʃuəl $ ˈvɚtʃuəl/ *adjective* **1** very close to being something: *Even a virtual beginner can use this computer.* **2** using virtual reality: *a virtual library* ➔ see Thesaurus at ARTIFICIAL

vir·tu·al·ly /ˈvɜːtʃuəli $ ˈvɚtʃuəli/ *adverb* almost completely: *The town was virtually empty.*

ˌvirtual reˈality *noun* (no plural) when a computer makes you feel as though you are in a real situation or place by showing pictures and sounds

vir·tue /ˈvɜːtʃuː $ ˈvɚtʃu/ *noun* a good quality in someone's character ANTONYM **vice**: *Honesty is a virtue I really admire.*

vir·tu·o·so /ˌvɜːtʃuˈəʊsəʊ $ ˌvɚtʃuˈoʊsoʊ/ *noun* (formal) someone who has great skill in music: *Nigel Kennedy, the violin virtuoso*

vir·tu·ous /ˈvɜːtʃuəs $ ˈvɚtʃuəs/ *adjective* behaving in a way that is morally good or kind ANTONYM **wicked**: *a decent virtuous man*

vi·rus /ˈvaɪərəs $ ˈvaɪrəs/ *noun* (plural **viruses**) **1** a very small living thing that causes diseases: *the flu virus* **2** a computer program that can destroy or damage information stored in the computer: *Many viruses are spread by software downloaded from the Internet.*

vi·sa /ˈviːzə/ *noun* an official document that allows you to enter or leave a country: *You need a visa to visit the US.* • *Have you got your entry visa yet?*

vis·i·bil·i·ty /ˌvɪzəˈbɪləti/ *noun* (no plural) the distance you are able to see ahead of you: *The pilot reported poor visibility before the crash.*

vis·i·ble /ˈvɪzəbəl/ *adjective* if something is visible, you can see it ANTONYM **invisible**: *The house was only just visible behind the trees.* —**visibly** *adverb*: *She was visibly upset.*

vi·sion /ˈvɪʒən/ *noun*
1 your ideas or hopes about what the world could be like in the future: *Gandhi had a vision of a better, more peaceful society.*
2 (no plural) your ability to see SYNONYM **sight**: *An airline pilot needs to have good vision.*

vis·it¹ /ˈvɪzɪt/ *verb*
1 to go and spend time with someone: *Granny is visiting us next weekend.* • *I went to visit Simon in hospital.* • *You must **come and visit** me some time.*
2 to go and spend a short time in a place: *We're hoping to visit Rome while we're in Italy.*
3 to look at a website on the Internet: *I visited their website to find out more about the company.*

visit² *noun*
an occasion when someone visits a place or a person: *The president made a speech during his **visit to** China.* • *I've just **had a visit from** Mr Heaney* (=Mr Heaney has just visited me).

vis·it·or /ˈvɪzətə $ ˈvɪzətɚ/ *noun* someone who visits a place or person: *Visitors to the building must wear a name tag.* • *I didn't realize that you had visitors.*

vi·sor /ˈvaɪzə $ ˈvaɪzɚ/ *noun* the front part of a HELMET (=hard hat) that comes down in front of your eyes to protect them

vi·su·al /ˈvɪʒuəl/ *adjective* related to your ability to see and things that you see: *an exhibition of visual arts*

ˌvisual ˈaid *noun* something that people can see, such as a picture or film, that is used to help them learn something

vi·su·al·ize also **visualise** *BrE* /ˈvɪʒuəlaɪz/ *verb* (formal) to imagine something: *I tried to visualize myself winning the race.*

vi·tal /ˈvaɪtl/ *adjective* very important: *It's vital to concentrate when you are driving.* ➔ see Thesaurus at NECESSARY

vit·a·min /ˈvɪtəmən $ ˈvaɪtəmɪn/ *noun* a natural chemical in food that keeps you healthy: *Oranges contain a lot of vitamin C.*

PRONUNCIATION
British people pronounce the first syllable of **vitamin** like 'lit'.
American people pronounce the first syllable of **vitamin** like 'light'.

vi·va·cious /vɪ'veɪʃəs/ *adjective* a vivacious person has a lot of energy and enjoys life SYNONYM **lively**

viv·id /'vɪvɪd/ *adjective* vivid descriptions or memories are very clear: *a vivid description of the accident* —**vividly** *adverb*: *I can remember my childhood vividly.*

vo·cab·u·la·ry /və'kæbjələri $ voʊ'kæbjəˌleri/ *noun* (plural **vocabularies**) **1** your vocabulary is all the words you know: *Our teacher wants us to improve our vocabulary.* **2** all the words in a language: *English has a very large vocabulary.*

vo·cal /'vəʊkəl $ 'voʊkəl/ *adjective* related to the human voice

vo·cal·ist /'vəʊkəlɪst $ 'voʊkəlɪst/ *noun* someone who sings with a group playing popular music: *She was a vocalist in a successful band.*

vo·cals /'vəʊkəlz $ 'voʊkəlz/ *plural noun* the part of a popular song that someone sings, rather than the part played by instruments: *The vocals were recorded separately.*

vo·ca·tion /vəʊ'keɪʃən $ voʊ'keɪʃən/ *noun* if you have a vocation, you have a strong feeling that you should do a particular job, especially a job that involves helping people: *He discovered his vocation as a nurse in a large hospital.*

vo·ca·tion·al /vəʊ'keɪʃənəl $ voʊ'keɪʃənəl/ *adjective* concerned with teaching or learning the skills you need to do a job: *vocational education and training*

vod·ka /'vɒdkə $ 'vɑdkə/ *noun* (no plural) a strong alcoholic drink from Russia that has no colour and looks like water

vogue /vəʊg $ voʊg/ *noun* **be in vogue** to be fashionable and popular: *Long hair is in vogue this year.*

voice /vɔɪs/ *noun* your voice is the sound you make when you speak or sing: *I could hear voices outside.* • *Lynda has a beautiful voice when she sings.*

PHRASES
keep your voice down (informal) to speak quietly: *Keep your voice down – I don't want them to hear us!*
lose your voice to not be able to speak, for example because of an illness: *The concert was cancelled when the lead singer **lost** his **voice**.*

voice·mail /'vɔɪsˌmeɪl/ *noun* (no plural) a system that records telephone calls so that you can listen to them later: *I left a message on your voicemail.*

void /vɔɪd/ *adjective* (formal) not legally or officially acceptable: *The result of the race was declared void.*

vol·a·tile /'vɒlətaɪl $ 'vɑlətl/ *adjective* **1** someone who is volatile often changes suddenly from being happy to being angry or upset: *The boss had a volatile temper.* **2** a volatile situation is one that is likely to change suddenly and become worse: *The stock market is very volatile at the moment.*

vol·ca·no /vɒl'keɪnəʊ $ vɑl'keɪnoʊ/ *noun* (plural **volcanoes** or **volcanos**) a mountain that sometimes explodes, sending out fire and hot rocks

vol·ley /'vɒli $ 'vɑli/ *noun* a volley of bullets or stones is a large number of them moving through the air at the same time

vol·ley·ball /'vɒlibɔːl $ 'vɑliˌbɔl/ *noun* (no plural) a game in which two teams hit a ball to each other across a high net with their hands and try to keep the ball off the ground

volt /vəʊlt $ voʊlt/ (abbreviation **v**) *noun* a unit for measuring the force of an electric current: *a 12-volt battery*

vol·ume /'vɒljuːm $ 'vɑljəm/ *noun* (no plural) the amount of sound a television, radio etc produces: *Turn up the volume – I really like this song.*

vol·un·ta·ri·ly /'vɒləntərəli $ ˌvɑlən'terəli/ *adverb* if you do something voluntarily, you do it because you want to, not because you have to: *She left the country voluntarily.*

vol·un·ta·ry /'vɒləntəri $ 'vɑlənˌteri/ *adjective* voluntary activities are ones that you do because you want to, not because you are being paid or forced to ANTONYM **compulsory**: *Have you thought of doing some voluntary work at the hospital?*

vol·un·teer¹ /ˌvɒlənˈtɪə $ ˌvɑlənˈtɪr/ *verb* to offer to do something without being told to: *I volunteered to clean the house.*

volunteer² *noun* someone who offers to do a job without being paid or forced to do it: *The shop is run by volunteers.*

vom·it /ˈvɒmɪt $ ˈvɑmɪt/ *verb* (formal) if you vomit, food comes up from your stomach and out of your mouth —**vomit** *noun* (no plural): *The car seats were covered in vomit.*

vote¹ /vəʊt $ voʊt/ *verb*

KEY PATTERNS
vote for someone/something
vote to do something
vote on a subject

to choose which person you want to elect or which plan you support by making a mark on a piece of paper or raising your hand: *Who are you going to vote for in the student elections?* • *The government has voted to increase taxes.*

vote² *noun*

KEY PATTERNS
a vote for someone/something
a vote against someone/something

1 a choice that you make to support a particular person or group of people by making a mark on a piece of paper or raising your hand in the air: *There were 603* ***votes for*** *Mr Jameson, and only 16* ***against.*** • *We spent three hours counting the votes.* • *The Communists won 22% of* ***the vote*** (=won 22% of the votes).
2 an occasion when people decide something by voting: *We* ***held a vote*** *to decide who would lead the team.* • *Since we can't agree, let's* ***take a vote on it.***
3 have the vote, get the vote people who have the vote are allowed to vote: *It was years before women* ***got the vote.***

vot·er /ˈvəʊtə $ ˈvoʊtɚ/ *noun* someone who votes or has the right to vote

vot·ing /ˈvəʊtɪŋ $ ˈvoʊtɪŋ/ *noun* (no plural) when people vote in an election or in a meeting: *Voting ends at 10.00 pm tonight.*

vouch /vaʊtʃ/ *verb* **1 vouch for something** if you vouch for something, you say that you know it is correct or true **2 vouch for someone** if you vouch for someone, you say that you know they are a good and honest person and people can trust them

vouch·er /ˈvaʊtʃə $ ˈvaʊtʃɚ/ *noun* a ticket that you can use instead of money: *free cinema vouchers*

vow /vaʊ/ *verb* (formal) to make a serious promise that you will definitely do something: *After he lost, he vowed that he would return for next year's championship.* ➔ see Thesaurus at PROMISE¹ —**vow** *noun*: *She made a vow to give up drinking.*

vow·el /ˈvaʊəl/ *noun* one of the sounds shown by the letters a, e, i, o, or u

voy·age /ˈvɔɪ-ɪdʒ/ *noun* a long trip in a ship or space vehicle: *a round-the-world voyage* • *the long voyage from Ireland to America* ➔ see Thesaurus at TRAVEL²

vs. a written abbreviation of VERSUS

vul·gar /ˈvʌlgə $ ˈvʌlgɚ/ *adjective* rude and likely to offend people: *Some of the language in the play is rather vulgar.*

vul·ne·ra·ble /ˈvʌlnərəbəl/ *adjective* not protected and therefore likely to be hurt or damaged: *Elderly people living alone are very vulnerable.* • *The town is very vulnerable to attack.*

vul·ture /ˈvʌltʃə $ ˈvʌltʃɚ/ *noun* a large wild bird that eats dead animals

vulture

Ww

W the written abbreviation of WEST or WESTERN

wade /weɪd/ *verb* to walk through deep water: *We waded across the river.*

wade

waft /wɑːft/ *verb* to move gently through the air: *The smell of cooking wafted in through the upstairs window.*

wag /wæg/ *verb* (**wagged, wagging**) if a dog wags its tail, it moves it from side to side

wage /weɪdʒ/ *noun* also **wages** the money that a worker gets for doing their job: *People who work in hotel kitchens often get paid low wages.* • *They promised us a wage increase.* ➔ see Thesaurus at PAY[2]

wag·on /ˈwægən/ *noun* a strong vehicle with four wheels that is pulled by a horse

wail /weɪl/ *verb* to cry loudly: *The children started to wail with hunger.* —**wail** *noun*: *the wails of the baby*

waist /weɪst/ *noun* the narrow part around the middle of your body: *She has a slim waist.* ➔ see picture on page A5

waist·coat /ˈweɪskəʊt $ ˈweskət/ *noun BrE* a piece of clothing with buttons down the front and no arms, which you usually wear over a shirt SYNONYM **vest** *AmE*

wait[1] /weɪt/ *verb*

KEY PATTERNS
wait for someone/something
wait to do something

wait

They are waiting for the bus.

to stay in one place because you are expecting a particular thing to come or happen: *I read a magazine while I was waiting.* • *Three people **were waiting for** the bus.* • ***Wait for me!*** • *He waited a few minutes **to** see what would happen.* • *We had to **wait until** the police arrived.*

PHRASES

can't wait (spoken) used when saying that you want to do something very much: ***I can't wait to** get back home.*

wait tables *AmE* to serve food in a restaurant to people who are sitting at the tables: *He got an evening job **waiting tables**.*

PHRASAL VERBS

wait around
to do nothing because you are waiting for a particular thing to happen: *We spent the afternoon **waiting around** at the airport.*

wait on
wait on someone/someone's table to serve food to someone at the table where they are sitting: *He got a job **waiting on** tables in a cafe.*

wait up
to not go to bed because you are waiting for someone to come home: *I'll be late, so don't **wait up**.* • *When I got back at midnight, my dad was **waiting up for** me.*

wait[2] *noun* (no plural) a period of time when you wait for something to happen: *You'll have a long wait for the next bus.*

wait·er /ˈweɪtə $ ˈweɪtɚ/ *noun* a man who serves food in a restaurant

ˈwaiting ˌlist *noun* a list of people who are waiting to have something that is not available for them now: *There's a long waiting list for eye operations.* •

We've been on the waiting list for a new flat for six months.

ˈwaiting ˌroom *noun* a room where people wait to see someone or do something: *the doctor's waiting room*

wait·ress /ˈweɪtrəs/ *noun* (plural **waitresses**) a woman who serves food in a restaurant

wake¹ /weɪk/ *verb* (**woke** /wəʊk $ woʊk/ **woken** /ˈwəʊkən $ ˈwoʊkən/) also **wake up** if you wake, or if something wakes you, you stop sleeping: ***Wake up****, Sam, your breakfast is ready.* • *Guy was woken by a loud noise.* • *Can you* ***wake me up*** *at 7.00 tomorrow?*

wake

wake² *noun* the waves that a ship leaves behind as it moves along

walk¹ /wɔːk/ *verb*

KEY PATTERNS
walk to school/the station
walk down the street
walk home

to move forwards by putting one foot in front of the other: *I usually* ***walk to*** *college.* • *I saw him* ***walking down*** *the street in front of me.* • *They* ***walked*** *home in silence.* • *Do you want to* ***walk*** *along the beach?* • *I* ***walked up*** *the steps to the front door.*

PHRASAL VERBS

walk away
to leave a difficult situation or problem and not try to deal with it: *Henry's marriage was not happy, but he couldn't just* ***walk away*** *and leave his children.* • *You can't deal with your problems by* ***walking away from*** *them.*

walk off with (informal)
walk off with something to steal something: *Someone* ***has walked off with*** *my camera.*

walk out on
walk out on someone to leave your family suddenly and go to live somewhere else: *Dad* ***walked out on*** *us when I was five.*

THESAURUS
march: *She* ***marched*** *into his office and demanded an explanation* (=walked in a quick, determined way). • *The soldiers* ***marched*** *along the road* (=walked with regular steps).
stroll: *You can* ***stroll*** *around the gardens* (=walk in a slow relaxed way).
trudge: *We* ***trudged*** *back home* (=walked with slow heavy steps because we were tired).

walk² *noun*
1 a journey that you make by walking: *We always* ***go for a walk*** *on Sundays.* • *The students* ***went on a long walk****.* • *The hotel is a ten-minute walk away* (=it takes ten minutes to walk there). • *It's only* ***a short walk to*** *the station from here.*
2 a path that people can walk along for pleasure: *There are some lovely walks in the area.*

USAGE
You say **go for a walk** or **take a walk**.
✘ Don't say 'make a walk'.

ˈwalking ˌstick *noun* a long stick that people who are old or ill use to help them walk

Walk·man /ˈwɔːkmən/ *noun* (trademark) a small machine that plays CASSETTES or CDs. You carry it with you and listen through EARPHONES SYNONYM **personal stereo**

wall /wɔːl/ *noun*
1 one of the sides of a room or building: *There was a map of the world on the wall.* • *The room had blue walls and a white ceiling.*
2 a narrow brick or stone structure that is built around an area of land or between two areas: *He crashed his car into a brick wall.*

wal·let /ˈwɒlɪt $ ˈwɑlɪt/ *noun* a small flat case that you use for carrying paper money

wallet

wall·pa·per /ˈwɔːlˌpeɪpə $ ˈwɔlˌpeɪpɚ/ *noun* (no plural) paper that you stick on the walls of a room to

A B C D E F G H I J K L M N O P Q R S T U V W X Y Z

decorate it —**wallpaper** *verb*: *Dad's wallpapering my bedroom this weekend.*

wal·nut /ˈwɔːlnʌt/ *noun* a type of tree that produces nuts, which are called walnuts → see picture on page A7

waltz /wɔːls $ wɔlts/ *noun* (plural **waltzes**) a dance with sets of three steps, or a piece of music for this dance: *the last waltz of the evening* —**waltz** *verb*: *They waltzed around the room.*

wan /wɒn $ wɑn/ *adjective* (written) looking pale, weak, or tired

wand /wɒnd $ wɑnd/ *noun* a long thin stick that you hold in your hand when you are doing magic tricks: *He waved his wand, and a rabbit appeared.*

wan·der /ˈwɒndə $ ˈwɑndɚ/ *verb*
1 to walk somewhere quite slowly and with no particular purpose: *A group of tourists* ***wandered around*** *the museum. • Derek stood up and* ***wandered over to*** *the window.*
2 if your mind or your thoughts wander, you stop paying attention to something and think about other things instead: *Her* ***attention*** *was beginning to* ***wander*** *and she looked around the room.*

wane /weɪn/ *verb* if someone's power, support, or interest wanes, it becomes less: *My enthusiasm for golf was starting to wane.* —**wane** *noun* (no plural): *His popularity is on the wane* (=becoming less).

wan·na·be /ˈwɒnəbi $ ˈwɑnəbi/ *noun* (informal) someone who tries to be like a famous person, although this is not sensible: *a Madonna wannabe*

want /wɒnt $ wʌnt/ *verb*

KEY PATTERNS
want something
want to do something
want someone to do something (for you)

to wish or need to have or do something: *What do you want for your birthday? • Do you want something to eat, Nancy? • She* ***wants to*** *be a doctor. • Do you* ***want me to*** *help you with your bags?*

USAGE
When you want to have something such as food or drink, don't say 'I want ...'. Say **I'd like** ... , for example: ***I'd like*** *some more tea.*
Often you use a question: ***Can I*** *have another coffee?*, or in more polite English: ***May I*** *have a glass of water?*

want·ed /ˈwɒntɪd $ ˈwʌntɪd/ *adjective* if someone is wanted, the police are looking for them because they may have done something illegal: *a wanted man • He is wanted for murder.*

war /wɔː $ wɔr/ *noun*

KEY PATTERNS
a war with another country
a war between two countries
the war against crime/drugs/terrorism

1 a period of fighting between two or more countries or states: *the* ***war with*** *Nazi Germany • the* ***war between*** *Greece and Troy • He was a prisoner during the Vietnam War. • The two countries* ***have been at war*** (=have been fighting) *for three years. • France* ***went to war with*** *England. •* ***War broke out*** (=started) *on August 4th.*
2 when people try to stop something bad from happening: *The police are losing* ***the war against crime.***

ward[1] /wɔːd $ wɔrd/ *noun* a room in a hospital with beds in it, where sick people stay

ward[2] *verb* **ward something off** to stop something bad from affecting you: *Keep warm in winter to ward off colds.*

war·den /ˈwɔːdn $ ˈwɔrdn/ *noun* someone whose job is to look after an area or the people who live in a large building: *He is the warden of a block of flats for old people.*

ward·er /ˈwɔːdə $ ˈwɔrdɚ/ *noun BrE* someone whose job is to guard people in prison

ward·robe /ˈwɔːdrəʊb $ ˈwɔrdroʊb/ *noun BrE* a large cupboard where you keep your clothes SYNONYM **closet** *AmE*

ware·house /ˈweəhaʊs $ ˈwerhaʊs/ *noun* a large building for storing materials or things that will be sold

war·fare /ˈwɔːfeə $ ˈwɔrfer/ *noun* (no plural) (formal) the fighting in a war: *We are all aware of the dangers of nuclear warfare.*

war·like /ˈwɔːlaɪk $ ˈwɔrlaɪk/ *adjective* warlike countries or people like fighting wars

warm¹ /wɔːm $ wɔrm/ *adjective*
1 quite hot: *It's lovely and warm in this room.* • *Cover the bowl to keep the soup warm.* • *It was a warm day, so we sat outside.* → see Thesaurus at HOT¹
2 warm clothes stop you from feeling cold: *I must buy a warm coat to wear this winter.*
3 friendly: *We gave the visiting students* ***a warm welcome.*** → see Thesaurus at FRIENDLY —**warmly** *adverb*

warm² *verb* **1** also **warm up** to make something warm, or to become warmer: *I can warm some soup if you're hungry.* • *The weather is expected to warm up this weekend.*
2 warm up to do gentle exercises to prepare your body before doing a sport, or exercising: *It's important to warm up before you start running.*

ˌwarm-ˈhearted *adjective* kind

warmth /wɔːmθ $ wɔrmθ/ *noun* (no plural) the heat that something produces: *the warmth of the sun*

ˈwarm-up *noun* a set of gentle exercises that you do to prepare for a sport: *We always do a ten-minute warm-up before the game.*

warn /wɔːn $ wɔrn/ *verb*

> KEY PATTERNS
> **warn someone that**
> **warn that**
> **warn someone about/of danger**
> **warn someone to do something**
> **warn someone not to do something**

1 to tell someone about a danger, so that they can be careful or can prepare for it: *The police* ***have warned*** *drivers* ***that*** *the roads are dangerous.* • *Scientists* ***have warned that*** *there will be more storms in future.* • *It is important that we* ***warn*** *young people* ***about*** *the dangers of drugs.* • *No one* ***warned*** *me* ***of*** *the risks of this treatment.*
2 to tell someone to do something or not to do something, because there is danger: *I* ***warned*** *you* ***to*** *drive slowly!* • *They* ***warned*** *us* ***not to*** *go out at night.*

warn·ing /ˈwɔːnɪŋ $ ˈwɔrnɪŋ/ *noun* something that tells you that something bad or dangerous is likely to happen: *The police* ***received a warning*** *just before the bomb exploded.* • *The wall collapsed* ***without warning.***

warp /wɔːp $ wɔrp/ *verb* if wood or metal warps, it becomes bent or twisted

war·rant /ˈwɒrənt $ ˈwɔrənt/ *noun* an official document that allows the police to search someone's house or take someone to a police station: *The police have a warrant for his arrest.*

war·ren /ˈwɒrən $ ˈwɔrən/ *noun* a group of holes underground where wild rabbits live

war·ri·or /ˈwɒriə $ ˈwɔriə/ *noun* a very brave person who fought in battles in the past

war·ship /ˈwɔːˌʃɪp $ ˈwɔrˌʃɪp/ *noun* a ship with guns that is used in wars

wart /wɔːt $ wɔrt/ *noun* a small hard raised spot that grows on your skin

war·y /ˈweəri $ ˈweri/ *adjective* (**warier, wariest**) careful because you think that someone or something may harm you: *Children should be wary of strangers.*

was /wəz; strong wɒz $ wʌz/ the past tense of BE which you use after 'I', 'he', 'she', and 'it'

wash¹ /wɒʃ $ wɑʃ/ *verb*

> KEY PATTERNS
> **wash your clothes/hands/hair**
> **wash the dishes**
> **wash something with soap**
> **wash something in (hot/cold) water**
> **get washed**

1 to clean something using soap and water: *Have you washed my shirt?* • ***Wash your hands with*** *soap after touching raw meat.* • *I had to* ***wash*** *my* ***hair in*** *cold water.* • *It's your turn to* ***wash the dishes*** (=wash the plates etc after a meal). → see Thesaurus at CLEAN²

A B C D E F G H I J K L M N O P Q R S T U V W X Y Z

2 if you wash or get washed, you clean your body with soap and water: *My brother **got washed** quickly and left for work.*

PHRASAL VERBS

wash away

wash something away if water washes something away, it removes it: *The heavy rains **washed away** the river bank.*

wash down

wash something down if you wash down food, you drink something while you eat, to help you swallow it: *Ari took a big bite of his sandwich, and **washed it down** with a mouthful of tea.*

wash up

1 wash up, wash something up *BrE* to wash the plates, dishes etc after a meal: *It's your turn to **wash up**. • Carrie was **washing** the cups **up**.*

2 wash up *AmE* to wash your hands

wash² *noun*

1 have a wash to wash your body with soap and water: *Isn't it time you **had a wash**?*

2 give something a wash to clean something with soap and water: *I'll **give** the car **a wash** later.*

3 be in the wash if your clothes are in the wash, they are being washed: *I can't wear my best shirt because it **is in the wash**.*

wash·ba·sin /ˈwɒʃˌbeɪsən $ ˈwɑʃˌbeɪsən/ *noun* a SINK that you use for washing your hands and face

washing

Sue is doing the washing.

Joe is washing up.

wash·ing /ˈwɒʃɪŋ $ ˈwɑʃɪŋ/ *noun BrE*

1 (no plural) clothes, sheets etc that you need to wash or have just washed SYNONYM **wash** *AmE*: *There were piles of dirty washing all over the flat.* **2 do the washing** to wash dirty clothes, sheets etc

ˈwashing maˌchine *noun* a machine that washes clothes

ˌwashing-ˈup *noun BrE* **do the washing-up** to wash the plates, dishes etc after a meal SYNONYM **do the dishes** *AmE*: *It's your turn to do the washing-up.*

was·n't /ˈwɒzənt $ ˈwʌzənt/ the short form of 'was not': *He wasn't happy.*

wasp /wɒsp $ wɑsp/ *noun* a flying insect with a black and yellow body, which can sting

waste¹ /weɪst/ *verb*

KEY PATTERNS
waste money/time/energy (on something)
waste money/time/energy doing something

if you waste something, you use more than you need to, or you do not use it in a sensible way: *I **wasted** £500 **on** that piano! • I don't want to **waste money** buying books I won't read. • Let's not **waste** any more **time** arguing. • Don't **waste** your **energy** worrying about things you can't change.*

PHRASAL VERBS

waste away

to slowly become thinner and weaker because of an illness: *Her muscles became weaker and gradually **wasted away**.*

waste² *noun*

KEY PATTERNS
a waste of money/time/energy

1 (no plural) when you use more of something than you need to, or you do not use it in a sensible way: *Buying expensive clothes for young children is **a waste of money**. • Don't leave the lights on – it's **a waste of** electricity. • Are you throwing that food away? What a waste!*

2 the parts of something that you have not used and do not need: *You can feed chickens on kitchen waste.*

→ see Thesaurus at RUBBISH

waste·bas·ket /ˈweɪstˌbɑːskɪt $ ˈweɪstˌbæskɪt/ *noun* a WASTEPAPER BASKET → see picture at BASKET

waste·ful /ˈweɪstfəl/ *adjective* using much more of something than you should: *a wasteful use of water*

waste·land /ˈweɪstlænd/ *noun* an area of unattractive land that is not being used for anything

waste·pa·per bas·ket /ˌweɪstˈpeɪpə ˌbɑːskɪt $ ˈweɪstˌpeɪpɚ ˌbæskɪt/ *noun* a container, especially one in a CLASSROOM or office, where you put paper and other small things that you no longer want

watch¹ → see box on page 756

watches

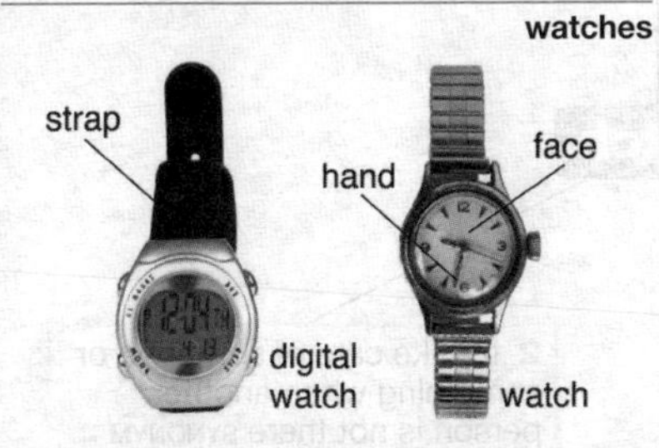

watch² *noun* (plural **watches**)
1 a small clock that you wear on your wrist: *It's 10 o'clock* ***by my watch.*** • *What time is it? I think my* ***watch has stopped*** (=is not working at the moment). → see picture at CLOCK
2 when you carefully watch a place or pay close attention to a situation: *Rosie stayed* ***on watch for*** *danger while her friends slept.* • *The president* ***is keeping a close watch on*** *the progress of the war.*

wa·ter¹ /ˈwɔːtə $ ˈwɔtɚ/ *noun*
1 (no plural) the clear liquid that falls from the sky as rain, and is in rivers and the sea: *a glass of water* • *I boiled some water to make tea.* • *She was struggling to keep her head* ***above water.*** • *The river flooded and the town was* ***under water.***
2 waters the sea, especially when it is close to a particular country: *The ship was not allowed to pass through French waters.*

water² *verb* **1** to pour water on a plant to help it grow: *George waters his roses every day.* **2** if your eyes water, they fill with tears because they are hurting: *The smoke made my eyes water.* **3** if food makes your mouth water, you want to eat it because it looks and smells good: *The smell of sausages made his mouth water.*

waterfall

wa·ter·fall /ˈwɔːtəfɔːl $ ˈwɔtɚˌfɔl/ *noun* water that is flowing over the edge of high rocks into a river or the sea

ˈwatering ˌcan *noun* a container that you use for pouring water on plants → see picture at GARDENING

wa·ter·logged /ˈwɔːtəˌlɒgd $ ˈwɔtɚˌlɔgd/ *adjective* waterlogged land is very wet: *After the rain, the football pitch was waterlogged.*

wa·ter·mel·on /ˈwɔːtəˌmelən $ ˈwɔtɚˌmelən/ *noun* a large round green fruit which is red inside with black seeds → see picture on page A7

wa·ter·proof /ˈwɔːtəpruːf $ ˈwɔtɚˌpruf/ *adjective* waterproof clothing or material does not let water in

ˈwater-ˌskiing *noun* (no plural) a sport in which someone wearing SKIS on their feet is pulled behind a boat over water

wa·ter·tight /ˈwɔːtətaɪt $ ˈwɔtɚˌtaɪt/ *adjective* a container that is watertight does not allow any water to get in or out

watt /wɒt $ wɑt/ *noun* a unit for measuring electrical power: *a 60 watt light bulb*

wave¹ /weɪv/ *verb*

> KEY PATTERNS
> **wave to/at someone**
> **wave goodbye to someone**
> **wave your arms/legs**
> **wave in the wind/air**

1 to move your hand from side to side in the air so that someone will see you: *The children* ***waved at*** *the queen as*

A B C D E F G H I J K L M N O P Q R S T U V W X Y Z

watch /wɒtʃ $ wɑtʃ/ *verb*

1 to pay attention with your eyes to something that is happening or moving: *All he does is **watch** television.* • *We **watched** a movie on TV.* • *I **went** to watch Jason play volleyball.* • *She **watched** him get out of the car.*

KEY PATTERNS
watch television/TV
watch a programme/film/game
watch someone do something

2 to take care of someone or something when another person is not there SYNONYM **look after**: *Carrie is going to **watch** the kids for me this afternoon.* • *Would you mind **watching** my bag for me? I'll be right back.*

3 to be careful about something, because you might have an accident or make a mistake SYNONYM **mind** *BrE*: ***Watch your head** – the ceiling's very low* (=be careful that you do not hit your head). • ***Watch** the traffic – cars drive very fast down here.* • *"Hey, **watch it!**" the truck driver yelled* (=be careful!).

WORD CHOICE
watch, **look at**, or **see**?
• You **watch** television, a film, an event, or a person. You usually **watch** things that are moving: *I like **watching** baseball.* • *I **watched** him get out of the car.* • *We spent the evening **watching** TV.* • *We **watched** television for a couple of hours.*
• You **look at** a picture, person, or thing deliberately, because you want to. You usually **look at** things that are not moving: *We **looked at** the map.* • *The man was **looking at** me.* • ***Look at** the view!*
• You **see** something or someone accidentally, or because you are trying to find them: *We **saw** some beautiful flowers.* • *I can't **see** her anywhere.*
✗ Don't say 'We looked at the television.'
Say: *We **watched** television.*

PHRASES

watch out
use this when someone should pay attention to what they are doing and be careful: *Charlie, **watch out!** The oven's hot.* • ***Watch out for** people trying to steal your wallet.*

watch your language
if you watch your language, you do not swear, especially because you do not want to offend the people you are with: *Mark, **watch your language** in front of Becky!*

her car passed. • *We* ***waved goodbye*** *to Dad.* • *The crowd waved and cheered when the singer appeared on stage.* • *His girlfriend came to* ***wave*** *him* ***off*** (=wave to him as he was leaving a place).
2 if you wave something, or it waves, it moves from side to side: *"Stop!" shouted Neil,* ***waving his arms.*** • *trees* ***waving in the wind***

wave² *noun*
1 a raised line of water that moves across the surface of a large area of water: *Big waves crashed against the side of the boat.*
2 the movement that you make with your hand when you wave to someone: *Dave* ***gave*** *us* ***a wave*** *as he passed.*
3 a sudden increase in a particular activity, especially one that is bad: *a crime wave* • *Who is responsible for the recent* ***wave of*** *bombings?*
4 the way that energy such as light and sound moves: *sound waves* • *radio waves*

wave·length /ˈweɪvleŋθ/ *noun* **1** the size of radio wave that a radio company uses to broadcast its programmes: *What wavelength is Radio 1 on?* **2 be on the same wavelength** (informal) if two people are on the same wavelength, they think about things in the same way: *We've never been on the same wavelength about music.*

wa·ver /ˈweɪvə $ ˈweɪvɚ/ *verb* to be uncertain about a decision for a short time: *Paul wavered for a few moments before accepting the offer.*

wav·y /ˈweɪvi/ *adjective* (**wavier**, **waviest**) **1** wavy hair has gentle curves and is not straight or curly: *wavy grey hair* **2** a wavy line has a series of curves in it

wax /wæks/ *noun* (no plural) a solid substance made of fats and oils which becomes soft when it is warm: *Wax polish protects your car against the weather.*

way → see box on pages 758 and 759

ˌway of ˈlife *noun* (plural **ways of life**) the typical or usual things that someone does: *The way of life in the countryside is different from the way that city people live.*

ˌway ˈout *noun* **the way out** a door through which you can leave a place SYNONYM **exit**

WC /ˌdʌbəljuː ˈsiː/ *noun BrE* a word for a toilet, which is used on signs

we /wiː/ *pronoun*
the person who is speaking and others: *We had a great time on holiday.* • *We had a maths test at school today.* • *We must protect the environment.*

weak /wiːk/ *adjective*
1 someone who is weak does not have much strength or energy ANTONYM **strong**: *At the end of the race he felt weak.*
2 if someone is weak, it is easy for other people to persuade them to do things ANTONYM **strong**: *He was too weak to say no.*
3 a weak student is not good at a subject: *The teacher gave special help to the weaker students.* • *Maths is my weakest subject* (=the one I am worst at).
4 a weak drink contains a lot of water and does not have a strong taste ANTONYM **strong**: *Do you like your coffee strong or weak?*

> **PRONUNCIATION**
> You pronounce **weak** like 'week'.

weak·en /ˈwiːkən/ *verb* to become less strong, or to make someone or something less strong ANTONYM **strengthen**: *Her long illness had weakened her.*

weak·ness /ˈwiːknəs/ *noun* **1** (no plural) when someone is not physically strong ANTONYM **strength**: *The illness causes tiredness and weakness.* **2** (no plural) when someone is not determined enough ANTONYM **strength**: *A strong leader does not show any sign of weakness.* **3** something that is bad about a plan, someone's character etc ANTONYM **strength**: *The system has both strengths and weaknesses.*

wealth /welθ/ *noun* (no plural)
the large amount of money and things that a rich person has: *She wanted to share her wealth with her friends.*

wealth·y /ˈwelθi/ *adjective* (**wealthier**, **wealthiest**) very rich: *a wealthy businessman* → see Thesaurus at RICH

way /weɪ/ *noun*

1 a method of doing something or the manner in which someone does something: *The Internet is a great* ***way to get*** *information quickly.* • *Can you think of any other* ***ways of*** *raising money?* • *I don't like* ***the way that*** *he treats people.* • *She was looking at me* ***in a strange way.*** • *I'm not sure that I'm doing this* ***in the right way.***

KEY PATTERNS
a way to do something
a way of doing something
the way (that) someone does something
in a particular way

way

2 the road, path etc that you must take in order to go to a place: *Excuse me, is this the* ***way to*** *the station?* • *He's trying to* ***find the way*** *on the map.* • *Why don't you drive, since you* ***know the way?***

He's trying to ***find the way*** *on the map.*

KEY PATTERNS
the way to the station/ hotel/airport
ask/tell someone the way

3 direction: *Is the TV aerial pointing* ***the right way?*** • *We must have gone* ***the wrong way.*** • *She turned and looked* ***the other way.*** • *The batteries are* ***the wrong way round*** (= they should be pointing in the opposite direction). • *Her house is* ***this way.***

4 distance: *It's* ***a long way*** *from my house to the station.* • *The park is just* ***a little way*** *up the road.* • *Becky ran* ***all the way*** *home.*

The park is just a ***little way*** *up the road.*

PHRASES

by the way (spoken)
say this when you want to tell someone about something you have just remembered: ***By the way**, have you heard from Tanya since she left?* • *Oh, Michael, **by the way**, Jim called about an hour ago.*

get in the way
if something gets in the way, it stops you doing what you want to do: *Hunger and tiredness can **get in the way** of learning anything at school.*

get out of the way
if someone or someone is out of the way, it is not stopping you from going somewhere, or seeing something: *She shouted, **"Get out of the way!"*** • *Here, let me move this bag **out of the way**.*

get your (own) way
to be able to do what you want, even when other people want to do something different: *If Hannah doesn't **get her own way**, she cries.*

in a way, in some ways
say this when you want to say something is true about a part of an event, a part of your feelings etc: *The holiday was great, but **in a way** I'll be glad to go back to work.* • ***In some ways**, we're a lot alike.*

in the way, in someone's way
if something is in the way or in your way, it is in front of you and stops you from going somewhere or seeing something: *A lot of people were standing **in the way**.*

no way! (spoken)
say this when you will not do or allow something: *You're not staying overnight at Ben's house. **No way!***

on the way, on someone's way
if you do something on the way or on your way to somewhere, you stop somewhere and do it when you are going to another place: *He stopped for a cup of coffee **on the way** to work.* • *I can pick Kerry up – her house is **on my way**.*

I can pick Kerry up – her house is ***on my way**.*

They stopped for a cup of coffee ***on the way** to work.*

on your way, on her way, on their way etc
if someone is on their way somewhere, they are travelling somewhere: *Jack's **on his way**; he called to say he'd be here by ten.*

way of life
how people live: *The **way of life** was very different in those days.*

GRAMMAR
✗ Don't say 'the way of living' when you mean **the way of life**.

weap·on /ˈwepən/ *noun* something that you use to fight with: *The weapon that he used was a knife.*

wear[1] /weə $ wer/ *verb* (**wore** /wɔː $ wɔr/ **worn** /wɔːn $ wɔrn/)
if you wear clothes, shoes, glasses etc, you have them on your body: *I decided to wear my blue dress.* • *Do you ever wear lipstick?*

PHRASAL VERBS

wear away

wear away, wear something away if something wears away, it slowly becomes thinner and disappears because something has rubbed it a lot: *The design on the necklace* ***has worn away.*** • *The movement of the waves* ***wears*** *the rocks* ***away.***

wear off

if a feeling or effect wears off, it slowly stops: *The effect of the drug takes a few hours to* ***wear off.***

wear out

1 wear out, wear something out if something wears out, or if you wear it out, it becomes damaged and useless because you have used it a lot: *One of the parts of the washing machine* ***had worn out.*** • *How do you manage to* ***wear out*** *your shoes so quickly?*

2 wear someone out (informal) to make someone very tired SYNONYM **exhaust**: *All these parties are* ***wearing*** *me* ***out!***

wear out

I have worn out my shoes.

PRONUNCIATION
You pronounce **wear** like 'air'.

WORD CHOICE
wear or **put on**?
• **Wear** means "to have clothes on your body": *She was* ***wearing*** *a long black dress.*
• **Put on** means "to put clothes on your body": *I* ***put on*** *a clean shirt.*

wear[2] *noun* **1 children's wear, women's wear etc** clothes for children, women etc: *The shop now has a very good women's wear department.* **2** (no plural) the damage that you cause to something when you use it a lot: *These old blankets are showing signs of wear.*

wear·y /ˈwɪəri $ ˈwɪri/ *adjective* very tired

wea·sel /ˈwiːzəl/ *noun* a small wild animal that looks like a long rat

weath·er /ˈweðə $ ˈweðɚ/ *noun* (no plural)

KEY PATTERNS
have good/bad weather
in good/bad weather

the weather in a place is the temperature and other conditions such as sun, rain, or wind: *Did you* ***have good weather*** *on your trip?* • *The weather was great!* • *You should drive more slowly* ***in wet weather.*** • *We had a week of lovely* ***hot weather.*** ➔ see picture on page A13

SPELLING
This word is often spelled wrongly. The correct spelling is: **weather**.

ˈweather-ˌbeaten *adjective* made rough by the wind and the sun: *a weather-beaten face*

ˈweather ˌforecast *noun* a report that says what the weather is expected to be like: *The weather forecast for tomorrow isn't very good.*

ˈweather ˌforecaster also **weath·er·man** /ˈweðəmæn $ ˈweðɚmæn/, **weath·er·girl** /ˈweðəɡɜːl $ ˈweðɚɡɚl/ *noun* someone whose job is to read the weather forecast on the television or radio

weave /wiːv/ *verb* (**wove** /wəʊv $ woʊv/ or **weaved**, **woven** /ˈwəʊvən $ ˈwoʊvən/ or **weaved**) **1** to make material by crossing threads under and over each other: *The women in the village sit together and weave rugs.* **2** to reach a place by moving around and between things: *Phil weaved through the crowd.*

web /web/ *noun* **1** a net of thin threads that a SPIDER makes **2 the Web** the WORLD WIDE WEB; a system that connects computers around the world so that people can use the INTERNET

webbed /webd/ *adjective* webbed feet have skin between the toes: *Ducks have webbed feet.*

web·cam /ˈwebkæm/ *noun* a video camera that shows what it is filming on a website: *You can watch the birds in their nest on a webcam.*

web·cast /ˈwebkɑːst $ ˈwebˌkæst/ *noun* a broadcast of an event such as a talk or a concert, which you can listen to or watch on the Internet: *A webcast of the lecture is available.*

web·log /ˈweblɒg $ ˈwebˌlɔg/ *noun* a webpage in which someone writes about their opinions, activities etc, which has the newest information first SYNONYM **blog**

web·page /ˈwebpeɪdʒ/ *noun* all the information that you can see in one part of a website

web·site /ˈwebsaɪt/ *noun* a place on the INTERNET where you can find out information about something: *For more information about the hotel, visit our website.*

we'd /wiːd/ the short form of 'we had' or 'we would': *We'd met her brother before.* • *We'd like to see a film tonight.*

wed·ding /ˈwedɪŋ/ *noun* a marriage ceremony: *I've been invited to Janet and Peter's wedding.*

ˈwedding ˌring *noun* a ring that you wear to show that you are married

wedge¹ /wedʒ/ *noun* a piece of something that is thick at one end and pointed at the other end: *a wedge of chocolate cake*

wedge² *verb* to force something into a small space: *I wedged the book in at the end of the shelf.*

Wednes·day /ˈwenzdi/ (written abbreviation **Wed**) *noun* the day of the week between Tuesday and Thursday: *Sorry, I can't go – I'm busy on Wednesday evening.*

> SPELLING
> This word is often spelled wrongly. The correct spelling is: **Wednesday**.

weed¹ /wiːd/ *noun* a wild plant that grows in gardens, where it is not wanted

weed² *verb* to remove weeds from a place: *Mum was outside, weeding the flower bed.*

week /wiːk/ *noun*
1 a period of seven days. A week is usually considered to start on Monday in Britain, and on Sunday in the US: *I won't have time to finish it* ***this week.*** • *The exams start* ***next week.*** • *She's been seeing her new boyfriend* ***for three weeks.*** • *I'll talk to you* ***later in the week*** (=in a few days).
2 the days from Monday to Friday, when people work or study: *My parents don't let me go out* ***during the week.*** • *I don't have much free time* ***in the week.***

week·day /ˈwiːkdeɪ/ *noun* any day of the week except Saturday and Sunday: *I work on weekdays.*

week·end /ˌwiːkˈend $ ˈwikend/ *noun* Saturday and Sunday. In British English you do things at the weekend, and in American English you do things on the weekend: *Did you have a good weekend?* • *We always go to a club* ***at the weekend.*** • *They play tennis* ***on the weekend.***

week·ly /ˈwiːkli/ *adjective, adverb* happening or done every week: *You will be paid weekly.* • *a weekly newspaper*

weep /wiːp/ *verb* (past tense and past participle **wept** /wept/) to cry: *Relatives were weeping outside the church.*
➔ see Thesaurus at CRY¹

weigh /weɪ/ *verb*

> KEY PATTERNS
> **weigh 10 grams/200 grams etc**
> **weigh something**
> **weigh yourself**

1 if something weighs a particular amount, it is that weight: *How much does she weigh?* • *My suitcase weighed 20 kilos.*
2 to use a machine to find out how much something or someone weighs: *They weigh all the parcels before loading them into vans.* • *He weighs himself every morning.*

PHRASAL VERBS
weigh down
weigh someone down if something heavy weighs you down, it stops you from moving easily: *I moved slowly along the street with my bags* ***weighing me down.***

weight /weɪt/ *noun*
1 how heavy someone or something is: *She worries about her weight.* • *What's the average* ***weight of*** *the parcels?*

2 weights heavy pieces of metal that people lift to make their muscles stronger

PHRASES

lose weight if you lose weight, you become lighter: *You need to **lose** some **weight**.*

put on weight if you put on weight, you become heavier: *John's **put on** a lot of **weight** since I last saw him.*

> PRONUNCIATION
> You pronounce **weight** like 'date'.

weight·lift·ing /ˈweɪtˌlɪftɪŋ/ *noun* (no plural) the sport of lifting heavy weights

weir /wɪə $ wɪr/ *noun* a wall that is built across a river to control the flow of water

weird /wɪəd $ wɪrd/ *adjective* (informal) unusual and strange: *It was quite a weird experience.* → see Thesaurus at STRANGE

> SPELLING
> This word is often spelled wrongly. The correct spelling is: **weird**.

wel·come¹ /ˈwelkəm/ *adjective*

> KEY PATTERNS
> **make someone welcome**
> **you are welcome to come/stay etc**
> **welcome to England!**

1 if you are welcome in a place, other people want you to be there and are friendly to you: *Strangers do not **feel welcome** in this town.* • *Everyone was kind and **made me welcome*** (=made me feel welcome).

2 if someone tells you that you are welcome to do something, they are telling you politely that you can do it: *You **are** all **welcome to** stay the night.*

PHRASES

welcome! (spoken) a friendly thing that you say to someone who has just arrived in a new place: ***Welcome to** London!*

you're welcome (spoken) used to reply politely to someone who has just thanked you: *"Thanks for the meal." "**You're welcome.**"*

> SPELLING
> This word is often spelled wrongly. The correct spelling is: **welcome**.

welcome² *verb*

1 to say hello in a friendly way to someone who has just arrived: *Josh welcomed us with a big smile.*

2 if you welcome something, you are happy if it happens because you think it is good: *The school always **welcomes** suggestions **from** parents.*

welcome³ *noun* the way that you behave towards someone when they arrive: *When we moved to Australia, everyone gave us a warm welcome.*

weld /weld/ *verb* to join metal objects together by heating them and pressing them together

wel·fare /ˈwelfeə $ ˈwelfer/ *noun* (no plural) **1** (formal) your welfare is your health, comfort, and happiness: *The teachers were concerned about the child's welfare.* **2** *AmE* money that the government gives to people who cannot work SYNONYM **benefit** *BrE*

we'll /wiːl/ the short form of 'we will': *We'll be late.*

well¹ /wel/ *adverb* (**better** /ˈbetə $ ˈbetɚ/ **best** /best/)

1 in a good or successful way ANTONYM **badly**: *I thought the whole team played well.* • *She **did** very **well** in her exams.* • *Did the meeting **go well**?*

2 a lot or completely: *Do you know him well?* • *I like my steak well cooked.*

PHRASES

as well also: *I bought a coat, and some shoes **as well**.*

as well as something in addition to something else: *He has been to Malaysia **as well as** Thailand.*

well done! used to tell someone that you are pleased with what they have done: *That was a great goal, Tim. **Well done!***

may as well, might as well (spoken) used to say that you think you should do something because there is nothing else you can do: *It's raining so we **may as well** go to the cinema.*

well after, well before (spoken) a long time after or before: *She didn't come home until **well after** 11.*

well² *adjective* (**better**)

healthy and not ill: *I don't **feel** very **well**.* • *Is he well enough to go to school?* → see Thesaurus at HEALTHY ILL

PHRASES

very well thank you, very well thanks (spoken) used to reply when someone asks how you are: *"Hello Clare, how are you?" "**Very well thanks**, how are you?"*

it's just as well (spoken) used to say that something that happens is lucky or good, after or before saying why: ***It's just as well** you're not hungry, because we haven't got much to eat.*

well³
used when you want to pause before saying something, for example because you are not sure what to say: *"Who should I ask to the disco?" "Well, how about Carla?"*

PHRASES

oh well used to show that you accept a situation, even though it is not a good one: ***Oh well**, I can take the exam again next year.*

well⁴ *noun* a deep hole in the ground from which water or oil is taken

ˌwell-'balanced *adjective* someone who is well-balanced is sensible and not easily upset: *a happy, well-balanced child*

ˌwell-be'haved *adjective* a well-behaved child is polite and behaves well

ˌwell-'being *noun* a feeling of being healthy and happy

ˌwell-'built *adjective* someone who is well-built is big and strong

ˌwell-'dressed *adjective* wearing good clothes: *a well-dressed TV presenter*

ˌwell-'fed *adjective* getting plenty of good food: *The local cats look well-fed and healthy.*

wel·ling·tons /'welɪŋtənz/ also **'wellington ˌboots** or **wel·lies** /'weliz/ (informal) *plural noun BrE* long rubber boots that you wear to keep your feet dry

wellingtons

ˌwell-'kept *adjective* a well-kept place is neat and tidy: *a well-kept garden*

ˌwell-'known *adjective* if someone or something is well known, a lot of people know about them: *a well-known singer* ➔ see Thesaurus at FAMOUS

ˌwell-'off *adjective* someone who is well-off has quite a lot of money SYNONYM **rich**: *She comes from quite a well-off family.* ➔ see Thesaurus at RICH

ˌwell-'paid *adjective* providing or getting a lot of money for a job: *Work in advertising is very well paid indeed.* • *a well-paid lawyer*

well-read /ˌwel 'red/ *adjective* someone who is well-read has read a lot and knows about many subjects

ˌwell-'timed *adjective* done at the best moment: *Ali scored a well-timed goal just before the final whistle.*

'well-ˌwisher *noun* someone who shows that they want you to succeed or be happy and healthy: *Money from well-wishers helped to raise the money for the little girl's operation.*

went the past tense of GO

wept the past tense and past participle of WEEP

we're /wɪə $ wɪr/ the short form of 'we are': *We're late.*

were /wə; strong wɜː $ wɚ/ the past tense of BE, which you use after 'you', 'we', and 'they'

weren't /wɜːnt $ wɚnt/ the short form of 'were not': *We weren't very impressed by the concert.*

west /west/ *noun* **1** (no plural) the direction that you look in to see the sun go down **2 the west** the western part of a country or area: *Rain is expected in the west.* —**west** *adverb, adjective*: *The house faces west.* • *Los Angeles is on the west coast.*

west·bound /'westbaʊnd/ *adjective* travelling towards the west: *westbound trains*

west·er·ly /'westəli $ 'westɚli/ *adjective* **1** towards the west: *They travelled in a westerly direction.* **2 westerly wind** a westerly wind blows from the west

west·ern¹ /'westən $ 'westɚn/ *adjective* **1** in or from the west part of a country or area: *western Canada*

A B C D E F G H I J K L M N O P Q R S T U V W X Y Z

2 also **Western** in or from Europe or the United States: *the Western way of life*

western² *noun* a film about life in the 19th century in the western part of the US

west·ward /ˈwestwəd $ ˈwestwərd/ also **west·wards** /ˈwestwədz $ ˈwestwərdz/ *adjective, adverb* towards the west: *We travelled westwards for three days.* • *Go in a westward direction for three miles.*

wet¹ /wet/ *adjective* (**wetter, wettest**)
1 covered in water or another liquid ANTONYM **dry**: *Her hair was wet.* • *We got wet in the rain.* • *Try not to get your shoes wet.*

wet

He got wet in the rain.

2 a wet day is a day when it is raining ANTONYM **dry**: *It was a horrible wet day.*
3 not yet dry: *My nail varnish is still wet.*
PHRASES
wet through, soaking wet very wet: *All my clothes were **soaking wet**.*

wet² *verb* (past tense and past participle **wet** or **wetted**, **wetting**) to make something wet ANTONYM **dry**: *Paul wetted his lips and blew the trumpet as hard as he could.*

we've /wiːv/ the short form of 'we have': *We've been playing basketball.*

whale /weɪl/ *noun* a very large animal that lives in the sea

wharf /wɔːf $ wɔrf/ *noun* (plural **wharves** /wɔːvz $ wɔrvz/) a structure that is built at the edge of a sea or river so that ships can stop next to it

what /wɒt $ wʌt/ *pronoun, determiner*
1 used to ask about something: *What did you tell him?* • *What's that noise?* • *What colour is your new car?* • *What time is it?*
2 used to talk about knowing or telling something: *I know what the answer is.* • *He told me **what to** do.*
3 the thing that: *I didn't like what he said.* • *What matters is that you tried.*
4 (spoken) used to say very strongly what you think: *What a great idea!* • *What a shame you were ill.*
5 (spoken) used to show, not very politely, that you did not hear what someone said: *"The game starts at 3." "What?" "I said the game starts at 3."*
6 (spoken) used when you are surprised or angry: *"The key isn't in the door." "What? It must be!"*
PHRASES
what for? (spoken) why: *"Take your shoes off." **"What for?"** • **What** did you tell her **for**?*
what if (spoken) used to talk about something that might happen: ***What if** someone finds out about the money?*

what·ev·er¹ /wɒtˈevə $ wʌtˈevər/ *pronoun, determiner* anything, or any kind of thing: *We could do whatever we liked.* • *Give him whatever he wants.* • *Whatever problems you have* (=it doesn't matter what they are), *we are here to help.*

whatever², what·so·ev·er /ˌwɒtsəʊˈevə $ ˌwʌtsoʊˈevər/ *adverb* (formal) used to say strongly that there is none of something: *There is no need whatever for you to worry.*

wheat /wiːt/ *noun* (no plural) a plant that is used to produce grain for making flour

wheel¹ /wiːl/ *noun* one of the round things under a car, bicycle etc that turn when it moves along: *A tricycle has three wheels.*

wheel² *verb* to push something that has wheels so that it moves along: *I had to wheel my bicycle home.*

wheel·bar·row /ˈwiːlˌbærəʊ $ ˈwilˌbæroʊ/ *noun* a container with one wheel at the front that you use outdoors for carrying heavy things

wheel·chair /ˈwiːltʃeə $ ˈwil-tʃer/ *noun* a chair with wheels that is used by someone who cannot walk → see picture at CHAIR¹

wheeze /wiːz/ *verb* to breathe with difficulty, making a whistling sound: *The old man coughed and wheezed.*

when /wen/ *adverb, conjunction*
1 used to ask or talk about a time: *When did you get back?* • *When's the next train?* • *She didn't tell us when she would be leaving.*

2 at the time that something happens: *I was very tired when I got home.* • *Call me when the programme starts.* • *When I was younger I hated football.*

when·ev·er /wen'evə $ wen'evər/ *conjunction*
1 every time: *This picture will remind me of you whenever I look at it.*
2 at any time: *The students can use the music rooms whenever they like.* • *We can go whenever you're ready.*

where /weə $ wer/ *adverb, conjunction*
1 used to ask or talk about a place: *"Where's Rosa?" "Upstairs, I think."* • *Where are you going for your holiday?* • *I don't know* ***where to*** *put everything.* • *This is where we hold our meetings.* • *I showed the police the place where the accident happened.*
2 used when talking about one part of a story: *I liked the scene where they were sleeping in the tent and it fell down.*

SPELLING
Don't confuse the spelling of **where** and **were** (=the past tense of the verb **be**).

where·a·bouts¹ /ˌweərə'bauts $ 'werəˌbauts/ *adverb* (spoken) used to ask about a place: *Whereabouts are you going in Spain?*

where·a·bouts² /'weərəbauts $ 'werəbauts/ *plural noun* (spoken) the place where someone is: *His exact whereabouts are unknown.*

wher·ev·er /weər'evə $ wer'evər/ *conjunction*
1 in every place: *They followed us wherever we went.* • *These plants grow wherever the ground is wet.*
2 in any place: *You can sit wherever you like.*

whet /wet/ *verb* (**whetted**, **whetting**) **whet someone's appetite** to make someone want more of something by letting them try it or see what it is like: *This book has really whetted my appetite for science fiction.*

wheth·er /'weðə $ 'weðər/ *conjunction*
used to talk about a question, or say that you do not know about something: *I asked Harriet* ***whether*** *she was coming to the party* ***or not.*** • *I'm not sure whether that would be a good idea.* • *I can't decide* ***whether to go or not.***

SPELLING
Don't confuse the spelling of **whether** and **weather** (=wind, rain, sunshine etc).

which /wɪtʃ/ *determiner, pronoun*
1 used to ask or talk about one member of a group: *Which book did you like best?* • *Which is your car?* • *I'm not sure which class she's in.*
2 used when giving more information about something: *Have you seen that new show which is on TV on Fridays?* • *This is the book which I was talking about.* • *Sheila was looking for her keys, which she had put down somewhere.* • *He'll be able to stay for two whole weeks, which will be nice.*

WORD CHOICE
which or **what**?
• You use **which** when the answer is one of a limited set of possible things: ***Which is Tom's house?*** • ***Which of these dresses do you like best?***
• You use **what** when the answer could be anything: ***What's the capital of North Korea?*** • ***What's your favourite food?***

which·ev·er /wɪtʃ'evə $ wɪtʃ'evər/ *determiner, pronoun*
any of the things or people in a group: *Use whichever shampoo suits you best.* • *I'll be happy whichever team wins* (=it does not matter which team wins).

whiff /wɪf/ *noun* a slight smell: *a whiff of cigarette smoke*

while¹ /waɪl/ *conjunction*
1 during the time that something is happening: *He started a business while he was still at school.* • *You must have phoned while I was asleep.* • *She listens to music while she works.*
2 (formal) although: *While it is possible to make a lot of money from writing, it's not easy.*

while² *noun* **a while** a short period of time: *We waited a while, but Anna didn't arrive.*

whilst /waɪlst/ *conjunction* WHILE

A B C D E F G H I J K L M N O P Q R S T U V W X Y Z

A B C D E F G H I J K L M N O P Q R S T U V W X Y Z

whim /wɪm/ *noun* a sudden feeling that you want to do something, without any particular reason: *I went to see the film on a whim.*

whim·per /ˈwɪmpə $ ˈwɪmpɚ/ *verb* to make gentle crying sounds: *The dog whimpered and looked at his master.*

whine /waɪn/ *verb* **1** to complain about something in an annoying voice SYNONYM **moan** *BrE*: *Stop whining and get on with your work!* **2** to make a long, high, unhappy sound —**whine** *noun*: *The dog gave a small whine.*

whinge /wɪndʒ/ *verb BrE* to complain in an annoying way about something unimportant SYNONYM **moan** *BrE*: *She's been whinging about the amount of homework she gets.*

whip¹ /wɪp/ *noun* a long thin piece of leather with a handle that is used for hitting people or animals

whip² *verb* (**whipped**, **whipping**) **1** to hit a person or animal with a whip **2** *AmE* (informal) to defeat someone easily: *The Dallas Cowboys whipped the Redskins last week.*

whir the American spelling of WHIRR

whirl /wɜːl $ wɚl/ *verb* to turn around quickly, or to make something turn around quickly: *Snowflakes were whirling down from the sky.*

whirl·pool /ˈwɜːlpuːl $ ˈwɚlpul/ *noun* water that turns around and around very quickly, pulling things towards it and then down into it

whirl·wind¹ /ˈwɜːlˌwɪnd $ ˈwɚlˌwɪnd/ *noun* a strong wind that turns around and around very quickly and causes a lot of damage SYNONYM **tornado**

whirlwind² *adjective* whirlwind events are exciting because they happen very quickly: *After a whirlwind romance, they got married.*

whirr *BrE*, **whir** *AmE* /wɜː $ wɚ/ *verb* if a machine whirrs, it makes a continuous low sound: *A helicopter whirred overhead.*

whisk¹ /wɪsk/ *verb* **1** to mix eggs or cream in a bowl very quickly so that air is mixed in: *Whisk the cream until it is thick.* **2** to take someone somewhere very quickly: *They whisked her to hospital.*

whisk² *noun* a small kitchen tool that you use to whisk eggs or cream

whis·ker /ˈwɪskə $ ˈwɪskɚ/ *noun*
1 an animal's whiskers are the long stiff hairs that grow near its mouth
2 whiskers the hair that grows on a man's face

whis·ky /ˈwɪski/ *noun* a strong alcoholic drink

whis·per¹ /ˈwɪspə $ ˈwɪspɚ/ *verb*

KEY PATTERNS
whisper something to someone

to say something very quietly to someone, so that other people cannot hear: *The girls were whispering at the back of the class.* • *James **whispered** something **to** Susie and she laughed.* • *What are you two **whispering about**?* • *He **whispered** something **in my ear**.*

whisper² *noun* a very quiet voice: *I can hear whispers at the back of the room.*

whis·tle¹ /ˈwɪsəl/ *verb*
1 to make a high sound or tune by blowing air out through your lips: *Terry **whistled a tune** as he worked.*
2 if something whistles, it makes a high sound because it is moving very fast: *The wind whistled in the trees.*

whistle² *noun*
a small object that makes a high sound when you blow into it: *The teacher **blew** her **whistle** for the game to start.*
→ see picture at BLOW¹

white¹ /waɪt/ *adjective* **1** something that is white is the colour of milk, snow, or salt **2** someone who is white has naturally pale skin **3** *BrE* white coffee has milk or cream in it

white² *noun* **1** a white colour: *She was dressed completely in white.*
2 the colourless part of an egg that becomes white when you cook it: *Whisk the egg whites until they are stiff.*
→ see picture at EGG²

white·board /ˈwaɪtbɔːd $ ˈwaɪtbɔrd/ *noun* a large white board, usually in a classroom, which teachers write on with a special pen → see Thesaurus at BOARD¹

white-ˈcollar *adjective* white-collar workers do jobs in offices, banks etc

whit·tle /ˈwɪtl/ *verb* **whittle something down** to gradually reduce a number or an amount: *I've whittled the list down to just four people now.*

whizz[1] *BrE*, **whiz** *AmE* /wɪz/ *verb* (informal) to move very quickly: *A bullet whizzed past his ear.*

whizz[2] *BrE*, **whiz** *AmE noun* (informal) **be a whizz at something** to be very good at something: *Peter is a whiz at math.*

who /huː/ *pronoun*
1 used to ask or say which person is involved: *Who told you that?* • *Who's your favourite singer?* • *I know who the card is from.*
2 used when giving more information about someone: *That's the girl who was nasty to me.* • *She's visiting her friend Deborah, who lives in London.*

who'd /huːd/ the short form of 'who had' or 'who would': *Nobody knew who'd done it.*

who·ev·er /huːˈevə $ huˈevɚ/ *pronoun*
1 the person who: *Whoever did this must be crazy.* • *There will be a reward for whoever finds the missing money.*
2 any person: *My parents said I could invite whoever I liked to the party.*

whole[1] /həʊl $ hoʊl/ *adjective* all of something SYNONYM **entire**: *I ate a whole loaf of bread.* • *We spent the whole day on the beach.* • *The whole class was shouting.*

whole[2] *noun*
1 the whole of something all of something: *The whole of my body ached.*
2 on the whole generally or usually: *On the whole, girls grow up faster than boys.*

> **PRONUNCIATION**
> In this word you do not pronounce the **w**, so it is pronounced exactly the same as 'hole'.

whole·heart·ed /ˌhəʊlˈhɑːtɪd $ ˌhoʊlˈhɑrtɪd/ *adjective* (formal) wholehearted support or agreement is total —**wholeheartedly** *adverb*: *I agree wholeheartedly with your mother.*

whole·meal /ˈhəʊlmiːl $ ˈhoʊlmiːl/ *adjective BrE* wholemeal flour, bread etc is made using all the parts of the grains of wheat SYNONYM **wholewheat**

whole·sale /ˈhəʊlseɪl $ ˈhoʊlseɪl/ *adjective* affecting a lot of things or people, often in a bad way: *the wholesale destruction that occurred during the war*

whole·sal·er /ˈhəʊlˌseɪlə $ ˈhoʊlˌseɪlɚ/ *noun* a person or company that buys things in large quantities and sells them to shops

whole·some /ˈhəʊlsəm $ ˈhoʊlsəm/ *adjective* good for your health SYNONYM **healthy**: *We eat only wholesome, natural foods.*

whole·wheat /ˈhəʊlwiːt $ ˈhoʊlwit/ *adjective* the American word for WHOLEMEAL

who'll /huːl/ the short form of 'who will': *Who'll be next?*

whol·ly /ˈhəʊl-li $ ˈhoʊli/ *adverb* (formal) completely: *The mistake was wholly my fault.*

whom /huːm/ *pronoun* (formal) used as the object of a verb or preposition to mean 'who': *To whom was the letter addressed?*

> **WORD CHOICE**
> **who** or **whom**?
> • **Whom** is used in formal English. In everyday conversation, people usually say **who**.

who're /ˈhuːə $ ˈhuɚ/ the short form of 'who are': *Who're you going to vote for?*

who's /huːz/ the short form of 'who is' or 'who has': *Who's your favourite film star?* • *Who's taken my pen?*

whose /huːz/ *determiner* **1** used when asking which person something belongs to: *Whose book is this?*
2 used when giving information about something that belongs to the person you are talking about: *He's the man whose car got stolen.*

> **SPELLING**
> Don't confuse the spelling of **whose** and **who's** (='who is' or 'who has').

who've /huːv/ the short form of 'who have': *people who've got problems*

why /waɪ/ *adverb*
used to ask or talk about the reason for something: *Why are you so late?* • *"I can't come to lessons tomorrow." "Why*

not?" • *He didn't know why they hated him.* • *I told her why I wanted to speak to her.*

PHRASES

why not, why don't you? (informal) used to make a suggestion: ***Why not** try giving up coffee?* • ***Why don't you** check the figures again? You might have made a mistake.*

why not (spoken, informal) used to accept an invitation or suggestion: *"Coming to the park with us?" "Yes, why not."*

wick·ed /ˈwɪkɪd/ *adjective* **1** very bad or evil: *Who would do such a wicked thing?* → see Thesaurus at BAD
2 (informal) very good: *We had a wicked time!*

wick·et /ˈwɪkɪt/ *noun* one of the sets of sticks that the BOWLER tries to hit with the ball in a game of CRICKET

wide[1] /waɪd/ *adjective*
1 measuring a large distance from one side to the other ANTONYM **narrow**: *a wide bed* • *a shirt with wide sleeves* • *The street is not wide enough to park in.* → see picture at NARROW[1]
2 used to talk about the distance from one side of something to the other: *The river is over a mile wide here.* • ***How wide** is the path?*
3 including a lot of different people or things SYNONYM **broad**: *You can study a **wide range** of subjects.*

wide[2] *adverb*
1 wide open, wide apart open as far as possible, or as far as possible apart: *The window was **wide open**.* • *She held her arms **wide apart**.*
2 wide awake completely awake: *Suddenly I was **wide awake**.*

ˌwide-ˈeyed *adjective, adverb* with your eyes wide open because you are very surprised or interested: *The children stared wide-eyed at the magician.*

wide·ly /ˈwaɪdli/ *adverb* in a lot of different places or by a lot of people: *Johnson was widely expected to be made team captain.*

wid·en /ˈwaɪdn/ *verb* to become wider, or to make something wider ANTONYM **narrow**: *The river begins to widen here.* • *They had to widen the entrance.*

wide·spread /ˈwaɪdspred/ *adjective* happening in many places: *The use of computers in classrooms is widespread in many countries.*

wid·ow /ˈwɪdəʊ $ ˈwɪdoʊ/ *noun* a woman whose husband is dead

wid·owed /ˈwɪdəʊd $ ˈwɪdoʊd/ *adjective* if someone is widowed, their husband or wife is dead

wid·ow·er /ˈwɪdəʊə $ ˈwɪdoʊɚ/ *noun* a man whose wife is dead

width /wɪdθ/ *noun* the distance from one side of something to the other: *He measured the length and width of the desk.*

wield /wiːld/ *verb* **1** to have and use power and influence: *The United States wields enormous political influence.*
2 to hold or use a weapon: *The police arrested the man for wielding a knife.*

wife /waɪf/ *noun* (plural **wives** /waɪvz/) the woman that a man is married to: *My brother and his wife came to visit us last week.*

GRAMMAR
The plural of **wife** is **wives**.
✘ Don't say 'wifes'.

WiFi /ˈwaɪfaɪ/ *noun* a way of connecting computers and other electronic equipment to a computer network using radio signals instead of wires: *Many schools are using WiFi technology to allow students to have easier access to the Internet.*

wig /wɪg/ *noun* something that is made to look like hair, which someone wears on their head

wig·gle /ˈwɪgəl/ *verb* (informal) to move part of your body from side to side or up and down: *She wiggled her bottom as she danced.*

wik·i /ˈwɪki/ *noun* a website that can be changed and added to by the people who use it

wild[1] /waɪld/ *adjective*
1 a wild animal or plant is living or growing in natural conditions, rather than being looked after by people: *A dingo is a kind of wild dog.* • *wild strawberries* → see picture at TAME[1]
2 very excited, angry, or happy, so that you cannot control your behaviour: *The children are a bit wild today.* • *When*

A B C D E F G H I J K L M N O P Q R S T U V W X Y Z

she saw them together she **went wild** (=behaved in a very angry way).
→ see picture on page A9

PHRASES

a wild guess a guess that you make without knowing any facts, so that it may be completely wrong: *He asked me how old I thought he was and I made a **wild guess**.*

be wild about something/someone (spoken) to like something or someone very much: *I'm not **wild about** rock music.*

wild² *noun* **1 in the wild** in natural conditions, not looked after by people: *In the wild, lions hunt in groups.* **2 the wilds** areas that are very far from towns and cities and where very few people live: *in the wilds of northern China*

wil·der·ness /ˈwɪldənəs $ ˈwɪldərnəs/ *noun* (no plural) a large natural area of land with no buildings: *Fifty years ago, this area was just a wilderness.*

wild·life /ˈwaɪldlaɪf/ *noun* (no plural) animals that live in natural conditions

wild·ly /ˈwaɪldli/ *adverb* in a way that is careless and not controlled: *He drives rather wildly.*

wil·ful *BrE*, **willful** *AmE* /ˈwɪlfəl/ *adjective* **1** doing what you want even though people tell you not to: *His daughter became a wilful teenager.* **2** (formal) done deliberately and without caring about the possible harmful results: *This act of wilful damage could have caused an accident.*

will¹ /wɪl/ *modal verb*
1 used for talking about the future: *Russ will be back next Tuesday.* • *Do you think she'll win?* • *The film will be showing at a cinema near you next week.* • *Greg won't manage to finish his course.*
2 used to say what you plan or agree to do: *"Someone's at the door." "I'll get it."* • *Sean won't play with the other boys.*
3 used to say what something can do: *The new plane will carry 550 passengers.* • *My car won't start.*
4 used to tell someone to do something: *Will you be quiet please, class.* • *Will you take me back to the hotel?*

GRAMMAR
The short form of **will** is **'ll**: ***We'll** be there in 20 minutes.*
The negative of **will** is **will not** or **won't**: *She **won't** tell me what's wrong.*

will² *noun*
a legal document in which you say who you want to have your money and property after you die: *Her grandfather left her some money **in his will**.*

PHRASES

against your will: *Nobody can make her get married **against her will*** (=if she does not want to get married).

of your own free will: *I came here **of my own free will*** (=because I wanted to, not because I was forced).

the/your will to do something if you have the will to do something, especially something difficult, you strongly want to do it: *She is very ill, but has not lost her **will to** live.*

will³ *verb* if you will something to happen, you try to make it happen by thinking about it very hard: *We were all willing England to win.*

willful the American spelling of WILFUL

will·ing /ˈwɪlɪŋ/ *adjective*

KEY PATTERNS
willing to do something

if you are willing to do something, you will do it if someone wants you to do it: *I am **willing to** help in any way that I can.* —**willingly** *adverb*: *I will willingly lend you the money for the car.* —**willingness** *noun* (no plural): *He wanted to show his **willingness to** change.*

wil·low /ˈwɪləʊ $ ˈwɪloʊ/ *noun* a tree with very long thin branches that hang down

will·pow·er /ˈwɪlˌpaʊə $ ˈwɪlˌpaʊər/ *noun* (no plural) the ability to make yourself do something even if it is difficult or unpleasant: *Losing weight takes a lot of willpower.*

A B C D E F G H I J K L M N O P Q R S T U V W X Y Z

wilt /wɪlt/ *verb* if a plant wilts, it becomes soft and bends because it needs water

wilt

wil•y /ˈwaɪli/ *adjective* (**wilier**, **wiliest**) clever at getting what you want

wimp /wɪmp/ *noun* (informal) someone who is afraid to do things: *Oh, come on. Don't be such a wimp!*

win[1] /wɪn/ *verb* (past tense and past participle **won** /wʌn/ **winning**)

KEY PATTERNS
win a race/competition/election
win at cards/cricket etc

1 to be the best or first in a game, competition, or fight ANTONYM **lose**: *Mark's team won the basketball tournament.* • *We always knew we would win the war.* • *Laurie always* ***wins at*** *tennis.* • *We* ***won*** *the quiz* ***by*** *12 points.* ➔ see Thesaurus at BEAT[1]
2 to get a prize in a game or competition: *I won a free trip to New York!*

PHRASAL VERBS
win over
win someone over to persuade someone to like you or support you: *It took me quite a while to* ***win*** *the children* ***over****.*

win[2] *noun* when a team or player wins something SYNONYM **victory** ANTONYM **defeat**: *We've only had two wins this year.*

wince /wɪns/ *verb* to suddenly change the expression on your face when you see or remember something painful or embarrassing: *He winced as he remembered his embarrassing mistake.*

wind[1] /wɪnd/ *noun*
1 air that you can feel moving around you: *A* ***cold wind was blowing****.* • *The flag on the church was waving* ***in the wind****.* • *The* ***strong winds*** *have caused quite a lot of damage.* ➔ see picture at BLOW[1]
2 (no plural) air or gas in your stomach that feels uncomfortable

THESAURUS
breeze: *The leaves on the tree fluttered in the* ***breeze*** (=a light, gentle wind).
gale: *We can't sail in this* ***gale*** (=a very strong wind).
hurricane: *The* ***hurricane*** *damaged many houses* (=a violent storm with very strong winds that move very fast).
typhoon: *The ship ran into a* ***typhoon*** *in the South Pacific* (=a tropical storm with very strong winds).
tornado: *They could see the* ***tornado*** *approaching and touching the ground* (=a strong wind that goes round and round).

wind[2] /waɪnd/ *verb* (past tense and past participle **wound** /waʊnd/)

KEY PATTERNS
wind rope/string etc around something
the road/river winds up/down/along etc somewhere

1 to wrap something long and thin around another thing many times: *I* ***wound*** *the bandage* ***around*** *his wrist.*
2 if a road or river winds somewhere, it goes in that direction and has many bends: *The path* ***winds up*** *the mountain.*
3 also **wind up** to make a machine or clock work by turning a small handle around several times: *You wind the toy using this key.* • *We had to* ***wind*** *the clock* ***up*** *once a week.*

PHRASAL VERBS
wind down
1 to gradually end: *After he left, the party started to* ***wind down****.*
2 to relax: *Exercise can help you* ***wind down*** *after work.*

wind up
1 wind something up to end something such as a meeting: *I think it's time to* ***wind up*** *the meeting.*
2 wind someone up *BrE* (informal) to make someone annoyed or angry SYNONYM **annoy**: *He deliberately says that to* ***wind*** *me* ***up****!*

PRONUNCIATION
Be careful how you pronounce this word:
wind[1] (*noun*) is pronounced like 'tinned'
wind[2] (*verb*) is pronounced like 'find'

wind·fall /ˈwɪndfɔːl/ *noun* an amount of money that you get when you do not expect it

wind·mill /ˈwɪndˌmɪl/ *noun* a tall structure with parts that are turned by the wind, which is used to crush grain or make electricity

win·dow /ˈwɪndəʊ $ ˈwɪndoʊ/ *noun*

> KEY PATTERNS
> **out of the window**
> **through the window**
> **at the window**

1 a space in the side of a building or car with glass across it, where light can come in: *I looked* ***out of the window***. • *You could see them* ***through the window***. • *She was standing* ***at the*** *kitchen* ***window***.
2 one of the areas on a computer SCREEN where you can do different types of work

ˈwindow ˌshopping *noun* (no plural) when you look at things in shops, without intending to buy them

win·dow·sill /ˈwɪndəʊˌsɪl $ ˈwɪndoʊˌsɪl/ *noun* a shelf at the bottom of a window

wind·screen /ˈwɪndskriːn/ *BrE*, **wind·shield** /ˈwɪndʃiːld/ *AmE noun* the large window at the front of a vehicle

ˈwindscreen ˌwiper *BrE*, **ˈwindshield ˌwiper** *AmE noun* a long object that moves across a windscreen to remove rain

wind·surf·er /ˈwɪndˌsɜːfə $ ˈwɪndˌsɝfɚ/ *noun* someone who goes windsurfing

wind·surf·ing /ˈwɪndˌsɜːfɪŋ $ ˈwɪndˌsɝfɪŋ/ *noun* (no plural) the sport of sailing across water by standing on a board and holding onto a sail: *I go windsurfing most weekends.* → see picture on page A14

wind·swept /ˈwɪndswept/ *adjective* a windswept place is very windy

wind·y /ˈwɪndi/ *adjective* (**windier**, **windiest**) if the weather is windy, there is a lot of wind: *It was too windy to go for a walk.* → see picture on page A13

wine /waɪn/ *noun* an alcoholic drink that is made from GRAPES: *a glass of red wine*

wing /wɪŋ/ *noun*
1 one of the two parts of a bird's or insect's body that it uses for flying: *The eagle* ***spread its wings*** *and flew away.* → see picture at BIRD
2 one of the two flat parts that stick out of the sides of a plane: *I had a seat next to the wing.* → see picture at AEROPLANE

wing·span /ˈwɪŋspæn/ *noun* the distance from the end of one wing to the end of the other

wink /wɪŋk/ *verb* to close and open one eye quickly, especially to show that you are joking or being friendly: *He winked at Eddie.* —**wink** *noun*: *"You might see Julie there," said Jon, with a wink.*

wink

win·ner /ˈwɪnə $ ˈwɪnɚ/ *noun* the person who wins a race, game, or competition ANTONYM **loser**: *The winner of each race will get a prize.*

win·nings /ˈwɪnɪŋz/ *plural noun* money that you win in a game or competition: *She went to collect her winnings.*

win·ter /ˈwɪntə $ ˈwɪntɚ/ *noun*

> KEY PATTERNS
> **in winter**
> **in the winter**

the season between autumn and spring, when the weather is coldest: *It gets very cold here* ***in winter***. • *This has been the coldest winter since 1947.* • ***In the winter***, *the temperature dropped to -20°.* → see picture on page A13

win·try /ˈwɪntri/ *adjective* wintry weather is cold or snowy weather

wipe /waɪp/ *verb*

> KEY PATTERNS
> **wipe the table/floor etc**
> **wipe the dirt from/off something**

1 to move a cloth or your hand over something, in order to clean it: *Sue wiped the table.* • *He wiped the sweat from his face with his hand.* • ***Wipe***

A B C D E F G H I J K L M N O P Q R S T U V W X Y Z

*those crumbs **off** the table.* ➔ see Thesaurus at REMOVE ➔ see picture at DUST[2]
2 to remove all the sound, film, or information from a tape or computer DISK SYNONYM **erase**: *I'm going to wipe this CD and record something else on it.*
PHRASES
wipe your feet to clean the bottom of your shoes by standing on something and rubbing your feet on it: *Wipe your feet before you come in the house.*
PHRASAL VERBS
wipe out
wipe something out (informal) to destroy something completely: *The bomb **wiped out** several buildings in the city centre.*
wipe up
wipe something up to remove liquid from a surface using a cloth: *I wiped up the water I had spilt.*

wip·er /ˈwaɪpə $ ˈwaɪpɚ/ a WINDSCREEN WIPER

wire¹ /waɪə $ waɪɚ/ *noun*
1 metal that is long and thin like string or thread: *We tied the posts together with wire.*
2 a long thin piece of metal that is used to carry electricity: *One of the wires was not connected correctly.*

wire² also **wire up** *verb* to connect electrical wires so that a piece of equipment will work: *Have you wired your new stereo system up to the speakers?*

wir·y /ˈwaɪəri/ *adjective* (**wirier**, **wiriest**) **1** someone who is wiry is thin but strong **2** wiry hair is stiff and curly

wis·dom /ˈwɪzdəm/ *noun* (no plural) **1** the ability to understand things and make good decisions because you have a lot of experience: *a man of great wisdom* **2** whether an action is sensible: *I was not sure about the wisdom of this plan.*

wise¹ /waɪz/ *adjective*

KEY PATTERNS
it is wise to do something

1 a wise decision or action is a sensible one: *Do you think that was a **wise decision**? • I think **it would be wise to** ask your parents for permission first.*
2 a wise person makes good decisions and gives good advice because they have a lot of experience: *Your grandfather is a very wise man.*
—**wisely** *adverb*: *She wisely decided to get the earlier train.*

wise² *verb* **wise up** (informal) to realize what is really true or what a situation is really like: *If you think college life is all drinking and partying, you'd better wise up.*

wise·crack /ˈwaɪzkræk/ *noun* (informal) something funny that someone says, especially when they should be more serious

wish¹ /wɪʃ/ *verb*

KEY PATTERNS
wish that

to want something to happen even though it is unlikely: *Sally **wished that** she had a sister like Kate. • I wish we lived in London.*
PHRASES
wish someone luck to tell someone that you hope they will have good luck and be successful: *I've got exams tomorrow – **wish me luck**!*
could wish for, couldn't wish for used to say strongly that something is as good as it could possibly be: *It was the best birthday that anyone **could wish for**. • I **couldn't wish for** a better friend.*

wish² *noun* (plural **wishes**)
1 make a wish to secretly say to yourself that you hope that something happens: *It was his birthday tomorrow, so Harry closed his eyes and **made a wish**.*
2 against someone's wishes if you do something against someone's wishes, you do it even though they do not want you to: *You took the car **against my wishes**.*
3 have no wish to do something to definitely not want to do something: *Dan **had no wish to** spend the summer holidays at home.*
4 best wishes a friendly phrase that you write before your name in cards and letters

wish·ful think·ing /ˌwɪʃfəl ˈθɪŋkɪŋ/ *noun* (no plural) when someone hopes that something good might happen, even though it is impossible

wisp /wɪsp/ *noun* **1** a small thin piece of hair **2** a small thin line of smoke or cloud: *They could see a wisp of smoke in the distance.*

wist·ful /ˈwɪstfəl/ *adjective* (written) a little sad because you know you cannot have something you want —**wistfully** *adverb*: *She looked wistfully back at the dress in the shop window.*

wit /wɪt/ *noun* **1** (no plural) the ability to say things that are clever and funny **2 wits** someone's ability to make good decisions quickly when they have to: *You have to use your wits in this job.* **3 scare someone out of their wits** to frighten someone very much

witch /wɪtʃ/ *noun* (plural **witches**) a woman who has magic powers

witch·craft /ˈwɪtʃkrɑːft $ ˈwɪtʃkræft/ *noun* (no plural) the use of magic, usually to do bad things

with /wɪð $ wɪθ/ *preposition*
1 used to say that people or things are together: *Can I come with you?* • *I'm going to the cinema with Jack.* • *We had chicken with rice.* • *Mix the paint with a little water.*
2 used to say who someone is arguing, fighting, or competing against: *He disagreed with me.* • *We used to fight with each other a lot.*
3 using something: *Cut round the shapes with scissors.* • *He pushed the door open with his foot.*
4 having something: *a girl with long blonde hair* • *a house with a garden* • *people with problems*
5 used to say who or what someone has a feeling about: *Why are you angry with him?* • *We were pleased with our performance.*
6 because of a feeling: *She was shaking with fear* (=she was shaking because she was so afraid).

with·draw /wɪðˈdrɔː $ wɪθˈdrɔ/ *verb* (formal) (**withdrew** /-ˈdruː/ **withdrawn** /-ˈdrɔːn/) **1** to take something out or away: *He withdrew £100 from the bank.* **2** if soldiers withdraw from an area, they leave it **3** to not take part in something that you intended to take part in: *He withdrew from the race because of a back injury.*

with·draw·al /wɪðˈdrɔːəl $ wɪθˈdrɔəl/ *noun* **1** when you take some of your money out of a bank: *You have made three withdrawals this month.* **2** when soldiers leave an area **3** (no plural) when someone who has been taking a drug regularly stops taking it and feels ill

with·drawn¹ /wɪðˈdrɔːn $ wɪθˈdrɔn/ *adjective* quiet and not wanting to talk to people: *He became very withdrawn after his father died.*

withdrawn² the past participle of WITHDRAW

withdrew the past tense of WITHDRAW

with·er /ˈwɪðə $ ˈwɪðɚ/ *verb* if a plant withers, its leaves become dry and it starts to die

withheld the past tense and past participle of WITHHOLD

with·hold /wɪðˈhəʊld $ wɪθˈhoʊld/ *verb* (formal) (past tense and past participle **withheld** /-ˈheld/) to not give something to someone: *The doctors decided to withhold treatment.*

with·in /wɪðˈɪn/ *preposition*
1 before the end of a period of time: *Your goods will be delivered within 28 days.*
2 less than a particular distance from something or someone: *I stood within two feet of him!*
3 (formal) inside: *Only a few people within the company knew about the plans.*

with·out /wɪðˈaʊt/ *preposition, adverb*
1 not having something: *I left home in the morning without my bag.* • *You can't travel on this train without a ticket.* • *people without jobs*
2 not having someone with you: *Sammy was late, so we left without him.*
3 used to say that someone does not do something: *He left without saying goodbye.* • *Suddenly, without warning* (=not telling other people), *the soldiers started shooting.*

with·stand /wɪðˈstænd $ wɪθˈstænd/ *verb* (formal) (past tense and past participle **withstood** /-ˈstʊd/) to not be harmed or affected by something: *These dishes can withstand high temperatures.*

withstood the past tense and past participle of WITHSTAND

A B C D E F G H I J K L M N O P Q R S T U V W X Y Z

wit·ness[1] /ˈwɪtnəs/ *noun* (plural **witnesses**) **1** (formal) someone who saw an accident or a crime: *There were no witnesses to the murder.*
2 someone who gives information in a court of law

witness[2] *verb* (formal) to see something happen, especially an accident or a crime: *Did anyone witness the attack?*

ˈ**witness** ˌ**box** *BrE*, ˈ**witness** ˌ**stand** *AmE noun* the place where someone stands to give information in a court of law

wit·ty /ˈwɪti/ *adjective* (**wittier, wittiest**) clever and funny: *He tried to think of a witty remark to make.*

wives the plural of WIFE

wiz·ard /ˈwɪzəd $ ˈwɪzərd/ *noun* **1** a man who has magic powers
2 (informal) someone who is very good at doing something: *a chess wizard*

wob·ble /ˈwɒbəl $ ˈwɑbəl/ *verb* to move from side to side in an unsteady way: *She wobbled along the lane on her bicycle.* ➔ see Thesaurus at SHAKE[1]

wob·bly /ˈwɒbli $ ˈwɑbli/ *adjective* (**wobblier, wobbliest**) moving from side to side in an unsteady way: *a wobbly chair*

wok /wɒk $ wɑk/ *noun* a large round pan used in Chinese cooking

woke the past tense of WAKE

woken the past participle of WAKE

wolf /wʊlf/ *noun* (plural **wolves** /wʊlvz/) a wild animal that is like a large dog ➔ see picture on page A9

GRAMMAR
The plural of **wolf** is **wolves**.
✘ Don't say 'wolfs'.

wolves the plural of WOLF

wom·an /ˈwʊmən/ (plural **women** /ˈwɪmɪn/) *noun* an adult female person: *Diana was a very beautiful woman.*

wom·an·izer also **womaniser** *BrE* /ˈwʊmənaɪzə $ ˈwʊməˌnaɪzər/ *noun* a man who has sexual relationships with a lot of women

womb /wuːm/ *noun* the part of a woman's body where a baby grows before it is born

PRONUNCIATION
In this word you do not pronounce the **b**.

women the plural of WOMAN

won the past tense and past participle of WIN

won·der[1] /ˈwʌndə $ ˈwʌndər/ *verb*

KEY PATTERNS
wonder why/where/what etc

to think about something you do not know, and want to know it: *We were wondering where you were.* • *I wonder what this switch does?*

wonder[2] *noun* **1** (no plural) a feeling of surprise or admiration: *The cathedral was huge, and she gazed at it in wonder.* **2 no wonder** (spoken) used to say that something does not surprise you: *No wonder you're cold if you didn't bring your coat!*
3 something that is very impressive: *the wonders of modern science*

won·der·ful /ˈwʌndəfəl $ ˈwʌndərfəl/ *adjective* extremely good SYNONYM **great**: *It was wonderful to see him again.* ➔ see Thesaurus at GOOD[1]

won't /wəʊnt $ woʊnt/ the short form of 'will not': *This won't take long.*

wood /wʊd/ *noun* **1** the material that trees are made of, which is used to make things: *All the furniture is made of wood.* **2** also **woods** a small forest: *We got lost in the woods.* ➔ see Thesaurus at FOREST

WORD CHOICE
wood or **wooden**?
• **Wood** is a noun: *The table is made of wood.*
• **Wooden** is an adjective: *a wooden chair.*

wood·ed /ˈwʊdɪd/ *adjective* covered with trees: *They walked through a wooded valley.*

wood·en /ˈwʊdn/ *adjective* made from wood: *a wooden door*

wood·land /ˈwʊdlənd/ *noun* an area of trees ➔ see Thesaurus at FOREST

wood·peck·er /ˈwʊdˌpekə $ ˈwʊdˌpekɚ/ *noun* a bird that uses its long beak to make holes in trees

wood·wind /ˈwʊdˌwɪnd/ *noun* woodwind instruments are musical instruments shaped like straight tubes which you blow into

wood·work /ˈwʊdwɜːk $ ˈwʊdwɚk/ *noun* (no plural) the parts of a building that are made of wood: *A lot of the woodwork was rotten and had to be replaced.*

wood·worm /ˈwʊdwɜːm $ ˈwʊdwɚm/ *noun* an insect that makes holes in wood

wool /wʊl/ *noun* (no plural) the soft thick hair of a sheep, which is made into thread: *She bought five balls of red wool.*

wool·len *BrE*, **woolen** *AmE* /ˈwʊlən/ *adjective* made of wool: *woollen socks*

wool·ly *BrE*, **wooly** *AmE* /ˈwʊli/ *adjective* (informal) made of wool: *a woolly hat*

word /wɜːd $ wɚd/ *noun*
a group of sounds or letters that have a particular meaning: *The only word she said was "yes". • I don't understand all these long words.*

PHRASES

not say a word, not understand a word to say nothing at all or understand nothing at all: *She's upset and she* ***hasn't said a word*** *all morning.*

a word of advice, a word of warning something that you say to advise or warn someone: *Here's* ***a word of advice*** *– never trust a salesman.*

have a word with someone (spoken) to talk to someone, usually about something that needs doing: *I'll* ***have a word with*** *my father, and ask if he can help you.*

in other words used when you are explaining what something means in a different way: *The car would cost £9,000;* ***in other words****, half her salary.*

word for word if you repeat something word for word, you say it using exactly the same words: *I want you to tell me what she said* ***word for word****.*

ˈword ˌprocessor *noun* a small computer that you use for writing

wore the past tense of WEAR

work¹ → see box on page 776

work² /wɜːk $ wɚk/ *noun*

KEY PATTERNS
do some work
be at work
go to work

1 (no plural) activity that involves effort: *You've* ***done*** *a lot of* ***hard work*** *today. • Come on – we still* ***have*** *a lot of* ***work to do****.*

2 (no plural) something that you do in order to earn money: *What kind of work would you like to do when you leave school?* → see Thesaurus at JOB

3 (no plural) the place where you do your job: *Paul isn't here, he's* ***at work****. • I* ***go to work*** *at eight o'clock.*

4 (no plural) the time when you are doing your job: *I'll meet you* ***after work****.*

5 (no plural) the things that you write or produce: *Your work is improving.*

PHRASES

work of art a very good painting, SCULPTURE etc: *He has a collection of* ***works of art****.*

a piece of work something that you have written or produced: *This essay is an excellent* ***piece of work****.*

be in work to have a job: ***Are you in work*** *at the moment?*

be out of work, be looking for work to not have a job: *Bill* ***has been out of work*** *for six months.*

work·a·ble /ˈwɜːkəbəl $ ˈwɚkəbəl/ *adjective* a workable plan or system will work effectively and be successful

work·a·hol·ic /ˌwɜːkəˈhɒlɪk $ ˌwɚkəˈhɔlɪk/ *noun* (informal) someone who spends all their time working

ˌworked ˈup *adjective* (informal) very upset or angry: *I don't see why you're getting so worked up about it.*

work·er /ˈwɜːkə $ ˈwɚkɚ/ *noun* someone who works for a company or organization, but is not a manager: *The workers at the factory are asking for more money.*

work·force /ˈwɜːkfɔːs $ ˈwɚkfɔrs/ *noun* all the people who work somewhere: *The bank has reduced its workforce by 3%.*

work·ing /ˈwɜːkɪŋ $ ˈwɚkɪŋ/ *adjective*
1 working people have jobs: *Working parents often have little time at home*

A B C D E F G H I J K L M N O P Q R S T U V W X Y Z

work /wɜːk $ wɚk/ *verb*

1 to do a job in order to earn money: *She* ***works in*** *a big office in New York. • He* ***works for*** *Microsoft. • Do you like* ***working for*** *your father? • I know someone who* ***works at*** *the Library of Congress. • Steve gave up farming and now* ***works as*** *an engineer.*

KEY PATTERNS

work in an office/a bank/a factory
work for a company/person
work at the museum/the hospital etc
work as a teacher/doctor/cook

work

2 to use effort in order to do something: *Tom was busy* ***working*** *in the garden. • You'll have to* ***work hard*** *to pass your exams.*

3 if a machine is working, it is not broken and you can use it without any problems: *My computer* ***isn't working*** *– can you check what's wrong with it? • Does that old radio still* ***work****?*

4 if a plan or method works, it is successful and gives you the results that you want: *She went on a diet to lose weight, but it* ***didn't work****. • The tablets should start* ***working*** *soon.*

PHRASAL VERBS

work on
to try to produce or repair something: *The band are* ***working on*** *some new songs. • Can I watch you* ***work on*** *your car?*

work out
1 to calculate an amount: *I will* ***work out*** *how much money each person owes. • Give me the calculator and I'll* ***work it out*** *for you.*
2 to find a solution to a problem or make a decision after thinking carefully: *We need to* ***work out*** *where we're going to live.*
3 if something works out, it gradually stops being a problem: *Everything* ***worked out*** *fine in the end.*
4 to do a series of physical exercises in order to keep your body strong and healthy: *I* ***work out*** *three times a week.*

work up to
to gradually do more of something so that finally you are doing a lot of it: *I'm* ***working up to*** *exercising four days a week.*

with their children. **2** relating to work: *What are your working conditions like?*

ˌworking ˈclass *noun* **the working class, the working classes** the people in society who do physical work or jobs for which they get low pay —**working-class** *adjective*: *He came from a working-class background.*

work·ings /ˈwɜːkɪŋz $ ˈwɚkɪŋz/ *plural noun* the way in which something works: *Students learn about the workings of the political system.*

work·load /ˈwɜːkləʊd $ ˈwɚkloʊd/ *noun* the amount of work that a person has to do: *My workload keeps increasing.*

work·man /ˈwɜːkmən $ ˈwɚkmən/ *noun* (plural **workmen** /-mən/) someone who does physical work such as building

work·man·ship /ˈwɜːkmənʃɪp $ ˈwɚkmənˌʃɪp/ *noun* (no plural) the skill with which something has been made: *I was impressed by the high standard of workmanship.*

workmen the plural of WORKMAN

work·out /ˈwɜːkaʊt $ ˈwɚk-aʊt/ *noun* a series of physical exercises that you do to keep your body strong and healthy

work·sheet /ˈwɜːkʃiːt $ ˈwɚkʃit/ *noun* a piece of paper with questions which helps students practise what they have learned

work·shop /ˈwɜːkʃɒp $ ˈwɚkʃɑp/ *noun* **1** a room or building where people make or repair things **2** a meeting at which people try to improve their skills by working together

work·sta·tion /ˈwɜːkˌsteɪʃən $ ˈwɚkˌsteɪʃən/ *noun* a desk and computer in an office

work·top /ˈwɜːktɒp $ ˈwɚktɑp/ also **ˈwork-ˌsurface** *noun* a flat surface in a kitchen on which you can prepare food

world¹ /wɜːld $ wɚld/ *noun*
1 the world the Earth and all the people and countries on it: *I think Paris is the best city* ***in the world.*** • *After university, she spent a year travelling* ***around the world.*** • *People* ***all over the world*** *are dying from this disease.*
➔ see Thesaurus at EARTH
2 things that are related to a particular type of business or activity: *the* ***world*** *of professional football* • *people from the fashion world*

PHRASES

the whole world everyone: *The whole world is trying to get tickets for this concert.*

the outside world the people and places outside the area where you live: *She wouldn't leave her house, she was afraid of* ***the outside world.***

world² *adjective* relating to the whole world: *the world heavyweight boxing champion*

ˌworld-ˈclass *adjective* one of the best in the world: *He has the ability to become a world-class footballer.*

ˌworld-ˈfamous *adjective* famous all over the world: *a world-famous writer*
➔ see Thesaurus at FAMOUS

world·wide /ˌwɜːldˈwaɪd $ ˌwɚldˈwaɪd/ *adjective, adverb* in every part of the world: *Pollution is a worldwide problem.* ➔ see Thesaurus at EVERYWHERE

ˌWorld ˌWide ˈWeb (written abbreviation **WWW**) *noun* **the World Wide Web** the system on the Internet that makes it possible to find information and pictures on computers in many parts of the world

worm¹ /wɜːm $ wɚm/ *noun* a small creature with a long soft body and no legs, which lives in the ground

worm² *verb* **worm your way** to move with difficulty through a narrow place: *Ron wormed his way into the tunnel.*

worn /wɔːn $ wɔːrn/ the past participle of WEAR

ˌworn ˈout, worn-out *adjective*
1 very tired, especially because you have been working hard SYNONYM **exhausted**: *I'm worn out – I need a holiday.* ➔ see Thesaurus at TIRED
2 too old or damaged to use any more: *You can't wear those old jeans – they're worn out.*

wor·ried /ˈwʌrid $ ˈwɚid/ *adjective*

> KEY PATTERNS
> **worried that**
> **worried about something/someone**
> **get worried**

A B C D E F G H I J K L M N O P Q R S T U V **W** X Y Z

if you are worried, you are not happy because you keep thinking about a problem or something bad that might happen: *Lucy **was worried that** the other girls would laugh at her.* • *I'm very **worried about** my exams.* • *I'm **getting** a bit **worried about** Jamie, he doesn't seem very happy.*

> **THESAURUS**
> **concerned**: *I am **concerned** that the aircraft may not be safe* (=worried).
> **anxious**: *Helen is always **anxious** about travelling alone* (=worried).
> **nervous**: *Before the interview, he felt very **nervous*** (=so worried that he could not relax).
> **uneasy**: *Something about his manner made her feel **uneasy*** (=slightly worried).

wor·ry¹ /ˈwʌri $ ˈwɚi/ *verb* (**worried, worries**)

> **KEY PATTERNS**
> **worry about something/someone**
> **worry that**
> **it worries me/him etc that**

1 to keep thinking about a problem or something bad that might happen so that you do not feel happy or relaxed: *My Dad **worries** a lot **about** money.* • *I sometimes **worry that** I won't get a good job.*
2 if something worries you, it makes you feel worried: ***It worries me that** my father lives alone now.*

worry² *noun* (plural **worries**) something that makes you feel worried, or the feeling of being worried: *It's a big worry when your children first leave home.* • *He couldn't sleep for worry.*

wor·ry·ing /ˈwʌri-ɪŋ $ ˈwɚi-ɪŋ/ *adjective* making you feel worried: *a worrying piece of news*

worse /wɜːs $ wɚs/ *adjective* more bad or more unpleasant ANTONYM **better**: *Your singing is even worse than mine!* • *The problem **is getting worse**.* • *If you **feel worse** (=feel more ill) tomorrow, go to the doctor.*

wors·en /ˈwɜːsən $ ˈwɚsən/ *verb* to become worse ANTONYM **improve**: *The hospital says his condition is worsening.*

ˌworse ˈoff *adjective* poorer, or in a worse situation ANTONYM **better off**: *Cheer up, we could be worse off.*

wor·ship /ˈwɜːʃɪp $ ˈwɚʃɪp/ *verb* (**worshipped, worshipping**) to express respect and love for God: *In my religion, we worship many gods.*
—**worship** *noun* (no plural): *an occasion for worship and prayer*

worst¹ /wɜːst $ wɚst/ *adjective* worse than any other person or thing: *Who is the worst player in the team?*

worst² *noun* **1 the worst** someone or something that is worse than every other person or thing ANTONYM **the best**: *Of all the exams, this one will be the worst.* **2 fear the worst** to be afraid that the worst possible thing has happened or will happen: *When Bob didn't come home, I began to fear the worst.*

worth¹ /wɜːθ $ wɚθ/ *preposition* if something is worth an amount of money, it has that value: *If the ring is really gold, it must be worth over £1,000.*

PHRASES
be worth doing if something is worth doing, it is interesting or useful to do: *The film's definitely worth seeing.* • *It's worth making sure you understand the question before answering it.*
be worth it, be worth your while if something is worth it, it is important enough or good enough to spend time and effort on: *I started running to catch the bus but then decided it **wasn't worth it**.* • *I think **it would be worth your while to** apply for the job.*

worth² *noun*
$10 worth, £500 worth etc an amount of something that has a value of $10, £500 etc: *He's just bought **£2,000 worth of** new computer equipment.*

worth·less /ˈwɜːθləs $ ˈwɚθləs/ *adjective* having no value: *It's just a worthless piece of rubbish.*

worth·while /ˌwɜːθˈwaɪl $ ˌwɚθˈwaɪl/ *adjective* if something is worthwhile, it is useful or enjoyable: *It's worthwhile checking the price of buying the camera online.*

wor·thy /ˈwɜːði $ ˈwɚði/ *adjective* (**worthier, worthiest**) good enough to have your respect or attention: *The* *opposing team were the worthy winners of the match.*

would /wʊd/ *modal verb*
1 used when saying what someone said or thought about the future: *Joe said he would think again about going to university.* • *The party went on till 2 o'clock, so I knew I would be tired the next day.*
2 used when talking about an event in a possible future situation: *If I won a lot of money, I would spend it on a huge house.* • *I wouldn't ever want to leave London.*
3 use **would have** when talking about an event that did not happen because something else did not happen: *If you had practised more, you **would have** won.* • *I **would have** fetched you from the station, but you didn't ring me.*
4 used to politely ask someone to do something: *Would you open the door, please?*
5 used to offer someone something: ***Would you like** a beer?*
6 used to make a suggestion or give advice: *I wouldn't worry too much about the test – it's easy.* • *I'd ask your teacher for help, if I were you.*

GRAMMAR
The short form of **would** is **'d**: ***I'd** like a cup of coffee.*
The negative of **would** is **would not** or **wouldn't**: *She **wouldn't** leave.*

would·n't /ˈwʊdnt/ the short form of 'would not': *He wouldn't do a thing like that!*

would've /ˈwʊdəv/ the short form of 'would have': *You would've enjoyed the film.*

wound[1] /wuːnd/ *noun* a deep cut made in your skin by a knife or bullet: *He had a deep wound in his side.*
➔ see Thesaurus at INJURY

wound[2] *verb* to injure someone with a knife or gun —**wounded** *adjective*: *Was he badly wounded?*

wound[3] /waʊnd/ the past tense and past participle of WIND[2]

wound up /ˌwaʊnd ˈʌp/ *adjective* very angry, nervous, or excited: *He gets really wound up when the other children tease him.*

wove the past tense of WEAVE

woven the past participle of WEAVE

wow /waʊ/ (spoken) used when you think something is impressive or surprising: *Wow, what a beautiful house!*

wran·gle /ˈræŋgəl/ *verb* to argue with someone angrily for a long time

wrap /ræp/ *verb* (**wrapped**, **wrapping**)

KEY PATTERNS
wrap a present
wrap someone in a blanket
wrap something around your head/shoulders etc

1 to cover a present with attractive paper ANTONYM **unwrap**: *I haven't wrapped the Christmas presents yet.*
2 to put a piece of cloth or paper around someone or something: *She **wrapped** the baby **in** a towel.* • *I bought some sandwiches **wrapped in** plastic.* • *She **wrapped** her scarf **around** her neck.*

PHRASAL VERBS
wrap up
1 wrap something up to completely cover something by putting paper or cloth around it ANTONYM **unwrap**: *They **wrapped** all the cups **up** in newspaper.*
2 wrap up to put on warm clothes: *Make sure you **wrap up well** if you're going out in the snow.*

wrap·per /ˈræpə $ ˈræpɚ/ *noun* the paper or plastic that covers something you buy: *The ground was covered in sweet wrappers.*

wrap·ping /ˈræpɪŋ/ *noun* paper or cloth that is put around something: *She took the present and tore off the wrapping.*

ˈwrapping ˌpaper *noun* coloured paper that you use to wrap presents

wreath /riːθ/ *noun* a circle of flowers and leaves that is used as a decoration or to show respect for someone who has died

wreck[1] /rek/ *verb* (informal) to destroy something completely SYNONYM **ruin**: *My drinking problem wrecked my marriage.*

wreck² *noun* **1** a car, plane, or ship that is very badly damaged **2 be a wreck** (informal) to be very tired, unhealthy, or worried **3** *AmE* a bad accident involving a car, train, or plane
SYNONYM **crash** ➔ see Thesaurus at ACCIDENT

wreck

wreck·age /ˈrekɪdʒ/ *noun* (no plural) the broken parts of a vehicle or building that has been destroyed: *She managed to pull the driver from the wreckage.*

wrench¹ /rentʃ/ *verb* to twist and pull something from somewhere, using force: *Tom wrenched the nail out of the wall.*

wrench² *noun* (plural **wrenches**) the American word for SPANNER

wres·tle /ˈresəl/ *verb* **1** to fight by holding someone and trying to push them to the ground **2 wrestle with something** to try to deal with something difficult: *I've been wrestling with this problem for days.*

wres·tler /ˈreslə $ ˈreslɚ/ *noun* someone who wrestles as a sport

wres·tling /ˈreslɪŋ/ *noun* (no plural) a sport in which two people fight and try to push each other to the ground

wretch·ed /ˈretʃɪd/ *adjective* **1** very unhappy or unlucky SYNONYM **miserable**: *He led a wretched life with his first wife.* **2** (informal) used when you feel angry with someone or something: *The wretched thing's broken again!*

wrig·gle /ˈrɪgəl/ *verb* to twist quickly from side to side: *She wriggled into the tight dress.*

wring /rɪŋ/ *verb* (past tense and past participle **wrung** /rʌŋ/)
1 also **wring out** to twist wet clothes etc to remove water from them
2 wring something's neck to kill an animal by twisting its neck

wring

wrin·kle /ˈrɪŋkəl/ *noun* a small line on your face that you get when you are old

wrin·kled /ˈrɪŋkəld/ *adjective* if someone's skin is wrinkled, it has a lot of lines on it because they are old

wrist /rɪst/ *noun* the joint between your hand and your arm ➔ see picture on page A5

wrist·watch /ˈrɪstwɒtʃ $ ˈrɪst-wɑtʃ/ *noun* (plural **wristwatches**) a watch that you wear on your wrist

write /raɪt/ *verb* (**wrote** /rəʊt $ roʊt/ **written** /ˈrɪtn/)

KEY PATTERNS
write a book/story/report etc
write something on a piece of paper
write (a letter/email) to someone
write someone a letter/email

1 to produce a book, song etc: *He wrote several books and many poems.* • *The Harry Potter stories are written by J.K. Rowling.* • *The article in the newspaper was very* ***well written.***
2 to make letters or words on paper, using a pen or pencil: *We teach children how to* ***read and write.*** • ***Write*** *your name* ***on*** *this piece of paper.*
3 to produce a letter or email to send to someone: *Will you* ***write to*** *me when you've gone?* • *I'm* ***writing*** *an email* ***to*** *Mum.* • *David* ***wrote me a letter*** *every week.*

PHRASES
write a cheque, write out a cheque to write information on a cheque as a way of paying money: *I* ***wrote a cheque for*** *£50 to pay for the meal.*

PHRASAL VERBS
write back
to answer someone's letter by sending them a letter: *Do you think Sarah will write back?*
write down
write something down to write something on a piece of paper: *Can you* ***write*** *your phone number* ***down*** *for me?*
write off
to send a letter to an organization, especially to ask them to send you something: *I've* ***written off*** *for an application form.*

THESAURUS
jot down: *I jotted down her phone number* (=wrote it quickly).
scribble: *He scribbled his address on a bit of paper* (=wrote it by hand in a quick and untidy way).
make a note of: *Make a note of the ingredients you will need* (=write them down so that you will remember).

'write-off *noun BrE* if a vehicle is a write-off, it is so badly damaged in an accident that it is not worth repairing

writ·er /'raɪtə $ 'raɪtɚ/ *noun* someone who writes books

writhe /raɪð/ *verb* (written) to twist your body, especially because you are in a lot of pain: *He lay on the ground, writhing in agony.*

writ·ing /'raɪtɪŋ/ *noun* (no plural) **1** words that are written by hand or printed: *I couldn't read the writing on the envelope.* • *I informed them in writing that I was going to leave.* **2** the activity of writing: *I'm hoping to do a course in creative writing.*

written the past participle of WRITE

wrong¹ /rɒŋ $ rɔŋ/ *adjective, adverb*

KEY PATTERNS
wrong about something
it is wrong to do something

1 not correct ANTONYM **right**: *That's the **wrong answer**.* • *You've added the numbers up wrong.* • *Mum was **wrong about** the train times and Dad was right.*
2 not morally right ANTONYM **right**: *Killing is wrong.* • *Some people think **it's wrong to** kill animals for food.* ➔ see Thesaurus at BAD
3 not suitable ANTONYM **right**: *You're wearing the wrong shoes for an exercise class.*

PHRASES
go wrong if something goes wrong, it starts to have problems or it is unsuccessful: *My washing machine **has gone wrong**.* • *His plan **went wrong**.*
something is wrong with something: ***Something's wrong with** my computer* (=my computer is not working correctly). • ***There's something wrong with** his heart.* • ***What's wrong with** you today* (=why are you not all right)?
get something wrong to make a mistake and say something that is not correct: *Did you **get** all the answers **wrong**?* —**wrongly** *adverb*

THESAURUS
incorrect: *That statement was incorrect* (=wrong).
false: *He lost his job because of a false accusation* (=not true).

wrong² *noun* **1** (no plural) behaviour that is not morally right ANTONYM **right**: *Children need to learn the difference between right and wrong.* **2** an action, decision, or situation that is unfair to someone: *Many wrongs were done to these people during the war.*

wrong·do·ing /'rɒŋˌduːɪŋ $ ˌrɔŋ'duɪŋ/ *noun* (formal) when someone does something illegal or wrong

wrote the past tense of WRITE

wrung the past tense and past participle of WRING

wry /raɪ/ *adjective* showing that you think that something is both funny and sad: *She made a wry comment about the state of his room.*

WWW the written abbreviation of WORLD WIDE WEB

Xe•rox[1] /ˈzɪərɒks $ ˈzɪrɑks/ *noun AmE* (trademark) **1** also ˈ**Xerox maˌchine** a PHOTOCOPIER **2** a PHOTOCOPY[1]

Xerox[2] *AmE* (trademark) *verb* to make a copy of a document using a PHOTOCOPIER SYNONYM **photocopy**

X•mas /ˈkrɪsməs/ *noun* an informal way of writing 'Christmas'

X-ray /ˈeks reɪ/ *noun* a photograph of the inside of someone's body, that you make using a special kind of light —**X-ray** *verb*: *The doctor X-rayed her broken leg.*

xy•lo•phone /ˈzaɪləfəʊn $ ˈzaɪləˌfoʊn/ *noun* a musical instrument with flat wooden or metal bars that you hit with a stick

xylophone

yacht /jɒt $ jɑt/ *noun* a boat with sails that people use for races or sailing for pleasure ➔ see picture at BOAT ➔ see Thesaurus at BOAT ➔ see picture on page A11

PRONUNCIATION
You pronounce **yacht** like 'hot'.

yachts·man /ˈjɒtsmən $ ˈjɑtsmən/ *noun* (plural **yachtsmen** /-mən/) a man who sails a yacht

yachts·wom·an /ˈjɒtsˌwʊmən $ ˈjɑtsˌwʊmən/ *noun* (plural **yachtswomen** /-ˌwɪmɪn/) a woman who sails a yacht

Yank /jæŋk/ *noun* (informal) someone from the US

yank /jæŋk/ *verb* (informal) to suddenly pull something hard: *The boy yanked at his mother's sleeve.*

yap /jæp/ *verb* (**yapped**, **yapping**) if a small dog yaps, it BARKS a lot

yard /jɑːd $ jɑrd/ *noun* **1** (written abbreviation **yd**) a length equal to 3 feet or 0.9144 metres: *The room was four yards wide.* **2** the American word for GARDEN: *Joey's out in the yard.* **3** an area of land with a wall around it, next to a building

yarn /jɑːn $ jɑrn/ *noun* (no plural) thick thread that you use for KNITTING

yarn

a ball of yarn

yawn

yawn /jɔːn/ *verb* to open your mouth wide and breathe deeply because you are tired or bored —**yawn** *noun*: *"I'm going to bed," he said with a yawn.*

yd the written abbreviation of YARD

yeah /jeə/ (spoken, informal) yes

year /jɪə $ jɪr/ *noun* a period of 12 months: *I have lived here* ***for two years***. • *We last saw Harry* ***three years ago***. • *Insurance costs* ***$100 per year*** (=for one year). • *She died* ***last year***. • ***Next year*** *I will be 16.*

PHRASES

for years (informal) for a long time SYNONYM **for ages**: *I haven't seen Ray for years.*

ten years old, 12 years old etc used for saying how old someone is: *My sister is only* ***two years old***.

year four, year six etc *BrE* used for saying what class someone is in in a school or college: *Ciara is in year seven.*

GRAMMAR
You use **in** with years: *I left college in 2006.*

year·book /ˈjɪəbʊk $ ˈjɪrbʊk/ *noun* a book that an organization or school produces every year, giving information about its activities

year·ly /ˈjɪəli $ ˈjɪrli/ *adjective, adverb* happening every year: *her yearly visit to her aunt* • *You can pay weekly, monthly, or yearly.*

yeast /jiːst/ *noun* (no plural) a substance that you use when you are making bread to make the bread rise

yell /jel/ also **yell out** *verb* to shout something very loudly: *"Come back!" he yelled.* ➔ see Thesaurus at SHOUT[1] —**yell** *noun*: *With a yell, she landed at the bottom of the stairs.*

yel·low¹ /ˈjeləʊ $ ˈjeloʊ/ *adjective* something that is yellow is the colour of a LEMON or BANANA

yellow² *noun* the colour of a LEMON: *Yellow is my favourite colour.*

A B C D E F G H I J K L M N O P Q R S T U V W X Y Z

yelp /jelp/ *verb* if a dog yelps, it makes a short high sound because it is in pain or excited

yes /jes/ *adverb*
a word you say when you agree with something or think that something is true ANTONYM **no**: *"Are you Ann?" "Yes, I am."* • *"This is great, isn't it?" "Yes, it is."* • *If I ask her to marry me, do you think that she will* ***say yes****?*

yes·ter·day /ˈjestədi $ ˈjestɚdi/ *adverb*
the day before today: *I went swimming yesterday.* • *Yesterday, the weather was fine.*

yet /jet/ *adverb*
1 also **as yet** (formal) use yet to ask if something has happened or to say that something has not happened up to the present time: *Have you had dinner yet?* • *I haven't finished my essay yet.* • *The school has not as yet decided how to deal with the problem.* • *Is Sharon back from town yet?*
2 use yet to say that someone cannot or need not do something now, although they may have to do it later: *I can't ask Mum yet – she's busy.* • *The train goes in two hours so we don't need to leave yet.*

PHRASES

biggest yet, best yet, most important yet etc used to say that something is the biggest, best, most important etc that has existed up to the present time: *I've read all her books, and this is the best one yet.* • *This is the most exciting game the Red Sox have played yet.* • *Everyone said that was the most difficult exam yet.*

yet another, yet more, yet again used to say that you are surprised that there is more of something or that something has happened again: *I watched as Bob took yet another slice of chocolate cake.* • *He's just been into town and bought yet more CDs.* • *You were late yet again this morning – that's the fourth time this week.*

yield¹ /jiːld/ *verb* (formal) to do what someone wants, although you do not want to: *The head teacher finally yielded to pressure and allowed students to wear casual clothes.*

yield² *noun* the amount that something produces: *Modern farming methods produce higher yields from crops.*

yo·ga /ˈjəʊgə $ ˈjoʊgə/ *noun* (no plural) a system of exercises which relax you and make your muscles stronger

yoga

yog·hurt, yogurt /ˈjɒgət $ ˈjoʊgɚt/ *noun* a thick white food that is made from milk

yolk /jəʊk $ joʊk/ *noun* the yellow part of an egg → see picture at EGG²

you /jə; strong juː/ *pronoun*
1 the person or people being spoken to: *Would you like some coffee?* • *I hate you!* • *What are you two doing?*
2 anyone: *Smoking is bad for you.* • *You can earn quite a lot of money being a salesman.*

you'd /jəd; strong juːd/ the short form of 'you would' or 'you had': *I know you'd like a drink.* • *I didn't think you'd finished.*

you'll /jəl; strong juːl/ the short form of 'you will': *You'll have to leave.*

young¹ /jʌŋ/ *adjective*
1 someone who is young has only lived for a short time ANTONYM **old**: *Do you enjoy working with* ***young children****?* • *The kids are still too young to stay at home on their own.* • *When my father was young he was very handsome.*
2 younger brother, younger sister a brother or sister who is younger than you

young² *plural noun* **1 the young** young people: *The BBC is planning more programmes for the young.*
2 young animals: *A mouse is capable of producing 150 young a year.*

young·ster /ˈjʌŋstə $ ˈjʌŋstɚ/ *noun* a young person

your /jə $ jɚ; strong jɔː $ jɔr/ *determiner*
1 belonging to the person or people being spoken to: *You can hang your coat up here.* • *Are your hands clean?* • *Have you all got your passports?*
2 belonging to anyone: *I believe you have to learn from your mistakes.*

SPELLING
Don't confuse the spelling of **your** and **you're** (=you are).

you're /jə $ jɚ; strong jɔː $ jɔr/ the short form of 'you are': *You're silly.*

yours /jɔːz $ jɔrz/ *pronoun* a thing belonging to the person or people being spoken to: *I wish I lived in a nice house like yours.*

your·self /jə'self $ jɚ'self/ (plural **yourselves** /jə'selvz $ jɚ'selvz/) *pronoun*
1 used when the same person that you are speaking to does an action and receives the action: *Be careful you don't hurt yourself.* • *What do you see when you look at yourself in the mirror?* • *You should all feel ashamed of yourselves.*
2 used to emphasize that you are talking about the person or people you are speaking to: *If you don't have a computer yourself, ask a friend if you can use theirs.* • *You have probably noticed this yourselves.*
3 used when talking about people in general, and they do an action and receive the action: *You can hurt yourself quite badly if you don't use the correct equipment.*

PHRASES
by yourself, by yourselves without anyone with you or helping you: *You'll have to wait there **by yourself** until the others get back.* • *See if you can manage to solve the problem **by yourselves**.*

youth /juːθ/ *noun* **1** (no plural) your youth is the time when you are young ANTONYM **old age**: *I lived in London in my youth.* **2** a young man: *There were three youths waiting outside.* **3** (no plural) young people in general: *We must do more for the youth of this country.*

'youth club *noun* a place where young people can meet, dance etc

youth·ful /'juːθfəl/ *adjective* seeming younger than you really are: *He has kept his youthful good looks.*

'youth ˌhostel *noun* a place where people who are travelling can stay cheaply

you've /jəv; strong juːv/ the short form of 'you have': *You've eaten it all!*

yo-yo /'jəʊ jəʊ $ 'joʊ joʊ/ *noun* a toy made of a round piece of plastic or wood that moves up and down a string

Zz

za·ny /ˈzeɪni/ *adjective* (**zanier**, **zaniest**) strange but amusing: *a zany comedian*

zeal /ziːl/ *noun* (no plural) (formal) great desire to do something: *When he was younger, he was full of zeal for learning.*

ze·bra /ˈzebrə $ ˈzibrə/ *noun* a black and white African animal, similar to a horse

zebra crossing

ˌ**zebra ˈcrossing** *noun BrE* a set of black and white lines painted on the road where vehicles are supposed to stop so people can cross safely SYNONYM **crosswalk** *AmE*

ze·ro /ˈzɪərəʊ $ ˈzɪroʊ/ (plural **zeros** or **zeroes**)
the number 0

zig·zag[1] /ˈzɪgzæg/ *noun* a line that goes first in one direction and then in the other, and continues in this way: *A zigzag of lightning lit up the sky.*

zigzag[2] *verb* (**zigzagged**, **zigzagging**) to move forward, going in straight lines first to one side, and then to the other: *The car zigzagged across the road.*

zinc /zɪŋk/ *noun* a blue-white metal

zip[1] /zɪp/ *verb* (**zipped**, **zipping**) also **zip up** to close or fasten something using a zip ANTONYM **unzip**: *She zipped the bag shut.*

zip[2] *noun BrE* a type of FASTENING made of two lines of small metal teeth and a sliding piece that joins them together SYNONYM **zipper** *AmE*: *The zip on my pencil case has broken.*

ˈ**zip code** the American word for POSTCODE

zip·per /ˈzɪpə $ ˈzɪpɚ/ the American word for a ZIP → see picture at FASTENING

zone /zəʊn $ zoʊn/ *noun* an area where a particular thing happens or where there are particular rules: *People are advised not to live in earthquake zones.* • *You're in a no-parking zone.* → see Thesaurus at AREA

zoo /zuː/ *noun* a place where different types of wild animal are kept so that people can see or study them

zo·ol·o·gy /zuːˈɒlədʒi $ zoʊˈɑlədʒi/ *noun* (no plural) the scientific study of animals

zoom /zuːm/ *verb* (informal) to travel somewhere very quickly: *Cars zoomed past us on the freeway.*

zuc·chi·ni /zʊˈkiːni/ the American word for COURGETTE → see picture on page A6

PRONUNCIATION
You pronounce **-cch-** as **k**.

A B C D E F G H I J K L M N O P Q R S T U V W X Y Z

Irregular verbs

This chart shows the verbs that have irregular forms for the **Past Tense**, **Past Participle**, or **Present Participle**. When a verb has more than one form that is used, the most common form is given first.

Verb	Past Tense	Past Participle	Present Participle
arise	arose	arisen	arising
awake	awoke	awoken	awaking
be	was/were	been	being
bear	bore	borne	bearing
beat	beat	beaten	beating
become	became	become	becoming
begin	began	begun	beginning
bend	bent	bent	bending
bet	bet	bet	betting
bid	bid	bid	bidding
bite	bit	bitten	biting
bleed	bled	bled	bleeding
blow	blew	blown	blowing
break	broke	broken	breaking
breed	bred	bred	breeding
bring	brought	brought	bringing
broadcast	broadcast	broadcast	broadcasting
build	built	built	building
burn	burned *or* burnt	burned *or* burnt	burning
burst	burst	burst	bursting
buy	bought	bought	buying
cast	cast	cast	casting
catch	caught	caught	catching
choose	chose	chosen	choosing
cling	clung	clung	clinging
come	came	come	coming
cost	cost	cost	costing
creep	crept	crept	creeping
cut	cut	cut	cutting
deal	dealt	dealt	dealing
dig	dug	dug	digging
dive	dived *or* dove *AmE*	dived	diving
do	did	done	doing
draw	drew	drawn	drawing
dream	dreamed *or* dreamt	dreamed *or* dreamt	dreaming
drink	drank	drunk	drinking
drive	drove	driven	driving
dwell	dwelled *or* dwelt	dwelled *or* dwelt	dwelling
eat	ate	eaten	eating
fall	fell	fallen	falling
feed	fed	fed	feeding
feel	felt	felt	feeling
fight	fought	fought	fighting

Verb	Past Tense	Past Participle	Present Participle
find	found	found	finding
fit	fitted or fit *AmE*	fit or fitted	fitting
flee	fled	fled	fleeing
fling	flung	flung	flinging
fly	flew	flown	flying
forbid	forbade	forbidden	forbidding
foresee	foresaw	foreseen	foreseeing
forget	forgot	forgotten	forgetting
forgive	forgave	forgiven	forgiving
freeze	froze	frozen	freezing
get	got	got *BrE or* gotten	getting
give	gave	given	giving
go	went	gone *or* been	going
grind	ground	ground	grinding
grow	grew	grown	growing
hang	hung	hung	hanging
have	had	had	having
hear	heard	heard	hearing
hide	hid	hidden	hiding
hit	hit	hit	hitting
hold	held	held	holding
hurt	hurt	hurt	hurting
keep	kept	kept	keeping
kneel	knelt *or* kneeled	knelt *or* kneeled	kneeling
knit	knit *or* knitted	knit *or* knitted	knitting
know	knew	known	knowing
lay	laid	laid	laying
lead	led	led	leading
leap	leaped *or* leapt	leaped *or* leapt	leaping
leave	left	left	leaving
lend	lent	lent	lending
let	let	let	letting
lie[1]	lay	lain	lying
lie[2]	lied	lied	lying
light	lit *or* lighted	lit *or* lighted	lighting
lose	lost	lost	losing
make	made	made	making
mean	meant	meant	meaning
meet	met	met	meeting
mislead	misled	misled	misleading
mistake	mistook	mistaken	mistaking
misunderstand	misunderstood	misunderstood	misunderstanding
outdo	outdid	outdone	outdoing
overcome	overcame	overcome	overcoming
overdo	overdid	overdone	overdoing
overhear	overheard	overheard	overhearing
overthrow	overthrew	overthrown	overthrowing
pay	paid	paid	paying
prove	proved	proved *or* proven	proving

Verb	Past Tense	Past Participle	Present Participle
put	put	put	putting
read	read	read	reading
redo	redid	redone	redoing
repay	repaid	repaid	repaying
rewrite	rewrote	rewritten	rewriting
ride	rode	ridden	riding
ring	rang	rung	ringing
rise	rose	risen	rising
run	ran	run	running
saw	sawed	sawed *or* sawn	sawing
say	said	said	saying
see	saw	seen	seeing
seek	sought	sought	seeking
sell	sold	sold	selling
send	sent	sent	sending
set	set	set	setting
sew	sewed	sewn *or* sewed	sewing
shake	shook	shaken	shaking
shed	shed	shed	shedding
shine	shone	shone	shining
shoot	shot	shot	shooting
show	showed	shown	showing
shrink	shrank	shrunk	shrinking
shut	shut	shut	shutting
sing	sang	sung	singing
sink	sank *or* sunk	sunk	sinking
sit	sat	sat	sitting
sleep	slept	slept	sleeping
slide	slid	slid	sliding
slit	slit	slit	slitting
sow	sowed	sown *or* sowed	sowing
speak	spoke	spoken	speaking
speed	sped *or* speeded	sped *or* speeded	speeding
spend	spent	spent	spending
spin	spun	spun	spinning
spit	spat *or* spit *AmE*	spat *or* spit *AmE*	spitting
split	split	split	splitting
spread	spread	spread	spreading
spring	sprang	sprung	springing
stand	stood	stood	standing
steal	stole	stolen	stealing
stick	stuck	stuck	sticking
sting	stung	stung	stinging
stink	stank *or* stunk	stunk	stinking
stride	strode	stridden	striding
strike	struck	struck	striking
strive	strove	striven	striving
swear	swore	sworn	swearing
sweep	swept	swept	sweeping
swell	swelled	swollen	swelling

Verb	Past Tense	Past Participle	Present Participle
swim	swam	swum	swimming
swing	swung	swung	swinging
take	took	taken	taking
teach	taught	taught	teaching
tear	tore	torn	tearing
tell	told	told	telling
think	thought	thought	thinking
throw	threw	thrown	throwing
thrust	thrust	thrust	thrusting
undergo	underwent	undergone	undergoing
understand	understood	understood	understanding
undo	undid	undone	undoing
unwind	unwound	unwound	unwinding
uphold	upheld	upheld	upholding
upset	upset	upset	upsetting
wake	woke	woken	waking
wear	wore	worn	wearing
weave	wove *or* weaved	woven *or* weaved	weaving
weep	wept	wept	weeping
wet	wet *or* wetted	wet *or* wetted	wetting
win	won	won	winning
wind	wound	wound	winding
withdraw	withdrew	withdrawn	withdrawing
withhold	withheld	withheld	withholding
withstand	withstood	withstood	withstanding
wring	wrung	wrung	wringing
write	wrote	written	writing

Labels used in the dictionary

AmE	American English
BrE	British English
formal	used in formal or official situations, but not usually in ordinary conversation
informal	used in conversations with friends and people who you know well, but not suitable for formal speech or writing
spoken	used mostly in spoken English
written	used mostly in written English
trademark	used as an official name of a product by a company

Parts of speech

noun	adjective	preposition	number
verb	adverb	plural	negative
pronoun	modal verb	past tense	past participle
present participle			

Answer key

Spelling

A

1 accommodation
2 government **3** beginning
4 address **5** until **6** pollution
7 accustomed **8** successful

B

1 receive **2** vegetable
3 guarantee **4** potatoes
5 mystery **6** grammar
7 friend **8** separate

C

1 grandmother **2** thank you
3 girlfriend **4** in spite of

Focus on grammar

A

1 reading **2** to lock **3** to fail
4 to speak **5** to do

B

1 at **2** at **3** to **4** in **5** at

C

1 He still hasn't answered my letter.
2 I don't agree with his opinion.
3 ✓
4 I love listening to music.
5 I'll call him when I get home.

D

1 Can you give me some advice?
2 I'd like some sugar, please.
3 We need to buy some furniture.
4 I need some information about train times.
5 Do you have a lot of homework to do?

Choosing the right combination of words

A

1 make a mistake – do the shopping – do your homework – take a bath – take some medicine – have a bath
2 make a (telephone) call – do (no combination) – take a shower – take a walk – have a shower – have a party – have a meeting

B

strong – coffee
deep – voice
rotten – apples strict – rules
heavy – traffic hard – work
stale – bread

C

1 bitterly **2** highly **3** heavily
4 strongly **5** bitterly **6** highly
7 absolutely **8** seriously
9 completely **10** absolutely
11 completely **12** deeply

Time, dates, and numbers

A

1 on **2** in **3** in **4** in **5** at
6 at (*BrE*)/on (*AmE*) **7** in
8 at **9** on **10** in **11** on **12** in

B

1 three forty *also* twenty to four *also* twenty of four (*AmE*)
2 five thirty *also* half past five
3 ten past nine *also* ten after nine

C

1 January the first/the first of January
2 ten sixty-six
3 two thousand and nine

D

1 one hundred and seventy-eight
2 five thousand, six hundred and twenty
3 zero double three double seven nine *also* oh double three double seven nine (*BrE*)
4 three zero *also* three nil (*BrE*)
5 zero point eight *also* nought point eight (*BrE*)

Choosing between similar words

A

1 furious **2** pleased
3 upset **4** exhausted
5 chop **6** well **7** latest
8 vast **9** get
10 disgusting **11** get

B

1 sensitive **2** borrow
3 lonely **4** economical
5 diary **6** stole **7** for
8 for **9** bored
10 principal's **11** its

Understanding signs and notices

A

1 You must not walk on the grass.
2 You can cross the road here.
3 You must not park here between 7 and 9 am and 4 and 6 pm, from Monday to Friday.
4 You must not drive at over 120 kilometres an hour.

B

1 D **2** E **3** A **4** C **5** F **6** B

Writing letters and filling in forms

Family name: COSKUN
First name: ASLI
Mr/Mrs/Miss/Ms: MISS (or Ms)
Date of birth: 5/5/91
Nationality: TURKISH
Email address: coskun.asli@hotmail.com
Daytime telephone number: 020 855005
What kind of course do you want? ELEMENTARY
When would you like to start your course? NEXT WEEK

Saying where things are in a room

1 above **2** on the right of
3 on **4** on the left of
5 under **6** next to
7 in front of
8 in the corner of